1986 Compton's Yearbook

A summary and interpretation of the events of 1985
to supplement Compton's Encyclopedia

Compton's Learning Company, a division of Encyclopædia Britannica, Inc.

CHICAGO

AUCKLAND · GENEVA · LONDON · MANILA · PARIS · ROME · SEOUL · SYDNEY · TOKYO · TORONTO

Library of Congress Catalog Card Number: 58-26525
International Standard Book Number: 0-85229-438-7
International Standard Serial Number: 0069-8091
Copyright © 1986 by Encyclopædia Britannica, Inc.
Printed in U.S.A.

1986 Yearbook Staff

Director of Yearbooks	Robert McHenry
Editor	Dale Good
Contributing Editors	David Calhoun, Charles Cegielski, Daphne Daume, Karen Jacobs Justin, Arthur Latham; *medical subjects:* Ellen Bernstein, Linda Tomchuck *geographical research:* Sujata Banerjee, William A. Cleveland, W. Peter Kindel
Editorial Assistant	Lavonne Nannenga
Art Director	Cynthia Peterson
Senior Picture Editor	Holly Harrington
Picture Editors	Rita Conway, La Bravia Jenkins, Mary S. Moss
Layout Artists	Anne H. Becker, John L. Draves
Cartographers	Gerzilla Leszczynski, Steven Bogdan
Art Staff	Daniel M. Delgado, Patricia A. Henle, Dale Horn, Raul Rios, Richard A. Roiniotis, Lillian Simcox
Director, Yearbook Production and Control	J. Thomas Beatty
Manager, Copy Department	Anita Wolff
Senior Copy Editors	Lawrence D. Kowalski, Barbara Whitney
Copy Staff	Anthony L. Green, Melinda Shepherd
Manager, Copy Control	Mary C. Srodon
Copy Control Staff	Marilyn L. Barton, Mayme R. Cussen, Timothy A. Phillips
Manager, Composition and Page Makeup	Melvin Stagner
Composition Staff	Duangnetra Debhavalya, Morna Freund, Van Jones, John Krom, Jr., Thomas Mulligan, Gwen Rosenberg, Tammy Tsou
Page Makeup Staff	Marsha Check, *supervisor* Michael Born, Jr., Griselda Cháidez, Arnell Reed, Philip Rehmer, Danette Wetterer
Director, Editorial Computer Services	Michael J. Brandhorst
Manager, Systems and Programming	I. Dean Washington
Computer Services Staff	Steven Bosco, Roland Garcia, Daniel Johnsen, Vincent Star
Manager, Index Department	Frances E. Latham
Assistant Manager	Rosa E. Casas
Senior Index Editor	Helen A. Peterson
Index Staff	Valerie Munei, Gayl Williams
Librarian	Terry Miller
Associate Librarian	Shantha Uddin
Assistant Librarian	David W. Foster
Secretary	Dorothy Hagen

Editorial Administration

Editor in Chief, Philip W. Goetz
Executive Director of Editorial Production, Karen M. Barch
Director of Budgets and Controller, Verne Pore

Encyclopædia Britannica, Inc.

Chairman of the Board, Robert P. Gwinn
President, Peter B. Norton

Contents

Pictured Highlights and Chronology of 1985

Events of the Year

Special Reports
49   *Biology:* Inhumane Treatment of Animals
65   *Canada:* A Mood for Change
79   *Computers:* The Homeless Computer
97   *Defense and Arms Control:* Intervention and Defense
        in Central America and the Caribbean
113   *Economic Affairs:* A Field Guide to Corporate Mergers
135   *Fashion:* The Street Scene—Pop, Glam, Androgyny
175   *International Trade:* The Case Against Protectionism: A U.S. View
200   *Latin-American Affairs:* The Swing Toward Democracy
247   *Newspapers:* Freedom of Information
289   *Religion:* As the "New Religions" Grow Older
299   *Social Services:* Homelessness
305   *South Africa:* South Africa's Apartheid Policy

Focus '85

Feature Articles
386   Kites: New Designs for New Uses
        by Miles L. Loyd
392   The New Asia-Pacific Era: A Perspective from an
        International Nation Building for the 21st Century
        by Yasuhiro Nakasone
405   The Center of the Milky Way
        by Gareth Wynn-Williams
412   The Soviet Union Under Gorbachev
        by Arkadi N. Shevchenko

427   **Asides**

431   **New Words**

433   **Biographies**

471   **Family Record**

483   **Calendar**

486   **Contributors and Consultants**

490   **Index**

pictured highlights and chronology

1985

2 Norway's defense ministry announced that what was believed to be a Soviet cruise missile had flown across Norway five days earlier before crashing in Finland. Evidence gathered at the crash site later showed that the weapon was an antiquated target missile that had simply malfunctioned.

Japanese Prime Minister Yasuhiro Nakasone arrived in Los Angeles to discuss bilateral trade and other issues with U.S. Pres. Ronald Reagan. Nakasone and Reagan approved high-level trade talks, which were expected to focus first on telecommunications and then to broaden to include such things as electronics, forest products, and medical supplies.

3 The Israeli government publicly confirmed rumors that some 10,000 Ethiopian Jews had been secretly flown to Israel in recent years, but it would give no details of the operation. An additional 10,000–15,000 black Jews were believed to be still living in Ethiopian villages and Sudanese refugee camps.

5 Four Colombians accused of international drug trafficking and money laundering were flown to the U.S. to face federal charges. This first-ever extradition of Colombian citizens to the U.S. was in effect a declaration by Pres. Belisario Betancur that he fully intended to continue prosecuting the war initiated by the minister of justice before he was murdered by members of the drug underworld in May 1984.

Egyptian Pres. Hosni Mubarak met with King Hussein in Jordan to discuss problems of the Middle East. They agreed that an international conference, attended by U.S. and Soviet representatives as well as by Arabs and Israelis, held the greatest promise for a comprehensive settlement of the area's many problems.

8 U.S. Secretary of State George Shultz and Soviet Foreign Minister Andrei Gromyko concluded two days of talks in Geneva after agreeing on the format, content, and objectives of arms control negotiations that were expected to get under way in a month or two. It was the first meeting between top officials of the two superpowers in more than a year.

10 In a modest ceremony Daniel Ortega Saavedra took the oath of office as president of Nicaragua. The presidential inauguration followed by one day the installation of a new National Assembly, which had been elected in November 1984.

14 The U.S. Department of Justice announced the indictments of 16 persons on charges of smuggling Central American aliens into the U.S. or giving them refuge after their arrival. Activists involved in what was called the sanctuary movement insisted that those being helped, sometimes in open defiance of the government, faced persecution and possible death at the hands of death squads in El Salvador and Guatemala.

15 Brazil's 686-member electoral college elected Tancredo de Almeida Neves the nation's first civilian president in 21 years. Gen. João Baptista de Oliveira Figueiredo, the outgoing president, said he would turn over the reins of government on March 15.

One day after Prime Minister Edward Seaga announced a 21% increase in the cost of gasoline and other fuels, Jamaicans took to the streets in protest. In Kingston, the capital, transportation was brought to a virtual halt by piles of debris and burning tires. The January 14 increase in fuel prices was but the latest of several steps Seaga had been taking, with the blessing of the International Monetary Fund, to alleviate Jamaica's financial problems.

18 The U.S. government formally announced it would participate no further in proceedings initiated against it by Nicaragua in the International Court of Justice because the issue was "an inherently political problem that is not appropriate for judicial resolution." The suit charged the U.S. with illegally supporting paramilitary attacks by rebels in Nicaragua and mining its harbors; it also sought millions of dollars in reparations.

19 French Pres. François Mitterrand made a 12-hour visit to New Caledonia, a French territory in the South Pacific, to urge an end to violence and an acceptance of a referendum to determine the island's political future. On January 20, during a televised address in Paris, Mitterrand said France intended to protect its strategic interests in the area by keeping out "whatever foreign power" might try to set up a presence on the island. He also indicated that France's military base in New Caledonia would be strengthened.

20 In a brief private ceremony, Ronald W. Reagan was sworn in for a second term as president of the United States. At 73 he was the oldest man ever elected to the nation's highest office. A public swearing-in ceremony was held the following day (Monday).

23 A panel of three government-appointed prosecutors announced in Manila that they had found ample evidence to charge 26 persons with involvement in the August 1983 assassination of Benigno Aquino, Jr., a leader of the opposition to Philippine Pres. Ferdinand Marcos. The accused included Gen. Fabian C. Ver, chief of staff of the armed forces and a close personal friend of President Marcos.

24 A federal jury in Manhattan reached a final verdict in the $50 million libel suit filed against *Time* magazine by Ariel Sharon, Israel's former defense minister. The trial focused on a paragraph in *Time*'s Feb. 21, 1983, cover story, which portrayed Sharon as indirectly responsible for the massacre of hundreds of Palestinian refugees by Lebanese Phalangist militiamen. After agreeing that the article was both defamatory and false, the jury found *Time* innocent of reckless disregard for the truth. Without a finding of malice, Sharon could not collect monetary damages.

26 Pope John Paul II arrived in Venezuela to begin a 12-day apostolic journey that would also carry him to Ecuador and Peru and then to Trinidad and Tobago, off the coast of Venezuela. It was the pope's 25th foreign trip since his elevation to the papacy in 1978.

30 The U.S. Department of Commerce reported that the nation's trade deficit for 1984 was a record $123.3 billion—nearly 78% higher than the previous record set in 1983. Analysis showed that more than half of the 1984 deficit was attributable to trade with Japan, Canada, and Taiwan.

The 13 oil ministers of the Organization of Petroleum Exporting Countries (OPEC) ended a three-day meeting in Geneva with nine nations agreeing to lower oil prices slightly. Algeria, Iran, and Libya placed OPEC unity in further jeopardy by refusing to cooperate.

(Above) Daniel Ortega Saavedra takes the oath of office as president of Nicaragua on January 10 in Managua. Cuban Pres. Fidel Castro (wearing hat) attended the ceremony. (Below) Kampuchean refugees stream into Thailand in the wake of a January offensive by Vietnamese troops against Khmer Rouge positions inside Kampuchea.

FEBRUARY

2 Gen. Augusto Pinochet, president of Chile's military government, ordered a 90-day extension of the state of siege that he had imposed on Nov. 6, 1984. The state of siege gave the government authority, among other things, to hold suspected dissidents without charge. It also extended the ban on specific publications, unauthorized gatherings, and political activities.

4 An Indian official told reporters in New Delhi that Coomar Narain, the alleged kingpin in a spy ring that was said to have been operating for some 25 years, had confessed to passing industrial, military, and political secrets to East German, Polish, and French diplomats.

The U.S. State Department announced that the ANZUS naval exercises scheduled for March had been canceled because Prime Minister David Lange would not permit a U.S. Navy destroyer to visit New Zealand unless the U.S. first certified that the ship carried no nuclear weapons.

5 Four Britons, taken hostage in Tripoli after Britain broke diplomatic ties with Libya in April 1984, were released after eight months of captivity. Col. Muammar Al Qadhafi, leader of Libya, expressed a hope that Britain would respond favorably by normalizing diplomatic relations and releasing Libyans held in British jails.

Spain officially removed all restrictions on travel to and from Gibraltar, the tiny British enclave on the southern tip of Spain. Gen. Francisco Franco had closed the border a decade and a half earlier, but limited pedestrian traffic had continued. In November 1984 Britain and Spain agreed that the time had come to initiate talks on the political future of the territory, which Britain had occupied since 1704.

7 A five-judge tribunal in Torun, Poland, found four security policemen guilty of abducting and murdering the Rev. Jerzy Popieluszko, an outspoken supporter of Solidarity. The two senior officers were given 25-year sentences; the two other men were ordered to prison for 15 and 14 years. Before the beginning of the trial, three of the four had admitted their roles in the crime. One defendant testified that his superior had ordered the kidnapping and murder, but no evidence was presented to support the allegation.

8 After spending two years in the U.S., South Korean dissident Kim Dae Jung returned to Seoul accompanied by two U.S. congressmen and other supporters. Tempers flared at the Kimp'o International Airport when policemen tried to separate Kim from those around him. After a scuffle with Kim's supporters, police drove the 59-year-old politician to his home, where he was placed under virtual house arrest.

10 Nelson Mandela, the imprisoned leader of South Africa's banned African National Congress, refused a government offer of freedom even though he had already been jailed for more than 20 years. The government had insisted that Mandela renounce violence as a condition for his release. Mandela's 23-year-old daughter quoted her father as saying: "Let him [Pres. P. W. Botha] renounce violence. Let him say that he will dismantle apartheid. . . . Let him guarantee free political activity so that the people may decide who will govern them."

15 After 12 years of military rule, Uruguay moved a step closer to democracy with the convening of a new Parliament. Julio María Sanguinetti Cairolo, who replaced Gen. Gregorio Conrado Álvarez Armelino as president on March 1, faced the immediate and delicate task of satisfying demands for the release of political prisoners without thereby angering the military officers who had imprisoned them.

16 Some 300 Israeli troops initiated the first stage of Israel's withdrawal from Lebanon by pulling out of the battered city of Sidon after 32 months of occupation. On February 18 armed Shi'ite fundamentalists poured into the city aboard hundreds of cars, buses, and trucks. They denounced Pres. Amin Gemayel as the "shah of Lebanon" and called for the establishment of an Islamic state.

18 Attorneys for Gen. William C. Westmoreland announced that the former commander of U.S. forces in Vietnam had withdrawn his $120 million libel suit against CBS. In a televised documentary, CBS had asserted that the general's command had deliberately underreported the number of enemy troops before their devastating Tet offensive of January 1968. The out-of-court settlement did not require CBS to pay damages or retract any part of its report.

20 The Irish High Court, acting in accordance with a law passed by both houses of Parliament the previous day after banking hours, seized more than $1.6 million said to belong to the outlawed Irish Republican Army. The minister of justice said the account represented extortion money obtained by threatening to kidnap or murder.

British Prime Minister Margaret Thatcher told a joint session of the U.S. Congress that she firmly endorsed President Reagan's plan to develop a space-based missile defense capability. "Let us be under no illusions," Thatcher said. "It is our strength, not their good will, that has brought the Soviet Union to the negotiating table in Geneva."

22 The trial of 26 men charged with complicity in the 1983 murder of Benigno Aquino, Jr., got under way in a Manila courtroom. The most prominent defendant was Gen. Fabian C. Ver, on leave of absence as chief of staff of the armed forces. An independent panel that had earlier conducted a long investigation had been told that Aquino was shot in the head by one of the military escorts leading him off the plane after it landed in Manila.

27 Israeli Prime Minister Shimon Peres accepted Egyptian Pres. Hosni Mubarak's suggestion that Israel enter into direct peace negotiations with a joint Jordanian-Palestinian delegation, or with Jordan alone if King Hussein consented and the Palestinians refused to participate. On February 28 a spokesman for the PLO criticized Egypt's call for direct talks and endorsed the notion of a UN conference as the proper framework for reaching a peace settlement. All interested parties, including the PLO, would participate.

28 Members of the Irish Republican Army killed nine constables when one of nine mortar shells they fired at a police base in Newry, Northern Ireland, hit a crowded cafeteria. It was the deadliest such attack since violence first erupted in 1969.

(Above) The trial of 251 suspected gangsters began in Naples, Italy, on February 4. The defendants were confined in 20 cages in a specially constructed courtroom. (Below) South Koreans voted in elections for their National Assembly on February 12. The opposition New Korea Democratic Party put in an unexpectedly strong showing.

MARCH

3 After three hours of heated debate, union representatives of Britain's coal miners decided in a close vote to end the strike that had kept thousands of miners out of pits for almost a year. The union was never able to work out an acceptable settlement with the National Coal Board, which insisted to the end that unprofitable coal mines had to be closed, even if it meant the loss of thousands of jobs.

4 West German Foreign Minister Hans-Dietrich Genscher flew to Moscow to discuss East-West relations with his Soviet counterpart, Andrei Gromyko. Though Genscher hoped his visit would begin to bring East and West closer together, little was accomplished.

6 The government of South Korean Pres. Chun Doo Hwan, noting that a new political climate "born of a harmonizing blend of freedom and order" had settled over the nation, announced that the political bans still affecting 14 politicians were being removed. Kim Dae Jung and Kim Young Sam, both internationally known dissidents, were among those pardoned.

President Reagan vetoed proposed legislation that would have provided federal loan guarantees to help farmers finance their spring planting and restructure their debts. Speaker of the House Thomas ("Tip") O'Neill, Jr., conceded that the farm bill was dead because there were not enough votes to override the presidential veto.

8 About 80 persons were killed and more than 200 injured when a car bomb exploded in a Shi'ite Muslim suburb of Beirut, Lebanon. The principal target was apparently Sheikh Muhammad Hussein Fadlallah, the spiritual leader of the Party of God, a fundamentalist Muslim group that endorsed Ayatollah Ruhollah Khomeini's pan-Islamic revolution. A spokesman for the sheikh claimed that Fadlallah had miraculously escaped injury.

10 Konstantin U. Chernenko, general secretary of the Communist Party of the Soviet Union and chairman of the Presidium of the Supreme Soviet (president), died in Moscow after a long illness. The 73-year-old leader had replaced Yuri Andropov as head of the Communist Party in February 1984. The official announcement of Chernenko's death was made on March 11, the same day 54-year-old Mikhail Gorbachev was named to succeed him as party secretary.

12 Soviet and U.S. officials came together in Geneva for their first formal arms control negotiations in 15 months. The seriousness of the talks was underscored by the fact that the Soviet Union did not ask for a postponement when news of Konstantin Chernenko's death on March 10 was announced.

15 With Brazil's 75-year-old President-elect Tancredo Neves critically ill, José Sarney was sworn in as the country's new vice-president and assumed responsibility for the government as interim president. The ceremony brought to an end 21 years of military rule in the largest country in South America. The civilian government's most urgent task was to find a way to solve the country's severe economic problems.

Raymond J. Donovan resigned as secretary of the U.S. Department of Labor after a New York State judge refused to dismiss an October 1984 indictment against him. As a consequence, a jury would decide whether or not Donovan was guilty of fraud and larceny. He was the first active member of a presidential Cabinet ever to be indicted.

17 Canadian Prime Minister Brian Mulroney announced in Quebec that he and President Reagan had, after brief consultation, appointed members to a joint team that would study ways of solving the problem of acid rain. "We have broken a three-year deadlock," he said, "by agreeing to our common and shared responsibility to preserve our common environment."

18 Leonard Goldenson, chairman and chief executive officer of ABC, one of three major television networks in the U.S., publicly acknowledged that he had accepted an offer from Capital Cities Communications Inc. to buy ABC. The deal, worked out with Thomas S. Murphy, the chairman and chief executive officer of Capital Cities, involved more than $3.5 billion. It thus became the largest business acquisition in U.S. history outside the oil industry.

The U.S. Supreme Court in a 7–2 vote upheld a lower federal court decision by ruling that the limit of $1,000 on the amount of money a political action committee could spend on behalf of a presidential candidate in a general election was a violation of constitutionally guaranteed free speech and association.

20 By a vote of 116 to 93, Belgium's Parliament approved the government's decision to deploy cruise missiles as part of its commitment to the North Atlantic Treaty Organization (NATO).

21 In one of South Africa's most violent racial incidents in many years, police shot and killed 19 blacks near Uitenhage, an industrial area northwest of Port Elizabeth. Black activists in the region were among the strongest supporters of the outlawed African National Congress. These latest killings in South Africa brought the death toll to nearly 250 in just over a year.

24 Arthur Nicholson, Jr., a major in the U.S. Army, was shot and killed while on patrol with his partner near Ludwigslurt, East Germany. A U.S. government spokesman claimed the team was 300 to 500 yd (270 to 450 m) away from a "permanent restricted area" when fired upon by a Soviet sentry. He called the shooting "totally unjustified" and tantamount to murder. The Soviets claimed that one of the Americans had penetrated a restricted area and had photographed combat equipment inside a military installation.

28 In their second and final vote on the issue, members of the U.S. House of Representatives approved, 217–210, President Reagan's request for 21 additional MX missiles at a cost of $1.5 billion.

29 After a marathon bargaining session in Brussels, representatives of the European Economic Community (EEC) announced that Spain and Portugal had agreed to become the 11th and 12th members of the organization on Jan. 1, 1986.

31 The Christian Democratic Party (CDP) of José Napoleón Duarte, president of El Salvador, claimed an unexpected victory in elections for the National Assembly and local offices. Initial results indicated that for the first time the CDP had won an absolute majority in the Assembly and had captured about 54% of the popular vote.

(Above) Canadian Prime Minister Brian Mulroney and U.S. Pres. Ronald Reagan take a stroll during their Quebec meeting on March 17. (Right) British coal miners return to work after nearly a year on strike. The strikers achieved none of their goals. (Below) The body of Soviet leader Konstantin U. Chernenko lies in state following his death on March 10. On March 13 he was buried in a ceremony attended by many heads of government.

APRIL

2 The Israeli Army announced that it had moved about 1,100 "violent" Lebanese prisoners from the Ansar detention camp in southern Lebanon to Israel so they could not disrupt the orderly withdrawal of Israeli troops from Lebanon. Israel later announced that 750 other prisoners would be released as a gesture of goodwill.

6 Gaafar Nimeiry, president of The Sudan, was overthrown in a military coup led by Gen. 'Abd ar-Rahman Siwar ad-Dahab, commander in chief of the armed forces and minister of defense. Nimeiry had named him to both posts just three weeks earlier. The military said it had seized power because of "the worsening situation in the country and the political crisis. . . ." On April 24 The Sudan announced that it would resume diplomatic relations with Libya.

8 The government of India filed suit in a Manhattan Federal District Court charging Union Carbide Corp. with responsibility for the gas leak at its plant in Bhopal, India, on Dec. 3, 1984. At least 1,700 people were killed and 200,000 more were injured.

9 In a nationally televised address, Japanese Prime Minister Yasuhiro Nakasone urged his fellow countrymen to buy foreign goods even though certain local industries would "suffer pain" as a consequence. He warned his audience that failure to resolve Japan's foreign trade surplus could affect "the life and death of our country," because Japan could not survive without free trade.

11 Enver Hoxha, Albania's 76-year-old Communist leader, died after a long, debilitating illness. As a World War II Communist guerrilla he had fought Italian and German occupation forces in his country, which had been annexed by Italy in 1939. After the war he established a Stalinist government, which he headed for 40 years.

15 The South African government announced that it would abolish laws that forbade marriage and sex between whites and nonwhites. Although many welcomed the announcement, antiapartheid activists said it was merely cosmetic, a minor concession since blacks were still not allowed to exercise any political power. The urgent need to find a solution for South Africa's racial problems had been underscored two days earlier when some 60,000 persons attended a funeral ceremony in Kwanobuhle township near Uitenhage for 27 blacks killed during riots in the past month in black townships.

17 The antidiscrimination section of Canada's three-year-old constitution became the law of the land even though many local laws had not yet been rewritten to conform to the principles laid down in the new Charter of Rights and Freedoms. The charter forbids discrimination on grounds of sex, color, race, ethnic origin, religion, or mental or physical disability.

19 During a visit to New Zealand, Hu Yaobang (Hu Yao-pang), general secretary of the Chinese Communist Party, told reporters that China would cut about one million troops from its army by the end of 1986. The reduction would affect about 25% of those now in military service.

20 At least 50 persons were killed and 250 injured during six days of riots in Karachi, Pak. The violence began on April 15 when a bus driver lost control of his vehicle and killed two female college students. Resentment against the Pashtun driver turned into anger against all Pashtuns, a minority group with ethnic ties to neighboring Afghans. Casualties mounted as rival groups attacked one another with guns, knives, and axes.

21 Tancredo Neves, Brazil's 75-year-old president-elect, died after intestinal surgery in São Paulo. On March 15 Vice-Pres. José Sarney had taken his oath of office and assumed the duties of president because Neves was hospitalized in critical condition. Sarney, who automatically became head of the government when Neves died, would be Brazil's first civilian president after five successive military regimes that held power for 21 years.

23 At least 15 persons were believed killed and about 100 injured as rival Hindu castes continued to clash in the state of Gujarat, India. In the industrial city of Ahmadabad, where much of the violence occurred, at least 55 persons had been killed in riots during the preceding two months. The intercaste troubles had begun after state authorities announced that nearly half of government-controlled positions would be reserved for lower caste Hindus, who up to that time had been allotted 31% of such jobs.

25 Peru's United Left coalition of Socialist and Communist parties decided to concede a scheduled runoff election between its Marxist candidate, Alfonso Barrantes Lingan, and Alan García Pérez, whose 46% of the popular vote in the April 14 presidential election was nearly twice that garnered by Barrantes.

Representatives from more than 80 nations ended a two-day meeting in Bandung, Indon., that commemorated the 30th anniversary of the founding of the nonaligned movement. In 1955 twenty-nine less developed African and Asian nations agreed not to become embroiled in the cold war that was being waged by the U.S. and the Soviet Union. One of many policy statements at that time was an evenhanded condemnation of "colonialism in all its manifestations." At both conferences China affirmed its intention to remain part of the nonaligned world.

26 Representatives of Bulgaria, Czechoslovakia, East Germany, Hungary, Poland, Romania, and the Soviet Union signed a 20-year extension of their Warsaw Pact treaty. Mikhail Gorbachev, the new leader of the Soviet Union, used the occasion to urge the U.S. again to accept a mutual cutback of nuclear weapons, but he noted that no such agreement was possible as long as the U.S. pursued plans to deploy nuclear weapons in space.

An estimated 100,000 Argentines heeded a call from Pres. Raúl Alfonsín and gathered in Buenos Aires's Plaza de Mayo to hear a plea for national unity and for support of an austerity program that held no promise "for a better standard of living this year."

29 Israel completed the second of a planned three-stage pullout from Lebanon by withdrawing its troops from the eastern and central sections of the country. Shi-'ite militiamen quickly moved to prevent the Palestine Liberation Organization from returning to three Palestinian camps in the vicinity.

(Above) Japanese Prime Minister Yasuhiro Nakasone conceded in a nationally televised address that some of Japan's import regulations had limited foreign access to Japanese markets. (Below) Brazil's newly sworn president, José Sarney, and his wife attend the state funeral of Tancredo Neves, Brazil's president-elect, who died on April 21.

MAY

2 Rebecca Quijano, a 32-year-old businesswoman, testified in a packed Manila courtroom that she was a passenger on the same plane that took Benigno Aquino, Jr., back to the Philippines in August 1983 and that she "saw a soldier holding a gun aimed at the back of Senator Aquino's head, and simultaneously I heard a gunshot."

E. F. Hutton, the fifth largest brokerage firm in the U.S., pleaded guilty in a Pennsylvania federal court to some 2,000 counts of mail and wire fraud. The company agreed to pay $2 million in criminal fines, $750,000 to cover the cost of the Justice Department's investigation, and as much as $8 million to about 400 banks that had been victimized over a 20-month period beginning in July 1980.

5 President Reagan, ignoring the protests of Jewish organizations, U.S. veterans' groups, and numerous congressmen, visited a military cemetery in West Germany in the company of Chancellor Helmut Kohl. When news spread that Reagan would visit the cemetery, a heated controversy had arisen because 49 Nazi SS graves were among the 2,000 graves of German soldiers in the Bitburg cemetery.

10 Sikh extremists killed at least 70 persons and injured about 150 others in terrorist attacks in New Delhi and the states of Haryana, Uttar Pradesh, and Punjab. Most of the casualties occurred in New Delhi, the nation's capital, where a series of explosions was set off, apparently by remote control.

11 Leftist guerrillas in El Salvador acknowledged in a radio broadcast that they had made mayors their new target because local government officials had become part of "counterinsurgency plans financed by the United States."

14 The Sri Lankan government reported that Tamil separatists disguised as soldiers had carried out several terrorist attacks killing nearly 150 persons in Anuradhapura, about 105 mi (165 km) north of Colombo, the capital. It was the first Tamil attack in an area heavily populated by Sinhalese.

17 The Japanese Diet (parliament) approved a bill that opened up new job opportunities for women by removing certain restrictions on the time of day and number of hours they could work. Starting in 1986 employers were expected to begin adopting new policies to eliminate sex discrimination in hiring, promoting, and assigning jobs.

19 Lebanese Shi'ite Muslim militiamen, mostly members of Amal, began a fierce battle to drive Palestinian forces, mostly Sunnite Muslims, out of three refugee camps—Sabra and Shatila in West Beirut and Burj al-Brajneh, south of the city. On May 23 more than 200 persons were reported to have been killed.

20 John A. Walker, a retired U.S. Navy chief warrant officer, was arrested by agents of the Federal Bureau of Investigation and charged with spying for the Soviet Union. Walker reportedly had in his possession classified documents passed to him by his 22-year-old son Michael, a yeoman third class, who was subsequently arrested aboard the aircraft carrier USS *Nimitz* and returned to the U.S. On May 29 Arthur Walker, a retired navy lieutenant commander and brother of John, was arrested and charged with espionage.

20 Under the supervision of International Red Cross officials, Israel released 394 guerrillas in Geneva and an additional 756 other prisoners in the Middle East in exchange for the last three Israeli soldiers still held by the Palestinians. The Israeli government was criticized by those who felt the nation had compromised its policy of never capitulating to terrorists. Japan, too, was upset because Israel had ignored a specific request not to release Kozo Okamoto, a member of the Japanese Red Army. He had been part of a three-man team of assassins who in 1972 killed 26 persons at the Lod Airport in Israel.

21 Indian Prime Minister Rajiv Gandhi arrived in Moscow for talks with Mikhail Gorbachev, the leader of the Soviet Union. During the visit two trade accords were signed guaranteeing India a credit of more than $1.1 billion to finance the buying of Soviet goods and services, especially in the area of energy.

23 About 70 South Korean university students began a peaceful occupation of the second-floor library of the U.S. Information Service Building in downtown Seoul. There was no effort to take hostages or restrict access to other parts of the building. The students demanded that the U.S. government apologize for its alleged role in suppressing the 1980 political upheaval in Kwangju that claimed some 200 lives. On May 26 the students left the building chanting "Down with the military dictatorship of Chun Doo Hwan" (president of South Korea). On May 28 the government arrested 25 of the protesters.

25 As many as 40,000 people in Bangladesh were believed drowned when a killer cyclone swept across the Bay of Bengal and drove a one-story-high wall of water across small inhabited islands in the delta of the Ganges River. Accurate figures on the number of those who lost their lives would probably never be known. When the fury subsided, countless human bodies were seen floating in the bay or strewn across the muddy terrain.

Sheikh Jabir al-Ahmad al-Jabir as-Sabah, the ruler of Kuwait, escaped serious injury when a bomb-laden car deliberately rammed his motorcade as it sped toward Al Sif Palace. The immediate motive for the attack was reinforcement of terrorist demands that 17 convicted Shi'ite Muslims held in Kuwait be exchanged for four Americans and two Frenchmen kidnapped in Lebanon.

28 Representatives of North and South Korea came together in Seoul to discuss possible ways of gradually moving toward reunification of their divided country. Although the parties could not agree on an agenda for the discussion, the mere fact that the two Koreas were holding formal talks for the first time in 12 years raised hopes that better relations might slowly be established if the talks continued.

President Reagan, in a nationally televised address, set forth his proposals for a new federal income tax plan that would be "clear, simple, and fair" and "reduce the tax burdens on the working people of this country." The new tax code, which would have to be enacted into law by Congress, would among many other things eliminate local and state taxes as deductible items.

(Above) On May 5 Pres. Ronald Reagan and West German Chancellor Helmut Kohl (center, left) visited Bitburg cemetery, where Nazi war dead were buried. (Below) Floodwaters stand in Bangladesh, where as many as 40,000 persons may have drowned when a cyclone drove a wall of water across settlements in the Ganges River delta.

JUNE

2 Incomplete election returns indicated that Pasok, the party of Prime Minister Andreas Papandreou, had won a majority of the seats in Greece's 300-member Parliament, but its percentage of the popular vote was somewhat less than in 1981. During the campaign the prime minister promised again to close down four U.S. military bases in Greece, but he conspicuously made no mention of an earlier pledge to withdraw from NATO and the European Communities.

3 The Vatican and Italy signed a concordat that replaced the Lateran Treaty of 1929 and significantly reduced the privileges the church had previously enjoyed in Italy. The new treaty no longer recognized Roman Catholicism as the state religion or Rome as a sacred city, but it affirmed the independence of Vatican City. Other provisions ended compulsory Catholic instruction in public schools and abrogated Vatican ownership of the Jewish catacombs.

8 In elections to the 352-seat Hungarian Parliament, 25 of 71 independent candidates waged successful campaigns. All were first obliged to pledge in writing that, if elected, they would not challenge the socialist structure of the government. Since 1949, when Hungary held its first election under Communist rule, only one candidate had been elected to Parliament without the endorsement of the (Communist) Patriotic People's Front.

10 Israel completed its three-stage withdrawal of combat troops from Lebanon but left an unannounced number of patrols, advisers, and observers in the "security zone" it had established in Lebanon along Israel's northern border. The feeling in Israel was one of general relief that the nation's three-year direct military involvement in Lebanon had ended.

11 Karen Ann Quinlan died in Morris Plains, N.J., at the age of 31. After she became irreversibly comatose on April 14, 1975, her parents sparked a long court battle when they urged the doctors to disconnect the respirator so that their daughter could die "with grace and dignity." The New Jersey Supreme Court decided in a unanimous opinion that the father had the right to seek out doctors who would remove the life-supporting systems. After the respirator was removed, Quinlan continued to breathe on her own and survived on only the food she received through a nasogastric tube.

12 The U.S. House of Representatives voted 248–184 to allocate $27 million in nonmilitary aid to Nicaraguan *contras* fighting to overthrow the country's Sandinista government. The bill stated that neither the Pentagon nor the Central Intelligence Agency could distribute the money, which would be dispersed over a period of nine months.

Indian Prime Minister Rajiv Gandhi was welcomed at the White House by President Reagan, who said that "shared democratic ideas serve as a bridge between us." The next day in an address before a joint session of the U.S. Congress, Gandhi said that India advocated independence and a nonaligned status for Afghanistan.

14 Two Shi'ite Muslims, said to be members of Islamic Jihad ("Islamic Holy War"), hijacked a Trans World Airlines plane after it left Athens on a scheduled flight to Rome. Of the 153 passengers and crew aboard, 104 were Americans. The pilot was forced to fly to Beirut, where one of the passengers, 23-year-old U.S. Navy diver Robert Stethem, was brutally beaten and then shot to death. The hijackers demanded that Israel free the more than 700 prisoners (mostly Shi'ites) it had captured in Lebanon. Finally, on June 30, the last 39 hostages were released. Though Israel released 31 prisoners on June 24, it insisted that the decision was in no way connected with the hijacking since it had long intended to release the prisoners.

Three political activists were sentenced to prison in Gdansk, Poland, after being found guilty of fomenting civil disorder. They had been accused of planning a nationwide 15-minute strike, which never took place, to protest against increases in food prices.

17 South Africa named a new multiracial administration in South West Africa/Namibia but retained the right to defend the country and dictate its foreign policy. In 1978 South Africa had attempted to defuse political unrest in Namibia by installing a surrogate regime, but when the plan collapsed in 1983, South Africa resumed direct control over the former German colony. By June 19 the UN Security Council had issued a weak statement calling for "appropriate measures" against South Africa if it did not respond to UN efforts to grant Namibia full independence.

20 After a series of protests directed at the regime of Pres. Augusto Pinochet Ugarte and the arrest of demonstrators in various parts of the country, five electricity transmitting towers were damaged by bombs in Chile's central valley. The saboteurs, who cut off power to some nine million people, were not identified. However, on May 24 the Manuel Rodríguez Patriotic Front, a leftist guerrilla organization, had claimed responsibility for a similar bombing that had damaged Chile's largest power station.

Seven judges of the Norwegian Crown Court convicted Arne Treholt, a 42-year-old former diplomat, of espionage and sentenced him to 20 years in prison. Treholt was found guilty of passing on classified or sensitive information to agents of the Soviet Union from 1974 until his arrest in January 1984.

21 An international team of forensic experts announced in São Paulo, Brazil, that the exhumed remains of a man who had reportedly died from drowning in 1979 were in fact those of Josef Mengele, the notorious Nazi doctor. Mengele, who had been hunted for years, had sent tens of thousands of men, women, and children to their deaths at the Auschwitz-Birkenau extermination camp in Poland and had personally selected others, especially twins, as subjects for sadistic experiments.

23 An Air India Boeing 747, on a flight from Toronto via Montreal and London to Bombay, plunged into the ocean off Ireland. There were no signs that any of the 307 passengers or 22 members of the crew had survived. The Indian minister of state for civil aviation said there was a distinct possibility that someone had placed a bomb aboard the aircraft. After the crash two groups claimed responsibility for destroying the aircraft and killing the 329 persons onboard: the Sikh Student Federation and the Kashmir Liberation Army.

(Above) Hooded Shi'ite hijackers of Trans World Airlines Flight 847 lead a demonstration against the U.S. and Israel at Beirut airport on June 21. (Below) Daniel Muñoz, a forensic specialist at the São Paulo, Brazil, coroner's office, exhibits a skull that he reported to be that of Josef Mengele, the notorious Nazi war criminal.

1 Eduard A. Shevardnadze was made a full member of the Soviet Communist Party Politburo, the fourth such appointment made by Mikhail Gorbachev since he came to power in March. On July 2 Shevardnadze replaced Andrei Gromyko as foreign minister. Gromyko, who was 75 years old, had been honored with the title of president of the Soviet Union after years of dedicated service.

6 The Zimbabwe African National Union-Patriotic Front won 63 of 79 contested seats allotted to blacks in Zimbabwe's 100-seat Parliament. Prime Minister Robert Mugabe interpreted the victory as a mandate to do away with the British-drafted constitution, which reserved 20 seats for whites, who comprised less than 2% of the population.

7 The 13 oil ministers of the Organization of Petroleum Exporting Countries (OPEC) ended a three-day meeting in Vienna without agreeing on any change in the price or production level of oil. Toward the end of the month the oil ministers met again, this time in Geneva. In a 10–3 vote they agreed to reduce some oil prices moderately, but Algeria, Libya, and Iran refused to endorse the decision of the majority.

9 David Stockman announced that he would resign on August 1 as director of the Office of Management and Budget for the Reagan administration. Stockman, who had fought tirelessly to control federal budget deficits by reducing government spending, had exercised exceptional power during his tenure.

10 Two explosions aboard the *Rainbow Warrior,* a ship belonging to an environmentalist group called Greenpeace, sank the 160-ft (49-m) vessel while it was moored to a wharf in Auckland, N.Z. A Portuguese-born photographer with Dutch citizenship was killed. The ship had been scheduled to sail to the South Pacific to disrupt French nuclear tests. On July 11 Auckland's detective superintendent reported that preliminary evidence indicated sabotage.

13 President Reagan underwent major abdominal surgery at the Bethesda (Md.) Naval Medical Center to remove a polyp found growing in his large intestine. Though the surgeons reported there was no visual evidence of cancer, a biopsy later revealed that the growth was malignant. On July 20 the president returned to the White House looking remarkably fit. Doctors expressed confidence that the timely surgery had prevented cancer cells from migrating to any other part of the president's body.

15 A 12-day women's conference opened in Nairobi, Kenya, to mark the end of the United Nations Decade for Women. The meeting was called to assess the achievements and failures of the past 10 years and to set goals for the next 15 years. More than 2,000 official delegates came from nearly 160 nations, 8 of which were not members of the UN.

17 The Japanese Supreme Court ruled that the 1983 elections to the Diet (parliament) were invalid because inequities in the procedures made some votes worth more than others and thus violated the constitution. The court, however, did not invalidate the results because, it said, it would not be in the public interest to do so. The ruling, which was the third such declaration since 1976, increased the likelihood that a special session of the Diet would be called to consider reapportionment.

18 The South Korean government announced that 56 student activists had been arrested in recent weeks and that 20 others were still being sought; all were said by the government to belong to a "pro-Communist organization" that planned the May 23 sit-in at a U.S. government building in Seoul.

20 The Organization of African Unity ended a three-day meeting in Addis Ababa, Eth., with a declaration that most African nations were on the brink of economic collapse. While acknowledging the existence of "some domestic policy shortcomings," the delegates placed most of the blame for Africa's problems on "an unjust and inequitable economic system."

22 An Israeli court sentenced 15 Jews to prison for crimes committed against Palestinian Arabs on the West Bank. On July 10 a panel of three judges had found the suspects guilty of a number of crimes, including murder, membership in a terrorist organization, and plotting to blow up Islam's holiest shrine in Jerusalem. Three of the 15 who stood trial were sentenced to life imprisonment; the 12 others received sentences ranging from three to ten years.

23 President Reagan, in an abbreviated ceremony, welcomed Chinese Pres. Li Xiannian (Li Hsien-nien) to the White House to mark the beginning of an official state visit. The most important event during Li's visit was the signing of a nuclear agreement between the U.S. and China. China would receive U.S. nuclear equipment and technology with the understanding that they would be used exclusively for peaceful purposes.

24 Indian Prime Minister Rajiv Gandhi told a surprised Parliament that an agreement had been reached with moderate Sikh leaders that was designed to lessen hostility toward the central government. Concessions included the enlargement of Punjab's boundaries to increase the Sikh population within the state and thus enhance Sikh political power in the area.

27 Ugandan Pres. Milton Obote was overthrown in a military coup led by Brig. Basilio Olara Okello. On July 29 Lieut. Gen. Tito Okello, who was not related to the leader of the coup, was sworn in as interim head of state.

28 Alan García Pérez, the 36-year-old leader of the Alianza Popular Revolucionaria Americana, replaced Fernando Belaúnde Terry as president of Peru. García confirmed his intention to deal directly with Peru's creditors rather than with the International Monetary Fund, which García claimed shared responsibility for many of Peru's current financial problems.

30 The foreign ministers of 35 nations convened in Helsinki, Fin., to mark the tenth anniversary of the signing of the Helsinki accords on security and cooperation in Europe. U.S. Secretary of State George Shultz used the occasion to accuse the Soviet Union of violating human rights; the new Soviet foreign minister, Eduard Shevardnadze (who had replaced Andrei Gromyko after his elevation to the presidency), denounced the U.S. for building up its military arsenal. The two men later met to discuss plans for the scheduled November meeting between Soviet leader Mikhail Gorbachev and President Reagan.

(Above) Chinese Pres. Li Xiannian (Li Hsien-nien) speaks at a White House ceremony marking the beginning of his state visit on July 23. (Right) U.S. Secretary of State George Shultz (right) greets new Soviet Foreign Minister Eduard A. Shevardnadze in Helsinki, Finland, on July 30. (Below) Sabotage was suspected in the sinking of the Rainbow Warrior, *flagship of the Greenpeace environmentalist group, in Auckland, New Zealand, on July 10.*

AUGUST

1 After months of haggling, the U.S. Senate and House of Representatives approved the basic outline for a 1986 federal budget that would trim $55.5 billion from the projected deficit and $276.2 billion from deficits over the next three years. Some members of Congress believed the latter projection was overly optimistic. The 1986 budget set spending at $967.6 billion, revenues at $795.7 billion, and the resultant deficit at $171.9 billion. Revenue sharing with the states was the only major federal program eliminated.

5 The trial of 16 black leaders, all charged with treason, got under way in Pietermaritzburg, South Africa. The accused were members of the United Democratic Front, which opposed the government of Pres. P. W. Botha. The defendants were accused of forming an alliance with the outlawed African National Congress, which was based in Zambia and was committed to overthrowing the white government of South Africa. Twenty-two other blacks were facing charges of treason in a separate trial.

Four members of a Puerto Rican terrorist group called the Armed Forces of National Liberation (FALN) were convicted of seditious conspiracy in a Chicago Federal District Court. The FALN had taken responsibility for some 120 bombings in U.S. cities between 1974 and 1983. Five persons had been killed and many buildings severely damaged. On October 4 three defendants were all sentenced to 35 years in prison. One defendant, who was judged to have been only peripherally involved, was placed on probation for five years.

7 King Hassan II of Morocco opened an emergency meeting of the Arab League hoping that frank discussions of issues that divided Arab nations, including all aspects of the "Palestinian question," would revitalize the organization. Algeria, Lebanon, Libya, South Yemen, and Syria boycotted the conference and only 10 of the 16 nations in attendance were represented by heads of state. In a final communiqué, the participants "took note" of the Jordanian-Palestinian plan for peace talks with Israel, thereby satisfying both those who supported talks and those who opposed them.

12 A Japan Air Lines jumbo jet crashed in central Japan after the pilot lost control of the disabled aircraft. Only 4 of the 524 persons aboard were found alive when rescue teams finally reached the site of the crash. It was the worst single plane disaster in the history of aviation.

13 The Philippine National Assembly's Committee on Justice, Human Rights, and Good Government rejected a motion to impeach Pres. Ferdinand Marcos for alleged graft and corruption, violations of the constitution, and other "high crimes." Sixteen of the 25 members of the committee belonged to the ruling New Society Movement (NSM). One member of the opposition remarked: "If this motion is overruled, it will not be by the merits of the case but by the tyranny of numbers."

14 The government of Vietnam turned over to U.S. officials what were said to be the remains of 26 Americans killed during the Vietnam war. The remains were then flown to Honolulu, where experts would attempt to make positive identifications. A Vietnamese deputy foreign minister pledged that Vietnam would exert every effort within the next two years to find the remains of all Americans still listed as missing in action so that the matter could finally be put to rest to the satisfaction of the U.S. government.

15 South African Pres. P. W. Botha, in a speech many hoped would signal a historic change in the country's system of apartheid, told an audience of 1,800 whites in Durban that he was "not prepared to lead the white South Africans and other minority groups on a road to abdication and suicide." The following day Bishop Desmond Tutu, the 1984 recipient of the Nobel Peace Prize, said he felt, after hearing Botha's speech, that the nation was "on the brink of a catastrophe."

20 Sant Harchand Singh Longowal, president of the moderate Sikh party Akali Dal, was assassinated by fellow Sikhs in Punjab. On July 24 Longowal and Indian Prime Minister Rajiv Gandhi had signed an accord that both hoped would end violence between Sikhs and Hindus in Punjab and quiet demands of Sikh extremists for total independence from India.

A car bomb detonated in Saddun Square in Tripoli, Lebanon, killed 44 persons and wounded 90. It was the fifth such explosion in Lebanon in a week and raised the cumulative death toll to about 150. In the latest incident the bomb-laden car had been parked near the home of Sheikh Kenaan Naji, the leader of the Soldiers of God. The group was a Sunnite Muslim fundamentalist militia backed by the Palestine Liberation Organization (PLO). There was speculation that Syria may have instigated the bombing as part of its effort to weaken the PLO. On August 17 at least 50 people had been killed when a car bomb was detonated in a Christian suburb of East Beirut. Two days later 29 persons died when a similar explosion took place in the Muslim section of the city.

23 West Germany reported that Hans J. Tiedge had defected to East Germany. He had held sensitive posts in West Germany's counterintelligence agency for two decades and knew the identities of numerous contact persons in East Germany. It seemed likely, therefore, that Tiedge had been at least partly responsible for the apprehension of scores of West German agents during the previous 18 months.

27 The U.S. Treasury Department announced that it had fined the Crocker National Bank of San Francisco $2,250,000 for failing to report some $3.9 billion in cash transactions over a period of four years. A Treasury spokesman said there was no evidence that bank employees had deliberately laundered money, even though the bank had unquestionably been used for that purpose by drug dealers from Mexico and the Far East.

31 An estimated 70,000 South African blacks gathered in the small township of Duncan Village for a mass funeral of 18 persons who had been killed in recent violence. It was believed to have been the largest funeral procession since violence began to sweep across the country 12 months earlier. The gathering also disregarded provisions of the state of emergency that Pres. P. W. Botha had declared in July. On August 9 officials had reported that 32 people had been killed in the Cape Town area in just 24 hours.

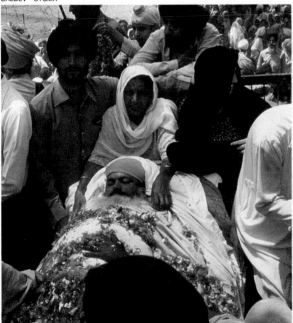

(Above) The body of moderate Sikh leader Sant Harchand Singh Longowal is borne to a funeral pyre following his assassination in India on August 20. (Right) Rescuers comb the wreckage of a Japan Air Lines jumbo jet that crashed in central Japan on August 12, killing 520 persons. (Below) About 70,000 South African blacks gathered on August 31 at the funeral of 18 persons killed in racial violence.

SEPTEMBER

1 A team of U.S. and French marine explorers positively identified the wreck of the luxury liner *Titanic,* which sank some 95 mi (150 km) off the coast of Newfoundland in 1912 with the loss of more than 1,500 lives. It did not appear likely that any effort would be made to bring the ship to the surface.

2 The Khmer Rouge announced that Pol Pot was retiring as leader of the Communist organization. He had ruled Kampuchea for four years until Vietnam invaded the country in 1979. As many as two million people were believed to have been killed during Pol Pot's reign of terror. Many tended to doubt that Pol Pot was relinquishing power, except perhaps in name.

6 The South African government announced the closing of 454 schools for students of mixed race in the Cape Town area because, it said, violence threatened the safety of those attending classes. Some 360,000 students were affected.

9 White and black youths began rampaging through the Handsworth area of Birmingham, Britain's second largest city, after firemen arrived to extinguish a blaze in an abandoned building. The area's population contained a high proportion of unemployed youths and drug users. The looting and arson, which were directed especially against Asians, continued the following day as police tried to protect themselves against rocks, bottles, and gasoline bombs and attempted to prevent the turmoil from spreading farther into nearby inner-city neighborhoods.

Some 400–500 soldiers, many said to have acted out of loyalty to former colonel Manoon Roopkachorn, initiated an early morning coup in Bangkok, Thailand, while the prime minister was in Indonesia and the head of the armed forces was in Europe. Troops loyal to the government ended the rebellion about ten hours after it began. At least four persons were killed, including two members of an NBC News television crew.

10 The eldest daughter of José Napoleón Duarte, president of El Salvador, was kidnapped outside a university on one of the main streets of San Salvador. One of her bodyguards was killed and another wounded in the attack. On September 13 and 14 an anonymous caller, claiming to represent the little-known Pedro Pablo Castillo Front, had said his group was holding the woman. The caller demanded freedom for certain imprisoned rebels and an end to government military operations against the guerrilla forces.

The foreign ministers of nine full members and two future members of the European Communities (EC) approved sanctions against South Africa in the hope that such action would induce the government to end its policy of apartheid. Though none of the sanctions was considered severe, South Africa was put on notice that even friendly nations supported the demands of South Africa's blacks for an end to apartheid.

11 Nine military officers who ruled Argentina during six years of extraordinary violence went on trial in Buenos Aires. They were charged with murder, torture, and kidnapping involving more than 9,000 citizens who "disappeared" during that period.

12 The British government announced that Oleg A. Gordievski, a high-ranking member of the Soviet intelligence agency (KGB), had defected in London and that 25 Soviet spies, identified by Gordievski, had been ordered to leave the country for activities "totally incompatible with their status and declared tasks." One report from Denmark claimed that Gordievski had been a double agent since the 1970s. On September 17 West Germans learned that a secretary in Chancellor Helmut Kohl's office had defected to East Germany with her husband. The first public revelation that Soviet spies had been operating at high levels in the West German government had occurred on August 27. Toward the end of September one senior Soviet military intelligence officer defected to the U.S., and it was also confirmed that another had defected to Greece in May. The former claimed that several employees of the U.S. Central Intelligence Agency were engaged in espionage for the U.S.S.R.

16 The Chinese Communist Party announced that 10 of the 24 members of the Politburo were retiring to make room for younger persons. China also confirmed that 64 of the 340 members of the Central Committee, which appoints members to the Politburo, were also being replaced. An additional 56 persons were named to the Central Advisory Commission and 31 to the Central Commission for Party Discipline Inspection. All replaced aging functionaries.

19 The first of two powerful earthquakes hit central and southwestern Mexico, causing huge buildings to crumble in ruins. The death toll, which was especially high in Mexico City, could not be immediately assessed because thousands of people were trapped alive beneath the rubble. Several times newly born babies were rescued alive from the ruins of a hospital, but it gradually became apparent that more than 20,000 people had lost their lives.

20 French Prime Minister Laurent Fabius accepted the resignation of Defense Minister Charles Hernu and fired Adm. Pierre Lacoste as head of the French intelligence agency as evidence mounted that top government officials had been involved in sabotaging a ship belonging to the environmentalist group Greenpeace that had been tied up at the New Zealand port of Auckland. The *Rainbow Warrior* had planned to sail to South Pacific waters to disrupt nuclear tests being conducted by the French government. A Portuguese-born photographer with Dutch citizenship was killed by the explosives.

26 The Tunisian government notified Libya that it was severing diplomatic relations. The rupture followed a bitter dispute over Libya's expulsion of some 30,000 Tunisian migrant workers from Tripoli and accusations that four Libyan diplomats had mailed more than 100 letter bombs to Tunisian journalists.

30 Four members of the Soviet embassy were kidnapped by gunmen in West Beirut, Lebanon. The terrorists later said they would kill all four hostages if Soviet- and Syrian-backed leftist militiamen continued to attack the northern Lebanese city of Tripoli, which was held by Sunnite Muslim fundamentalists. On October 2 the body of Arkadi Katakov, a secretary at the embassy, was found in an empty lot. He had been shot in the head. The remaining three hostages were released on October 30.

(Above) Smoke rises from damaged buildings in Birmingham, England, where unemployed white and black youths began rampaging on September 9. (Right) Rescuers in Mexico City search for persons trapped beneath rubble after a powerful earthquake struck central and southwestern Mexico on September 19, killing at least 20,000. (Below) Thai soldiers loyal to the government put down an attempted military coup in Bangkok on September 9.

OCTOBER

1 Israeli military aircraft flew across the Mediterranean to Tunisia, where they virtually obliterated the headquarters of the Palestine Liberation Organization (PLO) near Tunis. Some 60 persons were reported killed, but Yasir Arafat, chairman of the PLO, was not present at the time of the raid. Israel said the bombing raid was undertaken to avenge the murders of three Israelis who were gunned down by Palestinians in Larnaca, Cyprus, on September 25.

3 Mikhail Gorbachev, leader of the Soviet Union, told about 50 members of the French National Assembly that the time had come for the U.S.S.R., France, and Great Britain to negotiate their own separate arms agreement. During a news conference the following day, French Pres. François Mitterrand rejected Gorbachev's proposal for separate negotiations on arms reductions. Sir Geoffrey Howe, Britain's foreign secretary, said in London that no direct negotiations with the U.S.S.R. were possible until the Soviet Union and the U.S. had signed a strategic arms agreement.

7 Four Palestinian terrorists hijacked the Italian cruise ship *Achille Lauro* after it departed Alexandria, Egypt, for Port Said with 400 persons aboard. The terrorists threatened to blow up the ship unless 50 Palestinians were released from Israeli jails. The following day, while the ship was off the coast of Syria, the gunmen shot and killed a 69-year-old disabled American. The drama appeared to have ended when the terrorists surrendered to the Palestine Liberation Organization in Port Said on October 9. Then, on October 10, unscheduled news bulletins interrupted television and radio programs to announce that U.S. F-14 fighters had intercepted an Egyptian plane over the Mediterranean and had ordered it to land at a NATO base in Sicily. Intelligence agents had learned that the four hijackers of the *Achille Lauro* were aboard the aircraft and were being secretly flown to Tunisia. Hosni Mubarak, president of Egypt, expressed outrage that the U.S., a close ally, had "committed piracy"—especially after Egypt had been asked to act as a mediator in the crisis and had negotiated the safe release of hundreds of people, none of whom was Egyptian. U.S. relations with Italy were also strained when Italian officials refused to detain an Arab who, the U.S. said, was suspected of having organized the hijacking.

11 A U.S. State Department official acknowledged that nearly $1 million worth of nonlethal supplies had been flown to an undisclosed location in Central America to aid rebels fighting the Sandinista government of Nicaragua. The shipment, which consisted mainly of shoes, clothing, and medicines, was the first consignment of $27 million in supplies finally approved by the U.S. Congress in July. Though Congress had strictly forbidden the shipment of military supplies, the arrival of clothes and medicines would permit the rebels to use more of the money they had from other sources to satisfy their military needs.

15 Syria announced that Lebanese Christian, Druze, and Shi'ite Muslim militias—the principals in Lebanon's civil war—had for the first time reached basic agreement on a plan to end the decade of civil war. Previous settlements had been ineffectual because the politicians who drew them up had no control over the militias. Syria became directly involved in 1976 when the Arab League asked it to send troops into Lebanon to keep the peace.

The Japanese government of Prime Minister Yasuhiro Nakasone adopted a series of measures to stimulate the nation's economic growth and, it was hoped, curb its huge trade and capital surpluses. According to one estimate, the new policy would increase Japanese imports during 1986 by $2 billion. Some economists, however, were less optimistic because the program included neither tax cuts nor substantial increases in government spending.

16 U.S. Sen. Paul Laxalt held the first of several discussions with Philippine Pres. Ferdinand Marcos in Manila. Laxalt had delivered a message from President Reagan, who, it was reported, expressed grave concern over economic, social, political, and military developments in the Philippines and the need to take prompt action to avert an impending disaster.

21 Israeli Prime Minister Shimon Peres, in a speech before the UN General Assembly, appeared to be willing to accept the notion of an international conference if that seemed essential for Middle East peace negotiations involving King Hussein of Jordan. Israel, however, would insist that the Soviet Union first restore diplomatic relations with Israel if it wanted to participate in the negotiations along with the four other permanent members of the UN Security Council.

24 Salvadoran Pres. José Napoleón Duarte's eldest daughter, Inés Guadalupe Duarte Durán, was released by terrorists 44 days after she and a female companion were kidnapped in San Salvador. The exchange was part of a complicated agreement that included the release of 22 political prisoners and safe passage out of the country for 96 leftist guerrillas who had been disabled during the war. The rebels released the two women and more than 20 mayors of small towns who had been abducted.

The U.S. Senate approved a bill prohibiting the sale of advanced arms to Jordan before March 1, 1986. There was a proviso, however, that the proposed sale of up to $1.9 billion in jet fighters and air defense systems could proceed if Jordan began "direct and meaningful peace negotiations with Israel." King Hussein had held numerous but inconclusive discussions with Yasir Arafat, the chairman of the Palestine Liberation Organization, who represented Palestinian interests in Middle East peace talks. The two men, however, were unable to agree on basic principles before entering into negotiations with Israel.

The United Nations commemorated its 40th anniversary without being able to agree on a declaration to mark the special occasion. Numerous dignitaries from all over the world traveled to New York to address the General Assembly, but despite a shared hope that the special ceremonies at the UN would help revitalize the organization, old animosities surfaced.

26 France carried out its second nuclear test in three days at Mururoa Atoll in the South Pacific. New Zealand scientists, who monitored the explosions from the Cook Islands, estimated the yield to be between 12 and 14 kilotons.

(Above) Egyptian troops guard the Italian liner Achille Lauro *in Port Said after the four Palestinians who hijacked the ship were taken ashore on October 9. (Below) French Pres. François Mitterrand (right) and Soviet leader Mikhail Gorbachev review a color guard in Paris upon Gorbachev's arrival on October 2 for a state visit.*

NOVEMBER

2 The government of South Africa imposed broad restrictions on journalists, which forbade them, without explicit approval, to "make, take, record, manufacture, reproduce, publish, broadcast or distribute, or take or send to any place within or outside the Republic, any film . . . or any photograph, drawing or other representation, or any sound recording" that dealt with such things as public disturbances, riots, strikes, killings, and property damage. Violators could be imprisoned for up to ten years and fined $8,000.

3 Vitali Yurchenko, who was said to be a high-ranking Soviet KGB agent, astonished U.S. government officials by announcing that he wanted to return to the U.S.S.R. During a news conference held at the Soviet embassy in Washington, Yurchenko told reporters he had been kidnapped in Rome three months earlier and then transported in a drugged state to the U.S., where he was held prisoner by the Central Intelligence Agency. After the U.S. was satisfied that Yurchenko had freely decided to return home, he was allowed to depart by plane on November 6.

During a live television interview transmitted by satellite to the U.S. from Manila, Philippine Pres. Ferdinand Marcos surprised his audience by saying he was willing to support a "snap" presidential election in mid-January provided members of his New Society Movement party approved. On November 14 representatives of various political factions agreed that the election would not be held until sometime in February at the earliest.

7 Government troops and police in Bogotá, Colombia, virtually destroyed the Palace of Justice in an assault against leftist guerrillas of the April 19 Movement who had seized control of the five-story building the previous day and taken dozens of judges and government workers hostage. When the fighting was over, the president of the Supreme Court and 11 other judges were among the hundred persons who had lost their lives.

9 Miroslav Medved, a 25-year-old Ukrainian seaman, left Reserve, La., aboard a Soviet freighter after declaring to the satisfaction of U.S. officials that he had changed his mind about defecting to the West. On October 24 the seaman had jumped into the Mississippi River in an apparent attempt to defect. Though the man was interviewed on shore several times, some charged that U.S. authorities had badly mishandled the case.

11 Italian authorities issued arrest warrants for 16 Palestinians, all thought to have been directly involved in planning or carrying out the hijacking of the cruise ship *Achille Lauro* on October 7. The suspects were said to be members of the Palestine Liberation Front (PLF), one of several factions of the Palestine Liberation Organization. On November 19 authorities confirmed that Muhammad Abbas, the leader of the PLF, was one of those being sought. He had been detained earlier but was released.

12 Arthur Walker, a retired U.S. Navy lieutenant commander, was sentenced to life imprisonment after pleading guilty to charges of espionage. Walker, who was also fined $250,000, had been recruited by his brother to gather classified information.

13 The Nevado del Ruiz volcano, which had been dormant for nearly 400 years, came to life late at night with a violent explosion. An estimated 25,000 were killed as raging waters and a sea of mud swept through surrounding valleys and obliterated entire villages. The snow-capped volcano was located 85 mi (135 km) northwest of the Colombian capital city of Bogotá. Although rescue teams began work immediately, it was soon evident that most of those who had disappeared would never be found alive.

19 For the first time in six years, the leaders of the world's two most powerful nations met face to face in Geneva. The initial meeting between President Reagan and Soviet leader Mikhail Gorbachev continued for two hours. A second session later in the day also lasted two hours. The following day the two men met again. When the summit concluded the next day with a joint appearance, both leaders agreed that the meetings had been successful inasmuch as both sides had spoken frankly and left with a better understanding of each other's point of view. There was little progress in resolving such issues as arms control, human rights, U.S. plans to develop a space-based defense system, and regional conflicts that in various ways involved both countries, but the two men agreed to meet again in the U.S. in 1986 and in the Soviet Union in 1987.

22 Sir Roland Davison, the highest ranking judge in New Zealand, sentenced two French agents to ten years in prison for their roles in blowing up and sinking the *Rainbow Warrior* while it was at berth in Auckland Harbour. A photographer aboard the ship, which belonged to the environmentalist organization Greenpeace, was killed by the explosions.

23 An Egyptian Boeing 737 airliner, on a night flight from Athens to Cairo, was hijacked by terrorists who forced the pilot to land on the Mediterranean island of Malta. Egyptian commandos stormed the plane about 8:15 the next evening. Of the original 98 passengers and crew, 57 died in the gunfight and subsequent fire. The one hijacker who had not died was taken unconscious to a hospital. The hijacking was believed to have been organized by Abu Nidal, a pro-Libyan Palestinian.

27 Jonathan Pollard, a U.S. Navy counterintelligence analyst, appeared in a Washington, D.C., court after admitting he had provided Israel with huge quantities of classified military documents. The judge ordered Pollard held without bail. In a separate hearing in Baltimore, Md., Ronald Pelton, a former communications specialist at the National Security Agency, was also denied bond after being accused of spying for the Soviet Union. In a third court hearing the same day, this one in Alexandria, Va., Larry Wu-tai Chin, a retired analyst with the Central Intelligence Agency, was ordered to remain in custody until he stood trial on charges of spying for China.

The British House of Commons voted 473–47 in favor of giving Ireland a consultative role and official presence in Northern Ireland. It was hoped that such concessions would eventually end the bloodshed and sectarian violence that had plagued that part of the United Kingdom for many years.

(Above) Vitali Yurchenko, a Soviet KGB agent who allegedly defected to the U.S., waves as he boards a Soviet airliner on November 6 near Washington, D.C., before his return to the Soviet Union. (Below) Survivors rest before being evacuated from the site of the November 13 eruption of the Nevado del Ruiz volcano in Colombia.

DECEMBER

2 A three-judge court appointed by Philippine Pres. Ferdinand Marcos acquitted Gen. Fabian Ver and all of the other 25 defendants standing trial for involvement in the assassination of opposition leader Benigno Aquino, Jr., in August 1983. The judges totally rejected the conclusions of an independent panel of civilian investigators who had determined, after months of testimony, that there was convincing evidence that military personnel were involved in the murder.

Nine students, some carrying gasoline bombs, took over the office of the director of the U.S. Culture Office in Kwangju, South Korea. Nine hours later, after negotiations failed, the police moved in. This incident was but the latest in a long series of protests that had taken place in recent months against the government of Pres. Chun Doo Hwan and, in some cases, against U.S. policies.

Voters in the Canadian province of Quebec overwhelmingly backed candidates of the Liberal Party running for seats in the provincial National Assembly. The victory meant that 52-year-old Robert Bourassa, the leader of the Liberals, would once again head the provincial government even though he appeared to have lost the race for his district seat.

4 Gen. Wojciech Jaruzelski, Poland's head of state, met with French Pres. François Mitterrand for more than an hour in Paris. It was the first visit Jaruzelski had made to a Western capital since Poland suppressed Solidarity, the federation of trade unions, and placed the country under martial law in 1981.

6 The U.S. approved an agreement whereby Great Britain would have an active role in research projects linked to the development of a U.S. space-based missile defense system. It appeared that Britain would be awarded contracts to pursue specific intermediate goals that were considered vital to the overall success of the project.

8 Marco Vinicio Cerezo Arévalo, candidate of the Christian Democratic Party, defeated Jorge Carpio Nicolle of the National Union of the Center in a runoff election for the presidency of Guatemala. Cerezo captured two-thirds of the popular vote becoming the country's first nonmilitary president in years.

During a meeting in Geneva, the 13 oil ministers of OPEC agreed in effect that repeated efforts to maintain oil prices by curtailing production had been futile. Instead, OPEC would attempt to recapture its share of the world market by cutting prices as circumstances required.

9 A civilian court in Buenos Aires concluded that five members of two military juntas that ruled Argentina during the 1970s were guilty of serious crimes committed during their campaigns against urban guerrillas. During that period about 9,000 people disappeared and were never seen again. The trial, ordered by Pres. Raúl Alfonsín, was unprecedented in modern Latin-American history.

12 A chartered DC-8 aircraft operated by Arrow Air of Miami, Fla., crashed as it took off from an airport at Gander, Newfoundland. All 256 persons aboard were killed. The victims included 248 U.S. soldiers from the 502nd Infantry of the 101st Airborne Division who were returning home for Christmas after serving with the 11-nation peacekeeping force in the Sinai. There was no immediate explanation for the tragedy, and there were no apparent signs of sabotage.

21 Armed police forcefully removed Winnie Mandela from her home in Soweto, a black township in South Africa, when she refused to promise to observe new but less-restrictive limits on her movements. The next day she was arrested for slipping back into Soweto during the night. Eight days later she was arrested again while attempting to return to Soweto. After being banished to Brandfort eight years earlier, Mandela had complied with government orders until her home was gasoline bombed in September 1985.

Thousands of protesters in various cities and towns of Haiti continued to defy army troops by marching through the streets to demand an end to the dictatorial rule of Pres. Jean-Claude Duvalier. The unprecedented demonstrations were all the more remarkable because they continued even after several young protesters had been killed.

23 President Reagan signed into law two agriculture bills that together constituted the most fundamental change in U.S. government farm policy in half a century. The long-range purpose of the first bill was to make it more profitable and more necessary for U.S. farmers to compete for world markets because they would not be able to rely on generous federal income and price supports. The second bill, which reorganized the Farm Credit System, would permit a new agency to take over billions of dollars of delinquent loans and then resolve each case either by renegotiating the loans or by foreclosing.

24 For reasons that were not immediately clear, several thousand Zulus engaged in a bloody battle with a larger number of Pondo tribesmen near Durban, South Africa. Reports from the area indicated that 53 persons had been killed with spears, knives, and possibly firearms. The number of fatalities was far larger than in previous violent engagements between the two rival tribes.

27 In virtually simultaneous attacks, Palestinian gunmen hurled hand grenades and fired automatic weapons indiscriminately at civilian passengers congregated near El Al Israel Airlines counters at Leonardo da Vinci Airport in Rome and Schwechat Airport in Vienna. The terrorists killed 18 persons and wounded at least 110 others before four of their number were killed by security guards and the other three wounded and subdued. Evidence gathered from the belongings of the terrorists and from interrogations indicated that the men were members of a Palestinian group headed by Abu Nidal, who had broken away from the al-Fatah faction of the Palestine Liberation Organization (PLO) headed by Yasir Arafat. Experts on Middle East terrorism suspected the terrorists had been trained in Iran and had the backing of Libyan leader Col. Muammar Al Qadhafi.

31 Jordan's King Hussein ended a two-day visit to Damascus during which he and Syrian Pres. Hafez al-Assad exchanged views face to face for the first time in six years. No communiqué was issued at the end of the talks, and no details of the discussions were made public.

(Above) Snow-covered wreckage marks the site of the December 12 airplane crash that killed all 248 U.S. servicemen and 8 crew members on board. (Below) Members of Argentina's military listen to verdicts on December 9. Five were found guilty and four acquitted of charges of kidnapping, torture, and murder.

EVENTS
OF THE
YEAR

1985

ADVERTISING

After 99 years the Coca-Cola Co. announced in April 1985 that it was changing the formula for Coke. Industry experts believed the move was an attempt to counter Pepsi Cola's growing popularity. Coca-Cola had 21.8% of the $23 billion U.S. soft-drink market, compared with 17% for Pepsi, but Pepsi's share had been increasing. Coca-Cola had spent four years on research and development of the new beverage. However, strong consumer and bottler discontent forced it to reintroduce the original formula, and in July board chairman Roberto Goizueta announced that the reformulated drink would be sold as new Coca-Cola and the original as Coca-Cola Classic. Early figures suggested that Classic was leading new Coca-Cola in sales.

In May the U.S. Supreme Court upheld the right of a lawyer to present truthful newspaper and magazine advertising, including legal advice, to solicit clients on specific legal problems. The high court ruled 5–3 that the legal advice, as long as it is truthful and not deceptive, is protected by the guarantee of freedom of speech in the First Amendment to the Constitution. The case involved a lawyer whose ads advised women that they might be able to sue the manufacturer of the Dalkon Shield if they had been injured by the birth-control device. The decision overturned an Ohio state court ruling that the ads violated rules against offering unsolicited legal advice and against recommending oneself as a lawyer.

Each year *Advertising Age* publishes a list of the 100 leading national advertisers in the U.S. In 1984 these advertisers spent $22.5 billion, an increase of 16% over the 1983 total. Procter & Gamble was the biggest spender, followed by General Motors, Sears, Beatrice, and R. J. Reynolds Industries.

The five leading users of network television in 1984 were Procter & Gamble, AT&T, General Motors, General Foods, and American Home Products. Network television accounted for $6,460,000,000 of advertising spending by the 100 largest national advertisers. Procter & Gamble spent $412.7 million, or 47% of its advertising budget, on this medium.

Old Cola Drinkers of America founder Gay Mullins shows his distaste for newly formulated Coca-Cola. The manufacturer eventually restored production of "old" Coke, renaming it Coca-Cola Classic.

RICH FRISHMAN—PICTURE GROUP

General Motors was the largest user of newspaper advertising, while R. J. Reynolds was the largest magazine advertiser. With an increase of 71% over the previous year, AT&T moved to first place in expenditures for network radio advertising.

Advertising revenues were expected to increase by about 9% in 1985, but sales of network television time were expected to grow by only 3% because of advertiser dissatisfaction. In 1985 the average prime-time network commercial cost $180,-000, about three times more than in 1975, but only 7% more households were watching. Spending for ads on cable television was expected to rise by 20% in 1985, and advertisers were also turning to other types of media. Anheuser-Busch placed advertising on billboard-size video screens at sports stadiums. Packaged goods companies advertised on shopping carts at thousands of supermarkets. Campbell Soup placed ads in church bulletins and on parking meters, and companies such as Lever Brothers and General Foods paid fees starting at $50,000 to get their products used in movies.

In April the U.S. Federal Trade Commission (FTC) denied a request from 29 organizations to restrict the advertisement of alcoholic beverages. The groups had complained about advertisements directly associating drinking with driving and about company-sponsored beer-drinking contests on college campuses. A ban on beer and wine advertisements would cost broadcasters about $700 million a year. The National Association of Broadcasters (NAB) introduced public-service announcements for its members pointing out that driving and drinking do not mix. The FTC planned to review the alcoholic beverage industry's advertising and marketing practices on a case-by-case basis.

The Japanese government launched a major advertising campaign using television, newspapers, and posters to encourage its citizens to buy foreign products. The advertising effort was the result of U.S. pressure to allow more foreign products into the Japanese market. The TV ads reminded viewers that it was their responsibility to buy foreign products to maintain a free trade system.

AEROSPACE INDUSTRY

A succession of serious accidents in 1985 marred what had been a decade of steadily improving air safety. While not a single life was lost in a Western-built passenger jet during the first half of 1984, no fewer than 639 perished during the corresponding period of 1985. Worse was to follow: during August another 715 were killed, 520 of them in a single accident, the world's worst disaster in the air. There was no common factor, but two of the accidents involved Boeing 747s, an airliner that up to then had enjoyed an excellent safety record. Another 747 earlier in the year had a miraculous escape after falling uncontrolled from 37,000 ft (11,285 m) to 9,500 ft (2,898 m) with 273 people on board. Later, a DC-8 carrying U.S. soldiers home for the Christmas holidays crashed at Gander, Newfoundland, killing 256 passengers and crew.

Meanwhile, business continued to improve in the international air transport industry. Traffic maintained its upward trend, though profits were still weak. Nevertheless, recovery was sufficient to accelerate production rates among the major aircraft manufacturers. Boeing inevitably led the way and by the end of the year's third quarter had sold 184 new transports, more than all 1984 sales. In Europe demand for the Airbus A320 (the only completely new airliner) continued; PanAm placed orders for 28 A310s and A320s, enhancing their credibility in the U.S. market. Recovery was also marked by the brisk trade in used aircraft, and by the year's end stocks of popular models such as the Boeing 727 had rapidly diminished. A notable reason for this was the falling price of oil; a gallon of fuel costing $1 in January 1982 could be bought for only 72 cents three years later, making the less fuel-efficient but much cheaper secondhand airplanes increasingly attractive.

The same anticipated increases in oil prices that in the late 1970s had launched a new generation of fuel-efficient transports also spurred a new development in propulsion technology known as the prop-fan. Essentially sophisticated multiblade propellers, prop-fans were seen by manufacturers in both the United States and Europe as promising huge fuel savings even over the efficient existing high-bypass turbine engines. Others were not so sure, arguing against the greater technical risk and likely much higher initial cost of the prop-fans. First seen at the Farnborough Air Show in 1984, they were promoted to a much greater extent at the 1985 Paris International Air Show. The airlines themselves—the potential customers—were taking little interest in them, however, being too occupied with the slow climb back to profitability. The Paris show was also notable for the first appearance of the U.S.S.R.'s huge, 400-ton Antonov An-124 military transport, closely matching the United States military's Lockheed C-5 Galaxy in size. It was powered by the first Soviet high-bypass fan engines, disclosing that the U.S.S.R. was 20 years behind Western technology in this field.

The tiny Concorde fleet of Britain and France continued to service the two or three routes approved for the supersonic jetliners. Increasing demand, and the rise of the charter trade, prompted British Airways to bring out of mothballs its seventh Concorde, an encouragement to potential investors currently analyzing the airline's prospects as it headed for private ownership. In the U.S. the National Aeronautics and Space Administration (NASA) and a few enthusiastic research groups among the manufacturers continued to extol the virtues of supersonic or even hypersonic (five times the speed of sound) transport. They continued to be ignored by the airlines, put off by Europe's huge struggle to build just 16 Concordes.

AP/WIDE WORLD

The X-29, an experimental plane with forward-swept wings, underwent its second test flight during the year at Edwards Air Force Base in California.

In June the Douglas DC-3 reached its 50th birthday. For its contribution to aviation, the DC-3/C-47/Dakota was widely acknowledged the outstanding airplane of all time, and more than 700 continued to earn their keep around the world. Longevity had also become a characteristic of military aircraft, and words such as "updating," "enhancement," and "improvement" described the most important activities in this field. The most widely used combat aircraft were 15–25 years old, and even the newer types such as the F-16 Falcon and F/A-18 went back more than a decade. The time had long since gone when a new engine or weapon could justify the expense of a completely new aircraft, especially since progress in electronics was so rapid that the performance of equipment doubled every few years. Thus, entire fleets of such aircraft as F-111s, F-4 Phantoms, A-7 Corsairs, and even venerable B-52s were being reequipped with more capable black boxes or better and more reliable engines.

While the 30-year-old B-52 continued to be extensively updated, its successor, the B-1, reached the beginning of its service career; the first of a planned fleet of 100 aircraft was handed over to the U.S. Air Force in June. The B-1 had been canceled by U.S. Pres. Jimmy Carter in 1977 as part of a unilateral arms-reduction move, but it was reinstated by Pres. Ronald Reagan in 1981. Meanwhile, in the greatest secrecy, U.S. industry accelerated work on new "stealth" aircraft, the visibility of which to radar beams would be greatly reduced by the application of advanced electronic and structural techniques. However, there was considerable argument as to whether the money would be better spent on more B-1s.

A column of Afghan
mujahedeen rebels winds
through the countryside.
Despite a Soviet military
offensive during the year, the
rebels still controlled most
of Afghanistan outside the
largest cities.

ARTHUR CONNER/THE NEW YORK TIMES

AFGHANISTAN

Afghanistan was locked in military stalemate throughout 1985, with neither the Muslim insurgents nor the Soviet-backed government troops mounting any decisive military offensive, though there were numerous operations and clashes. The insurgents appeared better equipped than previously, with antiaircraft weapons in particular, in their efforts to counter government forces, who were aided by an estimated 115,000 Soviet soldiers. An antiguerrilla onslaught launched by the joint Soviet-Afghan military command in eastern Afghanistan in mid-August fell far short of success. However, the offensive, described by area experts as among the biggest since the Soviet intervention in 1979, brought the war closer to the Pakistani border, a fact that worried Islamabad. Afghanistan remained completely dependent on Moscow.

On the diplomatic front, the UN special representative for Afghanistan, Diego Cordovez, shuttled between Islamabad and Kabul. Three times during the year, in June, August, and December, he shuttled between separate rooms in the UN building in Geneva, meeting alternately with Afghan Foreign Minister Shah Mohammad Dost and his Pakistani counterpart, Sahabzada Yaqub Khan. The foreign ministers did not meet directly, since to do so would amount to recognition by Pakistan of Pres. Babrak Karmal's regime. The last round of talks adjourned on December 19 to allow the parties to study new UN proposals. Earlier, the United States announced its willingness to act as guarantor of a settlement that would involve Soviet troop withdrawal and an end to U.S. aid to the guerrillas.

Reports on the ongoing war in Afghanistan were sketchy and contradictory. In the absence of impartial reports, the world press gained its information largely from Western diplomats and Kabul Radio. News also reached the West from visitors who toured Afghanistan clandestinely. There were several major clashes during the year. In January Soviet-Afghan troops launched an offensive in three provinces in eastern Afghanistan and two in the west in an effort to cut off guerrilla supply routes. On March 23, according to resistance sources in Pakistan, some 400 Soviet and Afghan troops were killed when a series of explosions triggered by a time bomb engulfed a military convoy. In April Western diplomats claimed that several hundred civilians had been killed in late March during Soviet-Afghan attacks in four provinces. On June 12 at least 20 Afghan Air Force planes were blown up at Shindand air base in the western province of Farah. On September 4 an Afghan airliner traveling from Kabul to Farah crashed near Qandahar, killing all 52 people on board. The government blamed the guerrillas for the incident.

A UN report on human rights in Afghanistan accused Soviet forces in March of "bombarding villages, destroying food supplies, massacring civilians, and disregarding the Geneva convention." The report claimed that the government was holding 50,000 political prisoners and that tortures in jails were "commonplace." The government rejected the claims as "fabrication."

On January 10, Afghanistan marked the 20th anniversary of the founding of the ruling Communist Party. A three-day Loya Jirga (grand council) was held on April 23–25. This traditional national tribal assembly had not been convened since the 1979 coup.

On the international front, Kabul's relations with China and Iran deteriorated further. In August Foreign Minister Dost visited India, the only country outside the Soviet bloc with which relations improved.

AFRICAN AFFAIRS

The annual World Bank report warned of "the specter of disaster" confronting Africa and the international community. Although good rainfall in 1985 broke the five-year drought in the sub-Saharan region, the area's worst in 150 years, many of the 34 affected countries were not expected to produce sufficient crops before 1986. It was estimated that by then as many as 200 million people could be desperately short of food. Unless the level of international aid was increased substantially, the immediate prospect was of a situation worse than the acute 1973–74 famine disaster.

According to the UN Food and Agriculture Organization, 1,000,000,000 tons of topsoil were lost by means of erosion every year. During the previous 20 years food production in the continent had decreased by 20%. According to the UN Economic Commission for Africa (ECA), instead of the expected modest recovery of per capita income by 3.1%, the best that might be hoped for in 1985 was 2.6%, representing a continuing drop in real per capita income.

Organization of African Unity

The summit meeting of the Organization of African Unity (OAU) held in Addis Ababa, Eth., on July 18–20 devoted itself mainly to proposals for dealing with Africa's "unprecedented economic and social crisis." In his role as chairman, Pres. Julius Nyerere of Tanzania stressed that the continent was not only underdeveloped and poor but also too fragmented to organize its resources effectively. He argued that the dwindling external capital flows compelled the continent to base its development plans on its own internal resources. The OAU adopted a program for economic recovery centered on five main issues: action to rehabilitate agriculture and improve food supplies; a campaign to halt the advance of the desert; the achievement of an African common market by the year 2000; negotiations with the developed nations to ease Africa's external debt, which stood at about $170 billion; and a common platform for subregional, regional, continental, and international cooperation.

Among other major decisions taken were a call for sanctions against South Africa because of its racial separation policies, criticism of South Africa and the U.S. for obstructing the liberation of Namibia/South West Africa, and a new initiative to end the fighting in both Chad and the Western Sahara. The heads of state resolved the deadlock over the appointment of a new administrative secretary-general for the OAU by agreeing on Ide Oumarou, foreign minister of Niger. Pres. Abdou Diouf of Senegal was elected chairman for 1985–86.

Southern Africa

Predictions that the Nkomati accord that was signed in 1984 between South Africa and Mozambique would defuse the violence and instability of the region were not fulfilled. In spite of the accord, Mozambique's security problems became more acute because of attacks by the rebel Mozambique National Resistance (MNR). Mozambique's accusations that South Africa had failed to live up to its side of the agreement brought admissions that there had been some failures, described by South Africa as technical rather than deliberate breaches.

The 1984 cease-fire agreement between Angola and South Africa also failed to live up to its promise. Although South Africa's armed forces finally withdrew from Angola in April, their military attacks and sabotage activities continued. As Jonas Savimbi's National Union for the Total Independence of Angola (UNITA), which received strong support from South Africa, stepped up military pressures, Soviet support for the Angolan Army and the Cuban combat troops stationed in Angola also increased. The U.S. Congress moved toward giving greater support to UNITA by repealing the Clark amendment, which had precluded clandestine support for such movements.

Negotiations over Namibia's independence in terms of UN Resolution 435 reached a stalemate over the issue of the withdrawal of all Cuban troops from Angola. The Angolan offer, negotiated by the U.S., to begin phasing out the Cubans failed to satisfy South Africa. Although the armed struggle for independence of the South West Africa People's Organization (SWAPO) was blunted by Angola's decision not to allow incursions across its border, its international diplomatic offensive was effectively maintained. The new interim government installed in Namibia by South Africa was not accorded recognition by any Western power.

Meanwhile, the situation inside South Africa itself deteriorated seriously during the year with a significant rise in the level of violence.

Horn of Africa

The violent conflicts in and around Ethiopia showed no sign of lessening. Several military offensives mounted by the government against liberation movements in Eritrea and Tigre failed to break their resistance to Ethiopia's Marxist-Leninist regime. In a bid to force The Sudan to end its support for the Eritreans, the Ethiopians increased their aid to the rebel Sudan People's Liberation Army. Efforts by the new Sudanese military regime to end the hostilities with the SPLA were unsuccessful, and relations between The Sudan and Ethiopia remained uneasy.

Coups and Inter-African Affairs

After a period of fewer coup attempts, the number again increased in 1985. In April Pres. Gaafar Nimeiry of The Sudan was toppled in a military coup, led by Gen. 'Abd ar-Rahman Siwar ad-Dahab. In July Pres. Milton Obote of Uganda was overthrown by the Army, which installed Lieut. Gen. Tito Okello as head of state, and in August a struggle between rival factions of the Nigerian Army ended in the replacement of Maj. Gen. Mohammed Buhari by Maj. Gen. Ibrahim Babangida. The successful coups were all comparatively bloodless, unlike abortive coup attempts in Guinea and Liberia.

The tenth anniversary of the 16-nation Economic Community of West African States (ECOWAS) became an occasion to examine why the community had failed to achieve its earlier promise. One suggested reason was that governments were still too concerned about defending their sovereignty. The main achievements of ECOWAS were a protocol on free movement of people within the region, a major investment program to develop a regional telecommunications system, and a coordinated program to develop the trans-Sahara road network.

The 14-nation Southern African Development Coordination Conference (SADCC), in operation for five years, continued to make progress in fulfilling its major objective of lessening the dependence of its members on South Africa. Another practical example of cooperation among SADCC's members was Zimbabwe's decision to commit up to 7,000 troops to assist Mozambique in protecting its communication routes and in fighting the MNR.

Political Systems

Two African presidents voluntarily relinquished office during the year. Pres. Julius Nyerere of Tanzania was succeeded by Ali Hassan Mwinyi, and Pres. Siaka Stevens of Sierra Leone was succeeded by Maj. Gen. Joseph Saidu Momoh. The only other African leader who had previously stepped down of his own accord was Pres. Léopold Senghor of Senegal in 1980.

The first attempt in 15 years to hold multiparty elections in Lesotho was frustrated when all the opposition parties refused to participate because of objections to the new electoral system. The first elections in Liberia since the 1980 coup were con-

Members of the Organization of African Unity met in Addis Ababa, Ethiopia, in July in efforts to deal with their severe economic and social problems.

AP/WIDE WORLD

ducted in an atmosphere of controversy and bitter rancor. The incumbent head of state, Gen. Samuel Doe, who secured just over half of the votes cast in the presidential election, overcame an attempted military coup within weeks of his victory. After Zimbabwe's first elections since gaining independence in 1980, Prime Minister Robert Mugabe began negotiations with opposition leader Joshua Nkomo aimed at introducing a single-party system.

External Relations

The continent's economic crisis forced its leaders to look to the West for aid and understanding of their problems and needs and to accept Western, especially U.S., terms in order to improve their chances of getting support. One immediate consequence was the growing influence on African policies of such Western institutions as the World Bank and the International Monetary Fund (IMF). A number of countries such as Guinea, The Sudan, Zambia, and Tanzania, all formerly wedded to centralized economies, undertook to expand private-sector operations, a prerequisite for IMF and U.S. aid. This situation produced strongly ambivalent attitudes toward U.S.-supported international institutions, particularly the IMF.

The U.S. strengthened its position in Mozambique. U.S. Pres. Ronald Reagan seriously upset South Africa by signing an executive order for a program of selective sanctions against South Africa. Nevertheless, the OAU adopted a harshly critical resolution against the U.S. because of its failure to persuade Pretoria to implement the UN resolution on Namibia, while the possibility of the U.S. providing support for UNITA threatened to become a major point of new conflict between the majority of African countries and Washington.

Among Western European countries France continued to be the most politically active in the continent, as well as one of the largest donors of aid. Along with the Scandinavian countries, France led the Europeans in the militancy of its hostility toward South Africa. The interests of West Germany, like those of Japan, remained primarily in trade. The U.K. found itself almost isolated within the Commonwealth because of Prime Minister Margaret Thatcher's adamant opposition to economic sanctions against South Africa.

The Soviet Union, which played a relatively small part in African affairs during 1985, devoted most of its aid and attention to Ethiopia and Angola. It also contributed substantially to two liberation movements, the African National Congress of South Africa and SWAPO. The Soviet bloc suffered in the opinion of Africans because of its failure to measure up to the Western response in providing food and other aid programs to alleviate the famine conditions. Cuba withdrew all its troops from Ethiopia and announced its readiness to phase out its military presence in Angola once the issue of Namibian independence had been settled.

JUDY SLOAN—GAMMA/LIAISON

Thousands of angry U.S. farmers demonstrated in front of the White House on March 6 to denounce a presidential veto of a farm aid bill.

AGRICULTURE

The year 1985 was one of generally bountiful harvests throughout the world. Famine still stalked much of Africa after a succession of poor crops. Massive distribution of food aid helped alleviate the disaster, and recovery of crops around most of the region was beginning to cause attention to be turned to the rehabilitation of stricken areas. The availability of large supplies of agricultural products in the developed and exporting countries depressed the prices of many agricultural commodities and contributed to further trade confrontations. The U.S. agricultural sector faced a severe financial crisis just as the U.S. Congress enacted new basic farm legislation for the next five years.

Production

World agricultural and food production in 1985 increased somewhat over 1% from the previous year according to preliminary estimates of the U.S. Department of Agriculture's Economic Research Service. The strongest gains in output occurred in the less developed countries, especially those in Africa and western Asia. Harvests were better in the Soviet Union, and China consolidated most of the exceptionally large gains made in 1984. Although agricultural production fell in the European Communities (EC) and was only slightly larger in the United States, both regions faced problems of surpluses for many commodities. Per capita world food production was unchanged from that in 1984. It was little changed in the developed nations,

while gains in the less developed countries and the U.S.S.R. were offset by losses in China and Eastern Europe. The most heartening increases were in Africa south of the Sahara, where per capita food production rose about 2%.

Images of hunger and death poignantly conveyed the nature of the food situation in much of Africa during the last three years. Large-scale relief operations and generally favorable harvests throughout most of the continent brought substantial improvement in Africa's food situation in 1985. Of the 21 African countries on the "danger list" of the United Nations Food and Agriculture Organization (FAO) in 1984, only 6 remained there by the end of 1985. Despite a substantial recovery in food production, The Sudan remained on the list, as did Ethiopia, where growing conditions were improved in parts of the country. Elsewhere in East Africa average to above-average crops were harvested, and food supplies returned to normal. Total cereal production rose 50% in the seven previously afflicted countries of West Africa. All of the countries of the Sahel region (just south of the Sahara) except Cape Verde enjoyed above-average or record large crops. The fact that it was too early to forecast the size of the crops that were to be harvested beginning in April 1986 in southern Africa partly explained the continued presence on the danger list of Angola, Botswana, and Mozambique.

The FAO estimated in December that the 21 African countries that were on its danger list in 1984 would require total cereal imports of 6.6 million tons in 1985–86, 5.6 million tons less than the amount needed during the previous year. It estimated the total food-aid needs of those countries to be 3.4 million tons in 1985–86, compared with 7 million in 1984–85. Donor pledges and alloca-

Some 78,000 persons attended a Farm Aid concert in Champaign, Illinois, on September 22. Proceeds of the concert fell far short of organizers' early hopes.

AP/WIDE WORLD

tions through December totaled 2.7 million tons, including 1.2 million tons that arrived too late to be distributed in 1984–85. The FAO believed that additional financial aid was needed to move surplus grain from some African countries with bumper crops to food-deficit areas on the continent or to build up national and regional reserves. Surpluses totaling 1.8 million tons were estimated to be held in Zimbabwe, Kenya, Malawi, and parts of West Africa. The FAO saw some danger of surpluses and food aid flooding some markets and removing incentives for increased local production in 1986.

U.S. Farm Crisis

U.S. farmers at the end of 1985 were facing an accelerating crisis that approached the severity of that experienced during the Great Depression in the 1930s. At the year's end the U.S. Congress enacted new basic farm legislation intended to provide the ground rules for the nation's agriculture through 1990.

Prices received by farmers for all commodities fell by about 10% in 1985, the worst annual decline since 1953. Prices received for crops declined 13% in response to near-record production and stagnant domestic and foreign demand. The resulting huge carryover stocks for many commodities indicated little prospect for higher prices in 1986. Prices for grains, soybeans, and cotton fell to a level that triggered the government loan program to come to the aid of those commodities. Without a recovery of prices in 1986, this raised the possibility that government-owned stocks of these commodities could exceed even those that prompted the controversial PIK (payment-in-kind) program in 1983.

The lower prices were reflected in a decline in net farm income from $34.5 billion in 1984 to an estimated $25 billion–$29 billion in 1985. Real farm income (deflated to adjust for inflation) in recent years had been far below its peak of $20.3 billion (1972 prices) in 1975 and for 1985 was estimated at $10.8 billion–$12.6 billion.

The volume of farmers' debt in relation to assets had been rising steadily since 1979. It may have reached as high as 25% in 1985, compared with 23.2% in 1984 and 17% as recently as 1980. A study conducted by the United States Department of Agriculture surveying 1.7 million of the country's 2.3 million farms found that 12%—214,000 farms—began 1985 unable to pay the previous year's bills. Of commercial farms—those with annual sales in excess of $40,000, which represent one-third of all farms but 90% of all farm commodities sold—one in five had negative cash flow and a debt-to-asset ratio of over 40%.

Farmers were not just worse off in terms of lower current income and rising debt. In 1985, for the fifth year in a row, the total net worth of farmers fell, to $595 billion–$653 billion from $657 billion in December 1984. From 1980 to 1984 farmers' equity fell $180 billion, $100 billion alone in 1984. The average value of farm assets fell from a peak of $823 per acre in 1982 to $679 in 1985.

A decline in land values was the principal cause of the loss of farmers' equity. About three-quarters of farm real estate assets were land. Average values of farmland fell 12% between April 1984 and April 1985. The largest single-year losses—between 14 and 29%—were recorded in the Midwestern states. Iowa, Nebraska, Illinois, and South Dakota all lost

Grasshoppers hatched in record numbers in several Western states of the U.S., causing serious concern to farmers. To combat the hoards, the U.S. Department of Agriculture began a spraying program intended to cover more than 9 million acres (365,000 hectares) of farmland in 12 states.

more than one-quarter of their farm values in 1985 alone. Adding to the above list Texas, Ohio, Indiana, Minnesota, and Missouri would give those states whose land had depreciated between one-third and one-half since 1981. For all the states together, land values declined 19% between their peak in 1981 and 1985.

The drop in land values also endangered the farm banking system and led to new congressional legislation in December that reorganized the system and placed it under closer federal surveillance. The shrinkage of land values reduced sharply the value of bank assets that were based on loans to farmers with land as collateral. Banks also had less money to lend because many farm families had to withdraw personal and household savings to meet living expenses and farm debt payments. These circumstances made it increasingly difficult for the banks to refinance overdue farm debt. An American Bankers Association midyear survey estimated that 3.8% of all farmers filed for bankruptcy in 1985, compared with 0.7% in June 1982.

The Food Security Act of 1985, signed into law on December 23, was characterized by the chairman of the Senate Agriculture Committee as "the beginning of a slow, but decisive, transition to market-oriented farm policy." The act aimed at gradually reducing various large direct and indirect income aids to farmers while more rapidly allowing loan rates to fall as low as necessary to clear markets and make U.S. exports fully competitive. It also provided tools to promote agricultural exports, including several intended to reduce government stocks of surplus commodities. The eventual aim was for agriculture to respond more than it had in the past to prices determined by the basic balance between supply and demand rather than to government price and income programs.

During this transition, government seemed destined to play a very large role, one in which it would have considerable discretionary powers. The transition was also expected to be costly. For instance, the projected cost of the commodity programs administered by the Commodity Credit Corporation was about $52 billion for fiscal years 1986–88. A major uncertainty connected with the act was how it might be affected should the Gramm-Rudman act mandating a balanced federal budget be invoked to curb federal expenditures.

The major measure adopted for protecting farm income was the freezing of target prices for specified commodities at 1985 levels for the first one or two years; after that, reductions by the secretary of agriculture would be permitted within the following limits:

	1986	1987	1988	1989	1990
Wheat per bu	4.38	4.38	4.29	4.16	4.00
Corn per bu	3.03	3.03	2.97	2.87	2.75
Cotton per lb	0.810	0.794	0.770	0.745	0.729
Rice per cwt	11.90	11.66	11.30	10.95	10.71

AP/WIDE WORLD

French farmers spread liquid manure over the streets of Niort to protest drops in agricultural prices and the entry of Spain into the European Communities.

In addition, the support price for sugar was set at 18 cents per pound for the entire five years.

Farmers who entered the commodity programs received direct deficiency payments for the difference between the target price and the price at which they sold their commodities. They were obligated to accept acreage restrictions—many at the secretary of agriculture's discretion—that involved various combinations of mandatory or voluntary, unpaid or paid, removals of land from production. In the case of dairy farming a partially producer-funded program was authorized under which the government would buy entire dairy herds from farmers who were willing to quit milk production. Such production restraints would be necessary to keep output from rising and adding to surpluses as long as support payments remained far above world prices.

The provisions dealing with loan rates were complicated. For grains the rates were to be based on a historical average of grain prices with reductions of up to 5% permitted each year. However, the secretary of agriculture could under various conditions decide to operate under alternative provisions that permitted him to cut loan rates as much as an additional 20% in order to compete in world markets. Associated with these options were various payment-in-kind schemes.

Some of the provisions that were designed to promote agricultural exports included a bonus export program to use $2 billion in surplus commodities over the next three years to counter subsidies and unfair foreign trade practices; a minimum of $5 billion annually in short-term export credit guarantees; and $500 million annually in intermediate export credit guarantees through 1988 and up to $1 billion in 1989.

ALBANIA

On April 11, 1985, Enver Hoxha, leader of Albania for over 40 years and the longest-serving head of a Communist country, died after suffering a heart attack. Two days later he was succeeded as first secretary of the Albanian Party of Labor by Ramiz Alia, chairman of the Presidium of the People's Assembly since 1982. In his speech at Hoxha's funeral in Tiranë on April 15, Alia made it clear that no changes in Albanian domestic or foreign policy should be expected. Departing from international diplomatic practice, he did not allow representatives of foreign governments to attend the funeral, and the Soviet telegram of condolence was returned as "unacceptable." In August Alia said that moves to broaden ties with the outside world would not include the opening of diplomatic relations with either superpower.

In August U.K. Prime Minister Margaret Thatcher revealed that Britain was holding secret talks with Albania in an attempt to settle a 40-year-old diplomatic rift between the two countries. Britain was claiming nearly £850,000 in compensation for two destroyers mined off the Albanian coast, with the loss of more than 40 British lives, in 1946. Albania refused to pay until Britain handed over Albanian gold looted by the Germans during World War II. The gold, held jointly by Britain, France, and the U.S., was worth around £44 million at current prices. (For table of world currencies, *see* International Exchange and Payments.)

Albanian officials carry the coffin of Enver Hoxha, leader of the Albanian Communist Party for more than 40 years, during funeral rites in Tiranë.

AGENCE ALBANAISE/GAMMA/LIAISON

ALGERIA

During 1985 Algeria continued to concentrate on domestic affairs, particularly economic reorganization. In February Pres. Chadli Bendjedid instructed his administration to concentrate on developing the south of the country, revising the National Charter—the national development plan drawn up by his predecessor, Houari Boumedienne—and ensuring that his policies were properly understood by the population. The revision of the National Charter, which began in mid-July, was a potentially far-reaching move, since it implied the rejection of Boumedienne's legacy, and the former president was criticized in the media for the first time.

Algeria's economic problems stemmed from the fact that oil and gas revenues, while expected to maintain the 1984 level of around $12 billion, were substantially lower than they had been in the early 1980s. As a result, the 1985–89 plan was revised, and Algeria turned to international money markets for massive loans, making it one of the most heavily indebted nations in Africa. The foreign debt exceeded $16 billion by the end of the year. Algeria resisted price cuts proposed by the Organization of Petroleum Exporting Countries in December 1984 and January 1985, only reluctantly agreeing to a cut of $1 a barrel in March. Liquefied natural gas sales suffered from the decision of the U.S. company Distrigas to cancel its contracts. However, Spain agreed to pay $500 million in compensation for its failure to honor a 1975 gas purchase contract, and a revised agreement was signed.

The radical changes taking place inside Algeria were underlined in late April when serious riots broke out in Algiers to protest poor housing conditions. Riots in the southern town of Ghardaia in June were the result of a dispute over land distribution to the private sector. Islamic fundamentalism continued to pose a serious problem to Algerian authorities, despite the leniency shown during trials in Médéa in April, when 135 fundamentalists accused of involvement in the 1982 disturbances were either given light sentences or released. Algeria's accelerated arabization campaign was opposed by the Berber population and by elements in the administration who considered French a more appropriate official language.

In foreign affairs Algeria continued to support the Popular Front for the Liberation of Saguia el Hamra and Río de Oro (Polisario Front) in its struggle against Morocco for control of the Western Sahara. A proposed meeting of North African heads of state had to be abandoned in February when Algeria refused to exclude the Western Sahara issue from the agenda. Chadli tried to wean the United States from its support for Morocco during his state visit there in April. The subject also figured on the agenda when the president visited Madrid on July 1. Relations with France worsened during the year, partly because of France's close relations with Morocco.

REUTERS/BETTMANN NEWSPHOTOS

Jonas Savimbi, leader of the rebel group UNITA, tells reporters on October 7 how his troops repelled a major offensive by the Angolan government.

ANGOLA

In January 1985, Angolan Pres. José Eduardo dos Santos reaffirmed his government's commitment to Marxism-Leninism and to strengthening its links with the socialist world. In practice this did not prevent the development of economic relations with Western nations. Soon after making his speech, President dos Santos welcomed representatives of Gulf Oil and the Chevron Corp. to Luanda. During 1984 oil exports rose by 30%, and there was every prospect that output would be increased still further. The Movimento Popular de Libertação de Angola (MPLA) elected President dos Santos to a second five-year term on December 9.

Although the military activities of the National Union for the Total Independence of Angola (UNITA) rebels continued to be limited mainly to small-scale ambushes and raids, they were widespread enough to bring virtual devastation to much of the central region of the country. Acute shortages of fuel and essential foodstuffs were exacerbated by the disruption of communications, and hundreds of thousands of displaced persons placed a heavy burden on the nation's resources. In December 1984 UNITA forces attacked the diamond-mining town of Cafunfo in the north, claiming to have killed more than 100 government troops and to have captured a number of European technicians. However, President dos Santos refused to contemplate any coalition government that included UNITA representatives.

Some South African troops remained in southern Angola, ostensibly to guard against incursions by forces of the South West Africa People's Organization (SWAPO) into Namibia. The government believed, however, that South Africa's objective was to accomplish its overthrow and to ensure the withdrawal of Cuban troops from the country. U.S. mediation brought about an agreement in April by which Angola agreed to send home 10,000 Cuban troops and South Africa promised to withdraw its forces from Angola immediately.

It emerged that South Africa had not fully honored the agreement when a small South African raiding party was intercepted by Angolan forces in the Cabinda enclave in May. While South Africa described the party as a reconnaissance force seeking out SWAPO and African National Congress training areas, the Angolans believed that its aim had been to sabotage an oil refinery and accordingly announced their intention to break off negotiations with South Africa. There were subsequent raids into southern Angola by South African forces claiming to be in pursuit of SWAPO guerrillas in June and September. The government accused the South Africans of secretly assisting UNITA rebels, who had become increasingly hard-pressed during the year. As a result of improvements in training and equipment, government forces began to achieve a notable measure of success against UNITA. The Air Force, reinforced by a number of Soviet-made aircraft, struck several damaging blows in support of ground troops.

ANTARCTICA

Major events during the 1984–85 Antarctic summer field season included an international workshop on the Antarctic Treaty System held in Antarctica, the entrance of additional nations into Antarctic work, and the entrapment of a Soviet supply ship by late summer ice in the Amundsen Sea.

Fifty-seven persons from 24 nations met in early January at the Beardmore Glacier Camp only 400 mi (640 km) from the South Pole to examine the Treaty System and Antarctica's potential contributions to the nations of the world. The workshop, following the third world's challenge to the system in the UN, allowed treaty and nontreaty nations to better understand each other's views.

The Soviet vessel *Mikhail Somov* was trapped in the Amundsen Sea in March while conducting the annual resupply of Russkaya Station. The icebreaker *Vladivostok* from the Soviet Northern Sea Route fleet was sent to free the *Somov,* and by mid-July it had begun to break its way through some 400 mi of ice. On July 26 the *Vladivostok* took the *Somov* in tow, and by August 3, after a lengthy struggle against ice 12 ft (3.7 m) thick in places, the *Somov* had been freed.

Other nations displayed their interest in Antarctica by establishing bases. China established the Great Wall station on Fildes Peninsula on King George Island in the South Shetlands, only 1.2 mi (2 km) from Bellingshausen (U.S.S.R.) and Rodolfo Marsh (Chile). Two ships, carrying construction workers and a scientific staff, arrived on Dec. 30, 1984, and by mid-February 1985 the station had been completed. Brazil and Uruguay also established stations on King George Island. Commandante Ferray (Brazil) supported research programs in marine biology, geology, and geophysics during the summer. Artigas (Uruguay), in Collins Harbour near the Chinese station, was the seventh station on the island.

The international conservation organization Greenpeace announced plans to establish a small four-man station in Antarctica during the 1985–86 summer season. Cuba became the 32nd nation to accede to the Antarctic Treaty; 16 of the 32 had consultative status.

National Programs

Australia. Some 45 days were devoted to krill research in Prydz Bay from the *Nella Dan.* Geologic investigations concentrated on the Framnes Mountains of MacRobertson Land and on the detailed geologic mapping of the Stillwell Hills in Enderby Land.

Chile. The British Base T on Adelaide Island, unused since 1977, was transferred to Chile and renamed Teniente Carvajal. Three other bases were maintained, including Rodolfo Marsh on King George Island, where several families were living.

Japan. Marine geophysical surveys by the Japanese Agency for National Resources and Energy and the National Oil Corporation continued—in the current season, off Enderby Land. Two permanent stations were maintained, and a summer camp was established near the Sør Rondane Mountains.

New Zealand. Work began on the three-year CIROS (Cenozoic Investigations in the Ross Sea) offshore drilling project. A core was recovered through 554 ft (168.9 m) of glacial sediment down to bedrock before a major storm destroyed the drilling camp. The core was undamaged. Preliminary analysis suggested the scientifically rich samples are up to four million years old and contain evidence of a number of glacial events in the Ross Sea.

U.S.S.R. The 30th Soviet Antarctic Expedition continued wide-ranging exploration of Antarctica. Plans were announced for the establishment of an eighth permanent station, on Berkner Island in the Weddell Sea. A new summer-only station, Soyuz, was established at Beaver Lake in the Prince Charles Mountains. Station maintenance included the construction of a packed-snow airstrip at Novolazarevskaya, similar to the one in operation at Molodezhnaya. Vostok station, deep in the interior of Antarctica, was again supplied by a tractor train from Mirnyy.

United Kingdom. The British Antarctic Survey introduced helicopters to fieldwork but continued to prohibit women scientists from working in Antarctica. Field surveys were conducted to determine the feasibility of constructing a hard runway at Rothera, where the summer snow runway was used to support aircraft from British, Chilean, West German, and U.S. expeditions.

United States. Three permanent stations—Palmer, McMurdo, and Amundsen-Scott at the South Pole—were maintained, but Siple Station remained closed until late 1985. Major glaciologic work was concentrated at the Siple Coast on the eastern Ross Ice Shelf, where large ice streams drain the ice from Marie Byrd Land. The South Pole was the location for a major solar seismology project by U.S. and French scientists. The most significant geologic expeditions worked on Seymour Island searching for additional fossil deposits, in the Jones Mountains of Ellsworth Land, where detailed geologic mapping was emphasized, and near Mt. Takahe in Marie Byrd Land, where the volcanic geology of the area was investigated. Marine and oceanographic work was conducted from the Coast Guard icebreakers *Glacier* and *Polar Star* from the

Japanese researchers secure water samples from Don Quixote Pond in the Wright Valley of Antarctica. The unusual water formation consists of a layer of fresh water over a body of salt water.

LYNN JOHNSON—BLACK STAR

Antarctic Peninsula to Wilkes Land. The Seymour Island party also searched for Cretaceous-Tertiary boundary deposits to further study the theory that an asteroid hitting the Earth some 65 million years ago caused the extinction of the dinosaurs and other plant and animal life.

West Germany. Research continued at the permanent station, and the cooperative geologic and geophysical expedition Ganovex IV conducted research in North Victoria Land supported by two Dornier aircraft. While en route back to Germany one of the aircraft was shot down by guerrillas near Dakhla in the Western Sahara. Two pilots and the flight engineer were killed.

ANTHROPOLOGY

Examining the effects of apartheid (the policy of racial separation) in South Africa; working with tribal people displaced by hydroelectric development in Malaysia, India, and Canada; studying planned social change in Bulgaria; or reevaluating such basic concepts as culture and kinship; anthropologists continued to engage in a wide variety of research projects in 1985. Scholarly activity within the profession was stimulated by modest increases in research funding, growing graduate enrollments, and slightly improved employment opportunities. Declining undergraduate enrollments, persistently high unemployment rates, and increasing underemployment (large numbers of academically employed anthropologists were hired on a part-time or temporary basis) continued to be major problems. Fundamentalist Christian groups pressing for the teaching of the biblical version of creation as scientific fact in U.S. schools continued to challenge the legitimacy of anthropology as part of their effort to discredit evolutionary theory. Despite these problems the high level of scholarly activity maintained by anthropologists throughout the world testified to the vigor and vitality of the discipline.

Reexamination of basic anthropological concepts and renewed interest in humanistic aspects of the discipline were among the important theoretical developments in anthropology in 1985. Anthropologists had long debated the validity of such standard categories as culture, tribe, religion, government, and economics. Inspired by renewed interest in the concept of culture in anthropology and other disciplines, a group of ethnologists formed the Society for Cultural Anthropology. The society planned to provide an interdisciplinary forum for cultural studies in its forthcoming journal, *Cultural Anthropology.*

A new debate on another fundamental anthropological concept was sparked by the publication of David Schneider's *A Critique of the Study of Kinship.* Schneider claimed that uncritical assumptions based upon Western ideas of the nature of society had distorted the study of kinship since the 19th century. Noting that the Western concept of kinship was not shared by other cultures, he suggested abandoning the category as a cross-cultural construct.

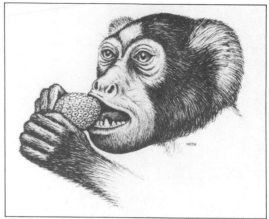

RECONSTRUCTION BY STEPHEN NASH AND RUSSELL CIOCHON, STATE UNIVERSITY OF NEW YORK AT STONY BROOK

Amphipithecus mogaungensis, which flourished about 40 million years ago, was nominated by some anthropologists as the common ancestor of Old and New World monkeys, apes, and humans.

Anthropology had long regarded itself as a social science. At the same time, anthropologists had never lost sight of their humanistic traditions. As Jacob Pandian pointed out, "Data may be produced by the scientific method, but it is the humanist who analyzes the data in relation to the quality and value of human life." Renewed interest in this aspect of the discipline led to the recent formation of the Society for Humanistic Anthropology. The society planned to sponsor symposia, organize meetings, and publish a newsletter and journal.

Small-Group Studies

The large number of papers devoted to applied, medical, urban, and political anthropology and the anthropology of development and education presented at the 1985 American Anthropological Association meeting vividly highlighted the growing emphasis upon practical applications of anthropological theory and method. Much of this effort was directed toward small-scale societies. Taking the traditional role of participant-observer, most anthropologists worked to study objectively the effects of change upon tribal people. Increasing numbers of field-workers, however, were taking a more active role. Malaysian anthropologists, for example, worked for three years to minimize the disruptions suffered by Iban tribespeople who had been displaced by the construction of the Batang Ai hydroelectric project on their lands. Other anthropologists, such as those working with Survival International, assisted tribespeople in their resistance to development projects in India, Namibia/South West Africa, Venezuela, and Brazil and to military repression in Nicaragua and Chile.

Anthropological research also influenced the work of others studying tribal societies. Anastasia Shkil-

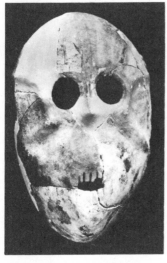

The oldest painted mask ever found, a limestone human face decorated in red and green, was one of several Neolithic artifacts from a cave near the Dead Sea that were displayed in April at the Israel Museum of Jerusalem.

DAVID HARRIS/TIME MAGAZINE

nyk, a policy adviser to the Canadian government, skillfully used anthropological methods to assess the effects of relocation, alcoholism, and the actual and potential losses caused by mercury pollution upon the Ojibwa of Grassy Narrows, Ont. Documenting the demoralization and disorientation of the Grassy Narrows community in her book, *A Poison Stronger than Love,* Shkilnyk showed that the problems of violence, illness, family breakdown, child abuse, and drug and alcohol abuse were not unique to the Ojibwa at Grassy Narrows or to other Canadian Indian groups but could be the common fate of all communities undergoing extraordinary change.

Effects of Modernization

Growing numbers of anthropologists also were turning their attention toward large-scale modern societies. In the United States June Nash studied the effects of the changeover from consumer-oriented heavy industry to production of high-technology equipment in Pittsfield, Mass. Susan Bourque and Kay Warren examined the ways in which the establishment of male-dominated cooperatives was causing rural Peruvian women to seek better economic opportunities as workers in provincial cities.

Problems associated with the rapid urbanization of a formerly rural agricultural population in Bulgaria were examined by Eleanor Smollett. Smollett's research traced the economic development of the country from pre-World War II peasant holdings to the establishment of present-day agro-industrial complexes and settlement systems, which integrated highly mechanized cooperative agriculture and industry in closely connected urban and rural areas. In this way Bulgarian social scientists and planners hoped to balance the attractions of village life with those of the city. If successful, those programs would enable Bulgaria to avoid the many problems associated with massive migration from the countryside to the city.

In his recent study *Waiting,* Vincent Crapanzano examined another society's efforts to deal with problems of modernization. Interested in the effect of domination on the people who dominate, Crapanzano conducted research in a small South African village in the Cape of Good Hope just before the recent declaration of a state of emergency. He studied attitudes of liberal (by South African standards) whites toward Coloureds (those of mixed race), blacks, and Asians. Interviewing both Afrikaners and other whites, he continually found "signs of anxiety, helplessness, vulnerability, and rage." Encountering a society simultaneously seeing itself as besieged and omnipotent, Crapanzano demonstrated how the stress of waiting while black unrest intensified affected every aspect of life in white South Africa.

Other changes associated with modernization were profoundly affecting the conduct of anthropological inquiry. Microcomputers were quickly becoming essential research and teaching tools. Computerized instruction programs were being adopted by growing numbers of instructors. Currently available packages ranged in complexity from simple administrative and testing programs to complex simulations allowing students to make decisions based upon knowledge of other cultural systems. The recent development of *World Cultures,* the first electronic journal for anthropologists, made the vast body of cross-cultural coded information contained in the Human Relations Area Files and other sources available on microcomputer diskettes.

ANTIGUA AND BARBUDA

An improved growth rate of 5% was forecast for 1985 in Antigua and Barbuda as tourist arrivals and earnings continued to increase. However, the government announced in April that it was preparing a structural adjustment plan aimed at dealing with the external debt and current account deficit. In January the government imposed an indefinite wage freeze for public employees, and in March it closed the country's only sugar factory, which had incurred substantial losses.

Efforts to attract foreign investment continued during the year. In February a U.S. company opened an electronics assembly plant, the first project to be established under the U.S. Caribbean Basin Initiative. Discussions were held with an Israeli company with a view to starting vegetable production for export. A visit by Deputy Prime Minister Lester Bird to China in June produced an aid package worth EC$5 million. (For table of world currencies, *see* International Exchange and Payments.)

In July Tim Hector, leader of the left-wing Antigua Caribbean Liberation Movement and a persistent critic of the government, was sentenced to six months in prison on a charge of undermining confidence in a public official. In March the National Democratic Party was formed, under the leadership of Ivor Heath, a surgeon.

ARCHAEOLOGY

The traditional archaeological activity in Egypt—the clearing, cleaning, and restoration of above-surface buildings and of tombs and the copying of inscriptions—proceeded, with archaeologists from an increasing number of nations being involved. There was interest in a new suggestion that the place of the missing (second) "solar boat" near the pharaoh Khufu's pyramid had been located. The first such boat was found in 1954, in a well-sealed pit. There was special interest in the possibility that, should this second example be likewise well sealed, it might yield uncontaminated samples of 4,600-year-old air for environmental analysis.

Both Israeli and foreign archaeologists were busy in Israel. A remarkable find, of approximately 9,000-year-old traces of cloth and a painted stone head, which had occurred in 1983 in a cave, Nahal Hemar, in the Negev, was put on display. Various biblical sites were being excavated, both in the Philistine (coastal) region and in the interior.

Both the Syrian and Iraqi governments were clearing and restoring around important old buildings in such towns as Aleppo, Damascus, Baghdad, and Mosul. In spite of the Iran–Iraq war, some brief fieldwork continued in southern Iraq.

In Turkey the joint Turkish-U.S.-West German expedition at Cayonu reported the final exposure of a nondomestic building of formal plan dating to about 9,500 years ago. It was the third such formally planned structure encountered, and it contained the burned skulls of some 50 humans. Built at a time when an effective food-producing way of life had only recently been developed, it suggested that the pace of cultural acceleration, given an assured food supply, was much faster than had been anticipated. The Turkish Antiquities Service began excavations at Harran, once visited by the biblical Abraham, and the long-range excavations by the Italians, West Germans, and Americans at Arslan Tepe, Bogazkoy, and Elmali continued.

In Greece and in Rome the various national "schools" proceeded with their long-range excavations on large sites with familiar names. There were a few exceptional finds. In European Turkey (Thrace) near Tekirdag a rich 2nd century BC tomb was found. At Paestum in southern Italy a University of Michigan expedition recovered new evidence of the secret women's cultic rites of the goddess known as Bona Dea.

The Pakistan antiquities service reported that significant progress had been made in stopping the degeneration of the building remains of the great site of Mohenjo Daro (about 2500 BC). The increase of groundwater with heavy salt concentration had been an acute problem. In Thailand, at the copper-mining site of Phulong, a University of Pennsylvania group examined the tracks of very early copper recovery and processing.

In North America, underwater investigations by a joint team of salvagers and archaeologists provided conclusive evidence that the sunken "treasure ship" found by private salvage divers in 1983 off the coast of Cape Cod was in fact the lost pirate ship *Whydah,* which sank with all hands after being commandeered in 1717, a year after its maiden voyage. A joint team of divers and archaeologists coordinated plans with Massachusetts state archaeologists to excavate and stabilize the wealth of discovered materials, valued at $10 million–$12 million.

The potential archaeological value of the offshore waters of the east coast of the U.S. was further highlighted in 1985 by a find in New York's East River. In September a group of salvagers reported the discovery of a sunken Revolutionary War frigate, the 26-gun *Hussar,* which sank in 1780. Although cold water and the depth of the find in 100 ft (30 m) of murky water prevented further investigation, available documents indicated that the British ship also contained 80 chained American prisoners of war and a payroll in gold now estimated to be worth millions of dollars.

In addition to these rather spectacular finds, ongoing work by U.S. archaeologists at the site of

University of Colorado archaeologists were embarrassed when their discovery of an "unknown" Inca city was revealed to be ancient news.

George Custer's last battle with Sioux and Cheyenne warriors at the Little Bighorn River in Montana Territory was causing scholars to reassess the events and tactics that took place at the battle. After carefully considering the identity and location of artifacts at the site, the archaeologists, led by Douglas Scott of the U.S. National Park Service, announced that the battle was lost both because of errors of strategy on Custer's part and because of the vastly superior numbers of both fighters and arms on the side of the Indians. Instead of attacking en masse, as had often been assumed, the Indians, according to the archaeologists, cautiously crouched and picked off the soldiers from at least six positions before finally annihilating them. The excavated battle debris also suggested that the Indians were equipped with large numbers of some of the most advanced weapons of the period, including at least 60 new 16-shot, lever-action rifles, while the U.S. soldiers were equipped with only army-issue single-shot Springfield carbines and Colt revolvers.

The vigilance of local inhabitants in the mountains of Guerrero in western Mexico who reported to authorities looting activities at an unstudied site resulted in one of the most important archaeological discoveries in that region in recent years. Located in the northern part of the state, inland from the resort of Acapulco, the site of Copalillo (currently being excavated under the auspices of the National Institute of Anthropology and History) contained on the surface a large platform and three large stone monoliths, each 5 ft (1.5 m) high, with Olmec designs inscribed on them. Ongoing excavations suggested that the site dates to between 2400 and 600 BC, that it is of Olmec cultural affiliation, and, at least tentatively, that this early Mexican civilization, previously thought to have developed on the country's east coast, may in fact have evolved simultaneously on both shores; such an interpretation would cause a drastic revision of old assumptions concerning the sources and direction of Mesoamerican culture.

Farther south, in the former Mayan territory of Belize, a husband-and-wife team, Arlen and Diane

A 9,500-year-old stone building uncovered in Turkey provided evidence of rapid cultural progress following the advent of farming in the ancient Middle East.

ROBERT J. BRAIDWOOD

Chase of the University of Central Florida at Orlando, announced through the U.S. National Science Foundation the discovery of two intact late postclassic Mayan tombs at the coastal site of Santa Rita Corozal. The first tomb contained elaborately decorated pottery and ornaments and the body of what was interpreted to be a king. The second tomb contained two individuals, one of whom had Aztec ear ornaments that were manufactured in central Mexico and the other consisting only of the remains of an unornamented skeleton that was riddled with sting-ray spines and a copper needle, associations in Mayan culture indicative of ritual bloodletting practices.

Untouched by looters, these unusual discoveries indicated that, contrary to current thinking that Mayan culture declined sometime after AD 600–900, Mayan rule in this region instead continued for hundreds of years with high-status nobility controlling large territories until just before the arrival of the Spaniards in the early 16th century.

The archaeology of Ecuador and of the Cauca River valley of Colombia had long been famous for the beautiful gold and ceramic artifacts of the highly publicized but poorly studied Quimbaya culture. Although the culture was well represented in private and museum collections, most pieces came from looted sites. Mostly by guesswork, it was estimated that they were made between AD 400 and 800, several thousand years after the appearance of the first gold technology in the south-central Andes of Peru. In 1985, however, long-overdue controlled archaeological excavations by John Isaacson of the University of Illinois at a small highland site near Quito yielded radiocarbon determinations from stylistically similar Quimbaya pottery that dated these artifacts at 600–1500 BC. These dates implied that the highlands of Ecuador were culturally and technologically advanced much earlier than had been assumed.

Events in South America of relevance to archaeology were overshadowed by a triumph of the Indiana Jones mystique over the conservatism of proper scientific data discovery and presentation. At a news conference the University of Colorado announced to a well-prepared media crowd the discovery of a pre-Inca city located on an eastern slope of the Peruvian Andes, and two faculty members, Tom Lennon and Jane Wheeler, explained their plans to study the site. News of the discovery was reported by many major media outlets, including the *Washington Post,* the television networks, and the wire services. The site was, however, not new and not unknown. Gran Pajaten had been explored by a Peruvian expedition in 1964 and by a U.S. explorer, Gene Savoy, in 1965; it was listed in the *South American Handbook,* was noted on current road maps, had been featured in a 1970 CBS documentary, and had been reported by Peruvian scientists and archaeologists in the national scientific literature over a 20-year period.

ARCHITECTURE

Controversy raged in New York City over the planned extension to the Whitney Museum of American Art, designed originally in the 1960s by Marcel Breuer. The Whitney had become a familiar and loved cultural landmark in the city, and any proposed alteration to its character attracted attention and comments. The extension, designed by Michael Graves, a leading exponent of "post-modernism," was very much larger and totally different in character from the existing building, although Graves had been concerned to ensure that the new extension harmonized with the old. The difficulty was that one person's harmony is another person's disharmony, and the controversy centered very much on this point.

Graves's design featured a massive wing joined to the original building by a curved element, both old and new structures being capped by an enormous stepped-back formal attic that totally altered the scale of the original Breuer building. Graves's design was geometric and formalist, and historical in reference, although uncompromisingly modern in concept. The addition would increase the height of the museum and extend it south at a cost of $37.5 million, adding 134,000 sq ft (12,060 sq m), of which 40,000 sq ft (3,600 sq m) would be exhibition space. The site itself was part of the Upper East Side Historical District. The new extension was to be clad in a grayish pink granite intended to harmonize with the dark gray granite of the older building. Those who opposed the scheme argued that, the suitability of the design aside, they were not convinced that a large-scale extension to the Whitney, which had always been one of the more manageable museums in terms of size and scale, was wholly desirable.

Yet another highly controversial project in which the same considerations were relevant was I. M. Pei's proposed modernization of the Louvre in Paris. Pei's plan featured a two-story underground central service and reception area with an entrance through a 70-ft (20-m)-high glass pyramid to be situated in the middle of the Cour Napoleon. The plan caused demands for a referendum and for a full-size model to be produced so that people could decide for themselves on its merits. In France the struggle seemed to be not only one between the conservationists and modernists but also a political controversy, as political conservatism was associated with conservationism in architecture whereas modernism was linked with socialism. Thus, a vigorous campaign against the scheme was mounted by the conservative newspaper *Le Figaro.*

Cultural Buildings

Design competitions remained popular in 1985, and a number of notable ones were under way. These were increasingly seen as useful exercises for fund-raising and publicity as well as encouragements for quality architecture. Landscapes as well as buildings provided subject matter, as for instance

A glass pyramid measuring 70 feet (20 meters) high was the focal point of a proposed modernization of the Louvre in Paris. Controversy both aesthetic and political surrounded the plan by Chinese-born U.S. architect I. M. Pei.

ROBERT COHEN—AGIP/PICTORIAL PARADE

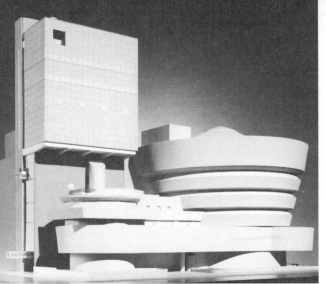

DAN CORNISH—ESTO

Rising above a model of New York's Guggenheim Museum, designed by Frank Lloyd Wright, is an addition proposed in 1985 by Gwathmey Siegel & Associates.

in Bellevue, Wash., where a competition was staged to provide a central park on a 17.5-ac (7.1-ha) midtown site. The winning design, by Beckley/Myers of Milwaukee, Wis., featured a central space within which would be an informal meadow.

The first prize in a competition funded by the National Endowment for the Arts to provide a master plan for Jacob's Pillow in the Berkshire Hills of Massachusetts, the site of a well-known summer dance festival, went to architects Stephen Furnstahl and Kenneth Warriner, Jr. Their plan featured a two-story arcade uniting the various areas of the site, including some historic structures that dated back nearly 200 years. A competition sponsored by the San Francisco Museum of Modern Art for a Napa Valley winery, intended to create a "landmark to viticulture," was won by Graves and artist Edward Schmidt. The site components included an operating winery, exhibition space for an art collection owned by the proprietors, a sculpture garden, an open-air theater, and a residence.

A plan for the extensive redevelopment of downtown Los Angeles would create a proposed Library Square including renovation and expansion of the city's 1926 Art Deco central library. Hardy Holzman Pfeiffer Associates were architects for the renovation and expansion of the library. Two linked commercial developments opposite the library site would provide the financing. They included a $315 million office tower designed by I. M. Pei and Partners and a $337 million tower by Philip Johnson and John Burgee. Pei's would be the city's tallest building when completed. The Johnson/Burgee design featured a historicist roofline with finials and a mansard roof. Two public spaces, one a garden for the library and the other the Bunker Hill Steps, would provide outdoor relaxation areas.

Richard Meier was chosen to design the $100 million J. Paul Getty Fine Arts Center in west Los Angeles. The complex was to include a museum,

an arts and humanities center, and a conservation institute. Construction was due to start in 1987, with completion planned for 1991. Also in the Los Angeles area, the new Filmcorp Center in Culver City would be a ziggurat-inspired terraced eight-story structure, designed by Maxwell Starkman Associates. An internal atrium lobby would rise 90 ft (27 m) to a sloping skyline. The exterior featured bands of light and dark granite alternating with gray solar glass. The project included offices, screening rooms, bars, restaurants, a library, and other facilities, totaling 400,000 sq ft (37,000 sq m).

Gwathmey Siegel & Associates were commissioned to design a six-story addition to the annex of Frank Lloyd Wright's Guggenheim Museum in New York City. The addition would provide extra gallery space, offices, and a restaurant, with a $9 million budget provided. Completion was scheduled for 1987.

Commercial Buildings

Towers were the most prevalent form of commercial office space in most modern developments throughout the world. Naturally enough, the U.S. led the way. Philip Johnson's American Telephone and Telegraph Co. (AT&T) Building in New York City continued to provide inspiration for roofline interest, as evidenced by the Johnson/Burgee building at 190 S. La Salle Street in Chicago. A 40-story office tower perched on a red granite base was crowned by steep and ornate gables, with arched vertical bays articulating the main block. The references to the famous Chicago buildings of Louis Sullivan were unmistakable.

The Civic Opera House in Chicago was the in-

The State of Illinois Center was dedicated in Chicago during the summer. The building contains state offices, shops, restaurants, and a 16-story atrium.

AP/WIDE WORLD

spiration for some of the historical allusions in another Chicago office tower, this one on Wacker Drive and designed by Perkins & Will of Chicago. The building featured an arcaded granite base and a pyramided top with a standard curtain-walled central area. Completion was projected for 1986. Skidmore, Owings & Merrill were designers of the 70-story Dearborn Center in Chicago, a building whose components seemed to be made up of various vertically stacked "segments," each with a separate "ground floor" and atrium; the building also featured multiple bay windows and large lower areas of skylit retail space. The same architects designed a 55-story office tower in Dallas, Texas, featuring a curved roofline punctuated by a six-story "window" or open space. A pedestrian plaza at street level was featured, and the sheathing was of the increasingly popular red granite, similar to that in the AT&T Building in New York.

The future of a 3½-ac (1.4-ha) tract at the southwest corner of Central Park in New York City, known as the Coliseum site, was decided in 1985 when it was sold to the developer Boston Properties in a complex deal. The development would provide retail, office, hotel, and residential space, and the design was by architects Moshe Safdie & Associates. There would be two granite towers of 57 and 72 stories, respectively, and a curved retail galleria. Features included setback structures with five-story prismatic greenhouses at the setback points. These glass "capsules" would provide gardens for apartment dwellers and office workers. A 30-ft (9-m)-high slot opening between the towers on the 59th Street axis was another visual feature. The towers were described by one critic as "expressionistic icebergs."

Many of the major commercial developments under way were multiuse projects. One of these was Skidmore, Owings & Merrill's design for Rowe's and Foster's Wharf on the Boston waterfront. Situated south of the Quincy Market area, the project featured a huge rotunda and a large plaza with housing built on piers jutting into the bay. The blocking of the view of the waterfront caused by the buildings was criticized by many, who felt that Boston's waterfront was a visual amenity that should be easily accessible to all residents, workers, and visitors and not just to the favored few who could afford waterside housing or office space.

Another high-class multiuse complex was Camelback Esplanade in Phoenix, Ariz., a development providing 2.4 million sq ft (216,000 sq m). Designed by the Zeidler Roberts Partnership in association with Cornoyer-Hedrick, the complex was reminiscent in form and material of Pueblo Indian adobe architecture. The project included four office towers, two condominium apartment buildings, a hotel area, and a retail galleria.

In Japan the Fujisawa Municipal Sports Center, some 50 km (30 mi) from Tokyo, of steel and reinforced concrete, was completed at the end of 1984 and was hailed as one of the most ambitious

KOKYU MIWA—HAZAMA-GUMI, LTD.

The Fujisawa Sports Center, designed by Fumihiko Maki, was made of steel and reinforced concrete and clad in stainless steel and gray porcelain tiles.

new Japanese buildings in years. The architect was Fumihiko Maki. The huge gymnasium complex took on a helmetlike form when seen from the air. The roof was covered with enormous stainless steel shingles, and the interior was reminiscent of an aircraft hangar in size. The exterior of the building was clad in gray porcelain tiles.

A sports stadium for a site in Queens, New York City, was planned to occupy the air rights above rail yards in the Long Island City neighborhood. Stephen Lepp Associates' design featured an 85,000-seat cable-supported domed stadium called the Appledome. The central portion of the dome would be removable during good weather to provide open-air sports facilities. An adjacent area, to be known as New York Garden, would provide an arena for ice hockey, basketball, indoor track, and boxing.

The U.S. received its first example of the British "high-tech" style as made famous in particular by architect Richard Rogers. This was the PA Technology Facility near Princeton, N.J., for which Kelbaugh & Lee were collaborating architects. The lightweight roof structure was suspended to provide a column-free interior space and—the usual Rogers trademark—mechanical services were hidden in brightly colored outer pipes. The cost of the building was high, $110 per square foot, and it would be interesting to see whether this mode of building would gain in popularity in the U.S. as it had done in Europe.

Awards

Richard Rogers received the Royal Institute of British Architects (RIBA) Gold Medal for 1985. The International Union of Architects awarded its first Gold Medal for outstanding architectural achievement to Egyptian architect Hassan Fathy, whose best known work was the New Gourna large-scale village relocation project in Luxor, begun in 1945.

AIA Honor Award winners in 1985 included Michael Graves's San Juan Capistrano (Calif.) Library; Richard Meier & Partners' Atheneum, in New Harmony, Ind.; and the Volvo Corporate Headquarters at Göteborg, Sweden, designed by

Mitchell/Giurgola Architects. *The Times* of London and RIBA announced a jointly sponsored new annual award for community architecture projects, with Prince Charles as patron. The first award was to be made in 1986.

ARCTIC REGIONS

Despite falling oil prices, the development of Alaska's North Slope continued. Production of 250,000 bbl of oil daily was expected to begin in 1986 from new developments, such as the Kuparuk and Lisburne fields, just when the giant Prudhoe Bay field would start to decline. Thus North Slope oil output, critical to Alaska's economy, should be stable at least through 1988–89. In February it was reported that the Sohio company estimated that up to 1,800,000,000 more barrels of oil should be recoverable from Prudhoe Bay than had originally been calculated, using new technology expected to be available within five years. Initial estimates of recoverable oil from the Prudhoe field were 9,600,-000,000 bbl, of which just over 3,000,000,000 bbl had been extracted by the end of 1984. In March ARCO Alaska announced that an $85 million pilot project had been undertaken to determine whether it was economically feasible to develop the oil-bearing sand 3,500 ft (1,065 m) beneath the Earth's surface at West Sak, on the North Slope.

In May two giant Korean and Japanese companies announced they were considering the feasibility of building an oil refinery at Valdez, the terminus of the trans-Alaska pipeline, to process products for the Far East. Processing the oil in Alaska would sidestep the U.S. ban on the export of crude oil from the North Slope. A potential roadblock was the fact that the state, which owned one-eighth of Prudhoe Bay's production, had already committed most of its oil in long-term contracts. Late in October Alaska Gov. William Sheffield announced an agreement between U.S. Pres. Ronald Reagan and Prime Minister Yasuhiro Nakasone of Japan to ship Alaskan crude oil to Japan starting early in 1986. The agreement, expected to earn the U.S. an estimated $461 million, involved oil from Cook Inlet and not from Prudhoe Bay.

The October issue of the journal *Alaska* reported that oil exploration in the Arctic National Wildlife Refuge had been completed in April. The program of oil and gas exploration had been mandated by the Alaska National Interests Lands Conservation Act of 1980. More than 1,200 mi (1,930 km) of seismic testing was done to determine how much oil and gas lie under the 1.4 million-ac (5.6 million-ha) coastal plain. Late in the year a federal appeals court issued a preliminary injunction prohibiting exploration for oil and gas on federally owned land on Alaska's outer continental shelf. The lawsuit had been brought by two native communities who argued that energy exploration would interfere with their aboriginal hunting and fishing rights.

After almost two years of study, the Alaska Native Review Commission, sponsored by the Inuit Circumpolar Conference and headed by Justice Thomas R. Burger, issued its review of the Alaska Native Claims Settlement Act (ANCSA) of 1971. In making his recommendations, Justice Burger listed the three main concerns of Alaska natives as land, self-government, and subsistence. The report, entitled *Village Journey: The Report of the Alaska Native Review Commission,* recommended that lands under the control of native corporations be transferred to tribal governments to keep the land in native ownership; that tribal governments established in all of Alaska's villages assert their native sovereignty; and that tribal governments have exclusive jurisdiction over fish and wildlife on native lands.

Canada

Canada's first major northern hydrocarbon development, the $530 million Norman Wells oil field expansion and pipeline project, reached production in May. While not big by world standards, its 25,-000 bbl a day made up 2% of Canada's crude oil requirements and would save Canada $250 million a year in imported oil.

Crewmen from the Soviet icebreaker Moskva *work to free some of the thousands of beluga whales that were discovered in February trapped by ice in the narrow Senyavin Strait off the Chukchi Peninsula of Siberia.*
APN/TASS/GAMMA/LIAISON

Early in the year the new Progressive Conservative government of Canada began to undo the regulatory regimes established by previous governments. The new regime was intended to reward drilling results, not drilling per se, and what this would mean for frontier exploration was not yet clear. In June the minister of energy told a gathering of businessmen in New York that Canada would continue to be a reliable, long-term energy supplier for the U.S. and that foreign investment in the energy sector would be encouraged by elimination of the government's right to take a 25% share of frontier discoveries without compensation. The minister said the best incentive for oil and gas development in the Mackenzie River-Beaufort Sea area would be a natural-gas pipeline from the Mackenzie to southern Canada or the extension of the Norman Wells oil pipeline into the Beaufort.

Important oil discoveries were being reported by several operators, including Panarctic Oils Ltd. at Cape Allison in the High Arctic and Esso Resources Canada Ltd. in the Beaufort Sea northwest of Tuktoyaktuk. The two-week voyage of the U.S. Coast Guard icebreaker *Polar Sea* in August through the Northwest Passage and the Canadian Arctic Islands led to a reaffirmation of Canada's claims to sovereignty over the passage.

In July the minister of Indian affairs and northern development announced that a task force would conduct a fundamental review of federal policy on native claims. The existing policy predated such developments as the 1982 and 1983 constitutional amendments on aboriginal rights, the report of a special committee on Indian self-government, and numerous court cases related to claims issues. In early January the Constitutional Alliance of the Northwest Territories (NWT) reached a tentative agreement on a boundary for division of the NWT into two separate northern territories. The federal government had already agreed in principle to the creation of a new territory in the eastern Arctic as a homeland for a majority of Canada's Inuit.

ARGENTINA

During 1985 public attention in Argentina was once again concentrated on the role that the armed forces had played in the "dirty war" against subversives in the 1970s. Worldwide attention was drawn to the trials on charges of murder and human rights abuses of nine former junta members who had governed Argentina during 1976–82. Public hearings began on April 22, 1985. The prosecution case lasted for five months, during which nearly 1,000 witnesses appeared before the tribunal to provide evidence of hundreds of cases of kidnapping, murder, and torture allegedly perpetrated by the security forces. The prosecution called for life imprisonment for five of the nine accused men and sentences of between 10 and 15 years for the other four. The case for the defense was based on the argument that the hearings were unconstitutional and politically

SYGMA

Former members of Argentina's military junta listen to testimony during their trial on charges of kidnapping, torture, and murder of hundreds of Argentine civilians.

orchestrated. The military remained unrepentant, claiming that its actions had been morally justified by the need to save Argentina from subversion. The verdict, issued December 9, resulted in the conviction of five of the defendants. Ex-president Jorge Videla and former navy commander Adm. Emilio Massera both received life sentences, while ex-president Gen. Roberto Eduardo Viola and two other former officers were given lesser prison terms. Four of the defendants, including ex-president Leopoldo Galtieri, were acquitted, although three of them (including Galtieri) remained in detention on charges connected with the 1982 Falklands war with Great Britain. A decision in that case was expected early in 1986.

While relations between Pres. Raúl Alfonsín and the military remained strained, the possibility of a coup was ruled out. The tactics of the alleged conspirators did not command wide support from the armed forces, and Alfonsín was seen to be popular and to have political and economic matters largely under control. The decree under which the 12 suspects were arrested was found to be unconstitutional by the judiciary, who ruled that they could be detained without trial only when a state of siege was in force. Principally in response to this ruling, the government declared a 60-day state of siege at the end of October. The courts then upheld the arrest order, and several of the suspects were detained again after having been freed. Alfonsín's Radical Civic Union (UCR) fared well in the November 3 elections, filling more than half of the 254-seat Chamber of Deputies (the first midterm congressional elections to be held for 20 years) and half of the seats in the provincial legislatures. Campaigning concentrated on economic issues such as inflation, the decline in real wages, and the rise in unemployment, calculated to have increased from 4.4% in May 1984 to 6.3%, the highest level in 11 years, by May 1985. The Peronists, the major opposition, were beset by divisions so deep that they presented two separate slates of candidates in the key electoral districts of Buenos Aires and its province. Both the Peronists and the UCR saw their share of the vote decline in comparison with the 1983 general elections. However, while the Peronists lost eight seats to emerge with a total of 103 in the Chamber of Deputies, the UCR increased its representation by one to 130.

Relations with the U.K. remained cool, and there was little progress on the Falkland Islands/Islas Malvinas dispute. In July the U.K. government lifted trade sanctions imposed on Argentina during the 1982 conflict over the islands, but the move was not reciprocated. Argentina refused to declare a formal cessation of hostilities unless the question of sovereignty of the islands was discussed.

Radical economic policy changes announced on June 14 marked an abrupt departure from the gradualist approach to economic decision making previously adopted by the Alfonsín administration. The Austral Plan introduced a new currency, the austral, pegged at U.S. $0.80. Other measures included an indefinite price and wage freeze, a severely restrictive monetary policy, and a move to stabilize public finance through spending cuts, higher public utility tariffs, and tax reforms. Automatic financing of the public-sector deficit by the central bank was suspended. The key objectives of the plan were to control inflation, which reached 1,129% in the year to June 1985, and to reduce the public-sector deficit from 12% of gross domestic product (GDP) in 1984 to 4.1% in 1985. The measures were in some instances even more stringent than those agreed upon with the International Monetary Fund (IMF).

The price freeze brought an immediate reduction in the inflation rate; the monthly rate declined in September to 2%—the lowest monthly increase for ten years—while the annual rate fell to 640% by the end of September and was officially forecast to drop to 150% by March 1986. The public-sector deficit was reduced from 13.1% of GDP in the second quarter of the year to 2% in the third. The spread between the official and the parallel rates of exchange was reduced, with the latter quoted at U.S. $0.90 in October.

Following the government's failure to reach IMF economic targets, in February the IMF suspended the credit facility agreed upon in December 1984. A bridging loan of $483 million, over one-third of which was provided by the U.S., was arranged in June to help meet interest payments and to keep repayment arrears within the sensitive 90-day period. After the implementation of the Austral Plan, the IMF allowed Argentina to resume drawing on its credit facility. The move unlocked the door for agreement with commercial bank creditors on a major rescheduling of debt.

AUTHENTICATED NEWS INTERNATIONAL

The "Rainbow Portrait" of Queen Elizabeth I, attributed to Marcus Gheeraerts, was one of hundreds of art objects on display at the National Gallery of Art in Washington, D.C., in the exhibition "The Treasure Houses of Britain."

ART AND ART EXHIBITIONS

Given the ever increasing cost of acquiring new works of art and the prohibitive sums needed for transport and insurance for loan exhibitions, in 1985 many museums and galleries concentrated resources on improving their own buildings and facilities and making their own collections available by way of special exhibitions. As always, however, there were notable extravaganzas. The National Gallery of Art in Washington, D.C., was host to one of the biggest, most complex, and most expensive shows ever to leave Britain. "The Treasure Houses of Britain," sponsored by the Ford Motor Co. and organized by the British Council, opened on November 3 and continued through the winter. Its theme was 500 years of private patronage and collecting as exhibited by individual treasures collected from country houses in Britain. Included were some 750 objects lent by 220 different British castles and stately homes, listed in a catalog that ran to over 600 pages.

Many organizations were involved in the planning and execution of the show, which was expected to bring a record million visitors to the National Gallery. The publicity was such that it sometimes appeared to be more an advertisement for Britain and the country-house way of life than an exhibition chosen for the merit of its objects. Nonetheless, the quality of the objects displayed was of the highest. They included tapestry and armor, along with family portraits, silver, jewelry, and furniture. The logistics involved in such an exhibition were overwhelming. Most of the items traveled on 16 separate scheduled flights. Exhibits had to be collected from locations as far apart as Cornwall and Scotland, and of course they would have to be returned after the exhibition ended.

Decorative items of painting, silver, porcelain, textiles, ivories, and furniture were included in an exhibition entitled "Baroque Splendors of Mexico" at the Denver (Colo.) Art Museum. The exhibition concentrated on the art of Mexico in its period of greatest cultural achievement—the 17th and early 18th centuries. Many of the items were drawn from the museum's own holdings, but others were lent from private and public collections. An exhibition in Paris devoted to the work of one of the leading artisans of the Art Deco period, Charlotte Perriand, was held at the Musée des Arts Décoratifs. It was the first such retrospective of the work of this designer, who spent ten years working in the studio of Le Corbusier and was a leading designer of furniture and interiors throughout the 1920s and '30s. She was a pioneer particularly in the use of metal in furniture.

As always, Paris played host to a number of important art exhibitions. One of the most interesting was a show devoted to Daniel-Henry Kahnweiler, the major avant-garde Paris art dealer of the first decade of the 20th century. The Kahnweiler exhibition was held at the Beaubourg (Pompidou Center) and was in two parts, the first part illustrating his career by means of photographs, books, and letters, and the second displaying his fine art collection,

which included works by his major patrons and friends, such as Picasso, Matisse, and Braque. It was an exhibition devoted to the history of collecting and taste as well as to a display of fine paintings.

At the Galerie Marigny the first major Parisian exhibition of miniatures since 1906 was mounted. On display were 200 portrait miniatures borrowed from more than 20 French private collections. Many of these were of considerable historical interest, among them a rare miniature of a child, "Blue Boy" by Horace Vernet. The centenary of the birth of Robert and Sonia Delaunay, pioneers of the early 20th-century Orphic style of Cubism, was celebrated with a show of paintings, drawings, watercolors, and artifacts at the Musée d'Art Moderne de la Ville de Paris.

Exhibitions devoted to French art and artists were shown in many other parts of the world. The theme of one at the National Gallery of Ireland in Dublin was 17th-century French classicism. It assembled works borrowed from the Louvre and other important French museums, and lesser known artists of the period were represented, as well as Claude and Poussin. "Master Drawings by Géricault," organized by the International Exhibitions Foundation, was shown first at the Morgan Library in New York City and later at the San Diego (Calif.) Museum of Art and the Museum of Fine Arts, Houston, Texas. Many of the drawings by the important 19th-century French Romantic artist were lent from foreign collections and had not been seen previously in the U.S. "Edgar Degas: The Painter as Printmaker" was shown at the Hayward Gallery in London from May to July. Organized by the Mu-

"Madame Charpentier and Her Children," painted in 1878 by Auguste Renoir, was part of a major retrospective exhibit of the artist's works. The exhibition traveled to London, Paris, and Boston.

THE METROPOLITAN MUSEUM OF ART, NEW YORK

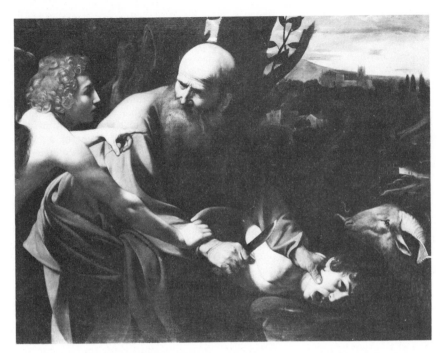

"The Sacrifice of Isaac," a painting by the Italian Baroque artist Caravaggio, was shown at the Metropolitan Museum of Art in New York City in an exhibition entitled "The Age of Caravaggio." The show later traveled to Naples, Italy.

UFFIZI; PHOTOGRAPH, SCALA/ART RESOURCE

seum of Fine Arts, Boston, and first shown there in 1984 to mark the 150th anniversary of Degas's birth, it displayed an aspect of his work less well known than his oils and pastels but one in which he was equally proficient. The chief aim was to show as many as possible of the stages of each lithograph and etching.

The 1985 Edinburgh International Festival had a French theme, and several of the art exhibitions echoed it. "Colour Since Matisse," an exhibition of exclusively French painting of the 20th century, focused on the use of color in painting, illustrated by the works of Bonnard and Delaunay and other artists up to those of the present day. The National Gallery of Scotland concentrated on a display of French art from its own fine collections, with works from the late 16th to the late 19th century. At the Scottish National Gallery of Modern Art, French art up to 1960 was the subject, with a survey of the work of the School of Paris. At the Royal Scottish Museum, "French Connections: Scotland and the Arts of France" focused on Scottish collections of French art, including the Hamilton Palace collection. Among the manuscripts, ivories, sculpture, furniture, and ceramics on show was a silver gilt tea service that had belonged to Napoleon.

At the Hayward Gallery in London, an exhibition devoted to the ever popular works of Auguste Renoir was mounted in the spring. With more than 90 paintings on display, it was the first important retrospective of Renoir's work to be seen in Europe since the show organized by the Arts Council of Great Britain for the Edinburgh International Festival and the Tate Gallery, London, in 1953. The show offered an opportunity to assess the works

of this artist on several levels and to examine his achievement, his contribution to Impressionism, and his place in the European figurative and landscape traditions. The range of color and light was extraordinary. Organized in collaboration with the Réunion des Musées Nationaux, Paris, and the Museum of Fine Arts, Boston, the exhibition later traveled to the Grand Palais in Paris, where it was one of the year's major events, and to Boston.

The Royal Academy in London was the venue for the first major retrospective devoted to the work of Marc Chagall to be seen in England since 1948. The exhibits, borrowed from collections worldwide, included theater designs, stained glass, oil paintings, and drawings. The show later traveled to the Philadelphia Museum of Art. Selections from the Cone Collection, Baltimore, Md., which included many fine French works, formed a traveling show seen at the Kimbell Art Museum, Fort Worth, Texas, and at the Los Angeles County Museum of Art. The Cone Collection, given to the Baltimore Museum of Art in 1949, was especially rich in paintings by Matisse, with Picasso, Cézanne, Renoir, and Gauguin also represented.

Italian Renaissance paintings and paintings of the 17th century were the theme of another group of 1985 art exhibitions. An exhibition of 87 Renaissance drawings from the Biblioteca Ambrosiana, Milan, Italy, was shown at the Los Angeles County Museum of Art from late January to the end of March. Included were works by Leonardo da Vinci, and Pisanello, as well as other masters of the 15th and 16th centuries in Italy. At the Prado in Madrid a winter exhibition featured three manuscripts by Leonardo, exhibited together for the first time in 400 years. They included the Codex Hammer (owned by Armand Hammer, the eminent U.S. collector; formerly the Codex Leicester), a scientific manuscript entitled *On the Nature, Weight and Movement of Water,* consisting of 36 folios dating from 1506 to 1510. The other two manuscripts belonged to the Biblioteca Nacional, Madrid.

"Baroque Portraiture in Italy: Works from North American Collections," organized by the John and Mable Ringling Museum of Art, Sarasota, Fla., was shown in the spring at the Wadsworth Atheneum, Hartford, Conn. Portraits in every medium including sculpture and portrait medallions were included among the works by 48 artists. "The Age of Caravaggio" was shown at the Metropolitan Museum of Art, New York City, and later at the Museo e Gallerie Nazionali di Capodimonte, Naples, Italy. It comprised 40 pictures either by or after Caravaggio, together with 60 paintings by artists who preceded him, followed him, or competed with him. Thus the exhibition was neither a monograph devoted only to Caravaggio nor solely a collection of works from his period. It afforded remarkable opportunities for visitors to compare and contrast Caravaggio with his contemporaries and his forerunners and also to study his very considerable influence on later artists. The show, which included works lent from collections in the U.S. and abroad, was sophisticated and thought-provoking.

A large exhibition devoted to the works of Vincent van Gogh at the Metropolitan Museum of Art, containing many of his best oils and a large selection of his drawings, showed particularly how strongly this artist was influenced by the Japanese tradition. The influence was especially noticeable in the brown ink drawings, less frequently seen and reproduced than some of the paintings.

To mark the Festival of India, which began in June in the U.S., the Metropolitan Museum of Art mounted a comprehensive show of the art of India from the 14th to the 19th century. About 350 works including paintings, jewelry, and tapestries were lent by collections in India, Europe, the U.S., and the Middle East. Indian shows were also held at the Asia Society in New York City and at the Cleveland (Ohio) Museum of Art. At the Fogg Art Museum at Harvard University, master drawings from the Woodner Collection were exhibited. Included were several recent acquisitions, notable among them a sheet of drawings by the 16th-century Italian artist and critic Giorgio Vasari. The sheet was from his *Libro dei Disegni* and was formerly in the collection of the duke of Devonshire at Chatsworth House, England.

At the Rijksmuseum, Amsterdam, an important exhibition of Rembrandt drawings from the museum's own collection was on show. It comprised the Print Room's entire collection of Rembrandt drawings, which were constantly being assessed, examined, and reattributed by experts. Sixty of the drawings were definitely attributed to Rembrandt, and 56 were ascribed to anonymous pupils or followers. An exhibition in Siena, Italy, devoted to Simone Martini (*c.* 1284–1344) was mounted at the Pinacoteca Nazionale and showed 28 works, mostly panel paintings but also a few detached frescoes. Items from Martini's workshop and entourage were included. Among the masterpieces on display was the Blessed Agostino Novello altarpiece from S. Agostino in Siena. The Canadian artist John O'Brien (1831–91), best remembered as Canada's first native marine artist, was the subject of an exhibition organized by the Art Gallery of Nova Scotia. The 28 paintings of this largely self-taught artist traveled to the National Gallery of Canada in Ottawa and later to other Canadian galleries. Both in the U.S. and in Canada, works by native artists continued to attract the attention of collectors and museums.

A number of important and thought-provoking exhibitions were mounted in London. One held at

An early 19th-century watercolor from Rajasthan, India, was part of an enormous collection of Indian art exhibited during the year as part of the Festival of India.

FINE ARTS MUSEUM OF SAN FRANCISCO, ACHENBACH FOUNDATION FOR GRAPHIC ARTS, KATHERINE C. BALL COLLECTION

the British Museum in early spring, entitled "The Golden Age of Anglo-Saxon Art: 966–1066," was jointly organized with the British Library. Many of the items, some of which had not been in England since the Middle Ages, were borrowed from foreign collections. The exhibition commemorated the 1,000th anniversary of the death of St. Aethelwold, bishop of Winchester, a key figure in the monastic reform movement out of which emerged the splendid illuminated manuscripts, ivories, and metal objects that dominated the show. The great quality and range of this period of art were well illustrated.

The Tate Gallery in London mounted a retrospective exhibition devoted to the works of the artist Francis Bacon, probably the most important living English painter, to celebrate 40 years of his work since 1944. The show, dominated by Bacon's powerful tormented expressionistic images, was later shown in Stuttgart, West Germany, and West Berlin. It was the second Tate retrospective of Bacon's work, the first having been in 1962. The centerpiece of the show was the display of 18 large triptychs completed since 1962. An exhibition of 36 paintings drawn from the Dulwich College Picture Gallery, London, entitled "Collection for a King," was sent to the U.S. and shown at the National Gallery of Art in Washington and later at the Los Angeles County Museum of Art. It was the first such display to travel from this gallery in some 40 years.

There was a discernible increase of interest in the Expressionist artists of the earlier 20th century. "Munch and the Workers," a major loan exhibition from the Munch-Museet in Oslo, consisting of over 100 works by the Norwegian Expressionist Edvard Munch, was shown at the City of Edinburgh Art Centre and later at the Barbican in London. The summer exhibition at the Museum of Fine Arts in Basel, Switz., was devoted to the same artist and entitled "Edvard Munch: His Work in Swiss Collections." It assembled paintings and graphics of the artist drawn from Swiss public and private collections, making many major works accessible to the public for the first time. Also in Switzerland, two major loan exhibitions were devoted to German Romantic painting. At the Kunstmuseum, Bern, "Traum und Wahrheit" included 290 paintings, watercolors, and drawings from collections in East Berlin, Leipzig, Weimar, and Dresden. At the Kunsthaus, Zürich, a group of 43 paintings by Caspar David Friedrich, K. F. Schinkel, and Carl Blechen was lent by the Nationalgalerie, West Berlin; 120 German Romantic drawings from the National Gallery, Oslo, were also exhibited.

"German Art in the 20th Century," which opened at the Royal Academy, London, in October, traced the development of German art from the pre-World War I Expressionist groups Die Brücke and Der Blaue Reiter through the satirical realism of the pre-Hitlerian Neue Sachlichkeit to the post-World War II Neo-Expressionism of the Neue Wilden. Finally, on a somber note, the Museum of Modern Art, Oxford, marked the 40th anniversary of the dropping of the atomic bomb on Hiroshima with "Hiroshima: Paintings by Survivors."

ASTRONOMY

Astronomers got their first close look at a comet in September, during a dress rehearsal for the interception of Halley's Comet in the spring of 1986. The International Cometary Explorer (ICE) satellite passed within 7,800 km (4,800 mi) of the core of the comet Giacobini-Zinner, a relatively bright comet that speeds by the Earth once every six and a half years. ICE had been launched by the National Aeronautics and Space Administration (NASA) in 1978, and the satellite was originally known as the International Sun Earth Explorer 3 (ISEE 3). It had been studying the interactions of the Earth and the solar wind—the gases that flow out from the Sun at about 400 km/sec (900,000 mph). In 1983 the craft was renamed ICE and sent on a series of maneuvers that used the gravitational pull of the Moon to sling it into the path of Giacobini-Zinner.

What ICE found surprised many of the scientists involved. In a 42-hour-long encounter with the comet, the space probe's instruments detected high energy ions (atoms with more or fewer electrons than electrically neutral atoms) as far away as 2 million km (1.2 million mi) from the comet's core. Apparently, the ions had been accelerated by the interaction between the solar wind's magnetic fields and the speeding comet.

In addition, ICE failed to find a clear-cut "bow shock" region where the solar wind first hits gases boiled off of the comet's icy core. Scientists expected a sharp jump in the strength of the magnetic field at the bow shock, similar to the mechanical shock wave produced by supersonic aircraft in the atmosphere. Instead of the neat shock front, ICE detected a complex, turbulent region of swirling ions and electrons. The interaction of solar wind and comets is clearly more complicated than had been thought.

In the meantime, Halley's Comet continued to speed toward its first close pass to the Earth in January 1986. By the year's end, it was visible with the unaided eye if the sky was sufficiently dark.

New observations of Jupiter's infrared light appeared to show that sulfur compounds cannot be the cause of Jupiter's multicolored clouds. On Earth sulfur can, depending on conditions, assume colors ranging from deep red to bright yellow—the right range for many of Jupiter's clouds. But University of Arizona scientists and other researchers flying in the Kuiper Airborne Observatory showed that the infrared spectrum of Jupiter has none of the characteristics of sulfur. This means that sulfur cannot be responsible for the colors in the clouds' upper regions. Two other possible coloring agents might be compounds of phosphorous or complex organic

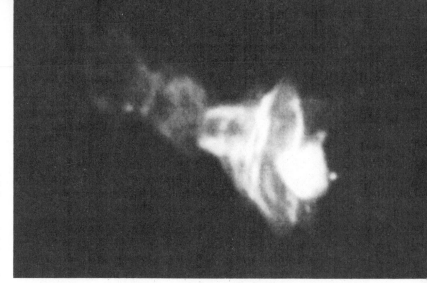

Astronomers at Columbia University, New York City, and the University of California at Davis announced the discovery of a new class of quasarlike celestial radio sources. The structures are tens of thousands of times closer to Earth than the nearest known quasar and may be associated with black holes or neutron stars.

AP/WIDE WORLD

molecules. At the moment, the puzzle of Jupiter's colors is deeper than ever.

Stars and Galaxies

It now appeared that most stars were not formed in a sudden burst of activity when galaxies first came into existence, as had previously been thought. New data collected by Stanislav Djorgovski and Hyron Spinrad of the University of California at Berkeley showed that about half of a galaxy's gas condenses into stars in the first billion years of its existence, half of the remainder in the next billion years, half of what is left in another billion, and so on. The scientists based their conclusions on detailed observations of extremely distant galaxies, up to 12,000,000,000 light-years away.

Closer to home, studies of our neighboring galaxy, the giant spiral M31, known as Andromeda, indicated that a relatively small spiral lies at the center of the huge system. Radio telescope observations analyzed by R. A. M. Walterbos of The Netherlands revealed a spiral pattern of hot gas almost identical in form to the larger spiral of stars that make up the galaxy itself. However, the inner spiral is only about 2,500 light-years across, while the galaxy itself is more than 150,000 light-years in diameter. Other optical observations confirmed the spiral orientation of the gases at the galaxy's heart. The gas, which is highly ionized, appears to be rotating around the center at about 200 km/sec (120 mi per sec), about the same speed that the galaxy as a whole is rotating. However, the inner spiral does not appear to be lying in the same plane as that of the galaxy itself but is tilted at a considerable angle.

Astronomers find the new data particularly fascinating in conjunction with the previous year's discoveries of objects at the center of our own Milky Way Galaxy. There, a complex pattern of arcs and filaments extends some 200 light-years from the center, while a dense ring of material about 12 light-years in diameter surrounds the nucleus of the Galaxy.

The features in Andromeda appear much more diffuse and far less bright than those in our own Galaxy, and the gas velocities are much lower. Andromeda's nucleus seems to be an example of one less active than that of the Milky Way, which in turn is weaker than many other galactic nuclei. However, the nuclei of both Andromeda and Milky Way are probably shaped at least as much by magnetic forces as by gravitational ones because their odd spiral shapes are hard to explain if only gravity is involved.

Our own Galaxy continues to reveal surprises as it is probed at different parts of the electromagnetic spectrum. The new EXOSAT X-ray satellite's survey of sources of radiation turned up not only a large number of discrete isolated sources, ranging from pulsars to old supernova remnants, but also a flat ridge or disk of X-radiation coming from the plane of the Galaxy. The disk extends about 20,000 light-years out from the center (about 40% of the distance to the edge or 60% of the distance out to our Sun) and is about 300 light-years thick. This is just a bit thicker than the disk of gas that runs along the galactic plane.

The X-ray ridge is pouring out about 100,000 times as much X-radiation as our Sun produces at all wavelengths. If the radiation is produced by hot plasma—ionized gases—the temperature of the plasma must be around 10 million to 100 million degrees Celsius and have a density one three hundredth that of the galactic gas as a whole. It is not clear what could produce this much hot plasma, or what could contain it to this narrow ridge. Alternatively, the X-rays might be produced by extremely energetic cosmic ray electrons spiraling around the galactic magnetic field. (When charged particles spiral through a magnetic field, they radiate energy—the higher their own energy, the higher the frequency radiated.)

Interstellar space not only is bathed in X rays but also is enshrouded in smog, according to Louis Allamandola of NASA's Ames Research Center. By analyzing infrared emission from various bodies of interstellar gas, Allamandola and his two colleagues concluded that the spectra matched those of extremely large and complex hydrocarbon molecules

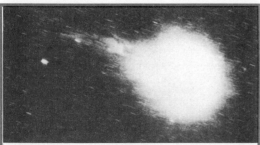

AP/WIDE WORLD

The Return of Halley's Comet

For at least the past 2,200 years Halley's Comet has swung into the inner solar system every 76 years or so. On Oct. 16, 1982, astronomers working with the Hale telescope atop Palomar Mountain spotted the comet once again, the first sighting since its last rendezvous with the Earth in 1910. This time it was due to make its closest approach to the Sun on Feb. 9, 1986.

Throughout 1985 growing popular excitement over Halley's coming manifested itself in the publication of at least 50 new books and thousands of articles about the comet, as well as the merchandising of Halley T-shirts, jewelry, posters, slide sets, stamps, coins, computer programs for orbital calculations, and the "proper" telescopes and binoculars. For those who could afford not to miss the best view of Halley, from the Southern Hemisphere, specially organized tours and cruises awaited. For the stay-at-homes there would be comet parties and other festivities, both indoors and under the stars.

Scientific excitement also swelled as a veritable armada of spacecraft sped to intercept the comet in the spring of 1986. First to be launched, in December 1984, were two Soviet spacecraft, Vega 1 and 2, whose dual mission comprised a visit to Venus in June 1985 and a rendezvous with Halley on March 6 and March 9, 1986. Japan launched the Sakigake spacecraft in January 1985 and another called Planet-A in August; the former was to fly into the comet's tail, the latter closer to the nucleus. In July 1985 the European Space Agency launched its Giotto space probe (named for the 14th-century painter who included the 1301 apparition of Halley's Comet in a Nativity scene). Giotto would pass within 500 km (310 mi) of the nucleus of the comet to provide the first pictures of how a comet really looks. The U.S., having no probe going directly to Halley, would observe the comet from a space shuttle orbiter. That country was also headquarters for the worldwide International Halley Watch, set up to help coordinate the ground-based observations planned and being carried out by more than a thousand professional and amateur astronomers.

called polycylic aromatic hydrocarbons, or PAHs. These molecules consist of some 20 to 50 carbon atoms linked together in several rings. On Earth, PAHs are produced in the exhausts of automobiles. How such quantities of smog are produced in interstellar clouds is not clear, but the discovery shows that ever more complex organic substances seem to be created in space, a conclusion that may affect theories about how life arose on Earth.

Cosmology

An important discovery in astronomy in 1985 was the detection of a supercluster of galaxies that stretched for well over a billion light-years across the sky. The supercluster is a collection of hundreds of thousands of galaxies formed into a filament about 10 million to 50 million light-years across, with clusters of galaxies dotted along it intermittently like beads on a string. It is located in the region of the sky covered by the Perseus and Pegasus constellations and includes the previously discovered Perseus supercluster. There is some evidence that this huge filament of galaxies includes our own Galaxy and the region around it and may, in fact, extend through our part of the universe to continue on the opposite side of the sky.

The supercluster, now the largest known structure in the universe, was discovered by Jack O. Burns of the University of New Mexico and a graduate student, David J. Batuski, during a systematic search with the 2.1-m (83-in) telescope at the Kitt Peak National Observatory. Since the supercluster extends out to the limits of Kitt Peak's view into deep space, it may well be longer than even a billion light-years. If it is, the Space Telescope, to be launched in 1986, might be able to trace it much farther into space.

The existence of such a large, filamentary structure seemed to support the theory of galaxy formation that assumes that large structures such as superclusters formed first, followed by clusters and then finally galaxies, rather than the opposite sequences. It also lent credence to speculations based on early supercluster discoveries that the universe is one big cosmic tapestry with almost all galaxies concentrated into a tangle of virtually endless filaments snaking across the sky.

One of the major puzzles that had intrigued astronomers over the past decade was the question of "missing mass." When the mass of clusters of galaxies is estimated by measuring the velocities of the galaxies that make them up, the mass seems as much as ten times more than that contained in the galaxies themselves. Even if the mass of the gas observed in the clusters is added in, there seems to be at least five times too little. The unaccounted for mass has been termed "missing." A similar but smaller problem seems to afflict the galaxies themselves. Their mass estimated from the velocities of the stars in them also seems too great for the number and size of stars contained in them.

Now two studies seemed to indicate that the "missing mass" just is not there at all. Mauri Valtonen of Turku University in Finland and Gene Byrd at the University of Alabama showed, with computer simulation, that groups of galaxies and clusters will tend to throw out member galaxies at high velocities, causing the cluster to slowly expand over time. (This happens when a smaller galaxy moves toward the strong gravitational field of a giant central galaxy and is slung away.) If the expelled galaxies are wrongly assumed to be still gravitationally bound, the mass of the cluster will be overestimated by two to five times.

A second very different study performed by scientists at Kitt Peak and AT&T Bell Labs analyzed thousands of images of distant galaxies that appeared close to much nearer galaxies. Einstein's theory of gravitation predicts that the nearby galaxies will distort the light from the distant galaxies, causing certain changes in the apparent shape of these galaxies' images. The more massive the nearby galaxy, the more the distortion. But the study found no such distortion. This seemed to limit the average mass of a galaxy to less than about 200,000,000,000 solar masses (about the mass of our own Galaxy). This is sufficiently small that there would be no need to hypothesize missing mass at the galactic level either.

Together, these results seemed to show that there is 30 to 50 times too little matter in the universe to eventually slow and reverse the current expansion of the universe. Since some current theories concerning the future of the universe assumed that there is just enough matter to "close" the universe, the recent results might lead to revisions of some cosmological theories.

AUSTRALIA

Support for the government of Prime Minister Robert (Bob) Hawke, which began 1985 in a strong position, deteriorated as the year progressed. After his Australian Labor Party (ALP) won a clear victory over the Liberal and National parties in the December 1984 general elections, Hawke strengthened his second ministry with some judicious appointments. Two senators who had made heavy weather of their Cabinet responsibilities were demoted; Gareth Evans was moved from the post of attorney general to become resources and energy minister, while Gordon Scholes, who was replaced as defense minister by Kim Beazley, left the Cabinet to become territories minister. By midyear, however, it was clear that the Cabinet reshuffle was not enough. Such serious defects had become evident in the Hawke government that public opinion polls suggested that the ALP would lose office to the Liberal Party should an election be held.

A series of disasters and policy turnabouts, especially in economic matters and foreign policy, led to a downward revision of popular support for the prime minister himself. Hawke accepted some of the blame but warned his ministers to think before they acted. Throughout 1985 Hawke and his Cabinet were clearly out of touch with public opinion. One of the first signs of this was the failure of the ALP to estimate correctly the strength of the antinuclear lobby. The Nuclear Disarmament Party (NDP), formed by a breakaway faction of the ALP and taking part in elections for the first time in December 1984, won a seat in the Senate. Nationwide, the NDP polled 6.8% of the Senate vote. However, at its inaugural national conference in April the NDP lost the support of several key figures, including the newly elected senator, Jo Valentine, because of fears that the party was being taken over by the Socialist Workers Party, a far-left group with an estimated national membership of only 300. Hawke's greatest failure during the year, however, was his ill-advised attempt to call a meeting of persons interested in tax reform.

The integrity of the government was damaged by two sensational court cases with political overtones. Norman Gallagher, general secretary of the Builders' Laborers Federation (BLF), was found guilty of accepting bribes and sent to prison. At the center of the case were two beach houses constructed for Gallagher by major building companies as insurance against disruptions at their work sites. Directors of the companies concerned were also found guilty and fined. The ALP tried desperately and, to some extent, effectively to distance itself from the problems of the BLF. Because of the sustained record of industrial lawlessness by the BLF, and despite warnings by the Australian Council of Trade Unions (ACTU) that it was hostile to the move, Minister for Industrial Relations Ralph Willis and Prime Minister Hawke decided to introduce a special law to deregister the union.

Far more serious for the government was the trial of Lionel Murphy, a former ALP federal attorney general and the first Australian High Court judge to face a criminal charge, who in September was found guilty of attempting to pervert the course of justice. He was sentenced to 18 months in prison for seeking to influence committal proceedings against Morgan Ryan, a solicitor charged with forging immigration documents. While Murphy appealed his sentence, Hawke appeared to vacillate when he failed to act in reply to a call from the Liberal Party that Murphy be sacked if he refused to step down from the bench. In November an appeal court granted Murphy the right to a retrial.

In September the leadership of the Liberal Party changed hands unexpectedly. In a stormy meeting of the parliamentary party, Andrew Peacock was unsuccessful in his attempt to obtain an undertaking from his deputy, John Howard, that he would not challenge him for the leadership. Peacock resigned, and Howard was elected to replace him by a convincing majority. A former treasurer in the administration of Malcolm Fraser, Howard was expected, by leading the party further to the right, to

An Australian police boat tows away a sailboat that attempted to obstruct a U.S. warship during an antinuclear demonstration in Sydney Harbor on March 4.

present a clearer alternative to the policies of the ALP government.

Foreign Affairs

The year 1985 was a bad one for Australia's policymakers. Apart from the disastrous foundering of the ANZUS defense treaty between Australia, New Zealand, and the U.S., foreign relations were seriously damaged when both Hawke and Foreign Minister William (Bill) Hayden made spectacular gaffes that tarnished that country's image abroad and contributed to a loss of confidence among foreign investors.

In February Hawke left for overseas talks planned to cement relations with the European Communities (EC) and the U.S. No sooner had he arrived in Brussels than word reached him that a storm had broken at home over the government's decision to help the U.S. test its MX intercontinental ballistic missile. In Hawke's absence, Minister of Defense Kim Beazley had revealed that deep-sea acoustic sensors necessary for the missile tests had already been laid in international waters about 200 mi (320 km) off the Tasmanian coast. Critics within the ALP were quick to point out that the government's efforts to assist the U.S. in developing the missile were inconsistent with its policy on the need for international disarmament.

Faced with the fury of his party and the condemnation of public opinion, Hawke backed down, changed the policy, and was fortunate that the U.S. administration, more concerned with the actions of New Zealand and their effects on ANZUS, tried to help Hawke out of his embarrassing loss of face. In explaining how he, along with Hayden and former minister of defense Scholes, had come to make the original decision on MX testing, Hawke said: "We have a security committee management which must obviously operate in certain sensitive areas. It is quite clear that not all decisions in this sort of area

are capable of being taken through the full committee and Cabinet process." Hawke paid a heavy price for the committee system by being publicly attacked and humiliated by his caucus colleagues, many of whom were frustrated and concerned that such a sensitive matter had not been brought before them.

Relations between Australia and the U.S. had more than their usual number of ups and downs in 1985. Another potentially serious dispute arose when the *National Times* published an article alleging that the U.S. government had repositioned a spy satellite controlled from its military base at Pine Gap, Northern Territory, so that it could spy on Greece and other Mediterranean countries. Australia's large Greek community was outraged, and Greek ethnic members of Parliament demanded that Hawke prevent the U.S. from spying on what was, after all, a friendly Western government. A third difficulty arose when Australia declined to assist the U.S. with the development of its Strategic Defense Initiative, or "Star Wars" program. The government's opposition was based on the argument that the current nuclear balance between the superpowers provided a reasonably stable deterrent, whereas the "Star Wars" program, if successful, would upset the balance.

Foreign Minister Hayden's problems concerned Australia's relations with the Association of Southeast Asian Nations (ASEAN). Hayden's situation was particularly unfortunate because he had made a point of stressing the need for Australia to have harmonious contact with ASEAN's member countries—the Philippines, Thailand, Singapore, Malaysia, Indonesia, and Brunei. The worst crisis in Australia-ASEAN relations developed when Hayden became involved in diplomatic quarrels between Thailand and Vietnam. Hayden believed Vietnamese leaders when they denied—falsely— that Vietnamese forces based in Kampuchea had made incursions into Thai territory to attack the forces of the Democratic Kampuchea government-in-exile. During his visit to Vietnam, Hayden also met with Kampuchean Prime Minister Hun Sen, thereby angering the leaders of ASEAN countries, who did not recognize the Hun Sen government. Ian McPhee, opposition spokesman for foreign affairs, described Hayden as an "amateur" and said that his poorly timed visit had undermined ASEAN's position at the United Nations and reduced Australia's credibility in the region. The Chinese government described Hayden as a "cat's-paw," and Hayden himself, with some chagrin, sent a stiff protest note to his Vietnamese counterpart, Nguyen Co Thach, regarding the misleading information he had received on Vietnamese troop movements.

The Economy

High unemployment and exchange-rate fluctuations proved difficult factors for the government to manage. Although the number of people out of work fell by 4,400 in May 1985, there were still more than 600,000 people registered as unemployed. The seasonally adjusted unemployment rate at that time was 8.4%, and it hovered around that figure throughout the year.

The Australian dollar suffered a major fall in value during the year. After beginning the year at U.S. $0.82, the Australian dollar reached its lowest value of U.S. $0.63 in late April before recovering slightly to around U.S. $0.70. It fell even further against the pound sterling and other currencies, losing about 20% of its value against the currency value of Australia's major trading partners. The dramatic and largely unpredicted decline was blamed on the country's poor international image, which, in turn, was blamed on various factors, including the Treasury's abandonment of money-supply targets, the crisis within ANZUS, the administration's strained relations with the U.S., and the triumph of the left-wing of the ALP, who prevented Hawke from reintroducing fees for university students. While in theory the depreciation of the currency might have offered unexpected relief from the widening trade deficit, in fact import businesses showed strong growth.

The dollar failed to rally and indeed might have been further harmed by Hawke's ill-advised conduct at a general meeting held in June to discuss tax reform. As part of his election policy, Hawke had pledged to gather together representatives of all sections of society—business people, trade unionists, economists, farmers, women, Aborigines, exporters, importers, and tax accountants—who together were expected, within the dignified confines of Parliament House in Canberra, to submerge their differences and agree on a consensus policy to achieve tax reform. By the time the so-called tax summit was held, seven months after the election, the economic climate had worsened to such an extent that it appeared extremely unlikely that any consensus could be reached. Matters were made worse when Treasurer Paul Keating signaled in advance his determination to introduce a broadly based consumption tax of 12.5% in return for income tax concessions.

When the tax summit began on July 1, Parliament House was guarded by baton-carrying police. Between 20,000 and 40,000 farmers gathered on the lawns outside, encouraged in their hostility to

Lionel Murphy, the first judge of the Australian High Court ever to face criminal indictment, speaks to reporters as he emerges from the courtroom. Murphy was convicted in September.

THE BULLETIN/AUSTRALIAN CONSOLIDATED PRESS, LTD.

the Hawke-Keating package by Sir Johannes Bjelke-Petersen, state premier of Queensland. Even before the summit began, public opinion polls showed that for the first time the leader of the opposition—at the time, Andrew Peacock—was more popular with the electorate than Hawke, who had hitherto been considered invincible. As the conference proceeded, the government abandoned its prepared position and fell in with the wishes of the ACTU. The views of all other participants at the meeting were ignored as Hawke retreated before the hostility of public opinion and dropped the idea of a consumption tax. Keating, who had staked his reputation on the acceptance of his consumption tax plans, quipped that the end of the conference was "like Ben Hur. We crossed the line with one wheel off the chariot." By the end of the summit, most interest groups and most members of the general public agreed that the summit had been largely a waste of time, while for both Hawke and Keating it was a political disaster.

The agricultural sector was troubled by the U.S. administration's moves to boost its own farm exports. The Australian Wheat Board warned that up to one-third of wheat export income could be under threat. Minister for Primary Industry John Kerin personally informed the U.S. administration of Australia's concern and its fears that a trade war between the EC and the U.S. would devastate Australia's primary producers.

The year saw strong increases in retail and motor vehicle sales, while private consumption and private business investment exceeded government targets of 2.5 and 5%, respectively. The budget, presented on August 20, contained little of significance apart from a promise to establish training schemes to fight unemployment among young people and a plan to provide rebates to farmers on diesel fuel excise.

AUSTRIA

During 1985 it was discovered that a "wine mafia" had been lacing local Austrian wines with harmful diethylene glycol, an automobile antifreeze additive that enhanced sweetness and alcoholic content. As doctored wines began turning up all over Europe and the U.S., the government was forced virtually to halt exports, and later in the year it introduced tough new wine laws.

The year had an unpropitious start with the welcome home after more than 30 years' imprisonment in Italy given to Nazi war criminal Walter Reder by Defense Minister Friedhelm Frischenschlager of the rightist Freedom Party of Austria, coalition partner of Chancellor Fred Sinowatz's Socialist Party of Austria. Reder had been jailed for his part in the massacre of 600 hostages in the northern Italian village of Marzabotto in 1944. The ensuing protests at home and abroad forced the minister to apologize, though he resisted pressure to resign.

Employment and conservation of the environment were prime concerns of Austria's policymakers. The government's conservation program pro-

GEORGE TAMES/THE NEW YORK TIMES

A chemist with the U.S. Bureau of Alcohol, Tobacco, and Firearms notes many instances of Austrian wine tainted with the toxic chemical diethylene glycol.

vided for the reduction of harmful emissions from vehicles and industrial plants, the purification of rivers, and protection of the countryside from dangerous chemicals. A priority was the provision of clean hydroelectric power. However, the strength of feeling among Austria's conservationists continued to hinder government plans for the Hainburg hydroelectric plant near the Czechoslovak border. The government postponed moves to restart operations after a serious political crisis threatened to erode Austria's traditional social consensus. In July the frustrated shareholders in the mothballed Zwentendorf nuclear power plant decided to dismantle it and sell off its components, arousing further fierce argument among the political parties.

On May 15 Austria celebrated the 30th anniversary of the State Treaty by which the nation had returned to full sovereignty after World War II. Eleven foreign ministers, including those of the signatory powers—Great Britain, France, the Soviet Union, and the U.S.—attended the celebrations in Vienna.

An Organization for Economic Cooperation and Development report in early 1985 welcomed Austria's overall economic performance, although it warned of possible longer-term dangers from increasing budget deficits, outmoded industrial structures, and distortions caused by industrial subsidies. Forecasts for 1985 estimated growth at 3%, investment up 4.5%, exports up 12.5%, inflation at 3.3–4%, and unemployment just under 5%. In October limited political and trade sanctions against South Africa were announced.

The worst floods since 1954 took many lives in August. Material damage amounted to billions of schillings. (For table of world currencies, *see* International Exchange and Payments.)

Billboards addressed to General Motors executives dotted freeways near Detroit in the spring as 38 states vied for the award of a new $5 billion auto-manufacturing complex. The plant, which would employ about 6,000 workers by the time the first cars rolled off the line in 1988, would produce 400,000 to 500,000 small Saturn cars that GM hoped would compete with Japanese cars.

PHOTOGRAPHS, PETER YATES

AUTOMOBILE INDUSTRY

World automobile and truck output in 1984, at 41,-282,000 vehicles, was 4.4% higher than in 1983 but still fell some 600,000 vehicles short of the record set in 1978. World car production, at 30,237,000, rose 2.2% from 1983 but fell short of the 1978 peak of 30,910,000. Commercial vehicle production hit a new high of 11,045,000 (1978, 10,982,000) and was 11% over 1983.

Major gains in both automobile and commercial vehicle output in North America largely offset losses elsewhere. The biggest increases were recorded in both cars and commercial vehicles in Canada and the U.S., with the latter regaining the world automobile production lead from Japan for the first time since 1979. U.S. car output in 1984 was 7,773,000, up from 6,781,000 in 1983, and U.S. commercial vehicle output rose from 2,444,000 to 3,151,400. In Canada car output rose from 969,000 in 1983 to 1,022,000, and commercial vehicle production increased from 545,500 to 808,000.

Japan continued its domination of world commercial vehicle production, rising to a new high of 4,392,000 from 3,960,000, but car output there dipped slightly from 7,152,000 in 1983 to 7,073,000. In the six vehicle-producing countries of the EC, total car and commercial vehicle output declined. Car output slipped from 9,645,000 to 9,172,000 and commercial vehicles from 1,124,000 to 1,086,-000. The only major European producer to increase both car and commercial vehicle output was Italy, while West Germany, France, and the U.K. all had declines in both categories.

Spain continued its strong growth in cars (a

record 1,177,000), consolidating its seventh place in the world behind the U.S., Japan, West Germany (3,790,000), France (2,713,000), Italy (1,439,000), and the U.S.S.R. (1.3 million). Canada (1,022,000) filled eighth place in 1984, relegating the U.K. (909,-000) to ninth. In Australia car output rose from the depressed 1983 figure of 317,000 to 370,000 and commercial vehicle production from 22,000 to 29,000; the latter included substantial numbers of vehicles assembled from virtually complete imported kits.

Total new car sales were higher in 1984 than in 1983 only in Italy, Sweden, Australia, and North America among the major motoring nations. Japan, West Germany, Belgium, France, and Spain all recorded lower 1984 car sales, and France, West Germany, and Spain also had lower commercial vehicle sales.

United States

In the U.S. 1985 was the year of Saturn as 38 states made presentations to General Motors Corp. in an attempt to win a new assembly plant. In July GM announced that tiny Spring Hill, Tenn., with a population of fewer than 1,000, would be the site of the plant to build 400,000 to 500,000 units annually of a new line of small cars starting with the 1989 model year.

The intent of the Saturn plant was to build small cars for less money in order to compete more effectively with Japanese producers. GM said that it hoped to reduce the cost of producing a car by $2,000.

While GM planned a new U.S. plant to combat

imports, several of the importing firms announced plans either to build U.S. assembly plants or to enter into joint ventures with U.S. producers to build cars in that country. Chrysler Corp. and Mitsubishi Motors Corp. of Japan chose a site outside the neighboring cities of Bloomington and Normal in central Illinois as the site of a plant to produce jointly from 180,000 to 240,000 subcompact cars annually starting in the 1989 model year.

Ford Motor Co. and Mazda Motors Corp. of Japan announced that Mazda would begin building a new line of luxury compact cars in the 1988 model year at a former Ford plant in Flat Rock, Mich. Mazda would build 200,000 cars a year and sell half of that output to Ford, which owned an equity interest in Mazda. Ford would sell the car under the Mustang nameplate.

Meanwhile, Honda, which was already building compact Accords in the U.S. in Marysville, Ohio, said that it would add production of its subcompact Civic to Marysville in 1986 and boost output of the two car lines from 150,000 to 300,000 annually within two years. Nissan, which had been producing compact pickup trucks in Smyrna, Tenn., began in 1985 producing its subcompact Sentra car at Smyrna as well.

Despite the unprecedented flurry of planned new plants, the industry hinted at even more activity in the near future as Ford announced that it had reached agreement with Kia Industries of South Korea to supply it with a new line of minicars for 1988. Also, GM's Pontiac Division said that Daewoo of South Korea would supply it with a minicar for the 1987 model year.

Yamaha of Japan and Ford reached agreement for Yamaha to sell high-performance engines to Ford for the 1988 models. Chrysler and Samsung Group of South Korea agreed that Samsung would supply Chrysler with parts and other components for the late 1980s. Chrysler and Maserati of Italy entered into an agreement whereby Maserati would design and build a two-seat roadster for Chrysler for 1987 using Chrysler engines and transmissions.

All these future production plans were made amid a good sales year for the automakers. During the 1985 model year, ended Sept. 30, 1985, U.S. automakers sold 8,380,000 cars, a 6% increase from the 7.9 million sold in the 1984 model year. This was the highest total since 8.6 million cars were sold in 1979. Imports, meanwhile, accounted for record sales of 2,670,000 cars, an 11.7% increase from the 2.4 million sold in the 1984 model year. Domestic and import sales combined reached 11,050,000 units, a 7% increase from the 10.3 million sold in 1984 and the highest total since 11,090,000 in 1983.

GM sold 4.7 million cars in the 1985 model year, up only slightly from the 4.6 million sold in 1984 but still its highest tally since selling 5.1 million cars in 1979. Ford sold 2,160,000 cars, a 13% increase from the 1.9 million sold in 1984 and its highest total since 2.2 million were sold in 1979. Chrysler sold 1,140,000 cars, up 21% from the 946,575 sold in 1984 and its best year since selling 1,180,000 cars in 1977. Chrysler had not sold one million cars in a single year since 1979, when it sold 1,120,000.

Honda laid claim to being the industry's fourth best-selling producer with sales of 147,674 units, a 24% increase from the 119,336 units sold in 1984. American Motors Corp. sold only 137,493 cars, a 32% decline from the 201,275 sold in 1984 and its lowest total since selling 99,300 in 1982. Volkswagen sales of cars made in the U.S. fell 17% to 71,884 units from 86,600 a year earlier, while in its first year in the U.S. Nissan sold 21,077 Sentras built in Smyrna.

Among the major imports—all Japanese—Toyota remained the top seller with sales of 456,561 units, a 10% increase from the 413,781 sold a year earlier. Nissan was second with sales of 407,733 units, up 11% from 367,029 in 1984.

Individually, the best-selling vehicle in the industry in 1985 was the F-series Ford pickup truck with sales of 581,767 units. The Chevrolet C/K pickup truck was second with sales of 498,525 units.

The Yugo, a tiny car imported from Yugoslavia, garnered much interest in the U.S. during the year as the least expensive new car on the market.

AP/WIDE WORLD

The best-selling car was the subcompact Chevrolet Cavalier with sales of 422,927 units. The subcompact Ford Escort was second at 410,978 units, and the midsize Chevrolet Celebrity was third at 360,167 units.

Rounding out the top ten were the Oldsmobile Cutlass Ciera in fourth with sales of 315,569; the Ford Tempo in fifth at 297,656; the Honda Accord in sixth at 259,937 (domestically produced and imported models combined); the Chevrolet Impala/Caprice seventh at 251,693; the Buick Century eighth with 239,570; the Oldsmobile Cutlass Supreme ninth at 234,242; and the Oldsmobile 88 tenth at 213,833.

Sales of all cars benefited from incentive programs undertaken by the manufacturers. These incentives for the most part were discounted automobile loan rates varying from 9.9 to 7.5%. The discount rates were offered by each automaker's financing subsidiary. The effect of the incentives was that new car sales rose sharply when the loans were offered but declined sharply when the programs ended.

For the new model year GM raised prices an average of $400, Ford by $350, Chrysler by $320, American Motors by $208, Volkswagen by $107, Nissan by $50, and Honda by $562 on its only U.S. model, the Accord.

With the 1986 model year came a variety of new cars, both domestic and imported. At GM the automaker's downsizing campaign continued with the introduction of a smaller Buick LeSabre and Oldsmobile 88 along with conversion of those cars from rear- to front-wheel drive. Both cars were built on 110.8-in wheelbases, 5.1 in shorter than on the previous rear-drive models, and were 196.2 in long overall, 22 in shorter than in 1984. Curb weight dropped by 400 lb.

GM also unveiled new downsized versions of the Cadillac Eldorado and Seville, Buick Riviera, and Oldsmobile Toronado. The wheelbases were shrunk 6 in to 108 in, and overall length was reduced 19 in to 187.2 in. The Cadillac models offered a 4.1-liter V-8 engine, but the others dropped V-8s and went to a 3.8-liter V-6 powerplant only.

At Ford the midsize, rear-wheel-drive Ford LTD and Mercury Marquis were replaced by a pair of front-wheel-drive cars called the Ford Taurus and Mercury Sable. They were offered in four-door sedan and station-wagon body styles. Both featured aerodynamic rounded body lines. In an unusual move Ford introduced the cars on December 26 rather than in the fall. Late in the summer Ford also introduced as a 1986 model the Aerostar minivan, a rear-wheel-drive van to compete with Chrysler's front-wheel-drive Dodge Caravan and Plymouth Voyager.

Chrysler added a new engine, a 2.5-liter four-cylinder, which took the place of a 2.6-liter four-cylinder that it had been importing from Mitsubishi of Japan. The 2.5-liter was used in cars only, while the 2.6-liter was still offered in vans.

Among the imports Toyota redesigned its subcompact Celica sports model and converted it to front-wheel drive. Nissan restyled its 300ZX sports model and added a four-wheel-drive Stanza to its compact station-wagon lineup. Honda restyled its compact Accord and lengthened the body by five inches. Mazda renamed its former GLC (Great Little Car) the 323 and installed a larger engine.

The new cars appeared under new federal fuel economy laws. The U.S. government, under its Corporate Average Fuel Economy (CAFE) regulations begun in the 1978 model year, had mandated that each automaker's fleet of cars obtain 27.5 miles per gallon (mpg) fuel economy in the 1985 model year and thereafter. However, after arguments by GM and Ford that demand for big cars by new car buyers was upsetting their CAFE and threatened to limit output of those models in order to conform to the law, the government rolled back the standard to 26 mpg for the 1986 model year. The automakers asked that 26 mpg be kept as the standard for at least two to three years, but the government did not respond immediately.

In the annual fuel economy ratings by the Environmental Protection Agency, the Chevrolet Sprint E/R was the most fuel-efficient car with a city rating of 55 mpg. Sprint was built by Suzuki of Japan, in which GM owned an equity interest, and was sold through the Chevrolet dealer network.

The only car in the top ten that was made in the U.S. was the subcompact Ford Escort FS with a 41-mpg city rating. However, Ford obtained the four-cylinder diesel engines for that car from Japan.

At the low end of the mileage ratings was the Rolls-Royce Silver Spur limousine, rated at 8 mpg in the city. The only U.S.-made cars in the bottom ten were the Chevrolet Caprice and Pontiac Parisienne station wagons, rated at 15 mpg in city driving.

Japan

During the year Toyota continued to be Japan's corporate giant. According to its financial statement for the year ended June 1985, Toyota sold a record 3,530,000 cars, trucks, and buses, amounting to 6,060,000,000,000 yen ($27.5 billion) with a sales profit of 505 billion yen.

Car production in Japan for 1985 was expected to achieve a record of 7.5 million units, up from 7,073,000 in 1984. This was mainly due to a large increase in exports to the U.S., where Japan's voluntary restriction quota was raised by 24% to an annual level of 2.3 million units beginning in April.

In the Tokyo motor show held during the autumn, Toyota, Nissan, and other major manufacturers displayed models featuring various new concepts for the next generation. High maneuverability and computerization were the highlights, and the future models were equipped with such technological advances as full-time four-wheel drive and four-wheel steering and were notable for their use of microchips for many purposes.

Danny Sullivan in car 5 slides in front of Mario Andretti during the Indianapolis 500-mile race. Both cars were able to continue racing after the spinout. Sullivan went on to win.

AP/WIDE WORLD

AUTOMOBILE RACING

The Roger Penske racing team in 1985 collected both the Indianapolis 500 and the Championship Auto Racing Teams (CART) crowns. The 1985 Indianapolis victory went to Danny Sullivan of Louisville, Ky., in a March-Cosworth by a margin of 2.47 seconds over Mario Andretti. Roberto Guerrero of Colombia finished third, and Sullivan's teammate, Al Unser, Sr., was fourth.

Al Unser, Sr., who drove at Indianapolis only because Rick Mears failed to recover sufficiently from injuries, won the CART crown on the final race of the season by finishing ahead of his son Al Unser, Jr. Andretti, best man in the Lola T-900 chassis, finished fifth in the season standings as the March-Cosworths proved dominant. Sullivan, fourth for the season, won the final race of the CART/PPG series at the new Tamiami, Fla., track before some 60,000 people. Third for the season was Bobby Rahal, who captured three races.

Bill Elliott, who drove in the Winston Cup series of the National Association for Stock Car Auto Racing (NASCAR), won the Elier driver of the year award over Sullivan and representatives from other forms of U.S. racing, but he lost the NASCAR season crown to Darrell Waltrip in the final race of the season 4,292 points to 4,191. Elliott, driving a Thunderbird, won 11 of 19 super-speedway events including the prestigious Daytona 500 and the Darlington Southern 500. His winnings for the year totaled over $2 million, more than any other driver had earned in one season. The steady Waltrip, driving a Chevrolet for Junior Johnson, won his third Winston Cup crown in five years. He also won three races plus the Winston invitational at Charlotte, N.C. But Elliott won the Winston Million, a $1 million bonus for victories at specified locales.

Porsche's 962 won 16 of the 17 International Motor Sports Association's Camel GT races, and Al Holbert, Porsche's U.S. competition director, won the season championship for Grand Touring prototypes. In the other GT classes, Jim Downing won the 750-kg prototype Camel Lights class in a Mazda-Argo; John Jones of Canada in a Ford Mustang won in the GTOver 2.8-liter class; and Jack Baldwin became the first IMSA GT repeat champion since 1968 by winning the GTUnder 2.8-liter category in a Mazda RX-7. In the 24 Hours of Daytona and in the 12 Hours of Sebring, a Porsche 962 driven by A. J. Foyt, Bob Wollek, and Preston Henn won for Henn's Swap Shop team. The races were more notable as the swan song of Chevrolet-powered cars for the 1985 season. Porsche 962 pilots occupied seven of the top ten driver positions. Jaguar drivers finished third, fourth, and ninth. In the new Firestone Firehawk Endurance series, Porsche 944 won car of the year honors over Toyota's MR2, the touring division champion. Walt Maas and Jon Milledge piloted the winning Porsche.

In the year's closest competiton, the Champion Spark Plug Challenge for small front-drive sedans, Mazda's Dennis Shaw defeated Dodge's Kal Showket in the final race of the season. Shaw won four races to Showket's seven but was more consistent.

Winning nine of a possible ten races, Tommy Riggins won the Kelly American Challenge title and his Buick Somerset took the manufacturers' crown. Irv Hoerr in a Chevrolet Camaro finished second.

The Sports Car Club of America's most successful professional series in 1985 was the Trans-Am. Two Ford-mounted drivers dominated the competition, with Wally Dallenbach, Jr., nipping Willie T. Ribbs for season honors. The new Playboy Endurance Series was totally dominated by Corvettes over Porsche 944s. The Can-Am series for prototypes was won by Lou Sell.

Grand Prix Racing

In international Formula One automobile racing in 1985, turbocharged 1½-liter engines predominated and road-holding capabilities were enhanced by the use of air foil wings. Tires were also crucial, and toward the end of the season Pirelli staged a comeback, competing against U.S. Goodyear. Michelin withdrew as a tire supplier. Engine power rose appreciably, to about 600 brake horsepower (bhp) at some 10,000 rpm from the better units. This resulted in speeds of more than 320 km/h (1 km = 0.62 mi) on the longer straightaways, as at Paul Ricard, France, and at Monza, Italy, where Nelson Piquet (Brazil) went through the speedtrap at 333.71 km/h in training for the Italian Grand Prix. Honda, in particular, was getting high power from its V6-cylinder engines.

The drivers' world championship was won by a Frenchman, Alain Prost. He clinched the title at Brands Hatch, England, in the European Grand Prix, with two more races still to be contested.

The first Grand Prix race took place at Rio de Janeiro, Brazil. Prost's McLaren-TAG-Porsche had the fastest lap at 187.292 km/h and won the race with an average time of 181.527 km/h. Michele Alboreto (Italy) placed second in a Ferrari, and Elio De Angelis (Italy) was third in a Renault-powered Lotus. The scene then moved to Portugal, at Estoril Autodrome. Ayrton Senna (Brazil) was the winner at 145.162 km/h after establishing the fastest lap at 150.404 km/h in a Lotus-Renault 97T. Alboreto's Ferrari was the only other car to complete the full distance, Patrick Tambay (France) finishing third in a Renault RE60, a lap behind. At Imola, Italy, in the San Marino Grand Prix, ten cars survived out of 25. The victor was De Angelis in his Lotus-Renault, at 191.798 km/h; Alboreto achieved the best lap speed, at 199.470 km/h. Thierry Boutsen (Belgium) finished second for Arrows, and Tambay's Renault was third.

In the tortuous Monaco street race, Prost (McLaren MP4) drove to a smooth victory, at 138.434 km/h; Alboreto finished second in his Ferrari, just ahead of De Angelis in the Lotus-Renault. A faulty track surface caused the Belgian Grand Prix at Spa to be postponed. In the Canadian Grand Prix at Montreal, Senna had the fastest lap at 181.554 km/h, and Alboreto won in his Ferrari at 174.688 km/h from teammate Stefan Johansson (Sweden); Prost's McLaren was third. The Detroit Grand Prix was won by Keke Rosberg (Finland) for the Williams-Honda team, at 131.486 km/h, ahead of the Ferraris of Johansson and Alboreto; Senna had the fastest lap, at 137.131 km/h.

In the French Grand Prix, Piquet finished just ahead of Rosberg, with Prost third—a varied trio of Brabham-BMW, Williams-Honda, McLaren-Porsche; Piquet's average speed was 201.323 km/h, and Rosberg had the fastest lap at 209.340 km/h. The British Grand Prix, at Silverstone, was notable for a remarkable 160-mph (257.6-km/h) qualifying lap and a race lap record of more than 150 mph (243.067 km/h) by Prost, who also won the race at 235.404 km/h over Alboreto and Jacques Lafitte (France) in a Ligier. A new, inferior, Nürburgring was the setting for the German Grand Prix, won by Alboreto, at 191.147 km/h, from Prost and Lafitte.

Niki Lauda (Austria) had the fastest lap, at 197.464 km/h. Prost then won the Austrian Grand Prix at 231.132 km/h from Senna and Alboreto and had the best lap at 239.701 km/h as well.

The Dutch Grand Prix at Zandvoort ended in a win for Lauda (McLaren), at 193.089 km/h, from Prost, who had the fastest lap, at 199.995 km/h; Senna was third. In the Italian Grand Prix, Prost was the winner at 227.565 km/h from Piquet and Senna; Nigel Mansell (Great Britain) had the fastest lap at 236.512 km/h. Spa then had its postponed Belgian Grand Prix, with Senna (at 189.811 km/h), Mansell, and Prost in the first three places; Prost had the fastest lap at 205.241 km/h. Mansell gained a convincing win at Brands Hatch in the European Grand Prix, averaging 203.625 km/h; Senna and Rosberg placed second and third. Lafitte had the fastest lap at 211.734 km/h.

The Williams-Honda FW10s came in first and second at Kyalami, South Africa, as Mansell won from Rosberg at 206.744 km/h. Prost was third, and Rosberg had the fastest lap at 215.536 km/h. In the final Grand Prix, over the excellent new Australian circuit near Adelaide, Rosberg gained the third consecutive victory for the Canon Williams-Honda team, at 135.168 km/h, and also achieved a lap record at 153.168 km/h.

Keke Rosberg of Finland steers his Formula One car past the "Spirit of Detroit" statue on June 23 on his way to a victory in the Detroit Grand Prix.

AP/WIDE WORLD

BAHAMAS, THE

Prime Minister Sir Lynden Pindling of The Bahamas remained securely in office throughout 1985 after defeating a parliamentary motion of no confidence in May. The motion was brought in the wake of the royal commission report on drug-related corruption, issued in December 1984, which recommended legal action against several people including a former Cabinet minister, George Smith. Following the commission's report, the government hired a U.S. lobbying firm to improve its image with the U.S. administration. The government cooperated with U.S. agents in a major operation against the drug trade in April.

Tourism, the mainstay of the economy, continued its upturn, with a 12% rise in stopover arrivals reported for the January–April period. Earnings for 1985 were projected at U.S. $900 million, against U.S. $820 million in 1984, and substantial investments were being made in the hotel industry by U.S. companies. In March The Bahamas was designated as qualifying for benefits under the U.S. Caribbean Basin Initiative.

In October the 1985 Commonwealth heads of government conference was held in Nassau, the first to be held in the Caribbean since the 1975 conference in Kingston, Jamaica.

BAHRAIN

The opening of the $1 billion Bahrain–Saudi Arabia causeway, rescheduled from December 1985 to December 1986 to allow for the completion of customs and immigration formalities, was expected to give a much-needed boost to the claims of Bahrain as a financial and services center for the Persian Gulf. The attractions of Bahrain as an offshore financial haven suffered a number of setbacks during the year. Three U.S.-based banks announced cuts in their establishments because of high operating costs. Officials countered by blaming the overall situation on declining bank profits worldwide and hoped soon to announce new banking licenses for institutions seeking representation in Bahrain. The local economy was helped by success in halting the decline of onshore oil production—output for the first half of 1985 stood at 41,744 bbl a day—although weak world oil prices were a depressing factor.

Intercommunal tensions continued between the politically dominant Sunnites, from whom the ruling family was drawn, and the Bahraini Shi'ites, constituting more than half the native population. A small minority of Shi'ites sympathized with the Iranian revolution and sought radical change in Bahrain, including discrimination against women and the closing of bars and nightclubs. On June 23 six Bahrainis were deported from the U.K. after being arrested on suspicion of plotting against the Bahraini government.

BANGLADESH

On May 25, 1985, Bangladesh suffered a devastating cyclone that drove huge tidal waves across the low-lying islands in the Ganges River delta. It was the worst natural disaster to hit the country since 1970. According to unofficial estimates the death toll was as high as 40,000, but the official report, released two weeks after the disaster, numbered the dead at 4,264, with 17,000 houses destroyed and another 123,000 damaged. The government appealed for $50 million worth of foreign assistance to aid recovery.

During the year Lieut. Gen. Hussain Mohammed Ershad brought some semblance of stability to his military regime and kept the fragmented opposition at bay. Following an opposition threat to boycott them, Ershad shelved plans to hold parliamentary and presidential elections in April. On March 1, Ershad reimposed full martial-law restrictions, including the banning of political activities. He claimed that he had conceded more to the opposition parties than was the case in any other country under martial law and berated the opposition for refusing to agree to his terms for holding elections in spite of this fact.

Ershad ordered a referendum to be held on March 21, when the people were asked to vote on the question of whether they wished the president

Two survivors of tidal waves that swept over a village on an island in the Bay of Bengal in May await a rescue ship to take them to the mainland of Bangladesh.

REUTERS/BETTMANN NEWSPHOTOS

to remain in office. He faced severe criticism from the opposition and from the international press, who alleged that the polls were rigged and that the turnout had been minimal, perhaps as low as 10 or 15%. They dismissed the referendum as a "farce." According to the official results, however, 72% of the electorate voted, and almost 95% of those, some 33 million people, cast their votes in favor of Ershad's remaining in office. There were reports of at least one death during referendum-related violence.

On May 16 and 20 elections were held for council leaders in the *upazillas* (subdistricts), the new units of local government. The elections were held on a nonparty basis. At least 11 people died in violence connected with the polling. Two major opposition leaders, who had been placed under house arrest on March 2, were freed on May 25.

In July Minister of Finance Mohammad Syed ud-Zaman presented the 1985–86 budget; it totaled $1,390,000,000, an increase of $111 million over that of the previous year. In the meantime, Bangladesh continued to be deeply dependent on foreign-aid disbursements, which in 1984 accounted for 40% of the government's total resources. The World Bank's International Development Association had approved 94 interest-free loans totaling $3 billion.

Bangladesh's relations with China continued to improve, with China pledging a loan worth 100 million yuan. (For table of world currencies, *see* International Exchange and Payments.)

BARBADOS

The sudden death of Prime Minister J. M. G. ("Tom") Adams on March 11, 1985, cast a shadow over the prospects of the governing Barbados Labour Party (BLP), which faced general elections in 1986. Under the new prime minister, Bernard St. John, there were reports that various groups within the BLP were maneuvering for position. In a reorganization of the Cabinet in June, St. John separated the posts of attorney general and foreign minister. The latter post went to former information minister Nigel Barrow, while the new attorney general was David Simmons, winner of a by-election held in May in the constituency left vacant by Adams's death.

With tourist arrivals declining and a continued slump in manufacturing, the government halved its 1985 economic growth target from 2 to 1% in June. Unemployment rose from 17.4 to 19.3% between March and June, following a number of factory closures. A major cause was the continuing trade impasse between Trinidad and Tobago and other members of the Caribbean Community (Caricom), including Barbados. The Caricom summit held in Barbados in July set a deadline of August 31 for implementation of a common external tariff and other measures. When Trinidad and Tobago failed to meet this deadline, St. John threatened to impose retaliatory trade restrictions.

BASEBALL

Though beset by problems such as a two-day strike and a drug investigation, major league baseball in 1985 produced an attendance record of 46,838,-819 spectators. There were also several landmark achievements and yet another new champion at the end of the longest season in history.

World Series

The Kansas City Royals, decided underdogs, won the first championship in their 17-year existence. They downed the St. Louis Cardinals four games to three in an all-Missouri World Series after trailing in the best-of-seven set three games to one. By rallying for their victory, the Royals became the first team in the 82-year annals of the World Series to triumph after losing its first two games at home.

In the Series opener at Kansas City on October 19, the Cardinals defeated the Royals 3–1 behind the strong pitching of John Tudor and Todd Worrell. One evening later the Royals appeared to have victory in hand, leading 2–0 after eight innings. But Kansas City left-hander Charlie Leibrandt, who had yielded only two hits until that time, was victimized by a four-run ninth inning, and the Cardinals prevailed 4–2 to assume what appeared to be an insurmountable 2–0 lead in games as the Series moved to St. Louis. There, during the regular season, the Cardinals had posted a 55–26 record.

However, in the third game of the Series on October 22, the Royals downed the Cardinals 6–1 on a strong six-hitter by right-hander Bret Saberhagen and three runs batted in by second baseman Frank White. On October 23 Tudor, considered the ace of the St. Louis pitching staff, surrendered only five hits and beat the visiting Royals 3–0. Willie McGee and Tito Landrum hit home runs for the Cardinals.

Anticipating a celebration the following evening, the Cardinals instead fell 6–1 as Kansas City's Danny Jackson worked a complete game. The Series now stood 3–2 in favor of St. Louis.

The Cardinals again appeared on the verge of their second World Series crown in four years and 14th in the franchise's history when they took a 1–0 lead into the bottom of the ninth at Royals Stadium on October 26. However, the resilient Royals scored two runs for a dramatic 2–1 victory. Pinch hitter Dane Iorg singled to drive in the runs soon after the Cardinals had argued heatedly about a call made at first base by umpire Don Denkinger. The Cardinals contended that Denkinger's "safe" ruling deprived them of a much-needed out and fueled the Royals' comeback aspirations.

The low-scoring pace of the World Series changed markedly on October 27, when the Royals treated a wildly cheering home crowd to an 11–0 rout at the expense of Tudor and six successors. Tudor was knocked out of the game in the third inning, his earliest departure in an otherwise splendid season. Joaquín Andújar, one of the Cardinal relief pitchers, was ejected from the contest, as was Car-

AP/WIDE WORLD

A jubilant Bret Saberhagen is mobbed by his Kansas City Royals teammates after pitching his second World Series victory in the deciding seventh game.

dinal manager Whitey Herzog. Saberhagen pitched a complete five-hitter in the final game and was voted most valuable player for the World Series, having won half of Kansas City's games.

All the Kansas City pitching staff was commended for restricting the Cardinals to a .185 batting average, the lowest mark ever recorded for a team participating in a seven-game Series. Moreover, the Cardinals, who led the National League in batting average (.264) and runs during the regular season, managed only one multiple-run inning in the Series.

The Kansas City triumph was the third straight World Series conquest for the American League. Beyond that, the success of the Royals underscored baseball's balance of power. Since the New York Yankees achieved consecutive World Series titles in 1977 and 1978, no champion had repeated.

Championship Series

In 1985 the intraleague championship series, or play-offs, were expanded from a best-of-five format to best-of-seven. Again, that afforded the Royals another opportunity to exhibit their special methods of survival.

The Toronto Blue Jays assumed a 3–1 advantage in games over the Royals, who then rebounded with three victories in a row to claim the American League pennant. The last two wins occurred at Toronto on October 15 and 16, by scores of 5–3 and 6–2. The Blue Jays, favored to prevail in that play-off, also had difficulties with the young, talented Kansas City pitching staff.

In the National League the St. Louis Cardinals began their championship series with the Los Angeles Dodgers by dropping the first two contests in Dodger Stadium. But after returning home to St. Louis, the Cardinals arose for three triumphs, the last being achieved on a tie-breaking home run in the ninth inning by normally light-hitting shortstop Ozzie Smith. His blow, off Tom Niedenfuer, gave the Cardinals a 3–2 decision and a 3–2 lead in the Series. Back at Los Angeles, on October 16, the Dodgers were clinging to a 5–4 margin when powerful Jack Clark clubbed a clutch three-run ninth-inning home run off the luckless Niedenfuer. The Cardinals won the contest 7–5 and the National League pennant in six games.

Regular Season

Undoubtedly, the most awaited event of the 1985 season took place in Cincinnati on September 11. On that evening the indefatigable Pete Rose, 44-year-old player-manager of the Reds, stepped up against Eric Show of the San Diego Padres and stroked his 4,192nd major league career hit. That broke a mark established more than a half century earlier by Ty Cobb. Rose, performing in his hometown, was accorded a standing ovation of several minutes.

Other veterans shared the limelight in a summer of touchstone achievements. On the same Sunday in August, Tom Seaver of the Chicago White Sox pitched his 300th career victory and Rod Carew of the California Angels garnered his 3,000th hit. On the last Sunday of the regular season 46-year-old Phil Niekro, the oldest player in the major leagues, notched his 300th victory as the New York Yankees beat the Blue Jays in Toronto.

That setback did not matter to the Blue Jays, for one day earlier they had clinched the American League East title after just nine years as a major-league team. The Blue Jays enjoyed a comfortable lead for most of the season and then fended off a late challenge by the Yankees. The defending World Series champion Detroit Tigers were never a factor in the race.

In the American League West division the Royals struggled with erratic hitting and were as many as 7½ games out of first place in late July. But they overtook the California Angels during a crucial four-game series in the last week of the regular season.

The Cardinals, picked to finish in fifth or sixth place, surprised most observers by winning 101 games during the regular season, the most in the major leagues. But, paced by the 24–4 record of their spectacular young pitching sensation, Dwight Gooden, the New York Mets won 98 and were a close second throughout the year.

The Dodgers, also dismissed as also-rans before the season, had few problems claiming first place in the National League West. Rose and the Reds were runners-up.

Willie McGee of St. Louis captured the National League batting crown with a .353 average. Resurgent Dave Parker of Cincinnati led the league with 125 runs batted in, and rookie Vince Coleman of the Cardinals accumulated 110 stolen bases (the

Cardinals had 314 as a team). Dale Murphy of the Atlanta Braves had 37 home runs to lead in that department. Besides Gooden, there were three other 20-game winners. Tudor and Andújar each collected 21 for St. Louis, while Tom Browning had 20 for Cincinnati.

St. Louis dominated the postseason awards in the National League, winning three of the four. Shortstop Willie McGee was named most valuable player; outfielder Vince Coleman was voted rookie of the year; and Whitey Herzog was manager of the year. Gooden of the New York Mets won the Cy Young award as the league's best pitcher. In the American League Kansas City's Bret Saberhagen was the Cy Young winner; first baseman Don Mattingly of the New York Yankees was the most valuable player; and shortstop Ozzie Guillen of the Chicago White Sox was voted rookie of the year. Bobby Cox of Toronto was named manager of the year.

Off-Field Problems

Baseball was girding itself for a protracted labor dispute when the players walked off the job in August. The two sides were quickly brought together, however, and the dispute lasted only two days. Much of the credit for the settlement was given to Peter V. Ueberroth, who in October completed his first year as commissioner.

Baseball's image was not so fortunate during a federal trial investigating the use of cocaine and other illegal drugs in the major leagues. Several present and past players testified under immunity. Based on their disclosures, it appeared that drugs constituted a serious problem for the sport. Ueberroth called on the major league players to submit to voluntary and random testing for drug use.

Toronto's Al Oliver (left) is greeted by his teammates after the Blue Jays beat the Kansas City Royals 3–1 in the fourth game of the American League play-offs.

AP/WIDE WORLD

AP/WIDE WORLD

A South Korean player slides home as the catcher on the Mexican team drops the ball during the championship game of the Little League World Series.

Little League

A team of 11- and 12-year-old boys from Seoul won the second consecutive Little League Baseball world series title for South Korea. It was the 15th title won by a Far East team in the series, which is played at Williamsport, Pa.

South Korea defeated a team from Mexicali, Mexico, by a 7–1 score. Because Mexicali is on the California border, it participates in the U.S. West play-offs and was the champion of that region.

The Korean pitcher hurled a one-hitter, struck out seven, and walked only one. The Mexican pitcher allowed five hits and walked five. Only two of Korea's runs were earned.

On its way to the title Korea beat Morristown, Tenn., which finished third, and Binbrook, Ont., the fourth-place team. Mexicali defeated Morristown and Staten Island, New York City. Teams from Maracaibo, Venezuela; Minnetonka, Minn.; and Al Khubar, Saudi Arabia, completed the eight-team field.

Series play determined five other champions in the spin-offs from Little League.

In the Senior League (ages 14–15) another Far East team, this from Taiwan, defeated Willemstad, Curaçao, Netherlands Antilles, the Latin-American entry, by a score of 3–2. In the Big League (ages 16–18), Broward County, Fla., defeated Carolina, P.R., 8–1.

In Little League Softball Brookfield, Ill., won the major division title for 10–12-year-olds with a 1–0 victory over Hawthorne, Calif. Des Moines, Iowa, was the senior division (ages 13–15) champion, by 10–7 over Minersville, Pa. Girls from Williamsport, the home of Little League, claimed their second straight Big League (ages 16–18) title with a 6–1 triumph over Dayton, Ohio.

RICHARD MACKSON/SPORTS ILLUSTRATED

Dwayne McClain (shooting) scored 17 points for Villanova, upsetting Georgetown in the National Collegiate Athletic Association championship.

BASKETBALL

The 1984–85 season belonged to Kareem Abdul-Jabbar. No stranger to the winner's circle, the 7-ft 2-in (2.19-m) center had helped the Los Angeles Lakers reach the NBA finals five times in six seasons. The 1985 triumph over the Boston Celtics, Abdul-Jabbar's third NBA championship as a member of the Lakers and the fourth of his career, was the sweetest one of all.

The superstar had turned 38 on April 16, two days before the Lakers opened their play-off schedule by crushing Phoenix 142–114 in a first-round game. For two straight years the Lakers had been humbled in the final play-off round, first by Philadelphia and then by Boston, and they hungered for revenge.

No one was more motivated than Abdul-Jabbar, who took it as a personal affront when the Celtics battered his team into submission in their seven-game 1984 showdown. He, Magic Johnson, and the rest of the Lakers endured taunts about being intimidated physically by the Celtics and mentally by boisterous crowds in Boston Garden.

So when the Celtics humiliated the Lakers 148–114 in the first game of their 1985 final round, it seemed like a replay of the previous year to elated

Boston backers and depressed Los Angeles fans. This was the second-worst margin of defeat ever in a game in the final play-off round, topped only by Washington's 117–82 rout of Seattle in 1978.

Undaunted, team captain Abdul-Jabbar held a players' meeting before the second game, aware that returning to Los Angeles with a deficit of 0–2 in the best-of-seven series would probably prove too big an obstacle to overcome. During the game, he silenced the packed Boston Garden with a 30-point, 17-rebound barrage. The Lakers survived 109–102 in what proved to be the pivotal contest of the series. They went to the West Coast, confidence restored, to take two of the next three confrontations with the Celtics, setting up the long-awaited final match in Boston on June 9. The Lakers climaxed their comeback by triumphing 111–100 in that contest. Never before had a visiting team won the decisive play-off game in Boston Garden. Abdul-Jabbar unleashed his fearsome skyhook, averaging 25.7 points per game against the Celtics while making 60.4% of his shots. He also became the leading all-time NBA play-off scorer, topping the record of 4,457 points set by the Lakers' Jerry West.

After being named most valuable player of the series, Abdul-Jabbar agreed that this had been his most satisfying moment in 16 pro seasons. In 1971, then known as Lew Alcindor, he first took play-off MVP honors for leading the Milwaukee Bucks to the NBA championship.

The exciting climax capped a successful NBA season, with attendance and interest on the upswing. The sensational debut of Olympic hero Michael Jordan was a major reason. Jordan drew huge crowds throughout the league, averaging 28.2 points per game, leading the Chicago Bulls into the play-offs, and outpolling Houston's Akeem Olajuwon for rookie of the year laurels.

College

Villanova's 66–64 triumph over Georgetown for the 1985 National Collegiate Athletic Association (NCAA) basketball championship was called the impossible dream, the classic upset, and many other things by stunned spectators and participants alike. The Wildcats, seeded 29th in the 64-team NCAA tournament field, had no business even reaching the final, according to most experts. They were given little chance of prevailing against mighty Georgetown, led by 7-ft (2.14-m) center Patrick Ewing.

Georgetown, top-ranked in every college basketball poll, had won 35 of 37 games, and the Hoyas were supremely confident of adding their second straight national title. With Ewing dominating the middle to block shots and intimidate foes, they had compiled a 121–23 record during the center's four years. And Georgetown needed just one more victory to become the first team since 1973 to wear back-to-back NCAA crowns.

But the Hoyas were stymied by Villanova coach Rollie Massimino and his aptly named Wildcats.

Beaten twice by the Hoyas during the regular season, Villanova also had lost eight other games before entering the NCAA tournament with an unimpressive 19–10 record. In semimiraculous fashion they then knocked off six straight favorites, becoming the first team not ranked among the nation's top ten to win the championship since City College of New York (CCNY) in 1950.

Every time Massimino's disciplined team faltered, 6-ft 10-in (2.08-m) center Ed Pinckney brought things under control. Still, conquering supposedly unbeatable Georgetown required a superb game from all the Wildcats, and they answered the challenge.

The sellout crowd of 23,124 at the University of Kentucky's Rupp Arena was only mildly surprised when Harold Pressley tipped in a basket to put Villanova on top 29–28 at halftime. Noted for strong finishes, Georgetown was accustomed to wearing down opponents in the closing minutes, cashing in on relentless defensive pressure throughout the game. The Hoyas' strategy usually forced critical turnovers at the moment of decision.

Besides, the underdogs had shot at a sizzling 72.2% in the initial 20 minutes, making 13 of 18 field goal attempts. Georgetown supporters were confident that no team could sustain that pace. But neither Hoya coach John Thompson nor anyone else expected what happened in the second half. Villanova made an unbelievable nine of ten shots, roared from behind in the closing minutes, and hung on for one of the biggest upsets in the history of college basketball. The new champions finished with 22 baskets in 28 tries, an NCAA tournament record shooting percentage of 78.6.

More than pinpoint shooting was needed. The Hoyas, expected to roll up a huge rebounding margin, were held to a 17–17 standoff on the backboards. Villanova's sticky 2–3 zone defense prevented Ewing from taking command under the basket. Most significant of all, the winners turned in a virtually flawless floor game.

The key man was Wildcat point guard Gary McLain. Despite being hounded all over the court by Georgetown's Tony Jackson, McLain brought the ball up with sure-handed grace, assuring good shots for Pinckney, who scored 16 points; Dwayne McClain, who got a game-high 17; and the unlikely Wildcat hero, guard Harold Jensen.

Coming off the bench, Jensen snapped a shooting slump by sinking all five of his field goal attempts, plus four of five free throws. Jensen clicked with the clutch 16-ft (4.9-m) jumper that put Villanova back on top for good with 2 minutes and 36 seconds left to play. He added four more points in the frantic closing minutes, frustrating repeated Georgetown rallies.

The National Invitation Tournament (NIT) was won by UCLA, which defeated Indiana 65–62 in the final. The women's NCAA basketball championship was won by Old Dominion (31–3) in a 70–65 decision over Georgia (29–5). Medina Dixon scored 18 points and added 15 rebounds for the Lady Monarchs, who took control with an impressive 57–30 domination of rebounds.

The NCAA rules committee voted to use the 45-second shot clock in 1985. Designed to eliminate stalling, it requires the offensive team to shoot within 45 seconds of gaining possession or surrender the ball.

World Amateur

The major confrontation in world basketball in 1985 took place at Kobe (Japan) University where a powerful U.S. collegiate team suffered a surprise 96–93 defeat by the Soviet Union in the men's final. Earlier in the tournament, during the preliminary games, the U.S. had beaten the Soviet Union 91–87, but the threat posed by the tournament-dominating 7-ft 3-in (2.21-m) Soviet center Arvidas Sabonis kept the outcome of the final an open question. The game was tied at 80–80 when Sabonis fouled out with 4½ minutes remaining. The lead then fluctuated until the score reached 93–93, when Vladimir Khomitchus sank a three-point jump shot from the corner with just two seconds on the clock

Kareem Abdul-Jabbar led the Los Angeles Lakers past Larry Bird and the Boston Celtics in the National Basketball Association championship series in June.

AP/WIDE WORLD

to clinch a Soviet victory. The Soviet Union also won the women's gold medal, defeating the U.S. 87–81 in the final. The first world championship for junior women took place at the Olympic Center at Colorado Springs, Colo., and completed a clean sweep for the Soviet Union, which beat Korea 80–75 in the final.

The world championship finals were scheduled to be held in Spain in 1986, and the European qualification system was based for the first time on qualifying groups playing their games on a home-and-away basis over a two-year period. Highlights of the first three rounds of matches were victories by England 69–68 over Czechoslovakia, by Greece 94–90 against France in overtime, and by The Netherlands 67–66 over Belgium.

The European men's championship finals were held in Stuttgart, West Germany. Once again the Soviet Union emerged the victors, beating surprise finalists Czechoslovakia 120–89. The women's European championship finals took place in Italy in September 1985. In the final the Soviets defeated Bulgaria 103–69. The third-place match was won by Hungary, which defeated Czechoslovakia 103–76.

The World Club Championship resulted in a win for the host club, FC Barcelona, which was victorious against Monte Libano of Brazil 93–89 in the final. The 1984–85 European Champions' Cup for men was won by KK Cibona of Zagreb, Yugos., which defeated seven-time previous winner Real Madrid 87–78 in the final at Athens. FC Barcelona took the Cup-Winners' Cup at Grenoble, France, with a 77–73 win over Zahlgiris Kaunas of the Soviet Union to gain a European cup for the first time after three times as finalists. In the women's European Champions' Cup final Fiorella Vicenza of Italy regained the title it had won in 1983 by defeating TTT Daugawa Riga of Latvia 63–55.

BELGIUM

The Belgian government of Prime Minister Wilfried Martens narrowly failed to complete its full four-year term of office when, on Sept. 2, 1985, King Baudouin I dissolved Parliament and called general elections for October 13. The results gave a slightly increased majority to the outgoing coalition of Flemish and French Social Christian and Liberal parties. The loss of six seats by the Flemish Liberals was more than compensated by the extra eight seats won by the Social Christian parties. While the Flemish Socialists increased their representation by six seats, the (Flemish nationalist) Volksunie and the Front Démocratique des Francophones both lost support.

The dissolution of Parliament was prompted mainly by tensions between the Flemish and French Social Christians. The latter refused to support a proposed constitutional amendment that would make communities responsible for educational matters. They believed the move would pose a threat to Roman Catholic schools in French-speaking Wallonia, where the Socialists, in opposition on the national level, were the major party.

Further tension resulted from the parliamentary inquiry into the riot in Heysel stadium, Brussels, that broke out before the start of the European Cup final soccer match between Liverpool (England) and Juventus of Turin (Italy) on May 29. The violence resulted in the deaths of 39 spectators. The inquiry concluded that the actions of the Belgian police had revealed serious shortcomings. When Interior Minister Charles-Ferdinand Nothomb, a French Social Christian, refused to assume responsibility, French Liberal Justice Minister Jean Gol tendered his own resignation, and a number of other French Liberal ministers followed suit. Martens offered the resignation of the entire government on July 16, but

A building housing the international secretariat of NATO's North Atlantic Assembly in Brussels was bombed on April 20 by a group calling itself the Revolutionary Front of Proletarian Action.

AP/WIDE WORLD

the king refused to accept it. Following the elections, Martens maintained the same Social Christian-Liberal coalition. In the new Cabinet sworn in on November 28, both Nothomb and Gol retained their posts.

Earlier in the year the government gave the green light to the installation of the first 16 U.S. cruise missiles at the Florennes air force base. The missiles arrived in March. Even after the installation, Flemish Socialists insisted on their withdrawal.

One of the left-wing terrorist groups, calling itself the Cellules Communistes Combattantes (CCC), attacked more than a dozen buildings, causing considerable damage. Its targets were the political headquarters of the Liberals and Social Christians and property belonging to U.S. "imperialists." Martens and Foreign Relations Minister Léo Tindemans made an official trip to the U.S. in January. Pope John Paul II visited Belgium in May during his tour of the Benelux countries.

BELIZE

At the start of 1985, the political climate in Belize was one of uncertainty because the United Democratic Party (UDP), which had won 21 of the 28 seats in the House of Representatives in the national elections on Dec. 14, 1984, was expected to chart a new course for the nation. Prime Minister Manuel Esquivel noted in his 1985 budget address that the government faced an enormous task in reviving the country's economy. During the months that followed, Belize found itself being drawn closer to the U.S. because U.S. markets accounted for about half of Belize's imports and exports. During the year Belize reportedly became the world's fourth largest exporter of marijuana. The U.S. agreed to spray toxic chemicals on the marijuana crop in an effort to control illicit trafficking in the drug.

The UDP was also committed to reaching an honorable settlement with neighboring Guatemala over the border dispute between the two countries. Hopes for an amicable agreement appeared to increase when the Guatemalan Assembly drew up a draft for a new constitution that contained no mention of the disputed territory. On October 9 Britain's Queen Elizabeth II began a three-day visit to Belize on her way to the Commonwealth heads of government meeting in The Bahamas. This was the first visit ever made to Belize by the queen.

BIOLOGY

The use of protein electrophoresis had dominated the study of ecological genetics in recent years, but another genetics technique—analysis of mitochondrial DNA—promised to provide an informative approach for some zoological questions. Some DNA (the material carrying the genetic code) is housed within the cell's respiratory organelles, or mitochondria. This mitochondrial DNA is transmitted by the female parent to her offspring through the cytoplasm contained in the egg. In 1985 knowledge of this process of maternal transmission across generations enabled scientists to apply mitochondrial DNA analysis to a specific problem in ecological genetics. Trip Lamb and John C. Avise of the University of Georgia examined populations of two frog species—green tree frogs and barking tree frogs—that had undergone extensive hybridization. Although the two species may breed at the same aquatic sites, they do not normally hybridize, presumably because male green tree frogs issue mating calls from shoreline shrubs and trees, whereas male barking tree frogs call to their females from the water itself. At the hybrid sites habitat maintenance practices had eliminated shoreline vegetation so that most green tree frogs called from the bare ground. It was suggested, therefore, that most mismatings resulting in hybrids would involve green tree frog males that intercepted barking tree frog females en route to the water to breed with their own males. Lamb and Avise confirmed this prediction by demonstrating that the mitochondrial DNA pattern in each hybrid was identical to that of the barking tree frog, indicating their maternal role in hybrid events. The results of this study demonstrated how the rigid mating behaviors characteristic of many animals can control genetic structure; even minor environmental perturbations might cause biologically significant changes.

Fossil finds and interpretations continued to add new spirit to inquiries about the origins and evolution of humans, apes, and other vertebrates. In Wyoming, at an Eocene Epoch site estimated to be 50 million years old, fossil vertebrates were examined by Leonard Krishtalka and Richard Stucky of the Carnegie Museum of Natural History, Pittsburgh, Pa. They had identified more than a dozen previously undescribed animal species, including primates similar to lemurs and tarsiers. The material from this site was expected to reveal much about the origin of modern mammals.

In the Old World, fossil evidence relating to human origins continued to accumulate. At a site in Kenya investigators from the National Museums of Kenya and Johns Hopkins University in Baltimore, Md., reported the unprecedented finding of a nearly complete human skeleton estimated to be 1.6 million years old. They concluded that the skeleton would further establish the modern human as a direct descendant of *Homo erectus.* Members of the team also reported the discovery of 18 million-year-old bones of *Proconsul africanus* on an island in Lake Victoria. The fossils revealed that *Proconsul,* regarded as a prehuman form of ape, was tailless. Because the remains of several individuals were excavated, the find should provide additional information about the biology of the species.

Perhaps the most significant scientific find relating to the early origin of prehumans was made by Russell L. Ciochon of the State University of New York at Stony Brook and colleagues, who reported that a 40 million-year-old Burmese fossil primate,

TRIP LAMB

A hybrid tree frog makes his mating call from dry ground, as do green tree frogs, rather than from the water, which is preferred by barking tree frogs. Scientists confirmed that hybrids are crosses of male green and female barking parents.

Amphipithecus mogaungensis, may be the oldest known common ancestor of monkeys, apes, and humans. The report was controversial in that the area of origin of the prehuman line had generally been thought to have been Africa rather than Asia. These investigators suggested that the higher primates evolved in Asia and later migrated to Africa and South America.

East Africa was hit by a new and potentially devastating pest of maize (corn)—the staple for much of the African population. *Prostephanus truncatus,* a grain-boring beetle that originated in Central America, gained entry to Tanzania probably some six years ago. By 1985 it had spread to Kenya and Burundi, had threatened Zambia and Malawi, and had most recently been found on the other side of the continent in Togo. In Africa it had so far avoided major enemies and had already caused average losses of 9% of grain stores.

Ornithology

During the decade since the end of the Cultural Revolution, there had been a resurgence of ornithological activity in China. Birdbanding was begun in 1983, and some 3,000 birds had been marked by the end of 1984. Bar-headed geese and brown-headed gulls were caught in considerable numbers at a breeding site on the Tibetan plateau. The biology of the white-rumped swift was under investigation in Shanghai.

In an imaginative experiment in economic ornithology, azure-winged magpies were trained by the forestry authorities in Shantong (Shantung) Province as "tree doctors"; the trees were suffering from the overattentions of the pine moth. First, nestling magpies were brought into captivity and reared to the fledgling stage. The birds were reared on a diet of adult moths or pupae (caterpillars), and every time a meal was made available, a whistle was

blown. After three years' training, the birds were taken to an infested part of the forest and released, and the whistle was blown. The birds were attracted to the vicinity of their trainer and at once began searching for the injurious insects. After 20 days, 18 birds had eaten 8,000 larvae, 1,700 pupae, and a number of full-winged adult moths.

By 1985 the five-year-old Ornithological Society of China had attracted 342 members. The new standard work on the birds of the republic listed 1,186 species, 20 of them new to China since 1976. Special attention was being paid to members of the pheasant family, no fewer than 16 of which were endemic to China. In Sichuan (Szechwan) the vocabulary of the brown-eared pheasant was extensively taped. A British ornithological expedition to China established a temporary observatory on the coast of the Yellow Sea during March–June 1985 and observed no less than half the world's population of Siberian cranes on migration from the Chang Jiang (Yangtze) marshes south to their breeding grounds in the U.S.S.R.

In the Soviet Union itself the first ornithological society was formed, with branches in even the most remote republics. Surprisingly, there were no fewer than 1,000 full-time ornithologists active in the U.S.S.R. Some notable studies, such as those of E. Panov on the wheatears (thrush species common to Eurasia), were outstanding in their excellence.

The theory that migratory birds from Europe and Soviet Asia fly nonstop across the Mediterranean and the Sahara in one "hop" en route to their winter quarters in Central Africa was disproved by researchers of the Max Planck Institute for Behavioral Physiology, Seewiesen, West Germany. After more than three months in the Libyan desert, investigator Herbert Biebach established that the genetically predetermined migration program of such birds as the spotted flycatcher is affected by climatic, ecological, and physiological factors. He set up two research camps in the desert, about 300 km (186 mi) south of the Mediterranean and 180 km (112 mi) west of the Nile; one camp was at an oasis, the other in the arid desert. At both camps Biebach spread mist nets. Many insectivorous migratory birds travel at night, and each dawn Biebach netted an average of 80–90 birds. For each specimen, body temperature and amount of subcutaneous fat were measured and recorded. Some birds were given blood tests to establish the level of their water reserves. They were then divided by species and weight. Biebach found that all desert-resting birds remained still for only 12 hours, from dawn till dusk, finding whatever shade they could. Significantly, the body weight of these birds was, on average, 10% higher than that of oasis-resting birds. No underweight birds landed in the desert; they flew on, presumably until they found food and water. At the oasis site, too, most birds stayed only for the day, but a significant proportion remained longer, some for weeks. These were predominantly underweight birds, who used the oasis to replenish their fat supplies and were prepared to interrupt their flight program to do so. The research emphasized that because there were very few oases in the Sahara to accommodate the estimated 5,000,000,000 land birds that crossed the Mediterranean and Sahara each year, it might be assumed that the overwhelming majority were forced to rest in the desert proper; in fact, however, only well-fed birds were found to do so. These findings were confirmed in the laboratory during simulated migration flights.

In *A Dictionary of Birds* (1985), edited by Bruce Campbell and Elizabeth Lack, 300 authors synthesized the current state of the science. Among the very recent discoveries published there for the first time, one of the more surprising was the slowness with which birds fly. The so-called swift was shown to be capable of only 40 km (24.8 mi) per hour. The fastest bird known to science (level flight, still air) was the eider duck, timed by radar at 72 km (44.7 mi) per hour.

Marine Biology

Ultraviolet light inhibits the growth of bryozoans and tunicates but not of corals on shallow Australian reefs; recent studies indicated that the corals have an ultraviolet blocking agent that might have potential as a sunscreen agent in paints and plastics. Studies of Caribbean reefs resulted in the construction of several coral reef "microcosms" at the Smithsonian Institution, Washington, D.C., which mimicked to an unusually successful degree the complexity and function of a natural coral reef and its lagoon. There were new insights into long-standing questions about the methods by which geologically recent and isolated coral reefs, such as those of the Hawaiian archipelago, had been colonized. One possible method might be via floating colonies

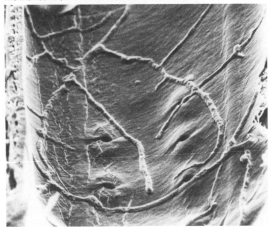

The enzyme lignase, secreted by the common white rot fungus Phanerochaete chrysosporium, *attacks lignin molecules in a pine-wood cell. The enzyme, whose structure had not been determined, also proved effective in degrading DDT, dioxin, and PCB.*

THOMAS KUSTER, U.S. FOREST PRODUCTS LABORATORY

of corals on logs, coconuts, and volcanic pumice. Another might be by mechanisms such as that described in *Pocillopora;* the planulae (free-swimming larvae), newly settled and metamorphosed, are able to re-form as secondary distributive planulae if subjected to stress within three days of settlement.

Extensive three-dimensional measurements of herring and mackerel shoals in large sea cages confirmed earlier predictions that fish in schools choose neighbors of similar body size. Juveniles of the solitary Red Sea blenny (*Meiacanthus nigrolineatus*) were found to possess a color pattern resembling that of various cardinal fish among shoals of which the blenny is often found; this discovery was the first example of school-oriented mimicry in a fish. Winter flounders (*Pseudopleuronectes americanus*) in North America cope with subzero temperatures by synthesizing blood-borne antifreeze peptides, which appear at different times of the year in different genetic races of fish, depending on local water temperatures. Juvenile menhaden (*Brevoortia*) in the eastern U.S., which feed on plants growing in coastal marshes, were shown to readily digest cellulose and other vascular plant material with 75% efficiency, thus providing the first example within a food web of a direct link from marsh-plan primary production to fishery use without intermediate steps involving microbial decomposition. A reduction of a giant kelp canopy off southern California from an area of 63 sq km (24.3 sq mi) in 1982 to 6 sq km (2.3 sq mi) in 1984 was attributed to temperature stress and nutrient starvation associated with the recent activities of El Niño, the periodic warming of the Pacific Ocean off the coasts of Peru and Ecuador. In 1982 and 1983 this increase in temperature was the most intense ever recorded.

Botany

In addition to the five groups of identified plant hormones (auxins, gibberellins, cytokinins, ethylene, and abscisic acid), there exists an array of chemical substances—referred to collectively as plant growth regulators, or PGRs—that affect plant growth and development. A PGR is a group of molecules that is chemically diverse and includes synthetically manufactured substances as well as natural products isolated from various plant tissues. These substances are useful in agriculture for a variety of purposes. Some PGRs act as dwarfing agents, allowing crop plants such as peanuts to be planted in closer rows, which results in increased yields. Others enhance storage quality of certain fruits such as apples, prevent sprouting of onions and potatoes, act as chemical hybridizing agents in wheat, or facilitate mechanical harvesting of crops such as cotton and potatoes.

In spite of the wide range of effects that both hormones and PGRs elicit in plants and the importance of PGRs in agriculture, discovery of their mode of action had been elusive—in part because application of PGRs to plants seemed to influence

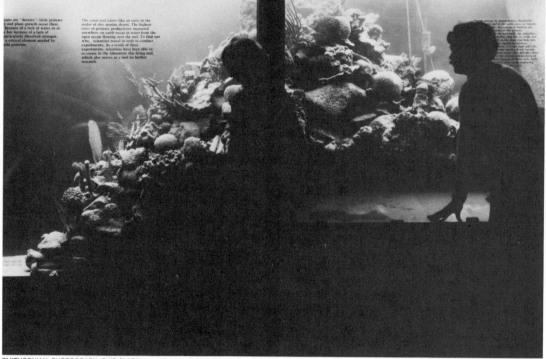

One of the Smithsonian Institution's new coral reef "microcosm" exhibits emphasizes the coral reef's ecological status as something of an oasis of life in the midst of the relative lifelessness of tropical oceans.

several developmental events at once. Furthermore, some aspects of development seemed to require the presence of more than one PGR, the right pH (degree of alkalinity or acidity), and other contributing substances as well.

Recently, however, a new group of molecules with perhaps more direct effects on morphogenesis was discovered. Surprisingly, this group includes naturally occurring carbohydrates, called oligosaccharins, that are components of plant cell walls. Oligosaccharins are short-chain sugars that can act as regulators of developmental processes. These substances were being studied for their ability to control a number of plant processes, including the production of phytoalexins (toxins that kill invading pathogens) and the control of certain symbiotic associations.

Most recently, experiments demonstrated the ability of oligosaccharins to control a number of developmental effects in tobacco tissue culture systems; for example, the promotion of both shoot and root development in undifferentiated tissue cultures and the regulation of the development of either flowers or vegetative buds. Previously these developmental processes had been shown to be influenced only by adjustment of the concentrations of auxin and cytokinin in the tissue culture medium. The demonstration of control of morphogenesis by molecules that are derived from the cell walls led investigators to suggest that the oligosaccharins may be in situ regulators of plant development.

Several toxic or carcinogenic compounds were known to persist in the environment as pollutants for extended periods of time, presumably because microorganisms either were unable to degrade them

or did so only very slowly. Some of these compounds, such as DDT, also showed a tendency to accumulate in the body fat of animals high in the food chain. It was recently shown that a common white rot fungus can be induced to secrete an enzyme that breaks down lignin, a complex component of plant cell walls. Because the complex lignin molecule contains structures similar to molecules of DDT, dioxin, and PCB (polychlorinated biphenyl), researchers decided to test the lignin-degrading enzyme against these substances and found it to be active in degrading them as well. While it was too early to determine the potential impact of this finding on the task of cleaning up contaminated environments, the investigators did suggest that inoculation of waste treatment water with the fungus that secretes the lignin-degrading enzyme might prevent the environmental accumulation of certain toxic wastes.

Efforts continued during the year to develop genetically engineered bacteria that would be beneficial to the plants on which they lived. Such symbiotic relationships had long been known in nature—for example, the association of nitrogen-fixing bacteria with the roots of certain plants. At least three newly engineered bacteria had been produced. One conferred frost resistance to the infected host; another produced an endotoxin that protects the host plant from invading insects; and a third conferred resistance to herbicide damage. However, as some doubt remained about the long-term effects of releasing genetically engineered organisms into the environment, the U.S. Environmental Protection Agency was continuing to evaluate the results of these experiments.

Special Report:
Inhumane Treatment of Animals

by Benedict A. Leerburger and Michael Allaby

The belief that animals are endowed with certain rights is not a new concept. However, when England enacted legislation in 1822 "to prevent cruel and improper treatment of Cattle," it became the first country to codify and define not only what rights animals possessed but which animals possessed them. Perhaps more important, the act established the authority of government to regulate the treatment of privately owned animals. The animal rights movement, in Britain as in most other Western countries, grew out of fears that working farm animals and circus animals were being ill-fed and that livestock destined for slaughter were being subjected to needless suffering. Until the completion of the British railway network, sheep and cattle were driven to market, often for hundreds of miles, and people saw them being openly whipped. Throughout the 20th century new laws were enacted to protect specific types of animals—livestock, race horses, zoo animals, wildlife—and to cover specific circumstances—transportation, caging, pet keeping. But while certain abuses were being dealt with by statute, new practices, not covered by existing law, were arousing the anger of animal protectionists. Thus public concern today focuses primarily on inhumane treatment of animals in intensive livestock husbandry and laboratory experimentation, illegal hunting practices, and the callous neglect inflicted in private by some pet owners. In the U.S. more than 400 groups with two million dues-paying members are involved in protesting these practices.

Animals in Service to Man

Perhaps the greatest source of anger to all animal rights groups is the treatment received by animals in scientific tests and experiments. It is estimated that in the United States alone up to 70 million animals are employed in research each year. Although the vast majority of these are specially bred mice and rats, the use of other animals—including rabbits, primates, bovids (cattle, sheep, and related animals), and impounded cats and dogs—has spurred animal rights organizations to take action. To dramatize their point of view, one group, the Animal Liberation Front, was involved on Dec. 25, 1983, in the theft of several dogs that were being used in medical research at a Los Angeles hospital.

One of the prime goals of many animal rights groups is the replacement of experimental animals with alternatives such as tissue cultures and computer models. The Draize test, a procedure widely used by drug and cosmetic manufacturers, is frequently cited by these groups as a typical instance of the needless suffering to which laboratory animals are subjected. In the Draize test, the chemical under scrutiny is dropped into the eyes of rabbits to measure its potential for causing irritation. An even more controversial procedure is the "Lethal Dose 50" (LD50) test, which measures the toxicity of a substance by determining the dose lethal to half of the animals in any test group. This process was designed in 1927 to standardize drug potency. Until 1983 federal agencies, including the U.S. Food and Drug Administration, demanded LD50 testing prior to accepting certain substances—including such household products as oven cleaners—as "safe." In 1984, however, several research groups developed a substitute procedure using computer models to predict toxicity.

The Mobilization for Animals (MFA), an international network representing several hundred animal-protectionist organizations, makes a particularly strong attack on the use of "higher" animals, especially primates, in various forms of psychological experimentation. The MFA states that "Of all experiments [using animals], those conducted in psychology are the most painful, pointless and repulsive." The MFA and other animal advocacy groups have alleged that animals are given "intense, repeated electric shocks . . . are deprived of food and water . . . and are mutilated to produce behavioral changes." However, a study by Rockefeller University psychologists D. Caroline Coile and Neal E. Miller takes issue with these charges. Coile and Miller evaluated each of the 608 articles involving studies in which animals were used that appeared over a five-year period in the journals of the American Psychological Association. They concluded that none of the MFA claims could be supported, noting that while unreported acts of cruelty may have occurred, "it is extremely misleading to imply that they are typical of experimental psychology."

Those who support the use of higher animals in experimental programs contend that psychological studies require the observation of the whole animal and its relationship to the environment. They claim that behavior problems cannot be observed in tissue cultures and do not lend themselves to computer models. Further, they point out that each year ten million dogs are destroyed by pounds, animal shelters, and humane societies, organizations often funded by animal protectionist groups. These scientists point out that in the U.S. there are existing mechanisms to ensure that research animals are treated in a humane way. Such mechanisms include the federal Animal Welfare Act, periodic inspection of all animal-research facilities by the Department of Agriculture, and personal inspections by representatives of federal agencies that fund animal research. In addition, most universities and research institutes have special committees that monitor animal research and care.

The Movement in Britain

The British animal welfare organizations fall into three main groups. There are those like the Royal Society for the Prevention of Cruelty to Animals that have a broad concern for all animals. They accept the need for some use of animals in scientific experimentation but seek to tighten controls over such procedures, to reduce the number of animals necessary, and, wherever possible, to adopt alternative techniques. Others, such as the Research Defense Society, the Humane Trust, and the other members of the so-called Moderate Coalition, concentrate on encouraging the development of laboratory procedures that eliminate the need for test animals.

The third group takes a more extreme position. They regard humans and nonhumans as moral equals and view all exploitation of animals as unjust. They would not permit the keeping of animals for meat, milk, or eggs, much less for furs, and they would ban all animal experimentation. One such organization is the British Union for the Abolition of Vivisection, which supports other "animal liberation" groups as well. It does not advocate violent protest but, like the Animal Liberation Front in the U.S., it supports those who enter premises illegally to destroy equipment and remove animals. In February 1985 its prosecution of the Royal College of Surgeons succeeded despite the fact that evidence produced by the union had been obtained illegally. The case, in which the college was found guilty of cruelty to a macaque monkey, was under appeal at year's end.

The Controversy over Hunting

Perhaps the question "To hunt or not to hunt?" best illustrates the controversy between advocates of animal rights and those who believe it is essential to permit limited killing. U.S. experts in wildlife management have urged the selective hunting of white-tailed deer to prevent overpopulation of the species. Biologists estimate that one square mile of range can support no more than 25 deer; when this number is exceeded, the food supply diminishes and, in turn, the herd's physical condition is directly altered. With hunting being either limited or curtailed, deer populations are increasing at an alarming rate, according to these authorities. Today, for example, more deer roam the state of Pennsylvania than existed in the entire country at the turn of the century.

In early 1985 state and federal wildlife managers agreed to open selected state and national preserves to limited deer hunting to thin the herds. Opposing this action is the Fund for Animals, which proposed instead a program of mass birth control—the implantation of time-release capsules that would prevent ovulation for several years. Although a similar method is used by zoos, it proved unsuccessful when tried in the wild on Angel Island, California, in the early 1980s. Says animal rights advocate Priscilla Cohn, "A lot of people say that hunting is as American as apple pie. But we're not living on the Plains with herds of buffalo anymore." Spokesmen for hunting organizations term such comments "Bambi hysteria." The Fund for Animals is also one of the leading animal rights organizations opposed to the killing of baby harp seals, which are "harvested" by Canadian Eskimos for their highly desirable downy-white fur.

The direct killing of animals is only one aspect of hunting objected to by animal rights groups. It has been estimated that each year U.S. hunters deposit some 3,000 tons of lead pellets in lakes, ponds, and marshes. Waterfowl accidently ingest these pellets while feeding, and this has led to increased mortality from lead poisoning. According to *Sports Illustrated,* "The mortality rate from lead poisoning is thought to be 2 to 3% of the fall population of all species, and that means that between 1.6 and 2.4 million ducks die each year."

A Growing Movement

In the U.S. those supporting a general policy of humane treatment of all animals have made significant inroads by their lobbying efforts with state and national lawmakers. Legislation now exists in many states governing the treatment and sale of pets. In some states, for example, rabbits and baby chickens—once bought in great numbers as Eastertime novelties—can no longer be sold as pets. And despite the guidelines issued by the U.S. Department of Agriculture for the humane raising and slaughter of domestic animals, animal protectionists continue to protest the abuses of "factory" farming, including the overcrowded caging of calves, hogs, and chickens. The international movement to assure the rights of all animals is active on all continents. Australian philosopher Peter Singer, author of *Animal Liberation,* observes that "we treat animals as if they were things to be used as we please, rather than as beings with lives of their own to live." If the advocates of animal rights are successful in their campaign, the lives of animals will be regarded with increased respect, and those who deal with animals, from pets to prey, will be increasingly subject to oversight and regulation.

A crew representing the U.S. (right) competes with a Swedish crew during the Liberty Cup yacht races in New York Harbor. The U.S. won the cup on July 2 by beating teams from seven other nations during the four-day regatta.

BOATING

In February 1985 the cream of the U.S. ocean-racing yachts, along with several boats from Europe, gathered in Florida for the Southern Racing Circuit competition. Charley Scott's J41 *Smiles* one-tonner took the overall honors.

With interest in the 1987 America's Cup series gathering momentum, more and more match-race series were being organized. In the Congressional Cup, sailed off Long Beach, Calif., three top U.S. helmsmen tied at the end of the regular series, and in the sail-off Rod Davis, the Soling class Olympic gold medalist, narrowly beat defending champion Dave Perry and John Kolius. The British match-race series was held off Lymington, Hampshire, in Westerley Fulmar yachts. Nine group races were sailed to select the four semifinalists. Iain Murray from Australia won the preliminary series with eight victories, ahead of Gary Jobson of the U.S. and Harold Cudmore, sailing for Ireland, and Chris Law of the U.K. Murray and Cudmore qualified for the finals, in which Murray badly lost the start and never recovered. Cudmore thus again won the Lymington Cup.

The Round Britain race took place again in 1985, and once more the big multihulled craft dominated the scene. Because of the vast difference in size and speed of the boats that were entered, the leaders finished before the smaller boats had gained the halfway mark. Most interest was naturally focused on the leading craft, with Michael Whipp and David Allen-Williams establishing a seven-hour lead in *BCA-Paragon* by the halfway stage, but soon afterward they had to retire into Peterhead. This left Tony Bullimore and Nigel Irons in the lead in *Apricot,* and they finished some 15 hours ahead of *Moor Energy* (Jeff Houlgrave and Bob Bradford), with *Marlow Ropes* (Mark Gatehouse and Peter Rowsell) a close third.

The field for the 1987 America's Cup challenge, due to be sailed in Australian waters, was whittled down to 14 teams: six U.S., two Canadian, two French, two Italian, and one each from Great Britain and New Zealand. The elimination series to determine the one challenger to sail against the Australian defender was scheduled to start with a round-robin series off Fremantle, Australia, on Oct. 5–20, 1986. The designs of keels and underwater shapes remained cloaked in secrecy, while technical advances in equipment continued unabated at huge costs.

In the Admiral's Cup series 18 teams entered. The British team was clearly a strong one, with three of the best one-tonners, including world champion *Jade* (Larry Wooddell), supported by *Panda* (Peter Whipp) and *Phoenix* (Lloyd Bankson). The West German team, holders of the cup, were in no mood to give the trophy up easily and had their boats *Rubin VIII* (Hans-Otto Schumann), *Outsider* (Tilmar Hansen), and *Diva (85)* (Diekel and Westphall Langloh) in top trim. The very windy channel conditions of late July and early August took a heavy toll of the fleet, particularly in the English Channel race. The Fastnet race was a rough one that caused many boats to retire, but the West German victory was in doubt until *Jade* suffered mast damage and had to withdraw. *Phoenix,* skippered by Cudmore, finished the series as top boat, and Great Britain took second place behind West Germany.

Motorboating

Lee ("Chip") Hanauer of Seattle, Wash., driver of the newly sponsored Miller American unlimited hydroplane, led the assault on the American Power Boat Association (APBA) record books in 1985, winning the coveted APBA Gold Cup for the fourth consecutive year. In doing so, Hanauer became the first driver since Gar Wood some 60 years earlier to win four Gold Cups in a row, surpassing the late Bill Muncey and Ron Musson, who each took three straight. Hanauer also set the sport's first lap record of more than 150 mph (240 km/h) in 1985, pushing his turbine-powered Lucero hull to a qualifying mark of 153.061.

Other unlimited newsmakers were the aircraft-powered *Executone* and *Miss Budweiser* teams. Drivers Scott Pierce and Jim Kropfeld fought off challengers and finished second and third, respectively, behind Hanauer in the national high point competition.

George Morales of Miami, Fla., continued his trek through the APBA record books with a record-breaking Offshore run from Miami to New York City. Morales's four 700-hp MerCruiser engines pushed his 14-m (46-ft) Cougar catamaran over the 1,257-mi (2,224-km) course in 19 hours, 38 minutes, and 35 seconds, chopping more than three hours off the former record set in 1974. Even the second-place finisher, Al Copeland of New Orleans, La., broke the former mark, finishing an hour behind Morales.

Morales added another gem to his Offshore crown in 1985, winning the world championship in the Superboat class, for his third championship title in

Lee ("Chip") Hanauer signals victory after becoming the first driver of a hydroplane in the unlimited class to break the 150-mph (240-km/h) barrier in competition.

as many years. Copeland, on the other hand, swept the Superboat class on the national circuit, winning the national high point title. Other 1985 national high point winners in Offshore competition included Miami's Sal Magluta in the Open class, Chris Lavin of Westport, Conn., in Modified, John Emmons of East Hanover, N.J., in Pro-Stock, Bob Erickson of Minnetonka, Minn., in Stock A, and Bill Kaye of Chicago in Stock B.

In the two-liter outboard tunnel boat class, the British International Harmsworth Trophy—known as the "America's Cup" of powerboat racing—remained on its home turf despite a hard-fought challenge by the U.S. The British team, led by Mark Wilson of Brighton, England, and Jon Jones of Cardigan, Wales, won convincing victories in both legs of the contest, clinching the historic prize for the second year in a row.

U.S. drivers fared better in the Formula One outboard season as Ben Robertson of Charleston, S.C., finished second in the international points competition, 11 points behind leader Bob Spalding of England. Robertson's teammate, Gene Thibodaux of Winter Haven, Fla., tied for third place with Sweden's Bertil Wik.

BOLIVIA

Pressure from within Congress and widespread discontent with the government's economic record forced Pres. Hernán Siles Zuazo of Bolivia to cut short his term of office by a year and call general elections for June 1985. The preelection period was marked by growing political unrest and rumors of a coup d'état, and these factors, combined with the slow registration of voters, served to delay the elections by a month. Foreign Minister Edgar Camacho Omiste resigned the day before polling to protest against the strengthening of relations with China and the consequent breaking of ties with Taiwan.

When polling took place on July 14, the right-wing Acción Democrática Nacionalista party, led by Gen. Hugo Banzer Suarez, Bolivia's military ruler during 1971–78, received 29% of the vote, as against 26% for the Movimiento Nacionalista Revolucionaria (MNR). Since no party gained an outright majority, the new president was chosen by congressional ballot. Víctor Paz Estenssoro, the MNR's centrist candidate, defeated Banzer by 94 votes to 51 and was inaugurated as president for the fourth time on August 6. Although he could count on the support of the left-wing parties, who were eager to keep the right out of power, his position in Congress was fairly weak, since he did not command a majority.

The year was one of continuing economic crisis, with inflation reaching an estimated 14,000% by midyear. Minimal growth of 1% in 1984 was mainly accounted for by the recovery in agriculture, as mining output fell to the lowest level since the 1930s. There was little evidence of improvement in 1985. The official exchange rate of 75,000 pesos

Mine workers in Bolivia began a month-long strike on August 31 to protest austerity measures taken by the new government of Pres. Víctor Paz Estenssoro to curb inflation.

NICOLE BONNET—GAMMA/LIAISON

to U.S. $1 was grossly overvalued when compared with the black-market rate of 1.4 million pesos to U.S. $1 (August figures). As a result, more and more business transactions were carried out on the black market, and Bolivians reverted to a barter economy. Bank deposits dwindled because of highly negative real interest rates, and traditional business ventures were being replaced by speculative activities.

At the end of August the new government announced a series of economic measures that included lifting exchange controls and introducing a "controlled float" to unify the free and official exchange rates. A new unit of currency, equivalent to 1 million pesos, was also promised. The government eliminated many price subsidies, raised domestic fuel prices, and imposed a four-month freeze on public-sector wages. A complete reorganization of public-sector companies, aimed at decentralizing control, was planned.

The package was greeted with protests from the workers. The Bolivian Workers' Central Labor Federation called a general strike in early September, and the government declared a state of siege. However, the business sector and foreign creditors welcomed the new government's stance, and debt negotiations resumed with optimism on both sides. Foreign governments also pledged aid to help with the implementation of the measures. The strike ended in early October with an agreement that included the release of detained labor leaders.

BOOK PUBLISHING

After posting a broad economic recovery in 1983 and the early months of 1984, U.S. book publishers turned in a mixed performance late in the year that resulted in modest forecasts for the industry's short-term future. The Association of American Publishers estimated total sales for 1984 at $9,120,000,000, a 6.2% increase over the previous year. By comparison, in 1983 the industry achieved a 9.5% increase. Overall bookstore trade sales rose 6.3% to $1.7 billion, compared with a 17% rise in 1983. Sales of

children's books rose almost 10% in 1984, but adult hardcovers and mass-market paperbacks made only slight gains—3.2 and 3.8%, respectively. The Book Industry Study Group (BISG), which monitored sales performances month by month, reported erratic figures early in 1985, with the first half of the year showing a 6.6% increase in total industry dollar volume over 1984. School textbook sales posted the largest sales gain—18%—and both adult hardcovers and trade paperbacks were up about 12% for the six-month period; however, mass-market sales declined 3.6% on a 12% drop in units sold. A five-year industry forecast by the U.S. Department of Commerce predicted only 3.5% growth through 1989, while the BISG, covering the same period, drew an even gloomier picture—with the exception of a 10% gain for trade books, no growth at all.

The big publishing conglomerates tended to become even bigger in 1985 as major mergers and acquisitions, a trend of the past 15 years, continued unabated. As the year began, the talk of book publishing was the purchase by Gulf and Western Industries in December 1984 of Prentice-Hall Inc., the nation's leading college textbook publisher, for $718 million. Gulf and Western, which already owned Simon & Schuster, thus became the nation's largest book publisher by a wide margin. (McGraw Hill Inc. had previously been ranked first.) In March Macmillan Inc., which bought the Scribner Book Co. in 1984, vaulted to fifth place among U.S. publishers by acquiring Bobbs-Merrill and six other companies from ITT. One month later Macmillan dissolved the 157-year-old Bobbs-Merrill in the name of business efficiency. Another venerable house, Dial Press, met the same fate when it was absorbed into the Doubleday corporate fold.

Grove Press was sold in March for $2 million to the Wheatland Corp., headed by Ann Getty, wife of an heir to the Getty oil fortune, and George Weidenfeld, a British publisher. Barney Rosset, Grove's founder and publisher, was to remain at the helm.

The line separating hardcover and paperback

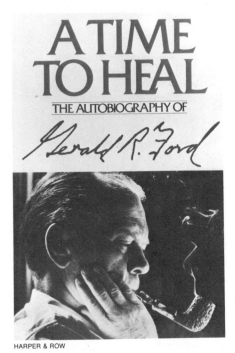

HARPER & ROW

The U.S. Supreme Court ruled that The Nation *exceeded the bounds of fair use in printing extensive quotations from former president Gerald Ford's memoirs.*

houses, once quite distinct, blurred even further in 1985. New American Library (NAL), a leader in paperbacks, acquired E. P. Dutton to complement its own hardcover imprint started in 1980. The move was part of a trend, born of high auction prices for reprint rights, in which paperback houses bought rights for both the hardcover and softcover editions of a book. The strategy seemed to have had the intended effect; rights auctions were generally lackluster in 1985. One of the biggest was Knopf's sale of *The Accidental Tourist* by Anne Tyler to Berkley for $962,500.

Paperback publishers were not the only ones to gain by eliminating the middleman. Best-selling authors realized larger profits, since by selling all rights to a single house they no longer had to split paperback revenues with the hardcover publisher. NAL granted the biggest deal of all when it guaranteed Stephen King, who topped the year's fiction lists with two titles, *Skeleton Crew* and *Thinner* (by the pseudonymous Richard Bachman), $10 million for a hardcover/paperback package on two novels due in 1987. Bantam made a similar deal for *Destiny* by the little-known British writer Sally Beauman, paying just over $1 million.

Memoirs and the prospect of memoirs made news repeatedly. Lee Iacocca's *Iacocca* sold more than two million copies in hardcover and shared the top spot on the nonfiction lists with Chuck Yeager's *Yeager.* In September Harper & Row agreed to pay $2 million for David Stockman's remembrance of his years in the Reagan White House. Later in the year Geraldine Ferraro's million-dollar *My Story* appeared, and Simon & Schuster was reported to be negotiating with Fidel Castro for his story.

Publishing's faltering love affair with the computer was not revived. Title output was reported down 43% for 1985; Harper & Row disbanded its software division after two years in the business; and one of the more successful specialty houses in the field, dilithium Press, filed for bankruptcy.

Free-speech guarantees were confirmed in the first test of a new kind of antipornography law. In Indiana a federal district court ruled unconstitutional an Indianapolis ordinance construing pornography as a violation of women's civil rights. Judges in Colorado and Virginia also struck down laws limiting minors' access to pornography.

In an unprecedented case a government effort to bring fraud charges against Antoni Gronowicz, author of *God's Broker,* a suspect biography of Pope John Paul II, was aided by a Court of Appeals ruling that Gronowicz had to obey a subpoena of his notes. The same court earlier had ruled that the author's notes were protected by the First Amendment. An appeal to the Supreme Court was expected.

There was an unexpected development in an antitrust suit brought by the Northern California Booksellers Association against Avon Publishers for granting preferential wholesale discounts to chain stores. As a result of a cost study undertaken to bolster its case—and without waiting for a verdict—Avon dropped 1,742 bookstore accounts that it deemed did too little business to justify the cost of service.

Meanwhile, chain stores were having their own battles over discounting. Waldenbooks, the nation's largest chain, entered the retail-discount wars with its Reader's Market outlets offering 35 and 25% off *New York Times* bestsellers and 15% off other titles. Crown Books responded by raising its discount rates. A February Gallup Poll revealed that 24% of paperbacks and 37% of hardbacks were bought at a discount.

Takeovers were the main feature of British book publishing in 1985. Associated Book Publishers bought Routledge & Keegan Paul; Century Publications merged with Hutchinson; Penguin acquired Thomson Books; Longmans took over Pitman; and Macdonald & Evans and Heinemann were absorbed into the new giant Heinemann-Octopus group. The realities of publishing now obviously favored the big battalions, both in terms of economies of scale and in securing an integrated line from hardcover into paperback rights.

The influence on sales impact of the main literary prizes, and most particularly the Booker-McConnell Prize, was spreading significantly overseas and in 1985 became a subject of interest and promotion in Australia, New Zealand, and North America.

The announcement by the U.K. chancellor of the Exchequer in his budget speech that the government had no intention of levying a value-added tax on books was regarded as a major triumph throughout the world book trade. In New Zealand, however, a threatened goods and services tax was almost certain to apply to books. New Zealand publishers and booksellers were deeply concerned with the likely impact on general book sales and were lobbying hard for additional educational budgets to cover the inevitable increased prices. Educational sales in the U.K. continued to suffer from government pressure on local-authority expenditures.

BOWLING

Championship match scores on the U.S. Professional Bowlers Association (PBA) tour in 1985 often disappointed viewers and sponsors, but Mike Aulby did not share the blame. Aulby had won five PBA titles going into the final weeks of the year, and the 25-year-old left-hander from Indianapolis, Ind., was consistently strong when first prize was at stake. In Union City, Calif., Aulby won his final match 245–190; in Toledo, Ohio, 253–211; in Garden City, N.Y., 233–220; in Denver, Colo., 210–159; and in Chicago, 245–189. In the PBA doubles championship in Las Vegas, Nev., Aulby and his brother-in-law, Steve Cook of Roseville, Calif., teamed for a 224–209 victory.

The six championships helped Aulby accumulate $199,800, surpassing Earl Anthony's one-year record of $164,735. Second on the money list was Pete Weber of St. Louis, Mo., 23-year-old son of Bowling Hall of Fame member Dick Weber, with $173,356. Missing from the list of 25 leading money winners was the 1984 Bowler of the Year, Mark Roth of Spring Lake Heights, N.J., who averaged 211.3 in 1985 but had little success during the tournaments.

A bowler who had long puzzled followers of the sport because of his inability to win a title despite numerous opportunities, Steve Wunderlich of St. Louis, won one of the year's richest events, the American Bowling Congress (ABC) Masters Tournament in Tulsa, Okla. In the final match Wunderlich defeated Tommy Kress of Rochester, N.Y., 256–171 and won $40,600.

In the ABC tournament for nonprofessionals in Tulsa, the Regular Division winners were: team, Terry's Pro Shop, Solon, Ohio, 3,233; doubles, Howard Higby and Clyde Gibson, Lake Jackson, Texas, 1,366; singles, Glenn Harbison, Pittsburgh, Pa., 774; all-events, Barry Asher, Anaheim, Calif., 2,033.

For the second time in three years Aleta Sill of Cocoa, Fla., won the biggest prize available to women bowlers when she topped Linda Graham 279–193 in the title match of the Maxim/Women's International Bowling Congress (WIBC) Queens Tournament in Toledo. Sill, who was runner-up to Japan's Kazue Inahashi in 1984, gained $20,700 for her victory. Graham, from Des Moines, Iowa, received $11,600.

Sill and Graham both were champions in the WIBC tournament in Toledo, with Sill taking the Open Division all-events honors with 1,900 for her nine games. Graham and Melody Philippson of Colfax, Iowa, each bowled 623 to win the doubles title with 1,246. A 2,934 total by a Toledo quintet, Don Redman Insurance, won the Open Division team crown, and Polly Schwarzel of Cheswick, Pa., rolled 694 for the singles championship.

Division I winners in the WIBC were: team, Taylor Chiropractic, Howell, Mich., 2,834; doubles, Sara Hennessey and Laura Lyons, Piqua, Ohio, 1,232; singles, Vicki Baker, St. Paris, Ohio, 656; and all-events, Barb Hansen, Marstons Mills, Mass., 1,800.

World Tenpins

The international tenpin season of 1985 opened with the eighth Asian Zone amateur championships of the Fédération Internationale des Quilleurs in Singapore in November 1984. Australia's John Sullivan and Thailand's Kunarksorn Luyong won the individual titles. Sullivan defeated Hiroshi Ishihara of Japan 211–196 in his final match, and Luyong defeated Bec Nautanabe of the Philippines in his final 204–170. The six-game singles was won by Ollie Reformado of the Philippines with a score of 1,390; the doubles went to Singapore with 2,532; Malaysia won the trios with a record high 3,666 series; and South Korea won the five-man event with 5,820. Paeng Nepomuceno of the Philippines won the all-events gold medal with 4,978.

In the women's division the Philippines' Bong Coo won the singles gold with 1,261; the Philippines took the doubles with 2,317, Australia the trios with 3,521, and Japan the five-game event with 5,827. The all-events gold went to Jeanette Baker of Australia, who totaled 4,689 for the 24 games.

The European amateur tenpin championships took place in Vienna in July 1985. From 12 events Finland, whose men won every team event, went home with four gold medals, four silver, and two bronze, while Sweden gained five gold medals, two silver, and two bronze. Tony Rosenqvist of Sweden was the champion above champions with victories in each men's individual event. In the women's events Finland won the trios; Italy claimed its first gold medal ever when Coletta Marcuzzo won the six-game event; the doubles competition was won by Åsa Larsson of Denmark and Lena Sulkanen of Sweden; France took the five-women team event; the 24-game all-events gold medal went to Great Britain with Meg Shaw; and in the match play final Larsson defeated Nora Haveneers of Belgium.

At the World Games II in or near London, bowlers of 24 nations took part in singles for men and women and mixed doubles. Dominique de Nolf and Haveneers of Belgium won the mixed doubles. The men's eight-game singles was won by Raymond Jansson of Sweden with 1,699 and the women's singles by Adelene Wee of Singapore with 1,601.

AP/WIDE WORLD

Marvelous Marvin Hagler (right) overpowers Thomas ("Hit Man") Hearns on his way toward winning the undisputed world middleweight championship in April.

BOXING

The biggest upset in heavyweight boxing in 1985 was the defeat of Larry Holmes (U.S.), by light heavyweight champion Michael Spinks (U.S.) on points over 15 rounds. Both fighters had been undefeated, and though Holmes had relinquished the World Boxing Council (WBC) title in 1983 to become International Boxing Federation (IBF; not internationally recognized) champion, he was still considered the world's top heavyweight. Earlier he had successfully defended his IBF crown by stopping David Bey (U.S.) in ten rounds and outpointing Carl Williams (U.S.). Holmes had won all of his 48 professional contests and was a firm favorite to beat Spinks. Spinks became the first light heavyweight champion to beat a heavyweight champion and, because Leon Spinks (U.S.) had won the heavyweight title from Muhammad Ali in 1978, it was the first time that two brothers could claim they had won the heavyweight championship.

Pinklon Thomas (U.S.) continued as WBC champion, knocking out former WBA champion Mike Weaver (U.S.) in eight rounds. Tony Tubbs (U.S.) became new WBA champion by outpointing Greg Page (U.S.).

The WBC cruiserweight championship changed hands twice. Alfonso Ratliff (U.S.) won it from Carlos de León (P.R.) but was then beaten by Bernard Benton (U.S.). Piet Crous (South Africa) retained the WBA title by stopping Randy Stephens (U.S.) in three rounds at Sun City, South Africa, but Dwight Muhammad Qawi (U.S.) later stopped Crous in 11 rounds, also at Sun City. Qawi was banned from appearing in WBC ratings for two years because he

had fought in South Africa.

Michael Spinks (U.S.) retained both the WBC and WBA light heavyweight titles, halting David Sears (U.S.) in three rounds and Diamond Jim McDonald (U.S.) in eight. However, after winning the IBF heavyweight title from Holmes, Spinks was stripped of his light heavyweight crown by the WBC and WBA. J. B. Williamson (U.S.) then won the WBC crown by outpointing Prince Mama Mohammed (Ghana).

Marvin Hagler (U.S.) remained the undisputed middleweight king, knocking out Thomas Hearns (U.S.), the WBC junior middleweight champion, in three rounds. Hearns remained the junior middleweight titleholder without making a defense during the year, but Mike McCallum (U.S.) made two successful defenses of the WBA version, stopping Luigi Minchillo (Italy) in 13 rounds and David Braxton (U.S.) in 8. Milton McCrory (U.S.) kept the WBC welterweight crown with two victories in France, outpointing Pedro Vilella (U.S.) and stopping Carlos Trujillo (Panama) in three, but then lost it on a two-round knockout by Don Curry (U.S.). Curry made only one defense of his WBA welterweight title, beating Colin Jones (Wales) in four rounds.

After retaining the WBC junior welterweight championship by outpointing Leroy Haley (U.S.), Billy Costello (U.S.) lost the title to Lonnie Smith (U.S.) after being knocked out in the eighth round. It was Costello's first defeat after 30 consecutive victories. The WBA championship at this weight passed from Gene Hatcher (U.S.), who was halted in nine rounds by Ubaldo Sacco (Arg.). The WBC lightweight title changed hands; Hector Camacho (P.R.) outpointed the titleholder, José Luis Ramírez (Mexico), but Livingstone Bramble (U.S.) retained the WBA version by outpointing Ray Mancini (U.S.). Julio César Chávez (Mexico) remained WBC junior lightweight champion in a busy year. He stopped Ruben Castillo (U.S.) in six rounds and Roger Mayweather (U.S.), the former WBA champion, in two; he then outpointed Dwight Pratchett (U.S.) to bring his record to 46 wins without a defeat. Rocky Lockridge (U.S.), having retained the WBA crown against Kamel Bou Ali (Tunisia), lost it to Wilfred Gómez (P.R.). Gómez thus joined the select number of champions who had won three titles, having previously held the WBC featherweight and junior featherweight crowns.

Azumah Nelson (Ghana) kept the WBC featherweight championship, stopping Juvenal Ordénes (Chile) in three rounds and dismissing Pat Cowdell (England) in the first. After retaining the WBA featherweight championship for the 19th time with a win on points over Jorge Lujan (Panama), Eusebio Pedroza (Panama) lost the title to Barry McGuigan (Northern Ireland) over 15 rounds. McGuigan then remained champion by stopping Bernard Taylor (U.S.), who had been undefeated in his previous 34 contests.

Michael Spinks (right) trades punches with International Boxing Federation heavyweight champion Larry Holmes during their championship fight on September 21. Spinks won a unanimous decision after 15 rounds to become the new IBF heavyweight champion of the world. Holmes, who had confidently expected to equal Rocky Marciano's record of 49 straight victories, had beaten Spinks's older brother, Leon, in a 1981 bout.

AP/WIDE WORLD

One of the biggest surprises of the year was the defeat of WBC junior featherweight champion Juan Meza (Mexico) by Lupe Pintor (Mexico), the former bantamweight champion. Pintor had been omitted from the world rankings for some time. The WBA junior featherweight crown remained with Víctor Callejas (P.R.), who outpointed Lee Seung Hoon (South Korea). Albert Davila (U.S.) relinquished the WBC bantamweight title, and this was later won by Daniel Zaragoza (Mexico) when Freddie Jackson (U.S.) was disqualified in the seventh round for butting. Zaragoza lost the crown in his first defense to Miguel Lora (Colombia). Richie Sandoval (U.S.) had no difficulty retaining the WBA title, stopping Cardenio Ulloa (Chile) in eight rounds.

World Boxing Champions
as of Dec. 31, 1985

Division	Boxer
Heavyweight	Pinklon Thomas, U.S.*
	Tony Tubbs, U.S.†
Cruiserweight	Bernard Benton, U.S.*
	Piet Crous, South Africa†
Light heavyweight	J. B. Williamson, U.S.*
	(vacant)†
Middleweight	Marvin Hagler, U.S.*†
Junior middleweight	Thomas Hearns, U.S.*
	Mike McCallum, U.S.†
Welterweight	Don Curry, U.S.*†
Junior welterweight	Lonnie Smith, U.S.*
	Ubaldo Sacco, Argentina†
Lightweight	Hector Camacho, Puerto Rico*
	Livingstone Bramble, U.S.†
Junior lightweight	Julio César Chávez, Mexico*
	Wilfred Gómez, Puerto Rico†
Featherweight	Azumah Nelson, Ghana*
	Barry McGuigan, Northern Ireland†
Junior featherweight	Lupe Pintor, Mexico*
	Víctor Callejas, Puerto Rico†
Bantamweight	Miguel Lora, Colombia*
	Richie Sandoval, U.S.†
Super flyweight	Jiro Watanabe, Japan*
	Kaosai Galaxy, Thailand†
Flyweight	Sot Chitalada, Thailand*
	Hilario Zapata, Panama†
Junior flyweight	Chang Jung Koo, South Korea*
	Yuh Myung-Woo, South Korea†

*Recognized by the World Boxing Council.
†Recognized by the World Boxing Association.

Jiro Watanabe (Japan), who had been stripped of the super flyweight championship by the WBA, was still recognized by the WBC and successfully defended this title three times, knocking out Payao Poontaret (Thailand) in 11 rounds, outpointing Julio Soto Solane (Dominican Republic), and stopping Katsuo Katsuma (Japan) in seven. The vacant WBA championship went to Kaosai Galaxy (Thailand) with a sixth-round win against Eusebio Espina (Dominican Republic). Kaosai followed this with victories against Lee Dong Choon (South Korea) in seven rounds and Rafael Orono (Venezuela) in five. Sot Chitalada (Thailand) continued as WBC flyweight champion by stopping Charlie Magri (England) in four rounds and drawing with Gabriel Bernal (Mexico). After defending the WBA flyweight crown for the ninth time by outpointing Antoine Montero (France), Santos Laciar (Arg.) relinquished the title and Hilario Zapata (Panama) won it.

Chang Jung Koo (South Korea) retained the WBC junior flyweight crown with wins against Germán Torres (Mexico) and Francisco Montiel (Mexico). Joey Olivio (U.S.) made boxing history in winning the WBA title from Francisco Quiroz (Dominican Republic), becoming the first American ever to win the junior flyweight championship. Later, however, he lost it to Yuh Myung-Woo (South Korea).

BRAZIL

The political year in Brazil was dominated by the transition to civilian rule and the unusual circumstances surrounding the presidential succession. On Jan. 15, 1985, the 686-member electoral college, made up of members of Congress together with representatives of the state assemblies, voted in the first presidential contest involving civilian candidates since the military came to power in 1964. The successful candidate was Tancredo de Almeida Neves, supported by the main opposition grouping, the

Brazilians celebrate the abolition of censorship announced July 29 by the new civilian government of José Sarney. Standing above signs that read in Portugese "Goodbye, Censorship" are (from left) Culture Minister Aluisio Pimenta, author Antonio Houaiss, Justice Minister Fernando Lyra, and author and Rio de Janeiro state Lieut. Gov. Darcy Ribeiro.

AP/WIDE WORLD

Brazilian Democratic Movement Party (PMDB), who received 480 votes to 180 for the only other candidate, Paulo Salim Maluf of the ruling Social Democratic Party (PDS). Neves was due to take office on March 15 but was prevented from doing so by an illness that required repeated surgery and eventually led to his death on April 21. José Sarney, who had been chosen as Neves's vice-president, was sworn in as acting president on March 15 and as president the day after Neves's death. Sarney was a leader of the Liberal Front Party, a breakaway faction of the PDS that had joined with the PMDB to sponsor Neves's candidacy.

In May Congress passed legislation that paved the way for direct presidential elections, legalized all political parties, and gave votes to illiterates. Direct elections took place in November 1985 for mayors in the state capitals, in those towns previously considered national security areas, and in other towns that had not held local elections since 1964. The PMDB suffered some unexpected defeats in the elections, losing a number of important towns to candidates of the extreme right and left.

Although not enjoying the same degree of popular support as Neves, Sarney steadily improved his position as the year progressed. After four months of deliberation Sarney announced the main lines of his economic strategy in a speech on July 22. Growth of 5–6% a year was to be fostered principally by the private sector, and the role of the state sector in the economy was to be progressively reduced. Inflation was to be tackled by price controls and measures to reduce prices of basic foodstuffs. Public spending would be redirected to social and small-scale projects and was expected to fall in real

terms in the long run. Programs to reduce poverty, particularly in the northeast, would take priority. The government would not adopt policies that would depress living standards and would honor all financial commitments at home and abroad.

On June 21 a group of forensic scientists announced that they had reached a "reasonable scientific certainty" that a body exhumed earlier in the month from a cemetery at Embu, Brazil, was that of Nazi war criminal Josef Mengele, the so-called Angel of Death of the Auschwitz-Birkenau concentration camp. The body was that of a man who had died in a drowning accident in 1979.

The Economy

Based on January–September figures, Brazil's $12 billion trade surplus target for the year was expected to be attained easily. Exports reached $18.4 billion, 7.6% less than in the same period of 1984, while imports were reduced by 10.3% to $9.2 billion. The balance of payments deficit in the first half of the year was $779 million, compared with $185 million in the first half of 1984. Gross international reserves stood at $11.6 billion in mid-1985.

Negotiations on rescheduling servicing of $45.3 billion of external debt due in 1985–90 remained. Although the government reached an agreement in principle with creditor banks in January, negotiations were cut short after the suspension of IMF credits in February. In October the U.S., creditor banks, and the IMF informed Brazil that a multiannual rescheduling could not be concluded without the IMF's stamp of approval. In November the government announced that it no longer intended to seek agreement with the IMF.

BUILDING AND CONSTRUCTION

In the United States during the year, higher dollar outlays for construction continued to provide support for the national economy. Despite concern over the nation's economic future, the continued lower rate of inflation and lower interest rates contributed to stronger consumer interest in housing and to investment in nonresidential building construction. The high level of residential construction was a major factor in the ongoing recovery in the construction industry, which had started in early 1983.

On the basis of a seasonally adjusted annual rate, the total value of new construction put in place in June 1985 was $343,837,000,000, according to the U.S. Department of Commerce. Monthly figures for the first nine months of 1985 indicated that the value of new construction put in place would reach a new record for the entire year of more than $340 billion. Outlays in 1984, the previous peak year, had totaled $312,988,000,000. Throughout the first nine months the Composite Construction Cost Index of the Department of Commerce fluctuated between a low of 166.2 (1977 = 100) and a high of 169.3, compared with an annual average of 163.7 in 1984. All the producer price indexes of materials used in building construction indicated that the rate of inflation in construction in 1985 was low.

Mortgage interest rates had moved slowly upward in 1984 until the last quarter of the year, when they turned down slightly, and these lower levels continued throughout 1985. The average effective commitment interest rate for 25-year conventional mortgages (75% loan-to-price ratio) was 11.75% in June 1985, compared with an average rate of 13.13% in 1984. The median sales price of a new home sold in July 1985 was $82,100, and it appeared that the median for the year would be slightly above that figure. The median price in 1984 was $79,900.

In Canada it was expected that the increase in the gross national product (GNP) would approach 3% in 1985, followed by a smaller increase in 1986. Consumer spending rose in early 1985, and housing investment was up sharply, but there was little change in business investment. In April and May, housing starts, responding to the fall in interest rates, were 20% higher than in the corresponding months of 1984. However, it did not appear that construction activity would improve further in the last half of the year.

Private investment in housing in Great Britain had fallen sharply in the last half of 1984. It increased in the first quarter of 1985, but this was attributable mainly to improvements made in existing housing, while investment in new housing continued to fall. Housing starts, which declined throughout 1984, rose sharply in the second quarter of 1985, but it appeared that neither private nor public investment in housing would increase during the remainder of the year. The French economy showed little vitality in 1985, and construction activity declined sharply in the cold winter months. Improvements in corporate profits during the year suggested that investments would rise, but with gross domestic product (GDP) growing at only a little over 1%, building and construction were expected to continue at low levels.

In West Germany the severe winter of 1984–85 had an adverse effect on construction. The industry had also experienced difficulty in 1984, when its contribution to GNP fell significantly. Despite large increases in orders for capital goods in mid-1985, the outlook for consumer spending was not good, and the overall outlook for the construction industry was unfavorable. Japan experienced an increase in residential construction in 1985, bolstered by a predicted growth of about 5% in GNP, stable prices for construction materials, and lower mortgage rates. A survey by the Bank of Japan indicated that nonresidential construction would also grow in 1985 and 1986 because of planned business expenditures on plant and equipment.

BULGARIA

The marked deterioration in relations between Bulgaria and Turkey that occurred during 1985 was deeply rooted in the past. An estimated one-tenth of Bulgaria's total population of almost nine million people consisted of ethnic Turks, a consequence of five centuries of Ottoman domination. Before 1944, the Turks had lived in relative harmony with the Bulgar population. In 1951 the Bulgarian Communist Party (BCP) began a campaign to bulgarianize the minority. In 1974 the government struck two major blows by prohibiting Turkish language teaching and closing down over 1,300 mosques.

Soviet leader Mikhail Gorbachev (left) and Bulgarian Pres. Todor Zhivkov lay flowers at Lenin's monument during a ceremony in Sofia between meetings of the Warsaw Pact in October.
TASS/SOVFOTO

In December 1984, according to the Turkish government, Bulgarians launched a campaign aimed at forcing the Turks to change their names to the Bulgarian equivalents. The Bulgarian authorities maintained that the Turks had adopted the new names voluntarily. Turkish Pres. Kenan Evren addressed a sharply worded letter of protest to BCP General Secretary Todor Zhivkov, and on Feb. 14, 1985, Turkey withdrew its ambassador to Sofia.

Turkey later applied economic pressure on Bulgaria by concluding an agreement to establish ferry services with Romania. Bulgaria responded in kind; during an official visit to Athens in July, Zhivkov and Greek Prime Minister Andreas Papandreou agreed to set up a train and ferry service that would provide both countries with access to Syria without passing through Turkey.

On February 10–11 Sir Geoffrey Howe became the first U.K. foreign secretary to pay an official visit to Bulgaria during the 100 years of diplomatic relations between the two countries. Zhivkov was the official guest of Gen. Wojciech Jaruzelski in Poland on April 2–3, and on October 21 Soviet leader Mikhail Gorbachev visited Zhivkov in Sofia.

BURMA

Rebels opposed to the Burmese government blew up a passenger train traveling between Rangoon and Mandalay on July 24, 1985, killing 67 people and injuring at least 100 others. The blast was caused by a land mine powerful enough to derail six coaches and the engine. Area experts believed that the explosion was the worst single act of sabotage against a civilian target during the rule of the Burma Socialist Program Party. In a similar incident, a troop train was blown up near Port Moulmein in May. Though no organization claimed responsibility for the explosions, the government believed that Karen insurgents were behind them. The Karens were one of several groups—others were the Burmese Communists, Kachin, Shan, Lahu, and Karenni (Kayah)— resisting the government, which was dominated by ethnic Burmese.

In February a security operation involving more than 3,000 troops was launched against insurgents who controlled the opium trade in eastern Burma. Though the outcome of the offensive was not made public, there were reports of clashes with rebels in several locations. Besides dealing in drugs, the smugglers exchanged Burmese gold, teak, gems, tin ore, and cattle for manufactured goods from Thailand and guns from unknown sources.

When Chinese Pres. Li Xiannian (Li Hsien-nien) visited Burma in March, the New China News Agency described the occasion as a "major event" in Sino-Burmese relations. In May Pres. Mohammad Zia-ul-Haq became the first Pakistani head of state to visit Burma in a quarter of a century. During his trip to Rangoon in July, Khurshi Alam Khan, India's junior external affairs minister, said Indo-Burmese relations were "excellent."

CANADA

The new Progressive Conservative administration headed by Brian Mulroney marked its first year in office in 1985. On Sept. 4, 1984, the Conservatives had triumphed in one of the most decisive electoral victories in Canadian history, winning 211 of the 282 seats in the House of Commons. Given this decisive mandate, Canadians had expected forceful leadership and sweeping change from the new government, but Mulroney, even though he concentrated executive power in the prime minister's office, proved a cautious leader. His legislative accomplishments during his first year were few, and he showed a tendency to retreat from policies when they proved to be controversial. The result was a first year in office for the Conservatives that many Canadians characterized as disappointing. Mulroney's personal standing declined in the polls, and the popularity of his party fell to 40% during the summer. This was a dramatic but perhaps inevitable contrast to the 50% rating the party had enjoyed on coming to power.

Mulroney, faced by an embarrassingly large group of followers in the Commons, chose 40 for his Cabinet, the largest number in Canadian history. He put real power in the hands of a veteran member from Yukon who was a shrewd parliamentary tactician, Erik Nielsen. Holding the honorific title of deputy prime minister, Nielsen was placed in charge of a task force to review government operations and propose reductions in personnel and expenditures. On February 27, after Robert Coates resigned as minister of national defense following a visit to a seedy West German bar (an episode the prime minister characterized as an error in judgment), Nielsen was named to that post as well, and he retained it in a minor Cabinet shuffle on August 20. Nielsen was also a member of the Priorities and Planning Committee, whose 16 members made the important decisions of the administration and reviewed the work of other Cabinet committees. In late September two senior ministers resigned: John Fraser from British Columbia, minister of fisheries, who admitted overruling fisheries inspectors in releasing a consignment of rancid canned tuna meat for public consumption, and Marcel Masse, minister of communications, who asked to be relieved of Cabinet duties while a complaint regarding the reporting of his election expenses was being investigated. Masse, a powerful figure on the Quebec political scene, was returned to the Cabinet on November 30 when the charges against him were determined to be unfounded. A new fisheries minister was appointed from British Columbia.

Parliament sat from Nov. 5, 1984, to June 28, 1985, when it adjourned for the summer recess. A total of 49 bills were approved, most of them housekeeping measures introduced by the previous Liberal administration. The Mulroney government moved swiftly to demolish one of the pillars of its predecessor's economic policy: the Foreign Invest-

U.S. Pres. Ronald Reagan (left) and Canadian Prime Minister Brian Mulroney shake hands at the start of a two-day summit meeting in Quebec City in March.
GAMMA/LIAISON

ment Review Agency (FIRA), a body set up in 1973, during a period of heightened concern over the effects of foreign investment in Canada. Its role was to screen investments from abroad and takeovers of Canadian businesses. The agency had been a source of contention with the U.S. during the early 1980s and was not popular with Canadian business. It was now replaced by Investment Canada, whose task was to encourage new investment, whether from foreign or domestic sources. The Conservatives also backed away from the Liberals' controversial metric policy, deciding that although metric measurement would continue to be mandatory in Canada, retailers could also use the imperial system.

The equality rights section of Canada's Charter of Rights and Freedoms came into effect on April 17, three years after the Charter had been formally proclaimed. The delay had been intended to give Parliament and the provincial legislatures time to bring their laws into conformity with the Charter. Seven of the ten provinces had taken the necessary steps or announced their intention of doing so. Quebec, which did not recognize the 1982 Charter, had its own comprehensive charter of rights. It was, however, an ordinary statute that could be repealed at any time, whereas the federal Charter was entrenched in the constitution.

Two important agreements were reached with the provinces during 1985. On February 11 Prime Minister Mulroney signed a 68-clause memorandum of understanding with Premier Brian Peckford of Newfoundland governing the management of oil and gas resources lying off the island-province's coast. Newfoundland was given the authority to tax these resources as if they were on land. The agreement was more generous to the province than one signed by the Liberal government in 1982 with Nova Scotia. That accord left ultimate power to manage offshore resources with the federal majority on the control board and with the federal energy minister. The Newfoundland document provided for the province and Ottawa each to appoint three members to the management board, which would have an independent chairman. Mulroney described

the Atlantic Accord as the most important agreement Newfoundland had entered into with Ottawa since it joined the Canadian confederation in 1949. Peckford went on to call an election for April 2, which he won, but with a reduced majority. His Conservative Party captured 36 of the 52 seats in the legislature.

An agreement relating to oil prices was signed with the western producing provinces of Alberta, Saskatchewan, and British Columbia on March 28. It provided for Canadian oil prices to be decided by the market rather than by government decree. Under the plan, Canadian oil prices were to be permitted to compete at world levels by June 1. The federal government agreed to eliminate five of its taxes and special charges on petroleum as soon as possible and to phase out its royalties on oil and

Hostages are released from the Turkish embassy in Ottawa, where they were held by Armenian nationals for four hours on March 12.
AP/WIDE WORLD

natural gas. The oil industry stood to gain a possible $1.3 billion in additional revenue during the first year of the pact. The agreement, called the Western Accord, effectively demolished most of the Liberal government's 1980 National Energy Program.

The Economy

The Canadian economy showed encouraging growth during 1985, with employment and incomes higher than the year before. Consumer demand, especially for automobiles, was the strongest component in the increase, although spending on plant and equipment (capital goods) was also strong. Exports to all major markets—the U.S., Europe, and Japan—were down. This condition contrasted with Canada's flourishing export performance in recent years. The gross national product, seasonally adjusted, was expected to reach $449 billion, representing an annual growth rate of about 4% in real terms in the first six months of the year. During the third quarter the rate increased to 6%. The Canadian dollar continued to feel the impact of high interest rates in the U.S. as it hovered between 71 and 73 U.S. cents during the year. Unemployment showed the usual regional and seasonal variations; in October it was running at 10.3%, compared with 11.2% in January. The jobless rate was still significantly higher in the 15–24-year age group, in Quebec, and in the outlying provinces of Canada. Inflation continued to be under control, with an annual rate of 4.2% recorded for October. Interest rates were also lower than they had been in previous years, the trend-setting Bank of Canada rate standing at 8.7% in mid-October.

Several major corporate takeovers occurred in Canada in 1985. On May 9 it was announced that British Telecom of London had acquired a controlling interest in Mitel Corp., a leading Ottawa-based telecommunications firm. On August 2 a Toronto financial group, Olympia & York Developments Ltd., purchased control of Gulf Canada, an oil company owned by Chevron Corp. of San Francisco, for $2.8 billion. Ten days later it was announced that Petro-Canada would buy Gulf Canada's petroleum refining and marketing assets west of Quebec. This would add 1,800 retail outlets to the 2,485 stations already owned by the state company, making Petro-Canada the largest gasoline retailer in the country.

An understanding was reached with Japan on July 3 by which Japanese car imports into Canada would be limited to 18% of the anticipated Canadian car market for 1985. The undertaking differed from those reached in previous years in that it did not specify the number of vehicles to be admitted into Canada. The new formula would allow Japanese manufacturers to increase the number of vehicles shipped to Canada in a year of strong consumer demand. A large Korean auto manufacturer, Hyundai, announced it would build an assembly plant at an undisclosed location in Canada, its first overseas facility. Korean cars had enjoyed booming sales in Canada since they were first introduced in 1984.

The Canadian banking system, long a symbol of stability, suffered a pair of shocks in September when two smaller banks failed. The Canadian Commercial Bank and the Northland Bank, both based in Alberta, dealt largely with business and institutional clients. The fall in value of real estate in western Canada and the recession in the oil industry in the early 1980s had left them holding nonperforming or troubled loans. The federal government promised to pay $900 million to the uninsured depositors in the two banks. At the same time, it set up a judicial inquiry to look into the factors that contributed to their collapse, the first in Canada since 1923.

A long-standing link between Canada and the U.S. was dissolved on March 30 when the Canadian branch of the United Automobile Workers (UAW) formally split from its international parent union. The Canadian union had unsuccessfully sought full autonomy for Canadian workers in 1984. The new Canadian union received $36 million as its share of UAW assets, thus providing a strike fund of $30 million, the largest of any union in Canada.

In his first budget, produced on May 23, Finance Minister Michael Wilson cut net spending by $1.8 billion and increased revenues by $200 million in the 1985–86 fiscal year. These measures were expected to reduce the deficit to $33.8 billion. Income and consumer taxes were raised, most notably through a 10% surtax on basic federal income tax on salaries of over $30,000, to last for 18 months from July 1. Large corporations were also to pay an income surtax of 5%, while the gasoline tax, excise taxes, and sales taxes were all increased or extended to formerly exempt items. A lifetime capital gains tax exemption of $500,000 was provided in an effort to instill investment incentives and create jobs. The most controversial section of the budget turned out to be a plan to partially deindex old-age pensions and family allowances paid by the state. Wilson proposed, beginning in 1986, to reduce indexing on these payments to the amount of the annual increase in the consumer price index that exceeded 3%. The proposal roused a storm of protest from citizens over 65, and on June 27 the finance minister announced that he would continue to index old-age pensions fully, offsetting the loss of savings through increases in corporate and gasoline taxes.

Foreign Affairs

The issue of trade with the U.S. gained public attention in Canada as protectionist proposals in the U.S. Congress were seen as threatening to jeopardize Canada's entry into the valuable U.S. market. (About 75% of Canada's trade is with the U.S.) When Pres. Ronald Reagan met Prime Minister Mulroney at the "shamrock summit" in Quebec City on March 17–18, the reduction of trade barriers was a major item of discussion. The two leaders agreed to work toward freer trade, the president reportedly telling Mulroney in a private session that he would "go to bat" for Canada in opposing protectionist measures.

In Canada a royal commission on the country's economic prospects appointed by former prime minister Pierre Trudeau recommended strongly in favor of a free trade agreement with the U.S. that would eliminate all tariffs over ten years. A joint committee of the Senate and the House of Commons, representing all three political parties, also reported in favor of "broad discussions with the United States to determine their receptivity to liberalizing bilateral trade." On September 26 Mulroney told the House of Commons that he had called President Reagan to inform him that he wished to begin negotiations on a broad package of tariff reductions. The 1965 pact allowing free trade in auto vehicles and parts was not to enter into the negotiations.

The Canadian Coast Guard cutter Sir John A. MacDonald (top) follows the U.S. Coast Guard icebreaker Polar Sea in Lancaster Sound in August. Polar Sea's journey through the Northwest Passage was denounced by many Canadians as an affront to Canadian sovereignty.

CANAPRESS

An auto buyer looks at Hyundai's Stellar. Hyundai, a large Korean auto manufacturer, and three Japanese firms announced plans to invest more than $800 million in assembly plants across Canada.

SIDNEY TABAK

Arrangements for strengthening North America's air defense were a more controversial topic in Canada. Although Canada permitted tests of free-flying cruise missiles over 1,550 mi (2,500 km) of its northern territory in late February, the government made it clear that U.S. nuclear arms could not be based in Canada without its consent. Air defense figured in the "shamrock summit" when the two leaders signed an agreement for a U.S. $1.5 billion upgrade to the northern radar defense system. It was made clear that there was no connection between the land-based radar system in the north, now 30 years old, and weapons in space that were aimed at antiballistic missiles. The matter was likely to be raised in parliamentary hearings dealing with renewal of the North American Aerospace Defense Command (formerly NORAD), due to expire in March 1986.

The March meeting between the two leaders referred the controversial acid rain issue to two high-profile former public officials, who were to study and report on the question before the next Mulroney-Reagan meeting in 1986: William Davis, Ontario's premier until February, and Drew Lewis, Reagan's transport secretary during his first term. The status of the historic Northwest Passage through Canada's Arctic islands was back in the news. Fifteen years earlier, Canada had asserted pollution-control regulations over the Arctic waters. The U.S. challenged this jurisdiction, claiming the waters were part of the international sea, and the issue of sovereignty remained uncertain. During early August the U.S. Coast Guard icebreaker *Polar Sea* made a successful transit of the occasionally ice-blocked passage. At first the Mulroney government reacted mildly to the voyage, but Inuit groups living along the route protested, and many Canadians felt that the government had not presented its objections forcefully enough to Washington.

On September 10, claiming that Soviet submarines had been operating in Arctic waters and citing the *Polar Sea* voyage, the Canadian government spelled out new measures to enforce its control in the Arctic. Straight baselines, authorized

in international law, would be drawn around the islands, giving Canada ownership of the internal waters they enclosed. Military surveillance flights over the Arctic would be increased, and the government would build a gigantic Class 8 icebreaker capable of crushing through ice 8 ft (2½ m) thick. More naval operations would also take place in the eastern Arctic in 1986. There would be an effort to cooperate more closely with the U.S. in the face of the common security concerns, but this cooperation would have to be based on a recognition of Canada's sovereignty in the area.

Measures to persuade South Africa to move away from its repressive racial policies were under intense consideration by the government during the year. On July 6 External Affairs Minister Joe Clark announced sanctions to discourage trade. The export of sensitive electronic equipment to South African government agencies would be banned, a double taxation agreement would be abrogated, Canadian banks would be encouraged not to sell South African gold coins, and Canada would terminate all contracts for the processing of uranium from South West Africa/Namibia when current agreements ended in 1988. Additional funds were to be provided to help in the training of black South African students in Canada and in their home country. On September 13 Clark announced that he was meeting bankers and businessmen to discuss further measures to influence the South African government. Canadian banks were also to be asked to ban new loans to the South African government or its agencies. In a strongly worded address September 25, Clark told the UN General Assembly that "measures to make all South Africans equal within their state must be pursued to the end." Prime Minister Mulroney carried the same message to the Commonwealth heads of government conference at Nassau in The Bahamas in the week of October 14. Mulroney helped to mediate between Britain and most other Commonwealth members in an effort to work out a single Commonwealth position on the vexed question of economic sanctions against South Africa.

Special Report: A Mood for Change

by Peter Ward

The overwhelming victory of the federal Progressive Conservative Party in the Canadian election of Sept. 4, 1984, seemed to open the floodgates, because the most constant thing about Canadian politics in 1985 was change. In some areas regional strongmen—allies or foes of former prime minister Pierre Trudeau—chose to leave public life, perhaps because the political wars had lost some of their zest. In other areas provincial governments were threatened by the same mood of discontent that had led voters to decimate the federal Liberals in 1984. Major upheavals took place or were threatened in Quebec, Ontario, New Brunswick, Manitoba, Saskatchewan, Alberta, British Columbia, and the Yukon Territory.

A Shift from Separatism

Perhaps the most significant change came in Quebec. Nine years earlier, in 1976, Quebecers had elected a provincial government dedicated to independence, headed by René Lévesque and his Parti Québécois (PQ). But in the 1984 federal election they did an about-face, giving a resounding victory to the federal Progressive Conservative Party and, by implication, support to continued adherence to the Canadian confederation. The fact that Prime Minister Brian Mulroney himself was from Quebec was a major factor in helping to solidify public opinion behind federalism. By early 1985 former premier Robert Bourassa and his rejuvenated Liberal Party—traditionally the party of federalism in Quebec—were far ahead in the public opinion polls.

With the next provincial election due no later than the spring of 1986, Lévesque realized his party could not win on an independence platform and sought a more moderate party stance, in line with the polls. The result was a high-level revolt within his government. Several senior Cabinet ministers, men who had been in the vanguard of the independence movement, resigned. Defections and resignations reduced the PQ majority on the Quebec National Assembly to the point where it was dangerously close to defeat. Discouraged by political developments and suffering from ill health, Lévesque resigned on June 20.

In the subsequent contest for leadership of the PQ, the choice of the moderates, Justice Minister Pierre-Marc Johnson, won handily. Such was his personal popularity that the PQ immediately passed the Liberals in the polls. However, hard-line party members were infuriated by the new leader's counsels of caution and his pledge to sign a constitutional agreement with Ottawa, provided Quebec was given jurisdiction over language and obtained certain other concessions recognizing its special status within Canada. Supporters of independence left the PQ to form the Parti Indépendantiste, which expected to field candidates in at least 15 constituencies.

Fall of a Machine

The most surprising change of the year came in Canada's largest province, Ontario, ruled by a succession of Conservative governments since 1943. In late 1984 William Davis, premier since 1971, resigned and called a leadership convention for early 1985. Cabinet veteran Frank Miller emerged victorious, but his tenure as premier was brief. From his accession to office on February 8 to the election on May 2, his fortunes went steadily downhill. Some blamed him for shunning the advice of the old provincial Conservative machine, which had been instrumental in Mulroney's victory. Others gave credit to the energetic and effective campaigning of the Ontario Liberal leader, David Peterson. In any case, election day resulted in a near stalemate, with the Conservatives capturing 52 of the legislature's 125 seats, the Liberals 48, and the New Democratic Party (NDP) 25.

After several weeks of negotiation, the NDP decided to support the Liberals, assuring the end of the Conservative monopoly of power in Ontario. The legislature met, and on June 18 Liberals, supported by the New Democrats, defeated the Miller government on a nonconfidence vote. Miller resigned as required, and after 42 years of Conservative rule, Liberal David Peterson became premier of Ontario. By the end of the summer Peterson was leading in the polls with 47% support, compared with 29% for the Conservatives and 23% for the NDP. Conservatives ended the year with a convention to choose a new leader. On the second ballot, Larry Grossman of Toronto, a former provincial treasurer, won by the narrow margin of 848 votes to 829 for Dennis Timbrell, formerly municipal affairs minister in the provincial government.

From Maritimes to Prairies

New Brunswick, ruled by Conservative Premier Richard Hatfield since 1970, also appeared to be heading for a change of governing parties, although a provincial election was not legally required until October 1987. In New Brunswick it was the alleged adventures of the premier that brought Conservative fortunes to a 15-year low. In September 1984 Hatfield, who had acquired a nationwide reputation for unconventional behavior, was accompanying Queen Elizabeth II on a tour of the province. Before their plane took off, police dogs, sniffing the baggage for explosives, discovered a political explosive in the form of marijuana in an outer pocket of Hatfield's suitcase. Hatfield was charged with possession.

He was acquitted in a sensational trial in January 1985, but within days of the verdict, newspaper stories appeared claiming Hatfield had picked up two young students and taken them to his home for a marijuana and cocaine party in 1981. Hatfield denied the allegations and claimed the Royal Canadian Mounted Police was out to get him. Nonetheless, the damage to his image was severe, and in August he had to face down demands from some fellow Conservatives that he resign. He was determined to lead his party in at least one more provincial election, and his political skills were such that observers hesitated to bet on the outcome.

In Manitoba, which since November 1981 had had Canada's only left-wing NDP government, Premier Howard Pawley was considering an election call, although polls showed his popularity about even with that of Conservative leader Gary Filmon. One of the biggest issues in Manitoba was bilingualism. The courts had ruled that a late 19th-century government acted illegally when it made Manitoba English-speaking and ordered all provincial legislation translated so it would be available in both English and French. Pawley favored seeking accommodation on the language issue and increasing the availability of French services in the province. This stand gave him political trouble in some rural areas, but the coming election appeared to be a toss-up.

Conservatives were the party with problems in Saskatchewan. Premier Grant Devine, who overwhelmed the NDP in an April 1982 election, had until April 1987 to call another one, but tradition favored a new election after four years. A summer sampling of public opinion in Regina, the provincial capital, showed the NDP ahead of the Conservatives—25% of the voters, compared with 16%—but 53% were undecided. The province led the country in economic growth, but a severe drought in traditionally Conservative southern Saskatchewan spelled economic disaster for farmers. Any massive provincial aid program for the farmers could signal an early election. At best, Devine was expected to lose some of the 56 Conservative seats in the 64-seat legislature.

No such troubles threatened the Conservative Party in Alberta, but there was a major change as Peter Lougheed, premier since September 1971, decided to retire. His departure marked the end of an era that had seen Alberta emerge as a major energy supplier. His successor, businessman Donald Getty, inherited a 65–4 majority in the provincial legislature. Once energy minister under Lougheed and a former teammate of the ex-premier on the Edmonton Eskimos professional football team, Getty was slightly to the right of Lougheed politically and could be expected to champion provincial rights in dealings with Ottawa. The new premier was expected to call an election sometime in 1986, though one was not due until November 1987.

Far West, Far North

British Columbia's Social Credit dynasty might be coming to a close. Premier William Bennett did not have to call an election until May 1988, but only two years after being returned to power by a healthy majority, his Social Credit Party (Socreds), out of power for only three years since 1952, was in trouble. A summer public opinion survey of the province's heavily populated lower mainland showed 25.7% of voters favoring the NDP to only 22.6% for the Socreds (9.6% supported the Liberals, 3% the Conservatives, and the rest were undecided).

Bennett's problems were economic. The world recession had devastated British Columbia's two chief industries, lumber and mining, and unemployment throughout 1985 hovered around 15%, compared with 10.5% for Canada as a whole. The NDP, gaining ground under its new leader, Robert Skelly, blamed Bennett for making things worse with his efforts to balance the provincial budget by raising taxes and cutting government services. In two years 12,686 civil servants and teachers had been dropped from the public payroll. Nor had Bennett achieved much success in recruiting federal aid to attract major industries to the province. His best hope, observers felt, might be to make capital from the public enthusiasm expected to accompany the Expo 86 world's fair in Vancouver.

Discontent with the political establishment extended far into the Canadian north in 1985. In a May election in the Yukon Territory the Conservatives, led by lawyer Willard Phelps, were defeated by the NDP under actor-playwright Tony Penikett. The Conservatives had been in power in the Yukon since 1978, the year party politics arrived in the territory, and they had been expected to win again. Phelps and his party captured only 6 of the 16 seats in the Legislative Council, to 8 seats for the NDP and 2 for the Liberals. The result was a setback for Erik Nielsen, the federal deputy prime minister and defense minister, who had been Conservative MP for the Yukon since 1957.

Meanwhile, the Mulroney government was vulnerable to the prevailing mood. A year after the 1984 election, a public opinion poll showed that 60% of those surveyed thought Mulroney had not kept his election promises. At the same time, 46% still said they would vote for him, compared with 29% for the Liberals and 21% for the NDP.

CERAMICS INDUSTRY

The strength of the U.S. economy in 1984 both helped and hurt U.S. ceramic companies. Low inflation and interest rates helped to keep costs low, but the value of the dollar in overseas markets hurt U.S. exports and favored foreign imports.

U.S. ceramic sales for 1984 were about $28 billion, up from $26 billion in 1983. Glass sales accounted for 63% of the market, porcelain enamel 15%, and advanced ceramics 14%. Whiteware sales, including ceramic tile, dinnerware, and artware, represented 8% of the total.

In the glass industry, containers accounted for 26% of all sales. However, volume was dropping steadily, primarily because of competition from plastics and legislation requiring the return of empty containers. Sales of flat glass, particularly for windows and doors, were 27% of all glass sales. They benefited from strong housing and automobile markets but were hurt by the energy-saving emphasis on smaller autos and fewer windows in buildings. The remaining glass sales were in fiberglass (18%), lighting (13%), consumer glassware (6%), cathode-ray tubes for television sets and computers (6%), and several smaller areas.

The porcelain enamel industry recorded sales of $4 billion in 1984. There were strong indications, however, that appliance enamels, 91% of all porcelain enamel sales, might suffer as appliance manufacturers turned to cheaper, more energy-efficient coating processes.

Advanced ceramic sales in the U.S., representing a wide variety of high-technology applications, totaled $3.8 billion in 1984 and appeared poised for great future growth. Low-voltage insulators represented 24% of U.S. sales in this category. Capacitors and electronic ceramic packages represented another 24%. Capacitor sales rose 31% over 1983 levels, with multilayer ceramic chip capacitors making particularly strong advances. The engineering ceramic segment, including heat-, wear-, and corrosion-resistant components; cutting tools; and bioceramics accounted for 18% of all U.S. advanced ceramic sales. Ferrites (12%), optical fibers (8%), high-voltage insulators (5%), and other electrical and electronic ceramics (9%) accounted for the remainder. Whitewares, including bathroom fixtures, floor and wall tile, artware, and dinnerware, maintained their sales level in the U.S. at $2.3 billion.

Forecasts for future worldwide ceramic sales were bright, especially for advanced ceramics. In this area growth estimates by the Japanese Ministry of International Trade & Industry and by A. R. C. Westwood of Martin Marietta Corp. suggested worldwide sales of $25 billion–$30 billion by the year 2000. Charles River Associates, in a report prepared for the National Bureau of Standards, predicted growth rates of 12–14% per year throughout the 1990s for some electronic ceramics to as much as 40% per year in the heat engine and integrated optics areas.

Japanese ceramic producers continued their strategy of early commercialization to assure a major share in future markets. They appeared willing to forgo early profits in exchange for the long-term advantages of high-volume production. During the year Toshiba introduced a spectrum analyzer that for the first time used integrated optic circuits based on advanced ceramics. Toshiba's unit appeared to be based on a U.S. (Westinghouse Corp.) design, but U.S. companies had been unwilling to sell the product without further development.

Japanese firms were also pursuing low-technology applications for advanced ceramics. For example, they began marketing, in the form of ceramic scissors, knives, and ballpoint pen tips, advanced ceramics that might be used in a few years in automotive engine parts.

The importance of these future advanced ceramic markets stirred action in Europe. In the U.K. two "clubs" consisting of companies that had agreed to pursue specific advanced ceramic applications cooperatively were formed. One was pursuing advanced ceramics for turbines and the other for reciprocating engines. In Sweden a group of companies was cooperatively emphasizing the application of hot isostatic pressing technology developed by the Swedish company ASEA.

CHEMISTRY

Organic Chemistry

Spurred by the successful introduction of aspartame as a commercial sweetener in the early 1980s, interest in the chemistry of sweet-tasting substances remained high during 1985. Scientists at the Research Triangle Institute in North Carolina, supported by the U.S. National Institute of Dental Research, synthesized D,L-amino malonyl-D-alanine isopropyl ester. This substance is nearly 60 times as sweet as sugar, although only half as sweet as aspartame. Nevertheless, at the weakly acidic conditions found in many soft drinks (pH 3.5), the new compound showed no degradation over a 36-day period. Under the same conditions 50% of a sample of aspartame degraded.

A natural compound about 1,000 times sweeter than sugar was discovered through the search of old texts and was then made synthetically. In a late 16th-century work on the natural history of New Spain by the physician Francisco Hernández, Cesar M. Compadre and colleagues at the University of Illinois, Chicago, found an account of a sweet-tasting herb used by the Aztecs. From the description they were able to identify it as *Lippia dulcis,* from which they extracted the new sweet compound, which they called hernandulcin.

New methods of organic synthesis appeared. In recent years many of these had aimed at improving the stereochemistry of organic syntheses; *i.e.,* the ability to control the spatial arrangement of the atoms in the molecular products. Chemists at

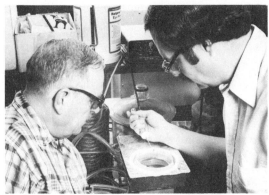

John Zeigler (right) injects a new compound into a spin caster as codeveloper Larry Harrah looks on. The new compound, a polysilane photoresist, could lead to improved microcircuits.

the Massachusetts Institute of Technology developed chiral boranes (boranes having left- and right-handed mirror-image forms, or stereoisomers) that convert olefins into alcohols with high specificity for left- or right-handed products. Saturo Masamune and his colleagues used *trans*-2,5-dimethylborolanes to convert both *cis*- and *trans*-1,2-dialkylethenes and 1,1,2-trialkylethenes into chiral alcohols. As an example of the power of this new reagent, Masamune synthesized the macrolide antibiotic 6-deoxyerythronolide B in 23 stages, with an overall yield of 5.7%, of which 85% was the desired stereoisomer. An earlier synthesis involved 49 steps and gave an overall yield of 0.3%, of which only 46% was the desired stereoisomer.

Chemists continued to investigate marine life as a potential source of new drugs. During the year compounds were isolated from the coral *Telesto riisei*. One of them, punaglandin 3, has potent antileukemic activity. Punaglandin 3 slightly resembles the prostaglandins, which are found widely in the body and exert many different effects upon it.

In the 1980s chemotherapy was still in its infancy in the treatment of viral diseases. Although there had been some successes, there was intense pressure for further advances, particularly in view of the worldwide attention being focused on acquired immune deficiency syndrome (AIDS), known to be caused by a retrovirus. In September the pharmaceutical company Burroughs Wellcome announced that it was starting clinical trials with 3-azido-3-deoxythymidine, a compound discovered at its Research Triangle Park, N.C., laboratories. This substance is converted into a triphosphate in the body, and the phosphorylated compound interferes with one of the enzymes needed by the AIDS virus for replication.

Physical Chemistry

The effects of near-zero gravity on chemical experiments were further explored. In August an or-biting U.S. space shuttle served as the laboratory for experiments by the 3M Co. on the physical vapor transport of organic solids. Shuttle astronauts operated equipment designed to grow crystals, in the form of thin films, from the vapors of materials that either do not dissolve or cannot exist in a molten state and that are impossible to combine by some alternate method in the gravity field of Earth. If manufactured as ordered thin films deposited on suitable substrates, they could have applications in optics and electronics. General Motors also planned space experiments to see whether nylon 6, one of nylon's most widely used forms, could be formed from caprolactam in the form of larger, more nearly perfect crystals than those obtainable on Earth. The physical and mechanical properties of such space crystals could have special advantages.

Catalysis interested many chemists because it helped them understand how molecules react and because it had enormous commercial potential. Most modern industrial chemical processes would be impracticable without catalysts. Richard Smalley and co-workers at Rice University, Houston, Texas, studied the catalytic behavior of small clusters of metal atoms produced by laser vaporization. They found that the size of the cluster affects its reactivity, although the reason was not yet known. With cobalt, for example, clusters of 3 to 5 atoms and 10 or more (but not 16) all react strongly with hydrogen. Single atoms of cobalt and clusters of two or six to nine atoms do not.

Robert E. Sievers of the University of Colorado explored the use of gold as a catalyst in reactions between nitrogen dioxide and organic compounds. One such reaction is the oxidation of alcohols to aldehydes. Many oxidizing agents, which do their work by removing electrons from a reactant, do not stop at this intermediate step but oxidize the alcohols to acids. Using gold—precipitated onto glass beads as gold chloride and then reduced with hydrogen to the free metal—and nitrogen dioxide, Sievers obtained a rapid and complete reaction without any significant by-products.

It would be useful for many purposes to be able to predict the solubility of one substance in another from basic principles. Mortimer J. Kamlet and Ruth M. Doherty of the Naval Surface Weapons Center, White Oak, Md., together with Michael Abraham of the University of Surrey, England, and Robert W. Taft of the University of California at Irvine, devised a universal equation for this purpose. The equation involves three different terms: a cavity term representing the energy required to make a hole in the solvent into which a molecule of solute can fit, a dipole interaction term, and a hydrogen-bonding term. This attempt to produce such an equation differed from predecessors in its use of the hydrogen-bonding term to replace terms based on acidity (proton transfer). Its usefulness in specific fields awaited the collection of sufficient data to establish meaningful coefficients.

Inorganic Chemistry

Life on Earth owes its existence to the tremendous combining ability of carbon atoms, which can link together into large molecules by means of both single (two-electron) bonds and stable multiple bonds. At one time it was thought that life elsewhere in the universe might be based on silicon, the abundant element that occurs directly below carbon in the periodic table of the elements. Silicon atoms, however, ordinarily are unable to form multiple bonds with one another. In recent years compounds had been made with silicon-silicon double bonds, but the molecules had to include bulky organic substituents to help hold the multiple bonds together. In 1985 scientists at the University of Frankfurt, West Germany, reported the first silicon-nitrogen triple bond. Heating of a triazidosilane compound gave an aromatic compound that appeared, from photoelectron spectroscopy, to contain a nitrogen atom attached by a single bond to one of the carbons in a benzene ring and by a triple bond to a silicon atom. The compound was isolated at a temperature near absolute zero; on warming it formed an insoluble polymer.

By contrast, the first stable compound containing a germanium-phosphorus double bond was isolated at Paul Sabatier University, Toulouse, France. Germanium falls directly below silicon in the periodic table and is therefore in the same family as carbon. This compound, isolated as orange crystals, had its double bond protected by bulky organic groups attached to both the germanium and the phosphorus atoms.

Another interesting inorganic compound reported during the year was the phosphorus analogue of benzene. Benzene is one of the commonest organic compounds, consisting of a six-membered ring of carbon atoms, to each of which is attached a hydrogen atom. The peculiar characteristic of benzene is the sharing of bonding electrons around the ring to form hybrid bonds that are intermediate between double and single bonds, an arrangement that confers particular stability on the compound. Chemists at the University of Kaiserslautern, West Germany, prepared a six-membered phosphorus ring by stabilizing it with two atoms of molybdenum, each of which was linked to a pentamethylcyclopentadienyl ion.

Analytical Chemistry

Sievers, whose work with gold catalysts is related above, was also exploring their potential for a new detection system in gas chromatography (GC), a technique used widely to separate complex mixtures. The key to successful GC is a suitable detector. The flame ionization detector had proved effective for many years, but it could not detect some types of compounds. Sievers's gold catalysts, used in a device called a redox chemiluminescence detector, induced such compounds to react with nitric oxide as they came out of the chromatographic column. Detection was based on a light-emitting reaction between the residual nitric oxide and ozone. Although the new procedure involved more steps than a conventional detector, it was highly specific. For example, when a flame ionization detector was used to find the antioxidant butylated hydroxytoluene (BHT) in aviation fuel, to which it is added at levels of about ten parts per million, the hydrocarbons in the fuel swamped any signal from the BHT. Sievers's system did not respond to hydrocarbons and showed the BHT clearly.

The uses of nuclear magnetic resonance (NMR) spectroscopy, which derives information from the way hydrogen, phosphorus, and certain other atoms respond to radio waves in the presence of a strong magnetic field, further expanded during 1985. Nino Yannoni and colleagues at IBM's research laboratory in San Jose, Calif., picked up an idea first discussed in the late 1940s as the basis for a new variation of NMR that could work out bond lengths between atoms in solids, such as powders, that have no long-range order. Nutation NMR used what was effectively a continuous field of radio waves rotating perpendicular to the applied magnetic field in an NMR machine. This arrangement had the effect of canceling out signals from various interactions among the atoms while emphasizing others, and it allowed bond lengths to be determined within 1%. The new technique did not apply to liquid or gaseous states. Nevertheless, it should prove useful as a research tool. For example, it was possible to show that the polymerization of acetylene catalyzed by molybdenum occurs via a mechanism different from that which operates with titanium catalysts.

CHESS

On Nov. 9, 1985, after 14 months and 72 games, Garri Kasparov of the U.S.S.R. became the chess champion of the world by defeating the titleholder, Anatoli Karpov, 13–11. At 22 Kasparov was the youngest world champion in the history of chess.

The long contest between the two Soviet grand masters began in September 1984. The first man to win six games was to be declared the champion. Karpov began strongly, winning four of the first nine games (the other five were drawn) in his effort to retain the title that he had held since 1975. But Kasparov became more cautious, and many of the subsequent contests ended in draws. Karpov eventually pulled ahead 5–0, but Kasparov then won one game and, in succession, two more, the 47th and 48th. At that time, in February 1985, the president of the International Chess Federation, Florencio Campomanes of the Philippines, halted the match on the grounds that both players were too exhausted to continue.

Both players at once protested against the decision, which was clearly against the rules as laid down by the chess federation congress. The president later said that he was acting in response to

Anatoli Karpov (left) looks away as challenger Garri Kasparov studies a move in their championship match. Kasparov went on to win the title.

a request from the Soviet Chess Federation, which believed that Karpov's health might suffer if the match were allowed to continue. But the correct procedure under the rules would have been for the Soviet Federation to submit its request to the match arbiter, who would then have advised Karpov to consult the match physician. If the physician thought that the world champion's health was endangered, he would then have advised him to resign the match. Eventually, nonetheless, both competitors said that they were prepared to abide by the president's decision.

In September 1985 the contest resumed in Moscow, with new scoring rules. The scores of the first round were canceled, and the two men were to play a maximum of 24 games, with one point awarded for a win and $\frac{1}{2}$ point given to each player for a draw. The first player to gain $12\frac{1}{2}$ points would win the match. Kasparov won the first two games and proceeded to play in brilliant style. The 16th game, a win for Kasparov, was a particularly interesting one. In the 19th game Karpov made a desperate attempt at a counterattack, but Kasparov refuted him and again won the game.

The 24th, and last, game of the match took place on November 9. Ahead 12–11, Kasparov needed only a draw to gain the championship. Karpov began play aggressively with a king-side assault, and Kasparov responded with a firm defense. But Karpov maintained his pressure, and Kasparov changed his tactics, adopting a more risky offensive style. The strategy was successful, and Karpov resigned the game and his title after 43 moves.

In other competition during the year, Evgeni Sveshnikov of the Soviet Union won the Hastings international tournament in the U.K. Sharing second place were Stefan Djuric of Yugoslavia, Jim Plaskett of the U.K., and Joel Benjamin and John Fedorowicz of the U.S.

At the Commonwealth championships in London, Kevin Spraggett of Canada and Praveen Thipsay of India tied for first place. Spraggett had tied for first in the event in 1984. At the Reggio Emilia

international tournament in Italy, Lajos Portisch of Hungary was the winner. Robert Hübner of West Germany and Ljubomir Ljubojevic of Yugoslavia tied for first in the Linares international tournament in Spain.

The Copenhagen international tournament in Denmark was won by Josef Pinter of Hungary, while second place was shared by two Danes, Curt Hansen and Bent Larsen, and an Icelander, Helgi Olafsson. Tied for first in the Windy City international tournament at Chicago were James Rizzitano and Vincent McCambridge, both of the U.S. Cris Ramayrat of the Philippines won the San Francisco international tournament; Jay Whitehead of the U.S. placed second. At the Baden-Baden international tournament in West Germany, Jan Smejkal of Czechoslovakia was the winner, and Efim Geller of the Soviet Union was runner-up. In one of the finest performances by a woman in the history of chess, Maya Chiburdanidze of the Soviet Union defeated an all-male opposition that included eight grand masters to win the Banja Luka international tournament in Yugoslavia.

The world junior championships, held in the United Arab Emirates, was won by Maxim Dlugy of the U.S. The world under-14 championships, which took place in Argentina, was also won by a U.S. player, Ilya Gurevich. Lev Alburt, a former Soviet grand master who moved to New York City, won his second consecutive U.S. championship.

Three interzonal tournaments were held in 1985. The top four finishers in each tournament qualified for the Candidates Tournament, the next round of competition for the world championship. In the first interzonal the four qualifiers were Artur Yusupov, Aleksandr Beljavski of the Soviet Union, and Aleksandr Chernin of the Soviet Union and Portisch. The top four finishers in the second interzonal were Jan Timman of The Netherlands, Jesús Noguieras of Cuba, Mikhail Tal of the Soviet Union, and Spraggett. Qualifying from the third interzonal tournament were Rafael Vaganian and Andrei Sokolov of the Soviet Union, Yasser Seirawan of the U.S., and Nigel Short of the U.K.

CHILE

The sacking of Interior Minister Sergio Onofre Jarpa Reyes and of Finance Minister Luis Escobar Cerda in February 1985 marked the end of an attempt by the Chilean regime of Pres. Augusto Pinochet Ugarte to negotiate with the political parties. Jarpa, who was replaced by Ricardo García Rodríguez, had been responsible for an initiative that was aimed at attracting and consolidating middle-class and right-wing support by promising an earlier return to democracy than was possible under the ruling constitution. However, after various interviews given by President Pinochet, the political parties involved in the dialogue with the government decided that the president had withdrawn his support from the initiative.

Membership in the Communist Party was once again declared illegal because of the party's endorsement of violent means to overthrow the regime. Repression of party members was on the increase. In March two Communist leaders and a left-wing dissident were found murdered after they had been kidnapped. Five months later, as a result of information made available by the state intelligence agency (the Central Nacional de Informaciones; CNI), 14 members of the police force were charged with the murders, while five police officials were accused of arranging the abduction of five teachers' union personnel in March. The accused belonged to the police force's intelligence division, the Dirección de Comunicaciones y Informaciones de Carabineros.

Attacks by unidentified persons on human-rights and trade-union organizers intensified just before the year's first organized day of protest, which took place on August 9. A three-day protest organized by the trade unions on September 4–6 was significant in that it drew support from middle-class shop owners, truck drivers, and taxi owners, previously strong supporters of the regime. Ten people were killed and 120 injured during September's demonstrations. As a result, the state of emergency, which had been partially modified in June, was reimposed for a further six months. Although President Pinochet had rejected the idea of dialogue with the opposition at the end of August, 11 political parties, claiming to represent 80% of the electorate, joined the church in sponsoring a petition calling for a rapid return to civilian rule. The document called for a return to democracy based on direct congressional and presidential elections in 1989.

The earthquake that hit Chile in the early evening on March 3 registered more than 8 on the Richter scale and caused at least 177 deaths and more than $1.8 billion worth of damage. The earthquake caused extensive damage to ports and infrastructure. Emergency relief was channeled by the government, while donations by friendly governments and loans from the World Bank were used to repair the damage.

On May 2 the Beagle Channel treaty between Chile and Argentina was formally ratified, ending six years of mediation by the Vatican. The agreement helped bring about a reduction of tension between the two countries. Chile's relations with the U.S. were more mixed. On the one hand, concern over the human-rights situation caused the U.S. to abstain in a vote to grant Chile an Inter-American Development Bank loan in February and to welcome the church-supported petition for a rapid return to democracy as "a positive step." On

Mothers and other relatives of desaparecidos, *"the disappeared ones" (persons believed to have been abducted by police and other government forces), organized a demonstration in Santiago on August 9.*
CARRION—SYGMA

the other hand, the U.S. supported a much larger World Bank cofinancing loan that allowed Chile to close its 1985 external financing program. In May it was disclosed that the U.S. had approached the government for permission to develop Easter Island as an emergency landing strip for the space shuttle program. Opponents of the government condemned the proposal on the grounds that it would ruin the island's environment, violate the island's sovereignty, and create a permanent U.S. military base that would make the area a possible target in the event of a war between the superpowers.

An external financing agreement and an arrangement with the International Monetary Fund (IMF) were reached in late June. The government agreed to guarantee private-sector debt if creditors so wished. Following the accord, the peso was devalued by 8.4% and import duties were reduced from an average of 30% to 20%. In spite of record low copper prices and a disappointing export performance in 1984, Chile was unusual among debtor nations in managing to meet the targets agreed on with the IMF. A $1 billion financing plan was signed with creditor banks in November.

CHINA

During 1985 China continued its pursuit of far-reaching reforms of the country's political and economic institutions and of expanded commercial and technical ties with the industrialized world. Under the guidance of elder statesman Deng Xiaoping (Teng Hsiao-p'ing), the Chinese Communist Party (CCP) accelerated the promotion of younger, better educated leaders into positions of political responsibility, hoping thereby to assure long-term policy continuity. But complications arose in China's departures from rigid central economic control, including, in particular, unchecked expenditures by individual enterprises and financial abuses by trading companies. Notwithstanding these difficulties,

the leadership reiterated its support for the economic reforms and the open-door economic policy. Relations with the United States encountered some difficulties but generally experienced stability and forward movement. Relations with the Soviet Union, although subject to larger differences and uncertainties, also made headway.

Domestic Affairs

Deng Xiaoping's principal energies in 1985 were devoted to further entrenching reformist policies by placing his supporters in key leadership positions. Deng engineered a major political victory at a special party conference held in September, when 64 members of the CCP Central Committee (including a number of senior officials considered unsympathetic to the political and economic reforms) relinquished their posts. Key backers of Deng's policies were also among those stepping down, reflecting the importance now attached to age and technical competence in leadership assignments.

However, Deng's decision not to relinquish his leadership position reversed his earlier intention to retire from political life by 1985 and indicated that his role remained vital to further development of the reforms. Despite evident good health at age 81, Deng increasingly sought to restrict his formal political activities. Principal responsibility for managing the reform program was delegated to Deng's chief lieutenants, 70-year-old party General Secretary Hu Yaobang (Hu Yao-pang) and 66-year-old Premier Zhao Ziyang (Chao Tzu-yang). But newly elected members of the Political Bureau, most notably 56-year-old Hu Qili (Hu Ch'i-li) and 57-year-old Li Peng (Li P'eng), were also entrusted with increased responsibility. The latter two officials (both trained as engineers) were expected to succeed to the top party and state posts, probably in 1987.

Leadership turnover at the top was paralleled by an effort to rejuvenate the CCP at other levels.

In front of the Gate of Heavenly Peace in Peking, two Chinese workers display headlines announcing September's shakeup in the Communist Party leadership.

AP/WIDE WORLD

Chinese shoppers crowd a Shanghai department store to buy television sets. An explosive demand for Japanese products had an adverse effect on China's balance of payments during the year.

JEAN-PIERRE LAFFONT—SYGMA

Since the institution of a mandatory retirement system in 1980, more than one million party officials had given up their posts. Despite a membership of more than 40 million, the CCP remained woefully short of personnel capable of overseeing China's ambitious plans for economic modernization. To fill this yawning gap between supply and demand, the CCP actively sought to recruit intellectuals and scientists into its membership. But many educated Chinese remained skeptical about these appeals and preferred to steer clear of political involvement.

Equally far-reaching steps were under way within the military establishment, long a source of resistance to Deng's reforms. In March plans were publicized to retire 47,000 veteran officers from active duty by the end of 1986, approximately 10% of the officer corps. Following a series of high-level leadership meetings in the late spring, it was announced that one million men (approximately one-quarter of present troop strength) would be pared from China's military establishment over the next two years. At the same time, the regional military commands were reduced from 11 to 7. The streamlining of the armed forces was intended to increase the combat effectiveness of all three services as well as to provide additional funds for the development of more modern weapons. Perhaps most important, Deng's allies within the senior military leadership hoped that these steps would provide increased opportunities for younger, better educated officers to advance to command positions.

But some of Deng's actions met with continued skepticism and resistance. Uneasiness about the potential implications of the economic reforms topped the list. Under Deng's aegis China's economic system had departed from many of the tenets of strict central planning and moved toward a combination of market and plan. The institution of an agricultural responsibility system in 1979, whereby farmers retain excess earnings after fulfilling their production quotas, significantly reduced state intervention in the rural sector, but implementation of equivalent industrial reforms announced in October 1984 was proving more difficult. Some top leaders, including veteran economic planner Chen Yun (Ch'en Yün), expressed serious reservations about excessive tampering with the urban industrial sector, the cornerstone of China's socialist economy. Chen warned that such reforms threatened the ability of central planners to oversee the directions of the economy as a whole. He also cautioned that excessive autonomy for individual enterprises could lead to unchecked expenditures and severe imbalances among sectors of the economy.

Other critics of Deng's policies focused on the potential for ideological deviations resulting from the open-door policy. China's encouragement of increased investment from abroad and the growing presence of foreign businessmen and tourists had created a more freewheeling atmosphere in China's cities, especially in the coastal provinces. Critics voiced concern about the undesirable side effects of an enhanced foreign presence, including the attraction of Chinese youth to foreign consumer goods and Western culture.

Although Deng and other reformers did not dispute the existence of such problems, they viewed them as difficulties to be overcome rather than as the portents of a major political or ideological crisis. Deng repeatedly made clear that serious political deviations from socialism would not be tolerated and that China's increased reliance on economic incentives and market mechanisms was not the precursor of the restoration of capitalism. He stated that the leadership would not permit the emergence of major polarities between rich and poor or a shift away from state ownership of the principal means of production. But at the same time, Deng saw the encouragement of individual initiative (including the profit motive) and increased economic ties with

Robert O. Anderson, chairman of ARCO, and Qin Wencai, president of the China National Offshore Oil Corporation, sign an agreement by which ARCO undertook to develop a natural gas field near Hainan (Hai-nan) Island.

the West as critical to enlivening the economic system and reviving public support for CCP policy.

The Economy

China was in important respects a victim of its own economic success in 1985. An extremely rapid growth rate in the first half of the year produced an overheated economy that threatened to overwhelm the country's severely burdened transportation and resource-allocation systems. A number of these problems were traceable to steps undertaken in late 1984 to free Chinese industry from the pervasive grip of central planning and to encourage increased innovation and risk taking. With many enterprises informed that they were now responsible for their own profits and losses, some factory managers aggressively pursued opportunities for increasing their market shares. But these actions produced a number of unwelcome consequences, including what Premier Zhao described as the "indiscriminate" issuing of bonuses to workers, an exponential growth in bank loans, and a rapid expansion of money supply. At the same time, the abrupt jump in industrial output—a rise of more than 23% in the first six months of 1985 alone, compared with a 14% increase for all of 1984—severely taxed China's energy resources and transportation system.

Some of the most acute problems concerned the rapid depletion of China's foreign exchange. Increased demand for consumer goods and the enhanced ability of provinces and some individual enterprises to make decisions on the spending of hard currency resulted in a ballooning international trade deficit and a 30% drop in China's foreign exchange reserves in the first six months of 1985 alone.

The biggest problems were associated with Japan, China's largest trading partner. An explosive demand for Japanese consumer items and industrial products and the importation of numerous production lines (especially in consumer electronics) contributed to a surge in China's imports that was not matched by comparable increases in exports. As a result China's 1985 trade imbalance with Japan was expected to exceed $5 billion, imposing a strain on relations between the two countries.

Unprecedented economic abuses also developed as a consequence of China's increased ties with the outside world. To attract foreign investment and technology, China in 1979 created a limited number of special economic zones in the country's southern coastal regions, where foreign firms were granted preferential tax treatment and related incentives for establishing factories and supplying advanced technology. Although many senior leaders (including Deng) had earlier deemed the special economic zones proof of the "correctness" of the open-door policy, mounting problems in the spring and summer produced a much more cautious view. Exposure of a major scandal on Hainan Island involving unauthorized imports of Japanese cars, motorcycles, and consumer electronics worth more than $1 billion graphically revealed the extent of such problems. The boomtown atmosphere in the zones not only created a ready climate for corruption but also raised the issue of whether the substantial costs required to develop new industrial areas had yielded a reasonable return on investment.

To cope with these problems, officials in Peking sought to curb much of the autonomy previously granted to the zones. A number of local officials were dismissed or reassigned, and far stricter controls on the expenditure of funds and disbursement of hard currency were imposed. In July it was announced that April 1984 plans to expand the zones to an additional 14 cities had been delayed, with near-term expansion to be limited to 4 major cities where the industrial and management infrastructure was already fairly well developed.

Foreign Affairs

Sino-Soviet relations were more active than at any point since the early 1960s, with both sides testing the opportunities for an expanded relationship in the aftermath of Mikhail Gorbachev's succession to power in the U.S.S.R. At Konstantin Chernenko's funeral in March, Gorbachev and Li Peng, leader of the Chinese delegation, both pledged renewed efforts to improve relations. In July Vice-Premier Yao Yilin (Yao Yi-lin) traveled to the Soviet Union, reciprocating the visit of Deputy Premier Ivan Arkhipov to China in December 1984. The two countries signed a long-term trade agreement for the 1986–90 period totaling $13.5 billion. Under the agreement two-way trade in 1990 was expected to reach $3.5 billion, more than double its present level. A separate agreement provided for the resumption of Soviet technical assistance to China for the first time since 1960, including the upgrading of 17 factories built by the U.S.S.R. in the 1950s and the construction of 7 new industrial plants. Official relations between the legislative bodies and the trade unions of the two countries were also restored, but China stated that it was not yet willing to consider the resumption of Communist Party ties. In December the two sides announced that the Soviet and Chinese foreign ministers would exchange visits to one another's capitals during 1986.

However, China repeatedly insisted that full political ties depended on elimination of the "three obstacles" to the normalization of relations: Moscow's occupation of Afghanistan, Soviet support for Vietnam's occupation of Kampuchea, and Soviet military deployments in East Asia, including the presence of ground forces in Outer Mongolia and 171 SS-20 intermediate-range missiles east of the Urals. Moscow not only remained unyielding on these issues but also stepped up the level of its military activity on all three fronts. Quite possibly because of the need for regional stability, China concluded that a less hostile relationship was nevertheless possible under those circumstances.

Sino-Soviet relations remained much more modest than the burgeoning ties between the United States and China. China continued to voice complaints about three areas of U.S. policy: U.S. dealings with Taiwan (especially continued arms sales to the island), restrictions on the sale of sensitive technologies to China, and protectionist sentiment that threatened to limit Chinese textile exports to the United States. Despite these differences China made clear its desire for expanded ties, with a particular emphasis on economic, scientific, and technical collaboration. U.S.-China trade reached a record $6.1 billion in 1984, and two-way trade for 1985 seemed certain to surpass it. U.S. investment in China (much of it in offshore oil exploration) exceeded $1 billion by 1985, well in excess of that of any other nation. Perhaps most important, an estimated 15,000 Chinese students were enrolled in U.S. universities, more than had been sent to all other countries combined.

High-level political visits took place and achieved important results. In July Pres. Li Xiannian (Li Hsien-nien) made the first visit ever of a Chinese head of state to the United States, reciprocating U.S. Pres. Ronald Reagan's April 1984 visit to China. The two countries signed a long-delayed accord on peaceful nuclear cooperation, which appeared to pave the way for sales of U.S. civilian nuclear-power technology to China. However, U.S. congressional concern about reports of Chinese assistance to Pakistan's nuclear program and the insistence of numerous legislators that China provide more binding pledges of its commitment to nuclear nonproliferation delayed final approval of the accord until December. President Li's visit to the U.S. was followed by Vice-Pres. George Bush's visit to China in October, at which time the U.S. announced new measures to expedite the flow of advanced Western technologies to China.

Sino-Japanese relations experienced some troubling moments during the year. An August visit by Prime Minister Yasuhiro Nakasone to a Tokyo shrine honoring Japan's war dead provoked a strong diplomatic reaction from China, and Nakasone later pledged not to undertake similar visits in the future. In September Chinese university students staged protests against China's growing trade dependence on Japan and the mounting influx of Japanese goods, which they described as a "second occupation." But senior officials quickly sought to prevent subsequent protests from assuming an anti-Japanese coloration. Admonitions to the students and reassurances to Tokyo reiterated that China's opening to the outside world remained unchanged but that ways had to be sought to achieve more balanced economic relations in the future.

Colombian army troops storm the country's Palace of Justice in November. The soldiers attempted to rescue 24 Supreme Court judges who were being held hostage by members of a terrorist group called M-19. About 100 persons died in the fighting including 11 judges. Another judge died later of a heart attack.

COLOMBIA

During 1985 events in Colombia were dominated by a resurgence of violence and increased social tensions arising from higher unemployment. Of the four main guerrilla movements, only one, the Colombian Revolutionary Armed Forces (FARC), upheld its cease-fire agreement made with the government in 1984. Some of its members later organized themselves into the Patriotic Union Party to participate in parliamentary and presidential elections scheduled to take place in 1986. The other guerrilla groups, notably the April 19 Movement (M-19), took advantage of the truce agreement to regroup, following the amnesty granted to their leaders. Claiming persistent attacks by the armed forces, M-19 intensified its guerrilla activity in southwestern Colombia, gained control of some of the slum areas of the main urban centers, and finally broke its cease-fire in June. The National Liberation Army resorted to new tactics of kidnapping and extorting money, and the Popular Army of Liberation continued its indiscriminate killings in the ranching districts of the northwest.

Violence also arose from the government's crusade against drug trafficking. As the U.S. began acting on its newly ratified extradition treaty with Colombia, some drug dealers fled the country, while others went into hiding and in some cases entered into alliances with guerrilla factions. That they continued to wield power was demonstrated by the killing in July of Tulio Manuel Castro Gil, the judge in charge of investigations into the murder of Minister of Justice Rodrigo Lara Bonilla in April 1984.

In a reshuffle of his Cabinet in August, Pres. Belisario Betancur Cuartas replaced the ministers of agriculture, education, and labor and social security. Pressure mounted later in the year for the replacement of Gen. Miguel Vega Uribe, appointed defense minister in January, because of his connection with the administration of former president Julio César Turbay (1978–82); at midyear the State Council, the highest court in the country, accused the Turbay regime of widespread human rights violations. Because ministerial posts were shared between the two main political parties, the Liberals and the Conservatives, further changes were expected to follow the New Liberal faction's break from the Liberal Party in August.

Despite economic growth in 1984, urban unemployment rose to 14.3% in June 1985. The rise was largely accounted for by the increase in the number of young people entering the labor force. The rising trend of unemployment was accelerated by the implementation of a tight austerity program in late 1984.

Disaster struck central Colombia on November 13 when the long-dormant Nevado del Ruiz volcano erupted, sending torrents of mud down the mountainside. The town of Armera was buried; the official death count was over 25,000, and some 60,000 persons were left homeless.

COMPUTERS

Virtually without warning the computer industry was rocked by a deep, prolonged slump in 1985. Manufacturers' inventories soared, resulting in the layoff of thousands of workers. Earnings of virtually every major vendor plunged, at times into the red, as even industry leader IBM Corp. struggled to avert its first earnings decline in four years.

The computer industry slump of 1985 had two

major causes, one being a pronounced downturn in corporate capital spending and the other a situation in which too many computer vendors were chasing too few buyers of equipment. U.S. government figures showed that the overall growth in the computer industry crawled ahead at an annual rate of under 2% during the first six months of the year, compared with annual growth of 15% in 1984 and 25% in 1983. Industry studies throughout the year bore witness to a continuing erosion in the confidence of computer users in their own systems' capabilities. An annual report conducted by the International Data Corp. on user spending on data processing showed a slowing of computer-related spending by major corporations for the second consecutive year.

Hardest hit by the slump were the semiconductor companies, whose silicon chips formed the processing and storage hearts of all computers and related equipment. In the third quarter of 1985 alone, National Semiconductor Corp. lost $53 million as sales plummeted more than $100 million, compared with the same quarter a year earlier. Intel Corp. posted its first quarterly loss in several years, cut the pay of its 14,500 U.S. workers by 4 to 8%, laid off some 1,850 workers throughout the year, and furloughed remaining employees for various periods. The semiconductor factory of Motorola Inc. announced layoffs that were to exceed 1,200 workers by the year's end. Japan's production of semiconductors in 1985 also was likely to fall short of the preceding year's level for the first time in a decade.

Also hard hit were the minicomputer companies as the U.S. market for midsized systems turned particularly soft. Wang Laboratories Inc., which had enjoyed several consecutive years of 30%-plus growth in both sales and profits, felt the sting of a $109 million quarterly loss during the second quarter of the year. The company trimmed its employment rolls by 5%, or 1,600 workers, and witnessed the departure of its president and chief operating officer and the return of founder An Wang as its de facto leader. Data General Corp. was hit with its first quarterly loss, $16 million, and first dismissal of workers, 7% of the total, or 1,300 in all. And AT&T, which just a year earlier had entered the computer market with a host of minicomputer offerings, announced plans to lay off 24,000 workers from its Information Systems group.

Even industry giant IBM saw its profits decline 15% through the first three quarters of the year, citing weak mainframe sales and even softer minicomputer sales as the reasons. Sperry Corp., Burroughs Corp., and Honeywell Inc. each posted declining profit figures, while Control Data Corp. canceled a $300 million bond offering at the last minute in the face of mounting losses in its computer unit that were expected to top $100 million by the year's end.

Microcomputer companies, those making home computers in particular, were also affected by the slump. Apple Computer Inc., second only to IBM in microcomputer sales, laid off 1,200 workers and completely overhauled its corporate structure, losing company founder Steven Jobs in the process. Commodore International Ltd., which boasted the largest installed base of computers in the world, posted a staggering $124 million third-quarter loss and laid off 700 workers in the face of a projected $80 million loss in the fourth quarter.

One glimmer of hope came from IBM, which unveiled critical elements of its long-term strategy to sell communications products capable of linking dozens of computers and peripherals in a cohesive

Two businessmen managed to make a profit in the computer industry during the year despite the prolonged slump in the manufacturing sector. Their success lay in buying surplus components in bulk and selling them at a discount.

network called a token ring local area network. The product ignited activity in literally dozens of communications product companies that sought to piggyback new product offerings onto IBM's network.

Technology

A technology that attracted considerable attention was that of reduced instruction set computer (Risc) architectures. Computers designed using these architectures contained relatively complex instructions within them relative to conventional computers, which often had many complex subroutines built into them. This simpler design characteristic of the Risc architectures made it possible for computers to execute certain applications much more quickly and efficiently than could conventional machines, which had to deal with more intricate architectures to execute programming instructions. Such new firms as Pyramid Technology Corp. and Ridge Computers unveiled computers based on Risc concepts. But the biggest boost for the concept came from Hewlett-Packard Co., which announced that it would base its future-generation computers around Risc architectures. Yet for all its promise, Risc architecture appeared destined to take a back seat to future computer designs built upon standard microprocessors, or single-chip computers, which, when stacked one atop another, promised quantum leaps in computing power at dramatically reduced prices.

One of the biggest breakthroughs in microprocessor design came from Intel Corp., which announced its 80386 microprocessor chip. Intel's 8086, 8088, and 80286-series microprocessors powered the entire line of microcomputers from IBM, which owned 20% of Intel. Breaking performance barriers, the 80386 32-bit chip could process three million to four million instructions per second. Moreover, the chip offered system developers, such as IBM and the makers of IBM-compatible computers, the ability to support multiple users performing separate tasks with one microcomputer, a performance domain reserved in the past for minicomputers and mainframes. The chip also allowed system developers to build machines that would run the thousands of programs already designed for the existing line of IBM and IBM-compatible microcomputers, only much faster. Introduction of the chip placed Intel in heated competition with Motorola and National Semiconductor, both of which had previously introduced high-speed, 32-bit microprocessors.

Amdahl Corp. enlarged its family of so-called supercomputers, machines designed almost solely for mathematics-intensive applications. Amdahl's additions, produced by Japan's Fujitsu Ltd., which owned controlling interest in Amdahl, included the model 1400, capable of performing 1,000,000,000 arithmetic operations per second. IBM also entered the supercomputer arena with its first so-called vector processing machine, although its entry was not nearly as powerful as Amdahl's or those of industry leader Cray Research, Inc.

In the market for home computers, the spotlight turned to two veterans of the home computer wars, Commodore International Ltd. and Atari Corp., owned and headed by former Commodore chief executive Jack Tramiel. Both companies began shipping new and technologically advanced microcomputers designed for both home and business use. Commodore's Amiga, priced at about $1,200, showcased features never before seen on a computer of that price, including advanced graphics capabilities based on a separate microprocessor designed to manage these graphics on the screen so as not to overtax the machine's basic microprocessor. However, early sales of the machine, greeted by industry watchers as a truly innovative and unique computer, were slowed by the reluctance of software developers to write programs for it. Atari's machine, the 520-ST, began arriving in stores in midsummer with very little software to run on it. Nonetheless, the machine, priced at only $700, had many features of computers costing twice as much and more.

In the software section of the industry, advances in artificial intelligence began to move that concept out of the laboratory and into mainstream data processing environments. Ansa Software, Inc., a company based in California, unveiled its Paradox data base management system, which offered microcomputer users the ability to query vast data bases and extract complex data with relatively simple English language commands.

Hitachi Ltd. announced in July that it would join with the Chinese government to develop Chinese-language computer software that would run on Hitachi's 16-bit personal computer, the B16/EX. The Tokyo firm planned to export 30,000 units of the PC to China in two years to July 1987. Ascii Corp., a Tokyo software developer, unveiled in May an enhanced version of the MSX software, an international unified standard for personal computers developed in 1983 by Ascii and its partner Microsoft Corp. of the U.S. Sony, Matsushita, and 13 other Japanese concerns were marketing MSX-based personal computers.

Bravice International Inc., a software firm in Tokyo, developed a Japanese-to-English machine translation system based on a personal computer. The software sold in Japan for less than one million yen. (For table of world currencies, *see* International Exchange and Payments.) Oki Electric Industry Co. announced the development of a Japanese-to-English translation system based on a workstation. Oki planned to start selling the system in early 1986.

NEC Corp. won three orders totaling 12 billion yen for its supercomputer, the SX-2, featuring a processing speed of 1,400,000,000 floating operations per second. Nippon Telegraph and Telephone Corp., which became a private firm on April 1, announced that it would purchase a Cray XMPI supercomputer.

Special Report:
The Homeless Computer

by R. L. Ashenhurst

The Computer Moves In
*By the millions, it is beeping its way
into offices, schools and homes*

WILL SOMEONE PLEASE TELL ME, the bright red advertisement asks in mock irritation, WHAT A PERSONAL COMPUTER CAN DO? The ad provides not merely an answer, but 100 of them. A personal computer, it says, can send letters at the speed of light, diagnose a sick poodle, custom-tailor an insurance program in minutes, test recipes for beer. Testimonials abound. . . .

Time, Jan. 3, 1983, cover story "Machine of the Year"*

The Computer Revolution can be dated from 1946, when the first electronic computer, the ENIAC, was completed. The growth of the computer industry since then is a remarkable phenomenon. The Microcomputer Revolution, a sort of "revolution within a revolution," essentially dates from 1975, when the Altair personal computer was introduced by the MITS company.

The size and price of that original personal computer (PC) made it possible for many people to envision having one in the home. Both size and price have diminished considerably since 1975, and the PC is now an established part of the information processing scene. Its role in "everyday life," however, remains a bit ambiguous.

It seems best to think of the "personal" aspect of a PC as meaning that one controls the machine on a personal level, whether in a business, professional, recreational, or other context, rather than as connoting the usual "personal versus business" dichotomy. Personal computers can in principle be used by a variety of people for many different purposes: by executives to do quick planning without recourse to their corporate data-processing departments; by managers of athletic teams to support playing-field decisions; by independent brokers to keep track of their clients, their portfolios, or both; by office workers to allow them to do a certain amount of their work at home; and by "family members at home" to play games and keep track of their Christmas lists and their household accounts.

The PC Marketplace

As anyone who has dabbled in computer stocks in the 1980s knows, a great many companies

whose focus is the personal computer industry have sprouted, bloomed, and in some cases died, or at least withered, during the first years of the decade. In trying to analyze the computer industry, however, a careful observer should distinguish between the hardware and the software marketplaces; this distinction is ignored at one's peril. Although some hardware companies started literally in a garage, today it takes substantial manufacturing and marketing organization for such a firm to be competitive. Software development can still be entrusted to the "superkid" working away back in the hills, but there, too, effective marketing is necessary. Liberal doses of venture capital are appropriate in either case.

When buying hardware, one must think not only about its compatibility (with various peripheral devices and software) but also about whether the particular model or brand contemplated has a reasonable chance for survival. Computers designed by one company to be functionally indistinguishable from those of another company are called "clones." Computers that belong to discontinued product lines, perhaps of defunct vendors, are called "orphans."

The compatibility problem also confronts the consumer who is acquiring software, but it pales beside the problem of determining, from among a

A freshman university student in Philadelphia begins to assemble her mandatory computer before writing her first English paper.

bewildering number of possibilities, which software program is the best for the envisioned application.

Computer Literacy

With the proliferation of computers there has developed something like a consensus that they should be worked into the educational process at all levels—primary, secondary, college, and graduate. From the beginning there has been confusion as to the best way to do this and even as to what exactly is to be the subject of instruction. On the one hand, computers can be used as tools in the learning process and adapted to any subject matter whatever; on the other hand, there is the process of learning about computers themselves and how to use them. The former use often is described as computer-assisted instruction. The latter must be considered on several levels, depending on the intended objective. The minimal objective, to impart "what every citizen should know" about computers, has come to be known as computer literacy.

Courses designed to impart computer literacy have been characterized (not always kindly) by the term "computer appreciation." The usual course tends to contain a little technical information (components of a computer, etc.), a little elementary programming (the computer language BASIC was developed with just this idea in mind), and a little about the wonderful world of applications (existing and potential). Missing is much of a sense of the complexity of modern computer configurations of hardware/software and, consequently, of the complexity involved in developing "real" applications on them. Also not included in such courses is the

revelation that, in a commercial or scientific setting, the end users and the system developers are two different sets of people, a fact that is largely responsible for many problems that arise.

Computer Competency

It is most useful to approach the subject of education about computers, and learning to deal with computers generally, as problems in achieving computer competency. Sidestepping the question of how college and graduate-school students should be prepared for the use of computers in business or a profession, and how grammar- and high-school students should be prepared to deal with computers in the workplace, one can instead look at the question of what a person needs to know to make reasonable use of a PC in the home.

Competition in the marketplace has resulted in considerable emphasis on the supposed simplicity of use of a PC. The popular term for such simplicity is "user-friendly." This can mean a variety of things, such as responses by computer with messages in English instead of in cryptic code and the inclusion of a great amount of "canned software" (already programmed applications), which allows a person to use a computer without knowing how to program. Much of this software has been written to ensure compatibility; that is, so that program X will run on computer Y as well as on computer Z. This requires the user to "tell" the software about the hardware on which it is going to operate.

Adapting a variety of packages to one's personal computer therefore requires remembering a lot of seemingly nit-picking rules of procedure, which must be brought into play whenever one is starting up or switching from one application to another. There is also the matter of files, remembering on which "diskette" one has stored this or that set of data. All of this, of course, takes place after the initial task of selecting the software that one will buy from among the aforementioned bewildering array of possibilities.

The effect of these complexities is to make the "casual" user of a home computer just that. After such an owner fiddles around with the PC for awhile, setting up a spreadsheet or two and seeing what there is in the games department, the computer often is left to sit in the corner. This results in a "homeless" computer. On the other hand, the person (the writer, the broker) who acquires a PC for one main purpose quickly finds that "logging in" becomes second nature. He or she soon is using the computer regularly.

Computer manufacturers are somewhat aware of this situation, and they have responded by trying to combine several different functions in one user-friendly package. However, these new products have so far not sold well. Evidently there must be a further period of accommodation before the occasional user feels sufficiently at home with the PC to set up housekeeping.

CONSUMER AFFAIRS

World Consumer Rights Day was celebrated on March 15, 1985, for the third consecutive year with a multitude of activities by the consumer movement worldwide. In April the UN General Assembly unanimously adopted the UN *Guidelines on Consumer Protection.* In a world where inconsistent standards in international trade—different safety measures, warnings, quality standards, and even different ethics—were common, the *Guidelines* represented a solid new basis for the work of consumer organizations and governments to make the marketplace, wherever it might be located, more uniformly safe and responsive to consumer needs.

International Cooperation

In December 1984 the UN General Assembly voted to continue to publish and expand a directory listing 500 potentially dangerous products that were banned, were restricted, or had failed to win approval in any of 60 countries. With the exception of the U.S., all UN members gave their backing to the consolidated list, which was promoted through the Consumer Interpol Program of the International Organization of Consumer Unions (IOCU). As of 1985 the Consumer Interpol Program numbered some 62 correspondents in 43 countries; its concerns ranged from the safety of consumer products to issues relating to the transfer and use of hazardous technologies.

During 1985 the IOCU's campaign to curb tobacco promotion—Action Groups to Halt Advertising and Sponsorship of Tobacco (AGHAST)—laid the foundation for strong support within the consumer movement and reached out to other antismoking groups. Aimed not at the smoker—the victim—but at the tobacco industry, the campaign was designed to promote the adoption of smoking control measures at the national level and to encourage consumer organizations to focus their efforts at that level.

Regional Developments

The safety of air travel was a major focus of attention in the U.S. as the crashes of several large scheduled airliners made 1985 the worst year in civil aviation history. These accidents raised growing concern about the effect of deregulation on the airline industry, lending support to the notion that deregulation had resulted in cost cutting that placed strains on airline equipment and personnel. Congressional critics questioned whether the Federal Aviation Administration (FAA) was doing everything possible to keep the skies safe. Inspectors' reports confirmed the FAA findings that the great majority of U.S. airlines were operating within the safety rules; however, the reports did reveal serious problems among the smaller regional and commuter carriers, which flew millions of passengers a year. In January 1985 consumer advocate Ralph Nader accused the FAA of underreporting the number of near collisions in the nation's airways. Nader said a spot check of documents from regional FAA offices revealed that more than 100 airborne close calls had not been included in official FAA data. In June 1985 the FAA issued a revised report, stating that there had been 592 near collisions of U.S. airliners in 1984, an increase of 293 over the previous estimate for the year.

In March and April six midwestern states were hit with an outbreak of salmonella food poisoning described as the worst of its kind in U.S. history. Altogether some 16,000 reported cases were traced to contaminated milk produced at a suburban Chicago dairy. Two valves had evidently allowed tainted raw milk to mix with pasteurized milk, thus causing the contamination.

In July California state agencies ordered grocers to destroy more than ten million watermelons on their stores' shelves after reports of more than 180 cases of sickness caused by watermelons treated with the pesticide aldicarb. The Environmental Protection Agency subsequently published a report stating that aldicarb would be banned because it is highly carcinogenic.

The closing in March of 71 Ohio savings institutions whose deposits were insured by a state-affiliated fund was thought to have been the most drastic action of its kind since the Great Depression. The decision to close the banks was made after the failure of a Cincinnati-based financial institution undermined the stability of the state's deposit insurance fund. Following the passage of emergency legislation requiring that these banks apply for federal insurance, several were allowed to reopen, and a feared run on state-insured savings banks in four other states was averted. A federal government report revealed that one-third of the 3,200 U.S. thrift institutions had liabilities that exceeded their tangi-

Bank customers await the reopening of a savings and loan in Delhi, Ohio. Seventy-one privately insured thrift units in Ohio were closed in March.

AP/WIDE WORLD

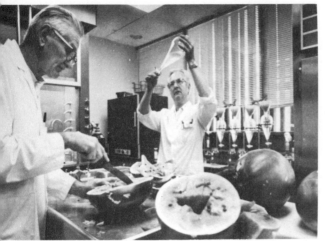

AP/WIDE WORLD

State chemists in Oregon test watermelons for pesticide residues following an outbreak of illness attributed to the use of the pesticide aldicarb.

ble assets. Many thrifts reported positive net worths (assets minus liabilities) by using special accounting techniques. The financial condition of the nation's thrifts posed questions about the stability of the Federal Savings and Loan Insurance Corporation (FSLIC), the unit of the Federal Home Loan Bank that insured thrift institutions.

In August the Manville Corp. offered to pay $2.5 billion to victims of asbestos-related health problems in the largest health-related settlement ever made by a U.S. company. Manville offered to set up a fund to which shareholders would surrender half the value of their stock and the company would give up a large part of its projected earnings for the next 25 years. For this offer to become effective, it would have to be accepted by shareholders, claimants, and the bankruptcy court.

A. H. Robins, manufacturer of the birth control device known as the Dalkon Shield, set up a $615 million reserve fund to settle legal claims from women who suffered injuries from the device. More than 12,000 users of the Dalkon Shield had already sued Robins. In 1984 the company had settled 8,300 claims for $314.6 million, but new lawsuits were being filed at an average of 300 a month. Robins asked for a federal court decision to consolidate all the suits into a single class action suit to determine the company's total liability.

In February, SmithKline Beckman Corp. was sentenced to two years' probation and ordered to spend $100,000 to establish a child abuse prevention program and to perform 500 hours of community service for having delayed reporting adverse side effects of Selacryn, a drug to control high blood pressure. It was the first time the U.S. Department of Justice had prosecuted a violator of reporting requirements under provisions of the Food, Drug, and Cosmetic Act.

In July 1985, after ten years of discussion, debate, and argument, the European Communities (EC) Council of Ministers adopted a product liability directive. This instrument, which had to be implemented by EC member states within three years, would make producers and importers throughout the Community strictly liable for damage caused by unsafe products. In September a new coalition of European and international consumer groups published *Cleared for Export,* a report examining the EC's pharmaceutical and chemical trade. The new coalition marked renewed, vigorous efforts to act against dangerous exports from European countries.

The Australian government increased its funding to the Australian Federation of Consumer Organzations (AFCO) by 41.6%, thus reflecting its growing commitment to consumer affairs generally. AFCO was closely involved in the collection of national statistics on injuries and deaths associated with consumer products. The data would be used to target areas where government action was needed to protect the health and safety of consumers.

COSTA RICA

The reality of Costa Rica's proclaimed neutrality came under attack during 1985 as relations with Nicaragua worsened and those with the U.S. strengthened. The Nicaraguan regime pointed out that politically active Nicaraguan refugees had been allowed asylum in Costa Rica and claimed that the country was being used as a base from which to attack Nicaragua. In February Costa Rica protested the abduction of a Nicaraguan draft resister from the Costa Rican embassy in Managua, where he had sought asylum. The arrival in Costa Rica of U.S. military advisers to train the civil guard was perceived as evidence of the government's gradual

Demonstrators outside Costa Rica's Legislative Assembly denounce in May the presence of U.S. military advisers in Costa Rica.

AP/WIDE WORLD

tilt toward the U.S., which supplied military assistance worth $9 million in 1985.

An upturn in the economy was evidenced by a growth of about 5% in 1984, despite the slowing of agricultural growth following a crippling strike in the banana industry. The strike cost the Compañía Bananera de Costa Rica some $12 million in lost production and spurred the U.S.-owned parent company, United Brands, to sell all of its banana plantations in Costa Rica, causing large areas to be taken out of banana production. Gross domestic product was expected to show a modest growth of 2–3% in 1985.

CRIME AND LAW ENFORCEMENT

With numbing frequency the world's media were dominated in 1985 by news of terrorist attacks. During one ten-day period alone, reports flowed in of an airplane hijacking near Athens, a bombing at the Frankfurt, West Germany, international airport, a possibly sabotaged jumbo jet falling in pieces into the Atlantic Ocean, and an explosion at Tokyo's Narita Airport.

For the passengers and crew aboard Rome-bound TWA Flight 847, a terrifying ordeal began on June 14 when the jet was hijacked shortly after takeoff from Athens. Seized initially by two gunmen, believed to be members of a militant pro-Iranian Shi'ite Muslim group, the plane shuttled for many hours between Beirut, Lebanon, and Algiers. Women, children, and elderly passengers were released, but the gunmen also beat and shot to death one passenger, Robert Stethem, a U.S. Navy diver. Eventually landed in the Lebanese capital and dispersed through the Muslim sector of the city to foil rescue efforts, Flight 847's remaining 39 passengers and crew became the subject of prolonged and tense negotiations for their release in exchange for more than 700 prisoners, mostly Shi'ites, held in Israeli prison camps. Negotiations proved successful, and the 39 hostages regained their freedom on June 30.

On June 19 a powerful bomb blast ripped through the international departure hall at Frankfurt's airport, killing two children and an adult and injuring 42 people. A terrorist cell calling itself the Arab Revolutionary Organization claimed responsibility. On June 23 an Air-India Boeing 747, bound for Bombay from Canada, disintegrated in midair and crashed into the sea 90 mi (145 km) off the coast of Ireland. All 329 people aboard, including 279 Canadians, perished in the worst airline disaster at sea to that date. On the same day, halfway around the globe, an explosion in a luggage container being unloaded at Tokyo's Narita Airport from a Canadian Pacific Air 747 just arrived from Vancouver, B.C., killed two baggage handlers and injured four others. Investigators began to explore the possibility that unidentified terrorists, from a base in North America, had planned to blow up two jumbo jets. Responsibility for planting explosives aboard the Air-India jet was claimed by two Indian terrorist

organizations. However, the cause of the crash was still unconfirmed at year's end.

In the Middle East three middle-aged Israelis were murdered on their yacht in the harbor of Larnaca, Cyprus, in September. A group calling itself Force 17 said it was responsible and claimed the Israelis were spies monitoring the movement of vessels carrying Palestine Liberation Organization (PLO) fighters from Cyprus to Lebanon. The same terrorist group was believed to have been involved in the hijacking on October 7 of the Italian liner *Achille Lauro.* The ship, with more than 400 passengers and crew aboard, was seized by four gunmen in the eastern Mediterranean. The gunmen, who demanded the release of Palestinians held prisoner by the Israelis, eventually surrendered to Egyptian authorities in Port Said after allegedly murdering a disabled U.S. citizen, Leon Klinghoffer. An Egyptian airliner was hijacked on November 23 by terrorists, thought to be Palestinians, and taken to Valletta airport in Malta. After two passengers were killed, Egyptian commandos, with the permission of the Maltese government, stormed the plane in a rescue attempt, but 57 of the 98 passengers and crew on board died in the gunfight and subsequent fire; one of the hijackers survived. In nearly simultaneous attacks at the Rome and Vienna airports on December 27, travelers at the counters of the Israeli airline El Al and others nearby were raked with machine-gun fire and grenades. Fifteen people (including 3 terrorists) were killed and 74 wounded at Rome, and 3 (including 1 terrorist) were killed and 47 wounded at Vienna. A PLO splinter group claimed responsibility.

Terrorism took an unexpected twist with the sinking on July 10 in New Zealand of the *Rainbow Warrior,* flagship of the international conservation group Greenpeace. The *Rainbow Warrior,* which was to have led a flotilla in the South Pacific to protest French nuclear weapons tests, sank in Auckland Harbour after mines ripped holes in its hull. One person aboard the vessel was killed. New Zealand authorities quickly arrested a man and a woman believed to be members of the General Directorate for External Security (DGSE), France's foreign intelligence agency. Despite initial denials by the French government, the *Rainbow Warrior* affair escalated into a major political scandal. In September Prime Minister Laurent Fabius placed the blame for the sinking on the defense minister, Charles Hernu, who resigned, and on the chief of the DGSE, Adm. Pierre Lacoste, who was removed from office. Further revelations were anticipated at the murder trial of the two suspects in New Zealand, but the proceedings ended when they pleaded guilty to the lesser charges of manslaughter and sabotage.

Murder and Other Violence

In the U.S. the FBI's Crime Index figures showed a 3% decline in serious crime during 1984. This was the third consecutive year in which the over-

At airport check-in areas in Vienna (left) and Rome (right), nearly simultaneous grenade and automatic-weapon attacks on December 27 resulted in 18 persons (including 4 terrorists) killed and at least 110 wounded.

all Crime Index had moved downward, although this encouraging news was tempered by the release in July of a U.S. Justice Department study that claimed the Crime Index, based on voluntary reports by approximately 15,000 law-enforcement agencies, was seriously flawed. The study proposed a number of reforms. Another study, *American Violence and Public Policy,* conducted by the Eisenhower Foundation, claimed that despite the continuing improvement in crime rates since 1982, as reported by the FBI, the level of violent crime in the U.S. remained at "astronomical" levels compared with other industrialized countries. Fear of crime in U.S. cities, said the study, was just as intense in 1985 as in the 1960s.

The case of Bernhard H. Goetz, the so-called subway vigilante, illustrated how anger and frustration about crime could affect city dwellers. On Dec. 22, 1984, four black youths (all of whom had criminal records) approached Goetz on a New York subway car and asked him for money. Goetz produced a .38-caliber pistol and shot each of the four, injuring one very seriously, before fleeing. He later surrendered to police. He was hailed as a vigilante hero by many New Yorkers and by the tabloid press, and a grand jury refused to indict him on charges of attempted murder or manslaughter, agreeing only to proceed against him for weapons violations. However, public sympathy for Goetz began to erode when it was revealed that, after shooting the four youths, he shot one again, saying, "You don't look so bad; here's another." Brought before a second grand jury in March, Goetz was indicted for attempted murder.

During the summer citizens of California were terrified by a serial killer, dubbed the Night Stalker, who was believed responsible for murdering as many as 16 people and gravely assaulting at least 21 others. In virtually every case the Night Stalker entered his victims' homes through unlocked doors and windows, killing men in their sleep and then raping women. The attacks were extraordinarily vicious. On August 31 Richard Ramirez was apprehended by angry citizens after he had tried to steal a car in a Mexican-American neighborhood of Los Angeles. Los Angeles police subsequently identified Ramirez as the man they believed to be the Night Stalker. In another troubling criminal case, an Illinois rape victim recanted testimony given originally at the trial of her alleged rapist in 1979. Cathleen Crowell Webb, now 23, claimed that in 1977 she had falsely accused Gary E. Dotson, now 28, of raping her because of fears that she was pregnant by her boyfriend. Dotson was convicted of the crime and sentenced to 25 to 50 years in prison. Deciding eventually to commute Dotson's sentence, Illinois Gov. James Thompson said he still believed Webb had been raped and Dotson properly convicted. Some observers feared the case could provoke a backlash against measures taken over the past decade to protect sexual assault victims.

Nonviolent Crime

A meeting of British Commonwealth heads of government held in mid-October in Nassau, The Bahamas, focused international attention on that Caribbean nation's involvement in massive drug-smuggling operations. Sir Lynden Pindling, The Bahamas prime minister, and members of his government faced continuing accusations of large-scale corruption linked to the island's role as a transit point for cocaine and marijuana sent from Latin America to the U.S. In March, in Miami, Norman Saunders, chief minister of the Turks and Caicos Islands, a British dependency south of The Bahamas, and three others were indicted on charges involving a plot to use the islands as a staging point for shipping drugs to the U.S.

In August Otto Lambsdorff, former economics minister in the West German government, went on trial in Bonn with two other defendants accused of corruption in connection with a payoff scandal. Lambsdorff, the first West German Cabinet minister to be indicted while in office, was alleged to have accepted $50,000 between 1977 and 1980 from Flick, a giant German corporation, in exchange for granting lucrative tax waivers. The trial was expected to last at least a year.

In the U.S. a wave of revelations concerning white collar crime touched some of the nation's largest business and financial institutions, including more than 40 of the top military suppliers, said to be the subject of ongoing criminal investigations. In May, following widespread allegations of massive fraud and mismanagement, the nation's third largest defense supplier, General Dynamics, suffered the cancellation of two contracts worth more than $22 million and the suspension of two of its divisions from obtaining fresh contracts until it repaid $75 million in cost overruns and installed a new code of ethics for its staff. In the same month, General Electric, the sixth largest U.S. military contractor, pleaded guilty to defrauding the Air Force of $800,-000 in 1980 on a Minuteman missile project.

Also in May, Wall Street's largest stockbroking firm, E. F. Hutton, pleaded guilty to a fraud that had bilked some 400 banks out of at least $8 million between 1980 and 1982. The firm agreed to pay a fine and court costs of $2,750,000 and to repay the banks, but no individual executives were prosecuted. The settlement was strongly criticized by congressmen and others who alleged that federal authorities were showing undue leniency toward corporate offenders. In marked contrast, former deputy secretary of defense Paul Thayer and a co-defendant were sentenced to a four-year prison term and fined $5,000 after pleading guilty to obstruction of justice charges relating to an insider trading investigation by the federal Securities and Exchange Commission. In August Crocker National Bank of San Francisco, the 11th largest U.S. bank, was fined $2,250,000 for failing to report almost $4 billion in foreign currency transactions. Federal authorities hoped the penalty, the most severe ever imposed under the U.S. Banking Secrecy Act, would ensure that law-enforcement officials received information required to trace laundered money involved with organized crime, drug deals, or corruption.

Maritime fraud cost the international shipping industry more than $13 billion per year, according to a report presented in August by the UN Conference on Trade and Development (UNCTAD) to the seventh UN Crime Congress in Milan, Italy. The largest fraud in shipping history, according to UNCTAD, occurred when an empty supertanker, the *Salem,* was scuttled in 1980 off the coast of Senegal as part of an elaborate scheme to cover up the theft of its original cargo of oil and to obtain $80 million in insurance. In April a Greek court

Reflections on the Bernhard Goetz Case

At a press conference shortly after his arrest, Bernhard Goetz was asked how it felt to be a celebrity, to have people interested in what he stood for. Goetz paused, then asked pointedly, "What *do* I stand for?" The precise answer to this question is still unclear. Perhaps of greater ultimate importance to society, however, are the insights that the case provided into the shortcomings of the criminal justice system and into some unfortunate aspects of media sensationalism.

That an act of vigilantism could garner such public support demonstrates the almost universal frustration with a system of criminal justice that is generally regarded as, at best, ineffective. Furthermore, the media took advantage of the situation, capitalizing on the feelings of many New Yorkers that crime was running rampant, that no place was safe. Goetz was hailed as a hero, a man who "finally decided to fight back." The perceived unresponsiveness of the police, prosecution, and courts to Goetz's plight only added to the outpouring of sympathy for him.

Interestingly, while Goetz was hailed as a man who justifiably had taken the law into his own hands, the mayor and other officials joined in the applause. Goetz was indicted only for illegal possession of a gun and was released on bail. Subsequently, however, additional information came to light. Goetz apparently had been prepared to fire in the face of questionable provocation. At later press conferences, he appeared somewhat unbalanced. The mayor and other officials withdrew their support; black leaders denounced Goetz's actions and the failure to prosecute as racist acts. A grand jury was reconvened and presented with "new" evidence. This time Goetz was indicted for attempted murder, aggravated assault, reckless endangerment, and illegal possession. Inevitably, questions were raised. Had the first indictment been a result of racist attitudes? Was the new indictment a pandering to the evident reversal of public opinion?

Had the Goetz case created a sustained media interest in solving the problems of the criminal justice system, the sensationalism and the injury to public confidence in the system might have been worthwhile. However, no such journalistic initiative has been forthcoming, and public anxiety about the court system is undiminished. Thus, unless the system itself takes corrective measures, society will have to cope with more vigilante justice, more media hype, and constantly frightened citizenry.

UPI/BETTMANN NEWSPHOTOS

Richard Ramirez (right), accused of being the Night Stalker murderer and allegedly slaying 16 persons, leaves court after being charged with one murder.

sentenced a shipping agent to 11 years in prison and four seamen to up to 4 years each for their complicity in the *Salem* fraud.

Law Enforcement

The importance of international cooperation in the fight against crime was underscored in March when President Reagan and Canadian Prime Minister Brian Mulroney signed a treaty designed to expedite criminal investigations involving their two countries. A key provision required the establishment in both nations' justice departments of central

Former U.S. Navy officer and accused spy ringleader John Walker (left) pleaded guilty in October to selling U.S. military secrets to the Soviet Union.

UPI/BETTMANN NEWSPHOTOS

clearinghouses for cross-border evidence, witnesses, and fugitives.

U.S. relations with Mexico were strained following the kidnapping and murder of a U.S. Drug Enforcement Administration (DEA) agent, Enrique Camarena Salazar. Camarena Salazar was abducted at gunpoint in February outside the U.S. consulate in Guadalajara. His body, and that of a Mexican pilot working for the DEA, were found several weeks later near Villahermosa. Suspicions by DEA officials that these murders could have occurred only with the knowledge and assistance of corrupt Mexican law-enforcement officials were confirmed late in March when six members of the Jalisco state police and a number of civilians were arrested by Mexican authorities in connection with the crimes.

The FBI announced in August that audits conducted in a dozen U.S. states indicated that at least 12,000 invalid or inaccurate reports on suspects wanted for arrest were transmitted each day to federal, state, and local law-enforcement agencies. The audits also brought to light problems with about 7,000 reports transmitted each day concerning stolen vehicles and license plates. The information, supplied to the bureau's National Crime Intelligence Center, was intended to give police officers speedy notice of whether a person stopped for a traffic offense was wanted on a criminal charge or whether a particular car had been reported stolen.

Law-enforcement officials in Pennsylvania were the subject of extensive investigations following a disastrous fire on May 13 that erupted after police dropped a bomb from a helicopter on a house in Philadelphia. The drastic action was taken by police in an attempt to end a two-day siege of the heavily fortified house occupied by members of a bizarre radical cult known as Move. The explosion set off an inferno that killed 11 people, 5 of them children, in the Move house and destroyed or damaged more than 60 surrounding houses.

In Poland, following an unprecedented public trial, four members of the secret police were convicted in February of the abduction and murder of a well-known Polish activist priest, Father Jerzy Popielusko.

Severe street rioting occurred in a number of British cities during the summer. In Brixton, a London suburb that was also the scene of major riots in 1981, the disturbances were sparked when police accidentally shot a black woman. A police officer was also killed during the rioting, leading to suggestions by police union leaders that their members be allowed to fire rubber bullets to disperse rioters—a crowd-control measure frequently used by British authorities in Northern Ireland. The continuing sectarian conflict in Northern Ireland produced more casualties, including the deaths in March of 9 police officers in a mortar attack on a police station in Newry; 37 others were injured.

A report prepared by researchers at the University of Cape Town's Institute of Criminology gave further credence to long-standing allegations of the use of physical and psychological torture by South African police. The study, which was supported by funds from the U.S.-based Ford Foundation, included interviews with 176 former political detainees, 83% of whom reported suffering some form of physical torture while in custody, and almost all of whom said that they had been subjected to psychological abuse. Police subsequently denied the allegations, although the South African government was known to have made an undisclosed number of out-of-court settlements with former detainees or their families who had brought civil legal proceedings.

CUBA

During 1985 there were signs of renewed life in the conduct of foreign policy as Cuba finally emerged from months of coming to terms with the shock of the U.S. intervention in Grenada in 1983. Diplomatic contacts were reestablished with a number of Latin-American nations, often for the first time since the 1959 revolution. Bolivia opened an embassy in Havana in May, Uruguay was planning to do the same, and commercial contacts were forged with several other countries, including Brazil, Argentina, and Ecuador. Pointing out that Cuba was also burdened with a large foreign debt, Pres. Fidel Castro skillfully increased his influence among Cuba's neighbors by calling for a debtors' strike. Though governments politely disassociated themselves from Castro's views, the idea struck a chord with many sections of Latin-American society. At the same time, it diverted some attention from Cuba's failure to influence events in Central America. The country's renewed standing among South American nations was highlighted by the success of the motion to admit Cuba to the Latin-American Parliament, approved by a vote of 140–25 at that body's meeting in June.

The promise of a slight thaw in relations between Cuba and the U.S. toward the end of 1984 proved false. The launching of the U.S.-sponsored anti-Castro Radio Martí took place on May 20. In retaliation, Castro suspended the immigration agreement reached with the U.S. in December 1984 and banned home visits by Cuban exiles. In fact, the output of the Florida-based station was noticeably short on political rhetoric, offering instead a safer diet of popular music and soap opera. Bilateral relations took another turn for the worse after Pres. Ronald Reagan accused Cuba of belonging to a "confederation of terrorist states" (along with Nicaragua, Libya, Iran, and North Korea). Castro responded by calling Reagan "the worst terrorist in the history of mankind . . . an imbecile . . . bum" and threatening to bolster Cuba's estimated 36,000-strong garrison in Angola and Ethiopia.

At home, a purge of pro-Moscow officials conducted in February was underlined by Castro's absence from Soviet Pres. Konstantin Chernenko's funeral in March. Many university-trained technocrats were later promoted to head key ministries. Few of Castro's old allies were sacked, however, and most of the changes appeared to reflect a general trend toward increased delegation of functions. Castro himself allowed his younger brother Raúl to run many areas of domestic policy, leaving him free to play a greater role on the international stage.

The economy grew by 7.4% in 1984, surpassing the target of 5%. The most important contributions were provided by industry and construction, which registered real output increases of 7 and 16%, respectively. Sugar production still dominated the economy, but its performance remained relatively disappointing. Output in both the 1983–84 and 1984–85 seasons was eight million metric tons. In 1984 Cuba sold 3,649,996 tons of sugar, or 52% of total exports, to the U.S.S.R. The price received for these sales was about seven times the average

One hundred Cuban military advisers arrive at Havana's José Martí Airport on May 2. They were returning from duty in Nicaragua, where 700 more Cuban military advisers remained.

AP/WIDE WORLD

free-market price of 5 cents a pound. Nevertheless, since Comecon sales were denominated in inconvertible rubles, Cuba valued its free-market sales as a source of hard currency. With free-market prices remaining depressed, Cuba's hard-currency trade deteriorated markedly. In 1984 the country ran a deficit in convertible currencies equivalent to 575 million pesos, compared with 45.8 million pesos in 1983. The measure of the slump in sugar sales to the West could be gauged by the fact that Cuba's resales of Soviet-supplied oil were by far its largest source of hard currencies, providing 434 million pesos in 1984. (For table of world currencies, *see* International Exchange and Payments.)

Cuba's convertible-currency debt reached $3,430,-000,000 by the end of 1984. In March 1985 Cuba's Paris Club creditors agreed to roll over $140 million in official debt, and in July commercial bank creditors agreed to reschedule $82 million in medium-term debts and $373 million of short-term obligations maturing in 1985. Cuba's first repayment to the U.S.S.R., equivalent to $125 million and falling due in 1986, had been rescheduled to 1990. Total debt to the U.S.S.R. and other Comecon members was unknown but was believed to be in the $8.5 billion–$23 billion range.

CYCLING

Bernard Hinault of France defied a broken nose and stitches in a head wound to win the 1985 Tour de France and join Jacques Anquetil and Eddy Merckx as the only riders to have won professional cycling's most important race on five occasions.

French cyclist Bernard Hinault (second from left) won the 1985 Tour de France. His teammate, Greg LeMond of the U.S. (not pictured) placed second.

VANDYSTADT/ALL SPORT

1985 Cycling Champions

Event	Winner	Country
WORLD AMATEUR CHAMPIONS—TRACK		
Men		
Sprint	L. Hesslich	East Germany
Tandem sprint	R. Tehounek, V. Voboril	Czechoslovakia
Individual pursuit	V. Ekimov	U.S.S.R.
Team pursuit	R. Amadio, G. Grisandi	Italy
	M. Brunèlli, S. Martinello	
1,000-m time trial	J. Glücklich	East Germany
50-km points	M. Penc	Czechoslovakia
50-km motor paced	R. Dotti	Italy
Women		
Sprint	I. Nicoloso	France
Individual pursuit	R. Twigg	U.S.
WORLD PROFESSIONAL CHAMPIONS—TRACK		
Sprint	K. Nakano	Japan
Individual pursuit	H.-H. Oersted	Denmark
50-km points	U. Freuler	Switzerland
One-hour motor paced	B. Vicino	Italy
Keirin	U. Freuler	Switzerland
WORLD AMATEUR CHAMPIONS—ROAD		
Men		
Individual road race	L. Piasecki	Poland
100-km team time trial	V. Jdanov, I. Sumnikov	U.S.S.R.
	V. Klimov, A. Zinoviev	
Women		
Individual road race	J. Longo	France
WORLD PROFESSIONAL CHAMPION—ROAD		
Individual road race	J. Zoetemelk	The Netherlands
WORLD CHAMPIONS—CYCLO-CROSS		
Amateur	M. Kluge	West Germany
Professional	K.-P. Thaler	West Germany
MAJOR PROFESSIONAL ROAD-RACE WINNERS		
Tour de France	B. Hinault	France
Tour of Italy	B. Hinault	France
Tour of Spain	P. Delgado	Spain
Paris–Nice	S. Kelly	Ireland
Milan–San Remo	H. Kuiper	The Netherlands
Tour of Flanders	E. Vanderaerden	Belgium
Paris–Roubaix	M. Madiot	France
Flèche Wallonne	C. Criquelion	Belgium
Liège–Bastogne–Liège	M. Argentin	Italy
Dauphiné–Libéré	P. Anderson	Australia
Bordeaux–Paris	B. Cornillet	France
G.P. de Midi Libre	S. Contini	Italy
Tour of Switzerland	P. Anderson	Australia
Circuit Het Volk	E. Planckaert	Belgium
Amstel Gold	G. Knetemann	The Netherlands
G.P. de Frankfurt	P. Anderson	Australia
Paris–Brussels	A. van der Poel	The Netherlands
Dunkirk 4-day	J.-L. Vandenbroucke	Belgium
Tirenno Adriatico	J. Zoetemelk	The Netherlands
Ghent–Wevelgem	E. Vanderaerden	Belgium
Tour of Romandie	J. Müller	Switzerland
Tour of Lombardy	S. Kelly	Ireland
Tour de l'Avenir*	M. Ramirez	Colombia
Tour of Britain*	E. van Lancker	Belgium
Berlin–Prague–Warsaw†	L. Piasecki	Poland

*Mixed professional and amateur.
†Amateur.

Hinault dominated the 3½-week race (June 28–July 21) despite the injuries he received in a crash at the finish of the 14th stage in Saint-Étienne. He also won his preparatory event, the Tour of Italy, and so completed the sport's most famous double—a feat achieved only by Fausto Coppi, Anquetil, Merckx, and Hinault himself—for the second time. English-speaking competitors enjoyed unprecedented prominence in the Tour de France. Runner-up Greg LeMond, riding for the same trade team as Hinault, recorded the first stage victory by a rider from the U.S. when he won the 47.5-km time trial at Lake Vassivière. The next three positions overall were filled by Ireland's Stephen Roche and Sean Kelly and Australia's Phil Anderson. Kelly won the Super Prestige Pernod trophy for the second consecutive year.

At the 1985 world championships in the Veneto

region of Italy, 38-year-old Joop Zoetemelk of The Netherlands won the professional road race title. Three other road titles were also decided there. After remeasurement of the course, the Soviet Union was credited with an Olympic-record-breaking average speed of 50.9 km/h (31.6 mph) in winning the team time trial. The amateur men's road race was won by Lech Piasecki of Poland, after a series of early crashes left 60 riders in need of medical treatment. Jeannie Longo of France took the women's title after previously winning three silver and three bronze medals on the road and track. The track program produced a world best of 5 min 43.02 sec from Hans-Henrik Oersted of Denmark during his successful defense of the professional 5,000-m pursuit title. Oersted returned to the 400-m cement track two weeks later and broke the nonaltitude world record for one hour, covering 48.149 km (29.852 mi). Two long winning sequences were extended when the seemingly invincible Japanese millionaire Koichi Nakano won the professional sprint for the ninth year, and Urs Freuler of Switzerland collected his fifth consecutive professional points race title as well as winning the keirin for a second time. Rebecca Twigg of the U.S. scored her third victory in the women's pursuit, but compatriot Connie Paraskevin lost the sprint title to Isabelle Nicoloso of France.

CYPRUS

There were high hopes for the January summit meeting in New York City between Pres. Spyros Kyprianou and Turkish Cypriot leader Rauf Denktash. The meeting was the culmination of efforts by UN Secretary-General Javier Pérez de Cuéllar to produce a draft agreement for a federal solution to end the division between the two communities. The summit collapsed, however, as it became clear that the two leaders were not of one mind. Kyprianou viewed the draft accord as nothing more than a basis for further negotiations. Denktash accepted the draft as a finished product, ready to be signed; he was willing to leave unresolved issues to be worked out later.

The talks ended amid bitter recriminations. Kyprianou returned home to severe criticism from the two powerful opposition parties, the Communist AKEL and the right-wing Rally. In an unprecedented move the executive president was censured by the House of Representatives, where his small Democratic Party, supported by three Socialists, was outvoted 23–12 in a motion calling for him to sign the draft agreement and submit to the will of the parliamentary majority or resign. Kyprianou refused to resign, as was his right, and the opposition proceeded to bring the legislature to a virtual standstill by blocking all measures sent to the House by Kyprianou's Council of Ministers.

In the north the ebullient Denktash was riding high as the Greeks squabbled. He proceeded to give the south a threefold lesson in democracy by

calling a referendum on a new constitution and then presidential and parliamentary elections. The constitution received 70% backing, and even Denktash himself confessed surprise when he won a six-way presidential race with a landslide 70% of the vote. In the northern assembly elections the National Unity Party (UBP), founded by Denktash, won 24 seats and formed an alliance with the 10-seat Communal Liberation Party (TKP). The left-wing Republican Turkish Party (CTP) won 12 seats, and New Dawn (YDP), a party of settlers from the mainland, won 4 seats.

In October the southern House unanimously voted to dissolve itself, setting parliamentary elections for December 8. The House was expanded from 35 to 56 seats. The elections were a personal triumph for Kyprianou. At the expense of AKEL, which won only 15 seats, the Democrats won 16, the Socialist EDEK won 6, and the Rally became the major party with 19.

The economy faltered but remained basically sound. Estimates for the growth of gross domestic product in 1985 showed a drop of 1.5% from the 6% of 1984. However, optimism surrounded 1986 forecasts, with agriculture, tourism, and service industries expected to continue booming. Inflation was reasonably stable at about 5.5%, as was unemployment at about 3%. In December Cyprus began detailed talks with the European Communities (EC) aimed at a transition to a full customs union with the EC.

CZECHOSLOVAKIA

Throughout 1985 the economy continued to occupy most attention in Czechoslovakia. It became evident to economists at home and abroad that no remedy had been found for the ills that had plagued the economy for years and that the outlook was bleak. Failure to modernize and to increase investment had left the country's once-modern industry resembling a 19th-century industrial scrap heap. Observers were particularly alarmed because Czechoslovak products were no longer always competitive within the Communist world. The diagnosis—overcentralization, excessive bureaucracy, insufficient market discipline, too much political interference in the running of the economy, high levels of waste—was widely accepted.

The Central Committee (CC) of the Communist Party of Czechoslovakia (CPC) projected a growth rate of 3.2% in net material product for 1985. Labor productivity was expected to rise by 4.7%. The 1984 growth figure of 2.8% barely prevented serious economic problems. Although the figure was on the positive side of the balance, it concealed deficits in a number of crucial economic areas. The gap between supply and demand in domestic trade remained unbridged. Shortages of energy resulted in shortened work time in several sectors.

Calls for changes in the economic system surfaced from time to time. The arguments of the reformers were restrained, however. They called for expansion of the service sector and attempts to curb the wastefulness of heavy industry by subjecting it to competition for resources. Valtr Komarek, one of the more prominent figures among the reformers, argued in a series of articles that the need for intensive, as opposed to extensive, methods was urgent, and that this need required a radical transformation of the approach to economics as a whole. However, Komarek came up against a political constraint—the refusal of the CPC leadership to contemplate economic reform for fear it would undermine the party's political position.

At a CC meeting in June 1985, CPC General Secretary Gustav Husak indicated once again that no market-oriented, decentralizing reform of the system was contemplated. A major anticorruption drive that led to a purge of CPC members was not expected to alter the balance of forces significantly, even though it claimed a number of relatively senior officials as victims.

The Charter 77 opposition group maintained its activities at, if anything, a somewhat higher level than in previous years. In November 1984 it issued a joint appeal with East German peace groups for "a missile-free Europe," the first time that such a joint appeal had been made. Charter later protested against the intensifying level of "disinformation" in the official press. The number of those who adhered to the Charter was growing slowly and had reached almost 2,000 by mid-1985. In October Charter sent an open letter to the Budapest Cultural Forum, one of the meetings held as part of the official follow-up to the 1975 Conference on Security and Cooperation in Europe. The letter contained accusations concerning the damaging effects of the Czechoslovak regime's repressive practices.

Vaclav Havel, the opposition dramatist, was increasingly emerging as a political thinker of considerable stature. The awarding of the 1984 Nobel Prize for Literature to the poet Jaroslav Seifert proved embarrassing to the authorities in view of Seifert's refusal to compromise with the government, and their response to the event was grudging. The popular response, however, was much more positive.

The year 1985 marked the 1,100th anniversary of the death of St. Methodius, regarded as the founding father of Christianity in the Czech and Slovak lands. Both the Roman Catholic Church and the state were determined to celebrate the event in their own ways. The authorities insisted that the significance of St. Methodius had been political. The church emphasized the religious content of the saint's message. The July 7 anniversary attracted around 150,000 pilgrims to Velehrad, site of the saint's tomb. This sizable public demonstration in the teeth of official disapproval indicated the depth of religious feeling. In April Pope John Paul II appointed Msgr. Jozef Tomko as the first Slovak cardinal.

DANCE

In a year dense with new productions and imports, the dance community in 1985 was beset with losses and changes that underscored the field's instability. In the U.S. three regional ballet companies (Los Angeles, Baltimore [Md.], and Connecticut) and American Ballet Theatre's second company (ABT II) were shut down. New York City lost critical rehearsal and teaching space to studio real estate interests. On the positive side, new initiatives—among them the National Choreography Project, the National Performance Network, and the public television series "Alive from Off-Center"—addressed the need for innovative programming.

It was the year of the full-length story ballet, with rival first U.S. productions of John Cranko's *Romeo and Juliet* (Joffrey Ballet) and Sir Kenneth MacMillan's version at ABT; Ballet West's "20th-century world premiere" of August Bournonville's 1855 work, *Abdallah;* and the first regional productions of George Balanchine's *A Midsummer Night's Dream* (Pacific Northwest and San Francisco).

At ABT, director Mikhail Baryshnikov pursued his commitment to the new by commissioning David Gordon's first ballet, *Field, Chair, and Mountain.* Debate over the decline of the star system continued even as ballerina Cynthia Gregory was given an old-fashioned gala commemorating her 20th year with the company. Alessandra Ferri was recruited from the Royal Ballet to dance with Baryshnikov, but knee surgery curtailed his appear-

The Feld Ballet staged Les Noces, *created by Bronislava Nijinska in 1923 and re-created by her daughter, Irina Nijinska.*

ROBERT R. MCELROY/NEWSWEEK

ances. In its 45th year, ABT drew fire for casting unripe dancers in major classical roles, giving short shrift to its Antony Tudor heritage—a revival of *Dim Lustre* was roundly criticized—and dismantling its school and junior company.

At the New York City Ballet (NYCB), Darci Kistler, Kyra Nichols, and Suzanne Farrell stole the season—Kistler in an exultant return as Titania, Nichols for her moody reverie in Peter Martins's trio *Poulenc Sonata,* and Farrell for transcendent artistry in Jerome Robbins's elegiac *In Memory of . . .,* to Alban Berg's *Violin Concerto.* NYCB's major Balanchine revival, after 20 years, was *Gounod Symphony;* the novelty was Martins's charity ballet for Ethiopian famine relief, *We Are the World.* Helgi Tomasson's *Menuetto* entered the repertory, and Tomasson himself retired, dancing his ardent signature role in the *Divertimento* from *Le Baiser de la Fée.* Later, following Michael Smuin's stormy departure, Tomasson was appointed artistic director of the San Francisco Ballet.

Ballet West's artistic coup restoring Bournonville's charming, opulent *Abdallah* was tempered by the untimely death of Toni Lander, who, with director Bruce Marks, had staged the reconstruction and whose impeccable coaching brought forth authentic results. Marks was appointed artistic director of the Boston Ballet; former Royal Ballet principal John Hart was named to succeed him at Ballet West.

Karel Shook, cofounder/director of the Dance Theatre of Harlem, died following the company's successful debut at the Metropolitan Opera House featuring David Gordon's companionate *Piano Movers.*

The Joffrey Ballet's first repertory season at Lincoln Center included a respectful 80th birthday celebration for Sir Frederick Ashton and impassioned dancing by James Canfield and Patricia Miller as Romeo and Juliet (the two subsequently left Joffrey and joined a small company in Oregon).

The Pennsylvania Ballet produced Peter Martins's modernized *La Sylphide* and commissioned Merce Cunningham's spare *Arcade.* Eliot Feld's new ballets included three to Steve Reich scores exploring motion on inclined surfaces. Feld's company performed ballets by Paul Taylor dancer David Parsons and the first New York City production of Bronislava Nijinska's landmark *Les Noces.*

The American Ballroom Theater brought the essence of couples dancing to the concert stage, and new Pilobolus repertory veered toward dance theater. On Broadway, Twyla Tharp directed and choreographed *Singin' in the Rain,* and Peter Martins choreographed *Song and Dance.* Baryshnikov and jazz tap virtuoso Gregory Hines won rave notices costarring in the Hollywood feature *White Nights.*

Alvin Ailey's company became the first modern dance troupe to visit China. Season highlights were his jazz dance tribute to Charlie Parker, *For Bird—With Love,* and Bill T. Jones and Arnie Zane's

JACK MITCHELL

Ballet West revived August Bournonville's Abdallah, *with the aid of a newly rediscovered musical score and notations on choreography.*

How to Walk an Elephant, a postmodern gloss on *Serenade.*

Merce Cunningham's emotionally resonant *Native Green* was among the year's masterworks. Paul Taylor celebrated his 30th anniversary with contrasting premieres—the romantic *Roses* (Richard Wagner) and the apocalyptic *Last Look* (Donald York/Alex Katz). Martha Graham unveiled *Song,* sensual and poetic, with Romanian folk music and spoken biblical text. Among numerous new works by David Gordon, *My Folks* and *Beethoven and Boothe* were outstanding. Mark Morris, the year's most sought-after choreographer, rekindled the spirit and audacity of early modern dance. Trisha Brown marked her 15th anniversary with *Lateral Pass,* a complex collaboration with composer Peter Zummo and artist Nancy Graves. Kenneth King's 20th anniversary concert was typically brain-teasing and mysterious. There was exciting new work from Karol Armitage ($-p = dH/dq$), Deborah Hay (a three-hour version of *Tasting the Blaze,* with composer Pauline Oliveros in Austin, Texas), and Dana Reitz (collaborating with light artist James Turrell on *Severe Clear* at Radcliffe College, Cambridge, Mass.). Los Angeles-based Rudy Perez helped the Dance Theater Workshop celebrate its 20th anniversary in his first New York appearance in a decade.

At the Brooklyn Academy of Music's third annual Next Wave Festival, Nina Wiener collaborated with the Miami, Fla., architectural firm Arquitectonica and composer Richard Landry, and Laura Dean premiered works with commissioned scores by Steve Reich and Anthony Davis.

From abroad came an influx of dance of all kinds. The Grand Kabuki brought its largest touring ensemble to three U.S. cities. *Tango Argentino,* offering an intense exploration of the genre, had an extended Broadway run. Pina Bausch's neo-expressionist Tanztheater Wuppertal drew throngs

David Gordon's Field, Chair, and Mountain *at the American Ballet Theatre featured Martine van Hamel and Clark Tippet in the lead roles and had a set designed by Santo Loquasto.*
MARTHA SWOPE

of admirers and detractors in a second Brooklyn Academy of Music engagement. The Festival of India brought assorted classical and folk artists. In a tragic performance accident in Seattle, Wash., Yoshiuki Takada of the Japanese Butoh group Sankaijuku fell to his death.

Proving the Canada Council's contention that dance was the fastest-growing art in that country, the year was rife with new work, festivals, and tours. The major event was Montreal's first Festival International de Nouvelle Danse. Eight modern Canadian companies were joined by six from the United States, Japan, Belgium, England, and West Germany. Merce Cunningham's pure movement pieces—not seen in Canada in two decades—contrasted with the prevailing international trend toward dance theater and expressive content.

Four rising choreographers contributed large-scale dramatic works. *Stella,* Jean-Pierre Perrealt's stark two-hour manifesto on women's regimentation, provoked controversy in Montreal. James Kudelka's *Dracula* for Les Grands Ballets Canadiens offered Margie Gillis a plum role. On tour, Edouard Lock's assaultive *Human Sex* (La La La Human Steps) combined punk rock, laser technology, and high-voltage scrimmages. Robert Desrosiers's surreal fantasy *Blue Snake* was a departure for the National Ballet of Canada (NBC). NBC director Erik Bruhn also commissioned contemporary work from David Earle, produced Constantin Patsalas's revised *Piano Concerto,* and took the company to Europe.

The peripatetic Royal Winnipeg Ballet premiered Sandra Neels's *The War Collection* and broke ground for a permanent home. Les Grands Ballets Canadiens, under new codirection of Jeanne Re-

naud and Linda Stearns, premiered a half-dozen works and performed at the Spoleto and Athens festivals. Les Ballets Jazz toured Africa and Central America, and a dozen smaller troupes made important debuts in the U.S. and Europe.

Several European countries received visits from

Cast members perform in Tango Argentino, *an unusual and exciting program of tango music and dancing that was a popular and critical success in New York City.*
BEATRIZ SCHILLER/TIME MAGAZINE

overseas companies: the National Ballet of Canada went to Luxembourg, West Germany, Switzerland, Italy, and The Netherlands; Les Grands Ballets Canadiens to Greece and Italy; the Ballets de Montreal and the Merce Cunningham company and several smaller U.S. groups to Britain and elsewhere; and the Martha Graham Dancers to Paris, where their celebrated founder, still creating new works at age 90-plus, received the French capital's highest civic award, the *Médaille de vermeil.* Japan's well-established Matsuyama Ballet from Tokyo traveled to London to demonstrate—in association with Rudolf Nureyev as guest principal—how such Western classics as *Swan Lake* and *Giselle* could acquire an Oriental tinge while preserving their choreographic character.

Sir Frederick Ashton's *Romeo and Juliet,* created originally for the Royal Danish Ballet and long thought to be lost, was reconstructed after 40 years for the London Festival Ballet. Danish-born Peter Schaufuss, giving new heart to the London company in his first season as director, restaged the ballet with the help of his father (who had danced the role of Mercutio, while his mother had been Ashton's first Juliet) and other diverse sources, including the 80-year-old Ashton himself, who aided in rehearsal and approved the final product. Never before given in London, the Ashton ballet showed a more lyrical than dramatic approach to storytelling, more dance than mime, more poetry than drama. Besides Schaufuss as Romeo, the work featured the 16-year-old U.S.-born Katherine Healy as a wonderfully assured Juliet, followed a few weeks later by the Spanish-born Trinidad Sevillano, performing her first Juliet on her 17th birthday.

DEFENSE AND ARMS CONTROL

U.S. Pres. Ronald Reagan's surprisingly successful summit meeting with Soviet leader Mikhail Gorbachev during November 19–21 in Geneva was the most important defense event of 1985. It symbolized the limited adversarial relationship between the two military superpowers that had dominated inter-

national affairs since World War II ended in 1945.

The competition between the two nations had been constrained by their possession of nuclear weapons and by the emergence of an increasingly stable balance of nuclear deterrence. Despite the acquisition by the U.S.S.R. of superior nuclear as well as conventional forces in the 1970s, Soviet leaders continued to believe that the potential costs of a nuclear war outweighed the potential gains. Significantly, the balance of nuclear deterrence between the U.S.S.R. and the three smaller nuclear powers—Britain, France, and China—also remained stable.

The result was an international system that was, in military terms, divided between the balances of nuclear deterrence and the balances of conventional deterrence. The nations within the nuclear balances were deterred by the threat of nuclear war from using force, nuclear or conventional, directly against one another. However, the emergence of the Soviet Union as a global military power, able to project its forces anywhere it wished, added a Soviet-U.S. dimension to the many existing regional conflicts, particularly in the Middle East. This increased the dangers that such conflicts could escalate or expand, dragging the superpowers into a conflict that neither had intended or wanted. The danger of international conflict was also increasing with the spread of nuclear weapons to other countries, now thought to include Israel, South Africa, India, and Pakistan. The proliferation of chemical and biological weapons (CBW) had also begun with their use in the continuing Iran-Iraq war.

The overriding defense problem facing the U.S. and Soviet leaders, therefore, was how to manage tneir competition in such a way as to prevent its leading to a major nuclear war through miscalculation. Their objectives were, however, very different. President Reagan, like his predecessors, wanted to contain the Soviets within the areas they already controlled, including Eastern Europe, and maintain the independence of the three other major power centers in the world—Western Europe, Japan, and China. By contrast, Gorbachev, like his predeces-

A U.S. F-15 fighter (left) launches an antisatellite missile during a test on September 13 over the Pacific Ocean. After being launched from the fighter, the missile (right) reached a U.S. satellite in orbit and smashed into it. The Pentagon described the test as "absolutely flawless."

PHOTOGRAPHS, AP/WIDE WORLD

sors, sought to expand the areas under direct and indirect Soviet control with the eventual objective of gaining control of one or more of those three power centers.

The Geneva summit was successful because the two leaders were able to discuss their differing interests honestly and to agree to meet again in Washington (1986) and Moscow (1987). This suggested that their competition would continue but would be controlled. The superpower relationship would thus remain a limited adversarial one.

United States

U.S. all-volunteer armed forces (AVF) in 1985 totaled 2,151,600 personnel (200,400 women). Retention rates remained high, as did personnel quality. The defense budget for fiscal 1985 was $292.5 billion, some 7.4% of 1985 gross domestic product (GDP) and about 30% of the federal budget.

Modernization of U.S. strategic and intermediate-range nuclear forces (S/INF) continued. In the Strategic Air Command (SAC) the first squadron of Rockwell B-1B strategic bombers was becoming operational. The aging B-52 bomber force had been reduced to 151 B-52Gs and 90 B-52Hs (first deployed in 1959 and 1962, respectively). Of the B-52Gs, 90 carried 12 AGM-86B air-launched cruise missiles (ALCM) each and 61 were used in a nonnuclear antishipping role with Harpoon missiles. SAC also had 56 FB-111A medium-range nuclear bombers. Development of the advanced technology (stealth) bomber and of the advanced cruise missile continued.

The vulnerability of the U.S. land-based fixed-silo intercontinental ballistic missile (ICBM) force remained a problem without a solution. At the end of 1985 this force comprised 1,000 silos containing Minuteman II and III ICBM. Only the 550 Minuteman IIIs were modernized missiles, each carrying three multiple independently targetable reentry vehicles (MIRV). The 450 Minuteman II missiles were nearly 20 years old. The last of the 26 Titan II missiles were scheduled to be retired.

Intense political debate continued on replacements for this force. Production of 48 MX Peacekeeper ICBM was approved. These were large missiles, each weighing about 195,000 lb (88,000 kg) and carrying ten MIRV. Tests of the MX Peacekeeper in 1985 were successful, but the Peacekeepers were to be deployed in existing Minuteman silos, which could not survive a Soviet attack.

Development of the small (weighing about 25,000 lb [11,350 kg]) single-warhead Midgetman ICBM was continuing. Deployment modes being considered included a land-mobile version carried in armored vehicles.

The ballistic missile nuclear submarine (SSBN) force rose to 37, carrying 640 submarine-launched ballistic missiles (SLBM). Six new Ohio-class SSBN each carried 24 Trident I/C-4s, which were to be replaced by the Trident II/D-5 SLBM in 1988–89.

Older SSBN comprised 12 of the Franklin class (192 Trident I/C-4s) and 18 of the Lafayette class (288 Poseidon C-3s).

Deployment of submarine-launched nuclear cruise missiles continued with four nuclear cruise-missile submarines (SSGN) so equipped. A total of 700 BGM-109A Tomahawk sea-launched cruise missiles (SLCM) was planned. An additional 2,300 conventionally armed Tomahawk SLCM were being deployed so that each vessel would carry a mix of nuclear and conventionally armed missiles. Dispersing the nuclear SLCM would enhance their survivability.

North American Aerospace Defense Command matériel remained minimal, with only 72 U.S. F-15 Eagle and 38 Canadian CF-18D (F-18) Hornet modern interceptors. To balance the Soviet antisatellite (ASAT) system, the U.S. was developing an ASAT system carried by F-15 Eagles. It was successfully tested in September, destroying a target satellite. Development continued on the components of the Strategic Defense Initiative (SDI) announced by President Reagan in his March 23, 1983, television address. Although popularly known as "Star Wars," only some components of the SDI would be space-based.

The U.S. Navy continued building toward a 600-ship goal, with 213 major surface combatants, 91 nuclear-attack submarines (SSN), and personnel totaling 568,800. These provided 13 carrier battle groups (to rise to 15), each with an attack wing of 70–95 aircraft plus escorting surface vessels and SSN. The modern (post-1955) aircraft carrier fleet of 11 comprised 4 nuclear and 7 conventionally powered carriers. Modern aircraft included 300 F-14A Tomcat interceptors, 166 A-6 Intruder and 84 F/A-18A Hornet strike planes, and 82 F-2C electronic warfare/airborne electronic warning aircraft. A third World War II battleship, *Missouri,* was being recommissioned with Tomahawk SLCM. The 9 nuclear and 20 conventionally powered guided weapons (GW) cruisers included three new Ticonderoga-class ships with the Aegis fleet air defense missile/radar system. Other major surface combatants included 37 GW and 31 gun/antisubmarine warfare (ASW) Spruance-class destroyers, plus 48 GW and 53 gun frigates.

The Marine Corps, with 198,200 personnel, formed with the Navy the main U.S. power-projection force. It was organized in three divisions, each with its integral air wing. Modern aircraft included 92 F-18 Hornet interceptor/strike aircraft, 69 A-6 Intruder, and 52 AV-8A/C Harrier vertical/short takeoff and landing (V/STOL) interceptor strike aircraft. The amphibious warfare ships carrying the Corps included five Tarawa and seven Iwo Jima helicopter/Harrier/troop carriers.

The 603,900-strong Air Force had approximately 3,700 combat aircraft. Modern types included F-15 Eagle interceptors, F-16 Fighting Falcon fighter-bombers, and 34 E-3A/8 Sentry airborne warning and control systems. Among older types were 1,212 F-4 Phantom fighter-bombers/reconnaissance, 230 F-111A/D/E/F medium bombers, and 555 A-10A Thunderbolt ground-support aircraft.

The Army, with 780,800 personnel, formed 16 divisions (18,500 men each): 4 armored, 6 mechanized, 3 infantry, 1 light infantry, 1 air assault, and 1 airborne. In addition, five new light infantry divisions were being formed. They were to be smaller (about 10,000 men each) and easier to transport. As part of the Rapid Deployment Force (RDF), they were intended for use outside NATO-Europe.

Armor included 2,833 M-1 Abrams tanks, 2,150 M-2/3 Bradley mechanized infantry combat vehicles (MICV), some 9,000 M-60A1, M-60A2, and M-60A3 Patton tanks, and 12,300 M-113 armored personnel carriers (APC). Missile systems included multiple-launch rocket systems and Patriot surface-to-air missiles (SAM). Secretary of Defense Caspar Weinberger canceled the Sergeant York divisional air defense system (DIVAD) as ineffective. The Army manned the two new INF systems, the Pershing II intermediate-range ballistic missile (IRBM; range 800 mi [1,800 km]) and the BGM-109A Tomahawk ground-launched cruise missile (GLCM; range 1,100 mi [2,500 km]).

U.S.S.R.

The Soviet military machine remained the most powerful in the world. Personnel totaled 5.3 million (including 1.3 million command and general support personnel) plus 25 million in the reserves. Defense spending remained high at about $295 billion, 12–17% of gross national product (GNP).

The Strategic Rocket Forces had 300,000 troops and continued to increase their superiority over U.S. and NATO S/INF in missile and warhead numbers and warhead yields and accuracy. As of 1985 the Soviets had a first-strike capability that the U.S. would not have during the rest of the 20th century. Estimates of Soviet strength often understate the Soviet advantage because they omit 1,000–3,000 reload missiles deployed by the Soviets for their ICBM, IRBM, and SLBM launchers. New systems being tested and deployed included two ICBM, the SS-X-24 and SS-X-25 (both mobile); five long-range cruise missiles, three similar to the U.S. Tomahawk—the SS-NX-21 SLCM, the SSC-X-4 GLCM, and the AS-X-15 ALCM (all in the 1,400-mi [3,000-km] range)—plus two long-range G/SLCM; and the SS-NX-23 SLBM carried in the DIV SSBN. The three new Typhoon-class SSBN, each carrying 20 SS-N-20 MIRVed SLBM, were the world's largest, displacing 23,000 tons.

The strategic aviation force comprised the new Blackjack A, larger than the U.S.'s B-1B; 125 older Bears plus resumed production of the Bear H as an ALCM launcher; and 130 Tu-22M Backfire B/Cs. Additional medium-range bombers included 130 Tu-22 Blinder A/Bs, 220 obsolete Tu-16 Badgers, and 450 Su-24 strike aircraft.

Soviet strategic defensive forces were also large. The Soviet National Air Defense Troops (APVO) formed a separate service with some 635,000 personnel, 1,200 interceptors, and 9,600 SAM launchers at 1,200 fixed sites. The latest SAM, the SA-X-12, had a tactical antiballistic missile (T-ABM) capability. Soviet upgrading of the ABM system around Moscow, plus the construction of other ABM radars, would enable the U.S.S.R. to field a nationwide ABM system.

The two million-strong Army was organized into 51 tank, 141 motor rifle (mechanized), 16 artillery, and 7 airborne divisions (10,500–12,500 men each). Equipment remained at much higher levels than for the U.S., its NATO allies, and China. It included 52,600 tanks (the modern types comprising 9,800 T-72/-80s and 9,300 T-64s, plus 33,500 older T-54/-55/-62s); 70,000 armored fighting vehicles; and 33,000 artillery pieces, including new self-propelled 203-mm, 152-mm, and 122-mm guns.

Deployment of the Soviet Army forces was roughly two-thirds against NATO-Europe and one-third against China. There were three Strategic Theatre Commands (GTVD), plus a central strategic reserve military district with 16 divisions. The Western GTVD controlled 28 Soviet divisions (14 tank, 12 motor rifle) and 45 non-Soviet divisions in Central and Eastern Europe, plus 62 divisions (31 tank, 29 motor rifle, 2 airborne) in the European U.S.S.R. The Southern GTVD controlled 30 divisions, mainly motor rifle, including some 115,000 troops occupying Afghanistan. The Far Eastern GTVD controlled 53 divisions (7 tank, 45 motor rifle). Large overseas deployments were in Syria (7,000), Vietnam (7,000), and Cuba (9,000),

A stationary missile is destroyed by a powerful laser in an experiment conducted September 6 under Pres. Ronald Reagan's Strategic Defense Initiative.
AP/WIDE WORLD

AP/WIDE WORLD

The first Israeli-made hydrofoil was unveiled on August 8. The missile-armed craft was expected to be effective in fighting seaborne guerrilla infiltration.

with smaller ones of 500–2,500 troops each in Algeria, Angola, Ethiopia, Iraq, Laos, Libya, Yemen (San'a'), and Yemen (Aden).

NATO

The five-year crisis caused by NATO's 1979 decision to deploy 572 new INF (108 Pershing II IRBM and 464 GLCM) was finally resolved by a decision in favor of deployment by the last two members who had promised to do so, Belgium and The Netherlands. Britain, Italy, and West Germany continued deployment. Although protests against deployment still occurred, they had become negligible by the end of 1985.

A new issue facing the NATO alliance was whether its members should participate in the U.S. SDI program. Those governments and groups opposing SDI argued that it was potentially destabilizing and threatened to leave NATO-Europe exposed to Soviet nuclear weapons while the U.S. sheltered behind its strategic shield. Those favoring SDI argued that it would be stabilizing because it would balance Soviet strategic defenses and would provide a shield for NATO-Europe as well as the U.S. The December 1985 U.S.-U.K. agreement that Britain would participate in SDI was a major advance in alliance cooperation. Canada, Denmark, and Norway decided that their governments would not participate but that private firms could do so.

NATO's major long-term problem remained its lack of political will to fund the emerging conventional weapons technologies, dubbed ET, needed to offset the buildup of the Soviet/Warsaw Pact forces. On the crucial Northern/Central Front, stretching from Norway to West Germany, the balance of forces was, in terms of total divisions (or equivalent) war-mobilized, for NATO, 54 divisions (19 tank, $19\frac{1}{3}$ mechanized, and $15\frac{2}{3}$ other) with 8,800 main battle tanks (MBT) and, for the Warsaw Pact, $113\frac{1}{3}$ divisions ($72\frac{1}{3}$ Soviet) comprising 43 tank, 55 mechanized, and $5\frac{1}{3}$ other with 24,200 main battle tanks. This gave the Soviet/Warsaw Pact forces an advantage of about 2:1 in divisions and 2.5:1 in battle tanks.

This military imbalance was accentuated by the imbalance in sharing the burden of military expenses. U.S. defense spending as a percentage of 1983 GDP was, at 7.4%, approximately twice that of France and West Germany (4.2 and 3.4%) and three times that of Canada, Denmark, and Italy. Only Britain's burden, at 5.5% of GDP, was comparable to that of the U.S.

Arms Control and Disarmament

The declining importance of arms control negotiations and agreements was dramatized by the expiration of the unratified 1979 Salt II treaty on Dec. 31, 1985. No replacement agreement was in sight. The Reagan administration was unlikely to extend the Salt II limits on U.S. forces because the Soviets had not observed them. A particularly blatant violation by the Soviets was their testing of two, instead of the one permitted, new ICBMs, the SS-X-24 and SS-X-25. Additional Soviet violations were detailed in the U.S. Department of Defense's November 1985 report.

Arms control attention was thus focused in 1985 on the future of the 1972 ABM treaty, the last major agreement of the 1970s still in force, and on the possibility of other limits on the deployment of strategic defensive systems. Soviet presummit propaganda had centered on stopping President Reagan's SDI, claiming that this was a precondition for progress in superpower relations. But the president had insisted he would not sacrifice SDI, and the Soviets had accepted this, though reluctantly. No agreement limiting strategic defenses or ASAT systems was expected. Soviet violations of the ABM treaty, particularly the continued construction of an illegal ABM radar at Krasnoyarsk, made it doubtful that the treaty could last indefinitely.

In light of these developments, the continued U.S.-U.S.S.R. negotiations in the talks covering strategic offensive forces (START), weapons in space, and INF were not expected to produce effective results. The proposals put forward by both sides, particularly the Soviet offer in September/October of a 50% reduction in strategic forces, seemed designed for propaganda purposes.

No progress was made in the other arms control negotiations, including the Vienna talks on mutual and balanced force reductions and the Stockholm Conference on Disarmament in Europe.

Special Report: Intervention and Defense in Central America and the Caribbean

by Robin Ranger

The continuing guerrilla wars in El Salvador and Nicaragua symbolized the problem of defense and military preparedness that has plagued much of Central America and the Caribbean region. In El Salvador the U.S. supported Pres. José Napoleón Duarte's democratically elected government against Soviet- and Cuban-backed guerrillas. In Nicaragua the U.S. assisted, with nonmilitary aid, guerrillas (*contras*) trying to overthrow the Sandinista government of Pres. Daniel Ortega Saavedra, a close Soviet ally. The basic problem was simple, although there was no simple solution to it: the weakness of the regional powers made them vulnerable to small military forces. Historically, these forces had been used by external powers or indigenous groups to seize and hold militarily and economically valuable resources. More recently, since 1962, the vulnerability of the governments has been exacerbated by Soviet and Cuban intervention to replace existing regimes with pro-Soviet revolutionary ones. The U.S. has tried to counter this intervention.

Small military forces (about 1,000 to 3,000 personnel) have been the traditional means of seizing and holding control of governments in Central America. The Somoza regime in Nicaragua gained control in 1933 because Anastasio Somoza García commanded the loyalty of the National Guard. His son, Anastasio Somoza Debayle, lost control (and later his life) in 1979 because his forces could not defeat the revolutionary guerrillas. Such guerrilla forces have been an equally traditional feature of regional politics because of the low level of economic and social development.

Soviet and Cuban Intervention

The first Soviet/Cuban offensive was launched after Fidel Castro seized control of the 1959 revolution in Cuba that overthrew Pres. Fulgencio Batista. In the early 1960s Cuba attempted to overthrow the governments of the Dominican Republic and Venezuela. Soviet concerns that Cuba was pushing this offensive too far and too fast led to a rift between the two countries from 1967 to 1969.

Then, between 1972 and 1974, the two launched a second South American offensive, paralleling one that they were undertaking in Africa. Both offensives took advantage of U.S. military and political weaknesses in the aftermath of the Vietnam war and the Watergate scandal. In Africa this offensive enabled the Soviets to gain control of Angola and Mozambique (1975–76) and Ethiopia (1977). In each case about 20,000 Cuban troops directed by Soviet generals were used, supported by 1,000–2,000 Warsaw Pact technical/security forces.

Revolutionary groups received Soviet and Cuban support in many parts of South and Central America. From the Soviet viewpoint this support was partially successful if it increased the political polarization in these societies, destroying the moderate center and pitting the military against the people. In Central America the first major Soviet/Cuban victory took place in Nicaragua in 1979. The two nations then aimed, apparently, to repeat this triumph by overthrowing the governments of El Salvador, Honduras, and others in the region and then taking control of their revolutionary forces. The ultimate objective was the establishment of a pro-Soviet government in Mexico.

In the Caribbean the first Soviet/Cuban victory was in Grenada, where the New Jewel Movement seized power in 1979. Covert Soviet/Cuban intervention seemed likely to bring about similar developments there in the late 1970s, but the plan was defeated by indigenous political groups.

The Soviets were pursuing traditional geopolitical objectives. They sought control of the Caribbean islands that in turn control the sea lines of communication, particularly the choke points through which shipping has to pass. In a major war the Soviets would be able to cut off such sea lines needed by the U.S., including important oil shipments, thereby forcing the U.S. and its allies to divert forces needed elsewhere to neutralize that threat.

Military Strengths

Cuba and Nicaragua are the regional military superpowers, with forces totaling 161,500 and 62,850 personnel. The Cuban forces in Nicaragua, estimated at 8,000–10,000 personnel, equal about one-quarter of El Salvador's armed forces of 41,650 personnel. Neighboring Honduras has only 16,600 armed forces, Panama and Costa Rica have about 12,000 and 8,000 each, and Guatemala 31,700.

These figures underestimate the military weakness of the region. Traditionally, its armies (plus small air and naval units) have been internal security forces. The rank-and-file soldiers were usually poorly equipped, trained, and led. The officers saw a military career as a route to personal wealth and political power. Such forces were adequate to deal with the traditional peasant revolts, but they could not deal with revolutionaries trained and equipped by the Soviets and advised by Cubans. The Soviets/Cubans could direct these revolutionaries because they badly needed the military supplies the Soviets/Cubans controlled.

The U.S. Response

For the U.S., Soviet/Cuban intervention in Central America and the Caribbean posed major new defense problems. The Reagan administration recognized that the military, political, and economic threat posed by Soviet/Cuban support for revolutionaries had to be neutralized. But it also recognized the basic truth that the U.S. could help regional powers help themselves but could not solve their security problems for them. The Reagan administration accordingly provided military and economic aid in El Salvador. Continued aid was made contingent on El Salvador's Army becoming an effective fighting force.

Although faulted by critics on the left and the right for intervening too much or too little, the Reagan administration's overall strategy seemed to be succeeding in El Salvador. President Duarte's forces were containing and wearing down the guerrillas. This strategy was supported by the Congress and the electorate. In other nations in Central America the U.S. was also successful in helping local governments to contain Soviet/Cuban attempts to overthrow them by aiding local revolutionaries. But the direct and indirect costs of these efforts were significant, particularly for the local populations. The region's existing minimal military forces had to be expanded. Guerrilla attacks on their economies increased, retarding economic and social development. These problems were marked in El Salvador's neighbor Honduras. There, the U.S. had obtained the government's reluctant consent to establish a series of temporary bases through which U.S. forces could be brought in if Nicaragua's attacks on El Salvador led to full-scale war.

This situation emphasized the basic limitation of the Reagan administration's strategy of containing Soviet/Cuban intervention in Central America: it forced the U.S. to react to their attacks without removing the source of the problem, the pro-Soviet Sandinista government in Managua. For this reason the administration supported anti-Sandinista Nicaraguan rebels, the *contras*. This was the most controversial of the U.S. policies. But the U.S. Congress approved nearly $27 million for 1985 nonmilitary aid to the *contras* after initial doubts about approving $14 million. A key factor in securing this authorization was President Ortega's April 1985 visit to Moscow, underlining his dependence on Soviet/Cuban support.

Military Outcomes

In military terms there were only two possible outcomes to the Soviet-U.S. conflict in Central America. One was that it would continue at its present level or escalate as Soviet aid to local revolutionaries, funneled through Cuba and Nicaragua, increased. The other was that the *contras* would overthrow the Sandinistas, establishing an independent democratic government allied with the U.S.

On balance the latter outcome seemed more likely. By the end of 1985 the Sandinista government had alienated most of its former supporters. Its attacks on the Roman Catholic Church and the Miskito Indians had been as counterproductive internally as its attacks on El Salvador and Honduras had been externally. For these reasons, the summer 1985 offensive by the *contras* against the Sandinistas was fairly successful, forcing the Sandinista government to declare a state of emergency in October.

An imminent *contra* victory would present the U.S.S.R. and Cuba with a defense dilemma. Major increases in Cuban combat forces in Nicaragua and the introduction of Soviet forces would trigger U.S. responses. These could include a naval blockade of Nicaragua and possibly of Cuba and intervention by the U.S. Army and Air Force. In geographic terms the Soviets would be challenging the U.S. in the latter's own hemisphere, where the U.S. was strongest and the U.S.S.R. was weakest. Yet the fall of the pro-Soviet Sandinista government would be a significant loss for the U.S.S.R., especially after the successful U.S. intervention in Grenada. The repercussions would be considerable in South America, Africa, and Asia, suggesting that other Soviet-imposed governments could be replaced by democratic ones. Militarily, the limits on the Soviet/Cuban ability to support their allies would be emphasized.

In the longer term the U.S. and its Latin-American allies would have to neutralize the threat to their security posed by the Soviets' Cuban outpost and the resulting joint intervention in support of revolutionaries throughout the region. The National Bipartisan Commission on Central America, chaired by former U.S. secretary of state Henry Kissinger, had concluded in 1984 that this Soviet/Cuban intervention was exacerbating the regime's economic and social problems, turning them into military ones. These military factors also explained the lack of success in the search for diplomatic solutions to the security problems of Latin America.

DENMARK

When Prime Minister Poul Schlüter delivered his speech at the opening of the Danish Folketing (parliament) on Oct. 1, 1985, he could claim that his four-party coalition government had fulfilled at least some of the promises made when it came to power three years earlier. During the first six months of 1985 the inflation rate was 2%. The Danish krone was among the world's strongest currencies, despite the large foreign debt and balance of payments deficit. Unemployment, though still acknowledged to be too high, had been reduced by 90,000 during the previous year. The deficit on the internal budget had been cut, and a majority in the Folketing had reached agreement in principle on tax reform.

The Achilles' heel of the government's economic policy was the balance of payments deficit. While the government aimed to achieve balance in this area by 1988, most economists believed it would take a year or so longer. The deficit for 1985 appeared likely to exceed the 1984 figure of 17 billion kroner, as well as government forecasts. (For table of world currencies, *see* International Exchange and Payments.) However, the government had no plans to intervene to slow the rise in the deficit, in the belief that it was an inevitable result of the recent boom in the economy and that intervention would threaten investment activity.

Paradoxically, in view of the 250,000 unemployed, certain industries were suffering from a lack of skilled workers. Official statistics, covering only a fraction of the job market, gave a strong indication of the trend; the number of unfilled jobs had risen to 2,000, compared with 200 at the end of 1982. The paradox led to debates about whether enough resources were being channeled into the education of unskilled labor.

At the end of March the failure of wage negotiations between trade unions and employers' federations sparked the worst wave of industrial unrest that Denmark had witnessed in over a decade. The government introduced an emergency package of austerity measures that included the limitation of wage increases to no more than 2% until 1987, cuts in social services, reductions in some social benefits in real terms, and an increase in company tax from 40 to 50%. The immediate result was an intensification of unofficial strike action among both public- and private-sector workers.

During the year there was a great deal of debate about the country's security policy and its attitude toward NATO, subjects on which there was dissent among the parties. There was general agreement, however, on the question of moves toward greater unity within the European Communities; Denmark was determined not to give up its right to a national veto on policy-making decisions.

DENTISTRY

Considerable commercial excitement was generated in 1985 about new oral hygiene products that claimed to prevent or control dental plaque, the colorless, sticky film of bacteria that forms on teeth and that is implicated in the development of gum disease. Although the effectiveness of these products remained questionable, the value of toothbrushing, a standard oral health technique, was reaffirmed during the year. In clinical examinations of students from two public schools in Ann Arbor, Mich., dental researchers from the University of Michigan found that brushing alone reduces gingivitis, the beginning stage of gum disease. When students were examined for gingivitis and plaque, those who had shown signs of the disease were given toothbrushes and a nonfluoridated toothpaste for use at least once daily. A nonfluoride toothpaste was chosen so that any possible effects of fluoride on plaque control could be avoided. Results showed that levels of plaque and gingivitis were distinctly lowered by regular brushing.

In a study involving 49 patients at the Louisiana State University School of Dentistry, New Orleans, researchers found that artificial tooth roots made of hydroxylapatite, an inert, bonelike plastic material, could aid denture wearers. Chemically similar to bone and tooth enamel, hydroxylapatite can be used in the surgical implantation of tooth replacements, thereby preventing the extensive bone loss that usually results from tooth extraction. The synthetic root implants preserved approximately twice as much bone as control sites on opposite sides of patients' mouths. Patients and dentists also observed that the oral discomfort that usually accompanies tooth loss was reduced with the use of hydroxylapatite roots implanted soon after the extractions.

Plastic sealants and fluoride, two important weapons used to fight tooth decay, were combined to produce anticavity protection that was potentially twice as strong as either substance alone. At the National Institute of Dental Research in Bethesda, Md., scientists combined fluorides and sealants into a fluoride-releasing sealant that appeared to provide children with nearly invincible armor against tooth decay. Similar to existing sealants, the new fluoride-releasing shield not only physically seals teeth from decay-causing oral bacteria but also continuously releases trace amounts of fluoride, adding increased protection against decay. The new fluoride-releasing coating, like conventional sealants, would be applied chiefly to pits and fissures, the biting surfaces of teeth where most decay occurs. The shielding of tiny predecay areas on other parts of a tooth may be accomplished by use of the new sealants.

DISASTERS

The loss of life and property from disasters in 1985 included the following:

Aviation

January 21, Reno, Nev. A four-engine Lockheed Electra charter airliner carrying 71 persons crashed moments after takeoff from Reno; the craft was

Firemen begin to remove bodies from the wreckage of a Boeing 737 that crashed during takeoff in Manchester, England, on August 22. Fifty-four persons were killed when the craft burst into flames after an engine exploded.

returning to Minneapolis after a gambling junket. Three persons survived the fiery crash.

February 1, Near Minsk, U.S.S.R. A Soviet TU-134 crashed shortly after takeoff; though no official casualty figures were released, the 80 to 90 passengers believed to be aboard were presumed dead.

February 19, Near Durango, Spain. A Spanish jetliner crashed into a mountain after striking a television relay tower some 18 mi (29 km) from the airport in Bilbao; all 148 persons aboard were killed.

February 22, Near Timbuktu, Mali. An Air Mali AN-24 turboprop passenger plane crashed and exploded on the Sahara shortly after takeoff; 50 of 51 persons aboard were killed, and the lone survivor was in critical condition.

March 28, Near San Vicente de Caguán, Colombia. A twin-engine turboprop commercial airliner slammed into a fog-shrouded mountain during a storm; all 40 persons aboard were killed.

May 3, Lvov, U.S.S.R. A Soviet airliner and a small military plane collided while approaching Lvov airport; 80 persons were reported dead.

June 23, Off the coast of Ireland. An Air-India Boeing 747 carrying 329 persons dived into the ocean, apparently after a bomb exploded aboard the aircraft; the crash, which claimed the lives of all aboard, was the worst disaster at sea in aviation history and the third worst aviation disaster to date.

July 10, U.S.S.R. A plane believed to have been carrying some 150 persons crashed between Karshi and Leningrad; all aboard perished.

July 24, Near Leticia, Colombia. A Colombian Air Force DC-6 carrying 79 persons crashed in the jungle; there were no signs of life near the wreckage.

August 2, Dallas-Fort Worth, Texas. A Delta Air Lines jumbo jet attempting to land at Dallas-Fort Worth Airport suddenly nosedived and struck several cars on Highway 114 (decaptitating one driver) before crash landing, breaking in half, and bursting into flames; 135 of the 162 persons aboard perished. Experts believed that wind shear, a sudden shift in wind direction and velocity, was responsible for the crash.

August 12, Gumma Prefecture, Japan. A Boeing 747SR Japan Air Lines jumbo jet, carrying 524 persons, crashed into Mt. Osutaka after the pilot reported that the right rear cabin door had broken and that he had lost control of the airliner; there were only 4 survivors in the worst single-plane disaster in aviation history.

August 22, Manchester, England. A Boeing 737 jetliner, carrying 137 persons, burst into flames after an engine caught fire and exploded; 54 persons were killed in the inferno.

December 12, Gander, Newfoundland. A DC-8 jetliner carrying 248 U.S. soldiers and 8 crew members crashed and exploded moments after taking off from a refueling stop; all aboard perished.

Fires and Explosions

April 21, Tabaco, Phil. A fire in a theater complex claimed the lives of 44 persons, most of them teenagers who were trampled to death when the audience panicked and rushed to the exits; 53 others were also injured, 20 of them seriously.

April 26, Saavedra, Arg. A three-hour blaze confined to the top two floors of a six-story mental hospital claimed the lives of at least 78 persons and injured 150 others.

May 11, Bradford, England. A flash fire in four minutes incinerated a 79-year-old wooden grandstand packed with some 3,500 soccer fans; 56 persons were killed, and 44 persons were in need of plastic surgery following the blaze.

Marine

January 12, Northeastern Peru. The 55-ton *Rosita* sank in the Amazon River some three hours after leaving Iquitos; 50 persons were missing and feared dead.

March 23, Near Dhaka, Bangladesh. A ferry capsized in the Buri Ganga River apparently after colliding with dredging machinery during a storm; at least 100 passengers were feared dead.

March 28, Off the coast of Guandong (Kwangtung) Province, China. A ferry carrying 228 persons capsized apparently after being buffeted by heavy winds; 77 persons lost their lives.

April 9, Saran district, Bihar, India. A boat capsized on the Ganges River, and 75 persons were feared drowned.

May 5, Sichuan (Szechwan) Province, China. A boat slammed into a rock in the Jinsha (Chin-sha) River, and 54 persons drowned.

May 26, Near Morena, India. An overcrowded boat carrying 90 passengers capsized in the middle of the Chambal River; 74 persons drowned.

Early June, Atlantic Ocean. An overloaded boat traveling from Ivory Coast to Ghana capsized and sank; 40 of the 75 persons aboard drowned.

Mid-August, Off the coast of The Bahamas. A rickety fishing boat loaded with Haitian refugees was found beached on a barren Bahamian island; seven refugees reported that smugglers had tossed at least 100 Haitians overboard, and they were feared drowned.

August 18, Near Harbin, China. An overcrowded ferry capsized after passengers ran to one side of the vessel to witness a brawl by two drunken riverboat pilots; 174 persons were feared drowned.

September 10, Bay of Bengal. Some 100 Bangladeshi crewmen were feared drowned after Thai fishermen threw them overboard and confiscated their catch, which presumably was going to be shared by the two nations.

October 5, Karnaphuli River, Bangladesh. A ferry carrying 200 persons split in half and sank after colliding with a fishing trawler; 100 persons were feared dead trapped inside the boat's hull or swept away by the strong current.

December 17, South China Sea. A boat carrying some 80 Vietnamese refugees was attacked by pirates; 50 refugees were slain and 10 women were raped.

December 18, Off the coast of Mindoro Island, Philippines. A ferry transporting some 200 persons between Palawan Island and Manila sank in the shark-infested China Sea; only 85 persons were rescued.

Mining

April 24, Off the coast of Nagasaki, Japan. An explosion in a coal mine on a small island killed 11 of the 501 workers in the mine at the time of the blast.

May 17, Hokkaido, Japan. An explosion in a coal mine, probably triggered by methane gas, killed 36 miners and injured 22 others, 7 of them seriously.

July 12, Guangdong (Kwangtung) Province, China. An explosion in a coal mine, possibly triggered by a gas leak, killed at least 47 miners; 8 others were missing and presumed dead in the blast, which blocked a tunnel entrance with some 2,000 tons of coal.

Late October, Diat and Diwata, Phil. Landslides at two gold mines buried some 300 to 400 prospectors; at least 150 miners and their families were missing and feared dead.

Miscellaneous

Late March–Early April, Somalia. A cholera epidemic, first detected at the Gannet refugee camp in northwestern Somalia, claimed the lives of more than 1,500 persons.

May 29, Brussels, Belgium. A group of drunken British soccer fans supporting the Liverpool team initiated a brawl with rival Italian fans supporting Juventus before the start of the European Champions' Cup soccer final; as the British fans attacked spectators, a concrete retaining wall collapsed and 39 persons were killed, 32 of them Italians.

Mid-June, California and Texas. An outbreak of listeria monocytogenes, linked to a Mexican-style cheese manufactured by Jalisco Mexican Products, claimed the lives of 62 persons, including at least 20 infants, some of whom were stillborn.

July 19, Stava, Italy. An earthen dam collapsed and sent a wall of mud and water cascading into an Alpine valley resort; some 250 persons died as three hotels were totally destroyed, a fourth was partially demolished, and some two dozen homes were leveled.

August 13, Bombay, India. An overcrowded three-story building in a slum collapsed during heavy monsoon rains; 52 persons were killed and 56 others were injured.

October 15, Dhaka, Bangladesh. Heavy rains gen-

Troops sift through the debris of a Boeing 747 airliner that crashed on a remote mountain in Japan on August 12, killing all but 4 of the 524 persons aboard.

REUTERS/BETTMANN NEWSPHOTOS

erated by a fierce storm in the Bay of Bengal caused the roof of the Dhaka University assembly hall to cave in on hundreds of students viewing a popular television soap opera; 71 persons were known dead and 300 others were injured.

Natural

January, Shaanxi (Shensi) Province, China. Two months of heavy rain precipitated thunderous landslides that buried entire villages; some 60 persons were killed.

January, Southern Brazil. Monthlong rains caused extensive flooding that claimed the lives of at least 71 persons and left thousands of others homeless.

Early January, Western Europe. A ten-day Arctic weather blast gripped France, Spain, Italy, and Portugal; some 200 deaths were attributed to the extreme cold.

Late January, U.S. A nationwide cold wave set record low temperatures in the East and Southeast, severely damaged Florida citrus crops, and was blamed for at least 128 deaths.

March 3, Chile. A powerful earthquake that measured 7.8 on the Richter scale at its epicenter near the village of Algarrobo shook an area of more than 1,000 mi (1,600 km) along the mountainous coast both north and south of Santiago; at least 177 persons were known dead, 2,000 others were injured, and some 150,000 persons were left homeless by the quake, which damaged some 60,000 buildings and knocked out communications.

More than 50 persons died in the crash of an express train near Viseu, Portugal, on September 11 when one train slammed into another.

AP/WIDE WORLD

Late March, Bangladesh. Early season monsoon storms flattened villages in northwestern and western Bangladesh with gigantic hailstones that took hours to melt; 750 persons succumbed and some 10,000 others were left homeless.

May 25, Bay of Bengal, Bangladesh. A devastating cyclone accompanied by 10–15-ft (3–5-m) tidal waves struck a cluster of islands at the mouth of the Ganges River, including Sandwip Island, North Hatia Island, South Hatia Island, Maiskhal Island, Bhola Char, Urrir Char, Char Clark, and Kutubdia Island; the storm's high winds reportedly swept thousands of people out to sea. Though the official death toll was placed at 2,540, some feared that as many as 11,000 people had perished.

May 31, Pennsylvania, Ohio, New York, Ontario. A 300-mi (483-km) frontal system spawned a pack of killer tornadoes that left a swath of death and destruction; at least 88 persons were known dead, hundreds were injured, and whole towns were virtually wiped out by the roaring twisters. Hardest hit were such Pennsylvania towns as Albion, Atlantic, Cherry Tree, Wheatland, and Beaver Falls.

June 6, Guangxi (Kwangsi) and Hunan provinces, China. Heavy rains sparked severe flooding that killed 64 persons and left thousands of others stranded.

June 16, Peru. A massive landslide near the Ucayali River in the Hoyada region killed scores of people.

Late June, Western India. Four days of monsoon storms battered the country, triggering landslides and heavy flooding; at least 46 persons were known dead, 50 others were injured, and 25,000 people were left homeless.

Late June, Northern Philippines. Monsoon rains precipitated three days of flooding that left at least 65 persons dead and more than 100,000 others homeless.

Mid-July, Punjab, India. Rising monsoon floodwaters claimed the lives of 87 persons and submerged at least 20 villages.

July 30, Zhejiang (Chekiang) Province, China. A deadly typhoon struck the country's eastern coast; 177 persons were known dead and at least 1,400 others were injured.

Late July–Early August, Near Dandong (Tantung), China. Two weeks of torrential rains caused raging floodwaters to slam through dikes along the China-North Korea border and the Yalu River to overflow its banks; two villages were swept away, 64 persons lost their lives, and thousands of others were left homeless.

Early August, China. Savage hailstorms, torrential rains, typhoons, and rampaging floodwaters killed more than 500 persons and left 14,000 others homeless.

August 23, Western China. A major earthquake measuring 7.4 on the Richter scale struck the sparsely settled agricultural Xinjiang Uygur (Sinkiang Uighur) autonomous region; 63 deaths were reported and about 16,000 people were left homeless.

September 19–20, Mexico City. Twin earthquakes, the first measuring 8.1 on the Richter scale and the second, the following day, measuring 7.5, reduced much of the city to rubble; more than 20,000 persons were killed, at least 40,000 were injured, and 31,000 others were left homeless.

October 7, Ponce, P.R. A two-day tropical deluge triggered a massive mud-and-rock slide that buried some 150 persons in their tin and wood shacks on the hillside in the shantytown of Mameyes.

October 18–19, India. Severe flooding, precipitated by raging storms, claimed 78 lives.

October 19, Luzon, Phil. Devastating Typhoon Dot battered the island and virtually demolished the capital city of Cabanatuan, destroying 90% of the buildings and causing an estimated $5.3 million in damages; 63 persons were known dead.

Early November, West Virginia, Virginia, Maryland, and Pennsylvania. A staggering 20 in (50 cm) of rainfall in a 12-hour period caused swollen rivers to overflow their banks, thereby destroying thousands of homes and killing at least 49 persons; property damage in the Virginias alone was estimated at half a billion dollars.

November 13, Armero, Colombia. The long-dormant snowcapped volcano known as Nevado del Ruiz came to life with a double eruption that melted the mountain's icecap and sent a liquid avalanche (lahar) of dirty water, gray ash, and mud cascading down its slopes, thereby burying the sleeping town of Armero; thousands were injured, 60,000 persons were left homeless, and more than 25,000 people were feared dead in one of the ten worst volcanic disasters in history.

Railroads

January 13, Near Awash, Eth. A five-car passenger train derailed while traveling over a bridge and plunged into a ravine apparently because the engineer, who was later arrested, had failed to slow the train as it rounded a curve; 392 persons were known dead and nearly 400 others were injured.

February 23, Near Raipur, India. A predawn fire aboard a packed passenger train claimed the lives of 50 persons, including a honeymoon couple and 18 members of their wedding party.

June 13, Agra, India. A passenger train and a freight train collided head-on near the Taj Mahal; 37 persons died in the crash.

July 24, Kywebwe, Burma. A passenger train derailed when rebels set off a land mine under the tracks; 67 persons were known dead and 112 others were injured.

August 3, Flaujac-Gare, France. A four-car passenger train and a local two-car "autorail" collided head-on apparently after the stationmaster gave the go-ahead for both trains to move toward each other on the same track; 35 passengers were killed and 165 others were injured in the crash.

AP/WIDE WORLD

Mudslides destroyed as many as 400 houses, killing some 150 persons, on October 7 in Puerto Rico following three days of torrential rains.

August 31, Near Argenton-sur-Creuse, France. A speeding passenger train, traveling in a repair zone at nearly three times the speed limit, derailed and then collided with a mail train traveling in the opposite direction; 49 persons were killed and nearly 100 others were injured, 10 of them critically.

September 11, Near Viseu, Port. An express train carrying laborers bound for France slammed into a local passenger train; at least 50 persons perished in the blazing wreckage.

Traffic

March 27, Near Johannesburg, South Africa. A double-decker school bus ran out of control presumably after a tire blowout, crashed through a fence, and plunged into the Westdene Dam reservoir; 39 high school students drowned and 28 others were injured, 5 of them critically.

September 1, Northern Pakistan. A speeding bus carrying 76 persons went out of control and plummeted into a mountain ravine in the remote Malakand region; 40 persons were killed.

November 21, Java, Indonesia. A truck carrying construction workers swerved to avoid a motorcycle, fell off a bridge, and plunged into a river in the southeastern district of Kepanjeng; 45 persons were killed and 13 others were injured.

DOMINICA

In general elections on July 1, 1985, the Dominica Freedom Party was returned to office with Eugenia Charles as prime minister. Her party won 15 of the 21 elected seats in Parliament, two fewer than it had won in the previous elections, held in July 1980. Among the candidates elected for the opposition Labour Party of Dominica was former prime minister Patrick John, who was facing retrial on a charge of conspiring to overthrow the government in 1981. In October John was sentenced to 12 years' imprisonment. Rosie Douglas, a left-wing independent and brother of Labour leader Michael

Douglas, defeated a government-backed independent, former acting president Jenner Armour.

Presenting the 1985–86 budget in August 1985, Prime Minister Charles stated that the government had achieved a surplus of EC$400,000 on the previous year's recurrent budget, compared with a deficit of EC$17.3 million in 1980–81, its first year in office. (For table of world currencies, *see* International Exchange and Payments.) The balance of payments deficit had been halved from EC$40.2 million in 1980 to EC$20.8 million in 1984. Inflation had declined from 30.5 to 2.2%, and unemployment had been reduced from 23 to 13%. The government indicated that during its second term it aimed to expand agricultural exports, agroprocessing, and tourism.

DOMINICAN REPUBLIC

Pres. Salvador Jorge Blanco's government appeared likely to pay a high political price for securing a 12-month standby loan worth 78.5 million Special Drawing Rights from the International Monetary Fund (IMF) in 1985. (For table of world currencies, *see* International Exchange and Payments.) At IMF insistence the government devalued the peso by 69% against the U.S. dollar when the official and parallel exchange rates were unified in January. There were echoes of the previous year's widespread rioting when, in February, violent protests against fuel price increases left at least four people dead. Faced with the threat of a general strike, President Jorge Blanco approved a 43% increase in the public-sector minimum wage in July.

With elections scheduled for May 1986, support for the political parties seemed finely balanced. The ruling Dominican Revolutionary Party was deeply divided, however, increasing the chances of victory for either the right-wing Reformist Party or the left-wing Dominican Liberation Party.

The trade deficit remained high, at $388 million, and the foreign debt had grown to $3.5 billion. In June commercial bank creditors rescheduled debts worth $787 million; the following month Paris Club creditors had agreed to reschedule $127 million over 11 years plus arrears amounting to $86 million over 6 years.

DRUGS

The most controversial drug issue during the year was the testing and availability of drugs to treat acquired immune deficiency syndrome (AIDS). According to the U.S. Centers for Disease Control, as many as one million U.S. citizens might already have been infected with the AIDS virus, and in the absence of a vaccine or therapy the number of cases of AIDS would continue to rise. While no medicine had yet been found to prevent or cure the disease, a number of encouraging developments emerged during 1985. The AIDS virus, HTLV-III, had been identified and a test approved for screening blood for presence of the HTLV-III antibody, thus indicating exposure to the virus. The U.S. Food and Drug Administration (FDA) approved a drug that effectively treats *Pneumocystis carinii,* which causes a fatal form of pneumonia that often strikes AIDS patients as well as other persons with disorders of the immune system. The drug was sold as Pentam 300 (pentamidine). Tests of three different kinds of drugs were under way. These were antiviral drugs that were shown to inhibit the replication of HTLV-III in a laboratory setting, immunoenhancer drugs, and, paradoxically, an immunosuppressive drug.

The experimental antiviral drugs included the following:
- Sodium suramin (Suramin), an antiparasitic drug used to treat African sleeping sickness and river blindness. Laboratory tests show that Suramin can block growth of the AIDS virus and inhibit its ability to attack the body's immune system. However, it has severe side effects.
- Ribavirin (Virazole), which was shown to inhibit the growth of HTLV-III in the laboratory. Side effects in some AIDS patients in a few studies conducted at university hospitals have included severe anemia.
- Azidothymidine (BWA509U), which was shown to inhibit both the infectivity and replication of HTLV-III. Studies to confirm laboratory findings were under way.
- HPA-23 was reported to inhibit the growth of HTLV-III in the laboratory. Made by a French pharmaceutical company, and reportedly used to treat U.S. movie star Rock Hudson, this drug was used on 46 other patients at the Pasteur Institute in Paris. It appeared to have no beneficial effect.

Among the immune-enhancing drugs being tested was interferon, a natural antiviral substance shown to have immune-stimulating and antitumor effects.

Reye's Syndrome

A pilot study reported by the U.S. Public Health Service strengthened evidence of an association between aspirin and Reye's syndrome. This acute, life-threatening condition sometimes develops in children between the stages of infancy and late adolescence who are recovering from a viral illness such as flu or chicken pox. The Department of Health and Human Services asked makers of aspirin products to voluntarily remove information on labels recommending that aspirin be used to treat flu or chicken pox in children and teenagers, and that an appropriate warning be added to the labels as well. The Aspirin Foundation of America, which represented major aspirin manufacturers, subsequently established a Voluntary Reye's Syndrome Precautionary Program that included label changes, warnings, and a major education program.

Warnings, Frauds, and New Drugs

A major study conducted in 1985 showed that women in the first trimester of pregnancy who take

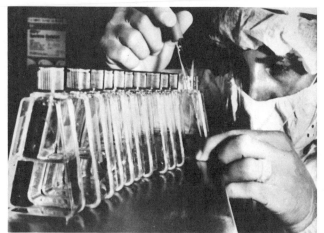

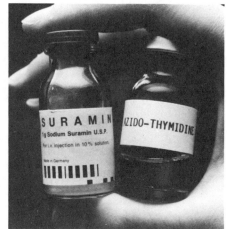

Concern over the medical and public policy issues surrounding AIDS increased during the year. (Above left) A drug technician prepares cell cultures used to develop a series of new AIDS diagnostic tests. (Above right) Among the many drugs tested against AIDS were sodium suramin and azidothymidine. (Right) French medical researchers claimed to have found a drug treatment that was very effective in stopping AIDS. Scientists in the U.S., however, were highly critical of the French claim, which they described as very premature.

(ABOVE LEFT) AP/WIDE WORLD; (ABOVE RIGHT) BILL BALLENBERG/DISCOVER MAGAZINE; (RIGHT) VIOUJARD—GAMMA/LIAISON

the antiacne drug Accutane (isotretinoin), a compound chemically related to vitamin A, have 25 times the normal risk of delivering a malformed baby. The drug, considered the medicine of last resort for those with severe acne, had been known to be dangerous to the early fetus when the drug was approved. Accordingly, the manufacturer had warned physicians and the general public of this danger from the outset.

During the year the National Institutes of Health suspended distribution of human growth hormone through the National Hormone and Pituitary Program. This hormone, prepared from human pituitary glands removed at autopsy, had been used to treat pituitary dwarfism. But the deaths from a rare affliction, Creutzfeldt-Jakob disease, of three men who had received the hormone suggested that the hormone could have become contaminated. This led to suspension of distribution of the hormone pending further evaluation of its safety. Fortunately for the 10,000 to 15,000 U.S. children who suffer from growth hormone deficiency, a genetically engineered growth hormone, somatrem (Protropin), was approved by the FDA during the year.

In accordance with its strengthened commitment against health fraud, the FDA took action during the

year to remove from interstate commerce a number of products. These included all so-called "chelation therapy" capsules and tablets promoted for home use to prevent or treat cardiovascular disease and touted as useful to prevent memory loss, senility, and gangrene and for promoting longevity and an enhanced sex life. These products usually consisted of vitamins, minerals, and amino acids and had no proven benefit for preventing or treating cardiovascular disease. Genuine chelation agents are substances that combine with metals and are used to combat poisoning from heavy metals, digitalis overdoses, and excess calcium. For such treatment physicians inject FDA-approved chelating drugs.

The FDA also acted to prevent the sale of two unproven drugs purported to produce weight loss. These drugs were CCK (cholecystokinin), a hormone involved in the human digestive system, and DHA (dehydroepiandrosterone or dehydroandrosterone), a steroidal hormone often sold as a food supplement. Neither substance had been shown to be safe or effective.

New regulations issued by the FDA were expected to dramatically speed the federal government's review of new drugs and upgrade drug safety monitoring. These regulations were expected to cut as much as six months or 20% on average from the two years or more now required for drug approval. One analysis showed that a speed-up of just two months for 15 therapeutically significant drugs per year would benefit more than 200,000 U.S. citizens.

Among the new drugs approved during the year, many under the new regulations, were Ridaura (auranofin), an oral gold compound to treat rheumatoid arthritis; Seldane (terfenadine), an antihistamine with little or no sedating side effects; a drug to treat the severe nausea often associated with cancer chemotherapy, Marinol (whose active ingredient, dronabinol, is a synthetic form of the principal active ingredient in marijuana); a new form of a 20-year-old anti-inflammatory drug, Indocin (indomethacin), found to correct a life-threatening heart defect, patent ductus arteriosus, that sometimes occurs in premature babies; and Lupron (leuprolide acetate), a self-injectable drug for managing advanced prostate cancer.

Another new drug includes the first oral medication, Zovirax (acyclovir), to prevent or reduce recurrent outbreaks of genital herpes, the second most common sexually transmitted disease, with 300,000 new cases each year.

An important new vaccine, b-Capsa I (Hemophilus b polysaccharide), was developed that protects against *Hemophilus influenzae,* type b (Hib), the most common cause of serious childhood bacterial meningitis. One of the leading infectious disease problems of childhood, each year Hib caused some 12,000 cases of meningitis, primarily in children under the age of five, as well as about 7,500 cases of pneumonia, infectious arthritis, blood infection, and epiglottitis, a swelling in the throat that can lead to suffocation. Hib infection led to an estimated 1,000 deaths each year and to neurological damage ranging from hearing impairment to some form of brain damage in some 3,000 to 4,000 children.

In addition to drugs already approved for marketing, a major government-sponsored study of a genetically engineered blood-clot dissolver showed it to be twice as effective as other medication used to halt heart attacks. Made from tissue plasminogen activator, or TPA, one of the substances found in the body in minute quantities as part of the normal clot-removal process, TPA theoretically offered a significant advantage over the other approved blood clot dissolvers, streptokinase and urokinase, in that these enzymes work throughout the body and thus can lead to unwanted bleeding. TPA, on the other hand, activates the clot-removing mechanism only in the immediate vicinity of the clot.

EARTH SCIENCES

In 1985 the Deep Sea Drilling Project and its research drilling ship *Glomar Challenger* were succeeded by the Ocean Drilling Program (ODP) and a new vessel, the *JOIDES Resolution.* Leg 100, the first cruise of the ODP, tested the drilling systems and the scientific laboratories on board. Results

from Leg 101, in the Bahama archipelago, favored the theory that isolated areas like The Bahamas are remnants of a vast carbonate platform, extending from Mexico to the eastern U.S., that was disrupted in the mid-Cretaceous Period (about 100 million years ago) over the theory that the topography formed much earlier when the African and North American continents were rifted apart 160 million years ago.

The recently proposed idea that clay minerals might serve as templates capable of self-replication and that these inorganic protoorganisms were the forerunners of later biomolecules, the primitive genes, found support in the discovery that clay has the ability to absorb, store, and transfer energy, which would be necessary for chemical reactions involving organic life. Energy storage in clays, perhaps achieved by capturing photons of light in lattice defects, was revealed by the slow emission of ultraviolet light when the clays were wetted, fractured, or irradiated.

The hypothesis that an event triggered by the collision of some astronomical body with the Earth caused the extinction of many life forms at the Cretaceous-Tertiary boundary, 65 million years ago, gained strength and supporters. Remarkable new evidence was reported in 1985 by Edward Anders and colleagues of the University of Chicago. They discovered concentrations of sooty carbon in the sediment layer corresponding to the time of impact that were 10,000 times higher than in sediments above and below. They concluded that the carbon came from global firestorms ignited by the fireball spreading out from the impact site. The recent discovery of spherules in some rocks that might be parts of ejecta blankets surrounding impact sites suggested that more detailed investigations might permit location of the impact site responsible for the Cretaceous-Tertiary event.

The idea that an earlier, larger impact on the Earth might have formed the Moon was discussed at the 16th Lunar and Planetary Science Conference in Houston, Texas, in 1985. According to the new impact-trigger hypothesis, a giant object perhaps as large as Mars smashed obliquely into the Earth near the end of its accretion period, after the core had formed and while the mantle was at least partly molten. The impact caused ejection of material from both the Earth and the other body, which subsequently aggregated in orbit around the Earth to form the Moon. Geochemists agreed that the mantles of the Earth and Moon have similar compositions and that most of the geochemical differences between the two are understandable in terms of the large-impact hypothesis. Dynamic and thermal modeling of the processes of impact, ejection, and aggregation supported the hypothesis, while dynamicists mounted strong arguments against the three classical hypotheses for origin of the Moon; *i.e.,* that it was a part of the Earth ripped away by tidal forces, that it was an independent body captured by the Earth's gravity, or that it formed in orbit around the Earth at the time of the origin of the solar system.

The large-impact origin requires a totally molten Moon to begin with, an idea consistent with the concept of a magma ocean that had been formulated to explain the origin of lunar rocks. The geochemical approaches, however, had not yet resolved the question of whether the magma ocean was confined to the outer several hundred miles or whether the Moon had been totally molten. In fact, some petrologists were abandoning the concept of a magma ocean in favor of a solid Moon, a position that appeared difficult to defend against the results of dynamic and thermal modeling.

The concept of a magma ocean was carried from the Moon to the Earth with a proposition that, if the density of magma at depth were higher than that of mantle rock, a layer of magma might remain below the lithosphere. The first relevant measurements were reported in a paper on "Densities of Liquid Silicates at High Pressures," which in 1985 earned the Newcomb-Cleveland Prize for the best paper in the periodical *Science* for S. Rigden, T. J. Ahrens, and E. M. Stolper of the California Institute of Technology (Caltech). The experiments were conducted in a shock-wave apparatus in which high-speed projectiles were fired for the first time at molten targets instead of solid material, and they permitted determinations of the density of the liquid at pressures equivalent to a depth of 435 mi (700 km). The results indicated that magmas that are formed by partial melting of mantle rock at depths greater than 155–215 mi (250–350 km) indeed may be more dense than the solid. Therefore, if melts formed in the Earth at these depths, they would sink rather than rise. Furthermore, they

would carry with them the heat-producing radioactive elements uranium and potassium-40, which were generally considered to be concentrated into the Earth's crust by rising magmas and volcanism. This process would require significant revision of interpretations of the geochemical and thermal evolution of the Earth and of other planetary bodies.

The Columbia Glacier, an ice mass 3 mi (4.8 km) wide near Valdez, Alaska, began to retreat in 1978 after at least 80 years of stability. Two years later the U.S. Geological Survey predicted on the basis of mathematical models that the glacier would begin to retreat more rapidly. The prediction was confirmed by 1985 when the glacier experienced a drastic retreat, with accelerating breakup. The models had successfully incorporated, for the first time, the effect of loss of ice due to calving from the glacier. Over the next 30–50 years the glacier could retreat as much as 19 mi (30 km).

Elsewhere in Alaska the Variegated Glacier experienced a forward surge in 1982–83, with an increase in flow speeds from about 0.7 ft (0.2 m) per day to as much as 213 ft (65 m) per day. The observation of this surge culminated a multiyear program of field measurements by Barclay Kamb of Caltech and coworkers. They explained the cause and mechanism of surging, a central unsolved problem in glacier mechanics, in terms of a physical model in a 1985 publication. Their measurements showed that the surge motion was due to rapid sliding at the base of the glacier, caused by high basal water pressure. In the nonsurging state water is transported by way of a few large basal tunnels, whereas in the surging state the tunnels are destroyed and water transport takes place through a linked-cavity system between the ice sole and the glacier bed. The role of water pressure is similar to its role in overthrust faulting of

More than 100 buildings collapsed in Mexico City on September 19 and as many as 20,000 persons were killed when an earthquake of magnitude 8.1 occurred a few miles onshore on the west coast of Mexico.

BARR—GAMMA/LIAISON

rocks and in landsliding. The advance of the surge front involves the development of a succession of thrust faults and folds in the ice, analogous to the imbricated (overlapping) structures in tectonic fold-and-thrust belts.

Geophysics

Along the southwest coast of Mexico the Cocos Plate, a massive slab of the Earth's crust, is sliding under the North American Plate at a rate of two to four inches (five to ten centimeters) per year. This subduction causes a very high level of seismic activity including frequent large earthquakes. In the late 1970s scientists discovered a gap, or locked section, of this boundary where seismicity was much lower than that of adjacent sections. Named the Michoacán Gap, it was postulated to be the most likely site for the next major earthquake. Accordingly the region was extensively instrumented with seismographs.

On the morning of Sept. 19, 1985, the long vigil produced results when an earthquake of magnitude 8.1 occurred at 18.2° N, 102.6° W, a few miles onshore. The nearest coastal cities and the towns and villages of the eastward mountains suffered some damage and a few fatalities, but minutes later, when the train of shock waves reached the alluvial lake bed upon which most of downtown Mexico City is built, about 230 mi (370 km) from the epicenter, a major disaster resulted. Of the wide range of frequencies in the train that passed through the alluvium, certain of them were attuned to the physical configuration of the lake bed, causing resonance and great amplification of the motion. When these movements were transmitted to the buildings, similar resonant vibrations were induced. As a result more than 100 buildings collapsed in the center of the city, and many more were either damaged beyond repair or rendered unsafe for habitation. Then, on the following day, amid massive rescue efforts, a very large aftershock of magnitude 7.5 endangered rescue workers and added to the destruction. Near the year's end the death toll was estimated at more than 20,000, and many hundreds were still missing.

Seismicity elsewhere during the year included several earthquakes of magnitude greater than 7.0 that resulted in death and property damage. One, of magnitude 7.8, occurred on March 3 near the coast of central Chile and was followed on April 9 by another shock, of magnitude 7.2, in the same area. An earthquake of estimated magnitude 7.4 occurred in the Hindu Kush on July 29, triggering avalanches in the epicentral area and in Tadzhikistan and northern India. On August 23 an earthquake of magnitude 7.5 struck near the Xinjiang-Kirgiz (Sinkiang-Kirgiz) Sino-Soviet border. The Wuqia-Shufu (Wu-ch'ia-Shu-fu) area of China and the Andizhan-Fergana-Namangan region of the U.S.S.R. were the most affected by the shock. At least eight other earthquakes, all of moderate size, also caused fatalities.

The first official earthquake prediction to be endorsed by the U.S. National Earthquake Prediction Evaluation Council and its California counterpart was issued during the year. Its forecast, that a shock between magnitude 5.5 and 6.0 would occur near Parkfield, Calif., before 1993, was based on the historical regularity of Parkfield earthquakes. Shocks had been reported in the vicinity in 1857, 1881, 1901, 1922, 1934, and 1966, with an average interval of 22 years. The council's panel members agreed that the potential existed for the next earthquake to be larger than magnitude 6.0 and for fault rupture to extend to the adjacent segment of the San Andreas Fault, but the data were insufficient to include these factors in the prediction.

One of the worst volcanic disasters in history took place on November 13 when the long-dormant Nevado del Ruiz, a 17,700-ft (5,400-m) peak in central Colombia, violently erupted, melting part of the mountain's ice cap and sending a flood of mud, ash, and stones down its flanks. The deluge poured into several river valleys located around the base of the mountain and buried almost all of the town of Armero on the Lagunilla River. Several other towns were also badly damaged. The Colombian government estimated the death toll at more than 25,000, with many thousands injured and homeless.

Nevado del Ruiz, about 90 mi (140 km) west

More than 25,000 persons died in November after the eruption of the Colombian volcano known as Nevado del Ruiz. A double eruption melted the mountain's ice cap and sent a liquid avalanche of dirty water, ash, and mud cascading down its slopes, burying the sleeping town of Armero.

BARR—GAMMA/LIAISON

The Columbia Glacier in Alaska began a drastic retreat and accelerated breakup during the year, thereby confirming a prediction made by the U.S. Geological Survey in 1980.

AP/WIDE WORLD

of Bogotá, lies at the northern end of a chain of two dozen active volcanoes along the Andean Cordillera Central. It was believed to have erupted at least six times in the past 3,000 years, including one in 1595 that was recorded by Spanish explorers and another in 1845 that produced mudslides and killed 1,000. In December 1984 the volcano began emitting large quantities of sulfurous gases, and in ensuing months seismographs detected numerous small tremors within the mountain. On September 11 a small explosion produced steam and ash. As a result the Colombian government, with the help of volcanologists from Costa Rica, Ecuador, and the U.S., began to monitor the volcano and to prepare warning and evacuation plans. Before these plans could be implemented, however, the disaster struck.

The November 13 eruption took the form of two directed blasts, about 90 minutes apart, on the northeast side of the volcano. These explosions dissolved a portion of the ice cap and sent mud and ash hurtling down the Azufrado riverbed on the eastern slope at speeds estimated at 20–30 mph (30–50 km/hr). The mudflow then pushed into the Lagunilla River, burst through a natural dam just upstream of Armero, and inundated the town. On the western side of the mountain, a second mudslide surged over hundreds of homes and killed as many as 1,000 in the town of Chinchiná.

In the early morning of December 25, Mt. Etna on the island of Sicily erupted, sending several rivers of lava down its flanks. Earthquakes triggered by the activity caused the collapse of a resort hotel on the mountain's slope, killing one person.

Following the designation by the U.S. in 1983 of an Exclusive Economic Zone (EEZ) extending 200 mi (320 km) from its shores, the U.S. Geological Survey (USGS) developed an important program, EEZ-SCAN, designed to map this zone systematically using long-range side-scan sonar equipment. The heart of the EEZ-SCAN program, in which the USGS was cooperating with the Institute of Oceanographic Sciences (IOS) in the U.K., was the Geological Long-range Inclined Asdic, the GLORIA II. The GLORIA II, developed by the IOS, was a two-ton side-scan sonar device, 26 ft (8 m) in length, which was towed 985 ft (300 m) behind the research ship at a depth of 165 ft (50 m). It could be towed at ten knots and could scan a swath of sea bottom 37 mi (60 km) wide. A row of 30 transducers on each side of the device emitted sonar pulses of 6.5 KHz. Return signals were recorded digitally and displayed visually as they were received.

By September 1984 the British research ship *Farnella* had completed four cruises with the GLORIA II and had mapped 250,000 sq mi (650,000 sq km) of Pacific seafloor between the Mexican and Canadian borders. This high-resolution system provided more intricate detail of submarine structures and much more thorough coverage than previously attainable. The data were being processed using computer-enhancement techniques developed by the USGS for space and planetary science programs and adapted for side-scan sonar use. An atlas of these interpretations consisting of 33 maps at a scale of 1:150,000 was scheduled for publication in early 1986. After several months of planning and preparation, the *Farnella* set sail in August 1985 to map the coast of the Gulf of Mexico.

ECONOMIC AFFAIRS

World economic growth during 1985 slowed significantly in comparison with 1984. During that year member countries of the Organization for Economic Cooperation and Development (OECD) recorded a gain in gross domestic product (GDP) of 4.5%. However, in 1985 business activity became weaker in most countries, and the latest available information suggested that growth for the full year was unlikely to exceed 3%. Some deceleration in growth also occurred in the principal oil-exporting and the less developed countries, although the extent of this could not be estimated meaningfully

STEVE SACK; REPRINTED WITH PERMISSION FROM THE MINNEAPOLIS STAR

owing to the unavailability of up-to-date statistical information.

The World Economy

The principal reason for 1985's relatively poor performance was the loss of momentum in the U.S. economy. In 1984 GDP in the U.S. rose by 6.8%, outperforming just about every comparable country. In 1985, however, growth was thought to have fallen back to about 2.7%. This was in spite of a relatively relaxed fiscal and monetary policy and a steady downward trend of interest rates. Inevitably, a slowdown of this magnitude in the world's most powerful economy could not but have an adverse effect on the performance of other countries.

Private consumption accounted for the largest single component of the expenditure on gross domestic product in all developed as well as most other countries. In 1984 private consumption was relatively sluggish everywhere except in the U.S. In 1985 the case was reversed, with consumers' expenditure growth slowing from 5.3 to about 3.5% in the U.S. but accelerating a little in Japan, West Germany, and the U.K.

A common feature of the world's economies during 1985 was a spectacular deterioration in foreign trade performance. On the basis of incomplete data, it was estimated that world trade, as measured by world exports, grew by approximately 4% in volume terms, compared with a gain in excess of 8% in 1984. It appeared that hardly any country enjoyed an increase in export sales and that a significant number faced a massive decline in the volume of merchandise sold abroad. Thus, Japanese exports, which were affected adversely by the weakness of the U.S. market, an increase in protectionist sentiments, and a strong appreciation in the external value of the yen, grew by some 8–9%, as against an increase of 16% in 1984. Exports by the U.S. rose by about 3–4%, as against more than 7% in the previous year, partly because the rapid rise in the value of the dollar to February 1985 made U.S. products less competitive. Oil-producing countries were confronted with reduced demand for energy in the industrialized world and therefore experienced a cutback in exports of about 4%. As in other areas of economic achievement, the larger European countries seemed to do relatively well, with both the U.K. and West Germany experiencing a decline of only some 2% from their 1984 growth rates to 6.5 and 7%, respectively.

Exports from the non-oil less developed countries appeared to be weaker in 1985 than in 1984. However, a development of even greater consequence for those countries was the weakness of commodity prices. Harvests and/or crop prospects were generally good in both 1984 and 1985. As a result both food commodities and agricultural raw materials were in good supply at a time when the slowdown in the developed world's growth created a weakness in demand. The result was a significant decline in prices (estimated at 13% in the case of food and 8–9% in the case of agricultural raw materials), which had an adverse effect on the foreign exchange earnings of the producing countries. Lower oil consumption and the reduction in the developed world's oil stocks caused a further decline of about 2% in the price of oil, but metal prices appeared to have suffered little or no decline. The effect of declining commodity prices on less developed countries was aggravated by the fall in value of the dollar (which raised the price of manufactured products in dollar terms) and resulted in a massive shift in the terms of trade in favor of the industrialized world.

In 1985, as in the previous year, the world financial scene was dominated by the massive fiscal and foreign payments deficits of the U.S. and the large surpluses of Japan and West Germany. Consequently, the U.S. remained a significant net importer of capital, making it more difficult for the weaker economies of the world, many of which faced problems in meeting their debt repayment and servicing schedules, to finance their deficits. Unlike 1984, however, most of 1985 was characterized by a gradual fall in the external value of the dollar. This was partly a result of the gradual decline in the level of U.S. interest rates as well as concerted action by the U.S. and other major industrial countries to force the dollar down to more realistic levels. As a result the trade-weighted value of the U.S. dollar in terms of the world's leading currencies was some 18% lower in early December than at the start of the year, more than offsetting the appreciation recorded during 1984.

Economic Policies of the United States

U.S. economic performance during the first half of 1985 was worse than most forecasters had projected at the start of the year. Expectations were raised by the robust growth in the gross national product (GNP) in the final quarter of 1984 (4.9% annual rate) that the economy had recovered from the summer slowdown. However, real GNP rose by a disappointing 0.3% annual rate during the first quarter of 1985 and by 1.9% in the second. Thus, the economy expanded by only 2% during the first half of 1985, compared with the same period a year earlier. A much faster than expected rebound in the economy pushed up the GNP growth rate in the third quarter to 4.3%. In the absence of clear economic indicators, however, expectations about the final quarter varied. The administration's view was that the economy had entered into a new growth phase, while many private economists and analysts believed that the underlying trend was still sluggish and that in the final quarter the growth rate would slip back to the 2.5–3% range. Even if the economy did not falter in the closing quarter, the GNP growth for 1985 as a whole would not exceed 2.7%, a far cry from the 6.8% registered in 1984.

The lackluster performance of the economy during the first half of the year hid the fact that real domestic demand was quite strong during that period. Personal consumption rose by 4%, fixed domestic investment by 6.8%, and government expenditure by 5.5%. The reason that the strength of the domestic demand was not fully translated into real GNP growth was the sharp deterioration in net exports and a deceleration in stockbuilding. Imports in the first half of 1985 rose by 11.3% over the same period of 1984, while exports on the same basis registered a decline of 2.5%.

It was not surprising that industrial output slowed dramatically during 1985 under the onslaught of cheap imports and the increased uncompetitiveness of U.S. exports in the world markets. At the beginning of 1984, industrial production stood 15% higher than at the beginning of 1983, but by the end of 1984, it was only 6.8% higher and the growth by August 1985 had all but evaporated to 1%. Growth in industrial production when measured against 1984 was expected to become negative before the end of 1985. New orders by manufacturers were affected by the same insidious process of domestic demand leaking out of the economy. After a poor performance during 1984, manufacturers' new orders rose by only 0.8% during the first ten months of 1985. Until the value of the dollar declined appreciably, no change in the state of the order books was expected.

While most output indicators during 1985 were faltering, housing starts maintained their strength. During the late summer they were about 10% above the level of a year earlier. It had been argued that the strength of housing starts is consistent with low utilization of industrial capacity, which frees capital and labor for the more speculative residential sector. It was also consistent with lower interest rates and the availability of credit, reflecting the less restrictive monetary policy.

The underlying personal income growth remained at a healthy rate of 0.3–0.4% per month for most of the year. This on its own would have maintained a reasonable momentum of retail sales, but it was reinforced by a sharp decline in the percentage of income that was saved as consumers reacted pos-

MICHAEL EVANS/TIME MAGAZINE

Sen. Bill Bradley, a Democrat from New Jersey, and Rep. Jack Kemp, a Republican from New York, confer during the U.S. Congressional Summit on Exchange Rates and the Dollar.

itively to price-cutting campaigns. In August, for instance, this savings ratio sank to 2.8%, the lowest level since the panic buying during the Korean War. However, the hectic growth pace of 8.3% in retail sales during the first nine months of 1985 was not expected to be maintained during the closing quarter of the year.

Consumer price inflation remained remarkably stable throughout 1985 at about 3.5%. In fact, during the second half of the year it even managed a slight reduction to 3%. Strong competition from cheap imports, which, in turn, was buoyed by the strong dollar, was the main reason. These competitive pressures caused the prices of manufactured goods to rise by less than 1%, while services, which are not prone to foreign competition, registered much higher price rises. Because services have a larger share in the consumer price index, virtually all of the consumer price increase in 1985 was attributed to rising prices in services.

The continued strength of domestic demand and the resilience of the dollar fueled an inexorable rise in imports, while exports stagnated. After trade deficits of $69.4 billion in 1983 and $123.3 billion in 1984, based on the figures available until September a record deficit of $150 billion for 1985 appeared inevitable. However, thanks to a moderation in the trade deficit during the final quarter, brought about by the unexpectedly large decline in the value of the dollar in November, a smaller deficit (perhaps as low as $138 billion) seemed probable. Inevitably the current account deficit widened and was expected to be in the region of $120 billion, nearly 20% higher than in 1984 and three times as high as the deficit in 1983. The ever rising current account deficit was financed largely by capital inflows from abroad attracted by high interest rates and the strength of the dollar.

In September the United States became a debtor nation for the first time since World War I. Foreign ownership of U.S. assets exceeded U.S. ownership of foreign assets by about $30 billion. Given the continually deepening trade deficit, it was not surprising that protectionist sentiment increased alarmingly. No fewer than 200 protectionist bills were brought before Congress in the autumn. Because many of them were designed specifically to reduce foreign competition rather than to open up foreign markets to U.S. exports, they conflicted with the administration's free-trade principles. The possibility of a presidential veto of such bills threatened a huge rift between the president and the Congress. The only long-term solution to the massive trade imbalance of the U.S. would be a lower exchange rate.

An agreement in September between the Group of Five—the five major industrial countries (U.S., Japan, West Germany, U.K., and France)—to step up their efforts to intervene in the foreign exchange market was another attempt to engineer a decline in the value of the dollar. In the short term this had the desired effect, and by December the dollar had depreciated by 20% against the yen, 14% against the Deutsche Mark, and 10% against the pound sterling.

While the decline in the value of the dollar marked the beginning of the correction of one of the imbalances in the economy, the trade deficit, by the year's end there was no real progress toward closing the federal deficit. Fiscal policy during 1985 remained expansionary. Increased defense spending and higher interest payments on the national debt reversed the previous year's trend.

Compared with a deficit of $175 billion during fiscal 1984 (ended Sept. 30, 1984), fiscal 1985 registered a deficit of $210 billion, nearly 5.4% of the GNP. The administration's budget proposals introduced in February envisioned reducing the budget deficit to $180 billion, or 4.5% of the GNP. Initially, the president proposed a 12.6% increase in defense expenditure. Apart from debt servicing most other programs were to be either frozen or cut

back. Based on an economic growth rate of 4% per year, the president's proposals envisioned a decline in the budget deficit to $144 billion, or 2.9% of the GNP, by the end of President Reagan's term. In the ensuing budget battle with the Congress, it was effectively agreed to freeze defense spending and not provide for indexation of Social Security in 1986.

When the economy entered into a growth recession in the second half of 1984, the Federal Reserve Board (Fed) relaxed its monetary stance to avoid sending the economy into an outright recession. The monetary growth targets announced at the beginning of 1985, while slightly lower than the previous year, were sufficiently high to accommodate an inflation rate of 3–3.5% and a similar growth rate without undue upward pressure on interest rates. In the opening months of the year, when monetary aggregates grew much faster than the upper limit of the target range, the response of the Fed was a modest tightening of its monetary growth policy; this led to slightly higher interest rates.

Later, as the economy was stunned into a growth recession by the strong expansionary forces generated by the huge budget deficit (which kept domestic demand growth strong) and the contractionary forces released by the overvalued dollar, the Fed shifted its policy to accommodate faster monetary growth. By adopting a policy of lower interest rates against a background of relatively fast monetary growth, it hoped to foster a downward trend in the value of the dollar. Although this policy was only moderately successful in the summer, it was perhaps instrumental in underpinning the flagging economy. After the September meeting of the Group of Five, however, the continuation of an accommodating monetary policy together with concerted intervention in the foreign exchange markets appeared to have been more successful in putting greater downward pressure on the dollar.

Leaders of the world's seven most advanced industrialized nations and a representative from the commission of the EC met in Bonn, West Germany, in May to discuss trade and monetary issues.

FRANCIS APESTEGUY/CHIP HIRES— GAMMA/LIAISON

Special Report: A Field Guide to Corporate Mergers

by Alan J. Auerbach

The heightened level of merger activity that began in the U.S. in 1984 continued into 1985, amid calls for increased regulation of the behavior of the corporations involved. Many attributed the increase in mergers to the liberalized antitrust position taken by the Justice Department under the Reagan administration, but there have been many other explanations as well, ranging from changes in industrial structure to innovations in the methods of financing acquisitions and changes in tax law.

Though there had been "merger waves" in the past, most recently in the late 1960s, many aspects of the current boom in corporate combinations made it different from and more controversial than those of earlier times. Chief among them were the enormous scale of the largest mergers, the spirited tactics adopted by managements in defending against hostile takeover attempts, the financial innovations that allowed small firms to gain control of much larger ones, and the potential tax benefits derived from merging. Particular attention focused on certain industries rife with mergers and takeovers. Members of Congress and other observers debated whether the current mergers were in the interest of the companies' shareholders and whether the common good more generally was being served.

Mergers: Good or Bad?

When two firms merge, is this good or bad? Orthodox economic theory says it is probably good for the owners of the firms concerned, or at least the owners believe it is. Evidence suggests that the combined value of the shares of stock in merging firms increases with the merger.

A merger may also be good for society as a whole, if synergy leads to innovation or increased production efficiency. Traditionally, the important policy question involving mergers has been whether these gains to the firms involved and, perhaps, to the economy as a whole, might be outweighed by the damage done through increased industrial concentration and reduced competition. This was the focus of "trust-busting" in the early years of the century and of the hearings conducted by the late Sen. Estes Kefauver in the 1950s.

With the increase in *conglomerate mergers* in the late 1960s, by which companies in unrelated businesses combined, the policy emphasis shifted from concern about reduced competition to the role of the corporate manager in serving the interests of shareholders. Some theories of corporate structure argue that the power of stockholders is diffuse, so when the interests of top-level managers diverge from those of the shareholders, the managers may have the ability to steer a course for the firm that is in their own favor. Such a course will involve preserving the existing power and influence of management and increasing it when the opportunity arises. Two types of behavior often held to support this view are the acquisition of other firms, at large premiums over their prior stock market value, even when evident economic reasons for joining the firms are few, and resistance to attempts by others to acquire the firm, even when the price offered for its shares is well above the market price.

Recent merger activity has been characterized by increased sophistication, both in the mounting of takeover attempts and in the resistance to such attempts. It also has included several extremely large mergers that increased industrial concentration.

The Rise in Hostile Takeovers

A merger occurs when two firms combine to form a new one; in a takeover, one firm absorbs another. While the distinction is often unimportant, it is crucial when corporate managements disagree about the course the companies should follow. This situation gives rise to the hostile takeover attempt, with one corporation seeking to purchase the shares of another in order to gain voting control and displace the target corporation's management. The hostile takeover has become much more a part of the merger scene than it was in the past, and it has spawned a series of defensive maneuvers used by the managements of target corporations to fend off unwanted takeover attempts.

Managements adopting such tactics argue that they are necessary to protect shareholders from being pressured to tender their shares at too low a price or to a purchaser who might harm the company. Critics contend that the primary aim of such behavior is the entrenchment of the firm's current managers, regardless of how poorly they may be operating the corporation.

A glossary of the terms for some of these defensive tactics indicates the bases for such arguments:

Greenmail. An agreement to purchase the outstanding shares of the pursuer at a price in excess of the market price of the shares. An example of this practice occurred when takeover specialist Saul Steinberg gave up his shares in the Walt Disney empire, at a substantial profit.

Poison Pill. A provision intended to make the company valueless in the event of a takeover, such as giving shareholders the right to purchase additional shares in the firm at a substantial discount should the contesting corporation succeed in gaining a controlling interest in the company. An example of this type of activity was provided when Unocal Corp. successfully fought off the tender offer of T. Boone Pickens. Unocal threatened to dissipate a substantial fraction of its net worth by purchasing its own shares at an elevated price from shareholders *other than* Pickens.

Golden Parachutes. Large severance benefits to be paid to corporate managers in the event of their displacement via takeover. In 1984 Congress introduced tax penalties on the use of such payments.

Supermajority Rules. When two-thirds or even 80% of all shareholders of a target corporation must approve a takeover.

Fair Price Provisions. When the use of other defensive tactics (such as a supermajority rule) is threatened unless all shareholders in the target company receive the same price for their shares in the event of a takeover.

In many cases, legal battles are part of the takeover process. Because so many U.S. corporations call the state home, Delaware's Supreme Court is often at the center of such activity. Its decisions, such as that in the Pickens–Unocal fight, have been watched carefully by those on both sides for portents of the future. In the current climate, corporate managements have a relatively free hand to take any defensive actions that have been sanctioned by a vote of their shareholders.

Giant Mergers: Oil Leads the Way

Merger activity in 1984 proceeded at a much faster pace than it had in earlier years. Well over $100 billion of corporate assets changed hands through merger activity in that year, more than double the level for 1983. Nearly $43 billion of this activity was in the oil industry. The year's three largest mergers each involved one oil company taking over another (Standard Oil of California–Gulf, Texaco–Getty, and Mobil–Superior). The popularity of oil industry mergers was explained in part by weak demand for petroleum, which led to depressed share values for firms in the industry. This gave firms the opportunity to "purchase" oil reserves at a cost below that of drilling for them by taking over another company and its oil fields. This was seen by some as an efficient contraction of an industry facing the need to reduce capacity. Others viewed it as an increase in the concentration of an already noncompetitive industry.

Other industries also played an important role in the current merger wave. Deregulation in the financial area helped spur mergers in banking and brokerage. Many airlines were in financial trouble, and mergers often were associated with attempts to reduce operating costs.

Junk Bonds and Leveraged Buyouts

One of the largest mergers of 1985 was the sale of the American Broadcasting Cos. to Capital Cities Communications for several billion dollars. Ted Turner tried to take over CBS, a company much larger than his own, but was rebuffed and turned elsewhere. The ability of Turner and others to mount such "David–Goliath" takeover attempts was attributable in part to the use of borrowed money. A small company may borrow substantial amounts to purchase a larger company, perhaps with the target company's assets used to back the loans. Such loans have frequently been termed *junk bonds* because of their riskiness.

An even more extreme case of borrowing to finance an acquisition is known as the *leveraged buyout,* in which a small group of investors, usually including the company's top management, purchases the stock of all the other shareholders and "takes the company private." When this has been accomplished, the company's shares are no longer traded publicly on a stock exchange, and no public reports on its operations need be issued. In 1984 approximately one quarter of all mergers and acquisitions over $1 million in value were leveraged buyouts.

Many voiced concern over the increased use of junk bonds and leveraged buyouts, arguing that it has a destabilizing influence on the country's financial structure. An additional fear about leveraged buyouts is that managers engaging in them might be using inside information about their companies to take advantage of the shareholders whose stock they are buying.

The Tax Motive

Many companies involved in mergers and acquisitions have tax deductions and credits they cannot use because of insufficient profits. By merging, they can effectively "sell" these benefits to other corporations. Especially after it liberalized the corporate tax law in 1981, Congress evinced concern that the trading of such tax benefits provided undue incentives for corporations to merge at the taxpayer's expense. Hearings were held in 1985 to determine whether the trading of tax benefits by merging should be curtailed.

This problem hit close to home in 1985, with the Department of Transportation's proposed sale of Conrail, the government-controlled railroad system, to the Norfolk Southern Corp. It was estimated that the sale could bring the acquiring corporation additional tax benefits worth nearly the entire purchase price to be paid to the government.

ECUADOR

For much of the first year after it came to power in Ecuador in August 1984, the government of Pres. León Febres Cordero faced severe problems in implementing policy in a Congress in which the opposition held an absolute majority. The single largest party was the opposition center-left Izquierda Democrática (ID), which held 25 of the 71 seats in Congress. A constitutional crisis was avoided in May 1985 when two ID members shifted their allegiance to the ruling right-wing coalition, the National Reconstruction Front. This shift, with that of five independents, gave the coalition 36 seats, a slim majority. The government then was able to introduce a 29% increase in the minimum wage, which failed to match either the 1984 inflation rate of 31% or the over 60% increase that had been advocated in Congress.

Following freak weather conditions in 1983, which had severely depressed output, a 3% growth in gross domestic product was achieved in 1984. The figure was higher than expected, and a further expansion of 2–3% was forecast for 1985. Ignoring output quotas and price levels set by the Organization of Petroleum Exporting Countries, Ecuador hoped to raise petroleum production to 300,000 bbl a day by the end of the year.

Foreign creditors were impressed by the government's success in meeting targets set by the International Monetary Fund (IMF) for controlling the public-sector budget and the inflation rate. A rescheduling agreement covering debts falling due in 1984 was followed by a much larger restructuring agreement, under the terms of which $4.6 billion of debt falling due between 1985 and 1989 was to be repaid over 12 years with a 3-year grace period. The IMF made available a standby facility of 105.5 million Special Drawing Rights. (For table of world currencies, *see* International Exchange and Payments.)

EDUCATION

In the U.S., schools opened in September on a rather peaceful note. The largest strike, which affected Chicago's 431,000 students, ended after only two days. Strikes of varying duration were called in other Illinois districts and in Rhode Island, Ohio, Pennsylvania, Michigan, Vermont, New York, and Washington.

The president of the National Education Association, Mary H. Futrell, urged her group to drop its longtime opposition to the testing of new teachers to assure that they had mastered both subject matter and professional competences. Albert Shanker, president of the American Federation of Teachers, declared that improved status for teachers could come only through a national examination that would limit entrance into teaching, student choice of schools they wanted to attend, evaluation of teachers by veteran teachers who could help to weed out incompetents, "career ladders" to permit experienced teachers to supervise novices, and encouragement of the brightest young persons to enter the teaching profession. In a Gallup Poll, conducted in cooperation with an education fraternity, Phi Delta Kappa, teachers reported that the main problems facing schools were parental indifference, limited financial support, lack of student interest, overcrowded classrooms, and discipline.

A number of reports on education were issued during the year, including two on the education of ethnic minorities, *Education for All* (the Swann Report) in the U.K. and *Equality and Excellence* in the U.S. In Japan Prime Minister Yasuhiro Nakasone's Ad Hoc Advisory Council on Education Reform issued its first report. The council had an all-embracing mandate to look into ways of reforming Japan's educational system, notably how to provide for the needs of the 21st century and how to deal with what the Japanese regarded as rising school violence, delinquency, and truancy. The council put forward the idea of establishing six-year specialist state secondary schools alongside the present three-year lower- and upper-level institutions. Critics argued that such schools would be used to prepare an elite for entry into prestigious universities and could threaten the legally enshrined principle of equal compulsory education for all up to age 15. They might also have the effect of pushing selection down from the secondary to the primary level, thus exacerbating the great pressure on Japanese schoolchildren. The Japan Teachers' Union de-

Preschoolers, mostly from poverty-stricken slums, eat lunch at a new public school in Rio de Janeiro, Brazil, in August. A concerted effort to bring poor children, who might not otherwise attend, into the schools achieved considerable success by the use of food—breakfast, lunch, snacks—as a lure.

AP/WIDE WORLD

AP/WIDE WORLD

*Therese Knecht Dozier is honored as the 1985
Teacher of the Year by Pres. Ronald Reagan on April
18 as Rep. Floyd Spence looks on.*

plored the report's failure to deal with industry's influence over the educational system but supported its call for greater emphasis on individuality.

Primary and Secondary Education

There were heartening accounts of progress in primary education from some parts of the world. From Brazil came the example of the Centros Integrados de Educacao Publica (CIEPs). Housed in simple, cheap, but highly distinctive buildings designed by the Brazilian architect Oscar Niemeyer, they were part of a program that aimed eventually to provide schooling for 300,000 children in the Rio de Janeiro area. The plan, strongly supported by the state governor, Leonel Brizola, was intended to tackle the interlinked problems of lack of schooling, juvenile delinquency, and malnutrition. The CIEPs provided not only full-time schooling from 7:30 AM to 5 PM but also three meals a day, clothing, and school materials. In an effort to revitalize teaching methods, a "cultural animator" was employed to incorporate popular culture into the curriculum, and dance and music were used extensively.

William J. Bennett, the new U.S. secretary of education, became an active spokesman for conservative views on the federal role in education and on education itself. He called for higher academic standards on all levels, firmer school discipline, more teaching of traditional morals and ethics, and greater emphasis on the humanities. A number of Bennett's pronouncements provoked controversy during the year, among them his recommendation that federal guidelines on bilingual education be eased. Current federal policy dictated that basic subjects be taught in the native language of children who speak little or no English. Bennett wanted local schools to determine the instructional methods to be used for such children, and he wanted the goal to be mastery

of English. The federal government had provided some $1.7 billion to fund bilingual programs since legislation on the subject was passed 20 years earlier. The largest group in bilingual programs was the Hispanics. Hispanic youth were described as "wasted" by a national study commission, which found that they had a 45% dropout rate.

Venturing into the delicate area of public aid to private schools, Bennett suggested that the federal remedial program aiding students with special learning problems be changed to a voucher system that would permit parents to select the school of their choice. This would enable parents to send their children to either a public or a private school. The recommendation was made after the U.S. Supreme Court ruled that public school teachers could not conduct special education classes in parochial schools. A Gallup Poll showed that Americans were divided on the subject, with 45% favoring government aid to parochial schools and 47% opposing it. In another decision upholding the "wall of separation" between church and state, the Supreme Court continued its mandate against Bible reading and prayer in public schools. An Alabama law authorizing a minute of silence "for meditation or voluntary prayer" was struck down because prayer was specifically mentioned as an option, though the court indicated that other approaches to the period of silence might be acceptable. Twenty-six states had "silence" laws in some form. Meanwhile, Congress passed a bill guaranteeing religious groups the same access to school property after school hours given to other groups that used school space for their meetings. In a move that might have

*Teachers in North Little Rock, Arkansas, were tested
in March to demonstrate their competency in reading,
writing, and mathematics.*
AP/WIDE WORLD

The Education of Ethnic Minorities

The educational needs of blacks and other ethnic minorities have been the subject of growing concern in many Western countries, whether their minorities are of long standing or the result of recent immigration. Two important reports on this topic appeared in 1985, one in the United States (*Equality and Excellence: The Educational Status of Black Americans*) and the other in the United Kingdom. (*Education for All*). The latter was widely known as the Swann Report, after Lord Swann, the chairman of the committee that produced it.

The U.S. report, prepared for the College Entrance Examination Board of New York by sociologist Linda Darling-Hammond, had a narrower focus than the Swann Report. It recognized that U.S. blacks had made great gains in education since the early 1960s, but since 1975 there had been some erosion of those gains, and the report even suggested that the movement toward educational equality was threatened with reversal. College attendance and completion rates for blacks had declined since 1975, and black participation in postgraduate education had declined since the early 1970s. All along the educational pipeline, from primary school to bachelor's degree, blacks had been losing ground relative to nonblacks. Furthermore, all minority students were disproportionately placed in vocational courses or low-track classes where they were not intellectually challenged and where teachers' expectations were low.

In part, this resulted from policy. Education was underfinanced because of federal aid cuts, the economic recession, and the property-tax revolt of the late 1970s. Also a factor was the decline in the morale and occupational prestige of the teaching profession. But there were also disturbing changes in the structure of black families that must provide part of the explanation. In the past decade the percentage of black households headed by females had risen from 28 to 41%, partly because of higher divorce rates and partly because of increases in the number of never-married mothers. Nearly one-half (47.6%) of all black children 18 years and under lived in households below the poverty line in 1982, compared with 17% of white children. The real median income of black families had been decreasing, both in absolute terms and as compared with whites.

In Britain the immigrant population was too recent for such trends to emerge so starkly. Moreover, the immigrants fell chiefly into two rather different groups—those from the Caribbean, and those from the Indian subcontinent. The first had what appeared on the surface to be a more flamboyant, extroverted culture; the second was more self-contained and, above all, Muslim. The stereotype of the Asian pupils was that they were well motivated, had strong parental support, and were relatively successful. In fact, the Swann Report found that children of Bangladeshi origin, in particular, were not doing at all well. The other stereotype was that the West Indian children were not achieving as might be expected, but it seemed that they were doing better (although there was still a great deal of room for improvement). The report rebutted the argument that some ethnic groups are innately less intelligent than others.

Perhaps the most important issue on which the U.S. and British reports found common ground was that education in a democracy must mean "education for all"—the Swann Report title. George Hanford, the College Board president, echoed this in his preface to the U.S. report: "The unique promise of the United States has been its commitment to extend opportunities to *all*—not just some—of its children. Since its earliest days, this nation has been dedicated to the principle that each generation deserves a fair start, and acting on this principle has served not only justice but the national well-being."

far-reaching consequences, the California Board of Education rejected all the science textbooks submitted for possible use in the seventh and eighth grades on the grounds that they "watered down" instruction on evolution. In doing so, the board bypassed objections by fundamentalists that the books overemphasized evolution at the expense of biblical creationism. Because California represented a large share of the national textbook market, the move could affect science textbooks nationwide.

In a case involving a student whose purse had been searched for cigarettes, the Supreme Court gave school officials authority to tailor Fourth Amendment provisions on searches and seizures to school settings if there was a reasonable suspicion that a law or school rule was being violated.

Media attention to some cases of child abuse in day-care centers and schools created considerable interest in new federal guidelines for child-care workers. While welcomed, the guidelines were criticized by some observers for not going beyond employment screening to keep out criminals and child abusers. Experts advocated efforts to improve staff and program quality. Interest in child care had grown as more and more mothers went to work and the number of child-care facilities increased to meet the demand. Other social concerns also reached into the schools. Controversy arose over the question of how to treat children with acquired immune deficiency syndrome (AIDS). Although the number of school-age children with AIDS was small, and experts insisted that the disease could not be spread by casual contact, the public's fear of the fatal ailment forced many school districts to establish policy on the issue. There was no consensus among districts. Los Angeles, for example, barred AIDS victims from the schools, while New York City admitted them on a case-by-case basis after an expert panel had made recommendations. The decision to admit one such student to a school in Queens led to a school boycott.

President Reagan's proposed tax reforms were seen by some critics as a threat to local and state school financing. Specifically under fire was the provision that would eliminate local and state taxes as federal income-tax deductions. The value of the deductions was estimated at $16.5 billion per year, constituting a form of federal subsidy. Without the deductions, it was feared, voters might revolt against school taxes, further hurting school districts already affected by declining federal dollars. Supporters of the president's reform believed that the effect would not be great, since only about one-third of taxpayers itemize deductions, and that, in any case, proposed reductions in the federal tax rate would free up more local tax dollars. They also claimed that polls showed that the public was willing to support the schools. The U.S. Department of Education, for example, released figures indicating that two-thirds of the people would pay higher taxes to raise teacher salaries and standards, increase teacher training, and lower class size. The survey sample was considered balanced except for the disproportionate number of college graduates among those responding.

The states were increasing their control over education, according to Terrel Bell, secretary of education during Reagan's first term. Bell noted that the states' share of school funding had exceeded the local share during the past five years and that hundreds of state laws regulating local schools had been passed. Much of this legislative activity had been inspired by the critical reports on U.S. public schools issued during the past few years and the resulting emphasis on excellence in education. The states were having a greater say about such matters as high school graduation requirements, testing, and teacher standards. Some states, however, were becoming very specific in their regulations; for example, by fixing the number of times announcements could be made over a school's public address system.

The Census Bureau released figures that showed that the U.S. school-age population overall had declined 5.3% over four years, to 44.8 million in 1984, but there was a 9% increase in preschool-age children during the years 1980–84. There were 17.8 million preschool children in 1984, and the population under the age of five was the high-

est since 1968. The Census Bureau attributed the increase to the larger number of mothers of child-bearing age rather than to an increase in fertility rates. A Gallup Poll showed that the level of public confidence in the schools had risen 11% and that 42% of Americans believed the schools were getting better. Achievement levels for U.S. elementary and secondary students improved again in 1985. Average scores on the Scholastic Aptitude Test, widely used as an admissions tool by colleges, rose for both verbal and mathematical skills. The Census Bureau found that U.S. children averaged more than an hour of homework per day, with white girls and all black students putting in more time than white boys.

In Australia the first primary school for Aborigines opened in South Australia amid some controversy. There were accusations of segregation, countered by arguments that the Aborigines were underachievers and needed special primary schooling. A movement toward segregated schools was apparent among Muslims in several countries. In England demands for Muslim schools established with government support were stimulated by one or two well-publicized examples of hostility toward immigrant children by head teachers in English schools.

In South Africa, where education was seriously disrupted by civil strife, there appeared to be some slight movement on the part of the white government to recognize the blacks' demand for reforms. There was no indication that the government would accede to the blacks' key demand for a single Ministry of Education and an end to separate educational systems. The situation was exacerbated by the fact that enrollment in white schools was diminishing while black schools were experiencing a population explosion. It was claimed that the enrollment figures in black schools were increasing at a rate of 250,000 a year, and the department in charge of black education had to provide for about six million pupils. The average pupil–teacher ratio in white schools was recorded as 20 to 1; in black secondary schools, 36 to 1; and in black primary schools, 52 to 1. It was estimated that the South African government spent seven times more on a white child's education than on that of a black child.

Higher Education

In keeping with the general upgrading of education in China, the Communist Party announced sweeping changes in higher education, some of which seemed to suggest a moving away from socialist ideals. An example was the introduction of a scholarship system linking grants to academic performance. Universities and colleges were to have greater autonomy in spending their funds, making appointments, and designing courses. It was also proposed to let universities select their own research projects, allowing them to engage in commercially profitable undertakings. As in the lower schools, there was emphasis on steering teaching away from the academic mold and toward the acquisition of practical skills for employment. Higher education in China had expanded from 400 higher education institutions with 584,000 students in 1977 to 800 institutions with 1,250,000 students in 1985.

Australia set about curbing spending on institutions of higher learning. The Tertiary Education Commission, an advisory body, issued a highly critical report on the lack of coordination in Australian higher education. In neighboring New Zealand a Maori study center was established in Victoria University of Wellington.

In the U.S. a proposed administration plan to cut $2.3 billion from college aid programs raised fears that many students could no longer afford to attend private colleges. Tuition at many colleges already exceeded the total a student could receive through a combination of federal grants, guaranteed loans, and work-study programs. Officials estimated that one million students would be affected by the changes. Meanwhile, federal officials claimed that student defaults on federally guaranteed loans administered by colleges had reached excessive levels.

EGYPT

Deteriorating economic circumstances and growing Islamic fundamentalism in Egypt were two factors worrying Pres. Hosni Mubarak as he began his fifth year in office in October 1985. They threatened to undermine the achievements of his presidency, which had been, first and foremost, his success in healing the wounds—both at home and abroad—of the turbulent years of his predecessor, Pres. Anwar el-Sadat.

The lifting of restrictions placed on Shenuda III, the spiritual leader of the Coptic Church, on January 1 represented a major reversal of policy adopted in the Sadat years. However, this gain for community understanding was offset by a worsening crisis in relations between the government and Islamic fundamentalists. In July Hafez Salama, the leader of a campaign to apply Shari'ah (Islamic law) in Egypt, was arrested along with 45 of his followers in the first crackdown on Muslim activists since Mubarak took office. In May the People's Assembly cut short a debate on the adoption of Shari'ah at the request of the ruling National Democratic Party. The government had determined to move slowly on the question of introducing Islamic law in a bid to please all parties.

Mubarak indicated his concern about internal developments with an angry speech on June 26 that was clearly directed against Islamic groups, whom—in a departure from his normally cautious style—he labeled "extremists." By promising a tough line against agitation, Mubarak put in doubt one of his earlier political goals—the creation of a wider and more active democratic franchise.

Underlying these political troubles were economic difficulties that provided the motivation for

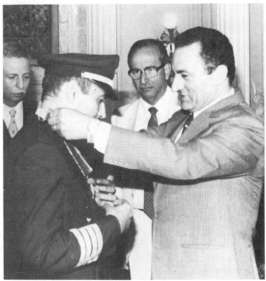

AP/WIDE WORLD

Egyptian Pres. Hosni Mubarak (right) honors for bravery the EgyptAir pilot whose craft was forced by U.S. Navy fighters to land in Sicily. The airliner carried the hijackers of the Italian cruise ship Achille Lauro.

the major new appointment in a reshuffle of the Cabinet announced in September. Former finance minister Ali Lutfi was appointed prime minister in place of Kamal Hassan Ali on September 4, following the resignation of Ali and his Cabinet. Lutfi was considered to be a close confidant of Mubarak, who had appointed him to a special committee on the economy established earlier in 1985. The Cabinet announced on September 5 involved few other changes, but one significant promotion was that of Kamal Ahmad al-Ganzouri, the minister of planning and international cooperation, who became one of four deputy prime ministers. A number of other moves served to diminish the influence of the military in the government.

The visit of U.K. Prime Minister Margaret Thatcher on September 16–18 was marked by the signing of a £12.5 million grant for the development of coal mining and the unveiling of a plaque opening the Greater Cairo Wastewater Project, in which British companies were participating. (For table of world currencies, *see* International Exchange and Payments.)

Two of Egypt's principal sources of revenue—income from oil exports and remittances from expatriate workers—were being curtailed by recession within the Gulf region and weak world energy prices. The country was suffering from a chronic shortage of hard currency at a time when talks with the International Monetary Fund (IMF) on financial aid were delicately poised. The government had resisted the IMF's earlier calls to end food price subsidies. Finance Minister Salaheddin Hamid and Ali Negm, governor of the central bank, took part

ANNA CLOPET—SIPA/SPECIAL FEATURES

Islamic fundamentalists demonstrate in Cairo in June demanding that the Egyptian government adopt the Shari'ah, Islam's 1,300-year-old legal code.

in talks with the IMF that began in Washington, D.C., on August 5. Their aim was to secure for Egypt a standby credit to support the balance of payments. It was believed the IMF acknowledged that the Mubarak administration had taken some steps toward easing public-spending burdens but considered that efforts by midyear had fallen short of what was required.

In a further move to come to grips with economic problems, Mubarak visited Spain on September 20–21 and France on September 29–30, where he discussed ways of reducing the arrears on Egypt's military debts to both countries. Prime Minister Ali announced in August that talks about rescheduling the $1.2 billion in military debt to the U.S.S.R. had been inconclusive but were to be resumed later in the year. On July 8 a trade protocol with Moscow valued at more than $800 million was ratified.

The introduction in January of a controlled floating exchange rate for the Egyptian pound and a new tariff system to restrict imports brought stability to the currency market, but this was threatened in September by a slide in the value of the pound. On September 18 Mubarak announced the suspension of all new credits or loans, apart from those for productive, profit-yielding schemes. The statement indicated the government's concern to reduce the widening trade deficit, which was estimated at $6 billion for the year to July 1985.

Egypt's consistent calls for higher oil prices upset the consensus on the matter among other Arab nations. When the petroleum and mineral resources minister, Abdel-Hadi Muhammad Kandil, attended a meeting of the Organization of Petroleum Exporting Countries (OPEC) as an observer in January, he criticized the OPEC resolutions as "indecisive."

President Mubarak continued his policy of improving relations with Arab nations, with the aim of maneuvering the country back into the Arab mainstream. Of great concern, however, was the move by Libya to expel hundreds of Egyptian expatriate workers, although the Cairo authorities said they could foresee no problem in integrating them.

On the wider question of bringing peace to the Middle East, in February Mubarak launched an initiative aimed at establishing a dialogue between the U.S. and a Jordanian-Palestinian delegation. This was viewed as a first step toward opening Arab-Israeli talks on the future of the West Bank and Gaza Strip. Mubarak pursued the idea when he visited the U.S. on March 9–13. Although any gains from his talks there were not immediately clear, the U.S. administration subsequently gave weight to attempts to revive the stalled peace process.

Egypt came under renewed pressure from the U.S. to normalize its relationship with Israel, which had been frozen since the Israeli invasion of Lebanon in 1982. However, Mubarak was seeking a more flexible attitude from Israel toward the Palestinian question, as well as the remaining bilateral territorial dispute (over Taba in the Sinai), before he would risk losing the diplomatic gains that came from better relations with moderate Arab states. On May 28 the petroleum minister visited Israel to discuss oil sales. This apparent improvement was spoiled, however, when an Israeli diplomat was assassinated in a Cairo suburb on August 20 by a group calling itself the Egyptian Revolution.

Egypt's relations with the U.S. suffered in the aftermath of the hijacking of an Italian cruise liner, the *Achille Lauro,* by Palestinians in October. On hearing that one passenger, a U.S. citizen, had been killed during the hijack, the U.S. administration was strongly critical of Egypt's decision to grant safe passage to the hijackers, and the Egyptian airliner carrying them to Tunisia was intercepted by U.S. military planes and forced to land at a U.S. base in Italy. Anti-U.S. demonstrations erupted in Cairo, and President Mubarak angrily demanded an apology to "all Egyptians." However, tensions over the incident had eased by year's end. In November the same EgyptAir plane involved in the *Achille Lauro* affair was hijacked by members of a Palestinian splinter group and flown to Malta, where Egyptian commandos stormed it with considerable loss of life.

EL SALVADOR

In 1985 a settlement of the six-year-old civil war in El Salvador seemed no closer. According to the Roman Catholic Church, an average of 200 people a week died in the fighting. Hope that a third round of the peace talks begun in 1984 would take place in January 1985 foundered when the parties failed to agree on a location and date for the talks and when the government rejected demands by the Farabundo Martí National Liberation Front (FMLN) guerrillas and the group's political wing, the Democratic Revolutionary Front (FDR), for discussion of a new constitution and a total reorganization of the armed forces.

In the face of heavy aerial bombardment, the relocation of civilians sympathetic to the guerrillas, and government efforts to encourage splits among the five groups that made up the FMLN, the rebels took steps in August toward unifying both the political wing and the revolutionary armies. The guerrillas concentrated on urban warfare, although in October, on the fifth anniversary of the formation of the alliance, the FMLN attacked a military base near the town of La Unión; 42 soldiers were killed and 68 were wounded.

The increase in the number of kidnappings strengthened the charge that the FMLN was merely a terrorist organization. The guerrillas demanded the release of 34 colleagues, a ban on house-to-house searches and arrests, and an end to government military operations in return for the release of Pres. José Napoleón Duarte's daughter, kidnapped on September 10. Government claims that nine of the guerrillas were not in their hands aroused suspicions that they had died in captivity. The president's daughter was released in a complex exchange after being held for six weeks. The final arrangement involved the release of Inés Guadalupe Duarte Durán and 23 mayors who had been abducted in previous months in exchange for the release of 22 guerrillas and the safe conduct out of El Salvador of 96 rebels disabled in the war. An urban guerrilla group affiliated with the FMLN claimed responsibility for the killing in San Salvador of 13 people, among them 4 U.S. marines, in June. The Army took retaliatory action in which 21 people were killed, and in late August 3 suspects were arrested. The new tactics adopted by the guerrillas and the improved training and better equipment available to the armed forces—in 1985 the U.S. supplied assistance worth $460 million plus $250 million in supplementary aid—suggested that the war of attrition would continue.

Congressional elections took place on March 31. The unexpected victory of President Duarte's Christian Democratic Party and a split within the main opposition party, the right-wing Nationalist Republican Alliance (Arena), led to the formation in early May of a new party, Patria Libre (Free Fatherland). Maj. Roberto D'Aubuisson was replaced as president of Arena in September by Alfredo Cristiani.

Pres. José Napoleón Duarte of El Salvador embraces his daughter (to his left) and her friend after the two women were released by antigovernment guerrillas.

CLAUDE URRACA—SYGMA

ENGINEERING PROJECTS

Work started in 1985 on building the second bridge across the Bosporus. A suspension bridge, its main span of 1,090 m (1 m = 3.3 ft) would be the fifth longest in the world when completed. Sited about five kilometers (three miles) north of the first Bosporus bridge (main span 1,075 m), it would form a vital section of a second peripheral road around Istanbul that would provide the main route for traffic moving between Europe and Asia. It would be a toll bridge with the single toll plaza located on the European side and, if traffic grew as fast as it did when the first bridge was opened in 1973, would pay for itself within three years of its scheduled completion in 1988. The bridge was being built by a consortium of major Japanese firms and an Italian organization. The Japanese were currently the most experienced builders of major bridges, but this would be the first really long-span suspension bridge they had built. It would provide the essential experience required to tackle the Akashi Kaikyo suspension bridge, the main span of which would exceed 1,700 m and which would form an essential part of the third crossing being built between the Japanese islands of Honshu and Shikoku.

Railway bridges present special problems to the engineer. China completed a steel box structure described as the longest of its type in the world. The deck box was a continuous girder 304 m long; the two end spans were 56 m long, and the central 192 m was supported at the third points by raking A-frames. It was an interesting, elegant, and economical design and was built of high-strength steel made in China and having good welding characteristics.

The Italian government announced that construction of a suspension bridge across the Strait of Messina would begin in 1988. The bridge, which would join the toe of the Italian peninsula to the island of Sicily in a single leap, would have a main span of 3,300 m, more than twice that of England's Humber Bridge (1,410 m), currently the longest bridge span in the world, and nearly three times the span of the Mackinac (Mich.) Bridge (1,158 m). The main girder of the Messina bridge would be a long steel box essentially triangular in cross-section, wide at the top and narrower below. Three traffic decks were planned to be inside the box, protected from the immediate effects of the wind. The top deck would carry four traffic lanes for road vehicles, the second deck two tracks for bicycles, and the third a single rail track. The structure would be massive, with the towers 380 m high. Each of the two main cables would measure 1,600 mm (62 in) in diameter and contain 45,000 5-mm (0.2-in)-diameter high-tension steel wires. Triangulated hangers, as used on the Humber Bridge, would be used to dampen any tendency of the bridge girder to oscillate; extensive tests in wind tunnels showed that the design could cope with gusts of up to 225 km/h (140 mph).

The Diplomatic Club in Riyadh, Saudi Arabia, made innovative use of fabric with concrete and stone. The structure, which contained restaurants, an auditorium, and sports areas, enclosed an open oasis of gardens and palm trees.

OMRANIA; PHOTOGRAPH, CRISPIN BOYLE PHOTOGRAPHY & ASSOCIATES

Buildings

Industry's demand for high-quality accommodations for manufacturing led to the continued development of medium-span structures with advanced environmental services. Construction of this type was reflected in the new laboratory facility for PA Technology in New Jersey. The building took the form of a central linear circulation zone with an approximately 24-m span of usable area on each side. The main structural support was a row of A-frames spanning the circulation zone; from the apex of the row ran ties that were divided at a lower level to provide end and intermediate supports to the roofs. Within the A-frame at the second-floor level was a continuous platform that supported the equipment for environmental services. Exposed ducting hung below the platform and dropped into the building just inside the circulation zone.

Similarly, at Cambridge, England, an advanced test station facility for Schlumberger Ltd. was completed. In this case the designers utilized Teflon-coated fiberglass fabric to form a row of three marquee-like enclosures of an approximately 24-m span. Instead of being supported on poles like a tent, however, the tops of the enclosures were suspended by cables from a system of columns, the tops of which were themselves stayed by cables. Along each side of the row was a single-story block of offices and laboratories, the roof of which was suspended from external trusses.

The Diplomatic Club in Riyadh, Saudi Arabia, was an example of fabric used with concrete and stone as opposed to fabric with steel. A relatively narrow three-story structure, snakelike in plan, enclosed an open oasis of gardens and palm trees. The Teflon-coated fiberglass fabric roof was supported by a radial tension cable system with anchor blocks at the perimeter. The reinforced concrete work was clad in stone, the roughness of which contrasted with the smoothness of the fabric roof. The completed building contained 24,000 sq m (258,000 sq ft) of floor area including a banquet hall, restaurants, an auditorium, and areas for sports.

Repairs to the (West) Berlin Congress Hall were under way following its collapse in 1980, when one of the inclined arches carrying the suspended roof failed. The new arch beams would have the same two-meter-square section but would be made of prestressed lightweight concrete and would not rely on the roof tendons to provide support. The roof itself, while suspended as before, would be lighter in weight. A similar roof in Milan, Italy, over the 126-m-diameter Palazzo dello Sport stadium, sustained comparable damage in January 1985. At the time, the roof was covered with some 750 mm (30 in) of snow, greatly in excess of the 100-mm (4-in) depth normally expected. The damage occurred when three 2.5-m-long sections of steel box-girder ring beam crushed. This caused the roof to sag some ten meters at the center.

Dams

A recent UN report claimed that by 1990 more than 1,200,000,000 people would be without water supplies and that in the early 1980s some 345 million people benefited from new water projects. The less developed countries continued to plan water resource developments, even at the risk of creating enormous debts, in the firm belief that such developments were essential for their survival. For example, Thailand was placing its hopes on the development of the lower Mae Ping project, which would supply 875 million cu m (1 cu m = 1.3 cu yd) of water for irrigation as well as 215 MW of generating capacity to meet power shortages. Ethiopia was planning a large dam on the Albera River, designed to irrigate 300,000 ha (1 ha = 2.5 ac) in the Gambela Valley. Nigeria started construction of the $90 million Jibiya Dam on the Gada River to provide drinking water for 200,000 people and to irrigate their farms.

Algeria announced a five-year plan to build 18 dams with an investment of $20 billion. This would double the domestic water supplies and irrigate more than 100,000 ha. Somalia started a 75-m-high concrete dam to irrigate 220,000 ha at a cost of $350 million. Angola, in need of a dam and hydroelectric plant but short of funds, arranged to have Brazil build the $1 billion Capana Dam on the Cuanza River in exchange for oil. Iran began work on a dam across the Abu Fares River at Ramhormoz. It was designed to provide irrigation for 1,500 ha, while another dam across the Marun River at Beh-

behan would irrigate 13,000 ha. Four dams were completed during 1985: the 63-m-high earth dam in the Baluchistan region, the 133-m-high Tiroft arch dam in Kerman Province, and the 65-m-high Toroq and Kabo dams in Khorasan Province.

The Soviet Union built four dams in Uzbekistan on the Amu Darya River. The capacity of the four reservoirs formed by the dams totaled 7,000,000,-000 cu m of water, enough to irrigate one million hectares of the Kara-Kum Desert.

The U.S.S.R. continued its interest in trying to blast the banks of a river to form a dam. Soviet engineers applied this technology to create a 16 million-cu m reservoir on the Alindzha River in the Nachicevan Republic.

The voices of environmentalists were heard during the year. India's Sardar Sarovar Dam, representing an ultimate investment of $5 billion, faced a restudy of the impact of relocating about 85,000 people. Dams on the Danube River in Europe were also being delayed because of objections of environmentalists to the possible loss of rare plants and animals in the floodplain.

Roads

Construction began on a segment of Interstate 80 (I-80) in Utah. When completed in 1986, it would provide the final link of the first intercontinental interstate highway in the U.S. Other major road projects begun during 1985 in the U.S. included the $1.3 billion 11.2-km (1 km = 0.62 mi) segment of I-90 through Seattle, Wash., including a floating bridge, a conventional bridge, and a tunnel; a 21.5-km segment of I-595 in Florida, with three four-level interchanges, costing $1.2 billion; the 29-km Century Freeway in Los Angeles, at $1 billion; and a 321-km segment of I-49 in Louisiana, also costing $1 billion.

Mexico planned to spend $1.6 billion on its current highway infrastructure program, which focused on trunk road modernization and the reconstruction and maintenance of rural roads. Chile was building 320 km of roads and upgrading 245 km of existing roads to serve regions in the south that previously were accessible only by air or sea. Construction started in 1985 on a 650-km highway from Puerto Lopez to Puerto Carreno in Colombia, linking the central mountain region with the Venezuelan border.

The Hume Highway between Sydney and the New South Wales border in Australia was being widened at a cost of $330 million, providing a four-lane highway between Australia's two largest cities, Sydney and Melbourne. A new five-year plan to guarantee road funding went into effect in Australia on July 1, 1985.

The United Nations Economic Commission for Africa initiated an African Highway Master Plan Study, which was to be completed in 1986. As of 1985 more than 3,000 km of the 6,399-km Trans-African Highway were in service, with the entire highway scheduled for completion in the 1990s. It would link Nigeria, Cameroon, the Central African Republic, Zaire, Uganda, and Kenya.

More than 1,700 km of the Trans-European Motorway were in service, with 500 km under construction. The 11,000-km system was planned to run through ten European countries. Also in Europe, Britain planned to renew and improve 112 km of motorways in the 1985–86 fiscal year at a total cost of $182 million.

Tunnels

Transport-related tunneling continued to feature prominently among the world's major underground projects. Work on mass transit systems in Singa-

Subway riders in Seoul, South Korea, pass through a newly constructed station. Station walls and ceilings were faced with rough-hewn granite to make the station look like a truly underground environment.

AP/WIDE WORLD

The one-kilometer (half-mile) Intercity Bridge across the Columbia River in the state of Washington, connecting the cities of Pasco and Kennewick, won a presidential award for design excellence.

pore; Lyon, France; Antwerp, Belgium; Washington, D.C.; Vancouver, B.C.; Seoul, South Korea; and Taipei, Taiwan, continued, while other large cities such as Los Angeles, Istanbul, and Shanghai were actively pursuing evaluations of the possible use of such systems.

In Western Europe, notably in West Germany and Switzerland, work on many road and rail tunnels continued or began during the year. The Sonnenberg mountain road tunnel near Lucerne, Switz., was equipped as a nuclear shelter for 21,000 people, complete with communal living facilities, hospital, police station, and bank. Austria adopted a $1,180,000,000 plan to divert all foreign truck transport onto railway transporter trains, thus relieving the heavy traffic on the national road network; the scheme would involve major enlargement of many rail tunnels and construction of new sections.

The 3,200-km Baikal-to-Amur railway in the U.S.S.R. became operative in 1985, having been officially inaugurated in 1984. This new trans-Siberian line had taken some ten years to complete. The greatest difficulties occurred in some of the nine tunnel sections, which totaled 30 km in length and where such diverse problems as permafrost, hot-water springs, and highly unstable geologic conditions had to be overcome or, in some cases, avoided. The Seikan Tunnel in Japan, whose pilot bore was completed in 1983 after some 19 years of construction, neared the final phase of conversion into a rail tunnel and service tunnel capable of accommodating the Shinkansen Bullet Train. An interesting revelation was that seismic observatories had recorded an earthquake registering 7.7 on the Richter scale in the vicinity of the tunnel, and no damage had occurred.

The British and French governments agreed to receive proposals for a commercially financed fixed link between their countries across the Strait of Dover. From a tunneling point of view, the most

appealing proposal publicized was one that envisioned a system of rail shuttle transporter trains carried in twin tunnels of 7.3-m diameter, with an additional 4.5-m-diameter service tunnel. The total tunneled length would be 150 km, and the intensive program necessary for early completion of the $3 billion project could result in the need for up to 12 tunnel-boring machines working simultaneously during peak program activity. Another proposal utilized a combination of bridges, artificial islands, and immersed-tube elements laid in a seabed trench and would also involve inland tunnels on the British coast. To supplement this road link, there would be a separate conventional passenger and freight train railway tunnel bored under the seabed between Dover and Calais. The cost of the total scheme was estimated at about $6.5 billion. A bigovernmental decision and approval for a fixed link was expected early in 1986. Sweden's Atlas-Copco company announced the arrival of its multipurpose Foro boring machine. Described as a "quantum leap forward" in tunneling technology, the new machine was said to be capable of excavating either vertical or inclined shafts (raise bores) or horizontal rock tunnels. It was computer controlled from a remote operator position and guided by the latest in inertial guidance systems of the type used in nuclear submarines.

ENVIRONMENT

When Pres. Ronald Reagan met Canadian Prime Minister Brian Mulroney in Quebec in March, acid rain was the main item on the agenda. The final agreement called for more research but not for controls. Canada continued to take unilateral action aimed at reducing wet sulfur deposition in the eastern provinces to 18 lb per ac (20 kg per ha) per year in a series of steps that would be completed in 1994. This would bring emissions of nitrogen oxides from cars and light trucks into line with

U.S. standards by September 1987. Acting under a court order, the U.S. Environmental Protection Agency (EPA) issued rules in November 1984 that would reduce sulfur dioxide emissions from power stations, mainly in the Ohio Valley. The regulations reduced the maximum permitted height for stacks and thus compelled power stations to burn low-sulfur fuel or install scrubbers if they were to meet ambient air quality standards.

In November 1984 acid rain was reported from two widely separated sites in the Northern Territories of Australia. Much less acid than rains in the Northern Hemisphere, the acidity in Australia was due to formic, acetic, and other weak acids. In September 1985 the U.S. government began a major survey of western lakes. Private researchers claimed to have found evidence of acidification in high-altitude lakes in the region.

Throughout the year the British government resisted pressures to order power stations to fit flue-gas desulfurization equipment to reduce sulfur dioxide emissions. The pressure came from the House of Commons Select Committee on the Environment, other members of the European Communities (EC), and voluntary groups, all of which urged Britain to join those countries pledged to reduce sulfur dioxide emissions by 30% over a ten-year period or to accept the EC proposal to reduce sulfur dioxide emissions by 60% and nitrogen oxides by 40% by 1995. The government view was supported by the Central Electricity Generating Board and the National Coal Board. The Forestry Commission reported in March that widespread damage to conifers observed in 1984 had occurred mainly as the result of harsh weather during the previous winter, not acid rain. On August 21 the commission published *Forest Health and Air Pollution: 1984 Survey,* which found no clear evidence of acid rain damage in British forests.

In West Germany the third annual Forest Damage Inventory, published in November 1984, showed that 50% of forests were affected by acid rain, compared with 34% in 1983. There were no reports of forest tracts in which all the trees were dead, but damage to broad-leaved species had increased. In August 1985 Otto Kandler of the Botanical Institute of the University of Munich suggested that disease might be responsible for the damage. He said several epidemics affected German forests, each with a cycle of peaks and troughs, and the "acid rain" phenomenon might be due to the coincidence of several peaks accompanied by a new disease that had not as yet been diagnosed. A virus causing damage similar to that seen in Germany had been isolated in Czechoslovakia. Chemists from the Institute of Ecological Chemistry in Munich advanced yet another theory in September, suggesting that certain unsaturated hydrocarbon compounds produced by the trees themselves could react with ozone to form substances that were able to destroy tree cells and enzymes.

The "Greenhouse Effect"

Scientists at the Climatic Research Unit, University of East Anglia, England, reported in March that the period from 1979 to 1984 was the warmest since 1851 over the land masses of the Northern Hemisphere, reversing the cooling trend observed between 1950 and 1970. Accumulating carbon dioxide was held to be the most plausible explanation, although in relation to natural climatic changes the warming was not sufficient to make this certain. A team at the National Center for Atmospheric Research, Boulder, Colo., led by Ralph Cicerone, warned in May that nitrous oxide and methane were also accumulating in the atmosphere at rates that could double the warming effect from carbon dioxide.

The Ozone Layer

Guy Brasseur and A. de Rudder of the Belgian Institute for Space Aeronomy reported in February that any threat to the ozone layer was sufficiently distant to allow time for further scientific evaluation. They calculated that if chlorofluorocarbon (CFC) emissions increased by 3% annually there might be some ozone depletion by the year 2034, but that if emissions were restricted the amount of ozone would increase. Further doubt was cast on the threat from CFCs in May when David Harper of Queen's University, Belfast, Northern Ireland, published his calculations of the rate at which chloromethane, similar chemically to a CFC, is released naturally by the common wood-rotting fungus *Phellinus pomaceus.* The fungus emits about 5 million metric tons annually, compared with an estimated release of 26,000 tons of industrial CFCs. He argued that if free chlorine were a genuine threat, the ozone layer should have been destroyed millions of years ago. In July, however, S. Lal, R. Borchers, P. Fabian, and B. C. Kruger, all of the West German Max-Planck-Institut, warned that bromine may catalyze the destruction of ozone more efficiently than chlorine. CFCs containing bromine, used mainly in fire extinguishers, release some 3,000 metric tons of bromine a year.

Marine Pollution

In a report published in June, the Fisheries Research Laboratory of the British Ministry of Agriculture, Fisheries, and Food warned that a scheme to treat sewage before discharging it into the Mersey estuary could cause serious heavy metal contamination of sediments in the Liverpool Bay area of the Irish Sea. Solids and heavy metals were being removed from sewage before its discharge into the estuary, but the residue was being dumped as a sludge in the bay some 12–18 mi (20–30 km) from the shore. Metal residues had increased from 220 parts per million in 1976 to 1,000 parts per million in 1980 as the sewage treatment plants came into operation.

In Poland it was reported in June that beaches

Photographs taken of the same spot in the Harz Mountains in West Germany in 1970 (left) and 1985 illustrate dramatically the severity of the forest damage that had become a matter of great concern in that nation.

at ten Baltic coast resorts near Gdansk were to be closed for the summer because of industrial pollution that could cause skin diseases.

Freshwater Pollution

A report issued in January said contamination of drinking water by supposedly "clean" high-tech industries may have contributed to high rates of birth abnormalities and miscarriages in Los Paseos, in California's "Silicon Valley." In 1980–81 there were 41 miscarriages in the town, compared with 23 in a control area, 13 birth defects compared with 5, and 30% of pregnancies ended in either miscarriage or a birth defect. In 1981–82 the proportion of Los Paseos children with congenital heart deformities was more than twice that in the county as a whole. The report suggested the cause was water contamination due to a leakage of 55,000 gal (250,000 liters) of 1,1,1 trichloroethane and dichloroethylene, both of which are degreasing agents, from storage tanks at a semiconductor factory 1,970 ft (600 m) from Los Paseos.

According to a policy statement issued by the Japanese Environment Agency in June, the migration of large numbers of people into new satellite cities with inadequate infrastructures was causing severe pollution of rivers and lakes. The pollution was said to be spreading to groundwater, which supplied 30% of Japan's drinking water.

July 18 was the deadline for the introduction of EC standards for drinking water, but as it approached several water authorities in the U.K. appealed for exemption or more time. Some used aluminum salts to treat water from acid peat moorland, and the aluminum content of the resulting water was very slightly higher than the EC limit. Others could not meet nitrate standards, and in July the government announced a three-year extension during which nitrate concentrations would be allowed to exceed the EC limit by 60 to 100% at 52 supply points serving 900,000 people.

There were fears of contamination of underground aquifers by chlorinated solvents when the contents of an unpublished Department of the Environment report were released in September. En-

gineers from the Imperial College of Science and Technology, University of London, who carried out the survey for the government, warned that 10% of aquifers could contain trichloroethylene and tetrachloroethylene in amounts exceeding limits recommended by the World Health Organization (WHO).

In May the Ganga Authority, whose nine-member committee was headed by India's Prime Minister Rajiv Gandhi, was given the five-year task of cleaning the Ganges. The river was polluted from the point where it enters Uttar Pradesh, at Hardwar, all the way to Calcutta, and some of the Ganges Basin was infertile because of salinity and metal contamination. The basin received one-third of all the fertilizer used in India and 3,000 metric tons of pesticides a year; 80% of the river pollution was caused by the discharge of sewage from 100 cities along the banks, and 20% from untreated effluent, cattle, farm fertilizers and pesticides, and incompletely cremated human corpses, hundreds of which floated in the river every day. A £180 million ($260 million) scheme to produce methane for fuel, fertilizer, and irrigation water from sewage was planned to reduce pollution by 75% in its first stage, which would treat sewage from the largest cities. The second stage would provide similar facilities for the smaller towns.

Air Pollution

In its report *Urban Air Pollution 1973–80,* published in October 1984, the Global Environment Monitoring System of the WHO listed the cities with the most polluted air. Measured in micrograms per cubic meter, and with a recommended limit of 60, sulfur dioxide was most serious in Milan, Italy (242), Tehran, Iran (160), Prague, Czech. (154), Santiago de Chile (137), and São Paulo, Brazil (135), while Helsinki, Fin., Glasgow, Scotland, and Warsaw and Wroclaw, Poland, were seriously polluted in winter. Measured in the same units, and also with a recommended limit of 60, smoke was worst in Tehran (222), Madrid (196), Bogotá, Colombia (120), Cairo (105), and Havana (101). Total particulate matter was worst in Lahore, Pak. (690), Baghdad, Iraq (563), Delhi (535) and

Calcutta (462), India, Accra, Ghana (398), Jakarta, Indon. (275), and Athens (235).

In the U.S. a survey of emissions from 80 of the country's largest chemical companies, made by the House Health and Environment Subcommittee, chaired by Rep. Henry Waxman (Dem., Calif.), reported on March 26 that hazardous substances were being released in more places and in larger amounts than had been suspected. Companies admitted discharging more than 200 substances they themselves classed as "hazardous," including acrylonitrile, ammonia, chloroform, vinyl chloride, ethylene oxide, and hydrochloric acid. Only asbestos, benzene, vinyl chloride, mercury, beryllium, and radionuclides were regulated federally, and the subcommittee was working on legislation that would require the EPA to produce regulations on a specific list of substances.

On January 17 a stage-two smog alert was imposed in North Rhine-Westphalia, West Germany. Private cars were banned during the morning and evening rush hours, and power stations were required to burn only light oil. For most of January 19 a stage-three alert caused a virtual shutdown of factories and a ban on all private cars in several cities, including Düsseldorf, Essen, Duisburg, Bottrop, Gelsenkirchen, and Oberhausen. Police were drafted to man smog barriers closing roads into the cities. The stage-two alert was lifted on January 20, but a stage-one alert remained in force. Citizens were asked to keep use of private cars to a minimum, and people with respiratory complaints were advised to remain indoors.

Land Conservation

The year was an exceptionally bad one for brush and timber fires in the western U.S. and Canada, where two years of dry weather had produced tinderbox conditions. During one period of high heat and humidity in the summer more than a million acres of 11 western states were ablaze, and fire fighters were brought in from as far away as Alaska. Electrical storms that produced lightning but little rain set off many of the fires, including most of those in wilderness areas, but arson was blamed for some of the blazes in California, where more than 170 homes were destroyed.

Despite opposition from environmentalists and an announcement in February that work had been halted, in August the Hungarian government decided to proceed with the construction of the Gabcikovo-Nagymaros hydroengineering project on the Danube. Opposition was based on fears that the "Danube Bend," a popular resort area for residents of Budapest, would be flooded, fears of the consequences for Budapest in the event of an earthquake, and doubts about the effects on wildlife of diverting 15.5 mi (25 km) of the river and its bayous through a concrete channel. The project would also divert the main navigational channel marking the border between Hungary and Czechoslovakia.

Nikolai Basiliev, the Soviet minister for land reclamation and water resources, announced on June 5 that the plan to divert the Irtysh and Ob rivers was essential to Soviet food production and would proceed. The scheme called for a 1,500-mi (2,400-km) canal and would reduce water flow into the Arctic, but Basiliev said scientists had concluded that any environmental effects would be merely local.

Radioactive Wastes

The trial of British Nuclear Fuels Ltd. (BNFL) began on June 5 at Carlisle Crown Court. BNFL faced six charges of contravening the Radioactive Substances Act 1960 and the Nuclear Installation Act 1965, arising from the accidental release of materials into the Irish Sea in November 1983. The company admitted one charge of failing to keep adequate records, and on July 9 the judge instructed the jury to acquit BNFL of two charges: failing to keep adequate records of radioactive materials stored on site, and failing to control material so it could not escape. The trial ended after eight weeks with the conviction of BNFL, although the judge stressed that the breaches of safety rules had not caused a discharge of material in excess of the authorized limits.

Toxic Chemical Wastes

Tanks at Union Carbide plants in West Virginia leaked twice in 1985, on August 11 at Institute and on August 13 at South Charleston. The first leak, caused by failure to contain a runaway reaction sim-

A mother comforts her daughters at an emergency treatment station after a large cloud of toxic gas leaked from a Union Carbide pesticide plant in Institute, West Virginia, on August 11.

REUTERS/BETTMANN NEWSPHOTOS

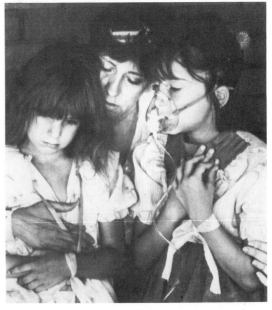

Sewage sludge is pumped into a barge at a site near New York City. Since 1924 sewage sludge had been dumped at a site just 12 miles (19 kilometers) offshore. Because of widespread contamination, however, a 1985 federal ruling required that future dumping be done at a site 106 nautical miles off the coast.

ilar to that at Bhopal, India, released aldicarb oxime gas, and 135 people received hospital treatment as a result. Following the Bhopal accident, the Institute plant had been modified to convert methyl isocyanate to the less dangerous aldicarb before it was transported across the country to make the finished pesticide Temik. The South Charleston incident released 418 gal (1,900 liters) of polyalkaline glycol (hydraulic brake fluid), isopropanol (solvent), and sulfuric acid into the Kanawha River. The chemicals were foul-smelling, but no one was injured.

In June the U.S. Economic Development Commission reported that exposure to toxic wastes in California would probably cause about 2,500 deaths annually for the next decade, and the cost of cleaning up the state would be about $4 billion a year. The oil refining, petrochemical, aerospace, defense, electronics, and agriculture industries, which were producing the wastes, also provided half the total employment in manufacturing in the state and 25% of state income. According to the head of the commission, Leo McCarthy, for every dollar invested, two more were spent managing toxic chemicals. The treatment of cancer caused by exposure to toxic wastes cost the state $1.3 billion a year; company lawsuits cost $2.7 billion a year; and replacing contaminated drinking water cost $32 million a year. The commission proposed seven immediate steps to deal with the problem, along with a five-year plan, based largely on treating wastes rather than dumping them.

In Britain the Hazardous Waste Inspectorate reported in June that many of the tips (dumps) receiving the 4.4 million metric tons of waste produced annually in England and Wales were badly managed and potentially dangerous. The report also warned of a shortage of incineration capacity for certain wastes, including polychlorinated biphenyls (PCBs). Britain was the only Western European country to rely on the private sector for industrial waste disposal, and many of the companies were in financial difficulties. The tips were licensed by local authorities, however, and in July the government told the county councils it expected better monitoring of the toxic waste tips they would inherit following abolition of the metropolitan counties. Re-Chem

International, one of the companies equipped to incinerate PCB, opened community relations centers at Pontypool and Fawley but failed to appease the public. Complaints of illness with symptoms similar to those previously reported from Bonnybridge, Scotland, were made by people living near the Fawley, Southampton, plant. Two scientific investigations reported in February that nothing unusual had been found in the health of humans or animals in the Bonnybridge area and that there was no evidence of high levels of PCB, dioxins, or furans near Bonnybridge or Pontypool.

In January a transformer containing insulation made from PCB exploded in the basement of an apartment building in Reims, France. The PCB burned to yield dioxins and furans. In August 343 people were told they had been contaminated, although no symptoms of injury had been reported. Bernard Paringaux, head of a waste disposal firm, was fined and sentenced to 18 months' imprisonment in June for receiving and concealing dioxin waste from Seveso, Italy, near Milan, where an explosion at the Icmesa chemical plant in July 1976 had caused widespread dioxin poisoning. At Seveso it was reported that the Icmesa factory site was being made into a park.

Lead

In November 1984 the British government asked the EC for permission to waive its compliance with a directive, due to come into force in July 1985, that would limit lead in tap water to 50 micrograms per liter. About five million people in Britain might be receiving water containing more lead. Although water authorities planned to install equipment to increase the alkalinity of acid waters and so reduce the amount of lead dissolved from pipes, the program would not be completed before 1989. In February 1985 the Paintmakers Association of Great Britain agreed to abandon all use of lead in paint by 1987. Regulations were laid before Parliament on June 24, and came into force on December 31, setting limits on the amount of lead permitted in canned food. The limit for most foods was one part per million, but corned beef and canned milk would have separate limits.

ETHIOPIA

A major development in Ethiopia during 1985 concerned a reassessment of the population in light of the country's first national census, conducted with UN assistance in May 1984. The census claimed to have covered 85% of the population. Estimates were made from various sources for the remainder, largely the population of rural highland regions in Eritrea and Tigre and pastoral lowland areas in all regions. The new total was declared to be 42,020,000, compared with the previous Statistical Office estimate of 34.6 million for the same date. The annual growth rate was put at 2.9%.

The distribution of population had been significantly altered in the aftermath of the 1983–85 drought, which affected virtually all regions, most seriously Eritrea, Tigre, Welo (Wallo), and certain areas of northern Shewa. Drought also hit regions such as Gojam, which previously had produced an exportable surplus of grain. In some areas the major factor in the disruption of the rural economy had been the uncertainty and inadequacy of rainfall in marginal areas of cultivation. It was also clear, however, that the northern regions had reached the end of a long historical period of traditional land use during which soil fertility had declined, and vegetation degradation had reached a point where long-term environmental upgrading would be required. In these circumstances the government was concerned to resettle people in more fertile areas. As of June 1985 more than 170,000 families had been resettled in the western provinces, and more than 300,000 families were to be resettled by year's end.

A French medical group, Médecins Sans Frontières, was ordered from the country after its chairman claimed that 100,000 people had died in the resettlement effort.

No figure had yet been put on the number of people who died during the famine. The problem had been compounded by the fact that extensive areas in the north were not under permanent government control as a result of secessionist activities. Figures released by the Relief and Rehabilitation Commission indicated that the total population requiring urgent relief supplies or supplementary feeding rose to nine million in July. The response was a large, if somewhat belated, program of support from the international community, contributed mainly through nongovernmental organizations.

The year brought rain to most regions in the country at the right time, but it remained to be seen whether the 1985 harvest would be sufficient. Grave doubts were expressed because the long period of food shortage and starvation had disorganized the agricultural economy. There was a shortage of seed grain; people were returning from feeding centers without farm implements or oxen; and the farming population in general was in a debilitated state. Further disruptions to food production occurred in the south where maize (corn) crops were attacked by an invasion of army worms, and the enset (false banana) plant, which provided the staple food for some three million people, was affected by disease. Herds had been seriously reduced by shortages of water and pasture. Finally, a battle was being waged against the coffee berry disease.

By May 1985 the world community had sent more than 500,000 tons of cereal grain to famine-wracked Ethiopia. Distribution of the food, however, was often hampered by the obstructive policies of the Ethiopian government.

RICHARD HOFFMANN—SYGMA

Against this background of rural disaster, which would require a considerable volume of external assistance to combat, the September celebrations of the Ethiopian new year and the 11th anniversary of the revolution were somewhat subdued. The expected announcement of the new constitution for a republic, following the formation of the Workers' Party of Ethiopia in September 1984, did not materialize.

There appeared to be no movement toward a settlement with the rebels in the north, where the continued fighting absorbed a significant proportion of government resources. Relations with Somalia also remained poor, and there were sporadic engagements along the lengthy border of the Ogaden during the year. The Ethiopian regime reacted with anger when news broke in January of Israel's secret evacuation of thousands of Ethiopian Jews from Ethiopia to Israel.

EUROPEAN AFFAIRS

Some further tentative steps toward greater political unity among member countries of the European Communities (EC; the European Economic Community [EEC], the European Coal and Steel Community [ECSC], and Euratom), together with continued failure to solve Western Europe's underlying economic ills, were the main characteristics of 1985. The year ended as it had begun with a serious unemployment crisis and further evidence that Western Europe was losing the industrial and technological struggle with the U.S. and Japan.

Although no clear or agreed strategy to make up lost ground had emerged, there was a growing consensus that existing policies had failed. There were signs of moves away from the monetarist orthodoxy that had guided national economic thinking in almost all Western European states from the beginning of the decade. There was also more questioning of existing trade and financial links binding Western Europe with the U.S. and the rest of the industrialized world.

Throughout the year Western Europe maintained pressure on the U.S. administration to act decisively to reduce its budget and balance of payments deficits. As the year drew to a close, however, there were fears that a new economic downturn in the U.S. might further delay and obstruct Western European efforts to reverse industrial stagnation and mass unemployment. The problems experienced by the U.S. dollar also exacerbated fears in Western Europe about the influence of third world indebtedness on international monetary and banking stability. This, in turn, revived Western European desires to strengthen and expand the European monetary system (EMS) as an autonomous element in the world monetary system.

The new EC Commission that took office in January under the presidency of Jacques Delors, former French finance minister, made the removal of internal economic and trade barriers one of its major priorities. With the total number of people out of work within the EC approaching 14 million, economists were gloomy about an early improvement in job prospects. Apart from encouraging faster technological innovation and development and strengthening the EMS, the EC committed itself in January to completing the internal Common Market. However, the task of removing institutional and other barriers to form a completely integrated European market appeared likely to require several years to accomplish.

Meanwhile, despite serious internal economic problems and unresolved issues affecting its political future, the EC pressed on with enlargement. After more than five years of negotiations, the EC summit held in Brussels on March 29–30 agreed to admit Portugal and Spain as new member states from Jan. 1, 1986. The treaties formalizing the accession of Portugal and Spain to the Community were signed at the EC summit held in Milan, Italy, on June 29.

In the same year that the decision was taken to increase substantially the geographic area and population of the Community, Greenland became the first territory to leave the EC. Greenland formally withdrew on February 1. In a referendum three years earlier, the majority of the tiny population of the self-governing Danish territory had voted to abandon membership because of dissatisfaction with the effect of EC fishing policy on its economy and the lack of development aid.

At the Luxembourg summit in December agreement was reached on a package of reforms that, if approved by national governments, would form the basis for amendments to the treaty. The package contained the prospect of a very limited extension in the use of majority voting on proposals designed to develop the internal market, an increased consultative role for the European Parliament, and "progressive realization" of economic and monetary union. However, while the U.K. emerged content with special provisions allowing it to retain border controls in view of its island status, in the opinion of some member countries the reform package was rendered ineffective by the number of national exemptions it contained.

Concern about the extent to which European industry was falling behind its major world industrial competitors surfaced regularly throughout the year. In April Pres. François Mitterrand of France proposed, with West German government support, a major project named Eureka, designed to keep Western Europe in the high-technology race by encouraging firms to coordinate high-technology research and development, particularly in the area of information systems, lasers, and artificial intelligence.

Trade frictions with the U.S., Japan, and some of the newly industrialized nations were another recurring source of concern in Western Europe. In October the U.S. and the EC each announced plans to bring action against the other under the General Agreement on Tariffs and Trade for unfairly subsidizing exports of cereals. Open trade conflict with the U.S. over steel exports was only narrowly avoided when, in November, an uneasy agreement was reached involving "voluntary restraint" of certain types of European steel exports to the U.S. The closing months of the year saw renewed pressure on Japan to further liberalize imports from Europe and to take action through exchange-rate policy to improve the balance of trade between Europe and Japan.

In May the EC and China signed a new trade agreement that greatly expanded cooperation in industrial research and development. During the year the Council for Mutual Economic Assistance, the Soviet-bloc trading organization, opened diplomatic contacts and sought a formal bilateral agreement with the EC. However, the Europeans, while eager to conclude separate agreements with individual Eastern-bloc countries on trade and other matters and encouraged over the U.S.S.R.'s apparent readiness to recognize EC institutions, indicated their desire first to observe the results of the U.S.-Soviet summit in November.

A major issue during September was the worsening unrest in South Africa and growing pressure within Western European countries for stronger action to express opposition to apartheid. The 12 EC governments (including Spain and Portugal, whose foreign ministers began attending discussions on political cooperation in midyear) agreed on largely symbolic trade and other sanctions against South Africa. Agreement came at the end of a three-week period during which the U.K. government had withheld its full support.

Much discussion took place during the year about the deterioration in relations between the nuclear superpowers. It was widely feared that U.S. Pres. Ronald Reagan's Strategic Defense Initiative, the so-called Star Wars proposal, might jeopardize the prospects for progress at the nuclear arms reduction negotiations between the U.S. and the U.S.S.R. in Geneva. There was relief during October when it emerged that Reagan and Soviet leader Mikhail Gorbachev would be meeting to try to give new impetus to the Geneva talks. On the other hand, it was felt that, in terms of Western European public opinion, the Soviet leader had stolen a march on the U.S. by making proposals for radical cuts in nuclear arms in the late summer. While no major breakthrough was achieved at the summit, both leaders reaffirmed their commitment to arms control negotiations. In December a meeting of foreign ministers from Western European countries expressed disappointment that the summit had not made concrete progress toward arms reductions.

During the year there were several meetings of the revived Western European Union, an association of the principal European members of the NATO alliance. This was interpreted by many on

CONTIFOTO/SYGMA

As Italian Prime Minister Bettino Craxi observes, Felipe Gonzáles, prime minister of Spain, signs the treaty that would admit his country and Portugal to membership in the European Communities.

both sides of the Atlantic as an indication that European members wanted to play a greater, and more independent, role within NATO and in their own defense decisions.

The European Court of Human Rights in Strasbourg was not in the headlines as often as in previous years. There were, however, significant rulings confirming the right of citizens in individual Western European countries to appeal to the court against decisions made by national governments and courts.

Further steps were taken to integrate the trading and financial systems of the European Free Trade Association, which linked non-EC countries of Western Europe, with the EC. The two organizations not only concerted their international policies on trade barriers, technical standards, and monetary cooperation but also discussed steps to tackle such problems as environmental pollution.

Eastern Europe

The central event of 1985 in Eastern European politics took place, as so often before, in the U.S.S.R. with the accession of Mikhail Gorbachev to the leadership of the Communist Party of the Soviet Union (CPSU) on March 11. Though Eastern Europe had become far more independent of Soviet desires than it had been under Stalin, it remained dependent on the Kremlin and on Soviet preferences. In this context the Gorbachev succession was important. Under his two short-tenured predecessors, Yuri Andropov and Konstantin Chernenko, the Soviet preference for the direction of Eastern European policies remained unclear. Gorbachev, it was expected, would change this. In particular, the new leader enjoyed something of a reputation as a reformer, a term that was undefined and open to interpretation.

By the end of 1985 there was little hard evidence of Gorbachev's true wishes for the future of Eastern Europe. Indeed, the picture was muddy and confused. Considerable alarm was occasioned in some Eastern European countries by an article published in *Pravda,* the CPSU daily newspaper, in June. The article was harshly critical of national deviations in Eastern European countries and asserted that the Soviet road to communism was the only true road. These were code words for centralization and reassertion of the supremacy of Soviet methods, something that several Eastern European countries were plainly reluctant to contemplate. Reactions to the article varied between those in Hungary, where it met with apprehension because it was felt that the entire Hungarian reform course was threatened by its implications, and those in Poland, where the article elicited barely a whisper.

Subsequent statements in the Soviet press—none of them, it should be noted, coming from politicians—served only to balance the picture. An article in *Kommunist,* the CPSU's theoretical monthly and, therefore, of high ideological persuasiveness, appeared to go in the other direction from the one in *Pravda* toward the acceptance of national differences in the "construction of socialism." There was no public statement from Gorbachev himself to clarify matters by the end of the year.

As against this, those Eastern European countries favoring relatively relaxed relations with the West, notably East Germany, Hungary, Romania, and, to a lesser extent, Bulgaria, took heart from the relatively optimistic note on which the Geneva summit between Gorbachev and U.S. Pres. Ronald Reagan in November ended. In terms of atmosphere, if not in content, the summit appeared to offer encouragement to those who favored easier contacts between East and West.

Yet, at the same time, the Budapest Cultural Forum, one of the meetings designed to maintain the process established by the 1975 Helsinki Accords by discussing, in this instance, East-West cultural relations and the political obstacles to them, ended in virtual failure when the delegates were unable to agree on any final document. With Western delegations stressing the unacceptability of Soviet and Eastern European restrictions on cultural contacts, there had been no doubt from the outset that the fairly tough Western line would make it difficult to reach agreement. Nevertheless, to end the forum without any kind of final document whatsoever reflected poorly on the six weeks of discussions. There was little doubt that the intransigent attitude of the Soviet and Czechoslovak delegations contributed materially toward the outcome, although at the end it was the Romanian delegation that vetoed the innocuous final communiqué drafted by the Hungarian hosts, mainly because Romania had been repeatedly pilloried during the forum for its discriminatory policies against its two million-strong ethnic Hungarian minority.

Celebration of the 30th anniversary of the signing of the Warsaw Treaty, which included a ceremonial renewal of the treaty at a Warsaw Pact summit in Poland in April, turned out to be a rather low-key affair. Despite the presence of all party leaders and heads of state and government from the seven Warsaw Pact countries, little more was done than to sign the text of the treaty, without amendments. The treaty itself was renewed for an additional 20 years with an automatic prolongation of another 10 years.

A clear new line was emerging in economic relations between the U.S.S.R. and Eastern Europe.

Members of the European Communities (EC) open a two-day summit on June 28. Delegates sought a joint strategy to deal with international terrorism and measures that would allow the EC to make important decisions more easily.

AP/WIDE WORLD

Evidently the Soviet Union was no longer prepared to accept the relatively low-quality goods that many Eastern European nations had grown used to delivering to Soviet purchasers. For decades the Soviet market had been regarded as "soft," that is, prepared to absorb goods of a quality that was well below the world level. The Soviet delegation to the Council for Mutual Economic Assistance meeting in June served notice that this would no longer be the case and that, as the U.S.S.R. delivered raw materials that were up to the standard expected in world markets, it would in the future expect the equivalent in manufactured goods. In several Eastern European countries the press carried reports warning that Soviet buyers were actually returning shoddy goods.

The implications of this move, which was clearly in line with Gorbachev's attempt to improve discipline within the U.S.S.R. itself, were disturbing for Eastern Europeans. In the medium term the change also had repercussions for investment, as it would evidently require the Eastern Europeans to retool and to introduce costly quality-control measures in order to upgrade the quality of their output.

FASHION

During the winter of 1984–85 that Japanese tendency to make all silhouettes, male or female, look alike still prevailed. Loose and slouchy jackets with broad, squared-off shoulders, borrowed from "Big Brother," were worn over fully gathered skirts that descended to below the calf, effectively camouflaging the body. This androgynous appearance was emphasized by the new cropped haircut. Previously, boy and girl had worn the same long, fluffy curls, but now, with hair closely trimmed over ears and neck, they were even more difficult to identify from the back.

On the Establishment side, ponchos and reversible lambskin coats did little to delineate the silhouette. However, the general look was livened by a great display of patterned stockings. Heavy black lace was the favorite and so important that boots were practically eliminated, except for short bootees. The low-heeled shoe, laced up the front and with side cutouts, soon became the hit for town wear. Black in winter, it turned white in the spring. Long, bright-colored, plain wool scarves replaced shawls. Hats were mainly the pull-on soft felt cloche type. From under the brim glittered heart-shaped diamond ear clips or swinging gold metal hoops—the larger the better.

Discarding the androgynous look, fashion turned to a new gentleness in the spring of 1985. This was achieved mainly through rounded instead of square padding at the shoulders, gathers and pleating at the sleeve tops on dresses and blouses, and very deep batwing armholes on everything including knitwear. Hemlines were a decision every woman made for herself. The very young, who had nothing to hide, jauntily paced the streets in tubelike skirts at mid-

AP/WIDE WORLD

Issey Miyake, a leading exponent of the so-called Japanese look, struck a bold note in his 1986 collection of ready-to-wear clothes for women.

thigh level, preferably in black leather or knitwear. Another influence came from the "flappers" of the '20s, revived in the film *The Cotton Club,* where the girls wore huge bows at hem or hip and at the side of the head. Another way of putting the accent on hips was to add a softly draped sash all around or to drape the lower part of a separate top to one side above a slim skirt. In this case the skirt could reach knee level or well below the calf.

A great display of color heralded the coming of spring. It started with pale apricot or melon, for everything from knitwear to knife-pleated crêpe skirts. Then came bright red, even for shoes. There followed a range of sherbet colors, pale pink, green, or yellow, before the all-white look took over for full summer. For town wear, white was worn with black accessories—bag, shoes, and jewelry, including jet eardrops and innumerable bracelets.

On the summer beaches, there were no more strings. Swimsuits were all in one piece, with shoulder straps, rounded neckline, and bare back. Swooping cutouts at the side, baring thighs nearly up to the waistline, turned them into real knockouts.

Thigh-baring cutouts were also applied to lingerie for all-in-one "bodies" in lace or plain stretch material with lace trimming. Abbreviated boxer shorts were the pick of all the youngsters, who fell for the imaginative prints. Borrowed from lingerie and revived from the 1950s were the "bustiers" or boned *guêpières,* with or without straps, worn on the beaches with tight miniskirts or boxer shorts. They topped long, fully gathered skirts for dancing in the evening.

The big, rounded shoulder line introduced in the spring pursued its natural course for autumn and winter. Contrasting with the pin-size head, top volume was the rule. Waists were belted or well defined. Shape was reinstated. Skirts were generally straight, but hemlines varied a great deal—from mini or mid-thigh to long and very long. In the autumn, colors switched to deeper, richer shades, as a counterpoint to black. A dark, inky blue was often the choice for the first autumn buy, the three-quarter-length jacket with deep armholes, large lapels or shawl collar, to be worn with a slim black skirt. The same deep blue was selected for blouses, sweaters, and wool scarves and again worn with black. Purple was also in the color race but more closely combined with black in weave or in print.

Short, narrow skirts put the emphasis on shoes and tights. Shoes were dressed up with bows—neat flat bows, pageboy style, or large draped bows over a covered instep and pointed toes. Heels were sometimes wide and flat, sometimes small or medium size, only occasionally really high, as for fancy sandals with draped straps. Tights were responsible for the big color splash and the touch of humor in winter fashion. With the miniskirt they either matched in plain color or contrasted in black. Lace patterns, dating from the previous winter in black or from the summer in white, were set aside. A multitude of jacquard patterns featuring plaids, checks, or light specks were suggested for daytime. There were also many pretty prints, such as allover paisley, feather, or marble effects or flowers. A scattering of rose bouquets was effective on black.

The color outburst in fashion was bound to influence makeup. The cheeks were brushed with pastel pink and the eyelids with smoky gray; lipstick was bluish red. The technicolor effect really began at night, with focus on the eyes. Eye shadow, eyeliner, and mascara for eyelashes all drew on parakeet yellow, green, blue, and red.

Men's Fashions

Designs and designers of fabrics and fashions were the key words in menswear in 1985. New patterns in natural and man-made fibers were largely the outcome of skillful variations of one or more standard weaves. In woolens and worsteds, these new and more colorful cloths, mostly in the now universally accepted lighter weights, provided international clothing designers with the foundations for their new fashions.

Conventionally styled suits, sports jackets, and topcoats, on the other hand, became even more conventional, with U.S. and British tailored and ready-to-wear fashions providing the classics for business and formal wear. The division between the conventional and the unconventional was also seen in footwear, where traditional full and semibrogue Oxford styles were worn for formal and business occasions, only to be replaced by the colorful track and running shoes for leisure and pleasure.

The "layered" looks of the previous year continued in both sports shirts and summer knitwear, much of it in cotton and some with blends of linen. Among younger men, the fashion of wearing the shirt outside the trousers led to many new lines of shirts especially designed for this purpose, with a short, squared front and a much longer, rounded shirttail at the back.

Byblos, one of Italy's most talented design studios, showed its facetious new menswear collection in Milan in July. Although clearly in tune with trends in Italian design, the two designers responsible for the look were actually English.

VINCENZO GIACO—A.R.T. FOTO

Fashion

Special Report:
The Street Scene—
Pop, Glam, Androgyny

by Suzy Menkes

Street style over the past decade has spawned many important fashion trends—the "retro" clothing revivals, deliberately torn, crumpled, and distressed clothes, androgyny, oversize. Where streetwise youth has led, mainstream fashion has followed, the ideas grasped, absorbed, and rehashed by dress manufacturers eager for profit. The concept of youth style was born out of the optimistic post-World War II years when a rising teenage generation was given its own cultural and commercial identity. The 1980s style was part of a harsher world in which unemployment and international upheaval bred insecurity. Against this background clothes became a form of tribal identity—a uniform in which to fight the generational war, a chance to escape, in the pleasure of dressing up, from too much reality.

Street fashion itself became the height of fashion by the spring of 1985, when established international designers declared the streets an inspiration. In Milan the Paris-based designer Karl Lagerfeld made a high-fashion fur collection in homage to wild street fashion, and Jean-Paul Gaultier in Paris re-created London street looks at couture prices.

The strongest single influence on the street scene as a manifestation of youth culture was pop music. With the growth of the pop video, identification of a singer and group with a particular clothing image reflected back on their fans. Many of the young British designers, products of a unique art college training system, were linked to the pop music world, so its stars now had personal image makers. The politically committed pop star expressed his ideals in clothes as well as lyrics; thus designer Katharine Hamnett created slogan T-shirts that were co-opted by Frankie Goes to Hollywood, and the streets were instantly beaming out messages like "Protest and Survive," "Frankie Say Arm the Unemployed," and "Save the Whales." Other designers captured the fragmented sequences of the pop video with visual disturbance prints, some in graphic patterns resembling computer printouts.

Androgyny was the buzz word in 1985. Women were taking control of their own lives and taking over the male wardrobe with its aggressive wide shoulder line and trousers. The most persistent street motif was the hanging shirttail, worn by both sexes. It was a conspicuous kind of dishabille, the

tails negligently but deliberately on show under a tailored, formal jacket—often bought from the flea market or thrift shop, important sources of street fashion.

Gender-bending, as Boy George showed, is a two-way street, and 1985 was also the year of the peacock male. Shiny and transparent fabrics revealing the male torso were a new interpretation of a theme familiar in women's clothes. Vivid colors and prints, often in floral and traditionally feminine patterns, made the young man more colorful

JOHN VOOS/THE TIMES

Hepburn's hooded headscarf, pointed pumps, and wrap sunglasses. Ray-ban glasses were the cult eyewear. Day-Glo colors lit up the street as sherbet-colored socks and accessories switched in and out of fashion like neon lights. Plastic sandals walked on and off just as rapidly. The dishabille look reached its zenith in the summer, with baggy oversize cottons and even silks, all deliberately crumpled and wrinkled. Yet at the same time, there was movement back toward the body, a rejection of natural fibers (the preoccupation of mainstream fashion), and a new emphasis on stretchy, clinging synthetics. Body-hugging leggings replaced the shirttail as a badge of style.

Both fashion and pop have a voracious appetite for change, and under the spotlight of media attention the street redefined its style by redefining gender. Pop heroes Michael Jackson, George Michael of Wham!, and Simon Le Bon of Duran Duran all turned elegantly tailored backs on hanging shirts and tailcoats. A strong return to tailoring was followed (or maybe led) on the streets, where 16-year-old boys wore for pleasure the smart suits their fathers had abandoned in favor of casual wear. At the same time, Madonna in the pop world and the TV stars of "Dynasty" suggested a new image for young women, in total contrast to the man-size collarless tweed jackets and overcoats, the straight pants and heavy boots of androgynous style. The sexist woman—tight black leather skirt and spiky high heels—had been a part of punk. In her new manifestation she was less aggressive, more overtly glamorous, in the pop tradition of glam rock.

than he had been since the 1960s. Cheeks contoured with blusher, discreet foundation, and subtle eye color (but not lipstick) were all seen among young men during the early part of 1985, but the identification of male makeup with the gay community discouraged the cosmetic companies from backing the trend.

The swinging '60s were now an inspiration to the children of the decade. The skinny rib polo neck, the miniskirt in moderation, op art and geometric patterns were all exuberantly rehashed. The trawl through times and closets past also brought back the ski-pant trouser (now for both sexes) and nostalgic re-creations of Grace Kelly's Capri pants, Audrey

FINLAND

Foreign ministers of the 35 countries that endorsed the Final Act of the Conference on Security and Cooperation in Europe met in Helsinki on July 30–Aug. 1, 1985, exactly ten years after the document was signed. Most important of some 200 bilateral and multilateral fringe meetings was the first meeting between U.S. Secretary of State George Shultz

and his new Soviet counterpart, Eduard Shevardnadze, who prepared the ground for the meeting between their respective leaders in November.

On January 2 Finnish defense staff announced that an "unidentified flying object" had penetrated Finland's airspace five days earlier. They gave the news only after the Norwegians revealed that a Soviet missile had crossed a neck of their territory

Finnish searchers inspect the wreckage of a Soviet cruise missile after it was recovered from the frozen Lake Inari. The missile went astray during exercises over the Barents Sea, and the Soviet Union subsequently apologized for the accident.

between the Arctic Ocean and Finland. Within 48 hours Moscow issued an unprecedented admission and apology to both Helsinki and Oslo, thereby defusing an incident that could have had serious consequences. The Soviets said the projectile had been "inadvertently" fired during shooting practice in the Barents Sea.

By the time Pres. Mauno Koivisto had his first full meeting with the new Soviet leader, Mikhail Gorbachev, in Moscow on September 19, two unforeseen problems had emerged to trouble bilateral relations. First, a nagging shortfall in Soviet crude-oil shipments to Finland had developed. Since Finland could not export more than it imported on bilateral account, the reassurances that Koivisto received on the oil flow were important. Second, the Soviets had issued a warning to the Finnish Communists that a split in their party would jeopardize interstate relations. At an extraordinary congress of the Finnish Communist Party in March, the national-minded majority had increased its influence at the expense of the pro-Moscow orthodox minority when the majority-controlled Central Committee (CC) was granted the power to eject district organizations that did not obey party rules. Despite Soviet intimidation, the CC later set October as the deadline to begin expulsions.

Pressure from the Kremlin proved abortive in another context. The Soviet news agency TASS pilloried a "peace and freedom" cruise mounted by exiles from the former Baltic republics of Estonia, Latvia, and Lithuania. Despite its embarrassment, the government allowed the ship to dock in Finland, and an unprecedented anti-Soviet march was staged in Helsinki on July 28.

There was concern about the government's handling of information during an incident in June in which 21 Finnish soldiers from the UN Interim Force in Lebanon were held captive for eight days by the Israeli-backed South Lebanon Army (SLA). After much official evasion, it was revealed that the troops had helped to stage-manage the desertion of 11 SLA militiamen.

FISH AND FISHERIES
The entry into the European Communities (EC) of Spain and Portugal, scheduled for Jan. 1, 1986, would have far-reaching repercussions, touching most fishing nations in some way in the years ahead. The Spanish fishing fleet almost equaled the combined EC fleets in size. Of its approximately 13,000 vessels, 11,000 were relatively small, but the remainder included many large ocean-ranging freezer trawlers and tuna boats. With the EC fleet virtually doubled, it would represent one of the world's largest fish-catching forces. At the same time, with the addition of Spain—a major seafood importer—the EC would constitute a single market of considerable size. Together, these two factors would enable the EC to exercise considerable influence at the international level. Also, Spain had

become highly specialized in setting up joint ventures with other countries worldwide. These would become increasingly integrated into the EC, and already Spain was offering its joint-venture expertise to its new partners.

There was also a move toward improving the quality of landed fish as a means of winning the high prices needed to compensate for smaller catches. The proportion of fish and shellfish undergoing processing before sale continued to rise. Food technologists were forecasting that most fish would eventually be sold as reformed mince, often utilizing those species less favored on the market, such as blue whiting and Norway pout.

During the year there was a fisheries exhibition at Vigo, Spain—Europe's largest fishing port. The Spanish government chose the occasion to mount a conference, to which some 30 fisheries ministers and high officials were invited, to discuss aid to third world countries' fisheries. China was also the venue for a fisheries exhibition and conference—an indication of that country's policy of expanding and modernizing its fishing industry and moving its fleets farther into international grounds. China was also exporting its undoubted expertise in multiple-species fish farming. In 1983 one-third of China's fish harvest had come from inland waters.

Japan continued to lead the world, both in size of catch and in fish and shellfish imports. Japan was also one of the nations taking an increased interest in fishing off the Falkland Islands—in this case for squid—and there were again demands in Britain for a 200-mi or similar exclusive economic zone around the Falklands that would enable stocks to be managed more efficiently. Peru was still recovering from the loss of the shoals of anchoveta that once brought the country more than ten million metric tons of raw material for its fish-meal plants. El Niño, the warm Pacific current that was blamed for the disaster, appeared to have subsided, and Peru's catch was climbing to three million metric tons—double the 1983 figure—20% of which consisted of food fish. Chile's catch rose 11% to 4.5 million metric tons. Mexico was still having problems marketing its shrimp, while U.S. shrimpers accused it of selling into a free U.S. market while maintaining its own high tariff barriers.

The U.S. industry took an upturn as the popularity of seafood rose on dietary grounds and the campaign for improved quality took effect. Stocks of frozen cod that had been jamming cold storage began to move, and imports of lobster, shrimp, scallops, and clams increased. On the U.S. West Coast fishermen were learning to diversify their catch and catching methods and were landing fish to foreign vessels under joint-venture agreements. Fresh optimism was demonstrated in orders for new boats, and the U.S. was at last getting tough with foreign vessels in order to support the newly burgeoning industry. Japan, the U.S.'s largest joint-venture partner, was told that it had to buy more

Crew members of a Japanese whaling ship, just returned to Tokyo from the Antarctic whaling grounds, clench their fists and shout in protest on learning that the Japanese government had agreed to close the whaling industry by 1988.

AP/WIDE WORLD

U.S.-produced *surimi* fish mince if it wished to keep its present quota of Alaska pollack. A new crab-stick plant, to be built in Seattle, Wash., would cut U.S. imports from Japan. Squid stocks off the northwest coast were also being exploited by the U.S., with 400 metric tons landed in three months at Oregon—yet another sign of increased versatility among traditionally conservative U.S. fishermen. A vote of confidence in the industry was the decision to build a new fish terminal in Brooklyn, N.Y.

Norwegian shipyards experienced a welcome return of orders, and in Scotland builders of fishing vessels were having a busy time as the fisheries successfully adapted to the EC common fisheries policy. Scotland was now the U.K.'s largest supplier of fish and shellfish. An increasing percentage of Scottish landings were being processed before sale, and new processing plants were proliferating. Scottish fishermen contrived to live in uneasy peace with North Sea oil. At a meeting in Aberdeen, concern was expressed over the extent of oil industry debris littering the seabed, to the detriment of fishing operations. There were also warnings of rising pollution levels in the North Sea, which could affect fishing.

According to a study by a U.S. team, export prospects for the Far East looked promising. The team forecast an increase in consumption that could not be satisfied by existing fishing grounds in the West. Fish farming in Europe could help to fill the gap, provided higher prices were obtained for currently less popular species that were good subjects for farming. The U.S. study also forecast greater use of fish-based products made from extruded fish mince, with flavors such as crab, lobster, and scampi superimposed by additives.

FLOWERS AND GARDENS

Weather strongly influenced U.S. gardening in 1985. With a late spring-summer drought in many sections, lack of rainfall reduced soil moisture, and growth of woody plants and seedlings was hampered. Water levels in civic reservoirs were down, and restrictions on water use made browned-off lawns the summer's norm. This was a significant problem for property owners; the Lawn Institute estimated that of the 83 million households in the United States, 53 million had lawns. Each lawn was about 4,000 sq ft (371 sq m) in size—nearly 5 million ac (about 2 million ha) of land, equivalent to six times the land area of the state of Rhode Island. Other weather factors also took their toll. Hurricane Gloria struck the northeastern coastal midsection with winds near 90 mph (145 km/hr), causing extensive property damage in eastern Long Island, central Connecticut, and into New England. Many heritage trees were lost.

But in spite of discouraging weather, the American Association of Nurserymen said that the garden market was growing rapidly, with a projected increase in sales of between 23 and 28%. The growth of the market was attributed to increased confidence in the economy as well as to homeowners' having more disposable income. The latter was evidenced during the year in a larger volume of residential landscaping contracts, plus higher sales for patio plants and vegetable garden seeds and seedlings. The effect of these trends was particularly marked in the post-World War II baby boom population, now centering between ages 30 and 40. Members of this group spent more than the average consumer on "self-help" products, including gardening tools and plants.

Tomatoes remained at the top of the vegetable popularity poll of crops grown at home. Next in popularity were peppers, green beans, cucumbers, and onions. Least popular with the U.S. gardener was the parsnip. Among flowers, petunias yielded first place to impatiens. Other popular flowers sold as seedlings at garden centers included marigolds, geraniums, sweet alyssum, and zinnias.

The national rose testing organization, All-America Roses, set an unusual precedent by giving its awards for the year exclusively to the hybrid tea class of roses. The three hybrid tea prizewinners, which were to be available for planting early in 1986, were Touch of Class (pink, shaded coral, and cream), Broadway, a bicolor (red-pink and yellow), and Voodoo (a blend of yellow, peach, and orange blushing to scarlet).

Indoor greenery remained a significant part of the U.S. life-style. At least 90% of homeowners surveyed by the Society of American Florists said that they had at least one plant in their homes, and of these, 57% said they had at least five plants.

An increased awareness of the effect of environmental stress on the nation's plant heritage was underscored by a new federal policy to eliminate the plant designation "rare" species, replacing it with the term "threatened" species. A threatened species is one that is likely to become endangered within the foreseeable future; an endangered species is one that is in danger of extinction throughout all or a significant portion of its range. Wildlife experts estimated that of the approximately 25,000 species of plants native to the U.S., one out of every eight—about 3,000—was currently rare or endangered. With these statistics in mind, the National Center for Plant Conservation was founded, made up of 20 national botanic gardens. The organization not only would monitor wild plant populations but would seek means to propagate the rarest species.

Eighty percent of British homes had gardens—the highest percentage in Europe. Not surprisingly, the garden market had continued to grow and now had an estimated value of $1 billion. Garden visiting continued to be a major reason for a day's excursion, and the numbers visiting gardens, both private and public, was still increasing.

New varieties of flowers that won awards after trials during the year included Summer Showers, an ivy-leaved geranium for raising from seed. The roses that received gold medals from the Royal National Rose Society were both hybrid tea types, as yet unnamed, and among certificate winners were Polar Star, another hybrid tea, raised in West Germany, and Princess Alice, a polyantha rose raised in Britain.

Two events that were of significance in the restoration of historic gardens were a large grant from English Heritage and the National Heritage Memorial Fund for the reclamation of the mid-18th-century landscape garden at Painshill, Surrey, and the opening of the walled garden at the royal palace at Apeldoorn in the east of The Netherlands. The garden at Apeldoorn, a 17th-century garden made for King William in the French style of the period, was the first of what are, in England, now called Dutch gardens. During the year the world-famous British nurseryman Sir Harold Hillier died. His chief legacies to gardeners were his arboretum, now in the care of Hampshire County Council, and his "Manual," which lists and describes most of the trees and shrubs that can be grown in Britain.

FOOD PROCESSING

A new preservation technology was being commercialized by a Belgian joint venture company formed between the Sud-Lait cooperative of Luxembourg and Oleofina, a subsidiary of the Petrofina Group. It involved the extraction of two naturally occurring bacteriocides from milk for use in infant foods and as a preservative in other food products.

Advances in genetic engineering and enzyme technology were providing new opportunities for food processors. Imperial Biotechnology of the U.K. developed a process for accelerating the ripening of cheese. Using enzymes extracted from selected strains of microorganisms, it could reduce the ripening time of cheddar cheese, normally nine months, to three months. A study by the market

The fruit of 13 years' labor by Adam Purple, the "Garden of Eden" in a burned-out area of New York City's Lower East Side was destroyed in September to make way for a low-income housing project. Purple had declined offers to move the garden because it was, he said, the center of the universe.

STEVEN FERRY—
GAMMA/LIAISON

analysts Frost & Sullivan published during the year estimated that the U.S. industrial enzyme market would grow at the rate of 6.5% a year, to a value of $255 million by 1988, with three-quarters of the market accounted for by the needs of the food industry. Enzymatically produced high fructose corn syrup, for example, was already replacing sugar as the prime sweetener in prepared foods and soft drinks in the U.S., and enzymes obtained from maize (corn) were making inroads in cheese making, meat tenderizing, brewing, and the manufacture of fish protein concentrates, where processors were increasingly turning away from traditional fermentation agents. In Europe, however, such developments were inhibited by punitively high levies on imports of maize products.

Enzyme technology was also making headway in the analytical field. Conventional procedures for detecting certain substances, such as trace contaminants, in foods were giving way, in certain circumstances, to techniques in which specific enzymes were made to react with the substances. Such enzymes are known as biosensors. In the U.K. workers at Cranfield Institute of Technology and at Imperial College, University of London, developed biosensors that rely on a direct interaction between the enzyme and an electrode. Such biosensors are immune from chemical interference, would be cheap to manufacture, and could be incorporated in compact, inexpensive instruments. It was envisaged that these instruments would be designed to predict the shelf life of food products and assess the microbial state or the progress of rancidity in a food well before spoilage.

The largest outbreak of salmonella food poisoning in U.S. history—some 16,000 cases reported—was traced to two faulty valves in this dairy in Melrose Park, Illinois.

JOSÉ MORÉ/CHICAGO TRIBUNE

Packaging Developments

The Coloreed bag-in-box packaging system used for Macphie's nondairy cream, which had been developed specifically for low-acid and nonacid products, used a new patented packaging principle that was said to eliminate the risk of product contamination and to provide improved operating efficiencies. Although Macphie was filling 10- and 25-liter packs (1 liter = 1.0567 qt [U.S.]), the technique could handle packs of any size between 2 and 50 liters, and similar systems were expected to find wide use in dairy-related industries for such products as milk, yogurt, cream, and soups.

Considerable publicity was given to the introduction by the U.K. company Crosse & Blackwell during the year of a line of shelf-stable soups in aseptic cartons. These were the first products of this type to be produced by the high-temperature short-time (HTST) process widely used for milk and fruit juices. According to the makers, the soups had a fresher and more natural taste than equivalent soups prepared by canning.

Within a few years, aseptic packaging had grown from relative obscurity into a billion-dollar industry. Its future looked bright, especially in the U.S., where, after a slow start, use of the technique was expanding at a faster rate than anywhere else in the world. Among the containers being used for aseptic packaging were paperboard cartons, plastic cups and bottles, and bag-in-box. During the year Tetra Pak opened its second factory in North America, in Toronto, complementing its factory in Denton, Texas, opened in 1984. The company claimed to be making 35,000,000,000 cartons annually.

More than 40% of U.S. homes now had microwave ovens. However, most food processors had not kept up with the trend and were having trouble developing "dual ovenable" products; that is, products that could be cooked in either a conventional or a microwave oven. The main difficulty was that because microwave ovens work through induction and not radiant heating, food cooked in them does not brown or crisp and sometimes has an unappetizing appearance. The Pillsbury Co. introduced a special package for a pizza product that overcame this difficulty. The package contained a "susceptor" to aid browning—a layer of powdered aluminum laminated under plastic. The aluminum absorbs the microwave energy and raises the temperature on the surface of the pizza sufficiently to brown and crisp the crust.

New Products

Fish and fish products were growing in popularity; major U.S. and Japanese food processors were flooding North American supermarkets with products made from *surimi,* a fish paste of Japanese origin. *Surimi* products could be flavored, shaped, and textured to resemble shrimp, lobster, and a host of other seafood products.

FOOTBALL

The Chicago Bears climaxed an 18–1 season and gained their first National Football League (NFL) championship since 1963 by defeating the New England Patriots 46–10 in the Super Bowl at New Orleans, La., on Jan. 26, 1986. The margin of victory was the largest in Super Bowl history. Dominating the game was the Bear defense, which allowed the Patriots only one first down during the first half and held them to only seven yards gained by rushing during the entire game. The Bears also tied a Super Bowl record by sacking the Patriot quarterbacks seven times. Voted the most valuable player of the game was Bear defensive end Richard Dent.

The Bears won the National Conference with the second 15-win season in NFL history. They captured the national fancy with an aggressive defense and William ("the Refrigerator") Perry, the 305-lb (138.5-kg) rookie defensive tackle who became the largest NFL player to score a touchdown on a planned offensive play. The Bears' only defeat, at Miami after 12 straight victories, drew the highest television ratings ever for a Monday night game. With help from four play-off teams in New York and Los Angeles, the NFL reversed its three-year decline in overall television viewership.

The Bears' defense allowed the fewest points (12.4 per game), total yards (258.4 per game), and rushing yards (82.4 per game) in the NFL. They were the first team to shut out two play-off opponents. Richard Dent led the NFL with quarterback sacks. The Bears' blitzing style became such an example for the league that five teams had at least 61 sacks, a total that was third highest in league history before 1984. Offensively, the Bears' 28.5 points per game ranked second in the league, and their 172.6 yd rushing per game ranked first for the third year in a row. Walter Payton had a record third straight 2,000-yd season on runs and catches. He set a record by rushing for at least 100 yd in nine consecutive games. Kicker Kevin Butler's 144 points led the league.

The Bears also led in possession time and turnover differential, taking the ball away 23 more times than they lost it. They swept the top individual awards with NFL coach of the year Mike Ditka, NFL defensive player of the year Mike Singletary, and NFC offensive player of the year Payton.

The Patriots were the third team to reach the Super Bowl as a "wild card," the term for two play-off teams in each conference that do not win division championships. They became the first team to win three play-off games on the road. They made 16 turnovers and lost only 2 in those victories, which included triumphs over the Los Angeles Raiders and the Miami Dolphins, regular season leaders of the American Conference with 12 victories and 4 defeats. The Patriots' stars included Andre Tippett, whose 16½ sacks led the American Conference, and Irving Fryar, who led the NFL with 14.1 yd per punt return.

The Cleveland Browns became the first NFL team to win a divisional championship without a winning record, taking the American Conference Central at 8–8. They produced the third pair of 1,000-yd rushers in league history, Kevin Mack and Earnest Byner. As division champions they went to the play-offs instead of the Denver Broncos, the first 11–5 team to miss postseason play.

The Bears and Dolphins were the only teams to repeat as division champions. The Dallas Cowboys had gone three years without a championship, the Browns four, and the Los Angeles Rams five. The Browns, Cowboys, Patriots, and New York Jets were the teams in the play-offs that had not qualified for them a year earlier. The San Francisco 49ers were the fifth defending champions in six years that failed to win their division or a play-off game.

The Raiders had the leading defense in the American Conference and their first NFL rushing leader, Marcus Allen. Allen tied Payton's record of nine straight 100-yd games in the last game of the regular season, when he finished with 1,759 rushing yards and passed National Conference leader Gerald Riggs of Atlanta by 40 yd. Allen's 2,314 yd on runs and pass receptions set a league record.

The Dolphins' Dan Marino led NFL passers with 30 touchdowns and 4,137 yd. San Diego was the best passing team, with league highs of 304.4 passing yards, 408.4 total yards, and 29.2 points per game. The leader in passing efficiency was the Jets' Ken O'Brien, with a 96.2 rating. San Francisco's Joe Montana led National Conference passers, and his .613 completion percentage led the league.

Fullback Roger Craig contributed 1,050 rushing yards and 1,016 receiving yards to the 49ers' National Conference-leading offense, becoming the first player ever to make more than 1,000 yd in both categories in one season and one of two backs ever to gain 1,000 yd receiving. The other was San Diego's Lionel ("Little Train") James, who set records with 1,027 yd receiving by a back and 2,535 total yards on runs, catches, and kick returns.

Craig led the NFL with 92 catches, and James the American Conference with 86. Washington's Art Monk led wide receivers with 91, and the Raiders' Todd Christensen led tight ends with 82. Seattle had two receiving leaders, Daryl Turner with 13 touchdowns and Steve Largent with 1,287 yd. Largent became the fifth and youngest player to gain more than 10,000 yd receiving during his career. Kansas City's Stephone Paige broke a 40-year-old record with 309 yd receiving in one game.

Paige's teammate Deron Cherry tied a record with four interceptions in a game. Everson Walls's nine interceptions for Dallas led the league a record-setting third time in only his fifth season.

The Rams' success stemmed largely from their kicking teams. Dale Hatcher led NFL punters with a 38-yd net average; Henry Ellard led National Conference punt returners with a 13.5-yd average; and Ron Brown led NFL kickoff returners with a 32.8-

Freshman quarterback Jamelle Holieway led the Sooners of Oklahoma to a 25–10 win over Penn State in the Orange Bowl. As the only one of the top four teams to win its New Year's Day classic, Oklahoma bagged its sixth national championship.

JOHN BIEVER/SPORTS ILLUSTRATED

yd average and three touchdowns. Nick Lowery's 58-yd field goal for Kansas City was the season's longest, and his .889 percentage (24 for 27) the league's highest. Minnesota's Jan Stenerud retired at 43 as the all-time field goal leader with 373.

Joe Morris led the NFL with 21 touchdowns for the Giants, all rushing. Washington allowed 171.6 passing yards per game, fewest in the league. The Jets had the best rushing defense in the American Conference, and the Pittsburgh Steelers led the conference in pass defense.

The United States Football League finished its third and last spring season with the Baltimore Stars winning their second straight championship 28–24 against the Oakland Invaders at East Rutherford, N.J., on July 14. The league planned to resume play in the autumn of 1986, but in the meantime it lost several star players, a handful of franchises, and its network television contract. It hoped to regain financial footing through a $1.2 billion lawsuit against the NFL, charging it with monopolizing network professional football telecasts.

Collegiate Football

Oklahoma won its sixth national U.S. college football championship when it was the only one of the four contenders to win a bowl game on Jan. 1, 1986. The Sooners finished with a won-lost record of 11–1 after defeating previously top-ranked Penn State 25–10 in the Orange Bowl. Penn State (11–1) fell to third in the Associated Press (AP) and United Press International (UPI) polls. Iowa and Miami (Fla.) also went into their final games hoping to rank first. But Iowa (10–2) lost 45–28 in the Rose Bowl to UCLA (9–2–1), and Miami (10–2) lost 35–7 in the Sugar Bowl to Tennessee (9–1–2), which thereby gained a ranking of fourth. Michigan (10–1–1) won second in the polls by beating Nebraska (9–3) in the Fiesta Bowl 27–23.

Florida (9–1–1) was ranked fifth by the AP but was ineligible for a bowl game or UPI ranking because of National Collegiate Athletic Association (NCAA) violations. The UPI's fifth-ranked team was Air Force (12–1), which tied Brigham Young for the Western Athletic Conference championship. Other top ten teams included Southwest Conference champion Texas A&M (10–2), Pacific Ten champion UCLA, Miami, Big Ten champion Iowa, and Nebraska.

Oklahoma won the Big Eight, and Tennessee took the Southeast Conference. Other conference champions were Maryland in the Atlantic Coast, Pennsylvania in the Ivy League, Bowling Green in the Mid-American, Fresno State in the Pacific Coast, and Furman in the Southern. Fresno State (11–0–1) was the only undefeated team in the NCAA's top Division I-A after its 51–7 California Bowl victory over Bowling Green (11–1) but was downgraded in the polls because it played against comparatively weak teams.

The highest individual honor, the Heisman Trophy, went to Auburn halfback Bo Jackson by three percentage points over Iowa quarterback Chuck Long, the closest margin in the award's 51 years. Jackson rushed for 1,786 yd, second in Division I-A to Michigan State's Lorenzo White with 1,908, and scored 17 touchdowns, second to Bowling Green's Bernard White with 19. Two defensive nose tackles won the awards for top linemen: Oklahoma's Tony Casillas the Lombardi Trophy and Boston College's Mike Ruth the Outland.

Navy's Napoleon McCallum was the Division I-A all-purpose running leader with 2,330 yd on rushes, pass receptions, and kick returns. He set a career record with 7,172 yd. Navy salvaged its 4–7 season with a 17–7 upset of Army, which finished 9–3.

Utah's Erroll Tucker became the first player to lead Division I-A both in average kickoff returns

(29.1 yd) and in punt returns (24.3 yd). He set a record with seven returns for touchdowns, including three on interceptions. John Lee of UCLA set career records with 79 field goals and an .859 accuracy rate (79 for 92). For the season his .875 percentage (21 for 24) tied Washington's Jeff Jaeger, while Ball State's John Diettrich led in total field goals with 25 and Tennessee's Carlos Reveiz had the most points on kicks, 102.

Division I-A passing leaders were Michigan's Jim Harbaugh with a 163.7 efficiency rating, Long Beach State's Doug Gaynor with a .710 completion percentage, Brigham Young's Robbie Bosco with 30 touchdowns and 4,273 yd, and Purdue's Jim Everett with 326.3 yd per game of total offense. The top pass receivers were Purdue's Rodney Carter with 98 catches, Kansas's Richard Estell with 1,109 yd, and Brigham Young's Mark Bellini with 14 touchdowns. Tennessee's Chris White and East Carolina's Kevin Walker tied for the interception lead with nine, and Air Force's Mark Simon had the highest punting average, 47.3 yd.

The Soccer Riot in Brussels

The European Champions' Cup final in Brussels on May 29, 1985, produced a major soccer tragedy when 39 people died as a result of injuries received in the Heysel Stadium. In addition, more than 200 people who had gone to see the game between Liverpool of England and Italian champions Juventus of Turin were hurt after a wall and a safety fence collapsed during a riot. At the subsequent inquiry English clubs were banned indefinitely from international competition by the Union of European Football Associations (UEFA), though it was thought that this ban might be lifted after three years.

The rioting started an hour before the evening kickoff, with drink inflaming the usual animosity between rival fans. Ugly scenes at the stadium were witnessed by millions worldwide on television. The kickoff was delayed for 85 minutes before the understaffed police and stewards could restore order sufficiently for the game to start. Opinion was divided as to whether UEFA officials should have allowed the match to go on, and the argument would long continue.

The high number of fatalities was caused by the collapse of a wall that crushed some fans and caused others to fall and pile up on one another; ambulance men had the hard task of extricating the dead, dying, and injured. Other injuries were occasioned by fighting between the two sets of supporters, with lumps of concrete and other missiles being hurled. The riot was believed to have begun when some Italian fans threw fireworks at the Belgian police. The British supporters, who already had a disgraceful reputation in Europe for unruly behavior, charged toward the sections reserved for the Juventus contingent. Thuggery followed as the rival factions clashed and the overworked and confused police were caught off guard. Moreover, there was no clearly defined segregation of the two sets of fans in the stadium. Yet no sociological arguments could excuse the terrible behavior of the British invaders. The Liverpool contingent was infiltrated, as were other British traveling football parties, by a hooligan element, which, fueled by liquor, wrought the most havoc.

British soccer hooligans on May 29 in Brussels touched off a riot that killed 39 persons.

DAVID CANNON—ALL SPORT/
SPORTS ILLUSTRATED

In Division III Augustana (Ill.) won its third straight national championship by beating Ithaca (N.Y.) College 20–7. North Dakota State (11–2–1) beat North Alabama 35–7 for the Division II crown, and Georgia Southern defeated Furman 44–42 for the Division I-AA title. Coach Eddie Robinson of 9–3 Grambling finished the year with 329 victories, exceeding Paul ("Bear") Bryant's former college record of 323 and George Halas's professional record of 326.

Canadian Football

The British Columbia Lions defeated the Hamilton Tiger-Cats 37–24 for the Grey Cup championship of the Canadian Football League (CFL) on November 24 at Montreal. Roy Dewalt was named the outstanding player after throwing touchdown passes of 84, 60, and 66 yd. Lui Passaglia of the Lions was the game's leading scorer with 19 points, including five field goals. The Lions, with a 13–3 record, won the Western Division for the third straight time. They had the season's most outstanding player, Mervyn Fernandez, who led CFL receivers with 1,727 yd and 15 touchdowns on 95 catches. Dewalt led league passers with 4,237 yd and 27 touchdowns. Defensive tackle Michael Gray was the most outstanding rookie.

The Tiger-Cats streaked from a 1–6 start to an 8–8 finish, still the CFL's worst division championship record ever. Tiger-Cat safety Paul Bennett was the most outstanding Canadian player and tied teammate Less Browne with 12 interceptions, the most in the league.

Winnipeg, second in the Western Division at 12–4, had the other two Schenley Award winners for top individual performances. They were linebacker Tyrone Jones for most outstanding defensive player and guard Nick Bestaja for most outstanding offensive lineman. Other leaders from Winnipeg were

Willard Reaves with 1,323 yd rushing and Trevor Kennard with 43 field goals and a record-setting 198 points. Saskatchewan's Craig Ellis led the CFL with 102 catches, 17 touchdowns, and 14 rushing touchdowns.

Association Football (Soccer)

Against the tragic backdrop of the events that preceded it, it was not surprising that the European Champions' Cup final at Brussels' Heysel Stadium lacked the sparkle that might have been expected of a match between Europe's top two clubs. It was settled by a single penalty goal scored by Michel Platini, the French midfielder and star of the Juventus effort, 12 minutes into the second half. Liverpool's Gary Gillespie had brought down Zbigniew Boniek as the Pole was dashing through, having headed in a long pass from Platini. Liverpool protested that the incident was outside the penalty box but to no avail, and Platini stepped up to do the rest. Liverpool had a penalty appeal turned down when Ronnie Whelan was brought down by Massimo Bonini, and goalkeeper Stefano Tacconi made several good saves in the last quarter of the game as Liverpool intensified its effort to score. But it was not to be; the Italians used both substitutes, thereby bringing on fresh legs, and held on for victory.

Everton, the English entry, proved equal to the task of returning the European Cup-Winners' cup to England after 14 years. The English team beat Rapid Vienna of Austria 3–1 in the final at Rotterdam on May 15. Everton built its game from a position of sound defense, and indeed all five members of that department, including goalkeeper Neville Southall, were international competitors. The Austrians realized that it would be a hard job to pierce so efficient a rear guard. Yet Rapid's manager, Otto Baric, also appreciated that Everton had plenty of goal potential and so planned a con-

Chicago Bear quarterback Jim McMahon executes a pitchout during the Super Bowl game on January 26. Execution, on offense and especially on defense, was the key to the Bears' 46–10 win over the New England Patriots.

AP/WIDE WORLD

taining strategy; this worked for almost an hour, though goalkeeper Michael Konsel was kept busy by the Everton raiders. Andy Gray of Scotland broke the deadlock after 57 minutes when Graeme Sharp collected a bad back pass from Leo Lainer and turned the ball back for Gray to shoot into an untenanted net. Then three minutes later Baric made his first substitution, sending in Hans Gross for Peter Pacult in an attempt to boost the attack; after another seven minutes Antonin Panenka joined the midfield to bolster the efforts of the lively Zlatko Kranjcar. After Konsel had made a fine save from Trevor Steven, the young attacking midfielder headed a second goal from a Kevin Sheedy corner. Everton's concentration lapsed momentarily in the closing minutes, and Hans Krankl, Rapid's danger man, topped off a fine pass by Gross, but within two minutes the energetic Irish winger Sheedy had restored the two-goal margin when he collected a through pass by Sharp and shot past Konsel.

The two-legged UEFA Cup final produced a reversal of the norm in 1985 in that the trophy was won by Real Madrid on the away leg rather than the home game. The Spanish team triumphed against Videoton of Hungary 3–1 on aggregate, having laid the groundwork with their triumph in Szekesfehervar on May 8. In the first encounter Real Madrid, after the usual exploratory feints and forays, started to get the better of a Videoton team crippled by injuries and suspensions. The Spaniards translated that superiority into tangible evidence with a goal by Miguel Gonzáles Michel from Ricardo Gallego's cross. Though Videoton increased its attacks, the Real Madrid defense, with Uli Stielike of West Germany as the pivot, maintained a firm grip, and some 20 minutes into the second half the Spaniards made their presence felt with a goal by Carlos Santillana after he had wasted an earlier chance to score. The long-serving Juanito (Juan Gómez), having entered the contest as a substitute, and Michel sprang the Hungarians' offside trap to present Jorge Valdano with a last-minute goal. In the return at Madrid two weeks later, Real could afford to squander a penalty, missed by Valdano, and two "goals" disallowed for offside. Though Real carried the major threat, the efforts of Miguel Ángel, their long-serving goalkeeper, foiled all that the Hungarians could throw at him except a rising shot from Lajos Majer four minutes before the end of the match.

Suffering from declining attendance in recent years, the North American Soccer League went out of existence in March and, consequently, had no season in 1985. Competition did continue in the Major Indoor Soccer League, however. Baltimore and San Diego were winners of the Eastern and Western divisions, respectively. In the play-offs San Diego emerged as champion by defeating Baltimore four games to one in the final round. San Diego's Steve Zungul was named the most valuable player in the play-offs.

FRANCE

At the start of the year, Pres. François Mitterrand launched a campaign to revive the failing electoral fortunes of the left, emphasizing the achievements of the Socialist Party (PS) government and appealing for unity. He was immediately countered by Georges Marchais, general secretary of the Communist Party (PC), who at the 25th PC congress in February attacked government policies over the previous three years. According to Marchais, most of the social reforms of 1981 had been gradually eroded before being abolished completely. On the grounds that "the class struggle is worldwide," Marchais refused to break with the countries of the Eastern bloc. The congress was an important one, leading to a radicalization of PC policies and confirming a state of war between it and the Socialist Party, following the breakup of the Union of the Left when the PC left the government in 1984.

In the cantonal elections, in which 2,044 seats, more than half the total, were contested, the right-wing opposition parties—the Rassemblement pour la République (RPR) and the Union pour la Démocratie Française (UDF)—won their fourth victory over the government since the start of President Mitterrand's seven-year term in 1981. In the second round, the right took 53.5% of the vote. The left gained control of Guadeloupe and French Guiana. Overall the PS took 424 seats, a loss of 155; the PC took 149 seats, a loss of 80; the Left Radicals (MRG) lost 13 seats; and various other left-wing parties gained 4 seats. Among the opposition parties, the RPR emerged with 400 seats, a gain of 155; the UDF took 525 seats, a gain of 102; various other right-wing parties increased their representation to 425 seats, a gain of 124; while the far-right National Front, lead by Jean-Marie le Pen, won a single seat. The right now controlled 69 départements, as against 26 for the left.

Meanwhile, the Cabinet made an important decision that was subsequently passed by Parliament: the 1986 legislative elections were to be held under a system of proportional representation in a single round of voting. Under the new system, the National Assembly would have its seats distributed, in each département, among the different party lists according to the highest average obtained. One round of voting would replace the two rounds under the existing majority-vote system, and consequently there would be no possibility of candidates standing down in favor of each other. The number of deputies was to be increased by 86, giving a National Assembly of 577 seats.

The legislative electoral reforms put great pressure on government solidarity. The first victim was Michel Rocard, who resigned as minister of agriculture in April on the grounds that he could not subscribe to a reform that he had always opposed. He was replaced by Henri Nallet, technical adviser at the Élysée Palace. Later, revealing that his decision to resign had another cause, Rocard announced

ORBAN—SYGMA

French Minister of Defense Charles Hernu (front center) was forced to resign in the wake of the "Greenpeace affair."

that he would be a candidate to succeed Mitterrand as president of the republic in 1988.

Despite profound differences within the party, the PS congress in October ended with a synthesis of the motions proposed by Lionel Jospin, PS first secretary, and Rocard. In response to President Mitterrand's appeal, unity was achieved by one means or another. After four and a half years in power, the Socialists had finally broken with the Communists, their former allies, and were attempting to regroup. Rocard did not win the day, but his cause moved forward; Jospin confirmed his position as party leader; and Prime Minister Laurent Fabius brilliantly stole the limelight and appeared the most likely Socialist candidate for the presidency.

The television confrontation between Prime Minister Fabius and opposition leader Jacques Chirac (RPR) at the end of October signaled the start of the election campaign for the following year. The tone of the debate was frequently heated. Chirac painted a picture of a country that was "disappointed, weakened, and uneasy," while Fabius took advantage of the opportunity to restate the main direction of his policies. Chirac discounted the possibility that his party would take part in a government that included the National Front, while Fabius, in his turn, said that he would not govern with the support of the Communists. The majority of viewers polled after the debate considered Chirac to have been the more convincing, clear, and competent of the two.

The second half of the year saw a slowing down of inflation, justifying the government's austerity policy. The rise in retail prices was virtually nil in September (0.1%), after a period of near stability in the preceding months. Consequently, the inflation rate for 1985 was expected to be barely over 5%, compared with 6.7% in 1984. On the other hand, unemployment remained a black spot, with the number of those out of work holding steady at around 2.5 million. Government measures to reduce unemployment were hampered by the size of the national debt. There was no improvement in foreign trade, and by September the cumulative balance of payments deficit since the start of the year had reached F 2.6 billion, equivalent to the total for all of 1984.

The territory of New Caledonia in the South Pacific Ocean, a French possession since 1853, was the scene of violent confrontations between Kanak (indigenous Melanesian) members of the Front de Libération Nationale Kanake et Socialiste (FLNKS) under Jean-Marie Tjibaou and the population of European (mainly French) descent, the *caldoches.* Faced with increased violence on the island, the government appointed Edgard Pisani first as high commissioner and then, in May, as minister for New Caledonia with a brief to speed up the process of granting self-determination. Despite a lightning visit by President Mitterrand on January 19, the state of emergency imposed a week earlier was extended and was not lifted until June. The French government decided to institute a transitional regime to allow the different population groups to express their views on the territory's progress toward independence in association with France. Four regions were set up—the Loyalty Islands, the Northern Region, the Central-Southern Region, and Nouméa and district—while France was to strengthen its military presence in the territory.

Regional elections took place as planned in September. Although the *caldoche* parties, which were opposed to independence, received 60.84% of the vote, as against 35.18% for those favoring independence, the pro-independence faction emerged with majorities in three of the four new regions; the Rassemblement pour la Calédonie dans la République, the main *caldoche* party, won control in Nouméa. Each side could claim a victory, and New Caledonia emerged from the elections more divided than ever. In the short term the new political regime was designed to effect a change in the balance in local public life in favor of the Kanaks and, in theory, lead to a referendum before Dec. 31, 1987, on the question of the territory's achieving independence in association with France. However, in the event of an opposition victory in the 1986 elections in France, this proposed new status for the territory was likely to be challenged.

Foreign Affairs

As usual, France's concerns and aspirations were centered mainly, though not exclusively, on Western Europe. The meeting of the European Communities (EC) Council (the heads of state or government of EC member countries) held in Brussels in March took place in a morose atmosphere, with differences of interest getting in the way of any agreement. Nonetheless, June 12 proved to be a red-letter day with the signing in Lisbon and Madrid of the act enlarging the EC from 10 to 12 members as of 1986. France believed that the enlargement of the Community would strengthen the position of Western Europe in relation to the superpowers.

At the Bonn summit of the seven most industrialized countries in May, there were considerable differences of opinion between President Mitterrand and U.S. Pres. Ronald Reagan, particularly over Reagan's Strategic Defense Initiative. Mitterrand remained opposed to the U.S. concept of "Star Wars" because, in his view, it would deprive Europe of its autonomy. Mitterrand went to West Berlin together with West German Chancellor Helmut Kohl to express France's continuing friendship toward the Federal Republic. He also spent four days in Brazil and Colombia. Much interest was excited by Mikhail Gorbachev's four-day visit to Paris in October, the Soviet leader's first visit to the West after he took power in March. Several private discussions between Gorbachev and Mitterrand made up what was described as "a dialogue, with no major concessions." On December 4 Gen. Wojciech Jaruzelski of Poland visited Paris. Fabius was among the French politicians who criticized Mitterrand for becoming the first Western head of state to meet the Polish leader since martial law was imposed on Poland in 1981.

French involvement in the "Greenpeace affair" was extensively covered by the world press. Agents of the Direction Générale de Sécurité Extérieure (DGSE), the French external security service, were responsible for sabotaging the *Rainbow Warrior,* flagship of the environmental movement Greenpeace, which sank on July 10 in the port of Auckland, New Zealand. In November two French agents, Maj. Alain Mafart and Capt. Dominique Prieur, received prison sentences of ten years after pleading guilty to charges of sabotage and manslaughter, the latter charge resulting from the death of a Greenpeace photographer. The pretext for their action was that the boat's mission was to spy on the firing ground for French nuclear tests at Mururoa Atoll, French Polynesia, although French Navy ships could easily prevent Greenpeace boats from entering Mururoa's territorial waters.

An official inquiry headed by Bernard Tricot issued a report exonerating the French government in August. The following month, however, Prime Minister Fabius admitted that Tricot had been misled and that the agents had indeed acted on government orders, though he did not reveal the source of the orders. Adm. Pierre Lacoste was dismissed as head of the DGSE and replaced by Gen. René Imbot, chief of staff of the Army. Minister of Defense Charles Hernu tendered his resignation and was succeeded by Paul Quilès, who had been minister for town planning, housing, and transport.

The other side of the matter emerged when President Mitterrand visited Mururoa Atoll on September 13 and presided over a meeting of representatives from French territories in the South Pacific. Twenty years after Gen. Charles de Gaulle, Mitterrand restated the need for a French presence in the Pacific and French determination to continue the subterranean nuclear tests at Mururoa for the sake of French independence. In general, France's right-wing opposition approved of the visit, thus demonstrating a degree of consensus over the country's policy of nuclear deterrence that had yet to be achieved in other fields.

Civil authorities in Paris begin to tow automobiles from the Champs-Élysées in August. The cars were left there by workers protesting the planned importation into France of cars assembled in Spain and other low-wage countries.

ROBERT COHEN—AGIP/ PICTORIAL PARADE

FUEL AND ENERGY

In 1985, for the third consecutive year, oil prices remained persistently weak. The Organization of Petroleum Exporting Countries (OPEC) remained incapable of coping with the situation or of enforcing internal discipline on its members, and the cumulative effect of events throughout the year threatened its very existence.

At the January meeting of OPEC, 9 of the 13 members agreed to a cut in official prices, the second such action in the organization's history. Non-OPEC exporters such as Mexico and Egypt promptly followed suit. In March it was announced that the British National Oil Corporation, the state trading concern handling one-half of all British North Sea oil production, would be abolished. This meant that from that time on, all such oil would be sold at spot market prices. This action occurred almost simultaneously with the ending of the British coal strike, which removed a significant portion of the world demand for the heavy fuel oil that had been substituted for coal in British electric power generators.

Market conditions worsened during the summer as oil production in non-OPEC countries (except for the U.S.S.R.) continued to increase by small but nevertheless significant amounts while demand continued to decline. Mexico cut its price a second time, as did OPEC. All members except for Saudi Arabia, however, continued to give hidden discounts from official prices and to produce in excess of their quotas. Saudi Arabia became increasingly dissatisfied with this state of affairs as it persisted alone in rigid adherence to official prices, producing well below its quota and very far below capacity; this caused the nation to incur increasingly large trade and budget deficits.

At the July OPEC meeting the Saudis threatened openly to increase their production, no matter what the effect would be on prices. The representatives at the meeting took no action, and neither did the Saudis. In September, however, they announced that henceforth they would no longer abide by official prices and were, in fact, signing new contracts for increased sales at prices determined by the market. Even this ominous development was not sufficient to produce agreement among the OPEC members. An OPEC meeting in October accomplished nothing.

The Saudi action raised fears among world oil producers of a price war that could lead to total market collapse. The immediate prospect of such an event was averted by a sudden flare-up of hostilities in the Iran-Iraq war. In a series of air raids Iraq seriously damaged Iran's only large oil-export facility, at Khark Island in the Persian Gulf, and severely curtailed Iran's export capability. The general consensus was, nevertheless, that the possibility of collapse had only been postponed and that everything would depend on whether world economic growth in 1986 would revive demand sufficiently to offset the normal spring decline at the end of the heating season.

In December the OPEC oil ministers, meeting in Geneva, agreed to abandon the strategy of defending a set oil price and to concentrate on defending the cartel's market share, cutting prices if this proved necessary. The new strategy, in effect, gave official recognition to the unofficial practice of most OPEC members.

In November the United States Department of Energy held its first test sale of crude oil from the Strategic Petroleum Reserve, as had been directed by the U.S. Congress in July. The purpose of the 1.1 million-bbl sale was to test the maximum rate at which oil could be drawn from the Reserve. At the time of the test the Reserve contained 490 million bbl, equivalent to approximately six months of crude oil imports.

In Canada the year was notable for governmental decisions affecting the petroleum industry. The federal government reached agreement with the province of Newfoundland on the management of offshore oil production, settling a 15-year dispute. In the so-called Western Accord reached with the provinces of Alberta, Saskatchewan, and British Columbia on March 28, the federal government agreed to the abolition of oil price controls and

Oil wells pump thick crude from oil sands at Imperial Oil Ltd.'s recovery facility at Cold Lake, Alberta. Cold Lake was Canada's largest site using conventional wells.

DOUGLAS MARTIN/THE NEW YORK TIMES

certain oil taxes, and the provincial governments reduced their royalties. The effect was a sharp stimulus to the Canadian oil and gas industries. By coincidence, the first commercial delivery of crude oil from the Canadian Arctic Islands to a Montreal refinery was made in September. In October the federal government completed the deregulation of oil and gas prices by abolishing controls on the domestic and export prices of natural gas. This action freed Canadian gas producers to compete in the decontrolled U.S. gas market.

A new record water depth for oil production was set by a well drilled in 2,470 ft (750 m) of water in the Mediterranean Sea off Spain. In April North Sea oil production exceeded that of Saudi Arabia for the first time. In the United States the Environmental Protection Agency announced a new rule further reducing the lead content of gasoline to 0.1 g per gal by the end of the year, with all lead to be removed by 1988. The European Communities announced that it had agreed to require all members to introduce lead-free gasoline by 1989. No date was fixed for the elimination of lead from gasoline, however.

In natural gas matters the major events of the year in the United States concerned regulation. On January 1 price controls on some 70% of natural gas sales were ended, under the provisions of the Natural Gas Policy Act of 1978. Owing to a general oversupply of gas, however, the effect on natural gas prices in general was negligible. In October the Federal Energy Regulatory Commission announced policy changes in the regulation of natural-gas pipelines. The new policies were designed to lower prices by giving consumers the chance to buy directly from producers.

Elsewhere, the United Kingdom ended several years of negotiations with Norway by declining to buy gas from the Sleipner field in the Norwegian North Sea, on the grounds that increased domestic reserves made the commitment unnecessary. Negotiations of several years between Australia and Japan, in contrast, were successful. Agreement was reached in 1985 to begin the export to Japan of liquefied natural gas from one of the world's largest gas fields, located off the northwest coast of Australia, by 1990. Fulfillment of the commitment would require completion of the largest resource project ever undertaken in Australia.

The most noteworthy event in coal was the ending of the British coal strike in March. Almost exactly a year in duration, it was the longest major national strike in British history. The strike was called in response to the National Coal Board's (NCB's) announcement that it intended to close 20 pits that were losing money. The strike was never fully effective, and when it ended the NCB was free to carry out its original intention. In the United States coal continued in general oversupply, with the market in the doldrums. Alaska, on the other hand, marked a notable event with the beginning

REUTERS/BETTMANN NEWSPHOTOS

Workers weld parts of a major pipeline in northeastern Colombia. The West German director of the project was asked to leave the country after being accused of paying protection money to leftist guerrillas.

shipment of coal to South Korea, the first export ever of Alaskan coal. The South Korean contract was expected to result in an eventual doubling of Alaskan coal production.

Electric utilities in four northeastern states were severely crippled by Hurricane Gloria in September. Although not an especially severe hurricane, the storm downed many power lines in Long Island, Connecticut, Massachusetts, and Rhode Island. At the storm's peak almost 2.5 million people were without electric power. Restoration of service took more than a week in some areas.

Other developments in the electric power industry concerned nuclear power. In October Three Mile Island Unit 1 in Pennsylvania began to produce power after being shut down for more than 6½ years. At the time of the accident to its sister unit in 1979, it was inoperative because of refueling; since that time all attempts to obtain permission to restart it had been vehemently opposed on the grounds that it was no safer than its ill-fated sister. Permission was granted for restarting after opponents had exhausted all avenues of litigation and the U.S. Supreme Court had refused to review the final decision. On the adverse side for nuclear power, the U.S. government announced that it was closing its original uranium-enrichment plant at Oak Ridge, Tenn., putting it on standby, and halting construction on a second plant near Portsmouth, Ohio. The announcement was part of a restructuring of U.S. enrichment facilities in the face of worldwide overcapacity and the development of a new, more efficient enrichment technology using lasers.

In the United Kingdom a public hearing on the proposal to build a pressurized water reactor next to an existing gas-cooled reactor came to an end

A technician makes an adjustment in a methanol plant in Jubail, Saudi Arabia. The plant, one of the world's largest, was just one indication of Saudi Arabia's emergence as a major force in the petrochemicals industry.

AP/WIDE WORLD

in March after 340 days of hearings and an estimated 16 million words of transcript. The Sizewell B public inquiry, as it was known, constituted the longest such inquiry in British history. A report on the findings was expected in 1986. The first high-temperature gas reactor in West Germany began operation in October. In France the world's largest fast-breeder reactor, the "Superphénix," was activated in September. The 1,200-MW unit was built with the participation of five other Western European countries.

Developments in the field of unconventional energy resources were both positive and negative. The largest commercial solar power plant, rated at 14.7 MW, began operation at Daggett, Calif. The largest geothermal power project, at the Geysers in central California, celebrated its 25th anniversary with the addition of two new units, bringing the total capacity of the project to 1,360 MW. Also in California the world's first commercial-size binary geothermal power plant began operation. Located in the Imperial Valley near Heber, the 45-MW unit uses geothermal brine at less than the boiling point to vaporize a second fluid that drives a turbine.

A French research ship completed successful testing of a "turbosail" wind-propulsion system. Large hollow cylinders, like smokestacks, are equipped with fans at the bottom. The fans draw air through the side of the cylinder to produce an effect, like an airplane wing, that moves the ship forward. The system was designed to supplement conventional screw propulsion and to save fuel. A research institute in the United States announced the successful production of synthetic methane (a constituent of natural gas) from water and carbon dioxide. This was the first synthesis of methane from inorganic compounds and was described as a significant first

step toward the ultimate commercial production of the gas from such sources.

The world's first fully commercial plant to convert natural gas to gasoline began operation during the year at Motunui, N.Z. (A similar plant in the United States built soon after World War II never achieved reliable operation.)

On the negative side were two project abandonments. Failure to receive sufficient subsidy caused sponsors of the Great Plains coal gasification plant at Beulah, N.D., to turn ownership of the plant over to the federal government. Completed in 1984 at a cost of $2 billion, the plant was intended to demonstrate the feasibility of large-scale gasification of lignite, processing 12,600 metric tons (14,000 short tons) per day to produce 125 million cu ft (3.5 million cu m) of synthetic gas a day. The plant continued operation under federal ownership while the government pondered whether to shut it down. In Israel the government stopped all work on a project to generate electricity by carrying water from the Mediterranean to the Dead Sea. Lower than expected prices for crude oil made the project uneconomic.

GERMANY

West Germany

Despite an economic upturn marred only by the high level of unemployment, the popularity of West Germany's center-right coalition government of the Christian Democratic Union (CDU), its Bavarian wing, the Christian Social Union (CSU), and the Free Democratic Party (FDP) decreased in 1985. This was largely the result of disappointment over the leadership of federal Chancellor Helmut Kohl, who showed an unsteady hand in his management of both domestic and foreign policies, though his position was not seriously challenged.

The biggest setback to the coalition parties was the outcome of the elections for the state parliament of North Rhine-Westphalia on May 12. Under the leadership of Johannes Rau, the charismatic state premier, the Social Democratic Party (SPD) won 52.1% of the vote. The CDU's share fell by almost seven percentage points to 36.5%, compared with the 1980 state elections. The Social Democrats won majorities in towns previously regarded as safe for the Christian Democrats. Roman Catholic industrial workers in the Ruhr deserted the CDU, while farmers in Westphalia who might have voted for the CDU showed their anger over reduced subsidies from the European Communities (EC) by staying home. It was assumed that Rau would be the party's choice as candidate for chancellor in the federal elections due to take place in 1987.

The first coalition between the Social Democrats and the Green Party was formed in October in the state of Hesse. The move, which brought the Greens into government for the first time, was forced on the Social Democrats because they lacked an overall majority in the state legislature. In Hesse the Greens took over the state Environment Ministry set up to run waste management, water pollution control, nature conservation, and general energy policy. The SPD remained responsible for nuclear energy policy decisions.

The 11th annual economic summit of seven industrialized countries (Canada, France, West Germany, Italy, Japan, the U.K., and the U.S.) took place in Bonn in May. A shadow was cast over the event by a row concerning an act of reconciliation at a German military cemetery to mark the 40th anniversary of Victory in Europe (VE) Day at the end of World War II. U.S. Pres. Ronald Reagan, who attended the summit, had accepted Kohl's invitation to visit the cemetery at Bitburg, not knowing that it contained the graves of soldiers of the Waffen SS, which had administered Hitler's concentration camps. Despite a storm of protest in the U.S., Kohl stuck to his plans, and Reagan felt obliged to go along with them.

President Richard von Weizsäcker made a strong attack on German attitudes toward Jews in the Third Reich in a remarkable speech on the anniversary of VE Day, May 8. He said that at the time, Germans with their eyes and ears open could not have failed to notice that Jews were being deported; at the end of World War II too many Germans had claimed they had not known anything. President Weizsäcker said that scarcely any country had remained free from blame of war or violence. The genocide suffered by the Jews was, however, unparalleled in history. While the perpetration of the crime had been in the hands of a few people, and had been concealed from the eyes of the public, every German could have seen for himself the misery of his Jewish compatriots.

West Germans, and their allies as well, were shaken by a series of spy scandals in August and September. The most serious of these was the defection to East Germany of Hans Joachim Tiedge, third in command of West German counterintelligence. In his position as head of a department of the Verfassungsschutzamt (the federal Office for the Protection of the Constitution), Tiedge had access to the most secret information. He had worked for the service for 19 years and was also well informed about the activities of allied counterintelligence organizations.

In the wake of the affair, Heribert Hellenbroich was dismissed as head of the Bundesnachrichtendienst (the West German intelligence organization) after only a month in office. Hellenbroich had previously been in charge of counterintelligence. Hans-Georg Wieck, West German ambassador to NATO, took his place as chief of the intelligence service.

Court proceedings against two former federal Cabinet ministers, Count Otto Lambsdorff and Hans Friderichs, in connection with the so-called Flick affair opened in August. The prosecution alleged that the Flick industrial concern had paid out large sums of money to buy influence in Bonn and that the two men had accepted bribes. Both strongly denied the charges. Lambsdorff had resigned as economics minister in June 1984.

In late September and early October a wave of violent protests that involved widespread looting and destruction of property swept through a number of West German towns and cities. The incident that apparently sparked the violence was the death of a demonstrator during a rally against neo-Nazism in Frankfurt on September 28. While Frankfurt was the scene of some of the worst incidents, riots

Johannes Rau (left) accepted in September his nomination by Social Democratic Party leaders, including party chairman Willy Brandt (right), as candidate for chancellor of West Germany.

DEUTSCHE PRESSE-AGENTUR/PHOTOREPORTERS

REUTERS/BETTMANN NEWSPHOTOS

Guards accompany former minister of economics Count Otto Lambsdorff on the walk from his lawyer's office to the court where he stood trial on corruption charges.

erupted in several other centers, including Hamburg, West Berlin, Hanover, and Stuttgart.

The level of unemployment, remained stubbornly unchanged at around two million. The inflation rate was about 2%; real gross national product was likely to rise by 2.5% for the year; export trade was increasing; and the health of state finances improved.

Chancellor Kohl's pronounced pro-U.S. stance at the Bonn economic summit in May irritated the French. Kohl sided with President Reagan on two key issues: European involvement in the Strategic Defense Initiative (SDI) research program, and the need for a new round of international trade talks under the auspices of the General Agreement on Tariffs and Trade (GATT). The French were afraid that the U.S., in a new round of GATT talks, would succeed in removing restrictions on trade in agricultural products. Should this happen, the EC common agricultural policy, which the French saw as the cornerstone of the Community, could no longer be maintained in its existing form.

A cautious willingness for West Germany to take part in the SDI research program could be detected in the Chancellor's Office, though Foreign Minister Hans-Dietrich Genscher was far from enthusiastic. Kohl had apparently been persuaded by West German industry that it stood to win lucrative contracts through collaboration with the project. Genscher feared that a bilateral agreement with the U.S. on "Star Wars" would place a further burden on West Germany's relations with its Communist neighbors. Genscher prompted Kohl to express support for West German collaboration in Eureka, the French-inspired project for a community of European technologies.

France continued to stress the importance of its relationship with West Germany. In October French Pres. François Mitterrand flew to West Berlin with Kohl to reaffirm France's commitment, as one of its guarantor powers, to the city's security. "You should interpret my presence here as a sign of solid, durable, and vigilant friendship," said Mitterrand at a welcoming ceremony. His visit, only the second by a French head of state, followed a meeting with Kohl in Bonn at which they discussed the implications of the forthcoming Geneva summit meeting between Reagan and Soviet leader Mikhail Gorbachev.

In October President Weizsäcker paid a visit to Israel, the first by a German head of state. Within the limits imposed by history, it was a success. Weizsäcker skirted sensitive questions about West German arms shipments to Saudi Arabia, saying policy-making was not part of his responsibility. It was a sensitive issue. Just before President Weizsäcker left Bonn, preliminary approval had been given to plans for a West German group to supply $2.5 billion worth of munitions plant to Saudi Arabia. Both the Social Democrats and the Greens denounced the possible contract, and Genscher was believed to have strong reservations about such a deal.

East Germany

The visit to East Berlin in June 1985 of French Prime Minister Laurent Fabius was an important milestone in East Germany's policy of improving relations with Western nations. Fabius was the first head of government of one of the three Western allied powers (the U.K., the U.S., and France, which, together with the U.S.S.R., had taken administrative control of Berlin at the end of World War II) to have political talks there.

One of the main purposes of the visit was to improve economic links between France and East Germany, the Eastern bloc's most powerful industrial country after the U.S.S.R. French interest in increasing trade was reflected in the unusually large French representation at the Leipzig trade fair in September.

East German leader Erich Honecker paid a state visit to Greece in October, reciprocating a visit by Prime Minister Andreas Papandreou to East Germany in 1984. In Athens they signed an agreement on industrial and technological cooperation, and both expressed concern at the prospect of the "arms race being extended to outer space."

In a speech on October 7, the 36th anniversary of the founding of the East German state, Honecker claimed that East Germany was making impressive economic progress. He said national income was up by 4.4%, productivity by nearly 8%, and retail trade turnover by 4.4%. Many thousands of apartments had been built or modernized, and the harvest of 11.6 million metric tons of grain was the biggest on record.

The Communist Party gave orders that each of its 2.2 million members be questioned "in a comradely atmosphere" about his or her political views, style of life, and attitude to work. A screening in 1980 had resulted in the expulsion of some 4,000 members; the biggest purge had been in 1951, when 150,000 members had been forced to leave the party.

Willy Brandt, former federal chancellor of West Germany, met Honecker on a semiofficial visit to East Berlin in September. According to West German sources, Honecker promised to make further "easements" in travel between East and West Germany. Brandt also received the impression that Honecker would like to visit Bonn.

On March 24 Maj. Arthur Nicholson, a member of the U.S. Army's military liaison mission in East Germany, was shot dead by a Soviet soldier near Ludwigslust, close to the border with West Germany. The incident provoked a row between the U.S.S.R., which claimed that Nicholson had been spying on a Soviet military installation in a restricted zone, and the U.S., which denied that the incident had taken place in an area that was restricted.

GOLF

Suspicions that the U.S. was not quite the force it had been in world golfing competition were confirmed in 1985. For the first time in 28 years, the U.S. was defeated in the Ryder Cup, though the team that beat it was admittedly European and not purely British, as had been the case in 1957. The agreed-upon base of selection, embracing the continent of Europe, had been made in 1977 because U.S. domination was undermining the match's appeal. Also, Sandy Lyle became the first British winner of the British Open since Tony Jacklin 16 years earlier, and Bernhard Langer of West Germany became only the third overseas player to win the U.S. Masters. Never in modern times had European golf enjoyed such a year of success.

It was Europe's Ryder Cup victory at the Belfry, near Birmingham, England, that most caught the public imagination, and the ultimate margin of $16\frac{1}{2}$–$11\frac{1}{2}$ was conclusive. No one derived greater satisfaction than Jacklin, the European nonplaying captain and winner of the British and the U.S. Open in 1969 and 1970, respectively. With his inspirational leadership, he outmaneuvered his opposite number, Lee Trevino.

Before record crowds (approximately 80,000 for the three days), Europe did not make the fast start that was thought to be important. The U.S. won the opening series of foursomes by 3–1 but, inspired by Severiano Ballesteros and his fellow Spaniard Manuel Piñero, with whom he won twice on that opening day, the Europeans closed the overall gap to a single point after the afternoon four-ball matches. A crucial small putt missed on the 18th green by Craig Stadler of the U.S. just before lunch on the second day brought the teams to a tie, and by nightfall Europe was ahead 9–7. Europe increased its advantage in the singles, again being given a fine example by the diminutive Piñero, who beat Lanny Wadkins in the top match. But it was Sam Torrance who had the distinction of holing the decisive putt for a birdie three to defeat Andy North, the U.S. Open champion, on the 18th green. At that moment the Ryder Cup, first contested in 1927, passed back into European possession. Among other winners of their singles were both Lyle and Langer, who thereby completed a notable season during which both had won their first major championships.

On the first day of the British Open championship at Royal St. George's, Sandwich, Kent, Christy O'Connor (Ireland) broke Henry Cotton's course record of 65 (which had also stood as a British Open record until 1977) with a 64 that included a run of seven consecutive birdies. Bad weather on the afternoon of the first day and morning of the second made conditions difficult for some players, among them Jack Nicklaus of the U.S., who failed to qualify for the last two rounds for the first time in his career. After three rounds the destiny of the title seemed to lie between Langer and Australia's David Graham, who in 1981 had won the U.S. Open. They were tied three strokes ahead of the field but, perhaps with eyes only for one other, fell away with last rounds of 75 apiece. This left the door open for their pursuers, and it was Lyle who stepped through it with a final round of 70 for a

British golfer Sandy Lyle kisses his trophy after winning the 114th British Open golf championship with a two over par on the course at Sandwich, Kent.

AP/WIDE WORLD

TONY TOMSIC/SPORTS ILLUSTRATED

Kathy Baker lines up a putt during the U.S. Women's Open in July. Baker, 24 years old, won the Open with an eight-under-par 280 for her first pro victory.

two-over-par aggregate of 282. He won by a stroke from Payne Stewart (U.S.), with Langer, Graham, O'Connor, Mark O'Meara (U.S.), and José Rivero (Spain) all sharing third place. Lyle's birdies on the 14th and 15th holes hoisted him to the top of the leader board, though he had an anxious wait after bogeying at the 18th.

Langer did the same thing at the last hole in the U.S. Masters at Augusta, Ga., as did North in the U.S. Open. The West German had nevertheless played beautifully over the last two rounds, scoring 68 each time and beating Ballesteros, Raymond Floyd, and Curtis Strange (both U.S.) by two strokes. Langer's total of 282 was six under par, while Strange's share of second place reflected a remarkable recovery. After an opening round of 80, he had booked a flight home the following evening. Instead he came back with a 65, followed it with a 68, and went into the last round only a stroke off the lead.

North, standing 6 ft 4 in (1.93 m) tall, gained his second U.S. Open victory in eight years. He had won at Cherry Hills Country Club near Denver, Colo., in 1978 and now did so again at Oakland Hills Country Club near Detroit by a stroke from Denis Watson of South Africa. A total of 279 for the four rounds left North the only player under par. For a time there had been the distinct possibility that a player from Asia would win the championship, because at one stage in the last round, T. C. Chen of Taiwan led by four strokes. However, he foundered at the fifth hole when, in chipping to the green, he hit the ball twice and took an eight. It was also an agonizingly near miss for Watson, whose first round of 70 included a two-stroke penalty when he waited beyond the permitted ten seconds for a putt that had stopped on the edge of the hole to drop. Except for that penalty he would have finished a stroke ahead of North.

North, at 35, was hardly one of the rising generation of U.S. golfers. Nor was Hubert Green, 38, who won the U.S. Professional Golfers' Association (PGA) championship at Cherry Hills by two strokes from the defending champion, Trevino, seven years his senior. Throughout the tournament it was nearly always a two-horse race, Trevino leading through the first two days but Green overtaking him in the third round before being caught again with nine holes to play. However, it was Green, the 1977 U.S. Open champion, who had the stronger finish. He had a total of 278, six under par, on a course that drew much criticism for its severity.

The U.S. Tournament Player's Championship at the Tournament Players' Club course, Ponte Vedra, Fla., was won in fine style by Calvin Peete, the tournament having some claim to being the world's fifth "major." But the player of the year was Strange, who won three tournaments—the Honda Classic, the Panasonic Las Vegas International, and the Canadian Open—on the way to becoming the leading money winner with a record of $542,321. But he decided not to enter the British Open, and at the year's end he had not yet won a major championship.

A remarkable feature of U.S. golf was the success of the Seniors' tour for players over 50. Peter Thomson of Australia, who had won the British Open five times during the 1950s and '60s, was so dominant that his earnings of $386,724 were exceeded only by Strange and Wadkins on the main tour.

Lyle, who won only one other tournament—the Benson and Hedges International—besides the British Open, was nevertheless the leading money winner in Europe with £162,552, well ahead of Langer. It was the third time that he had headed the money list since 1979, and in those seven seasons he had not once finished outside the top five. In third place was Ballesteros, whose five victories included yet another in the Suntory world match-play championship at Wentworth, England. He had now won this event four times in five years. The event promised an epic final when Ballesteros came face to face with Langer, as he had done 12 months earlier. But the West German was well below his best, his defeat by six and five being the most conclusive since the match-play competition was launched in 1964.

The U.S. was beaten by Australia in the new Dunhill Cup, a medal match-play event at St. Andrews, Scotland, with teams of three men on each side. Graham Marsh, David Graham, and Greg Norman defeated Raymond Floyd, Mark O'Meara, and Curtis Strange by 3–0 in the final.

It was therefore left to the U.S. amateurs to restore some pride as they defeated Great Britain and Ireland in the Walker Cup at Pine Valley, Clementon, N.J. The margin of 13–11 was, however, much closer than most people had expected and contrasted sharply with the whitewash inflicted on the British when last the Walker Cup was played at Pine Valley, in 1936. After the first day the two teams were even, and the turning point came in the second series of foursomes, which the Americans took by 3–0 with the other game halved. The British managed to close the gap in the last series of singles and, for their tenacity, made a big impression on crowds that had to be limited to 3,000 each day because of the difficulties of spectator control on a notoriously difficult but scenically beautiful course. On the victorious U.S. team was Scott Verplank, who a few weeks earlier had become the first amateur in 29 years to win a professional event when he took the Western Open at Butler National Golf Club in Oak Brook, Ill. Verplank failed, however, in his defense of the U.S. amateur championship at Montclair, N.J., the title going to Sam Randolph, another Walker Cup player, who defeated Peter Persons on the last green in the 36-hole final.

The British amateur championship broke new ground at Royal Dornoch, Scotland, and it produced in Garth McGimpsey the first Irish champion since Joe Carr in 1960. He beat Graham Homewood, a little-known Englishman, by eight and seven over 36 holes.

Nancy Lopez enjoyed her best year for some time. She won five tournaments, was leading money winner for the third time in her career with an astonishing $416,472, and was named Ladies Professional Golf Association golfer of the year. However, it was Kathy Baker who took the most treasured prize, the U.S. Women's Open at Baltusrol, N.J., finishing three strokes ahead of Judy Clark. The British Women's Open championship went to an American, Betsy King, who beat Marta Figueras-Dotti of Spain by two strokes.

GREECE

Political developments in Greece in 1985 were dominated by two events: the sudden resignation of Pres. Konstantinos Karamanlis on March 10, and the decisive victory of the ruling Panhellenic Socialist Movement (Pasok) in the general elections on June 2. Economic difficulties forced the government to introduce a program of rigorous economies. Frequent incidents of international terrorism on Greek territory induced the government to tighten security and coordinate counterterrorist action with other Western law-enforcement services.

Prime Minister Andreas Papandreou's sudden decision to withdraw his promised support for President Karamanlis, former New Democracy Party

(conservative) prime minister, who was seeking reelection by Parliament for a second five-year term, forced Karamanlis to resign. Taking his own Pasok parliamentary group by surprise, Papandreou nominated instead Christos Sartzetakis, a Supreme Court judge, as the next chief of state. At the same time, he put forward proposals for a revision of the constitution in order to curtail presidential prerogatives. Employing methods whose legitimacy was questioned by the opposition as well as by constitutional experts, Papandreou succeeded in securing the required three-fifths majority to elect Sartzetakis as president in the third round of voting. When the New Democracy Party challenged the legality of the new president and called for general elections, Papandreou obliged, but not before Parliament approved the constitutional reforms. The reforms would go into effect only if the next Parliament endorsed them.

The results of the elections of June 2 proved that Papandreou was right to discount the theory that, by withdrawing support from Karamanlis, he would lose the moderate vote. The Greek countryside, once the stronghold of conservatism, went solidly behind Pasok for the second time, despite Pasok's opposition to Greece's membership in the European Communities (EC), which had brought

Greek Prime Minister Andreas Papandreou casts his ballot in general elections in June. His ruling Panhellenic Socialist Movement was victorious.
AP/WIDE WORLD

increased prosperity to the agricultural sector. Pasok took nearly 46% of the vote and 161 seats, and New Democracy nearly 41% and 126 seats, while the pro-Moscow Greek Communist Party (KKE) won 12 seats and the Eurocommunists one seat.

Still suffering from the shock of its second successive electoral defeat, New Democracy faced a new crisis when its leader, Konstantinos Mitsotakis, resigned abruptly in the belief that his leadership was being put in question by his parliamentary deputy, Kostis Stefanopoulos. The party's parliamentary group promptly reelected Mitsotakis. Stefanopoulos, who did not turn up to challenge him, left the party and, along with nine other dissident deputies, formed the Democratic Renewal Party, whose conservative platform was spiced with populism.

There was speculation about whether Pasok, in its second four-year term, would reach out for its more radical strategic objectives. However, it soon became clear that the constraints that had tempered Papandreou's aims during his first term remained in place and were, if anything, stronger. An abrupt deterioration in the economy was evidenced by rising unemployment, two-digit inflation, and soaring foreign and domestic debts. After some hesitation, Papandreou shuffled his Cabinet to bring in a new economic team under former agriculture minister Kostas Simitis, who became minister of national economy, and on October 11 he launched a rigid austerity program. The government resisted the wave of strikes and protests that followed and disciplined its own party's recalcitrant trade union leaders. The austerity budget for 1986 introduced in November included proposals to increase tax revenues and cut government spending.

At the same time, Papandreou turned to both the EC and the U.S. for support in the form of loans and investments that would inject some life into the stagnant economy. Rapprochement with the U.S. was a difficult objective, however. Incensed by years of anti-U.S. rhetoric from Papandreou, Washington was not eager to help. Indeed, following the hijacking on June 14 of a Trans World Airlines passenger aircraft that had taken off from Athens airport, U.S. Pres. Ronald Reagan admonished Papandreou for showing laxity toward terrorists and declared Athens airport unsafe. A dramatic decline in arrivals of U.S. tourists was estimated to have cost Greece about $300 million in lost revenue. Furthermore, the U.S. Defense Department withheld approval of the sale of 40 F-16 fighter aircraft to the Greek Air Force on the grounds that Greece was suspected of leaking Western high-technology secrets to the U.S.S.R. The revelations of Sergei Bokhan, a Soviet diplomat who defected to the U.S. from Athens in May, seemed to corroborate the existence of such leaks.

In both instances, the government acted promptly. It stepped up its counterterrorist activities and warned its Arab friends that illicit activity conducted through Greece would no longer be toler-

ated. At the same time, a naval officer and two civilian electronics experts named by Bokhan were arrested and charged with selling defense secrets to the Soviets. However, Washington's main concern focused on whether Papandreou could be induced to drop his threat to expel the U.S. from its military bases in Greece when the current agreement expired in 1988.

GRENADA

During 1985 the New National Party government, which came to power in Grenada's general elections of December 1984, faced major economic problems. Despite substantial aid from the U.S. and other countries, Grenada remained heavily in debt, with arrears amounting to EC$8 million in July 1985. (For table of world currencies, *see* International Exchange and Payments.) The main thrust of economic policy was to develop tourism. In September it was announced that a new airline, Grenada Airways, would be launched in December in conjunction with a French company, which also planned to build a 750-room hotel.

With the exception of a team of security specialists, the last U.S. forces left Grenada on June 11. Some Jamaican troops remained to carry out duties at Richmond Hill prison. The trial of 19 former ministers and other officials of the People's Revolutionary Government, charged with the murder of former prime minister Maurice Bishop and others in October 1983, underwent a number of adjournments, with the result that little progress was made during the year.

Disagreements among factions within the government were reported in midyear, but Prime Minister Herbert Blaize survived challenges to his leadership. During her visit in October, Queen Elizabeth II praised Grenada's return to democracy.

George Louison (right), a leader of the opposition Maurice Bishop Patriotic Movement in Grenada, leads a rally marking the March 13, 1979, coup on the island.
AP/WIDE WORLD

AP/WIDE WORLD

Marco Vinicio Cerezo Arévalo, Guatemala's president-elect, waves to supporters at a victory rally in Guatemala City on December 9 after defeating Jorge Carpio Nicolle.

GUATEMALA

Following congressional and presidential elections on Nov. 3, 1985, Guatemala was to return to civilian rule with the inauguration of the elected administration in January 1986. However, no candidate gained the 50% majority necessary to secure the presidency in the first round of voting, but in a second round on December 8, Marco Vinicio Cerezo Arévalo of the Christian Democrats (DCG) easily defeated Jorge Carpio Nicolle of the Union of the National Center (UCN).

During the final months of military rule, political instability was exacerbated by the worsening economic crisis. While gross domestic product showed marginal growth in 1985, led by the recovery of agriculture, other sectors of the economy remained depressed. Petroleum output plummeted from 10,-000 bbl a day to 3,000 bbl a day, and construction problems delayed the completion of the Chixoy and Aguacapa hydroelectricity schemes. The resulting power shortages led to electricity rationing.

Foreign-exchange reserves fell to perilously low levels as a result of high debt servicing, estimated at over 35% of exports, and increased oil imports. In July Guatemala sold one-fifth of its gold reserves in order to finance imports, and the government increased gasoline (petrol) prices in an effort to ease the cash shortage. However, when bus fares were raised to cover the increase, Guatemalans took to the streets in protest, forcing the government in September to rescind the fare increase and freeze the prices of basic goods.

GYMNASTICS

Gymnasts from the Soviet Union regained their top world ranking by winning both the men's and women's team titles, the all-around titles, and more individual championships than competitors from any other country. The world championships, held November 4–10 at Montreal, climaxed the Soviet renaissance, which also included the women's European championship and the male and female all-around champions in the World University Games at Kobe, Japan.

For the first time in the history of the world championships, there was a tie for the all-around title. A pair of 16-year-old Soviet newcomers, Elena Shoushounova and Oksana Omeliantchik, finished even. Two East German gymnasts, Dagmar Kersten and Gabriele Fahnrich, trailed the Soviet duo. In winning the uneven parallel bars, Fahnrich had the highest individual score in the apparatus finals, 19.950 out of a possible 20.000.

In the men's competition at the world championships, Valentin Moglinyi of the Soviet Union and Sylvio Kroll of East Germany shared the parallel bars title, and Moglinyi also won the pommel horse. Tong Fei of China won the floor exercise, and Li Ning of China shared the rings title with Yuri Korolev of the Soviet Union. Korolev won the side horse vault outright.

In the women's events Shoushounova won the vault, and teammate Omeliantchik was the gold

Chinese gymnast Li Ning won three medals, including a share of the rings title, at the world gymnastics championships in Montreal in November.

AP/WIDE WORLD

medalist in the floor exercise. Fahnrich was the winner on the uneven parallel bars, and Romania's Daniela Silvas defeated her more experienced teammate Ecaterina Szabo on the balance beam.

Few gymnasts were scored "ten" by the judges in comparison with the comparatively large number of perfect marks at the 1984 Olympic Games. There were two tens in the women's apparatus finals. Silvas received a perfect score on the balance beam, and Omeliantchik received a perfect mark for her routine in the floor exercise.

In the men's competition the U.S.S.R. won a total of nine medals to seven for China, and by a margin of seven to four the Soviets outscored Romania in the women's competition. Only one United States gymnast qualified for the apparatus finals; Sabrina Mar tied for sixth place in the vault.

Natalia Yurchenko of the U.S.S.R. retained her all-around honors in the World University Games, while teammate Dmitri Bilozerchev won the men's all-around title. A broken leg sidelined Bilozerchev for the world championships.

HAITI

A national referendum held on July 22, 1985, endorsed constitutional changes that set guidelines for the formation of political parties, restored the office of prime minister—to be filled in 1987—and confirmed Jean-Claude Duvalier as president for life, with the power to appoint his successor. The authorities stated that over 99.9% of the electorate had voted in favor of the changes, but reports from authoritative sources suggested that widespread voting malpractices had occurred. The new constitution incorporating the amendments had already become law following its approval by the National Assembly on June 6. The Parti Nationale Progressiste was formed in late August.

In September Duvalier forced the resignation of Roger Lafontant, the hard-line minister for the interior and national defense, in a move to improve relations with more moderate elements in the country in general and the Roman Catholic Church in particular. The church had become the chief channel for the expression of opposition. Lafontant was replaced by François Guillaume. In a Cabinet reshuffle December 31, 14 new ministers were appointed and 4 were given diplomatic appointments abroad.

The economy showed a slight improvement in 1985, primarily as a consequence of a recovery in manufacturing and coffee exports. However, government finances remained unstable.

HONDURAS

Political wrangling in Honduras during the months preceding the November 1985 general elections provoked a constitutional crisis. The central issue was opposition in the National Assembly to Pres. Roberto Suazo Córdova's attempts to manipulate his own Liberal Party and the rival National Party

to ensure that only presidential candidates who met with his approval were nominated. A related issue was the fight for control of the Supreme Court; when the Assembly dismissed several pro-Suazo Supreme Court justices for alleged corruption, the president imprisoned the replacement Supreme Court president and charged him with treason. Pressure from the Assembly, the Roman Catholic Church, the trade unions, and the U.S. administration forced Suazo to accept a compromise on May 21. It included reform of the Supreme Court and of the electoral system, to allow candidates chosen by party factions to run for office. The Supreme Court president was released the following day. In the November 24 balloting Rafael Leonardo Callejas of the National Party was the leading candidate with about 41% of the vote. However, under the new electoral system victory went to the leading candidate of the party gaining the most votes for all its candidates as a group, making José Azcona Hoyo of the Liberal Party the winner.

The presence in Honduras of Nicaraguan Democratic Forces guerrillas (*contras*) heightened tension between Honduras and Nicaragua. The U.S. embassy in Tegucigalpa was forbidden to distribute aid to the *contras* because the Honduran government would not admit officially that the guerrillas operated from its territory.

Recruits of the Nicaraguan Democratic Forces train in Honduras. The presence of the FDN, an anti-Sandinista contra *group, increased tension with Nicaragua.*

CLAUDIO URRACA—SYGMA

HORSE RACING

Winners in five of the seven Breeders' Cup races were named divisional champions in the Eclipse Award voting conducted by the Thoroughbred Racing Associations, the National Turf Writers Association, and the *Daily Racing Form.* They included: two-year-old colt, Tasso; older filly or mare, Life's Magic; male turf horse, Cozzene; female turf horse, Pebbles; and sprinter, Precisionist.

Other horses earning Eclipse Award honors were: two-year-old filly, Family Style; three-year-old colt, Spend a Buck; three-year-old filly, Mom's Command; older male horse, Vanlandingham; and steeplechaser, Flatterer, which had won the previous two years. Life's Magic, champion three-year-old filly in 1984, was the only other Eclipse Award winner to repeat. Spend a Buck and Mom's Command, which had been retired because of injury, did not take part in the Breeders' Cup competition.

Other Eclipse Award winners included: owner, Mr. and Mrs. Eugene Klein; trainer, D. Wayne Lukas; breeder, Nelson Bunker Hunt; jockey, Laffit Pincay, Jr.; and apprentice jockey, Art Madrid, Jr. The Kleins, who raced Family Style, Life's Magic, and Lady's Secret, established a record for stable earnings with $5,446,401. Lukas, who trained for the Kleins and others, had a record total of 70 stakes victories for the year. He saddled horses that nearly doubled his record 1984 earnings by accumulating $11,160,111. Pincay, previously named champion jockey in 1971, 1973, 1974, and 1979, became the first individual to win five Eclipse Awards. In 1985 his mounts earned $13,353,299 to smash the record of $12,045,813 established in 1984 by Chris McCarron.

Probably the outstanding champion of the year was the English-bred four-year-old filly Pebbles, Europe's best female Thoroughbred. Racing as the 2.20–1 favorite, the daughter of Sharpen Up defeated 13 male rivals in the Breeders' Cup Turf at 1½ mi. Because that was Pebbles's only start in the U.S., many voters ignored her in the Eclipse Award competition.

Lady's Secret was successful in eight consecutive stakes, which included three Grade I events—the Maskette, Ruffian, and Beldame—but was outvoted by Mom's Command. The latter, owned and bred by Peter Fuller and ridden by his daughter Abby, won seven stakes in nine starts and finished second in two others. Her victories included the Triple Crown for fillies—the Acorn, Mother Goose, and Coaching Club American Oaks.

Spend a Buck, which won the Kentucky Derby and Garden State's $2 million bonus for victory in a series of races, set a single-season earnings mark of $3,552,704. The three-year-olds comprised a vintage crop. Besides Spend a Buck they included Proud Truth, winner of the Breeders' Cup Classic; Chief's Crown; Creme Fraiche, winner of the Belmont Stakes; Stephan's Odyssey; and Tank's Prospect, winner of the Preakness Stakes.

AP/WIDE WORLD

Spend a Buck, jockeyed by Angel Cordero, Jr., approaches the finish to win the 111th running of the Kentucky Derby in Louisville, Kentucky, on May 4.

Spend a Buck and Mom's Command were among the contenders for horse of the year honors, won in 1984 by John Henry. That marked a record seventh Eclipse Award for the then nine-year-old gelding and his second prize as horse of the year. John Henry was retired in 1985 with record earnings of $6,597,947.

The versatile Vanlandingham scored in four stakes, including the Suburban, Jockey Club Gold Cup, and the Washington, D.C., International. The International was his first start on turf. Family Style finished second to stablemate Twilight Ridge in the Breeders' Cup race for two-year-old fillies but won three stakes, including the Spinaway, the Arlington-Washington Lassie, and the Frizette.

Sam-Son Farm's Imperial Choice was the unanimous choice as Canada's horse of the year. The gelding also was named champion grass horse and champion three-year-old male. Imperial Choice's victories included the Prince of Wales Stakes, one of Canada's Triple Crown races for three-year-olds. In the others, the filly La Lorgnette won the Queen's Plate (she also took the Canadian Oaks), and Crowning Honors was first in the Breeders' Stakes.

Sam-Son Farm raced another champion, Grey Classic, in the two-year-old male division. Other Sovereign Award winners included: two-year-old filly, Stage Flite; three-year-old filly, La Lorgnette; older male, Ten Gold Pots; older mare, Lake Country; and sprinter, Summer Mood.

Almost all of the quality events in European racing take place between mid-April and late October, but the proliferation of valuable international prizes at the end of the year was altering the shape of the European season in 1985. It was becoming

AP/WIDE WORLD

Prakas, piloted by Bill O'Donnell, won the $1,272,000 purse at the Hambletonian race at the Meadowlands track in East Rutherford, New Jersey, on August 3.

increasingly worthwhile to concentrate on the big autumn prizes, the most important of which were provided by the Breeders' Cup program in the U.S., run in 1985 at Aqueduct Race Track in New York City. There, on November 2, Pebbles set a new course record of 2 min 27 sec for the 1½ mi in the Breeders' Cup Turf. Pebbles had started her season on April 26, when she won the newly instituted Trusthouse Forte Mile at Sandown Park, but the Aqueduct race was only her fifth of the year. She was beaten 1½ lengths by the 33–1 Bob Back in the Prince of Wales's Stakes at Royal Ascot but avenged that defeat in beating Rainbow Quest and Bob Back by 2 lengths and 1½ lengths in the Coral-Eclipse Stakes on July 6. Pebbles became ill soon afterward and did not race again until October 19, when she gained an impressive success in the Dubai Champion Stakes at Newmarket, beating the Epsom Derby winner, Slip Anchor, by three comfortable lengths.

Harness Racing

In 1985 Nihilator, son of the record-breaking Niatross and himself holder of the two-year-old and three-year-old mile pacing track records of 1 min 52⁴/₅ sec and 1 min 49³/₅ sec, respectively, won the $350,730 Little Brown Jug. Later in the year, however, Falcon Seelster won an invitational pace in a world record 1 min 51 sec for a competitive race. The two-year-old trotting fillies' Breeders' Crown of $632,803 was won by Caressable, and the $367,850 Kentucky Pacing Derby by Sherman Almahurst; Prakas won the World Trotting Derby of $553,750 in 1 min 53²/₅ sec, a new world's three-year-old record, and then went on to win the Hambletonian. The Roosevelt International Trot of

$250,000 was won by Lutin d'Isigny of France for the second time. The $1,344,000 Woodrow Wilson final for two-year-old pacers was taken by Grade One. Nihilator won the $1,018,000 Meadowlands Pace, and Chairmanoftheboard the $600,000 Cane Pace. The richest Standardbred of all time, On The Road Again, with earnings of more than $2,750,000, swept the World Cup Series of pacing with a 1-min 52²/₅-sec final at the Meadowlands. Meadow Road of Sweden made a clean sweep of the $320,000 International Statue of Liberty Trot, winning the second leg in a world record 1 min 54⁴/₅ sec from Sandy Bowl (U.S.) and Mon Tourbillon (France), and also won the Meadowlands $400,000 International Series.

In voting by the United States Trotting Association and the United States Harness Writers Association, Nihilator was selected harness horse of the year and pacer of the year. Prakas was voted trotter of the year. Divisional winners for pacers were: Barberry Spur, two-year-old colt; Follow My Star, two-year-old filly; Nihilator, three-year-old colt; Stienam, three-year-old filly; On the Road Again, aged pacer; and Green With Envy, aged mare. Divisional trotting winners included: Express Ride, two-year-old colt; Britelite Lobell, two-year-old filly; Prakas, three-year-old colt; Armbro Devona, three-year-old filly; Sandy Bowl, aged trotter; and Babe Kosmos, aged mare.

Champion trotting mare Scotch Notch took the Inter-Dominion Trotters championship in Australia. Preux Chevalier won the Inter-Dominion Pacing championship final of $A180,000 from Village Kid and Game Oro. (For table of world currencies, *see* International Exchange and Payments.) West Australian-bred two-year-old Prince of Princes paced a world record mile rate of 1 min 59.6 sec in a 2,100-m race. Anne Frawley became the first woman to drive a Derby winner in Australia when she won the New South Wales Pacers' Derby with Vanderport. Australia's greatest money winner, Gammalite, retired with $A1,386,480 from 94 wins. In New Zealand the premier two-year-old Sapling Stakes was won by Sir Alba. New Zealand's famous pacer Roydon Glen made it 12 in succession when he broke the track record at Cambridge in 1 min 57 sec. Juvenile champion Nardinski won the $NZ120,000 Great Northern Derby. The $NZ125,000 New Zealand Pacing Cup went to Camelot, while the Trotters Free for All was won by Sir Castleton.

In Sweden Legolas won the Swedish V65 final. The Onion won the Gold Divison at Göteborg, and Meadow Road took the Elitlopp final in a world record 1 min 55.2 sec (5/8-mi track) from Rosalind's Guy and Brandy Hanover. In Denmark Minou du Doujon won the Copenhagen Cup, and the Tuborg Open Trot went to Norway's Victoria S. In Norway the Oslo Grand Prix was won by French-owned Ogorek; Toyota Moulin captured the Gold Division final, and Jarlsberg took the Grand International from The Onion.

HUMAN RIGHTS

Human rights may be defined either narrowly or broadly. In the usage of the information media and of major "human rights organizations" such as Amnesty International, the primary denials of human rights are those that punish individuals by imprisonment, torture, execution, exile, or travel restrictions for their nonviolent expression of opinion or organizational activities. Torture for any reason is, of course, opposed by all human rights advocates. Human rights as defined in United Nations documents, and especially in a growing academic literature on human rights, include a wide variety of "rights" to organize, to express opinion, to exercise cultural choice, as well as to receive specified levels of nutrition, health care, and education. The denial of human rights may be by governments, societies, or dissidents, but the struggle for human rights is primarily a struggle against the unjustified expression of the power of the state.

A survey of the year's record in human rights will necessarily concentrate on those areas that have received greatest attention in the press. Human rights violations in countries where the mechanisms of repression are most thoroughly established are infrequently reported.

Communist Societies

For the purpose of assessing human rights performance, Communist societies may be divided into traditional Marxist-Leninist societies, including the U.S.S.R., Cuba, Vietnam, North Korea, and Albania, and evolving Communist societies, such as China, Poland, Hungary, and Yugoslavia. In the traditional Communist societies, there is no assumption of individual rights against the state. In such states there are thousands of prisoners of conscience, and the least hint of dissent or of organizational independence from the regime is severely punished. The traditional Communist denial of the cultural and religious rights of selected peoples was exemplified in 1985 by reports of a Bulgarian campaign to forcibly change the names of all citizens of Turkish background.

In the evolving Communist states, alongside the maintenance of many repressive Marxist-Leninist practices, governments allow individual activity and criticism greater scope. Polish society, for example, shows a somewhat higher degree of pluralism.

Latin America

Many Latin-American countries persevered in their attempt to institutionalize respect for human rights. The trial in Argentina of military leaders for their part in torturing and executing thousands of citizens ended with the conviction of five former military junta members and the acquittal of four others. Similar investigations of former military rulers began in Brazil and Uruguay, although not on the same scale. Peru managed a fair election amid staggering economic and security problems; the new government moved quickly to reassert civilian control over counterinsurgency forces. Elections in El Salvador confirmed civilian control and were followed by a reduction in the brutal killings attributed to the right wing.

Mexico and Chile failed to follow the trend to greater democracy among the larger countries of the hemisphere. Mexican elections were reported to have been more questionable than ever, while Chile's Gen. Augusto Pinochet Ugarte resisted the society's desire to return to democracy with detention, internal exile, and murder. The murder of those thought to be opposed to the system continued in Guatemala, much of it attributable to security forces. In Nicaragua there was strong evidence that the Sandinista government was carrying out a clandestine policy of executing suspected opponents, and toward the end of the year a pretext was found for the further reduction

South African children, packed in an army armored personnel carrier, wait to be driven to a police station after soldiers swept through Soweto arresting children who were not attending school. Some 800 children were arrested in August for boycotting classes as a protest against South African racial policies.

AP/WIDE WORLD

of the civil liberties of the internal opposition. Institutionalized repression continued in Cuba, Haiti, and Paraguay.

Middle East

In the Middle East violence and terror—by both governments and their opponents—were the order of the day in many societies. An attempt to set up a human rights organization in relatively moderate Algeria was met by imprisonment of its leaders, but even the attempt would have been impossible in half of the countries of the region. In Lebanon, where contestants appeared to have decided that only weapons could be decisive, there could be little expectation of respect for human rights. The Kurdish people's right to self-determination continued to be denied by Turkey and Iraq—Iran denied Kurdish rights within its borders but supported them within those of its neighbors. The quest for Arab self-government in territories occupied by Israel helped to keep the region in ferment. There were positive trends, however, in Jordan, Egypt, and Kuwait.

Executions of political opponents, violent and nonviolent, were once again reported to be common in Iran. Women of the Middle East continued to fight a losing battle against their second-class citizenship. New and revised laws in Algeria and Pakistan reinforced discrimination in family life and court testimony. In Egypt a legislative attempt to cancel gains achieved in the Sadat era was only partially blocked.

Africa South of the Sahara

In sub-Saharan Africa many governments again failed to meet their elementary responsibilities to serve the interests of their starving and uneducated peoples. Most flagrant was the willingness of the Ethiopian government to put the suppression of dissident peoples and the celebration of the new Communist Party ahead of famine relief. Many parts of the continent, such as Chad, southern Sudan, and much of Uganda, relapsed during the year into general anarchy.

The denial of equal rights to people of a different ethnic, religious, or racial group that claimed major international attention in 1985 occurred in South Africa. In an effort to meet the rising tide of internal and external criticism, the South African government, over the past few years, had enacted reforms in petty apartheid—marriage laws, residence rights, constitutional change. Real power remained with the whites, however, and reforms only served to fan the flames of dissent, which in 1985 broke out in sustained riots, boycotts, demonstrations, and the inevitable violent police reactions. This crisis was not caused by increased denials of human rights—in many ways the denials had been marginally eased—but by the buildup in South Africa of the struggle for equal rights that had taken place over many years.

Asia

In Asia, India moved effectively to overcome the challenging problem represented by the demand of many Sikhs for greater self-determination. The minority problem in Sri Lanka seemed more intractable. Government forces continued to kill civilians in revenge for attacks against its forces, and Tamil rebels replied in kind. Authoritarian regimes in the Philippines and Taiwan continued to repress the legitimate opposition. In the Philippines the problem was compounded by the existence of revolutionary Communist forces. Killing and torture by security forces and by fanatic outlaw gangs allied with them had become an escalating part of the human rights problem in the Philippines, although the country continued to have strong and well-organized groups campaigning for fair elections and other human rights. In Indonesia suppression of the East Timorese was most often in the news, but the government's suppression of the people of West Irian represented a more serious violation of the right to self-determination. The Melanesian peoples of the province were in danger of being submerged in a tide of Javanese settlement.

Western Democracies

Against this background, the continuing human rights problems of the Western democracies appeared less significant. Aside from the continuing and intractable case of Northern Ireland, the most obvious problems concerned immigrants and aliens, problems that now affected nearly all industrialized democracies. The U.S. struggled with an inconsistent immigration policy that allowed easy entry for people from countries whose governments the administration did not like, such as Iran or Poland, but severely limited entry from countries it wished to support, such as El Salvador or Guatemala. In Great Britain continued rioting in areas of recent immigration pointed up the difficulty of accommodating people from quite different cultural backgrounds.

The development and expression of human rights concerns appeared to be growing in many countries. The annual report of the U.S. State Department on human rights conditions in all countries continued its year-by-year improvement. "Helsinki watch" groups brought out a number of reports on human rights issues associated with the Helsinki process; these same issues were considered at an "experts meeting" of the Helsinki Accords countries in Ottawa, Ont. The Inter-American Commission on Human Rights of the Organization of American States became more active during the year, preparing several detailed studies of human rights problems in the hemisphere. Amnesty International continued its well-publicized campaigns, emphasizing its commitment to ending the practice of torture by issuing reports on torture occurring in the U.S.S.R., Mozambique, Turkey, and other countries.

HUNGARY

The 13th national congress of the Hungarian Socialist Workers' (Communist) Party took place in Budapest on March 25–28, 1985. The congress, the first to be held since 1980, was attended by 935 delegates representing the 871,000 party members, as well as by delegates from 50 other Communist parties around the world. In his opening address, General Secretary Janos Kadar made a passionate defense of his government's program of reform aimed at decentralizing and liberalizing the economy, promised an improvement in living standards, and pledged to continue contracts with Western nations. His speech included dismissive references to dissident Hungarian intellectuals.

The Soviet representative at the congress was Grigori Romanov, at the time still a senior Soviet Politburo member. His speech indicated that the Kremlin extended cautious approval to Hungary's economic reforms. He noted that the U.S.S.R. approved of closer links with capitalist nations in order to prevent a situation in which "imperialist forces" could apply economic pressure as a means of interfering in internal affairs.

Kadar's concern to reassure the people of Hungary that the reforms had a long-term future led the Communist Party to become the first in Eastern Europe to create the post of deputy party leader. The appointment went to Karoly Nemeth, a loyal supporter of Kadar on the Politburo and an opponent of both right-wing and left-wing deviation. The congress reelected Kadar as general secretary and approved a Politburo in which 3 of the 13 members were replaced.

Elections to the 387-seat National Assembly took place on June 8. A second round of voting on June 22 was necessary in those constituencies where no candidate won an outright majority. Each voter had two ballot papers, one for 35 unopposed deputies on a list of national candidates, the other to select a single deputy to represent the constituency, of which there were 352 in all. A new electoral law stipulated that at least two candidates must contest each constituency. Before the elections, each candidate was obliged to sign a declaration of support for the program of the Patriotic People's Front. Dissident groups were unsuccessful in their efforts to have candidates nominated. The results showed that independent opposition candidates secured 25 seats. The new Assembly returned Pal Losonczi for a further five-year term as chairman of the Presidential Council on June 28.

During Kadar's working trip to Moscow on September 25, he and Soviet leader Mikhail Gorbachev issued a joint communiqué stating that Hungary and the U.S.S.R. intended to continue their collaboration according to the principles of "Marxism-Leninism, democratic centralism, and socialist internationalism." On January 21 Minister of Foreign Affairs Peter Varkonyi met with his Romanian counterpart, Stefan Andrey, in Bucharest.

INTERFOTO MTI/EASTFOTO

Janos Kadar, general secretary of the Hungarian Socialist Workers' Party, opened the party's national congress with a defense of his policies.

They discussed the problem of Romania's Hungarian minority of 1.7 million to 2 million.

Returning Prime Minister Margaret Thatcher's 1984 trip to Hungary, Kadar paid a three-day visit to the U.K. beginning on Oct. 31, 1985. During his European tour, U.S. Secretary of State George Shultz visited Hungary, where he met Kadar and discussed trade issues with government ministers.

ICE HOCKEY

The Edmonton Oilers in 1985 once more proved their dominance over the National Hockey League (NHL) by winning their second straight Stanley Cup, this time by beating the Philadelphia Flyers in the final series four games to one. The speedy, high-scoring champions dropped the series' first game in Philadelphia but then reeled off four straight victories, ending with an 8–3 win at their home rink. Invincible at home, the Oilers compiled a record 16 straight play-off victories there.

The Flyers' appearance in the finals was testimony to the managerial skills of Bobby Clarke, the former player and Flyer captain, in his first year as general manager. The recharged team had finished the regular season with the best overall record in the league. On the way to the Stanley Cup series the Flyers defeated two formidable foes, the New York Islanders in the quarterfinals and the Quebec Nordiques in the semifinals.

But Edmonton, with youth, depth, experience, and confidence, claimed the cup. Wayne Gretzky, the incomparable center, once more set several scoring records, but there were other outstanding Edmonton players as well.

The 24-year-old Gretzky achieved a record sixth consecutive Hart Trophy as the league's most valuable player. In the National Hockey League only Bobby Orr had won any award for more than six straight years, having been named top defenseman for eight seasons beginning in 1967. Gretzky also won a fifth straight league scoring championship,

AP/WIDE WORLD

Edmonton Oiler center Wayne Gretzky scores his third goal of the first period, setting a National Hockey League record, as the Oilers beat Philadelphia on May 25.

surpassing the mark of four that he shared with Detroit's Gordie Howe and Boston's Phil Esposito. Gretzky had 73 goals and 135 assists in the regular season for a total of 208 points. In the play-offs Gretzky scored 47 points on 17 goals and 30 assists, the most points and assists ever achieved by one player in one play-off season. That feat earned him the Conn Smythe Trophy as the play-offs' most valuable player.

Gretzky's teammate Paul Coffey won the Norris Trophy as the league's best defenseman. Jari Kurri, another Oiler and a native of Finland, won the Lady Byng Award as the league's most gentlemanly player.

Pelle Lindbergh of the Philadelphia Flyers won the Vezina Trophy as the league's best goaltender. Lindbergh missed the final game of the Stanley Cup series with a knee injury. Tragedy struck, however, on the morning of November 10 when Lindbergh, driving home intoxicated after a team party, lost control of his sports car and crashed into a concrete wall. The 26-year-old player died of brain and spinal cord injuries.

Flyer coach Mike Keenan, in his rookie NHL season, won the Adams Trophy for coach of the year. The William Jennings Trophy for the goaltending team with the fewest goals scored against it went to the Buffalo pair of Tom Barrasso and Bob Sauve. Mario Lemieux, a 6-ft 4-in (1.93-m) center for the Pittsburgh Penguins, was named rookie of the year. Lemieux had been selected first overall in the previous year's amateur draft and had signed the richest rookie contract in NHL history. He led the Penguins in regular-season scoring with 43 goals and 57 assists.

The Buffalo Sabres' Craig Ramsay won the Selke Award as the league's best defensive forward. Anders Hedberg of the New York Rangers, whose last

year before retirement was cut short by an eye injury, won the Bill Masterton Trophy for sportsmanship and dedication to hockey.

In accepting his trophies, Gretzky criticized an NHL rule change set for the 1985–86 season that would virtually eliminate the four-on-four skating situations on which Gretzky has thrived. The new rule would allow teams to remain at full strength when coincidental minor penalties were assessed—as had been the case with coincidental major penalties. (In a coincidental penalty each team loses the same number of players for the same amount of time.) Gretzky said the rule change would rob the game of some excitement.

The 1984–85 season was marked by the retirement at age 33 of the great Guy Lafleur, one of the legendary "Flying Frenchmen" who propelled Montreal Canadiens to five Stanley Cup championships during the 1970s. One of the most graceful and exciting skaters ever to play the game, Lafleur retired in November. The right wing's accomplishments included six straight seasons (beginning in 1970) with 50 or more goals.

A dizzying flurry of coaching changes took place during the 1984–85 season. In Boston Gerry Cheevers resigned during the season, and general manager Harry Sinden took over. At the season's end a newly retired player, Butch Goring, was named head coach. In Buffalo general manager Scotty Bowman, who had also been coaching the team, replaced himself with Jim Schoenfeld, a recently retired player. Bowman's 17-year coaching career had included guiding the Montreal Canadiens to five Stanley Cup championships. He went to Buffalo as coach and general manager in 1979.

Orval Tessier of Chicago, who was named coach of the year in 1983, was dismissed by general manager Bob Pulford, who then took over as coach. In

Before his tragic death in a car crash, Philadelphia Flyer goalie Pelle Lindbergh (center) is congratulated following a 3–0 shutout of the Quebec Nordiques.
AP/WIDE WORLD

Detroit coach Nick Polano was dismissed after the season and replaced by Harry Neale.

Neale had been general manager of Vancouver. During the season Neale fired Vancouver coach Bill LaForge and took over himself behind the bench. But after Vancouver's poor finish, Neale was fired as general manager. Named as Vancouver's new general manager was Jack Gordon, and the new coach was Tom Watt. Minnesota general manager Lou Nanne fired coach Bill Mahoney early in the season and replaced him with Glen Sonmor as interim coach. After the season Lorne Henning was named head coach. In Montreal coach Jacques Lemaire resigned and was replaced by Jean Perron. Herb Brooks was fired as coach of the New York Rangers during the season. General manager Craig Patrick took over himself. At the season's end he named a new coach, Ted Sator.

In the minor leagues the Sherbrooke Canadiens won the American Hockey League championship. The Peoria Rivermen won the International Hockey League title.

It became compulsory during the year for all world junior championship players to wear face masks. The International Ice Hockey Federation (IIHF) expressed the hope that the juniors would continue wearing such masks after becoming seniors. Studies showed that the number of serious injuries had declined since the players had become better protected.

It was decided by the executive board of the International Olympic Committee that professionals would be eligible to participate in the 1988 Winter Olympic Games in Calgary, Alta., provided that they were younger than 23 on February 1 of that year. Former professionals would also be eligible if they held no contract after Sept. 1, 1987.

ICELAND

Throughout 1985 the Icelandic economy experienced moderate growth, largely under the influence of a limited fish catch, while other industries performed only passably well. Real gross national product (GNP) rose by an estimated 1.5% in volume, following a 2.5% rise in the previous year and a 5.7% decline in 1983. Despite the slow rate of growth in 1985, the economy was under considerable demand pressure, which found an outlet in substantial wage and price increases and a sizable current account deficit. Inflation averaged 31%, and the current account deficit was estimated at some 5% of GNP.

Iceland's relations with the U.S., which over the years had been excellent, were soured in 1985 by the fact that the U.S. base in Iceland ceased using Icelandic vessels for its freight import needs and resorted instead to using ships of U.S. registry, thus depriving two local shipping companies of important revenue. The matter was taken up directly by Foreign Minister Geir Hallgrímsson with U.S. Secretary of State George Shultz. The latter did his utmost to smooth over the issue by visiting Iceland twice during the year, in March and again in November. Soviet Foreign Minister Eduard Shevardnadze also paid a goodwill visit to the country in November.

The long-running dispute between the Icelandic government and Alusuisse, the Swiss corporation that owned an aluminum smelter in Iceland, was finally resolved in July when the Icelandic government signed an agreement settling all outstanding issues. The agreement increased the price of electric power supplied to the smelter and at the same time settled a dispute over the amount of tax that the smelter was to pay.

The Althing (parliament) dealt with two unusual bills early in 1985. The first, which called for abolition of the state monopoly of radio and television, was passed; the second called for an end to the ban on alcoholic beer and was rejected. Both issues were hotly contested.

The right-of-center coalition government of the Progressive Party and the Independence Party, led by Prime Minister Steingrímur Hermannsson of the Progressive Party, continued in office throughout the year. In October the Independence Party, which held six of the ten posts in the Cabinet, reshuffled its ministers. The major objective of the reshuffle was to facilitate the entry into the Cabinet of Thorsteinn Pálsson as finance minister.

On October 24 the women of Iceland staged a one-day strike as they had done ten years earlier on the same date. The strike was intended to emphasize the role and importance of women in the economy and everyday life. Factories and offices were largely shut down and, since housewives also participated in the strike, most husbands had to take over the duties of cooking and child care.

ICE SKATING

A profusion of new indoor rinks throughout the world underlined a continuing upsurge of recreational and competitive participation in all branches of ice skating. A higher standard of competition was particularly evident in Japan, corresponding with that country's improved instructional facilities. The popularity of ice dancing widened, while a decline in the number of pair skaters was attributed to the increased risk of the sport brought about by the attempt to perform more ambitious lifts and jump throws. Speed skating seemed likely to benefit from a decision by the International Skating Union to introduce a World Cup series in 1986 and by the addition of an extra Olympic Games women's event, the 5,000 m, as well as through an increasing interest in short-track indoor racing.

Figure Skating

The departure from competition of several stars after the 1984 Winter Olympics sparked a fascinating new cycle of growth, with highly promising challengers to the more established performers en-

Katarina Witt of East Germany skates to her second consecutive victory in the world figure skating championships.

hancing the drama of top-level contests. The men's technical progress was especially noticeable, with an added degree of athleticism. The triple axel jump was now being seen more than once in a performance; other triples became more commonplace, and even an occasional quadruple toe loop jump was landed correctly.

There were 117 competitors in the four events of the 75th world championships in Tokyo on March 4–9. Aleksandr Fadeev captured the vacant men's crown, resisting strong late challenges from Brian Orser, the Canadian runner-up in the 1984 Winter

Andrea Schöne of East Germany set a world record for the 5,000-meter event at the women's speed skating world championship in Yugoslavia in February.

Olympics, and Brian Boitano, who won the bronze for the U.S. Six judges gave Fadeev a score of 5.9 (out of a possible 6.0) for technical merit despite his touching down from a double salchow. Orser collected the same mark from four judges for presentation, three more than the Soviet victor. Each achieved a clean triple axel.

Katarina Witt, the East German Olympic gold medalist, came from behind to retain the women's title. Not for the first time, she showed a champion's cool when the chips were down, overtaking Kira Ivanova of the Soviet Union and third-place Tiffany Chin of the U.S. with a personal best performance that inspired five judges to award her 5.9 for presentation.

In a generally improved women's competition, runner-up Ivanova came within an ace of completing an unprecedented Soviet sweep of the four titles. Chin, a U.S. resident of Chinese parentage, proved a powerful jumper and elegant spinner. Her fall from a double axel near the end surely cost her the silver medal. The host country suffered a harsh setback when Midori Ito, the great local hope who had been the outstanding jumper in the previous year's contest, had to withdraw after breaking her ankle in training while attempting a triple toe salchow.

With superior overhead lifts and well-landed triple throws, Oleg Vasiliev and Elena Valova recaptured the pairs title they had previously won in 1983. They overhauled their Soviet compatriots Oleg Makarov and Larissa Selezneva in spite of a touch down from a double axel by Vasiliev. Lloyd Eisler and Katherina Matousek, the Canadian bronze medalists, led a significant challenge to Eastern European dominance by three North American partnerships.

After three frustrating years as runners-up to Britain's invincible Christopher Dean and Jayne Torvill, who had turned professional, Andrei Bukin and Natalia Bestemianova succeeded to the ice dance title. Sergei Ponomarenko and Marina Klimova, also of the Soviet Union, finished second. Michael Seibert and Judy Blumberg of the U.S. won the bronze medal for a third time.

Speed Skating

Hein Vergeer of The Netherlands outpaced the Soviet defender, Oleg Bozhiev, to capture the men's world championship in Hamar, Norway, on February 16–17. Another Dutchman, Hilbert van der Duim, the 1982 winner, gained the bronze medal. In the individual events Vergeer won the 5,000 m and Bozhiev the 1,500 m, with Gaetan Boucher of Canada and Geir Karlstad from Norway taking the 500 m and 10,000 m, respectively.

In the women's world championship at Sarajevo, Yugos., on February 9–10, Andrea Schöne of East Germany regained the title she had held in 1983, this time dominating the competition with wins in all four distances. In the 5,000 m she set a world record time of 7 min 32.82 sec. Gabi Schönbrunn, also of East Germany, finished second in the overall competition, with Sabine Brehm completing an East German clean sweep.

In the separate world sprint championships, at Heerenveen, Neth., on February 23–24, Igor Zhelezovski of the U.S.S.R. gained the men's title, with Boucher, the defending champion, finishing in second place and Dan Jensen of the U.S. in third. Christa Rothenburger defeated her fellow East German Angela Stahnke to take the women's title, with Erwina Rys-Ferens of Poland third.

At the fifth world short-track (indoor) championships, in Amsterdam on March 15–17, Toshinobu Kawai won the men's title for Japan, followed by his compatriot Tatsuyoshi Ishihara, runner-up for a second successive time; Louis Grenier from Canada finished third. Japanese ascendancy was further emphasized by the victory in women's competition of Eiko Shishii, who proved too good for Bonnie Blair of the U.S. and Nathalie Lambert of Canada, second and third, respectively.

INDIA

In India 1985 was the year of Rajiv Gandhi, of political reconciliation, and of new moves in economic policy. Succeeding his murdered mother, Indira Gandhi, on Oct. 31, 1984, the young prime minister established himself within 12 months as a resourceful, dynamic, and farsighted leader. The election he ordered in December 1984 to the Lok Sabha (lower house of the national Parliament) gave his party, the Congress (I), a record 401 seats out of the 515 for which polling took place—a higher proportion than it had secured under either Jawaharlal Nehru or Indira Gandhi. The Council of Ministers that he formed on December 31 confirmed that Rajiv Gandhi was a man with a mind of his own.

He followed this up by announcing that finding solutions to the problems of Sikh separatism in the Punjab and agitation against immigrants in Assam would be his highest priority. Another early move of the new government was a bill to ban defections from parties. The bill was unanimously adopted by Parliament in January.

Negotiations undertaken through the governor of Punjab resulted in the signing on July 24 of an agreement between Sant Harchand Singh Longowal, president of the Akali Dal (which was agitating for an autonomous Sikh state), and Prime Minister Gandhi. The agreement reaffirmed that the city of Chandigarh would go to Punjab and that certain Hindi-speaking areas of Punjab would be transferred to neighboring Haryana state on the advice of a commission. It also entrusted to a Supreme Court judge the question of the sharing of river waters between Punjab and Haryana.

While the agreement was widely welcomed, it was not to the liking of extremists. Terrorists continued their attacks throughout the year, one of their victims being the head priest of the Akal Takht in the Golden Temple, Amritsar. Nearly 80 people were killed in New Delhi, Haryana, and Uttar Pradesh in simultaneous bomb explosions on May 10. The country was stunned when an Air-India jet crashed into the Atlantic Ocean off Ireland on June 23 with 329 persons aboard. There were no survivors. It was widely believed that the aircraft had been blown up by Sikh extremists, although commissions of inquiry had not given their verdict by the end of the year. The chain of killings did not stop with the signing of the accord. On July 31 Lalit Maken, a member of Parliament, was gunned down; and on August 20, three days after plans to hold elections

Surjit Singh Barnala (right), the Sikh leader of the Akali Dal party, was sworn in as chief minister of Punjab on September 29 by Punjab Gov. Arjun Singh at a ceremony in Chandigarh.

AP/WIDE WORLD

in Punjab were announced, Sant Longowal was assassinated while addressing a meeting.

Elections in Punjab went ahead as planned on September 25. Polling proved to be peaceful and heavy, in spite of a boycott call by extremists. The Akali Dal secured 73 out of 117 seats in the state assembly as against 32 seats won by Congress (I). A Dal government, headed by Surjit Singh Barnala, was sworn in. Although Sant Ajit Singh did not take up a post in the government, he was regarded by many as the natural successor to Sant Longowal as leader of the Sikhs. Elections were also held to fill Punjab's 13 seats in the Lok Sabha; the Dal won 7 and the Congress (I) 6.

On August 15 a settlement of the long-drawn-out problem of foreigners (emigrants from Bangladesh) in Assam was reached. It was decided that for the purpose of detecting foreigners and deleting their names from the electoral roll in the state, Jan. 1, 1966, would be regarded as the base date. The names of foreigners who had entered the state between then and March 24, 1971, would be deleted from existing electoral rolls and would be restored on the expiration of a ten-year period. Foreigners who had arrived after March 25, 1971, would be expelled. Elections were held to the state assembly on December 16. The Assam Gana Parishad, formed by the parties and groups that had carried on the agitation, won 63 of the 125 seats, while Congress (I) won 23 and the United Minorities Front 17.

On September 25 Rajiv Gandhi carried out a major reshuffle of the Council of Ministers. Bali Ram Bhagat, Narayan Dutt Tiwari, and A. B. A. Ghani Khan Chowdhury were made ministers of external affairs, industry, and program implementation, respectively. Gandhi took over the defense portfolio from P. V. Narasimha Rao, who was appointed to the newly created Ministry of Human Resource Development. In November Arjun Singh resigned as governor of Punjab to take up the post of minister of commerce.

Among other major political moves during the year was the enactment of a bill to permit donations from companies to political parties and the introduction of a bill to appoint an ombudsman to investigate complaints against holders of high political office. A bill to prevent terrorist and disruptive activities was also enacted, and a stringent law was adopted to deal with the drug menace.

In January India was rocked by the revelation that secret papers had been stolen from the Prime Minister's Office and given to foreign governments. Many employees were arrested. In an important verdict the Supreme Court ruled that women divorced under Muslim law were entitled to maintenance. The Jawaharlal Nehru award for international understanding was conferred upon Bruno Kreisky, former chancellor of Austria, and, posthumously, on Indira Gandhi. She was also awarded the Lenin Prize by the U.S.S.R. and the José Martí Order of Cuba. India filed a suit in the U.S. against Union Carbide Corp. for compensation for the victims of the poison-gas tragedy at Bhopal in 1984. Celebrations of the centenary of the Indian National Congress, the first session of which had been held on Dec. 28, 1885, took place in December.

The Economy

The union government budget, presented on March 16, contained a new approach to direct taxes. It reduced the highest income-tax level to 50% and raised the exemption limit. Total receipts during 1985–86 were set at Rs 479,460,000,000, including Rs 3,110,000,000 from new taxes and Rs 21,440,000,000 from external loans. (For table of world currencies, see International Exchange and Payments.) Total disbursements were estimated at Rs 512,950,000,000, leaving a deficit of Rs 33,-490,000,000. The allocation for defense was Rs 93.9 billion and that for the development plan Rs 185,090,000,000.

A meeting of the national development council in November adopted the draft of the seventh five-year (1985–90) plan. The plan envisioned an outlay of Rs 1.8 trillion by the union and state governments during the five-year period, with priority being given to agriculture, industrial modernization, and programs providing direct assistance to the poor. The plan aimed at an annual growth rate of 5% and the creation of 40 million jobs over five years.

Foreign Policy

A conference of India, Argentina, Greece, Mexico, Sweden, and Tanzania was held in New Delhi in January to pursue a six-nation disarmament initiative. It called on nuclear powers to halt all tests, refrain from adding to their stockpiles, and start a dialogue on disarmament. In March Prime Minister Gandhi attended the funeral of Soviet leader Konstantin Chernenko in Moscow. He paid an official visit to the U.S.S.R. in May and held wide-ranging talks with the new leader, Mikhail Gorbachev. A 1 billion ruble credit and an agreement on scientific and technical cooperation until the year 2000 were signed.

The following month Gandhi visited Egypt, France, Algeria, the U.S., and Switzerland. In Washington, D.C., he held talks with Pres. Ronald Reagan and also addressed a joint session of the U.S. Congress. Discussions were held on closer cooperation between the two countries in several fields of advanced technology, for which a memorandum was signed. Gandhi also paid brief visits to Bangladesh and Bhutan. In October he went on a visit to the U.K., The Bahamas (to attend the Commonwealth heads of government meeting), Cuba, the UN (for its 40th anniversary celebrations), and The Netherlands. On his return trip he went to Moscow. In November he visited Vietnam and Japan.

The desire to improve relations with Pakistan appeared to be blocked by concern about Pakistan's intentions regarding the production of nuclear weapons and its alleged support of extremists. Talks were held with a Chinese delegation in November on the border question. The trouble in Sri Lanka between Tamils, whose traditional home was India, and the government of Sri Lanka continued to cause anxiety. The two sides held several meetings under Indian auspices, and a cease-fire was arranged. An extraordinary meeting of the coordinating bureau of nonaligned countries was held in April in New Delhi. India also participated in the formal inauguration of the South Asian Association for Regional Cooperation in Dhaka, Bangladesh, in December.

INDONESIA

The main theme of Indonesia's domestic affairs in 1985 was the government's ongoing campaign to bring all spheres of national life under its secular ideology, *pancasila* (the five principles: belief in a supreme deity, nationalism, democracy, humanitarianism, and social justice). A climax was reached in May when a controversial law was passed by Parliament requiring all civic and religious bodies to adopt *pancasila* as their sole guiding principle within two years. Groups that received funds from abroad without official clearance, aided foreigners threatening to harm the nation's interests, or professed anti-*pancasila* doctrines (Communism was the only one named outright) could be disbanded. Though the law stipulated that the state creed would not regulate the observance of religious duties, some faith-based groups and political parties remained concerned about interference, noting that the government was empowered to "guide" organizations. Such worries were widely believed to have been a key motivation behind a series of mysterious bombings and fires that began in late 1984 and continued into 1985. However, most groups apparently sympathized with the authorities' underlying goal of preserving national unity by dampening Muslim fundamentalist or secessionist ambitions.

The government's determination to act against extremist-inspired violence became apparent when the trials of more than 40 people charged with involvement in the bombing incidents began in January. The testimony indicated that the violence had been sparked by a volatile mix of emotions: frustration that the authorities were taking control of Islam and resentment that Indonesia's ethnic Chinese continued to dominate the national economy. After five months of court hearings, nine defendants were found guilty of participation in the bomb attacks, including H. M. Sanusi, a former Cabinet minister.

Having consolidated its position at home, President Suharto's administration clearly indicated its desire to play a more prominent role on the international stage. The highlight of the year took place in April when Indonesia was host to the commemoration of the watershed Afro-Asian Conference held in Bandung, Java, 30 years earlier. Some 240 delegates, representing more than 80 nations, 4 liberation movements, and three-quarters of the world's population, gathered in Java to draft a new Bandung declaration. Of particular interest was the presence of Chinese Foreign Minister Wu Xueqian (Wu Hsüeh-ch'ien). His talks with Suharto marked the first contact at such high levels between the two governments since bilateral relations were frozen 18 years earlier, after Jakarta accused Peking of fomenting an abortive coup attempt. Later in the year the two countries agreed to reopen bilateral trade links.

The year was one of continued moderate economic growth, despite soft world oil prices and rising protectionism in the developed countries. In his budget for fiscal 1985–86, Suharto set total expenditure at 23,046,000,000,000 rupiah, an increase of 12% over the previous year. (For table of world currencies, *see* International Exchange and Payments.) Growth in gross domestic product recovered in 1984 to about 5%. The Indonesia Commodity Exchange began trading in April, and in the same month the new $600 million international airport opened at Cengkareng, some 15.5 mi (25 km) west of Jakarta.

INTERNATIONAL EXCHANGE AND PAYMENTS

Contrary to the fears expressed toward the end of 1984, a relatively stable world financial climate characterized 1985. In spite of a slowdown in the growth of the world economy, a marked deceleration in the rise of world trade, a sharp fall in commodity prices, and continuing concern about the volume and nature of deficit financing in some countries, the problems of the principal debtors remained under control, and there were no crises of significant international proportions. This, to a large extent, was a tribute to the degree of cooperation between the major financial powers as well as to the efficiency and sophistication of both national and international financial institutions in managing a potentially troublesome situation. In terms of solving the underlying problems of world finance, however, only limited progress was made.

As in 1984, the international financial scene was characterized by major imbalances. The U.S. administration continued to run a huge budget deficit and, despite some attempts to reverse the trend, there was a further increase in the current account deficit from approximately $102 billion to an estimated $120 billion. Furthermore, as in the previous year, a very large part of the U.S. deficit was financed by an inflow of foreign funds, making it more difficult for other, less powerful economies to cover their funding requirements. By contrast, a significant rise in their trade and current account surpluses took place in Japan and West Germany, with the performance of the former giving rise to growing international criticism and a further strengthening of protectionist sentiment. At the same time, preliminary figures available in late 1985 suggested that, partly because of a deceleration in the growth of imports by the developed world and a sharp decline in commodity prices, the external payments position of the less developed countries deteriorated. This was disappointing in the wake of the sharp reduction (from $70.5 billion to $43.9 billion) in their current account deficits that had occurred from 1983 to 1984—a development that, together with further debt rescheduling, had contributed heavily to the relative financial stability experienced during 1984.

The existence of these large imbalances had serious implications for exchange and interest rates, debt financing, international capital flows, and national economic policies. By far the most important aspect was the presence of the huge U.S. budget and external deficits that led to a competition for funds within the developed world and tended to make it more difficult to finance the needs of the less developed countries. This was spelled out strongly at the annual meeting of the International Monetary Fund (IMF) in Seoul, South Korea, in October, where the U.S. came under heavy pressure to take corrective measures. Although U.S. officials could point to proposed budget cuts of $55.5 billion for fiscal 1986 approved by Congress in May, there was considerable skepticism about the chances of an early and substantial reduction.

There was, however, a degree of satisfaction about the trend of the external value of the dollar. In recent years the liberalization of world financial markets and a range of technical and technological advances had made capital flows from country to country considerably easier. The result was that, unlike the situation in the age of strict national controls on external capital transactions, it became relatively simple for countries to attract external finance in order to cover their deficits as long as they provided a sufficiently high reward/risk ratio to foreign holders of capital. This created a situation in which the traditional weapons of dealing with national deficits—deflation, currency devaluation, and restrictions on the outflow of capital—became less relevant. On the contrary, as long as a sufficient flow of funds from abroad was maintained, it was possible for a country to run large external deficits and at the same time ensure an appreciation in its currency.

Such an appreciation, however, made imports cheaper and exports more expensive, and this in turn tended to make the achievement of external equilibrium more difficult. The recent U.S. experience was a case in point. Under the influence of relatively high interest rates, continued confidence in the growth prospects of the economy, and fears about the financial stability of some less developed countries, a strong flow of international capital to the U.S. had taken place during the past few years. This not only financed the huge U.S. budget and external deficits but also resulted in a significant appreciation in the external value of the dollar during 1984 and the first two months of 1985, tending to impair U.S. trade performance even further. From February 1985, however, the underlying trend in the dollar was in a downward direction, largely as a result of a reduction in interest rate differentials as well as an increasing degree of national and international intervention in foreign exchange markets aimed at pushing the U.S. currency down to more realistic levels.

As a result, by the second quarter of 1985 the trade-weighted value of the dollar was 2.7% below the average for the previous three-month period. This was followed by a further significant depreciation in the wake of the September agreement

(continued on page 172)

More than 100,000 members of labor unions marched through Buenos Aires, Argentina, in August to denounce the government's compliance with austerity measures proposed by the International Monetary Fund.

SIPA/SPECIAL FEATURES

WORLD CURRENCIES
Foreign Units and Their Value in United States Dollars

After 1934, when the United States and most other nations went off the gold standard, the nominal values of foreign moneys and their exchange quotations came to differ widely; these also changed frequently. Quotations for this table were supplied by the *London Financial Times*. They were effective on Dec. 31, 1985. Newspapers or banks should be consulted for the latest values of foreign money.

The Special Drawing Right (SDR) is a unit of credit granted by the International Monetary Fund. SDRs, in effect, enlarge a nation's foreign reserves without draining it of gold or national currency, thereby expanding international liquidity in matters of debt. The SDR rate per U.S. dollar as of Dec. 31, 1985, was 0.91040, according to *International Financial Statistics*.

Country	Local Unit	Value of U.S.$1	Country	Local Unit	Value of U.S.$1	Country	Local Unit	Value of U.S.$1
Afghanistan	Afghani	68.49	Gibraltar	Pound	0.69	Paraguay	Guaraní[12]	239.09
Albania	Lek	7.01	Greece	Drachma	147.24		Guaraní[8]	640.06
Algeria	Dinar[1]	4.77	Greenland	Danish Krone	8.92	Peru	Sol[1]	13,889.73
Angola	Kwanza	29.57	Grenada	EC* Dollar	2.69	Philippines	Peso	18.21
Antigua and			Guadeloupe	Franc	7.50	Poland	Zloty	145.80
Barbuda	EC* Dollar	2.69	Guatemala	Quetzal	1.00	Portugal	Escudo	158.08
Argentina	Austral	0.80	Guinea	Syli	22.58	Qatar	Riyal	3.63
Australia	Dollar	1.47	Guyana	Dollar	4.10	Romania	Leu[2]	3.97
Austria	Schilling	17.21	Haiti	Gourde	4.98		Leu[7]	11.09
Bahamas, The	Dollar	1.00	Honduras	Lempira	2.00	St. Christopher		
Bahrain	Dinar	0.38	Hong Kong	Dollar	7.80	and Nevis	EC* Dollar	2.69
Bangladesh	Taka	30.61	Hungary	Forint	47.11	St. Helena	Pound	0.69
Barbados	Dollar	2.00	Iceland	Króna	41.94	St. Lucia	EC* Dollar	2.69
Belgium	Franc[2]	50.05	India	Rupee	11.98	St. Pierre and		
	Franc[3]	50.40	Indonesia	Rupiah	1,120.72	Miquelon	Franc	7.50
Belize	Dollar	1.99	Iran	Rial[10]	83.36	St. Vincent		
Benin	CFA† Franc	374.96	Iraq	Dinar	0.31	and the		
Bermuda	Dollar	1.00	Ireland	Pound	0.80	Grenadines	EC* Dollar	2.69
Bhutan	Ngultrum	11.98	Israel	Shekel	1,497.75	San Marino	Italian	
Bolivia	Peso[4]	1,556,057	Italy	Lira	1,670.53		Lira	1,670.53
Botswana	Pula	2.15	Jamaica	Dollar[10]	5.46	São Tomé and		
Brazil	Cruzeiro	10,473.88	Japan	Yen	200.28	Príncipe	Dobra	41.38
Brunei	Dollar	2.12	Jordan	Dinar	0.37	Saudi Arabia	Riyal	3.65
Bulgaria	Lev	0.99	Kampuchea	Riel	n.a.	Senegal	CFA† Franc	374.96
Burkina Faso	CFA† Franc	374.96	Kenya	Shilling	16.22	Sierra Leone	Leone[4]	5.26
Burma	Kyat	7.84	Korea, North	Won	0.93	Singapore	Dollar	2.12
Burundi	Franc	111.28	Korea, South	Won	891.37	Somalia	Shilling	36.46
Cameroon	CFA† Franc	374.96	Kuwait	Dinar	0.29	South Africa	Rand	2.58
Canada	Dollar	1.40	Laos	Kip	34.87	Spain	Peseta	153.06
Central African			Lebanon	Pound	18.03	Sri Lanka	Rupee	27.23
Republic	CFA† Franc	374.96	Liberia	Dollar	1.00	Sudan, The	Pound	2.49
Chad	CFA† Franc	374.96	Libya	Dinar	0.29	Suriname	Guilder	1.78
Chile	Peso	181.01	Liechtenstein	Swiss Franc	2.06	Swaziland	Lilangeni	2.58
China	Renminbi		Luxembourg	Franc	50.05	Sweden	Krona	7.58
	(Yuan)	3.20	Madagascar	Franc	529.14	Switzerland	Franc	2.06
Colombia	Peso[5]	166.23	Malawi	Kwacha	1.65	Syria	Pound[1,9]	6.23
Congo	CFA† Franc	374.96	Malaysia	Ringgit, or			Pound[2]	3.91
Costa Rica	Colón[6]	53.20		Malaysian		Taiwan	New Taiwan	
Cuba	Peso	0.89		Dollar	2.42		Dollar	39.76
Cyprus	Pound	0.55	Maldives	Rufiyaa	6.97	Tanzania	Shilling	16.22
Czechoslovakia	Koruna	10.77	Malta	Lira	0.42	Thailand	Baht	26.34
	Koruna[2]	6.47	Martinique	Franc	7.50	Togo	CFA† Franc	374.96
	Koruna[7]	11.26	Mauritania	Ouguiya	76.71	Trinidad and		
Denmark	Krone	8.92	Mauritius	Rupee	14.33	Tobago	Dollar	3.58
Dominica	EC* Dollar	2.69	Mexico	Peso[5]	451.77	Tunisia	Dinar[10]	0.75
Dominican				Peso[11]	356.94	Turkey	Lira	565.03
Republic	Peso[4]	1.00	Monaco	French Franc	7.50	Uganda	Shilling	1,383.54
	Peso[8]	2.93	Mongolia	Tugrik	3.34	Union of		
Ecuador	Sucre	95.39	Morocco	Dirham[10]	9.55	Soviet Socialist		
Egypt	Pound[4]	0.83	Mozambique	Metical[1]	41.40	Republics	Ruble	0.76
	Pound[9]	1.34	Namibia	South		United Arab		
El Salvador	Colón[4]	2.50		African Rand	2.58	Emirates	Dirham	3.67
	Colón[5]	4.86	Nepal	Rupee	20.42	United Kingdom	Pound	0.69
Equatorial			Netherlands, The	Guilder	2.76	Uruguay	New Peso	122.91
Guinea	Ekwele	374.96	New Caledonia	CFP‡ Franc	138.36	Venezuela	Bolívar[13]	4.28
Ethiopia	Birr	2.08	New Zealand	Dollar	1.99		Bolívar[14]	7.27
Finland	Markka	5.39	Nicaragua	Córdoba[4]	27.89		Bolívar[15]	14.65
France	Franc	7.50	Niger	CFA† Franc	374.96	Vietnam	Dong[4]	14.20
French Guiana	Franc	7.50	Nigeria	Naira[10]	0.99	Yemen (Aden)	Dinar	0.34
French			Norway	Krone	7.59	Yemen (San'a')	Rial[1]	6.98
Polynesia	CFP‡ Franc	138.36	Oman	Rial	0.34	Yugoslavia	Dinar	310.86
Gabon	CFA† Franc	374.96	Pakistan	Rupee	15.72	Zaire	Zaire	54.46
Germany, East	Mark	2.51	Panama	Balboa	1.00	Zambia	Kwacha	5.50
Germany, West	Mark	2.51	Papua New			Zimbabwe	Dollar	1.65
Ghana	Cedi	59.97	Guinea	Kina	1.00			

[1]Approximate. [2]Commercial rate. [3]Financial rate. [4]Official rate. [5]Free rate. [6]Unified rate. [7]Noncommercial rate. [8]Parallel rate. [9]Tourist rate. [10]Selling rate. [11]Controlled rate. [12]Rate for exports. [13]Preferential rate for public sector debt and essential imports. [14]Preferential rate. [15]Free rate for luxury imports, remittances of money abroad, and foreign travel.
*East Caribbean. †Communauté Financière Africaine (African Financial Community). ‡Comptoir Français du Pacifique (French Bank of the Pacific).

(continued from page 170)
reached by the so-called Group of Five—the five major industrial countries (U.S., Japan, West Germany, U.K., and France)—to take further steps to push the dollar down. As a result, the average for the July–September quarter revealed a further decline of 4.8% from the preceding quarter. The downward trend was confirmed in October and November, and it was widely anticipated that by the end of the year the external value of the dollar would be some 20% lower than in January 1985. Nevertheless, many observers believed that even at that level the dollar was overvalued and that a further reduction would be required in order to make significant inroads into the large U.S. trade deficit.

In terms of the dollar, most major currencies appreciated significantly. The most spectacular increase occurred in the dollar value of sterling, which was some 32% higher in November 1985 than in February of the same year. Between February and October the value of the West German Deutsche Mark rose by some 20% and that of the Japanese yen by 24%. As the year drew to a close, the trend was still upward, although in some countries, notably the U.K., there were growing fears that a further appreciation would have a serious adverse effect on exports.

During 1984–85 the International Monetary Fund confirmed its efforts to ease the problems of weaker debtor countries by rescheduling their debts and mobilizing support from commercial banks and other nongovernmental sources. The most important agreements negotiated during this period included a major multiyear rescheduling plan for Mexico that involved a total of $49 billion, the stretching of repayment over 14 years, and an improvement in the terms of the loan. Another $21 billion agreement was reached with Venezuela, and progress was also made with other smaller rescheduling agreements. However, although these and other, similar steps helped to defuse a number of particularly difficult and potentially dangerous situations, they failed to solve the underlying problem of the huge debts that had been incurred by the less developed countries.

With the downturn in the growth of world trade and the weakening in commodity prices, many debtor nations were likely to face renewed problems and display growing resistance to the inevitable economic sacrifices involved in meeting IMF requirements. During 1985 Peru failed to comply with the IMF's terms and called for the debt-servicing terms of a less developed country to be related to its export performance. Brazil, too, failed to meet its obligations and declared a 140-day moratorium on debt repayments, while Pres. Fidel Castro of Cuba called for the unilateral repudiation of the debts of the less developed countries. Another difficulty was South Africa's inability to meet its debt obligations, and while this was regarded as a problem of a less fundamental nature, it served to underline the potentially destabilizing effects that adverse economic and political developments could have for countries with large debts.

It was feared that one consequence of this situation would be a growing reluctance on the part of commercial banks to adopt a flexible approach to countries with debt problems and to the granting of new credit. This, in turn, could restrain the growth of the comparatively poor and unstable economies, which not only would affect growth in the rest of the world but might force those poorer nations to take extreme steps detrimental to world financial stability. Recognizing these dangers, the October IMF conference held in Seoul devoted considerable attention to the problem of world debt.

In addition to agreeing (as it always did) to the key importance of rapid economic growth in the industrialized world, to the rejection of protectionism, and to continuing efforts to increase the volume of investable savings generated within less developed countries, the conference also discussed a specific proposal put forward by the U.S. Known as the Baker Plan (after U.S. Secretary of the Treasury James Baker), this would provide some $20 billion over three years, largely through commercial banks, to the large debtor countries, including Mexico, Brazil, Argentina, and Yugoslavia. The plan would also provide for additional lending of $9 billion by the World Bank and regional development banks over and above the $18 billion that would, under present policies, have been lent anyway. At the same time, it was suggested that the bulk of the repayments due to the IMF Trust Fund should be re-lent to particularly poor countries with serious external payments difficulties. Both the president and the managing director of the IMF gave strong support to the plan, although commercial bankers, already overexposed in terms of lending to the third world, greeted the proposals with a distinct lack of enthusiasm.

INTERNATIONAL TRADE

During 1985 economic growth in Organization for Economic Cooperation and Development (OECD) member countries was estimated at about 3%, representing a marked deceleration from the rise of 4.5% achieved a year earlier. In the same period, however, the slowdown in the growth of world trade was much more pronounced. At the end of 1985 it was estimated that the volume of world exports for the entire year would register a gain of 4–5%, as against a rise of 8% in 1984. By far the most important reason for this was the unexpectedly large cutback in oil imports. Mainly because of continued energy conservation, aided by several years of heavy investment in energy-saving equipment, Western industrialized countries used significantly less oil in 1985 than in 1984. During the first six months of 1985 oil usage was approximately 3% below that of the corresponding period of the preceding year, and the estimated outcome for the whole of 1985 was a reduction of some 2.5%. At the same time, oil stocks were depleted in anticipation of a further weakening of oil prices.

The effect of these developments was reflected in OPEC (Organization of Petroleum Exporting Countries) exports. In volume terms these were believed to have declined 4%, compared with an increase of 1.6% in 1984. Another reason for the relatively slow growth in world trade was the weakness of commodity prices. This had an adverse effect on foreign exchange earnings and, therefore, on the ability to afford imports of a number of less developed countries. As 1985 drew to a close, only partial statistics were available, but the initial estimates suggested that imports by the less developed countries would grow by only some 4.5%, as against just over 5% in 1984.

The cutback in OPEC exports had a marked adverse effect on imports by OPEC members. These were believed to have fallen by 5% in 1985, as against a cutback of 3% during the preceding year. This decline, which weakened the import capacity of the non-oil less developed countries, had a significant effect on the exports of the industrialized world. Thus, total exports from the OECD area were estimated to have risen by only about 5.5%, compared with a gain of 9.5% in 1984. Most OECD members faced a deceleration in their export growth, with West Germany and the U.K. losing comparatively little momentum but with Japan and the U.S. experiencing less than half their 1984 growth rates. Although the centrally planned economies appeared to have maintained their import growth at about the 1984 level, their exports were heading for an increase of little more than 5%, as compared with 7.5% in 1984. This was the result of the generally lower level of economic activity in the world's principal markets as well as a reduction in exports of Soviet fuel.

During 1985 the terms of trade moved sharply in favor of the industrialized countries. Despite a cutback in OPEC oil production in response to reduced world demand, the average price of crude oil declined by about 2% in the wake of a 4% decline

in 1984. At the same time, non-oil commodity prices did even worse, recording a fall of 9–10%, as compared with a modest gain of 1% in 1984. The weakest area was food. As a result of good harvests in 1984 for most food crops, 1985 opened with weakening prices and fairly large supplies. During the year output (and crop prospects) remained strong, and prices declined rapidly. At the end of the year the average fall in the price of the principal food commodities—grains, sugar, coffee, tea, and cocoa—was about 13%, as against an increase of 5% in 1984.

A substantial decline, perhaps about 8–9%, was also registered in prices of agricultural raw materials such as wool, cotton, and rubber. This compared with a decline of only 2% for those goods in 1984 and was the result of the high level of output in both 1985 and the preceding year. By contrast, the trend of metal prices was comparatively encouraging. Although these exhibited (the customary) widespread fluctuations from period to period and product to product, it seemed that on average they lost no significant ground in 1985, after declining about 6% in 1984.

The figures available at the end of 1985 suggested that the trade deficit of the OECD area could total some $50 billion for the year. This was about $10 billion more than the deficit recorded in 1984 ($41.3 billion) but more than double the shortfall in 1983. Just as the 1984 explosion was the result of a severe deterioration in U.S. foreign trade performance, the unexpected increase in 1985 owed much to U.S. developments. In 1984 a rapidly appreciating dollar made imports relatively cheap and exports expensive for the U.S. Combined with a rapid growth in domestic demand, this resulted in a massive 24% gain in the volume of imports and a relatively modest rise of 7% in exports. This pushed the U.S. trade balance into deficit to the tune of $123 billion, compared with $69 billion in 1983. Although the dollar continued to strengthen during the first quarter of 1985, it weakened markedly against most other currencies during the remainder of the year. This reduced the attraction of foreign

Keijiro Murata (standing, left), Japan's minister of international trade and industry, asks executives of 60 major Japanese companies to increase imports in response to Prime Minister Yasuhiro Nakasone's appeal to the nation to buy more imported goods in order to reduce trade frictions.

AP/WIDE WORLD

products, which, together with weaker demand for oil and a less buoyant growth in the economy, led to a cutback in the rise of imports to a level of about 7–8%.

Nevertheless, although the weaker dollar also made U.S. exports more competitive, it was not possible to gain the full benefit of this in view of the slowdown in world economic growth and the weakening of import demand in the oil-producing nations and, to a lesser extent, in the non-oil less developed countries. As a result the volume of U.S. exports during 1985 was estimated to have risen by only some 3–4% and, combined with the fall in the external value of the dollar, the net effect of those developments was a further, but relatively modest, increase in the U.S. trade deficit. On the basis of the figures for the first three quarters of 1985, the outcome for the year was projected to be a deficit of around $135 billion, representing an increase of some 10% over the 1984 figure.

In sharp contrast to the U.S., Japan experienced an additional rise in its already excessive trade surplus, although the rate of increase slackened as the year went on and was not as pronounced as in 1984. During that year the volume of Japanese exports had risen just over 16% as a result of a weak yen and little growth in domestic demand. During 1985, however, partly in response to growing foreign criticism of Japanese trade and economic policies, the yen appreciated sharply and domestic demand rose somewhat. This had a marked effect on the volume growth of Japanese merchandise sales overseas, with the latest available projections pointing to an increase amounting to only some 8–9%.

Unfortunately, and unexpectedly, there was also a significant slowdown—from 10.8% in 1984 to perhaps 6% in 1985—in the volume growth of imports, with much of the weakness coming from goods supplied by the U.S. and OPEC. The net result was a further rise in the trade surplus to an estimated $50 billion, an increase of approximately 12% over the preceding year. The Tokyo government, therefore, remained under considerable international pressure to take effective steps to reduce this imbalance by restraining the growth of Japanese exports and by enhancing domestic demand in combination with further measures to open up its markets to overseas exporters.

While there was some increase in OECD trade between 1984 and 1985, the current account of the balance of payments deteriorated somewhat. This was the result of a significant increase in the deficit on invisible transactions—shipping, tourism, receipts, and remittances of profits on foreign investments—from $24 billion in 1984 to approximately $33 billion in 1985. The main reason for this was the trend in the U.S., where there were indications of a substantial decline in the traditional invisible surplus as a result of a cutback in the net inflow of investment income.

In Japan the position appeared to be the reverse. Japanese business had been investing large sums abroad in recent years as a means of reducing the country's external surplus and thus lessening protectionist sentiment among its trading partners. As a result profits earned from foreign investments rose rapidly, offsetting an increasing proportion of the traditional deficit in such invisible items as transportation and tourism. The last available forecast suggested that the 1984 invisible deficit of $9.3 billion might have been cut back by about $1 billion in 1985. Most other major members of the OECD performed about as they had in 1984; West Germany and Canada recorded large but broadly unchanged deficits, while the U.K., France, and Italy earned modest surpluses.

For the OECD as a whole, the visible and invisible trade developments gave rise to a current account deficit of about $83 billion. This represented an increase of some 33%, compared with the gain of 160% in 1984. In relative terms, therefore, the 1985 performance represented a significant improvement, although the absolute level of the deficit was more than three times as high as the 1982–83 average. As has already been pointed out, this was entirely due to the U.S. performance; in fact, apart from the U.S., with a deficit of around $120 million, the only major member of the OECD recording a current account deficit during the year was Italy, where the total was estimated at around $4 billion. In contrast, Japan and West Germany were heavily in surplus, and small positive balances were also earned by the U.K., France, Spain, The Netherlands, and Canada.

On the basis of incomplete figures available in late 1985, OPEC countries seemed to have secured an improvement in their external payments position. Although both the price of and the demand for oil were weak in 1985, OPEC countries cut back their imports and managed to enlarge their trade surplus from $55 billion to $60 billion. As in the past, however, this was more than offset by the deficit incurred on invisible transactions, and the current account was heading for a net deficit of about $5 billion. This, however, represented a marked improvement over 1984, during which the deficit was $10 billion; in 1983 it had been $20 billion.

In contrast with the performance of OPEC, the non-oil less developed countries faced a deterioration in their external payments position, reversing the steady improvement they had made between 1980 and 1984. Their overall current deficit was expected to reach $30 million, as against $24 million, partly because of weaker demand for their products and a significant shift in the terms of trade in favor of the industrialized countries. There was little up-to-date information about the external accounts of the centrally planned economies, but the early expectations were that there would not be a significant change in 1985 from the current account surplus of $9.6 billion achieved in 1984.

Special Report: The Case Against Protectionism: A U.S. View

By Senator Charles McC. Mathias, Jr.

The issue of trade protectionism has gathered political force in many countries beset with continuing economic problems. It is proving increasingly difficult to craft sound national and international trade policies at a time of low or uneven global economic growth. The seemingly simple solution of restricting imports to protect certain domestic workers and industries has had considerable appeal to politicians unable or unwilling to act decisively with respect to fundamental economic problems. Yet the prospects for stimulating and perpetuating economic growth in the future will be jeopardized by trade-restricting measures that are currently under consideration in many capitals.

The GATT Regime

Current sentiment favoring trade protectionism flies in the face of the dominant direction of informed opinion in free market economies since World War II. This opinion has advocated, and political leaders have sought, reductions in the barriers to the free flow of goods across international borders. The framework for this effort has been the General Agreement on Tariffs and Trade (GATT).

The GATT was first negotiated in 1947. The sorry experience with trade restrictions during the Great Depression of the 1930s provided the impetus for implementing tariff reductions and establishing orderly trade arrangements. The GATT contains a list of negotiated tariff schedules and principles and rules governing the trade of the signatory countries. These elements have been modified in seven rounds of trade negotiations since the 1940s. The unifying concept governing the GATT system is the most-favored-nation principle holding that contracting parties will conduct their commercial relations with each other on the basis of nondiscrimination.

Annual world merchandise exports reached $2 trillion in the 1980s, aided by a generally receptive global trading environment and a framework of accepted rules. Nonetheless, the 1980s have witnessed a significantly lessened commitment in the U.S. and elsewhere to expanding the free-trade system. In part, this is because the evolution in the GATT has not kept up with the evolution in the global economic environment.

The global economy has changed significantly since the first GATT negotiations took place in the 1940s. Trade in goods has been swamped by short-term financial flows ($2 trillion versus approximately $40 trillion annually). Floating exchange rates have disrupted the exchange markets. The debt crisis of the 1980s has exacerbated the uncertainties in the global economy. Lowered growth in industrialized countries has focused greater attention on persistent unemployment problems.

Moreover, GATT member governments have not fully subscribed to the nontariff barrier agreements or codes established in 1979. Successful tariff negotiations have exposed nontariff barriers to trade. Significant areas of global trade are not covered by GATT. And there are a rising number of bilateral agreements and understandings, such as voluntary restraint agreements, that circumvent GATT rules.

The New Wave of Protectionism

More important, in terms of the U.S. commitment to free-trade principles, has been the recent emergence of three economic factors that have sent the U.S. trade deficit to unprecedented heights and weakened opposition to import restrictions. These factors are the global debt crisis, the appreciation of the U.S. dollar, and faster U.S. economic growth relative to other major economies.

The Latin-American debt crisis has been a disaster for U.S. exporters. In 1981 U.S. exports south of the border totaled $42 billion; two years later this figure had dropped to $25.5 billion. But, if the Latin Americans could not buy, others would not buy because an overvalued U.S. dollar made U.S. products uncompetitive abroad. By March 1985, when the value of the dollar peaked, it had risen 98% in less than five years against a trade-weighted average of ten major currencies. Finally, relatively greater U.S. growth in 1983 and 1984 helped to bid up the value of the dollar and attracted imports.

These factors merged to drive the U.S. trade deficit from a modest $25 billion in 1981 to a projected $150 billion in 1985, with no end in sight. The U.S. current account went from a positive $6.3 billion in 1981 to a negative $101.6 billion in 1984. The trade balances of virtually every U.S. industry have deteriorated since 1980. The free-trade community in the U.S. has retreated in the face of a rising chorus of voices favoring protectionist measures of one sort or another. The benefits to the U.S. economy from imports, such as lowered inflation, have been submerged by the distress of the exporting sectors and of industries competing with imports.

Inevitably, the issue of trade protectionism has become politically charged. It arises at a time of difficult transition for certain U.S. industries and their workers. The understandable political reaction to the pain experienced by U.S. textile and steel workers is to seek to protect them from the pressures of imports. Moreover, there is an understandable tendency to see their problems as resulting from the unfair practices of others. In response to these pressures, numerous trade-restricting bills have been introduced into both houses of Congress. Much of this legislation is based on unilateral reciprocity, discrimination, and threats of retaliation that fly in the face not only of U.S. GATT obligations but of economic good sense as well.

The protectionist analysis of U.S. trade problems is faulty, and therefore the proposed remedy of restricting imports is incorrect and ultimately dangerous. The root of the problem is that Americans do not save enough. There is a gap between what they save as a nation and what they invest. That gap is being filled through foreign borrowing. But this means that foreigners are purchasing dollars, thus keeping the value of the dollar high, and investing these dollars in the U.S. market. In the process U.S. exports stagnate and imports soar.

Much has been made of the so-called "Japan problem." The U.S. trade deficit with Japan continues to worsen, rising from $15.8 billion in 1981 to an annual rate of over $45 billion in 1985. Some in the U.S. point to Japanese barriers to imports. Barriers exist, but no one argues that the increase in the trade deficit between the two countries is due to an increase in Japanese restrictions on imports. Even if all the barriers were removed, a sizable trade deficit would exist, the result of comparative U.S.-Japanese rates of productivity and unit labor costs as well as comparative savings rates. The Japanese, quite simply, produce more, for less money, and save more and consume less than Americans.

Dealing with the Trade Deficit

In order to deal with the trade deficit, the U.S. must deal with its saving-investment problem. It must reduce the federal budget deficit, which is maintaining upward pressure on U.S. interest rates and increasing the need to borrow abroad. Productivity must be increased. Domestic savings must be encouraged. Furthermore, the U.S. must encourage growth in other countries that will strengthen their currencies and raise their demand for imports.

The U.S. must do so because self-interest demands it. A nation must export to grow. Moreover, others look to the U.S. for leadership in this area.

Protectionists want tariffs. They argue that not only would domestic workers and industries be protected from unfair competition but revenue would be raised to put against the budget deficit and so reduce pressure on U.S. interest rates. These benefits must be weighed against the costs of tariffs, which would include:

- Higher prices and, therefore, reduced national output;
- Reduced economic activity for countries exporting to the U.S., including major debtor nations;
- Possible retaliation against U.S. exports;
- Increases in the dollar exchange rate and therefore lower U.S. exports.

These costs argue not for more barriers to trade but for fewer. The needs of workers in vulnerable industries should be met by retraining, not by putting workers in other industries on the unemployment rolls. The U.S. should also seek negotiated reductions in the remaining barriers to trade. This means a new round of GATT negotiations.

The obstacles to another round, however, are formidable. As in the past, the U.S. would have to be the moving force behind a new round of negotiations. However, the U.S. no longer dominates the global economy as it once did. High U.S. unemployment in key industries such as textiles and steel, whose products might be subject to negotiation, complicates the task of consensus building. The administration, in seeking authority from Congress to proceed, would have to indicate both what it wants to obtain in a new round and what it might be prepared to give up.

There are numerous agendas for a new round in circulation. Generally they seek to (1) reverse the trend to protectionism, (2) involve less developed countries in the process, and (3) deal with nontariff barriers. Ideally, a new round would strengthen the existing trading system by dealing more substantively with agriculture, textiles, and steel. It would extend GATT to new areas, including trade in services, high tech, investment, and intellectual property. Beyond that, it would improve the existing safeguard system intended to provide troubled industries with temporary relief from import competition through protection implemented on an evenhanded basis against all foreign suppliers. Further, the process of dispute settlement in the GATT system would be improved. The subsidies, government procurement, and standards codes negotiated during the Tokyo Round of trade negotiations concluded in 1979 need to be fully implemented, enforced, and extended as well.

These efforts should constitute the priorities of wise U.S. trade policy, not erecting dangerous barriers to trade.

IRAN

Pressures arising from the continuing Gulf war between Iran and Iraq permeated all aspects of Iranian life during 1985. Iran remained firmly locked in the conflict, which entered its sixth year in September. Furthermore, the Iranian regime remained internationally isolated. The major powers were without exception aligned against the Iranian struggle to bring about the downfall of Iraqi Pres. Saddam Hussein At Takriti and to seize part or all of Iraq. Iran was all but denied access to the arms, financial credits, and diplomatic support that were channeled to Iraq by the U.S.S.R., France, and the Arab nations. Among the few countries offering support to Iran were Syria and Libya; on June 23 the latter concluded an agreement providing for close political and military cooperation with Iran.

In March the Iranians launched a major new land offensive in the southern marshlands of Iraq. Iranian forward troops succeeded in crossing the Tigris River. However, lacking logistical support and air cover, the attack fell victim to punishing countermoves by the Iraqis. The campaign resulted in heavy losses on the Iranian side, and any possibility that the Iranians might have regained the initiative in the war receded. The Iraqis mounted a number of air raids against Iranian cities, bombing civilian targets in Tehran, Esfahan, Tabriz, Shiraz, and many other settlements. By April the "war of the cities" had developed into a series of exchanges in which the Iranians shelled Basra and Baghdad and bombed Iraqi border areas. With neither side apparently able to sustain the war against city populations, the attacks faded out in mid-April, though there were reports of further intensive air raids by the Iraqis on Tehran in June.

As a counterstrategy to Iraqi control of the air war, Iran adopted a tactic of small-scale attacks along the 900-mi (1,450-km) frontier with a view to undermining Iraqi morale. Attacks on the northern front and, later, in the central sector were augmented by infiltration of Iraqi positions in the marsh areas of the south during late April and May. The Iraqis responded by carrying out a series of intensive air raids on the Khark Island oil terminal beginning on July 15. For the first time, considerable damage was inflicted, and Iraq maintained an intermittent bombardment of the terminal throughout the remainder of the year. The Iraqi raids, though they did not bring Iranian oil exports to a complete halt, succeeded in making the operation extremely difficult. There were reports that Iranian troops were again massing in preparation for an offensive in the southern marshlands in late December.

Representing a marked change, there was open debate in Iran about the issues involved in the war and the need for peace. Nevertheless, Iranian conditions for peace were relaxed scarcely at all. Efforts at mediation came to nothing despite a clear desire on the part of Iraq for an end to the confrontation.

Sayyed Ali Khamenei was returned for a second

AP/WIDE WORLD

Civilians watch rescue workers in Nahavand following a bombing attack by Iraqi warplanes. Air attacks by Iran and Iraq killed at least 100 on March 11.

four-year term as president when he won over 85% of the vote in elections held on August 16. Speculation that the prime minister might be replaced ended when Mir Hossein Moussavi was reappointed to the post in October. He brought a number of new ministers into his Cabinet and promised a more radical program for the coming year. In November it was announced that the Council of Experts had designated Ayatollah Hussein Ali Montazeri to succeed Ayatollah Ruhollah Khomeini as the country's supreme spiritual leader, although there were no signs that Khomeini would step down in the near future.

Economic conditions deteriorated considerably as a result of the demands of the war budget. Foreign exchange receipts fell in response to the softening international market for crude oil and difficulties in exporting oil. The country's ability to pay for its imports declined as reserves of foreign exchange fell below $3 billion.

IRAQ

The Gulf war entered a new phase in mid-1985 when Iraq stepped up its attacks on the Iranian oil terminal at Khark Island. Iraqi raids on a steel complex in Ahvaz and a partially constructed nuclear power plant in Bushehr on March 4 led to an Iranian attack on the city of Basra. Using this breach of an earlier pledge to avoid civilian targets as justification, Pres. Saddam Hussein At Takriti launched the "war of the cities" campaign and ordered attacks on 30 cities. In the same month, after intensive fighting on the ground, Iranian forces briefly held a section of the road from Baghdad to Basra before they were driven back. During five years of hostilities 70,000 Iraqis had been killed, 150,000 wounded, and 50,000 taken prisoner by Iran. Some $35 billion in foreign-currency reserves had been spent on the war, and the government had accumulated more than $40 billion in foreign debt.

In order to fuel the war effort, Iraq sought an increase in its oil-exporting quota from the Organization of Petroleum Exporting Countries in Vienna on October 4. Oil Minister Qasim Ahmad Taqi argued that new development projects had rendered its 1.2 million-bbl-a-day quota unrealistic. The first phase of a new pipeline to link Iraq's southern oil fields with the Saudi Arabian pipeline was commissioned on October 4. On June 2 Taqi announced that the latest estimate of Iraq's oil reserves was 145,000,000,000 bbl, a figure that, if confirmed, would put them second only to those of Saudi Arabia in world terms. On July 17 President Hussein claimed that he expected oil production would soon return to the levels attained before the start of the Gulf war.

The government faced difficulties in repaying in full rescheduled debts to its trading partners. While Iraq owed some $25 billion to the Arab Gulf states, principally Kuwait and Saudi Arabia, other creditors included France, West Germany, the U.K., and Japan. The surge of oil through the Saudi pipeline, estimated at 500,000 bbl a day by late 1985, was expected to help settle these accounts, but not before 1986.

The five-year (1986–90) plan was described by First Deputy Prime Minister Taha Yassin Ramadan as "the beginning of a new era." Development plans concentrated on improving and extending infrastructure and social services. Investment in oil was to remain a high priority, but diversification into the agricultural and light industrial sectors was also to be encouraged.

President Hussein continued to command a large degree of support at home. However, a bomb attack

Iraqi soldiers guard Iranian prisoners of war following an Iranian offensive across the Tigris River in March. Iranian casualties reportedly numbered in the thousands.

PIERRE PERRIN—GAMMA/LIAISON

on the Rafidain Bank headquarters on March 14 indicated the existence of local opposition in Baghdad. In September the leader of the Democratic Party of Kurdistan, Masoud Barzani, claimed that his forces controlled much of the area around Iraq's northern border with Syria.

The government took heart from the support offered by the Gulf Cooperation Council countries and by the Arab summit that took place in Morocco in August. On June 27 an economic, cultural, and scientific agreement was signed with Egypt. On June 26 Iraq suspended diplomatic relations with Libya after the latter joined Iran in a strategic alliance with the aim of resisting any effort by Egypt, Iraq, Jordan, and the Palestine Liberation Organization to seek an accommodation with Israel. An indication of the improvement in Iraq's relations with the U.S. came in September when the two countries initialed a wide-ranging trade agreement. There was also evidence of better relations with nonaligned countries, particularly India and Yugoslavia, and with Soviet-bloc countries, from whom Iraq received military equipment.

IRELAND

The Irish government, midway through its term of office, faced economic difficulties that showed little sign of improvement during 1985. The foreign debt, at 70% of gross national product, reached Ir£2,000 million. Unemployment continued to rise and in mid-1985 stood at 17.7% of the work force. (For table of world currencies, *see* International Exchange and Payments.) With one million people totally or partially dependent on social-welfare payments, and one-half of the population below the age of 25, the burden of taxation continued to be borne by the middle-income groups. There was considerable discontent over the policies being pursued by the government, and demands were made throughout the year for a change in the taxation system, under which the average wage earner paid tax at around 40%. Discontent reached acute levels in October when the public-service unions confronted the government by staging the country's first comprehensive strike in the public sector.

Though inflation, down to 5.2% and falling, was below the average for the European Communities (EC), improved industrial performance did little to help the economic situation. Government strategy, which hoped to combine modest cuts in taxation with curtailment of public expenditure, failed to reach the targets set in the January budget. More significantly, performance was well short of the targets set by the government for the three-year period 1985–87. Agriculture was adversely affected by the worst summer in 30 years as widespread flooding destroyed grain and hay harvests. Despite government and EC measures to aid the worst-affected areas, the general mood of discontent spread to rural areas.

The ruling coalition of Fine Gael and the Labour

Prime Ministers Garret FitzGerald of Ireland (left) and Margaret Thatcher of Great Britain signed a treaty on November 15 giving the Irish government a formal consultative role on issues relating to Northern Ireland.

Party lost some parliamentary support early in the year over its measure designed to liberalize the availability of contraceptives. The new law allowed the sale of nonmedical contraceptives to persons over the age of 18, whereas previously contraceptives had been available only to married people on prescription. The bill passed the Dail (lower house of parliament) in February, despite the fact that some members of both government parties refused to support it, and became law in March.

The introduction of the new legislation was followed by a severe political setback for the coalition in local elections held in June. The main opposition party, Fianna Fail, made substantial gains throughout the country and took control of a number of local authorities, councils, and corporations. The reverse was heralded by the declining fortunes of the administration in the opinion polls, in which Fianna Fail was seen to lead the combined coalition partners by as much as 18 percentage points. Riding on this tide of public popularity, Fianna Fail leader Charles J. Haughey forced the expulsion of his main rival, Desmond O'Malley, from the party.

The trend in political affairs toward divergence and confrontation hindered progress in the talks between the British and Irish governments on a new initiative aimed at solving the problem of Northern Ireland. While Prime Minister Garret FitzGerald, together with Deputy Prime Minister Dick Spring and Foreign Affairs Minister Peter Barry, worked throughout the year to ensure that the Republic of Ireland would have a say in Northern Ireland's future, the opposition leader declared himself to be increasingly opposed to any approach that was not structured toward eventual achievement of a united Ireland. His stance placed considerable strain on

negotiations and led to delays in the planning of a summit meeting between FitzGerald and U.K. Prime Minister Margaret Thatcher. When the summit took place at Hillsborough Castle, County Down, Northern Ireland, on November 15 the two leaders signed an agreement setting up an Anglo-Irish Conference for Northern Ireland that would bring together, as joint chairmen, the U.K. secretary of state for Northern Ireland and the Irish Republic's foreign minister. The principle behind the plan was that the Republic of Ireland representative, accompanied by additional aides, would act as guarantor for the minority nationalist community in Northern Ireland. The concept received widespread support in both the U.K. and the Republic, although it was accompanied by considerable risks and earned growing opposition among the unionists in Northern Ireland as the details emerged. The Hillsborough agreement was approved by both the U.K. and Irish parliaments by year's end.

IRON AND STEEL INDUSTRY

The improvement in world steel activity that began in late 1983 continued and broadened in 1984. Output for 1984 was about 710 million metric tons, which represented a gain of 7% over 1983 and 10% compared with the exceptionally low level in 1982. Moreover, this advance was experienced in all regions, including the large traditional non-Communist producing areas (Japan, the European Coal and Steel Community [ECSC], and the U.S.), whose share of the world total rose to 44% from 42% in 1983.

The welcome recovery in 1984 had to be seen in perspective, however. World output in that year was no more than at the start of the decade, before the severe downturn of 1982, and was only marginally higher than in 1974. Thus an entire decade of growth anticipated in the early 1970s before the first oil crisis had failed to materialize. On the other hand, not only did investment plans made by established producers in the earlier, more buoyant era come to fruition in due course, but many countries also began steel production or greatly expanded it during the decade. The latter development, however, was expected to exacerbate the problem of structural excess capacity.

By late 1984 the recovery in production had lost momentum, and output in 1985 was likely to be little changed or might indeed be lower. That was certainly expected to be the case with the U.S., where production in the first three quarters of 1985 was more than 8% less than during the corresponding period in 1984. This decline, together with the strength of the U.S. dollar, increased the pressure for protection of the U.S. market, which had been a persistent and increasingly critical factor on the world steel scene in recent years.

Recent U.S. steel import protective measures centered on the presidential decision of Sept. 18, 1984, on the import relief case brought by U.S. steel producer and steel labor union interests earlier in the year. The U.S. trade representative was charged by the president with reaching voluntary restraint arrangements with main supplying countries in order to reduce the total import share of the U.S. market from about 24% at that time to 18.5%. In subsequent months eight such arrangements were concluded with major supplying countries, including Japan, to run to October 1989. These arrangements were estimated potentially to involve some three million metric tons of finished steel imports into the U.S. The displacement of such a large tonnage would clearly have appreciable effects on other markets.

Treated somewhat apart from the above arrangement were imports to the U.S. from the ECSC. These had been subject, in the case of most general steel products, to the U.S.-ECSC General Steel Arrangement concluded in October 1982 to run to the end of 1985. In the early part of 1985 a parallel arrangement was reached on tubes and pipes, and in August a similar agreement was concluded on so-called consultation products, a range of steel products referred to in the October 1982 arrangement but not made subject to licensed quotas thereunder.

During autumn 1985 the U.S. and European Communities (EC) authorities were engaged in negotiations for the extension of the October 1982 arrangement to embrace also the "consultation products," stainless steel products currently subject to a range of separate unilateral U.S. import restraints, and semifinished steel. Agreement was reached in early December on a new arrangement to run to September 1989 covering most products, except semifinished steel, on which the U.S. authorities had announced unilateral restrictions.

In the EC the end of 1985 marked a watershed in the development of special measures to combat the long steel crisis. First, the Steel State Aids Code, defined in its existing form in August 1981, expired. Under its terms EC governments were permitted to

Automation is evident in a small steel mill run by Chaparral Steel Co., which could now produce steel with 22% less labor than its Japanese rivals.

CHARLES THATCHER

make public funds available to steel companies, to an extent authorized by the European Commission, in return for capacity reductions to total 26.7 million metric tons of hot rolled products for the ECSC as a whole by the end of 1985 from a 1980 baseline. At a meeting of the ECSC Council of Ministers on Oct. 29, 1985, the terms by which state funds could be made available to steel firms for an additional three years were unanimously agreed upon. These were stringent: essentially for research and development and for environmental protection measures on the same basis as for other industries within the EC, and for certain direct costs involved in further plant closing. At the same meeting agreement was also reached on extension of the quota system for another two years to the end of 1987. This was to be on a modified basis, with certain products taken out of the system. More products were likely to be freed from quotas at the end of 1986.

The statutory minimum price system that had applied to a range of products since the beginning of 1984 was to be suspended from Jan. 1, 1986. The EC was expected to decide before the end of November 1985 on the 1986 regime of voluntary restraint arrangements for imports of steel into the ECSC from the principal supplying countries. The agreed-upon tonnages would almost certainly be increased to some extent. However, any long-term strengthening of the world steel market was rendered uncertain by a continuing excess of capacity.

ISRAEL

Israel embarked on an entirely new political experience in September 1984 when the government of national unity—in which neither the Labor Party on the left wing nor Likud on the right was dominant—took office. To the surprise of many, the government survived throughout 1985. In accordance with the coalition agreement, Prime Minister Shimon Peres and Deputy Prime Minister and Foreign Minister Yitzhak Shamir were to exchange portfolios at the midpoint of the government's term of office in October 1986. The prospect of the moderate, flexible Peres being replaced by the hard-line, unbending Shamir preoccupied politicians at home and both friends and adversaries of Israel abroad. It also brought a sense of urgency to the efforts of Peres to resolve Israel's economic crisis and to search for a peace settlement in the Middle East. In the opinion of Peres, the central issue was the rehabilitation of the economy, which was a necessary prerequisite to restoring Israel's position on the international scene. In his view, once the former was achieved, the latter would take care of itself.

The events of 1985 made sense only when interpreted against the background of the drama being acted out between the two major parties, each of which—while rarely losing sight of the national interest—sought a position of advantage. There were, moreover, domestic complications for the leaders of both the major parties. When Prime Minister

MOSHE MILNER—SYGMA

Ethiopian Jews, brought to Israel in a secret airlift, stand at the Western Wall in Jerusalem in July and demand that Israeli rabbis stop forcing them to undergo conversion rites.

Peres (Labor) had taken office, his own standing in the country had not been particularly high. Furthermore, a strong element within the Labor Party leadership believed that Labor should seek fresh elections before the time came to hand over the office of prime minister to Likud. For his part, Peres insisted that he would honor the agreement to hand over leadership to Shamir after 25 months unless in the meantime Likud decided to withdraw from the government and abandon the agreement.

Shamir was concerned with preserving conditions that would allow the fulfillment of the agreement and the rotation of portfolios. This fact clearly inhibited his opposition to government measures that were unpalatable to the Likud rank and file, especially the more extreme nationalist and religious groups who saw their views better represented by the populist Likud politicians and rivals of Shamir, deputy party leader and Housing and Construction Minister David Levy and Trade and Industry Minister Ariel Sharon. However, their radicalism was also tempered by the ultimate threat available to Peres: to dissolve the agreement and call for new elections.

During the course of 1985, the personal popularity of the prime minister soared, while that of Shamir and other Likud leaders declined. The opinion polls gave Peres an all-time-high rating for a prime minister of 67%. Shamir and his colleagues barely reached 20%. Similarly, in terms of popular-

ity Labor was drawing away from Likud and began to appear the major party most likely to attract the necessary support from the smaller parties to form a coalition government that was not based on national unity. Likud leaders therefore decided not to risk the probable consequences for their party of an election challenge. The government survived an early threat to its unity in December 1984 when Yitzhak Peretz, leader of the Shas Party, resigned from the government in protest against not being offered the religious affairs portfolio; he withdrew his resignation, however, on being offered the interior ministry. A more serious crisis began to develop in mid-October 1985 when Sharon and Levy led Likud's criticism of Peres for speeches, made during a visit to the U.S., in which he suggested that Israel might respond to Jordan's call for an international conference to discuss the Middle East peace process. Likud ministers were completely opposed to the idea of Israel's making any territorial concessions. Later, in particularly vitriolic language, Sharon publicly accused Peres of seeking secret talks with Syria, of conducting secret negotiations with Jordan, and of being prepared to enter into negotiations with the Palestine Liberation Organization (PLO). Peres responded by demanding that Sharon either apologize or resign. On November 15 Peres accepted a letter of apology from Sharon and withdrew the threat of dismissal, thus averting the collapse of the government.

In July, 15 members of the so-called Jewish underground, among them prominent members of the orthodox settlers movement, the Gush Emunim, were found guilty of terrorist acts against Palestinians on the West Bank. The trial had become a focus of intensified controversy following the government's release on May 20 of 1,150 Palestinians held in Israel in exchange for three Israeli soldiers held by a PLO group based in Damascus, Syria. Among the freed Palestinians were many convicted terrorists and murderers. Their release may have eased security problems in Israel's overextended prison system, but it undermined the country's hitherto firm stance against terrorism both at home and abroad. In the view of some, the release of the Palestinians was an outstanding political blunder.

The government's new austerity measures announced on May 28 made a sharp impact on the entire nation; the cost of subsidized food was increased by 25%, fuel by 25%, and gasoline by 45%. By mid-July the government had begun to implement its fairly ruthless economic emergency plan, the principal features of which were a three-month price freeze, an 18.8% depreciation of the shekel, a freeze on the new exchange rate and on salaries, and savage cuts in government budgets and public-sector staffing levels. Banks were ordered to restrict credit and to take other measures to control and encourage growth rather than inflation. A new shekel worth 1,000 old shekels was introduced on September 3. By the end of the year, there was evidence of the first signs of improvement in the economy.

Peres summarized his objectives in his speech to Israeli industrialists and foreign investors who met in Jerusalem on September 10. He told them that, despite the generous aid Israel received from the U.S. (some $3.5 billion overall in 1985) and from

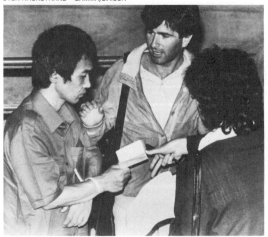

Japanese terrorist Kozo Okomato, who took part in a bloody attack on Tel Aviv's Lod International Airport in 1972, was released on May 20 along with 1,150 Palestinians in exchange for three Israeli soldiers.

SVEN NACKSTRAND—GAMMA/LIAISON

world Jewry, the country had to turn inward "to conquer the ruinous phenomenon of inflation, to alter the structure of our economy, to curtail government expenditure, to do without and to save—in order to reduce our dependence on foreign aid to a minimum."

Foreign Affairs

From the first day of 1985, uncharted and unforeseeable problems emerged and demanded instant attention, rather than long-term plans, from government ministers. The year had hardly dawned when premature publicity endangered the secret airlift of Ethiopian Jews carried out by Israel with some assistance from the U.S.; some 7,000 Ethiopian Jews, members of an ancient community of Jews reputedly dating back to the days of the queen of Sheba, had already been transported from Ethiopia via the Sudan to Israel, and more were to come later.

On January 14 the government announced plans for the total withdrawal of Israeli troops from Lebanon, to commence within five weeks and to be concluded in three phases. Following the commencement of the withdrawal, a small number of Shi'ite militants apparently organized from the Iranian embassy in Damascus began to launch hit-and-run attacks on Israeli troops. While they inflicted almost daily casualties, the effect of their actions was greatly magnified by the massive coverage provided by the Israeli press and television of grieving families at funerals. The theme was taken up worldwide and exploited most effectively in militant Shi'ite propaganda from Damascus. Even serious Western commentators accepted at face value claims by Shi'ite militants that they were "chasing" the Israelis from southern Lebanon. The PLO and the West Bank Palestinians were enjoined to emulate this most effective Shi'ite uprising, which was said to have forced the Israelis to flee. By early May, however, the Shi'ite "uprising" had evaporated. It emerged that barely 20 or 30 of the 200 or more Shi'ite villages in southern Lebanon had given succor to the militants. What had seemed to be a crisis turned out to be little more than a swiftly forgotten incident.

The country heaved a collective sigh of relief when the withdrawal from Lebanon was completed in early June. Few had time to give due consideration to the fate of those Lebanese who had allied themselves to the Israelis, especially the Christian community in the areas now threatened by Druze and Shi'ite militias. Prime Minister Peres announced that the Lebanese would have to look after themselves.

The proposals for peace in the Middle East revealed in February by King Hussein of Jordan and Yasir Arafat, chairman of the PLO, were presented as a dramatic initiative to bring Jordan, the Palestinians, and Israel to the negotiating table for a settlement that would exchange peace for territorial concessions by Israel. As the year unfolded, the

by Israel and claimed by both countries, made only limited progress. Nevertheless, after all the gloom at the start of the year, Israel appeared set to end 1985 on an upbeat note. Southern Lebanon had been quiet for months. The Galilee was no longer threatened, and there was a dialogue of sorts with Jordan and the West Bank Palestinians. However, developments at the end of the year curbed the mood of optimism. Israel claimed that Syria's deployment of surface-to-air missiles along its border with Lebanon posed a threat to Israel's security. Then on December 27 terrorists attacked the Israeli airline check-in desks at the Rome and Vienna airports; 18 people were killed. Israel refused to accept the PLO's claim that it was not involved in the attacks, which were blamed by some sources on a Palestinian group, led by Abu Nidal, opposed to the PLO.

ITALY

Italy's coalition government of Christian Democrats, Socialists, Republicans, Social Democrats, and Liberals, in office since Aug. 4, 1983, faced a severe crisis that forced Socialist Prime Minister Bettino Craxi to offer his own and his government's resignation on Oct. 17, 1985. The first link in a chain of events that precipitated the crisis was the hijacking of the Italian cruise ship *Achille Lauro,* with over 400 people aboard, by four Palestinians claiming to be members of the Palestine Liberation Front (PLF), a splinter group of the Palestine Liberation Organization (PLO). The hijacking took place on October 7 as the ship was sailing in the Mediterranean Sea between Alexandria and Port Said, Egypt. Craxi, who had held several friendly meetings with PLO chairman Yasir Arafat, turned to him to use his good offices. Fifty-two hours later the four hijackers surrendered to the Egyptians, and Rome celebrated Craxi's triumph.

As the four Palestinians were being flown in an Egyptian aircraft to Tunisia as part of the surrender pact, however, their plane was intercepted by U.S. Tomcat fighters operating from an aircraft carrier. U.S. Pres. Ronald Reagan telephoned Craxi for permission to force the Egyptian plane to land at the NATO base at Sigonella, Sicily. With Craxi's consent, the plane landed, bringing the four hijackers physically under Italian jurisdiction. Italy already had legal jurisdiction over them for the crimes they had committed aboard the Italian ship, including the murder of one U.S. passenger. Also aboard the aircraft, as it turned out, were Arafat's negotiator, Abul Abbas, and another aide. The U.S. claimed that Abbas, a PLF leader, had been responsible for planning the original objective of the mission, which apparently had been to attack the Israeli port of Ashdod. Already frustrated by Craxi's refusal to turn over the four hijackers, Reagan again telephoned Craxi and demanded the arrest and extradition of Abbas. Craxi, instead, allowed him and the other Arafat aide to leave the country, arguing that they were under Egypt's protection and that

AP/WIDE WORLD

Ultraconservative Rabbi Meir Kahane (center foreground) and some of his followers dodge stones during a demonstration against Kahane at the Hebrew University in Jerusalem, where he tried to speak on February 28.

initial euphoria was progressively tempered by unresolved ambiguities concerning the position of the PLO and the willingness of Hussein to enter into direct negotiations with Israel.

In the second half of the year, Israel appeared to be benefiting from a change in the international climate. Israel's retaliatory attack (a response to the killing of three Israelis in the Cypriot port city of Larnaca) on the PLO headquarters near Tunis on October 1 did not evoke the storm of condemnation that it would have done earlier. Peres's leadership was apparently bringing dividends for Israel and benefits for Peres and his party at home. The failure of the PLO leadership to embarrass Israel also contributed to a new confidence in the Israeli government. However, a rare opportunity for dissent between Israel and its closest ally, the U.S., was afforded in November when it was revealed that a U.S. citizen, a civilian intelligence analyst with the U.S. Navy, had been accused of supplying Israel with classified military information. The prime minister apologized, and the Israeli government promised a full-scale investigation.

Talks with Egypt about the disputed Taba enclave in the Sinai Peninsula, which was controlled

Premier Bettino Craxi (standing) addresses the Italian Chamber of Deputies before resigning in the wake of the crisis caused by U.S. actions in the Achille Lauro affair.

Abbas also carried an Iraqi diplomatic passport.

Defense Minister Giovanni Spadolini, claiming he had not been consulted on the decision to allow Abbas to depart, led his fellow Republicans out of the Cabinet, forcing Craxi to offer his resignation. However, Pres. Francesco Cossiga, only four months into his term of office, neither refused nor accepted the proffered resignation. By the end of October, following talks with the various party leaders, Craxi was in a position to assure Cossiga that he could continue with the same coalition. On November 6 Craxi won a vote of confidence in the Chamber of Deputies by a secure margin.

Regional and municipal elections took place in most of the nation in May. The results brought a return to the status quo of the previous decade. The Communists, who had shown a fractional lead over the Christian Democrats in the 1984 elections to the European Parliament, received only 30% of the national vote while the Christian Democrats' share increased to 35%. The Christian Democrats also regained control of Rome's city administration after nine years of Communist domination.

Pres. Alessandro Pertini's seven-year term of office ended in July. On June 16 Pertini announced that he would not seek reelection. On June 24 Parliament elected Cossiga, a Christian Democrat who was chairman of the Senate at the time.

Two trials that took place during the year attracted much public attention. The first, which began in February, was of 251 defendants accused of crimes related to the activities of the Camorra, the Neapolitan-based organization of criminal gangs.

The second trial was that of four Turks and three Bulgarians whom Mehmet Ali Agca, the Turk who was serving a life sentence for his 1981 attempt to kill Pope John Paul II, accused of being his accomplices and paymasters. Ably presided over by Judge Severino Santiapichi, the trial nevertheless rapidly turned into farce. Agca, the sole accuser, retracted much that he had said in pretrial sworn statements, and on several occasions he announced that he was Jesus Christ incarnate. As he named additional Turks as his accomplices, evidence of the existence of a Bulgarian connection in the plot diminished.

Terrorism did not cease, but some of the acts perpetrated on Italian soil were "imported" and apparently related in different ways to the Palestinian conflict. Two Jordanians were killed in an ambush in Rome; hand grenades thrown among the tables of an outdoor café injured approximately 40 people; and in September a 16-year-old Arab was apprehended after a bomb exploded in the British Airways ticket office in Rome, injuring 13 people and killing an Italian woman clerk. On December 27 Palestinian gunmen using grenades and machine guns attacked passengers at the Israeli airline check-in desk at Rome's Leonardo da Vinci Airport.

On July 19 an earthen dam gave way in the Fiemme Valley, near Trento in the Dolomite Alps, releasing a flood of mud and water that killed some 250 people. However, the tragedy that left an indelible impression upon Italians because it was transmitted live on television was the death of 31 Italian football fans, who were among those who died in Heysel soccer stadium, Brussels, on May 29. The fans had gone there to support Juventus of Turin in the European Cup final match against the English club Liverpool. The deaths, most of them caused by crushing and suffocation, were blamed primarily on the hooliganism of the English fans and secondarily on the seating arrangements and inadequate policing in the stadium.

Though the government's goal was to bring inflation down from its 1984 level of 10% to 7%, Italy seemed certain to close the year with double-digit inflation again. The 1984 record budget deficit of 93.9 trillion lire, representing 16.7% of the gross domestic product, seemed sure to be overtaken by the 1985 fiscal deficit. (For table of world currencies, *see* International Exchange and Payments.)

During the year imports grew faster (by 5%) than exports (down by 7.3%), reflecting the facts that the percentage of dollar-determined prices was higher for imports than for exports and that Italy had to import most of its prime materials and 80% of its energy supplies.

JAMAICA

Street demonstrations in January 1985, in which seven people died and considerable property damage was caused, ushered in a turbulent year for the Jamaica Labour Party government of Prime Minister Edward Seaga. The demonstrations were in protest against a rise in gasoline (petrol) prices. At the end of June the major trade unions organized a short-lived general strike to demand wage increases, an end to public-sector layoffs, and a change in government policy to moderate the rate of price increases. Seaga withstood the pressure from the unions and stated that there would be no change in his policies. During the year, however, the opposition People's National Party rallied strongly in the opinion polls.

In July the International Monetary Fund agreed to a new U.S. $115 million standby arrangement for the period up to March 31, 1987, and a debt rescheduling agreement with foreign governments and commercial banks followed shortly afterward. The government nevertheless faced a worsening trade deficit, caused mainly by a slump in the bauxite industry. Gross domestic product was expected to decline by at least 4% in 1985, while inflation was running at about 31%. The exchange rate slid from J$5 to almost J$6 to the U.S. dollar between January and October. (For table of world currencies, *see* International Exchange and Payments.)

The burned-out hulk of an automobile marks the aftermath of serious rioting in the Jamaican capital of Kingston that was sparked by an increase in the price of gasoline early in the year.

UPI/BETTMANN NEWSPHOTOS

JAPAN

In October 1984, despite intraparty criticism, Yasuhiro Nakasone had been reelected president of Japan's ruling Liberal-Democratic Party (LDP) and was thus assured of continuing as prime minister. He appointed a new Cabinet, in which portfolios were distributed among recent rivals and LDP faction leaders. On Jan. 25, 1985, in a speech at the resumption of the 102nd session of the Diet (parliament), Nakasone promised to continue, during his second term, policies pressing for nuclear disarmament, free trade, and domestic reforms, including further deregulation of public corporations, reduction of the deficit, and alteration of the system of education. The prime minister would not rule out the possibility that defense spending in fiscal 1985 might exceed the politically established limit of 1% of Japan's gross national product (GNP). On October 16, in the lower house, Nakasone suggested elimination of the ceiling.

Meanwhile, there were behind-the-scenes moves in the LDP toward a "post-Nakasone" era. On February 7 a member of Nakasone's Cabinet, Finance Minister Noboru Takeshita, announced the organization of a study group (the Soseikai), in effect a faction within a faction. It brought together 40 members of the Diet, one-third of the powerful 123-man Tanaka faction. Former prime minister Kakuei Tanaka, found guilty in the Lockheed aircraft procurement case, was not technically an LDP member while his case was on appeal, but he still managed the largest party faction. He denounced Takeshita's move, as did LDP Vice-Pres. Susumu Nikaido, nominal head of the Tanaka faction and a possible successor to Nakasone.

LDP Secretary-General Shin Kanemaru openly stated that the inauguration of the study group signaled Takeshita's intention to be a contender for the presidency of the LDP in the election scheduled for November 1986. The faction led by former prime minister Zenko Suzuki reaffirmed its ties with the Tanaka group. Suzuki backed a senior faction member and former chief Cabinet secretary, Kiichi Miyazawa, for future leadership. Foreign Minister Shintaro Abe was also considered a "new leader," along with Takeshita and Miyazawa.

On February 27 Tanaka suffered what at the time was called a "mild stroke," but on March 4 doctors reported that his condition was worse than announced. Masayuki Fujio, a leader of the faction attached to former prime minister Takeo Fukuda, stated openly in April that Tanaka had a slim chance for political recovery. On June 6 Tanaka was moved to a villa in Karuizawa, and his Tokyo political office was closed. At first these developments seemed to presage additional intraparty friction, since Prime Minister Nakasone had originally been raised to power by the Tanaka faction.

Indeed, LDP leaders were revealing sharp policy differences. Miyazawa, for example, called for government measures to stimulate domestic demand.

So did State Minister Toshio Komoto, who argued that Japan had to alter its economic structure from one that relied heavily on imports. Ippei Kaneko, director general of the Economic Planning Agency (EPA), urged that business stimulation be incorporated in the fiscal 1986 budget. Chief Cabinet Secretary Takao Fujinami, however, stated that the government had no intention of taking drastic steps to stimulate demand. Takeshita stated that the Finance Ministry was opposed to issuing additional deficit-financing bonds. Kanemaru urged that the introduction of indirect taxation to restore fiscal balance not be ruled out. Meanwhile, Takeshita's new group and non-Soseikai members led by Nikaido groped for a compromise that would guarantee unity in the Tanaka faction. In April a Kyodo opinion survey reported that the prime minister enjoyed the highest level of support (at 58.7%) in his 28 months in office. Despite his popularity, Nakasone faced opposition within the party to any plan to amend LDP rules so that he could run for a third term.

The Nakasone administration also faced stiff opposition in the Diet. In late January and again in late February, the Japan Socialist Party (JSP) brought parliamentary debate to a halt in protest against Nakasone's apparent intention to exceed the 1%-of-GNP ceiling on defense spending. On March 6 opposition parties accepted a compromise worked out by Kanemaru, who promised that the LDP would "earnestly" consider tax reduction and would also try to hold down defense costs.

On April 5, four days after the beginning of the new fiscal year, an austere budget bill received the approval of the Diet. General account expenditures totaled 52,499,600,000,000 yen, an increase of 3.7% over the previous year. (For table of world currencies, *see* International Exchange and Payments.)

Debt service expense, which topped 10 trillion yen for the first time, and defense expenditure, which rose 5.1%, accounted for the increase. Otherwise, the LDP draft budget placed emphasis on research toward the construction of new bullet-train lines and technology fitted to the 21st century. According to the EPA, Japan's real GNP for calendar 1984 totaled 223,056,600,000,000 yen ($857.9 billion) at 1975 prices, an increase of 5.8% (the sharpest annual rise since 1973). Exports expanded 16.2% and accounted for much of the gain. Imports rose only 11.2%.

On June 25 the 102nd Diet closed its 207-day session, carrying over such controversial legislation as an antiespionage bill, revision of the election law, and a measure for reforming the public pension law. As of early July party strength in the (lower) House of Representatives was: LDP (including New Liberal Party allies) 262; JSP 112; Clean Government Party (Komeito) 59; Democratic Socialist Party (DSP) 38; Japan Communist Party (JCP) 27; independents 8; vacancies 5 (total 511). In the (upper) House of Councillors it was: LDP 139; JSP 42; Komeito 27; DSP 13; JCP 14; independents 13; vacancies 4 (total 252).

On May 31 the LDP had submitted to the Diet its "6–6 plan" to rectify disproportionate representation in the lower house. The bill would add one seat to each of the six most densely populated districts and decrease one in each of the six most sparsely populated areas. Opposition parties rejected the plan. In any case, on July 17 the Supreme Court ruled that the last general election was unconstitutional because of disproportionate distribution of votes. The court did not, however, set aside the results of the 1983 poll. The LDP "6–6" bill was resubmitted to an extraordinary session of the Diet that opened October 14.

Thousands of paper lanterns are set adrift on the Motoyasu River at Hiroshima's Peace Memorial Park on August 6 to commemorate those who died when an atomic bomb was dropped on the city that day in 1945.

REUTERS/BETTMANN NEWSPHOTOS

The Nakasone administration was more successful with other reforms. On April 1, under a law passed in 1984, Nippon Telegraph & Telephone Public Corporation (Denden Kosha) was deregulated and became a private joint-stock firm, NTT Corp. (Shindenden), with 318,000 employees and capital of 780 billion yen (one-third of its stock was held by the government). Similarly, on April 1 the Japan Tobacco & Salt Public Corporation was changed into a private concern. On June 25 Prime Minister Nakasone replaced Iwao Nisugi as president of Japanese National Railways (JNR) with Takaya Sugiura, former vice-minister of transportation. Nisugi had opposed a plan to deregulate the deficit-ridden JNR. On July 26 a government committee recommended that the JNR be split into 24 regional, private companies. Sabotage to rail communications and signal systems that disrupted Tokyo commuter traffic during the morning rush hour on November 29 was thought to have been perpetrated by a far left group to protest the privatization scheme. The government also had plans to privatize Japan Air Lines (JAL).

In June Michio Okamoto, chairman of the Ad Hoc Advisory Council on Education Reform, presented his first set of recommendations. His report praised the present system of education for its egalitarian nature but called for deemphasis on examinations and reform of the system's uniformity and parochial outlook. Ichiro Tanaka, president of the Japan Teachers Union (Nikkyoso), attacked proposals made by the council, which, he said, was determined to privatize and commercialize education.

On August 12 a JAL domestic flight to Osaka crashed in rugged mountains 70 mi (110 km) northwest of Tokyo. All but 4 of the 524 persons aboard perished. It was the worst single-aircraft accident in history.

Foreign Affairs

In 1985 Japan used a world's fair to advertise its own progress and to forecast a worldwide high-tech transition to the 21st century. Officially known as the International Exposition-Tsukuba, Expo '85 opened March 17 for a six-month run in the science city of Tsukuba, about 30 mi (50 km) northeast of Tokyo, already the site of 46 Japanese research institutes. Expo '85 included exhibits from 49 nations, 37 international organizations, and 28 private corporations.

Meanwhile, back in the 20th century, in 1984 Japan produced a record annual trade surplus of $44,350,000,000 (current account surplus of $35,020,000,000). Japan's reserves in gold, currencies, and International Monetary Fund Special Drawing Rights stood at $27,330,000,000 at the end of May 1985. This position exacerbated trade friction with the U.S., the Western industrial democracies, and the members of the Association of Southeast Asian Nations (ASEAN). However, because Japan had initiated a market-opening package in April in

Prime Minister Yasuhiro Nakasone shops for imported goods in a Tokyo department store in April. He had appealed to his fellow citizens to buy more imports.

an effort to increase imports, the leaders attending the May 2–4 Bonn summit of major industrialized nations held back criticism of Nakasone.

Nevertheless, relations with the U.S. were dominated by trade considerations. In 1984 exports to the U.S. (about one-third of Japan's total) soared 40% to a record high of $60 billion. At their meeting in Los Angeles on Jan. 2, 1985, U.S. Pres. Ronald Reagan pressed Nakasone for steps that would increase Japan's imports. Nakasone agreed to take such measures in several categories: telecommunications, computers, forestry products, pharmaceuticals, and medical equipment. When Vice-Foreign Minister Nobuo Matsunaga was appointed the new ambassador to the U.S. on January 29, he stated that his biggest task was to head off protectionist sentiment in the U.S. Congress.

On March 2 the minister of international trade and industry, Keijiro Murata, called on Japanese automakers to exercise moderation in exports to the U.S., even after "voluntary restraints" expired. The government announced on March 28 that auto exports would be limited to 2,330,000 units (a 24% rise over the 1984 quota). Also in March, the prime minister asked Murata and State Minister Komoto to coordinate all agency negotiations with the U.S. on trade. On April 9 Nakasone unveiled his "substantial" package of measures. Late in June the government announced another package featuring a uniform 20% tariff reduction on 1,790 items. On July 29 the administration adopted measures to ease standards and certification and other procedures.

When the two leaders met in January, President Reagan asked Nakasone for an "understanding" of the U.S. Strategic Defense Initiative (SDI). Back in Japan, the prime minister was much more cautious in comments on the "Star Wars" proposal, indicating that he would abide by Japan's constitution and remember the Diet's 1969 resolution against military use of space. As to more conventional weapons, in April and in September some 26 U.S. F-16 fighter-bombers were deployed at Misawa in Aomori Prefecture. A second squadron was scheduled to arrive in 1987 to enhance—according to the Japan Defense Agency (JDA)—the "American-Japanese deterrent" against a potential Soviet threat from the north.

Relations with the Soviet Union remained tentative. On February 7 the Japanese observed "Northern Territories Day," a government-sponsored campaign designed to publicize Japan's claim to four islands northeast of Hokkaido still occupied by the U.S.S.R. 40 years after the end of World War II. Prime Minister Nakasone told an audience that Japan "is fully resolved to regain Habomai, Shikotan, Kunashiri, and Etorofu by peaceful means." When Nakasone met the new Soviet leader in Moscow on March 14, however, Mikhail Gorbachev refused to discuss the territorial issue.

On March 11 the new Soviet ambassador to Tokyo, Petr Abrasimov, proposed to Foreign Minister Abe that they address four issues: (1) promotion of bilateral trade; (2) cultural exchange (among major nations only Japan and the U.S. had no treaty on this subject with the U.S.S.R.); (3) a tax treaty to avoid double levies; and (4) a proposal to lift the Soviet embassy personnel ceiling. On June 6, more than five years after the Soviet invasion of Afghanistan prompted Japan to cut off all talks, the Foreign Ministry handed Abrasimov a revised draft for a comprehensive cultural exchange treaty.

Trade between Japan and China during 1984 set a record high, with Japanese exports totaling $7.2 billion and imports, $5.9 billion. On March 27 LDP Vice-President Nikaido began a five-day visit to China, his sixth trip since 1972 when he accompanied Prime Minister Tanaka to start negotiations toward normalization of relations.

Since 1965 Japan had had normal relations with South Korea, despite various strains in the relationship. On February 7 South Korean opposition leader Kim Dae Jung made an overnight stopover in Tokyo on his way home. He was reported as saying, "I am overwhelmed to be setting foot on Japanese soil again, almost 12 years after I was kidnapped and taken away to Korea from Japan." The Japanese press and public watched developments carefully as Kim was placed under house arrest immediately upon his arrival in Seoul. As of January 1 the government lifted the sanctions imposed against North Korea to protest the 1983 terrorist bombing that killed 17 South Korean officials in Rangoon, Burma. Tokyo had not, however, established official relations with Pyongyang.

A Pacific Basin Cooperation Plan was accelerated by Nakasone's eight-day trip to Oceania beginning January 13. His tour included Australia, New Zealand, Papua New Guinea, and Fiji. Prime Minister Rajiv Gandhi of India arrived in Japan for a four-day visit in late November.

AP/WIDE WORLD

King Hussein (right) of Jordan greets Egyptian Pres. Hosni Mubarak on the latter's arrival in Amman to discuss efforts for a Middle East peace.

JORDAN

During 1985 King Hussein of Jordan was at the center of efforts to secure a lasting peace in the Middle East. In partnership with Palestine Liberation Organization (PLO) chairman Yasir Arafat, he proposed that Israel relinquish "in exchange for peace" the territories that it had occupied since 1967. The two leaders also declared that the future of the Israeli-occupied territories lay in the setting up of an autonomous Palestinian entity in confederation with Jordan. The agreement between Hussein and Arafat, announced in February, had the aim of bringing the U.S. into the peace process as a first step toward securing an international conference, at which direct Arab-Israeli talks could take place.

King Hussein journeyed to the U.S. at the end of September to promote his initiative in an address to the UN and talks with U.S. Pres. Ronald Reagan. Hopes were raised when, following her visits to Jordan and Egypt in mid-September, U.K. Prime Minister Margaret Thatcher invited to London a joint Palestinian-Jordanian team that was to include two members of the PLO executive. However, when the talks were called off at the last minute—amid a welter of recriminations from both British and PLO representatives—the initiative was dangerously undermined. An Israeli peace proposal, presented in October at the UN, was regarded by Hussein as "positive" in spirit but brought no forward movement in negotiations between the two countries.

Thatcher's visit to Amman culminated in the signing of a $350 million arms deal in which the U.K. agreed to supply military vehicles, radio equipment, tank ammunition, patrol boats, and battlefield command systems. The U.S. administration was eager to cement relations with Jordan by supplying military interceptor aircraft and other air defense equipment, but the U.S. Congress voted to refuse any arms sales to Jordan before March 1, 1986, unless in the interim Jordan and Israel were to begin "meaningful" peace negotiations. In January the Jordanians announced that the U.S.S.R. had agreed to supply ground and air defense systems. The deal followed the U.S. refusal in 1984 to supply Jordan with Stinger antiaircraft missiles.

On April 5 Zaid ar-Rifai, newly appointed prime minister, swore in a new Cabinet in which only five ministers were retained from the previous government. Rifai placed priority on improving relations with Syria and stimulating the private sector of the economy. On September 16–17, following mediation by Saudi Arabia, talks took place in Jidda between Rifai and his Syrian counterpart, Abdul Rauf al-Kasm. The growing rapprochement between the two countries was underlined by the meeting between King Hussein and Syrian Pres. Hafez al-Assad in Damascus on December 30, the first time the two leaders had met since 1979.

The 1985 budget called for a 5% increase in public spending and set total expenditure at 811.2 million dinars ($2.2 billion). Foreign finance was vital to the success of the program. In 1984 Arab aid totaled $606 million, showing a decline for the fourth consecutive year, but remittances from Jordanians working abroad increased because of the strong dollar. Economic growth of nearly 2% in 1984 was the result of higher industrial and mining output and growth in the financial sector.

KAMPUCHEA

Events in Kampuchea during 1985 were again dominated by the struggle for control of the country's political destiny. Kampuchea's Vietnamese occupiers launched unprecedentedly fierce and successful attacks against Democratic Kampuchea (DK) resistance bases on the border with Thailand. The tripartite resistance coalition—made up of the (Communist) Khmer Rouge, the (non-Communist) Khmer People's National Liberation Front (KPNLF), and the Armée Nationale Sihanoukist

(ANS)—was forced to rethink its military strategy. Hanoi's forces began their annual dry-season assault on the resistance earlier than usual. Their successes of the last two months of 1984, when they gained control of four important KPNLF camps, continued in 1985. In January nearly 4,000 Vietnamese troops overran Ampil camp, the KPNLF's political, military, and social nerve center. The following month the Vietnamese won control of the Khmer Rouge mountain redoubt of Phnom Malai, and in March the frontier stronghold of the ANS at Tatum fell.

The conflict sent some 250,000 Khmer civilians fleeing across the border to Thailand, greatly exacerbating that country's refugee problem. In addition, Vietnam's military strikes often penetrated into Thai territory, resulting in clashes with the Thai Army. The offensive also brought forth threats of military retaliation from China, chief backer of the Khmer Rouge. Analysts surmised that China's apparent restraint was motivated by a desire to encourage a thaw in relations with the U.S.S.R., Vietnam's principal ally. The Association of Southeast Asian Nations (ASEAN), main supporter of the KPNLF and the ANS, reacted with concern to the collapse of the guerrilla bases but did not waver in its pledge to continue backing the resistance.

The DK abandoned its attempts to defend stationary camps in favor of guerrilla tactics in the Kampuchean interior. The switch had little effect on the Khmer Rouge, who were used to the rigors of jungle operations, but experts predicted that the adjustment would be more difficult for their non-Communist partners. Faced with the prospect of losing credibility, DK forces launched numerous pinprick attacks on the Vietnamese and their installations. Resistance leaders, meanwhile, traveled to sympathetic countries in search of assistance.

China was quick to deliver fresh supplies of arms not only to the Khmer Rouge but to the other two factions as well. After intensive lobbying by former prime minister Son Sann, the KPNLF leader, and Prince Norodom Sihanouk, president of the DK government-in-exile, the U.S. Congress changed its policy and authorized $5 million in assistance.

Some 250,000 refugees fled across the border from Kampuchea to Thailand in January as Vietnamese troops overran camps of the chief anti-Vietnam resistance organizations in Kampuchea.

ROLAND NEVEU—GAMMA/ LIAISON

In August a meeting of Indochinese foreign ministers pledged that Vietnamese troops would leave Kampuchea by 1990. It was the first time that Hanoi had publicly announced a specific date for withdrawal. It was believed the process might begin even sooner if the Khmer Rouge and its notorious leader, Pol Pot, were "eliminated." Barely two weeks later, Khmer Rouge radio announced that Pol Pot had retired as military chief to assume an "advisory" position. Though the statement was received with skepticism in Hanoi, ASEAN officials welcomed it.

KENYA

The setbacks caused by three years of drought in Kenya were compounded in January 1985 when about 90,000 ac (36,500 ha) of land were devastated by army worms. By April, however, following plentiful and widely dispersed rainfall, the situation had improved greatly. In 1985 the country as a whole was self-sufficient in food production, with food supplies from more fertile districts being diverted to areas badly hit by prolonged famine. In order to reimburse farmers affected by the drought, the prices of milk, tea, sugar, rice, and beef were raised in February. Later in the year, higher production costs led to price increases of 16% for bread and more than 20% for maize (corn) meal.

Prices offered on the world market for the main export crops, tea and coffee, were low. However, a loan of more than $40 million from a consortium of British banks allowed the government to finance existing coffee stocks until a market could be found for them. As a result, in spite of the reduction in the 1984–85 coffee crop, Kenya met the export quota permitted by the International Coffee Organization in full. The government's close adherence to the stabilization program prepared by the International Monetary Fund maintained economic growth and brought a reduction in the trade deficit, along with a proportionate fall in the inflation rate.

The reopening of the rail link between Taveta, Kenya, and Kahe, Tanzania, in February provided evidence of the improving relations between the two countries. Initially, only freight trains operated across the border. However, both passengers and freight were carried on the weekly steamer service across Lake Victoria connecting Kisumu, Kenya, and Mwanza, Tanzania, which was restored at the same time. The following month, under pressure from the European Communities, ministers met with their counterparts from Tanzania and Uganda and agreed to the revival of a number of joint projects. Initially, they planned to work out means of cooperation in transport and communications, tourism, and scientific research. Then, in October, the three heads of government met to consider the wider implications of cooperation, though it was clear that there was no intention of reviving the East African Community, which had linked the three countries before it broke up in 1977.

June elections within the ruling Kenya African National Union introduced a number of new members into the party hierarchy. In August there was a reshuffle of the Cabinet with a view to increasing efficiency in economic planning. Of particular importance was the appointment of Robert Ouko as minister of planning and national development. Ouko had considerable experience as foreign minister and as minister of labor and was well known to a number of international financiers.

In February students at the University of Nairobi once again came into conflict with the government after three of their leaders were expelled without explanation and five others were deprived of their scholarships. In the course of the demonstrations that followed, a student was killed when riot police tried to disperse protesters. Some 2,500 students were ordered to leave the university and report to their local chiefs.

The conference ending the UN Decade for Women was held in Nairobi in July.

KOREA

During 1985 there were unprecedented developments in the relationship between the two governments of Korea. In September 1984 North Korea had offered relief aid to its rival regime after floods devastated many areas in South Korea. The offer was, surprisingly, accepted. Discussions on economic cooperation begun by the two sides in 1984 continued into 1985. On the agenda were such topics as trading complementary items, reopening railway links severed decades ago, opening ports, pursuing joint ventures in mining, and setting up standing consultative committees. However, North Korea continued to protest fiercely against the annual military exercises conducted jointly by South Korean and U.S. forces.

A significant breakthrough occurred in May when North and South Korea agreed to resume bilateral Red Cross talks. The two-day sessions, characterized by a rare lack of rancor, focused on the prospect of exchange visits among some ten million Koreans who were separated from relatives by the division of their country. Follow-up negotiations in midyear eventually produced results. In September 50 ordinary citizens from each side, accompanied by performing artists, journalists, and officials, crossed the demilitarized zone for reunions with their kinfolk. The occasion, lasting four days and three nights, marked the first time such an exchange had taken place since the nation was divided in 1945.

North and South Korea also opened dialogues on parliamentary affairs. In addition, both governments agreed to discuss a possible role for North Korea in the 1988 Olympic Games, to be held in Seoul, South Korea. The Japanese press carried a surprising report that Ho Dam, a member of the North Korean Politburo, had visited Seoul in September for secret talks with Pres. Chun Doo Hwan. Both sides, however, denied the story.

Republic of Korea (South Korea)

In South Korea the year began with two highly significant political events: the return from exile of leading dissident Kim Dae Jung and the elections for a new National Assembly. On February 8, under the glare of extensive media publicity, Kim arrived in Seoul after two years of self-exile in the U.S. "I am coming home to join my people's struggle for democracy," he declared. With 17 years left of a 20-year jail sentence on sedition charges, Kim was immediately escorted to his home and placed under house arrest. The standing ban against his participation in political activities meant that he could not become directly involved in the parliamentary elections.

On February 12 South Koreans went to the polls to elect the 276-seat unicameral legislature, which constitutionally shared power equally with the executive branch of government. President Chun's Democratic Justice Party (DJP), as expected, topped the lists by taking 35% of the popular vote. Much to the government's consternation, however, a newly formed opposition party performed unexpectedly well. Backing both Kim Dae Jung and another outspoken opposition leader, Kim Young Sam, the uncompromisingly antigovernment New Korea Democratic Party (NKDP) gained 29% of the vote. The return of Kim Dae Jung had apparently provided a significant morale boost to the opposition.

Clearly taken aback by the election results, President Chun reshuffled both his Cabinet and the top leadership of the DJP. The new prime minister was Lho Shin Yong, former head of national security, while Rho Tae Woo, head of the National Olympic Committee and a close friend of the president, took over as DJP chairman. Both Lho and Rho were considered political moderates.

A new challenge to Chun's authority arose in April when the NKDP merged with the smaller Democratic Korea Party, a moderate opposition party. Together they commanded the one-third majority needed to call an extraordinary session or block constitutional changes in the National Assembly. Chun's response was to make conciliatory overtures. He also lifted the political ban from 14 opposition leaders, including both Kim Dae Jung and Kim Young Sam.

Another political storm blew up in August when Chun tried to introduce a law under which students found guilty of having engaged in "violent" demonstrations would be sent to detention centers for ideological "reorientation." However, opposition to the bill was so broad and so heated that the president shelved it, at least temporarily.

Although South Korea had no diplomatic ties with China, both had clearly indicated a desire in recent years for improved relations. Two incidents during the year tested South Korea's attitude toward the matter. In March a Chinese torpedo boat drifted into Korean waters following a mutiny during which a number of crew members died. Three Chinese warships that entered Korean waters in search of the vessel were "strongly invited" by Seoul to leave. China quickly obliged and even apologized. In return, South Korea sent back the boat and the survivors, among them an unknown number believed to have requested passage to Taiwan. The latter, a friend of South Korea, expressed its "profound discontent." When a comparable incident occurred in August, however, the Koreans appeased Taiwan. The defecting pilot of a Chinese air force bomber was allowed to go to Taiwan, though the damaged plane and a second crewman were returned to China.

A weakening of the exporting and industrial prowess that in recent years had powered South Korea's growth took place during the year. Though the government initially projected a 7.5% expansion in gross national product (GNP) for the year,

South Korean chief delegate to the North-South Korean Red Cross talks, Song Young Dae (right), and his North Korean counterpart Park Yong Su greet each other as they start a meeting on July 19 at the truce village of Panmunjom.

AP/WIDE WORLD

the estimate was revised to 6.5% and then to 5–6% as overseas markets remained depressed and protectionist sentiment continued to gain ground in the developed countries. Particularly hard hit were the construction and shipbuilding industries. Concern was also mounting over the country's huge external debt of $45 billion, and targets for trimming the current account deficit were not being met. The government was obliged to moderate its tight monetary policies in an effort to stimulate the domestic economy.

Democratic People's Republic of Korea (North Korea)

The political scene in Pyongyang continued to be dominated by speculation about when 73-year-old Pres. Kim Il Sung would pass power on to his son, Kim Chong Il. While the timing remained uncertain, the course itself was further confirmed during massive celebrations surrounding the president's birthday on April 15. Eulogies of the "Great Leader" (the father) invariably referred to the "Dear Leader" (the son) as well. The younger Kim, already supreme commander of the armed forces, had reportedly taken over the day-to-day management of the Workers' (Communist) Party, the government, and the military establishment. Though some resistance to his accession apparently remained among veteran generals, these opponents were expected to be retired or otherwise swept aside before long.

North Korea had long practiced a delicate balancing act in keeping roughly equidistant relations with its giant neighbors, China and the U.S.S.R. However, in 1985 there was evidence of a distinct tilt toward the Soviets. The first hint that something was afoot came in May when China disclosed that Chinese Communist Party General Secretary Hu Yaobang (Hu Yao-pang) had made a sudden, secret trip to meet Kim Il Sung in North Korea. The next day a squadron of Soviet MiG-23 fighter aircraft landed outside Pyongyang; later it was reliably reported that the Soviets had left behind ten of the aircraft, probably as a gift to the Kim leadership. Shortly afterward, in an unprecedented gesture of friendship, both Kims appeared separately at special functions at the Soviet embassy in Pyongyang. In September the Soviets were allowed to conduct at least one reconnaissance flight against China over North Korean air space.

The economy continued to perform indifferently. The second seven-year (1978–84) plan had aimed to achieve a 9.6% annual growth in GNP, but most independent experts estimated the attained figure to be 4–5%. The delay in announcing a third plan prompted some analysts to suggest that unforeseen problems had arisen. North Korea, which spent 20–25% of its GNP on the armed forces, had been obliged to seek foreign investment during the previous two years. However, President Kim's personal approaches to Japan and his government's traditional archenemy, the U.S., met with cool responses.

KUWAIT

An attempt on the life of Emir Sheikh Jabir al-Ahmad al-Jabir Al Sabah of Kuwait narrowly failed when a suicide bomber drove a vehicle into a motorcade in which the emir was traveling on May 25, 1985. Two bodyguards, a passerby, and the suicide driver, who was a member of the underground Iraqi radical group al-Dawa, were killed, and 12 others were injured. The attack was believed to be linked to demands by the terrorist group Islamic Jihad ("Islamic Holy War") for the release of 17 Shi'ite Muslims convicted of involvement in bomb attacks on Kuwait City in 1983. On July 11 two bomb explosions in seaside cafés in the capital killed 9 people and injured more than 80. Authorities believed that they were the work of al-Dawa, although a little-known group based in Beirut claimed responsibility. On July 17 a bill calling for the death penalty for terrorist acts was overwhelmingly passed in the National Assembly. By early September over 6,000 people had been deported.

Elections to the National Assembly, in which only Kuwaiti males could vote, took place on February 20. Among the 50 directly elected members of parliament, the veteran nationalist Ahmad al-Khatib and 11 of his supporters were returned to office. Although conservatives retained their majority, the opposition made unexpected gains. Crown Prince Sheikh Saad al-Abdullah as-Salim Al Sabah formed a new government in which he remained prime minister, but a number of his ministers came under attack, including Oil and Industry Minister Sheikh Ali al-Khalifah Al Sabah.

In 1984 Kuwait's petroleum production totaled 1,160,000 bbl a day, slightly more than the quota set by the Organization of Petroleum Exporting Countries. Despite cutbacks attributable to lower income from oil exports, Kuwait remained the world's leading donor to the third world, giving 3.8% of its gross national product in aid during 1984.

Four persons were killed in an assassination attempt on Emir Sheikh Jabir. The emir escaped with minor cuts and 11 others were injured in the attack.

KUNA—GAMMA/LIAISON

Members of the United Auto Workers union walk a picket line at an entrance to Chrysler Corp. headquarters in Highland Park, Michigan, on October 16. Some 80,000 union members in the U.S. and Canada struck the automaker in an effort to win back concessions made when the company was trying to avert bankruptcy.

AP/WIDE WORLD

LABOR AND EMPLOYMENT

In 1985 few of the industrialized market economies were without massive, or at least high, unemployment. While modest economic growth was achieved generally, in most of those countries somewhat austere economic policies continued to be judged necessary. The feeling grew, in Europe particularly, that lack of competitiveness owed much to rigidities in both industrial structure and the labor market. Comparison between economic and employment performance in the U.S. and Japan on the one hand and in Europe on the other reinforced the feeling that in Europe payroll taxes and constraints relating to employment, working conditions, and working practices had made many industries uncompetitive. Hence, interest grew in ways to increase labor market flexibility without sacrificing social benefits.

United States

The 30th anniversary of the merger of the American Federation of Labor (AFL) and the Congress of Industrial Organizations (CIO) found the united AFL-CIO short of the goals set when the old AFL's president, George Meany, and the CIO's president, Walter Reuther, jointly wielded a merger gavel in a cavernous armory in New York.

The coming together of the two large federations—the AFL dating back to 1886 and the CIO to 1935—resulted largely from a growing concern over the future of American labor. Unions were struggling, and often competing, to organize millions of unorganized workers. In a premerger year, $4.5 million was spent to add a scant 8,000 to union rolls. Standing in front of a banner proclaiming "All Trades—All Crafts—All Creeds—Together," Meany and Reuther put aside old animosities to predict that the future would see fewer unions representing millions more workers.

The number of unions has declined through mergers, but slowly, from about 125 to 96. And while membership figures showed dramatic gains at first, from 15 million at merger time, the total has declined steadily during the last decade, to 13.7 million in 1985. Along with membership losses, the AFL-CIO suffered losses of public influence, bargaining strength, and political and legislative power.

Ten years earlier an AFL-CIO convention had recognized the problems arising from shrinking membership rolls. It called for more effective and innovative programs to spur union growth, particularly in the crafts and among blue-collar industrial workers. The calls in 1975 and subsequent biennial conventions projected nothing new. The shrinkage continued.

Since 1980, membership in the AFL-CIO and outside unions had dropped 14% to 17.3 million, or 18.8% of the U.S. work force in 1984. While leaders gave assurances that organized labor was alive and effective, Thomas R. Donahue, AFL-CIO secretary-treasurer, warned grimly, "We have to grow."

In February 1985, AFL-CIO top policymakers guided by Lane Kirkland, president, and Donahue received a two-year study on the changing situation of workers and their unions. This study was an unusually candid look at the labor movement by the AFL-CIO. It proposed "really significant changes" in the structure and policies of American labor.

Some union leaders objected to study proposals as an infringement of the rights of autonomous labor organizations. Others were skeptical about the effectiveness of planned changes. However, delegates to the AFL-CIO's convention in Anaheim, Calif., in October 1985 formally adopted the federation's most sweeping program of changes in its 30 years.

It could bring about AFL-CIO unions' biggest offensive for new members since the 1950s by ending a federation policy against active AFL-CIO organizing aid to affiliates.

Much of the program remained vague at the end of the year. Kirkland described it as "a living document" whose details would be worked out as new policies were put into effect. Among things that could be tried were a plan for associate memberships for those not in union job jurisdictions, low-cost insurance and consumer services to be offered by unions to members—perhaps including a labor credit card—and development of job issues and contract proposals "responsive to employees who have values and needs different from those of current union members."

One "voice of the future" supporting the program, Linda Puchala, president of the Association

Striking United Airlines pilots picket at O'Hare International Airport in Chicago on May 23 during the seventh day of their walkout. The airline's demand that beginning pilots be paid on a wage scale different from that for more senior staff proved to be the main obstacle in the negotiations.

of Flight Attendants, welcomed the AFL-CIO's "giant step" in developing new ideas and concepts. "The new worker we need to attract more often than not is a female, is a minority, is well educated and is sophisticated," she said.

Labor Unions. Lane Kirkland said in opening the AFL-CIO's 1985 convention that organized labor "still is around, live and kicking," although its "obituary has been written at least once" for every year of the AFL-CIO's history.

There was less reason for optimism in 1985. The federation reported 13.2 million members in affiliated unions. Industrial unions had continued to lose ground, the result of profound changes in the economy, technological changes that reduce manpower needs, and strong competition from imports. Manufacturing jobs were disappearing; blue-collar (factory or industrial plant) unions were showing sharp membership losses.

The United Steelworkers was down from a peak of 1,062,000 in 1975 to 572,000 ten years later. The United Auto Workers was down from a 1,260,-000 peak in 1955 to 974,000. Among other major unions, the International Association of Machinists & Aerospace Workers slumped from 780,000 in 1975 to 520,000, the International Ladies' Garment Workers' Union from 363,000 to 210,000, and the United Rubber Workers from 173,00 to 106,000.

At the same time, a number of unions reported increases in expanding government employment and service and communications industries.

The American Federation of State, County & Municipal Employees grew from 647,000 in 1975 to 997,000, the Service Employees International Union from 480,000 to 688,000, and the Communications Workers of America (which now includes groups of government workers) from 476,000 to 524,000.

AFL-CIO unions and independent unions such as the International Brotherhood of Teamsters, the National Education Association, the United Mine Workers, and the United Electrical Workers had a total membership of 13.7 million, a decline of more than one million in the 1980s. The 18.8% ratio of union members in the U.S. labor force was not much higher than the percentage during the Great Depression of the 1930s. Aided by the National Labor Relations Act, which was 50 years old in 1985, the level had risen above 30% in the early 1950s. With the labor force expanding faster than union memberships, the ratio then had begun dropping, to 24.1% in 1979 and, with year-to-year declines, to 18.8% in 1984.

Fewer than one worker in five eligible for union membership now wore a union button. That meant that more workers were nonunion. According to government estimates, about 90% of new jobs in expanding service and high-technology industries were nonunion. Many of these jobs were in rural areas or in the South and Southwest, where unions were relatively weak, and many were being filled by women and members of minorities, often at lower wages.

Such groups ordinarily were hard to unionize, and the percentage of representation elections won by unions dropped in 1984 to 46% of those conducted by the National Labor Relations Board.

Winning an election did not necessarily mean winning a contract; government figures showed that in 1984 unions were able to negotiate contracts for only 65% of new bargaining units after winning organizing elections.

Bargaining and Strikes. Strong bargaining pressures on unions continued to hold down wage settlements in 1985, with average increases below those of 1984. This would mean a fifth consecutive year of settlements at a lower price than in the previous year.

During the first six months of 1985, average wage adjustments in major bargaining (1,000 employees or more) were for 2.8% raises in the first year and 2.9% annually over the term of contracts. Settlements in 1984 averaged 3.1% for the first year and 2.8% annually thereafter.

Typical of major settlements, General Electric and its unions agreed on cash payments of 3% of projected wages for 12 months, an average of about $675 to each employee, then 3% raises in 1986 and 1987, a total of 9%. Westinghouse Electric signed similar contracts.

Railroads and their unions continued negotiating in late 1985 on "responsible" contracts covering 350,000 workers. Work rules were eased, and initial agreements were for about 10.5% over 40 months.

Construction settlements remained low, some with pay cuts or freezes. The spread of nonunion building contributed to union bargaining moderation.

The Teamsters took pay cuts from $13.21 to $11 an hour to help at least one group of major employers survive. United Auto Workers locals in two American Motors plants also accepted cuts to avert threatened plant closings.

Lump-sum wage payments that did not increase hourly rates also showed up in a two-year contract negotiated by the Amalgamated Clothing & Textile Workers, with payments of $500 in December 1985 and $600 to be made in December 1986.

The United Rubber Workers settled with major companies in the industry for 43 cents an hour in increases spread over three years, 115,000 New York City employees for wage and benefits gains of 19.1% over three years, and the Service Employees International Union for raises of $20 a week in 1985 and 1986 and $21 a week in 1987 for 30,000 employees.

The year was for the most part relatively free of large strikes, but 13 unions, led by the United Steelworkers, continued a long walkout (since July 1983) against the Phelps Dodge Corp.

Labor and Government. The AFL-CIO continued strongly opposed to the Ronald Reagan administration in 1985, but relations improved in one area, between labor and the U.S. Department of Labor. After Secretary of Labor Raymond J. Donovan resigned under pressure of criminal charges, President Reagan named William E. Brock to be his successor. Lane Kirkland welcomed him as one who "has earned our respect" despite a generally conservative voting record over 14 years in the House and Senate. As U.S. trade representative, Brock had had an open-door policy toward unions on trade matters related to job-threatening imports.

There had been no open lines of communication between the Reagan administration and the AFL-CIO since the early days of Reagan's presidency; Brock immediately initiated friendly talks with Kirkland, Donahue, and other labor leaders. In October he became the first secretary of labor to appear before an AFL-CIO convention or council meeting since 1978, although labor secretaries traditionally had been guests.

In a further move to improve relations with unions, Stephen L. Schlossberg, labor lawyer and former union organizer, was named deputy under secretary of labor for labor-management affairs, an appointment welcomed by unions but called "outrageous" by Reed Larson, head of the National Right to Work Committee and high on labor's list of conservative foes.

Although AFL-CIO relations with the Reagan administration eased a little, the president's economic, trade, and social policies remained a barrier. Labor faulted the president for continuing high unemployment, despite improvements in job statistics. It criticized lack of action to stop a decline in U.S. manufacturing leading to plant closings and losses of jobs.

It also blamed the president for "foot-dragging" in enforcing occupational safety & health standards and, at the 1985 AFL-CIO convention, drafted a "bill of particulars" against President Reagan, among other things against his tax-reform position, his civil rights record, his "pro-business conservative government," and what the AFL-CIO called the president's "lack of social consciousness."

Unemployment. The U.S. Department of Labor reported that November unemployment dropped to 7% nationally, down from 7.1% in the previous month, while employment gains pushed the number working to just over 107.9 million. The 7% rate matched the lowest unemployment level of Reagan's presidency. Employment gains lifted the total of new jobs added since the recession to 10.1 million, a new record for the first three years of a U.S. economic recovery.

Although the drop in the number of jobless was hardly significant, only slightly below the 7.1% figure of a year earlier, a White House spokesman said it was "good news" that the country was con-

Hundreds of people in Detroit turned out for a march on August 21 to show support for workers striking the Phelps Dodge Corp. in Arizona. The strike of some 2,400 workers in 13 unions had been in effect since July 1983.

UPI/BETTMANN NEWSPHOTOS

tinuing "on a steady course in job creation and employment."

The AFL-CIO replied that government estimates of 8.1 million unemployed were too low, that another 1.2 million "discouraged workers" wanted jobs but had given up looking for them, and that 5.6 million were working only part-time because full-time jobs were not available.

By labor's reckoning, more than 15 million were suffering "serious joblessness and income problems." Adult men were 6% unemployed, adult women 6.8%. Black unemployment was 15.3%, that of Hispanics 10.4%. The rate for teenagers was 17.9%, but for black teenagers it was 38.3% in November.

United Kingdom

The long-running strike in the coal mines gradually crumbled until more than half of the nation's miners were working. The British National Union of Mineworkers (NUM) called off the strike, without any last-minute attempt to achieve an agreement, and work was resumed on March 5, almost a year after the stoppage began. Miners in some areas where dissatisfaction with the way the strike had been called was particularly great decided to break away from the NUM. In September 1985 the NUM joined with the Communist mining unions (acting as a group), the small Australian mineworkers' union, and some left-wing unions from third world countries to form a new International Mineworkers Organization, with headquarters in Paris and the NUM's Arthur Scargill as president.

In October miners in Nottinghamshire and South Derbyshire, with some Durham miners, voted to create the Union of Democratic Mineworkers, which quickly gained recognition from the National Coal Board. The NUM, meanwhile, at a national delegate conference in July, had strengthened the powers of its executive body, thus further antagonizing the dissidents.

The provisions of the Trade Union Act 1984 requiring a ballot to be held before a strike if legal immunity was to be retained were tested on numerous occasions during the year and proved more successful than had been expected. Unions became increasingly hesitant about calling a strike without a ballot.

LANDMARKS AND MONUMENTS

The fifth General Assembly of nations that were parties to the International Convention Concerning the Protection of the World Cultural and Natural Heritage met in November 1985 in Sofia, Bulg., in conjunction with Unesco's 23rd General Conference. The latest adherents to the convention were the Dominican Republic, Hungary, and Sweden, bringing to 87 the total number of countries that had ratified or accepted it. Subsequently, in December, the convention's World Heritage Committee held its ninth session in Paris. After careful evalu-

ation of national recommendations, 30 properties were added to the World Heritage List, bringing the total to 216 sites in 55 countries.

Additions to the list included, among other sites, the historic center of Salvador (16th–18th century), Bahia state, Brazil; the historic area of Quebec City (17th–19th century), Canada; the "Pont du Gard" (the Nîmes aqueduct, 1st century BC), département of Gard, France; the archaeological site of Petra (ancient capital of the Nabataeans, 4th century BC to 2nd century AD), district of Ma'an, Jordan; the rock drawings of Alta Fjord (4200–500 BC), Finnmark County, Norway; the Altamira cave (prehistoric wall paintings of the Solutrean and Magdalenian periods), near Santander, Cantabria, Spain; the historic district of Segovia (primarily medieval and Renaissance periods) and the Roman aqueduct (1st–2nd century), Segovia, Spain; and the historic district of Santiago de Compostela (11th–18th century), Galicia, Spain.

As well as studying nominations to the list and making decisions for or against inclusion, the World Heritage Committee played an important role by ensuring that action was taken at the national level to protect the monuments and sites listed. When adding a new entry, the committee often at the same time made recommendations on the safeguarding or restoration of the site. This procedure helped to make the convention an effective instrument for the protection of the common heritage. Moreover, the committee tried to ensure that the World Heritage List was as representative as possible of different types of cultural and natural property.

Two international campaigns to safeguard the cultural heritage were launched by the director general of Unesco in 1985. The first, in Bangladesh, was for the restoration and preservation of two sites, Paharpur and Bagherhat, which were also inscribed on the World Heritage List in 1985. The monastic site of Paharpur was perhaps the largest Buddhist monastic complex south of the Himalayas. The Somapura Mahavihara ("great monastery") became a renowned intellectual center, attracting monks, scholars, and pilgrims from the 8th until the 17th century. From Paharpur, monks were also sent to Central Asia and the Far East. The monastery was notable for its monumental architectural organization, which influenced later Buddhist architecture in Burma, Java, and Cambodia, and for its carved stone bas-reliefs and terra-cotta panels. The Bagherhat remains, dating from the first half of the 15th century, included a remarkable number of Islamic religious monuments such as the mausoleum of the founder, the Turkish general Ulugh Khan Jahan, and the Shait Gumbad mosque, renowned for its large prayer room divided into 7 longitudinal aisles and 11 deep bays. More than 50 monuments were identified for preservation and restoration.

The second Unesco campaign, for the restoration of the architectural heritage of Guatemala, was aimed particularly at providing assistance for Span-

The Paharpur Buddhist Monastery in Bangladesh, which dates from the 8th century AD, was one object of an international campaign during the year to restore and preserve the world's heritage.

J. SANDAY—UNESCO/
AUTHENTICATED NEWS
INTERNATIONAL

ish colonial structures damaged by the earthquake of Feb. 4, 1976. However, an integral part of the campaign was also the preparation of a detailed inventory of Guatemala's architectural patrimony. This would assist in the protection of Maya monuments and sites such as Tikal, Quirigua, Kaminaljuyu, and Iximche.

LAOS

Attracting much attention throughout 1985 were the tense and apparently deteriorating relations between Laos and its larger neighbor Thailand. A dispute between the two governments over three strategically located border hamlets that began in 1984 simmered well into 1985. By August the issue had provoked more than 120 armed encounters between Laotian and Thai troops. Bangkok put the casualties at 2 Thai soldiers killed and 11 wounded and 8 Laotians dead and an unspecified number injured. Intermittent diplomatic attempts to resolve the dispute came to nothing. There were reports that villagers living in the vicinity had been killed, and Thailand accused the Laotians of sending "spies" trained by Vietnam into its territory in an attempt to convert its hill-tribe people to Communism.

Vietnam's involvement in Laos was the subject of two documents issued early in the year. A paper on the "Soviet-Vietnamese condominium" in Laos was the work of a former senior official of the ruling Pathet Lao who had received training in Vietnam and the U.S.S.R. The author, now based in Paris, asserted that his country was home to 8,000 Vietnamese and 1,600 Soviet advisers as well as 400,000 Vietnamese settlers. The second document, a White Paper issued by the Thai Foreign Ministry, also decried the vietnamization of Laos and claimed that Hanoi cadres had infiltrated every government organization. The report noted that since the Communists came to power in Laos a decade earlier, more than 280,000 Laotians had fled to Thailand. After slowing in recent years, the exodus picked up again in 1984 and 1985, with more than a thousand refugees crossing the border in some months. Laotian officials blamed the departures on "Western policies" aimed at "parasites who don't want to work, preferring to be unemployed in the United States."

Opponents of the Vientiane regime who stayed behind posed no real threat. Some 6,000 were still believed to be in two dozen "reeducation" camps. Resistance groups, spearheaded by borderland minority tribes such as the Hmong, the Yao, the Khmu, and the Muser, remained fragmented and lacked the resources to mount a serious challenge to the Laotian Army, which was strengthened by the presence of 60,000 Vietnamese troops.

The government continued to rely heavily on foreign aid for economic development. In 1984 and 1985, however, the amount declined some 15–20% from the annual average of around $100 million during 1978–82 because lack of infrastructure and expertise slowed absorption. The funds came mostly from the Soviet bloc, the UN, and a handful of Western countries. Socialization of agriculture remained slow, but the country maintained self-sufficiency in food production. More than $20 million worth of hydroelectricity, representing 90% of exports, was sold to Thailand.

LATIN-AMERICAN AFFAIRS

In 1985 Latin America's economic difficulties showed few signs of abating, and its external indebtedness gave grounds for concern. Elections in several countries continued a trend toward civilian rule that had begun in 1980. Following presidential and general elections held in Peru and Bolivia in April and July, the new presidents, Alan García Pérez and Víctor Paz Estenssoro, respectively, took office in July and August. Presidential and general elections also took place in Guatemala and Honduras in November and December. The victor in the second round between the two leading presidential contenders in Guatemala was Vinicio Cerezo, who was to take office in January 1986. In Honduras, after legal wrangles delayed the announcement of official results, José Azcona Hoyo was declared the winner at year's end. Legislative and state gubernatorial elections held in Mexico in July were won by the government party, the Partido Revolucionario Institucional. In November Pres. Raúl Alfonsín's Radical Civic Union in Argentina increased its majority by one seat in midterm elections for the Chamber of Deputies. Also in November, in elections for mayors of state capitals in Brazil, the Brazilian Democratic Movement Party, chief party in the governing coalition, won an overall victory but lost in São Paulo, Rio de Janeiro, and several smaller cities.

No solution to the Falkland Islands/Islas Malvinas dispute between Argentina and the U.K. was in sight, although during President Alfonsín's official visits to France and Spain in September and October, he held meetings with U.K. opposition party leaders. On November 25 the UN General Assembly adopted an Argentine-backed resolution calling for talks between the two countries.

Central America remained subject to political and social disorders, with guerrilla activity continuing in El Salvador, Guatemala, and Nicaragua. Peace initiatives were in progress throughout the year. The Contadora Group, formed in January 1983 by Colombia, Mexico, Panama, and Venezuela, presented the second draft of a peace and cooperation treaty for the region to the governments of Costa Rica, El Salvador, Honduras, Guatemala, and Nicaragua and to the UN in October. It proposed that military activity of all kinds be monitored by an international corps of inspectors. The Contadora Group announced that it would not persist with negotiation efforts if the treaty was not accepted. The previous proposed treaty, prepared in 1984,

had been accepted by Nicaragua but was rejected by El Salvador, Honduras, Costa Rica, and the U.S.

In November the European Communities (EC) formalized links with Central America by signing a five-year cooperation agreement. It granted most-favored-nation status to Costa Rica, El Salvador, Guatemala, Honduras, Nicaragua, and Panama and committed the EC to increasing substantially its aid to the region, which stood at about $30 million a year.

On October 1 the Central American Common Market (CACM) countries—Costa Rica, El Salvador, Guatemala, Honduras, and Nicaragua— began implementing a new set of customs nomenclature and import tariffs, based on the EC nomenclature. Negotiations were completed in July on 85% of the new tariffs, which were to range between 5 and 80%. The lowest were to be for capital goods, raw materials, and inputs for the productive sectors. The agreement was one of the most important initiatives designed to revive the moribund CACM since the late 1970s.

In February the state-owned banks in Argentina, Brazil, and Mexico established Latinequip, a trinational company, to try to increase Latin America's share in the market for capital goods and engineering services. Latin-American industrial concerns were to draw on lines of credit from the founder banks, while the World Bank and the Inter-American Development Bank (I-ADB) were to be approached for funding.

When heads of government of the 13-nation Caribbean Community (Caricom) met in July in Bridgetown, Barbados, trade was the main item on the agenda. They agreed to raise the common external tariff by 15% as of the end of August on imports of cement, steel products, automotive parts, and a range of other goods from outside the Caricom area. The U.S. Caribbean Basin Initiative

While Pope John Paul II looks on, Chile's foreign minister, Jaime Del Vallo (left), and his Argentine counterpart, Dante Caputo (right), sign a Vatican-mediated pact on May 2 ending a border dispute over the Beagle Channel.
AP/WIDE WORLD

(CBI) functioned fitfully throughout the year. The CBI, which had become law in January 1984, was an integrated program of tax and trade measures that included an agreement offering duty-free access to the U.S. market for 12 years for a wide range of Caribbean and Central American products, mainly manufactured goods. In 1984 only 7.5% of exports from Caribbean Basin countries to the U.S. carried the CBI's duty-free status, and all exports from those countries in the period January–June 1985 were down, compared with the same period in 1984. In November Canada announced a plan, designed to help make up for the CBI's shortcomings, that would allow duty-free entry into Canada for a wide variety of Caribbean and Central American goods, including textiles, cigars, footwear, and rum.

An upturn in the world economy in 1984 helped Latin America to reverse somewhat the declines registered during the period 1980–83. A growth in gross domestic product of 3.1% in 1984 resulted in an increase in per capita product of 0.6%, compared with a decline in the latter of 10% in 1982–83. Increased demand for imports in the U.S. and Japan helped exports from Latin America reach $99 billion, as against $89 billion in 1983, while tight controls contributed to imports of $61 billion, compared with $59 billion in 1983. The increase in the external debt slowed to 5.6% during the year, compared with 6% in 1983. The region's total external debt reached $360 billion by the end of 1984 and was estimated at $370 billion in mid-1985. Interest payments on the debts amounted to $38 billion in 1984, as against $35 billion in 1983 and $36 billion in 1982. Inflation remained a major problem as the average regional rate reached 175.4% in 1984, up from 130.8% in 1983. Preliminary estimates indicated that in 1985 the growth rate would be lower than that of 1984 and that exports would be reduced significantly because of a fall in demand from advanced industrialized countries and because of depressed commodity prices. Inflation was expected to remain at a high level.

Although Latin-American governments expressed increased anxiety about the foreign debt, no coordinated approach to tackling the problem emerged. On taking office in Peru in July, President García stated that his country's debt repayments during the upcoming 12 months would be limited to 10% of export earnings, although in fact the policy was not strictly adhered to later. Several Latin-American leaders, including Pres. José Sarney, new leader of Brazil, pointed out that concessions on repayments were necessary to help foster internal development and growth. Representatives of the Cartagena Group, comprising the 11 principal debtor countries in the region, held talks on the debt problem with the EC in April. A call by Pres. Fidel Castro of Cuba in July for a regionwide default was rebuffed by other governments in the area.

The region's two largest borrowers were in disagreement with the International Monetary Fund

UPI/BETTMANN NEWSPHOTOS

Argentina's economics minister, Juan Sourrouille (right), and a Citibank official, William Rhodes, sign a new external financing agreement in New York City in August.

(IMF). In September the IMF declared Mexico out of compliance with austerity objectives and suspended payment of $900 million in pending loans; however, a rapprochement was likely in view of the large expenditures involved in repairing damage caused by the Mexico City earthquake during the same month. The Brazilian government, the IMF, and creditor banks failed to agree on economic policy and the rescheduling of $45.3 billion of debts due in 1985–89, despite the fact that concurrence in principle on the latter point had been reached with creditor banks in February. On the other hand, after Argentina began implementing an austerity program that was even more severe than that previously agreed upon with the IMF, Argentina and creditor banks signed a contract in August that provided for the rescheduling of debts and provision of $4.2 billion in new credits.

U.S. Secretary of the Treasury James Baker presented a "Program for Sustained Growth" to the IMF/World Bank meetings at Seoul, South Korea, in October. The program aimed to encourage less developed countries with recent debt-servicing problems (reportedly including Argentina, Bolivia, Brazil, Chile, Colombia, Ecuador, Mexico, Peru, Uruguay, and Venezuela) to follow market-oriented economic policies promoting growth, as well as IMF fiscal, monetary, and exchange-rate policies. In return they would be eligible for enhanced assistance from international financial institutions. The World Bank and the I-ADB were requested to increase disbursements by 50% in 1986–88, and commercial banks were asked to increase their lending by some 2½% a year during the same period.

Special Report: The Swing Toward Democracy

by George Philip

Between 1980 and 1985 military government went into retreat across Latin America. Although Maj. Gen. Augusto Pinochet Ugarte in Chile and Gen. Alfredo Stroessner in Paraguay remained, the list of countries that underwent transitions toward civilian and democratic rule included Argentina, Bolivia, Uruguay, Brazil, Peru, Panama, and Honduras. In Ecuador an elected civilian president replaced a military junta in 1979, and in Guatemala elections took place in late 1985. Although civilian rule remained precarious in a number of the countries where it had been instituted, the cumulative effect of this transformation was considerable. In most of these countries, moreover, the military showed no particular wish to force its way back into power.

There was no single or simple explanation for this trend. Some cases of democratization owed much to particular historic experiences. These included the military defeat of the Argentine junta in the South Atlantic in 1982, the cocaine connection in Bolivian politics, and the near defeat of the Salvadoran military by Marxist insurgents in 1981–82. It should also be remembered that almost every South American country had enjoyed periods of democratic rule in the past. There had been many swings between civilian and military rule, although recent military governments had tended to be more technocratic, more durable, and often more repressive than their predecessors. The return to the barracks, therefore, was by no means definitive, but in many cases it seemed to have been established more firmly than in prior years.

Forces for Change

Circumstances differed in each country, but there were two general factors behind the recent democratizing trend. One was that, in South America, recession and economic setbacks were, perhaps surprisingly, democratizing forces. The other was that the U.S. had been pressing for democratization in Central America as part of its response toward the Sandinista revolution in Nicaragua.

Recent military regimes generally projected a technocratic image and pretended that they were superior to civilians at economic management. When international conditions were favorable, this pretense could be sustained; when export prices fell and international interest rates rose, the bluff was called. Faced with the need to impose unpopular austerity measures, military authorities often

sought (with some success) to limit popular unrest by promising an eventual return to democracy and easing political conditions generally.

The original supporters of military rule, seeing that political conditions were changing, sought to find a basis for compromise with the opposition. Where this was achieved, as in the case of Brazil, the transition to democracy was relatively smooth. Where it was not, as in Chile, the dictatorship was able to continue. In most cases, however, the military failed to control its own succession and eventually was forced to return power to moderate opposition figures: Fernando Belaúnde Terry in Peru (whom the military had overthrown in 1968), Tancredo Neves in Brazil (before his unexpected death), and Raúl Alfonsín in Argentina. Civilian politicians who had maintained too close an association with the military regime suffered some notable setbacks when democracy returned.

In Central America, the early 1980s were dominated by the various responses to the Nicaraguan revolution. Some countries in the region, notably El Salvador, became heavily dependent on U.S. support to combat Marxist insurgents. Although the U.S. had not always been an unqualified supporter of Latin-American democracy, Washington was anxious to ease out the hard-line military dictatorships that had provided rebel movements with recruits and grist for propaganda. U.S. pressure, therefore, played a major part in democratizing El Salvador and in persuading the Guatemalan government to agree to hold elections. Interestingly enough, the U.S. government proved unable fully to control the outcome of these democratic openings; Washington was unenthusiastic about José Napoleón Duarte until he was elected president of El Salvador in 1984 and won an outright congressional majority in 1985. Continuing U.S. support for democratic reform was crucial if the military was to be kept out of presidential palaces.

The Road Ahead

Democratization was taking place at a particularly difficult time for Latin America. The very factors that precipitated military withdrawal from office—high inflation, domestic recession, a severe foreign debt problem—were burdens on incoming civilian regimes. In addition, these civilian governments often had to face insurgencies originally directed against the military rulers, and they had

DEMOCRACY IN LATIN AMERICA, 1985

UNITED STATES

THE BAHAMAS

Tropic of Cancer

Puerto Rico (U.S.)
British Virgin Islands (U.K.)
ST. CHRISTOPHER AND NEVIS
ANTIGUA AND BARBUDA
Guadeloupe (France)
DOMINICA
Martinique (France)
ST. LUCIA
BARBADOS
GRENADA
TRINIDAD AND TOBAGO

CUBA
DOMINICAN REPUBLIC
HAITI
JAMAICA
Virgin Islands (U.S.)
ST. VINCENT AND THE GRENADINES

MEXICO

BELIZE
HONDURAS
GUATEMALA
EL SALVADOR
NICARAGUA
COSTA RICA
PANAMA

CARIBBEAN SEA
Netherland Antilles (Neth.)

NORTH ATLANTIC OCEAN

NORTH PACIFIC OCEAN

VENEZUELA
GUYANA
SURINAME
French Guiana (France)

COLOMBIA

ECUADOR

Equator

Galápagos Islands (Ecuador)

PERU

BRAZIL

SOUTH PACIFIC OCEAN

BOLIVIA

PARAGUAY

CHILE

Tropic of Capricorn

ARGENTINA

URUGUAY

SOUTH ATLANTIC OCEAN

Falkland Islands / Islas Malvinas (U.K.)

Status:
- Democratic
- Partially democratic
- Not democratic
- Dependent state

Source: The Economist.

0   200   400   600 mi
0   400   800 km

In the past decade Latin America experienced a notable democratizing trend, with more and more governments changing through an electoral process in which opposing parties vied for votes. It continued to be true, however, that most of the countries in the region moved toward only partial democracy, with opposition parties having political influence but not being allowed to win elections and thereby to come to power.

to decide how far to pursue cases of human rights abuses committed by the military. Prolonged recession, in particular, might intensify the disillusionment already common enough in Latin America with regard to democratic institutions.

Despite these difficulties, some civilian presidents were surprisingly successful in maintaining domestic confidence while, at the same time, tackling their countries' most severe outstanding problems. They were helped by the fact that the political atmosphere had quieted down since the 1960s. Hopes and fears that Cuban-style revolution was imminent in South America had largely evaporated. The armed left remained active only in Chile, Colombia, and in Peru. Even in Central America, the armed left had little prospect of short-term success outside its existing bastions in Cuba and Nicaragua.

In the larger South American countries, right-wing hopes of a military-technocratic miracle had been effectively dashed by the world recession. In some countries (notably Argentina), relations between the military and the business sector broke up amid some acrimony as a result. There was now a more realistic appreciation of the limits of what was politically possible in Latin America. This, however, did not necessarily entail political quiescence. The more successful democratic leaders were those able to maintain a degree of presence and to exercise leadership; Argentina's Alfonsín and El Salvador's Duarte were good examples. Now that the nonsolution of military rule had been largely discredited, political leaders would have a better chance of coming to grips with the many problems confronting them.

LAW

In 1985 the various judicial tribunals throughout the world decided a number of important cases, most of which involved civil rights, criminal law, and business matters.

Religious Freedom

Three cases handed down by the U.S. Supreme Court, regarded by scholars as that court's most important decisions during the year, clarified the meaning of the "establishment of religion clause" of the First Amendment to the U.S. Constitution. That clause prevents states and the federal government from establishing an official religion in the U.S. *Wallace* v. *Jaffree* involved a challenge to the constitutionality of an Alabama statute that authorized a one-minute period of silence in all public schools "for meditation or voluntary prayer." The court held that the purpose of the statute was to endorse religion rather than some secular interest; that the establishment clause requires the government to pursue a course of complete neutrality toward religion, including the right of individuals to select any religious faith or none at all; and that, therefore, the statute was unconstitutional.

For similar reasons, the "Community Education and Shared Time" program adopted by the city of Grand Rapids, Mich., was held unconstitutional in *Grand Rapids School District* v. *Ball*. The program provided classes to nonpublic school students at public expense and was intended to supplement the core curricula of the private schools so that their students could meet the requirements of an accredited school program, as mandated by the state of Michigan. Among the subjects offered were remedial and enrichment mathematics and reading, art, music, and physical education. Most of the nonpublic schools involved in the programs were sectarian religious schools. The court held that these programs impermissibly involved the government in the support of sectarian religious activities and thus violated the "establishment clause" of the First Amendment.

In *Aguilar* v. *Felton,* the Supreme Court also struck down, on "establishment clause" grounds, a program developed by New York City that was similar in a number of respects to that of Grand Rapids.

Freedom of Speech

Significant cases on freedom of expression were handed down by the U.S. Supreme Court. *Federal Election Commission* v. *National Conservative Political Action Committee* entangled the U.S. Supreme Court in a political fight between the Republican and Democratic parties concerning campaign financing through political action committees, known familiarly as "PACs." A federal law offered presidential candidates the option of receiving public financing for their general election campaigns, but it provided that, if the candidate elected such financing, it was a criminal offense for an independent political committee to expend more than $1,000 to further the candidate's election. Believing that a particular PAC intended to violate this law on the grounds that it was invalid, the Democratic Party brought an action to have it declared constitutional. The court found the statute unconstitutional as a violation of free speech guaranteed by the Constitution.

Harper & Row v. *National Enterprises* attracted worldwide interest, though scholars tended to agree that it had little legal significance. The case involved the theft and publication of portions of former U.S. president Gerald Ford's unpublished memoirs, including his account of the pardoning of former president Richard Nixon. The unauthorized publication was held to be a violation of the copyright laws.

Criminal Law

Anderston v. *Ryan,* decided by the House of Lords, the highest court in the Commonwealth, fascinated criminal law experts throughout the common law world. The case dealt with the criminal law of "attempt," generally defined as any overt act

A police van carries four terrorists, the hijackers of the Achille Lauro, *from Sicily to Spoleto, one of four Italian cities that claimed jurisdiction in the case.*

ARAL—SIPA/SPECIAL FEATURES

that is done with the intent to commit a crime but is prevented from commission by the interference of some independent cause. Unanswered by this definition is the question: Can one with criminal intent "criminally attempt" to do something that is lawful? The House of Lords said no. The case involved the buying of a video recorder by a person who erroneously believed it was stolen. The court said this could not be a crime because the factual circumstances made the intended offense incapable of fulfillment.

But what about the thief who puts his hand into an empty pocket? This, said the court, does involve a "criminal attempt." Buying goods is not illegal, standing alone. When this activity is done in connection with an "illegal" intention, no crime occurs. But putting one's hand into another's pocket is illegal and, when this activity is combined with a criminal intention, a crime occurs, even though the intended result of the act was impossible from the start. In view of the doctrinal importance of *Anderston* v. *Ryan* to common law countries, including the U.S., scholars were eagerly awaiting possible clarification from the House of Lords through a pending case dealing with a person convicted of "smuggling" tea leaves in the belief that they were a controlled drug.

In *Winston* v. *Lee,* the Supreme Court held that a person could not be required to undergo surgery in order to produce evidence of his guilt or innocence of a crime. A shopkeeper had been wounded during an attempted robbery but, being armed with a gun, wounded his assailant in the left side. The assailant then ran from the scene. Police officers found the accused eight blocks away from the shooting suffering from a gunshot wound to his left chest area. He was arrested, and the state moved for an order directing him to undergo surgery to remove a bullet lodged under his left collarbone, asserting that the bullet would provide evidence of his guilt or innocence. The court held that the proposed surgery would violate the accused's right to be secure in his person and that, consequently, the proposed "search" was unreasonable and in violation of the Fourth Amendment to the Constitution.

Tennessee v. *Garner* was concerned with whether the use of deadly force could be employed by police to prevent the escape of an apparently unarmed felon. The U.S. Supreme Court held that it could not, because such activity is proscribed by the Fourth Amendment to the Constitution. The court concluded that such force may not be used unless it is necessary to prevent the escape of the suspected felon and the officer has probable cause to believe that the suspect poses a significant threat of death or serious physical injury to the officer and others.

Business Matters

Banking law in the U.S., almost from the start, was dominated by the idea that a bank in one state, whether chartered by the federal or state government, could not conduct business in another. This idea was threatened by the emergence of bank holding companies, separate corporate entities that acquired banks in many states. To deal with this threat, the "Douglas Amendment" was passed in 1956. Under it, the Federal Reserve Board was charged with approving or disapproving bank holding companies and, significantly, a holding company located in one state was prohibited from acquiring a bank in another state unless such acquisition was specifically authorized by the laws of that state. Beginning with Massachusetts in 1982, several states enacted laws lifting the Douglas Amendment ban on a reciprocal basis within geographic regions, and these laws had spawned an impressive literature as to their legality and constitutionality.

One such law, enacted by most New England states, permits holding companies to establish banks in their states provided that other New England states accord reciprocity. This kind of law, passed by Massachusetts, was attacked by New York banks and others as discriminatory. In *Northeast Bancorp, Inc.* v. *Board of Governors,* a case of major importance to the U.S. economy and the banking community, the Supreme Court sustained the Massachusetts statute. In this opinion, Justice William Rehnquist established guidelines for interstate banking that, in the view of many experts, would dominate for the remainder of the century.

International Law

The nature of world violence took a new turn in 1985, although the signs had been visible in previous years. Whereas in the past breakdowns in international law and order were localized in wars, interventions, and traditional border incursions, there now emerged a broader willingness on the part of major powers to disregard the territorial sovereignty of other states and, as a matter of deliberate policy, to place military or police expediency above compliance with international law. This applied not only to the improper use of force and to unauthorized incursions by state instrumentalities (military ships and aircraft) into the territory of foreign friendly states but also to the extended exercise of criminal or quasi-criminal jurisdiction, and the application of domestic criminal law, against foreign nationals living in their own country and in respect of acts carried out there. These trends began to raise the question of whether the basic concept of classic international law as a system governing relations between independent sovereign states was beginning to dissolve as greater regional and global interdependence and the increasingly hegemonic attitudes of the two superpowers diluted the old concept of the nation-state.

The most dramatic example of this trend involved a very complex legal situation. An Italian cruise liner in the Mediterranean, the *Achille Lauro,* was seized by four Palestinian terrorists and held to ransom for the release of 50 Palestinians held in an

Israeli prison camp. This was the first extension of aerial hijacking to the sea, and there was dispute among lawyers as to whether the law of piracy would apply in such a case; some still restricted the crime of piracy to robbery at sea, thus excluding acts of violence for political purposes. While in control of the ship, the captors murdered a U.S. passenger. The Egyptian president negotiated the release of the ship, and the captors, having been promised transport to "neutral" territory, embarked on an Egyptian civil aircraft for Tunis. U.S. Navy fighter aircraft then approached the Egyptian plane in international airspace off Crete and compelled it to fly under escort to the NATO air base at Sigonella in Italy. There the Palestinians were taken into Italian custody, after an attempt to keep them in U.S. military custody had been disallowed. Although the U.S. action had some similarity to a classic "intervention," it was the first example of such a seizure on the high seas or in international airspace outside a contiguous zone or in the absence of a state of war and in an area remote from the territory of the seizing state.

A similar extension of the intervention concept had taken place a week earlier when Israeli war planes breached Tunisian airspace 1,500 mi (2,400 km) away and bombed the headquarters of the Palestine Liberation Organization near Tunis. In July French government agents, using explosives, clandestinely sank the ship *Rainbow Warrior,* belonging to the environmental organization Greenpeace, in Auckland Harbour, New Zealand. The ship had been about to lead a demonstration against French nuclear weapons tests at Mururoa Atoll in the Pacific. The French agents breached New Zealand territorial sovereignty as well as engaging in unlawful violence against a British-registered ship. The accidental death of a photographer in the explosion ensured that the affair would become a major diplomatic incident, which led to the resignation of the French minister of defense.

Less dramatic was the extension of breaches of territorial waters and airspace by foreign submarines and military aircraft. In October a Czechoslovak fighter fired on a U.S. military helicopter, the 17th

violation of West German airspace by Warsaw Pact aircraft in six months; in April a U.S. helicopter had been buzzed by Soviet fighters after itself crossing into Czechoslovak airspace. In the Aegean, Greece protested vigorously against multiple violations of its airspace by U.S. and Turkish aircraft during a military exercise. A potentially worrying type of air violation occurred at the turn of the year when a Soviet cruise missile (unarmed), launched from a submarine in the Barents Sea, unlawfully crossed Norwegian territory into Finland, where it crash-landed; the Soviet government apologized.

Scandinavian maritime boundaries were also the site of two incidents. In the Barents Sea a Norwegian seismic research ship had its cable cut deliberately by a Soviet naval vessel 30 mi (50 km) within the Norwegian boundary. In the eastern Baltic the U.S.S.R. had long claimed that the border with Sweden should follow the median line between the two coasts, while Sweden had claimed that the line should be calculated from the coast of the island of Gotland (not from the Swedish mainland). In the resulting disputed area, Soviet fishery-protection vessels boarded and expelled numerous Swedish, Danish, and West German fishing boats. A more serious incident occurred in October when a Soviet minesweeper collided with a Swedish electronic surveillance ship, the *Orion,* which was monitoring signals from a Soviet Kilo-class submarine; this took place not in the disputed zone but on the high seas.

Discussions were proceeding on the drafting of an arbitration agreement between the U.K. and Ireland to settle the matter between them. Farther west, Canada in September drew a straight baseline around the whole of its Arctic archipelagic territory, thus affirming that all the sea between the islands constituted internal waters and was under the complete sovereignty of Canada. This followed a voyage made through the Northwest Passage by the U.S. Coast Guard icebreaker *Polar Sea* without first obtaining the permission of the Canadian government, pursuant to U.S. policy, which regarded the Northwest Passage as an international strait.

The most noteworthy boundary settlement during the year was the agreement between Chile and Argentina on their boundary in the Beagle Channel, following lengthy mediation by the Vatican. The two countries exchanged instruments of ratification in May. Guinea-Bissau and Senegal agreed to submit their maritime boundary dispute to arbitration, after a similar dispute between Guinea-Bissau and Guinea resulted in an arbitration award in February. In December 1984 Australia and Papua New Guinea signed a treaty settling their mutual boundary in the Torres Strait. The UN preparatory commission for the future International Sea-Bed Authority reached a compromise agreement on the delimitation of the seabed exploitation areas between the U.S.S.R. and Japan; no agreement could be reached, however, on the more complex dispute between the U.S.S.R. and France, since 80% of their claims overlapped. The U.S., the U.K., and West Germany were unable to take part in such proceedings because they had refused to sign the Law of the Sea Convention.

Boundary treaties were concluded between North Korea and the U.S.S.R.; Algeria and Mauritania; France and Spain (an adjustment of the Treaty of the Pyrenees of 1659 resulting in the transfer of 3,230 sq ft (300 sq m) of the town of Agullana and 600 of its inhabitants from Spain to France); Italy and Switzerland (border adjustments agreed on in 1981 but not ratified or entering into force until January 1985); and Sweden and Finland (the boundary in the Torne River, affecting fishing rights). Relaxation of border controls was agreed on between Italy and France and Italy and Austria; the Albania-Greece border was at last opened; and a commission was set up under the auspices of the Contadora Group (Colombia, Mexico, Panama, and Venezuela) to establish the Costa Rica-Nicaragua border.

A new president, Judge Nagendra Singh (India), and a new vice-president, Judge Guy Ladreit de Lacharrière (France), were appointed to the International Court of Justice. For the first time in its history, the court would also include a woman member, Mme Suzanne Bastid (herself daughter of a former president of the court, Jules Basdevant).

The decision of the International Court in November 1984 to accept jurisdiction in Nicaragua's action against the U.S., alleging interventionist acts against Nicaraguan territory, had two consequences. The U.S., which bitterly disputed the correctness of the judgment, withdrew its acceptance of the "optional clause" as from April 1986, since continued acceptance of the court's compulsory jurisdiction would be "contrary to our commitment to the principle of the equal application of the law, and would endanger our vital national interests." Second, the U.S. refused to participate further in the proceedings brought by Nicaragua. Oral argument took place in September, but in the absence of U.S. rep-resentatives. However, the U.S. was not boycotting the court as such, and it reached an agreement with Italy to submit to the court a dispute involving Italian subsidiaries of two U.S. companies.

The Iran-U.S. Claims Tribunal resumed sittings early in the year, after its work had been interrupted by an assault by two Iranian judges on a neutral Swedish colleague. The two were recalled and replaced.

LEBANON

The withdrawal of the Israeli Army from Lebanon and plans for closer cooperation between Pres. Amin Gemayel and Syria's Pres. Hafez al-Assad took place against a background of continued sectarian fighting in Lebanon during 1985. Beirut airport was the scene of an international hostage drama involving a Trans World Airlines passenger airliner hijacked on June 14 by Shi'ite gunmen demanding the release of some 700 Shi'ite Lebanese and Palestinians being detained by the Israelis. One U.S. passenger, a navy diver, was shot dead by the hijackers. A solution to the crisis, resulting in the release on June 30 of the 39 remaining U.S. hostages, was brought about through the mediation of Nabih Berri, leader of the Amal, Lebanon's dominant Shi'ite militia. All of the detainees were released by Israel before the end of the year, but the hostage incident inevitably provoked some discomfort for U.S. Pres. Ronald Reagan and the Israeli leadership. The hijack had been masterminded by a semiautonomous wing of Amal led by Akel Hamiyeh, who was also prominent in the earlier month-long attack on Palestinian refugee camps in Beirut.

The Israeli withdrawal from Lebanon, reportedly completed on June 10, did not end Israel's involvement in Lebanon's internal affairs; Israeli military advisers were to remain behind to assist the South Lebanon Army, a 2,000-strong militia composed mainly of Maronite Christians, which the Israelis supported as a buffer against violence that would otherwise be directed at their own country. Earlier,

A convoy of Red Cross vehicles bearing released U.S. hostages crosses Beirut on its way toward Damascus, Syria, and freedom. The 39 hostages had been held for 17 days after the hijacking of a TWA Boeing 727 over Europe by Shi'ite gunmen on June 14.

ALAIN NOGUES—SYGMA

FRANK VIELJEUX—SYGMA

Children in the Palestinian camp of Borge Barajni in Lebanon huddle in a building that was pocked by bullets during fighting between Palestinians and Shi'ites.

in mid-February, Israel had pulled out of Sidon after 32 months of occupation. The Shi'ites, a minority in Sidon itself, were seen as having mounted a successful guerrilla campaign that greatly influenced Israel's decision to withdraw. On the strength of this success, the Shi'ites began to press more strongly for an end to their inferior status under the constitution.

Syria's central role in the forging of a settlement between rival Lebanese Christian and Muslim factions emerged clearly during the year. The Syrian government made its most determined effort to end the ten-year-old civil war since Damascus sent its troops into Lebanon in June 1976. The peace initiative made a promising start in July when West Beirut militia leaders agreed to keep their fighters off the streets. Syrian officers then organized a meeting of Muslim and Druze leaders in the Bekaa Valley. At the meeting it was agreed that plans would be drawn up for a conference between all of Lebanon's factions to decide on a new power-sharing formula. These hopeful moves were thwarted by a new outbreak of violence that included a spate of murderous car bombings in Beirut and Tripoli. The explosions were sufficient to trigger the heaviest artillery exchanges experienced in the capital for some months. In early October, following three weeks of fighting between Muslim fundamental-

ists and Syrian-supported leftist militias, the Syrian Army took over the Lebanese port of Tripoli. The fighting in Tripoli resulted in at least 200 dead.

The Lebanese relationship with the U.S.S.R. was another casualty of the hostilities in Tripoli. In October four officials of the Soviet embassy in Beirut were kidnapped. One was killed, the others held hostage but released unharmed on October 30. Responsibility for the incident was claimed by Sunnite Muslims who were demanding Syrian intervention to end the fighting in Tripoli.

On April 17 Prime Minister Rashid Karami announced the resignation of his nine-member Cabinet, but the collapse of his national unity government was avoided when, a week later, he agreed to remain in office. The government, which had been formed in May 1984, gave factional leaders ministerial responsibilities, but it had failed to influence greatly the political deadlock or Lebanon's economic misery. Complicating factors were the revolt of the Christian militia against President Gemayel's Christian Phalange Party and the emergence of a semiautonomous Druze statelet in the Shuf Mountains.

On October 16 it was announced that Christian, Druze, and Shi'ite militia representatives had agreed on draft proposals for political reforms at talks chaired by Syria's Vice-Pres. 'Abd al-Halim Khaddam. The proposals called for the gradual abolition of Lebanon's Christian-dominated system of government. An accord incorporating the proposals and providing for the disbanding of the militias was signed in Damascus on December 28 by Berri, Druze leader Walid Jumblatt, and Elie Hobeika, commander of the (Christian) Lebanese Forces.

In January, following a serious slide of the Lebanese pound against the U.S. dollar, the Karami administration decided to seek assistance from the International Monetary Fund. The economy had declined markedly in 1984. The balance of payments deficit reached $1.4 billion, and foreign-exchange reserves dwindled alarmingly. Industrial production fell by 4% to $250 million. Despite attempts by Lebanese authorities to tighten security at Beirut international airport, by late 1985 the national carrier, Middle East Airlines, was the only airline serving the airport; passenger traffic had slumped to its lowest level since 1953, with slightly more than 1,000 passengers a day using the facility.

President Gemayel made an urgent appeal to Saudi Arabia's King Fahd for economic aid, but it was noted that Saudi Arabia delayed disbursement of $460 million worth of aid promised at the 1979 Arab summit held in Tunisia. The industrial sector suffered from factors other than the direct effects of the conflict, including the increased cost of raw materials, a rise in energy prices, high interest rates, and recession in the Gulf states, the destination of many Lebanese exports.

The fate of six U.S. citizens, some missing since June 1984, remained uncertain. They were believed to be captives of the group known as Islamic Jihad ("Islamic Holy War"). The murder of one of the six, William Buckley, an officer of the U.S. embassy in Beirut, was announced in October, but the report was not confirmed. A seventh U.S. prisoner, a Presbyterian minister who had been held for 16 months, was freed in September. Other kidnapped or missing foreign nationals, some British and French, were still unaccounted for at year's end.

LIBRARIES

In the U.S. strong local and state funding brightened the public-library picture. The Miami-Dade County, Fla., public library system opened a new 200,000-sq ft (18,600-sq m) central library in a Mediterranean-style cultural plaza in Miami on July 19; the Los Angeles City Council approved a $110.4 million, 200,000-sq ft expansion and rehabilitation of the landmark 1926 central library; the Atlanta-Fulton (Ga.) Public Library won a $38 million bond referendum in October for new library buildings and improvements; and the New York Public Library began converting its ten million-card catalog into book and on-line formats and renovating its main library facade as part of a $45 million restoration program. Major library renovations were under way or announced in Baltimore, Md., Chicago, and Boston. In general, however, according to 1984 figures reported in mid-1985, public libraries were struggling with an 11.5% rise in expenses.

School libraries, still limited to some $4.62–$6.41 per pupil for books, according to a University of North Carolina survey, got moral support from the first National School Library Media Month, designated in a joint congressional resolution introduced by Sen. Daniel P. Moynihan (Dem., N.Y.) and celebrated April 1 on the U.S. Capitol steps. Biennial statistics from the Association of College and Research Libraries showed members' interlibrary lending up 21% and borrowing up 28%, reflecting the current emphasis on cooperative activity among academic and research libraries. A showcase on-line catalog system at the University of Illinois at Urbana began operation in April, giving users quick access not only to the university's holdings but, through interlibrary loan, to the collections of 25 other Illinois libraries.

Among current trends, job vacancies for children's librarians were going unfilled in several regions and public libraries were lending large numbers of videocassettes—for example, some 100,000 loans a year at the Thousand Oaks, Calif., and Findlay-Hancock, Ohio, libraries. Robert Wedgeworth stepped down as director of the American Library Association after 13 years and was succeeded by Thomas J. Galvin, formerly dean of the University of Pittsburgh library school. During Wedgeworth's tenure, ALA membership climbed from 31,580 to 42,017. The National Commission on Libraries and Information Science estimated the number of U.S. libraries at 103,774, including the 70,854 school libraries counted in 1978.

In Europe widespread disillusionment with education was affecting the finances of university and college libraries. Librarians were being asked to provide ever more effective and efficient services, often with fewer resources. This frequently resulted from a lack of national library and information policies, which were difficult to formulate in developed countries where diverse agencies had grown up over the past 50 or more years. In less developed countries the major problems were the scarcity of hard currency and of adequate professional training. Lack of books continued to plague African countries in particular; efforts were being made to help through charities like the Ranfurly Library Service, Books for Development, and recent initiatives

A patron at the New York Public Library consults the new computerized catalog from one of 50 terminals in the system. The electronic system was to replace some ten million cards and the nearly 9,000 drawers that contained them and greatly shorten the time it took to search for a book.

JOHN MCGRAIL/TIME MAGAZINE

of the Nordic countries to provide works in science and technology.

The International Federation of Library Associations and Institutions turned its attention to the problems of transborder information flow and to another new preoccupation of librarians, conservation. While greater and better provision of books had been called for during recent decades, little account had been taken of the state of the books themselves. These, made for the past century or so of chemical papers and for the past 30 years bound in impermanent bindings, were in imminent danger of disintegrating. Conservation had therefore become a pressing concern, particularly of librarians dealing with collections of major national importance.

Library automation and on-line services for bibliographical information continued to play an increasing part in library development. There were now nearly 3,000 data-base services, covering most disciplines.

LIBYA

During 1985 Libya suffered from the slack world demand for oil and the consequent drop in prices. The value of oil exports was further eroded from midyear by the long-anticipated fall in the value of the U.S. dollar, the currency in which oil was traded. Observers put the annual level of oil revenues as low as $8 billion, compared with the peak of $23 billion in 1980. The consequences for all aspects of the economy were severe. New investment in the development of infrastructure virtually ceased as the bills for medium-term and long-term projects in industry, agriculture, and infrastructure initiated in the boom years of the late 1970s fell due. Some major projects retained a prominent place, among them the "great man-made river" water pipeline scheme for the transportation of water from the southeast of the country to the coast at the Gulf of Sidra; but the future of this project, estimated to cost a minimum of $11 billion, was precarious.

The cost of the large immigrant work force could not be sustained, and it was reported that more than 100,000 foreign workers were expelled or laid off during the year. In August an estimated 25,000 Tunisians and a smaller number of Egyptians and African nationals were ordered to leave on very short notice. Domestic consumption was also restricted, and widespread shortages were reported in the shops as a result of the disruption of imports by overseas suppliers dissatisfied by delays in payment. Restrictions on the movement of capital out of Libya were increased, and international flights were reduced.

Libyan leader Col. Muammar Al Qadhafi attempted to improve relations with the U.K. government, which had severed diplomatic relations after the shooting of a policewoman outside the Libyan People's Bureau (embassy) in April 1984. Four Britons detained in Libya since May 1984 were sent home in February 1985. The Libyans tried, unsuccessfully, to secure the release of a number of Libyans accused of involvement in a series of bombings aimed at anti-Qadhafi Libyans in London and Manchester in March 1984. Four of the accused were found guilty and given prison sentences ranging from 5 to 15 years.

A number of terrorist attacks in Rome and Bonn were directed at Libyan diplomats serving overseas and at opponents of the Qadhafi regime. In June a member of the Libyan mission to the UN was expelled from the U.S., charged with involvement in plots against Libyan dissidents there. Relations with the U.S. remained cool and deteriorated markedly at the end of the year when the U.S. accused Libya of involvement in terrorist attacks at airports in Rome and Vienna on December 27. While relations with the U.S.S.R. continued to be cordial, during Qadhafi's visit to Moscow in October it was clear that Libya's economic role was no longer as valued as it had been in the 1970s, when it had been a particularly useful customer because of its ability to settle in hard currency.

LITERATURE

The 1985 Nobel Prize for Literature was awarded to the French novelist Claude Simon. He was remembered as a representative of the *nouveau roman* ("new novel") mode of the 1950s, a method of writing without regular construction or punctuation, to give the impression of a stream of consciousness. As this technique had never been widely admired or emulated in the English-speaking world, there was a reaction of surprise at the Stockholm committee's decision and a feeling that, if it was France's turn for the prize, Marguerite Yourcenar might well have been the recipient.

United States

Fiction. Perhaps the most notable literary event in the United States during 1985 was the appearance of a new novel by William Gaddis. *Carpenter's Gothic* was his first since *JR,* which won the National Book Award in 1976, and only his third in a 30-year literary career. Although considerably briefer than its massive predecessors, *Carpenter's Gothic* certainly approached them in artfulness and originality.

Among the most enthusiastically praised fiction of the year was Anne Tyler's tenth novel, *The Accidental Tourist.* Set in her now familiar literary landscape of middle-class Baltimore, Md., Tyler's crisply written comedy of manners once again displayed her brilliant gift for rendering dialogue and the details of domestic life. Ann Beattie, another writer who had marked out a fictional territory, in her case the world of the upwardly mobile members of the baby-boom generation, returned to it in her third novel, *Love Always.* As adept as Tyler at amusing dialogue and relentless in amassing sharply observed details of everyday life among the yuppies,

(Left) Anne Tyler;
(right) Elmore Leonard

(LEFT) DIANA WALKER/TIME
MAGAZINE; (RIGHT)
THOMAS VICTOR

Beattie was less successful in making use of these gifts to delineate convincing character, and *Love Always* degenerated into self-parody.

Two of American literature's foremost practitioners of black comedy produced notable examples of the genre during the year. In *Stanley Elkin's The Magic Kingdom* the author employed his idiosyncratic prose style to brilliant comic effect on what would seem an impossible subject, a trip to Disneyland for a group of terminally ill children. *Galápagos,* the best of Kurt Vonnegut's recent novels, returned to one of his familiar themes, apocalypse. An account of the founding of a colony on one of the Galápagos Islands by the survivors of a sunken luxury liner in the wake of various planetary disasters, Vonnegut's new novel was typically inventive, digressive, and funny.

Gloria Naylor's first book, *The Women of Brewster Place,* a powerfully written series of connected short stories about the black inhabitants of a poor neighborhood, won the 1983 American Book Award for first fiction. In her ambitious and effective novel *Linden Hills,* she moved up the social ladder to explore the stressful world of upper-middle-class black professionals. *Betsey Brown,* a second novel by poet and playwright Ntozake Shange, was a vivid account of the life of a black middle-class family in St. Louis, Mo., in 1959—the year that city began to integrate its schools—seen through the eyes of its 13-year-old heroine. Full of the lyrical passages that marked her first novel, *Sassafrass, Cypress & Indigo,* it was more conventional in its storytelling than her eccentric earlier book.

The latest American writer to emerge from the confines of genre fiction and into the awareness of a larger public was Elmore Leonard, whose 19th crime novel, *Glitz,* was widely and extravagantly praised by the reviewers and spent many weeks on the best-seller list. Science-fiction writer Ursula K. Le Guin's latest novel, *Always Coming Home,* was an intriguing multimedia experiment. The entire ethnography of the Kesh, a people dwelling in the far-distant future, including everything from their myths to their recipes, was accompanied by a cassette containing the music of the Kesh, the work of composer Todd Barton.

The new celebrity among U.S. humorists was radio monologist Garrison Keillor, whose eminence was confirmed by his appearance on the cover of *Time* magazine. Keillor demonstrated a broad range of comic tone in *Lake Wobegon Days,* his account of the doings of the stoic locals in a small Minnesota town, from the poignant absurdity of the sad tale of the rise and fall of local baseball great Wally ("Hard Hands") Bunsen to the epigrammatic daffiness of his description of a religious neighbor who "thought cards were okay so long as you didn't play with a full deck." *Crows,* a fine second novel by Charles Dickinson, author of the much-praised *Waltz in Marathon,* demonstrated the same strengths as his first book—convincing, attractive, well-drawn characters, a strong pictorial quality, a droll humor, and considerable stylistic resource. His affection for the engaging eccentrics of Mozart, Wis., was as appealingly obvious as that of Keillor for Lake Wobegon, Minn.

Carolyn Chute's impressive first novel, *The Beans of Egypt, Maine,* an account of life in the rural slums of the Northeast, was an extraordinary mixture of poverty, squalor, violence, and hilarity. Louise Erdrich's first novel, *Love Medicine,* forcefully employed multiple narrators in the creation of the fictional tapestry blending past and present with which Erdrich expressed contemporary Native American life; it won the National Book Critics Circle's award for fiction. *In Country,* a first novel by Bobbie Ann Mason, dealt movingly with the legacy of the Vietnam war and confirmed the high reputation established by her first book, *Shiloh and Other Stories.*

There was continuing evidence of the revival of interest in short fiction that had marked recent American literature. E. L. Doctorow's sixth book was a collection of short fiction. *Lives of the Poets: Six Stories and a Novella* contained some of the best writing Doctorow had done. Philip Roth appended a brilliant comic novella, *The Prague Orgy,* as an epilogue to a new, single-volume edition of his three Zuckerman novels. The American Book Award for fiction went to Ellen Gilchrist's collection of short stories, *Victory over Japan.* Tobias Wolff's brief, brilliant first novel, *The Barracks Thief,* won the year's PEN/Faulkner award for fiction.

History, Biography, and Belles Lettres. The revival in popularity of narrative history continued during the year. The figures of Theodore Roosevelt and Woodrow Wilson dominated the seventh volume of Page Smith's *People's History of the United States. America Enters the World: A People's History of the Progressive Era and World War I* was a comprehensive, highly readable narrative of two critical decades during which the U.S. emerged as a world power. Well-handled narrative also dominated *The Workshop of Democracy,* the second volume of *The American Experiment,* James McGregor Burns's projected three-volume history of the U.S., which covered the period from the Civil War to the early years of the Great Depression.

Having extensively studied World War II "from the rarefied perspective of the Supreme Commander" in producing his definitive biography of Dwight D. Eisenhower, historian Stephen E. Ambrose felt the desire to get closer to the action "because at Ike's level one did not hear the guns, see the dead, feel the fear, know any combat." The result of the desire was an interesting essay in narrative history, *Pegasus Bridge: June 6, 1944,* a skillful minute-by-minute account of a single military operation, the seizure of a critical bridge in Normandy by British gliderborne troops who were the first Allied soldiers to touch French soil on D-Day. Another well-written account of World War II combat was *Iwo Jima: Legacy of Valor* by Bill D. Ross. Far larger in scope than *Pegasus Bridge,* Ross's book exhaustively considered both the background and the impact of one of the bloodiest campaigns in U.S. military history.

Perhaps the most debated book of the year was *Losing Ground: American Social Policy 1950–1980* by neoconservative intellectual Charles Murray. A compelling if tendentious piece of revisionism, it detailed its author's view that the liberal social programs that had shaped U.S. domestic politics for the last several decades had had a perverse effect. Focusing his study on American blacks, Murray amassed a great deal of data to demonstrate that, despite the fact that welfare spending was 20 times greater in 1980 than in 1950, the same period had

also seen enormous increases among blacks in unemployment, crime, and illegitimacy and decreases in educational levels and family stability. Another absorbing study of the unintended consequences of liberal social programs was J. Anthony Lukas's *Common Ground,* a brilliantly written account of what happened in Boston between 1968 and 1978 as a result of court-ordered busing to integrate the city's schools.

Hemingway: A Biography by Jeffrey Meyers was only the second full-scale life of the writer to have appeared since his death in 1961. While in no way replacing Carlos Heard Baker's massively detailed 1969 volume, *Ernest Hemingway: A Life Story,* Meyers's book was generally well done and did contain revealing new material. Peter Griffin's study, *Along with Youth: Hemingway, the Early Years,* dealt in an interesting way with the writer's childhood and youth and carried its account of Hemingway forward to the time of his first marriage. Griffin's book included five previously unpublished short stories by the young Hemingway. *Dateline: Toronto,* edited by William White, was an interesting collection of articles written by Hemingway for the *Toronto Star* between early 1920 and late 1924. Norman Mailer, whom Jeffrey Meyers termed "the hip-pocket Hemingway of our time," was himself the subject of a huge, gossipy biography by Peter Manso. *Mailer: His Life and Times* was an inevitably intriguing patchwork pieced together from the tape-recorded recollections of scores of the writer's friends and enemies. James Baldwin's *The Price of the Ticket: Collected Nonfiction, 1948–1985,* which included such polemical classics as his book-length essay from 1963, *The Fire Next Time,* gave powerful testimony to his stature as a literary stylist and social critic.

Poetry. Certainly the major event in American poetry during the year was the appearance of Allen Ginsberg's *Collected Poems 1947–1980,* which both fully displayed his evolution and achievement as a poet and offered substantial evidence of the importance of his role in the literary and political history of the last several decades. James Merrill's *Late Settings,* his tenth collection of poetry and his first since his highly regarded metaphysical epic *The Changing Light at Sandover* in 1982, was more relaxed in its virtuosity but confirmed his reputation as one of America's foremost poets. Galway Kinnell's new collection, *The Past,* his first since his Pulitzer Prize-winning *Selected Poems* in 1982, dealt strongly with Kinnell's most persistent theme, the transience of existence. In *Black Hair,* Gary Soto continued his examination of the experience of being Mexican in the U.S., but the tone of his latest verse was far less bleak than that of his earlier work. John Updike's fifth collection of poetry, *Facing Nature,* demonstrated once again his mastery of, among many other things, light verse.

Literary Awards. Pulitzer Prizes were awarded in 1985 for work published in 1984. The winners included: fiction—Alison Lurie, *Foreign Affairs;* history—Thomas K. McCraw, *The Prophets of Regulation;* biography—Kenneth Silverman, *The Life and Times of Cotton Mather;* general nonfiction—Studs Terkel, *"The Good War": An Oral History of World War Two;* poetry—Carolyn Kizer, *Yin;* drama—Stephen Sondheim and James Lapine, *Sunday in the Park with George.* The 1985 Bollingen Prize in Poetry was awarded jointly to John Ashbery and Fred Chappell. Both were honored for the body of their work. Pamela Alexander's *Navigable Waterways* was a somewhat controversial choice for Volume 80 of the prestigious Yale Series of Younger Poets. The Library of Congress named Gwendolyn Brooks as poetry consultant for 1985–86.

United Kingdom

Fiction. Among the most ambitious and impressive novels of the year were three historical romances, all of them expressing or implying strong views about the 20th century. *Gentlemen in England,* by the often mordant and morbid A. N. Wilson, expressed a real affection for the year 1880, which he found preferable to the present day. "Gentlemen in England now a-bed," he began (quoting *Henry V*), "Shall think themselves accurs'd they were not here"—in 1880. The hero of the story was Lionel Nettleship, a young man striving to become a priest in the Church of England, against the will of his atheistic father, a learned geologist. Arguments and eccentricities within the Anglican Church and its Catholic Revival combined with tales of 19th-century painting, courtship, and simple gossip to present an agreeable and historically credible reconstruction.

With *A Maggot* John Fowles offered a historical mystery about the disappearance of a dissident, visionary young nobleman while traveling with a prostitute, a mute manservant, and two men of the London theater in the year 1736. The manservant is found hanged, prompting a legal inquiry into his death. Much of the book was presented in the form of an 18th-century report of a lawyer's interrogation, credibly imitated by the author. The title referred to the archaic use of the word maggot to mean a whim or a quirk. Nevertheless, the word maggot was used in at least two different senses in the book, helping *A Maggot* to take on a persuasively occult or metaphysical authority.

Also set in the 18th century, for the most part, was Peter Ackroyd's eerie mystery *Hawksmoor,* concerning a 20th-century policeman of that name (which was also the name of an 18th-century church architect) investigating a series of child murders that somehow relate to the satanic activities of another 18th-century church architect. This complex, unhinging story gave many readers horrid but pleasurable thrills, and it was one of the winners of the important Whitbread Prize.

Iris Murdoch, with *The Good Apprentice,* offered a novel about a group of confused people, unsure about the meaning and use of the words good and evil in a world without God. The godless ones, wrote Victoria Glendinning, "all want to worship, to confess . . . and they turn to spiritualism, . . . or to sex, romantic love, drugs or psychiatry. . . . Stuart, who wants to be good without recourse to any such devices, operates in a sterile vacuum until he realizes that he can't begin to be good without recognizing his capacity for evil. Stuart is the good apprentice who, like Doris Lessing's 'good terrorist,' has got it all a bit wrong." This was a novel with relevance to Murdoch's work as a scholarly philosopher.

Discovered in the archives of Metro-Goldwyn-Mayer was a novel by Graham Greene, written in

(Left) Garrison Keillor; (right) Grace Paley

PAUL ORENSTEIN

Robertson Davies

1944 as the draft for a film script. It was published as *The Tenth Man,* with a preface by Greene, who was surprised to find "this forgotten story very readable—indeed I prefer it in many ways to *The Third Man.*" It was the story of a Frenchman called Charlot (the French name for Charlie Chaplin), held as a hostage during the Nazi occupation, making a disgraceful bargain to save his life and finally making a good death. The pressure of Roman Catholicism in the story disconcerted many critics but did not detract from its appeal to the general reader.

Lives, Letters. To commemorate the career of Earl Mountbatten, assassinated by Irish terrorists in 1979, Philip Ziegler offered *Mountbatten: The Official Biography.* Roy Jenkins, a former home secretary, opined that "Mountbatten, for good or ill, was decisive in replacing the old, fairly tight-knit white family with the loose new multi-racial Commonwealth."

Winston Churchill, inevitably, was prominent again in *The Fringes of Power,* diaries kept between 1939 and 1955 by his secretary, Sir John Colville. The published diaries of poet Stephen Spender also had a strong political tinge, taking him from his pro-Communist youth in prewar Germany through his work for the anti-Communist journal *Encounter* and his international campaigning against political censorship.

There were new lives of two British cardinals of the Roman Catholic Church, Henry Manning and Arthur Hinsley, two composers, Schubert and Schumann, and two Victorian prophets, Charles Darwin and John Ruskin. Tim Hilton's *John Ruskin: The Early Years, 1819–1859* was especially admired. With *Chaplin: His Life and Art* David Robinson added a weighty tome to the library of books about the great man. Robinson's book looked like the definitive biography, the end of the whole story, but immediately after its publication some long-lost reels of old Chaplin movies were discovered, thus adding new material for future writers. Another distinguished actor, Sir Alec Guinness, presented his memoirs as *Blessings in Disguise,* with characteristic elegance and mysterious self-effacement.

Among the new series of feminine biographies was "Lives of Modern Women," which got off to a good start with four books (all by women) about the novelists Jean Rhys and Rebecca West, the singer Bessie Smith, and the intrepid traveler and Arabist Freya Stark. The collected letters of Dylan Thomas were published and mocked by Kingsley Amis for their "lyric flights of imitation pathos and real cadging," reminding readers of a good, new, Amis-like novel about Thomas-haunted Swansea, *Banana Cat* by Christopher Hood.

Poetry. Sir Stephen Spender published, as well as his diaries, a new version of his *Collected Poems,* much trimmed and refined, and his translation, as a stage version, of three plays by Sophocles to be performed together in one evening. Ted Hughes, the new poet laureate, published two poems of public statement and national concern. One addressed the issue of conservation, supporting Prince Philip's argument that to "preserve" game birds for shooting parties was a reputable and coherent policy. The other, "For the Duration," concerned an old soldier whose grim silence about his wartime exploits combined with his nighttime shouting during nightmares to suggest that "his war was more unbearable than anybody else's."

Canada

It was exciting to see how Canada's social and cultural mosaic was increasingly reflected in the works of new writers. In 1985, for example, there were *Digging Up the Mountains: Selected Stories* by Neil Bissoondath, with stories set in the West Indies, Canada, and anonymously violent countries throughout the world; a different slant on the experience of West Indians in Canada in the eight stories comprising Austin Clarke's *When Women Rule;* and *Darkness* by Bharati Mukherjee, another collection of short stories, in which the cruelty of some Canadians toward people from Pakistan and India is incised on the reader's consciousness with ironic precision. Books dealing with the experiences of European immigrants in Canada included *My Harp Has Turned to Mourning,* Al Reimer's poignant exploration of the ways in which Mennonites adapted—or did not adapt—to their new lives.

Other significant prose works published during the year were Janette Turner Hospital's third novel, *Borderline,* in which two strangers, meeting at the

Canadian border, create an international incident out of a flurry of misunderstandings; Margaret Atwood's *The Handmaid's Tale,* a grim fable of the puritanical theocratic dictatorship that could develop if certain current trends were taken to one of their possible logical extremes; and Ann Ireland's *A Certain Mr. Takahashi,* winner of the 1985 Seal First Novel Award. There were also new works by Hugh Hood, a collection of short stories and a novella entitled *August Nights;* David Donnell, *The Blue Ontario Hemingway Boat Race,* in which the protagonist of a series of linked stories is based on Hemingway during the 1920s when he worked on the *Toronto Star;* Mavis Gallant, *Overhead in a Balloon: Stories of Paris;* Robert Harlow, *Felice: A Travelogue;* and Edna Alford, *The Garden of Eloise Loon.*

Notable new poetry collections included Phyllis Webb's *Water and Light: Ghazals and Anti Ghazals,* an imaginative gambol through the rigors of poetic form; Doug Fetherling's *Variorum: New Poems and Old, 1965–1985,* dissecting his subjects with a critical eye and a manic tongue; *Silk Trail* by Andrew Suknaski, contrasting the high sheen of Chinese culture with the harsher aesthetic of the West; P. K. Page's *The Glass Air: Poems Selected and New,* containing eight of her drawings as well; *A Linen Crow—A Caftan Magpie,* in which Patrick Lane provides much lyrical material for thought; Anne Marriott's explorations of connections from both psychic and physical distances in *Letters from Some Island;* Joy Kogawa's haunting evocations of the primitive within each of us in *Woman in the Woods;* and Joe Rosenblatt's *Poetry Hotel: Selected Poems 1963–1983,* containing some of his best and most whimsical works. Robert Kroetsch fearlessly continued to give *Advice to My Friends,* while Erin Mouré waxed incandescent on love in *Domestic Fuel.* In bill bissett's *Canada Geese Mate for Life,* the great white light of urban consciousness is refracted through the poet's crystal of introspection. Lorna Crozier creates an equally brilliant scene in *The Garden Going On Without Us.*

Ursula K. Le Guin

LITERATURE FOR CHILDREN

Despite the buffeting of the publishing industry by mergers and takeovers, high prices, and terminal attrition of backlists, once the solid base of children's book publishing, the industry flourished. Enough specialty book stores existed to have led to the formation, in 1985, of the Association for Booksellers to Children. The numbers of new titles, both hardbound and paperback, stayed at the level of the previous year, while prices rose. Also continued were trends of the previous year in format (toy books, pop-ups, board books) and in subjects such as child abuse, sugary romance, nuclear war, frontiers in science, and handicaps. There was an encouraging surge of high-quality fantasy.

For Younger Readers

The simplicity and directness of traditional tales have a perennial appeal to young children, and some of the most familiar appear in Helen Oxenbury's *The Helen Oxenbury Nursery Story Book.* Another new edition was Charles Perrault's *Cinderella,* smoothly adapted by Amy Ehrlich and handsomely illustrated by Susan Jeffers. A less well-known story is a tale of unselfish brotherly love, Florence Freedman's retelling of *Brothers: A Hebrew Legend,* illustrated by the sensitive paintings of Robert Andrew Parker.

Among the best of the new stories of modern fantasy for younger children was Chris Van Allsburg's *Polar Express,* in which a visit to Santa Claus is capably told and is illustrated with paintings of breathtaking beauty and power. In a similar style of illustration, Antony Browne tells a touching story of a child's need for love in *Gorilla.* Humor plays a large part in *Hazel's Amazing Mother* by Rosemary Wells.

There were several good poetry books for very young children. One was Arnold Lobel's *Whiskers and Rhymes,* with verses that are lilting, brief, and occasionally in parody of Mother Goose rhymes. Animal poems, simple and brief, are often humorous in Karla Kuskin's *Something Sleeping in the Hall. The Oxford Book of Children's Verse in America,* edited by Donald Hall, should appeal to readers of all ages.

Realistic stories for younger children reflect the way in which their circle of awareness widens, from home to the extended family and then to school and friends. Shirley Hughes, a skilled author as well as artist, in *An Evening at Alfie's* tells a cheerful story about a babysitter who capably copes with a household emergency. Exuberant color pencil drawings by Stephen Gammell illustrate a story about a family visit, *The Relatives Came,* told by Cynthia Rylant with affection and humor. Riki Levinson's *Watch the Stars Come Out* extends concepts of time as a child listens to her grandmother tell the story of her own mother's immigration to America as a small child.

As there were for readers of all ages, there were

SAINT GEORGE AND THE DRAGON ADAPTED BY MARGARET HODGES © 1984 LITTLE, BROWN AND COMPANY

Saint George and the Dragon, *adapted by Margaret Hodges and illustrated by Trina Schart Hyman, received the American Library Association's 1985 Caldecott Medal for illustration.*

several books about child abuse for the read-aloud group. One of the best was Betty Boegehold's *You Can Say "No": A Book About Protecting Yourself,* which is candid but not frightening.

Since many children are introduced to computers at the kindergarten level, they should appreciate a book that is written simply and authoritatively: Seymour Simon's *How to Talk to Your Computer.* An excellent introduction to large numbers is *How Much Is a Million?* by David Schwartz, whose vivid examples are imaginatively interpreted in drawings by Steven Kellogg.

For the 8–11 Group

Few books of folktales for the middle grades, the greatest consumers of this genre, have substantial illustration; an exception is *The People Could Fly: American Black Folk Tales,* in which material from a number of sources is beautifully retold by Virginia Hamilton and handsomely illustrated by Leo and Diane Dillon. A noted British author, Alan Garner, has fluently adapted over 20 stories in rich and varied styles in *Alan Garner's Book of British Fairy Tales.* Children looking for active female protagonists will find them in *The Woman in the Moon and Other Tales of Forgotten Heroines,* in which James Riordan has compiled stories from many parts of the world. *The Random House Book of Fairy Tales* has romantic pictures by Diane Goode for a selection of old favorites adapted by Amy Ehrlich.

Diana Wynne Jones consistently produced books that are polished in style, inventive in plot, and sound in structure; her book of short stories *Warlock at the Wheel and Other Stories,* is exemplary fantasy. Another fine collection of tales was *Uninvited Ghosts and Other Stories* by Penelope Lively.

Of the poetry books published in 1985 for this age group, among the best were John Ciardi's *Doodle Soup,* a mixture of narrative poems and poetic jokes; the humor in Felice Holman's *The Song in My Head* is of a gentler kind, with poems that are often written from a childs' viewpoint.

There was a broad range of realistic fiction for this age group, from brief stories like Eth Clifford's *The Remembering Box,* a touching testament to the love between a small boy and his grandmother, to the intricate subtlety of Nina Bawden's *The Finding,* the story of an orphaned child who runs away in the mistaken belief that he is protecting his family.

Historical fiction was a genre that seemed to be gaining popularity. An outstanding example was Patricia MacLachlan's *Sarah, Plain and Tall,* the story of a mail-order bride who wins the hearts of the prairie family with whom she is spending a trial period. Another fine book was *The Bombers' Moon* by Betty Vander Els, in which two children of a missionary family are sent away from danger during the Japanese invasion of China in 1942.

It is not easy to write a biography that is simple, thoughtful, and comprehensible about a philosopher like Henry Thoreau, but in *A Man Named Thoreau* Robert Burleigh did just that by clarifying concepts and showing how they are pertinent today. In contrast, Janet Caulkins wrote about a contemporary figure in *A Picture Life of Mikhail Gorbachev.* It is a useful book, a balanced account that is respectful but that lacks the adulatory note that mars so many biographies for younger children.

Indicative of the broadening range of interests for this middle group of readers are some informational books that are typical of the best in nonfiction writing. In Nate Aaseng's *Baseball: It's Your Team* the reader is presented with a series of problems (real major league teams, real problems) and asked to make a choice of proffered solutions. Photographs by Christopher Knight extend Kathryn Lasky's informative text, *Puppeteer,* about a man who makes hand puppets, Paul Davis, and about the mounting of a production. Of the many fine books commemorating the centennial of the Statue of Liberty, Mary Shapiro's *How They Built the Statue of Liberty* was one of the most outstanding, in large part because of the detailed drawings of the statue's construction by Huck Scarry.

For Older Adolescents

Of the more effective fantasies of 1985 for older readers, several relate to nuclear war. In *Children of the Dust* by Louise Lawrence, the few survivors of a series of atom bomb attacks struggle to exist in an almost sterile universe and find that some of the mutants they have spurned have made a better adjustment than they have. Stories about shifts in time were plentiful and popular; Lois Duncan's *Locked in Time* has an unusual twist as the protagonist slowly comes to realize that the woman her father has married (and the woman's two children) are immortal and have existed through a string of murdered husbands used for cover. Another unusual story is *BAAA* by David Macaulay. In a world in which people have disappeared, sheep go through the cycle of becoming civilized and then moving toward their self-destruction. It is barbed, but both text and illustrations are very funny.

Among the books of realistic fiction was an outstanding volume of short stories, Janni Howker's *Badger on the Barge and Other Stories,* in which the young protagonist of each story has a special relationship, subtly perceptive, with an elderly person. Two other books are also more concerned with relationships than plot although both are adequately structured. One is about a family of country music singers, Katherine Paterson's *Come Sing, Jimmy Jo.* In *Thunderbird* by Marilyn Sachs there is a nice role switch, for it is Tina whose hobby is repairing cars and Dennis, intellectual and activist, who cannot tell one car from another.

An unusual historical novel is *Mountain Light* by Laurence Yep; it is set in China in the mid-19th century, and it has a broad sweep of action and strong characters whose adventures reveal rather than compete with the historical background of martial conflict in China and racial conflict encountered in the United States after the hero emigrates. Set earlier in the century, Paul Fleischman's *Coming-and-Going Men* has four linked stories about traveling men who go to a small Vermont town, each making a deep impression on at least one of the residents.

Like the book about the Statue of Liberty cited earlier for the middle group, Leonard Fisher's *The Statue of Liberty* gives excellent background information based on plentiful source material; here there is fine illustration and many photographs. With the passing of Halley's Comet, many books appeared on the subject during the year. Isaac Asimov's *Asimov's Guide to Halley's Comet* is perhaps the most informative among them, since it gives

scientific information that is both accurate and comprehensive and is written in a casual, conversational style. Problems and issues in our society were often addressed in books for older children; among them this year was *Dark Harvest: Migrant Farmworkers in America.* Using information based on research and interviews, Brent Ashabranner presents the devastating facts about migrants' lives. Its incisive text is complemented by Paul Conklin's excellent photographs. One of the year's outstanding biographies was James Lincoln Collier's *Louis Armstrong: An American Success Story.* It is written with candor, enthusiasm, and an appreciation of Armstrong's importance in jazz history.

Awards

The Book of the Year for Children Award given by the Canadian Library Association was conferred on Jean Little for *Mama's Going to Buy You a Mockingbird.* The Canadian prize for illustration, the Amelia Frances Howard-Gibbon Award, went to Ian Wallace for *Chin Chiang and the Dragon's Dance.* The award given every three years by the National Council of Teachers of English to a children's poet went to Lilian Moore for the body of her work. The award given by the International Reading Association to an author for a first or second book went to Janni Howker for *Badger on the Barge and Other Stories.*

Robin McKinley's The Hero and the Crown *won the 1985 Newbery Medal for the most distinguished contribution to children's literature.*

THE HERO AND THE CROWN BY ROBIN MCKINLEY © 1984
GREENWILLOW BOOKS

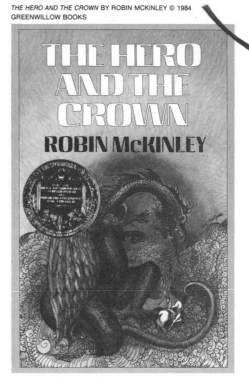

MACHINERY AND MACHINE TOOLS

Worldwide machine-tool production was estimated to have totaled $20 billion in 1984. This was up slightly from $19.4 billion in 1983 but below the high of $26.5 billion reached in 1980. In 1984 Japan accounted for $4.5 billion of the total, while the Soviet Union ranked second with production estimated at nearly $3 billion. Third was West Germany with production of $2.8 billion, while the United States was fourth with $2.4 billion.

The U.S. total was down from the high of $5.1 billion in 1981 but up from the $2.1 billion of 1983. Orders for U.S.-built machine tools in 1984, as contrasted to shipments, totaled $2.9 billion. This included $1.9 billion in orders for metal-cutting machines such as lathes, milling machines, and drilling machines and $1 billion for metal-forming machines such as brakes, presses, and shears. Total orders and exports of U.S.-built machine tools in the first half of 1985 remained at about the same levels as for the first half of 1984, but shipments were up about 10% and imports rose 48%.

Imports of machine tools to the U.S. during the first half of 1985 totaled $880 million and were supplied principally by Japan, West Germany, Taiwan, and the United Kingdom in that order. Imports from Japan in that period totaled $450 million, up 50% from the first half of 1984. Imports from West Germany during the first half of 1985 reached nearly $120 million, an increase of more than 40% over the first half of 1984. Imports from Taiwan, which were predominantly metal-cutting machines, rose over 60% from 1984 to $78 million. U.S. imports from the United Kingdom during the first half of 1985 rose about 33% from the prior year's level, to nearly $48 million.

Exports of U.S.-built machine tools during the first half of 1985 had a total value of approximately $200 million and were primarily to Canada, Mexico, the United Kingdom, Japan, Singapore, and China. Exports to Canada, exceeding $38 million, accounted for nearly 20% of the total. Exports to Mexico were 12% of the total, while the United Kingdom and Japan each accounted for 8%.

The technology of machine tools had advanced considerably during recent years with the advent of better metal-cutting materials, the use of less vibration-prone machine-tool structures designed by computers, the use of advanced servomechanisms to control the relative positions of tools and workpieces, and the development of techniques for efficient integration and common control of machine tools, tool-changing mechanisms, material-handling systems, and workpiece inspection equipment. These advances in the design and technology of computers and factory communications systems allowed many machine tools to be combined into commonly controlled cells and systems, and these, in turn, allowed the concept of the unattended or nearly unattended manufacturing facility to become a reality.

MAGAZINES

Court cases dominated magazine news during the year. In 1979 *The Nation* had published an article based on the memoirs of former U.S. Pres. Gerald Ford, which were copyrighted by the book publisher Harper & Row. In 1985 the U.S. Supreme Court ruled that *The Nation* had infringed the copyright law, thus overturning a Court of Appeals ruling that the use by *The Nation* of 300 words from the memoirs constituted "fair use." *The Nation* claimed that public officials had no right to withhold public information for profit, but the court said that what was being protected was Ford's own personal viewpoint.

Time scored only a partial victory over Gen. Ariel Sharon. The end of the trial found that the magazine was guilty of "false and defamatory" accusations against the former defense minister of Israel but was innocent of libel. Soon after General Sharon lost his $50 million libel suit, a second general, William Westmoreland, dropped his $120 million suit against CBS.

The thousands of investment newsletters apparently need not worry about libel. Where no malice is intended, a newsletter may advise someone not to invest in a particular stock, bond, or other financial instrument. This was the ruling by a federal judge, who said that negative ratings by the *Hulbert Financial Digest* were not libelous.

Considered by many to be the world's best general magazine, *The New Yorker* had its 60 years of independence ended when it was bought in 1985 by Samuel I. Newhouse, Jr., for $142 million. The arbiter of good taste and superior fiction was guaranteed continued freedom by the new owner, and its well-known editor, William Shawn, was retained. Among other major sales was the $362 million purchase of the Ziff-Davis Publishing Co. by CBS. The magazine titles that CBS thus acquired included *Car and Driver, Modern Bride, Stereo Review,* and *Yachting.*

Most magazines reporting to the Audit Bureau of Circulation noted circulation increases for the second half of 1984 and continued gains in 1985. Subscription gains were posted by 65% of the magazines, but 53% reported declines in single-copy (at the newsstand) sales.

In the 1985 National Magazine Awards, *American Heritage* and *The Washingtonian* magazine led the ten winners. *The Washingtonian* won for public service and for an article on medical care. *American Heritage* won for general excellence and the best single-topic issue, on medicine. Among the other winners were *Time* and *American Health* for general excellence, *Texas Monthly* for reporting, and *Life* for photography.

Essence, the first magazine for black women, celebrated its 15th birthday in 1985. With a circulation of more than 800,000, it covered such subjects as fashion, beauty, food, health, and child care from a black perspective.

COVER PHOTOGRAPH BY BILL WEEMS

GEO, *a glossy rival to* National Geographic *and* Smithsonian, *ceased publication in February 1985.*

Among the new entries of the year were *Manhattan, inc.,* the first magazine in the U.S. published expressly for Yuppies (young urban professionals). It told those with an income of at least $50,000 how to dress for success and make the right connections. Among the failures during the year was *GEO,* a glossy rival to *National Geographic* and *Smithsonian* brought to the United States in 1979 by a German publisher. After six years it ceased publication because of heavy costs and persistent inability to gain U.S. readers.

For the second year in a row, *McCall's* was the best place for a free-lance writer to place an article. According to a *Writer's Digest* poll, the magazine paid a minimum of $1.25 a word, compared with *Redbook,* which paid a minimum of 25 cents but a maximum of $2. Among other top markets were *Reader's Digest,* the *New York Times Magazine, Travel & Leisure,* and *Sports Afield.*

The British magazine market continued to ride a wave of activity, and several new titles were introduced in 1985. There were some notable failures, too, and the year ended with a clear indication of strain as International Publishing Corp. (IPC) Magazines, the biggest publisher in the market, announced a package of economies including a list of specialist titles to be eliminated or offered for staff buyout. This confirmed the trend in which smaller energetic publishing operations were scoring greater successes than the giant created in the 1960s; one

of IPC's new titles, *The Hit,* aimed at the teenage male market, ceased publishing after six weeks.

The main center of activity continued to be the younger woman. IPC and the D. C. Thomson group launched new titles aimed at teenage girls, *Mizz* and *Etcetera,* respectively. Each made respectable debuts, but the star continued to be East Midlands Allied Press's (EMAP's) *Just Seventeen,* launched in 1983 as a fortnightly with spectacular success and switched to weekly publication in February 1985 without denting its upward sales graph. In September EMAP introduced *Looks,* aimed at picking up the sister magazine's readers as they grew out of it.

Publishers had been awaiting a decision from official regulatory bodies that had been considering the practice whereby the British Broadcasting Corporation (BBC) and Independent Television (ITV) could claim a copyright on their schedules, thereby protecting their own *Radio Times* (BBC) and *TV Times* (ITV) as the largest and most profitable magazines in the country. Several contenders hoped to have the chance to run an equivalent of the U.S.'s *TV Guide.* However, the networks' copyright was upheld.

She celebrated its 30th anniversary and *The Lady* ("A Journal for Gentlewomen") its 100th, while the 143-year-old *Illustrated London News* was bought from International Thomson Publishing Ltd. by U.S. businessman James Sherwood. A famous French title spread its wings. *Elle,* the Paris-based fashion magazine published by Hachette, introduced English-language editions in the U.S. and the U.K. through a deal with the Murdoch empire.

In West Germany Gerd Heidemann and Konrad Kujau were convicted on charges arising from the 1983 "Hitler Diaries" fraud perpetrated on *Stern* magazine. They received prison sentences of more than four years but were released pending appeal.

MALAYSIA

Though Malaysian Prime Minister Mahathir bin Mohamad was not required to call general elections until April 1987, he had been expected to do so before the end of 1985. The chief reason that he did not was the continuation throughout the year of a bitter leadership dispute within the Malaysian Chinese Association (MCA), the country's largest Chinese-based political party and a key member of the ruling National Front coalition. The MCA feud was touched off in March 1984 when Neo Yee Pan was challenged for the job of party president by his deputy and rival, Tan Koon Swan. In February 1985 an accord was signed in which Neo agreed to reinstate Tan and 13 of his associates in the party and to clean up the party membership rolls, while Tan promised not to contest the MCA presidency in party elections to be held later in the year.

By April, however, the rivals were again publicly blaming each other for breaching terms of understanding over the question of the party rolls. Under the mediation of National Front leaders, they set-

REUTERS/BETTMANN NEWSPHOTOS

A patrol of Malaysian soldiers keeps watch on the road leading to Betong, Thailand. The frontier crossing was heavily used by Communist guerrillas.

tled on a second compromise in May; Tan would withdraw a proposed motion of no confidence in Neo, a special committee would be formed to clean up membership lists, and the MCA presidential election would be open to all contestants, including Tan. When barely three months later disagreements between Neo and another party stalwart, Mak Hon Kam, again split the MCA, Mahathir dismissed Neo from his Cabinet post as minister of housing and local government, and the MCA was given a three-month period to put its house in order.

Prime Minister Mahathir's standing within his own United Malays National Organization (UMNO), the dominant party within the National Front, remained strong. Moderation emerged as the country's political keynote—a trend that influenced even the fundamentalist Partai Islam.

An unexpected political storm blew up in the state of Sabah. In state assembly elections held in April the ruling Berjaya Party of Chief Minister Harris Salleh was defeated by the Partai Bersatu Sabah (Sabah United Party; PBS), a new grouping led by Joseph Pairin Kitingan. The PBS took 25 seats, while Berjaya dropped from its previous tally of 44 to 6, and the United Sabah National Organization (USNO) garnered 16. The success of PBS was attributed by analysts to the growing feelings of alienation and discrimination among Christian Kadazans, Sabah's largest single ethnic community.

Like many less developed countries, Malaysia felt the economic impact of sluggish commodity prices. The gross domestic product was expected to achieve a 4–5% growth in 1985, compared with 7.3% a year earlier. In the first quarter government debt increased slightly, but external debt declined by a small amount for the first time. Inflation remained low at just over 4%.

Prime Minister Mahathir paid an official visit to China in November.

MATHEMATICS

An important new discovery in topology during the year illustrated the increasing use of computers in mathematics. David A. Hoffman of the University of Massachusetts and William Meeks III of Rice University, Houston, Texas, found a third type of "minimal" surface—the first such surface discovered in nearly 200 years—and they did it with the help of a sophisticated computer graphics program that showed them what the surface looked like.

Minimal surfaces are surfaces that span a given curve with the minimum possible surface area. A soap film stretched across a wire frame automatically assumes the shape of a minimal surface. While there are an infinite number of such minimal surfaces, only a very few fit certain mathematical restrictions, such as "completeness" and "embeddedness." A complete surface is one that extends to infinity, such as a plane, and an embedded surface is one that does not fold back or intersect itself.

Until recently, only two embedded, complete minimal surfaces were known: the catenoid, the surface created by stretching a film between two parallel circles as the circles are moved to an infinite distance, and the helicoid, the surface stretching along the curve of an infinitely long helix or spiral. Some mathematicians thought that these might be the only such surfaces possible.

But Hoffman suspected otherwise. He started with a surface defined by a Brazilian graduate student, Celso J. Costa, which the student had proved was minimal and complete. The surface extended to infinity at two ends and around its middle— like a plane joined to a catenoid. But it was not clear from the equations whether the surface intersected itself or was embedded. With the help of a computer graphics program, Hoffman was able to plot the surface on a computer screen as if it were

A third type of "embedded minimal surface" was discovered in 1985. Computer graphics aided in visualizing the equations that define the surface.

© 1985 DAVID HOFFMAN AND JAMES T. HOFFMAN

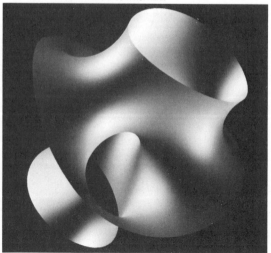

a real object. By viewing the surface from various angles, he could see that it was indeed embedded. The computer-generated image gave Hoffman and Meeks enough clues to formulate a mathematical proof that the surface was embedded. They went on to show the existence of infinitely many examples of this type of surface.

A second major development in topology during the year concerned distinguishing between different kinds of knots. Topologists define a knot as any simple closed curve embedded in a three-dimensional space. This definition means, in part, that topological knots have no free ends, unlike knots tied with rope. Two topological knots are equivalent if there is some way of bending and twisting them, without breaking them, so that one knot is transformed into the other.

In the past, topologists had come up with ways of determining in advance if two knots were equivalent. Starting in the 1920s they discovered ways of associating a polynomial with a certain type of knot (such as t^2-t+1, the polynomial for the trefoil). If two knots had the same polynomial, they were equivalent. The polynomial was termed an invariant because it did not change when the knot was transformed.

However, the key previously existing polynomials, the Alexander and Jones polynomials, could not be used to distinguish among all known knots. The newly developed polynomials can. Each knot is associated with a unique function P, which is a polynomial in three variables (such as $x^{-2}z^2-2x^{-1}y-x^{-2}y^2$, which is the polynomial for a left-handed trefoil).

The new polynomials were not only more useful but also simpler and easier to use than the old ones. Yet the ideas involved seemed, to topologists, so simple that they could have been discovered many years earlier. The discovery seemed to be an extreme case of an idea whose time had come. In a period of a few days in late 1984, the *Bulletin of the American Mathematical Society* received papers from four separate authors or teams, each describing the same discovery of the polynomials. It was clear that the six mathematicians (Peter Freyd and David Yetter; Jim Hoste; W. B. R. Lickorish and Kenneth C. Millett; and A. Ocneanu) had arrived at the discovery independently. Each paper used a different proof and elaborated the main theorems in separate ways. When informed of the coincidence the six cooperated on a joint paper published in early 1985. A fifth proof, submitted by a pair from Poland, arrived too late because of slow mail to be included in the group paper.

MEDICINE

The health and medicine news in 1985 was dominated largely by the acquired immune deficiency syndrome (AIDS). It was the fourth year since the disease had been recognized and named, and the number of AIDS victims had at least doubled in each subsequent year. By December 1985 nearly 16,000 AIDS cases had been reported in the U.S.; more than 8,000 Americans had died from AIDS, and an estimated 50,000–100,000 showed possible early signs of the disease—the "AIDS-related complex," or ARC. In March the U.S. Food and Drug Administration (FDA) licensed a test to be used to screen all blood donors for the AIDS virus (HTLV-III, also called LAV). It was estimated that as many as one million people in the U.S. had antibodies to AIDS in their blood, an indication that they had been exposed to the virus. According to the U.S. Centers for Disease Control (CDC), 5 to 10% of homosexual men who had positive blood tests for viral antibodies would develop the full-blown disease within three to five years. By this sort of calculation, 100,000 people in the U.S. alone might come down with AIDS in the next five years. The campaign to find better treatment methods and, ultimately, a vaccine to prevent AIDS was given tremendous added impetus by the death in October of film star Rock Hudson, the first celebrity to become an acknowledged victim of the disease.

The spread of AIDS in Great Britain and other parts of Europe paralleled the earlier development of the epidemic in the U.S. As the epidemic spread, it was becoming clear that the disease was not confined to homosexual men, intravenous drug users, and hemophiliacs and other recipients of blood or blood products—the first major groups to be identified. The disease was also appearing in children of AIDS patients and persons at risk and in sexual partners of patients and people in high-risk groups. Several studies indicated that the prevalence of AIDS antibodies in female prostitutes—many of whom are also drug abusers—was considerably higher than in the general population. A study conducted by the U.S. Army identified a number of cases of AIDS in military personnel in which heterosexual contact was the sole identifiable risk factor. The possibility that the virus could be transmitted through heterosexual relations was further substantiated by reports from Africa, which showed almost equal numbers of men and women affected by the disease.

Several findings published during the year further extended the scientific knowledge about AIDS. One of the discoverers of the AIDS virus, Robert Gallo, and his colleagues found the virus in the tears of one out of seven AIDS patients tested. The investigators concluded that although no transmission of disease had been traced to this source of virus, professionals concerned with eye care and treatment should minimize direct contact with tears. Researchers at several institutions reported the discovery of virus in the cerebrospinal fluid and brain tissue of AIDS patients. These findings raised the prospect that the virus can infect cells other than lymphocytes (the type of white blood cell characteristically attacked by the virus).

Although medical investigators and government

health officials emphasized that AIDS is not a casually transmitted disease and that it is spread through contact with a patient's body fluids, fear of the disease gripped portions of the U.S. public. The Pentagon announced that it would begin testing all military personnel for antibodies to the AIDS virus. For the first time, parents and school boards grappled with the problem of whether to allow children with AIDS to attend regular classes in public schools. In New York City a decision by officials to allow a seven-year-old AIDS victim to attend classes led to a boycott involving some 12,000 students. Other school boards reached varying decisions on how to treat children with AIDS—some decided to bar them from the schools; others agreed to consider the question on a case-by-case basis.

Public concern in Great Britain also spurred government action. New regulations enacted in 1985 gave British magistrates increased authority to protect the public from AIDS. These included the power for local authorities to order hospitalization of an AIDS patient and to prevent relatives of a deceased AIDS victim from taking possession of the body.

In the U.S. one consequence of public awareness of the AIDS threat was that people were apparently changing their behavior to avoid exposure. The most profound change was among homosexual men, more and more of whom were reportedly using condoms, avoiding multiple sexual relationships, and avoiding bathhouses and other sites of casual encounters. Many heterosexuals also seemed to be reevaluating their attitudes toward casual sex, and the incidence of venereal disease generally declined during the year.

Heart Disease

The artificial heart was a center of controversy in 1985 as researchers and medical ethicists began

President and Mrs. Ronald Reagan greet well-wishers from the window of the hospital room where he was recovering from surgery to remove a cancerous polyp.

AP/WIDE WORLD

to question the high incidence of complications in recipients of the device. By year's end, surgeon William C. DeVries of the Humana Heart Institute in Louisville, Ky., had implanted permanent artificial hearts in four patients, all of whom had suffered from complications involving bleeding and blood clots. A Swedish man who had been making remarkable progress in the six months since he had been given a Jarvik-7 heart (the same kind used by DeVries) suffered a stroke in September and subsequently died.

Despite these setbacks, supporters of the artificial heart argued that it might at least prove useful as a temporary device to keep a patient alive until a human heart could be found. Critics said that unless the problems could be resolved, even this use would remain questionable. In late August physicians at the University Medical Center in Tucson, Ariz., implanted an artificial heart in a 25-year-old man, Michael Drummond, to tide him over until a suitable human heart could be found. Drummond subsequently suffered a series of strokes that impaired his speech and led his doctors to speed up the search for a human heart; he received a transplanted human heart within ten days of the implantation of the artificial heart.

As a result of Drummond's experience, however, researchers thought they had discovered one cause of the problems with the artificial device. After examining the heart removed from Drummond, Donald Olsen of the University of Utah concluded that a plastic connection between the artificial heart and Drummond's artery was the source of the clotting problems that may have caused strokes in the artificial heart patients. Olsen planned to begin testing a new connecting system in animals, and Robert Jarvik, inventor of the Jarvik-7, the most widely used artificial heart, said he was considering some design changes in the device. In October a man awaiting human heart transplantation received a temporary implant from doctors at the Pennsylvania State University Medical Center. The device used in this case—a slightly different model known as the "Penn State heart"—functioned satisfactorily for the 11 days that elapsed before a suitable human heart was found, but the patient died several days after receiving the transplanted human organ.

Several major studies concluded during the year extended the knowledge of coronary heart disease and its prevention. An analysis of middle-aged men in Boston and Ireland showed that those who for 20 years had been consuming a diet high in saturated fats and cholesterol were more likely to have suffered a fatal heart attack during the intervening period. The influence of diet on heart disease was confirmed by several other studies. In one, the Leiden Intervention Trial, 39 patients with stable angina pectoris (chest pain) and evidence of an arteriosclerotic lesion were monitored over a two-year period during which they ate a vegetarian diet low in cholesterol and high in polyunsaturated fats.

Ryan White (left), who contracted AIDS through a blood transfusion, was refused admittance to a Kokomo, Indiana, school in August. A special telephone line was installed to allow him to take part in his seventh-grade classes, but neither he nor his mother thought it an adequate substitute for the classroom.

UPI/BETTMANN NEWSPHOTOS

Eighteen of the 39 experienced no worsening of the arteriosclerosis.

The health value of fish received considerable attention during the year. Investigators in The Netherlands and the U.S. suggested that people could reduce their risk of succumbing to heart attack by increasing their intake of fish oils. Even the consumption of only one or two servings of fish per week might confer a protective effect. The 1985 Nobel Prize for Physiology or Medicine was awarded to Joseph L. Goldstein and Michael S. Brown, U.S. researchers whose work over the past two decades had significantly advanced the understanding of cholesterol metabolism.

The results of a study from the Multicenter Post-Infarction Research Group in the U.S. contradicted some earlier theories about the adverse effects of so-called type A behavior (characterized by easily aroused hostility and high-pressure dedication to achievement) on cardiovascular health. Among 516 heart attack victims monitored for one to three years after the event, survival and long-term outcome were not related to the factors associated with type A personality. On the other hand, a British study of 192 test subjects judged to be at risk for heart disease (because of high blood cholesterol, heavy smoking, or severe hypertension) showed that a combination of relaxation training, breathing exercises, and medication reduced the individual's chances of developing coronary disease.

Cancer Research and Treatment

The year 1985 saw the conclusion of two major U.S. cancer studies that helped to resolve professional disagreements about the most appropriate surgical treatment for breast cancer. Both were conducted at U.S. hospitals under the auspices of the National Surgical Adjuvant Breast Project. One study compared ten-year survival rates in mastectomy patients whose tumors had not spread to the axillary (underarm) lymph nodes. It showed that

simple removal of the breast was as effective as the more extensive and disfiguring surgical procedure known as radical mastectomy. The other survey, based on five years' experience, revealed equally satisfactory results from the even more limited segmental mastectomy. Together, these studies indicated that breast cancer could be dealt with by much less mutilating surgery than was thought necessary in the past.

A trial organized by the Swedish National Board of Health and Welfare demonstrated the benefits of mass screening for breast cancer using the technique of mammography. The results of a study initiated in 1977 showed a 31% reduction in mortality from the disease and a 25% reduction in stage 2 (more advanced) breast cancer among women offered screening every two or three years, compared with those who were not offered screening.

Negative findings emerged from an investigation conducted at the Mayo Clinic, Rochester, Minn., to confirm or refute earlier claims that high doses of vitamin C have a beneficial effect on people suffering from advanced cancer. In a double-blind study, 100 patients with large colorectal tumors were given considerable quantities of either vitamin C or a placebo; results showed that the vitamin treatment had no effect on patient survival.

In July U.S. Pres. Ronald Reagan was operated on for colon cancer. During a routine physical exam in March, Reagan's physicians had found a noncancerous polyp in the lower portion of his colon. Four months later, during what was expected to be routine surgery to remove that growth, doctors, using a colonoscope (a flexible fiber-optic viewing device), examined the entire large intestine. They found another, larger growth in the cecum, the junction between the large and small intestines. In a subsequent operation this tumor, along with 18 in (46 cm) of intestine, was removed. The excised tissue showed some evidence of cancer. Nonetheless, the president's doctors were optimistic, predicting that

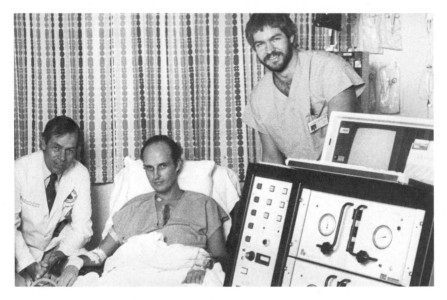

Michael Drummond (center) chats with hospital staff as a Jarvik-7 artificial heart beats in his chest, controlled by the apparatus at right. Drummond later suffered a series of strokes before he received a human heart transplant.

UNIVERSITY MEDICAL CENTER, TUCSON

he had a 95% chance of being cancer-free five years from the date of the operation.

Although the surgery was considered successful, Reagan's physicians were criticized by some for not having been more diligent in their routine examinations. Despite a family history of colon cancer and two earlier tests that had shown blood in his stool, Reagan had not undergone any of the more definitive diagnostic procedures (barium X-rays, colonoscopy) that might have revealed the tumor at an earlier stage.

Every year the U.S. National Institutes of Health (NIH) sponsored consensus panels—meetings in which a panel of experts determined medical advice that established a national standard of care. In 1985 one such panel, considering cancer treatment, recommended hormonal therapy for certain postmenopausal breast cancer patients whose disease had spread to the lymph nodes. Taximofen—a hormonal therapy that blocks the actions of estrogens—should be given, the panel said, if tests of the cancerous tissue showed that it would be responsive to the drug.

Hereditary Disorders

The year saw considerable progress in methods of prenatal detection of serious congenital conditions. One such advance was based on the use of extremely pure monoclonal antibodies (artificially produced antibodies with particular ability to target specific tissues). David Brock and colleagues at the Western General Hospital, Edinburgh, employed one monoclonal antibody to reveal neural tube defects such as spina bifida in the early fetus. The new technique had two important advantages over current methods: it was more reliable, and it required less technical skill to perform. Later in the year Brock's group announced a similarly successful method for the prenatal diagnosis of cystic fibrosis.

There were also major developments in genetics based on the application of DNA probes—short pieces of DNA (the material that carries the genetic code) that are capable of identifying other pieces of DNA by sticking to them very specifically. Geneticists in Sardinia reported success in using a DNA probe to identify the particular genetic mutation responsible for most local cases of β-thalassemia, a hereditary anemia fairly common in Mediterranean countries. The technique could not be applied universally because any of a number of mutations can cause the underlying error in hemoglobin synthesis that is characteristic of the thalassemias. By using several different probes, however, a team from the University of Oxford subsequently showed that they could identify the majority of cases of β-thalassemia in two Mediterranean populations.

The use of DNA probes was instrumental in several successful attempts at prenatal diagnosis of hereditary disorders. International collaboration among geneticists in The Netherlands, Canada, England, and the U.S. led to the development of a probe capable of identifying carriers of Duchenne muscular dystrophy and detecting the disorder in male fetuses at 12 weeks of gestation. Duchenne dystrophy is one of the most common sex-linked (*i.e.,* carried on the X chromosome) disorders. Fifty percent of the male offspring of a female carrier of the disease may potentially be affected. With no method of prenatal diagnosis, some women who knew they were carriers had relied upon selective abortion of male fetuses to ensure that their children would not suffer from the disease. The new technique would enable parents to determine whether or not a male fetus was affected.

Also in 1985, specialists at Baylor College of Medicine, Houston, Texas, announced the creation of a DNA probe for the prenatal diagnosis of phenylketonuria, a congenital enzymatic deficiency.

Groups in France, Italy, Great Britain, and the U.S. reported success in using DNA probes to identify carriers of classical hemophilia (hemophilia A, also known as factor VIII deficiency) and to detect the disease in a fetus during the first trimester of pregnancy.

Fertility and Maternal Health

What was hailed as a major triumph in helping women who experienced repeated spontaneous abortion was accomplished by a team at St. Mary's Hospital Medical School, London. Their technique was to immunize female patients by injecting them with purified white blood cells from their male partners. Of 22 women so treated, 17 proceeded to enjoy a successful pregnancy immediately after undergoing the procedure. Scientists were not entirely certain how the method worked. One theory was that the man's white blood cells can induce antibodies that, in turn, protect parts of the fetus that would otherwise be attacked by the maternal immune system. However, 10 of 27 women injected with their own white cells also had normal pregnancies, suggesting the possibility of a placebo effect.

The adverse effect of cigarette smoking on fertility was highlighted by a survey of more than 17,000 women conducted at the Radcliffe Infirmary, Oxford. Five years after stopping contraception, 10.7% of women who smoked more than 20 cigarettes a day still had not given birth; among nonsmokers, the rate of infertility was only 5.4%.

Drug treatment of infertility was a subject of some controversy during the year. In May, Patti Frustaci, a California woman who had been treated with the fertility drug Pergonal, gave birth to septuplets. Although the birth was 12 weeks premature and one of the infants was stillborn, the parents were initially buoyant. However, three of the remaining six babies died within weeks. In October, only a few days after bringing the last of the three surviving babies home from the hospital, Frustaci and her husband filed a lawsuit charging the doctor and clinic with prescribing "excessive and inappropriate dosages" of fertility drugs. The surviving infants had multiple medical problems that might require years of costly treatment.

Reye's Syndrome

The possible link between aspirin and Reye's syndrome was the source of another lawsuit during the year. In January 1985 the results of a small pilot study on the association between aspirin use and Reye's syndrome were released by the CDC, spurring a demand by consumer groups for warning labels on aspirin bottles. Reye's syndrome is a potentially fatal viral illness that may be accompanied by vomiting, fever, convulsions, and coma. The pilot study, which was to precede a larger scale investigation, showed that youngsters who were given aspirin when they were suffering from flu or chicken pox ran a sharply increased risk of developing Reye's syndrome, compared with similar patients not treated with aspirin. Margaret Heckler, U.S. secretary of health and human services, requested that aspirin manufacturers voluntarily put warning labels on their products, and while many proceeded to comply, in the summer of 1985 the first suit was filed against a drug company by parents of a child who had developed Reye's syndrome.

Nutrition

Two NIH panels focused on nutrition-related topics. The first recommended that the entire U.S. population strive to lower blood cholesterol levels by reducing consumption of saturated fats and cholesterol. The panel endorsed a diet similar to the one proposed by the American Heart Association, which emphasized fresh fruits and vegetables, restricted consumption of egg yolks to no more than two a week, and specified lean meat, skim milk, and low-fat cheeses. Another panel, considering the "Health Implications of Obesity," attempted

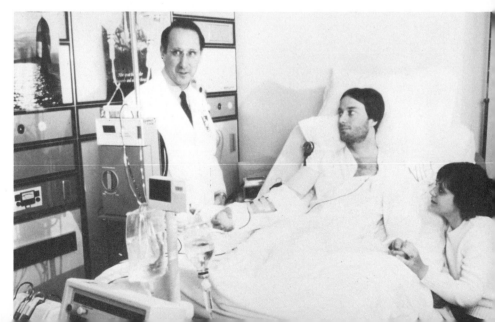

Steven A. Rosenberg (left) of the National Cancer Institute stands beside a cancer patient who is receiving an experimental therapy. In this new therapy, the patient's own white blood cells are treated with a growth factor called interleukin-2 (IL-2). The cells are then returned to the patient's blood stream along with more IL-2. Preliminary results were encouraging.

WALLY MCNAMEE/NEWSWEEK

to define obesity and to consider its influence as a risk factor in relation to other conditions such as hypertension and diabetes. The 14-member panel concluded that any level of obesity constituted an increased health risk, but it identified a level of 20% or more above "desirable" body weight as the threshold for medical intervention.

MENTAL HEALTH

According to research conducted by two British medical institutions during 1985, some barriers that formerly segregated the mentally ill were being removed. A pioneering study at Amersham General Hospital in Buckinghamshire, England, showed that children with psychiatric illnesses could be treated successfully in a general ward instead of being relegated to facilities solely for the mentally disturbed. During four years of treatment all of the children, who had illnesses varying from psychoses to anorexia, showed considerable improvement and were later discharged. A second study, reported by London's Institute of Psychiatry, showed that in recent years there had been an unprecedented movement of psychiatric specialists into community-based services. Of the 811 psychiatrists and psychotherapists surveyed, approximately one-fifth said that they no longer worked only in hospitals, spending at least some time working with physicians in general practice.

A report about adolescent suicide released by Lee Salk and colleagues at Cornell University Medical College in New York City and other research institutions revealed previously unsuspected influences and risk factors. The child's condition at birth and the mother's health during pregnancy were identified as significant influences in the lives of the teenagers who took their own lives. The Cornell researchers compared the records of 52 adolescent suicides with those of matched controls. The study

Volunteers receive nose drops containing cold virus. Researchers have concluded that introverts tend to have worse colds than extroverts.

C. STEELE PERKINS

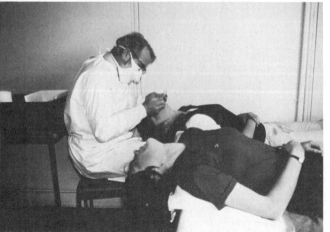

identified three factors that were clearly linked with suicide: respiratory distress for over an hour at birth, lack of antenatal care before 20 weeks of pregnancy, and chronic illness of the mother during pregnancy. Although he was unable to explain the mechanisms behind these relationships, Salk pointed out that at least the recognition of specific risk factors broadened the possibilities for prevention.

Alcoholism continued to be a major health concern for most of the Western world, the U.S.S.R., and some Eastern-bloc countries. Results of a collaborative study conducted by Columbia University, New York City, and the Royal Perth (Australia) Hospital confirmed that brain shrinkage occurred in chronic alcoholics. The recent findings were linked to previous research showing that these people were at risk of developing Korsakoff's syndrome, a form of brain damage resulting in severe memory loss. In experiments on drinkers conducted at the University of Modena, Italy, researchers found that even in drinkers who showed no detectable brain damage, memory was affected. In performance tests comparing men who had been consuming at least two liters of wine per day for five years or more and a control group who consumed a maximum of two glasses per day, the first group showed poorer memory performance.

At Britain's Common Cold Unit, near Salisbury, England, a 21-month study also showed a relationship between psychological factors and the severity of physical disease symptoms. In the experiment, volunteers were given personality questionnaires and inoculated with cold viruses. To ensure objectivity, the clinicians assessing the volunteers' symptoms were not shown the psychological findings. The results showed that introverts suffered much more severe colds than extroverts. The controversy surrounding cancer and mental attitude was renewed when research at King's College School of Medicine and Dentistry, London, supported the theory that an individual's mental outlook may have a significant influence on the outcome of a malignant disease. In studies of women with breast cancer, ten years after the initial diagnosis many more deaths had occurred among those women who had responded with feelings of helplessness or hopelessness than among those whose reactions had been to deny the disease or to fight it. At the University of California School of Medicine, researchers raised the possibility that endorphins, opiumlike substances that occur naturally in the brain, may affect the body's immune system and may even function as the mechanism by which the mind can alter the course of a physical illness.

Electroconvulsive therapy, a controversial treatment for the most severely mentally ill, was cautiously endorsed by a National Institutes of Health consensus panel. The panel concluded that the therapy could be beneficial for severely depressed individuals or for those who did not respond to other treatment or drugs.

The usual delay of 20 minutes stretched to seven hours at the border crossing from Tijuana, Mexico, to San Ysidro, California. U.S. customs officials slowed down the processing of vehicles crossing the border from Mexico as part of a campaign to pressure Mexican authorities in the case of a kidnapped U.S. narcotics agent.

BILL NATION—SYGMA

MEXICO

In Mexico 1985 was ushered in with reports of violent protests in the northern states against alleged electoral fraud, a topic that dominated the political scene throughout the year. Municipal elections held on Dec. 2, 1984, gave widespread victory to the ruling Partido Revolucionario Institucional (PRI), although the opposition Partido de Acción Nacional (PAN) claimed to have won several mayoral races. The refusal to recognize PAN's claim to victory in Piedras Negras, on the border with Texas, resulted in violence that left two people dead. The Army was brought in to restore order.

These incidents heightened worries about the fair and peaceful conduct of elections due in July to fill the Chamber of Deputies (lower house of Congress) and 7 of the 31 state governorships. Many commentators saw the elections as the most important in the PRI's 56-year rule, as they were the first major elections since the economic crisis of 1982. The PRI was vulnerable, since the previous two to three years had witnessed falling real wages, rising unemployment, and high inflation rates. The PAN, which received most of its support in the prosperous americanized north, benefited from a growing dissatisfaction with the government despite lacking a coherent program of its own. However, its voters were predominantly urban, whereas PRI support continued to be strong among rural and southern voters. Although the opposition did not constitute a serious threat to the PRI's overall support, there was some evidence that the PRI went to great lengths to hinder the PAN's performance in the elections.

Polling took place on July 7. The official results, announced a week later, revealed a landslide victory for the PRI, despite indications that its support was at an all-time low. The PRI won all seven state governorships and 289 of the 300 directly elected seats in the Chamber of Deputies. (The remaining

100 were allocated by a system of proportional representation.) In a turnout of 50%, some 65% of voters supported the PRI and 16% the PAN. Allegations of fraud were strengthened by the fact that in some areas the PRI candidate announced victory before the polls closed. There were isolated incidents of clashes with the police and protests by the PAN, but the aftermath was marked by a lack of protest. During his state of the nation address in September, Pres. Miguel de la Madrid Hurtado admitted that there had been "deficiencies and electoral irregularities in some electoral districts."

In the Central American region, Mexico continued to provide economic support to Nicaragua, which it supplied with petroleum, while at the same time maintaining its support for regional groupings such as the Contadora Group and the Cartagena Agreement. The government was careful not to antagonize creditors by making radical statements on debt. President de la Madrid's 18-day visit to Europe in June, aimed at increasing trade and investment, gained him valuable media coverage at home.

A spurt of growth during the latter part of 1984, resulting in part from the relaxing of austerity but also fueled by export growth, contributed to a 3.5% growth in gross domestic product (GDP) for the year as a whole; this followed a contraction of over 5% in 1983. The growth was accompanied by an acceleration of the inflation rate to 65% and a public-sector deficit of 7% of GDP, well beyond the target of 5.5% set by the International Monetary Fund (IMF). In 1985 the government restored its austerity policy with the implementation of large spending cuts. An austerity program announced in January included a freeze on public-sector employment. The government wanted to assure its creditors that fiscal discipline would continue even after IMF involvement ceased in 1985. The theme

(continued on page 227)

A newborn child is rescued alive from the ruins of a Mexico City hospital.
ALON REININGER—CONTACT PRESS IMAGES

The Mexican Earthquake

The earthquakes that shook Mexico City in the early morning of Sept. 19, 1985, and during the evening of the following day left thousands dead or dying in collapsed buildings in the city center. Initial estimates of the total death toll varied hugely, from 5,000 to 20,000. The worst damage was relatively localized in the central part of the city, which housed hotels, apartment buildings for middle-income workers, some government offices, and historic buildings. It was suggested that Spanish colonial buildings withstood the quakes far better than modern structures. While the imagination of the world was captured in the immediate aftermath of the disaster by dramatic rescues of newborn babies who survived for almost two weeks before being retrieved from the ruins of collapsed hospitals, the personal, economic, and political ramifications of the tragedy would continue to affect the Mexican people for years to come.

The government soon came under pressure for its alleged mishandling of the rescue operation. The military, who were called in to help, received no instructions on how to proceed, and during the first few days after the earthquake, foreign assistance was turned down. Civilians who formed their own rescue teams lacked technical expertise in dealing with a crumbling city and might in fact have caused more lives to be lost than would otherwise have been the case. Civilians continued to play a major role in the rescue even after international aid, both economic and technical, was accepted.

The disaster brought to light several cases of corruption, in the construction industry in particular. A commission was set up to study construction codes for the city and examine cases of noncompliance with existing building regulations. The government's failure to act on its policy of decentralization was also highlighted. The uncontrolled growth of Mexico City had been allowed to continue, and the resulting overcrowding no doubt added to the number of deaths.

By its actions immediately after the disaster, the government lost an opportunity to win back popularity, both at home and abroad, and as a result it was likely to remain constrained in its future activities. The economic cost, in terms of both reconstruction and lost revenue, was considerable. Estimates of the cost of rebuilding ranged from $2 billion upward.

The International Monetary Fund (IMF) was on the verge of demanding new, stricter economic measures from the government when the earthquake struck. Although the IMF then tempered its demands, there nevertheless remained uncertainty about Mexico's relationship with its creditors. In the weeks that followed, Mexico received special aid and loans from multilateral agencies, including a $300 million loan from the World Bank and emergency assistance from the IMF. There were calls, mainly from the country's trade unions, for a debt moratorium, but the government itself made no request of this nature and appeared to be trying to honor its commitments, at least in principle.

A major problem facing Mexico was the need to ensure that foreign aid and other inflows would not leave the country again in the shape of capital flight. Financial crisis loomed as the value of the peso plummeted, and the hoped-for boom in construction was overshadowed by external payment difficulties. Mexico's economy, pushed even closer to collapse by the disaster, could recover only through careful control of foreign aid and concessions in the reconstruction period that would follow.

(continued from page 225)
dominated the president's state of the nation address, when he warned that there was no prospect of an early end to the country's problems and that the inflation rate had to be brought down. While speaking out against confrontation and ultimatums over debt repayments, he stated that better terms and larger inflows of capital were required if Mexico was to maintain its debt servicing.

With the decline in world oil prices seriously affecting the balance of payments, the 1984 current-account surplus was expected to be replaced by a deficit in 1985. The growth of nontraditional exports, mainly to the U.S., slowed down. Although the daily slippage of the peso was increased in February, the currency remained overvalued. In June, as pressure mounted, the government recognized the existence of a "super-free" rate by allowing banks to use it for certain transactions. Finally this rate was fully integrated, and the "official-free" rate was abolished. On July 25 the controlled rate was devalued by 17%, and on August 5 a regulated float replaced the daily slippage. These changes were expected to keep inflation high in 1985.

Mexico's economic and political problems were overshadowed to a great extent by the disastrous earthquake that struck Mexico City and the surrounding area on September 19 and left many thousands of people dead, injured, or homeless.

MICROELECTRONICS

The year 1985 was one of extremes for the microelectronics industry. Economically, it was one of the worst in the 40-year history of the industry. But from a technological standpoint the year was a ringing success.

After two years of tremendous growth—in 1984 United States semiconductor sales totaled $25.9 billion—1985 sales tumbled 25% to $19.5 billion.

A 32-bit microprocessor manufactured by Motorola Corp. was among the first semiconductor chips to be registered with the U.S. Copyright Office.

AP/WIDE WORLD

Part of the slump was due to overordering of semiconductors by such customers as personal computer makers, who also saw the market for their products crash in 1985. Another reason for the poor results was the downward pressure on prices of such items as dynamic random-access memories (DRAMs) and erasable programmable read-oniy memories (EPROMs). Japanese companies were selling these memories at such low prices that three major U.S. semiconductor houses asked the International Trade Commission to levy a dumping tax on eight Japanese companies. (Dumping is the illegal selling of products below the cost of manufacturing them.)

The U.S. was not alone, however, in suffering from a frigid economic climate. In Europe growth was a minuscule 2%, and in Japan it was even less.

In regard to technological development, major strides were made during the year in both the memory and logic segments of the microelectronics industry. One-megabit (one million bits) dynamic RAMs were announced by both Japanese and U.S. companies; some even had samples to deliver. This led some analysts to believe that the life of the 256-kilobit (256,000-bit) DRAMs would be short. But the one-megabit RAMs presented their designers with testing problems that they had not encountered with memories of lower capacity. Until those problems were solved, mass production could not begin.

Both U.S. and Japanese companies announced or were delivering small quantities of 256-kilobit static RAMs. Static RAMs differ from DRAMs in that they do not need to be continually refreshed (or recharged) in order to retain the data that they hold. Thus, if a battery is designed into a system with static RAMs, then the memories can keep the data even when the power is shut down.

A new kind of memory, a hierarchical RAM, was developed in 1985. It combined both dynamic and static features; the cells were dynamic, but the memory was addressed as though it were static.

The workhorse of microelectronics remained the microprocessor. During 1985 all of the major firms introduced 32-bit processors; such processors took instructions and processed data in chunks that were 32 characters (or bits) wide.

The 32-bit processors, coupled with the high-capacity memory chips, produced powerful but inexpensive desktop computer systems. Just ten years earlier, systems with comparable processing power cost millions of dollars and were so large and power hungry that they needed to be kept in special air-conditioned rooms.

A British firm introduced what it called a transputer. Essentially a system on a chip, the transputer consisted of a 32-bit microprocessor, four communications links, memory, and a memory interface on one chip. Unlike computers, which process instructions one at a time, the transputer executed a number of instructions simultaneously.

MIDDLE EASTERN AND NORTH AFRICAN AFFAIRS

The year brought little hope of an end to the long conflict between Iran and Iraq. Iran maintained its insistence that its objective was to overthrow Iraq's Pres. Saddam Hussein At Takriti. In March fighting flared to a pitch of ferocity rarely seen since the early weeks of the conflict. The move to escalate the fighting came initially from Baghdad as Iraqi bombers attacked first the Iranian petroleum-exporting terminal at Khark Island and then Iranian cities, breaking an agreement made in June 1984 not to attack civilian targets. Iran opened an offensive on March 12 that aimed to establish a bridgehead on the west bank of the Tigris River to cut the Baghdad–Basra road, a principal communications artery. The attack was repulsed by Iraq, which also stepped up its raids on oil tankers. Despite possessing superior air power, Iraq was unable to halt loading at the Khark Island terminal for more than short periods. Although a moratorium on air and missile strikes on civilian targets was announced on June 14, Iraq renewed the onslaught on July 1, claiming that the attacks would continue until a just and honorable peace had been reached on terms to be set by President Hussein.

Iraq's main financial support was from the Gulf Cooperation Council (GCC) member states, which continued to help their "Arab brother" with oil swaps and direct subsidies. Iran maintained its war effort through income from petroleum exports and

by making use of its larger population and more plentiful natural resources. Iran was confident of being able to maintain its 2.3 million-bbl-a-day quota set by the Organization of Petroleum Exporting Countries (OPEC). In early October Iran mounted naval maneuvers in the Strait of Hormuz, through which tankers enter the Gulf. Iranian Pres. Sayyed Ali Khamenei warned Western powers against military intervention; Iran made it clear that it was determined to close the strait if its own oil supply lines were cut. Iraq immediately retaliated on November 6 with a strike on Iran's Ahwaz pipe mill.

At the GCC summit held in Muscat, Oman, in November, GCC leaders showed some signs of taking a more neutral stance on the war. However, mediation initiatives taken by the GCC after its summit were rebuffed by Iran, which declined to meet the GCC envoy, Omani Minister of State for Foreign Affairs Yusuf al-Alawi.

Gulf Cooperation Council

Defense and security were the major concerns voiced by leaders of the GCC countries—Saudi Arabia, Kuwait, Bahrain, Qatar, Oman, and the United Arab Emirates (U.A.E.)—at the 1985 summit in Oman. Their talks ended on November 6 with renewed calls for an end to the Gulf war and pledges to stop the spread of terrorism. In May Emir Sheikh Jabir of Kuwait survived unhurt when a bomb attack was made on his motor cavalcade in Kuwait's normally peaceful Corniche. Preoccupa-

Fierce religious and political sectarianism in Lebanon created intense factional fighting. After the Israeli invasion of Lebanon on June 6, 1982, there was a major shift in the power balance in favor of Syria. Other groups gaining political influence were the Druze and the Shi'ites, while the Maronites and the Sunnites were the losers.

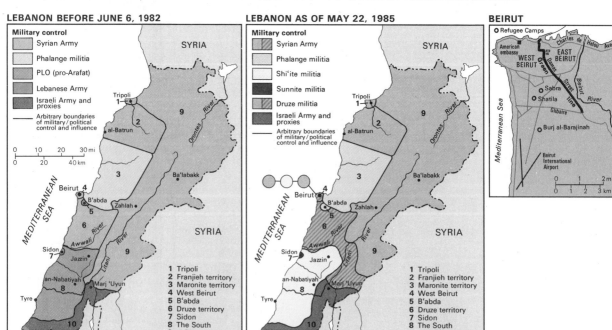

Source: *The Economist.*

tion with these subjects pushed to one side regional topics, including economic integration and industrial strategy, which had been expected to dominate the summit agenda. The final communiqué used two UN Security Council resolutions on the war—Resolution 540 of October 1983 and Resolution 552 of June 1984—as points of departure for renewed contacts between the GCC and the warring parties. Both resolutions had been rejected by Iran.

In August the defense forces of the six GCC states held joint exercises at the King Khalid Military City in northeastern Saudi Arabia. It was also understood that progress was being made on the idea of forming a GCC rapid-deployment force that could assist in the event of a localized emergency, such as the attempted coup in Bahrain in December 1981. While contacts between GCC members remained good at the government level, private-sector interests in the richest of the GCC states—Saudi Arabia and Kuwait—still favored a nationalist and protectionist approach to trade policies. It was decided to postpone until December 1986 the opening of the $1 billion road causeway linking Bahrain with Saudi Arabia to allow more time to study its social and economic impact.

In what could be regarded as diplomatic gains for the U.S.S.R. in its superpower rivalry with the U.S., two GCC member states announced their decision to recognize the Soviet Union during the year. Oman made the announcement on September 26, and the U.A.E. made a similar statement on November 15. Each country affirmed that its decision was a strictly bilateral one. Oman's rapprochement with the U.S.S.R. represented a major policy reversal; relations between the two countries had been poor since the 1970s, when the U.S.S.R. had supported a guerrilla insurgency movement in the Dhofar region of Oman from bases in Marxist-led South Yemen. Diplomatic sources in Muscat said that Oman's decision reflected a desire to establish credentials as a nonaligned state, an interpretation that was reinforced by the invitations to many third world leaders to attend the 15th anniversary celebrations for Sultan Qabus ibn Sa'id of Oman on November 18. The diplomatic initiatives brought to three the number of GCC states that recognized the U.S.S.R.—Kuwait had already done so—but it was considered unlikely that Qatar and Saudi Arabia would follow suit because of their distaste for the treatment of Muslims in the U.S.S.R.

GCC states remained on excellent terms with most Western countries, although relations were soured by the move by the European Communities (EC) to put tariffs on methanol and polyethylene imports from the GCC to Europe. A meeting in Luxembourg in October revealed a lack of communication between the EC and the GCC.

The PLO and Arab-Israeli Relations

A major development during 1985 was the Jordanian-Palestinian response to U.S. moves to break

REUTERS/BETTMANN NEWSPHOTOS

The last Israeli tank in Lebanon returns to Israel on June 10. Israel withdrew its last troops but left military advisers behind in a newly created security zone.

the deadlock between Arab countries and Israel over the Palestine issue. In February it was announced that King Hussein of Jordan and Palestine Liberation Organization (PLO) chairman Yasir Arafat had reached agreement on a joint peace initiative based on urging Israel to hand over the occupied territories in exchange for peace. Throughout the year King Hussein was at the forefront of efforts to arrange a meeting between a joint Palestinian-Jordanian team and U.K. Secretary of State for Foreign Affairs Sir Geoffrey Howe as a first step toward a meeting between a Jordanian delegation and U.S. representatives. Although the meeting with Howe was called off at the last minute, assurances were given on November 4 that the EC would receive a joint Jordanian-Palestinian delegation. On the same day, Luxembourg's Foreign Minister Jacques Poos said that King Hussein's plan also involved recognition of Israel by the PLO and a meeting between a Palestinian-Jordanian group and U.S. negotiators that would take place within the framework of an international conference including all five permanent members of the UN Security Council.

Arafat disputed this interpretation when, in a speech in Cairo on November 5, he described the demand for PLO recognition of Israel as amounting to a precondition to negotiations and, as such, unacceptable. He maintained that the PLO had no intention of renouncing violence outside Israel and the occupied territories and claimed that the demand for the PLO to halt military action outside Israel was "unreasonable" as long as Israel continued to attack Palestinians "all over the world."

The Arab summit conference in Casablanca, Morocco, ended on August 9 with a resolution that gave implicit backing to the joint Jordanian-PLO peace initiative with Israel. However, the significance of the meeting was diminished by the fact that it was attended by fewer than half the Arab heads of state, while five countries boycotted the meeting altogether. Later in the year a rapprochement between Syria and Jordan increased Arafat's isolation. During Jordanian Prime Minister Zaid ar-Rifai's visit to Damascus, Syria, on November 12–13, both Jordan and Syria rejected any bilateral deal with Israel and called for an international conference on the Arab-Israeli conflict. This was followed by a two-day meeting between Hussein and Syria's Pres. Hafez al-Assad in Damascus at the end of December.

Many Israeli officials were convinced that King Hussein was serious in his commitment to reviving peace talks. They believed that moderate Arab nations would have more success in curbing the activities of the PLO following its implication in the *Achille Lauro* affair. Israel's Prime Minister Shimon Peres made a significant move to assist King Hussein by embracing the idea of convening some kind of international meeting to begin peace talks. As a result Peres faced, and overcame, an internal government crisis in November.

Peres insisted that the U.S.S.R. mend fences with Israel before taking part in such an international conference, and beginning in midyear there were reports suggesting that Moscow was stepping up its contacts with Israel. The Soviet Union had severed diplomatic ties with Israel following the 1967 Arab-Israeli war. Since assuming power in March 1985, Soviet leader Mikhail Gorbachev was understood to have initiated moves to bring the U.S.S.R. into a central role in Middle Eastern diplomacy. Peres was sharply criticized, however, by Israeli Foreign Minister Yitzhak Shamir in July for sending a goodwill message to Gorbachev through Edgar Bronfman, president of the World Jewish Congress. In return for Israeli help, King Hussein was attempting to find a solution to the main problem facing Peres by seeking Palestinian negotiators who would be acceptable to the Israeli prime minister. In the fall of 1986 Peres was due to hand over power to the Likud, who were regarded as being hostile to any deal with the Palestinians; this fact brought a sense of urgency to negotiations.

U.S. Policy

The U.S. resumed its role as broker in the cause of peace in the region when during May 10–13 U.S. Secretary of State George Shultz visited Israel, Egypt, and Jordan. Although the tour was regarded as having been fruitless in terms of major achievements, it provided the backdrop to the meeting between King Hussein and U.S. Pres. Ronald Reagan on May 29. With Pres. Hosni Mubarak of Egypt already supporting his stand, King Hussein was anxious to secure the involvement of the U.S., which was regarded by many moderate Arab countries, including Saudi Arabia, as being indispensable to any major peace initiative. President Reagan subsequently yielded to pressure from Republican senators to block a proposed sale of weapons, worth $1.9 billion, to Jordan unless Jordan and Israel began direct talks. Speaking at the UN General Assembly on October 21, Peres appeared to acknowledge the progress made by U.S. diplomacy when he agreed to entertain the Jordanian idea of an international peace conference while continuing to push for bilateral talks between Israel and Jordan. Israel's air strike on the PLO headquarters near Tunis, Tunisia, on October 1, carried out in revenge for the murder of three Israelis in Cyprus, was not well received in Washington. However, U.S. outrage over the *Achille Lauro* seizure just one week later did much to redress the balance.

The U.S. had insisted since 1975 that it would negotiate with the PLO only after the guerrilla organization recognized Israel and pledged support for UN resolutions 242 and 338, which were generally interpreted as implying recognition of the Jewish state. What appeared to be a softening of this stance in 1985 was interpreted by hard-line Likud politicians as merely a "flexing of commitment," which would not be followed by any real change in U.S. support for Israel.

Terrorism

The rash of terrorist attacks affecting civilians, particularly U.S. citizens, was a feature of the year's events that worried Western leaders. On June 14 a U.S. Trans World Airlines passenger aircraft flying from Athens to Rome was hijacked by Lebanese Shi'ite Muslims, who demanded the release of prisoners held by the Israelis. One U.S. passenger was killed and a number were held hostage for two weeks in Beirut before the crisis was ended following negotiations conducted by Nabih Berri, Lebanon's minister of justice and political leader of the Lebanese Shi'ite community. Shi'ite gunmen later kidnapped four officials of the Soviet embassy in Lebanon; they killed one diplomat before releasing the others at the end of October after holding them for a month.

The Italian cruise liner *Achille Lauro* was seized on October 7 off the coast of Egypt by four gunmen who were reported to be members of the Palestine Liberation Front, a splinter group of the PLO. The gunmen killed one U.S. passenger, 69-year-old Leon Klinghoffer, before surrendering to the Egyptian authorities on October 9. As part of the surrender pact the gunmen were to be flown to Tunisia, but their plane was intercepted by U.S.

fighters and forced to land in Sicily, bringing the Palestinians to trial in Italy. The Italian authorities who took charge of the investigations were reported to be seeking at least 16 other Palestinians in connection with the incident.

An EgyptAir airliner flying from Athens to Cairo on November 23 was hijacked to the airport at Valletta, Malta. During the hijacking and the ensuing gun battle as Egyptian troops stormed the plane, 57 of the 98 passengers and crew were killed. It was the heaviest loss of life ever suffered during an airliner hijack. Responsibility for the hijacking was claimed by the group led by Abu Nidal, a Palestinian faction opposed to Arafat's leadership of the PLO and to any rapprochement between Jordan, the PLO, and Israel. The Abu Nidal group was believed by some sources to be based in Libya. The same group was reported to have carried out attacks on Israeli El Al check-in counters at airports in Rome and Vienna on December 27.

The Economy

Saudi Arabia appeared to be prepared to break ranks with OPEC by increasing its petroleum extractions toward its OPEC quota of 4.3 million bbl a day and so abandoning its pivotal role as OPEC's "swing producer." Speaking in Mecca on September 22, Saudi Arabia's King Fahd underlined his country's continued support for OPEC, but he also warned that Saudi Arabia would increase its output if other members raised their production quotas. At the December OPEC meeting in Geneva the oil ministers agreed to cease defending the $28-a-barrel price in favor of increasing sales.

North Africa

The year was marked by the growing ostracism of Libya and by a polarization among the nations of the Maghrib—Morocco, Algeria, Tunisia, and Libya. The crisis began on August 5 when Libya, following the example of Nigeria, started sending foreign workers home. The country most affected was Tunisia, which retaliated by expelling more than 250 Libyans, including some diplomats. Tunisia also claimed that Libya was massing troops on its border and subsequently called for all its nationals to return home and halted all economic cooperation with the regime of Col. Muammar Al Qadhafi. With Libya and Morocco allied by the Oujda accord of 1984, Algeria was moving closer to Tunisia. When Algerian Pres. Chadli Bendjedid visited Tunis on September 2, he assured Pres. Habib Bourguiba of Tunisia of Algeria's support.

On October 23 Moroccan Prime Minister Mohammad Karim Lamrani told the UN that Morocco wished the UN to organize a referendum in January 1986 about the future of the disputed Western Sahara. Morocco had declared a unilateral cease-fire in the territory, where it had been fighting guerrillas from the Polisario Front independence movement since 1975.

MINES AND MINING

In many respects experience in the mining industry worldwide was quite uniform during 1984 and 1985. Market pressures to obtain the lowest price possible for raw materials required mine operators to seek every economy of operation they could identify, including reduction of costs for labor, energy, transportation, and processing and concentrating activities. Furthermore, marketing arrangements, currency movements, and research and development to identify new product applications, as well as accommodation of conservation, environmental, and safety legislation without loss of profits, all demanded attention if a company or mineral sector were to remain healthy. For many countries, however, constraints of capital, manpower, extent and geologic implacement of resources, energy costs, and aging physical plant meant loss of traditional markets or of market share to new producers, inability to fully exploit certain kinds of operations, or inability to undertake new operations.

Exploration

As was the case in 1983, exploration and development projects in 1984 and 1985 concentrated heavily (to the extent of perhaps a third of all new properties) on gold-mining operations. Some of the more active areas included the Casa Berardi locality in northern Quebec, the Milot area of Haiti, and Obenemase, Ghana; and there were extensions of existing properties in Australia, Canada, and South Africa. Even Czechoslovakia, which had ceased gold mining some 20 years earlier, announced plans to reopen its Celina Mokrsko facility and to develop new facilities by 1990 at Slate Hory in Moravia.

United Mine Workers members demonstrate near Lobata, West Virginia, against the A. T. Massey Coal Co., which was resisting the union's demand for a single contract covering all the company's divisions and affiliates.
AP/WIDE WORLD

Of particular interest in the U.S. Geological Survey's report for fiscal 1984 were the descriptions provided of several new instrumental techniques for exploration (a coaxial-loop, extra-low-frequency electromagnetic sounder, for locating sulfide mineral deposits as deep as 2,790 ft [850 m]), mapping (the APT, or Aerial Profiling of Terrain, System, a laser terrain profiler with extraordinary capacity for detail), and interpretation of potential mineralization via analysis of paleothermal anomalies (identifying ancient heating events with mineralizing potential by identification of fluid inclusions, fission tracks, and alteration of organic materials).

Mine Operations

The coal miners' strike in the U.K. that had begun in March 1984 was settled partially by a return to work on March 5, 1985, but the fundamental issues of mine closures on economic grounds remained unresolved. The year-long strike was among the most bitter, divisive (among Britain's labor unions), and destructive in that nation's history.

In South Africa the mines were one of the principal centers of labor and social unrest during the year. Repercussions included, from the South African side, threats by authorities to consider means of repatriating jobs, especially those in the mines, held by expatriate workers (from Lesotho, Botswana, Swaziland, and the black states that South Africa had declared independent) and, from abroad, the imposition of additional economic pressure by countries outside South Africa to force movement away from apartheid (racial separation). Among these measures were the banning of Krugerrand sales in the U.S. by Pres. Ronald Reagan from October 11 and the announcement by France late in the year that contracts for coal purchases from South African producers would not be renewed.

New Caledonian mine properties were attacked during the year by Kanak (indigenous Melanesian) militants attempting to disrupt nickel mining operations at Thio by blockades (beginning in November 1984) and sabotage. By the year's end this violence had reduced production targets for 1985 by more than 40%.

Safety

Two elements of the overall problem of mine safety gained attention in 1985. In July the collapse of two tailings dams holding fluid wastes from a fluorite mine in the Dolomite Mountains above Stava, Italy, caused the loss of some 250 lives when 53 million cu ft (1.5 million cu m) of water and tailings destroyed the village, a tourist-oriented center with many hotels. The responsibility of the Italian government and Trentino provincial authorities to inspect and of the mine owners to build and maintain such structures properly all came immediately into question, but by year's end no clear assignment of culpability had taken place.

The first International Conference on the Health of Miners, held in Pittsburgh, Pa., June 2–7, drew speakers from 15 nations and more than 200 representatives of union, government, industry, and health groups. Problems discussed included occupational injury and exposure to toxic substances, dust, heat, noise, and a variety of other factors that were serious enough concerns in those countries having worker protection laws but were far more destructive in countries with child labor, endemic ill health among workers, or a lack of protective legislation. Health problems related to mining were said to be as bad in the third world in the 1980s as they were in Europe during the Industrial Revolution.

Technology

The relatively small contribution of the U.S. to worldwide technological innovation in mining was troubling to many. Research and development investment did not suffice either to gain ground on other nations or to maintain position in fields of past importance. Computerization, artificial intelligence, and robotics were prominent examples. Japanese and Western European advances in such areas as mechanization of dangerous tasks, safety monitoring equipment (especially rapid analysis and warning systems), work scheduling and process control (using fifth-generation artificial-intelligence systems), and new mining technologies were both aggressive in scope and long-term in outlook.

The Mining '85 exhibition held in Birmingham, England, June 10–14 displayed many examples of advanced or new technology for mine work. Equipment shown included several advanced submersible pumps for mine drainage; slurry pumps, including a gravel pump; alignment, orientation, and remote-control systems for large equipment like shearers, both to control working of the mine face and to permit operations in dangerous areas; and support equipment capable of remote operation.

MOROCCO

During 1985 events in Morocco were once again dominated by the country's continuing struggle with the Popular Front for the Liberation of Saguia el Hamra and Río de Oro (Polisario Front) and its associated government-in-exile, the Saharan Arab Democratic Republic (SADR), for control of the Western Sahara. Morocco tightened its hold on the territory by building two new defensive walls that extended and consolidated its control eastward and southward. The Polisario Front continued its attacks and shot down several aircraft, including a Belgian civilian plane in January and a West German plane in February.

Morocco's diplomatic isolation increased as the number of states recognizing the SADR rose to 64. The Organization of African Unity (OAU), from which Morocco had withdrawn in protest in 1984, confirmed the member status of the SADR by electing the SADR president as OAU vice-president at its summit in July 1985. During an address to the

UN on October 23, Prime Minister Mohammad Karim Lamrani announced that his government had declared a unilateral cease-fire in the area and was willing to allow the UN to organize a referendum to decide its future. The speech made no move toward recognizing the validity of Polisario claims to represent the Western Saharans.

Anxious to maintain good relations with Morocco in view of its claims on the Spanish enclaves of Ceuta and Melilla, Spain expelled Polisario Front representatives in September. Following a visit by French Prime Minister Laurent Fabius in April, France agreed to provide F 1 billion in development aid and 1.3 million metric tons of cereals by the end of the year. (For table of world currencies, *see* International Exchange and Payments.) Relations with the U.S. continued to be threatened by Morocco's treaty of union with Libya. King Hassan II canceled plans to visit Washington. The rapprochement with Libya was itself somewhat soured by King Hassan's decision to call an Arab summit in August to discuss the proposed Jordanian-Palestinian Middle East peace initiative, which Libya opposed, and by Morocco's disapproval of the closer links between Libya and Iran.

The majority opposition party, the National Union of Popular Forces, was critical of the administration's willingness to follow requirements laid down by the International Monetary Fund (IMF) for restructuring the economy. The government's 1986–88 plan underlined this commitment by reducing the role of the public sector, while in September subsidies on essential foodstuffs were cut by up to 20%. Foreign debt stood at almost $12 billion at the start of the year. In September the IMF renewed its standby credit at 315 million Special Drawing Rights, while official creditors in the Club of Paris agreed to reschedule $1 billion of debt.

Pope John Paul II (left) is escorted by Morocco's King Hassan II (third from left) on the pope's arrival in Casablanca on August 19.

FRANCOIS LOCHON—GAMMA/LIAISON

MOTION PICTURES

Hollywood production in 1985 seemed to be principally aimed at a teenage market, with a proliferation of comedies, romances, gory horrors, and even science fiction (John Hughes's *Weird Science*) set in colleges and high schools. This apparently wholesale surrender to those under 18 caused *Variety,* the venerable show-business journal, to declare: "When the causes of the Decline of Western Civilization are finally writ, Hollywood will surely have to answer why it turned one of man's most significant art forms over to the self-gratification of high-schoolers."

Undoubtedly the tastes of this same youthful audience dictated the box-office winners of the year: boisterous comedies like the execrable *Police Academy 2* and *Pee-Wee's Big Adventure;* comedy-dramas such as John Hughes's *The Breakfast Club;* and fantasies like Robert Zemeckis's *Back to the Future,* the top commercial success of 1985, in which a time machine carries a teenager, played by Michael J. Fox, back to the 1950s and his parents' own teenage days. The popularity of films in which violent, unconquerable, fabulous heroes commit wholesale slaughter, in defense of American values, against enemies within and without— Sylvester Stallone in *Rambo: First Blood Part II* and Chuck Norris in *Missing in Action* and *Invasion U.S.A.*—seemed to be connected to the same teenage phenomenon.

The taste for fantasy, whether set in the future or in the past, strongly marked the year's films; Ridley Scott's *Legend* was an example of a sophisticated fairy tale picture, showing off the work of special-effects experts, while Richard Donner's *Ladyhawke* was one of the better examples of the "sword and sorcery" genre. There were attempts to revive older Hollywood styles. Bruce Beresford's return to biblical spectacular in *King David* failed to excite audiences, but Clint Eastwood's *Pale Rider* and Lawrence Kasdan's *Silverado* showed that the traditional Western maintained its appeal.

Few of the older major Hollywood directors were in evidence, though 78-year-old John Huston had a major success with his suave and ironic reading of Richard Condon's comic novel about a Mafia family, *Prizzi's Honor.* Woody Allen, too, made one of his most inspired comedies, *The Purple Rose of Cairo,* a fantasy about a sad, movie-crazed waitress of the Depression era and a screen character who comes to life, walking out of the film to woo her. Martin Scorsese's black comedy of paranoia in New York City, *After Hours,* was about a bored young man who one night strays from his Manhattan apartment to SoHo and becomes involved with a series of bizarre characters and nightmarish situations.

Of the newer directors, Ron Howard followed *Splash* with *Cocoon,* another modern fable, about a group of elderly citizens who find a fountain of youth. Susan Seidelmann also scored at the box

Kathleen Turner and Jack Nicholson starred as rival professional killers who become lovers in Prizzi's Honor, *an unconventional comedy directed by John Huston.*

office with *Desperately Seeking Susan,* a fast-paced farce set in New York City about a young, repressed suburban housewife who loses her memory and becomes convinced that she is Susan, an eccentrically dressed free spirit. In his second feature film Wayne Wang achieved success with *Dim Sum—A Little Bit of Heart,* which related the small adventures, hopes, and fears of a Chinatown family.

Among foreign directors working for major U.S. film companies, the Australian Peter Weir made *Witness,* a stylish movie about the events that ensue after a small boy from an Amish community witnesses a murder. For *The Emerald Forest,* an adventure story with a touch of Tarzan and a strong ecological message, the English director John Boorman led a film expedition into the fast-vanishing rain forests of Brazil.

Unusual in the Hollywood context, Paul Schrader's *Mishima* was a stylized, impressionistic biography of the controversial Japanese writer Yukio Mishima, made in Japan in the Japanese language. Another exceptional exercise in film biography was Peter Bogdanovich's *Mask,* a dramatized account of the life and death of Rocky Dennis, a lively, intelligent California boy who battled to overcome the handicaps of a severely disfiguring disease. The popular success of the film was a tribute to Bogdanovich's management of sentiment without mawkishness.

Among the films released near the end of the year were Steven Spielberg's *The Color Purple,* Alice Walker's novel about the lives of southern rural blacks some 50 and 60 years ago; Sydney Pollack's *Out of Africa,* based on the experiences of the Danish author Isak Dinesen; Jonathan Lynn's *Clue,* based on the popular board game; Lewis Teague's *Jewel of the Nile,* a sequel to the 1984 hit *Romancing the Stone;* Sir Richard Attenborough's adaptation of the hit Broadway musical *A Chorus Line;* Sylvester Stallone's latest in his series about the boxer Rocky Balboa, *Rocky IV;* and Taylor Hackford's cold-war drama with dancing, *White Nights.*

A notable development of the year was a rise in feature-length documentaries, aimed at the ever growing international television market. Among the most distinguished were Fred Wiseman's *Racetrack;* Martin Bell's *Streetwise,* about runaway children in Seattle, Wash.; Christine Noschese's *Metropolitan Avenue,* about the battle of an inner-city commu-

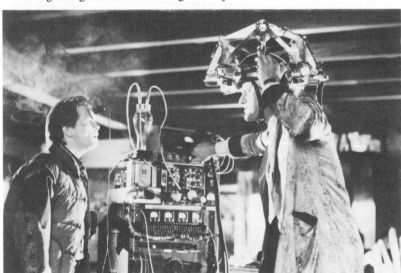

In Back to the Future, *Michael J. Fox (left) portrayed a teenager who travels back to 1955 and finds that he must serve as a matchmaker to the young man and woman who are to become his parents. Christopher Lloyd played the inventor of the time machine.*

nity in Brooklyn to retain its identity; and Lee Grant's *What Sex Am I?,* about transsexuals.

At the annual awards ceremony of the Academy of Motion Picture Arts and Sciences in Hollywood in March, *Amadeus* received awards for best film, best director (Milos Forman), best actor (F. Murray Abraham), best screenplay adaptation (Peter Shaffer, from his own play), art direction, sound, and makeup. Sally Field was adjudged best actress, for *Places in the Heart,* which also won the award for best original screenplay (Robert Benton). Dame Peggy Ashcroft's performance in *A Passage to India* earned her the Oscar for best supporting actress. Haing S. Ngor was best supporting actor, for his role in *The Killing Fields,* a British film that also received Oscars for cinematography and editing. The best feature documentary was Robert Epstein's *The Times of Harvey Milk.* The Swiss *Dangerous Moves* was the best foreign-language film.

Other English-Language Films

The best British productions during the year were to be found among low- and medium-budgeted features, many of them partly or wholly funded by television networks. Several of the best of these were comedies, including *Letter to Brezhnev,* a first film by Chris Bernard, which inaugurated an authentic regional and popular cinema. Describing the troubled romance of an unemployed girl who falls in love after a brief encounter with a Soviet sailor, it managed at once to be richly comic and to treat vital topics of the social and political life of contemporary Britain. Hanif Kureishi's fine script for Stephen Frears's *My Beautiful Laundrette* touched upon issues of race, sex, ambition, and racketeering in contemporary Britain. *Brazil,* directed by Terry Gilliam of Monty Python fame, was an imaginative, futuristic comedy featuring elements of *1984* and traditional theatrical satire with a screenplay written, in part, by Tom Stoppard.

The past continued to preoccupy British filmmakers. Mike Newell's *Dance with a Stranger* returned to the 1950s to reconstruct the story of Ruth Ellis, the last woman to be hanged in Britain for murder. Gavin Millar's inventive *Dreamchild* portrayed, as an old lady, the Alice that inspired *Alice in Wonderland,* reflecting on her relationship with the complex Rev. Charles Dodgson, alias Lewis Carroll. In *The Assam Garden,* a promising debut by Mary McMurray, the odd friendship of an elderly widow and an Indian woman immigrant afforded insights into Britain's colonial past. U.S. history figured in Nicolas Roeg's *Insignificance,* based on Terry Johnson's metaphorical play, imagining a New York City encounter, one night in the early 1950s, between Albert Einstein, Marilyn Monroe, Sen. Joseph McCarthy, and Joe DiMaggio.

Australia's major commercial successes of the year were *Mad Max: Beyond Thunderdome,* directed by George Miller and George Ogilvie, the third in a series of dynamic and visually inventive

MATSUMOTO—SYGMA

Ran, *a film based on Shakespeare's play* King Lear *by Japanese director Akira Kurosawa, received high critical acclaim in 1985.*

films picturing a future world of violent punk subcivilization, and Graeme Clifford's *Burke and Wills,* a spectacular, well-researched epic about the disastrous expedition of the two Australian explorers in 1860. Among other interesting productions, *Unfinished Business,* a witty romantic comedy about middle-aged people, marked the directorial debut of the noted screenwriter Bob Ellis. John Hughes's *Traps* was an essay on the decline of parliamentary democracy, combining news film with a fictional framing story. Dennis O'Rourke's *Half Life* was a distinguished feature-length documentary about the effects of the 1954 hydrogen-bomb tests on the people of the Marshall Islands.

While the hopes of many Canadian filmmakers were set on breaking into the U.S. market with low-budget horror films and youth comedies, one or two films of indigenous character emerged. Two of these were comedies: Giles Walker's sophisticated and funny *Ninety Days,* about the problems of a shy suitor and a mail-order bride, and John Paizs's debut feature *Crime Wave,* which dealt with a man suffering a creative block. Mort Ransen's appealing *Bayo* set its story of a seastruck boy and his crusty grandfather on the Newfoundland coast.

France and West Germany

Commercial production continued to be dominated by comedies and police thrillers. Of the latter, one of the most engaging was Jacques Deray's *On ne meurt que deux fois.* Two major directors tried variations on that genre, Jean-Luc Godard with the perverse and whimsical *Détective* and Maurice Pialat with *Police.*

Agnès Varda's *Sans toit ni loi,* an unsparing study of the last days of a runaway girl, won the Golden Lion of the Venice Film Festival. This festival also screened two marathon French productions: a painfully static version of Paul Claudel's *Le Soulier de satin,* directed by Manoel de Oliveira, and *Shoah,* a nine-and-a-half-hour documentary on the Holocaust, directed by Claude Lanzmann.

The novelist-director Marguerite Duras, in collaboration with Jean-Marc Turin and Jean Mascolo, made a whimsical-absurdist essay on the human condition, *Les Enfants,* about a seven-year-old (played by a grown man) who announces that he will leave school because they teach him only what he does not know. Jacques Rivette made *Hurlevent,* a cool, elliptical adaptation of *Wuthering Heights* transposed to France of the 1930s, while Claude Chabrol directed a rural murder mystery, *Poulet au vinaigre.*

The West German phenomenon of the year was the overwhelming box-office success of *Otto—Der Film,* directed by Xaver Schwarzenberger and starring a popular comedian, Otto Waalkes. Clearly, comedy was in demand, and another hit of the season was Christian Rateuke and Dieter Hallervorden's *Didi und die Rache der Enterbten,* starring Hallervorden. Art and "authors' " films were eclipsed at the box office by comedies and thrillers, though Percy Adlon's *Zuckerbaby,* a whimsical romantic comedy about a mortuary attendant and a subway driver, was well received.

Eastern Europe

There were signs in 1985 of a more relaxed atmosphere for Soviet cinema. Sergei Paradjanov, after years of inactivity and imprisonment, completed a strange and visionary epic, *Legend of the Suram Fortress.* Eldar Shengelaya made a witty satire about bureaucrats in a crumbling state publishing house, *The Blue Mountains.* Nikolai Gubenko's *Love, Life and Tears,* set in an old peoples' home, was a sharp attack on uncaring bureaucracies. The outstanding film of the year, well timed for the 40th anniversary of the end of World War II, was Elem Klimov's *Go and See,* an epic tragedy of the Nazi massacre of a Belorussian village in 1943.

Gradual relaxation led to the release of films that had been shelved since the introduction of martial

Whoopi Goldberg plays the part of Celie in The Color Purple, *which was adapted from Alice Walker's novel of the same title and directed by Steven Spielberg.*

law, and new films were increasingly outspoken. Krzysztof Kieslowski's *Without End* dealt allegorically with events of recent years, describing a woman's efforts to continue her dead husband's support of illegal labor movements. Wieslaw Sanievski's *Custody,* shown in 1985 after being shelved since 1981, exposed the unproductive inhumanity of the prison system through the story of a young woman condemned to life in prison for petty embezzlement. Radoslaw Piwowarski's *Yesterday* was a melancholy anecdote of the crushed dreams of youth and, incidentally, an homage to the Beatles era.

Hungarian cinema offered fewer highlights than in most recent years, though Istvan Szabo's *Colonel Redl,* a coproduction with West Germany, enjoyed major international success. As in *Mephisto,* Szabo brought his own imaginative interpretation to historical events—in this case an army scandal that shocked Imperial Vienna during the last years of the Austro-Hungarian Empire. Gyula Gazdag's *Package Tour,* a remarkable cinéma vérité about a group of elderly Jewish Holocaust survivors revisiting the Nazi death camps, was a powerful commentary on that somber piece of history.

The emergence of an innovative new generation of Yugoslavian filmmakers was underlined by the award of the Cannes Festival Grand Prix to Emir Kusturica (whose *Do You Remember Dolly Bell?* took the Venice Golden Lion in 1981). His winning film, *When Father Was Away on Business,* treated a previously taboo era of Yugoslavian history, the imprisonment of Stalinists in the early years of Yugoslavia's breakaway from Soviet domination, viewing it from the standpoint of the six-year-old son of a small-town family. The Grand Prix of the Mannheim Festival went to Filip Robar-Dorin's *Sheep and Mammoths,* an ebullient comic essay on nationalist prejudice in a multinational state. Bora Draskovic's *Life Is Beautiful* was a vivid but more elusive film metaphor set in a country inn where travelers who provide a microcosm of an entire society are stranded.

Latin America

Peru enjoyed an international success with Francisco J. Lombardi's *The City and the Dogs,* adapted from a novel that uses a military college as a microcosm of a corrupt society. A Franco-Venezuelan coproduction, *Oriana*—an atmospheric story about the memories that haunt an old country house—also achieved an international market.

Rapidly recovering from the years of the generals, when major talent was blacklisted, the Argentine cinema was immeasurably helped in its efforts at renascence by the worldwide success of María Luisa Bemberg's *Camila* in 1984 and of Luis Puenzo's *La historia oficial* in 1985. For her role in the latter film, which tells how a liberal-minded housewife and history teacher gradually recognizes the extent to which she had been implicated in the events of the bad years, Norma Aleandro was awarded the best actress prize at the Cannes Festival in May.

Brazilian production was undergoing both economic and artistic crisis. Growing political censorship tended to drive filmmakers to find outlets in eroticism, and the resulting proliferation of pornography proved bad for the box office. The best film of the year, Hector Babenco's *Kiss of the Spider Woman*, succeeded in combining political and sexual motives. Based on a story by Manuel Puig, it told of the mutually enlightening relationship that develops between a homosexual and a political prisoner sharing a prison cell.

The most striking film to emerge from Cuba during the year was a coproduction with Italy and Spain, Fernando Birri's *Mi hijo el "Che."* This was a 60-minute portrait of the aged but still sprightly father of "Che" Guevara, through whose memories and old home movies emerges an impression of his son, not as a legend but as a vital, likable, idealistic young man.

Asia

The major event of the year in Japanese cinema was Akira Kurosawa's spectacular *Ran (Chaos)*, which translated *King Lear* to 16th-century Japan and changed the monarch's daughters to sons. The film opened the Tokyo Film Festival, promised great commercial success, and, according to the 75-year-old director, was the renascence of his career. Another veteran, Kon Ichikawa, remade his 30-year-old classic *The Burmese Harp*, but color could not recapture the poetic qualities of the original. Masaki Kobayashi's *The Empty Table* related the disastrous effects upon an ordinary middle-class family when the eldest son becomes a terrorist. Kobayashi also completed *The Tokyo Trial*, a remarkable 265-minute compilation on the International Military Tribunal for the Far East of 1946–48.

Political relaxation in China was reflected in the enlarged range of subjects; China even embarked on martial arts films with Tsui Siu Ming's *The Holy Robe of the Shaolin Temple*. The outstanding production, however, was Chen Kaige's *Yellow Earth*, a film of classic style, about a Communist soldier traveling in Shaanxi (Shensi) Province in the 1930s and befriending poverty-stricken peasants.

MOTORCYCLE RACING

In 1985 Freddie Spencer of the U.S. became the first man to win both the 500-cc and 250-cc motorcycle world championships in the same road-racing season. Riding a Rothman's Honda, he defeated the 1984 500-cc champion, Eddie Lawson (U.S.; Yamaha), who finished second, and mastered the West German Anton Mang (Honda) in the 250-cc series. Spencer recorded 14 wins and 4 seconds in 21 grand prix starts. In the 250-cc competition he won six consecutive races.

Fausto Gresini (Italy; Garelli) was the 125-cc champion, with countryman Pierpaulo Bianchi (MBA) finishing second. The 80-cc class was won,

for the second year, by Stefan Dörflinger (Switz.; Krauser). World Formula One champion was Joey Dunlop of Northern Ireland (Honda).

The 1985 world champion endurance team was Gerard Coudray and Patrick Igoa (France; Honda). The Le Mans, France, 24-hour event was won by the team of Guy Bertin, Bernard Millet, and Philippe Guichon (France; Suzuki).

In world motocross competition the 500-cc title went to Britain's Dave Thorpe (Honda). Heinz Kinigadner (Austria; KTM) was the 250-cc champion, and Hansi Bachtold and Fritz Fuss (Switz.; EML) took the sidecar class.

Thierry Michoud (France; Fantic), who set a record in winning 9 of the 12 rounds in the contest, was world trials champion. Eddie Lejeune (Belgium; Honda) finished in second place.

Winners of the main World Trophy in the International Six Days Enduro, held in Spain, were the Swedish team; East Germany took the subsidiary Junior Trophy contest. Erik Gundersen (Denmark) retained his world speedway championship.

MOUNTAINEERING

The Union Internationale des Associations d'Alpinisme (UIAA) held its annual General Assembly for 1985 in Venice, Italy, in October. The Chinese Mountaineering Association was elected to membership, and so the national mountaineering bodies of all the major Himalayan countries had become members of the UIAA. The new president was Carlo Sganzini (Italy), and Maj. Gen. Ali Mizrah (Pakistan) and Jaromir Wolf (Czechoslovakia) were elected vice-presidents. A main topic for discussion at the assembly was that of proposals to develop competition climbing. After previous unsuccessful proposals to introduce it as a sport in the Olympic Games, the Mountaineering Federation of the U.S.S.R. proposed a European cup competition in the Crimea under the existing Soviet competition rules and with UIAA patronage. This was rejected by the assembly, but individual countries were left to accept or reject Soviet invitations.

The UIAA approached the Himalayan countries with two requests: to reduce the compulsory personnel for lightweight expeditions, and to introduce a winter climbing season in India and Pakistan (previously Nepal had been the only country with such a season). The Indian government announced limited arrangements for climbing in the eastern Karakoram, to be undertaken by joint Indian-foreign expeditions. Noteworthy new routes were on Masherbrum northwest side by a Japanese party and on Gasherbrum I northwest face by Poles.

In Nepal in 1984 after the monsoon, 49 expeditions took place. Particularly noteworthy was the completion by a Spanish party of a route on the south face of Annapurna I. In 1985 before the monsoon, only 26 expeditions took place, including several on Mt. Everest (among them a successful ascent by British mountaineer Chris Bonnington);

Everest was fully booked until 1997. The Nepalese government announced a 10% increase in the royalty charge after the 1985 monsoon. Reinhold Messner of Italy climbed Annapurna I and Dhaulagiri I and so had only two 8,000-m (26,200-ft) peaks still to climb.

A new development in the Alps in 1984–85 was the wholehearted application of modern rock-climbing techniques and attitudes in the higher mountains, particularly in the Chamonix Aiguilles. Also noteworthy on Mont Blanc was the climbing of several difficult routes by one party in one day, such as the north face of the Grand Pilier d'Angle, the 1961 Freney route, the Freney-Bardill direct route, and the Innominata Arête in one day of 22 hours.

MOZAMBIQUE

The year 1985 began with sporadic acts of violence by the Mozambique National Resistance (MNR, or Renamo). The attacks were a repetition and escalation of similar acts that had, over several years, contributed to the breakdown of the country's economy and left most rural areas in a state of insecurity and urban centers virtually under siege. The government believed that funds and matériel were being supplied to the guerrillas from Portuguese and South African sources. In January, after some hesitation due to the constitutional principles involved, Portuguese Prime Minister Mário Soares responded to complaints from Mozambique by placing restrictions on MNR activists who had previously operated freely in Lisbon.

The South African government insisted that it was attempting to act as mediator between the government of Mozambique and the MNR and was fulfilling the terms of the 1984 Nkomati accord, under which it had promised not to give assistance to the MNR. After a meeting of the joint South African-Mozambican security commission in February, however, South African Foreign Minister R. F. ("Pik") Botha admitted that his government found it difficult to prevent supplies of aid from reaching the guerrillas by way of Portuguese who had left Mozambique and taken refuge in his country. Although Mozambican Pres. Samora Machel appeared skeptical about South Africa's sincerity and declared that in his opinion the Nkomati accord had failed, both countries reaffirmed their commitment to it in March.

The People's Assembly in June approved incentives to encourage Western investment in Mozambique and, simultaneously, the government signed its first loan agreement with the World Bank. The U.S. and the U.K. then made limited offers of assistance to areas affected by drought and of nonlethal military supplies, while the U.K. also promised to provide a training program for the Army. Machel visited both countries in September. In July an estimated 5,000 Zimbabwean troops joined the 2,000 already stationed in Mozambique to help protect the railway and the petroleum pipeline running from the Zimbabwean border to the Mozambican port of Beira.

Accusations of complicity with the guerrillas were again leveled against South Africa by the government. In reply the South African government admitted on September 19 that it had violated the Nkomati accord but had done so only in a technical sense and with the clear aim of bringing the MNR into meaningful negotiations with the government of Mozambique. As if to signal their continuing opposition, MNR representatives in Lisbon claimed that their movement had been responsible for huge explosions in a military arsenal near Maputo.

The MNR actions, together with the effects of the drought conditions suffered during the previous year, resulted, according to Finance Minister Rui Baltazar, in a 22% decline in the value of exports in 1984 and a 25% drop in industrial production.

MUSEUMS

At the Virginia Museum of Fine Arts in Richmond, a new $22 million west wing would hold the modernist decorative arts and paintings from the Mellon and Lewis collections. The National Building Museum, housed in the Pension Building in Washington, D.C., opened its exhibition galleries. Perhaps the most active museum in the U.S., the Whitney Museum of American Art in New York City opened its fourth satellite branch in the lower floors of the Equitable Life Assurance Society Building. The Whitney also revealed plans for a controversial expansion, a block-long, $37.5 million, ten-story addition by the postmodernist architect Michael Graves, which would engulf its main structure. Another mid-Manhattan expansion was announced by the Guggenheim Museum, which planned to build an 11-story, $9 million extension to its present 4-story annex in a style sympathetic to its famous Frank Lloyd Wright structure. The Isamu Noguchi Garden Museum, endowed by the sculptor and featuring his works, opened in Long Island City, N.Y.

The planned move of the International Museum of Photography from Eastman House in Rochester, N.Y., to the Smithsonian in Washington, D.C., was halted by a public outcry and subsequent refunding. The Kodak Co. donated property valued at $15 million to form an endowment for the museum. In Dallas, Texas, the Museum of Art unveiled its new 15,000-sq ft (1,395-sq m) decorative arts wing, which would house the Reeves Collection of 1,400 works. B. Gerald Cantor established an outdoor garden at Stanford University in which to display the 19 large sculptures of Auguste Rodin that he had given the university.

In Britain a consultation paper issued by the Office of Arts and Libraries in the autumn was designed to give the institutions greater incentives for raising cash from the public. This was thought by some to point toward eventual privatization of mu-

TIMES NEWSPAPERS LTD.

Actor Colin Welland expresses his opinion concerning the institution of a voluntary admission charge at the Victoria and Albert Museum in London.

seums. Admission charges were again a controversial subject as the Victoria and Albert Museum in London introduced "voluntary" charges in November. The V & A also announced the formation of a merchandising company whose purpose would be fund-raising. Following the example of a number of U.S. museums, the new company would produce and sell consumer goods based on objects in the museum's collection. The National Gallery of Art in Washington, D.C., announced that its Patrons Permanent Fund, which solicited small donations, had exceeded $50 million. The Art Institute of Chicago became the first U.S. cultural institution to issue short-term demand bonds.

The financial future of the National Gallery, London, seemed more secure following the announcement of a gift of £50 million by J. Paul Getty II. (For table of world currencies, *see* International Exchange and Payments.) The gift would help to fund acquisitions, perhaps keeping treasures in Britain that otherwise might have gone abroad.

In London's East End the Whitechapel Gallery reopened after having been closed more than two years for renovation. The Prado in Madrid opened its recently doubled floor space with an exhibition of Neapolitan paintings. The exhibition was the first to be held in the Villahermosa Palace, formerly a bank headquarters, acquired for the Prado by the Ministry of Culture. More than 12 years after the artist's death, the Picasso Museum in Paris was completed and opened to the public in September. It was housed in the 17th-century Hôtel Sâlé in the Marais district, restoration of which had cost F 80 million. At the British Museum the Wolfson Galleries of Classical Sculpture and Inscriptions were opened formally in April. The renovated area comprised eight basement-level galleries, including the Duveen Gallery displaying the Elgin Marbles.

In Scotland a major new museum complex was formed by the amalgamation of the Royal Scottish Museum and the National Museum of Antiquities of Scotland in Edinburgh, to be known as the Royal Museum of Scotland.

New Acquisitions

At Colmar, France, the "Isenheim Altarpiece," with panels by Matthias Grünewald and sculptures by Nicholas de Haguenau, was reassembled and went on view at the Musée d'Unterlinden. The sculptures had been purchased by the Badisches Landesmuseum, Karlsruhe, West Germany, in 1977 and after years of negotiations had finally returned to Colmar. The National Gallery, London, purchased a major painting by Van Dyck, "Charity." The V & A acquired the Rodney Searight Collection of watercolors, drawings, prints, and illustrated travel books depicting the Middle East as it appeared to travelers of the past. With the help of public donations, the British Museum raised £200,-000 for the purchase of a Samuel Palmer watercolor, "Moonlight with Evening Star." The painting had been sold to a U.S. buyer, but an export license was refused.

The J. Paul Getty Museum, with its huge endowment, bought two of the year's most expensive paintings: an "Adoration of the Magi" by the 15th-century Italian master Andrea Mantegna, for $10.4 million; and "The Annunciation" by Dirck Bouts, a later 15th-century Flemish artist, for at least $6 million. The Museum of Art in Philadelphia acquired 43,000 European Old Master and 19th-century prints through purchase and exchange with the Pennsylvania Academy of the Fine Arts.

Michael Graves's design for an addition to the Whitney Museum in New York City provoked controversy during the year. The original structure, designed by Marcel Breuer, comprises the lower left portion of the model.

PASCHALL/TAYLOR

A robbery in October at the Musée Marmottan in Paris resulted in the disappearance of one of the most important pictures in the history of modern art: Claude Monet's celebrated "Impression, Soleil Levant," from which the Impressionist movement derived its name. In an even more spectacular robbery, some 140 priceless pre-Columbian artifacts were stolen from the National Museum of Anthropology in Mexico City on Christmas Eve.

MUSIC

Classical

Symphonic Music. The year's most important symphonic premiere was that in Manchester, England, of British composer Peter Maxwell Davies's sinuously powerful Third Symphony. A BBC commission designed to mark the 50th anniversary of the BBC Northern Orchestra (since renamed the BBC Philharmonic), the symphony had been inspired by certain principles of Renaissance architecture. Its London premiere (at the Henry Wood Promenade concerts) confirmed earlier impressions of a work of striking potency and creative vigor.

Further premieres (of a sort) came in the shape of a performance and subsequent recording, at the small town of Odense in Denmark, of what might (or might not—scholars remained divided) be a previously unknown symphony by the young Mozart, the orchestral parts for which had been discovered in the Odense Symphony's library by orchestra archivist Gunnar Thygesen; and a concert performance at Bristol, England, under the baton of Carl Davis of a suite of incidental music written in 1967 by Sir William Walton for the film *The Battle of Britain* but subsequently jettisoned by producer Harry Saltzman.

More than 72,000 rock fans jammed the Live Aid concert in Wembley Stadium in London, and another 90,000 filled John F. Kennedy Stadium in Philadelphia as international pop stars raised money for African famine relief.

SYNDICATION INTERNATIONAL/PHOTO TRENDS

Principal interest in the U.S. centered on the Paris Orchestra's visit (their sixth to date) with chief conductor Daniel Barenboim and the spectacular progress of the previously shabby-sounding St. Louis Symphony under the increasingly impressive charge of Leonard (son of Felix) Slatkin. A European tour had yielded plaudits from even the most seasoned critics.

Also in the U.S., Lorin Maazel succeeded André Previn as principal conductor with the Pittsburgh Symphony, Previn having returned full time to Britain and a rapidly improving Royal Philharmonic Orchestra. Herbert Blomstedt took charge of the San Francisco Symphony from Edo de Waart (who had traveled home to assume control of the troubled Netherlands Opera). In Canada exiled Soviet conductor Rudolf Barshai was appointed principal conductor of the Vancouver Symphony, at the same time retaining a similar post with England's Bournemouth Symphony. Mstislav Rostropovich and the Washington National Orchestra scored a particular triumph in Paris, as did Sir Georg Solti and the Chicago Symphony in London.

U.S.-born James Conlon succeeded Hans Vonk as conductor in chief of The Netherlands' Rotterdam Philharmonic, Dutchman Vonk moving sideways with his appointment as music director of both the Dresden (East Germany) State Opera and Staatskapelle Orchestra. British conductor-scholar Norman del Mar replaced Ole Schmidt as principal at Denmark's Aarhus Symphony.

Opera. The biggest operatic news in the U.S. was perhaps the San Francisco Opera's lavish staging of Wagner's *The Ring* tetralogy (an event heavily advertised and promoted as far away as London and Paris). Principal singers included sopranos Helga Dernesch, Gwyneth Jones, and Eva Marton; contralto Hanna Schwarz; tenors Peter Hofmann and René Kollo; and basses Walter Berry and Thomas Stewart. Departing San Francisco Symphony music director Edo de Waart was the conductor.

The New York City Metropolitan Opera's season included a new production of *Khovanshchina* (the Shostakovich version), with Dernesch, in her Met debut, as Martha, Martti Talvela as Dositheus, Aage Haugland as Khovansky, Wieslav Ochman as Golitsin, and Alan Monk as Shaklovity. Among concert opera performances the Philadelphia Orchestra (conductor, Riccardo Muti) presented *Rigoletto* at Carnegie Hall in New York City, using Martin Chusid's new interpretation of the score. In the name part was Renato Bruson; Cecilia Gasdia made her U.S. debut as Gilda.

At the Bayreuth Festival in West Germany it proved to be conductor Giuseppe Sinopoli's year, with a strikingly somber new production (by Wolfgang Wagner) of Wagner's *Tannhäuser* and the customary *Ring* cycle, in which soprano Hildegard Behrens's assumption of the role of Brunnhilde was considered to be one of the most impressive, vocally, of recent years. The 1985 Bayreuth Festival witnessed also the last scheduled stagings of Harry Kupfer's fiery *The Flying Dutchman* production.

In Britain the Royal Opera House at Covent Garden in London crossed its fingers and hoped for the best with productions of such curiosities as Stockhausen's untranslatable *Donnerstag aus Licht,* produced by the National Theatre's Michael Bogdanov and conducted by Pierre Boulez protégé Peter Eotvos; and Alexander von Zemlinsky's *The Birthday of the Infanta,* and *Florentine Tragedy,* adapted from Oscar Wilde and produced in association with the West German Hamburg State Opera. The English National Opera's characteristically innovative season showcased, among more familiar fare, Handel's *Xerxes,* Sir Michael Tippett's *The Midsummer Marriage,* and (an increasing rarity in the unsentimental 1980s) the sweetly saccharine nonsense of Gounod's *Faust.* Other operatic delights enjoyed by Londoners in 1985 included productions of two rarities of Puccini's youth, *Le Villi* ("The Spirits") and *Edgar,* at the Bloomsbury Theatre and, at the Camden Festival, even more offbeat offerings, among them Caccini's *Euridice,* Boito's *Nerone,* and Richard Strauss's *Friedenstag.*

Recordings. After many seasons of recession, 1985 ranked as the audio and record industry's most important year in decades. CD (laser-read compact disc) came of age, consolidating throughout the Western world the previous three years of progress; in Europe and especially in the U.S. the new medium made its mark to the extent that current world production capacity (calculated at some 50 million units annually) proved inadequate, and demand began steadily to outstrip supply. As a result, the recording industry took on an almost jaunty air for the first time in more than a decade, a state of affairs reflected in RCA's sudden reemergence from its slumbers and subsequent lightning takeover of France's Erato.

Of particular interest to classical collectors was the quantity of back-catalog material already finding its way (by means of some highly sophisticated digital remastering techniques) onto compact discs. Classics such as Benjamin Britten's composer-conducted *War Requiem* (London-Decca), Karl Böhm's 1966 Bayreuth *The Ring* (Philips), Otto Klemperer's Beethoven symphony cycle (Angel-EMI), Sir Georg Solti's Richard Strauss *Salomé* (London-Decca), and many Wilhelm Furtwängler (Angel-EMI Japan) and Bruno Walter (Columbia-CBS Japan) reissues found their way (to spectacular effect) onto CD.

Under the circumstances the standard microgroove LP disc was obliged to take something of a back seat. Significant developments continued in this area, however. PRT (Precision Records and Tapes) unlocked in England a particularly valuable collection of reissues that returned to the catalog at budget prices a treasure trove of material that featured such figures as conductors Sir Adrian Boult and Sir John Barbirolli, cellist André Navarra, and

JIM WILSON/THE NEW YORK TIMES

Leontyne Price rehearses with James McCracken for a Metropolitan Opera production of Verdi's Aïda. *Price sang her farewell performance in her role as* Aïda.

pianist Bela Siki. Transfer and pressing quality were of a high order, as they were in Angel-EMI France's "Références" series. The latter continued to provide valuable material from the Angel-EMI lists, much of it unavailable for half a century and more.

Important first recordings included Bizet's *The Fair Maid of Perth* (Angel-EMI); Leonard Bernstein's complete *West Side Story,* conducted by the composer (Deutsche Grammophon); complete cycles of Bizet and Musorgski piano music (both Melodiya); Rutland Boughton's *The Immortal Hour* and Holst's *The Dream City* (both Hyperion); Francesco Cavalli's *Xerxes* (Harmonia Mundi); Gottfried von Einem's *Danton's Death* (Orfeo); Elgar's early cantata *King Olaf* (Angel-EMI); Ferenc Erkel's *Hunyadi László* and Respighi's *The Flame* (both Hungaraton); Josef Förster's *Eva* (Supraphon); Philip Glass's *Satyagraha* (Columbia CBS); Kalomiris's *Mother's Ring* (Concert Athens); a complete five-disc set of Sibelius songs (London-Decca); Richard Strauss's *Guntram* (Columbia-CBS); Tchaikovsky's *Iolanthe* (Erato); and the collected symphonies of Eduard Tubin.

Jazz

The most striking young player to become visible in 1985 was guitarist Stanley Jordan, 26, whose unorthodox approach to his instrument (he tapped the strings rather than plucking them) found favor with the public. His debut album, *Magic Touch* (Blue Note), was the year's best-selling jazz LP and also placed on the pop charts.

A new sextet, OTB (for "Out of the Blue"), made up of gifted players in their 20s, was launched by Blue Note, a label reactivated with much fanfare and a marathon New York concert featuring many of the luminaries associated with it in the 1950s and 1960s. It quickly assumed a leading position in the field.

Only a few months before its 50th birthday, George Gershwin's Porgy and Bess *had its first Metropolitan Opera performance in New York City in 1985.*

BEATRIZ SCHILLER

Trumpeter Wynton Marsalis repeated his astonishing feat of 1984 by winning Grammy awards as best instrumental soloist in both the jazz and classical categories. No new classical record by Marsalis was issued in 1985, but his jazz album *Black Codes (from the Underground)* (Columbia) was hailed as his best yet.

While Marsalis separated his jazz and classical careers, some notable "crossing over" took place between these musics. The San Francisco-based Kronos String Quartet recorded music by Thelonious Monk (for Landmark Records) and premiered, at New York City's Carnegie Recital Hall, new works by Muhal Richard Abrams, Anthony Braxton, Leroy Jenkins, and Leo Smith, noted composer-instrumentalists who all emerged from Chicago's AACM (Association for the Advancement of Creative Musicians) in the 1960s. An opera by composer and pianist Anthony Davis, *"X"* (based on the life of Malcolm X), was presented in Philadelphia in October and was scheduled for full-scale production at the New York City Opera in 1986. Classical and jazz works by Ornette Coleman were performed at a week-long event in his honor in Hartford, Conn.

Two of the most respected saxophonists in modern jazz, Sonny Rollins and Wayne Shorter, made news in 1985. Rollins gave the first solo concert of his long career at New York City's Museum of Modern Art. It was recorded (by Fantasy) and was a milestone in the annals of unaccompanied jazz performances. Shorter, to the delight of his many admirers, detached himself from Weather Report, the successful jazz-fusion band he had led with Joe Zawinul since 1970, and toured with his own quartet in the wake of the release of his first album as a leader in a decade (*Atlantis;* Columbia).

In the field of big-band jazz, trumpeter-composer-arranger Thad Jones was appointed leader of the Count Basie Orchestra. Though best known as coleader (with drummer Mel Lewis) of one of the most innovative big bands of the 1960s and '70s, Jones declared himself proud to perpetuate Basie's legacy, which also was celebrated by the publication of *Good Morning Blues,* Basie's posthumous autobiography, as told to essayist, novelist, and jazz historian Albert Murray. One of the few surviving stars of the golden age of big bands, Benny Goodman, resumed active performing after a lengthy layoff. At the helm of a big band borrowed from a young tenor saxophonist, Loren Schoenberg (which itself made its recording debut in 1985), Goodman led a tribute to Fletcher Henderson at Waterloo Village in New Jersey and gave a concert at Yale University. With the band, and such noted alumni as Teddy Wilson, Red Norvo, and Slam Stewart, he also taped a television special. On drums for that occasion was Louie Bellson, whose own big band was among the several active in Los Angeles.

Among other veteran jazz performers, Joe Williams had an outstanding year. The singer won his first Grammy award; saw the publication of his biography, *Every Day* (by Leslie Gourse); and joined the cast of the nation's most popular television series, "The Cosby Show," portraying Bill Cosby's father-in-law. Also conspicuously active was Benny Carter. A mere 78, the saxophonist, trumpeter, and arranger toured Europe and the U.S. and made his first album as a leader since 1976 (*A Gentleman and His Music,* Concord Jazz).

Previous attempts at organizing the jazz community had not been notably effective, but some promising developments occurred in 1985. The formation of the National Jazz Service Organization, based in Washington, D.C., and supported by the National Endowment for the Arts, was announced in the spring. It was to function as a national advisory center and planned to establish a permanent jazz repertory ensemble and an archive. Also formed during the year was the American Federation of Jazz Societies, dedicated to setting up a national touring network for jazz performers and to the general promotion of jazz.

Popular

The biggest pop music event of the year—indeed, the most spectacular event in the entire history of pop—was very much a triumph of this new idealism. On July 13, some 72,000 people packed Wembley Stadium in London, and a further 90,000 packed the John F. Kennedy Stadium in Philadelphia, for a 16-hour concert that took place on both sides of the Atlantic and was televised live around the world. In all, it was watched by over 1,500,000,000 people. More remarkable still was the fact that this was a charity concert, at which all performers and technicians gave their services free, to raise money for the Band Aid fund to combat starvation in Ethiopia. The two Live Aid shows raised over $71.5 million from viewers around the world. The extraordinary event had been arranged by Bob Geldof, the singer with the Boomtown Rats, who immediately became an international celebrity.

Live Aid, along with the earlier Band Aid appeal in Britain and USA for Africa in the U.S., showed that musicians could still be as socially concerned as they had been in the 1960s; now, however, they were better organized and more powerful as a result. After Live Aid, musical benefits for different causes began to spring up in Britain and the U.S. After turning their thoughts to those suffering abroad, U.S. musicians began to concentrate on those suffering at home. Bob Dylan had commented on the plight of U.S. farmers during Live Aid, and Willie Nelson later organized his own Farm Aid concert. Meanwhile, Bruce Springsteen, undoubtedly the most successful U.S. pop musician of the year, went from publicizing the plight of the Vietnam veterans to publicizing the problems of hunger in the U.S., promoting Food Bank programs and donating money to them in towns where he performed.

Along with the social concern came political involvement. In Britain a year-long miners' strike ended in March. Many musicians had been politicized by the strike, giving benefit shows for the miners, and this in turn led to musical support for Britain's Labour Party. Soloist Billy Bragg invited members of Parliament from the Labour Party to his "Jobs for Youth" tour in March and later started an organization called Red Wedge, pledged to win youth votes for Labour at the next election. Renewed interest in international politics helped organizations in Britain and the U.S. fighting apartheid (racial separation) in South Africa. In Britain Robert Wyatt and Jerry Dammers from The Specials collaborated with students from South West Africa/Namibia on the *Wind of Change,* a record that became a minor hit and raised money

for the South West Africa People's Organization. In the U.S. a whole set of musicians—Dylan, Miles Davis, Springsteen, and Bobby Womack, along with such British artists as Pete Townshend and Ringo Starr—collaborated in an even more commercial antiapartheid fund-raiser, *Sun City.*

While the musical causes of 1985 were easy to spot, the musical trends that went with them were not so obvious, as must have been clear to anyone watching the Live Aid concert. On show, after all, were grand old bands from the 1960s, like The Who, alongside newer, established superstars like U2 and Simple Minds or brand new contenders like Madonna. One of the stars of Live Aid was Phil Collins, who flew by Concorde across the Atlantic during the show and so managed to appear in both London and Philadelphia. His enormous success during the year with the album *No Jacket Required* reflected one clear trend—for well-known performers with a particular band to go off on a solo career of their own. Mick Jagger (who sang solo and with Tina Turner at Live Aid) released his first solo album during the year, to only moderate critical acclaim. He then returned to recording with the Rolling Stones. Sting, the lead singer with The Police, also went solo during the year with an album, *The Dream of the Blue Turtles,* and a world tour. He was accompanied on both by musicians from the black American jazz scene and reflected the new socially concerned trend in music with songs about miners and the arms race.

The year's best-sellers in the U.S. came mostly from these well-established artists, along with other veterans such as John Fogerty, once the leader of Creedence Clearwater Revival. The most successful black U.S. artists were also mostly well-established names, including Tina Turner and Stevie Wonder; the latter contributed to the antiapartheid trend with one of the songs on his album *In Square Circle.*

New developments on the white American rock scene included the continued resurgence of guitar bands like R.E.M., while the most inventive U.S. album of the year was Tom Waits's *Raindogs,* a mixture of blues, Kurt Weill, and Broadway. Newcomers who did well in the U.S. ranged from the British duo Tears for Fears, who sold more than six million copies of their album *Songs from the Big Chair,* to a new U.S. rock queen, Madonna. An established British group that enjoyed a big success in the U.S. was Dire Straits with *Brothers in Arms.*

In the far more fluid and volatile British home market, there was no one clear trend but a whole variety of styles. Favorites of previous years like Frankie Goes to Hollywood and Culture Club slipped from favor, and in their place came everything from the mournful self-pitying balladry of The Smiths to the cool soulful balladry of Sade or the far more chaotic but exhilarating blend of punk and Irish traditional styles offered by The Pogues, one of the more unexpected successes in a colorful year.

Demonstrators in Utrecht denounce Pope John Paul II's visit to The Netherlands in May. The pontiff's trip was marred by demonstrations and riots.

FRANCOIS LOCHON—GAMMA/LIAISON

NETHERLANDS, THE

During 1985 three issues dominated public life in The Netherlands: the visit of Pope John Paul II; the decision regarding the deployment of U.S. medium-range cruise missiles; and the "Elfstedentocht," a traditional ice-skating race around 11 cities in Friesland Province. A cold spell allowed the race to take place on February 21 for the first time in 22 years. Attracting 16,000 competitors, the event caused skating fever to grip the country. The race was won by Evert van Benthem, a 26-year-old farmer, in a time of 6 hr 46 min 46 sec. He received a wreath of honor from Queen Beatrix and became a national hero, at least for a time.

Pope John Paul received rather less attention when he paid a four-day official visit in May. The majority of Dutch people had mixed feelings about his visit; on the one hand, they appreciated his disarming nature and his efforts to deliver his speeches in Dutch; on the other, they disapproved of the Roman Catholic Church's views on divorce, abortion, contraception, and the role of women in the church. In the face of protests that began a week before his arrival and continued throughout his visit, the pope remained firm. Among several groups who declined to meet him were the Dutch Jews, who refused because he chose not to apologize for the fact that the church did not speak out against Nazi persecution of Jews during World War II. The pope's reception revealed the independent nature of Dutch culture more clearly than Catholic officials could express it to the Vatican.

On November 1 Prime Minister Ruud Lubbers announced that the government had agreed to sign a treaty with the U.S. allowing NATO to deploy 48 cruise missiles in The Netherlands by 1988 and guaranteeing its permission for five years. The agreement, expected to come into force in 1986, marked the end of more than six years of emotional political discussion and followed an attempt in June 1984 to link the decision with the progress of East-West arms-control negotiations. Days earlier Lubbers had been handed a petition signed by some 3,750,000 people opposed to deployment. In October the U.S.S.R. launched an intensive political offensive aimed at influencing the government. At the last minute the government was invited to discuss disarmament proposals with the Soviets if it would abandon its intention to accept the missiles.

The government decision was strongly opposed by the Socialist Party (PVDA) and the smaller left-wing parties, which claimed that it was unconstitutional and that the government had not tried to negotiate with the U.S.S.R. The two major government parties favored the decision. The Liberals (VVD) were satisfied that the move showed The Netherlands to be a reliable member of NATO, while the Christian Democratic Appeal accepted it as the inevitable consequence of the failure of its attempt to influence arms-control negotiations.

Queen Beatrix and Prince Claus paid an official visit to Spain on October 8–10, returning the visit by King Juan Carlos to The Netherlands in 1980. The occasion was seen as a final gesture of reconciliation. After more than three centuries, the war in which The Netherlands won independence from Spain was banished to the history books.

NEWSPAPERS

At a ten-minute ceremony in New York City in September, Rupert Murdoch, the Australian-born publisher whose holdings included more than 80 newspapers and magazines on three continents, became a U.S. citizen. Murdoch took that unusual step to complete a deal he had made earlier in the year to purchase six television stations from Metromedia Inc., a major U.S. broadcasting firm. U.S. Federal Communications Commission regulations barred foreigners from holding more than 20% of a broadcast license. At the same time, other FCC rules prohibited simultaneous ownership of a TV station and a daily newspaper in the same city, and so it appeared that Murdoch would have to dispose of two major dailies he owned in cities with Metromedia outlets: the *New York Post* (circulation 930,000) and the *Chicago Sun-Times* (circulation 650,000).

Even before the Metromedia purchase, however, Murdoch had sold another of his newspapers, the *Village Voice* (circulation 164,000), a weekly published in New York City. The buyer was Leonard Stern, president of Hartz Mountain Industries, manufacturers of products for pet animals, and the purchase price was slightly more than $55 million. Murdoch had acquired the paper in 1977, when he bought *New York* and *New West* magazines. Though the publisher would not have been required to dispose of the *Voice* under FCC rules, it was widely assumed that he sold it to raise cash to buy the Metromedia stations.

In any case, the *Village Voice* sale and the prospect that the *Post* and the *Sun-Times* would soon change hands made 1985 a busy year for newspaper buying and selling. Much of it was done by a single firm, Gannett Co., the nation's sixth largest media company (86 daily newspapers, 6 television stations, and 14 radio stations). Gannett bought the respected *Des Moines* (Iowa) *Register* (circulation 238,000) and three sister papers for $200 million from the Des Moines Register and Tribune Co. Then Gannett spent $42 million for *Family Weekly,* a magazine supplement inserted in the Sunday editions of more than 300 newspapers that had a combined circulation of more than 12 million. The supplement was subsequently renamed *USA Weekend,* prompting many subscriber newspapers to stop carrying it. The papers objected that the redesigned supplement was too similar to Gannett's three-year-old national daily, *USA Today* (circulation 1,247,000), which many of the papers considered a direct competitor. In perhaps the biggest newspaper transaction of the year, Gannett acquired the Evening News Association, parent firm of the *Detroit News* (circulation 656,000), which had been controlled by the Scripps family for 112 years. The price was $717 million and included lucrative television stations in six cities. Under FCC rules against cross-ownership, Gannett could keep all of the stations only if it disposed of several newspapers, most notably the *Tucson* (Ariz.) *Citizen* (circulation 61,000).

Newspaper readership and advertising revenues had another record-breaking year in 1984. Average daily circulation hit an all-time high of 63,081,740 according to the 1985 *Editor & Publisher International Year Book.* That represented an increase of 437,137 over 1983. A preliminary report of the Newspaper Advertising Bureau revealed a 15% increase in advertising dollars spent in newspapers.

An exact comparison with the previous period was difficult to make because 1985 was the first

full year in which column inches replaced agate lines in the U.S. as the standard unit for measuring newspaper advertising. An overwhelming majority of U.S. dailies agreed to the change, which was the first such move toward standardization since 1820, when the agate line was first adopted.

Despite the industry's evident prosperity, the number of daily newspapers in the U.S. declined in 1985 to 1,688, a net loss of 13. Nineteen dailies switched to morning publication, bringing the total of morning papers to 458 and total morning circulation to 35,424,418. The number of evening papers dropped to 1,257, and evening circulation declined to 27,657,322.

In Canada average circulation rose in 1984 by 78,969 copies, or about 1½%, to 5,339,712. Morning circulation increased by 85,014 to 2,574,174, while evening distribution dropped by 6,045 to 2,765,538. The number of dailies declined by one, to 114.

The gold medal for public service, most prestigious of the Pulitzer Prizes, went to the *Fort Worth* (Texas) *Star-Telegram* for a series by its Defense Department reporter, Mark Thompson, about defects in U.S. Army helicopters that had been cited as a cause in 67 crashes and had killed nearly

The staff of the Des Moines Register *await word of the paper's fate in January. The highly regarded* Register *and three sister papers were bought by the Gannett Co.*
AP/WIDE WORLD

AP/WIDE WORLD

Cape Times *editor Tony Heard leaves Magistrates' Court in Cape Town after being arrested for publishing quotes attributed to Oliver Tambo, a leader of the African National Congress and a "banned" person.*

250 servicemen. The medal was especially gratifying to journalists at the paper, which had been the target of an advertising boycott organized by the Fort Worth-based firm that manufactured the helicopters.

None of the usual Pulitzer-winning papers—the *New York Times,* the *Washington Post,* and the *Wall Street Journal*—won a prize in 1985. Instead, the *Philadelphia Inquirer* and Long Island's *Newsday* each took home two Pulitzers. In addition, Jon Franklin of the *Baltimore* (Md.) *Evening Sun* received an award in the newly created category of explanatory journalism for his seven-part series on molecular psychiatry. Alice Steinbach of the *Baltimore Sun,* the *Evening Sun*'s sister paper, won a Pulitzer for feature writing. Thomas Knudson of the *Des Moines Register* was cited for a six-part series on the occupational hazards of farming, while Lucy Morgan and Jack Reed of the *St. Petersburg* (Fla.) *Times* won a prize for their investigation of alleged corruption in a local sheriff's office.

In other Pulitzer awards Jeff MacNelly, political cartoonist for the *Chicago Tribune,* received his third prize; Studs Terkel was cited for his nonfiction book *"The Good War": An Oral History of World War Two;* Alison Lurie won a prize for her novel *Foreign Affairs;* and *Sunday in the Park with George,* with music by Stephen Sondheim and book by James Lapine, was awarded the Pulitzer for drama.

In the last quarter of 1985 ownership of 5 of Britain's 17 national newspaper titles changed hands, the staff on three others agreed to cuts of up to one-third in manpower levels, and a long-awaited change in printing union attitudes to the less labor-intensive new technologies seemed well under way. One of the most important catalysts in this ferment of change was the arrival on the national newspaper scene of Eddie Shah, publisher of a small chain of free newspapers in northwestern England. He had first come to prominence in 1983 by means of a long industrial confrontation and legal battle with the printing union, the National Graphical Association, that had ended with the union's being heavily fined for contempt of court under new trade union legislation. Early in 1985 Shah announced his intention of setting up a new national daily newspaper, which by printing outside London would escape the union rules on manpower and use of electronic technology that had made the "Fleet Street" nationals so unprofitable and slow to change. This gave existing owners both reason and excuse for speeding technological change and forced the unions to negotiate seriously with national newspapers over the changes already being accepted in the regional and local press.

Each publisher took a different approach, but most involved investing in new production facilities away from the traditional central London area of Fleet Street. The most ambitious of these plans ended the reign, with dramatic swiftness, of one of the oldest Fleet Street proprietors, the Berry family, who in December had to yield a controlling interest in the Telegraph group to Canadian businessman and publisher Conrad Black.

The Guardian, which had shared printing in London with *The Times,* was building its own center on the Isle of Dogs in London's East End. Murdoch's News Group sought to activate its Wapping center, mothballed for several years because of a failure to agree on terms with the unions, by announcing another new title, the *London Post,* planned as an evening paper but with 24-hour capacity. The *London Post* had as editorial director Charles Wilson, but he returned to *The Times* in November, as editor, on the death of Charles Douglas-Home.

There were many instances during the year of tighter controls on the media. In South Africa Anthony Heard, editor of the *Cape Times,* was arrested after publishing an interview with Oliver Tambo, "banned" president of the African National Congress, and faced a maximum three-year prison sentence if convicted under the Internal Security Act. South Africa's leading liberal newspaper, the 83-year-old *Rand Daily Mail,* closed in April.

Special Report: Freedom of Information

by Harold Evans

Tension between government and press is a healthy commonplace in all the political democracies. Terrorism has given it a new twist. Both the British and U.S. governments accuse television of sustaining terrorists with the oxygen of publicity. In the United States the Reagan administration condemned the television interviewing of American hostages held by Lebanese Shi'ites in Beirut in 1985 as "terribly harmful" in the negotiations. In Britain shortly afterward, Prime Minister Margaret Thatcher's government intimidated the lay governors of the British Broadcasting Corporation into banning a documentary program featuring a leader of the Irish Republican Army.

The issues of public policy that provoke charges of irresponsibility and countercharges of censorship are similar in all the political democracies, but the grounds of the debate, and the consequences of it, are very different. The difference is notable between the U.S. and the two European countries most closely associated with the early republic, Britain and France. It is greatest between the U.S. and Britain, which are thought to share a common heritage of law and language.

Free Debate Versus Free Inquiry

Europeans go to the barricades for the right to free speech. Americans talk more often of "the right to know." The insufficiently appreciated distinction between these two ideas is at the heart of the matter. It is a distinction between opinion and fact. The coercive power of the state and the law is seldom brought to bear against the utterance of an opinion. The teachings of Milton, Locke, and Mill are embedded in everyone's consciousness. In Britain a beaming policeman protects speakers at Hyde Park Corner, within earshot of Buckingham Palace, who incite the violent overthrow of the monarchy. In the U.S. the lawns opposite the White House are frequently ablaze with banners denouncing the administration. Nothing is sacred in Voltaire's France; debate there is more catholic than in the U.S., where Constitution, church, and capitalism are secure from satire. But this tolerant convergence on free speech does not apply to free inquiry. U.S. law obliges government agencies to disclose official information. The law of Britain punishes disclosure. The French leave it to custom and practice, which is usually just as restrictive.

The differences are apparent at once in the nomenclature. The relevant statute in the U.S. is the Freedom of Information (FOI) Act; in Britain it is the Official Secrets Act. The Freedom of Information Act, 20 years old in 1986, lays it down that all records in the possession of the executive branch of the federal government must be provided to anyone on request unless they can be withheld by one or more of nine specific tests (concerning mainly national defense, privacy, privileged or confidential trade secrets, or the regulation of financial institutions). The Official Secrets Act, betraying its origins as a weapon against espionage in World War I, threatens jail or heavy fine for officials who give information without approval and for those who receive it.

In two recent cases the British prosecuted officials for revealing information that was politically embarrassing but, on the government's own admission, posed no threat to national security. A junior clerk in the Ministry of Defence was jailed for six months for passing a document to *The Guardian* newspaper discussing how the government proposed to handle public relations for the deployment of cruise missiles. A senior civil servant was prosecuted for sending a document to a member of Parliament that showed how Parliament itself had been deceived by ministers during the 1982 Falkland Islands/Islas Malvinas war about the sinking of the Argentine cruiser *General Belgrano.* The jury acquitted, though the judge instructed the jury to convict on the grounds that the interests of the state and of the government of the day are one and the same thing.

The authoritarian overtones of this view were widely criticized, but the British political and legal establishment places high value on confidentiality and secrecy in government and business. There has been talk about freedom of information legislation since the Fulton Report in the '60s, through the Franks Report, Labour manifesto promises, draft Civil Service codes, private members' bills, and an abandoned Conservative Party measure entitled *The Protection* (author's italics) of Official Information Bill; a new all-party campaign for a freedom of information act was launched in 1982. All these efforts have foundered on two things: a genuine belief in Lord Salisbury's dictum that government must be private to be good; and an anxiety to do nothing to disturb the supremacy of Parliament. Even the sovereign body of Parliament is restricted in the right to know. Successive administrations have refused to answer questions from members of Parliament on rent for government offices, telephone tapping, Cabinet committees, forecasts of future trends in incomes, the names of nonmedicinal and cosmetic products containing hexachlorophene, and many more such subjects remote from any question of national security.

Opinion Versus Information

The roots of the striking difference between Britain and the U.S. go back further than 1966, for the U.S. Freedom of Information Act is no more than a legislative embodiment of the prescription of James Madison: "A people who mean to be their own governors, must arm themselves with the power knowledge gives. A popular government without popular information or the means of acquiring it, is but a prologue to a farce or a tragedy or both." This was the logic of the First Amendment to the Constitution that "Congress shall make no law . . . abridging the freedom of speech, *or of the press*" (author's italics). The emphasis on popular sovereignty was, of course, a reaction to the suppressions of the British crown. In Britain itself there was nothing to disturb the assumption of the classical philosophers that free speech was underpinned by a free flow of facts.

The assumption that the facts on which to base an opinion were available was tolerable in a society with very small conglomerations of power and a ruling elite, certainly as tolerable as the assumption of the classical economists that there was a free flow of goods and services in a perfect market. But in Britain the citizen's access to knowledge failed to keep pace with the vast expansion of state and corporate power. Two attitudes seem to underlie the restriction of freedom of information.

First, information is frequently referred to by judges and politicians as if it were the property of the government and not of the people. This lends substance to Thomas Jefferson's conviction that in Britain the Tory or Norman concept of rights is dominant: that they are grants from the crown, as distinct from the Whig or Saxon concept that they are natural to the people and the crown has no powers except those expressly granted.

Second, in cases where free publication has been challenged, the British courts have fallen back on common law precedents rooted in the rights of property. There is no Bill of Rights to put personal rights into the balance, and a Bill of Rights is rejected on the grounds that it would limit the supremacy of Parliament.

The Right to Know

The First Amendment has been the principal bulwark against censorship in the U.S., but the right to publish is not the same as access to official information, a concept that seems to have originated in Scandinavia. Though the principle of freedom of information has long been accepted in the U.S., it took many years of campaigning by press, lawyers, and members of Congress to gain the Freedom of Information Act. Before 1966 the American citizen had to prove his right to look at governmental records. The revolution of the Freedom of Information Act was to shift the burden of proof from the individual to the government. Congress enacted a series of amendments in 1974 that encouraged even more disclosure. Inquiries have run around 150,000 a year. They have uncovered an astonishing diversity of information of public importance, from illegal FBI harassment of domestic political groups to congressional and executive abuse of travel funds. As a result of news reports based on FOI information, legislation and court rulings have brought about the overhaul of the nursing home industry, the removal of unsafe drugs from market shelves, and a closer examination of irregularities in defense contracting.

The Reagan administration has sought to reverse this process, by seeking lifetime secrecy pledges from government employees, by lobbying in Congress for amendment of the act, and by discretionary executive action that has made exploitation of the act much more costly and time-consuming. Delays of 6 to 9 months have become common, 14 months with the CIA. The federal courts, with an increasing number of Reagan appointees, also have cut down on the availability of information. Recent decisions have allowed officials to remove records from agency files, thereby precluding access under the act; permitted the director of the CIA to protect any intelligence source or method without any showing of harm to national security; and made all documents that are privileged in civil litigation unavailable under FOI. A comprehensive package of 40 amendments has been proposed by Sen. Orrin Hatch (Rep., Utah), principally on the grounds of enabling business to protect its commercial secrets and preventing access by organized crime. The Reporters' Committee for the Freedom of the Press in Washington says the package will increase delays and costs still further.

In its efforts to curb the flow of information, the philosophical approach of the Reagan administration, contrary to the American tradition, is that government information is government property. There is an echo of the dominant attitude in Britain and France (though not in Denmark or Sweden, or in Canada, Australia, and New Zealand, where Conservative administrations have brought in freedom of information legislation). The Reagan campaign has had limited success, but the proven value of openness, the robustness of the judiciary, the existence of the First Amendment, and the spirit of the country seem likely to sustain the U.S. as the most open of the democracies, convinced still, in the words of Justice Louis Brandeis, that "sunlight is the best of disinfectants and electric light the most efficient policeman."

NEW ZEALAND

In 1985 New Zealand's Labour Party government, brought to power in the July 1984 general elections, introduced measures to cut income tax and impose a 10% goods and service tax (GST). The move followed years of complaint over the stifling effect of higher levels of the income-tax system and of speculation as to when politicians would act on the findings of a formal inquiry recommending that taxation be based on spending. Finance Minister Roger Douglas presented the budget proposals in two parts, on June 13 and August 20. They provided for a $NZ1.5 billion reduction in the budget deficit to $NZ1.3 billion, which, at 2.8% of gross domestic product, would make it the lowest for 12 years. (For table of world currencies, *see* International Exchange and Payments.) Corporate taxes were increased slightly, and companies were to be taxed on the value of perks such as cars and loans given to staff.

The introduction of GST, originally planned for April 1986, was postponed until October 1986. Low-income families were to receive support to deal with the expected 5% rise in prices that GST would bring. Labour faced criticism from its own industrial wing, which feared that low earners would suffer from the changes and fought to exclude essential foods from the tax, despite the government's determination to tax all goods. The government urged restraint in wage demands as the wage freeze imposed by the previous administration came to an end. In September 1985 independent economists from the Institute of Economic Research predicted that the annual average wage increase would be 13%. The inflation rate dropped from a record 5.1% in the quarter ended in June to 2.8% in the following quarter.

By the end of its first 12 months in office, the Labour Party government had, among other things, floated the New Zealand dollar, introduced a bill of rights, provided schools with more teachers, set up new ministries for women and the environment, reopened a mission in New Delhi, India, with Sir Edmund Hillary as ambassador, and cut overseas borrowing. It attracted criticism for imposing a special tax on old-age pensions, despite an earlier resolve not to do so; for identifying itself closely with a controversial campaign to decriminalize homosexuality; and for failing to control soaring interest rates. The government's 17-seat majority was reduced when it lost a by-election in what was previously considered a safe Labour seat.

From an international perspective, the most newsworthy event of 1985 in New Zealand was the bombing and subsequent sinking of the *Rainbow Warrior,* flagship of the Greenpeace organization, in Auckland Harbour in July. Prime Minister David Lange led the government's outraged response to the act, the responsibility for which was subsequently attributed to two French secret service agents. Lange continued to promote his government's decision

REUTERS/POPPERFOTO

The Most Rev. Sir Paul Reeves (left), the first person of Maori descent to be named governor-general of New Zealand, is offered a traditional Maori greeting by Prime Minister David Lange before his installation in Parliament.

to ban nuclear-powered and nuclear-armed vessels from the country's ports in a significant show of independence and challenge to the U.S., the country that in practice would be most affected by the ruling. The prime minister was criticized at home for a tour of African countries that was considered by some New Zealanders as pointless. Nonetheless, Lange maintained a high profile, even as the opposition National Party lamented the failure of its new leader, former justice minister Jim McLay, to match the impact of former party leader and prime minister Sir Robert Muldoon.

Sir Basil Arthur, speaker of the House of Representatives, died in office in May and was succeeded by Gerald Wall. Paul Reeves, Anglican archbishop of New Zealand, resigned his church office to take up appointment as governor-general, becoming the first person of Maori descent to fill the post.

NICARAGUA

The Sandinista National Liberation Front government of Nicaragua decided in May 1985 to step up military action against its opponents by launching punitive strikes against the Honduran bases of the largest *contra* grouping, the Nicaraguan Democratic Force (FDN). Tens of thousands of people were moved out of areas in northern Nicaragua in order to deprive the *contras* of local support and to create "free-fire zones" that would enable the Army to operate freely. The morale of the *contras* was boosted by the U.S. administration's total embargo on trade with Nicaragua, imposed as of May 7, and by the vote in the U.S Congress on June 12 that approved

TASS/SOVFOTO

Nicaragua's Pres. Daniel Ortega Saavedra (left) is greeted by Soviet leader Mikhail Gorbachev during his visit to the Soviet Union in May.

the release of $27 million in "nonlethal" aid to the rebels. Although apparently unable to retain control of captured areas, *contra* forces, particularly those based in Honduras, remained a potent threat. The effectiveness of the Democratic Revolutionary Alliance (ARDE) rebels, based in Costa Rica, was reduced by Costa Rica's stated neutrality, by their own internal divisions, and by successful Sandinista raids. Opposition groups attempted to present a united front by forming the United Nicaraguan Opposition, but the presence within the FDN of former national guardsmen who had been supporters of the late president Anastasio Somoza was deeply resented by other anti-Sandinista groups.

Following the November 1984 elections, the swearing in of the new National Assembly and the inauguration of Daniel Ortega Saavedra as president took place in January 1985. On October 15 the government reimposed the state of emergency that had been lifted shortly before the elections.

Nicaragua's economic difficulties posed a more direct threat to the government than did the actions of the *contras,* although problems were compounded by the fact that 40% of government spending was devoted to counterinsurgency operations. On February 8 the government announced a package of austerity measures that included production incentives for agriculture, a freeze on nonmilitary public-sector hiring, salary increases of 47–60%, the termination of most subsidies, and the devaluation of the córdoba, the unit of currency. The value of coffee exports fell by 20.5% to $119.2 million in 1984, while sales of cotton rose by 27.5% to $133.8 million, making it the most important export.

Pressure from the U.S. forced the government to abandon its application for a $58 million loan from the Inter-American Development Bank in March 1985. In its search for multilateral credits, the government was showing greater willingness to pay its debts; for example, in April the $7.5 million outstanding to the International Monetary Fund under a loan granted to the Somoza regime was repaid. President Ortega's trip to Europe in April–May apparently raised credits worth $402 million, one-half of which came from Western countries. The U.S.S.R. promised to supply from 80 to 90% of the country's petroleum needs.

NIGERIA

Maj. Gen. Mohammed Buhari, Nigeria's leader since the Army seized power on the last day of 1983, was himself toppled from power on Aug. 27, 1985, in a bloodless coup. During 20 months in power the Buhari administration had clearly been unsuccessful in its efforts to solve Nigeria's pressing economic problems. At the same time it had become deeply unpopular as a result of its severely repressive tactics.

The new leader was Maj. Gen. Ibrahim Babangida, who declared on coming to power: "We recognize that a government, be it civilian or military, needs the consent of the people to govern if it is to reach its objectives." The Supreme Military Council was replaced by the Armed Forces Ruling Council and the Federal Executive Council by a National Council of Ministers. Six of the previous ministers were retained. The majority of ministers were military officers. Two important new appointments were those of Bolaji Akinyemi as external affairs minister and Kalu Idika Kalu as finance minister. The new regime replaced 13 of the 19 state governors.

Nigerians had been prepared for sacrifices and accepted austerity measures imposed by the Buhari regime. They found, however, that individual freedom was also curtailed, in particular the right to comment upon government actions, and that the regime showed a marked unwillingness to take public opinion into account. Its most unpopular measure was Decree 4, which effectively muzzled the press. The new government at once repealed Decree 4 and released about 100 detainees, many of whom had been in prison for 20 months without charge or trial. In addition, the powers of the much-criticized and feared Nigerian Security Organization were greatly reduced.

Although the Buhari government blamed its predecessors for the state of the economy, both unemployment and prices continued to rise. The question of whether or not to accept a loan from the International Monetary Fund (IMF), together with the conditions that would be attached to it, had been under debate for three years. Babangida at once invited a public debate on the issue. Public opinion was overwhelmingly hostile; opponents of the IMF loan insisted that Nigeria opt for a policy of self-reliance that would also entail rejecting ex-

In the second wave of mass expulsions in two years, the Nigerian government rounded up tens of thousands of illegal aliens and trucked them, along with what household goods they could carry, to border points for repatriation.

JOHN CHIASSON—GAMMA/ LIAISON

ternal borrowing from other sources. The external debt amounted to just short of $21.4 billion at the end of 1984.

Setting out the objectives of his government, Babangida emphasized economic reconstruction, social justice, and self-reliance. It became clear to Nigerians that the military would be in power for a considerable time and that all decision making would be dominated by economic factors. On October 1, the 25th anniversary of independence, Babangida declared a state of economic emergency for the next 15 months, during which time the aim would be to turn the economy around and lay the foundations for long-term development.

NORWAY

Parliamentary elections held on Sept. 9, 1985, returned to power the three-party, right-of-center coalition led by Kåre Willoch, who thus became the first Conservative in the 20th century to win a second term as Norway's prime minister. Willoch's government, in which the Christian Democrat (Christian People's) and Center (agrarian) parties were junior partners, lost ground, however, in terms of both parliamentary strength and share of the total vote. It emerged with a lead of only one seat over the Socialist opposition, comprising the Labor and Socialist Left parties. The balance of power in the Storting (parliament), expanded from 155 members

Former Norwegian diplomat Arne Treholt (center) was convicted on June 20 of spying for the Soviet Union and Iraq and was sentenced to 20 years in prison.

AP/WIDE WORLD

to 157, was held by the right-wing Progress Party, although its representation shrank from four seats to two. The new Storting contained the highest proportion (35%) of women of any national assembly in the world.

Increased support for the Labor and Socialist Left parties reflected widespread discontent with government spending curbs, aimed at slowing inflation, which had adversely affected health and social services in particular. The budget for 1986, introduced on October 14, sought to repair the damage by sharply increasing expenditure in these sectors.

During the year gas exports began flowing to the U.K. and other countries in Europe from the Anglo-Norwegian Statfjord field. The mainland economy prospered. Gross national product was expected to show 3.75% growth over the previous year, with industrial output up 3%. Unemployment dropped from an average of 3% in 1984 to 2.25%, and industrial wages rose by over 9%. Expansionist fiscal policies, adopted with an eye to the elections, partly accounted for the boom. Another factor was the strong U.S. dollar in the first part of the year, which boosted krone revenues from exports.

The weakening of petroleum prices, and the fall in the value of the dollar in the latter half of the year, seemed likely to continue into 1986 and were expected to reduce state revenues from petroleum to 35.8 billion kroner in 1986, down from an estimated 46 billion kroner in 1985. (For table of world currencies, *see* International Exchange and Pay-

ments.) The 1986 budget foresaw a deficit of almost 1 billion kroner, compared with an expected 1985 surplus of 19.3 billion kroner. Modest personal income tax concessions were aimed at encouraging moderation in 1986 wage demands.

A news event of international interest during the year was the trial on spying charges of former diplomat and government minister Arne Treholt. In June a tribunal found Treholt guilty of spying for both the U.S.S.R. and Iraq. He was sentenced to 20 years' imprisonment and ordered to pay costs of 100,000 kroner, as well as the 1 million kroner he allegedly received from the Soviet and Iraqi secret services. Treholt appealed to the Supreme Court.

NUCLEAR INDUSTRY

The most commonly used type of nuclear reactor in the world was the pressurized light-water reactor (PWR), accounting for over half of all reactor types. The PWR enjoyed a significant improvement in average performance in 1984 as judged from figures for 1984 published during 1985. The average capacity factor (energy produced as a percentage of the maximum possible) for all PWRs in 1984 was 68.9%, compared with 61.9% for the previous year. The rise in average performance figures for the PWR had, with some minor variations, occurred steadily each year since 1979, and by 1985 average PWR performance exceeded that of other reactor types.

Performance figures for pressurized heavy-water

In addition to simulating the 1979 Three Mile Island accident, the Loss-of-Fluid-Test facility in Idaho also produced simulations of cooling system accidents, studies of which would benefit nuclear reactor operations in ten nations.

UPI/BETTMANN NEWSPHOTOS

reactors (PHWRs) for the year dropped considerably, to 62.1% in 1984, compared with 72.2% in 1983. The decline was due mainly to the shutdown for replacement of the pressure tubes in two of the reactors at Pickering, Ont. Boiling-water reactors (BWRs) had annual capacity factors of 64.1% in 1984, compared with 60.1% the previous year.

Two Canadian Candu PHWRs achieved the best individual annual performances of the 263 reactors worldwide (rated at 150 MW or more and excluding those in Soviet-bloc countries). They were followed by a Japanese PWR. Two Canadian PHWRs also headed the lifetime performance list, followed by a Swiss PWR.

The total operating nuclear power capacity in the world at the beginning of 1985, based on International Atomic Energy Agency (IAEA) figures for 1984, was 220,407 MW, and an additional 175,-729 MW of plant was under construction. Under a new agreement with the Soviet Union, IAEA inspectors, including those from Western countries, began inspection of Soviet PWR installations during the year. However, the inspection agreement did not cover the U.S.S.R.'s water-cooled graphite-moderated reactors, which produce high-quality plutonium, or that nation's fuel-fabrication facilities. Later in the year the Chinese delegation to the IAEA general conference pledged to place some of its civilian nuclear installations under IAEA safeguards "at an appropriate time."

In the U.S., with the cancellation of the Clinch River fast-breeder project, the Department of Energy began letting development contracts for advanced breeder concepts. The department invested $14 million during the year in design work by General Electric Co. and Rockwell International Corp. for small fast-breeder reactors that could be assembled to suit the overall rating required.

Early in October, after several legal battles, appeals, court orders, and a ruling by the U.S. Supreme Court, the unharmed Unit 1 at Three Mile Island finally resumed operation. The Tennessee Valley Authority, one of North America's largest electricity utilities, applied a self-imposed shutdown of its nuclear plants because of inadequate record keeping relating to some aspects of safety procedures. The utility blamed this on poor management and shut down its nuclear plant while new management training was carried out.

Nuclear power had a clear cost advantage over coal in Western Europe, according to reports presented to the International Union of Electricity Producers (Unipede) and by the Organization for Economic Cooperation and Development's Nuclear Energy Agency. This advantage applied even if loadings of the nuclear plant were as low as 3,000 hours a year, and even if nuclear costs rose substantially. The Unipede report found a wide variation in capital costs among the countries studied. In North America the west coasts of Canada and the U.S. still could obtain coal-fired electricity at prices lower than from nuclear power. In the U.S. this was due mainly to the increasing costs of nuclear power, brought about by a decade of growing project delays, high interest rates, and inflation.

In a review of energy development to the year 2000, the International Energy Agency forecast a "massive expansion" of nuclear power in each of the 21 member countries. Nuclear power generation was predicted by member governments to grow from the thermal equivalent of 156.8 million tons oil equivalent (mtoe) in 1983 to 460 mtoe by 2000, or 25% of all fuels used for electricity generation.

OCEANOGRAPHY

In the early morning of April 15, 1912, the ocean liner *Titanic* sank about 95 mi (150 km) south of the Grand Banks of Newfoundland after striking an iceberg. At the same location and at nearly the same time of day on Sept. 1, 1985, video images transmitted by the underwater search vehicle *Argo* to researchers on the U.S. research vessel *Knorr* showed a ship's boiler with three fire doors. The wreck of the *Titanic* had been found.

The successful search, led by Robert D. Ballard of the Woods Hole (Mass.) Oceanographic Institution, was a joint undertaking between U.S. and French researchers using very different techniques. The French ship *Le Suroit* towed a high-resolution acoustic scanner in a regular pattern about the search site—chosen on the basis of the estimated position of the *Titanic* when it sank and of the ships that came to its aid—continuously imaging the seafloor. U.S. researchers made use of a remotely controlled underwater search vehicle developed jointly by Woods Hole and the U.S. Navy. The wreck lay at a depth of about 13,100 ft (4,000 m). The hull had evidently broken in two, and debris was scattered over a wide area.

The Strait of Gibraltar is a narrow (8-mi; 13-km) and shallow (about 1,000-ft; 300-m) passage, bounded by Spain and Morocco, through which the Mediterranean Sea and the Atlantic Ocean exchange water. Because insolation and evaporation are high in the Mediterranean, its water is saltier than that of the open Atlantic. Between one million and two million cubic meters per second of this saline water spill out of Gibraltar along the bottom of the strait into the north Atlantic. Although the flow rate is only 1–2% of that of a major ocean current such as the Gulf Stream, the resulting increase in salinity of the intermediate and deep waters of the Atlantic was believed to lead to important differences in the subsurface circulations of the Atlantic and the Pacific. In spite of the importance of this flow, scientists did not know what determines its rate or how it fluctuates.

In late 1985 scientists from the U.S., Spain, Morocco, Canada, and France began a year-long study of the flow in the strait. Moored current meters, to be maintained in the strait for an entire year, would measure the flow directly, while repeated research cruises would observe the temperature and salinity of the water in the strait from shipboard. Although these measurements would describe the flow over the year of the experiment, they were too costly and time-consuming for monitoring the flow over longer periods. Hence, an array of bottom-mounted pressure sensors as well as an array of coastal sea-level (tide) gauges were also being maintained. These devices were easier to operate over long periods, and their ability to monitor the flow and its variations could be carefully evaluated by comparison with the results of the current-meter array and the shipboard observations. If they proved able to monitor the flow, then it also was possible that existing tide-gauge records contained useful information about the variation of the flow in past years. The age of the outflowing water would be estimated by measuring its content of chlorofluorocarbons (CFCs, or freons) and of tritium.

Global measurements of CFCs and of tritium would be an important part of the World Ocean Circulation Experiment (WOCE), the first truly global survey of ocean circulation, for which planning took place in 1985. Interest in WOCE was sparked by the fact that far less was known about the circulation of the southern oceans than of the northern oceans, and hardly anything was known about the variability of basinwide circulation in either hemisphere. WOCE necessarily would be a many-year effort lasting into the 1990s. By then satellites dedicated to oceanographic research should be in orbit, and in 1985 it was not possible to foresee what studies would then be undertaken. But powerful new techniques for observing the circulation directly were being developed; their global application would be an important part of WOCE.

One such was the measurement of CFCs and of tritium in the oceans. Chlorofluorocarbons F-11 and F-12 have no natural sources. They have entered the ocean primarily from the atmosphere since the mid-1930s, when F-12 became industrially important in refrigeration; F-11 was introduced later but in greater quantity. The ratio of F-11 to F-12 in ocean water was thus a sensitive indicator of when in the past few decades the water was last in contact with the atmosphere. Tritium is a by-product of atmospheric nuclear-weapons testing. It entered the ocean from the atmosphere in the Northern Hemisphere and was being spread throughout the deep ocean by the processes WOCE was intended to study. Both CFCs and tritium were unusual tracers of water motion because scientists expected to see their global distribution change measurably in a few decades and so directly see the deep circulation at work.

Other new techniques included the possibility of constructing "pop-up" floats. These would follow the deep circulation at a preset depth for a period of weeks or months, pop up to the surface to report their position to a satellite, and then descend to the preset depth for another period of deep movement. Oceanographers recently began following surface floats from satellites, and they also tracked floats ballasted to remain at depths of 3,300–9,850 ft (1,000–3,000 m) from acoustic listening stations. The pop-up float combined both of these capabilities into a new instrument for describing the deep circulation.

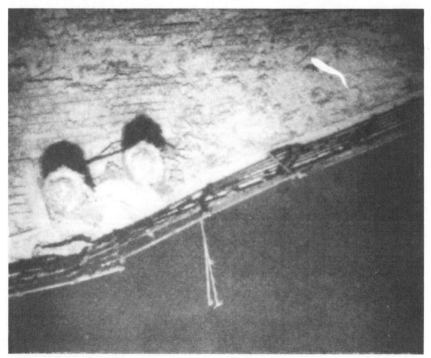

The wreckage of the Titanic was discovered at a depth of more than 13,000 feet (4,000 meters) by a joint U.S.-French oceanographic team. A deepwater rattail fish can be seen swimming above the wooden deck of the bow of the ship.

AP/WIDE WORLD

A traffic accident in Karachi, Pakistan, in April turned into a six-day riot whose targets were chiefly Pashtuns, an ethnic minority with ties to Afghanistan. At least 50 persons died and 250 were injured.

SANDRO TUCCI—GAMMA/ LIAISON

OMAN

The announcement on Sept. 26, 1985, that Oman and the U.S.S.R. were to establish diplomatic relations was regarded as a coup for Soviet diplomacy in the Middle East, given the past opposition of Sultan Qabus ibn Sa'id to Communist regimes. Until then Kuwait had been the only Gulf Cooperation Council country with an ambassador in Moscow. Minister of State for Foreign Affairs Yusuf al-Alawi said that Oman's relations with the U.S. and other Western countries would not be affected. The position of the U.S. and the U.K. as the country's principal suppliers of weapons appeared unlikely to be changed by the Soviet move. Oman was expected to take delivery in 1986 of 300 U.S.-made Sidewinder missiles, to be deployed on Tornado fighter-aircraft supplied by the U.K. under a multimillion-dollar deal signed in London on August 14.

Petroleum production reached record levels during the year as the government made preparations for a new five-year (1986–90) plan. The third plan, based on a production level of 450,000 bbl a day, involved a shift in emphasis from infrastructure to non-oil income-generating schemes as part of a long-term strategy to prepare for the time, 20 or 30 years ahead, when petroleum supplies would be exhausted.

Relations with Yemen (Aden; South Yemen), a supporter of the Dhofar rebellion against the sultan in the 1970s, continued to improve, following the resumption of diplomatic ties in 1983. In April Radio Oman reported that South Yemen had agreed to a proposal that ambassadors be exchanged. South Yemen later appointed a nonresident ambassador.

PAKISTAN

Official results of the referendum held in Pakistan on Dec. 19, 1984, revealed that 97.7% of voters in a turnout of 62% had approved the islamization policy of Pres. Mohammad Zia-ul-Haq and the continuation of his chosen course in transferring power to an elected assembly. Zia interpreted the vote as a mandate to remain in office as president for a further five years. However, opposition leaders accused the government of ballot rigging on a massive scale.

Undeterred by opposition criticism, on Jan. 12, 1985, Zia announced a six-point islamization plan and elections to provincial and national assemblies. The 11-party opposition grouping, the Movement for the Restoration of Democracy (MRD), boycotted the elections because the ban on political activities had not been lifted. In a government crackdown during the week before polling day, many MRD leaders were jailed or placed under house arrest. The government admitted that 369 people had been arrested, but the MRD alleged that the total was at least 1,500. At least ten people died in election-day violence. Although elections to the National Assembly, which took place on February 25, were conducted on a nonparty basis, an official analysis of the results revealed that the greatest number of seats had been won by supporters of the Pakistan People's Party (PPP)—the party of the executed former prime minister Zulfikar Ali Bhutto—and the Muslim League. Voters expressed disapproval of the government by failing to return five of the nine ministers in the Cabinet.

Before Parliament assembled on March 23, Zia restored some of the suspended 1973 constitution; he also introduced constitutional amendments that increased the power of the president at the expense of the prime minister and prevented any presidential order that Zia had made since coming to power in 1977 from being altered or repealed without the sanction of the president. On March 24 the National Assembly gave a vote of confidence to the new prime minister, Mohammad Khan Junejo. Opposition leaders were again placed under house arrest in September when the Assembly debated the controversial indemnity bill, which sought to legalize all decisions that had been made by Zia and

255

the military courts during the years of martial law. The bill was passed on October 16 after the government offered a compromise amendment limiting the power of the military in future administrations. Zia officially declared martial law at an end on December 30.

Benazir Bhutto, daughter of the late prime minister and leader of the PPP, ended 19 months of self-imposed exile when she returned to Pakistan on August 21. She returned for the burial of her brother, Shahnawaz Bhutto, a leader of the Al Zulfikar guerrilla group, who had died under mysterious circumstances the previous month in Cannes, France. Benazir Bhutto was placed under house arrest within days of her return, after calling for the lifting of martial law. The military courts handed down stiff punishments on a number of occasions during the year to people found guilty of plotting against the regime. In March life sentences (25 years under Pakistani laws) were passed on 54 people, allegedly members of Al Zulfikar.

Relations with India, increasingly uneasy during the year, were improved by Zia's visit to New Delhi in December, during which he and Prime Minister Rajiv Gandhi pledged not to attack one another's nuclear installations. In September the U.S. revealed a proposal to sell $103 million worth of arms to Pakistan. Although the conflict in Afghanistan advanced closer to Pakistan's borders during the year, this produced no discernible change in relations with the U.S.S.R. There was marked improvement in relations with China.

The economy performed well in 1985. On May 23 a balanced budget with no deficit financing was presented for 1985–86. The Aid-to-Pakistan Consortium met in Paris on May 6–7 and pledged assistance worth $2.1 billion; Pakistan had requested $1.8 billion.

PANAMA

When Nicolás Ardito Barletta assumed the duties of the presidency of Panama in October 1984, he was confronted by a national debt that reached well over $3 billion, which prompted the quick passage of austerity laws, including tax increases, cuts in expenditures by government departments, a freeze on the wages of government employees, and a reduction in the privileges of labor unions. Mass demonstrations and protests followed. So great was the pressure of discontent that the president agreed to repeal the laws.

Gen. Manuel Antonio Noriega, the commander of the defense forces, felt compelled to strengthen his control over the government in May by requiring the president to remove six Cabinet members and to fill those places with figures more to his liking. New austerity measures accompanying a $60 million loan to Panama in June produced a general strike of laborers on July 1 and 2. Their chief demand was for a freeze on payments of the national debt, but they eventually were forced to retreat.

CLAUDE URRACA—SYGMA

Gen. Manuel Antonio Noriega, commander of Panama's defense forces, consolidated his rule by forcing Pres. Nicolás Ardito Barletta to resign in September.

When General Noriega openly criticized the president, the signal for Ardito Barletta's resignation was clear. Called back to Panama from his travels, the president stepped down on September 28. The first vice-president, Eric Arturo Delvalle, was sworn in at a late-night meeting of the Legislative Assembly. His initial address was a plea for democracy and an end to divisiveness.

PARAGUAY

The government of Pres. Alfredo Stroessner of Paraguay unleashed a new wave of repression against unofficial opposition party leaders and also increased censorship. Opposition calls for a national dialogue were rejected by the government in July, and Radio Nandutí was accused of subversion and closed down for ten days in mid-August. The Roman Catholic Church became more outspoken in denouncing human rights violations and growing socioeconomic inequalities.

Unrest among young army officers was triggered by corruption in the higher ranks. The ruling Colorado Party was split over the question of what should happen in the post-Stroessner era. The *tradicionalistas,* who still controlled the party executive, were reported to favor a military-civilian government for a transition period to democracy. On the other hand, the *oficialistas* took advantage of the August celebrations of Stroessner's 31 years in office to proclaim his son, Gustavo Stroessner, an air force officer, as his eventual successor.

The country's involvement in the narcotics trade prompted the U.S. administration to adopt a less sympathetic stance toward the Stroessner regime. Harsh criticism by the West German public about the harboring of Nazi war criminal Josef Mengele forced Stroessner to postpone a vist to West Germany.

PEOPLE

Among the milestones in the lives of people making news in 1985 were the following:

Births

To singer **Glen Campbell** and his wife, on Jan. 15, a son.

To entertainer, composer, and prexy of Nightstar Productions, **Donny Osmond,** and his wife, on Jan. 29, a son.

To Greek shipping empress **Christina Onassis** and her fourth husband, Thierry Roussel, on Jan. 29, a daughter.

To rock performer **Pat Benatar** and her husband, producer and guitarist Neil Giraldo, on Feb. 16, a daughter.

To actress **Susan Sarandon** and Italian writer Franco Amurri, on March 8, a daughter.

To Rolling Stones guitarist **Keith Richards** and his wife, model Patti Hansen, on March 18, a daughter.

To television actress **Rhea Perlman** ("Cheers") and her husband, actor **Danny DeVito** ("Taxi"), on March 25, a daughter.

To television actress **Shelley Long** ("Cheers") and her husband, Bruce Tyson, on March 27, a daughter.

To television host **Bill Boggs** and his wife, actress Linda Thorson, on April 23, a son.

To Olympic gold-medalist **Evelyn Ashford,** world-record holder in the women's 100-meter dash, and college basketball coach Ray Washington, on May 30, a daughter.

To television commentator **Cathy Rigby McCoy** and her husband, Tom McCoy, on June 23, a daughter.

To actress **Jane Seymour** and her husband, David Flynn, on July 31, a son.

DAVID HUME KENNERLY/TIME MAGAZINE

Actress Amy Irving cradles her son, Max, who was born on June 13. Max's father, film producer and director Steven Spielberg, directed The Color Purple.

To Rolling Stones lead singer, **Mick Jagger,** and model Jerry Hall, on Aug. 28, a son.

To actress **Melanie Griffith** and her husband, actor Steve Bauer, in August, a son.

To Canadian Progressive Conservative Prime Minister **Brian Mulroney** and his wife, Mila, on Sept. 4, a son.

To country-pop singer **Barbara Mandrell** and her husband, Ken Dudney, on Sept. 6, a son.

To pop drummer **Zak Starkey** (son of Beatle Ringo Starr) and his wife, on Sept. 7, a daughter.

To one-time Bendix Corp. vice-president **Mary Cunningham** and her husband, William Agee, on Sept. 30, a daughter.

Farrah Fawcett and Ryan O'Neal pose with their son, Redmond James Fawcett O'Neal, who was born on January 30.

RICHARD D'AMORE—TANNER ASSOCIATES

MARK CARDWELL—UPI/BETTMANN NEWSPHOTOS

New Jersey Generals quarterback and Heisman Trophy winner Doug Flutie and his bride, Laurie Fortier, kiss after their wedding in Natick, Massachusetts, in August.

To retired Swedish tennis star **Bjorn Borg** and his wife, Swedish model Jannike Bjorling, in September, a son.

To **Joe Namath,** former New York Jets quarterback (pro football hall of fame) now sports broadcaster and his wife, actress Deborah Mays Namath, on Oct. 12, a daughter.

To television actor **Jerry Mathers** ("Leave It To Beaver") and his wife, on Oct. 23, a daughter.

To actress and author **Candice Bergen** and her husband, French director **Louis Malle,** on Nov. 8, a daughter.

To model **Christie Brinkley** and singer-songwriter **Billy Joel,** on Dec. 29, a daughter.

To Polish union leader **Lech Walesa** and his wife, Danuta, in December, a daughter.

Marriages

American running star **Mary Decker,** 26, to British discus thrower Richard Slaney, 28; Jan. 1, Eugene, Ore.

Record-breaking Miami Dolphins quarterback **Dan Marino,** 23, to Claire Veazey, 22; Jan. 30, Pittsburgh, Pa.

Former football star running back, sports commentator **O. J. Simpson,** 37, to interior decorator Nicole Brown, 25; Feb. 2, Brentwood, Calif.

Film director **Martin Scorsese,** 42, to film production worker Barbara DeFina, 38; Feb. 9, New York City.

Television actor **Charles Haid,** 41, of "Hill Street Blues," to actress Debi Richter, 25, also of "Hill Street Blues"; in February, Malibu, Calif.

Model **Christie Brinkley,** 31, to singer-songwriter **Billy Joel,** 35; March 23, New York City.

Television talk-show host **Christina Ferrare,** 34, to television executive Anthony Thomopoulos, 47; April 20, Beverly Hills, Calif.

Singer and songwriter **Bruce Springsteen,** 35, to model-actress Julianne Phillips, 25; May 13, Lake Oswego, Ore.

Princess **Yasmin Aga Khan,** 35, daughter of actress Rita Hayworth and the late Prince Aly Kahn, to Greek shipping heir Basil Embiricos, 36, May 15, New York City.

Poultry firm owner **Frank Perdue,** 65, to investment banker Kathleen M. Markey, 37; in May, New York City.

Television actress **Victoria Principal** ("Dallas"), 35, to Beverly Hills plastic surgeon Harry Glassman, 42, on June 22, Dallas, Texas.

Television actor **Gavin MacLeod** ("Love Boat"), 54, remarried to Patti Steele MacLeod, 54 (his wife of seven years whom he divorced in 1982); in July, at the annual convention of Born Again Marriages, Omaha, Neb.

Norwegian actress and writer **Liv Ullmann,** 46, to Boston real estate broker Donald Saunders, 50; Sept. 7, Rome, Italy.

Singer and actress **Diana Ross,** 41, to Norwegian shipping tycoon and mountaineer, Arne Naess, Jr., 47; Oct. 23, New York City.

Actress **Joan Collins,** 52, to Swedish pop star, now businessman, Peter Holm, 38; Nov. 6, Las Vegas, Nev.

Movie mogul **Steven Spielberg,** 37, to actress **Amy Irving,** 32; Nov. 27, Sante Fe, Calif.

Actor and director **Sylvester Stallone,** 39, star of the *Rocky* and *Rambo* series of hit movies, to Danish model Brigitte Nielsen, 22; Dec. 14, Beverly Hills, Calif.

Singer and songwriter **James Taylor,** 37, to actress Kathryn Walker, 42; Dec. 14, New York City.

Author and radio personality **Garrison Keillor,** 43, to Ulla Skaerved, 42; Dec. 29, Copenhagen, Denmark.

Rock singer Madonna Louise Ciccone (upper left, on balcony) stands by her husband, actor Sean Penn, during their August 16 wedding in Malibu, California.
AP/WIDE WORLD

Obituaries

Abruzzo, Ben, U.S. balloonist (b. June 9, 1930, Rockford, Ill.—d. Feb. 11, 1985, Albuquerque, N.M.), was a wealthy land developer turned daredevil who captured the imagination of the world when on Aug. 17, 1978, together with Maxie Anderson and Larry Newman, he completed the first crossing of the Atlantic Ocean in a balloon after piloting the *Double Eagle II* 3,000 mi (4,800 km) in six days from a clover field in Presque Isle, Maine, to a barley field in Miserey, France.

Ashley, Laura, British fashion designer (b. Sept. 7, 1925, Dowlais, Glamorgan, Wales—d. Sept. 17, 1985, Coventry, England), founded the internationally famous soft furnishings and women's clothing empire using Victorian-type prints on natural fabrics that produced flowing feminine garments flattering the middle-aged and the young alike.

Bailey, Sir Donald Coleman, British civil engineer (b. Sept. 15, 1901, Rotherham, England—d. May 5, 1985, Bournemouth, England), originated the bridge design that bears his name and that played an important role in the Allied advance through Europe toward the end of World War II.

Baxter, Anne, U.S. actress (b. May 7, 1923, Michigan City, Ind.—d. Dec. 12, 1985, New York, N.Y.), best remembered for her portrayals of seemingly sweet yet conniving women, won an Academy Award for best supporting actress as the tragic Sophie in *The Razor's Edge* (1946) and was again nominated for best actress in 1950 for her role as the smiling schemer bent on replacing an aging star (played by Bette Davis) in *All About Eve.*

Beard, James Andrews, U.S. gastronome and author (b. May 5, 1903, Portland, Ore.—d. Jan. 23, 1985, New York, N.Y.), was a culinary expert who took an epicurean delight in preparing meals and dining as evidenced by both his corpulence (6 ft 3 in tall, 275 lb [1.9 m, 125 kg]) and his authorship of more than 20 best-selling cookbooks.

Böll, Heinrich Theodor, West German novelist (b. Dec. 21, 1917, Cologne, Germany—d. July 16, 1985, Hürtgenwald-Grosshau, West Germany), was one of the two leading literary figures in West Germany (the other being Günther Grass) and was internationally respected for his Catholic humanism and his democratic and conscientious stands on public issues. Böll was awarded the 1972 Nobel Prize for Literature.

Braudel, Fernand, French historian (b. Aug. 24, 1902, Luméville-en-Ornois, Meuse, France—d. Nov. 28, 1985, Savoie, France), was one of the most prominent exponents of the method of historical study that focused on all social and cultural events and not solely on political events. Braudel was elected to the French Academy in 1984.

Brooks, Louise, U.S. actress (b. Nov. 14, 1906, Cherryvale, Kan.—d. Aug. 8, 1985, Rochester, N.Y.), was a strikingly beautiful star of the silent screen who evoked a sensual eroticism with her smoldering countenance and helmet of bobbed brunet hair, which became her trademark.

Brynner, Yul, U.S. actor (b. July 11, 1920?, Sakhalin Island, U.S.S.R.—d. Oct. 10, 1985, New York, N.Y.), became a romantic sex symbol with his magnificent performances as the virile, bald, pompous yet lovable potentate in *The King and I,* the hugely successful Broadway musical that was made into a motion picture in 1956. Brynner garnered a Tony award for his Broadway performance and earned an Academy Award for best actor for his motion picture portrayal. Although he had major roles in other films, he would forever be identified with his role as the king, which he performed 4,625 times, the last on June 30, 1985.

Burnet, Sir (Frank) Macfarlane, Australian virologist (b. Sept. 3, 1899, Traralgon, Victoria, Australia—d. Aug. 31, 1985, Melbourne, Australia), made important contributions to knowledge about viruses and was joint winner (with Peter Medawar) of the 1960 Nobel Prize for Physiology or Medicine for the discovery of acquired immunological tolerance to tissue transplants. Burnet was elected a fellow of the Royal Society in 1942, knighted in 1951, and awarded the Order of Merit in 1958.

Burrows, Abe (ABRAM SOLMAN BOROWITZ), U.S. writer and director (b. Dec. 18, 1910, New York, N.Y.—d. May 17, 1985, New York), as the coauthor of such Broadway smash hits as *Guys and Dolls* (1950), *Can-Can* (1953), and *How to Succeed in Business Without Really Trying* (1961), for which he won a Pulitzer Prize, was one of the pioneers of musical comedy.

JOHN TIMBERS—CAMERA PRESS, LONDON
LAURA ASHLEY

PETER ABBEY—CAMERA PRESS, LONDON
SIR DONALD COLEMAN BAILEY

AP/WIDE WORLD
JAMES BEARD

People

UPI/BETTMANN NEWSPHOTOS

LOUISE BROOKS

AUSTRALIAN INFORMATION SERVICE
PHOTOGRAPH, ERIC WADSWORTH

SIR MACFARLANE BURNET

KARSH OF OTTAWA—CAMERA PRESS, LONDON

MARC CHAGALL

Caldwell, Taylor (JANET MIRIAM TAYLOR HOLLAND CALD-WELL), U.S. writer (b. Sept. 7, 1900, Manchester, England—d. Aug. 30, 1985, Greenwich, Conn.), was the indomitable and pro-lific author of 33 best-selling novels, including *Dynasty of Death* (1938), *Testimony of Two Men* (1968), *Captains and the Kings* (1972), and *Answer as a Man* (1981). Although her books were not critically acclaimed, they were so popular among readers that they were translated into 11 languages.

Calvino, Italo, Italian novelist (b. Oct. 15, 1923, Santiago de las Vegas, Cuba—d. Sept. 19, 1985, Siena, Italy), was a prominent figure in post-World War II Italian fiction with tales that com-bined fantasy, humor, and irony. Perhaps his greatest achieve-ment was to have crossed the divide between experimental literature and the traditional novel. Calvino's interest in science and his ability to incorporate contemporary scientific philosophi-cal and linguistic concerns into his work led him to be compared to the French 18th-century writer Voltaire. He was awarded the Premio Riccioni and the Premio Feltrinelli per la Narrativa.

Cameron, (Mark) James Walter, British journalist (b. June 17, 1911, London, England—d. Jan. 26, 1985, London), was considered by many to be one of the most distinguished and controversial correspondents of his day. His work was a com-bination of brilliant and intuitive writing with an outstanding integrity and a preoccupation with the human condition. In the words of Lord Beaverbrook, Cameron wrote "the grim hard truth from the heart."

Chagall, Marc, Russian-born painter (b. July 7, 1887, Vitebsk, Russia—d. March 28, 1985, Saint-Paul-de-Vence, Alpes-Maritimes, France), was one of the most original and most outstanding figures in 20th-century art. His work, nourished by Jewish tradition and by childhood memories of Russian village life, had a unique quality of naive poetry. Though influenced by Cubism, Fauvism, and Surrealism, Chagall adapted their discov-eries to suit his own imaginative vision, which was characterized by a range of colors and subject matter drawn from Jewish folk-lore, Hasidic mysticism, and peasant life.

Chernenko, Konstantin Ustinovich, Soviet chief of state (b. Sept. 24, 1911, Bolshaya Tes, Krasnoyarsk region, Siberia—d. March 10, 1985, Moscow, U.S.S.R.), served as general secretary of the Communist Party of the Soviet Union from Feb. 13, 1984, and as chairman of the Presidium of the Supreme Soviet from April 11, 1984, until his death.

Claire, Ina (INA FAGAN), U.S. actress (b. Oct. 15, 1892, Washington, D.C.—d. Feb. 21, 1985, San Francisco, Calif.), was a bubbly comedienne who specialized in sophisticated comedy featuring well-bred, bad-mannered characters whose spiteful be-havior gave her ample opportunity to showcase her quicksilver wit. One of her most famous roles was Greta Garbo's nemesis in the 1939 classic film *Ninotchka.*

Clarke, Kenny ("KLOOK"; KENNETH SPEARMAN CLARKE), U.S. jazz drummer (b. Jan. 9, 1914, Pittsburgh, Pa.—d. Jan. 25, 1985, Paris, France), was a gifted jazz innovator who as the foremost drummer in the development of bebop during the 1940s was credited with breaking the traditional four-beat rhythm from the bass drum to the cymbal, thereby permitting the use of the bass and snare drums for independent counterrhythms in support of improvising soloists.

Cole, Lester, U.S. screenwriter (b. June 19, 1904, New York, N.Y.—d. Aug. 15, 1985, San Francisco, Calif.), was the prolific writer of 36 scripts before being branded one of the "Hollywood Ten"—writers and directors who refused to testify before the House Committee on Un-American Activities and were sen-tenced to a year in prison. After his release Cole was unable to find work as a screenwriter and held a variety of jobs before helping to write the screenplay for *Born Free* in 1965 under the name Gerald L. C. Copley.

Douglas-Home, Charles Cospatrick, British journalist (b. Sept. 1, 1937—d. Oct. 29, 1985, London, England), was editor of *The Times* of London from 1982 until his death from cancer. He had previously worked as the newspaper's defense correspon-dent, as editor in various departments, and as deputy editor to Harold Evans.

D'Oyly Carte, Dame Bridget, British theater and hotel director (b. March 25, 1908, London, England—d. May 2, 1985, Shrubs Wood, Chalfont St. Giles, Buckinghamshire, England), for over 30 years successfully carried on her family's presentation of the

Gilbert and Sullivan comic operas, in the U.S. and Canada as well as in Britain. The last London presentation was made in 1982. She was made a Dame Commander of the Order of the British Empire in 1975.

Dubuffet, Jean, French painter (b. July 31, 1901, Le Havre, France—d. May 12, 1985, Paris, France), created powerful and naive images through the use of various materials in his paintings and constructions, which he classified as *art brut.* Characteristic early works show figures executed with apparently childlike outlines moving across a surface where the addition of glass, sand, and other materials to the paint exhibits Dubuffet's delight in textures.

Eisenhower, Milton Stover, U.S. diplomat and educator (b. Sept. 15, 1899, Abilene, Kan.—d. May 2, 1985, Baltimore, Md.), was an astute and levelheaded adviser to six U.S. presidents, including his brother Dwight, and served as president of Kansas State College (1943–50), Pennsylvania State University (1950–56), and Johns Hopkins University (1956–67 and 1971–72).

Ervin, Samuel James, Jr., U.S. politician (b. Sept. 27, 1896, Morganton, N.C.—d. April 23, 1985, Winston-Salem, N.C.), was a crusty Democratic senator from North Carolina (1954–74) who as an expert on the U.S. Constitution achieved national prominence in 1973–74 while presiding as chairman of the Senate Select Committee on Presidential Campaign Activities, popularly known as the Senate Watergate committee.

Gordon, Ruth (RUTH GORDON JONES), U.S. actress (b. Oct. 30, 1896, Quincy, Mass.—d. Aug. 28, 1985, Edgartown, Mass.), was a vivacious and determined personality who used her boundless energy to help write such successful screenplays as *A Double Life* (1948), *Adam's Rib* (1949), and *Pat and Mike* (1952) and to perform onstage and in motion pictures, notably *Rosemary's Baby* (1968), for which she won an Academy Award for best supporting actress for her spooky portrayal of a devil worshipper.

Gould, Chester, U.S. cartoonist (b. Nov. 20, 1900, Pawnee, Okla.—d. May 11, 1985, Woodstock, Ill.), as the creator of "Dick Tracy"—a hawk-nosed square-chinned detective whose adventures pitted him against such rogues as Flattop, the Mole, Mumbles, B-B Eyes, Pruneface, and the Brow—introduced crime and violence to the comic strip pages. Gould retired in 1977 after masterminding the strip for 46 years.

Graves, Robert Ranke, British man of letters (b. July 24, 1895, Wimbledon, London, England—d. Dec. 7, 1985, Deyá, Majorca, Spain), a writer of immense versatility, received the greatest acclaim for his poetry but was generally best known for his historical novels, of which *I, Claudius* and *Claudius the God* (both 1934) achieved the widest renown after they were brilliantly adapted for television in 1976.

Guarnieri, Johnny, U.S. jazz pianist (b. March 23, 1917, New York, N.Y.—d. Jan. 7, 1985, Livingston, N.J.), as a virtuoso keyboard specialist, was one of the foremost jazz pianists of the swing era and was credited with the first jazz harpsichord solos. A leading exponent of Fats Waller's Harlem stride style, Guarnieri was also influenced by Teddy Wilson and Count Basie.

Hamilton, Margaret, U.S. actress (b. Dec. 9, 1902, Cleveland, Ohio—d. May 16, 1985, Salisbury, Conn.), rode to fame on a broomstick with her frightening portrayal of the green-skinned, cackling Wicked Witch of the West, who terrorized Dorothy and her dog, Toto, in the 1939 motion picture classic *The Wizard of Oz.* She was a superb character actress whose sharp-featured looks marked her for such roles as stern spinsters, pushy town gossips, and puritanical aunts. She appeared in some 75 motion pictures.

Harris, Patricia Roberts, U.S. lawyer and educator (b. May 31, 1924, Mattoon, Ill.—d. March 23, 1985, Washington, D.C.), was a dynamic civil rights activist and the first black woman to hold a Cabinet post or serve as a U.S. ambassador. Harris became a political figure in 1965 when Pres. Lyndon B. Johnson appointed her ambassador to Luxembourg. During Pres. Jimmy Carter's administration she served as the secretary of housing and urban development (1977–79) and then as the secretary of health, education, and welfare (1979–80); she continued in the latter post (1980–81) after the department was renamed health and human services. She later became dean of the law school at Howard University.

Hoxha, Enver, Albanian Communist Party leader (b. Oct. 16, 1908, Gjirokaster, Albania—d. April 11, 1985, Tiranë, Albania),

FRED FEHL

INA CLAIRE

THE TIMES/CAMERA PRESS, LONDON

CHARLES DOUGLAS-HOME

AP/WIDE WORLD

SAM ERVIN

People

AP/WIDE WORLD

MARGARET HAMILTON

AP/WIDE WORLD

PATRICIA ROBERTS HARRIS

GAMMA/LIAISON

ENVER HOXHA

was for 42 years the dominant personality in his country. During the last decade of Hoxha's tenure in power, there were numerous purges within the party leadership.

Hudson, Rock (b. ROY SHERER, JR.; later adopted surname of his stepfather, Wallace Fitzgerald), U.S. actor (b. Nov. 17, 1925, Winnetka, Ill.—d. Oct. 2, 1985, Beverly Hills, Calif.), was a tall, dark, and handsome Hollywood superstar who became a matinee idol with his romantic melodramas of the 1950s and his bubbling sex comedies of the 1960s, many featuring co-star Doris Day.

Hu Feng, Chinese writer (b. 1903, I-tu, Hupeh [Hubei] Province, China—d. June 8, 1985, China), was a left-wing critic, poet, and essayist who followed Marxist theory in political and social matters but insisted on individual freedom to foster creativity in literature.

Jones, Jo (JONATHAN JONES), U.S. drummer (b. Oct. 7, 1911, Chicago, Ill.—d. Sept. 3, 1985, New York, N.Y.), was the heartbeat of the Count Basie band from 1935 to 1948 and a major innovator who revolutionized jazz percussion with his steady four-beat rhythm on the high-hat cymbal. Jones, also known as Kansas City Jo Jones and Papa Jo Jones, was sometimes confused with jazz drummer Philly Joe Jones. When Jo Jones joined Basie's band in 1935, he contributed a new light, graceful rhythm to the otherwise heavy jazz beat, shifting the pulse from the bass drum to the high-hat.

Jones, Philly Joe (JOSEPH RUDOLPH JONES), U.S. drummer (b. July 15, 1923, Philadelphia, Pa.—d. Aug. 30, 1985, Philadelphia), was one of the greatest hard bop drummers of all time and gave the influential 1950s Miles Davis quintet its distinctive sound with his combination of deep-toned tom-tom and bass drums with subtle swirls of cross-rhythm on cymbals. Jones, who helped make the transition from prewar big band sounds to postwar "cool" jazz, contributed to more than 500 record albums.

Kertész, André, U.S. photographer (b. July 2, 1894, Budapest, Hung.—d. Sept. 27, 1985, New York, N.Y.), as one of the most influential lyrical photojournalists of the century, inspired such photographers as Henri Cartier-Bresson, Robert Capa, and Brassaï with his pioneering use of the small hand-held 35-mm camera. He first gained renown with his black and white pictures, in which he recorded the street life of Paris and Greenwich Village for more than 50 years.

Kimball, Spencer W., U.S. religious leader (b. March 28, 1895, Salt Lake City, Utah—d. Nov. 5, 1985, Salt Lake City), as the 12th "prophet, seer, and revelator" of the 5.8 million-member Church of Jesus Christ of Latter-day Saints, the Mormons, instituted such momentous changes as allowing blacks to hold the Mormon priesthood (a decree that struck down the church's 148-year-old policy excluding black men from full participation in the church), retiring elderly church leaders, and adding the first non-Americans to the modern church hierarchy.

Kuznets, Simon (Smith), Ukrainian-born economist (b. April 30, 1901, Kharkov, Ukraine—d. July 8, 1985, Cambridge, Mass.), won the 1971 Nobel Prize for Economics for his use of sophisticated statistical analysis to compute the gross national product (GNP), total market value of the final goods and services produced by a nation's economy during a specific period of time, computed before allowance is made for the depreciation or consumption of capital used in the process of production. Kuznets's extensive research on the economic growth of nations ushered in the era of quantitative economics.

Lander, Toni, Danish ballerina (b. June 19, 1931, Gentofte, Den.—d. May 19, 1985, Salt Lake City, Utah), achieved international fame as a dancer with the American Ballet Theatre, the London Festival Ballet, and the Royal Danish Ballet. Probably her finest and most exacting role was in Harald Lander's *Études*. Born Toni Petersen, she married the Danish choreographer Harald Lander in 1950. She was a leading dancer with the American Ballet Theatre (1960–71) and returned to the Royal Danish Ballet (1971–76) as dancer and teacher, making her farewell performance in *The Moor's Pavane*.

Langer, Susanne Knauth, U.S. philosopher and educator (b. Dec. 20, 1895, New York, N.Y.—d. July 17, 1985, Old Lyme, Conn.), assigned unprecedented importance to signs, symbols, and feelings in her philosophical approach to such things as language, art, and psychoanalysis. In *Philosophy in a New Key: A Study in the Symbolism of Reason, Rite, and Art* (1942), she rejected the premise that language is the only means of articulating thought and that everything that is not speakable thought is feeling.

Larkin, Philip Arthur, British poet (b. Aug. 9, 1922, Coventry, Warwickshire, England—d. Dec. 2, 1985, Hull, England), produced only five small collections of poetry but became recognized by critics as perhaps the most gifted living English poet and as a result enjoyed considerable popularity. He won the Queen's Gold Medal for Poetry (1965) and in that year was asked to edit *The Oxford Book of Twentieth Century Verse* (1973). Larkin, who many had expected would succeed Sir John Betjeman as poet laureate, was made a Companion of Honour in 1985.

Lodge, Henry Cabot, U.S. politician and diplomat (b. July 5, 1902, Nahant, Mass.—d. Feb. 27, 1985, Beverly, Mass.), was a Boston aristocrat who served (1937–44 and 1947–53) as a three-term Republican senator from Massachusetts, as longtime delegate to the UN (1953–60) during the cold war, and as ambassador to South Vietnam (1963–64 and 1965–67). He was later ambassador to West Germany (1968–69), chief negotiator at the talks in Paris on peace in Vietnam (1969), and special envoy to the Vatican (1970–77).

Longowal, Sant Harchand Singh, Indian Sikh priest (b. 1928, Laungowal, Punjab, India—d. Aug. 20, 1985, Sherpur, Punjab), as a moderate leader of the Sikh political party, the Akali Dal, was assassinated by Sikh extremists resentful that he had signed an agreement with India's Prime Minister Rajiv Gandhi.

Lon Nol, Kampuchean army officer and politician (b. Nov. 13, 1913, Kampong Leon, Prey Veng Province, Cambodia—d. Nov. 17, 1985, Fullerton, Calif.), was a prime architect of the March 1970 coup that overthrew Prince Norodom Sihanouk and from then until 1975 was one of his country's most prominent leaders, serving as premier (until 1972) and then as president of the Khmer Republic (1972–75).

MacInnes, Helen Clark, U.S. novelist (b. Oct. 7, 1907, Glasgow, Scotland—d. Sept. 30, 1985, New York, N.Y.), was dubbed "the queen of international intrigue" as the best-selling author of 21 spy novels, notably *Above Suspicion* (1941), *Assignment in Brittany* (1942), *The Venetian Affair* (1963), and *The Salzburg Connection* (1968), all of which were made into motion pictures.

Maltz, Albert, U.S. screenwriter (b. Oct. 28, 1908, Brooklyn, N.Y.—d. April 26, 1985, Los Angeles, Calif.), won two Academy Awards for the documentary films before gaining notoriety as one of the "Hollywood Ten," who refused to answer questions posed to them by the House Committee on Un-American Activities. The ten were blacklisted by the U.S. motion picture industry. Maltz also wrote the classic thriller *This Gun for Hire* (1942), such patriotic films as *Destination Tokyo* (1944) and *Pride of the Marines* (1945), and *The Naked City* (1948).

Maris, Roger Eugene, U.S. baseball player (b. Sept. 10, 1934, Hibbing, Minn.—d. Dec. 14, 1985, Houston, Texas), was an exceptional defensive outfielder and a powerful hitter who in 1961 surpassed Babe Ruth's 1927 season home run record of 60 by slamming 61 homers for the New York Yankees; because Maris's one-season total was accumulated during a 162-game schedule and Ruth's was accrued during a 154-game season, the baseball commissioner, Ford C. Frick, ruled that Maris had not broken Ruth's record. Maris retired in 1968 with 275 home runs, 851 runs batted in, and a lifetime batting average of .260.

Martin, John Joseph, U.S. dance critic (b. June 2, 1893, Louisville, Ky.—d. May 19, 1985, Saratoga, N.Y.), fostered the development of modern dance in the U.S. by promoting the new art form's importance in his dance critiques for the *New York Times* (1927–62).

Moncreiffe of that Ilk, Sir (Rupert) Iain Kay, 11TH BARONET, Scottish genealogist (b. April 9, 1919, Hampton Court, Middlesex, England—d. Feb. 27, 1985, London, England), was a notable eccentric whose books on genealogy brought him international fame. He was, from 1961, Albany Herald in the court of Scotland's Lord Lyon King of Arms. His serious study of genealogy and heraldry began with his doctoral thesis on the Scots law of succession to peerages. Moncreiffe served in the court of Lord Lyon as Falkland Pursuivant (1952–53), Kintyre Pursuivant (1953–55), and Unicorn Pursuivant (1955–61). He succeeded his cousin to the baronetcy (created 1685) in 1957.

Naipaul, Shivadhar Srinivasa, West Indian writer (b. Feb. 25, 1945, Port-of-Spain, Trinidad—d. Aug. 13, 1985, London, England), was not overshadowed by, but had yet to match the

FRED FEHL

TONI LANDER

AP/WIDE WORLD

HENRY CABOT LODGE

PATRICE HABANS—SYGMA

SANT HARCHAND SINGH LONGOWAL

People

CAMERA PRESS, LONDON

SIR IAIN MONCREIFFE OF THAT ILK

TARA HEINEMANN—CAMERA PRESS, LONDON

SHIVADHAR SRINIVASA NAIPAUL

PHIL BURCHMAN—PICTORIAL PARADE

LLOYD NOLAN

achievement of, his elder brother, the novelist V. S. Naipaul. His novels earned him an impressive array of literary awards, including the Royal Society of Literature's Winifred Holtby Memorial Prize, the Jock Campbell New Statesman Award, the John Llewellyn Rhys Memorial Prize, and the Whitbread Literary Award.

Nash, Clarence ("DUCKY"), U.S. vocal impressionist (b. 1904, Watonga, Okla.—d. Feb. 20, 1985, Burbank, Calif.), created the squawking voice of the irascible Donald Duck and served as the cartoon character's only spokesman for over 50 years in more than 150 cartoons and motion pictures. Nash, who once had ambitions to become a doctor, by his own admission became the nation's leading quack. Perhaps Nash's greatest challenge occurred when Donald's cartoons were dubbed in French, Spanish, Portuguese, Japanese, Chinese, and German and Nash had to learn to quack in those languages.

Nolan, Lloyd Benedict, U.S. actor (b. Aug. 11, 1902, San Francisco, Calif.—d. Sept. 27, 1985, Los Angeles, Calif.), was a reliable character actor who portrayed secondary gangsters and tough policemen. Though he turned in impressive performances in such films as *A Tree Grows in Brooklyn* (1945) and *The House on 92nd Street* (1945), he did not win recognition for his accomplishments until he starred as the neurotic Captain Queeg in the stage and television versions of *The Caine Mutiny Court Martial*. In 1955 he won an Emmy, his only national award, for his sterling portrayal of Queeg in a television adaptation of the play. Nolan appeared in more than 70 films, including *Bataan* (1943) and *Guadalcanal Diary* (1943).

O'Brien, Edmond, U.S. actor (b. Sept. 10, 1915, New York, N.Y.—d. May 9, 1985, Inglewood, Calif.), specialized in portrayals of tough guys in such films as *The Killers* (1946), *A Double Life* (1948), *D.O.A.* (1950), *The Great Imposter* (1961), and *Birdman of Alcatraz* (1962) and garnered an Academy Award as best supporting actor for his role as the venal Hollywood press agent in *The Barefoot Contessa* (1954). He also turned in notable performances in *The Man Who Shot Liberty Valance* (1962) as the frontier newspaper editor, in *The Wild Bunch* (1969) as a grizzled old man and the only gang member to survive, and in *Seven Days in May* (1964) as an aging, alcoholic senator.

Ormandy, Eugene (JENO BLAU ORMANDY), Hungarian-born conductor (b. Nov. 18, 1899, Budapest, Hung.—d. March 12, 1985, Philadelphia, Pa.), as the principal conductor of the Philadelphia Orchestra from 1938 until his retirement in 1980, was credited with elevating the ensemble to one of the finest symphonies in the world, with a repertoire that featured Late Romantic and early 20th-century works.

Pritikin, Nathan, U.S. nutritionist (b. Aug. 29, 1915, Chicago, Ill.—d. Feb. 21, 1985, Albany, N.Y.), was a best-selling author who in such books as *Live Longer Now* (1974) and *The Pritikin Program for Diet & Exercise* (1979) advocated a controversial low-cholesterol, low-fat diet to reverse the symptoms of heart disease, hypertension, and diabetes.

Redgrave, Sir Michael Scudamore, British actor (b. March 20, 1908, Bristol, England—d. March 21, 1985, Denham, Buckinghamshire, England), was a superb actor on both stage and film and was noted in particular for his intelligence and for his extraordinary portrayals of strong characters fatally flawed. In his best performances, on stage as Uncle Vanya in 1962 or on film as the schoolmaster in *The Browning Version* (1951), he achieved a tragic poignancy that was enhanced by his regal bearing and sonorous voice. Redgrave was knighted in 1959.

Richter, Charles Francis, U.S. seismologist (b. April 26, 1900, near Hamilton, Ohio—d. Sept. 30, 1985, Pasadena, Calif.), in 1935, together with Beno Gutenberg, developed the scale of earthquake magnitude that became known as the Richter scale, a measure of the movement of the Earth as recorded on seismographs.

Roy, Maurice Cardinal, Canadian prelate of the Roman Catholic Church (b. Jan. 25, 1905, Quebec, Canada—d. Oct. 24, 1985, Montreal, Que.), served as archbishop of Quebec (1947–81) and primate of Canada (1956–81) after gaining distinction as chief of chaplains of the Canadian Armed Forces during World War II.

Ryskind, Morrie, U.S. playwright and newspaper columnist (b. Oct. 20, 1895, Brooklyn, N.Y.—d. Aug. 24, 1985, Crystal City, Va.), shared the 1932 Pulitzer Prize for drama with George S.

Kaufman and Ira Gershwin for the Broadway musical *Of Thee I Sing* and showcased his comic writing talents as a collaborator on such classic Marx Brothers films as *Coconuts* (1929), *Animal Crackers* (1930), and *A Night at the Opera* (1935).

Scott, Francis Reginald, Canadian poet, lawyer, and politician (b. Aug. 1, 1899, Quebec City, Que.—d. Jan. 31, 1985, Montreal, Que.), was a distinguished member of the Montreal group of poets in the 1920s and used his creative genius to help shape Canadian constitutional law and to draft the Regina Manifesto, the founding document of the Co-operative Commonwealth Federation (CCF) party (which merged with the labor movement in 1961 to form the New Democratic Party).

Scourby, Alexander, U.S. actor and narrator (b. Nov. 13, 1913, Brooklyn, N.Y.—d. Feb. 22, 1985, Boston, Mass.), was a seasoned stage performer and motion picture character actor who was most famous for his mellow voice, which was heard most notably in the offscreen narration of the television series "Victory at Sea," first shown in 1952. For the blind he recorded more than 400 of the world's great works of literature.

Segal, Walter, Swiss-born architect (b. May 15, 1907, Ascona, Switz.—d. Oct. 27, 1985, London, England), was influential in his profession and a pioneer in building low-cost nonprofessionally assembled houses. He was also known for his severe and now vindicated criticism of high-rise tower blocks put up by British housing authorities after World War II. His prototype house, a bungalow, was built for only $2,240 in the early 1960s; he cut costs by calculating quantities, using modern materials in standard production measurements, and eliminating the use of professional builders.

Sessions, Roger Huntington, U.S. composer (b. Dec. 28, 1896, Brooklyn, N.Y.—d. March 16, 1985, Princeton, N.J.), was an important modern composer of orchestral, vocal, chamber, and instrumental works and had been influential since the 1920s in the development of serious American music both as a teacher of composition and as a composer of his own complex works. He was named to the National Institute of Arts and Letters in 1938 and to the American Academy of Arts and Sciences in 1961. Sessions was awarded a Pulitzer Prize in 1974 for the body of his work and a second in 1981 for *Concerto for Orchestra*.

Signoret, Simone, French actress (b. March 25, 1921, Weisbaden, Germany—d. Sept. 30, 1985, Eure, France), matured from the young star of *Casque d'Or* (1952) to an actress with the potential to play women with the warmth and courage evident in her private life. Signoret won critical acclaim for her best-selling books, including her second novel, *Adieu, Volodia*, which appeared in 1985.

Silvers, Phil, U.S. comedian (b. May 11, 1912, New York, N.Y.—d. Nov. 1, 1985, Los Angeles, Calif.), endeared himself to millions of television viewers as the blustering, conniving, and goldbricking Master Sergeant Ernie Bilko in the hit comedy "You'll Never Get Rich," which was rechristened "The Phil Silvers Show" (1955–59). The series, which garnered three Emmy awards, featured Silvers as a master con artist barking orders at a ragtag platoon.

Sims, Zoot (JOHN HALEY SIMS), U.S. saxophonist (b. Oct. 29, 1925, Inglewood, Calif.—d. March 23, 1985, New York, N.Y.), was the renowned swinging tenor saxophonist with big bands led by Benny Goodman and Stan Kenton and was one of the legendary "Four Brothers" who made up the saxophone line with Stan Getz, Herbie Steward, and Serge Chaloff in Woody Herman's Second Herd band. He also played an elegant soprano saxophone but was better known for his buoyant tenor saxophone. Sims's more than 40 recordings include *Jive at Five, Zootcase, Joe & Zoot,* and *Soprano Sax.*

Smith, Samantha, U.S. peace advocate (b. June 1972, Maine—d. Aug. 25, 1985, Auburn, Maine), captured the imagination of the world when, as an 11-year-old schoolgirl, she wrote a letter to Soviet Pres. Yuri V. Andropov expressing her fear of nuclear war. She achieved international celebrity status when she accepted Andropov's unexpected invitation to visit the Soviet Union for an all-expenses-paid trip. She was accorded VIP treatment when she visited the Soviet Union in 1983. Smith was killed, together with her father and six others, when their plane crashed and exploded on their return trip to Manchester, Maine, from London. Her death was mourned both in the United States and in the Soviet Union.

JANE BROWN—CAMERA PRESS, LONDON

SIR MICHAEL REDGRAVE

AP/WIDE WORLD

SIMONE SIGNORET

YVONNE HEMSEY—GAMMA/LIAISON

SAMANTHA SMITH

UPI/BETTMANN NEWSPHOTOS

XUAN THUY

MARTINE PECCOUX—GAMMA/LIAISON

ORSON WELLES

UPI/BETTMANN NEWSPHOTOS

COOTIE WILLIAMS

Sondergaard, Gale (EDITH HOLM SONDERGAARD), U.S. actress (b. Feb. 15, 1899, Litchfield, Minn.—d. Aug. 14, 1985, Woodland Hills, Calif.), launched her motion picture career by winning the Academy Award for best supporting actress for her first film, *Anthony Adverse* (1936). During the 1930s and '40s she specialized in villainous roles. During the early 1950s her career was interrupted when she refused to testify before the House Committee on Un-American Activities; she did not return to the screen until 1969.

Stewart, Potter, U.S. judge (b. Jan. 23, 1915, Jackson, Mich.—d. Dec. 7, 1985, Hanover, N.H.), as associate justice of the U.S. Supreme Court (1958–81) served as the crucial "swing vote" on close court decisions involving the exercise of government powers during the Warren Court era (1953–69); he then became a centrist when the more conservative Burger Court assumed power in 1969.

Tabouis, Geneviève, French journalist (b. Feb. 23, 1892, Paris, France—d. Sept. 22, 1985, Paris), was respected during the 1930s for her reports in the newspaper *L'Oeuvre* and inspired awe for the accuracy of her predictions, including the Nazi occupation of Austria and Czechoslovakia. She was also an Officer of the Légion d'Honneur.

Taniguchi Masaharu, Japanese religious leader (b. 1893, Hyogo Pref., Japan—d. June 17, 1985, Nagasaki, Japan), was the founder of Seicho-no-Ie ("House of Growth"), a religious organization that boasted some 3.5 million followers and espoused the principles of Buddhism, Christianity, and Shintoism. He elaborated on the movement in 20 volumes, which had a seven million-copy printing.

Thuy, Xuan, Vietnamese politician (b. Sept. 2, 1912, near Hanoi, French Indochina—d. June 18, 1985, Hanoi, Vietnam), served as vice-speaker and secretary-general of Vietnam's National Assembly but became internationally known when he was the North Vietnamese foreign minister (1963–65) and his country's chief delegate (with Le Duc Tho, who negotiated separately with Henry Kissinger) at the Paris peace talks that ended U.S. involvement in Vietnam.

Tillstrom, Burr, U.S. puppeteer (b. Oct. 13, 1917, Chicago, Ill.—d. Dec. 6, 1985, Palm Springs, Calif.), delighted millions of television viewers, children and adults alike, as the creator and voice of a gallery of puppets whose antics were showcased on the "Kukla, Fran, and Ollie" television program. The character of Fran was played by Fran Allison, the only visible human member of the troupe. The show was canceled in 1957 but was later syndicated. The multitalented Tillstrom gained five Emmy awards, two Peabody Awards, and more than 50 other honors for his imaginative work.

Turner, Big Joe (JOSEPH VERNON TURNER), U.S. blues singer (b. May 18, 1911, Kansas City, Mo.—d. Nov. 24, 1985, Englewood, Calif.), helped usher in the era of rock and roll as the "blues shouter" of such classic rhythm and jump songs as "Shake, Rattle and Roll," "Corrina, Corrina," and "Flip, Flop and Fly." Turner, who was dubbed the "Boss of the Blues," was widely imitated by a string of white performers including Bill Haley and the Comets.

Welles, (George) Orson, U.S. director, producer, screenwriter, and actor (b. May 6, 1915, Kenosha, Wis.—d. Oct. 10, 1985, Los Angeles, Calif.), was a maverick genius "boy wonder" whose extraordinary artistic talents included those of actor, director, producer, and filmmaker. His classic *Citizen Kane* (1941) came to be considered a cinematic masterpiece and possibly the greatest film ever made, although at the time of its release it was a box-office flop.

Williams, Cootie (CHARLES MELVIN WILLIAMS), U.S. trumpeter (b. July 24, 1908, Mobile, Ala.—d. Sept. 15, 1985, New York, N.Y.), was identified by his growling, muted horn and, as the last surviving member of the classic Duke Ellington bands of the 1920s and '30s, played a key role in maintaining the inflections and nuances of the original band.

Zimbalist, Efrem Alexandrovich, Russian-born violinist (b. April 9, 1890, Rostov-na-Donu, Russia—d. Feb. 22, 1985, Reno, Nev.), was a violin virtuoso whose unhurried tempos and refined performances were underscored by an emotional understatement and high technical polish; he was also an important composer of songs and chamber music and from 1941 to 1968 headed Philadelphia's Curtis Institute.

PERU

On July 28, 1985, Pres. Fernando Belaúnde Terry became Peru's first freely elected ruler since 1945 to hand over power to a democratically chosen successor. General elections held on April 14 gave the center-left Alianza Popular Revolucionaria Americana (APRA) absolute majorities in both houses of Congress. However, there was no outright winner in the presidential contest, although APRA candidate Alan García Pérez fell just short of the target with 48% of the vote. In second place with 23% was Alfonso Barrantes Lingán, candidate of the Marxist coalition Izquierda Unida (IU) and mayor of Lima, while the ruling right-wing Acción Popular (AP) party was pushed into fourth place by the Convergencia Democrática, a coalition of right-wing parties. In the event, the need for a second round was obviated by Barrantes's withdrawal from the contest on April 25 and the National Election Board's announcement on June 1 that a runoff was no longer necessary.

APRA now held undisputed power for the first time in its long history. García possessed youth and dynamism, in sharp contrast to the outgoing government, and this was apparently of greater importance to the electorate than his lack of experience. The swing to the left was also the result of the Belaúnde government's failure to deal with the country's ever worsening political and economic situation. The last year of Belaúnde's term was marked by an increase in protests by workers and in violent acts perpetrated by the Maoist guerrilla group Sendero Luminoso (Shining Path).

An Amnesty International report, estimating that over 1,000 people were missing after being detained by the security forces, elicited official denials. In September García dismissed three top army generals held responsible for the massacre of some 40 peasants by counterinsurgency forces.

The government also faced an economic crisis. Growth in gross domestic product of 3.5% in 1984 had to be judged in the light of a contraction of almost 12% the year before. The modest recovery was led by the fishing and agricultural sectors, which had plummeted in 1983 following freak weather conditions. The new government announced an economic package aimed at "austerity without misery." The main elements were the freezing of the exchange rate, a reduction in interest rates, a price freeze, and a wage rise of 18%.

The measures were announced on the heels of a radical pronouncement by García on the subject of the external debt: Peru was to restrict repayments on its $13.6 billion foreign debt to 10% of export earnings, and commercial banks were asked to grant a six-month freeze on repayments. The government was already heavily in arrears. García repeated his strong views in his address to the UN General Assembly in September when he pointed out that austerity measures could threaten the stability of a country. On December 17 President García an-

NICOLE BONNET—GAMMA/LIAISON

Peru's new president, Alan García Pérez, speaks at his swearing-in ceremony on July 28. He succeeded Pres. Fernando Belaúnde Terry.

nounced that his government was seizing the assets of the U.S.-based Belco Petroleum Corp. because Belco had not met his demand that money from tax exemptions be invested in exploring new areas.

PHILIPPINES

A year of increasing Communist guerrilla activity and worsening economic conditions ended in December 1985 with a presidential election campaign. Pres. Ferdinand E. Marcos, seeking reelection, was opposed by Corazon C. Aquino, who blamed him for the 1983 murder of her husband, opposition leader Benigno S. Aquino, Jr., despite a court finding that a lone Communist gunman was probably responsible.

Marcos arranged to have the election more than a year ahead of schedule. On Aug. 25, 1985, the presidential palace had said that public opinion reports showed "an overwhelming rejection" of an early election, but on December 2, amid mounting domestic and U.S. criticism of his regime, Marcos signed a National Assembly bill calling for elections to be held on Feb. 7, 1986. U.S. Pres. Ronald Reagan had sent a close friend, Sen. Paul Laxalt (Rep., Nev.), to Manila in October to express concern over deteriorating conditions and to urge reforms.

The constitutionality of the early election was challenged because the presidency was not vacant, but Marcos said he would resign only when a winner was ready to be sworn in. A prominent critic of this arrangement was national assemblyman Arturo Tolentino, who had been fired from the post of foreign minister on March 4 for criticizing Marcos's retention of power to rule by decree after martial law ended in 1981. Nevertheless, on December 11 Marcos chose Tolentino, the ruling New Society

AP/WIDE WORLD

Opposition presidential candidate Corazon Aquino shares a joke with her vice-presidential running mate, Salvador Laurel, during a campaign rally on December 26.

Movement's best vote getter, as his vice-presidential candidate.

Marcos signed the election law a few hours after a special court acquitted 26 persons accused of conspiracy to murder Aquino. The government had contended that Aquino was shot by a man acting on Communist orders, who was then killed by security forces. However, a year-long investigation led to the indictment of one civilian and 25 security men, including Gen. Fabian C. Ver, the armed forces chief of staff. The Supreme Court barred from their trial some of the evidence the investigation had used, weakening the prosecution's case that a Manila policeman accompanying Aquino had shot him. Ver, who had been suspended during the trial, was reinstated by Marcos as chief of staff and immediately began reorganizing the armed forces. Although ostensibly done in response to U.S. pressure for reform, the changes were described by foreign observers as tightening Marcos's personal control.

The head of a 12-party opposition coalition, Salvador Laurel, announced his candidacy for president, as did Mrs. Aquino. The archbishop of Manila, Jaime Cardinal Sin, interceded to avoid a splitting of the anti-Marcos vote, and Laurel agreed to run for vice-president with Mrs. Aquino.

Marcos said on December 14 that 10,000 "innocent civilians" had been killed during 1985 by guerrillas of the Communist New People's Army (NPA). A government White Paper issued in May estimated NPA strength at between 10,000 and 12,000, but Communists claimed 30,000. The U.S. Defense Department warned that within three years the guerrillas could achieve military parity with government forces.

The insurgency fed on economic distress. Falling world prices for sugar and coconuts cut farmers' incomes, and industry was in recession. The average person's income dropped 6.9% between the first half of 1984 and the same period of 1985.

PHOTOGRAPHY

Among new designs for 35-mm SLRs, Minolta decisively led the way with its new Maxxum line. Not since Canon introduced its landmark AE-1 in 1976 did an SLR have such an impact on the photographic industry and marketplace. The Maxxum 7000 established its commanding position by being the first production-line interchangeable-lens 35-mm camera to provide fast, accurate automatic focusing at even relatively low light levels by incorporating electronic distance detectors and a focusing motor within the camera body rather than within individual lenses. To function with these components, Minolta designed a family of new dedicated lenses that coupled to the shaft of the built-in motor and supplied focal-length and f-stop data to the camera via five gold contacts. Twelve A-mount autofocusing lenses having focal lengths from 24 mm to 300 mm were introduced initially.

The Maxxum 7000 offered a variety of other features including multimode, multiprogrammed exposure automation, optional manual operation, automatic film loading, automatic setting of ISO (International Standards Organization) film speeds based on Kodak's DX cartridge and film coding system, LCD (liquid-crystal-display) function readouts on the camera deck, a variety of push-button controls, and motorized film transport and rewind. Also available was a Maxxum 2800 AF flash unit, which focused in the dark by infrared light.

Later in the year the company introduced a second, professional model, designated the 9000 in the U.S. Whereas the original Maxxum had a top shutter speed of 1/2,000 second, the professional Maxxum provided a 1/4,000 second. Other features unique to the 9000 included an automatic-exposure metering system that allowed the photographer to choose among a center-weighted average reading, a conventional spot reading, a spot highlight reading (plus 2 1/4 stops) or a spot shadow reading (minus 2 3/4 stops). While the 7000 model allowed the shutter to be tripped only when the subject was in focus, the 9000 permitted this option with an FP (focus-priority) setting.

A new 35-mm SLR from Olympus, the OM-PC, offered a novel feature called ESP (for electro-selective-pattern) metering. When the ESP button was set, the camera's metering system automatically compensated for difficult lighting situations such as backlighting or a very light or very dark background. Otherwise the user could choose conventional center-weighted average metering. The OM-PC offered three exposure modes: program, aperture-priority, and full manual control. A DX-capable camera, it had a top shutter speed of 1/1,000 second.

Models of compact 35-mm "auto-everything" cameras continued to proliferate during the year. The Olympus Quick Flash was the first compact to use a new cartridge-packaged six-volt lithium battery to power the camera's various electronic func-

Photographs by Stan Grossfeld of illegal aliens on the Mexico–U.S. border were among the pictures that earned 1985 Pulitzer Prizes for feature photography.

STAN GROSSFELD/THE BOSTON GLOBE—AP/WIDE WORLD

tions. The lithium cells provided an estimated five years of performance with ordinary use, gave rapid flash-recycling time, and, unlike earlier types, could be replaced easily by the user. To increase picture-taking versatility some manufacturers of compact cameras introduced dual-lens models. For example, the Fuji TW-300 allowed the user to switch between a 38-mm *f*/3.5 and a 65-mm *f*/5.6 telephoto, while the Minolta AE-Tele provided, at the flip of a switch, a choice between a 38-mm *f*/2.8 and a 60-mm *f*/4.3.

A number of new color-printing papers were introduced, including an Agfacolor Type 8 for making prints from negatives and Agfachrome Color Reversal Paper for prints from color slides. Eastman Kodak delivered Ektacolor Professional Paper as a replacement for Ektacolor 74 (and also celebrated

the 50th anniversary of Kodachrome film). Fuji Photo Film introduced Fujicolor Paper Type 02 (prints from negatives) and Fujichrome Paper Type 33 (prints from color slides).

The new series of autofocus A-mount lenses for the Minolta Maxxum was the most innovative development in consumer camera lenses during the year. Added to the 12 models mentioned above was a giant 600-mm *f*/4 apochromat telephoto with internally focusing elements that quickly and efficiently responded to the small motor built into the Maxxum's body. Camera manufacturers and independent lens makers introduced numerous new zoom lenses, especially in the popular range covering wide-angle (28-mm or 35-mm) to moderate telephoto (70-mm to 135-mm). An even longer range was offered by some models, including the

Angolan women harvesting corn greet soldiers with chants and songs. A series of photographs from Angola and El Salvador depicting their war-torn inhabitants earned a 1985 Pulitzer Prize for feature photography for Larry C. Price of the Philadelphia Inquirer.

LARRY C. PRICE/THE PHILADELPHIA INQUIRER—AP/ WIDE WORLD

André Kertész (right) attended the opening of a retrospective of his work at the Art Institute of Chicago, where he was greeted by the Institute's curator of photography, David Travis.

35–200-mm *f*/3.5–4.8 Soligor one-touch zoom and Vivitar's 28–200-mm *f*/3.8–5.6.

Kodak began test marketing two new photo/video still-image systems. One, the Color Video Imager, enabled the user to select a scene from a videocassette recorder, video camera, or computer or TV monitor and make a 1/10-second exposure of it on Kodak Trimprint film, which produced a fully developed color print in less than two minutes. Kodak's second system comprised two parts: a photo-laboratory-based transfer station that stored the images of 50 35-mm color negatives (converting them to color positives) on a video floppy disc and a home player/recorder unit that displayed the positive images on a standard color television set.

Cultural Trends

"André Kertész: Of Paris and New York," a major retrospective exhibition of the Hungarian-born master photographer's work, opened at the Art Institute of Chicago and later at the Metropolitan Museum of Art in New York City. (Concurrently a book with the same title was published.) Kertész, at age 91, was present at the Chicago opening but did not live to see the New York premiere. Kertész was highly regarded in Paris during the 1920s and 1930s as a creative artist and a photojournalist, but after moving to the U.S. in 1936 he felt that he was misunderstood and unappreciated. From the 1960s on, however, he received much recognition and eventually was showered with honors.

The Amon Carter Museum in Fort Worth, Texas, displayed two documentary exhibitions. One was a selection of work by former *Life* staffer Carl Mydans during his years with the U.S. Farm Security Administration and as a combat photographer in World War II. The second was the result of an unusual project in which the museum assigned fashion photographer Richard Avedon to document the people of the western U.S., which he proceeded to do with an 8×10-in view camera over a period of six years. The exhibition, "In the American West" (also the title of a book published concurrently), was a deromanticized record of harsh aspects of life and work among ranchers, miners, oil-field hands, carnival people, and drifters. The larger-than-life-size prints had visual power, but some viewers criticized Avedon for exploiting his subjects to create his own myth of the West.

The International Center of Photography in New York City displayed the work of Robert Capa in a retrospective that ranged from his early photojournalism in Paris to the last frame he exposed moments before being killed by a land mine in Vietnam in 1954. Two books were published in conjunction with the exhibition: *Robert Capa Photographs,* edited by Cornell Capa and Richard Whelan, and *Robert Capa: A Biography,* by Richard Whelan. The Philadelphia Museum of Art showed "W. Eugene Smith: 'Let Truth Be the Prejudice'," with 250 master prints on loan from the Center for Creative Photography of the University of Arizona.

Coinciding with the run of the Tsukuba World Expo '85, a large photo exhibition was held in nearby Tsukuba City, Japan, from March 9 to September 16. Although not permanent in character, it was heralded as a significant event in view of the fact that there were so few photo museums in Japan. The exhibition presented 450 original prints by 170 well-known photographers from Japan and elsewhere.

At the 42nd Pictures of the Year competition sponsored by the National Press Photographers Association and the University of Missouri School of Journalism, Fred Comegys of the *Wilmington* (Del.) *News Journal* was named Newspaper Photographer of the Year; Steve McCurry of *National Geographic* was named Magazine Photographer of the Year; and Stan Grossfeld of the *Boston Globe* received the Canon Photo Essayist Award. The 1985 Pulitzer Prize for spot news photography went to the staff of the *Santa Ana* (Calif.) *Register* for "Olympic Games." The Pulitzer for feature photography was given to Stan Grossfeld for "Famine in Ethiopia" and "Illegal Aliens from the Mexican Border" and to Larry C. Price of the *Philadelphia Inquirer* for "War-Torn Inhabitants of Angola and El Salvador."

The World Press Photo of the Year Award went to Pablo Bartholomew of Gamma agency. In Japan Keiichi Tahara received the tenth Ihei Kimura prize for his "Eclat" and other aesthetic works. The W. Eugene Smith Memorial Grant in Humanistic Photography was split between Donna Ferrato for "Domestic Violence" and Letizia Battaglia for "The Mafia in Sicily." The Hasselblad Award for photography given by the Hasselblad Foundation in Göteborg, Sweden, went to Irving Penn.

PHYSICS

In the world of theoretical particle physics, scientists had been attempting for decades to devise a way of uniting the four basic forces of nature: gravitation, electromagnetism, the weak force that is responsible for radioactivity, and the strong, or nuclear, force that binds atomic nuclei together. Nearly all such efforts had run into insurmountable difficulties in the past. In 1985 the latest such effort aroused considerable enthusiasm among theoreticians. It was called superstring theory, and it abandoned a key assumption of most earlier theories—that the elementary particles of which the universe is composed are point particles; that is, mathematical points without any extent. Instead, superstring theory hypothesized that everything is ultimately composed of tiny, infinitely dense strings that have a finite extension in one dimension—their length.

The new theory, initially developed by Michael Green of Queen Mary College in London and John Schwarz at the California Institute of Technology, and subsequently elaborated by many others, assumed the existence of a ten-dimensional space rather than the four-dimensional one of space and time that we perceive. Several earlier theories had also tried to use a higher number of dimensions as a way of pulling the many different forces together. The superstring theory, however, appeared to have one large advantage over earlier efforts—it eliminated the infinite quantities that kept popping up in the equations.

Because earlier theories assumed point particles, and because all forces, such as electricity and gravitation, grow stronger the closer to a particle one gets, the forces at the particle itself were calculated to be infinite. This implies infinite energy bound up in holding the particle together and, therefore, infinite mass, according to Albert Einstein's theories of the equivalence of energy and matter.

When theorists tried to formulate a theory of gravity compatible with the quantum theories of electromagnetism and nuclear forces, the problems got worse. Each infinitely massive particle so distorted space-time around itself that it would become a self-contained bubble, or black hole. The very structure of space-time would tend to shred into tiny independent pieces, something that obviously does not occur in the real universe.

Although the strings in the new theory were very tiny—only 10^{-33} cm long, far smaller than the nucleus of an atom (10^{-12} cm)—the fact that they had any extent at all eliminated the problems of infinite energy and mass. In one version of the theory the strings were imagined to be little loops 10^{-33} cm across, whose behavior was governed by the ways in which they can vibrate.

While the theory looked attractive to many physicists, it could not yet be verified by experimental data. For one thing, no one yet had proposed a way of relating the ten-dimensional space of the theory to the perceived space of four dimensions.

Second, the differences between the tiny strings and point particles show up most clearly at distances of 10^{-33} cm. To probe to such tiny scales, extremely high energies on the order of 10^{28} electron volts are required, far beyond the capabilities of particle accelerators or even cosmic rays. (A particle of that energy would have as much energy as 400 lb [182 kg] of TNT.) Therefore, extrapolations of the theory down to energies reachable by current machines would be necessary before the truth of the superstring idea could be tested. One of the theory's initial predictions was that a "shadow" world of matter could exist, detectable only by its gravitational interactions. However, such matter by its nature would be difficult to find.

While some scientists were busy seeking predictions from new theory, others were coming up with results that challenged existing theories of matter. Current theories of nuclear forces were based on the idea that nuclear particles consist of smaller units called quarks. But recent experiments might have undermined this concept.

The experiments were done by a team led by Alan Krisch of the University of Michigan working at the Brookhaven National Laboratory's particle accelerators on Long Island, New York. They showed that when protons collide at high energies, the results are influenced by which direction the particles are spinning, a situation that sharply contradicted the predictions of quark theory.

All protons spin, but in most high-energy exper-

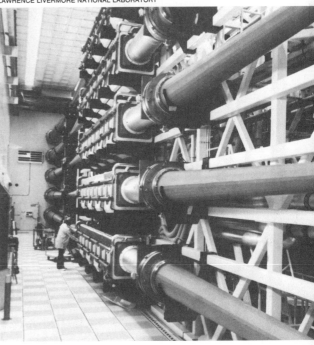

A technician makes adjustments on Nova, the world's most powerful laser, which began operating at Lawrence Livermore National Laboratory in California in April.

iments the protons in the accelerated beam and those in the stationary target are unaligned; that is, they spin in every possible direction. Krisch, however, aligned all the protons' spins by using magnetic fields, thereby creating a polarized target and a polarized beam. He and his colleagues found that when the beam protons were spinning in the same direction as the target protons, far more were scattered at high angles than when the spins were opposed. Even more surprising, he found that when the target protons were aligned in the "up" direction, more protons were scattered to the right than to the left.

The mathematical formulation of the quark theory, called quantum chromodynamics (QCD), predicts that at high energies the three quarks that are assumed to make up a proton would act independently, so that the overall spin of the proton would have a negligible effect. But Krisch's results showed that the higher the energy, the greater the spin effects. Whether the spin results would prove a mortal blow to QCD theory or whether new calculations would bring the theory into line with experiments was not clear at year's end.

New Type of Material Discovered

A crystal is distinguished from other solids by the regular pattern in which its atoms are stacked. Crystals can be based on any shape—such as a cube, a hexagonal solid, or a tetrahedron—that can be neatly stacked to fill a space completely. Physicists had long thought that they knew all the forms that crystals could take. It was "known" that just as one cannot tile a floor with only pentagons, there existed no crystals with fivefold symmetry.

At the end of 1984, however, Dan Shectman and his colleagues at the National Bureau of Standards (NBS) discovered a material with just this forbidden fivefold symmetry. The group was studying rapidly cooled crystals made from a mixture of aluminum and manganese. Shectman produced electron diffraction patterns by putting the crystals in an electron beam, a standard research technique. To his amazement, the patterns showed the sharp peaks characteristic of a crystal with a regularly repeating structure, yet the pattern for peaks had a fivefold symmetry, which seemed impossible.

The new structure appeared to be neither regularly structured, like a true crystal, nor random, like glass. Instead, it was a new material, a "quasi crystal" with "quasi-periodic" structure that almost but not quite repeats throughout the material. Mathematicians had previously found that patterns can be built up out of pentagons and icosahedrons (three-dimensional shapes with pentagonal faces) that are rigidly determined, although they do not repeat. The patterns are part of a class of objects termed Penrose tiles, which use two different shapes—icosahedrons and another shape that fills the spaces between the icosahedrons. Two theoretical physicists, Paul Steinhardt and Dov Levine at the University of Pennsylvania, had previously derived diffraction patterns of a hypothetical fivefold quasi crystal. The patterns predicted were almost identical to those actually found at NBS. During the year scientists began to examine the properties of and to search for potential uses for these materials that are neither crystal nor glass.

New Tools for Physics

During 1985 five important new tools for studying matter were put to work. In April the world's largest and most powerful laser, Nova, began operating at Lawrence Livermore National Laboratory in California. The laser's ten beams, each emanating from an amplifier as long as a football field, could concentrate for an extremely short amount of time 100 trillion watts, ten times the world's total supply of power, on a microscopic target. The new laser was intended for work in controlling nuclear fusion reactions for energy production and for military work simulating the detonation of fusion bombs. It was predicted that with its immense power, Nova should be able to crunch tiny pellets of fusion fuel to 10,000 times the density of water and heat them to several tens of millions of degrees, replicating the conditions in the center of the Sun.

Two groups of scientists, one at Livermore and another at Princeton University, developed lasers that emit X-rays. An X-ray laser, once perfected, could be a valuable instrument in making smaller integrated circuits for computers, in studying biologically important molecules such as DNA, and in studying atomic structure. The Livermore version focused Nova's smaller sibling, Novette, on a thin foil of selenium, thereby creating a hot dense ionized gas called plasma. As the ions collided with one another they were raised to a higher energy level. When they dropped out of this higher level, the plasma emitted a beam of X-rays of short duration. Princeton's device used a commercial carbon dioxide laser and a thin carbon filament.

Scientists had long tried to trap single atoms in motionless suspension. With such isolated and motionless atoms, significant studies could be conducted. The light emitted from such motionless atoms could improve the accuracy of standard atomic clocks by a hundredfold. In April William Phillips of NBS reported that his group had finally succeeded in trapping sodium atoms in a simple magnetic field. Their technique was to slow the atoms, initially traveling at about 1,000 m per second (3,280 ft per second), by shining laser light up the atomic beam. The light pressure gently slowed the atoms and could be precisely controlled to stop the motion of the atoms.

At the other extreme of the energy spectrum, the world's newest and most powerful particle accelerator came on line at Fermi National Accelerator Laboratory. There scientists activated a one-trillion electron volt beam of antiprotons and sent them colliding into a similarly energetic beam of protons.

PLASTICS

In the plastics industry, overall growth—modest but real—in 1985 was of the same order as that experienced in 1984, and the downturn in the world business cycle that many expected did not occur. Competition was especially fierce in commodity plastics, and Western Europe continued to be the most critical area. Polyvinyl chloride (PVC) consumption, and consequently prices, rose during the year, giving a measure of relief to its hard-pressed suppliers, and polystyrene (PS) business stayed generally stable. The situation with low-density polyethylene (LDPE) was more turbulent.

The completion of large petrochemical and plastics plants in the Middle East (especially Saudi Arabia), based on cheap and abundant supplies of petroleum-associated gas, had long been feared by manufacturers in less favored areas. In 1985 the threat became a reality, so far almost entirely in the form of linear low-density polyethylene (LLDPE). The Organization for Economic Cooperation and Development estimated that exportable surpluses of ethylene derivatives such as LLDPE from the Middle East to Europe and Japan might amount to 3–3.5% of their total consumption by 1990, with the remainder going largely to less developed countries. This nevertheless represented a considerable tonnage of extra material in saturated markets. The first LLDPE that arrived in Europe helped to create downward pressure on LDPE prices as a whole because these two varieties of polyethylene were largely in competition.

A number of important intercompany deals were announced in the second half of 1985. Imperial Chemical Industries (ICI) of the U.K. and Enichem of Italy revealed that they were considering collaboration in the PVC field. The combined capacities of these two producers amounted to over 1.3 million metric tons a year. Similarly, Borg-Warner Chemicals of the U.S. and CdF Chimie of France said they were planning to merge their European acrylonitrile-butadiene-styrene (ABS) plastics businesses. Hoechst of West Germany, having sold its PS facilities in the U.S. to Huntsman Chemical, discussed the disposal of its share in a joint PS manufacturing venture in The Netherlands to its partner, Shell. Also under discussion was the acquisition by Shell of an ICI LDPE plant in France.

Polypropylene (PP) and, to a lesser extent, high-density polyethylene (HDPE) continued to fare better than the other commodities. ABS also had a good year, largely because of further expansion in the automotive, telecommunications, electronics, and appliance fields. Manufacturers continued to seek high-priced specialty plastics that might profitably replace or supplement less attractive commodity business, and interest in the products of new chemistry intensified. For instance, liquid crystal polymers with self-reinforcing properties were shown for the first time in Europe by Celanese Corp. at the Interplas 85 exhibition.

POLAND

General elections took place in Poland on Oct. 13, 1985. In previous elections all candidates had been approved by a special committee of the Front of National Unity, composed of delegates from the three existing political parties: the Polish United Workers' (Communist) Party (PUWP), the United Peasants' Party, and the Democratic Party. The 1985 elections were the first to be held under a new electoral law. Each eligible citizen had two votes: one for 50 unopposed candidates on a national list, and the other for one of two candidates in local constituencies, of which there were 410 in total. The national list of candidates was prepared by the Patriotic Movement for National Renaissance (PRON), a government-appointed body set up in 1983 under the chairmanship of Jan Dobraczynski, a nonparty man of letters. The list comprised 22 candidates from the PUWP, 8 from the Peasants' Party, 4 from the Democratic Party, and 16 independents, with the notable lack of an independent sponsored by the Roman Catholic Church. All candidates in the elections pledged loyalty to the existing political system.

Official results of the elections published on October 16 revealed a turnout of 78.64%. The final distribution of seats among the three parties was close to that in the previous Sejm (parliament), with a slight increase in the number of independents. The government, pointing to the fact that more than three-quarters of the electorate had voted, claimed that it had triumphed over the boycott called by Solidarnosc (Solidarity), the banned trade union movement, and urged Western nations to drop remaining economic sanctions in view of the approval that it had won from the voters. Solidarity in turn expressed skepticism about the election results; Solidarity leader Lech Walesa claimed that in his hometown of Gdansk 50% of the voters had boycotted polling, while the government claimed a 66% turnout.

Significant shifts in the mechanism of power were announced on November 6, the date that the new Sejm was inaugurated. Gen. Wojciech Jaruzelski stepped down as premier and handed over the reins of government to Zbigniew Messner, an economist, who was a member of the PUWP Politburo and had been one of Jaruzelski's deputy premiers. The Sejm elected a new Council of State in which Jaruzelski succeeded Henryk Jablonski as chairman (head of state). Since Jaruzelski also retained the post of first secretary of the PUWP, he remained, incontestably, Poland's leader. At its second sitting on November 12 the Sejm approved a new Council of Ministers, reduced from 27 to 26 members. Messner dismissed nine ministers, principal among them being Janus Obodowski, who had been deputy premier in charge of planning, and Stefan Olszowski, foreign minister, who had resigned from the Politburo the previous day. The latter was replaced by Mar-

(continued on page 275)

Col. Adam Pietruszka *(left) and Capt. Grzegorz Piotrowski (right), both in civilian clothes, stand in a Polish court on February 7 as a judge announces their convictions in the murder of the pro-Solidarity priest Father Jerzy Popieluszko.*

AP/WIDE WORLD

The Popieluszko Trial

The trial that followed the vicious murder in October 1984 of the pro-Solidarity Polish priest Father Jerzy Popieluszko was seen in the West as an unprecedented event in a Communist country within the Soviet orbit. The four accused men were members of the state security police—generally considered to be above the law—and the trial was open to the public and to Western reporters, with the proceedings broadcast live by Polish Radio. No evidence emerged to implicate high-ranking officials directly, while both the presiding judge and counsel for the defense took every opportunity to mention the hostility of some Roman Catholic priests toward the socialist state.

The events leading to the trial began on October 19, when Father Popieluszko and his driver, Waldemar Chrostowski, were intercepted late at night en route from Bydgoszcz to Warsaw by three of the accused, Capt. Grzegorz Piotrowski and Lieutenants Waldemar Chmielewski and Leszek Pekala. Popieluszko was savagely beaten and, bound and weighted with rocks, thrown into a reservoir. But Chrostowski managed to escape, with the result that, by the following morning, both the ecclesiastical and state authorities were aware of the crime.

Interior Minister Gen. Czeslaw Kiszczak, appointed by Premier Gen. Wojciech Jaruzelski to investigate the circumstances of Popieluszko's disappearance, announced on October 27 that Piotrowski, Chmielewski, and Pekala had been arrested and reduced to the ranks. On December 27 they and their immediate superior, Col. Adam Pietruszka, were brought to trial in Torun,

charged with the murder of Popieluszko, whose body had been found on October 30. State Prosecutor Leszek Pietrasinski, demanding the death penalty for Piotrowski, called him "a cold, calculating, merciless murderer." For the other three defendants he demanded 25-year prison terms—the maximum under Polish law. Dismissing the death penalty as a "sign of vengeance," Presiding Judge Artur Kujawa, on Feb. 7, 1985, sentenced Piotrowski to 25 years' imprisonment. Pietruszka also received 25 years, but Pekala and Chmielewski—"victims of their superiors' action"—were given sentences of 15 and 14 years, respectively.

Who authorized the action that resulted in Father Popieluszko's murder? No clear answer emerged. The most senior official to give evidence at the trial was Gen. Zenon Platek, head of the Interior Ministry department concerned with monitoring church affairs. Platek's questioning by the prosecution was perfunctory, but his probable complicity was indicated by his suspension from duty before the trial opened and his subsequent dismissal from his post. More importantly, Gen. Miroslaw Milewski, a Politburo member and Central Committee secretary, resigned from all his positions on May 14.

Soviet reaction to the affair could be gauged by *Pravda*'s reference, in a report of the trial, to the Polish church's support for "hostile activities against the socialist state." Some weeks before the crime, on Sept. 11, 1984, *Izvestiya* had rebuked the Polish government for weakness in its dealings with "anti-Soviet provocateurs such as Jerzy Popieluszko."

(continued from page 273)
ian Orzechowski, a professor of history and deputy member of the Politburo.

On his first visit to the West since he became premier in February 1981, General Jaruzelski flew to New York City on September 24 to attend the UN General Assembly. The visit did not fulfill any expectations he might have entertained that it would end the period of diplomatic isolation imposed by the U.S. and its European allies when martial law was declared in December 1981. On August 31 the U.S. administration announced that Pres. Ronald Reagan would refuse to meet Jaruzelski during the visit. The snub was in protest against the continuing arrests of supporters of Solidarity.

In his address to the UN General Assembly on September 27, Jaruzelski deprecated the "correctors of history" who were trying to undermine the existing frontiers enacted at the Tehran, Yalta, and Potsdam conferences during and at the end of World War II. During his five-day stay in New York he met many foreign statesmen. Talking to U.S. journalists, Jaruzelski admitted that Poland's relations with the U.S. were as bad as they had ever been but maintained that Poland was not to blame. "We are prepared for full normalization in our bilateral relations. . . . But this has to be paralleled by a return to elementary political realism," he stated.

There were signs that some Western European nations were prepared to seek an improvement in relations. In April U.K. Foreign Secretary Sir Geoffrey Howe visited Poland, and on December 4 Jaruzelski arrived in Paris for a meeting with French Pres. François Mitterrand. Mitterrand's decision, announced only days before the visit, to become the first Western head of state to agree to meet the Polish leader since December 1981 provoked deeply hostile reactions at home.

Although officially banned, Solidarity remained active. May Day demonstrations in support of Solidarity took place in Warsaw and several other Polish cities. While Walesa himself was prevented from joining the march in Gdansk, two leading dissidents, Jacek Kuron and Seweryn Jaworski, received prison sentences of three months for organizing the Warsaw demonstration. However, arguing that he had been attempting to negotiate a peaceful end to the rally, Kuron appealed successfully against his sentence. In June three Solidarity activists, Adam Michnik, Bogdan Lis, and Wladyslaw Frasyniuk, arrested in Gdansk in February, were found guilty of attempting to incite public unrest and received jail sentences ranging from $2\frac{1}{2}$ to $3\frac{1}{2}$ years. The number of political prisoners in Poland rose from 25 at the end of 1984 to some 370 by mid-November 1985. In that month, following the elections, the authorities granted a limited amnesty to political prisoners; because it excluded those freed under earlier amnesties and subsequently rearrested, it did not extend to most imprisoned Solidarity activists. After the Sejm passed a controversial law in July

INTERPRESS/SYGMA

Poland's premier, Gen. Wojciech Jaruzelski (right), raises a toast with Soviet leader Mikhail Gorbachev after the April 26 renewal of the Warsaw Pact treaty.

granting the government greater power of control over the universities, the minister of education in November dismissed the rectors of a number of academic institutions, including the universities of Poznan, Gdansk, and Wroclaw. According to Solidarity sources, those dismissed were Solidarity sympathizers. The trial of four state security police charged with the murder of pro-Solidarity priest Jerzy Popieluszko in October 1984 attracted intense interest both at home and abroad.

POPULATION

World population stood at 4,842,042,000 at mid-1985, according to the latest estimate of the UN Population Division, up 79 million from 4,763,004,000 at mid-1984. The annual growth rate was expected to decline from 1.7 to 1.5% by the year 2000, but because of the growing base population, 89 million would then be added annually. The UN projected world population at 6,127,000,000 in 2000 and 8,177,000,000 in 2025. Between 1985 and 2025, 93% of world population growth would occur in the less developed countries of Africa, Asia (minus Japan), and Latin America. These countries would account for 83% of world population in 2025, compared with 76% in 1985. The proportion of population living in urban areas in 1985 was estimated at 41% for the world as a whole, 32% in less developed countries, and 72% in more developed countries. Regionally, Asia's population was the least urbanized (28%) and Europe's the most (73%).

According to the U.S. Census Bureau, the U.S. population (including armed forces overseas) was 238,816,000 on July 1, 1985, an increase of 2,135,000 over a year earlier. About 1.6 million of this was due to natural increase (excess of births over deaths), and the remainder (about 500,000) was accounted for by legal immigration. Illegal immigration added more to the U.S. population each year, but that figure was unknown. In 1985 the urban proportion of the U.S. population was 74%.

Birth Statistics

The National Center for Health Statistics reported that 3,697,000 births occurred in the U.S. in 1984, 2% more than in 1983. The birthrate was 15.7 live births per 1,000 population, and the fertility rate was 66 births per 1,000 women aged 15–44, both 1% higher than the rates for 1983. The increase continued into 1985. For the 12-month period ended in May, there were 2% more births than in the same period a year earlier. This trend was attributed to increases in birthrates for older women. Detailed data showed that birthrates were stable for women aged 15–29 from 1975 to 1982 but rose 23% for women aged 30–34. During this period the proportion of all births occurring to women age 30 and older increased from 17 to 22%. The rate of first births for women aged 30–34 more than doubled between 1972 and 1982.

In 1982 the total fertility rate, which indicates the average number of lifetime births per woman if current fertility rates were to continue, was 1.8 births for all women, 1.7 for white women, and 2.2 for black women. For U.S. women as a group, this rate had been below the "replacement" level of 2.1 births per woman since 1972. There were 715,-227 births to unmarried women in 1982, 4% more than in 1981. Almost 20% of all births occurred to unmarried women, and the birthrate per 1,000 unmarried women aged 15–44 was 30, the highest ever recorded. In 1982, 12% of white births, 57% of black births, and 51% of all births to adolescents under age 20 were to unmarried mothers.

Although the overall U.S. birthrate was low, the Alan Guttmacher Institute reported that adolescent women in the U.S. had higher rates of pregnancy, abortion, and childbearing than adolescent women in 37 developed countries studied, and the U.S. was the only developed country where adolescent pregnancy (though not fertility) had increased in recent years. Details from six countries showed that in 1981 the pregnancy rate per 1,000 women aged 15–19 was 96 overall and 83 for whites in the U.S., compared with 45 in England and Wales, 44 in Canada, 43 in France, 35 in Sweden, and 14 in The Netherlands.

Recent estimates reported by the Population Reference Bureau put the world birthrate at 27 per 1,000 population in 1985, down from 28 a year earlier. The average was 31 in less developed countries and 15 in more developed countries. Africa had the highest regional rate, 45, and Kenya the highest country rate, 54. The regional rates were 31 in Latin America, 28 in Asia, 15 in North America (Canada and the U.S.), and 13 in Europe. Total fertility rates continued to fall in most parts of the world except sub-Saharan Africa, but slowdowns in the decline

were observed in several less developed countries. China reached the replacement level of 2.1 births per woman in 1983, but there were reports that it was easing its one-child-per-family policy. The total fertility rate for less developed countries about 1985 was estimated at 4.2, on average, with Kenya highest at 8. For developed countries, the estimated average was 2, with West Germany lowest at 1.3.

According to the "State of World Population 1985" report of the UN Fund for Population Activities, which focused on women to mark the end of the UN Decade for Women, the total fertility rate in less developed countries would fall only to 3.2 by 2000 and would still be as high as 5.8 in Africa. At the world conference ending the women's decade, held in Nairobi, Kenya, in July 1985, 153 official delegations called on governments to strengthen family planning and maternal and child health programs and to ensure women a free choice in family-size decisions, and they urged efforts to raise the age of entry into marriage "in countries in which this age is still quite low" and to provide adolescents with adequate family planning information and education.

Death Statistics

Provisional estimates put deaths in the U.S. at 2,047,000 in 1984 and the death rate at 8.7 per 1,000 population, 1% more than the rate of 8.6 in 1983. The leading causes of death in 1984 were:

	Causes of death	Estimated rate per 100,000 population
1.	Diseases of the heart	324.4
2.	Cancers	191.6
3.	Stroke	65.6
4.	Accidents and adverse effects	40.1
5.	Chronic obstructive lung diseases	29.8
6.	Pneumonia and influenza	25.0
7.	Diabetes mellitus	15.6
8.	Suicide	12.3
9.	Chronic liver disease and cirrhosis	11.3
10.	Atherosclerosis	10.4
11.	Diseases of the kidney	8.5
12.	Homicide and legal intervention	8.3
13.	Diseases of newborn infants	8.0
14.	Septicemia	6.4
15.	Birth defects	5.6

Heart disease, cancer, and stroke accounted for over two-thirds (67.1%) of all deaths. Between 1983 and 1984, death rates rose for cancer and declined for heart disease and stroke.

Worldwide, the death rate averaged 11 per 1,000 population, unchanged from the previous two or three years. Death rate declines offset birthrate declines in many less developed countries, so natural increase remained at relatively high levels. In eastern Africa, for example, a death rate of 17 and a birthrate of 48 resulted in an annual increase of 3.1%. At that rate a population would double in 23 years. In Western Europe, by contrast, the death rate was 11 and the birthrate 12, resulting in an annual increase of 0.1%. These countries would take more than 1,000 years to double if this rate continued. Deaths exceeded births in Denmark and East and West Germany.

Infant Mortality

The infant mortality rate in the U.S. in 1984 was the lowest U.S. rate ever recorded: 10.6 deaths of infants under one year per 1,000 live births. Detailed data for 1982 showed that the mortality rate for black infants was almost twice that of white infants, as it had been 20 years earlier.

Recent estimates put infant mortality rates at 81 per 1,000 live births worldwide, 18 in more developed countries and 90 in less developed countries—all lower than previous estimates. The rates were lowest in Finland (6), Japan (6.2), Sweden (7), and Iceland (7.1). The rate for Africa, although declining, remained regionally the highest at 119.

Life Expectancy

Average life expectancy in the U.S. in 1984 was the same as the record high set in 1983—an estimated 74.7 years for the total population. New highs were recorded in 1984 for white women (78.8 years), white men (71.8), and black men (65.5). Life expectancy for black women declined slightly, from 74 to 73.7.

Worldwide, life expectancy was estimated at 62 years, a slight improvement over recent years, but there was still a 15-year gap between the estimated average for less developed countries (58 years) and that of more developed countries (73). Japan claimed to have set a world record life expectancy of 80.18 years for girls born in 1984, the first time the 80-year mark had been topped by so large a major population group. Japan also claimed the highest rate for males born in 1984, 74.54 years. Africa had the lowest life expectancy (50 years).

Marriage and Divorce Statistics

The number of marriages in the U.S. rose 2%, from an estimated 2,444,000 in 1983 to a record 2,487,000 in 1984. Because population also increased, the marriage rate per 1,000 population was the same in both years, 10.5. The median age at first marriage in 1982 was 22.3 for brides and 24.1 for grooms, compared with 20.6 and 22.5, respectively, in 1970. About 45% of marriages in 1982 were remarriages for one or both partners, up from 31% in 1970.

The number of divorces in the U.S. declined for the third consecutive year to 1,155,000 in 1984. The divorce rate of 4.9 per 1,000 population in 1984 was the lowest since 1975. Final figures for 1982 showed that the median duration of marriages ending in divorce was seven years. The number of children involved in divorce declined from 1,180,000 in 1981 to 1,108,000 in 1982.

Surveys

Findings reported by the National Center for Health Statistics from the latest U.S. national fertil-

World's 25 Most Populous Urban Areas[1]

Rank	City and Country	City proper Population	Year	Metropolitan area Population	Year
1	Tokyo, Japan	8,362,000	1985 est.	29,002,000	1981 est.
2	New York City, U.S.	7,164,742	1984 est.	17,807,100	1984 est.
3	Mexico City, Mexico	8,831,079	1980 cen.	17,321,800	1985 est.
4	Osaka, Japan	2,631,000	1985 est.	16,224,000	1983 est.
5	São Paulo, Brazil	10,036,900	1985 est.	15,143,000	1985 est.
6	Los Angeles, U.S.	3,096,721	1984 est.	12,372,600	1984 est.
7	London, England	6,756,000	1984 est.	12,231,200	1983 est.
8	Cairo, Egypt	5,881,000	1983 est.	12,001,000	1983 est.
9	Shanghai, China	6,320,872	1982 cen.[2]	11,940,000	1983 est.
10	Rhine-Ruhr, W.Ger.	[3]	[3]	10,984,000	1982 est.
11	Paris, France	2,149,900	1984 est.	10,210,059	1982 cen.
12	Buenos Aires, Arg.	2,924,000	1984 est.	9,677,200	1981 est.
13	Peking, China	5,597,972	1982 cen.[2]	9,541,000	1983 est.
14	Seoul, South Korea	[4]	[4]	9,501,413	1984 est.
15	Calcutta, India	3,305,006	1981 cen.	9,194,018	1981 cen.
16	Rio de Janeiro, Brazil	5,090,700	1980 cen.	9,014,274	1980 cen.
17	Moscow, U.S.S.R.	8,275,000	1984 est.	8,537,000	1984 est.
18	Bombay, India	[4]	[4]	8,243,405	1981 cen.
19	Chicago, U.S.	2,992,472	1984 est.	8,035,000	1984 est.
20	Nagoya, Japan	2,112,000	1985 est.	7,968,000	1981 est.
21	Tianjin, China	5,142,565	1982 cen.[2]	7,880,000	1983 est.
22	Jakarta, Indonesia	[4]	[4]	7,585,000	1985 est.
23	Manila, Philippines	1,725,500	1983 est.	6,914,581	1985 est.
24	Chongging, China	2,673,200	1982 cen.	6,511,100	1983 est.
25	Istanbul, Turkey	3,017,940	1985 est.	5,758,743	1985 est.

[1]Ranked by population of metropolitan area.
[2]Preliminary census figures.
[3]An industrial conurbation within which no single central city is identified.
[4]City proper not identified by reporting countries.

ity survey revealed that in 1982 contraception was used by 55% of all U.S. women aged 15–44, including 68% of currently married women, 54% of previously married women, and 35% of never-married women. Sterilization was the leading contraceptive method, used by 33% of all who practiced some form of contraception (22% female sterilization; 11% male sterilization), followed by the pill (29%).

The World Fertility Survey of 1972–84 reported that in seven of ten sub-Saharan African countries surveyed, fertility had increased in the 15 to 20 years before the surveys (conducted in the late 1970s and early 1980s). The proportion of married women using contraception ranged from 1% in Ivory Coast and Mauritania to 10% in Ghana. Overall, the average number of children the women said they would like to have was eight.

PORTUGAL

Factional squabbling within the Social Democratic Party (PSD), which, together with the Socialist Party (PSP), formed Portugal's coalition government, led the PSD leader, Deputy Prime Minister and Defense Minister Carlos Mota Pinto, to resign both his party and government posts in February 1985. Mota Pinto, who died three months later, was replaced in both capacities by Rui Machete. Machete's following in the PSD was weak, however, and on May 19 he himself was replaced as head of the party by Aníbal Cavaço Silva, leader of the party's right wing. Socialist prime minister Mário Soares, who had been counting on the PSD to support his aspirations in the presidential elections due in January 1986, was angered by the PSD's choice of candidate. The PSD faction headed by Cavaço Silva was strongly opposed to PSP policies, especially on the subjects of labor and agrarian reform.

On June 3 the political committee of the PSD met and decided to pull the party out of the coalition on June 13, the day after the country signed its accession treaty with the European Communities (EC). Meanwhile, the Communist-led unions staged nationwide strikes in the industrial and transport sectors and organized demonstrations calling for an end to the coalition government. They were joined in this demand by the right-wing Democratic and Social Center (CSD), whose leader, Francisco Lucas Pires, called for snap elections. Pres. António dos Santos Ramalho Eanes asked the Assembly if it could muster a new Cabinet without elections. Prime Minister Soares offered his resignation on June 25; the Assembly was dissolved on July 12; and general elections were set for October 6.

In the general elections the PSD overtook the PSP to become the largest single party in the 250-seat Assembly. While the PSD increased its representation from 75 to 88 seats, the PSP, whose representation dropped from 101 to 57 seats, lost support largely to the Democratic Renewal Party (DRP), which emerged with 45 seats. Both the (Communist) United People's Alliance and the CSD lost seats. A constitutional crisis threatened when, immediately after the polling, Prime Minister Soares announced that he was handing over his official duties to PSD Deputy Prime Minister Machete. President Eanes stepped in and secured a promise from Soares that he would continue as caretaker prime minister until a new government had been formed.

Aníbal Cavaço Silva, president of the Social Democratic Party, votes in parliamentary elections on October 6. He became prime minister in November.

AP/WIDE WORLD

After receiving the endorsement of his party on October 20, Cavaço Silva was appointed prime minister of a minority PSD government on October 28. The CSD offered working support, and the DRP declared that it was "not opposed." Cavaço Silva's Cabinet, sworn in on November 6, retained three ministers from the previous coalition administration and included two independent ministers.

Despite a security crackdown in 1984 against suspected members of the Popular Forces of April 25 (FP-25) urban guerrilla group, acts of terrorism continued. The FP-25 had claimed responsibility for a series of bomb attacks on banks, property, and NATO installations and the killing of 14 people since 1980. In February 1985 the FP-25 carried out a bomb attack on the West German air base at Beja in southeastern Portugal. Among those detained in 1984 was Lieut. Col. Otelo Saraiva de Carvalho, a major figure of the revolution. During his trial, which began in July 1985, he admitted that FP-25 forces had infiltrated his organization and that some of his own men had carried out acts of violence, but he denied that terrorism was part of his plan. Carvalho revealed that since 1978 he had been preparing the ground for a resistance movement opposed to the return of fascism. To that end, he had set up a four-tier organization that comprised the Forces of Popular Unity, a grouping of seven radical left-wing parties; Carvalho himself; the Civilian Armed Structure, which was to recruit workers for armed struggle; and a fourth structure known by the code name Barracks, which was to recruit military personnel. According to the prosecution, the third-named part of the organization was, in fact, the FP-25.

U.S. Pres. Ronald Reagan visited Portugal during his European tour in May. As he prepared to deliver an address to the Assembly, Communist deputies walked out to protest U.S. policy toward Nicaragua.

PRISONS

The swing in emphasis from reformation to punishment, now called "the new realism" by European penologists, continued and accelerated in 1985. In his state of the union speech, U.S. Pres. Ronald Reagan noted that, despite a fall in the crime rate, there were record numbers in U.S. prisons. Popular support for tough treatment of criminals was shown by the acclaim given Bernhard Goetz for shooting four youths who he thought were mugging him in the New York subway. In the U.K., where prison numbers also broke records, Prime Minister Margaret Thatcher called for sterner sentences for violence and proposed legislation allowing the Court of Appeal to review overlenient sentences. From Islamic countries there were continued reports of floggings, the chopping off of fingers and hands, public hangings, and beheadings. In Tehran, Iran, a woman whose husband had blinded her was allowed by judicial order to cut out his eyes. The

Inmates in the Tennessee State Prison in Nashville state their grievances at a press conference during disturbances on July 2. The prisoners' hostages were released during the conference.

AP/WIDE WORLD

Ministry of Justice in China claimed that its new policy of harsh punishment had helped to reduce the number of reported serious crimes from 800,-000 to 500,000.

Graeme Newman's book *Just and Painful: A Case for the Corporal Punishment of Criminals* advocated the punishment by electric shock of men, women, and children convicted of crime. Susan Jacoby's *Wild Justice: The Evolution of Revenge* considered the legitimacy of vengeance as an element in judicial punishment. While both books attracted as much censure as praise, their significance for Western penology lay in opening up for discussion ideas thought scarcely mentionable for many decades. Penal reformers in the U.S. advocated compensation for people imprisoned pending trial and subsequently acquitted; this was available in most European countries but not generally in Britain or the U.S. British government proposals to extend compensation for victims of crime seemed to arouse greater support.

Capital Punishment

Amnesty International reported worldwide growth in the number of executions. It had documentary evidence of 1,500 in 40 countries in 1984 but thought the real total to be many times higher. In the U.S. individual executions became less newsworthy, attracting widespread public attention only when they were particularly macabre. Abolitionists began to focus less on individual executions and more on the broad social and moral issues involved in capital punishment; for example, that it discriminated against black people: 42% of the 1,400 people on "death row" in 1984 were black, according to the American Civil Liberties Union, whereas blacks constituted only 12% of the general U.S. population. Supporters of capital punishment, meanwhile, protested strongly when the California Supreme Court overturned four death sentences in June 1985; the court had already overturned 29 and

affirmed only 3 since the reinstatement of capital punishment in the U.S. in 1976.

In the U.K. those favoring restoration of the death penalty found support for their cause in Home Office figures showing that 33 people had been convicted of a second homicide between 1973 and 1983, and that an estimated 4,000 to 5,000 convicted killers were at large in England and Wales in 1985. In Ireland the government announced its intention to abolish capital punishment.

Prisons

In many countries, including the U.S. and the U.K., the trend to severer sentencing led to greater prison overcrowding, often producing squalid physical conditions. Sharp rises in the number of juveniles in custody, despite the decline of this age group in the general population, caused particular concern, as did the growing practice reported from the U.S. of incarcerating "difficult" juveniles in hospital "secure units" at the expense of insurance companies and without court hearings. Fear of AIDS (acquired immune deficiency syndrome) added new terrors to life in prisons, where homosexual behavior is common. When a homosexual prison chaplain died from AIDS in February at Chelmsford, England, movements in and out of prisons were restricted, known homosexual prisoners were threatened, and the Prison Department was blamed for employing the chaplain. Most Western countries also reported growing drug problems in prisons. Alcohol and heroin were said to be so readily available in British prisons that attempts at treatment were useless. Serious rioting in protest against prison conditions occurred in many countries. At Spike Island, Ireland, a new prison modeled on Alcatraz, inmates drove the staff and their families off the island and destroyed all the buildings. Prisoners at Belo Horizonte, Brazil, began the regular killing of inmates, chosen by lot, as a protest against conditions.

Unprecedented prison overcrowding, public pres-

Private Means to Public Ends

During the early 1980s, few proposals in the field of corrections stimulated as sharply divided opinions as the prospect of contracting with the private sector for the management of prison and jail facilities. Some saw a chance to introduce efficiency and innovation to a field laboring under the burden of outmoded facilities, unprecedented population increases, and declining resources. Others feared that the profit motive would interfere with professional corrections practice.

The propriety of delegating matters of social control proved to be the most controversial issue. In a facility operated by the private sector, a range of quasi-judicial functions would be delegated to the contractor. The deprivation of liberty, the administration of discipline, the capacity to use restraining or deadly force, control over decisions that could affect how much time an inmate served and the conditions of his or her confinement—all would be transferred to managers in the private sector. Those who questioned the propriety of such a shift argued that the administration of justice is a raison d'être of government and neither can nor should be delegated.

In this view, imprisonment serves broad social interests; to the extent that private purposes are superimposed, justice is compromised. The compromise might take many forms. Economic motives might conflict with the need to provide decent conditions of confinement. Private contractors might skim off the cream of the inmate crop, leaving the public corrections system with the most expensive inmate-management problems. Paid on the basis of the number of in-mates housed, contractors might maintain high occupancy rates, even in the absence of demonstrated need.

In rebuttal, others argued that policy development—and not the execution of policy—is the central role of government. In this view, private motives would conflict with the public interest only if public-sector managers failed to establish appropriate performance standards and to closely supervise their contractors. Indeed, because a private vendor would be under competitive pressure to perform, the quality of privately provided services would probably be superior to the same services dispensed in the monopolistic environment of government. Left unanswered was whether there would be sufficient market pressure to sustain any improvements over the long term or whether competition would be stifled—either because few providers were attracted to the field or because it was impractical to turn contracts over often enough to maintain competition.

Questions of economic efficiency also remained largely unanswered. After considering all the hidden costs of contracting (including the burden of supervising the private contractors), would proprietary facilities save the government any money? Many public-sector prisons and jails were underfunded in relation to the number of offenders in custody. Was it really possible for the private sector to provide more service for less money? Or would time simply reveal that more prisoners require more resources and that, if public-sector managers could negotiate the same deal as private contractors, they might do just as well?

sure for more and longer prison sentences, and general opposition to increased public spending combined to present governments and prison authorities with a dilemma. One solution tried in the U.S. was "privatization." More traditional penal reformers sought the solution in reduced prison numbers. The National Association for the Care and Resettlement of Offenders, London, demonstrated that, relative to populations, the U.S. imprisoned about twice as many people as the U.K. and the U.K. twice as many as France. Reformers also urged reduction in the use of pretrial detention, which accounted for half the prison population in Italy and France. French Minister of Justice Robert Badinter announced his government's intention to restrict examining magistrates' power to remand in custody. Another attempt to reduce prison numbers was by the "tracking" of offenders set at liberty. In New Mexico surveillance was effected by nonremovable bracelets transmitting radio signals.

During the year many European countries, the U.S., and Canada signed the Council of Europe's Convention on the Transfer of Sentenced Prisoners, allowing prisoners to serve or complete sentences in their home countries. The convention did not extend to African, Arab, Asian, or South American countries.

QATAR

During 1985 Qatar maintained petroleum production at or close to the 280,000-bbl-a-day quota set by the Organization of Petroleum Exporting Countries. Almost all of the petroleum came from the onshore Dukhan Field. Proven reserves would be sufficient to last for 40 years at current levels of extraction. Japan, the largest customer, took almost half of petroleum exports in 1984.

The most important economic project was the development of the North Field. Lying off the northeast coast of Qatar, it contained the world's largest known reserves of natural gas. The project was expected to require investment of up to $6 billion. In September it was announced that the Japanese Marubeni Corp. had taken a 7.5% stake in the company established to develop the find, a tripartite venture of the Qatar government, British Petroleum, and the Compagnie Française des Pétroles-Total. Following the government's purchase of 14 French-built Mirage F-1C jet fighters in 1984, the construction of a military air base had become a priority.

In February 1985 Emir Sheikh Khalifah ibn Hamad ath-Thani opened an extension of the University of Qatar. When it first opened, for the 1973–74 academic year, the university had 150 students; by 1985 there were over 4,500. Accompanied by senior ministers, Sheikh Khalifah visited the U.K. on November 12–15 and then went on to tour France.

RACE RELATIONS

More than 90 church leaders from Belgium, Britain, and The Netherlands signed a declaration in 1985 acknowledging that, in their view, racial prejudice and racist practices were to be found in all parts of Europe and admitting that "the churches have failed to resist this evil adequately." The evidence of continuing racial discrimination and racist violence lent added weight to this declaration. In the U.S., according to the National Urban League, progress made by the black community during the 1960s had peaked in the 1970s and declined since then. On the other hand, international condemnation of apartheid—institutionalized racism—in South Africa gathered force during the year; but some Western governments, notably that of the U.K., refrained from bringing to bear on South Africa the economic pressure called for by apartheid's most vocal opponents.

United States

Pres. Ronald Reagan's administration continued to focus attention on civil rights programs and laws of the 1960s. On Sept. 26, 1985, Secretary of Education William Bennett declared that over the last two decades federal policies concerning bilingual education had become "confused as to purpose and overbearing as to means." He claimed that $1.7 billion had been wasted and proposed new legislation to allow local school districts virtually complete autonomy in deciding how to teach children whose first language was not English.

Also undergoing reconsideration were affirmative-action programs that set specific targets and guidelines for black and other minority employment. The Department of Justice filed a brief supporting white teachers who were appealing against a layoff plan adopted by the school board of Jackson, Mich., that gave preference to members of minority groups over whites with more seniority. In its brief in *Wygant* v. *Jackson* the department asked the

U.S. Supreme Court to hold that all governmental preferences based on race were unconstitutional, whether they benefited blacks, whites, or others. U.S. Attorney General Edwin Meese III triggered a storm of controversy when, in a speech on September 17, he likened supporters of racial quotas to Americans who once argued "that slavery was good not only for the slaves but for society."

In another case before the Supreme Court, *Thornburg* v. *Gingles,* the Department of Justice supported the state of North Carolina in its appeal against a lower court ruling that the state's 1982 redistricting plan violated the rights of black voters. This was the first major test of the 1982 amendments to the Voting Rights Act. These actions reinforced the gulf between the administration and the black community and illustrated the divergence of views that led Urban League president John Jacob to describe President Reagan's record on civil rights as "deplorable."

Despite a drop of just under one percentage point in the poverty rate from 15.3% in 1983 to 14.4% in 1984, the poverty rate for blacks remained nearly three times the white rate—33.8% to 11.5%. Of the 404,000 families who moved over the poverty-line definition, more than one-quarter were black.

Great Britain

The Policy Studies Institute found that at least one-third of employers discriminated against black job applicants, the same proportion found in a previous study in 1974. John Cordrey of the Commission for Racial Equality (CRE) said that throughout

Police armed with riot shields make an arrest during the second night of rioting in the Handsworth area of Birmingham, England, on September 11.

REUTERS/BETTMANN NEWSPHOTOS

AP/WIDE WORLD

Leading a 20th-anniversary commemoration of the famous march from Selma to Montgomery, Alabama, were the Rev. Jesse Jackson (left) and Coretta Scott King (right), widow of the 1965 march's leader.

the country, "The whole of the recruitment situation . . . is riddled with discrimination." The CRE found that Asians were twice as likely to be refused a mortgage as were whites, and a number of studies on public housing documented racist practices. Studies of the government's Youth Training Scheme found extensive discrimination against black youths. A number of establishment figures, including judges and the president of the Royal College of Physicians, reported racial discrimination in the legal and medical professions. The report of the committee headed by Lord Swann, on the education of ethnic minority children, found racism to be a major factor in the poor showing of black and Asian pupils. In the face of this evidence and of specific policy recommendations, the government continued its opposition to strengthening the enforcement powers of the CRE, to the establishment of affirmative-action and contract-compliance procedures, and to increased expenditures.

In September and October 1985 major outbreaks of violence took place in a number of British cities with large nonwhite communities: the Handsworth district of Birmingham; Toxteth in Liverpool; and Brixton, Peckham, and Tottenham in London. All of these areas suffered from high levels of unemployment, urban blight, and homelessness. Relations with the police had deteriorated in the wake of charges of lack of police protection of the black communities against an increasing incidence of racist violence, combined with what was seen as an increasing level of victimization by the police themselves. Each of the riots was triggered by a police-community interaction, including the shooting of a black woman in a dawn raid on her home by police in Brixton and the death of another black woman (apparently as the result of a heart attack)

after a police search of her home in Tottenham. After the Brixton violence nine Brixton Anglican priests issued a public statement in which they declared: "We deplore the conditions of life which have persisted and worsened in Brixton since the 1981 riots. We deplore the fact that no effective steps have been taken by the government in the past four years to alleviate unemployment."

Continental Western Europe

In November an all-party committee of the European Parliament reported a rise of racism and neofascism throughout Europe. The evidence cited for this conclusion included instances of violence against members of ethnic minorities, the revival of "scientific" racist theories, and growing support for ultraright and neofascist political parties.

In France the National Front (NF) gained 10.4% of the vote in constituencies in which its candidates campaigned in the first round of the March 1985 cantonal elections. They gained their highest votes in Toulon (31%), Marseille (30%), Cannes (26%), and Seine St. Denis (17%). Pres. François Mitterrand's suggestion in April that France's four million immigrants be given the right to vote in local elections was denounced by the NF and other opposition parties.

The increase in racist violence against "guest workers" in Denmark was such that Queen Margrethe referred to the problem directly in her 1985 New Year speech. In Geneva a right-wing group, the Vigilance Party, based its campaign on the repatriation of foreign workers and won 19 seats in the cantonal parliament in the October 1985 elections, tying for first with the Liberals.

South Africa

The South African Institute of Race Relations calculated in November 1985 that 834 people had died in racial violence in the 14 months since the arrests on charges of treason of the leaders of the United Democratic Front in September 1984. On July 21, 1985, the South African government imposed a state of emergency that led to a doubling of the number of deaths. Police and army activity accounted for more than 50% of the deaths. More than 6,000 antiapartheid activists had been interned without trial by mid-October 1985.

Pres. P. W. Botha's control over the white minority was challenged in 1985 on a number of fronts. Large numbers of white students took part in demonstrations against the state of emergency and following the hanging of the black activist and poet Benjamin Moloise, convicted of complicity in the 1982 murder of a policeman, on October 18. Seven of South Africa's leading white businessmen and newspaper editors defied President Botha and met with the leaders of the outlawed African National Congress (ANC) in Zambia on September 13. The government subsequently had to withdraw the passports of a number of white student and church leaders to prevent them from meeting with ANC leaders. On November 4 the *Cape Times* published an interview with ANC leader Oliver Tambo despite the risk of prosecution and imprisonment of its editor, Tony Heard. Along with the protests, however, there was an increase of more than 200% in support for two ultraright parties in the October "mini election" in five constituencies. In Sasolburg the Herstigte Nasionale Party (HNP) won its first parliamentary seat ever on a platform of opposition to all reforms and concessions to the country's black majority. Louis Stofberg, the Sasolburg victor and general secretary of the HNP, declared that his victory "heralded the resurrection of the Afrikaner nation as a free and independent entity."

Botha's reforms had apparently frightened some sections of white Afrikanerdom, but he continued to resist demands for a fundamental overthrow of apartheid, legalization of the ANC, and the release of Nelson Mandela and other ANC leaders from prison. In a major address in August he declared that he "could not accept the principle of one man, one vote. That would lead to the domination of one [race] over the others." Faced with an increasingly serious sanctions campaign throughout the world, a sharp drop in the value of the rand and a major threat to the South African banking system, and an increasingly determined militant African majority, Botha announced on November 1 the prohibition of the televising, photographing, recording, or even drawing of conflict situations in the 38 magisterial districts covered by the state of emergency except with the permission of the commissioner of police.

REFUGEES AND MIGRANTS

Hopes that 1985 could be a year for the consolidation of attempts to achieve durable solutions for refugee problems were dashed by the dramatic crisis in Africa, where over a million persons were displaced by unprecedented drought and famine as well as civil and political disturbances. UN High Commissioner for Refugees Poul Hartling had launched his first Africa Emergency Appeal in November 1984 for $8 million, but as UNHCR found itself obliged to organize a vast emergency relief operation—at the expense of its ongoing programs—in the Central African Republic, Djibouti, Ethiopia, Somalia, and The Sudan, successive appeals raised the target by the end of 1985 to $107 million. While the crisis was largely brought under control, it stretched the financial and human resources of UNHCR and had serious repercussions on the organization's ability to push forward with durable solutions in Africa and elsewhere in the world. In addition, contributions made by the international community to the African emergency came at the expense of UNHCR's general programs, with the result that UNHCR entered the last quarter of 1985 in the midst of an unprecedented financial crisis. At the end of October it faced a shortfall of $40 million in its reduced program budget of $319 million.

Elsewhere in Africa, the voluntary repatriation of Ugandans took place from Rwanda, The Sudan, and Zaire, and UNHCR participated in negotiations between Rwanda and Uganda to find a solution to the problem of some 40,000 displaced persons and asylum-seekers who crossed from Uganda to Rwanda in 1982. A major new influx from Angola into Zaire's Shaba Province began in late 1984 and continued throughout the first half of 1985; by midyear UNHCR was assisting over 60,000 refugees in the area. The highlight of the year was the handing over to the government of Tanzania in July of the rural refugee settlement of Mishamo; this marked the achievement of a durable solution to at least one refugee problem in the troubled continent.

In Southeast Asia resettlement remained the main durable solution for refugees in camps, though an increasing number of Indochinese "long-stayers" awaiting resettlement caused concern. The Orderly Departure Program from Vietnam maintained a rate of over 2,000 legal emigrants a month, which made it likely that the milestone of 100,000 orderly departures would be reached by year's end. Progress was also made in the areas of rescue-at-sea and antipiracy activities, though pirate attacks on boat people continued. The Anti-Piracy Program concluded with Thailand was renewed in June.

In Latin America, while progress toward durable solutions was recorded in Mexico and to some extent in Costa Rica, the situation in Honduras remained difficult, particularly for refugees from El Salvador. Efforts to relocate refugees away from the border were planned; similar efforts were successful in Mexico, where some 45% of the 45,000 Guatemalan refugees assisted by UNHCR were relocated in new agricultural settlements. Large numbers of refugees returned to Argentina, Bolivia, and Uruguay following the restoration of democratic forms of government in those countries.

In Europe the increasingly negative public reaction to the arrival of larger numbers of refugees and asylum-seekers from other continents, some of them by irregular means, prompted UNHCR to convene intergovernmental consultations on the problem in May. The discussions at this meeting were widely seen as a useful basis for further action.

The year marked the end of the second term of office of High Commissioner Hartling, who had first been elected to the post in December 1977. On December 10 the UN General Assembly unanimously elected Jean-Pierre Hocké of Switzerland as Hartling's successor.

Migration

The determination of the governments of the richer countries to control immigration from the poorer ones remained unshaken during 1984–85. In the U.S. there was continuing controversy over immigration, particularly from the Western Hemisphere and Asia, and an increase in violence directed against Asian immigrants. During the 1985 legislative session, Congress debated the Simpson-Rodino bill, which represented another attempt to pass a comprehensive immigration statute. On September 19 the Senate passed the immigration bill, which included an amendment establishing a "guest worker" program allowing up to 350,000 aliens into the U.S. to harvest perishable fruit and vegetable crops, on the grounds that there was a shortage of domestic farm workers. This argument was challenged in testimony by Dolores Huerta, vice-president of the United Farm Workers, who pointed out that more than 14% of domestic farm workers were unemployed—twice the national unemployment rate.

Refugees from Central America and their supporters continued to protest the U.S. administration's refusal to grant political asylum to Salvadoran and Guatemalan refugees; the rate for Salvadorans was 3% of those applying. Refugees at the El Centro detention camp in California carried out a hunger strike in protest against mistreatment and U.S. immigration policy, beginning on Memorial Day, May 27, and ending on June 4. Lawyers acting for refugee children won a legal victory in a Los Angeles federal court when, on September 20, U.S. District Judge Edward Rafeedie ruled that deporting minors without allowing them to contact a parent, relation, friend, or lawyer was unconstitutional.

In France and West Germany immigration restriction was reinforced by offers of money to encourage unwanted foreign workers and their families to return to their countries of origin. These policies were accompanied by increasing levels of anti-immigrant agitation, notably in the French right-wing press.

In Britain the Commission for Racial Equality (CRE) reported that immigration policy placed an "excessive" emphasis on "detecting and preventing evasion and abuse." This overrode the "interests and welfare of those with a rightful claim to come to the U.K." and exacted "an unacceptable cost to genuine families and to race relations generally." These conclusions were given added weight by the leak of a confidential Home Office briefing to ministers, which stated that long lines of people claiming a legal right to enter Britain from the Indian subcontinent were maintained deliberately to regulate numbers. The number of clearance officers dealing with the demand for entry was "the primary regulator of the number of husbands, wives, children, and male fiancés admitted from the Indian sub-continent in any one year." This led to waiting times in 1984 of 22 months for those applying from Bangladesh, 11 months for Pakistanis, and 12 months for Indians. As a result, there were 19,400 women and children in the subcontinent waiting to join family members already in Britain.

The number of immigrants allowed to settle in the U.K. in 1984—51,000—was the lowest since statistics were first compiled in 1962 and 2,500 below the 1983 figure. The number of people accepted from the New Commonwealth (nonwhite Commonwealth) and Pakistan fell for the eighth successive year to 24,800—2,750 fewer than in

Refugees covered by the UNHCR and the UNRWA mandates numbered an estimated ten million people in 1984. Standards of treatment and of protection of refugees varied widely; while in some areas prospects for repatriation or integration into host societies were improving, in others camps were frequently under threat of military attack.

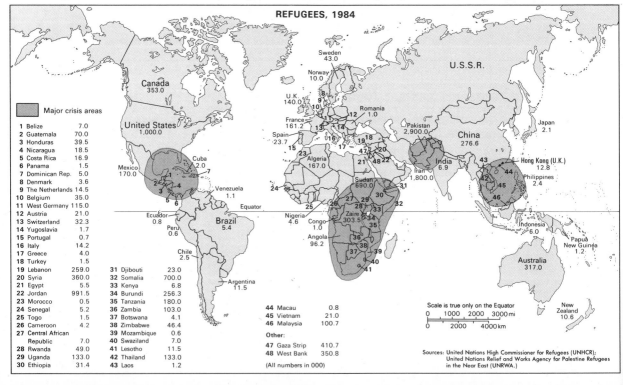

REFUGEES, 1984

Major crisis areas

1	Belize	7.0
2	Guatemala	70.0
3	Honduras	39.5
4	Nicaragua	18.5
5	Costa Rica	16.9
6	Panama	1.5
7	Dominican Rep.	5.0
8	Denmark	3.6
9	The Netherlands	14.5
10	Belgium	35.0
11	West Germany	115.0
12	Austria	21.0
13	Switzerland	32.3
14	Yugoslavia	1.7
15	Portugal	0.7
16	Italy	14.2
17	Greece	4.0
18	Turkey	1.5
19	Lebanon	259.0
20	Syria	360.0
21	Egypt	5.5
22	Jordan	991.5
23	Morocco	0.5
24	Senegal	5.2
25	Togo	1.5
26	Cameroon	4.2
27	Central African Republic	7.0
28	Rwanda	49.0
29	Uganda	133.0
30	Ethiopia	31.4
31	Djibouti	23.0
32	Somalia	700.0
33	Kenya	6.8
34	Burundi	256.3
35	Tanzania	180.0
36	Zambia	103.0
37	Botswana	4.1
38	Zimbabwe	46.4
39	Mozambique	0.6
40	Swaziland	7.0
41	Lesotho	11.5
42	Thailand	133.0
43	Laos	1.2
44	Macau	0.8
45	Vietnam	21.0
46	Malaysia	100.7

Other:

| 47 | Gaza Strip | 410.7 |
| 48 | West Bank | 350.8 |

(All numbers in 000)

Canada 353.0
United States 1,000.0
Mexico 170.0
Cuba 2.0
Venezuela 1.1
Ecuador 0.8
Peru 0.6
Brazil 5.4
Chile 2.5
Argentina 11.5

Sweden 43.0
Norway 10.0
U.K. 140.0
France 161.2
Spain 23.7
Algeria 167.0
Romania 1.0
Nigeria 4.6
Congo 1.0
Angola 96.2
Zaire 303.5
Sudan 690.0

U.S.S.R.
Pakistan 2,900.0
China 276.6
India 6.9
Iran 1,800.0
Japan 2.1
Hong Kong (U.K.) 12.8
Philippines 2.4
Indonesia 6.0
Papua New Guinea 1.2
Australia 317.0
New Zealand 10.6

Scale is true only on the Equator
0 1000 2000 3000 mi
0 2000 4000 km

Sources: United Nations High Commissioner for Refugees (UNHCR); United Nations Relief and Works Agency for Palestine Refugees in the Near East (UNRWA.)

The Sanctuary Movement

On Oct. 22, 1985, 11 clergy and laity, indicted on more than 50 felony counts of conspiracy, smuggling and transportation, concealing, harboring, and shielding, as well as encouraging the entry of illegal aliens into the U.S., went on trial in federal court in Tucson, Ariz. There had been two prior court proceedings against activists of the Sanctuary Movement, but it was the Tucson case that attracted national attention to Sanctuary's efforts to assist refugees from El Salvador and Guatemala in finding a haven in the United States.

The number of undocumented Salvadorans and Guatemalans in the U.S. was unknown but, whatever the actual figures, the reach of the Sanctuary Movement was limited to a small fraction of them. However, its influence far exceeded its scope, as reflected in the endorsements it received from national religious bodies or their affiliates. A denominational breakdown of Declared Sanctuaries as of Dec. 1, 1985, prepared by the Chicago Religious Task Force on Central America, listed 259 church facilities, of which 44 were Roman Catholic, 43 under Quaker auspices, 40 Unitarian/Universalist, 26 Presbyterian, 15 Jewish, 13 United Church of Christ, 11 Lutheran, 11 Methodist, and 10 Mennonite. They were located in 33 states, with the heaviest concentration (98) in California.

Officially, the movement began on March 24, 1982, when the Southside Presbyterian Church of Tucson declared itself a Public Witness Sanctuary and so advised the Immigration and Naturalization Service. Clandestine transport of refugees across the Mexican border had been going on since 1981. By moving into the open, Sanctuary meant to publicize its work, challenge the administration, and, as was freely acknowledged, influence U.S. policy in Central America. The Justice Department at first refrained from entering churches to search for illegal aliens. It was unclear why this policy was abandoned or why undercover agents and informers were infiltrated into the movement, since its activities were quite open.

In practice, the Sanctuary Movement did not reach out to exiles from all of Central America but only to those from El Salvador and Guatemala. The position of the government was that, with a few exceptions, the Salvadorans and Guatemalans entering from Mexico were economic migrants rather than political refugees, victims not of persecution but of poverty. And as economic migrants they could not be fitted into the legal guidelines controlling the granting of asylum. Echoing the finding of the UN High Commissioner for Refugees that some people who might not meet the definition of the UN Convention on Refugees were leaving their countries of origin to escape severe internal upheavals or armed conflict and, therefore, should not be returned to areas where they might be exposed to danger, the Sanctuary Movement advocated the granting of extended voluntary departure (EVD) to Salvadorans and Guatemalans. EVD is an administrative remedy previously granted to nationals of several countries who were permitted to remain and work in the U.S. until conditions in their home countries returned to normal. The Sanctuary Movement did not admit or accept the consequences of deliberate defiance of legal authority. In this sense its stated rationale was not civil disobedience. It nevertheless was within the tradition of conscientious objection to laws perceived as oppressive and in conflict with religious and ethical imperatives.

1983. The refusal rate for applicants from the Indian subcontinent was one in three.

British immigration rules were again declared unlawful in a unanimous ruling by the European Court of Human Rights on May 28, 1985. The court found that the rules introduced by the Conservative government in 1980, which denied to foreign women with full residency rights in the U.K. the right to bring in their husbands or fiancés (a right allowed to men), violated Art. 13 of the European Convention on Human Rights because they discriminated against women. The British government responded to the court's ruling on July 10 by amending the restrictions on entry to include foreign wives and fiancées, thus ending sex discrimination but extending the already long waiting lists for entry certificates. These applications would be considered as nonpriority cases, and the applicants would have to prove that "immigration is not the primary purpose of the marriage." In the past this requirement had led to a rejection rate of 45% of husbands and fiancés from the Indian subcontinent, and it was feared that wives and fiancées would also have problems in this area.

Chris Hurford, the Australian minister for immigration and ethnic affairs, announced on June 3 a series of changes in Australian immigration policy to take effect on July 1. The number of immigrants targeted to settle in Australia in 1985–86 was increased to 84,000 from the 80,000 targeted for 1984–85; this was a significant increase from the 70,000 expected to be granted permanent residence in 1984–85. A major feature of the new program was a doubling in admissions of migrants with business and professional skills from the estimated 9,000 visas issued in 1984–85 to a target of 18,500.

WILLIAM E. SAURO/THE NEW YORK TIMES

Amy Eilberg, the first woman Conservative rabbi, was ordained in May at the Jewish Theological Seminary of America in New York City.

RELIGION

The day before he was scheduled to go on trial, a defiant Denis Hurley, Roman Catholic archbishop of Durban, South Africa, told a cheering crowd in his cathedral that "the Gospel is political." Hurley, accused by the South African government of making unlawful remarks about alleged police atrocities in neighboring Namibia, was acquitted in February 1985, but this dispute was only one of many clashes between religious and government leaders during the year.

The competing claims of the "sacred" and "secular" spheres were drawn most sharply in South Africa, the scene of massive protests against the government's apartheid (racial separation) policy. Church leaders were in the forefront of the struggle. Among the most radical and visible was Allan Boesak, president of the World Alliance of Reformed Churches. Boesak, classified by the government as "Coloured" because of his mixed racial descent, was detained, then arrested after he called for black boycotts of white businesses and the withdrawal of foreign investments from the country. He also was accused of participating in public gatherings defined as illegal by the nation's strict security laws.

Allied with Boesak was black Anglican Bishop Desmond Tutu, winner of the 1984 Nobel Peace Prize. As a peacemaker, Tutu often was caught in the middle. In August he drew criticism when he refused to join other South African religious leaders in a meeting with Pres. P. W. Botha. After a five-day trip to South Africa, Jerry Falwell, fundamentalist leader of the Moral Majority in the U.S., said that "if Bishop Tutu maintains he speaks for the black people of South Africa, he's a phony." Falwell later softened his accusations but remained opposed to the many religious leaders who were active in antiapartheid protests. At an emergency meeting in Harare, Zimbabwe, in December, the World Council of Churches called for church pressure and economic sanctions against South Africa.

In the U.S. the so-called wall of separation between church and state was the site of many battles. One of the most protracted resulted from the decision by more than 200 churches and synagogues to provide "sanctuary" for illegal aliens from Central America, whom they regarded as victims or potential victims of persecution in their homelands. In Brownsville, Texas, Lorry Thomas, a Sanctuary leader, was sentenced to prison after telling a judge she would continue violating federal immigration laws. In Tucson, Ariz., 11 persons—including a Protestant minister, 2 Roman Catholic priests, and a nun—faced federal charges of transporting and concealing illegal aliens. Before the trial opened in October, the defendants accused the government of violating their constitutional right to freedom of religion by having agents infiltrate their churches.

Several church-state issues were on the docket of the U.S. Supreme Court. In two 5–4 decisions, the court ruled that public school officials in New York City and Grand Rapids, Mich., should not permit public school teachers to lead special education classes in parochial schools. In other rulings the court invalidated a Connecticut law that gave employees an unqualified right to observe their Sabbath as a day off from work and struck down an Alabama law that allowed a moment of silence for prayer in public schools. Such decisions prompted William J. Bennett, the U.S. secretary of education, to accuse the court of displaying a "fastidious disdain for religion." Throughout the year the Cabinet official drew both praise and blame as he lashed out at those he held responsible for "a new aversion to religion."

Some public policy issues not only drove a wedge between church and state but also created divisions within the church. In Pennsylvania an activist Lutheran minister incurred the wrath of both civil and religious authorities. After serving a jail term for contempt of court, D. Douglas Roth was defrocked by an ecclesiastical court convened by the Lutheran Church in America. The church court decided that Roth had acted in "willful disregard and violation" of church law when he refused to obey his bishop's order to vacate his pulpit. Roth's congregation in Clairton, Pa., was divided over the role the radical minister played in an ecumenical campaign to combat the causes of unemployment in the steel mill area.

Debate over the proper role of the church in the public arena divided ranks in the Roman Catholic Church. Following precedents set down in the early days of his pontificate, Pope John Paul II continued to insist that priests and nuns stay out of public office. In February four priests in Nicaragua lost their priestly status, on orders from the Vatican, when they refused to give up their prominent positions in that nation's Marxist-oriented Sandinista government. In other ways, however, Catholic leaders, from the pope on down, tried to influence political decisions by vigorously articulating the church's teaching on abortion, nuclear warfare, birth control, human rights, and economic justice. During a 12-day trip to Latin America in January and February, John Paul went out of his way to visit regions of extreme poverty. Wherever he went, he championed the cause of "authentic liberation" that leads to social justice without resorting to violence. On the eve of his departure in August for a 12-day trip to Africa, he condemned South Africa's apartheid system. In May, however, during his 26th trip abroad, sparse crowds and hostile street demonstrations marred his visit to The Netherlands, where there

was strong opposition to his strict orthodox views.

In Rome, John Paul took several steps to put his own "household of faith" in order. His most decisive step resulted in the convening of an Extraordinary Synod of Bishops. In the months prior to the 13-day meeting in November and December, Catholic leaders anticipated the event with a combination of hope and dread. In particular, progressive Catholics feared that the Synod would set in motion policies that would roll back reforms of the Second Vatican Council (Vatican II). By the time the Synod ended, however, a synthesis of views was achieved that enabled both progressives and conservatives to go home with the feeling that at least some of their views had been incorporated into the final document. Far from being dismissed as a historical aberration, Vatican II was hailed as

Liberation Theology

"Liberation theology" was born in Latin America in the late 1960s. Its advocates insist that it is not a theology "about" liberation but a theology "for" liberation. It is politically committed. It is deliberately partisan. It has made what it calls the "option for the poorest," by which is meant that one has a better chance of understanding the Christian gospel if one is on the side of the oppressed.

Adopt this point of view and familiar Gospel texts take on a new meaning. A favorite text is Luke 4:18, in which Jesus quotes Isaiah: "The Spirit of the Lord is upon me, because he has anointed me to preach good news to the poor. He has sent me to proclaim release to captives." The Magnificat, which speaks of God casting "down the mighty from their thrones" (Luke 1:52), is read in the same light.

But it is the idea of God that changes most radically. While the traditional Christian God is seen by liberationists as the prop of an unjust social system, with a message of resignation in this world and hope only in the next, the God of liberation theology leads his new People of God out of slavery in Egypt. The God of liberation theology brings hope into the here and the now.

Liberation theology came about partly because Latin-American theologians felt they had reached maturity. No longer dependent on Europe, they opened their eyes to their own situation. At Medellín, Colombia, in 1968, the Latin-American bishops denounced "social sin" and "structural injustice." This paved the way for the Peruvian Indian Gustavo Gutiérrez to write *Teología de la liberación* (1971; Eng. trans. *A Theology of Liberation,* 1973). Countless other works in the same genre followed. The best-known authors were the Jesuits Juan Segundo

(Uruguay) and Jon Sobrino (El Salvador) and the Brazilian Franciscan Leonardo Boff, together with his brother Clodovis. The development of liberation theology was patchy, but it was by definition a local matter—a Christian reflection on political oppression as sin.

Pope Paul VI was not unsympathetic to liberation theology. Some of its ideas influenced the Roman Synods of 1971 and 1974. The idea that preaching justice was not a postscript to the Gospel but a constitutive dimension of it came from Latin America. Many of the issues raised by liberation theology were considered by the third Conference of Latin American Bishops held in Puebla, Mexico, in 1979. The bishops strongly endorsed the church's involvement in social problems, but warned of "the risk of ideologization of theological thought when Marxist analysis is used as its starting point." In 1974 Karol Cardinal Wojtyla (later Pope John Paul II) criticized liberation theology as too this-worldly, and he subsequently criticized liberationists' substitution of the concept of class struggle for the traditional Christian idea of charity. Too many theologians, he said in Venezuela in January 1985, "proclaim not the truth of Christ but their own theories."

An Instruction of the Sacred Congregation for the Doctrine of the Faith, the watchdog of orthodoxy, released Sept. 3, 1984, roundly condemned the Marxist elements in liberation theology. The theologians concerned denied that the occasional use of Marxist methods of analysis necessarily led to Marxist conclusions. They denied, too, that they had tried to create a "popular church" at odds with the hierarchy. But the disciplinary measures taken suggested that the weight of the evidence was to the contrary and that these protests would be disregarded.

Ezra Taft Benson (center) was named president of the Church of Jesus Christ of Latter-day Saints in Salt Lake City, Utah, on November 11. He succeeded Spencer W. Kimball, who died November 5.

a "gift of God to the church and to the world," and champions of "collegiality" were gratified that regional and national bishops' conferences were endorsed as "useful, even necessary." Conservatives and progressives came together to support the development of a "universal catechism" of official Catholic teaching. In his closing homily, John Paul declared that "at the end of the 2nd millennium, the church truly desires to be the church in the modern world."

The pope continued to meet resistance from members of religious orders, especially women's orders in the U.S. A focus of controversy was a December 1984 decree by the Vatican's Congregation for Religious and Secular Institutes that threatened to expel from their orders 24 nuns who signed a newspaper ad stating that "a diversity of opinions regarding abortion exists among committed Catholics." The contest of wills simmered throughout 1985.

The pontiff deepened his personal imprint on the church by naming 28 new members of the College of Cardinals. All the appointees echoed in their own statements the pope's conservative theological views. Many of the new cardinals were distinguished chiefly by their opposition to Marxist regimes or by their outspoken denunciation of Christians who, in the Vatican's judgment, had compromised their faith by capitulating to the secular "spirit of the times." Outside the Vatican walls, the Italian Chamber of Deputies ratified a concordat that brought to an end Roman Catholicism's status as the official religion of the state.

In spite of strong opposition by veterans and Jewish groups, U.S. Pres. Ronald Reagan carried out his controversial plan to visit a West German cemetery at Bitburg, the burial site for 2,000 German soldiers, including 49 members of the Nazi's Waffen SS, which was responsible for the deaths of 12 million persons, including 6 million Jews, in World War II death camps. Reagan hoped to depict the visit as an act of reconciliation designed to close the book on German-American tensions left over from World War II, but many citizens believed that Reagan had failed to understand the depth of survivors' feelings about the horrors of the Holocaust. In the White House to receive an award, author Elie Wiesel, a Holocaust survivor, told Reagan that his proper place was not with the SS at Bitburg but "with the victims of the SS."

Relationships between blacks and Jews in the U.S. continued to be somewhat strained, despite efforts by leaders on both sides to rebuild the "coalition of goodwill" forged during the civil rights campaigns of the 1960s. In Los Angeles black Muslim leader Louis Farrakhan inflamed Jewish feelings when he told Jews: "Don't push your 6 million [Holocaust victims] when we lost 100 million [in slavery]." His remarks drew a stern rebuke from Tom Bradley, Los Angeles' black mayor. The controversy soon intensified when Farrakhan, addressing 25,000 supporters in New York's Madison Square Garden, accused his critics of aiming to murder him.

Insurgency in the ranks of Orthodox Jews aggravated tensions within the Jewish community. In Israel the Knesset (parliament) narrowly defeated a bill that would have recognized as Jews only those converts to Judaism instructed by an Orthodox rabbi. The bill was strongly opposed by Reform and Conservative rabbis, and Prime Minister Shimon Peres pleaded with the legislature to turn its attention to other, "more weighty problems."

In India attempts to resolve tensions between Sikhs and the Hindu majority received a setback in August when the moderate Sikh leader Sant Harchand Singh Longowal was slain. Shortly before, he had signed an agreement with Prime Minister Rajiv Gandhi that proposed giving more power to Sikhs but stopped short of granting them autonomy. In Lebanon Hizbollah, the "Party of God," an Islamic fundamentalist movement with strong ties to Iran, was believed to be chiefly responsible for the hijacking of a Trans World Airlines jet aircraft. Egyptian Pres. Hosni Mubarak took steps to curb the activities of Islamic fundamentalists. One phase of his campaign called for drivers whose vehicles carried religious bumper stickers to be fined and subject to having their licenses revoked for a year. In another effort to control social unrest, Mubarak released Shenuda III, leader of Egypt's Coptic Church, from house arrest.

Christian fundamentalists continued to play a major role in American religion. In Dallas, Texas, hard-line fundamentalists clung to control of the Southern Baptist Convention (SBC), the nation's largest Protestant denomination, when Charles Stanley was reelected SBC president. One of the few religious liberals who made news was Edmond L. Browning, the bishop of Hawaii, who was elected to a 12-year term as presiding bishop of the Episcopal Church.

Special Report: As the "New Religions" Grow Older

by Martin E. Marty

When Minister Louis Farrakhan filled Madison Square Garden in New York City in the early autumn of 1985, he drew attention to the Nation of Islam, a group that had split off from the American Muslim Mission. Controversy over his anti-Semitic remarks tended to obscure awareness that he led a small, intense religious group of the sort that several years earlier would have been called a "cult." When, in November, the Oregon commune of Rajneeshpuram announced plans to dissolve after its founder, Bhagwan Shree Rajneesh, left the country, it appeared that another such group would soon vanish.

Where Have They Gone?

Such events as these occasionally kept the issue of "cults" and "the occult" before the public. For the larger part they had slipped from view, or at least from the attention they had commanded in the media 15 years earlier. Almost a generation had passed since 1969, when a California professor, Theodore Roszak, had described *The Making of a Counter Culture,* a youthful movement that provided the context for the "cults." A year later another California professor, Jacob Needleman, called his book on Meher Baba, Subud, Transcendental Meditation, and the like *The New Religions,* even though some of them had ancient roots. In the United States they were new, and they were news.

Fifteen years later, despite the occasional front-page story, it had become appropriate to ask, "Whatever happened to the 'New Religions' in America?" The Evangelical magazine *Christianity Today* consulted counsellors who deal with members of these groups. They contended that the groups were as strong as ever. A scholarly conference in April at the University of Nebraska attracted scores of researchers who found plenty of groups to study. But something *had* happened. By 1985 attention focused more on the legal rights of "cults" than on their promise, more on how to study them objectively than on what to study.

Hard evidence on cultural trends such as these is always difficult to amass; much of it comes from

impression. Thus campus bulletin boards, once crowded with notices about Eastern religious groups and their meetings, now usually had only a few yellowing placards on the subject. Visual images of saffron-clad young people on street corners and in airports were dimming as the surviving members of the groups donned business suits or disappeared. Suburban conversations about young family members "lost" to intense religious groups were less frequent. Had the groups risen to a crest, only to decline and begin to slip away?

Such a question is hard to answer because it could be that the media and the public simply take the once-new phenomena for granted. It could also be that a different sort of expertise was now needed to cope with stories on the subject. Thus legal experts and reporters had to cover the news when the Rev. Sun Myung Moon, founder of the Holy Spirit Association for the Unification of World Christianity, the "Unification Church," was released in August from a Danbury, Conn., prison where he had served time for federal tax violations. At the time of his release some reporters noted that his church claimed 45,000 members. Many observers thought it numbered only 5,000 to 15,000.

The Numbers Game

In 1974 psychiatrist Harrison Pope, Jr., in *The Road East* admitted that it was hard to count the members of the New Religions in general. Yet Nichiren Shoshu Buddhism then claimed 100,000 American practitioners; followers of the Guru Maharaj Ji were said to be approaching 100,000; and Transcendental Meditation listed 232,118 initiates by 1973. In 1981 James Ogilvy and Philip Kohlenberg in *Religion and Values* cited a Gallup Poll that found six million in Transcendental Meditation, four million in Yoga, and a million interested in other Asian traditions. "These statistics reveal a mass movement toward Eastern thought." By the mid-'80s there was no more talk of such a mass movement, and suspicion about inflated statistics became widespread.

To the direct question "How many Americans

are members of New Religion groups?" the answer is clear: "No one knows and no one can know." The U.S. Census dare not ask detailed questions about religion. Churches and religious movements need not release figures about membership. The New Religions do not report to the *Yearbook of American and Canadian Churches*. Only Transcendental Meditation released accurate statistics, and they revealed a drastic drop in initiates in the 1980s.

Leaders of the groups have good reason to inflate statistics. It gives them encouragement, suggests that they are to be reckoned with, and hints that joining them is the thing to do. Enemies of the groups organized in the Anti-Cult Movement (ACM), made up in part of parents who "lost" children to "cults," have reasons to suggest that huge numbers are involved. Such statistics would impel others to regard cults as threats to their families and country. Scholars of New Religions, many of them fair-minded in their researches and not a few of them empathic with and even congenial to New Religions, might be expected to work with inflated statistics to show that their subject matter is important.

Despite all this, more and more experts now take low membership figures seriously. In *The Cult Experience* (1982), J. Gordon Melton and Robert L. Moore, two not unfriendly scholars, suggested, on the basis of the best available data, that the two largest New Religions, Scientology and the Unification Church, seemed to have each not "much more than 5,000 and certainly than 8,000 to 10,000 active members (*i.e.,* persons who would consider themselves Scientologists or Unificationists)." They note that many mainline Christian congregations are larger than the largest of these movements. In 1978 the Church of Satan claimed 10,000 members, but "fewer than 2,000 seem to have been active at any given time," and by 1979 only three "grottoes" (congregations) remained at all active. "By the best estimates several hundred thousand persons could be considered members of alternative religions."

The Gallup Poll had gone wrong, Willa Appel contended in 1983 in *Cults in America,* for "puzzling" reasons, partly because it had to count not only members but also those peripherally involved. She phoned a Hare Krishna employee about the 1978 Gallup Youth Survey projection of 250,000 teenagers in the group. After some hesitation the employee estimated 5,000 full-time members in the United States. Scientologists had an accountable membership not of three million but of about 6,500.

End of a Phase

No one knows, one must repeat, how many are involved, but one can now speak of the rise of the New Religions as an episode in one stage of American culture. Many of the new groups arrived in the late 1960s, when the youth culture was large, when the "counterculture" of drugs, hippies, and experimenters with "alternative life-styles" thrived in the midst of economic prosperity. In the early 1970s the New Religions had grown, established themselves, and become lures for many searching young people.

In the course of the 1970s many things changed. Most scholars list several reasons for the arrested growth of the movements. First, faddism. The young are "into" one thing one year and into another the next year. Joining became no longer the thing to do. Second, the economy. Recession in the 1970s removed the luxury of experiment, and young people lined up straight and square, as it were, in college, there to pursue careers that might assure them prosperity in harder times. Esoteric religions became a luxury and a distraction. Third, there was a documentable high attrition or "dropout" rate, so the groups did not hold the converts whose arrival they advertised.

Later in the decade other factors became significant. The mass suicide of 913 emigrants at Jonestown, Guyana, made "People's Temple" a term with which to stigmatize cults and drive people off. Sometimes declining groups were drastically altered and became less noticeable. Thus the Transcendental Meditation movement put its energies chiefly into its university in Fairfield, Iowa, and impressed townspeople as being generally respectable, though nationally the group was suspect for claiming that initiates could or did "levitate." Others, like the Children of God, faced decline and criticism by moving to Africa and Europe.

One trend, as New Religions turned old, was that old religions turned new. They cut into what some scholars call the recruiting "market." Born-again Christians, Catholic Pentecostals, and groups of Hasidic Jews reached for enthusiastic and exuberant forms that were congenial with home-grown religious traditions. Young people, without ranging so far, could have intense experiences, find new authorities in their lives, gain an identity in a group.

It would be foolish to predict the disappearance of the New Religions. They meet the needs of too many citizens for that. Their leaders have often shown ingenuity at adapting. They have a way of reappearing in new guises when old ones no longer attract. They are likely to remain a permanent part of the religious scene. It is not easy to picture a nation of 240 million people all of whom would be "secular" on the one hand or satisfied with conventional religion on the other. But clearly one stage of New Religion, one episode, is passing.

One might picture the movement as a glacier that moves on. It leaves a moraine, an altered landscape. In this case, the altered landscape alerts observers to at least one grand theme: people and cultures are more diverse and complex than most analysts of 20 years ago had thought. Not all are satisfied with a world in which signals of the sacred are said to disappear, or in which they are channeled into routine institutions. Such seekers will continue to search for outlets, in the New Religions grown older or the Old-Time Religions striving to be renewed.

ROMANIA

Official results revealed a turnout of 99.9% in general elections held on March 17, 1985, to fill Romania's 369-seat Grand National Assembly (parliament). All candidates were nominated by the Socialist Democracy and Unity Front, which included the Romanian Communist Party (RCP) and various other Communist organizations. While 97.7% of votes were cast in favor of candidates, the percentage voting against was 2.3%, compared with 1.5% in the previous elections in 1980. The new National Assembly convened on March 29 and reelected Nicolae Ceausescu for another five-year term as president of the republic and thus, automatically, as president of the State Council.

During the year a number of changes were made to the Council of Ministers. In December Gen. Constantin Olteanu was replaced as defense minister by his former deputy, Gen. Vasile Milea. On October 17 Ioan Avram, deputy prime minister responsible for supervision of the energy sector, Nicolae Busui, minister of electric power, and Marin Stefanache, minister of mines, were dismissed, and at about the same time, high army officers were placed in command of coal-burning power stations. The moves were occasioned by a crisis in the energy sector. The winter of 1984–85 had been the most severe in four decades, and long periods of dry weather in both 1984 and 1985 had depleted water supplies in rivers and reservoirs, resulting in an unprecedented slump in hydroelectric power production. At the same time, production in the coal-mining industry failed to reach targets, and the country's petroleum extraction was on the decline.

During the early months of 1985, the authorities took drastic action to save fuel. Romanians were barred from using many electrical appliances; private cars were banished from the streets; and only minimal street lighting was permitted. Later in the year some of those measures were reintroduced as the country took steps to guard against the effects of another hard winter. The shortages of fuel and food were aggravated by Ceausescu's drive to reduce the foreign debt. From a peak in 1982, when some estimates put the total at $14 billion, the foreign debt had been reduced to $4 billion by late 1985 according to the government.

The extension of the Warsaw Pact treaty was signed by Ceausescu along with leaders of the six other Warsaw Pact countries at a summit meeting in Warsaw on April 26. Ceausescu paid his fourth official visit to China in October. In December he visited Yugoslavia. During U.K. Foreign Secretary Sir Geoffrey Howe's visit to Bucharest in February, he and Ceausescu discussed trade links between the two countries. On December 15 U.S. Secretary of State George Shultz made the first stop of his European tour in Romania. Shultz reportedly warned Ceausescu that unless his government improved its human rights record, the U.S. would withdraw Romania's "most-favored-nation" trade status.

SAINT CHRISTOPHER AND NEVIS

Despite a positive economic performance in 1984, with real growth of 4% in the gross national product, the government of St. Christopher and Nevis (St. Kitts-Nevis) warned early in 1985 that the continued world recession made it increasingly difficult to maintain public services. Stamp duty and taxes on travel, vehicles, alcoholic drinks, and other items were increased in the 1985 budget to raise an extra EC$1.3 million. (For table of world currencies *see* International Exchange and Payments.) The weak international sugar market continued to give cause for concern.

Strong sectors included tourism, which in 1985 maintained the momentum of the previous year, when arrivals increased by 16.3% to almost 40,000. Trade in manufactured goods, principally electronic components, also increased. New direct air links with Canada were opened in September.

The opposition Labour Party, which had suffered a crushing defeat in the 1984 general elections, retained its leader, Lee Moore, at the 1985 party convention but indicated a desire to rejuvenate its image by electing a young lawyer, Henry Browne, as deputy leader.

SAINT LUCIA

Increased investment in St. Lucia's industrial and tourist sectors, much of it from the U.S., held out the prospect of an economic upturn in 1985, despite continuing difficulties in the country's trading relations with fellow members of the Caribbean Community.

Tourist arrivals, which rose 13% in 1984, appeared set to continue increasing.

Nevertheless, Prime Minister John Compton, presenting the 1985–86 budget, warned that difficult times lay ahead. Staffing levels in the public services were to be frozen for the coming year and reduced over the next three years; wages in this sector accounted for 55% of total current government spending. In 1984 the budget was in deficit by EC$13.1 million, while the trade deficit of EC$191.7 million reflected the fall in exports to Guyana, Jamaica, and Trinidad and Tobago. (For table of world currencies, *see* International Exchange and Payments.) The garment industry in particular was affected by new import restrictions introduced by Trinidad.

At its party convention in August 1985, the opposition St. Lucia Labour Party (SLP) rejected a proposal from the Progressive Labour Party (PLP), led by George Odlum, to form an electoral pact. The PLP had been formed in 1981 by a breakaway faction of the SLP.

SAINT VINCENT AND THE GRENADINES

The New Democratic Party (NDP), which gained office in St. Vincent and the Grenadines in the July 1984 general elections, consolidated its position in February 1985 when it won a by-election in the East St. George constituency. The seat, made vacant by the retirement of former prime minister Milton Cato of the St. Vincent Labour Party, went to the NDP with a majority of 700 and brought its strength to 10 of the 13 seats in the National Assembly. Labour elected Hudson Tannis as its national leader to replace Cato.

During 1985 the government concentrated on reorganizing public enterprises and finances. The sugar industry, which had debts of EC$42 million, was closed down at the end of the 1985 season. (For table of world currencies, *see* International Exchange and Payments.) In May the government bought the Commonwealth Development Corporation's majority holding in the country's electric power company. The 1985 budget offered tax incentives aimed at stimulating investment in the productive sector and the construction industry. Prime Minister James Mitchell pointed to reduction of the 40–50% unemployment rate as his government's highest priority.

SAUDI ARABIA

Saudi Arabia's decision in 1985 to increase oil production to close to its Organization of Petroleum Exporting Countries (OPEC) quota of 4.3 million bbl a day put strains on the unity of OPEC during a year that was increasingly dominated by Saudi Arabian moves to improve its security. In taking this fresh direction in its oil policy, Saudi Arabia triggered debate about the need for OPEC to find market-related pricing mechanisms, while also throwing down the gauntlet to non-OPEC producers who had come to depend on the kingdom's acting as a "swing producer" to avoid oversupplying the market. The agreement at the December OPEC meeting to stop defending oil prices in favor of defending the cartel's market share in essence legitimized recent practices. The Gulf Cooperation Council (GCC) summit in Oman ended on November 8 with renewed calls to end the Gulf war and prevent terrorism. Saudi Arabia reiterated that these issues were of more importance to the GCC than the secondary goal of economic integration.

Following a visit by U.K. Prime Minister Margaret Thatcher in April, on September 26 Defense and Aviation Minister Prince Sultan Salman ibn Abdel-Aziz as-Saud and U.K. Secretary of State for Defense Michael Heseltine signed a memorandum of understanding on the purchase of military aircraft from British Aerospace. Valued at some $4.2 billion, it was described as the largest export order ever negotiated by Britain. Part of the payment was to be met through oil barter, and the deal might also be linked with an offset investment program similar to one already agreed on with the U.S. for the "Peace Shield" defense program. In February the Ministry of Defense and Civil Aviation awarded the U.S. company Boeing Aerospace Corp. three contracts valued at $1.1 billion under the offset

KEYSTONE

Sheikh Ahmed Zaki Yamani, Saudi Arabia's oil minister, speaks to the press in Geneva during meetings of the Organization of Petroleum Exporting Countries.

program, which was now monitored by a Saudi government committee; 35% of the value of the contracts had to be reinvested in the kingdom in high-technology ventures in which Saudi Arabian investors would match the investment.

The government was eager to diversify its sources of weapons supplies in order to avoid dependence on the U.S., where the pro-Israel lobby had often blocked sales of advanced weapons to the kingdom. Nevertheless, according to a *New York Times* report on September 5, the government had made a verbal commitment to allow U.S. forces to operate from its bases in the event of Soviet aggression or if the kingdom was unable to handle a Gulf crisis on its own. While informal contacts had taken place between the government and Moscow, no progress was made toward establishing formal links.

The Hajj (pilgrimage to Mecca) passed off peacefully in August. Some 1.6 million people took part, including 150,000 pilgrims from Iran. On May 18 two explosions rocked the Sulaymani district of Riyadh, killing one person and injuring three. Responsibility was claimed by the externally based Islamic Jihad ("Islamic Holy War") group. The incident was the first serious terrorist attack since the 1979 siege of the Grand Mosque in Mecca. Religious sentiment in Saudi Arabia remained extremely conservative. In June prominence was given in the media to a statement by Islamic leader Sheikh Abdel-Aziz ibn Baz that allowing men and women to mix at work would open an evil door that would be hard to close. Young Saudi Arabians of both sexes were inspired by the example of Prince Sultan Salman ibn Abdel-Aziz as-Saud, who in June became the first Arab astronaut when he joined the crew of the U.S. space shuttle *Discovery.*

In 1984 Saudi Arabia moved up to 11th place among the world's top 20 trading nations in terms of both imports and exports, according to a General Agreement on Tariffs and Trade assessment. After two years in which the kingdom balanced its budgets by drawing down its foreign-exchange reserves, the government determined to take tough action to keep spending under control. Both the 1985–86 budget and the fourth five-year (1985–90) plan were based on oil production of not less than 3,850,000 bbl a day. The 1985 budget included cuts in nearly every spending department. At a meeting with representatives of the private sector in Riyadh on March 27, King Fahd called for greater commitment by the private businessman in his own country. The largest project to be affected by the new mood of realism was the proposed refinery at Qassim. Development of the $1 billion project was suspended by royal decree on March 11. It was later announced that work would resume within five years. During the plan period, some subsidiaries of the state hydrocarbons agency, Petromin, were expected to be privatized, along with the national airline, Saudia.

Although King Fahd had previously championed the cause of joint ventures between home and foreign businesses, in 1985 he came under growing pressure from the business lobby to support protectionist legislation. In June he issued a royal decree urging government departments to heed earlier orders to award more contracts to local companies. Under the five-year plan, production and private initiative replaced construction and public enterprise as key themes. The plan envisaged a cut of 600,000 jobs, mainly in the unskilled categories, in the expatriate population by 1990 and the creation of 375,000 new jobs for Saudi Arabians.

The difficulties faced by Saudi Arabia in its industrialization drive were highlighted by a growing atmosphere of confrontation with the European Communities (EC). On August 3 the EC slapped 13.4–14% tariffs on imports of Saudi Arabian polyethylene. The Saudi Basic Industries Corporation claimed that the duty was based on "exaggerated data and unfounded fears regarding the purported impact of Saudi exports." The government was understood to be reviewing its options, including the possibility of imposing retaliatory tariffs on imports of manufactured goods from the EC. Industry and Electricity Minister Sheikh Abdel-Aziz az-Zamil told the *Al-Riyadh* daily newspaper in January that the kingdom should aim at 50% self-sufficiency in industrial goods. Total imports were now running at more than $40 billion a year.

The Eastern Province, home of the petroleum industry and the major industrial complex of Jubail, was expected to benefit from the road causeway link with Bahrain; the opening of the causeway, scheduled for December 1985, was postponed until December 1986. On September 30 the industrial city of Yanbu on the Red Sea coast received its first shipment of crude oil from Iraq via the new pipeline linking Iraq with Saudi Arabia's main east-west pipeline.

The kingdom was the sixth largest contributor to the International Monetary Fund, and the Saudi Arabian Monetary Agency (SAMA) was one of the largest institutional investors outside the industrialized countries. Commercial banking in the kingdom remained profitable, although some foreign banks experienced difficulties in securing judicial recognition of loan defaults because of Islamic strictures against usury. During 1985 the Saudi Fund for Development, an aid agency, agreed to provide India, Senegal, Niger, Rwanda, and Mali with loans, largely to assist construction of infrastructure and improvement of social welfare. Prime Minister Turgut Ozal of Turkey, who concluded a six-day visit on March 22, claimed that he had secured an agreement to encourage joint production of sophisticated weapons and spare parts for military equipment.

SHIPS AND SHIPPING

Gross overcapacity within the world shipbuilding industry continued to make survival difficult for shipyards. Although few yards were closed down, there was a vast reduction in the number of people employed in ship construction. With no recovery in shipbuilding demand in sight and the productivity level within existing yards constantly improving, there appeared to be little hope of reversing the decline in European shipbuilding unless shipbuilding capacity in the Far East was drastically reduced. For most of 1985 the world total of new orders for ships remained at the same low level as in the corresponding period of 1984. Only 14% of the new

Even the Hyundai shipyards in South Korea, considered among the world's most efficient, were forced into heavy layoffs by the downturn in shipbuilding.
IAN STEEL

JOE TRAVER/THE NEW YORK TIMES

Workers repair a 180-foot (55-meter) section of wall that collapsed in Lock Seven of the Welland Canal near Thorold, Ontario, on October 14.

orders went to European shipyards, while Japan took 44% and South Korea 16%.

The Association of West European Shipbuilders pointed to the cheap credits offered by the Export-Import Bank of Japan that had attracted many orders, while South Korean yards had been accepting new orders at well under realistic prices. Although there were moves throughout the European Communities to make member governments reduce the level of subsidies to either shipbuilders or shipowners, it became clear that European governments were not in general prepared to see their industries driven out of the market. It appeared that subsidies to European yards would not be reduced until Japanese and South Korean shipyards quoted what the Europeans would consider to be fair prices.

At mid-1985 the tonnage of new ships on order was 47,749,261 tons deadweight (dw), compared with 58.5 million tons dw at the same time in 1984. By the autumn the figure had fallen again to 46,-990,304 tons dw. At midyear bulk carriers led the list of new tonnage with 444 vessels totaling 25,-727,724 tons dw, followed by 284 tankers totaling 12,972,882 tons dw. Dry cargo ships (not bulk carriers) totaled 3,092,638 tons dw and containerships 3,956,285 tons dw.

Japan continued to gain the bulk of the new orders at 19,449,570 tons dw (down from the 1984 figure of 26.3 million tons dw), followed by South

Korea with 9,009,188 tons dw (10 million tons dw in 1984); Brazil retained third place with 2,395,437 tons dw. There was a surprising rise in the amount of new tonnage won by shipyards in Taiwan, which secured 2,016,900 tons dw and went into fourth place, followed by China with just over 1.5 million tons dw. Poland took sixth place with 1,332,660 tons dw. Seventh and eighth were Yugoslavia with 980,846 tons dw and Spain with 845,300 tons dw. During the year several yards closed in Western European countries, particularly France and The Netherlands.

Orders for large and sophisticated cruise liners were again a feature of world shipbuilding activity, and by the end of the summer there were nine passenger liners on order totaling 314,000 gross registered tons (grt), with orders for at least three more to come. One of the largest orders was placed in July by Norway's Royal Caribbean Cruise Line for a 70,000-grt vessel costing $170 million and with a capacity of 2,500 passengers. Earlier in the year the same line had ordered two 40,000-grt cruise liners at a total cost of $200 million, each ship to carry 990 passengers. Contessa Cruise Line placed an order for two 18,000-grt passenger vessels with Marine P. & E. Inc.—one of the very few orders for merchant ships to be won by a U.S. shipyard. The Soviet Union broke ground by ordering four 20,000-grt cruise liners from a Polish shipyard.

There were signs by midyear that prices for new building had bottomed out and were very slowly moving upward and that contracting activity was beginning to improve. Despite the prevailing low prices, however, shipowners were not tempted to order in any strength because the market outlook appeared to be uncertain and financing had become more difficult to obtain.

Shipping and Ports

Hopes generated during the previous year that some sectors of the world shipping industry might be emerging from the recession in freight rates were dashed in 1985. As a result of inaccurate projections, wrong incentives, and doubtful national policies, the world's merchant fleet had doubled since the mid-1970s, while the growth in the amount of trade carried by sea was less than one-third of the increase in capacity. During 1985 several major shipping companies went out of business, the largest being Japan's Sanko Line. Behind all the shipowners' problems was the still massive amount of tonnage that was not being used. At midyear the number of tankers in lay-up was 343 vessels with an aggregate of 53.6 million metric tons dw; the number of dry-cargo ships laid up numbered 969, totaling 10.5 million metric tons dw. Governments continued to make the situation worse by providing financial subsidies, and many shipyards offered vessels for sale at well below their true cost. A positive development was the rise in the volume of tonnage scrapped. This reached a record level of more than

40 million metric tons dw and included four of the world's largest tankers, all over 500,000 tons dw.

The total tonnage of the world merchant fleet fell slightly from 419 million gross registered tons (grt) to 395 million grt. Liberia's remained the largest national fleet with 58 million grt, and Panama (40.6 million grt) took second place from Japan (39.9 million grt). Greece remained in fourth place with 31 million grt. The U.K., which had once had one of the largest merchant fleets in the world, was in ninth place with 14.3 million grt.

New investment in port development continued unabated, particularly in China, despite the unstable conditions in world shipping. Access to the port of Amsterdam was improved to enable ships of 150,000 tons dw to enter via the North Sea Canal. To serve the massive coal project of El Cerrejon, Colombia, the port of Puerto Bolívar was equipped to handle up to 10,000 metric tons per hour of highly volatile bituminous coal suitable for U.S. eastern seaboard and Western European markets. Because of the high cost of providing deeper water at their berths, many ports invested in bulk loading and discharging operations offshore, using a transfer rig stationed in sheltered or even in open waters.

SKIING

The worst weather and snow conditions for many decades early in the 1984–85 season failed to block the major contests. Spectator attendance understandably fell in December and early January but then rose to unprecedented heights in North America during March. Some 1,800 Alpine and Nordic competitions were held worldwide.

Alpine Racing

At the 28th world championships, at Bormio, Italy, from January 31 to February 10, Pirmin Zur-

Pirmin Zurbriggen of Switzerland won the men's downhill and the combined downhill and slalom and placed second in the giant slalom during competition at the Alpine skiing world championships held in Bormio, Italy.

DAVE CANNON—DUOMO

briggen of Switzerland won the 60th men's downhill and the combined downhill and slalom and finished second in the giant slalom—all within weeks of having undergone knee surgery.

Markus Wasmaier of West Germany, a noted downhiller, unexpectedly won the giant slalom title. Peter Müller, another Swiss, and Doug Lewis of the U.S. finished second and third in the downhill. Jonas Nilsson of Sweden won the slalom, followed by Austrian-born Marc Girardelli of Luxembourg and Robert Zoller of Austria. Girardelli took the bronze medal in the giant slalom, but though he was the top-seeded skier of the season, he failed to win a gold. Second and third to Zurbriggen in the combined event were an Austrian, Ernst Riedlsperger, and a Swiss, Thomas Bürgler.

Swiss racers won two of the four women's events. The Olympic gold medalist, Michela Figini, took the downhill with a convincing margin of 1.61 sec over her compatriot Ariane Ehrat and Katrin Gutensohn of Austria, who tied for second. The experienced Erika Hess, who had won three gold medals in 1982, took the combined event for Switzerland, ahead of Sylvia Eder of Austria and Tamara McKinney of the U.S.

A Hess fall allowed Perrine Pelen and Christelle Guignard to gain the first and second slalom spots for France, followed by Paoletta Magoni of Italy. A surprise giant slalom winner was 17-year-old Diann Roffe of the U.S. Second-place Elisabeth Kirchler of Austria denied a U.S. clean sweep, with Eva Twardokens and Debbie Armstrong finishing third and fourth.

The 19th Alpine World Cup series concluded on March 24 at Heavenly Valley, Calif. The winners in the men's and women's divisions were Girardelli and Figini. Girardelli won the overall, slalom, and giant slalom titles, finishing first in

seven slalom races during the series to equal the record set by the Swedish skier Ingemar Stenmark. Zurbriggen, the defending champion, was second in the overall standings, followed by Andreas Wenzel of Liechtenstein.

Figini showed exceptional all-round talent, taking the women's overall and downhill titles and sharing the giant slalom with Marina Kiehl of West Germany. Hess won the slalom and Brigitte Oertli took the combined. Oertli was overall runner-up to Figini, with Maria Walliser finishing third to complete a Swiss clean sweep. The concurrently decided Nations Cup was retained by Switzerland, ahead of Austria and West Germany.

Nordic Events

Norway, the most successful nation in Nordic competition, took 5 of the 13 gold medals in the 35th world championships, at Seefeld, Austria, on January 18–27. Two cross-country superstars were Gunde Svan of Sweden, winner of the 30 km and 50 km, and Anette Boe of Norway, the fastest woman in the 5 km and 10 km.

Kari Haerkoenen of Finland won the men's 15 km, and Norway took the team relay. Per Bergerud of Norway proved the outstanding jumper, winning the 90-m event and finishing third in the 70 m, which was won by Jens Weissflog of East Germany. The individual Nordic combination went to a West German, Hermann Weinbuch, who was also one of his country's victorious trio in the team event.

Grete Nykkelmo of Norway won a gold medal in the women's 20 km and also finished third over each of the distances won by Boe. In the team relay the U.S.S.R. outpaced the Norwegian runners-up despite the presence of Boe and Nykkelmo.

Svan retained the men's title in the sixth Nordic World Cup competition for cross-country racing, a series of events spanning four months. Tor-Haakon Holte was runner-up for Norway, with third place shared by Thomas Wassberg (Sweden) and Ove Robert Aunli (Norway). Boe captured the women's crown, with Nykkelmo and Britt Pettersen completing a Norwegian grand slam. The Nations Cup went to Norway, followed by Finland and Sweden.

The second World Cup in Nordic combination, linking cross-country and jumping, was gained by Geir Andersen of Norway. Weinbuch and Hubert Schwarz finished second and third for West Germany, and a Nations Cup for this competition went to Norway, with West Germany second and East Germany third.

In the world biathlon championships, combining cross-country skiing with rifle shooting, at Ruhpolding, West Germany, on February 14–17, Frank-Peter Rötsch of East Germany won the 10-km event from Erik Kvalfoss of Norway. Rötsch took the silver medal in the 20 km, which was won by Yuri Kaschkarov of the Soviet Union. The team relay went to the U.S.S.R., with East Germany runner-up and West Germany third.

SOCIAL SERVICES

An old social program and two relatively new ones shared the spotlight in the U.S. in 1985, while the debate over poverty and how to deal with it became more acrimonious. The old program was Social Security, which celebrated its 50th anniversary in apparently solid financial and political shape. Total income for the year for the Social Security system was expected to be $199.5 billion, with disbursements (benefit payments and administrative costs) of $193.2 billion. After years of concern over the future, the system was said to be fiscally sound for at least the next half century. According to Census Bureau estimates, beneficiaries would more than

Diann Roffe of Williamson, New York, speeds to a gold medal in the women's giant slalom event during the Alpine skiing world championships.

STEVE POWELL/SPORTS ILLUSTRATED

More than one-third of all persons labeled poor in a U.S. Census Bureau study were children, and a similar proportion were from single-parent homes. Of minority children under six years of age, over half were considered poor.

CHESTER HIGGINS, JR./THE NEW YORK TIMES

double by the year 2035—from 36,683,000 in 1985 to 79,843,000—and disbursements were expected to increase 25-fold, to more than $5 trillion. However, assets were also expected to soar during those 50 years, from $35.6 billion to $11,428,700,000,-000, although critics claimed that this projection was far too optimistic.

In the political arena, Congress moved to make the Social Security Administration more independent and to free its old-age and disability trust funds from future budget battles. Efforts to freeze the annual cost-of-living adjustments (COLAs) failed, as the House of Representatives and the Reagan administration prevailed over the Senate. As a result, Social Security beneficiaries would receive a 3.1% cost-of-living increase as of Jan. 3, 1986, raising the monthly benefit from $464 to $478 for the average retired worker and from $788 to $812 for the average couple. The maximum benefit for a person who retired in 1985 at age 65 would be $739. To finance the increase, Social Security taxes would go up in 1986 to 7.15% on the first $42,000 of a worker's salary, compared with 7.05% on the first $39,600 in 1985.

In another victory for beneficiaries, the Reagan administration announced that it would generally follow court precedents requiring the payment of Social Security disability benefits. The government had tried to cut disability payments to almost half a million people, usually on grounds that they were no longer too ill or injured to work. The courts, however, had ruled in thousands of cases that the benefits were ended improperly.

Two relatively new social experiments gained attention. One of these was "workfare," which tied welfare benefits to work. It had been tried on a small scale in the 1960s and 1970s with the federal Work Incentive Program and in California when Ronald Reagan was governor. As president, Reagan proposed a national mandatory work requirement for welfare recipients in 1981, but Congress rejected the idea in favor of state programs. By the end of 1985, at least 23 states were experimenting with the idea on a limited basis. Programs varied from state to state, but most offered participants help in finding jobs or getting job training before requiring them to work for their monthly assistance. Although the number of participants was still only a small proportion of the total welfare rolls, it was growing. The nation's two most populous states, New York and California, initiated mandatory workfare programs in 1985. New York's plan, considered the most comprehensive of its kind in the U.S., would require an estimated 220,000 welfare recipients (mothers with children under age six were exempted) to take a job or enter a job-training program; failure to do so would result in a reduction of benefits.

The second stepped-up program was the crackdown on parents—almost all of them fathers—who failed to pay child support. A federal law that was enacted in 1984 and went into effect Oct. 1, 1985, required states to go after delinquent child-support payments or face the loss of up to 5% of their federal welfare funds. The law ordered states to provide for mandatory wage withholding as soon as an absent parent fell 30 days behind in payments. States would also have to arrange to withhold tax refunds from parents who were delinquent in payments and place liens on their property. As of October 1, 21 states had already adopted the required regulations. A Census Bureau study said that half of the four million parents who were legally entitled to child support from an absent spouse in 1983 did not receive the full payment.

Meanwhile, the debate over poverty and what to do about it intensified. The Census Bureau reported that the nation's poverty rate dropped to 14.4% in 1984 from 15.3% in 1983, the largest one-year decline in more than a decade. A total of 33.7 million Americans lived below the poverty level ($10,609 for an urban family of four). The Census Bureau attributed the drop to economic recovery and low inflation. While applauding the decline, skeptics pointed out that the percentage of poor was still at its highest level since 1966, except for 1982 and 1983, and that the gains registered in 1984 were uneven. For example, the poverty rate for black children under age six rose slightly, to 51.1%, the highest since figures were first kept in 1970. More than one-third of the poor were children, and 35% were from one-parent homes.

Congress's first fiscal 1986 budget resolution provided funding that would allow most programs for the poor to keep pace with inflation. A report from the House Ways and Means Committee indicated that the value of combined food stamp and welfare benefits for a family of four with no other income fell 22% nationwide between 1972 and 1984. The main reason, according to the committee, was that cash welfare payments failed to keep up with inflation.

Other Developments

Some countries managed to improve their systems. Finland, for example, passed legislation making retirement age more flexible under both the national pensions scheme and the earnings-related pension scheme for private-sector employees. In France a new benefit was introduced for parents who stopped work or reduced their working hours by half following the birth of a child, when that birth brought the total number of dependent children to three or more.

Earnings-related unemployment benefits were introduced in Portugal. The new benefit was paid at the same rate as sickness benefit (60% of previous earnings) and was payable for six months to unemployed workers who had been in employment for at least three years.

In most other countries, governments attempted with varying degrees of success to reduce their social security commitments. As part of an austerity program introduced in May, the government of Chile announced a freeze on old-age pensions that continued to be paid under the pre-1981 social security system and cut unemployment benefits by half.

In Japan a major pension reform was enacted in April, for implementation in April 1986, designed to reduce the rise in social security costs expected to take place over the next 40 years because of the aging of the population and the maturing of the country's system. The accrual rate for earnings-related pensions for employees would decrease gradually from 1 to 0.75% of covered earnings per year; the accrual rate for flat-rate pensions, both for employees and for the rest of the population, would also decrease, so that it would take 40 years rather than 25 years to earn a full pension. The retirement age for employed women would be increased gradually from 55 to 60, the age applying to men. Finally, all wives would be compulsorily covered by the National (flat-rate) Pension Program. These measures would be phased in over a period of 20 years. It was also the government's intention to increase the retirement age to 65, but no date for this was specified in the 1985 reform.

Social security benefits in The Netherlands were further reduced in the course of 1985. At the beginning of the year, unemployment and disability insurance benefits, which had amounted to 80% of previous earnings until the end of 1983, were lowered to 70%, and in May sickness benefits were cut from 80 to 75% of earnings, with a further reduction to 70% planned for January 1986. Legislation was passed making the duration of unemployment benefit dependent on age. At a later stage, benefit duration would be related not only to age but also to the duration of previous employment.

In the U.K. a government review of social security declared that the system had "lost its way" and proposed the phasing out of the State Earnings Related Pension Scheme, established with the agreement of all parties in 1978. The proposal elicited an overwhelmingly hostile reaction not only from the trade unions and poverty pressure groups but also from the Confederation of British Industry, whose members believed that it would increase total employment costs and create instability in the pension system. As a result, the government backed down on its abolition proposal while leaving the way open for some cost-cutting modifications.

A second major proposal contained in the U.K. social security review was to replace the supplementary benefit system by a new system of income support, under which benefits would be determined by age and family responsibilities. Single payments made under the existing regulations to persons lacking clothing, furniture, and other necessities would be abolished and replaced by discretionary payments from a social fund. In October an important change took place in the financing of the British social security system. The contributions ceiling, previously fixed at earnings of £265 (about $385) per week, was abolished as far as employers' contributions were concerned, and the extra revenue was used to reduce the contributions payable by low-paid employees and their employers.

Special Report: Homelessness

by Peter Hall

Preparations were under way during 1985 for the International Year of Shelter for the Homeless in 1987, designated by the UN General Assembly with the aim of improving the housing of the poor. In many third world cities projects were being undertaken to achieve the UN's objective: that by 1987 at least some poor people would enjoy better shelter and upgraded neighborhoods. In this context there was no little irony in the fact that a mere three blocks from the UN's New York headquarters, in one of the richest cities in the world, scores of homeless people were sleeping each night on the floors and in the telephone booths of Grand Central Terminal.

A Growing Problem

During the first half of the 1980s, homelessness—especially big-city homelessness—had become a major focus of U.S. media attention and public concern. In December 1982, and again in January and May 1984, the House of Representatives Subcommittee on Housing and Community Development had received expert testimony on the subject, with the most graphic coming from the victims themselves. Committee members heard of people sleeping under freeways, in tent cities and makeshift shanties, in their cars, even—on the evidence of a Salvation Army major from Cleveland, Ohio—in the boxes maintained by the Army to receive donations of discarded clothing. They heard from the mayors of some of the nation's leading cities, and from Gov. Mario Cuomo of New York, that the problem was becoming much worse.

Just how many homeless there were was the subject of fierce controversy. *Homelessness in America: A Forced March to Nowhere,* a widely publicized report by Mary Ellen Hombs and Mitch Snyder of the Community for Creative Non-Violence, based on interviews with local experts, put the figure at 2.2 million nationally. The federal Department of Housing and Urban Development (HUD) commissioned its own study, which used a variety of methods to produce a range of from 192,000 to 586,000 on any one night in early 1984; within that range, the consultants thought the most reliable estimates were between 250,000 (quoted by local observers) and 350,000 (from operators of shelters). HUD Secretary Samuel R. Pierce used his department's report to cast doubt on the Hombs-Snyder figure. In turn, at the House subcommittee hearing, Rep. Barney Frank (Dem., Mass.) condemned the HUD report as "intellectually shoddy, methodologically lacking, morally incredibly callous."

If there was no consensus on figures, there was at least some agreement on causes. The HUD investigators confirmed the testimony of many local observers before the House subcommittee: within the homeless population, certain groups—the mentally ill, alcoholics and drug abusers, ethnic minorities, young single men—were overrepresented. They differed from much congressional evidence, however, in finding that most homeless persons had been on the fringes of society for some time. Congressional witnesses had suggested a recent sharp upswing in homelessness among the "new poor": families, especially those belonging to ethnic minorities, who had lost their homes as a result of unemployment or the steady erosion in the supply of low-rent homes and cheap hotels. Their numbers, the witnesses suggested, were augmented by two other groups: mental patients discharged from hospitals under deinstitutionalization programs, accounting for perhaps 30–40% of the total, and some 350,000 people taken off disability assistance rolls during 1981–83 because of more stringent eligibility rules.

The response to the problem was varied, and

As part of an outreach project administered by a hospital in New York City, a worker offers lunch to a man who lives in a box in one of the city's parks.

PATRICK AVENTURIER—GAMMA/LIAISON

The rise in the number of urban homeless was a growing concern of a great many nations, developed and less developed alike. During a January cold snap, this French train station became a refuge.

some witnesses argued strongly that it was inadequate. Coping with homelessness in the U.S. is strictly a matter for the cities themselves. In general, state law gives little guidance, although in New York a legal action of 1979 led to the signing of a consent decree that, in effect, committed the city to providing shelter. In any case, most U.S. cities can do little more than furnish emergency shelter, because their stocks of low-rent public housing are so limited.

Britain's Homeless

At first sight, the situation in Britain would appear to be very different. In 1983, despite sales of some 500,000 units of public housing to the occupiers in the previous three years, 32% of all households still rented from local authorities or other public bodies. This meant that while the typical low-income U.S. household had to find private rental housing, often in bad condition and at rents that were high in relation to income (resulting in a constant risk of eviction for nonpayment of rent), its British counterpart would be housed in fairly modern public housing, with all the necessary amenities, at a subsidized rent, and with a considerable degree of security against eviction.

The most notable difference, however, is that Britain has national legislation to provide for homeless people. The Housing (Homeless Persons) Act, 1977 (in England and Wales; the equivalent Scottish act dates from 1978), requires borough or district authorities with responsibilities for housing to take specific action to help the homeless. For certain groups in "priority need"—those with dependent children, pregnant women, the aged or handicapped, victims of disasters—the local housing authority has a responsibility to find secure accommodation.

Some limitations were written into the act by Parliament. The most important is that if a person becomes homeless "intentionally," through something he or she did or failed to do, the authority must provide advice but does not have to find housing. However, a Code of Guidance, which accompanies the act, specifically states that certain cases—mortgage arrears, marital disputes leading to violence on a wife, simple lack of money—do not fall under the category of "intentional." Although the code is not legally binding, it is fairly clear that in many—though by no means all—cases the courts regard it as such. In the early years of the act's operation, only 3–4% of applicants were declared intentionally homeless.

The number of those accepted as homeless under the act has increased steadily year by year, from 57,200 in 1979 to 83,190 in 1984. Furthermore, these figures represent only about half of those who apply; the majority of single homeless people and couples without children have no right to permanent accommodation under the act, although they may get temporary shelter. The voluntary housing organization Shelter argues that the official figures represent only "the tip of the iceberg," because they ignore those who do not apply but are living with relatives or friends, or in poor conditions.

Mainly because of this, nearly half the households accepted under the act are placed not in local authority housing but in temporary bed-and-breakfast type accommodations, sometimes for long periods. There have been numerous accounts in the media of poor conditions and huge profits accruing to some proprietors of cheap hotels. Yet local authorities are understandably reluctant to place homeless families in public housing immediately, ahead of others who may have been on the waiting list for months or years.

Once rehoused, the former homeless still must pay the rent for their new accommodations. If they qualify on the basis of low income, they will receive help from the unified housing benefit introduced by the British government in 1982. This is not paid by the Department of the Environment, the department responsible for local housing policies, but by the Department of Health and Social Security, and it is administered by local authorities. It has been the subject of considerable criticism on the grounds of complexity, delay, and the financial worries of tenants whose allowance has not arrived.

Britain, then, has not solved the problem entirely and, indeed, a perfect solution may be impossible in an imperfect bureaucratic world. Urban poverty and homelessness in Western societies spring from deeper economic and social conditions—unemployment, especially among the unskilled, marital breakdown, drug dependence. Housing policies, however well intentioned and economically administered, cannot cure these ills, and as long as they continue to fester, so will the housing problem. If public expenditures are cut as a reaction to economic recession, even greater human suffering will be the sure result.

SOMALIA

Following general elections in Somalia on Dec. 31, 1984, 46 new members took their seats in the 171-member People's Assembly. The elections were the second to take place since the Somali Revolutionary Socialist Party (SRSP) was established as the country's sole legal party in 1976.

Antigovernment forces based in Ethiopia maintained their attacks during the year. The Somali Democratic Salvation Front (SDSF), one of the main rebel groups, continued its occupation of the strip of land on the Somali-Ethiopian border that it had occupied with the backing of Ethiopian troops in 1983. Meanwhile, divisions within the SDSF led to internecine violence. In October Col. Abdullahi Yusuf, leader of the SDSF, was arrested by Ethiopian authorities.

An estimated 700,000 refugees originally made homeless by the 1977–78 war with Ethiopia over the Ogaden region were housed in more than 30 camps throughout Somalia. Early in the year a fresh influx of refugees, reportedly fleeing from political and religious repression in Ethiopia, began arriving in the northeast of the country. By March the new arrivals numbered some 45,000. There followed an outbreak of cholera that spread through the refugee camps and to the general public. By mid-May, as the result of a government quarantine and immunization measures supported by the efforts of International Red Cross teams, the outbreak was reported to be under control.

In a speech to the SRSP Central Committee in February, Pres. Muhammad Siyad Barrah referred to Somali-U.S. relations as "limping," apparently because of U.S. reluctance to supply more than minimal military aid. On the same occasion, he spoke of his desire to "normalize" relations with the U.S.S.R., a former ally with whom relations had been severed in 1977 when Moscow backed Ethiopia in the Ogaden war. Nevertheless, Somalia during 1985 remained firmly within the Western camp.

The effect of government policy was increasingly to move away from central control toward a free-market economy. Throughout 1984 the government was involved in negotiations with the International Monetary Fund (IMF) to establish terms for an extended credit facility. After agreement had been reached in principle, the government in January introduced a dual exchange rate for the Somali shilling and allowed exporters to retain 65% of profits, compared with 35% previously. The IMF provided a standby credit worth $54 million in February. Meanwhile, a special meeting of aid donor countries pledged an estimated $80 million over and above their previous aid commitments in order to help Somalia meet its balance of payments requirements in 1985.

There was an exceptionally good grain harvest in midyear. This ended a five-year period of drought and shortages.

SOUTH AFRICA

In January 1985, opening the first full session of the tricameral Parliament created under the controversial Constitution Act of 1983, executive State Pres. Pieter W. Botha spoke of the National Party (NP) government's plans for constitutional development and racial reform. In the eyes of most South Africans and of other observers throughout the world, however, the government proposals were completely overshadowed by unrest in the black townships. Beginning in the Vaal Triangle in September 1984, the unrest continued unremittingly in one part of the country or another throughout 1985. In response, the government declared a state of emergency in 36 districts of the Transvaal and Eastern Cape on July 20. The state of emergency was lifted in six districts but on October 25–26 was extended to an additional eight in the Western Cape.

Botha's proposals included setting up an "informal, nonstatutory" negotiating forum for discussion with black leaders, removing the "negative and discriminatory" aspects of influx control, restoring South African citizenship to residents of the former homelands, and granting freehold rights to Africans in urban areas. In later speeches during the year, Botha and other government ministers stated that the government was considering including African members on the appointed President's Council and that it intended to repeal the only remaining statutory job color bar, contained in the Mines and Works Act. At the same time, the government continued to defend residential and school apartheid (racial separation) and the separate political identity of the homelands.

Parliament repealed the Prohibition of Mixed Marriages Act and sections of the Immorality Act and also the Prohibition of Political Interference

Winnie Mandela, wife of African National Congress leader Nelson Mandela, attends the funeral of a 19-year-old who was stabbed to death by a prison warden.

AP/WIDE WORLD

Elijah Barayi, the newly elected president of the Congress of South African Trade Unions, is carried aloft by jubilant workers at the launching of South Africa's biggest trade union federation in Durban in December.

Act, which had prohibited multiracial political parties. Parliament also passed the Regional Services Council Act, providing for the creation of multiracial metropolitan councils. The President's Council issued a report whose most publicized recommendations were that influx control, "as applied at present in terms of Act 25 of 1945, be abolished . . . in an orderly manner" and that uniform identity documents be issued to all citizens. The report was under consideration by the government.

While there were many localized causes for the unrest, it was rooted in opposition to apartheid policies and in the nation's worsening economic conditions. Protest took many forms, including mass boycotts of school classes, rent strikes, work stay-aways, and street fighting against government security forces. By November, for example, some 350,000 residents of Vaal Triangle townships had been on a rent strike for 14 months, and such strikes were also widespread in the Eastern Cape. In November it was estimated that more than 90% of the eligible students were boycotting matriculation exams.

The government claimed that the unrest was created by a small minority of "Communist-inspired agitators" of the banned African National Congress (ANC). However, the most marked feature of the situation in the townships—not only in major centers but in tiny towns throughout the country—was the spread of grass-roots organizations, in many cases embracing entire communities, and the involvement in protest actions of blacks of all ages, including boys and girls in primary school. Organization took place largely under the banner of the United Democratic Front (UDF), which had

spearheaded the widespread boycott of the 1984 elections to the Coloured and Asian chambers of Parliament and was demanding political rights for all South Africans. Opinion polls conducted among blacks during the year showed the huge popularity of leaders identified with the ANC, in particular the imprisoned Nelson Mandela.

In dealing with the unrest the police were increasingly reinforced in the townships by units of the South African Defence Force (SADF), following the precedent established in Sebokeng and Sharpeville in October 1984. The use of troops and security-force methods and the imposition of the state of emergency were factors leading to the nationwide spread of a boycott of white businesses that was launched, and remained most effective, in the Eastern Cape. There was widespread criticism of police methods. Among the most publicized incidents were police shootings in Uitenhage on March 21, which resulted in 19 deaths according to official sources and 43 according to others, and the "Trojan Horse" affair in the Western Cape in October, when police hiding in containers on the back of a delivery vehicle emerged to open fire on demonstrators. The government-appointed commission inquiring into the Uitenhage incident made some criticisms of the police but concluded that they had had no option but to open fire, although the commission also pointed out that the majority of the victims had been shot in the back.

According to the Institute of Race Relations, there were 825 deaths resulting from the unrest between September 1984 and the end of October 1985. Official sources claimed, up to the same date, 504 deaths from security-force action and 232 others. Among other ominous developments were disappearances, murders, and mutilations allegedly carried out by white "death squads." By Nov. 8, 1985, the number of people who had been detained without trial under the state of emergency had reached 5,253, of whom 3,063 had been released. Thousands of other blacks had also been arrested, and there were widespread allegations of torture.

During the year a number of UDF leaders were charged with treason, which on conviction carried a maximum penalty of death. In December charges were dropped against 12 of the 16 defendants in one trial; a further 22 UDF leaders faced the same charge in a separate trial. In August the Rev. Allan Boesak, patron of the UDF, was charged with subversion. Winnie Mandela, wife of Nelson Mandela, was arrested twice in late December for defying a banning order forbidding her to enter Soweto, which she regarded as her home. She was released under bail conditions that repeated the ban.

In an attempt to curtail the worldwide publicity that the situation was receiving, the government on November 2 prohibited foreign journalists from filming, or being present at, scenes of unrest. During the same month, Anthony Heard, editor of the *Cape Times,* was charged under security legislation for publishing an interview with exiled ANC leader Oliver Tambo.

The government argued that much of the township violence was directed by blacks against other blacks. It appeared for the most part, however, to be directed against blacks who were regarded as "collaborators" with apartheid—those who had taken office in the unpopular local community councils, black policemen, and blacks regarded as police informers. In Natal in August there was a severe outbreak of violence between Africans and Indians. While Gatsha Buthelezi, head of the KwaZulu government and of the Inkatha movement, blamed the violence on black youths from outside Natal, UDF leaders in Natal identified its roots in the violent hostility of Inkatha vigilante groups toward the UDF. At the end of December there were violent clashes between members of the Zulu and Pondo tribes south of Durban. Over 50 people died in the fighting, which was apparently unrelated to the year's political violence.

The political strife entered a new phase in December with an increase in the number of attacks on whites. The most serious incident took place on December 23 when a bomb exploded in a crowded shopping center at Amanzimtoti, a resort south of Durban. The government blamed the ANC for the attack, which killed five people, all white.

Throughout the year there were growing indications of dissatisfaction among influential sections of white opinion with the NP government's handling of the situation. This increased during the state of emergency and also following President Botha's speech on August 15 to the Natal NP congress, in which he failed to announce anticipated new initiatives. In September Frederick van Zyl Slabbert, leader of the opposition Progressive Federal Party (PFP), together with Chief Buthelezi, launched the National Convention Alliance. Its aims were to persuade the government to repeal all discriminatory legislation, to legalize all banned organizations, to set free unconditionally all political prisoners and detainees, and to allow free political association as the basis for calling a representative national convention to formulate a new constitution.

A surprising new development was the decision of major business leaders to fly to Lusaka, Zambia, on September 13 for informal talks with leaders of the ANC, including Tambo. The business leaders rejected calls for government based on one person, one vote in a unitary South Africa, favoring instead a "federal" system reflecting the "plural" character of the population. At the same time, recognizing the popularity of the ANC, they wished to ascertain from its leaders the conditions under which they would enter negotiations. Besides enumerating preconditions for negotiations, ANC leaders stated that the only matter for negotiation was "the transfer of power to the majority." They also stated that they were not willing to abandon their strategy of armed struggle.

The Conservative Party and Herstigte Nasionale Partij (HNP), both to the right of the NP, played on white fears by blaming the unrest on the government's reform policies. By-elections in May showed only a slight swing to the right, but in by-elections held on October 30 the HNP won its first seat in Parliament.

A major development during the year was the decision by the majority of nonracial (predominantly African) trade unions to unite as the Congress of South African Trade Unions. Initial membership was estimated at more than 500,000, making the organization the largest trade-union coordinating body in the country.

Foreign Relations

The major feature of the year was the intensified international isolation of South Africa. A number of Western countries instituted or intensified sanctions on investment, trade, and military-related transactions and withdrew their ambassadors. In partial reversal of his previous policy of "constructive engagement" with the apartheid government to encourage reform, U.S. Pres. Ronald Reagan in September restricted new bank loans and banned sales of computer systems to the security forces, sales of nuclear technology, and the importation of Krugerrands. The move came after strong pressures from the U.S. Congress, whose members were in turn affected by widespread antiapartheid campaigning in the U.S. Most strongly resistant to any form of sanctions was Prime Minister Margaret

A youth carries the coffin of a two-month-old child during a funeral procession for 12 persons killed on November 21 in clashes with South African police.
AP/WIDE WORLD

AP/WIDE WORLD

South African Pres. P. W. Botha (center) held a meeting on November 21 with the presidents of the four black homelands given independence by South Africa but not recognized abroad. They are (from left) Pres. Patrick Mphephu of Venda, Prime Minister George Matanzima of Transkei, acting president Bernard Motsatse of Bophuthatswana, and Pres. Lennox Sebe of Ciskei.

Thatcher's Conservative government in Britain. However, the British government came into line with mild sanctions measures instituted by the European Communities and with similar measures agreed upon by the Commonwealth conference.

Within southern Africa the Nkomati agreement with Mozambique and negotiations with Angola in 1984 had appeared to herald a halt to the armed conflict punctuating South Africa's relations with those countries. However, such hopes proved overoptimistic. The Mozambique National Resistance (MNR) movement continued its insurgency against the Mozambique government, and increasing evidence emerged that there was continued support for it from within the South African regime, particularly with the publication in October by the Mozambique government of diaries captured from MNR leader Alfonso Dlakhama. The South African government admitted that "technical violations" of the accord had occurred. Military officers alleged to be responsible for the violations were moved to other posts, and Gen. Constand Viljoen, chief of the SADF, retired prematurely.

SADF troops withdrew from Angola in April but were again in action in the country in subsequent months. In September–October the SADF openly admitted its support for the National Union for the Total Independence of Angola (UNITA) rebels, who were fighting the Angolan government. Its troops were involved in operations to defend UNITA bases against a government offensive, in which there was evidence of intensified military assistance from the U.S.S.R.

Pressures were maintained internationally for the

implementation of UN Resolution 435, calling for independence for South West Africa/Namibia from South African control and for democratic elections. After April, however, the South African government unilaterally went ahead with the establishment of a transitional government in Namibia formed from the six parties of the Multi-Party Conference on the basis of a 62-person legislature. An eight-member Cabinet was appointed and began to take steps toward drawing up a new constitution.

On June 14 in South Africa's first military offensive against Botswana, SADF commandos raided houses in Gaborone that allegedly served as bases for ANC guerrilla activity. At least 15 people were killed. The ANC and the Botswana government vigorously denied the charges, and the raid was widely condemned internationally. In response to pressure for increased international sanctions, South African government spokesmen on several occasions appeared to threaten retaliation against the country's southern African neighbors in the form of cutting economic ties and repatriating foreign migrant workers.

The Economy

At the beginning of 1985 the economy was suffering severely from the effects of anti-inflationary austerity measures, including spending cuts and raised interest rates, that were instituted in August 1984. The consequences were considerable rises in unemployment and a marked increase in the number of bankruptcies. In the year to June 1985 some 48,400 jobs, almost two-thirds belonging to blacks, were lost in manufacturing. Official statistics on unemployment among blacks were unreliable, but it was widely estimated that the total exceeded three million. The March budget continued the austerity policies and raised the general sales tax to 12%.

The slowing down of economic activity, by reducing the demand for imports, created a massive turnaround in the current account of the balance of payments. An annualized deficit of more than R 2 billion in the third quarter of 1984 was replaced by an annualized surplus of R 5.4 billion in the second quarter of 1985. (For table of world currencies, *see* International Exchange and Payments.) Important contributions came from gold exports and a revival in agriculture. (While the dollar gold price remained relatively static, rand earnings rose to record levels because of the decline in value of the rand.) At the same time, there was a steady net outflow of capital, amounting to some R 2 billion during the year.

The austerity measures were markedly unsuccessful in diminishing inflation, which reached a record rate of 16.8% in October. Nevertheless, because of internal pressures, during the second half of the year the government embarked on mildly reflationary measures, including a reduction of interest rates and an injection of R 900 million into job-creation measures.

Special Report: South Africa's Apartheid Policy

by Colin Legum

South Africa entered the most difficult period of its modern history in 1985 when its government formally committed itself to unscrambling the policy of apartheid (racial separation) that it had pursued with vigor and ruthlessness throughout the years since the National Party came to power in 1948. The core of apartheid ideology was the belief that peaceful racial coexistence could be secured only by separating the country's four communities—the 23.9 million blacks, 4.8 million whites, 3 million Coloureds (people of mixed race), and 1 million Asians (mainly Indians)—into different social and political societies that would nevertheless remain economically interdependent. The objective was to be achieved by dividing the country between whites, who were allocated more than two-thirds of the territory, and blacks. It was proposed that the blacks should achieve their separate political independence within ten ethnic homelands scattered across the remaining one-third of the nation; those blacks living in the designated white area, who were roughly equal in number to the total white community, would be treated as "temporary sojourners" whose political rights would be restricted to their own ethnic homelands. Such a policy called for, among other things, a major effort to reverse the influx of blacks into the economically prosperous white areas by removing all black workers surplus to the needs of the white economy, a policy that involved uprooting millions of people.

Apart from the moral questions that it raised, this policy of reshaping the country's demography ran up against a number of practical difficulties. For example, insufficient land was allocated to absorb the "surplus" black labor; a rapidly expanding industrial society called for many more, not fewer, black workers in the white-designated areas; and millions of urban blacks had long since lost all contact with their ethnic roots. These basic fallacies in the ideology of apartheid, long recognized by its critics, finally also came to be acknowledged by the South African government.

In a speech in August executive state Pres. Pieter Botha announced that he was "not prepared to lead white South Africans and other minority groups on a road to abdication and suicide." The U.S. and other foreign governments were dismayed; they had been led to expect an announcement of significant reforms that would lead to the end of apartheid. In September Botha made some concessions to mounting pressure at home and overseas and promised to grant citizenship to blacks who lived in urban areas but were nominally citizens of "independent" homelands and to scrap the law that required blacks to carry passes designed to restrict "unauthorized" blacks from white-designated areas.

During the 37 years of apartheid rule, the political attitudes of black South Africans had been transformed: a largely quiescent people had been politicized; an entire new generation of young blacks had been radicalized by their struggle against discriminatory laws and an inferior education system; and an increasing number of blacks had come to believe that their only hope for change was through a violent struggle. They were inspired by the success of the armed struggles in neighboring countries and by the example of Umkonto We Sizwe (Spear of the Nation, underground military wing of the banned African National Congress [ANC]), which had been launched by Nelson Mandela in 1961. Mandela, in the 21st year of a life sentence in prison, had come to be regarded as the symbol of African resistance. Successive public opinion polls showed that he commanded the support of 70% of all black South Africans, as well as that of a significant number of whites. Botha himself recognized Mandela's importance by offering to release him from prison to allow him to enter into the process of negotiations, provided only that he undertook to renounce violence, a condition that Mandela rejected.

A revolt of young black militants, which had first manifested itself in Soweto in 1976, spread across South Africa in 1985. Angry young people, many still teenagers, took over the leadership of some communities. They organized school and consumer boycotts and began a campaign to make the black ghettos ungovernable by attacking police and others who collaborated with the system. This forceful black resistance called forth strong police and military reaction by the authorities. There were also other centers of black opposition led by such movements as the Zulu-dominated Inkatha, whose leader was Chief Gatsha Buthelezi, and the newly legalized black trade unions. Hopes of peaceful reform were frustrated.

South Africa's leaders also came under greater

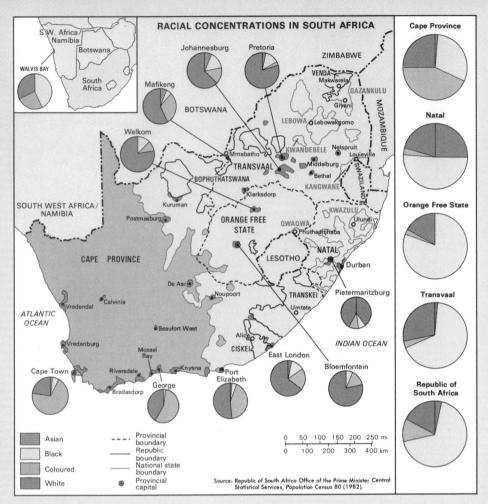

RACIAL CONCENTRATIONS IN SOUTH AFRICA

Cape Province

Natal

Orange Free State

Transvaal

Republic of South Africa

Asian
Black
Coloured
White

Provincial boundary
Republic boundary
National state boundary
Provincial capital

0   50 100 150 200 250 mi
0 100 200 300 400 km

Source: Republic of South Africa Office of the Prime Minister Central Statistical Services, Population Census 80 (1982).

South Africa in 1985 consisted of three groups of territorial units: four provinces for settlement by whites under apartheid laws (Cape, Natal, Orange Free State, and Transvaal); six black national states that had not yet achieved "independence" under South African law (Gazankulu, Kangwane, Kwandebele, Kwazulu, Lebowa, and Qwaqwa); and four republics that had become formally "independent" under South African law (Bophuthatswana, Ciskei, Transkei, and Venda). The last two groups were at first called Bantu homelands, but were later redesignated as black national states. Although only 14% of South Africa's area is assigned to areas of black settlement, more than 72% of the population in South Africa as a whole is black. The populations of each of the national states and republics in 1980 was more than 98% black. The effect of South Africa's racial policies was to reduce the apparent black population of the Republic of South Africa by nearly 4,000,000 at the census.

pressure from an increasingly hostile Western community. Until 1985 foreign investors had viewed South Africa as a stable country, but with the increase in racial tensions and the evident difficulties of reforming the system, doubts crept in. Western governments, including those of the U.S. and Britain, showed their concern over the slow progress in ending apartheid; though they remained opposed to blanket economic sanctions, they began to favor the idea of adopting a program of selective sanctions as a way of exerting pressure on President Botha to defuse the danger of catastrophic violence by moving more decisively in implementing his promise to scrap apartheid.

In the United States the movement in favor of disinvestment had grown rapidly to the point where Congress was ready to support this and other measures, a move that was preempted by Pres. Ronald Reagan's surprising decision to sign an executive order, which, in effect, applied a series of selective sanctions against South Africa. The country's economic problems were accelerated throughout the year by a number of foreign banks that refused to renew loans to South Africa. On August 27 South Africa suspended trading on the stock and currency markets after the rand fell in value by nearly 60%. On September 1 the country announced a four-

month freeze on repayments of principal on the foreign debt. The South African business community, which had long shared the sense of impatience over the government's failure to end apartheid, acted in defiance of the government by sending an influential delegation to Zambia for talks with leaders of the ANC.

The détente between powerful South African business leaders and the ANC, coming on top of growing Western hostility and escalating political violence at home, increased the pressure on President Botha to stop talking about reforms and to begin to implement them by starting negotiations with such black leaders as Mandela. However, he continued to delay action, partly because of the climate of violence but, more importantly, because of signs of growing opposition to his policies among the Afrikaner electorate in particular. He felt himself trapped; on the one hand, pressures at home and abroad urged him to move faster in ridding the country of apartheid and, on the other, he risked a right-wing white backlash. The transition period away from apartheid to a new political system based on power sharing demanded rare skills in crisis management. It remained to be seen whether President Botha possessed the statecraft needed to accomplish this.

SOUTHEAST ASIAN AFFAIRS

During 1985, for the seventh successive year, the diplomatic calendar of Southeast Asia was dominated by efforts to resolve the conflict over Kampuchea, where the regime was supported by some 170,000 Vietnamese troops. This activity intensified after Hanoi mounted its fiercest ever dry-season military offensive against Khmer resistance guerrillas between November 1984 and April 1985 and knocked out all their major bases near the border with Thailand. A number of political initiatives issued from both major camps involved in the conflict: the Association of Southeast Asian Nations (ASEAN), which supported the Democratic Kampuchea (DK) resistance coalition, and Vietnam-led Indochina.

Sensing military victory, the foreign ministers of Vietnam, Laos, and the Phnom Penh regime met in Ho Chi Minh City, Vietnam, in mid-January to chart a diplomatic course. They put forward what they described as a new proposal to break the deadlock. Its chief elements were a withdrawal of Vietnamese forces from Kampuchea and the holding of internationally monitored elections, provided the "genocidal clique" headed by Pol Pot of the Khmer Rouge, one of the three parties in the DK resistance coalition, was eliminated. The foreign ministers also suggested an international conference on Kampuchea, to consist not only of regional and global powers but of other nations, such as Australia and Sweden, that had "contributed to peace in Southeast Asia." However, ASEAN officials were skeptical about the plan, seeing little in it that was new.

Australian Foreign Minister William (Bill) Hayden tried to mediate the dispute by flying to Indochina in March and giving the proposal a sympathetic hearing. Not surprisingly, Hayden met a cool reception when he subsequently arrived in Thailand to elaborate on the Indochinese plan. That same week Thailand had complained that Vietnamese troops had entered its territory and clashed with its Army. Hanoi's leaders had denied the allegation to Hayden. After being shown videotaped evidence supporting Thailand's claim when he was in Bangkok, Hayden admitted that he had been misled by Vietnam. The Australian initiative stalled.

In April an ASEAN effort was launched when Malaysia suggested proximity talks between representatives of the UN-recognized DK resistance coalition and the Phnom Penh regime. The proposal was designed to overcome Phnom Penh's refusal to meet the Khmer Rouge by bringing the two sides to a common venue but keeping them in different rooms, where communications would be effected through a neutral mediator. Although ASEAN governments showed interest, at the end of May Indonesian Foreign Minister Mochtar Kusumaatmadja proposed a separate peace plan, with the normalization of relations between Vietnam and the U.S. as its centerpiece. Seen at first as a competitive move on Jakarta's part, Mochtar's proposal was later presented as being complementary to the Malaysian one.

Initially the proposal to hold proximity talks envisaged discussions between the two warring Khmer sides only. By the time it had been officially endorsed at the annual meeting of ASEAN foreign ministers in July, however, it had undergone a significant change. The modified version proposed that DK representatives meet officials not only from Phnom Penh but also from Hanoi. A senior ASEAN official said the DK had rejected the original initiative on the grounds that it was not involved in a civil war, and therefore it wished to talk directly with the aggressor, Vietnam. Though Hanoi did not formally reject proximity talks, the Vietnamese media referred to the idea in derogatory terms. According to well-informed sources, the Vietnamese had been interested in the first version but found the second unacceptable.

The communiqué issued at the end of the ASEAN foreign ministers' conference included other references to Indochina. It deplored the latest Vietnamese dry-season offensive that had driven a quarter of a million Khmer refugees into Thailand and drew attention to their plight. It also noted "with serious concern" Hanoi's use of Kampuchean forced labor in war zones.

Indonesia further developed its designated role as ASEAN's interlocutor with Vietnam on the Kampuchean issue. Relations between Jakarta and Hanoi continued to improve, culminating in November in reciprocal visits by trade delegations and a deci-

Members of Thailand's elite border patrol police fortify their defensive positions at a strategic pass near the Thailand-Kampuchea border. Thailand deployed army and border patrol units along the 450-mile (725-kilometer) border to face Vietnamese forces in Kampuchea.

AP/WIDE WORLD

sion to resume direct commerce. However, controversy broke out within ASEAN earlier in the year when Gen. Benny Murdani, chief of the Indonesian armed forces, remarked after a visit by Vietnamese Defense Minister Gen. Van Tien Dung that Jakarta would step up its military ties with Hanoi.

The U.S.S.R., already involved in the Kampuchean conflict through its ally, Vietnam, sought a higher diplomatic profile in the region to complement its broadened military presence. During a month-long tour of Southeast Asian capitals, Soviet Deputy Foreign Minister Mikhail Kapitsa said that Moscow was prepared to act as a guarantor of peace once the region's key nations had settled the Kampuchean issue. The offer, however, was not well received. ASEAN members became increasingly uncomfortable as the U.S.S.R. continued its military buildup at strategic points in the Indian Ocean, the sea-lanes of East Asia, and the former U.S. naval base at Cam Ranh, Vietnam. To meet the perceived threat to security posed by the arrival of Soviet MiG-21 and MiG-23 fighter aircraft in Ho Chi Minh City and Kampuchea, the Malaysian Air Force was to buy 40 Skyhawks over several years, while Thailand was seeking to acquire sophisticated F-16 jet fighters from the U.S. With virtually full access to the Cam Ranh and Da Nang bases on Vietnam's coast, the Soviets were able to maintain medium-range Tu-16 Badger bombers, long-range patrol craft, and several submarines in the Pacific Ocean. They were also well positioned to conduct maritime surveillance and to gather intelligence on radar and air defenses throughout Southeast Asia.

The increase in Soviet activities put pressure on the U.S. to raise its own profile in the region, which had been low ever since the U.S. military withdrawal from Vietnam in 1975. In July the U.S. Congress passed a bill that would allow $5 million in aid to the two non-Communist partners of the DK resistance coalition. In a significant shift from its previous stance, the U.S. administration stated that it would no longer refuse military assistance to the resistance forces.

While busily cultivating trade and business links with non-Communist Southeast Asia, China was less active than usual on the diplomatic scene. Nonetheless, a significant milestone was passed when Chinese Foreign Minister Wu Xueqian (Wu Hsueh-ch'ien) went to Indonesia in April to meet President Suharto and Foreign Minister Mochtar. Though the meetings produced no substantive breakthrough, they marked the first time since bilateral relations were suspended in 1967 that top-level officials from the two countries had met on either's home territory. Later, Jakarta and Peking announced the resumption of direct trade links. The progress of Sino-Indonesian relations was watched closely by the other members of ASEAN.

Links between Japan and the region were bedeviled by growing frustration over the trade pattern that had developed between them. At a meeting in June of economics ministers from all the nations concerned, ASEAN officials characterized the pattern as "distorted" and "lopsided." Some 90% of ASEAN's exports to Japan consisted of raw materials and primary products, while a similar proportion of Japanese exports to the region was made up of manufactured goods. The conference even heard references to Tokyo's wartime attempt to colonize Southeast Asia.

Though ASEAN's economic performance in 1985 remained superior to that of the rest of the world, it slipped noticeably from the levels of the previous year. For much of 1985 growth rates for exports and gross national product fell short of projections. Prime reasons included sluggish commodity prices and slow economic performance by ASEAN's major trading partners. The latter factor in turn fueled a high tide of protectionist sentiment in Western countries, particularly the U.S. Throughout the year ASEAN countries joined the chorus of protest from Asia against the protectionist laws being introduced by the U.S. Congress. The battle against a controversial bill that threatened to cut deeply into East and Southeast Asia's textile exports to the U.S. was especially heated. In October, just before the House of Representatives voted on the bill, Prime Minister Lee Kuan Yew of Singapore made an impassioned, lucid speech on the dangers of protectionism before the full U.S. Congress. The bill passed, but it failed to muster the two-thirds majority needed to override the veto that Pres. Ronald Reagan had promised to exercise if necessary.

SPACE SCIENCE AND EXPLORATION

As 1985 began, the second meeting of ministers from the 11 member nations and 3 associate member nations of the European Space Agency (ESA) took place in Rome on January 30. At the meeting the members agreed to participate in the program proposed by U.S. Pres. Ronald Reagan to launch a permanent space station into Earth orbit in the 1990s. The ESA contribution would be a manned scientific module named *Columbus.* It could be detached from the space station to form a building block in an ESA space station if the need arose.

Also early in 1985 Great Britain announced that it would establish the British National Space Centre, probably at the Royal Aircraft Establishment at Farnborough. Its mission would be to foster the development of space technology within the U.K. and coordinate a national space policy. In October ESA member nations unanimously approved the acceptance of Austria and Norway to full membership status. The two countries had been associate members since 1981.

Manned Flight

In Japan the National Space Development Agency announced that three astronauts had been selected from 533 applicants. One of them would be tapped to fly aboard the U.S. space shuttle in January 1988.

In April the U.S.S.R. invited Japan to provide an astronaut to fly aboard a Soviet spacecraft at some future time.

After extensive screening by the U.S. National Aeronautics and Space Administration (NASA), a schoolteacher was selected to undertake astronaut training in preparation for a space shuttle mission in early 1986. She was Sharon Christa McAuliffe of Concord, N.H. NASA also announced in June that 13 new astronauts had been selected, bringing the total to 103.

On Jan. 24, 1985, space shuttle orbiter *Discovery* lifted off from the Kennedy Space Center in Florida. The crew was all military, as was the mission. Few details about the flight were released by the U.S. Department of Defense.

Informed sources in the technical and scientific media reported that the primary purpose of the mission was to place in orbit a satellite designed to track Soviet missile tests and intercept military and diplomatic communications in the U.S.S.R. and elsewhere. In addition to the secret satellite, *Discovery* also carried an Australian blood experiment that was not military. The experiment, provided by Sydney Hospital, was designed to investigate how zero gravity affects human blood. *Discovery* returned to Earth on January 27, landing at the Kennedy Space Center.

Discovery again was launched from the Kennedy Space Center on April 12. The primary mission was to launch the Anik C-1 and Leasat 3 satellites, which was accomplished. However, Leasat 3 failed to activate in orbit. A variety of scientific experiments were performed aboard the *Discovery* orbiter, including one involving electrophoresis that had potential commercial applications in pharmacology. On board was U.S. Senator Jake Garn, who participated as a subject in several medical experiments. The shuttle orbiter returned to the Kennedy Space Center on April 19.

On April 29 the *Challenger* shuttle orbiter took off from Kennedy Space Center with a crew of seven, including scientists from The Netherlands and the U.S. The flight was dedicated to materials processing and life sciences experiments in the first operational Spacelab. While the materials-processing experiments went well, a life sciences project to evaluate an animal holding cage stocked with two monkeys and 24 rats did not fare as well. It indicated the need to improve the design for such a facility. A crew member took a series of spectacular photographs of auroras within the Earth's atmosphere while looking down upon them. *Challenger* returned to Earth on May 6, landing at Edwards Air Force Base in California.

Discovery was launched from the Kennedy Space Center on June 17. In addition to the flight crew there were two payload specialists: Prince Sultan Salman ibn Abdel-Aziz as-Saud, a nephew of King Fahd of Saudi Arabia and an experienced jet pilot, and Patrick Baudry of France.

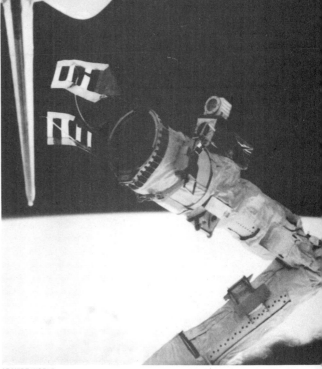

Two "swatters" on the robot arm on the space shuttle Discovery *were broken in a vain attempt to activate a switch on the Leasat 3 satellite in April.*

It was a busy mission. The Arabsat 1-B, Morelos 1, and Telstar 3D communications satellites were launched. A small, free-flying platform, Spartan 1, was deployed from the shuttle cargo bay by the craft's remote manipulator arm. It made astronomical measurements and was later retrieved. On June 24 *Discovery* landed at Edwards Air Force Base.

Next in the busy schedule for the space shuttle was the launch of *Challenger* on July 29 from the Kennedy Space Center. The primary mission was to perform a series of scientific experiments on the first pallet-only flight of the Spacelab 2. *Challenger* landed at Edwards Air Force Base on August 6.

Discovery was launched on August 27 from the Kennedy Space Center. In one of the busiest missions to date, *Discovery* launched three satellites and retrieved an inoperative one, repaired it, and redeployed it. Several scientific experiments were also on board. In addition, crew members used a 70-mm movie camera to take footage for a film to be released later as *The Dream Is Alive*.

Launched as planned were the Aussat 1 (Australia), ASC 1, and Leasat 4 communications satellites. The high point of the mission, however, was the capture and repair of the Leasat 3, which had failed during an earlier mission. For two days astronauts James van Hoften and William F. Fisher spent hours in the cargo bay of the shuttle orbiter. With the repairs completed, van Hoften mounted supports on the end of the remote maneuvering arm and manually deployed the satellite into space after spinning it by hand to 3 rpm. The success of the repairs was not known until late in October when

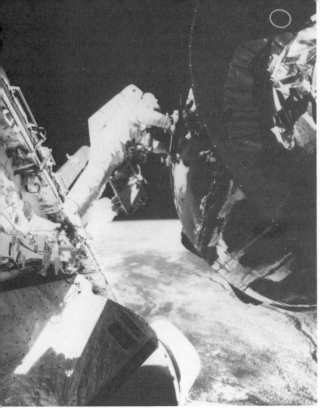

(LEFT) UPI/BETTMANN NEWSPHOTOS; (RIGHT) AP/WIDE WORLD

Discovery astronaut William Fisher (left) prepares to redeploy the $85 million Leasat 3 communications satellite in September. While in space Fisher had repaired a faulty electronic device on the satellite. James van Hoften (right) stands on the end of Discovery's robot arm after heaving the device back into space.

Earth controllers of the Leasat 3 fired the satellite's perigee kick motor to place it into the desired orbit. The highly successful mission ended with a landing at Edwards Air Force Base on September 3.

The shuttle orbiter *Atlantis* was launched for the first time on October 3. Even though the details of the flight were classified by the U.S. Department of Defense, it was believed that an objective of the mission was to launch two Defense Satellite Communications System (DSCS, phase 3) satellites. They were successfully placed in orbit. *Atlantis* landed on October 7 at Edwards Air Force Base.

Atlantis was launched into orbit again on November 26 from the Kennedy Space Center. During the mission the crew successfully launched into orbit Morelos-B, a Mexican communications satellite; Australia's Aussat-2 communications satellite; and a Satcom K-2 for RCA American Communications Inc. On November 29 and December 1 astronauts Jerry Ross and Sherwood Spring stepped out of *Atlantis* into space to practice construction techniques that would be used to build future space stations. *Atlantis* returned to Earth on December 3, landing at Edwards Air Force Base.

Also during the year the Soviet Union continued its program of manned spaceflight, concentrating on the further development of activities that would lead to larger and more versatile space stations. On June 6 Soyuz T-13 was launched from Tyuratam with two cosmonauts aboard. Their mission was to accomplish repairs on the Salyut 7, which had

been seriously disabled. Soyuz T-13 returned to the Earth on September 26 with two cosmonauts, while three remained on the Salyut 7.

Soyuz T-14 was launched from Tyuratam on September 17 with three cosmonauts on board. They took supplies and supplemented the crew aboard the space station.

On July 19 a new type of spacecraft was launched from Tyuratam and docked with the Salyut 7 space station. Cosmos 1669 was apparently a free-flying, unmanned module that could be used to enlarge the Salyut. The Soviets said that it was based on the *Progress* unmanned ferry spacecraft. It was detached from Salyut 7 on August 29, reentered the atmosphere, and was destroyed.

Yet another extension module was added to Salyut 7 on September 27 when Cosmos 1686 was launched from Tyuratam by a Proton launch vehicle. On October 2 it docked with the space station. The new addition more than doubled the length of the space station, to 115 ft (35 m). On November 21 the three cosmonauts aboard Salyut 7 returned to the Earth because one was ill.

West Germany paid NASA $64 million to fly *Challenger* on a mission that lasted from October 30 to November 6. The U.S. flight crew, West German physicists Ernst Messerschmid and Reinhard Furrer, and Dutch physicist Wubbo Ockels were on board. The first manned spaceflight to be managed by a country other than the U.S. or U.S.S.R., the mission was dedicated to scientific experiments.

Unmanned Satellites

The year 1985 was notable for demonstrating the utility of unmanned satellites in saving human life. A young Belgian race car driver owed his life to the combined efforts of the U.S. NOAA 9 and Soviet Cospos 1 satellites when they fixed his position after his race car had an accident in a remote area of Somalia. Rescue teams dispatched by French authorities found the man and evacuated him to a hospital in Brussels, where he later recovered. By the end of May more than 400 lives had been saved by the network of three Soviet and two U.S. search-and-rescue satellites.

ATS 3 in 1985 performed yeoman's duty during the disastrous September earthquake in Mexico City. The 18-year-old satellite was pressed into service through its control center in Malabar, Fla. It supported relief operations of the American Red Cross and the Pan-American World Health Organization. The satellite was also used by CBS to relay commercial communications and news to the U.S. from its reporters in Mexico.

On June 21 the U.S.S.R. provided the world with a mystery satellite. It broke into three pieces while in orbit. The largest piece reentered the Earth's atmosphere on June 24, and the other two followed on June 28. The largest piece was estimated to be approximately 3.3 ft (1 m) long. Western experts were puzzled by the fact that the Soviets, for only the second time since their space program began, did not give the launch from Tyuratam a name or number. They theorized that it was an antisatellite test or possibly a new launch vehicle that exploded prematurely.

In September the ESA Ariane III launch vehicle suffered a setback. It veered off course from the launch site in French Guiana and had to be destroyed two minutes into the mission. Lost were the ECS 3 and Spacenet 3 satellites. It was the third failure in 15 attempts for Ariane.

Probes

During the year both the U.S.S.R. and the U.S. announced plans for future probes. The Soviet announcement was couched in terms that showed that considerable planning had gone into the future missions. Scheduled for a June 1988 launch were two probes to Mars and a rendezvous with and possible landing on its satellite Phobos. If the landing attempt succeeded, the second probe would go on to rendezvous with the planet's other satellite, Deimos. Other Soviet probes planned for 1989 and 1990 included a polar-orbiting Mars probe to study the geochemical makeup of the surface and ice caps in the dark polar caps.

As 1984 ended, the Soviets launched two probes, Vega 1 and Vega 2, to visit Venus and then ren-

Astronaut Lieut. Col. Sherwood Spring of the U.S. Army stands on the end of the robot arm as he maneuvers a 45-foot (13.7-meter) truss above the cargo bay of the space shuttle Atlantis. He and Maj. Jerry Ross of the Air Force assembled the truss on December 1. The structure was built to test construction techniques for use in assembling possible future space stations.

AP/WIDE WORLD

dezvous with Halley's Comet. Each probe consisted of a main body, a landing module, and a helium-filled balloon. The instrumented ten-foot (three-meter)-diameter balloon deployed from Vega 1 in the Venusian atmosphere was tracked for 46 hours by an international network of ground stations on Earth in June. There were also 11 radio telescopes around the world receiving data from the balloon's instrumented gondola. Transmission failed when batteries in the gondola were exhausted. The balloon drifted through the atmosphere at an altitude of 34 mi (54.7 km) above the surface.

The balloon from Vega 2 was deployed on June 15 and transmitted data until June 17. Its gondola also transmitted data for 46 hours until its batteries failed. At the altitude above Venus's surface of 34 mi (54.7 km), preliminary analysis of data indicated an atmospheric temperature of 100° F (37.8° C) and a wind velocity of 148.5 mph (239 km/h).

Both Vega 1 and 2 also ejected landing modules to the surface of Venus. They were instrumented to telemeter atmospheric pressure, temperature, X-ray fluorescence, and gamma-ray radiation. Because of the extreme heat and high atmospheric pressure on the surface, the landers transmitted data for only about 20 minutes.

Meanwhile, the main bodies of the Vegas continued on their trajectories for their rendezvous with Halley's Comet in March 1986. Other probes to Halley's Comet included two by Japan and one by ESA. The contribution of the U.S. to cometary exploration took place on September 11 when ICE (International Cometary Explorer) flew through the tail of the distant Comet Giacobini-Zinner.

SPAIN

The Cabinet reshuffle announced by Prime Minister Felipe González Márquez of Spain in July 1985 included the surprise resignation of Miguel Boyer, minister of economy and finance, who reportedly quit after failing in his attempt to persuade González to appoint him as his deputy. Instead the prime minister closed ranks with Deputy Prime Minister Alfonso Guerra González, arguing that Guerra commanded support from various parts of the ruling Partido Socialista Obrero Español (PSOE; Spanish Socialist Workers Party) machine. Foreign Minister Fernando Morán was also dismissed, mainly because of his anti-NATO attitude. Morán was replaced by Francisco Fernández Ordóñez, while Boyer was succeeded by Carlos Solchaga, former minister of industry and energy. The fact that four other posts were filled by technocrats rather than by politicians was taken by the press as an indication that early elections were likely in the event of a government defeat in a referendum planned for early 1986 on the question of Spain's membership in NATO. The González government, now in favor of NATO membership, had suspended it upon coming to power in December 1982.

The efforts of Gerardo Iglesias, secretary-general

of the Partido Comunista Español (PCE), to set up a new broadly based left-wing front, Convergencia de Izquierda, were publicly opposed by his predecessor, Santiago Carrillo. In order to reduce Carrillo's considerable support among party members, Iglesias resolved to have his supporters elected to regional power centers. Carrillo and several of his supporters were dropped from the PCE Central Committee in April. Ramón Tamames, who left the PCE at the end of 1984, set up the Federación Progresista, which defined itself as federalist and progressive.

A general strike supported by both the Communist-led Comisiones Obreras and the Socialist Unión General de Trabajadores took place in mid-June. The strike and demonstration signaled the growing impatience of the unions with official economic policy and with the government's impotence in the face of a 22% unemployment rate. Pressure from union members to abandon the national wages accord grew more intense, especially after the employers' federation threatened to withdraw from the accord when it became evident that the government would not concede further tax cuts or incentives to increase jobs. The general strike was the first since the death of Gen. Francisco Franco ten years earlier. In November the anniversary of Franco's death was commemorated by a demonstration in Madrid, attended by at least 50,000 right-wing Spaniards and led by one of Franco's daughters.

The government was also unpopular with environmentalists, who teamed up with anti-NATO demonstrators to hold a weekend of street parties and protests in November. While reiterating his own and his party's commitment to NATO, González announced that he would seek a reduction in the number of U.S. troops stationed in Spain. At the same time, Spain was reportedly upgrading the naval base at Rota to prepare for its use in conjunction with NATO partners and bringing the armed services up to NATO standards.

King Juan Carlos confers with U.S. Pres. Ronald Reagan during their walk through the garden of El Pardo near Madrid on the second day of Reagan's visit.
AP/WIDE WORLD

Near Paranthan in northern Sri Lanka, a group of young Tamil recruits learn the use of automatic rifles and grenade launchers as part of a six-month training course conducted by a Tamil separatist organization opposed to the Sinhalese-dominated national government.

AP/WIDE WORLD

As a result of a series of agreements signed between the Basque and Catalan regional governments on the one hand and the central government and local Socialist parties on the other, relations between the central and autonomous governments improved markedly. In the Basque Country the Basque Nationalist Party (PNV) began the year without a working majority in the regional parliament. The endorsement by the parliament of José Antonio Ardanza, a moderate PNV member, as premier of the regional government led to the Basque Socialist Party's agreeing to support the PNV and paved the way for a formal statement, issued by the PNV in March, urging Basques to assist efforts to end violence in the region. The PNV, however, avoided entanglement in negotiations between Madrid and the military wing of the Euzkadi ta Azkatasuna (ETA; Basque Homeland and Liberty) aimed at facilitating the return of former ETA members to the region after standing trial and formally abjuring violence.

Early in the year there were major demonstrations against a proposed law to reform the education system; the changes would make the state more responsible for education at the expense of the Roman Catholic Church. Demonstrations against a law allowing abortion in strictly limited circumstances were backed by certain members of the medical profession who refused to implement the provisions for reasons of conscience.

At the end of March the European Communities (EC) Council of Ministers released a statement noting that key issues such as fisheries, agriculture, and social affairs (emigration) had been resolved and that enlargement of the EC to include Spain and Portugal could take place as planned on Jan. 1, 1986. At the end of April an agreement was reached regulating bilateral Spanish-Portuguese trade relations within the EC context during the next ten years. Despite a last-minute rush to complete negotiations, there were unresolved issues—and therefore blank pages in the treaty—when it was formally signed in Madrid in June.

SRI LANKA

Sri Lanka entered its third successive year of emergency rule during 1985 as a section of the Tamil community continued its ten-year-old campaign for an autonomous Tamil state in the north and east of the country. The first half of the year was dominated by fierce clashes between Tamil militants and the national security forces, most of whom were drawn from the country's Sinhalese majority, and the second half by negotiations aimed at resolving the ethnic conflict. In July the government claimed to have foiled a Tamil attempt to assassinate Pres. Junius Jayawardene.

On June 18 the government and a number of Tamil guerrilla groups agreed to cease hostilities until mid-September in an effort to reach a peaceful settlement. Peace talks took place in July and August at Thimphu, Bhutan, under the auspices of the Indian government. However, the second round broke down on August 17 when all six participating Tamil organizations walked out in protest after the two sides traded charges of truce violations. Although the talks failed to produce results, they at least succeeded in bringing each side to a greater understanding of the other. On September 16 the government announced a unilateral extension of the cessation of hostilities for an indefinite period, and later it accepted in part a Tamil proposal to enlarge the multiracial committee that was monitoring the cease-fire.

The government admitted that defense spending had increased tenfold to almost $600,000 a day since the start of the upsurge in ethnic violence. The economy was also suffering from a slump in tourism and from the disruption of road, rail, and sea transport.

STAMPS AND COINS

There was further improvement in the market for rare stamps and postal history material during 1985, but dealing at the general collector and junior level remained quiet. In the U.S. the Postal Service worked closely with the Council of Philatelic Or-

313

The U.S. Postal Service announced in November that it would issue a booklet of commemorative stamps in January 1986 in celebration of the hobby of stamp collecting.

U.S. POSTAL SERVICE

ganizations to stimulate interest among the general public, especially children. In the U.K. the Stamp Collecting Promotion Council became part of the British Philatelic Federation (BPF).

Among the large number of internationally famous one-country collections sold at auction for high totals were the Benwell Barbados, £67,000 [1£ = U.S. $1.45]; Dunstan Uganda, £117,300; and Crabb Tristan da Cunha, £60,000. The postponed (second) sale of surplus archival material held at London's National Postal Museum proved disappointing, and the third sale was incorporated in a Phillips auction of Great Britain stamps from various owners, an experiment that improved realizations.

A Boston collector discovered the 16th example of the Falkland Islands 1964 6*d* stamp featuring HMS *Glasgow* in error for HMS *Kent*. The original sheet of 60 had been broken up and distributed as a normal new issue before the error was discovered. Newly discovered errors were color trials of the Australian 1982 60-cent humpback whale stamp accidentally included in the printers' delivery to the Australian Post Office. Argyll Etkin Ltd. of London began handling the Ishikawa collection of U.S. classic stamps valued at £11.4 million, the most valuable private collection of these issues ever marketed. The Philatelic Foundation of New York discovered more than 200 fakes of its Expert Committee certificates. Charges were brought against an employee of the foundation and three others.

Several rare stamps and covers made record realizations: Western Australia 1854 4*d* deep blue "inverted swan" error, £60,000 (estimate, £35,000); Bermuda 1861 "Perot" postmaster provisional, one of five now known and the only unused example, £33,000 (£20,000); India 1854 4 annas (cut to shape) error "inverted head," used, a new find,

The People's Bank of China issued a pure gold coin bearing a design of the Qiniandian (Ch'i Nien Tien) of the Temple of Heaven and a panda eating bamboo as part of an international campaign to save the panda.

CAMERA PRESS, LONDON

£12,000 (£7,500); U.S. 1918 24-cent airmail error, inverted center, $88,000 (estimated to $100,-000); Confederate States cover with a pair of Livingston, Ala., 5-cent blue, $176,000 (estimate, $160,000); Baden, Germany, 1851 9-kreutzer black on blue-green color error (only three known), on cover, £615,000; Tristan da Cunha cover with ½*d* and 1*d* King George V Great Britain with typed overprint, £12,000 (£6,000); Great Britain 1840 2*d* blue, Plate 1, mint marginal block of four, £20,350.

The BPF congress was held in Oxford for the first time. Three collectors signed the Roll of Distinguished Philatelists: Carl Richard Brühl (West Germany), author of a newly published two-volume history of philately; Roberto M. Rosende (U.S.), a leading authority on Cuban philately; and W. Raife Wellsted (Great Britain), an internationally known postal historian and curator of the National Postal Museum. The BPF Congress medal was awarded to A. Herbert Grimsey, honorary secretary of the BPF and collector of musical philately.

The major Fédération Internationale de Philatélie (FIP) international stamp exhibition of the year was held in Tel Aviv, Israel, in May. The FIP Grand Prix d'Honneur was awarded to Jochen Heddergott (West Germany) for a collection of classic Indian stamps; the Grand Prix National to "Manuela" (Italy) for Holy Land Forerunners; and the Grand Prix International to L. Kapiloff (U.S.) for U.S. postal history of 1847.

Coins and Paper Money

In October U.S. Pres. Ronald Reagan banned the importation of South African Krugerrands, the world's most widely traded gold coin. The ban was one of several economic sanctions imposed on the government of South Africa for its racial policies. Some other nations also prohibited—or considered a prohibition of—Krugerrand imports during 1985. South Africa first minted the one-ounce Krugerrand in 1967, and by 1971 it had become the dominant gold coin on international bullion markets. In 1984 the Krugerrand accounted for about two-thirds of all bullion coins sold in the world, compared with 27% for its nearest rival, the Canadian maple leaf. However, many bankers and metal dealers thought the maple leaf might emerge as the world's top seller in 1985. On December 17 President Reagan signed legislation authorizing the issuance of four U.S. bullion gold coins ($5, $10, $25, and $50) to compete with the Krugerrand. The Australian government made plans to issue a bullion gold coin during 1986.

On Oct. 18, 1985, the U.S. Mint began striking three different coins to commemorate the Statue of Liberty's centennial in 1986. Coin sales to collectors could raise as much as $137.5 million for repairs to the statue and to the old immigration facilities on nearby Ellis Island in New York Harbor.

Throughout 1985 the U.S. Treasury continued to study ways to protect paper money from would-be counterfeiters operating improved color copying machines, which were expected to be widely available later in the decade. Under serious consideration was the use of watermarks or thin metal security threads in the paper, as well as other subtle changes. The Bank of England distributed new £20 notes with a revised watermark and other changes in an effort to thwart counterfeiters. Also, the bank quit printing one-pound notes on Jan. 1, 1985, forcing British citizens to use a one-pound coin introduced in 1983. Officials said the move would lower the cost of producing money because each coin should remain in circulation for about 40 years, while the typical note lasted ten months.

Australia continued to replace its one-dollar notes with a one-dollar coin first minted in 1984, and the Canadian government studied the feasibility of making a new one-dollar coin and eliminating the one-dollar bill. In September, Canada unveiled the first two silver coins of a ten-piece set commemorating the 1988 Winter Olympics in Calgary, Alta. The Bank of Israel released into circulation new shekel notes worth 1,000 times the old notes.

Rare coin prices increased 11.5% in the 12 months ended June 1, 1985, according to a Wall Street securities firm, putting them fourth on a list of 14 investment vehicles. Nonetheless, the values of many old coins remained below the highs set during the market boom of 1979 and 1980. Two U.S. rarities brought impressive prices at a 1985 auction; one of five known 1913 Liberty nickels sold for $385,000, and an 1804 silver dollar fetched $308,000.

STOCKS AND BONDS

Stock exchanges throughout the world generally staged broad-based advances in 1985. All of the major stock price indexes except one registered gains, with many reaching new all-time highs. World commodity prices also experienced gains but remained well below their record highs set in 1980.

Stock price movements are generally determined by a mixture of economic developments and psychological factors. In 1985 the favorable conditions outweighed the negative influences. Real gross national product in most countries was modest but on the upswing. Corporate profits were rising, and consumer confidence about the outlook for world peace was generally high. Moreover, substantial surpluses existed worldwide in manufacturing capacity; wage costs were stabilizing; and new wage settlements were down significantly from the early 1980s. In an environment of relatively slow economic growth and subdued inflation, both short- and long-term interest-rate levels tended to enhance the relative attractiveness of equity securities and reduce the appeal of investing in tangible assets, such as precious metals, stamps, rare coins, and art.

The widespread bullish performance of stock prices throughout the industrialized world in 1985 was also influenced by growing economic and political conservatism and by the apparent success of the private sector in adjusting to the structural imbalances caused by the long and painful process of moving from inflation to disinflation. The adoption of policies and programs by major industrial nations to give higher priority to increasing productivity and boosting corporate profits began to bear fruit. The new entrepreneurial spirit and profit-oriented business philosophy was reflected not only in the trend toward the sale of state-owned assets, public distribution of the shares of denationalized enterprises, and increased incentives for equity investment but also in a greater willingness by the electorate and their representatives to accept relatively high unemployment in return for slow and consistent economic performance. Moreover, the extensive restructuring efforts undertaken by many companies improved earnings prospects and enhanced their competitive standings.

As 1985 drew to a close, the constant flow of positive economic and political news produced a salutary environment for equity investment. Yet the outlook for the world economy was clouded by uncertainties over potential turmoil in currency exchange markets, the mounting debt burden of third world countries, high levels of bankruptcies, rising protectionist sentiment, and the effects of the precipitous drop in selected commodity prices.

The U.S. stock market posted the most profitable year in its history in 1985. The value of common stocks rose $462 billion, with most of the gain in the final quarter. The Dow Jones Industrial Average rose irregularly during the first three quarters of the year before achieving a dramatic record-breaking spurt in the fourth quarter. From a low of 1,184.96 at the beginning of 1985, the index reached an all-time high of 1,553.10 in December. Volume on major exchanges reached record levels, with 50,-200,000,000 shares changing hands, as compared with 39,600,000,000 in 1984. The bull market also boosted trading in stock index options, while volume on individual equity options was little changed from 1984 levels. In the bond market, prices soared as interest rates on fixed-income securities dropped to their lowest levels in six years.

Investor uncertainty about economic prospects at the beginning of the year gave way to a growing perception that high interest rates and the threat of inflation were gone and, as interest rates fell, increasing numbers of investors began shifting funds into the stock market. After the September

Nomura Securities Co. of Japan, which grew to be the world's largest brokerage house partly on the strength of a 2,300-woman sales force that sold mutual funds and bonds in the home, was poised to become a major U.S. investment power, but the move from the tightly regulated Japanese financial market to Wall Street would not be simple.

HITOSHI FUGO

22 Group of Five finance ministers' meeting took action to reduce the value of the dollar, a record-breaking rally began.

The stock market rally was fueled by a growing conviction among investors that corporate profits would rise because of lower interest rates and controlled inflation. A declining dollar, growth in the money supply, takeovers, corporate buyouts and stock repurchases, steady economic growth, an improved profit outlook, falling oil prices, and an influx of Individual Retirement Account funds into the market were all bullish factors. Analysts were more cautious in their forecasts because of continuing uncertainty about the course of interest rates, high consumer debt, possible defaults on some bonds, major changes in Federal Reserve policy, and a surplus of confidence by investors.

Corporate mergers and buyouts were among the major stock market developments in 1985. RCA was acquired by General Electric Co. in a $6.2 billion deal; Beatrice Companies Inc. agreed to a leveraged buyout by Kohlberg Kravis Roberts & Co. for a similar amount; Royal Dutch Shell purchased 30.5% of Shell Oil Co. for $5.7 billion; General Foods Corp. was acquired by Philip Morris Inc. for $5.6 billion; and Hughes Aircraft was bought by General Motors Corp. for $5 billion. Texaco Inc., which attempted to intervene in a Getty Oil Co. acquisition by Pennzoil Co., was sued successfully, with Pennzoil obtaining a judgment for $11.1 billion, the largest such judgment in history.

Salomon Brothers Inc. was the leading underwriter of securities sold by U.S. issuers in 1985, with 20% of the volume. They managed more than $34 billion of underwritten public offerings by U.S. issuers worldwide. Drexel Burnham Lambert Inc. managed 56% of the "junk bonds," high-yielding bonds issued in leveraged buyouts and corporate takeovers. The total of taxable securities underwritten was $138,530,000,000, breaking the previous record of $97,280,000,000 set in 1983.

The prime rate began the year at 10.75%, fell to 10.5% in January, to 10% in May, and to 9.5% in June, its lowest level in many years. On May 20 the discount rate was cut by the Federal Reserve Board to 7.5% from 8%, the lowest since August 1978. Interest rates generally fell throughout the year with few interruptions. The consumer price index rose only 3.5%, down from 4.3% in 1984. The unemployment rate declined from 7.5% in 1984 to 7.1% in 1985. The dollar dropped 18.5% for 1985 against all major world currencies, its lowest level in 2½ years. Real economic growth, as measured by gross national product, was the slowest since 1982 according to the U.S. Department of Commerce.

Volume on the New York Stock Exchange (NYSE) rose 19% in 1985, with a turnover of 27,510,706,353 shares, as compared with 23,071,-031,447 a year earlier. The number of stock issues traded was 2,332 in 1985, slightly less than the comparable figure of 2,351 in 1984. A survey estimated the number of Americans owning stock at 47 million, up 12% from 1983. Most of the growth was among stock mutual funds, which accounted for 30.3% of the total number of shareholders in 1985. Bond sales totaled $9,046,453,000 in 1985, a rise of 30% from the $6,982,291,000 achieved in 1984.

The NYSE averaged close to 115 million shares a day traded in 1985, up from 92 million in 1984. Among industry groups the best performers in 1985 were savings and loans, up 859% in earnings; oil service companies, up 188%; leisure-time, up 90%; real estate, up 70%; and drugs, up 59%. The worst performers were electronics, down 29%; automotive products, down 21%; general machinery, down 18%; and conglomerates, down 16%. A study group was set up in June to examine the creation of a common trading system that could lead to broad trading ties with the London Stock Exchange.

Turnover on the American Stock Exchange (Amex) totaled 2,100,860,000 shares in 1985, up 36% from the 1984 figure of 1,545,010,000 shares. Daily volume on the Amex averaged a record 8.3 million shares, compared with 6.1 million shares in 1984. The number of traded issues rose from 924 in 1984 to 936 in 1985, with 74 new companies being listed for a total of 941. Bond trading on the Amex rose to $645,182,000 in 1985, an increase of 73% over the prior-year figure of $371,990,000. Options trading volume totaled 45 million contracts in 1985, compared with 40 million in 1984 and as few as 3.5 million in 1975. In September the Amex became the first exchange to open two-way trading with a foreign market when it linked up with the Toronto Stock Exchange. Volume on the Midwest Exchange rose 27% for the year, while the Pacific Stock Exchange boosted its volume by 35% to a level of 1,361,368,015 shares traded.

Mutual fund sales in 1985 totaled $110.5 billion, compared with the previous record of $45.9 billion in 1984. Sales were bolstered by the rising stock market as well as by keen investor interest in high-yielding funds. Total assets of mutual funds in 1985 were $495 billion, a 34% increase over the $370,-680,000,000 in 1984. The return on mutual funds was 27.45%, compared with 4.88% in 1984.

The Standard & Poor's Index of 500 stocks climbed 26.3% in 1985, with a total return of 31.57%, compared with 6.10% in 1984. The high for the year was 212.02 and the low 163.68. During January the average jumped from the 1984 year-end level of 164.48 to 171.61; it then moved to 180.88 in February, slid briefly in March, and moved ahead in April to 180.62, peaking by July at 192.54 (Table I). Stock price averages gained across the board, with the industrials leading the other stock groups with a rise of 25.86%. The average price-earnings ratio on the S & P 500 was 13.69 at mid-December, compared with 10.09 a year earlier.

While short-term interest rates were stable in 1985, with three-month Treasury bills trading between 7% and 7.3% and Federal Funds trading within a narrow range of 8%, the Treasury bond yield on 30-year bonds dropped from 11.7% in January to 9.5% by year-end. U.S. government long-term bond yields (Table II) in 1985 were well below the levels of 1984. From 11.15% in January they rose to 11.78% in March, drifted lower to 10.36% in June, and then remained in a narrow range before declining below 10% in December. Bond yields on the long-term Treasury issues fell to a six-year low of 9.3% in 1985.

The year was also a record one for corporate bond issues. Volume rose $96 billion. Yields on most taxable bonds were at the lowest levels since 1979, with many medium-term issues falling below the 10% barrier. From a level of 12.08% in January 1985, the yield on U.S. corporate bonds rose to 12.56% in March before beginning its irregular decline to 10.94% in June; after a rise to 11.07% in September (Table III), the index fell in the last quarter of the year.

The options and futures markets were volatile in 1985. The year's most popular futures were in Treasury bonds traded on the Chicago Board of Trade, where the average daily volume of 154,-592 contracts represented a rise of 29% over 1984. The year's most popular options were Standard & Poor's 100 traded on the Chicago Board Options Exchange, with an average daily volume of 347,791 contracts for a gain of 30% over 1984. Seat prices on most U.S. commodity exchanges fell during 1985 because of competition from the stock market and a glut of failures and consolidations among futures brokerage firms.

The securities industry recorded its second best year in earnings, with $3.5 billion in pretax profits, because of rising stock prices and falling interest rates. Fees from corporate takeovers contributed at least $425 million of the total.

Traders crowd the floor of the New York Stock Exchange on December 11 as the Dow Jones industrial average closed for the first time above 1,500. Analysts said that the market benefited from a continuing drop in open-market interest rates.

AP/WIDE WORLD

Table I. U.S. Stock Market Prices

Month	Railroads (6 stocks) 1985	Railroads (6 stocks) 1984	Industrials (400 stocks) 1985	Industrials (400 stocks) 1984	Public utilities (40 stocks) 1985	Public utilities (40 stocks) 1984	Composite (500 stocks) 1985	Composite (500 stocks) 1984
January	111.65	112.90	191.64	187.50	75.83	68.50	171.61	166.39
February	120.18	102.29	202.13	177.14	78.14	66.25	180.88	157.25
March	114.15	103.41	200.42	177.85	78.89	65.25	179.42	157.44
April	113.56	103.58	201.13	178.57	81.25	64.34	180.62	157.60
May	117.19	100.93	204.83	177.60	83.60	64.94	184.90	156.55
June	121.48	94.36	208.50	174.20	86.90	64.00	188.89	153.12
July	130.00	90.53	212.90	171.70	87.22	64.66	192.54	151.08
August	125.85	100.83	209.40	186.86	83.21	68.11	188.31	164.42
September	123.58	103.03	205.15	188.10	81.46	69.71	184.06	166.11
October	...	101.35	...	185.44	...	72.02	...	164.82
November	...	101.47	...	186.57	...	73.58	...	166.27
December	...	102.16	...	183.62	...	74.43	...	164.48

Sources: U.S. Department of Commerce, *Survey of Current Business*; Board of Governors of the Federal Reserve System, *Federal Reserve Bulletin*. Prices are Standard & Poor's monthly averages of daily closing prices, with 1941–43 = 10.

Table II. U.S. Government Long-Term Bond Yields

Month	Yield (%) 1985	Yield (%) 1984	Month	Yield (%) 1985	Yield (%) 1984
January	11.15	11.29	July	10.51	12.82
February	11.35	11.44	August	10.59	12.23
March	11.78	11.90	September	10.67	11.97
April	11.42	12.17	October	...	11.66
May	10.96	12.89	November	...	11.25
June	10.36	13.00	December	...	11.21

Source: U.S. Department of Commerce, *Survey of Current Business*. Yields are for U.S. Treasury bonds that are taxable and due or callable in ten years or more.

Table III. U.S. Corporate Bond Yields

Month	Yield (%) 1985	Yield (%) 1984	Month	Yield (%) 1985	Yield (%) 1984
January	12.08	12.20	July	10.97	13.44
February	12.13	12.08	August	11.05	12.87
March	12.56	12.57	September	11.07	12.66
April	12.23	12.81	October	...	12.63
May	11.72	13.28	November	...	12.29
June	10.94	13.55	December	...	12.57

Source: U.S. Department of Commerce, *Survey of Current Business*. Yields are based on Moody's Aaa domestic corporate bond index.

The Securities and Exchange Commission stepped up its inspection of financial advisers and investment companies in 1985 with a well-publicized campaign against insider trading and financial fraud. A major development was the decision by the SEC to extend its regulatory scope over the stock-brokerage activities of approximately 2,000 banks. The SEC took the position that the stock-brokerage activities of banks should be subject to the same rules as any brokerage firm.

SWEDEN

General elections held in Sweden on Sept. 15, 1985, resulted in the widely predicted return to power of Prime Minister Olof Palme's Social Democratic Party government for another three-year term. Less predictable were the narrow margin of the Socialist victory and the sudden reemergence of the Liberals as a force to be reckoned with. The Social Democrats won 159 seats in the Riksdag (parliament). However, in losing seven seats they no longer commanded a majority over the combined forces of the three non-Socialist parties (the Conservative, Center, and Liberal parties) and were forced to rely on the Communists, who won 19 seats, for support.

AP/WIDE WORLD

Sweden's Liberal Party leader Bengt Westerberg, who more than doubled the share of votes for his party in the general election, signals victory on election night.

Every party lost support except the Liberals, who, under their new leader, Bengt Westerberg, won 51 seats, a gain of 30. Westerberg's rapidly rising star eclipsed the two other non-Socialist leaders. The Conservatives, under Ulf Adelsohn, won 76 seats, a loss of 10, while the Center Party, led by former prime minister Thorbjörn Fälldin, won 44, a loss of 12.

Palme had also suffered a partial eclipse and was clearly irked. He described the election as "an enormous victory," declared that reliance on Communist support was nothing new for his party. Communist leader Lars Werner was in the Eurocommunist mold, having denounced the Soviets for alleged incursions by their submarines into Swedish territorial waters and for their involvement in Afghanistan. However, he declared that his party would seek to move the Social Democratic Party's policies further to the left.

The election indicated that, while the average Swede feared the erosion of the welfare state, the Social Democrats were unlikely to see a return to the days before 1976 when for 44 years their election victories had been virtually automatic. An echo of those days was sounded earlier in the year when more than 50,000 people paraded through the streets of Stockholm to pay tribute to the memory of Tage Erlander, prime minister during 1946–69, who died on June 21.

At the beginning of May some 20,000 public-sector employees, including air-traffic controllers, customs officials, and postal workers, began one of the most disruptive labor disputes in Sweden's post-World War II history. Air traffic came to a halt, and the land borders were virtually closed to imports. A compromise agreement on wage increases was reached on May 20 following secret meetings between Palme and trade-union leaders.

A speech to Sweden's Young Socialists during which Palme criticized U.S. policies in Central America brought a strong reaction from the U.S.

State Department, which labeled the speech "one-sided and provocative." Palme was more cautious in his conduct of domestic affairs. The economy experienced moderate expansion, while unemployment remained steady at around 3%.

SWIMMING

The first world record of 1985 was established in the annual dual meet between the Soviet Union and East Germany at Erfurt, East Germany. There on March 3 Igor Polianski of the Soviet Union lowered the 200-m backstroke record to 1 min 58.14 sec. At the East German national championship competition in June at Leipzig, Silke Hoerner lowered the world-record 200-m breaststroke to 2 min 28.33 sec. This was the only world record set by women in 1985.

West Germany's Michael Gross, winner of two gold medals in world-record time at the 1984 Olympics, shaved 0.52 sec off the world mark to 3 min 47.80 sec in the 400-m freestyle at the West German championships at Remscheid on June 27. Two days later he regained the 200-m butterfly world record, slicing 0.03 sec from the old mark for a time of 1 min 57.01 sec. On August 10 in the XVII European Championships at Sofia, Bulg., Gross again lowered the 200-m butterfly mark by 0.36 sec with a time of 1 min 56.65 sec, thereby equaling Mark Spitz's feat of holding four world records at the same time.

Matt Biondi, a junior at the University of California, in only his third year of major swimming competition, lowered the 100-m freestyle world record of 49.36 sec set by Olympic champion Rowdy Gaines in 1981. Biondi's 49.24 sec was set in a preliminary of the 1985 U.S. swimming long course championships at Mission Viejo, Calif., August 6. In the final Biondi set a new record of 48.95 sec. With the exception of Biondi's outstanding performance, lackluster swims were the rule in almost every male event in the U.S. championships. In the women's competition this was even more evident. Mary T. Meagher, an Olympic champion, was the only woman to have a better time than the Germans, achieving this in the butterfly. Mark Schubert coached his Mission Viejo Nadadores to the women's team and combined team championships, making him the most successful coach in U.S. swim history.

Two world records were set by the U.S. men's national team in the Pan Pacific meet, held in August at Tokyo. On August 17 the quartet of Scott McCadam, Mike Heath, Paul Wallace, and Biondi were timed at 3 min 17.08 sec for the 4 × 100-m freestyle relay, taking nearly two seconds off the previous mark set in 1984. A day later the team of Rick Carey, John Moffet, Pablo Morales, and Biondi took 1.02 seconds off the 4 × 100-m medley relay with a time of 3 min 38.28 sec.

The XVII European Championships, held at Sofia in August, was marked by the absence of So-

viet champion Vladimir Salnikov, holder of three world records. East Germany dominated the women's events, winning 14 out of 15. However, it was the first time since 1977 that East Germany had lost a gold medal, as Bulgaria's Tania Bogomilova won the 200-m breaststroke. Heike Friedrich was the outstanding competitor at the meet, winning the 100-m and 200-m freestyle events and swimming on three winning relays. The East German women also won ten silver and three bronze medals.

In the men's European competition, Igor Polianski of the U.S.S.R. won both the 100-m and 200-m backstroke races, setting a European record of 55.24 sec for the shorter event. Michael Gross was the outstanding male competitor, winning six gold medals: the 200-m freestyle, 100-m and 200-m butterfly, and three relays. This effort contributed to West Germany's medal count of six gold, two silver, and three bronze. East Germany was runner-up with two gold, six silver, and two bronze medals. For the first time since 1970 France won a gold medal as Stephan Caron took the 100-m freestyle.

At the Pan Pacific meet, out of 16 events U.S. men won 12 gold, 6 silver, and 5 bronze medals, outdistancing Australia with 2 gold, 5 silver, and 5 bronze. Matt Biondi paced the Americans with five gold medals, one silver, and one bronze, winning the 50-m and 100-m freestyle and anchoring three winning relays. The U.S. women surpassed the men, winning 13 gold, 8 silver, and 4 bronze medals. Canada was their nearest rival, with two gold, one silver, and five bronze. Olympic 100-m champion Carrie Steinseifer of the U.S. was the outstanding female, winning a gold medal in the 200-m freestyle, a silver in the 100-m freestyle, and golds in two relays. A U.S. record was set in the 4 × 200-m freestyle relay as Mary Wayte, Trina Radke, Laura Walker, and Steinseifer were timed in 8 min 6.74 sec, taking 0.57 second off the previous time.

Diving

The Federation Internationale de Natation Amateur (FINA), the world governing organization for amateur aquatics, conducted the IV World Cup diving championships, held in April at Shanghai. The event attracted 67 divers representing 14 nations, competing as teams and in individual events.

Michael Gross of West Germany strokes to a victory and a new world record in the 200-meter butterfly at the West German championship meet in Remscheid in June.
AP/WIDE WORLD

AP/WIDE WORLD

Matt Biondi of California wins the 100-meter freestyle event in the Pan Pacific championship in Tokyo on August 16, finishing the race in 49.17 seconds.

The overall team trophy was captured by the host nation, China, with a total of 4,334.07 points. The Soviet Union was second, and the United States finished third. The women's team trophy and men's team trophy were each won by China, followed by the U.S.S.R. and the U.S. In the women's 3-m springboard the winner was Li Yihua of China, followed by teammate Li Qiaoxian. Brita Baldus of East Germany finished third. Michele Mitchell of the U.S. defeated Chen Xiaoxia of China to win the platform competition; Alla Lobankina of the U.S.S.R. was third. In the men's 3-m springboard Tan Liangde of China defeated Mark Bradshaw of the U.S., with Ron Meyer of the U.S. third. Tong Hui of China won the platform over Viacheslav Troshin of the U.S.S.R., giving China three of the four gold medals. Third place in the platform went to Li Kongzheng of China.

At the McDonald's International Diving Invitational, at Fort Lauderdale, Fla., in May, Li Yihua again won the women's 3-m springboard event, followed by the U.S. pair of Kelly McCormick and Michele Mitchell. Mitchell won the platform,

upsetting Chen Xiaoxia, with Veronica Ribot of Argentina third. Tan Liangde won the men's 3-m springboard, outpointing Niki Stajkovic of Austria and Ron Meyer. Li Kongzheng defeated Tong Hui in the platform with Bruce Kimball of the U.S. placing third.

Following the McDonald's meet, the U.S. defeated China in a dual competition at Orlando, Fla., in May. McCormick and Mitchell won the women's 3-m springboard and platform, respectively. Tan Liangde and Li Kongzheng won the men's 3-m springboard and platform for China.

At Clayton, Mo., in August at the U.S. outdoor diving championships, McCormick won the 3-m springboard and Mitchell the platform. Greg Louganis, who sat out the international tournaments because of a shoulder injury, continued his unbeaten season by winning both the 3-m springboard and platform.

The Soviet Union won three of the four European contests. Zhanna Tsirulnikova won the women's 3-m springboard, followed by teammate Irina Sidorava, with Heidemarie Grecka of Czechoslovakia third. Anjela Stasyulevi of the U.S.S.R. outpointed Ramona Patow-Wenzel of East Germany for a Soviet victory in the women's platform. Alla Lobankina of the U.S.S.R. placed third. In men's diving Nikolai Drozhzhin of the U.S.S.R. won the 3-m springboard, with Bulgaria's Peter Georgiev and West Germany's Dieter Doerr placing second and third. Thomas Knuths of East Germany prevented a Soviet sweep by diving off the platform with enough consistency to outpoint the runners-up, Albin Killat of West Germany and Domenico Rinaldi of Italy.

Synchronized Swimming

At the U.S. championships, held in Fort Lauderdale, Fla., from June 30 to July 7, Sarah Josephson of Ohio State University won the solo event. Mary Visniski of Walnut Creek, Calif., barely outpointed Karen Josephson of Ohio State University for the silver medal. The Josephson sisters won the duet title, followed by Kristen Babb and Michelle Svitenko of Walnut Creek, Calif. Alice and Margarita Smith of the University of Arizona were third. Walnut Creek won the team crown with 138.679 points, followed by Ohio State with 137.541 and Santa Clara, Calif., with 135.872.

In the II FINA World Cup at Indianapolis, Ind., in August, Canada swept all three titles; Carolyn Waldo of Montreal was almost perfect in her solo routine, receiving five scores of 9.9 out of a possible 10; after winning that title she then paired with Michelle Cameron to win the duet. Canada edged the United States for the team victory, with Japan third. Winners at the European championships were Carolyn Wilson of Great Britain in solo competition, Alexandra Worisch and Eva-Marie Edinger of Austria in the duet, and France as the team champion.

World Swimming Records Set in 1985

Event	Name	Country	Time
MEN			
100-m freestyle	Matt Biondi	U.S.	49.24 sec
100-m freestyle	Matt Biondi	U.S.	48.95 sec
400-m freestyle	Michael Gross	F.R.G.[1]	3 min 47.80 sec
200-m backstroke	Igor Polianski	U.S.S.R.	1 min 58.14 sec
200-m butterfly	Michael Gross	F.R.G.	1 min 57.01 sec
200-m butterfly	Michael Gross	F.R.G.	1 min 56.65 sec
4 × 100-m freestyle relay	U.S. national team (Scott McCadam, Mike Heath, Paul Wallace, Matt Biondi)	U.S.	3 min 17.08 sec
4 × 100-m medley relay	U.S. national team (Rick Carey, John Moffet, Pablo Morales, Matt Biondi)	U.S.	3 min 38.28 sec
WOMEN			
200-m breaststroke	Silke Hoerner	G.D.R.[2]	2 min 28.33 sec

[1]Federal Republic of Germany (West Germany).
[2]German Democratic Republic (East Germany).

As preparations for the summit meeting between U.S. Pres. Ronald Reagan and Soviet leader Mikhail Gorbachev were completed, some 10,000 advocates of peace and other causes marched quietly through the streets of Geneva.

GAMMA/LIAISON

SWITZERLAND

Switzerland experienced another year of political, economic, and social stability in 1985. Political affairs were dominated by a proposal to revise the constitution. The existing constitution, dating from 1848 and revised for the first time in 1974, was a bewildering mixture of basic principles and detailed amendments on a wide range of matters that in other countries were left to legislative procedure. A draft revision submitted in 1977 had met with considerable opposition from those who favored increased powers at the cantonal level and supporters of free enterprise. Toward the end of 1985 Elisabeth Kopp, minister at the Department of Justice and Police, submitted for parliamentary discussion a report incorporating a revised version of the earlier draft and two other proposed models for revision. Public reaction reflected the view that the existing constitution worked, despite its drawbacks, and that there were far more urgent problems to be tackled. In December Parliament elected Minister of the Interior Alphons Egli, a Christian Democrat, to serve as president for 1986.

Kopp's department was at the center of controversy surrounding refugees from third world countries. The granting of asylum to persons whose lives were endangered by political persecution in their own countries, on condition that they did not threaten Switzerland's security or public order, was a sacrosanct principle of Swiss tradition and constitutional practice. At first Kopp allowed a liberal interpretation of these laws. However, she changed her approach rapidly and without hesitation when it was discovered that numerous refugees had sought asylum on the basis of insufficient or fraudulent information and documents.

Gross domestic product appeared set to maintain a modest growth rate of about 2%, while the inflation rate remained unchanged at about 3%. Unemployment did not exceed the comparatively moderate proportions of the previous few years, although the watch and precision-instrument manufacturing industries were still experiencing serious difficulties in adapting to pressure from foreign competition.

A subtle but significant change appeared to be under way in the conception and application of Switzerland's time-honored principle of neutrality. This conclusion could be drawn from the unprecedented appearance at the UN of a highly placed Swiss diplomat, Edouard Brunner, who accepted an invitation to address the UN during its 40th anniversary celebrations in October. His speech contained a lucid statement of Switzerland's combination of neutrality and increasingly intense participation in the international scene, a practice that was proving useful to the international community as a whole. A plebiscite on Switzerland's proposed accession to full membership in the UN was to take place in 1986.

SYRIA

On Feb. 11, 1985, Gen. Hafez al-Assad won a third seven-year term as president of Syria when he secured 99.97% of the votes cast in a national referendum in which 99.38% of eligible voters took part, according to official figures. At the ruling Ba'ath Party congress in January, the first in five years, Assad was endorsed by the party as secretary-general. Five members of the party's 21-member Regional Command were replaced at the 16-day congress; President Assad's younger brother, Rifaat al-Assad, previously thought to be in disgrace, was reappointed to both the Regional Command and the 90-member Central Committee. President Assad's position was considered to have been greatly enhanced by his show of strength at the congress, coming as it did after a period during which he had reportedly suffered from poor health. A revised government list revealed on April 8 contained few significant changes apart from a reshuffle of economic portfolios.

Syria made its most determined effort since its army intervened in Lebanon in 1976 to bring about a settlement between the warring Christian and Muslim factions in that divided country. On December 28 an agreement was signed by leaders of Christian, Shi'ite, and Druze militia following talks chaired by Syrian Vice-Pres. 'Abd al-Halim Khaddam. The agreement called for a gradual phasing out of the built-in Christian majority in Lebanon's Chamber of Deputies (parliament). In early October the Syrian Army took control of the northern Lebanese port of Tripoli following three weeks of fighting between Muslim fundamentalists and Syrian-backed leftist militia. Syria was widely believed to have been behind Shi'ite attacks on Palestinian refugee camps in Lebanon that followed the withdrawal of the Israeli Army. Syria firmly denied the charge, blaming the violence at the camps in May and June on the Palestine Liberation Organization (PLO). Damascus was opposed to the efforts of PLO chairman Yasir Arafat and King Hussein of Jordan to revive peace negotiations with Israel, though at the same time there was a marked improvement in relations between Syria and Jordan. The meeting between Hussein and Assad in Damascus on December 30 was the first in six years.

Syria's radical stance in Arab and Middle Eastern affairs continued to be reflected in support for Iran in the Gulf war, opposition to any rapprochement with Israel, and close friendship with the U.S.S.R. and other Soviet-bloc countries. Assad refused to attend the emergency Arab summit called by King Hassan II of Morocco in August because, in Damascus's view, the summit was designed to justify the Jordanian-Palestinian peace moves. Assad visited Moscow on June 19–22 for talks with Soviet leader Mikhail Gorbachev. In May Syria signed an economic and technical cooperation agreement with the U.S.S.R., and in September a separate agreement covering Soviet aid for petroleum exploration was concluded. Expectations of petroleum production from the recently discovered field in the Deir az-Zor region were revised downward to some 50,000 bbl a day. Total crude petroleum production

stood at around 170,000 bbl a day, while 200,000 bbl a day were imported for use in local refineries. Most of the imports were supplied by Iran at concessionary rates in return for Syria's decision to deny Iraq the right to export its crude petroleum through Syrian territory.

Syria received assurances from Kuwait that it intended to honor its aid obligations, despite a vote to the contrary in the Kuwait National Assembly. In 1985 Syria was scheduled to receive $186 million from Kuwait. The 1985 budget, passed by the People's Council in June, reflected the government's commitment to tight control over public spending. Defense spending accounted for more than 50% of current expenditure, while the investment budget gave priority to the agricultural sector.

TAIWAN

The year 1985 proved to be a trying one for leaders on Taiwan. Economic uncertainties combined with mounting concern about the political succession to Pres. Chiang Ching-kuo, 75 years old and in questionable health. The increasing presence of China on the world scene accentuated Taiwan's growing diplomatic isolation. Officials in Taipei continued to resist pressures from the government in China to reach a political accommodation, regarding China's overtures as a subterfuge for Taiwan's eventual incorporation under Communist control. But trade tensions with the United States also clouded the island's position and long-term prospects, a fact underscored by the U.S. government's repeated denials of Taiwan's requests for new, advanced military hardware.

Some of the 39 U.S. citizens who had been held by hijackers in Beirut held a press conference in Damascus after their release in June. Syrian Pres. Hafez al-Assad had played a key role in obtaining their release.

FRANK VIELJEUX—SYGMA

Two alleged Taiwan gangsters were charged with the murder of Henry Liu, a California writer who was critical of the Taipei government.

The behavior of Taipei's internal security apparatus also proved highly vexing at home and abroad. A court found the former head of Taiwan's intelligence forces guilty of involvement in the late 1984 murder in California of Henry Liu, a Chinese-American writer who had written a highly critical book about Chiang Ching-kuo and his family. During a September visit to the island, a Taiwan publisher, now residing in the U.S., was arrested for allegedly distributing propaganda from the Chinese mainland, charges that she denied following her release on lesser charges. These activities prompted protests from the U.S. Department of State and the Congress and suggested erosion in U.S. political support for Taiwan, a crucial factor in maintaining the island's viability.

Major economic uncertainties were also of great concern to the leadership. Protectionist sentiment and reduced external demand for Taiwan's products slowed economic growth from a robust 11% in 1984 to less than 5% in 1985. Taiwan was also under mounting pressure to open its markets much more fully to U.S. goods and services in the expectation that such steps would reduce a trade surplus with the United States that exceeded $10 billion in 1984. However, the small size of the domestic market precluded the possibility that increased internal demand could compensate fully for lost sales abroad. Business failures increased substantially, especially among firms already heavily in debt.

To counteract these trends and the continuing flight of capital, the government announced plans to spend approximately $20 billion for 14 major construction projects between 1985 and 1991. But this commitment to key projects was not expected to settle the uncertain economic outlook in the immediate future.

Despite these setbacks and the generally low morale among senior officials, the ruling Kuomintang (Nationalist Party) demonstrated continued political strength in November elections for local and provincial government offices, garnering nearly 70% of the vote. However, in more politically active Taipei the 11 opposition candidates all won handily, reflecting the growing vigor and assertiveness of nonparty politicians. Nor did the Kuomintang's electoral successes obscure the potential crisis associated with the impending succession to Chiang Ching-kuo. Although 62-year-old Vice-Pres. Lee Teng-hui (a Taiwan native and U.S.-trained agronomist) seemed a logical successor to some observers, others doubted that the former mainlanders, who had long been dominant within the Kuomintang, would permit it.

Underlying these domestic uncertainties was the challenge posed by the growing power of China. In the spring the government publicly acknowledged the existence of an increasingly robust trade (estimated as high as $1 billion) between China and Taiwan, which authorities in Taipei no longer actively curtailed. In late November Taiwan received a major setback when the Asian Development Bank announced plans to admit China to full membership.

TANZANIA

On Nov. 5, 1985, Julius Nyerere, who had led the country since independence, resigned as president of Tanzania and handed over the office to his elected successor. As chairman of the sole party, Chama Cha Mapinduzi (CCM), a post that he planned to retain until 1987, Nyerere would continue to exert considerable influence over Tanzanian affairs.

At a special congress of the CCM in August, Ali Hassan Mwinyi was chosen ahead of Prime Minister Salim Ahmed Salim and Rashidi Kawawa, the CCM general secretary, as sole candidate to succeed Nyerere. He received the endorsement of the electorate in presidential elections on October 27. Elections to the National Assembly took place on the same day. Mwinyi, who had taken over the joint offices of Tanzanian vice-president and president of Zanzibar following the resignation of Aboud Jumbe in early 1984, had achieved considerable success in improving Zanzibar's economy and handling its potentially delicate relations with the mainland.

As president of Tanzania, Mwinyi inherited a unified country with no organized opposition but with serious economic problems that provided a possible breeding ground for discontent. Not least among them was the shortage of food. Potentially capable of supplying all its own food requirements, Tanzania was forced to use some of its meager foreign-exchange reserves to pay for imported maize (corn). At the same time, the fall in prices offered for its main cash crops (sisal, cotton, and cashew nuts) reduced reserves still further. Nyerere had consistently refused to accept aid from the International Monetary Fund (IMF) because he rejected the conditions imposed by that organization.

Nyerere felt impelled by circumstances to permit some relaxation of his principles. He ordered the sisal industry, nationalized in 1967, returned to private ownership because state control had proved unsuccessful. Controls on imports were relaxed to a limited extent to reduce public discontent, while private enterprise was allowed to take over certain areas of business. However, Nyerere insisted that the government would continue to control the most important sectors of the economy. On taking office, President Mwinyi promised to adhere to the program of socialism and self-reliance drawn up by his predecessor in his Arusha Declaration of 1967. However, the steadily worsening balance of payments deficit, coupled with rising inflation, rendered the need for an accommodation with the IMF increasingly urgent.

Addressing the Southern African Development Coordination Conference summit in August, Nyerere attacked the U.S., the U.K., and West Germany for their failure to impose economic sanctions on South Africa. He urged African nations to mount a trade boycott against South Africa, while stressing that such action would invite retaliation that could have a serious effect on the countries concerned.

TELECOMMUNICATIONS

In 1985 both telecommunications developers and users had a mixed year. The makers of the equipment that transmits voice and data around the world enjoyed some successes, such as the slow but continuing evolution of the International Telegraph and Telephone Consultative Committee's integrated services digital network (ISDN). And they enjoyed the further advances in the wide-bandwidth fiber-optics technology. Cellular telephony also continued to grow.

On the other hand, insurance firms balked at backing communications satellites that seemed to have more than their fair share of launch aborts, and local network technology was further saddled with a host of offerings that left buyers confused as to which system to purchase. Indeed, users continued to be confused by a variety of new offerings for their every voice and data telecommunications need. These were not always dependable; for example, private branch exchange manufacturers went in and out of business as they attempted the complex job of simultaneously handling voice and data. Adding to the problems, government and standards agencies had the most influence in determining who built what equipment and what services consumers would have from which organizations.

In the long run ISDN would replace the still mostly analog worldwide telecommunications net-

FRED PROUSER

Bell Telephone Co. of Pennsylvania began a trial using telephones that display the phone numbers from which incoming calls originate, allowing subscribers to decline to receive unwanted calls.

work with a digital technology-based network that would provide voice, television, videotext, data, and a host of other telecommunications services to users in a home, office, and factory world that would be wired together. Necessary to the success of this idea was that users would control their ISDN interface and select the services they needed from a catalog of offerings. While some circuits were designed and some products were made available in 1985, the massive undertaking was expected to require additional years of development.

A bright spot on the local network scene was the rapid progress of the factory network standard known as manufacturing automation protocol (MAP). Unique in that it was a network standard promoted by communications and computer equipment users rather than by manufacturers, MAP was enjoying rapid development. One reason for the rapid pace was the economic strength of its main backers, such as General Motors Corp.

MAP was based on the International Standards Organization's work in defining how computers should communicate in both local and global networks. ISO's standards for software and hardware to allow easy communication enjoyed success in 1985. For example, several major communications and computer firms in the U.S. and Europe announced that their products would be ISO-compatible by late 1985 or 1986.

U.S. telecommunications users continued to suffer with AT&T as that firm endured its second year as a deregulated activity. Continued layoffs plagued AT&T as it persisted in its attempts to enter the computer industry and strengthen its position in the telecommunications industry with the introduction of several new products. Also using its great strength in telecommunications, the firm made new local network and service offerings in such fields as teleconferencing and videotext. AT&T also continued to lead in the use of fiber-optic technology in both local and global networks, although Japanese firms were a close second if not equal. The goal of this work was to adapt the hair-thin glass fibers to ever more uses in transmitting telecommunication signals with minimal attenuation and, compared with any other technology, with a maximum number of different signals on one cable. Both the U.S. and Japan were also active in using new kinds of single-mode fiber that introduced less distortion to the signals being transmitted.

Fiber was so cost-effective that it could compete with satellites for transatlantic telecommunications coverage. And in 1985 the possibility of laying fiber cable under the ocean rather than launching communications satellites by rocket or space shuttle got a boost when several such satellites were lost, causing insurance carriers to raise their premium rates and thereby introducing a major new cost factor into satellite communications. Even the comparatively inexpensive Ariane rocket used in Europe for launches suffered failures and financial reverses.

TELEVISION AND RADIO

Some form of radio and television service was available in all major countries in 1985. Approximately 980 million radio sets were in use throughout the world, including 554 million, 56% of the total, in the United States. There were about 475 million television sets, of which approximately 175 million, or 37%, were in the U.S. The Soviet Union, with 75 million, or 16%, ranked second, and Japan was third with 30.2 million, or 6.4%, according to estimates published in the 1985 *Broadcasting/Cablecasting Yearbook*. Other *Broadcasting* estimates of television sets by country included West Germany, 21.8 million; Brazil, 21.4 million; France, 19 million; United Kingdom, 18.6 million; Italy, 13.6 million; Canada, 12.4 million; Spain, 11.6 million; China, 9.7 million; Poland, 8.2 million; Mexico, 7.6 million; Australia, 6.5 million; The Netherlands, 6.2 million; Argentina, 5.9 million; East Germany, 5.8 million; Yugoslavia, 4.4 million; Czechoslovakia, 4.3 million; Egypt, 3.9 million; Turkey, 3.6 million;

Saudi Arabia, 3.5 million; and Sweden, 3.2 million.

Television stations on the air or under construction throughout the world numbered approximately 8,300. About 2,200 were in the Far East, 2,110 in Western Europe, 1,492 in the U.S., 920 in Eastern Europe, 180 in South America, 105 in Mexico, 100 in Canada, and 50 in Africa. There were about 18,000 radio stations, most of which employed the amplitude-modulation (AM) system of transmission, but the number of frequency-modulation (FM) stations was growing. In the U.S. there were about 10,610 radio stations, of which 5,641 (53%) were FM.

Organization of Services

In the U.S. Pres. Ronald Reagan's deregulation policies continued to ease restrictions on broadcasters and cable operators, but by 1985 much had already been done and further opportunities were diminishing. The regulatory body, the Federal Communications Commission (FCC), found one major opportunity for deregulation but could not take action on it. Finishing a proceeding that it originated the year before, the FCC in August concluded that the so-called fairness doctrine—a long-established policy that required a station to present all sides of important controversial issues if it presented any side—was contrary to the public interest, inhibiting rather than encouraging the presentation of public issues, as it had been intended to do. But the doctrine had been approved by the U.S. Supreme Court in a 1969 decision, and the commission therefore would continue to enforce it.

What might prove to be the most significant deregulatory move of the year came not from the FCC but from a U.S. appeals court in Washington, D.C. To the delight of cable operators and the consternation of broadcasters, the court ruled in July that the FCC's "must-carry" rules, which for 20 years had required local cable systems to include the programming of local TV stations on their cable channels, were too broad to meet the requirements

The rapid proliferation of satellite-dish television antennas for private use—about 1.2 million of them had been installed in the U.S. so far—prompted some 700 exhibitors to show their wares at an industry convention in Nashville, Tennessee, in September.

STEVE HARBISON/TIME MAGAZINE

One of the bright spots in network television programming in 1985 was the return of Mary Tyler Moore in a comedy series, simply called "Mary." The show also featured John Astin.
CBS

of the First Amendment to the Constitution. Many cable operators had long wanted to be free of the rules, which they said deprived them of channels they wanted to devote to other programs, while broadcasters insisted that the rules were essential to them in maintaining the availability of local broadcast service to cable subscribers as well as nonsubscribers. The court's decision left the way open for the FCC to try to redraft the rules, but many commission officials doubted that the commission could do it in a way that would meet the court's criteria. The FCC at first said that it would not appeal the court's decision, but later, under pressure from broadcasters and a number of congressmen, it said that it would call a hearing to see what might be done and would welcome proposals. Broadcasters, in the meantime, opened a campaign to repeal or modify the compulsory license under which cable companies gained access to broadcasting and other programs in return for a modest fee, and at the end of November the National Cable Television Association tentatively empowered its officers to talk with broadcasters about the possibility of finding a "mutually tolerable" alternative to the must-carry rules.

The financial structure of some of broadcasting's oldest, biggest, and most prestigious companies underwent basic changes in 1985, a year marked by takeovers and mergers. The American Broadcasting Cos., owner of the ABC-TV network, a variety of radio networks, television stations in five of the largest U.S. markets, and 12 important radio stations, agreed to be acquired by the much smaller but prestigious Capital Cities Communications, a major broadcaster, publisher, and cable TV operator, in a cash-and-stock transaction valued at $3.5 billion. The first transfer of a network's ownership since ABC itself was formed more than 30 years earlier, the transaction was approved by the FCC in November on condition, as expected, that the merged company dispose of enough stations and

other interests to bring it into compliance with the FCC's various multiple-ownership rules.

The ABC-Capital Cities deal, impressing investors with the value of broadcasting stocks, was one of many takeovers, attempted takeovers, bidding wars, and straightforward acquisitions undertaken during the year. CBS, a broadcasting leader since its formation in the late 1920s, finally succeeded in fighting off a takeover bid by the relatively small Turner Broadcasting System, but only at the expense of more than $1 billion in debt (from buying up 21% of its own stock); this led to the sale of several of its major nonbroadcasting properties, disposal of the limited cable TV interests that it owned, a commitment to reduce 1987 expenses by 20%, extensive personnel layoffs, and an offer of early retirement that was accepted by more than 500 of its executives. Turner Broadcasting, meanwhile, turned its acquisitive attentions elsewhere and came up with a deal to buy the Metro-Goldwyn-Mayer/United Artists (MGM/UA) film company in a cash-and-stock transaction valued at about $1.5 billion. And in December a second change in network ownership was set in motion when RCA, owner of the NBC network, agreed to be acquired by the General Electric Corp. for something over $6 billion, the most money ever paid for a non-oil company.

Cable television continued to expand. The A. C. Nielsen Co., the leading TV audience measurement service, estimated that in July the number of cable-equipped U.S. homes totaled 38,955,150, or 45.7% of all U.S. television homes, compared with 36,-105,500, or 42.9%, in July 1984. Cable was still experiencing growing pains, however. Many system operators were uncertain as to whether the fundamental business should be basic cable (supported by advertising) or pay cable, or part of a new trend, "pay per view," in which cable homes could order—and pay for—only those movies or other special events they particularly wanted to see.

Cable also had another problem: program piracy. More and more homes were buying small satellite receiving antennas, or "backyard dishes," that enabled them to receive cable programs without paying for them. A number of pay cable services were beginning to "scramble" their signals to thwart these interceptions, and an industrywide movement was under way late in the year to develop a single scrambling policy applicable to all.

Videocassette recorders (VCRs), the devices that record TV programs and play them back later and also play prerecorded movies and other programs, were again television's biggest growth area. Industry estimates put the total of VCR-equipped homes in 1985 at about 28.1% of all U.S. TV homes, more than double the 13% estimated in 1984. A. C. Nielsen Co. found that in July the average VCR was used for 2 hours 14 minutes a week for recording and 4 hours 18 minutes for playback.

Programming

Comedies and other programs intended primarily for the young adult viewer gained new emphasis in the prime-time television schedules that the major U.S. networks offered for the 1985–86 season. The number of half-hour situation comedies, relatively small only a few years earlier, increased 10% over the previous season, reaching 24 a week; in addition, there were two new comedy series, "Stir Crazy" and "Hometown," of an hour each, an uncharacteristically long form for comedy. Action-adventure dramas, which dominated the 1984–85 schedules, increased by one, to 36. Together, the three networks introduced 20 new series totaling 16½ hours.

The 1984–85 season had produced a major turnaround in the network audience rankings. CBS again finished first, but NBC, which for years had seemed to have permanent possession of third place, continued a dramatic rise and not only ousted ABC from second place but gave CBS a close run for first. The new rankings were reflected in the amount of new programming introduced for 1985–86. ABC replaced more than one-third of its prime-time schedule, with eight new programs totaling 7½ hours; CBS introduced six new series, adding up to 5 hours; while NBC, confident of the momentum in its current schedule, made the fewest changes it had undertaken in 15 years, deciding to get by with six new series totaling 4 hours, or 18% of its prime-time lineup.

In nonseries programming, made-for-television movies and miniseries continued to play a greater role, while the use of theatrical motion pictures declined. Because of the motion picture industry's practice of releasing movies so that they could be shown on pay cable six months in advance of their network release—and with pay cable's habit of showing each movie several times—most theatrical pictures had been seen by large audiences by the time the networks could broadcast them, and their ratings were far below what they would have been otherwise. For the most part, therefore, the networks found that they could attract larger audiences with made-for-TV movies.

In cable, too, the trend toward creation of special programming continued. As the supply of new theatrical movies dwindled, more and more of the large pay-cable operators, such as Home Box Office, Cinemax, Showtime, and The Movie Channel, were producing or underwriting the production of new comedy, drama, and children's series, miniseries, and specials for their own use. By 1985 some of these shows, especially situation comedies, had become so successful that their owners were considering syndicating them to broadcast TV stations after their cable runs.

The most widely seen and heard program of 1985, and perhaps of any year, was the 16-hour Live Aid concert on July 13, a multinational, multimedia event. The concert, organized by Bob Geldof to raise money for famine relief in Africa, was held simultaneously in Philadelphia and London. Produced by Worldwide Sports & Entertainment and featuring some 60 contemporary rock and country music acts, it was carried in whole or in part by—

Robin Bailey and Diana Rigg were Lord and Lady Dedlock in "Bleak House," another brilliant British production brought to U.S. audiences as part of the Public Broadcast System's "Masterpiece Theatre" series.

WTTW, CHICAGO

among others—ABC-TV, ABC Radio, the Music Television cable network, the BBC, and more than 100 independent stations. It was beamed live via satellite to more than 110 countries and on a tape-delayed basis to about 40 others. In all it reached more than 1,500,000,000 people throughout the world.

The summit conference between President Reagan and the Soviet Union's Mikhail Gorbachev in Geneva in November was among the most extensively covered events of the year, though it was far from the newsiest, thanks to a news blackout imposed by both sides until the meetings were over. The hijacking of TWA Flight 847 by terrorists in the Middle East in June and the plight of the passenger-hostages became the subject of continuous reporting, much of it live, for more than two weeks and led to a public controversy—and to introspection by the networks themselves—as to whether so much coverage, especially so much live coverage, had played into the hands of the terrorists and delayed a resolution of the crisis.

In the 37th annual Emmy awards, the Academy of Television Arts and Sciences named "Cagney & Lacey" as the outstanding drama series and "The Cosby Show" the outstanding comedy series. "Motown Returns to the Apollo" won for variety, music, or comedy programs; "The Jewel in the Crown" for limited series; "Do You Remember Love?" for drama/comedy specials; and "Garfield in the Rough" for animated programs.

Emmys for lead actor and actress in a drama series went to William Daniels of "St. Elsewhere" and Tyne Daly of "Cagney & Lacey." Robert Guillaume of "Benson" and Jane Curtin of "Kate & Allie" won for lead actor and actress in a comedy series, while lead actor and actress awards for limited series or specials went to Richard Crenna of "The Rape of Richard Beck" and Joanne Woodward of "Do You Remember Love?" Outstanding supporting actor and actress Emmys were won by Edward James Olmos of "Miami Vice" and Betty Thomas of "Hill Street Blues" in the drama series category, John Larroquette of "Night Court" and Rhea Perlman of "Cheers" for comedy series, and Karl Malden of "Fatal Vision" and Kim Stanley of "Cat on a Hot Tin Roof" for limited series or specials. In the 12th annual Emmy awards for daytime programming, top honors went to "The Young and the Restless" as the outstanding drama series, "$25,-000 Pyramid" in the game show category, "Sesame Street" for children's series, "Donahue" for talk/service shows, "Jim Henson's Muppet Babies" in the animated program classification, and "All the Kids Do It" in the children's specials category.

In radio, music and news remained the staples. Listeners could find stations that catered to an almost endless variety of tastes: jazz, classical, country, or rock music; ethnic, religious, talk, and information combinations; and all news. Among radio stations generally, country music was first in popularity, with adult contemporary second, and middle-of-the-road/nostalgia third.

The Public Broadcasting Service (PBS) reported that during the 1984–85 season its programs reached 48,050,000 homes and 95,145,000 viewers in an average week, or 75% more homes and 86% more people than in 1977–78, when PBS started regular audience measurements. In prime time the totals were 28,870,000 homes and 53.7 million people, for gains of 113 and 120%, respectively.

Amateur Radio

The number of amateur ("ham") radio operators continued to grow. The American Radio Relay League, the leading organization of ham operators, put the U.S. total in October 1985 at 413,127, up from 410,066 in October 1984. Throughout the world licensed ham radio operators were estimated to number 1,511,000 in 1985.

Ham operators provide vital communications links in emergency or other conditions when normal communications lines are down. In the fall of 1985, for example, when an earthquake killed thousands of people in Mexico, and in November, when thousands more died in mud slides triggered by a volcanic eruption in Colombia, ham operators provided communications between the devastated areas and the outside world.

TENNIS

Dominance in men's tennis in 1985 shifted from the U.S. to Europe. In the three leading championships, those of France, Wimbledon (England), and the U.S., the only men's title exclusively won by Americans was the U.S. doubles. In singles a Swede, Mats Wilander, won the French title; a West German, Boris Becker, won at Wimbledon; and a native of Czechoslovakia, Ivan Lendl, won the U.S. In addition, West Germany beat the U.S. in the second round of the Davis Cup. Spectator interest increased at the main events. Total paid attendance at the U.S. Open in New York City was a record 409,455.

Concern about possible adverse effects of intensive play at too young an age resulted in restrictions for both boys and girls in the rules of the respective Men's and Women's International Professional Tennis councils. In Grand Prix events all boys under 14 were made ineligible; those aged 14 were restricted to 8 tournaments in a year and the 15-year-olds to 12. Girls under 15 were limited to 10 international series tournaments in a year; those aged 15 to 16 could play only 12; and all girls under 16 were limited to three successive tournaments and had to take at least two rest periods of 30 days. No minimum age limit was imposed.

The Wimbledon championships produced the youngest men's singles champion of all time. Becker was 17 years 227 days old; the previous youngest winner was Wilfred Baddeley of Great Britain, who in 1891 was 19 years 175 days old—nor was any men's singles champion of France or the U.S. younger.

Unacceptable court behavior caused problems throughout the year. Following the defeat of the U.S. by Sweden in the Davis Cup final in Göteborg in 1984, the U.S. Tennis Association took the unprecedented step of requiring its players to sign an agreement to conform to a code of good sportsmanship. Neither John McEnroe nor Jimmy Connors signed, and they were not selected for the 1985 Davis Cup team. In September Connors was suspended from Grand Prix competition for 42 days; it was an automatic suspension when fines for violations of the code of conduct totaled $7,500. McEnroe was asked to resign his honorary membership in Queen's Club, London, after complaints about his language.

Men's Competition

McEnroe was again named as "world champion" by the International Tennis Federation (ITF). He ended 1984 as leader of the Grand Prix series and earned the top bonus of $600,000. The last major tournament of the season, the Australian championships in Melbourne in December 1984, was won by Wilander. He beat Kevin Curren (South African-born, naturalized U.S.) 6–7, 6–4, 7–6, 6–2 in the final.

McEnroe won the Grand Prix Masters' event in Madison Square Garden, New York City, in January. He defeated Wilander 6–1, 6–1 in the semifinals and Lendl 7–5, 6–0, 6–4 in the final. McEnroe's form subsequently declined. In the finals of a tournament in Dallas, Texas, in April, the most important of World Championship Tennis (WCT) events and, in 1985, part of the Grand Prix series, Joakim Nyström (Sweden) beat McEnroe in the opening round. In the final Lendl defeated Tim Mayotte (U.S.) 7–6, 6–4, 6–1. In another WCT event, the Tournament of Champions at Forest Hills, N.Y., in May, Lendl defeated McEnroe 6–3, 6–3 in the final. Wilander won the French championship for the second time, defeating McEnroe 6–1, 7–5, 7–5 in the semifinal and Lendl 3–6, 6–4, 6–2, 6–2 in the final.

Wimbledon had not only its youngest but, uniquely, an unseeded winner in Becker. That the West German was unseeded was due to the logic of the computer ranking list rather than the sharp form he had revealed two weeks earlier when he won the Queen's Club, London, tournament. Even so his victory at Wimbledon was unexpected. There were many other surprises at Wimbledon. Wilander lost in the first round to Slobodan Zivoyinovic (Yugos.), and Henri Leconte (France) beat Lendl 3–6, 6–4, 6–3, 6–1 in the fourth round. Curren beat McEnroe 6–2, 6–2, 6–4 in the quarterfinals.

Becker beat Nyström, seeded seventh, by 3–6, 7–6, 6–1, 4–6, 9–7 in round three and Mayotte by 6–3, 4–6, 6–7, 7–6, 6–2 in the fourth. He was a winner in four sets in the later rounds, 7–6, 3–

AP/WIDE WORLD

Boris Becker of West Germany makes a characteristic lunge for the ball on his way to a stunning victory in the men's singles event at Wimbledon in July.

6, 6–3, 6–4 in the quarterfinal against Leconte, 2–6, 7–6, 6–3, 6–3 against fifth-seeded Anders Jarryd (Sweden) in the semifinal, and 6–3, 6–7, 7–6, 6–4 in the final against Curren, the eighth seed.

Becker did not rise to the same heights in the U.S. Open at the National Tennis Center in Flushing Meadow, New York City, in September. Nyström beat him 6–3, 6–4, 4–6, 6–4 in the fourth round. McEnroe in turn defeated Nyström 6–1, 6–0, 7–5 and then triumphed over Wilander 3–6, 6–4, 6–3, 6–3 in the semifinals. Lendl defeated Connors 6–2, 6–3, 7–5 in the other semifinal and won his first U.S. Open by beating McEnroe 7–6, 6–3, 6–4 in the final. No pair dominated doubles. The outstanding pair, Peter Fleming (U.S.) and McEnroe, won the Masters' tournament in January 1985 for the seventh consecutive year but later split. The Australian title for 1984 went to Mark Edmondson (Australia) and Sherwood Stewart (U.S.), and Edmondson also won the French title with Kim Warwick (Australia). Heinz Günthardt (Switz.) and Balazs Taroczy (Hung.) won the Wimbledon championship. The U.S. title was taken by Ken Flach and Robert Seguso (both U.S.).

The World Team Cup, with eight nations qualifying by the world ranking of their players, was staged in Düsseldorf, West Germany, in May. In the final the U.S. (McEnroe, Connors, Flach, Seguso) beat Czechoslovakia (Lendl, Miroslav Mecir, Tomas Smid) 2–1 to win for the third time.

The Davis Cup attracted an entry of 62 nations. The four zonal sections were won by Denmark, Great Britain, Mexico, and New Zealand; as a result of their victories each of those nations gained promotion to the World Group for 1986. In the World Group of 16 nations, Japan, Argentina, France, and Chile lost in the first round and the subsequent play-off and so were relegated to the zonal sections for 1986. The most notable casualty was France, which first lost to Paraguay 3–2 in Asunción and then to Yugoslavia 4–1 in Belgrade. Surprising, too, was the defeat of the U.S. in the second round. Without its best singles players the U.S. (Eliot Teltscher, Aaron Krickstein, Flach, Seguso) beat Japan 5–0. In the second round, however, West Germany (Becker, Hans Schwaier, Andreas Maurer) beat the U.S. 3–2 in Hamburg. Becker's powerful play then helped West Germany defeat Czechoslovakia, with Lendl able to play only in doubles, 5–0 in Frankfurt.

The defending champion, Sweden (Wilander, Jarryd, Stefan Edberg, Henrik Sundström), beat Chile 4–1 in Santiago, India 3–0 at Bangalore, and Australia 5–0 in Malmö to reach the final against West Germany. It marked the fourth time that Sweden had reached the final round. West Germany's only previous appearance was in 1970. In the final round Sweden successfully defended its championship by defeating West Germany 3–2. With the two nations tied 2–2, Edberg defeated West Germany's Michael Westphal in the final singles match 3–6, 7–5, 6–4, 6–3.

Women's Competition

Martina Navratilova (Czechoslovakian-born, naturalized U.S.) was again the outstanding player but by a less wide margin. She was declared "world champion" for the fourth time. After success in six

Hana Mandlikova of Czechoslovakia exults after defeating former compatriot Martina Navratilova for the U.S. Open championship in New York in September.

AP/WIDE WORLD

straight "Grand Slam" (Wimbledon, French, U.S., and Australian championships) singles titles, she lost in the Australian semifinals in December 1984. Helena Sukova (Czech.) defeated her 1–6, 6–3, 7–5. Chris Evert Lloyd (U.S.) then beat Sukova 6–7, 6–1, 6–3 to win the title for the second time.

Navratilova won the Virginia Slims series, which ended in March, and won a bonus of $185,000 for her triumphs in singles and doubles. In the concluding tournament at Madison Square Garden, she won the final 6–3, 7–5, 6–4 against Sukova. Evert Lloyd won the West German championship in Berlin, defeating a young West German, Steffi Graf, in the final.

Evert Lloyd's greatest triumph came in the French Open, where she ended a long series of losses to Navratilova by defeating her 6–3, 6–7, 7–5 in an exhilarating final. It was Evert Lloyd's sixth French title win. At Wimbledon, however, Navratilova reasserted her dominance. She defeated Evert Lloyd 4–6, 6–3, 6–2 in the final for her sixth singles championship in that tournament.

The U.S. Open at Flushing Meadow had a more surprising victor. With disciplined, brilliant strokes, Hana Mandlikova (Czech.) beat Evert Lloyd 4–6, 6–2, 6–3 in the semifinals and Navratilova 7–6, 1–6, 7–6 in the final. As a youngster in Prague, Mandlikova had been a ball boy for Navratilova before the latter became a U.S. citizen.

Navratilova was also less dominant in doubles. She and Pam Shriver (U.S.) retained only the Australian and French titles. In winning the French doubles in June, they gained their eighth successive Grand Slam crown. At Wimbledon Kathy Jordan (U.S.) and Elizabeth Smylie (Australia) defeated them 5–7, 6–3, 6–4 in the final. In the U.S. Open final Claudia Kohde-Kilsch (West Germany) and Sukova beat them 6–7, 6–2, 6–3.

Navratilova expanded her activities by competing in mixed doubles. She won at Wimbledon with Paul McNamee (Australia). Because of rain they played the last three rounds in one day. They won the semifinal 6–7, 7–5, 23–21 against Scott Davis (U.S.) and Betsy Nagelsen (U.S.), the longest mixed doubles ever staged at Wimbledon, and played a total of 117 games in the seven sets. Navratilova also won the mixed doubles in the U.S. Open with Heinz Günthardt (Switz.).

The Federation Cup, the women's world team championship, was held in Nagoya, Japan, in October with an entry of 38 countries. Czechoslovakia (Mandlikova, Sukova, Andrea Holikova, Regina Marsikova) beat the U.S. (Kathy Jordan, Elise Burgin) 2–1 in the final to win the title for the third straight year and the fourth time in all.

The U.S. beat Great Britain 7–0 at Williamsburg, Va., for the Wightman Cup. It was the 47th win in 57 contests for the U.S. (Evert Lloyd, Shriver, Kathy Rinaldi, Betsy Nagelsen, Anne White). Great Britain (Annabel Croft, Jo Durie, Ann Hobbs, Virginia Wade) last won in 1978.

To cope with a growing flood of imports—which doubled between 1980 and 1984 and continued to grow—U.S. textile firms were investing heavily in technology and automation.

NANCY PIERCE

TEXTILES

A growing trend throughout the textile industries of industrialized countries was the appearance of numerous small organizations that, rather than manufacturing massive volumes of low-priced goods, sought to provide goods with a high added value and at prices that generated good profit margins. There were fewer very large factories employing perhaps several thousand operatives, and the organizations of this kind that did survive were concentrating on increasing automation, with the aim of achieving faster production and better quality with much less labor. The new smaller concerns—often family owned—specialized in specific areas. The so-called management buyback or buyout was an effective method of making a small company out of a large one, reducing labor and overhead and enabling it to compete on more favorable terms.

World currency changes in 1985 were the dominant force in governing wool prices. Normal market forces were distorted, and floor prices were effectively raised or lowered for overseas buyers. Despite currency-related problems, a reasonable long-term supply-demand balance was maintained. Finer merinos showed outstanding price strength in 1984–85 because of fashion demand and limited supply. Consumption by the main wool-textile industries continued on an upward trend in 1984. World production of wool in the 1984–85 season was 1,668,000 metric tons clean, compared with 1,646,000 tons in 1983–84. The forecast for 1985–86 was 1,670,000 metric tons clean.

World cotton production in the 1984–85 season totaled nearly 84 million bales (a bale = 217.7 kg or 480 lb), compared with only 68 million bales in the previous growing season. China led with nearly 28 million bales, followed by the U.S. with 13 million and the U.S.S.R. with 12 million.

New highly sophisticated, high-speed spinning processes were appearing in various parts of the world, and machine builders warned cotton growers that as a result there was likely to be a growing demand from textile manufacturers for finer cottons. Man-made fiber producers were already offering exceedingly fine regenerated and synthetic fibers for blending with cotton, which were better suited for such processes as open-end spinning. However, the breeding of new strains of cotton would take time.

During 1984–85 the silk industry was dominated by fluctuating exchange rates and the strength of the dollar. In the spring of 1984 China decided to base its silk export prices on the dollar. As the dollar strengthened, the silk price was artificially inflated, causing strong buyer resistance. The Chinese revised this policy, which revived demand during the winter of 1984–85.

Meanwhile, consumption in Western European countries held up well as the strong dollar enabled them to increase their exports of high-quality fabric and garments to the U.S. Because of fashion as well as U.S. customs regulations, demand for silk blended with other fibers such as wool continued, creating shortages. Prices rose but demand appeared to remain unsatisfied.

Japan continued to suffer decreasing demand, and steps were taken to reduce the mountain of government-held silk. Raw silk prices were reduced on Nov. 16, 1984, by 2,000 yen per kilogram, the first such step in 26 years. (For table of world currencies, see International Exchange and Payments.)

During 1983 world production of raw silk totaled 54,551 metric tons, with China producing 28,169 tons and Japan 12,456 tons. Consumption was greatest in Japan, at 13,222 tons. Silk of Chinese origin accounted for 90% of the international silk trade.

As in other sectors of textile manufacture, producers of man-made fibers were concentrating on expensive specialities, and increasing numbers of modified fibers were appearing. In the U.S. and Japan there was a move toward an elastic form of polyester fiber.

The aerospace industry was laying down very strict flammability rules, and this was forcing the creation of "fire blocking" materials, often based on carbon fibers or mixes with aramids, glass, or even ceramic fibers. The objective was to enable a fire to be extinguished or at least retarded before it reached the foam fillings, which release toxic fumes when they burn. Weight for weight, aramid fibers were stronger than steel. Now some even stronger fibers based on polyethylene were being produced.

THAILAND

On Sept. 9, 1985, Thailand was shaken by the 16th attempted coup d'état since the abolition of absolute monarchy in 1932. Some 500 rebel soldiers, backed by 22 tanks, proclaimed on radio at 7:30 AM that "the Revolutionary Party, which comprises military, police, and civilian parties, has seized national sovereignty." Barely eight hours later, however, the rebellion had fizzled out, aborted by an evident lack of support both within the powerful military establishment and among the public. In the meantime, however, two bloody battles in the streets of Bangkok involving tanks and small arms killed 5 people, including 2 foreign journalists, injured approximately 60 others, and caused damage amounting to several million baht. (For table of world currencies, *see* International Exchange and Payments.) Thailand's recent record of political stability received a sharp jolt.

The coup attempt was apparently masterminded by Manoon Roopkachorn, a charismatic former army colonel who had been cashiered after leading a similarly unsuccessful revolt in 1981, and his brother Manas, an officer in the Air Force. Among those who reportedly gave their support once the

coup was under way were former prime minister Kriangsak Chamanand, Gen. Serm Na Nakhorn, a former supreme commander of the armed forces, and Gen. Yos Thephasdin, a former deputy commander in chief of the Army. It soon became clear, however, that dominant forces within the military remained loyal to Prime Minister Prem Tinsulanond. Manoon negotiated with government authorities to secure safe passage out of the country in return for a prompt, peaceful conclusion to the rebellion. Following the surrender he flew to Singapore and then to West Germany, after U.S. authorities had denied his request for asylum.

The government arrested Kriangsak, Serm, and Yos, despite their protests that they had been forced to support the coup, as well as some 100 others. Chief motives for the coup attempt were widely believed to be economic hardship and Manoon's own ambitions.

Long-standing tensions between the military and the politicians also came to the fore in July when Parliament passed the most controversial bill of the 1985 session. The constitutional amendment, which would change the country's electoral system, had been introduced by the Social Action Party, the largest partner in the ruling coalition. It provided for provinces to be divided into constituencies in a way that many believed would improve the chances of smaller parties against bigger ones and against individual candidates backed by the military.

The readings on Thailand's economy were mixed. There was concern about falling exports, rising unemployment, and slow growth, but both the World Bank and the government were cautiously optimistic. Though it passed a zero-growth budget of $8 billion for 1985–86, the government set an av-

Thai army soldiers loyal to the government battle rebel troops, estimated at some 500 strong. The rebels supported an unsuccessful coup attempt on September 9 led by a former army colonel and an air force officer.

SYGMA

Athol Fugard (left) and Zakes Mokae starred as South African brothers divided by skin color in a 25th-anniversary production of Fugard's The Blood Knot at the Yale Repertory Theatre in New Haven, Connecticut.

ROBERT E. MCELROY/NEWSWEEK

erage growth target of 5% a year in its sixth (1987–91) development plan. Some economists criticized the goal as unrealistic, noting that such major commodity exports as rice, sugar, tapioca, and maize (corn) were expected to face soft prices for some time into the future.

THEATER

The death of Yul Brynner late in the year symbolized the state of Broadway in 1985. For the first time in memory even the producers in New York City were forced to concede that Broadway was not in good health, and as evidence of this, for the first time in their history, the major performance categories of the annual Tony awards were reduced for want of deserving nominees. The central question was crucial: Was this crisis just the cyclical one, to be survived as usual by this "fabulous invalid," or had the commercial theater undone itself with unrecoupable production costs and unaffordable ticket prices?

The situation was not helped by a hitless musical year. More than ever, Broadway's morale was determined by its musical stage, and New York City was offering a menu only of old hits, one of them (A Chorus Line) ten years old. Indeed, the most popular musical of the year was over 30 years old—the endlessly popular revival of The King and I—and it closed only because the star, Brynner, was mortally ill.

If there was any sunshine in Broadway's wintry year, it came from Neil Simon's delightful Biloxi Blues. The second in a projected autobiographical trilogy that had been inaugurated in 1983 with Brighton Beach Memoirs, this play took its youthful protagonist from his Brooklyn adolescence into the maturing ritual of military basic training in the 1940s. Few disagreed that here was Simon's most substantial and well-wrought play, a thoughtful and touching study of a young man's confusion and his struggle toward adulthood. Simon was rewarded with a Tony award for the best play of the year—astonishingly enough, the first ever won by this author of Barefoot in the Park, The Odd Couple, and Plaza Suite, among others.

Another of the few bright spots in the 1985 Broadway year was, of all things, a revival of Frederick Lonsdale's 1923 drawing-room comedy Aren't We All?, starring the redoubtable Claudette Colbert and Rex Harrison. Some took this success to suggest an audience hungry for sophistication and the traditional values of wit, civility, and polish. That would be reassuring were it true, but it was difficult to make out any current young Claudette Colberts, Rex Harrisons, or, for that matter, Frederick Lonsdales.

The musical show that did win the year's Tony award, if merely for want of competition, was the decidedly un-Broadway Big River. This adaptation of The Adventures of Huckleberry Finn emanated from the American Repertory Theatre at Harvard University. It was not produced by people associated with Broadway, nor was it created by them, and it did not have the brash music or the tough glitter of traditional Broadway shows. It was not so wonderful either, but if Big River was not a great show, it did teach a valuable lesson—that there are musical theater languages that audiences can appreciate other than that of orthodox show business.

As for the failures in the Broadway year, they were at least more diverse than the hits. The once infallible producer-director Harold Prince continued his catastrophic downslide with the $5 million *Grind.* Other musical flops ranged from the vaudevillian *Harrigan 'n Hart* to the rock-and-rolling *Leader of the Pack.* There were also unsuccessful Broadway revivals of Peter Nichols's *Joe Egg,* Rod Serling's *Requiem for a Heavyweight,* and Eugene O'Neill's *Strange Interlude,* although in October Jason Robards propelled another marathon O'Neill play, *The Iceman Cometh,* to a successful Broadway engagement. If theater lovers hoped that this signaled a new fall season and a fresh start, their hopes were dashed. Not that there were many failures in the fall of 1985. Worse, there were few attempts, although Lily Tomlin did make a great hit with her appropriately titled one-woman show, *The Search for Signs of Intelligent Life in the Universe.* It certainly was the year's most intelligent Broadway entertainment. Too, a most unlikely hit turned out to be *Tango Argentino,* an evening devoted entirely to tangos played by a small onstage orchestra, sung by several ardent vocalists, and, most importantly, danced by a company of middle-aged, overdressed, and gloriously sensual ballroom dancers. This was the sort of unpredictability that should characterize a healthy theater.

Off-Broadway in New York City the year was not much more encouraging except that serious dramas, which had all but disappeared from the uptown theaters, were regularly settling down for long runs in the smaller houses. Sam Shepard, who had yet to be produced on Broadway, had three plays running in smaller theaters at various times during the year: *Fool for Love, Curse of the Starving Class,* and *A*

William Petersen performed in the Wisdom Bridge company's production of In the Belly of the Beast. *The Chicago company won international praise in 1985.*

WISDOM BRIDGE THEATRE; PHOTOGRAPH, JENNIFER GIRARD

Lie of the Mind. Herb Gardner's *I'm Not Rappaport,* thanks to a charming script and ingratiating performances by Cleavon Little and Judd Hirsch, survived unkind reviews to settle down for a run off-Broadway and then in a big house. Perhaps the season's most disturbing play was *Orphans* by Lyle Kessler. It was typical of the dramas that seemed to be appealing to audiences across the country—tense, threatening, darkly comic plays dealing with family relationships. Such works, inspired most notably by Harold Pinter via Sam Shepard, were particularly propagated by the Steppenwolf Theatre Company of Chicago, which produced both *Orphans* and a recent successful revival of Shepard's *True West.*

Indeed Chicago, once clucked over by show folk as a bad theater town, had developed into one of the nation's most active stage centers. In addition to Steppenwolf, the city offered such professional and ambitious production companies as the Organic Theatre Company, the Body Politic, Wisdom Bridge, and, of course, the celebrated Goodman Theatre. Indeed, when New York City's repertory theater in Lincoln Center was finally started anew after several years of shameful inactivity, it was the Goodman Theatre's artistic director, Gregory Mosher, who was called in to run the place. Lincoln Center reopened its doors at the year's end with a double bill of plays by David Mamet, *The Shawl* and *Prairie du Chien.* Mosher had originally staged them at the Goodman.

Los Angeles had long since developed into one of the nation's busiest stage centers, originating commercial productions as well as institutional ones. One of the year's most interesting stage events, in fact, occurred there with the autumn revival of Harold Pinter's *Old Times,* starring Liv Ullmann, Nicola Paget, and the playwright himself. As actor, Pinter was not equipped to communicate his lines well, and the production's projected tour was canceled following a tepid Los Angeles reception.

Canada

In Canada the Stratford Festival continued to endure endless crises while appearing prosperous. Artistic director John Hirsch, who had rescued this most prestigious of North American theaters when it was said to be on the brink of disaster five years earlier, announced his resignation at the end of the summer. The 1985 season had been acceptable for this major but tourist-oriented festival theater. It might have been accused of a certain commercialism, presenting *The Pirates of Penzance* and a punk version of *Measure for Measure,* but a perking up was welcome after years of deadly institutionalism. The year's rising attendance and dropping deficits surely eased the threat of governmental interference that always seemed to overshadow Stratford's well-trimmed lawns.

Other production choices for the Canadian institution's 1985 season were unexceptionable: *King*

Roshan Seth (foreground), as an urbane Indian novelist in Britain, was one of the chief figures in David Hare's A Map of the World, *an exploration of relations between developed and third world nations that had its U.S. debut off-Broadway.*

MARTHA SWOPE/TIME MAGAZINE

Lear, Twelfth Night, Oliver Goldsmith's *She Stoops to Conquer,* and, for a contemporary touch, Tennessee Williams's *The Glass Menagerie.* John Neville was engaged to succeed Hirsch in 1986, and that at least ensured a smooth transition of administrations unlike several confused ones in the past.

Great Britain and Ireland

Conflicts involving the Arts Council of Great Britain (ACGB) and its clients became more acute as the arts minister, Lord Gowrie, increased the ACGB's grant for 1985–86 by 2% to £106 million, which was well below the inflation rate. (For table of world currencies, *see* International Exchange and Payments.) There was additional criticism of the ACGB's apparent acceptance of this defeat and of the ensuing demise of several theatrical companies. Government policy was opposed by the new National Campaign for the Arts, members of Parliament, and such public figures as Sir Peter Hall, head of the National Theatre (NT).

Condemnation by subsidized theaters in Britain and the resignations of half of the ACGB's drama panel, its drama director, and its financial director forced a reversal of policy. The ACGB's demand for £161 million for 1986–87 was in keeping with Lord Gowrie's pledge that the arts world would not be let down after the abolition in April 1986 of the Greater London Council (GLC) and six regional metropolitan authorities. Yet the government broke its promise, increasing the grant to £135 million, far below the figure required to make up the shortfall or to enable the ACGB to help launch the new South Bank Board as successor to the GLC.

A number of official surveys upheld the case for the arts establishment, and this was strengthened when the Policy Studies Institute revealed that box-

office receipts in the state-subsidized theaters had been steadily rising. Nonetheless, the first of these theaters to have their grants axed were five leading "touring date" theaters, headed by the historic Sadler's Wells in London.

Sir Peter Hall's concerns on behalf of the NT and the theater in general were echoed everywhere. They led to the closing of the Cottesloe Theatre, where the prizewinning *The Mysteries* (later transferred to the Lyceum) won for NT director Bill Bryden prizes from all four award juries—the Laurence Olivier (LO), London Standard (LS), *Plays and Players* (P&P), and *Drama Magazine* (DM) awards. A special grant from the GLC reopened the Cottesloe, where the NT group led by Ian McKellen and Edward Petherbridge excelled in Mike Alfreds's unconventional production of *The Cherry Orchard.* The NT annual report for 1984–85 showed an excellent record, with earned income rising to £7.5 million against a grant of £7.8 million.

At the Lyttelton *Mrs. Warren's Profession* featured a superb performance by Joan Plowright in the title role. The best of two award-winning productions at the Olivier was Alan Ayckbourn's comedy of backstage amateur theatricals, *A Chorus of Disapproval,* in which Michael Gambon as a much-harassed director and Imelda Staunton as his patient wife won several awards. As the Machiavellian newspaper proprietor in David Hare and Howard Brenton's award-winning satire on Fleet Street, *Pravda,* Anthony Hopkins won the new LO Ken Tynan award. Other prizes went to designer William Dudley for his innovative work on *The Mysteries,* to David Essex's *Mutiny!* at the Piccadilly Theatre, to *The Merry Wives of Windsor* at the Stratford home of the Royal Shakespeare Com-

(continued on page 337)

Raw Power on the Stage

To begin with, it's the ultimate in-the-round performance. Viewers not only are on all four sides of this stage; they are practically on top of it. Here Bertolt Brecht's platform stage is brought to perfection; here the reductio ad absurdum trappings of the likes of John Napier (the brilliant environmental designer of *Cats, The Life and Adventures of Nicholas Nickleby,* and other wonders) is at its simplest, cleanest, most bare visual elegance.

Theatrical visionaries, in stripping away lighting, elaborate scenery, and all those three-dimensional nooks and crannies of a Broadway stage, are trying to make a point about drama, and the point is this: The mythic power of the art form, the elemental heroes and forces that the best dramas succeeded in illustrating, thunder forth at their loudest and most subliminal when their surroundings are unadorned and spartan. Give me a bare stage and a few great actors, and I can show you life in a handful of magic stardust.

All this is in reference to a just completed evening of drama, which, to recall now, more than an hour after its conclusion, still makes my fingers tremble at my typewriter, still makes my spine tingle as I sit in my swivel chair. It was one of those rare evenings—so startling, so moving, so total, and so innovative—that critics (and, naturally, press agents) live for. It is called *Wrestling,* and although I saw it at a theater called the Rosemont Horizon near Chicago, I'm told it's available as well through any number of cable and local television outlets throughout the land.

In any event the mastermind or minds behind *Wrestling* (the program credits no author—come to think of it, the usher neglected to give me a program) have stripped theater bare and dished up its essence. Even the performers are virtually stripped, clothed in brilliantly simple bathing-trunk attire that reveals most of their rolling flesh, warts and all.

The plot is base, vile, combative. Four characters—bearing such cartoon names as Hulk Hogan and Mighty Manfred—leap onstage and attack each other. What begins as a kind of fracas of brute fisticuffs soon grows into a verbal tirade without bounds. (Hogan at one point implies an illicit tie between Manfred and his sister, an obvious allusion to Oedipus.)

But the performance doesn't stop at name-calling and assault. In the midst of the conflict—an obvious allegory of the raging forces at war in the heart and soul of mankind—these characters erupt in breathless, athletic choreographic reveries. Hogan leaps over Manfred, landing on the palms of his hands and then pushes back up in a springboard antic, as if at loose in a buoyant rubber landscape. I haven't seen ballet as spartan and deft as that since Edward Villella last leapt his way across the stage of the Auditorium Theatre in Chicago.

Wrestling then introduces the innovative touch of a microphoned narrator—this in a work so simple that a narrator is the last imaginable adornment. But there he is, a kind of inverse absurdist symbol of our desire to understand, even that which ought to appear so obvious. These are dramatists (when will we be given their names?) whose levels simply don't quit. Does a backyard brawl need a narrator? Does, in fact, the human condition?

Human and dramatic traditions, present in both poetic bareness and satiric sting; stage simplicity and stage expansiveness; elemental conflicts and up-to-the-minute technology; all are combined in one breathless story and performance, one as simple as a neighborhood melee and as moving and poetically sparse as something by Samuel Beckett.

Critics, of course, are not supposed to sully their hands with discussions of commercial prospects for a work; their realm is properly aesthetic. But some theatrical endeavors demand a breaking of the rules, and I, for one, wish to go on record predicting: *Wrestling* is one drama whose run will last forever.

Hulk Hogan and other dramatis personae: no sets, no props, no script, no dialogue, hardly any costume; just drama.

WALLY MCNAMEE—WOODFIN CAMP & ASSOCIATES

Amanda Plummer and Will Patton were among the actors who performed A Lie of the Mind *by U.S. playwright Sam Shepard. The critically acclaimed play opened in New York City in December.*

MARTHA SWOPE

(continued from page 335)

pany (RSC), and to the uproarious NT double bill at the Olivier of *The Critic* and *The Real Inspector Hound.* Opinion was divided on Peter Shaffer's Bible-inspired *Yonadab.*

Like that of the NT, the RSC's annual report deplored the ACGB's grant increase of 1.9% as insufficient to maintain standards. The RSC's awards were fewer in 1985; the LO best comedy prize was given to Peter Barnes's religious satire *Red Noses,* and the best actress in a musical award went to Patti LuPone of the U.S. in *Les Misérables* (at the Barbican) and in Marc Blitzstein's *The Cradle Will Rock,* one of several U.S. plays at the Old Vic. The LO and LS best actor awards went to Antony Sher as Richard III and as the camp hero of *Torch Song Trilogy,* both RSC productions.

Bill Hamon, author of *Grafters,* a social drama at the Hampstead Theatre, was named most promising playwright (LS), and Gary Oldman was voted most promising actor (*DM*) in Edward Bond's *The Pope's Wedding* at the Royal Court. Two *P&P* "most promising" awards were won at the Royal Court, by Timberlake Wertenbaker for her pastiche 18th-century drama, *The Grace of Mary Traverse,* and by Janet McTeer in its title role. *DM* selected Espen Skjønberg of Norway as best supporting actor in his role as Chebutykin in *Three Sisters* at the Royal Exchange Theatre in Manchester and gave a new general merit award to the Kick Company's *King Lear.* Another "most promising" (LO) award went to the Cheek by Jowl company in three plays at the Donmar Warehouse.

Awards in the private sector went to Vanessa Redgrave (best actress: *DM,* LS, and *P&P*) in *The Seagull;* the shared *P&P* newcomer award to her daughter Natasha Richardson in the same play; the LS best musical to Alan Bleasdale's biography of

Elvis Presley (from Liverpool), *Are You Lonesome Tonight?;* and to *Me and My Girl* for best musical (LO) and best actor in a musical (LO) to its star, Robert Lindsay. There were memorable performances by Liv Ullmann in *Old Times;* Charlton Heston in *The Caine Mutiny Court-Martial;* Michael Denison in *Twelfth Night* (at the Open Air Theatre); Sian Philips in a musical of *Gigi;* Maggie Smith as a lovelorn Foreign Office interpreter in Ronald Harwood's *Interpreters;* and the hilarious Donald Sinden in *The Scarlet Pimpernel,* from Chichester.

Though Ted Nealon, the arts minister, admitted that Irish arts were underfunded and advocated a lottery, and Joe Dowling resigned as head of the Abbey Theatre in protest against cuts in funding, the Dublin Festival, under Michael Scott, was able to present a bumper program of new Irish works from both North and South. Also, the Abbey, with Christopher Fitz-Simmons as new head and with a £100,000 Arts Council grant, yielded a fine dramatic crop, including Siobhan McKenna in *Long Day's Journey into Night;* a revival of John B. Keane's modern classic *Sive;* Marie Keane in a Beckett double bill; Ulick O'Connor's Irish Republican Army (IRA) drama of 1922, *Execution;* Frank McGuinness's play on Ulster Protestantism, *Observe the Sons of Ulster Marching Towards the Somme* (also seen at the Belfast Festival); Tom MacIntyre's *Rise Up Lovely Sweeney;* Maureen Toal in McGuinness's monodrama *Baglady;* Thomas Murphy's saloon-bar comedy *Conversation on a Homecoming;* and Eoghan Harris's 1840 potato famine drama *Souper Sullivan.* The best Lyric Belfast Players' productions were Brian Moore's *Catholics;* Martin Lynch's *The Minstrel Boys,* about the hunger strike by IRA prisoners; and Stewart Parker's historical *Northern Star,* also seen at the Dublin Festival.

YES, OUR TRIP TO PARIS WAS LOVELY, AND WITH THE INCREDIBLY STRONG U.S. DOLLAR WE PICKED UP SOME BARGAINS YOU WON'T BELIEVE!...

TOURISM

According to World Tourism Organization (WTO) estimates, international travel and tourist volume in 1985 increased by 4% to a new record of 325 million arrivals. Dollar receipts were worth $105 billion, an increase of 4% over 1984. Although high unemployment in many countries acted as a brake on leisure and holiday travel, business travel boomed. The strength of the U.S. dollar early in the year helped to stimulate Americans' foreign travel. Western European countries welcomed 5% more U.S. visitors than in 1984. These 6.6 million tourists spent over $5 billion. But although U.S. resident travel grew by 9% in the first half of 1985, Americans cut back 6% on travel plans for the second half of the year, partly in response to the weakening of the dollar's international value.

Spain retained its preeminent position in world tourism. Although arrivals at 42.9 million were roughly equal to the 1984 total, visitors from abroad spent 4% more in dollar terms. A record eight million visitors traveled in Spain in August alone— more than some leading countries received in the entire year. Italian arrivals rose strongly and the arrival of travelers from the United States improved by 16%. Spain also remained the premier destination for tour operators, though other countries experienced faster growth rates. British tourists, however, perhaps deterred by reports of crime and terrorism in tourist areas, stayed away from Spain until an unprecedentedly wet British summer prompted a flurry of late bookings.

Along with Tunisia and Yugoslavia, Greece reported a boom in inclusive tours, although the luxury hotels in Athens suffered a drop in bookings following U.S. State Department warnings about airport security after the TWA hostage crisis in June. London welcomed 8.8 million overseas visitors in 1985 as well as 15 million from Britain itself. The British Tourist Authority expected a 10% growth in arrivals and a 25% jump in receipts to reach £600 million for the year. But soaring hotel prices worried operators, and the British government moved to introduce simplified planning procedures to promote new accommodations and leisure projects. In Sweden 29-year-old tennis star Björn Borg signed a contract with the Swedish Tourist Board to market Sweden as a travel destination.

Portugal had a strong growth in tourism with 20% more West Germans and Britons and 26% more travelers from Spain. Italy's good summer weather helped that country enjoy a good season. Austria promoted Vienna as the "lively capital" and planned to act as host to the first World Cup ski race in 1986. Austria's traditional winter tourism remained highly successful, but a 12% drop in overnight stays had taken place between 1980 and 1984.

In Eastern Europe Hungary offered possibly the widest choice of international hotels in Budapest, where the Spring Festival was helping to lengthen the tourist season. Hungary's state tour operator handled 724,000 foreign visitors in 1985 alone. Israel's $300 per person travel tax seriously affected outgoing tourism in 1985, with a 30% drop in departures in the early part of the year. The tax was lowered to $100 in October.

China received more than 50,000 European tourists in 1985. With 89% hotel occupancy in 1984, Hong Kong expected its boom in visitors to run out of steam in late 1985 owing to tight capacity and a strong currency. Sri Lanka's dependence on leisure travel (88% of arrivals) explained the 17% drop in total arrivals by July in the face of continuing political unrest. In Japan a hotel boom was under way with 82 new hotels offering 20,300 rooms due to open between 1985 and 1987; the aim was to strengthen Japan's position as a convention destination.

Theme parks were a popular tourist attraction, and 400,000 visitors were expected to visit New Zealand's Heritage Park in the year following its formal opening by Prime Minister David Lange in December 1984. In Africa, Mauritius expected a 15% increase in arrivals from the 140,000 recorded in 1984. A new hotel and conference center opened in Zimbabwe's capital, Harare, in October 1985. In the Caribbean, Cuba embarked on a five-year program intended to double tourist accommodations.

TOYS AND GAMES

There was a continuing decline in 1985 in world demand for video and electronic games and an increasing call for basic toys. Plush toys—especially teddy bears—dolls, and other traditional items returned to favor, and there was a rise in the shipment of board games. The previous year's success of "GoBots," produced by the Bandai Co. of Japan, and Hasbro Bradley's "Transformers"—robot figures that can be transformed into vehicles—had encouraged some U.S. and European manufacturers to make parallel items, while a number of import firms placed orders with factories in the Far East for similar products. Consequently, at the U.S. and European trade fairs at the beginning of 1985, there was an explosion in the availability of those toys.

The enormous popularity of Coleco Industries' "Cabbage Patch" dolls and Hasbro Bradley's "My Little Pony," both of which were launched in 1983, influenced other leading U.S. toymakers to develop their own characters. Lewis Galoob Toys, Inc., and Mattel Inc. both chose to produce new action toys for girls. Galoob introduced "Golden Girl and the Guardian of the Gemstones," a concept of fantasy-adventure figures and accessories, while Mattel produced "She-Ra," a sister for "He-Man" of the "Masters of the Universe" series. Coleco introduced a line of fantasy dolls called "Sectaurs," and L.J.N. Toys Ltd. decided to capitalize on the popularity of televised professional wrestling by making a series of action figures based on the wrestlers.

The penetration of Western markets by toys manufactured in the Far East continued to increase in 1985. Hong Kong strengthened its position as the world's leading toy exporter, increasing its total in 1984 by 30%. The U.S. absorbed 58% of Hong Kong's total export figure of $1,447,000,000. As of late 1985, there were 2,600 toy factories in Hong Kong, employing 56,000 workers. The toy and other industries were given stimulus by the signing in December 1984 of the Sino-British accord over the future of the crown colony's economy after it reverted to China in 1997. However, there was some speculation about the amount of manufacturing that would continue in Hong Kong. During the last five years labor costs had increased, and there was the tempting prospect of a vast amount of cheaper labor available in China. Some forecasters believed that international business agencies and design consultants would continue to operate in Hong Kong

WALTER NEAL/CHICAGO TRIBUNE

Nathan Bitner of Naperville, Illinois, was one of five young finalists in a contest to design a new cast member of the popular children's toy line "Masters of the Universe." His entry, Fearless Photog, ultimately won.

but that much labor-intensive production would move to China.

The subject of counterfeiting dominated the 11th annual meeting of the International Committee of Toy Industries, held at Windsor, England, in May and attended by representatives from eight national toy manufacturers' associations. U.S. manufacturers, who asked for the subject to be placed on the agenda, claimed to be the main victims of counterfeiting, and according to their representative the chief offending countries were Taiwan, South Korea, and Hong Kong. The Toy Manufacturers of America (TMA) decided to make 1985 a year of action against counterfeits. A declaration was to be written into exhibitors' contracts at the American International Toy Fair in New York City to the effect that immediate action would be taken against items found to be counterfeit. The Consumer Product Safety Commission (CPSC) was to be informed by the TMA of all counterfeit products; the CPSC had reported that 65% of calls it received on its hotline arose from counterfeit toys that failed to meet safety standards. At the Congress of the European Toy Institute, held in Edinburgh, Scotland, in June, the subject of counterfeiting was also discussed at length by delegates of European manufacturers. Their main complaint was against the activities of importers and retail buyers who took European-designed toys to the Far East to be copied.

A new Toy Safety Act became law in the U.S. at the end of 1984. The act amended the Federal Hazardous Substances Act and gave the CPSC the authority to notify the public and immediately recall potentially hazardous toys. According to the

TMA, the previous recall procedures used by the CPSC were too time-consuming.

Toys "R" Us, the giant U.S. toy retail chain, opened the first five of its European megastores in the U.K. in the autumn of 1985. In the U.S. the chain had 14% of the retail toy market, and its entry into the U.K. was viewed with understandable concern by independent toy retailers, whose share of this national market had declined from 35% in 1975 to 22% in 1984. Each of the five new stores occupied a one-acre (0.4-ha) site and carried 19,000 product lines, a stock far in excess of the capability of the majority of specialist toy retailers in the U.K. In 1986 Toys "R" Us planned to open a number of megastores in West Germany.

TRACK AND FIELD

Three new worldwide competitions graced the 1985 track and field season. Added to the schedule of the worldwide governing body, the International Amateur Athletic Federation, were the first World Indoor Games, World Cup marathon, and the Grand Prix invitational circuit. All were pronounced successes by the IAAF and were to be scheduled regularly, with the indoor meet becoming an official world indoor championship in 1987.

Men's International Competition

Two young but experienced middle-distance runners provided much of the excitement during the year as they competed against each other and the clock with equal vigor. They were Steve Cram of Great Britain, the 1983 world champion at 1,500 m, and Said Aouita of Morocco, the 1984 Olympic champion at 5,000 m. Born just 19 days apart in late 1960, the pair accounted for five world records in four events and for near misses at two other distances.

The stage was set early in the European season when the two clashed at 1,500 m on July 16 at Nice, France. Both smashed Steve Ovett's two-year-old world record, with Cram hanging on for the win in 3 min 29.67 sec and Aouita just 0.04 sec behind. Both claimed a world record 11 days later in separate events at Oslo. Cram took away the one-mile record of Britain's Sebastian Coe, the improvement again being more than a second as Cram clocked 3 min 46.32 sec. It was the first loss for Coe in a record-breaking race; previously he had won nine contests in world best time. The Oslo track also was kind to Aouita as he claimed his first world record. He covered 5,000 m in 13 min 00.40 sec, bettering David Moorcroft's three-year-old mark, made on the same track, by the narrowest possible margin, 0.01 sec.

Cram and Aouita then went their separate ways but remained aware of each other as each continued to seek additional triumphs. The Briton was the first to score as he added the less frequently run 2,000-m mark to his collection. At Budapest, Hung., on August 4, Cram ran the 2,000 m in

4 min 51.39 sec, surpassing John Walker's nine-year-old record by 0.01 sec. Just five days later, at Gateshead, England, Cram narrowly failed to collect his fourth world record in 24 days. He ran 1,000 m in 2 min 12.85 sec, missing Coe's mark of 2 min 12.18 sec while running the second fastest time ever. This, however, marked the end of fast racing for Cram in 1985, as an injury did what no opponent was able to do.

The spotlight then shifted to Aouita, who made clear his determination to hold all world records from 1,500 m to 5,000 m. He first went after Cram's new mile mark. He barely missed it on August 21 at Zurich, Switz., running 3 min 46.92 sec; this was 0.61 sec short of Cram but the second best time ever recorded. At West Berlin, two days later and reportedly suffering leg problems, Aouita earned his second world record by overtaking Cram's 1,500-m mark. Aouita covered the distance in 3 min 29.46 sec, 0.21 sec faster than Cram. Next Aouita turned his attention to the 3,000-m record of 7 min 32.1 sec. At Brussels on August 30 he missed by less than a second, and his 7-min 32.94-sec time was the third fastest ever. Hurting badly, Aouita missed Cram's new 2,000-m record by a substantial margin in September, but his 4 min 54.02 sec still was the fourth fastest ever.

As the season neared its end, Cram was left with world records in the mile and 2,000 m and the second best performances in history in the 1,000 m and 1,500 m. Aouita also had two world marks, in the 1,500 m and 5,000 m. His mile time was the

Steve Cram of Great Britain edges Said Aouita of Morocco by just 0.04 second in the 1,500-meter race in Nice, France, on July 16 to set a new world record.
AP/WIDE WORLD

second best ever, his 3,000-m mark the third best, and his 2,000-m time the fourth.

Three of the five field-event records went to Soviet athletes. In the high jump little-known Rudolf Povarnitsin improved his personal pre-1985 best by 0.19 m (7½ in) when he jumped 2.40 m (7 ft 10½ in). This surprising record was achieved August 11 at Donyetsk, U.S.S.R., but Povarnitsin was destined to hold it for just 24 days. Then on September 4 Igor Paklin of the U.S.S.R. won the World University Games at Kobe, Japan, with a leap of 2.41 m (7 ft 10¾ in). The new pole vault mark was far from surprising, as it was made by Sergei Bubka, who had scored four world records in 1984. His 1985 feat took place on July 13 in Paris and broke a major barrier. It was the first 6-m (19-ft 8¼-in) vault ever.

There was considerable surprise surrounding the triple jump record. Willie Banks of the United States had fallen to sixth in the 1984 Olympics and, as he had reached the age of 29, there was considerable speculation that his prime had passed. The first intimation that this was not true came when Banks jumped 17.67 m (57 ft 11¾ in), the second best leap in history, on June 8. Just eight days later, in the U.S. national championships in Indianapolis, Ind., Banks astounded everyone by reaching 17.97 m (58 ft 11½ in). The lone throwing record of the year was set by East Germany's Ulf Timmermann, who put the shot 22.62 m (74 ft 2½ in) on September 22. This broke the previous mark by 0.40 m (15¾ in) and brought the amateur record to within 0.24 m (9½ in) of the all-time best made by professional Brian Oldfield in 1975.

The World Cup brought together at Canberra, Australia, eight national and regional teams. The 1985 winner of this quadrennial affair was the United States, while the best individual performance belonged to Ben Johnson of Canada. His 10.00 sec for 100 m was the fastest time ever for a race into a head wind.

The World Indoor Games in Paris came too early (January 18–19) for peak performances, but the interest shown by 75 competing countries spoke well for the first World Indoor Championships, to be held in 1987. World indoor best performances during the year (there were no new official indoor world records) included two in the 400 m; the first was set by Thomas Schonlebe of East Germany (45.60 sec), and it was then broken by Todd Bennett of Great Britain (45.56 sec). Greg Foster of the United States lowered the 50-m hurdle best to 6.35 sec, and Timmermann put the shot 22.15 m (72 ft 8 in). The high jump best fell twice, Patrik Sjoberg of Sweden leaping 2.38 m (7 ft 9¾ in) and Dietmar Moegenburg of West Germany, the 1984 Olympic titlist, clearing 2.39 m (7 ft 10 in).

Women's International Competition

Winning the World Cup with a record score and accounting for half of the ten world records set dur-

JOHN IACONO/SPORTS ILLUSTRATED

Mary Decker Slaney (14) of the U.S. moves ahead of Zola Budd (4), who runs for Britain, on her way to win a 3,000-meter race in London on July 20.

ing the year, the women of East Germany had an outstanding season. Furthermore, they accounted for all five of the world records set at recognized Olympic distances. Leading the way was veteran champion and record breaker Marita Koch. She climaxed her season on October 6 by regaining the 400-m record, which had been regarded as somewhat untouchable after Jarmila Kratochvilova of Czechoslovakia lowered the mark to 47.99 sec in 1983. Koch, however, ran the distance in 47.60 sec. And as a fitting climax to a season during which she also had come within 0.07 sec of her own 200-m world record of 21.71 sec, she ran a fast 47.9-sec leg on the winning 4 × 400-m relay team. The World Cup also produced an international record in the 4 × 100-m relay, the East German quartet of Sabine Rieger, Silke Gladisch, Ingrid Auerswald, and Marlies Gohr running 41.37 sec.

The East Germans also produced two world records in a September 22 meeting. Moving from the 400 m to the 400-m hurdles, Sabine Busch climaxed a successful debut in that event when she ran 53.56 sec. And in the long jump Heike Drechsler (Heike Daute when she won the world championships in 1983) leaped 7.44 m (24 ft 5 in). Petra Felke achieved two world javelin marks on June 4, throwing first 75.26 m (246 ft 11 in) and then 75.40 m (247 ft 4 in).

Also earning a record under a new married name

AP/WIDE WORLD

Soviet pole vaulter Sergei Bubka clears 6 meters (19 feet 8¼ inches) on July 13, breaking his own outdoor world record and becoming the first vaulter to clear that height.

was Mary Slaney of the United States, known as Mary Decker until 1985. She lowered the record in the mile, a non-Olympic event, to 4 min 16.71 sec. Zola Budd, who had collided with Decker in the 1984 Olympic 3,000 m, claimed a record in the 5,000 m, which was not scheduled for the Olympics. She ran the distance in 14 min 48.07 sec. Ingrid Kristiansen of Norway ran two world bests, but the 10,000 m had not yet been run in the Olympics, and no world records were recognized for the marathon. She ran the 10,000 m in 30 min 59.42 sec and the marathon in 2 hr 21 min 6 sec. In the infrequently contested 5,000-m walk, Maryanne Torrellas of the United States earned a record with her performance of 22 min 51.10 sec.

Indoors there were three world bests of note. Drechsler long jumped 6.99 m (22 ft 11¼ in) but lost the record two weeks later when Galina

Chistyakova of the Soviet Union leaped 7.25 m (23 ft 9½ in). And Koch dashed 60 m in 7.04 sec.

U.S. Competition

U.S. men produced only one world record in 1985 but did achieve 16 national records in nine events. As with the world records, the U.S. successes were almost entirely in the middle distances and jumps. Sydney Maree led the way, establishing U.S. records in the 1,500-m, 2,000-m, and 5,000-m events. A former world record holder at 1,500 m, Maree lost his U.S. mark to Steve Scott but gained it back with a time of 3 min 29.77 sec, the third best time ever. He ran the 2,000 m in 4 min 54.20 sec, the fifth fastest ever, and pushed Aouita to the latter's record in the 5,000 m. In that race Maree was timed in 13 min 1.15 sec, a mark bettered only by two others.

Banks scored two U.S. bests in the triple jump. Two others broke U.S. standards twice or more. Jud Logan upped the hammer throw best four times, finally reaching 77.24 m (253 ft 5 in). And Joe Dial twice cleared heights never before attained by U.S. vaulters, leaping 5.83 m (19 ft 1½ in) and 5.85 m (19 ft 2¼ in). Two names were recorded in the U.S. high jump record book when Dennis Lewis tied the previous best with 2.34 m (7 ft 8 in) and Jim Howard then cleared 2.35 m (7 ft 8½ in). On the track Johnny Gray improved on his own 800-m national best, running 1 min 42.60 sec, and veteran Henry Marsh recorded a time of 8 min 9.17 sec in the steeplechase, the fifth fastest in history.

A dozen national records were earned by U.S. women. Slaney led the way with her world mile best and U.S. records in the 800 m (1 min 56.90 sec), the 3,000 m (8 min 29.69 sec and then 8 min 25.83 sec), and the 5,000 m (15 min 6.53 sec). Three new marks were set in the 400-m hurdles, Latanya Sheffield and Judi Brown-King each running 54.66 sec and then Brown-King completing the season with 54.38 sec. The long jump also produced three new bests, Carol Lewis leaping 7.01 m (23 ft) and 7.04 m (23 ft 1¼ in) only to see Jackie Joyner stretch out to 7.24 m (23 ft 9 in). Ramona Pagel completed the national record activity with a shot put of 19.13 m (62 ft 9¼ in).

U.S. indoor records went to Foster with 6.35 in the 50-m hurdles, Gray with 1 min 46.9 sec for 800 m, Doug Padilla with 7 min 44.9 sec for 3,000 m and 8 min 15.3 sec for two miles, and Howard twice in the high jump with a best of 2.35 m (7 ft 8½ in). For the women Diane Dixon and three-time Olympic gold medalist Valerie Brisco-Hooks took turns breaking the 400-m mark, each doing it twice with Dixon finally bringing the time down to 52.20 sec. Lewis long jumped 6.78 m (22 ft 3 in).

The National Collegiate Athletic Association indoor and outdoor men's championships were won by Arkansas. For the women Florida State won the indoor team title and Oregon the outdoor championship.

Marathon Running and Cross Country

The first World Cup marathon ever to be held took place in Hiroshima, Japan, and resulted in very fast times. The surprising individual and team wins came from the African country of Djibouti, which never before had produced outstanding runners. Ahmed Salah won the race in 2 hr 8 min 9 sec, the second fastest time ever, and teamed with two countrymen to win the team title by more than 4 1/2 minutes over Japan. The women's race, held a day earlier on April 13, was won by Katrin Dörre of East Germany in 2 hr 33 min 30 sec, and Italy was the winning team.

The men's world marathon best performance (there are no official world records inasmuch as conditions vary considerably from race to race) was achieved by 1984 Olympic Games marathon champion Carlos Lopes of Portugal. Running at Rotterdam, Neth., on April 20, Lopes took 53 seconds off the previous best time with a performance of 2 hr 7 min 12 sec. The former world's best, Steve Jones of Great Britain, made a brilliant effort to regain his record but lost by one second while winning at Chicago on October 20. And at London on April 21 the women's best time was lowered to 2 hr 21 min 6 sec by Kristiansen.

Valerie Brisco-Hooks sets a U.S. indoor record time of 52.99 seconds in the women's 440-yard race on February 2 at the Dallas Times Herald Invitational track meet.
AP/WIDE WORLD

The men's world cross-country championship was won by Lopes, the defending champion, and the women's title went to Budd. Ethiopia won the men's team race for the fifth year in a row, defeating Kenya and the United States, while the U.S. women's team won its third consecutive championship. In college competition Wisconsin won both the men's and women's team title and also the individual men's race, which went to Tim Hacker. Suzie Tuffey of North Carolina State became the women's winner.

TRANSPORTATION

The African famines and the Latin-American natural disasters highlighted the costs of inadequate transport in times of distress, and the spate of airline crashes and hijackings that led to more than 1,900 passenger fatalities served as a reminder of the millions of people who are killed and injured in transportation accidents every year. Paradoxically, the relative number of deaths from air accidents remained small, and long-term risks were still of the order of one fatality in one million passenger journeys.

Aviation

The year was a poor one for airline safety. Among the major disasters, on June 23 an Air-India 747 crashed in the Atlantic southwest of Ireland with the loss of all 329 on board. Sabotage was suspected but at year's end was unproved. On August 2 an L-1011 of Delta Air Lines crashed while on its final approach to the Dallas-Fort Worth (Texas) Airport. The death toll was 135 on board and one person on the ground. Investigation centered on the possibility that the aircraft encountered severe wind shear. On August 12 a Japan Air Lines 747 crashed in mountainous country in Japan. Of the 524 passengers on board, 4 survived. The aircraft was disabled in flight and became uncontrollable, possibly because the rear bulkhead of the pressurized fuselage failed. On August 22 a British Airtours 737 caught fire during the takeoff run at Manchester (England) International Airport. The captain brought the aircraft to a halt, but it was engulfed by the fire, which had begun when an engine combustion chamber failed. There were 55 fatalities, and 14 were seriously injured. On September 6 a DC-9 of Midwest Express crashed shortly after takeoff from Milwaukee, Wis., with the loss of 31 lives, and on December 12 a chartered DC-8 operated by Arrow Air of Miami, Fla., crashed just after taking off from Gander, Newfoundland; all 256 on board, including 248 U.S. soldiers, were killed.

In 1984, by contrast, the International Civil Aviation Organization (ICAO) had reported 224 passenger fatalities on scheduled services, with a fatality rate of 0.02 per 100 million passenger-km (per 63.75 million passenger-mi), both figures the lowest for many years. The 1985 fatality total surpassed that of 1974 when there were 1,299 passenger fatalities

AP/WIDE WORLD

Travelers at Boston's Logan International Airport endure long lines at the Pan American check-in area on February 28 as a strike by Transport Workers Union members virtually halted the carrier's domestic service.

and a fatality rate of 0.24. Traffic then was at less than half the level of 1985, however, so the 1985 fatality rate was likely to be substantially lower.

Despite continued growth in traffic during 1985, there were renewed fears about financial prospects for the airlines. The International Air Transport Association (IATA) reported a growth of 8.5% in scheduled international passenger traffic during the first seven months of the year and a 6.3% increase in capacity. The strong growth in freight reported in 1984 for international traffic—14.3%—dwindled during the first seven months of 1985 to 2.8%. As a result, although total traffic was up 6.4%, it was outstripped by capacity, which rose 6.9%.

Financial results for IATA airlines in 1984 were considerably worse than anticipated. The association in October of that year, had predicted an operating profit of $2.9 billion on international services and a profit after interest of $1.2 billion. The actual result was an operating profit of $2.2 billion, which became $500 million after interest payments. The forecasts were scaled down appropriately, and the after-interest result for 1985 might prove to be little more than one of breaking even. The situation was all the more disappointing because the 1984 forecasts, coming after the severe losses of 1979–83, had foreseen profits improving into 1986 at least.

For once the deterioration could not be laid at the door of fuel prices. Fuel accounted for 25% of IATA members' operating costs, the highest single item, but prices had been stable and even decreasing slightly. Alarm expressed by U.K. airlines in particular during October about sudden and major price increases before the end of the year could not immediately be confirmed as a general trend, and some oil industry analysts argued that it was a local and temporary phenomenon.

A steady reduction in yield—the rate of revenue per unit of traffic—during 1980–84 had been matched by a fall in unit operating costs, achieved largely through improved staff productivity and the introduction of more efficient aircraft. However, this trend could not be maintained in 1985, when yield became static but costs began to rise.

In the U.S. traffic growth appeared to slow toward the end of 1985, but during the first nine months of the year there was a 14.3% increase in passenger traffic over the same period of 1984. Capacity grew only by 8.4%. International passenger traffic of the 20 Western European flag carriers in the first eight months of 1985 was 8.5% above that for the same period of 1984, while international freight traffic rose 3.6%.

In the U.S. Pan American agreed to sell its profitable Pacific division to United Air Lines. Control of TWA was won by financier Carl Icahn in a contest with Texas Air. Frontier Airlines was taken over by the fast-growing People Express.

Freight and Pipelines

Freight traffic was relatively buoyant during the year, with European air cargo up by more than 14% and European rail traffic up 11%. More countries were planning larger trains; 10,000-metric-ton coal trains were being planned for China's Datang (Ta-t'ang) to Guangzhou (Canton) line, which was being electrified. Generally, freight packaging was being made more efficient.

As of the end of 1985 there were 193,000 km (1 km = 0.62 mi) of pipelines in the construction, planning, and study phases, with starts in 1985 on 32,000 km of new construction. Despite this, the capacity of the world's pipeline construction industry was not being fully utilized; pricing was, therefore, competitive, and there was sustained innovation in construction techniques in hostile environments such as deep waters, where an increasing proportion of new pipelines was being laid.

Among major projects completed in 1985 was the 3,380-km, 140-cm (56-in)-diameter oil line between Novosibirsk and Yelets in the U.S.S.R.; in the same area a 250-km coal slurry pipe was opened. In Utah a 153-km phosphate slurry line was commissioned, and a 217-km carbon dioxide pipe was brought into service in the U.S. Central Basin area. A growing proportion of new pipelines in the Middle East was for water rather than for oil or gas. An example was the 345-km pipeline to Asir in Saudi Arabia.

The biggest pipeline project started in 1985 was the $1.7 billion, 1,600-km Indian oil and gas line from the western offshore fields to inland fertilizer plants to the north.

Roads and Traffic

The shift in policies toward deregulation and private ownership appeared to have boosted interest in toll roads. As of the end of 1985 there were more than 4,000 km of toll roads in Japan, and 900 km were planned in Malaysia. China was building a toll expressway to link Shenyan (Shenyen)-Guangzhou (Canton) and Zhuhai (Chu-hai) at a cost of $900 million. The Turkish government planned a $500 million toll road to run from Bulgaria over the second Bosporus crossing to Ankara in Turkey. In the U.S. 27 km were in the planning stage in the Chicago area, and the Dallas (Texas) North Tollway was under construction. Perhaps the most impressive toll facility that was opened in 1985 was the 8.4-km Penang Bridge linking the island of Penang to the mainland of Malaysia.

Other major highway facilities opened in 1985 were the 480-m Iguaçu Bridge linking Argentina and Brazil, the Fort McHenry Tunnel under the Baltimore, Md., harbor, the cross-Denmark motorway between Vejle and the West German border, and the Ali Ayub expressway in Iraq. At $750 million for 218 km, the four-tube Fort McHenry Tunnel was one of the most expensive sections of highway ever built.

Traffic growth appeared to be greater in 1985 than in recent years. This was consistent with the increased demand for new vehicles, with the U.S. automobile industry again profitable. Concerns about oil supplies and prices persisted, and the use of alcohol-based fuels was spreading among less developed countries that had little or no indigenous oil.

Maintaining the growing length of heavily traveled superhighways continued to be a major problem, as illustrated by the shutdown of a section of Britain's busiest motorway, the M-1, for two weeks for reconstruction. Standards were being revised upward, and new motorway pavements in the U.K. were to be built to provide an 85% chance of lasting 20 years without requiring strengthening.

Intercity Rail

In a year marking the 150th anniversary of the first German railway (Nürnberg to Fürth), the West German rail system was being electrified at a rate of 280 km per year, and its intercity experimental train was unveiled. In Japan the main bore of the Seikan Tunnel was completed, and another section of the Tohoku Shinkansen line was opened. In France the Lille-to-Lyon Train à Grande Vitesse (TGV) service began operating, and work started on the 280-km TGV-Atlantique, scheduled for completion in 1990. In the U.S.S.R. the Baikal-to-Amur railway was fully operational, reducing rail hauls between European Russia and Western Siberia by 200 to 450 km. The project had necessitated the construction of 32 km of bridges and 25 km of tunnels.

As of 1985 China had one of the world's busiest railway systems. Extending over 56,000 route-km, it carried 220,000,000,000 passenger-km and 800,000,000,000 metric ton-km in 1985. Chinese passenger trains consisted of as many as 25 coaches; to help cope with the growth in demand, 420 diesel and 150 twin electric locomotives, along with double-decker passenger coaches, were ordered. In Denmark the world's first three-phase asynchronous 25-kv locomotives were in service, and in the U.K. the High Speed Train set a new world record for a diesel-hauled train by covering the 432 km between Newcastle and London at an average speed of 186 km/h and achieving a maximum speed of 232 km/h. Electrification projects were being implemented in most industrialized countries and increasingly were introduced in less developed countries.

Serious train crashes occurred in Portugal, where at least 50 people were killed, and in Ethiopia,

U.S. Secretary of Transportation Elizabeth Dole and Robert B. Claytor, Chairman of Norfolk Southern Corp., hold a press conference on February 8 to announce the sale of Conrail, the U.S.-subsidized freight rail system, to Norfolk Southern Corp. if approved by Congress.

AP/WIDE WORLD

SUSAN GREENWOOD/THE NEW YORK TIMES

The new elevated mass transit system in Miami, Florida, was widely admired for design, cleanliness, and efficiency, but fiscal problems and low ridership clouded its future.

where 392 people died. The latter was one of the worst disasters in railway history.

Urban Mass Transit

One of the most far-reaching changes in urban transit policy in industrial countries occurred with the passing of the Transport Act 1985 in the U.K. Essentially, this gave the market prime place in providing local transport services, with publicly sponsored services occupying a secondary role.

Recent innovations in bus transport included reopening of the defunct Trinidadian railways as busways and the opening of new busways in Ottawa, Ont., and Pittsburgh, Pa. Bus transportation projects were being planned in five other U.S. cities. Energy conservation systems on buses, using high-speed flywheels and compressed gases, were tried successfully, and electrically steered buses were being tested in Fürth, West Germany. The strong interest in light rail (a railway system equipped to carry only light traffic) over recent years resulted in the opening of several new systems in 1985. In Vancouver, B.C., a 23-km system began operation and would serve Expo 86—the 1986 World Exposition of Transport and Communications—when it opened in May 1986. In Buffalo, N.Y., the first ten kilometers of the city's $530 million system was operating. Other light railways recently opened included the Island Line in Hong Kong, the central section of Pittsburgh's South Hills Line, the first half of Manila's 15-km system, the Scarborough, Ont., 7-km system, and a new line in Volgograd, U.S.S.R. Work was under way on new lines in Strasbourg, Grenoble, and Paris in France and in Los Angeles and Dallas, Texas, in the U.S. The Dallas system would eventually extend to 258 km.

New subways were opened in Tianjin (Tientsin), China, and Odessa, which became the 19th city in the U.S.S.R. to have a subway. Extensions to existing systems were opened in Washington, D.C., Miami, Fla., Atlanta, Ga., Asphoro, Japan, Seoul, South Korea, Paris, and in the U.S.S.R. in Leningrad, Novosibirsk, and Moscow (whose system was now 200 km in length). London's subway stations were being extensively modernized, and automatic ticketing programs were under way. In New York City one-fifth of the 6,200 subway cars were being replaced, and extensive modernization of the Paris and Madrid systems was under way.

TRINIDAD AND TOBAGO

The National Alliance for Reconstruction (NAR), formed a year earlier by four of Trinidad and Tobago's opposition parties, was officially launched in September 1985. The NAR comprised the Democratic Action Congress, the United Labour Front, the Organization for National Reconstruction, and the Tapia House Movement. It was expected to present a strong challenge to the governing People's National Movement in general elections due to take place before February 1987.

The government's economic austerity measures showed some success in increasing the trade surplus and slowing the decline in international reserves. A trade surplus of TT$708 million was achieved in the first six months of 1985, compared with TT$467 million for all of 1984. (For table of world currencies, *see* International Exchange and Payments.) Petroleum production averaged 177,639 bbl a day in the first half of the year, a 9.4% increase over the corresponding period in 1984. Despite a rise in sugar production from 64,800 metric tons in 1984 to 81,200 metric tons, the state-owned Caroni company announced a package of economy measures in October to deal with immediate cash-flow problems arising from reduced domestic demand and low world sugar prices. There were a number of labor disputes over pay and job security issues.

In July and August Prime Minister George Chambers toured the U.K., Japan, China, India, Hong Kong, South Korea, and Austria to promote trade and investment.

TUNISIA

At a meeting of the Central Committee of the ruling Parti Socialiste Destourien (PSD) on March 9, 1985, Tunisia's Pres. Habib Bourguiba gave the clearest indication yet that his successor, "when the time came," would be Prime Minister Mohammed Mzali. In a ministerial reshuffle on October 23 Zine El Abidine Ben Ali was promoted from state secretary to minister-delegate in charge of national security, and Nourredine Hached, ambassador to Algeria, was appointed minister of labor.

Meanwhile, the government faced increasing opposition. The year began with a strike by students at the University of Tunis to mark the anniversary of the previous year's "bread riots." Local elections on May 12 were boycotted by opposition parties. Tension between the government and the labor union organization, the Union Générale des Travailleurs Tunisiens (UGTT), grew throughout the year. In October the UGTT headquarters in Tunis was closed by government order, and in November UGTT Secretary-General Habib Achour was placed under house arrest. Following an agreement reached on December 4 between the UGTT and Minister of Labor Hached, Achour was replaced as secretary-general by Sadok Allouche.

The government also had to contend with two crises in Tunisia's foreign relations. The first of these arose in August when Libya began to expel Tunisian workers (of whom there were some 80,000–90,000 in Libya). In all, some 30,000 were expelled, adding to Tunisia's already severe economic problems. Relations worsened with the expulsion by Tunisia of 253 Libyans accused of espionage. Efforts at mediation were made by the Arab League, and Tunisia was supported by Algeria, whose Pres. Chadli Bendjedid visited Bourguiba at Monastir on September 2. On September 26 Tunisia severed relations with Libya.

The second crisis involved Tunisia's relations with the U.S., previously a trusted ally. Tunisia was outraged by Pres. Ronald Reagan's initial approval of the Israeli air raid on the headquarters of the Palestine Liberation Organization on the outskirts of Tunis on October 1, when many Tunisians were among those killed or injured. The visit to Tunis on October 21–23 of U.S. Deputy Secretary of State John C. Whitehead, with an offer of increased U.S. aid, helped to repair the rift.

Franco-Tunisian relations remained cordial. French Foreign Minister Roland Dumas visited Tunis twice during the year. In June, when Bourguiba visited France privately, Pres. François Mitterrand met with him at the Tunisian embassy. In August Edith Cresson, French minister of industrial redeployment and foreign trade, visited Tunis for discussions on economic cooperation.

TURKEY

During 1985 the political scene in Turkey changed as the opposition to the government of Prime Minister Turgut Ozal, leader of the right-of-center Motherland Party, chose new leaders and regrouped. On the left the extraparliamentary Social Democratic Party merged with the main opposition party in Parliament, the Populist Party, under its new leader, Aydin Guven Gurkan. However, a further division was introduced by the formation on November 14 of the Democratic Left Party, based on the personal following of Bulent Ecevit, former prime minister, who had been banned from political activity for ten years under the 1982 constitution. In the ranks of the right-wing opposition, the Nationalist Democracy Party, under its new leader, Umit Soylemezoglu, drew closer to the extraparliamentary Right Path Party, led by Husamettin Cindoruk, a supporter of former prime minister Suleyman Demirel, also barred from taking a political role.

Restrictions imposed after the 1980 military takeover continued to be eased. At the end of the year only 9 of the country's 67 provinces remained under martial law, while in 16 others civil administrators still held emergency powers. The area still under martial law was in the southeast, where the outlawed Kurdish Workers Party (PKK) continued its campaign of violence. Launched in August 1984, by the end of November 1985 the campaign had caused 241 deaths, 59 of them among the security forces.

The government was preoccupied with the plight of ethnic Turks in neighboring Bulgaria, who had allegedly been subjected to forcible assimilation. Notes of protest and offers to take in the Bulgarian Turks failed to produce results. Following the temporary partial closure of the frontier, the mutual blockading of consulates, and the suspension of sporting contacts, the Turkish government voiced its complaints at international gatherings and canvassed other Muslim countries for support.

There was no improvement in relations with Greece, which accused both Turkish and U.S. air-

Workers begin to sift through the rubble left after Israeli jets bombed the headquarters of the Palestine Liberation Organization near Tunis in October.

AP/WIDE WORLD

craft of violating its airspace during periodic maneuvers. During his visit in November, Michael
Armacost, U.S. assistant secretary of state for political affairs, discussed the revision of the U.S.-Turk-
ish defense and economic cooperation agreement,
which was to expire in December. A $100 million
economic aid agreement between the two countries
was signed at year's end. The consolidation of
the self-proclaimed Turkish Republic of Northern
Cyprus was supported by Turkey, the only country
to recognize the state. At the same time, Turkey
continued to support the efforts of the UN to solve
the Cyprus dispute.

The economy continued to grow, although at a
slower rate than in 1984. The trade balance improved, and Turkey was able to service its foreign
debt and to obtain further external finance. Inflation hovered around 40%. Prime Minister Ozal's
primary concerns during his visits to the U.S. in
April and the Far East in July were to promote
trade and to attract foreign investment.

UGANDA

The steady economic recovery that had taken place
with the support of the World Bank and the International Monetary Fund since Pres. Milton Obote
was returned to office in Uganda in 1980 was increasingly threatened in the early months of 1985
by the activities of antigovernment rebels and the
heavy-handed reprisals of government troops. In
response to a request from Obote, the U.K. government agreed in April to renew and increase military
assistance; at the same time, the British voiced their

Truckloads of freed political prisoners arrive in
downtown Kampala after their release on October 10
by the new military government. Pres. Milton Obote,
who had jailed them, was ousted in a July 27 coup.
AP/WIDE WORLD

disquiet over reports of army excesses. Hopes of a
more stable future were undermined when the National Resistance Army (NRA), the main guerrilla
force, opened a new front in the Western Province.
In the eyes of many Ugandans, the new offensive
gave credence to the rebels' claim that they were
not merely conducting a tribal struggle for power in
support of the interests of a section of the Baganda
people who had opposed Obote ever since he drove
their ruler, the kabaka, into exile 20 years earlier.

During a visit to the U.K. in June, Paul Ssemogerere, leader of the main parliamentary opposition, the Democratic Party, pleaded with the British
government to intervene to protect democracy in
Uganda. He claimed that half a million people,
more than during the years (1971–79) of former
president Idi Amin's tyrannous rule, had died since
Obote took office. Shortly afterward Amnesty International published a report in which detailed
charges of torture were leveled against the security
forces. Obote invited Amnesty representatives to
examine the situation for themselves, but before
the offer could be taken up, his government was
overthrown by a military coup on July 27. Obote
fled first to Kenya and later to Zambia.

The origins of the coup lay in the disaffection
among Acholi members of the Army who were
critical of the favored treatment that, they said, was
given to soldiers from Lango, Obote's own tribal
district. The northern brigade, under Brig. Bazilio
Olara Okello, mutinied and advanced southward to
Kampala, which they seized without much resistance but with an excess of looting.

The NRA, which claimed foreknowledge of the
coup, hoped to take a share in government. They
were angry, therefore, when, without consultation,
the mutineers appointed a Military Council under
Gen. Tito Okello, the army commander, to supervise the government of the country for a year. They
were even more disturbed when Paulo Muwanga,
vice-president under Obote, whom they distrusted
as much as Obote himself, was appointed prime
minister of an interim government on August 1, and
when the Military Council enlisted the aid of some
of Amin's former soldiers. While the NRA threatened to continue its military activities, Ssemogerere
accepted office as minister of internal affairs. His
first duty was to release more than 1,000 prisoners
detained by the Obote regime.

The dismissal of Muwanga within a month did
little to reassure the NRA. However, talks between
the leaders of the Military Council and the NRA began in Kenya in August, with Kenyan Pres. Daniel
arap Moi as mediator, and on December 17 a peace
treaty was signed in Nairobi. Under the agreement,
power in the Military Council would be shared by
the NRA, and the guerrillas would be absorbed
into the national army. A four-nation observer
force would monitor the accord. On December 11,
the government announced that elections would be
held in July 1986.

The body of Konstantin Chernenko is borne in a funeral procession in Moscow in March. Chernenko, who had held the general secretaryship of the Communist Party for just over a year, became the third Soviet leader to die in 28 months.

JEAN-CLAUDE FRANCOLON—
GAMMA/LIAISON

UNION OF SOVIET SOCIALIST REPUBLICS

The death of Konstantin Chernenko on March 10, 1985, was a watershed in Soviet politics, representing the final passing from the scene of a generation of leaders who had come to power under Leonid Brezhnev. The new general secretary of the Communist Party of the Soviet Union (CPSU), Mikhail Gorbachev, was at 54 the youngest man to become leader since Joseph Stalin. In nominating Gorbachev as the new general secretary at a meeting of the CPSU Central Committee (CC) on March 11, Foreign Minister Andrei Gromyko stated that Gorbachev had taken the chair at CC Politburo meetings when Chernenko had been too ill to attend. Of Gorbachev's chairmanship he said: "Without exaggeration, he conducted himself brilliantly"; he also praised the flexibility and lack of dogma in his approach to problems.

There was little doubt that Gromyko's praise was genuine, and it underlined the fact that Gorbachev was the most able man in the Politburo. The succession battle had been between him and Grigori Romanov, the only other CC secretary who was a full member of the Politburo. Since Gorbachev had been running the CC Secretariat in Chernenko's absence, he was ideally placed to take over. In contrast to his three aged predecessors, Gorbachev presented a picture of health, vitality, dynamism, and, despite his limited experience of life among Moscow's political elite, remarkable self-confidence.

Because the CPSU had changed only its leader and not its policies, Gorbachev could not make sweeping changes in the Politburo, but he was in a stronger position to bring new people into the Secretariat. In order to build up his own authority, he needed to bring in those who shared his own vision of the future. Yegor K. Ligachev became a full member of the Politburo and was responsible in the Secretariat for personnel appointments. As such, he emerged as Gorbachev's deputy.

Since 1977 the general secretary of the CPSU had always been chairman of the Presidium of the Supreme Soviet (president) as well, but in July this vacant post was filled by Gromyko, who thus ended 28 years as foreign minister. If this was a surprise—most foreign observers had expected Gorbachev to become head of state—the appointment of Eduard A. Shevardnadze to replace Gromyko as foreign minister astonished many. The Georgian had little experience of the outside world and was a beginner in foreign affairs. The effect of these two appointments was to increase Gorbachev's authority and allow him greater flexibility in external policy. Gromyko appeared to be a stopgap president, and it seemed likely that in the near future Gorbachev would add the post to those he already held, those of head of the CPSU and chairman of the Defense Council. Another significant promotion was that of Anatoli Dobrynin, long-time Soviet ambassador in Washington, who became first deputy foreign minister. Dobrynin's considerable ability and expertise made him a key adviser to Gorbachev on United States policy.

While there were many changes at the top of the party in 1985, there were even more lower down. Over 40% of the first secretaries of oblasts or *krai*s (provinces) changed between March and December. Directed by Ligachev, the aim was to sweep away the old guard and install able, technically competent functionaries capable of increasing the effectiveness of Soviet economic life. Another reason for removals was the pervasiveness of corruption, which had spread rapidly during the final years of the Brezhnev era.

Marshal Nikolai Ogarkov, dismissed as chief of general staff in September 1984, appeared to make a comeback as commander in chief of the Western

V. KUZMIN—TASS/SOVFOTO

In the Kremlin on March 12, Soviet official Vasili Kuznetsov (right) greets Zhang Chengxian (Chang Ch'eng-hsien), leader of a delegation from China.

theater of military operations. The post probably also included command over the Northwestern theater and Warsaw Pact forces. In the event of a conflict with NATO forces, Ogarkov would be the key field commander. His thinking on military strategy, operational art, and tactics was systematically implemented in the Soviet armed forces throughout the year. It appeared certain that the reason for Ogarkov's dismissal in 1984 concerned disagreements over resource allocations and not over military doctrine. Ogarkov wanted more high-technology weapons immediately, whereas the CPSU leadership judged that such a demand would impose too great a burden on the civilian economy. The leaders were willing to produce the weapons but only in limited quantities.

A new generation of military and naval commanders took over, although not all of them could be connected with Ogarkov. There were new commanders in charge of almost all 16 Soviet military districts, all four groups of Soviet forces (in East Germany, Poland, Czechoslovakia, and Hungary), all theaters of military operation, and the Baltic, Northern, and Black Sea fleets. These changes represented the most rapid turnover at the top of the Soviet military since 1945.

Gorbachev began to develop a distinctive style of leadership. On walkabouts in Leningrad, Tselinograd, and other cities, he sought to communicate directly to the citizens his views about how the U.S.S.R. should develop. When editors and journalists from the press and television were invited to see him, he greeted them not with the long speeches they had come to expect but with requests for their own opinions, telling them that he had come to listen. He was critical of poor discipline in all its guises, be it overconsumption of alcohol, poor time-keeping, or failure to meet one's obligations. As a nondrinker as well as a nonsmoker, Gorbachev led the campaign against alcoholism. The general secretary castigated those who were capable of making long-winded speeches but were quite incapable of fulfilling their plans.

The number of Jews and Germans permitted to emigrate declined to a trickle during the year. It was thought, however, that Gorbachev's desire to improve relations with Israel, the U.S., and West Germany might result in an increase in 1986. Yelena Bonner, wife of the dissident Soviet physicist Andrei Sakharov, was granted permission to journey to the West to seek medical treatment. The draft version of a new program and statute of the CPSU, due to be presented to the 27th congress in February–March 1986, was published for discussion in October. A new party program had been promised for years and was certainly necessary in the light of promises made in the previous program, published in 1961, which had looked forward to the Soviet public living under communism in the 1980s. The new program was intended to guide the population through to the year 2000. It forecast that over the 15-year period economic output would double and living standards would rise substantially. There was sharp criticism of the Brezhnev leadership, which was accused of failure to assess "in due time and proper manner alterations in the economic situation and the need for profound change in all spheres of life." The optimistic objective was an annual growth of 4.7% over the 15-year period. The key to the future was declared to be scientific and technical progress. However, the program contained few tangible suggestions as to how the country's economic problems were to be solved. Generalizations were the rule. Since Soviet industry was incapable of supplying all the new equipment necessary to achieve such progress, an increase in East-West cooperation appeared probable.

The Economy

The increase in industrial production between January and September was 3.7% over the same period in 1984, while labor productivity grew by 3.3%. In the third quarter of 1985 the daily rate of output rose by 5%; in the energy and electrification sector production was up by 4%, and in chemicals and the oil machinery industry it rose 5% over the same quarter of 1984. The oil industry achieved 96% of its plan target and mineral fertilizers 97%, but the coal industry recorded a 1% growth to achieve 100.2%—quite an achievement given the great problems of the industry. However, coal output was well below the original goals set in the five-year (1981–85) plan. Light industry also failed to meet its target. The transportation sector continued to experience difficulties, with only air transport and the merchant marine fulfilling plan objectives. The railroad network was overburdened and would require considerable investment.

In October the government newspaper *Izvestiya* stated that those ministries, associations, and enterprises selected to participate in the "economic experiment" had done especially well. This factor was increasingly significant in assessing economic performance, as some 2,300 enterprises, accounting for over 12% of Soviet output, now worked under "new conditions." However, the performance of some ministries failed to live up to expectations. While the Belorussian Ministry of Light Industry and the Ukrainian Ministry of the Food Industry were praised, the Ukrainian Ministry of Local Industry did not fulfill its goals. A decree issued in August stated that selected enterprises were to be permitted to use their own profits to renew equipment during the 12th five-year (1986–90) plan, and enterprise funds were to be channeled into the construction of homes and recreational buildings for workers.

The harvest attained an estimated 180 million metric tons, greater than that achieved in 1984 but nevertheless disappointing because it fell short of expectations. Output and economic efficiency in the agricultural sector remained generally unsatisfactory despite some trends for the better. Besides problems in grain production, the output of sugar beets, sunflowers, and cotton remained inadequate. Animal products improved, thanks mainly to imported fodder, but productivity remained low. In 1984 grain imports reached 45 million metric tons, including 26.4 million metric tons of wheat; the importation of 5.5 million metric tons of sugar made the Soviet Union the leading importer of sugar on the world market. Imports of agricultural products over the years 1982–84 cost an estimated $16.1 billion. A new agreement on agricultural cooperation concluded with the U.S. included a new five-year pact on grain sales that foresaw Moscow purchasing at least nine million metric tons of grain a year from the U.S.

While Gorbachev hinted that fewer resources might be devoted to the rural sector, he did not articulate any solutions to the perennial problems that have faced agriculture. Waste was still evident on a massive scale. In July *Pravda* revealed that since 1981 in Chimkent oblast, Kazakhstan, almost one billion rubles had been invested in agriculture, and yet the output of grain, potatoes, vegetables, and milk yield per cow had declined. Not surprisingly, overall agricultural output in the oblast had also dropped. In November it was announced that a superministry of agriculture was to be formed by merging the Ministries of Agriculture, Agricultural Procurement, the Meat and Dairy Industry, and the Food Industry, as well as the State Committee for the Production and Technical Supervision of Agriculture.

Foreign Affairs

The year was dominated by the summit meeting between Gorbachev and U.S. Pres. Ronald Reagan in Geneva on November 19–20. It was the first meeting between the superpower leaders since 1979. Given the poor state of Soviet-U.S. relations, such a meeting had appeared improbable earlier in the year. It appeared that the Soviets agreed to the con-

In a Moscow parade marking the 68th anniversary of the Bolshevik Revolution, workers carry a sign calling on the "peoples of the world" to unite in opposition to the "militarization of space."

AP/WIDE WORLD

ference mainly because of their apprehension about the U.S. Strategic Defense Initiative (SDI), popularly known as the "Star Wars" defense system.

The shooting of Maj. Arthur Nicholson, a U.S. military liaison officer, by a Soviet guard in East Germany in March angered the U.S. administration. It was the first U.S. fatality in 40 years of liaison work with the Soviet Army. Later the U.S. accused the Soviet Union of using "spydust" to keep track of U.S. diplomats in the U.S.S.R. Then the U.S.S.R. accused the U.S. of "kidnapping and terrorism" when Vitali Yurchenko, a KGB officer, appeared in the Soviet embassy in Washington in November claiming that he had been held in the U.S. against his will. At a press conference in Moscow on his return, Yurchenko stated that he had been seized in Rome on August 1 and taken to the U.S., where he had been put under pressure to betray his country. The U.S. Central Intelligence Agency claimed that Yurchenko had been a genuine defector but had changed his mind; another possible interpretation of events was that Yurchenko had been sent on a reconnaissance mission by the KGB in order to learn about CIA debriefing techniques and also to permit the U.S.S.R. to attack the U.S. on human rights.

In the weeks preceding the summit the Soviet Union conducted a fierce campaign against SDI, skillfully utilizing opposition to the program in the West to bolster its position. Gorbachev's visit to France in October revealed the Soviet leader to be highly persuasive. His wife, Raisa, charmed Western viewers even more. President Reagan was considered to be at a disadvantage; an old U.S. leader pitted against a young Soviet leader provided quite a contrast to the recent past.

At Geneva long discussions between the two leaders established a basis for mutual trust that augured well for the future. Although Gorbachev had stated beforehand that only an agreement to halt SDI would represent success, and Reagan refused to make any concessions on this point, the summit was a success. In a joint statement both sides agreed that a nuclear war could not be won and must not be fought. Neither side would seek to achieve military superiority. They called for early progress in arms control negotiations and supported the idea of an interim agreement on intermediate nuclear forces. Further steps would be taken to reduce nuclear risk. Both underlined their commitment to the nuclear non-proliferation treaty. Bilateral discussions involving technical experts would aim to achieve a ban on chemical weapons, including the questions of verification that would ensue. Both sides favored positive results from the NATO-Warsaw Pact talks on mutual and balanced force reductions in Vienna. The U.S. and the U.S.S.R. intended to facilitate an early and successful conclusion to the Stockholm Conference on Confidence- and Security-Building Measures and Disarmament in Europe. Dialogue between the superpowers was to be intensified at

both foreign minister and other levels. Safety on air routes in the northern Pacific was to increase. Air services between the two countries were to resume. A Soviet consulate general was to open in New York City and a U.S. one in Kiev. There was to be cooperation on environmental protection, while educational and cultural exchanges were to be expanded. Both countries favored the expansion of international cooperation in utilizing controlled thermonuclear fusion for peaceful purposes. The two leaders agreed to meet again in Washington in 1986 and in Moscow in 1987.

Anglo-Soviet relations reached a new low in September when 31 Soviet diplomats and media people were expelled from the U.K. and the same number of Britons were ordered out of Moscow. The Soviets expelled by Britain were accused of spying on the evidence of Oleg Gordievski, KGB head in Britain, who had defected in August. British intelligence claimed that Gordievski had been a double agent for 19 years, during which time he had provided much valuable information. He was the highest ranking KGB officer ever to defect to Britain. However, relations between the two countries recovered rapidly, and by the end of the year Soviet visas had been granted for some replacement British diplomats.

Sino-Soviet relations improved slightly during the year. Yao Yilin (Yao Yi-lin), Chinese vice premier, visited Moscow and signed a new five-year trade agreement; he was the highest ranking Chinese official to visit the U.S.S.R. in more than 20 years. However, while relations at the state level improved, contacts at party level made little progress.

The war in Afghanistan continued into its sixth year with no military or political victory in sight. The Soviet Union suffered a humiliating defeat at the UN in November when a record 122 nations censured its occupation of Afghanistan, with only 19 countries supporting Moscow and 12 abstaining. The subject caused sharp disagreements at the Geneva summit, and Gorbachev was apparently well aware that the issue had become a liability.

In the Middle East Oman established diplomatic relations with Moscow in September, and the United Arab Emirates did so in November. Kuwait, which had already recognized the Soviet Union, deployed the first of its Soviet missiles, bought in 1984 for $325 million. Saudi Arabia and its allies were considering establishing diplomatic relations with the U.S.S.R. The Soviet Union continued its policy of cultivating better relations with Israel in an effort to increase its influence in the area. When Col. Muammar Al Qadhafi of Libya visited Moscow in October, attempts were made to persuade him to moderate his anti-Israeli stance.

The U.S.S.R.'s charmed existence in Lebanon ended when three diplomats and an embassy physician were kidnapped in September by left-wing guerrillas. One diplomat was murdered before the release of the others was negotiated.

UNITED ARAB EMIRATES

Two developments in 1985 strengthened the regional position of the United Arab Emirates (U.A.E.). A new national airline, called Emirates Airlines and based in Dubai, began operations in October with initial traffic rights to Kuwait (later withdrawn), Pakistan, and India. The new carrier was in competition to some extent with Gulf Air, in which the U.A.E. was a shareholder. The Dubai National Travel Agency began promoting "winter sunshine" package tours to the U.A.E. with a view to boosting tourism from Europe. The second development, announced on April 23, was the setting up of a free-trade zone authority at the Jebel Ali port area outside the town of Dubai. Although Abu Dhabi remained the most important member of the federation in terms of its petroleum production and influence on policy-making, Dubai moved ahead as a commercial center.

The aim of a number of mergers among local banks during the year was to restrain the unfettered growth of the banking sector. In June the Petroleum and Mineral Resources Ministry revealed a multi-million-dollar plan to stockpile enough petroleum to meet the country's needs for at least 45 days.

In November the U.A.E. announced that it was establishing diplomatic relations with the U.S.S.R. Before 1985 only Kuwait, among the Gulf emirates, had maintained relations with the Soviets.

UNITED KINGDOM

On March 5, 1985, with bands playing and heads held high, the striking miners marched back to their pits. For the defeated strikers it was a day of bitterness and humiliation. For the government of Prime Minister Margaret Thatcher it was the moment of victory. The strike ended a year almost to the day after it had begun with the announcement by the National Coal Board (NCB) of a plan to close 20 uneconomic pits and thereby make redundant some 20,000 of the industry's 186,000 workers. Throughout the bitter and often violent dispute, Arthur Scargill, president of the National Union of Mineworkers (NUM), had insisted that there was no such thing as an uneconomic pit. But the strike was about more than the economic future of the British coal industry. It was about the constitutional and political authority of the government; it was about the rule of law over disorder; and it was about the cohesion of the Labour movement—the Trades Union Congress (TUC) and the Labour Party—and the power of the trade unions.

For Scargill the strike was a single battle in a revolutionary class struggle. This viewpoint had given the strike a political character from the outset and had increased the government's determination to win and to be seen to win decisively. Not least this was because folk memories of the events of 1974—when the Conservative Party government of Edward Heath had been destroyed at the hands of the miners, or had perhaps destroyed itself with their

GROENDHAL-BLUE—GAMMA/LIAISON

After a strike of nearly a year, most British miners returned to work on March 5. A few pits remained closed, however, as miners demanded that arrested co-workers be freed in order to return to work, too.

aid—were still strong. For Thatcher the strike was also a trial of will.

By the beginning of the year the outcome of the dispute was no longer in doubt. The miners were effectively beaten. Coal stocks were more than sufficient to see the winter through; not an electric light bulb had been extinguished, in contrast to the blackouts of 1974, when industry had been reduced to a three-day working week. Moreover, once the New Year arrived the drift back to work of defeated or disaffected miners gathered pace until, toward the end of February, the NCB could claim that more than 50% of the miners were at work, including the 26%, mainly in Nottinghamshire, who had refused to join the strike in the first place. In the end, at a delegate conference of the NUM, the miners voted by the narrowest margin for a return to work without any terms at all. In effect, it was unconditional surrender. Nevertheless, Scargill claimed victory. "All our future struggles will be stronger as a result," he declared. Few other leaders of the Labour movement agreed with him.

From the government's point of view, the government was seen to govern, as Thatcher had resolved would be the case, and the ghosts of 1974 were laid at last. Furthermore, victory over the miners confirmed and dramatized the tilt in the balance of power against the trade union movement in general that had been evident since the Conservatives came to office in 1979. The defeat of the miners left the unions in disarray.

After the strike, normality returned to British political life, although there were some surprising, and unforeseen, consequences. One was a sharp decline in the government's popularity. Any hope that the "Scargill factor" would do for the prime minister's popularity what the "Falklands factor" had in 1982 was soon dispelled.

In January the government's average standing in the three major opinion polls was 41% to Labour's 33% and the Liberal-Social Democratic Party Alliance's 24%. By May, in which month the Conservatives experienced severe setbacks in local elections to fill the nonmetropolitan county councils, the government's standing had fallen to 36%. On July 4 the Alliance narrowly won a parliamentary by-election in the constituency of Brecon and Radnor, Wales, in which the Conservative candidate was relegated to a humiliating third place.

Was this merely a case of "midterm blues" or something more serious? Thatcher was not bound to fight another general election until May 1988, but with unemployment still well above the three million mark and showing little sign of improvement, an increasing number of Conservative members of Parliament began to wonder whether the party could win again on its existing economic policies. Following the local elections, doubts were openly expressed as to whether the prime minister remained an electoral asset to her party. A standard of rebellion was raised by Francis Pym, former foreign secretary whom Thatcher had sacked from her Cabinet after the 1983 election victory. Pym placed himself at the head of a new grouping, launched in May, of traditional and progressive Conservative backbenchers that called itself Centre Forward.

Apart from a brief spurt in its popularity rat-

A masked demonstrator hurls a gasoline bomb toward British security troops during violence in the Bogside area of Londonderry, Northern Ireland, in August.

AP/WIDE WORLD

ings in March, coinciding with the ending of the miners' strike, the Labour Party was not the chief beneficiary of the government's sagging popularity. Its weighted average standing in the polls remained around the 36% mark. In contrast, the Alliance began the year at 25% and by September was leading the field with 35%. Opinion-poll projections suggested that a "hung" or minority Parliament was likely after the next elections, and at the time of the party conferences in the autumn, there was much talk of coalitions.

Yet even while the opposition parties were benefiting from the media exposure during their annual conferences, a quiet recovery was taking place in the government's standing. Compared with the low point in August, by the end of November it had recovered by some four percentage points to run neck and neck with Labour, while support for the Alliance quickly subsided to little more than it had been at the beginning of the year. Conservative spirits brightened, Thatcher's popularity ratings rose again, and any suggestion that she might not lead her party into the next elections was dispelled along with the autumn mists.

During the first half of September, Thatcher announced a number of new government appointments and a major reshuffle of her Cabinet. Within the Cabinet, Douglas Hurd moved to the Home Office from the Northern Ireland Office, where he was replaced by Tom King. Hurd succeeded Leon Brittan, who took over as trade and industry secretary from Norman Tebbit. Tebbit remained in the Cabinet as chancellor of the duchy of Lancaster and also took over from John Selwyn Gummer as chairman of the Conservative Party. Lord Young of Graffham replaced King as employment secretary. Kenneth Baker entered the Cabinet as environment secretary in place of Patrick Jenkin, who left the government. In what was to prove a controversial party appointment, Jeffrey Archer was chosen to be deputy chairman of the Conservative Party.

Whatever the cause of the recovery in the government's popularity, it was clear that the "Scargill factor" continued to haunt the Labour movement. Both the TUC and the Labour Party were split down the middle on the question of whether to support retrospective reimbursement of legal fines and penalties incurred by the NUM during the strike. At the Labour Party conference in October, Labour leader Neil Kinnock was defeated on this electorally embarrassing issue, but he resolved to leave no doubt as to where he, and a future Labour government, would stand. He denounced both Scargill and, in a stirring piece of oratory, the leaders of the Liverpool city council, members of the Trotskyist Militant Tendency faction of the Labour Party, who, in protest against the government's policy of limiting the local rates (property taxes) that local councils could levy, were following a course that would bankrupt the city. (A compromise was later reached that allowed the city's immediate financial crisis to be resolved.) Kinnock's speech won him personal kudos but could not dispel the spectacle of a Labour Party divided and preoccupied with internal issues, plagued by extremists, and ambivalent in its attitudes toward the rule of law.

According to the pollsters, more than 80% of the population believed that unemployment was the chief issue facing the country, but all the while the average real living standards of those who did have jobs was increasing. It had been rising by about 2% a year since the end of the recession in 1981, and in 1985 the increase may have been a little greater. The budget introduced in March was a cautious one in which the overriding priority remained the further reduction of inflation. Chancellor of the Exchequer Nigel Lawson was widely regarded as having laid the ground for substantial tax cuts in the years leading up to general elections in 1987 or 1988. In the meantime, the chancellor was clearly taking no chances. In his 1985 budget, tax thresholds were lowered by £730 million—less than half the sum that had been talked about a few months earlier—and some £2,000 million was set against future government spending to allow for a fall in the value of the U.S. dollar and declining oil revenues. (For table of world currencies, *see* International Exchange and Payments.)

In general the British financial community applauded the budget, while Conservative backbenchers were content that their lobbying endeavours had headed off further radical reforms of the kind that might upset the Conservative middle classes, notably the taxation of private pensions. There was talk of "Thatcherism" being dead. Financial pundits concluded that monetarism in the technical sense was dead when it became clear that the government's interest-rate policy was geared to controlling the exchange rate of sterling rather than the money supply. However, there was more to "Thatcherism" than monetarism. In early June the government published its long-awaited review of the social security system, billed as the most important exercise of its kind since the original Beveridge report of 1942. This was expected to show whether political caution had taken over from radical reforming zeal—and so it did, although not immediately.

Concern about the emphases of economic policy was matched by concern about its social consequences. These reached a new pitch in the autumn when a series of unconnected disturbances brought violence to the inner cities once more. In Handsworth, an inner-city area of Birmingham, a whole street was destroyed in an orgy of gasoline bombing on September 9. Brixton, in south London, scene of some of the worst riots in 1981, exploded a few weeks later after a black woman was shot and injured by police during a dawn raid on her home. On October 6 there was a similar but even more violent outburst in Tottenham, in north London, following the accidental death of another

ARAL—SIPA/SPECIAL FEATURES

Terry Waite (upper left), special envoy of the archbishop of Canterbury, conducted private and quite hazardous diplomacy on behalf of hostages in Lebanon.

black woman, who suffered a heart attack during a police raid. During the Tottenham riots a police officer was stabbed to death. Although in Handsworth, for example, 50% of black youths were out of work, government ministers were quick to assert that unemployment was not the cause of the violence; they attributed it rather to criminal behavior. These disturbances prompted renewed concern about inner-city conditions. In December a commission set up by the archbishop of Canterbury published a report called "Faith in the Cities" that listed familiar but costly measures for dealing with the physical decay and human despair in inner-city areas.

The riots increased concern not only about the social condition of the poor and unemployed but also about the general tide of violence in British society. The government's political recovery after September owed at least something to its firm handling of the disturbances. The year had already been marred by an appalling outbreak of hooliganism on May 29 when Liverpool soccer fans ran amok before the start of a match against the Italian club Juventus in Heysel Stadium, Brussels. The violence resulted in 39 deaths. These images of violence, later reinforced by the riots and reminiscent of the picket-line clashes of the previous year, were linked in people's minds with what appeared to be a contagion of violent crime, gratuitous violence to individuals, child abuse, and rape.

The horror of the Heysel Stadium riot was made worse because it took place just over two weeks after another soccer ground had provided the setting for what was on this occasion a tragic accident. On May 11 fire engulfed a spectators' stand during a match at Bradford City soccer club. The blaze killed 56 people and injured more than 200 others.

Foreign Affairs

Thatcher was more active than usual in foreign affairs. In April she toured Malaysia, Singapore, Brunei, Indonesia, Sri Lanka, India, and Saudi Arabia. During her trip to the Middle East in September, she agreed that her government would meet representatives of the Palestine Liberation Organization, but the meeting was later canceled. The government gave conditional support to U.S. Pres. Ronald Reagan's Strategic Defense Initiative (known as "Star Wars") and toward the end of the year reached an agreement for British industry to participate in the research program.

Thatcher suffered a setback at the Milan summit of the European Communities (EC) in June when her pragmatic approach to reforming the EC's decision-making machinery was overruled by those who wanted more ambitious revisions to the Treaty of Rome. By the time EC leaders met again in Luxembourg in December, however, realism and national interests had prevailed over European idealism and, although the British made some concessions, the resulting compromise was closer to Thatcher's view than to the declarations made in Milan. At the biennial Commonwealth heads of government conference in Nassau, The Bahamas, in October, Thatcher was forced to give some ground—although not much—in agreeing to economic measures against Pres. P. W. Botha's regime.

Northern Ireland

The most potentially important development of the year in foreign affairs was the accord signed in November with the Republic of Ireland giving the latter a consultative role in the governing of Northern Ireland. The Hillsborough agreement was reached after long and painstaking secret diplomacy between Dublin and London. In effect, it exchanged a role for the Republic on behalf of the nationalist minority in the north for a de facto recognition by Dublin of Northern Ireland's union with Britain. It was hoped that the agreement would result in a more coordinated and effective drive against the Irish Republican Army (IRA) while at the same time preventing the alienation of Roman Catholics from the political process and keeping them from voting for Sinn Fein, political wing of the IRA. At the end of December 18 prominent members of Sinn Fein were arrested and charged with possession of explosive substances.

Although London insisted that the Hillsborough agreement did nothing to alter the status of Northern Ireland as a province of the U.K., the Ulster loyalists exploded in predictable wrath, crying treason and threatening to overthrow the agreement by whatever means. The government had prepared itself on this occasion to face down or defeat a Protestant backlash of the kind that had wrecked the Sunningdale agreement in 1974, but as 1985 ended, that confrontation was still to come.

UNITED NATIONS

In October 1985 the UN commemorated its 40th birthday in a ten-day celebration at UN headquarters. On UN Day itself (October 24), Secretary-General Javier Pérez de Cuéllar reminded the delegates of their "single, collective constituency," the human race, that "vast, silent majority which wants peace with justice and dignity, with freedom from fear and the hope of a better tomorrow."

The anniversary Preparatory Committee had wanted the General Assembly to adopt a celebratory declaration but was unable to agree on a text. The Assembly did, however, proclaim 1986 the "International Year of Peace."

Middle East

On October 21 Shimon Peres, Israel's prime minister, called for immediate termination of the state of war between Jordan and Israel. Peres offered to go to Jordan or to any other mutually acceptable place to attend a peace conference with King Hussein, a Jordanian-Palestinian delegation, or even with the U.S.S.R. if the Soviet Union restored diplomatic relations with Israel. Hussein praised Peres as a "man of vision."

On a U.S. initiative and with the support of the U.S.S.R., the Council on December 18, for the first time in its history, unanimously and "unequivocally" condemned all acts of "hostage-taking and abduction" and called for the "immediate, safe release of all hostages. . . ." On December 6 the Assembly had adopted a similar resolution.

On October 1 the Council debated Israel's air strike on Palestine Liberation Organization (PLO) headquarters near Tunis, Tunisia. Israelis called the attack "an act of self-defense" because the PLO allegedly had used the base for planning terrorist operations against Israel and Jews everywhere. On October 4 the Security Council condemned (14–0–1, the U.S. abstaining) "Israel's armed aggression" and asserted Tunisia's "right to appropriate reparations." On December 16 the Assembly declared that Israel was not "peace-loving" and urged (86–23–37) members "totally to isolate" it.

Lebanon

After Israel announced (January 14) a plan to withdraw its troops from southern Lebanon, where they had been stationed since 1982, Undersecretary-General Brian Urquhart went to the Middle East to coordinate Israel's troop movements with those of the UN Interim Force in Lebanon (UNIFIL). He also tried unsuccessfully to persuade Israel to allow UNIFIL to patrol the border, replacing the South Lebanon Army (SLA), an Israeli-backed 2,000-man Christian militia that the Shi'ite Muslims distrusted.

On February 16 Israel completed the first phase of a three-stage withdrawal. Six days later Lebanon complained to the secretary-general about Israeli "raids, arrests, killings, and repression." Israeli officials called their "iron fist" essential to thwart

Shi'ite attacks on their troops. On March 2 UNIFIL reported that Israel was mounting a huge crackdown, and on March 6, fearing Shi'ite reprisals if the U.S. vetoed a Council resolution criticizing Israel, UNIFIL relieved its U.S. nationals of field responsibilities. On March 12 the U.S. did veto an anti-Israeli draft resolution, preferring an alternate text expressing regret for the violence in Lebanon.

On May 31 the Council unanimously called on all concerned "to end acts of violence against the civilian population . . . particularly in and around Palestinian refugee camps," which still housed over 100,000 people. Israel withdrew its last units from Lebanon on June 10 but left military advisers and plainclothes agents to watch over a "security zone" 8 to 12 mi (13 to 19 km) deep in Lebanon.

On June 7 Finnish soldiers of UNIFIL turned over to the Shi'ite Muslim militia, Amal, 11 SLA militiamen who wanted to defect. The SLA accused UNIFIL of forcing the men to leave and took 21 UNIFIL soldiers, all Finns, hostage. The Finns were freed on June 15 after representatives of the International Committee of the Red Cross convinced the SLA that the militiamen were genuine defectors.

Iran–Iraq War

The UN conducted its first on-site investigation of prisoner-of-war (POW) camps, and three experts concluded, in a report made public February 21, that both parties had violated the Geneva Convention, though neither side treated POWs as badly as the other side alleged. The experts asked both sides to release as many of the estimated 60,000 prisoners as possible. Iraq's foreign minister urged the Security Council on March 4 to arrange a prisoner exchange, but Iran, which claimed that the Council favored Iraq, asked the secretary-general to work for an exchange independent of the Council. On December 12, however, Iran's UN delegate said he would join in Council deliberations if the Council condemned chemical weapons and the bombing of civilian targets.

Afghanistan

Undersecretary-General Diego Cordovez conducted "proximity talks" with Pakistani and Afghan officials in Geneva in June about Afghanistan, which Soviet troops, estimated to number about 115,000, had entered in December 1979. Afterward, he expressed his growing conviction that parties to the Afghan war now agreed that a military solution was unattainable. He held further talks in June, August, and December, but the core issue, establishing a timetable for withdrawing Soviet troops, remained. On December 11, however, the U.S. endorsed a draft treaty negotiated with UN help between Afghanistan and Pakistan that incorporated Soviet guarantees to withdraw its troops from Afghanistan in exchange for U.S. pledges to stop siding with the Afghan rebels. In the December round of proximity talks, the Afghans informally

AP/WIDE WORLD

Harold Stassen (left) of the U.S., Charles H. Malik (center) of Lebanon, and Gen. Carlos Romulo (right) of the Philippines were among the original signers of the UN Charter who met to mark the 40th anniversary of the event in San Francisco in June.

showed Cordovez a timetable for Soviet troop withdrawal, to be considered officially at meetings in early 1986.

South Africa

South Africa's policies of apartheid (racial separation), intervening militarily in neighboring states, and refusing to grant independence to South West Africa/Namibia were condemned frequently by the Security Council. On April 15 South African Foreign Minister R. P. ("Pik") Botha said that South Africa would pull its forces out of Angola, where they were fighting guerrillas of the South West Africa People's Organization. He hoped this would lead Cuban troops to withdraw from Angola. On May 22, however, Angola announced that it had killed two South Africans and taken one prisoner when they tried to sabotage oil installations in Cabinda Province. Angola then broke off negotiations on Cuban troop withdrawal.

South African troops continued operating in Angola, and on June 20, September 20, and October 7 the Security Council unanimously condemned the Pretoria government's actions. On June 21 the Council condemned South Africa for mounting an "unprovoked . . . military attack" on Botswana one week earlier. On December 6 the Council again condemned South Africa's "continued and unprovoked acts of aggression" against Angola, and on December 30 it demanded compensation for "killings and . . . unprovoked and premeditated violence" on December 20, when South African commandos invaded the Lesotho capital of Maseru.

On June 17 South Africa installed an interim

Both the British and U.S. ambassadors to the UN raise their hands to veto a Security Council resolution on November 15 to impose mandatory sanctions against South Africa. The proposed sanctions were in response to South Africa's delay in granting genuine independence to the territory of South West Africa/Namibia.

AP/WIDE WORLD

administration in Namibia that the UN Council for Namibia characterized as a "puppet regime." Two days later the Security Council mandated the secretary-general to resume immediate contact with South Africa to implement a UN plan for Namibian independence and "strongly" warned (13–0–2, the U.K. and U.S. abstaining) that South Africa's failure to cooperate would "compel" the Council to consider sanctions. On November 15 Britain and the U.S. vetoed a draft resolution seeking to impose "mandatory selective sanctions" (France abstained).

On March 12 the Council unanimously condemned South Africa for killing 18 blacks at a squatter camp in clashes with police and for detaining 16 leading opponents of the white minority government. On July 26 it censured South Africa for imposing a national state of emergency and urged states to apply sanctions, and on August 21 it strongly condemned South Africa for continued killings and mass arrests.

Economic and Social Problems

The World Health Organization (WHO) convened a two-day conference in Geneva on September 25 on acquired immune deficiency syndrome (AIDS). In October the UN Office of Emergency Operations in Africa said that, although Africa's need for international food aid would decline in 1986, more than $1 billion in drought-related assistance and supplies was required to assist 19 million people still facing famine. The UN Commission on Environment and Development, meeting in São Paulo, Brazil, on October 28, received a new multi-billion-dollar plan to save the world's rapidly disappearing tropical forests.

On November 9, as the Unesco General Conference ended, delegates unanimously approved a proposed work program. The $398 million budget for 1986 and 1987 was cut by 25% to make up for the loss of contributions by the U.S., which resigned at the end of 1984. Despite these reforms, the U.K. announced on December 5 that it would withdraw at the end of the year.

UNITED STATES

Foreign Affairs

Thinking perhaps about how his administration would be judged by historians of a future day, U.S. Pres. Ronald Reagan indicated a yearning for lasting global peace in his second inaugural address, Jan. 21, 1985. He accused the Soviet Union of mounting "the greatest military buildup in the history of man" but pledged to "meet with the Soviets hoping that we can agree on a way to rid the world of the threat of nuclear destruction."

This offer led eventually to a summit conference in Geneva on November 19–20 between Reagan and Soviet leader Mikhail S. Gorbachev. In a nationally televised address five days before the meeting, the president said: "My mission, stated simply, is a mission for peace. It is to engage the new Soviet leader in what I hope will be a dialogue for peace that endures beyond my presidency. It is to sit down across from Mr. Gorbachev and try to map out, together, a basis for peaceful discourse even though our disagreements on fundamentals will not change."

The actual encounter went much as President Reagan evidently had envisioned it. Appearing together on a stage in the Swiss city on November 21, the two leaders voiced their determination to restrain the arms race and to "improve U.S.-Soviet relations and the international situation as a whole." But they made no mention of any specific steps to limit or reduce their respective nuclear arsenals. Instead, they acclaimed the reaching of agreements on cultural exchanges and stressed their concurrence on the need for a fresh start in East-West relations.

On his return to the United States, Reagan delivered a generally optimistic report to a November 21 joint session of Congress. "It was a constructive meeting," he said. "So constructive, in fact, that I look forward to welcoming Mr. Gorbachev to the United States next year. And I have accepted his invitation to go to Moscow the following year." On the other hand, the president acknowledged that "We remain apart on a number of issues, as had to be expected."

Much of the potential drama of the Geneva summit had been undercut by previous developments. In a September 9 *Time* magazine interview that caused consternation in official Washington, Gorbachev took the Reagan administration to task for playing down the Geneva meeting as a "get-acquainted" session. And in a speech to the United Nations General Assembly on October 24, Reagan urged the Soviet Union to join the U.S. in finding peaceful solutions to five regional conflicts—in Afghanistan, Angola, Cambodia (Kampuchea), Ethiopia, and Nicaragua—that involved regimes supported by Moscow.

However, the main breakthrough in U.S.-Soviet relations in 1985 was not the Reagan-Gorbachev meeting but the resumption of talks, also in Geneva, between lower-level representatives of the two superpowers on reduction of nuclear arms. Renewal of the negotiations was agreed upon in early January by U.S. Secretary of State George P. Shultz and Soviet Foreign Minister Andrei A. Gromyko. The Soviets had withdrawn from the Intermediate Nuclear Forces talks in November 1983 and from the Strategic Arms Reduction Talks the following month. The resumption of negotiations was made possible when the Soviets agreed to drop their earlier insistence that they would not return to the bargaining table unless the U.S. halted its deployment of medium-range cruise and Pershing II missiles in Western Europe.

The renewed bilateral arms discussions got under way at the insistence of the U.S.S.R. on March 12 despite the death two days earlier of Soviet Pres. Konstantin U. Chernenko. The two sides agreed on March 14 to divide their negotiating teams into subgroups on strategic nuclear weapons, intermediate-range nuclear arms, and space-based weapons. The talks were adjourned for a month on April 24 amid reports that no progress had been made because of a continuing dispute over how the talks should be conducted.

Resumption of the Geneva arms talks on May 30 brought no improvement in atmosphere. It soon became obvious that the main sticking point was the U.S. position on its Strategic Defense Initiative (the so-called Star Wars plan). The Soviets continued to insist that the United States make "necessary adjustments" in this program, while the U.S. made it clear that Star Wars was a nonnegotiable issue.

Given these inflexible positions, the second round

of arms talks ended July 16 with no apparent progress. White House spokesman Larry Speakes asserted that Soviet negotiators preferred to explore "concepts" rather than "deal in concrete terms and with hard numbers." Speakes expressed hope that the Soviet Union would be "more forthcoming" in the next round of discussions.

The third round opened September 19 amid a mood of pessimism. At the end of the month Soviet negotiators proposed a 50% reduction in the strategic nuclear arsenals of both countries. Viktor P. Karpov, head of the Soviet team, called the proposal a "well-balanced package of drastic new arms-control measures." U.S. negotiators responded by offering on November 1 a disarmament package that included a new limit on the maximum number of nuclear warheads in the arsenals of the United States and the Soviet Union. The U.S. offer contained no Star Wars concessions, and U.S. officials privately acknowledged that the proposals amounted to a "repackaging" of previous offers.

The generally favorable media coverage of Reagan's meeting with Gorbachev contrasted sharply with the negative commentary that accompanied the president's trip to Western Europe in May in connection with observances commemorating the 40th anniversary of the end of World War II in Europe. Reagan came under fire when it was disclosed that he intended to lay a wreath at a military cemetery in Bitburg, West Germany, where the graves included those of some members of the Waffen SS, Hitler's elite troops.

Announcement of the president's plans, which

Most of the 39 U.S. citizens who had been held hostage in Beirut, Lebanon, arrive at Andrews Air Force Base, Maryland, after their release in June.
AP/WIDE WORLD

UPI/BETTMANN NEWSPHOTOS

President and Mrs. Ronald Reagan welcome Li Xiannian (Li Hsien-nien), president of China, and his wife to a state dinner at the White House in July.

the White House refused to alter, elicited sharp complaints from Jewish and veterans' groups. Far from disavowing his plans, however, Reagan said on April 18 that German soldiers had been "victims" of the Nazis "just as surely as the victims in the concentration camps." But he blunted criticism of his visit to Bitburg by stopping earlier the same day at the nearby Bergen-Belsen Nazi prison camp.

The controversy over Bitburg overshadowed what was supposed to have been the highlight of the president's trip to Europe—his participation in the 11th annual summit meeting of the seven major industrial democracies, held May 2–4 at Bonn, West Germany. The communiqué issued by the summit leaders on May 4 asserted that "world economic conditions are better than they have been for a considerable time," that inflation had been reduced, and that the "recovery in the industrial countries has begun to spread to the developing world." The leaders agreed to work to strengthen their individual economies, halt protectionism, improve world monetary stability, increase job opportunities, and reduce social inequities.

Another focus of concern for U.S. foreign-policy makers in 1985 was South Africa. Early in the year it seemed that the troubles in that country could possibly be turned to the Republican administration's advantage. This was because of the unexpected hostility that greeted the visit to South Africa on January 5–13 of Sen. Edward M. Kennedy (Dem., Mass.). Kennedy had been invited to the country by Bishop Desmond Tutu, winner of the 1984 Nobel Peace Prize, and the Rev. Allan Boesak, president of the World Alliance of Reformed Churches.

Kennedy's reception was chillier than expected. Both black and white South Africans accused him of making the trip to stage a "media event" that would help his chances of gaining the Democratic

Party's presidential nomination in 1988. Leading newspapers reminded their readers of controversial incidents in the senator's past and called him a "morally inept" politician with no standing to speak to South Africans on morality.

The Kennedy trip soon faded into insignificance, however, as a nationwide movement aimed at pressuring South Africa to dismantle its apartheid system of racial separation gathered momentum. Protest demonstrations held almost daily outside the South African embassy in Washington, D.C., were augmented by similar activities on college campuses and elsewhere across the country.

In Congress, meanwhile, more than 20 bills were introduced with the aim of persuading South Africa to abandon apartheid. Reagan, succumbing to the pressure, reversed his previous position and on September 9 ordered limited trade and financial sanctions against the country. Among other measures he ordered a ban on trade in nuclear technology, on computer sales to South African government security agencies, and on bank loans to Pretoria, except for those that financed projects that clearly benefited all racial groups.

Reagan, however, remained firm in his opposition to the leftist Sandinista government of Nicaragua. The Department of State announced on January 18 that the United States would not participate in proceedings in the International Court of Justice (World Court) concerning Nicaragua's suit against U.S. aggression. Administration officials said the same day that the U.S. had suspended talks with the Sandinista government, begun in June 1984, on easing tensions between the two countries. And on October 7 the United States announced that it would no longer automatically comply with World Court rulings, stating that the tribunal had been "abused for political ends" by nations such as Nicaragua.

Reagan ordered an embargo on trade with Nicaragua on May 1 and banned Nicaraguan aircraft and ships from the United States. In an executive order and accompanying letter to Congress, he justified the moves by charging that Nicaraguan policies and actions constituted a threat to U.S. security. The measures followed a decisive defeat in Congress during the previous week of Reagan's request for $14 million in aid to the Nicaraguan *contra* rebel forces.

Congress subsequently had a change of heart. In a major victory for the White House, the House of Representatives voted June 12 to provide $27 million in humanitarian aid to the Nicaraguan *contras.* The Senate had voted June 6 to approve $38 million in nonmilitary aid to the *contras* and also voted to bar the use of U.S. funds for operations against Nicaragua that would flout international law or the charter of the Organization of American States.

U.S.-Canadian relations took a turn for the better with Reagan's meeting in Quebec City March 17–18 with Prime Minister Brian Mulroney. The meeting was named the "shamrock summit" since it began on St. Patrick's Day and both participants were of Irish descent. The two leaders signed an agreement to upgrade the North American radar defense system, known as the Distant Early Warning (DEW) Line, and also agreed to appoint "special envoys" to search for solutions to the problem of acid rain. In addition, Reagan and Mulroney signed agreements on trade, fishing, space projects, and coordination of law-enforcement efforts in cross-border criminal investigations.

Domestic Affairs

Economic policy dominated the Reagan administration's domestic program in 1985 as the White House pursued the twin goals of tax reform and a program to achieve a balanced federal budget. The president referred indirectly to those objectives in his second inaugural address when he declared: "We must act now to protect future generations from government's desire to spend its citizens' money and tax them into servitude when the bills come due. Let us make it unconstitutional for the federal government to spend more than the federal government takes in."

It was not until four months later, however, that Reagan outlined his tax reform proposals in detail during a nationally televised address on May 28. He called the current tax system "unwise, unwanted, and unfair" and said that his own plan would "reduce tax burdens on the working people of this country, close loopholes that benefit a privileged few," and simplify the U.S. tax code.

The plan, based on a set of Treasury Department recommendations made public in November 1984, proposed to merge the existing 14 personal income-tax brackets into just three, with a substantial lowering of the maximum tax rate. It would, the administration said, mean a tax reduction for virtually all of the two-thirds of U.S. taxpayers who did not itemize deductions. It would cut overall personal income taxes by 7% while collecting 9% more revenue from business. And it would eliminate a variety of credits, deductions, incentives, and preferences.

As expected, the president's tax proposals came under attack from special interest groups and members of Congress. The battle was joined in earnest on September 26, when Rep. Dan Rostenkowski (Dem., Ill.), chairman of the tax-writing House

Protesters aboard a small boat approach the Soviet freighter Marshal Koniev *near Reserve, Louisiana, in November. They were demonstrating against the U.S. Immigration Service's actions in returning to Soviet authorities a Ukrainian sailor who had twice jumped ship in attempts to defect but then apparently changed his mind about seeking asylum in the U.S.*

AP/WIDE WORLD

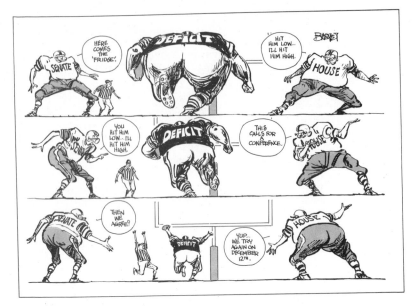

Ways and Means Committee, unveiled his plan for overhauling the federal tax code. Rostenkowski's proposals followed the general outline of Reagan's but modified them in a number of respects. Though the Rostenkowski plan retained the overall personal tax rate structure advanced by the Reagan administration, it allowed less generous personal exemptions for taxpayers who itemized deductions than did the president's plan, and it proposed a scheme that would continue to allow individuals to deduct a portion of their state and local income taxes from federal taxable income. It also called for a higher maximum tax rate on capital gains. On December 18 the House passed a bill that incorporated most of Rostenkowski's proposals and sent the legislation to the Senate.

In the meantime, Congress was wrestling with its annual round of appropriations legislation, including a measure requiring a balanced federal budget by fiscal year 1991. The balanced-budget proposal, a program of forced deficit reductions, took the form of an amendment to legislation raising the ceiling on the federal debt from $1,824,000,000,000 to $2,079,000,000,000. Congress approved the bill on December 11, just in time to forestall a possible December 12 default by the federal government on its existing debt obligations.

Approval came shortly after Reagan said that he would sign the measure despite provisions that could lead to substantial reductions in defense spending. Department of Defense officials calculated that the potential cuts could amount to as much as $18 billion.

In another major economic development the U.S. took part in international efforts to check the long rise in the value of the U.S. dollar against other major currencies. On February 27 the U.S. Federal Reserve Board and the central banks of six European countries—Austria, Belgium, the U.K., France, Italy, and West Germany—intervened in world currency markets in a successful attempt to force the dollar down.

A new campaign to lower the dollar's value began on September 22 in New York City at a meeting of central bankers and finance ministers of the five leading non-Communist industrial nations—the U.S., West Germany, Japan, France, and Britain. On the next day, intervention in the international currency markets by some or all of the so-called Group of Five nations helped to cause a record one-day decline in the value of the dollar. By the end of the week the dollar had fallen 5.2% in value against major currencies, according to the Federal Reserve Board.

The decline of the dollar from what many economists regarded as an unrealistically high value was seen as one factor in the stock market surge that occurred at the end of the year. Also contributing to the steep rise in share values were continued low inflation and declining interest rates. In November alone the closely watched Dow Jones average of 30 industrial stocks exceeded the 1300 and then the 1400 level for the first time in Wall Street history. Then, on December 11, the Dow broke the 1500 barrier. At that point the average was almost twice as high as it was in early August 1982, just before the start of the current bull market.

The year was a busy one for corporate merger activity, much of it involving well-known print or broadcast media properties. For example, the magazine publishing world was surprised on March 8 by the news that directors of *The New Yorker* had agreed to sell the periodical for $142 million to Samuel I. Newhouse, Jr. It was the first time that the magazine had changed hands in its 60-year history. In a takeover attempt that many did not take seriously at first, Atlanta broadcaster Ted Turner announced in April that he would ask CBS Inc. shareholders to sell him a controlling interest in the television network. The proposed deal eventually fell through after CBS announced plans to buy back nearly $1 billion worth of its own stock from shareholders, a defensive maneuver that left the company with a heavy burden of debt and forced it to introduce a series of painful cost-cutting measures.

The two other major national commercial TV networks did change ownership during the year, however. The sale of American Broadcasting Cos. for at least $3.5 billion to Capital Cities Communications Inc. was announced March 18. Then, on December 11, it was disclosed that General Electric Co. had agreed to purchase RCA Corp.— parent company of the NBC television network— for $6,280,000,000. The merger was expected to produce a defense, communications, and consumer products powerhouse with few equals anywhere. In yet another takeover involving a group of television stations, the owners of Twentieth Century-Fox Film Corp. agreed in May to buy the seven independent television stations owned by Metromedia Inc. for $2 billion.

The turnover of television properties had its analogue in the upper reaches of the Reagan administration, which experienced substantial personnel changes. One of the earlier and more unusual shifts involved the exchange of jobs, announced on January 8, between White House Chief of Staff James Baker and Secretary of the Treasury Donald Regan. Baker was designated to head the Treasury, a Cabinet post that required Senate confirmation, which was forthcoming January 29. No such action was needed for Regan to take over as the top White House aide in Reagan's second term.

A week after clearing Baker's appointment, the Senate confirmed three other new Cabinet appointees: William J. Bennett as secretary of education, Donald P. Hodel as secretary of the interior, and John S. Herrington as secretary of energy. Seeking speedy action on the Bennett nomination, Reagan had assured Congress that he had dropped plans to abolish the Education Department "at this time."

Further high-level changes in the executive branch were to come. Secretary of Labor Raymond J. Donovan resigned March 15 after a New York State judge refused to dismiss fraud and larceny charges pending against him. Donovan was the first Cabinet member ever to be indicted while in office. He was succeeded as labor secretary by U.S. Trade Representative Bill Brock.

By far the most controversial Cabinet confirmation of the year was that of Edwin Meese III as attorney general on February 23. The Senate vote was 63 to 31, with Democrats casting all the nays. The confirmation came more than a year after Meese, a former White House counsel, had been nominated by Reagan to succeed William French

ANDERSON—GAMMA/LIAISON

The tenth anniversary of the end of the Vietnam war was marked in New York City in May with a parade of veterans on Broadway and the dedication of a memorial.

Smith in the post. Opponents of the nomination argued that Meese was insensitive to civil rights and the concerns of minority groups generally.

Meese subsequently made headlines by attacking certain opinions of the U.S. Supreme Court. In a speech before the American Bar Association July 9, he admonished the court for what he called "policy choices" instead of decisions based on "constitutional principle." He specifically condemned recent rulings concerning school prayer, government aid to religious schools, and a state law giving employees the right to a day off to observe their Sabbath. The attorney general later described as "wrong" the court's decision in *Miranda* v. *Arizona,* a celebrated 1960s case that established the right of a criminal defendant to have a lawyer present before questioning by police. In turn, Meese's views on constitutional law were publicly assailed by Supreme Court Justices John Paul Stevens and William Brennan, Jr.

President Reagan announced on October 1 that Health and Human Services Secretary Margaret Heckler had agreed to leave her Cabinet post and become ambassador to Ireland. Though the White House took pains to portray the move as a "promotion," it followed weeks of rumors that Regan was seeking her ouster. Regan also was reported to have engineered the departure from the White

House of Robert McFarlane, Reagan's national security adviser.

In a move that was not unexpected, UN Ambassador Jeane Kirkpatrick told the president on January 30 that she was leaving government to "speak out clearly" on U.S. foreign policy. She was succeeded in the post by Lieut. Gen. Vernon Walters, who had been deputy director of the Central Intelligence Agency under presidents Richard Nixon and Gerald Ford.

Budget Director David Stockman, one of the leading architects of the administration's campaign to reduce federal spending, quit his post effective August 1 to join the New York investment banking firm of Salomon Brothers Inc. Succeeding him as head of the Office of Management and Budget was James C. Miller III, who was chairman of the Federal Trade Commission at the time of his appointment.

One of the year's most disconcerting developments was the large number of espionage cases that came to light. Of particular interest was a spy ring including three members of the same family: John Walker, Jr., a retired navy warrant officer, charged in May with spying for the Soviet Union for nearly 20 years; Michael Walker, John Walker's son and a navy yeoman aboard the aircraft carrier USS *Nimitz,* charged with providing classified documents to his father; and Arthur Walker, John Walker's brother and a retired navy lieutenant commander, also charged with delivering classified documents to his brother. The fourth principal figure in the case—described by federal officials as the largest and most damaging in recent U.S. history—was Jerry Whitworth, a former navy enlisted man charged with passing classified materials to John Walker.

The U.S. citizens implicated in other spy cases in 1985 included: Sharon Scranage, a clerk in the CIA's Ghana station, charged with passing classified intelligence information to her Ghanaian lover; Edward Howard, a former CIA officer charged with passing intelligence information to the Soviet Union;

Jonathan Jay Pollard, a civilian employee of the Naval Investigative Service, charged with spying for Israel; Larry Wu-tai Chin, a retired CIA analyst accused of spying for China for 30 years; and Ronald Pelton, a former communications specialist for the National Security Agency, charged with spying for the Soviet Union from 1965 to 1979. Commenting on this in a nationwide radio address on November 30, Reagan said: "Some of you may be wondering if the large number of spy arrests in recent weeks means that we are looking harder or that there are more spies to find. Well, I think the answer to both questions is yes."

At least as worrisome to the public as revelations of espionage were incidents and threats of terrorism. One such drama began to unfold on October 7 when Palestinian terrorists hijacked an Italian cruise ship with more than 400 passengers and crew off Egypt and demanded that Israel free Palestinian prisoners. After a two-day ordeal during which a wheelchair-bound U.S. tourist was slain by the hijackers, they surrendered in Egypt in exchange for a pledge of safe conduct out of the country. When an Egyptian jet tried to fly the terrorists to a safe haven on October 10, U.S. Navy F-14 fighters intercepted the craft and forced it to land in Sicily. The incident strained relations between the United States and both Egypt and Italy.

In an earlier hijacking episode that lasted far longer, two Lebanese Shi'ite gunmen on June 14 commandeered a Trans World Airlines passenger jet carrying 153 passengers and crew, 104 of them American, shortly after takeoff from Athens airport. Over the next two days, as the plane was forced to shuttle back and forth across the Mediterranean between Beirut and Algiers, one U.S. passenger was killed and more than 100 others were freed by the hijackers. The remaining 39 U.S. hostages were freed on June 30. On July 8 Reagan accused Cuba, Iran, Libya, Nicaragua, and North Korea of making up a "confederation of terrorist states" guilty of "outright acts of war" against the U.S.

A potentially more serious assault on the country, in the opinion of many health professionals, was the growing incidence of acquired immune deficiency syndrome (AIDS), an almost invariably fatal condition caused by a virus that attacks and destroys the body's defenses against disease, leaving it vulnerable to a host of common and exotic infections. Concern about AIDS, mounting in some urban areas for the past several years, gained a national focus in July with the disclosure that film and television actor Rock Hudson was suffering from the ailment. In the United States most AIDS patients had been male either homosexuals or intravenous drug users. According to the federal Centers for Disease Control in Atlanta, Ga., nearly 16,000 AIDS cases had been diagnosed by December, and more than 8,000 persons had died of complications arising from the condition. Hudson died October 2, some 15 months after his case had been diagnosed.

THE 13 EXECUTIVE DEPARTMENTS
as of December 1985

Secretary of State . . . . George P. Shultz
Secretary of the Treasury . . . . James A. Baker III
Secretary of Defense . . . . Caspar W. Weinberger
Attorney General . . . . Edwin Meese III
Secretary of the Interior . . . . Donald P. Hodel
Secretary of Agriculture . . . . John R. Block
Secretary of Commerce . . . . Malcolm Baldrige
Secretary of Labor . . . . William E. Brock III
Secretary of Health and
    Human Services . . . . Otis R. Bowen
Secretary of Housing and
    Urban Development . . . . Samuel R. Pierce, Jr.
Secretary of
    Transportation . . . . Elizabeth Hanford Dole
    ...etary of Energy . . . . John S. Herrington
    ...etary of Education . . . . William J. Bennett

Developments in the States in 1985

Severe deficit problems restricted the federal government's ability to develop innovative solutions to national problems during 1985, allowing state governments to share the spotlight in a variety of areas. The states moved forward on such concerns as education reform and child abuse, and accelerated attempts to find common solutions to environmental and taxation problems. Preoccupation with problems of federalism and education typically made 1985 a quiet year for structural changes in state governments.

Government Relations

The year was a tumultuous and historic one in regard to state relationships with other levels in the federal system. In an unexpected development the U.S. Supreme Court reversed a precedent of only nine years and ruled that states must be held subject to certain federal laws, such as wage and hour strictures. The 5 to 4 vote in *Garcia* v. *San Antonio Metropolitan Transit Authority* occurred because a single justice, Harry Blackmun, changed his position on the issue. Late in the year the U.S. Congress approved a bill exempting state and local governments from most federal wage laws, thus saving state governments from $1 billion to $3 billion annually in higher labor costs, but the judgment diminishing state powers remained.

State officials were badly split over a federal tax-reform plan, initially proposed by the administration of Pres. Ronald Reagan, that would have eliminated the deduction for state property and income taxes. A survey of 38 governors found 24 opposing the Reagan proposal and only 9 favoring it; leaders of high-tax Northeastern and Midwestern states were vigorous in their opposition to it, saying that the measure amounted to "double taxation." Supporters of the Reagan plan argued that it would broaden the federal tax base (to which many state income tax schemes are tied) and increase state tax receipts. State and local tax deductibility was restored in the reform plan reported out by the Democratic-controlled House Ways and Means Committee.

A proposed state call for a constitutional convention to write a balanced-budget amendment remained stalled during the year, with no states joining the 32 demanding the convention; convention resolutions failed during the year in Michigan, Hawaii, Illinois, Maine, Minnesota, Montana, and Washington.

Despite adverse court decisions and reduced federal assistance, state leaders expressed confidence during the year that state governmental powers and prestige were enjoying a substantial resurgence as deficit problems forced the federal government to reduce its activism on domestic issues. The U.S. government has "no choice but to unload substantial responsibilities" onto the states, Virginia Gov. Charles Robb declared. It thus appeared that the Reagan administration's "New Federalism" program, widely scorned after its 1982 publication, might become national policy by default as a result of fiscal and deficit pressures.

Finances

As the nation's economic recovery completed its third year, pressures on state treasuries eased, making the year an unremarkable one for tax legislation. Overall, tax rates in the 50 states were modestly lowered during 1985, with only inflation and economic growth pushing revenues higher. A survey by the Tax Foundation found that eight states (Michigan, Minnesota, New Jersey, New York, North Carolina, Ohio, Oregon, and Pennsylvania) had cut taxes by $100 million or more, while only five (Florida, Illinois, Indiana, Oklahoma, and Tennessee) had raised taxes by a similar amount. Several states found it necessary to cut spending during the year, often by the use of hiring freezes; Arkansas, Colorado, Illinois, Idaho, Iowa, Nebraska, and Louisiana were among states trimming budgets in order to balance year-end books.

Oregon voters for the seventh time rejected a proposed state sales tax, leaving the number of states without such a levy at five. New Hampshire, New Jersey, and Vermont abandoned the federal surplus food program as U.S. funds for food distribution ran out. Six farm states—Minnesota, Illinois, Wisconsin, Indiana, Ohio, and North Dakota—initiated interest-rate subsidy programs to assist hard-pressed farmers.

Figures compiled in 1985 revealed that state revenue from all sources totaled $397.1 billion during the 1984 fiscal year, an increase of 11% over the preceding 12 months. General revenue (excluding state liquor and state insurance trust revenue) was $330.7 billion, up 13.9%. Total state expenditures rose only 5.2% to $351.4 billion, the smallest percentage increase in 23 years and one creating a technical surplus of $45.7 billion for the year. General expenditures, not including outlays of the liquor stores and insurance-trust systems, amounted to $309.7 billion, up 8.6% over fiscal 1983. Of general revenue, 59.6% came from state taxes and licenses, 15.8% from charges and miscellaneous revenue, including educational tuition, and 24.6% from intergovernmental revenue (mostly from the federal government).

The largest state outlay was $116.1 billion for education, of which $40 billion went to state colleges and universities and $67.5 billion to local public schools. Other major outlays included $62.7 billion for public welfare, $28.9 billion for highways, and $24.9 billion for health and public hospitals.

Ethics

An extraordinary outbreak of criminal and ethical accusations against current and past state officials took place in 1985. The most sensational involved Louisiana Gov. Edwin W. Edwards, indicted February 28 on 50 fraud and racketeering counts centering on state approval for hospital and nursing-home construction. A mistrial was declared in December after a federal jury was unable to agree on a verdict.

Retired Hawaii Supreme Court Justice Kazuhisa Abe was indicted on theft and conspiracy charges in connection with alleged fraudulent sales of commodities. Minnesota Supreme Court Justice John Todd resigned after being accused of cheating on a Florida bar examination. A grand jury investigated, but absolved, West Virginia Chief Justice Richard Neely, who admitted firing his secretary because she refused to baby-sit for his son. Rhode Island's chief justice, Joseph A. Bevilacqua, was suspended for four months and publicly censured for bringing his office "into serious disrepute" by his friendships with reputed mobsters. A New York jury convicted state Supreme Court Justice William C. Brennan of taking bribes in return for fixing four criminal cases.

Nebraska's attorney general, Paul Douglas, resigned in December 1984 after being convicted of perjury before a state legislative committee; in March 1985 he was ordered to perform 1,500 hours of volunteer work and to pay a $25,000 fine. Mississippi state Sen. Thomas N. Brooks was indicted and convicted of attempted extortion in soliciting $50,000 in return for helping to pass a horse-racing bill.

Kansas Attorney General Robert T. Stephan dropped his gubernatorial election bid after it was revealed that his supporters had paid more than $20,000 to settle a sexual harassment suit against him brought by a former employee. Two ranking New Mexico treasury officials, Kenneth Johnson and Philip Troutman, were convicted in federal court of attempting to extort payoffs from a New York bank.

Education

Numerous educational reform measures, including upgrading of teacher pay and of teacher examinations, were proposed in most state capitols during 1985. One survey found that all but five states were in the process of testing teacher competency despite vigorous objections from some teacher groups. Results of the first serious teacher literacy and competency exams, in Arkansas, revealed that more than 95% passed. Georgia, South Dakota, Illinois, and Kentucky were among states taking major educational reform steps during the year.

New Hampshire moved to equalize spending among school districts of varying economic resources. A federal appeals court ruled unconstitutional Louisiana's "creationism" law; it had required that the biblical theory of creation be taught alongside evolution. Similar creationism bills were considered by 31 states during 1985, but none was approved.

Health, Welfare

Thirteen additional states approved "living will" laws during 1985, bringing to 35 the number of jurisdictions where individuals could forbid heroic lifesaving measures in the event of terminal illness. New Mexico and West Virginia regulated smoking in public, bringing the number of states with such laws to 38; New Jersey and Washington toughened existing smoking regulations. California became the first state to attack problems associated with Alzheimer's disease, appropriating $5 million for treatment and research.

Seeking to combat problems associated with the growing numbers of the homeless ill, Georgia joined North Carolina and Hawaii in allowing courts to require mandatory outpatient services for the mentally afflicted. Texas and Washington required school postural screening for spinal curvatures, bringing to 19 the states with such laws. Virginia, Louisiana, and South Carolina experimented with helping pregnant teenagers by hiring unemployed mothers to counsel them.

Oregon and New York became the first states to require hospitals to ask survivors of terminally ill patients for organ donations. Massachusetts became the first state to require labels on snuff cans warning of possible addiction, oral cancer, and other diseases associated with smokeless tobacco.

Illinois experienced a virulent outbreak of food poisoning, with several thousand cases of salmonella and 3 deaths attributed to a couple of faulty valves at a dairy. Although the office of state health director Thomas Kirkpatrick published releases in-

A group of 21 workers in Mount Vernon, New York, bought one of three tickets that shared the state's biggest lottery prize ever, a $41 million jackpot.

JOYCE DOPKEEN/THE NEW YORK TIMES

dicating that he was holding daily meetings on the problem, Kirkpatrick was fired by Gov. James Thompson after it was revealed that he had left the state on vacation in mid-crisis.

Law, Justice

Reacting to national outrage over abuse and victimization of children, many states stiffened their laws governing day care, exploitation of minors, and courtroom requirements for children during the year. A dozen states provided for videotaped testimony by underage witnesses in child-abuse cases, and Florida, Nevada, Washington, Tennessee, Alabama, Utah, New Mexico, and Alaska were among states that expanded and toughened their child-abuse statutes. Several states innovated in publicizing missing children; Georgia helped place photographs of such children in monthly gas bills, and New York printed their pictures on state tollway tickets.

Drugs

Under the threat of a cutoff of federal highway funds, 13 more states—New York, Connecticut, Alabama, Florida, Georgia, Kansas, Mississippi, New Hampshire, Maine, North Carolina, South Carolina, Texas, and Virginia—raised their minimum drinking age to 21 during the year, undoing a move in the 1970s toward lower age minimums for alcoholic consumption. A total of 33 states had returned to 21 years by the end of 1985; the deadline for doing so in order to avoid congressionally mandated cuts in highway funding was Oct. 1, 1986. After several years of nationwide grass-roots campaigning against drunk driving, Oregon emerged as the toughest enforcement state; inebriation was classified there as a blood alcohol content of only 0.08%, and first-time offenders would have their licenses suspended for a year.

Arizona, Indiana, Kansas, and Oklahoma moved to curb "happy hour" drink promotions, but there were signs that the antidrinking campaign was meeting opposition. Illinois, Rhode Island, and South Dakota moved to set limits on their "dram shop" acts, which hold bar owners liable if they serve patrons too much liquor.

Prisons

The population of state prisons rose to another record level during 1985, forcing more than $200 million worth of new construction. A midyear census by the Bureau of Justice Statistics found 452,372 inmates in state prisons, up from 419,968 a year earlier. Officials attributed the continued increase, which was occurring at a period of generally declining crime rates, to tougher state laws, hardened judicial attitudes, and a cutback in early-release programs for prisoners.

A federal judge, citing delay and official indifference to overcrowding, ordered a closing of Tennessee prisons to new convicts, throwing them en-

Governors of the States
(With Party Affiliations and Current Terms)

Ala.	George C. Wallace (D), 1983–87
Alaska	Bill Sheffield (D), 1982–86
Ariz.	Bruce Babbitt (D), 1983–87
Ark.	Bill Clinton (D), 1985–87
Calif.	George Deukmejian (D), 1983–87
Colo.	Richard D. Lamm (D), 1983–87
Conn.	William A. O'Neill (D), 1983–87
Del.	Michael N. Castle (R), 1985–89
Fla.	Robert Graham (D), 1983–87
Ga.	Joe Frank Harris (D), 1983–87
Hawaii	George Ariyoshi (D), 1982–86
Idaho	John V. Evans (D), 1983–87
Ill.	James R. Thompson (R), 1983–87
Ind.	Robert D. Orr (R), 1985–89
Iowa	Terry Branstad (R), 1983–87
Kan.	John Carlin (D), 1983–87
Ky.	Martha Layne Collins (D), 1984–88
La.	Edwin Edwards (D), 1984–88
Maine	Joseph E. Brennan (D), 1983–87
Md.	Harry R. Hughes (D), 1983–87
Mass.	Michael S. Dukakis (D), 1983–87
Mich.	James J. Blanchard (D), 1983–87
Minn.	Rudy Perpich (D), 1983–87
Miss.	William A. Allain (D), 1984–88
Mo.	John Ashcroft (R), 1985–89
Mont.	Ted Schwinden (D), 1985–89
Neb.	Bob Kerrey (D), 1983–87
Nev.	Richard H. Bryan (D), 1983–87
N.H.	John H. Sununu (R), 1985–87
N.J.	Thomas H. Kean (R), 1986–90
N.M.	Toney Anaya (D), 1983–87
N.Y.	Mario M. Cuomo (D), 1983–87
N.C.	James G. Martin (R), 1985–89
N.D.	George Sinner (D), 1985–89
Ohio	Richard F. Celeste (D), 1983–87
Okla.	George Nigh (D), 1983–87
Ore.	Victor G. Atiyeh (R), 1983–87
Pa.	Richard L. Thornburgh (R), 1983–87
R.I.	Edward DiPrete (R), 1985–87
S.C.	Richard W. Riley (D), 1983–87
S.D.	William J. Janklow (R), 1983–87
Tenn.	Lamar Alexander (R), 1983–87
Texas	Mark White (D), 1983–87
Utah	Norman H. Bangerter (R), 1985–89
Vt.	Madeleine M. Kunin (D), 1985–87
Va.	Gerald L. Baliles (D), 1986–90
Wash.	Booth Gardner (D), 1985–89
W.Va.	Arch A. Moore, Jr. (R), 1985–89
Wis.	Anthony S. Earl (D), 1983–87
Wyo.	Ed Herschler (D), 1983–87

WILLIAM E. SAURO/THE NEW YORK TIMES

In June 1985 Gov. Mario Cuomo signed a bill that raised the drinking age in New York to 21 from 19, thereby averting a cutoff of federal highway funds.

tirely on city and county jails. State officials rushed new funds into prison construction and considered the possibility of having a private, profit-making corporation take over the operation of state prisons.

Gambling

State-run games of chance continued to gain public acceptance, with Iowa becoming the 22nd state to authorize a state lottery. Three New England states started the first multistate lottery as a means of boosting prizes to compete with neighboring games in Massachusetts and New York; Maine furnished the computer for the "megabucks" game, New Hampshire conducted the drawing, and Vermont handled the administration.

Environment

States continued to band together to combat perceived environmental threats, either bypassing or combating the federal government in pursuing polluters vigorously. Connecticut, Massachusetts, Maine, New Hampshire, New York, New Jersey, and Vermont sued the U.S. Environmental Protection Agency over its failure to impose emission controls on acid rain suspects in the Midwest. Six Northeastern states signed an agreement with five Canadian provinces to reduce sulfur dioxide emissions. The governors of Illinois, Indiana, Michigan, Minnesota, New York, Ohio, Pennsylvania, and Wisconsin initialed a pact with Canadian officials to register and monitor major freshwater withdrawals from the Great Lakes.

Following a major leak at a Union Carbide Corp. facility at Institute, W.Va., officials approved a law requiring that stores of hazardous substances be reported to local health and fire officials. Vermont approved major legislation protecting groundwater and providing for the cleanup of toxic-waste sites. Maine voters insisted on approving any future low-level radioactive-waste storage plan.

Equal Rights

Comparable worth, a concept that calls for equal pay for jobs requiring similar training and responsibility, received a major judicial blow during the year when a federal appeals panel threw out a major Washington State claim. California state workers had earlier filed the largest gender discrimination wage claim in history on behalf of 38,000 female workers in 400 job categories, but the court decision cast doubt on its legal merit. After several years of examination, five states (Iowa, Massachusetts, Minnesota, Washington, and Wisconsin) were providing some funding for equalizing female state workers' pay, and seven more states were on record favoring it. But governors in Ohio and Oregon vetoed similar expenditures, and experts doubted whether additional states would agree to the expensive proposition.

Consumer Protection

Following the lead of New York and New Jersey, 14 additional states made the use of seat belts mandatory for adult automobile passengers during 1985. Transportation Secretary Elizabeth Dole had asserted that unless 67% of the population was covered by strict seat-belt laws by 1989, she would require that 1990 automobiles throughout the nation have automatic seat belts or air bags. Many of the state laws did not provide for the $25 fine specified in the Dole order, however, and it appeared that air bags would be required eventually.

There was much additional action on auto safety. Massachusetts became the first state to require use of the seat belts in both front and rear passenger areas, and 21 states required their employees to wear belts at all times when driving or riding in a car. North Carolina and Wyoming became the 49th and 50th states to require seat belts for minors, and several states raised the age limit for those covered.

Maine sued Sears, Roebuck and Co. over its sale of service contracts, which state investigators said often duplicated warranty coverage. Iowa declared a state of economic emergency, allowing farmers to obtain a one-year reprieve from foreclosure on their homesteads.

Ohio and Maryland, two of five states furnishing extensive state insurance to savings and loan associations, experienced a serious loss of investor and saver confidence during the spring, leading to a shutdown of all privately insured thrift institutions in both states. Ohio Gov. Richard Celeste managed to reopen most of the institutions after 11 days, but depositors were still barred from full access to their funds at a half dozen Maryland thrifts at the year's end.

Members of the Congress of the United States

2nd Session, 99th Congress*

The Senate

President of the Senate: George Bush

State	Senator	Current Service Began	Current Term Expires	State	Senator	Current Service Began	Current Term Expires
Ala.	Howell Heflin (D)	1979	1991	Mont.	John Melcher (D)	1977	1989
	Jeremiah Denton (R)	1981	1987		Max Baucus (D)	1978	1991
Alaska	Ted Stevens (R)	1968	1991	Neb.	Edward Zorinsky (D)	1976	1989
	Frank H. Murkowski (R)	1981	1987		J. James Exon (D)	1979	1991
Ariz.	Barry Goldwater (R)	1969	1987	Nev.	Paul Laxalt (R)	1974	1987
	Dennis DeConcini (D)	1977	1989		Chic Hecht (R)	1983	1989
Ark.	Dale Bumpers (D)	1975	1987	N.H.	Gordon J. Humphrey (R)	1979	1991
	David Pryor (D)	1979	1991		Warren Rudman (R)	1980	1987
Calif.	Alan Cranston (D)	1969	1987	N.J.	Bill Bradley (D)	1979	1991
	Pete Wilson (R)	1983	1989		Frank R. Lautenberg (D)	1982	1989
Colo.	Gary W. Hart (D)	1975	1987	N.M.	Pete V. Domenici (R)	1973	1991
	William L. Armstrong (R)	1979	1991		Jeff Bingaman (D)	1983	1989
Conn.	Lowell P. Weicker, Jr. (R)	1971	1989	N.Y.	Daniel P. Moynihan (D)	1977	1989
	Christopher J. Dodd (D)	1981	1987		Alfonse M. D'Amato (R)	1981	1987
Del.	William V. Roth, Jr. (R)	1971	1989	N.C.	Jesse A. Helms (R)	1973	1991
	Joseph R. Biden, Jr. (D)	1973	1991		John P. East (R)	1981	1987
Fla.	Lawton Chiles (D)	1971	1989	N.D.	Quentin N. Burdick (D)	1960	1989
	Paula Hawkins (R)	1981	1987		Mark Andrews (R)	1981	1987
Ga.	Samuel A. Nunn (D)	1972	1991	Ohio	John H. Glenn, Jr. (D)	1974	1987
	Mack Mattingly (R)	1981	1987		Howard M. Metzenbaum (D)	1976	1989
Hawaii	Daniel K. Inouye (D)	1963	1987	Okla.	David L. Boren (D)	1979	1991
	Spark M. Matsunaga (D)	1977	1989		Don Nickles (R)	1981	1987
Idaho	James A. McClure (R)	1973	1991	Ore.	Mark O. Hatfield (R)	1967	1991
	Steven D. Symms (R)	1981	1987		Bob Packwood (R)	1969	1987
Ill.	Alan J. Dixon (D)	1981	1987	Pa.	H. John Heinz, III (R)	1977	1989
	Paul Simon (D)	1985	1991		Arlen Specter (R)	1981	1987
Ind.	Richard G. Lugar (R)	1977	1989	R.I.	Claiborne Pell (D)	1961	1991
	Dan Quayle (R)	1981	1987		John H. Chafee (R)	1976	1989
Iowa	Charles E. Grassley (R)	1981	1987	S.C.	Strom Thurmond (R)	1956	1991
	Tom Harkin (D)	1985	1991		Ernest F. Hollings (D)	1966	1987
Kan.	Bob Dole (R)	1969	1987	S.D.	Larry Pressler (R)	1979	1991
	Nancy Landon Kassebaum (R)	1978	1991		James Abdnor (R)	1981	1987
Ky.	Wendell H. Ford (D)	1974	1987	Tenn.	James R. Sasser (D)	1977	1989
	Mitch McConnell (R)	1985	1991		Albert Gore, Jr. (D)	1985	1991
La.	Russell B. Long (D)	1948	1987	Texas	Lloyd M. Bentsen (D)	1971	1989
	J. Bennett Johnston, Jr. (D)	1972	1991		Phil Gramm (R)	1985	1991
Maine	William S. Cohen (R)	1979	1991	Utah	Jake Garn (R)	1974	1987
	George J. Mitchell (D)	1980	1989		Orrin G. Hatch (R)	1977	1989
Md.	Charles McC. Mathias, Jr. (R)	1969	1987	Vt.	Robert T. Stafford (R)	1971	1989
	Paul S. Sarbanes (D)	1977	1989		Patrick J. Leahy (D)	1975	1987
Mass.	Edward M. Kennedy (D)	1962	1989	Va.	John W. Warner (R)	1979	1991
	John F. Kerry (D)	1985	1991		Paul S. Trible, Jr. (R)	1983	1989
Mich.	Donald W. Riegle, Jr. (D)	1976	1989	Wash.	Slade Gorton (R)	1981	1987
	Carl Levin (D)	1979	1991		Daniel J. Evans (R)	1983	1989
Minn.	David Durenberger (R)	1978	1989	W.Va.	Robert C. Byrd (D)	1959	1989
	Rudy Boschwitz (R)	1978	1991		John D. (Jay) Rockefeller, IV (D)	1985	1991
Miss.	John C. Stennis (D)	1947	1989	Wis.	William Proxmire (D)	1957	1989
	Thad Cochran (R)	1978	1991		Robert W. Kasten, Jr. (R)	1981	1987
Mo.	Thomas F. Eagleton (D)	1968	1987	Wyo.	Malcolm Wallop (R)	1977	1989
	John C. Danforth (R)	1976	1989		Alan K. Simpson (R)	1979	1991

*Convened January 1986.

369

The House of Representatives*

Speaker of the House: Thomas P. O'Neill, Jr.

Alabama
Sonny Callahan, 1 (R)
William L. Dickinson, 2 (R)
Bill Nichols, 3 (D)
Tom Bevill, 4 (D)
Ronnie G. Flippo, 5 (D)
Ben Erdreich, 6 (D)
Richard C. Shelby, 7 (D)

Alaska
Don Young (R)

American Samoa
Fofo I. F. Sunia (D)†

Arizona
John McCain, 1 (R)
Morris K. Udall, 2 (D)
Bob Stump, 3 (R)
Eldon D. Rudd, 4 (R)
Jim Kolbe, 5 (R)

Arkansas
Bill Alexander, 1 (D)
Tommy F. Robinson, 2 (D)
John P. Hammerschmidt, 3 (R)
Beryl Anthony, Jr., 4 (D)

California
Douglas H. Bosco, 1 (D)
Gene Chappie, 2 (R)
Robert T. Matsui, 3 (D)
Vic Fazio, 4 (D)
Sala Burton, 5 (D)
Barbara Boxer, 6 (D)
George Miller, 7 (D)
Ronald V. Dellums, 8 (D)
Fortney H. (Pete) Stark, 9 (D)
Don Edwards, 10 (D)
Tom Lantos, 11 (D)
Ed Zschau, 12 (R)
Norman Y. Mineta, 13 (D)
Norman D. Shumway, 14 (R)
Tony Coelho, 15 (D)
Leon E. Panetta, 16 (D)
Charles (Chip) Pashayan, Jr., 17 (R)
Richard H. Lehman, 18 (D)
Robert J. Lagomarsino, 19 (R)
William M. Thomas, 20 (R)
Bobbi Fiedler, 21 (R)
Carlos J. Moorhead, 22 (R)
Anthony C. Beilenson, 23 (D)
Henry A. Waxman, 24 (D)
Edward R. Roybal, 25 (D)
Howard L. Berman, 26 (D)
Mel Levine, 27 (D)
Julian C. Dixon, 28 (D)
Augustus F. Hawkins, 29 (D)
Matthew G. Martinez, 30 (D)
Mervyn M. Dymally, 31 (D)
Glenn M. Anderson, 32 (D)
David Dreier, 33 (R)
Esteban Edward Torres, 34 (D)
Jerry Lewis, 35 (R)
George E. Brown, Jr., 36 (D)
Alfred A. McCandless, 37 (R)
Robert K. Dornan, 38 (R)
William E. Dannemeyer, 39 (R)
Robert E. Badham, 40 (R)

Bill Lowery, 41 (R)
Dan Lungren, 42 (R)
Ron Packard, 43 (R)
Jim Bates, 44 (D)
Duncan Hunter, 45 (R)

Colorado
Patricia Schroeder, 1 (D)
Timothy E. Wirth, 2 (D)
Michael L. Strang, 3 (R)
Hank Brown, 4 (R)
Ken Kramer, 5 (R)
Dan Schaefer, 6 (R)

Connecticut
Barbara B. Kennelly, 1 (D)
Sam Gejdenson, 2 (D)
Bruce A. Morrison, 3 (D)
Stewart B. McKinney, 4 (R)
John G. Rowland, 5 (R)
Nancy L. Johnson, 6 (R)

Delaware
Thomas R. Carper (D)

District of Columbia
Walter E. Fauntroy (D)†

Florida
Earl D. Hutto, 1 (D)
Don Fuqua, 2 (D)
Charles E. Bennett, 3 (D)
Bill Chappell, Jr., 4 (D)
Bill McCollum, 5 (R)
Buddy MacKay, 6 (D)
Sam Gibbons, 7 (D)
C. W. (Bill) Young, 8 (R)
Michael Bilirakis, 9 (R)
Andy Ireland, 10 (D)
Bill Nelson, 11 (D)
Tom Lewis, 12 (R)
Connie Mack, 13 (R)
Dan Mica, 14 (D)
E. Clay Shaw, Jr., 15 (R)
Lawrence J. Smith, 16 (D)
William Lehman, 17 (D)
Claude Pepper, 18 (D)
Dante B. Fascell, 19 (D)

Georgia
Robert Lindsay Thomas, 1 (D)
Charles F. Hatcher, 2 (D)
Richard Ray, 3 (D)
Patrick L. Swindall, 4 (R)
Wyche Fowler, Jr., 5 (D)
Newt Gingrich, 6 (R)
George Darden, 7 (D)
J. Roy Rowland, 8 (D)
Ed Jenkins, 9 (D)
Doug Barnard, Jr., 10 (D)

Guam
Ben Blaz (R)†

Hawaii
Cecil Heftel, 1 (D)
Daniel K. Akaka, 2 (D)

Idaho
Larry E. Craig, 1 (R)
Richard H. Stallings, 2 (D)

Illinois
Charles A. Hayes, 1 (D)
Gus Savage, 2 (D)
Marty Russo, 3 (D)

George M. O'Brien, 4 (R)
William O. Lipinski, 5 (D)
Henry J. Hyde, 6 (R)
Cardiss Collins, 7 (D)
Dan Rostenkowski, 8 (D)
Sidney R. Yates, 9 (D)
John Edward Porter, 10 (R)
Frank Annunzio, 11 (D)
Philip M. Crane, 12 (R)
Harris W. Fawell, 13 (R)
John E. Grotberg, 14 (R)
Edward R. Madigan, 15 (R)
Lynn M. Martin, 16 (R)
Lane Evans, 17 (D)
Robert H. Michel, 18 (R)
Terry L. Bruce, 19 (D)
Richard J. Durbin, 20 (D)
Melvin Price, 21 (D)
Kenneth J. Gray, 22 (D)

Indiana
Peter J. Visclosky, 1 (D)
Philip R. Sharp, 2 (D)
John Hiler, 3 (R)
Dan Coats, 4 (R)
Elwood Hillis, 5 (R)
Dan Burton, 6 (R)
John T. Myers, 7 (R)
Frank McCloskey, 8 (D)
Lee H. Hamilton, 9 (D)
Andrew Jacobs, Jr., 10 (D)

Iowa
Jim Leach, 1 (R)
Tom Tauke, 2 (R)
Cooper Evans, 3 (R)
Neal Smith, 4 (D)
Jim Ross Lightfoot, 5 (R)
Berkley Bedell, 6 (D)

Kansas
Pat Roberts, 1 (R)
Jim Slattery, 2 (D)
Jan Meyers, 3 (R)
Dan Glickman, 4 (D)
Bob Whittaker, 5 (R)

Kentucky
Carroll Hubbard, Jr., 1 (D)
William H. Natcher, 2 (D)
Romano L. Mazzoli, 3 (D)
Gene Snyder, 4 (R)
Harold Rogers, 5 (R)
Larry J. Hopkins, 6 (R)
Carl C. Perkins, 7 (D)

Louisiana
Bob Livingston, 1 (R)
Lindy (Mrs. Hale) Boggs, 2 (D)
W. J. (Billy) Tauzin, 3 (D)
Buddy Roemer, 4 (D)
Jerry Huckaby, 5 (D)
W. Henson Moore, 6 (R)
John B. Breaux, 7 (D)
Cathy (Mrs. Gillis) Long, 8 (D)

Maine
John R. McKernan, Jr., 1 (R)
Olympia J. Snowe, 2 (R)

Maryland
Roy Dyson, 1 (D)
Helen Delich Bentley, 2 (R)
Barbara A. Mikulski, 3 (D)
Marjorie S. Holt, 4 (R)

Steny H. Hoyer, 5 (D)
Beverly B. Byron, 6 (D)
Parren J. Mitchell, 7 (D)
Michael D. Barnes, 8 (D)

Massachusetts
Silvio O. Conte, 1 (R)
Edward P. Boland, 2 (D)
Joseph D. Early, 3 (D)
Barney Frank, 4 (D)
Chester G. Atkins, 5 (D)
Nicholas Mavroules, 6 (D)
Edward J. Markey, 7 (D)
Thomas P. O'Neill, Jr., 8 (D)
Joe Moakley, 9 (D)
Gerry E. Studds, 10 (D)
Brian J. Donnelly, 11 (D)

Michigan
John Conyers, Jr., 1 (D)
Carl D. Pursell, 2 (R)
Howard Wolpe, 3 (D)
Mark D. Siljander, 4 (R)
Paul B. Henry, 5 (R)
Bob Carr, 6 (D)
Dale E. Kildee, 7 (D)
Bob Traxler, 8 (D)
Guy Vander Jagt, 9 (R)
Bill Schuette, 10 (R)
Robert W. Davis, 11 (R)
David E. Bonior, 12 (D)
George W. Crockett, 13 (D)
Dennis M. Hertel, 14 (D)
William D. Ford, 15 (D)
John D. Dingell, 16 (D)
Sander M. Levin, 17 (D)
William S. Broomfield, 18 (R)

Minnesota
Timothy J. Penny, 1 (D)
Vin Weber, 2 (R)
Bill Frenzel, 3 (R)
Bruce F. Vento, 4 (D)
Martin Olav Sabo, 5 (D)
Gerry Sikorski, 6 (D)
Arlan Stangeland, 7 (R)
James L. Oberstar, 8 (D)

Mississippi
Jamie L. Whitten, 1 (D)
Webb Franklin, 2 (R)
G. V. (Sonny) Montgomery, 3 (D)
Wayne Dowdy, 4 (D)
Trent Lott, 5 (R)

Missouri
William (Bill) Clay, 1 (D)
Robert A. Young, 2 (D)
Richard A. Gephardt, 3 (D)
Ike Skelton, 4 (D)
Alan Wheat, 5 (D)
E. Thomas Coleman, 6 (R)
Gene Taylor, 7 (R)
Bill Emerson, 8 (R)
Harold L. Volkmer, 9 (D)

Montana
Pat Williams, 1 (D)
Ron Marlenee, 2 (R)

Nebraska
Douglas K. Bereuter, 1 (R)
Hal Daub, 2 (R)
Virginia Smith, 3 (R)

Nevada

Harry M. Reid, 1 (D)
Barbara F. Vucanovich, 2 (R)

New Hampshire

Robert C. Smith, 1 (R)
Judd Gregg, 2 (R)

New Jersey

James J. Florio, 1 (D)
William J. Hughes, 2 (D)
James J. Howard, 3 (D)
Christopher H. Smith, 4 (R)
Marge Roukema, 5 (R)
Bernard J. Dwyer, 6 (D)
Matthew J. Rinaldo, 7 (R)
Robert A. Roe, 8 (D)
Robert G. Torricelli, 9 (D)
Peter W. Rodino, Jr., 10 (D)
Dean A. Gallo, 11 (R)
Jim Courter, 12 (R)
Jim Saxton, 13 (R)
Frank J. Guarini, 14 (D)

New Mexico

Manuel Lujan, Jr., 1 (R)
Joe Skeen, 2 (R)
Bill Richardson, 3 (D)

New York

William Carney, 1 (C-R)
Thomas J. Downey, 2 (D)
Robert J. Mrazek, 3 (D)
Norman F. Lent, 4 (R)
Raymond J. McGrath, 5 (R)
Joseph P. Addabbo, 6 (D)
Gary L. Ackerman, 7 (D)
James H. Scheuer, 8 (D)
Thomas J. Manton, 9 (D)
Charles E. Schumer, 10 (D)
Edolphus Towns, 11 (D)
Major R. Owens, 12 (D)
Stephen J. Solarz, 13 (D)
Guy V. Molinari, 14 (R)
Bill Green, 15 (R)
Charles B. Rangel, 16 (D)
Ted Weiss, 17 (D)
Robert Garcia, 18 (D)
Mario Biaggi, 19 (D)
Joseph J. DioGuardi, 20 (R)
Hamilton Fish, Jr., 21 (R)
Benjamin A. Gilman, 22 (R)
Samuel S. Stratton, 23 (D)
Gerald B. H. Solomon, 24 (R)
Sherwood L. Boehlert, 25 (R)
David O'B. Martin, 26 (R)
George C. Wortley, 27 (R)
Matthew F. McHugh, 28 (D)
Frank Horton, 29 (R)
Fred J. Eckert, 30 (R)
Jack F. Kemp, 31 (R)
John J. LaFalce, 32 (D)

Henry J. Nowak, 33 (D)
Stan Lundine, 34 (D)

North Carolina

Walter B. Jones, 1 (D)
Tim Valentine, 2 (D)
Charles Whitley, 3 (D)
William W. Cobey, Jr., 4 (R)
Stephen L. Neal, 5 (D)
Howard Coble, 6 (R)
Charles Rose, 7 (D)
W. G. (Bill) Hefner, 8 (D)
J. Alex McMillan, 9 (R)
James T. Broyhill, 10 (R)
William M. Hendon, 11 (R)

North Dakota

Byron L. Dorgan (D)

Ohio

Thomas A. Luken, 1 (D)
Willis D. Gradison, Jr., 2 (R)
Tony P. Hall, 3 (D)
Michael G. Oxley, 4 (R)
Delbert L. Latta, 5 (R)
Bob McEwen, 6 (R)
Michael DeWine, 7 (R)
Thomas N. Kindness, 8 (R)
Marcy Kaptur, 9 (D)
Clarence E. Miller, 10 (R)
Dennis E. Eckart, 11 (D)
John R. Kasich, 12 (R)
Donald J. Pease, 13 (D)
John F. Seiberling, 14 (D)
Chalmers P. Wylie, 15 (R)
Ralph Regula, 16 (R)
James A. Traficant, Jr., 17 (D)
Douglas Applegate, 18 (D)
Edward F. Feighan, 19 (D)
Mary Rose Oakar, 20 (D)
Louis Stokes, 21 (D)

Oklahoma

James Rogers Jones, 1 (D)
Mike Synar, 2 (D)
Wes Watkins, 3 (D)
Dave McCurdy, 4 (D)
Mickey Edwards, 5 (R)
Glenn English, 6 (D)

Oregon

Les AuCoin, 1 (D)
Robert F. Smith, 2 (R)
Ron Wyden, 3 (D)
James Weaver, 4 (D)
Denny Smith, 5 (R)

Pennsylvania

Thomas M. Foglietta, 1 (D)
William H. Gray III, 2 (D)
Robert A. Borski, 3 (D)
Joe Kolter, 4 (D)
Richard T. Schulze, 5 (R)
Gus Yatron, 6 (D)

Robert W. Edgar, 7 (D)
Peter H. Kostmayer, 8 (D)
E. G. (Bud) Shuster, 9 (R)
Joseph M. McDade, 10 (R)
Paul E. Kanjorski, 11 (D)
John P. Murtha, 12 (D)
R. Lawrence Coughlin, 13 (R)
William J. Coyne, 14 (D)
Donald L. Ritter, 15 (R)
Robert S. Walker, 16 (R)
George W. Gekas, 17 (R)
Doug Walgren, 18 (D)
William F. Goodling, 19 (R)
Joseph M. Gaydos, 20 (D)
Thomas J. Ridge, 21 (R)
Austin J. Murphy, 22 (D)
William F. Clinger, Jr., 23 (R)

Puerto Rico

Jaime B. Fuster (D)‡

Rhode Island

Fernand J. St. Germain, 1 (D)
Claudine Schneider, 2 (R)

South Carolina

Thomas F. Hartnett, 1 (R)
Floyd Spence, 2 (R)
Butler Derrick, 3 (D)
Carroll A. Campbell, Jr., 4 (R)
John M. Spratt, Jr., 5 (D)
Robin Tallon, 6 (D)

South Dakota

Tom A. Daschle (D)

Tennessee

James H. Quillen, 1 (R)
John J. Duncan, 2 (R)
Marilyn Lloyd, 3 (D)
Jim Cooper, 4 (D)
Bill Boner, 5 (D)
Bart Gordon, 6 (D)
Don Sundquist, 7 (R)
Ed Jones, 8 (D)
Harold E. Ford, 9 (D)

Texas

Jim Chapman, 1 (D)
Charles Wilson, 2 (D)
Steve Bartlett, 3 (R)
Ralph M. Hall, 4 (D)
John Bryant, 5 (D)
Joe Barton, 6 (R)
Bill Archer, 7 (R)
Jack Fields, 8 (R)
Jack Brooks, 9 (D)
J. J. Pickle, 10 (D)
Marvin Leath, 11 (D)
Jim Wright, 12 (D)
Beau Boulter, 13 (R)
Mac Sweeney, 14 (R)
E. (Kika) de la Garza, 15 (D)
Ronald D. Coleman, 16 (D)

Charles W. Stenholm, 17 (D)
Mickey Leland, 18 (D)
Larry Combest, 19 (R)
Henry B. Gonzalez, 20 (D)
Tom Loeffler, 21 (R)
Tom DeLay, 22 (R)
Albert G. Bustamante, 23 (D)
Martin Frost, 24 (D)
Michael A. Andrews, 25 (D)
Richard Armey, 26 (R)
Solomon P. Ortiz, 27 (D)

Utah

James V. Hansen, 1 (R)
David S. Monson, 2 (R)
Howard C. Nielson, 3 (R)

Vermont

James M. Jeffords (R)

Virginia

Herbert H. Bateman, 1 (R)
G. William Whitehurst, 2 (R)
Thomas J. Bliley, Jr., 3 (R)
Norman Sisisky, 4 (D)
Dan Daniel, 5 (D)
James R. Olin, 6 (D)
D. French Slaughter, Jr., 7 (R)
Stan Parris, 8 (R)
Frederick C. Boucher, 9 (D)
Frank R. Wolf, 10 (R)

Virgin Islands

Ron de Lugo (D)†

Washington

John R. Miller, 1 (R)
Allen Swift, 2 (D)
Don Bonker, 3 (D)
Sid Morrison, 4 (R)
Thomas S. Foley, 5 (D)
Norman D. Dicks, 6 (D)
Mike Lowry, 7 (D)
Rod Chandler, 8 (R)

West Virginia

Alan B. Mollohan, 1 (D)
Harley O. Staggers, Jr., 2 (D)
Robert E. Wise, Jr., 3 (D)
Nick Joe Rahall, 4 (D)

Wisconsin

Les Aspin, 1 (D)
Robert W. Kastenmeier, 2 (D)
Steven Gunderson, 3 (R)
Gerald D. Kleczka, 4 (D)
Jim Moody, 5 (D)
Thomas E. Petri, 6 (R)
David R. Obey, 7 (D)
Toby Roth, 8 (R)
F. James Sensenbrenner, Jr., 9 (R)

Wyoming

Dick Cheney (R)

*Numbers after names indicate congressional districts; where no number is given, the representative is elected at large.
†Nonvoting elected delegate.
‡Nonvoting elected commissioner.

AP/WIDE WORLD

Julio María Sanguinetti Cairolo (right), the new president of Uruguay, is congratulated by U.S. Secretary of State George Shultz upon his inauguration on March 1.

URUGUAY

Following 12 years of military government, Uruguay returned to civilian rule on March 1, 1985, when Julio María Sanguinetti Cairolo was sworn in as president. Soon after his victory in the November 1984 elections, Sanguinetti began attempts to establish political consensus. His aim to form a government that would include all the major parties as well as his own Colorado Party was limited to the extent that members of the opposition generally declined Cabinet positions. However, the defeated presidential candidate of the Unión Cívica, Juan Vicente Chiarino, and two National (Blanco) Party sympathizers, Enrique Iglesias and Raúl Ugarte, accepted Cabinet appointments. Representatives of the parties, trade unions, and employers met early in the year and reached broad agreement on most political and economic issues, except for labor relations and amnesty for political prisoners.

The new government immediately lifted bans on several organizations, relaxed laws restricting freedom of the press, and allowed political exiles to return to the country. However, frustrated expectations of immediate increases in wages led to a series of damaging strikes. The militancy of labor demands ended the national dialogue and resulted in a one-day general strike in September. At the same time, efforts continued to bring army officers accused of human rights violations to justice.

VENEZUELA

In January 1985 Luis Matos Azócar resigned as minister in charge of Venezuela's state coordination and planning office (Cordiplán) after he had been outspokenly critical of the economic austerity measures imposed by Pres. Jaime Lusinchi's government. The result of this move and a Cabinet reshuffle announced in March was to strengthen the economic hand of Minister of Development Héctor Hurtado Navarro. Leopoldo Carnevalli was transferred from the Central Budget Office to become the minister in charge of Cordiplán. A new appointment to the Cabinet was that of Carmelo Lauría Lesseur, former governor of Caracas, as secretary to the presidency. The new foreign minister was Simón Alberto Consalvi, who had held the same position under former president Carlos Andrés Pérez in the 1970s.

In August President Lusinchi vetoed a series of reforms that would have established a primary-style system for choosing presidential candidates in place of a system controlled by the parties at the national level. The change in policy was advocated by supporters of Pérez, who had begun an informal campaign for the presidency. Lusinchi's reaction was to speak out against the reelection of any former president. He feared that the Pérez campaign would create added potential for divisions within his administration.

The debate had the effect of diverting the attention of the ruling Acción Democrática (AD) party from the opposition Social Christian Party (COPEI). In September COPEI proposed a new labor law that was more favorable to workers than was the existing AD-sponsored legislation. The labor vote had been instrumental in sweeping the AD to power in the 1983 elections. The ruling party could not therefore reject the proposed legislation without the risk of alienating the unions and compromising its pro-labor stance. A congressional committee was set up to study the proposed legislation.

In March Hemmy Croes, a leading trade unionist and member of the Central Committee of the Venezuelan Communist Party, was shot dead outside his home in Caracas. This followed the murder during the previous month of Juan Luis Ibarra Riverol, the lawyer representing Lieut. Col. Luis Alfonso Godoy, who had brought charges of corruption against three former defense ministers in the government of Lusinchi's predecessor, Luis Herrera Campíns. Godoy attributed "intellectual responsibility" for the death to the three men. It later emerged that the murder had been carried out by military personnel, apparently in revenge for the fact that they had not been paid for information supplied in support of the charges. Godoy was compulsorily retired from the Army for upsetting military discipline and promoting scandal.

In mid-May the government and its committee of advisory banks reached agreement for restructuring national debts of $21.1 billion. The agreement sanctioned the rescheduling of the debt over 12½ years at 1.125% above the London interbank rates or above the basic interest rate of the national bank of the country concerned. Venezuela was to pay $750 million to the banks once the rescheduling agreement came into effect.

At the end of June new rules amending the

Pope John Paul II accepts gifts from representatives of the Amazon Indians of Venezuela during his January visit to that nation. During the visit the pope spoke out strongly in support of traditional church teachings.

AP/WIDE WORLD

country's restrictive foreign-investment laws were issued. Special incentives were introduced for foreign-owned firms that exported more than 80% of their production outside the Andean Group of countries; their obligation to sell shares to domestic investors was lifted, as was the limit placed on profits they could remit from their exports.

VIETNAM

In 1985 Vietnam experienced a quiet year in terms of developments at the top levels of political power. Though 77 years old and ailing, Communist Party Secretary-General Le Duan remained firmly in control. Hanoi's decision to seek more normal economic links with the outside world was largely motivated by years of economic stagnation at home. An even more significant shift was under way in the diplomatic field. Spurred by a growing need for development aid as well as by a desire to lessen its dependence on the U.S.S.R., Vietnam's leaders launched initiatives to repair its long-frayed relationship with the U.S.

Throughout the year Le Duan maintained his characteristic low profile. However, suspicions that he might be losing his grip were dispelled by the reinstatement of Nguyen Van Linh, a confidant of Le Duan, in the Communist Party's 15-member Politburo. A veteran revolutionary, Linh had been expected to fade into obscurity when he was dropped from the Politburo in 1982. The importance of another center of Vietnamese power, the Army, was underscored in December 1984 during commemorations of the 40th anniversary of its founding, when two senior officers were promoted; Le Duc Anh, in charge of military operations in Kampuchea, and Le Trong Tan, chief of general staff, became only the fifth and sixth men to attain the rank of full general.

During 1985 Hanoi marked the 40th anniversary of the August Revolution, which brought the late president Ho Chi Minh to power in the north, and the 10th anniversary of Hanoi's conquest of the south. The latter celebration was attended by a phalanx of U.S. press and television journalists compiling in-depth retrospectives on their country's fateful involvement in Vietnam.

A major current in the social and religious life of Vietnam went largely unnoticed in the outside world. The authorities stepped up the political crackdown launched the previous year against major religious groups in the south, especially Buddhists and Christians, who had long constituted an important political force in that part of the country. During 1984 some leading Buddhist figures were retired, many others were jailed, and a few died mysteriously. In 1985 the authorities extended their suppression to grassroots elements. According to Vietnamese exiles in clandestine contact with Buddhists at home, the campaign was a "systematic" part of Hanoi's policy to curb criticism of the state. Only 15,000 or so monks remained in the temples and monasteries of southern Vietnam, compared with more than 100,000 a decade earlier. The authorities withdrew the traditional exemption of clergy from service in the armed forces; placed pliant monks, often from the north, in key positions in leading Buddhist organizations; disseminated revised, party-sanctioned versions of Buddhist teachings; and required monastery schools to teach Marxism-Leninism to their pupils. Monks were also removed from monasteries to work in factories or the fields.

Christians were not spared. A number of Roman Catholic leaders were detained because of their opposition to government-controlled religious committees. Constant pressure was applied against the

Under a portrait of Ho Chi Minh,
troops representing Vietnam's 1.2
million-man Army march past a
reviewing stand full of dignitaries.
The Liberation Day parade in Ho
Chi Minh City (formerly Saigon)
marked the tenth anniversary
of North Vietnam's victory over
the south.

EDDIE ADAMS—GAMMA/LIAISON

Evangelical Church of Vietnam, the nation's largest and oldest Protestant church. Some 100 pastors were reportedly confined to camps. One result was that Christianity was beginning to go underground.

Meeting at the end of 1984, the seventh plenum of the Communist Party's Central Committee concentrated on economic matters. It identified the need to boost food production and the manufacture of consumer goods as major priorities. Though food output in 1984 had grown by 300,000 metric tons, the total fell short of the target of 18 million metric tons. The plenum blamed inclement weather, bad management, and disruptive efforts by China. The agricultural sector faced further setbacks in the third quarter of 1985 when several typhoons destroyed large areas of rice paddy.

Faced with a foreign debt estimated at more than $6 billion and meager reserves of $16 million, Hanoi began actively to solicit closer ties with the international financial community. At a conference of Southeast Asian central bankers in Malaysia in February, Hanoi's representatives announced that they intended to seek $200 million in loans from the International Monetary Fund. Officials of the IMF were noncommittal, pointing out that the Fund had stopped lending to Vietnam three years earlier.

The plenum endorsed a policy aimed at improving diplomatic relations with Western countries, especially the U.S. The strategy involved fostering the normalization of ties with Washington by being more cooperative on bilateral matters and encouraging the U.S. to play a more active role in Southeast Asia in order to counter China's influence. Besides softening its customary anti-U.S. rhetoric, Vietnam made a significant gesture on the unresolved, emotional issue of U.S. servicemen who remained missing in action (MIA) from the Indochina wars. During talks in Hanoi in August, Vietnamese negotiators promised that their government would unconditionally complete the search for MIAs within two years. Previously, Vietnam had always demanded in return that the U.S. declare willingness to normalize relations, deliver fi-

nancial aid, or stop "colluding" with China. On this occasion Hanoi announced that it would conduct investigations of crash sites and carry out necessary excavations on its own, but the U.S. offered to bear the costs of the digging and proposed joint searches. The first such search, at the crash site of a B-52 bomber about 9 mi (14 km) north of Hanoi, was completed December 1. Human remains were found and removed for possible identification.

Spurred perhaps by an apparent thaw in Sino-Soviet relations, Vietnamese officials repeatedly stated that their government attached no preconditions to renewed amity with China, although the latter, like the U.S., continued to insist on a withdrawal of Vietnamese troops from Kampuchea. There was some evidence of easing in the troubled relationship, but analysts agreed that substantive improvement probably remained some way off.

WEATHER

Hurricanes dominated the weather scene in 1985. Six hurricanes and two tropical storms made landfall along the U.S. coast, giving that country its most active hurricane season since 1916. Two of the hurricanes, Elena and Gloria, were major storms that caused evacuation of an estimated two million people from the Gulf of Mexico and Atlantic coastlines. The death toll was held to four in Elena and nine during Gloria's sweep up the heavily populated East Coast.

The year's first hurricane, Bob, briefly reached hurricane force before moving inland across South Carolina on July 25. Hurricane Danny reached a maximum strength of 90 mph (145 km/hr) near the time of landfall on August 15 along a sparsely populated coastal region of Louisiana.

Elena formed off Cuba on August 28 and finally went ashore at Biloxi, Miss., on September 2 with winds as high as 125 mph (200 km/hr). Its exceptionally erratic movement in the Gulf of Mexico had it going first toward the northwest, then east; then it stalled off the western coast of Florida and finally moved to the west, threatening the Florida

panhandle for the second time in a week. Before it was over, about 1.5 million residents had been safely evacuated (some of them twice) in communities along the coast of Florida, Alabama, Mississippi, and Louisiana. Damage was estimated as high as $1 billion in the four-state area.

Hurricane Gloria reached hurricane status on September 22. Three days later, when it hung 150 mi (240 km) east of The Bahamas, it was the most intense hurricane in recent history. Its central pressure was measured at 27.43 in (929 millibars) with winds up to 150 mph (240 km/hr). The entire coastal area from just south of Charleston, S.C., to Eastport, Maine, came under a hurricane warning. A half million residents were evacuated to safety. Gloria skirted the coastline, brushing Cape Hatteras, but its most dangerous core remained offshore. When it made landfall in Long Island and Connecticut, it did so at low tide, minimizing the feared death and destruction. Damage was estimated at $350 million.

Two tropical storms, Henri and Isabel, also affected the U.S. coast but inflicted little damage and no deaths in the U.S. The tropical wave that later developed into Isabel dumped as much as 15 in

(380 mm) of rain in Puerto Rico, causing major flooding and landslides on the south central coast and killing at least 180 people. Damage was estimated at $500 million.

A late-season hurricane, Juan, created havoc in southern Louisiana. It moved inland southwest of New Orleans on October 29, was downgraded to a tropical storm, moved back to the central Louisiana coast on October 30, looped into the Gulf, and made landfall a second time just west of Pensacola, Fla., on October 31. Between 9 and 13 in (230 and 330 mm) of rain fell in southern Louisiana, causing extensive flooding. At least seven people died, and damages neared the $1 billion mark.

Just when it seemed the hurricane season was over, Kate formed north of Puerto Rico on November 16. It passed near The Bahamas, crossed the northern coastline of Cuba leaving at least ten dead, sideswiped the Florida Keys, and then burst into the Gulf of Mexico with winds of 115 mph (185 km/hr). Kate made landfall in the Florida panhandle between Panama City and Apalachicola on November 21. More than 100,000 residents heeded the advanced warning and again evacuated. Seven people were reported dead as a result of Kate's

The Shenandoah River floods buildings in Harpers Ferry, West Virginia. Widespread flooding in West Virginia and Virginia and parts of Maryland and Pennsylvania in early November took more than 40 lives and resulted in damage of about $1 billion.

AP/WIDE WORLD

passage. During the 1985 hurricane season parts of every coastal state from Texas to Maine received hurricane warnings.

On May 25 a tropical cyclone (hurricane) struck Bangladesh's eastern delta region with a huge storm surge that left 2,540 persons dead by one official estimate; some believed as many as 11,000 died. It was the world's deadliest storm since 300,000 were drowned in that same area in the 1970 cyclone. There were also numerous typhoons (hurricanes) in the western Pacific in 1985, which caused widespread flooding and damage in China, Japan, and the Philippines.

Drought continued to afflict Africa in 1985, especially the nations along the southern border of the Sahara known as the Sahel. Its extreme severity marked it as one of the most significant climatic events of modern times. While patterns of alternating wet and dry episodes are typical of most semiarid regions of Africa, it was the long-term variations such as those affecting the Sahel that concerned global meteorologists. A turn toward more arid conditions in the Sahel had been observed for the past three decades, and some scientists speculated that a deterioration might have been under way there for as long as a century. Some climatologists were concerned that it could be an early indication of the global effects of rising carbon dioxide in the atmosphere.

WILDLIFE CONSERVATION

On Jan. 13, 1985, ornithologists counted 1,350 great white cranes (*Grus leucogeranus*) at Poyang Lake Bird Sanctuary in China, which was established in 1983. It was belived to be the largest flock of cranes in the world. Also in January, China reported a survey revealing 700 black-necked cranes (*Grus nigricollis*) in the country; previously there were thought to be only 300–400 left in the wild. Efforts were made in Ladakh, India, to protect 14–16 pairs of black-necked cranes by placing armed guards at the breeding areas. Chicks were ringed

in order to locate the wintering area of the Indian flock, believed to be in China or Bhutan. In North America the whooping crane (*Grus americana*) conservation program suffered a setback at the end of 1984 when 7 members of the captive flock of 37 birds died of eastern equine encephalitis. This left a total of 148 whooping cranes alive, including birds in captivity.

A fire broke out on Isabela, the largest island in the Galápagos archipelago, on February 26. It was started accidentally by farmers burning diseased coffee bushes and spread into the national park, where it burned intensely, fueled by the abnormally heavy growth of vegetation induced by the 1983 El Niño current and dried by the 1984 drought. Ecuador mobilized soldiers and local residents to fight the fire and in March appealed for international aid. Both Canada and the U.S. responded, Canada sending flying boats to bomb the critical areas with tons of seawater, and the U.S. contributing troops and fire-fighting experts. There were fears for the island's wildlife, particularly for the Sierra Negra race of giant tortoises, whose habitat was in the path of the fire. An airlift rescue operation was planned for them, but the fire-fighting efforts and rains in April brought the fire under control before it became necessary. The fire, which was still smoldering in June, destroyed approximately 98,-800 ac (40,000 ha) of scrub and grassland. It would be some time before the full effects on the wildlife were known.

The Californian condor (*Gymnogyps californianus*) census in April revealed that 7 of the 15 birds alive the previous autumn were missing. Only one breeding pair remained among the surviving eight, and it produced three eggs, all of which were taken for captive rearing, although one chick subsequently died. In December only six were left in the wild, and the U.S. Fish and Wildlife Service recommended that they be taken into captivity for breeding in a last attempt to save the species from extinction.

The white-tailed sea eagle (*Haliaeetus albicilla*) reintroduction project on the Scottish island of Rhum had a success in 1985 when the first bird to be bred in the wild in Britain for 70 years took flight. Thailand reintroduced sarus cranes (*Grus antigone*) to the Bang Phra Wildlife Sanctuary after receiving three pairs from the U.S.-based International Crane Foundation. In New Zealand a new population of the world's heaviest parrot, the kakapo (*Strigops habroptilus*), was discovered; only about 50 kakapos were known to exist. In the New Zealand Parliament the death was announced of "Old Blue," a female Chatham Island black robin (*Petroica traversi*), which was, in 1980, among the last five of the species. All but 2 of the 30 black robins alive at the end of 1984 were Old Blue's direct descendants.

The parties to the Convention on International Trade in Endangered Species of Wild Fauna and Flora (CITES) assembled in Buenos Aires, Arg., in April for their fifth biennial conference. The resolutions approved included one, put forward by 12 South American countries, to reject all wildlife shipments originating in Bolivia until that country reorganized its permit system. Bolivia had been strongly criticized early in the meeting for exporting large quantities of specimens taken illegally in other countries, in contravention of the CITES. Another resolution approved establishment of a special Ivory Unit to scrutinize the trade in African elephant ivory more closely; the proportion of poached ivory entering the trade was estimated at up to 80% in recent years. The meeting decided to relax controls on trade in Nile crocodile hides for those countries able to demonstrate that they had healthy crocodile populations and the means of controlling the trade effectively.

The International Whaling Commission (IWC) held its 37th annual meeting in Bournemouth, England, in July, the last meeting before the indefinite moratorium on commercial whaling due to begin at the end of 1985. The U.S.S.R., Japan, and Norway remained formally opposed to the moratorium, but the U.S.S.R. announced that it would halt Antarctic whaling in 1987. The meeting voted to give full protection to Norway's severely depleted stock of minke whales in the northeast Atlantic, making it unlikely that Norway would continue whaling. Japan showed no signs of ceasing whaling. In the 1984–85 season it took 400 sperm whales in defiance of the IWC's zero quota. The U.S., required by law to impose sanctions on nations contravening IWC decisions, privately agreed with Japan not to impose sanctions if Japan promised to cease whaling by 1988. In late 1984 conservationists had taken the U.S. government to court over this agreement. A district court ruled that the government had acted illegally, and the ruling was confirmed in August by the Federal Court of Appeals. The government appealed the decision to the Supreme Court. Iceland and South Korea did not formally oppose the moratorium but announced their intention to take 200 whales each year for the next four years, using an IWC clause that allowed governments to grant themselves special permits to take any number of whales for scientific research.

In February hundreds of white whales (*Delphinapterus leucas*), trapped in the Bering Sea by ice since mid-December, were freed by a Soviet icebreaker, which broke open an 11.8-mi (19-km)

A humpback whale nicknamed Humphrey frustrated scientists, environmentalists, and well-wishers for over three weeks in October after it swam into San Francisco Bay and up the San Joaquin and Sacramento rivers. The whale, a member of an endangered species, ignored all efforts to drive it back to the safety of salt water but was finally coaxed back to sea by recorded sounds of humpbacks feeding.

AP/WIDE WORLD

KEITH ROBERT WESSEL/TIME MAGAZINE

Lan-lan, a black-necked crane, dances with a Chinese official at the International Crane Foundation in Baraboo, Wisconsin. Lan-lan and another crane were sent by China to aid in a captive breeding program.

channel and lured them through it into open water by playing classical music through a loudspeaker.

Plans to breed Sumatran rhinos (*Dicerorhinus sumatrensis*) in captivity were announced in August. With fewer than 800 individuals in existence, this rhino was one of the 12 animals identified by the International Union for Conservation of Nature and Natural Resources (IUCN), at its general assembly in Madrid in November 1984, as among

the world's most endangered species. As part of an IUCN-coordinated project, an agreement was made between Indonesia and the U.K. under which two pairs of the rhinos would be captured and taken to two British zoos for captive breeding. The status of rhinos in parts of Africa became critical in 1985. Kenya decided to round up its last black rhinos to keep them in heavily guarded sanctuaries. Rhinos in Zimbabwe's Middle Zambezi Valley, once considered safe because of their remoteness, became the latest target of armed poaching gangs, which killed 18 rhinos in early 1985 alone.

On September 27 the ban on imports of baby harp and hooded seal skins to the EC, imposed in 1983 and due to expire on Oct. 1, 1985, was extended for four years.

YUGOSLAVIA

In 1985 Yugoslavia grappled with serious economic and financial problems against a background of growing political ferment at home, while in foreign policy the country maintained its nonaligned stance. Premier Milka Planinc visited the U.S. in May for talks that chiefly concerned the country's financial position. In July she visited Moscow, and in the same month Gen. Wojciech Jaruzelski, Poland's premier, visited Yugoslavia. In November Bulgarian Premier Grisha Filipov journeyed to Belgrade to return Planinc's visit to Bulgaria in 1984. He was followed in December by Romanian Pres. Nicolae Ceausescu and U.S. Secretary of State George Shultz.

Relations with Albania improved slightly after the death of Enver Hoxha, the Albanian Communist Party leader, in April. In November the two countries signed an agreement to open the railway linking Shkoder with Titograd, Albania's first direct rail link with the outside world, in early 1986. Trade between the two countries doubled in 1985. However, polemics continued about the situation in Yugoslavia's Kosovo Province, with its predom-

A researcher prepares a Californian condor for its trip to a California zoo. In December the U.S. Fish and Wildlife Service recommended that the last six Californian condors still living in the wild be snared and sent to California zoos where 21 other captive condors resided. Although the program was opposed by several environmental groups, the Wildlife Service felt that its decision to attempt to breed captive condors was the last hope for the survival of the species.

DAVID A. CLENDENEN/TIME MAGAZINE

V. KOSHEVOI—TASS/SOVFOTO

Premier Milka Planinc (far right) of Yugoslavia meets with Mikhail Gorbachev (far left), general secretary of the Communist Party of the Soviet Union, during her visit to Moscow in July.

inantly Albanian population. Albania complained of the oppression of Albanians in Kosovo, while Yugoslavia accused Albania of interfering in its internal affairs.

The situation in Kosovo remained Yugoslavia's main internal security problem. Throughout the year there were trials of Kosovo Albanians who were agitating for the province to be made a full federal republic. Emigration of Serbs and Montenegrins from Kosovo continued against a background of complaints that they were leaving under pressure. In Serbia there was growing demand for revision of the 1974 constitution, which had granted considerable autonomy to the two provinces of Kosovo and Vojvodina, both part of Serbia.

Three of six accused dissidents were sentenced in February to prison sentences ranging from one to two years; one was released for lack of evidence, and the trial of the other two was postponed. Others arrested at the same time, including Milovan Djilas, Yugoslavia's best-known dissident, had already been released. In spite of the continuing crackdown against the Roman Catholic Church in Croatia and Bosnia, some 15,000 young Croatian Catholics attended a rally in Zagreb Cathedral at the end of October. Pope John Paul II was refused permission to attend the ceremonies in July marking the 1,100th anniversary of the death of St. Methodius, the Greek-born missionary who for a time had been

bishop of what is today a part of Yugoslavia. A large crowd attended the rededication in Belgrade on May 12 of the foundations of the Serbian Orthodox Church of St. Sava, patron saint of Serbia.

In July two draft laws on the redistribution of hard currency failed to receive the required two-thirds majority in the federal Parliament, largely because of opposition from Croatia and Slovenia. They objected to a larger share of hard-currency earnings being handed over to the National Bank for general needs, including debt repayment, on the grounds that the move would discourage exports. Negotiations begun in 1984 with Western banks about Yugoslavia's $19.5 billion debt resulted in agreement in September 1985 to reschedule $3.5 billion worth of repayments falling due in the period 1985–88. The agreement cleared the way for payment of a further installment of an International Monetary Fund credit. In the first six months of 1985, exports to the hard-currency area increased by only 2%, instead of the planned 15%, while those to member countries of the Council for Mutual Economic Assistance rose 15%. In the same period, imports from both East and West went up 7% and industrial output rose 2.9% as compared with the first half of 1984. The inflation rate reached 80% in the second half of 1985, while unemployment exceeded one million and the number of strikes was double the 1984 level.

ZAIRE

Fighting in the town of Moba, Shaba Province, in mid-November 1984 was attributed by the government of Zaire to the activities of rebels based in Tanzania. However, the Tanzanian government denied that it harbored Zairian rebels, and opposition groups in Brussels said that the fighting was the result of a mutiny in the Zairian Army. It was significant, therefore, that shortly afterward Pres. Mobutu Sese Seko retired six generals and five lieutenant colonels and announced that a new army unit was to be set up with the special task of providing information for the head of state. A subsequent attack on Moba in June 1985 was blamed once again on "hostile elements" from Tanzania.

In late 1984 and early 1985 Mobutu carried out a substantial reorganization of his Cabinet. On February 1 he himself assumed the justice portfolio, and on April 12 he made three further significant changes affecting the ministries of finance, economy and industry, and external trade. The government's adherence to the austerity program laid down in the 1985 budget evoked confidence in the economy and induced the International Monetary Fund to agree to a standby credit arrangement of $160 million in April. Other sources of foreign aid also remained available. Italy offered a loan to promote agricultural development in the Bas-Zaire (Lower Zaire) and Bandundu regions, and the U.S. Agency for International Development offered a further loan for road building and for medical and water projects in Shaba region. The UN Development Program and Food and Agriculture Organization also agreed to make a grant of $1.9 million to assist in administrative and agricultural reforms.

Zaire was granted an increase in its coffee export quota under the International Coffee Agreement, a concession granted to only two other African countries. In February it was announced that Zaire

Pres. Mobuto Sese Seko of Zaire reviews an honor guard on his arrival in Israel May 12, his first visit since Zaire restored ties with Israel in 1982.

AP/WIDE WORLD

expected to meet its domestic petroleum needs from its own resources by exchanging its light, sulfur-free crude oil for imports of heavier oils and refined products. Like neighboring Zambia, Zaire had suffered for nearly a decade from the low price paid for copper on the world market, but there was a modicum of encouragement to be gleaned from the announcement that Western European countries intended to increase their consumption of copper by 2–3%.

In June several members of the banned Zairian Union pour la Démocratie et le Progrès Social (UDPS) who had been under house arrest since 1982, when they campaigned against the government's one-party policy, were released. They claimed that the government had agreed to release all political prisoners and to halt political arrests in return for the cessation of public activity by the UDPS. On July 18, however, a Belgian employee of the European Parliament, Ronald van den Bogaert, was arrested on his arrival in Kinshasa and charged with possessing seditious material intended for members of the UDPS. He was tried and sentenced to ten years' imprisonment, though both the trial and sentence were fiercely criticized by Belgium's Flemish Socialist Party, of which he was a member. Shortly afterward the UDPS charged the government with failing to respect the truce. On October 9 a UDPS meeting in Kinshasa in the home of the party chairman, Kibassa Maliba, was broken up by government troops; the UDPS claimed that 13 of its members had been arrested, though the government said only one person had been detained. At the end of June former prime minister Nguza Karl-I-Bond was reported to have renounced his opposition to Mobutu and returned to Zaire, ending four years of voluntary exile in Belgium.

Relations with Zambia continued to be strained because of the expulsion by each country of nationals belonging to its neighbor, a situation that was aggravated by the influx of hundreds of refugees into Zambia after the fighting in Moba in 1984. On February 9, at the end of a visit to Kinshasa by Pres. José Eduardo dos Santos of Angola, Zaire signed a number of bilateral agreements with Angola covering defense and security, trade, conservation, and health. Each country agreed to prevent the launch of attacks against the other from within its borders, and the two presidents also discussed the question of refugees.

In September Minister of Foreign Affairs Mokolo wa Mpombo paid an official visit to South Korea, where he sought that country's participation in agricultural and hydroelectricity projects and urged South Korea to import Zairian cobalt and zinc. The two countries reaffirmed their desire for bilateral cooperation in the fields of economics, technology, and culture.

In May President Mobutu paid a six-day official visit to Israel, where he reportedly secured favorable credit terms for the purchase of military hardware from Israel. In 1982 Zaire had been the first of the black African nations to break a boycott of Israel. During the course of his African tour in August, Pope John Paul II visited Zaire for the second time.

ZAMBIA

Austerity was the theme of all the Zambian government's pronouncements in 1985. Estimates of expenditure for the year rose by $55.5 million, all of it attributable to debt servicing. Although Pres. Kenneth Kaunda deplored the "terrifying" demands attached by the International Monetary Fund to its loans, the government found it essential to borrow. When the value of the kwacha, Zambia's currency, was more than halved in October, the finance minister declared he was confident that it would stabilize at a higher level once the business sector calmed down. Speaking at the opening of the 20th national council meeting of the ruling United National Independence Party in October, Kaunda said that industry had become too capital intensive and urged that the importation of capital equipment be discouraged.

Over the recent years of drought, Zambia had found it necessary to use its scarce supplies of foreign currency to import maize (corn). With the drought broken, the potential benefits were threatened by low prices offered by the government to producers and by the danger that a fuel shortage might hamper harvesting. The fuel crisis was averted when a new loan was raised from a consortium of banks.

ZIMBABWE

During the opening months of 1985 Joshua Nkomo, leader of Zimbabwe's main opposition party, the Zimbabwe African People's Union (ZAPU), experienced increasing difficulty in addressing public meetings because of the violent intervention of supporters of the ruling Patriotic Front party, the Zimbabwe African National Union (ZANU [PF]). At the end of February five supporters of another party, the United African National Council (UANC), led by former prime minister Bishop Abel Muzorewa, were shot dead at Hwange railway station after a party meeting, while on the same day, supporters of ZAPU and ZANU (PF) fought pitched battles in the streets of Bulawayo. On March 2 Bulawayo was sealed off by hundreds of troops who then spent two days searching the city for antigovernment rebels in an attempt, they claimed, to prevent a recurrence of the previous week's violence. Nkomo, who had already complained of mass abductions of his supporters, described the military action as another attempt by the government to demoralize his followers. His complaint was reinforced a few days later when the Roman Catholic Church's Commission for Justice and Peace handed the government its report on violent incidents by supporters of the government and ZANU (PF) against their critics in Matabeleland.

Parliamentary elections planned for the end of March were postponed because electoral registers had not been completed in time to allow the delimitation commission to define new constituency boundaries. The new date for voting was fixed for June, but when, after further delays, legislation was passed in May to hasten the electoral process, opposition parties were vocal in their criticism because they believed the new measures did not allow them adequate time to choose and allocate candidates. The High Court rejected an application from ZAPU to postpone the closing date for nominations, but the date was postponed by one and a half days by presidential order. Elections were fixed for June 27 for voters on the white roll and July 1–2 for voters on the common roll.

In the elections on the white roll, Ian Smith's Conservative Alliance of Zimbabwe won a surprisingly convincing victory, taking 15 of the 20 seats reserved for whites in the National Assembly; the breakaway Independent Zimbabwe Group won 4, and the final seat was taken by an independent. The result did not please Prime Minister Robert Mugabe, who was highly critical of the lack of cooperation shown to the government by Smith and his supporters. Claiming that the trust bestowed by the government upon the white minority clearly had not been deserved, the prime minister promised to abolish white representation at an early date.

When the black voters went to the polls, clumsy polling procedures caused lengthy delays with the result that the period allowed for the elections had to be extended by two days. Although there had been some harassment of opposition supporters in the days leading up to the elections, the voting went off without incident. However, the militancy of some ZANU (PF) members was demonstrated in areas near Harare and Kwekwe, where members of the opposition were threatened with eviction from their homes if they did not join the government party. As expected, Mugabe's ZANU (PF) won an overwhelming victory, polling half a million more votes than in 1980 and increasing its representation from 57 to 63 seats. ZAPU secured 15 seats in Parliament, 5 fewer than in 1980. Even in Matabeleland, where support for ZAPU remained strong, there were some ZANU (PF) gains. Worst hit of all the parties was Muzorewa's UANC, which failed to win a single seat in Parliament.

As a snub to those who voted for Smith, Mugabe dropped Denis Norman, minister of agriculture, from his Cabinet, though he appointed Chris Andersen, the only independent white member of Parliament, to a ministerial post. ZAPU leaders were angered by the appointment of Enos Nkala as minister of home affairs in charge of police. Though Ndebele himself, Nkala had always advocated harsh measures against the government's opponents in Matabeleland. Nkala responded to criticism of his appointment by threatening to ban, and later to destroy, ZAPU.

AP/WIDE WORLD

Prime Minister Robert Mugabe of Zimbabwe speaks to the press on July 6 after winning a landslide victory in Zimbabwe's first postindependence elections.

Following the elections the government began to take a more lenient line toward Conservative Alliance supporters, though a televised talk by Smith, during a November visit to the U.K., aroused strong resentment. Subsequently, a parliamentary committee was established to consider reprimanding Smith for making derogatory remarks about Zimbabwe's government and its black population. Douglas Collard ("Boss") Lilford, former chairman of the Rhodesia Front, the forerunner of the Conservative Alliance, and a major political figure during the period of Rhodesia's unilateral declaration of independence, was found murdered on November 29. Whites were more affected than blacks by a constitutional amendment that, as of early December, barred Zimbabweans from holding dual nationality.

The pressure on ZAPU was sharply increased by a number of incidents, including the arrest of Sydney Malunga, a senior ZAPU official and member of Parliament, and of Nick Mabodoko, mayor of Bulawayo; the eviction of ZAPU from its Harare headquarters; and the seizure of Nkomo's passport. Muzorewa's retirement from politics in November further weakened opposition to the government, but hopes of a more stable future were raised by talks between Mugabe and Nkomo with a view to a merger between their two parties.

At the beginning of the year the first steps were taken to implement the leadership code laid down by ZANU (PF) in August 1984 that banned party officials from receiving more than one salary, owning more than 50 ac (20 ha) of land, or engaging in any form of business activity. A month later Wiriddzayi Nguruve, commissioner of police, was sus-

pended from office pending an inquiry into charges of serious misconduct. Mugabe was criticized by trade unionists within his party for labor legislation that outlawed strikes and gave the labor minister power over union finances and officeholders—measures seen as constituting a denial of the Socialist policies that ZANU (PF) professed to uphold.

There was better news for the government on the agricultural front when it was announced in March that the maize (corn) crop seemed likely to reach a record three million metric tons. The tobacco crop, an important source of export earnings, was also expected to reach record levels. As a gesture of goodwill, 25,000 metric tons of maize were promised to famine-stricken Ethiopia, while the government paid $1 million to the emergency assistance fund set up by the Organization of African Unity in 1984. As a further response to the improved economic outlook, and with an eye to the parliamentary elections, in April Mugabe announced a 15% increase in the wages of the lowest paid workers to take effect July 1. At the same time, allocations of foreign currency for imports were increased by 30%, and restrictions on payments to foreign shareholders living abroad were relaxed in an effort to encourage foreign investment.

The budget introduced by Finance Minister Bernard Chidzero on July 30 provoked a mixed response. The public was relieved that no obviously oppressive measures appeared to be contemplated, but economists feared that the proposed 28% increase in the budget deficit might adversely affect relations with the International Monetary Fund. They also forecast considerable increases in the prices of food and fuel.

ZOOS AND BOTANICAL GARDENS

One of the major justifications for keeping animals in zoos was to promote the conservation of species. Not only could they be used to demonstrate the need for conservation, particularly of species liable to become extinct in the rapidly diminishing wild, but they could also be used as the nucleus of reintroduction programs.

There was encouraging news of the 1984 reintroduction of the golden lion tamarin (*Leontopithecus r. rosalia*) to a reserve in Brazil; by 1985 there had been three births, all from animals bred in zoos and released in 1983, and in July a further two family groups from zoos were sent for release into a neighboring area. Other current examples of reintroduction projects that were under way or planned included: Przewalski horse (*Equus przewalskii*) from collections in the U.S. and U.K. to reserves in Mongolia and, possibly, Kazakhstan, U.S.S.R.; Père David's deer (*Elaphurus davidianus*) from Whipsnade Zoo and Woburn Park, England, to reserves in China; scimitar-horned oryx (*Oryx dammah*) from collections in Britain to a national park in Tunisia; Jamaican hutia (*Geocapromys browni*) from Jersey Zoological Park (Channel Islands) to private estates in Jamaica; European otter (*Lutra l. lutra*) from the Otter Trust, Bungay, Suffolk, to reserves in East Anglia, England; Somali ostrich (*Struthio camelus molybdophanes*) from Oklahoma Zoo to the Shaumari Wildlife Reserve in Jordan; eastern sarus crane (*Grus antigone sharpii*) from the International Crane Foundation, Baraboo, Wis., to the Bang Phra Wildlife Sanctuary in Thailand; cheer pheasant (*Catreus wallichi*) eggs from the World Pheasant Association, Basildon, England, to a reserve in Pakistan; white-headed duck (*Oxyura leucocephala*) eggs from the Wildfowl Trust, Slimbridge, England, to a reserve in Hungary; Philippine crocodile (*Crocodylus mindorensis*) from Silliman University, Dumaguete City, Phil., to the Calauit Wildlife Sanctuary in northern Busuanga Island, Calamian Group, Philippines.

Reintroduction programs needed the cooperation of zoos and conservation bodies. Careful planning and monitoring were essential; so was the availability of scientific data on zoo animal populations and on individual animals not only for reintroduction projects but also for many aspects of zoo animal management, husbandry, and breeding. In 1985 three conferences underlined and endorsed these needs: the International Union of Directors of Zoological Gardens and the Captive Breeding Specialist Group both met in Calgary, Alta., and the American Association of Zoological Parks and Aquariums met in Columbus, Ohio.

Further progress was reported in the use of artificial breeding techniques. The Zoological Society of London announced the successful birth in June of a zebra foal to a domestic pony. This birth was the result of work involving the nonsurgical collection of an embryo and transfer to a surrogate mother. In March the New York Zoological Society reported from its breeding facilities on St. Catherine's Island the first birth of a gemsbok (*Oryx g. gazella*) following artificial insemination. In June, Ueno Zoo in Tokyo announced the birth of a giant panda (*Ailuropoda melanoleuca*) after artificial insemination, and in November the official Chinese news agency reported the birth, to a twice-artificially inseminated panda, of seven cubs, five of which survived. Notable among more straightforward breedings were the first captive breedings of a Commerson's dolphin (*Cephalorhynchus commersoni*) at Sea World, San Diego, Calif.; the false gharial (*Tomistma schlegelii*) at the Bronx (N.Y.) Zoo; Papuan pythons (*Liasis papuanus*) at Knoxville (Tenn.) Zoological Park; and twin giant pandas (one survived) in Chapultepec Zoo, Mexico City.

Recent new zoo buildings and exhibits included "Jungle World" at Bronx Zoo; Asian elephant breeding facilities at San Diego Wild Animal Park; "Alaska Tundra" at Washington Park Zoo, Portland, Ore.; "Wings of Asia" at Metrozoo, Miami, Fla.; "The Predators" at Birmingham (Ala.) Zoo; "Great Cat Complex" at Perth (Western Australia) Zoo; and "The Ark" at Paignton (England) Zoo.

AP/WIDE WORLD

Katja holds her baby, Mueseli, at the San Diego Zoo's koala enclosure. The zoo announced a two-year loan program that would send koalas to other U.S. zoos.

Botanical Gardens

Increasing awareness of the need to address world-scale problems such as plant utilization for food was galvanizing the more forward-looking gardens into action. National and international policies were slowly being formulated to increase the degree of cooperation between gardens, and there was significant activity on this front. In October 1984 the Royal Australian Institute of Parks and Recreation published a report on the collection of native plants in Australian botanical gardens and arboretums. The report emphasized the need to ensure that Australian flora were preserved and protected for posterity. One way to do this was to set aside in cultivation, in professionally designed and managed botanical gardens, a collection of indigenous Australian plants. The report, submitted to the federal and state governments, recommended a national network of 39 botanical gardens and arboretums. A program of assistance to smaller supporting gardens was also recommended, with a national committee, made up of heads of major state botanical gardens, to coordinate joint programs.

The European and Mediterranean Regional Group of the International Association of Botanic Gardens (IABG) held its second meeting, in Durham, England, during September 1985. The main theme of the meeting was botanical gardens in the 21st century. Inadequate funding and lack of coordination—both nationally and internationally—were identified as the major constraints on development. Clearly defined objectives related to specific research and educational programs were recognized as being of immediate priority. In this context the cooperation between the Utrecht, Leiden, and Wageningen botanical gardens in The

ROYAL BOTANIC GARDENS, KEW

A striking new display complex was nearing completion at the Royal Botanic Gardens at Kew, England. It would house many plants requiring special environments.

Netherlands and within the newly formed Ibero-Macronesian Association exemplified the successful utilization of common resources.

In November 1985 the International Union for the Conservation of Nature and Natural Resources sponsored a conference entitled "Botanic Gardens and the World Conservation Strategy," held at Las Palmas, Gran Canaria (Spain). The objective of the conference was to review the involvement of botanical gardens in complementing world conservation

strategy, in particular by considering their function as centers of information and education and their capacity to carry out both ex situ and in situ conservation. Recommendations were made to enable botanical gardens to formulate arguments for additional funding to meet essential commitments in the field of conservation activity.

The introduction into Europe of many exotic species during the 18th and 19th centuries led to the construction of large conservatories and greenhouses. However, many of these structures were now in urgent need of renovation. The palm house in Göteborg, Sweden, was one of those currently being restored. Built in 1878 and situated in a municipal park in the city center, it was a building of considerable architectural importance, and the restoration specification had to be carefully drafted to ensure that the integrity of the original structure was preserved. Completion was scheduled for 1986. At the Royal Botanic Gardens, Kew, England, restoration of the world-renowned Palm House dating from 1848 proceeded. A large new development nearing completion at Kew was a 48,-600-sq ft (4,500-sq m) display complex that would provide ten separate compartments to grow extensive collections of tender herbaceous plants such as ferns, orchids, cacti, and succulents. Of contemporary design, the structure reflected the form of the original greenhouses it replaced, but modern materials and up-to-date technology were being used to create environments that would satisfy the most demanding plant groups.

Shamu, born September 26 at Sea World park in Orlando, Florida, was the first killer whale calf to successfully nurse in a zoo, gaining 50 pounds in one week.
AP/WIDE WORLD

85

FOCUS

Feature Articles

386 Kites: New Designs for New Uses
     by Miles L. Loyd

392 The New Asia-Pacific Era: A Perspective from an
     International Nation Building for the 21st Century
     by Yasuhiro Nakasone

405 The Center of the Milky Way
     by Gareth Wynn-Williams

412 The Soviet Union Under Gorbachev
     by Arkadi N. Shevchenko

427 **Asides**

431 **New Words**

433 **Biographies**

471 **Family Record**

483 **Calendar**

486 **Contributors and Consultants**

490 **Index**

Kites:
New Designs for New Uses

by Miles L. Loyd

Recreational kites have stirred the imagination and excited people throughout the world for at least 2,000 years. The scientific investigation of kites began with an English schoolmaster about 1820. George Pocock applied the existing understanding of these soaring devices to drive a carriage, called a *char-volant,* through the countryside around Bristol. Pocock fully appreciated the significance of extracting energy from the wind with his kites, and he made great improvements in their configuration and control. However, his greatest contribution may have been in documenting his adventures in *The Aeropluestic Art, Or Navigation in the Air, by the Use of Kites, or Buoyant Sails.* Pocock would surely be amazed by the science that has grown out of his modest beginning, for his purpose of providing energy is being dramatically advanced by new kite designs.

Kites featuring remarkable new designs are probing the atmosphere to improve our understanding of the kinetic energy in the wind. Experimental kites, similar to large airplanes and helicopters, are preparing the way to tap the energetic winds of the upper atmosphere. Kites deployed from the space shuttle can skim through the outer atmosphere at 25 times the speed of sound, improving the efficiency of shuttle maneuvers. These kites would provide an aerodynamics research facility that is unmatched on Earth. The science of the design of these new kites includes elements of aerodynamics, materials science, structural design, stability theory, and controls. Advancement in these fields has been essential in progressing to today's designs.

Current Use and Design

During the last two decades kites have been revolutionized by advances in materials science. Kite shops offer exotic designs rendered on spars of laminated fiberglass using films of ripstop nylon. Kites are made of plastic films and extruded plastic spars that were unknown 20 years ago. There are many variations in these new materials, and today the classic wood and paper kite is almost extinct. The new kites are lighter and stronger. Today children are flying as many as 15 controllable kites linked together so that their flowing tails give the illusion of a grand flag. This has become possible through the development of materials and structures that

enable these kites to withstand ground impact without damage. Modern kites also can retain their shapes when they are wet. To the scientific workers in the early 1900s, these features would be miracles. In both the elaborate controlled kites and the toy-store variety, the advances in materials science are enriching the experiences of those who fly kites for recreation.

The ultimate in recreational kites may be those that are able to lift a person off the ground, a notion that has inspired adventurers throughout history. Such kites have been more than exciting toys. The Wright brothers learned to fly on large kites before they achieved powered flight. Man-lifting kites were used as observation platforms for military reconnaissance in World War I. A dramatically different kite design was used in World War II, when the Germans used man-lifting autogiro kites towed by surfaced submarines for observation at sea. Later, recreational autogiro kites were produced in the United States by the Bensen Aircraft Corp. Autogiro kites are unique because the circular area swept by the kite's rapidly turning rotor is the effective area of the surface of the kite. This swept area is many times the actual area of the rotor blade. The motion of the rotor provides control that is not possible with other kite designs. An autogiro kite is stable when landing vertically, and the kinetic energy stored in the flywheel action of the rotor provides power for limited maneuvers, such as slowing the descent just before landing or hopping off the ground on takeoff.

Advances in kite design have been most remarkable during the past 30 years. Man-lifting kites gained a surge in popularity in the 1950s when an Australian, Bill Bennett, and several others throughout the world demonstrated that they could ride kites pulled by boats. Man-lifting kites were soon added to the water-ski shows at Cypress Gardens in Florida. The kites used in these shows reflect three eras of design, progressing from flat kites through aerodynamic sails to modern wings.

The flat kites of the first era had relatively poor aerodynamic performance and stability. The kite structure was designed with straight spars crossed near the center of the kite and a fabric cover that was stretched tightly over the windward face. The location of the spars interfered with the airflow over the surface, limiting the kite's lift and increasing its drag. The flat surface provided no inherent stability, so constant vigilance was required by the flyer to maintain control. Although limited by their design, these kites did work.

With the introduction of sails the aerodynamic characteristics of the kites improved significantly. In the late 1940s and early 1950s Francis Rogallo, an aeronautical engineer with the U.S. National Aeronautics and Space Administration (NASA), developed kites with well-formed airfoil sails that provided greater lift and less drag than could be produced by the flat kites. For the right and left wings Rogallo kites use a pair of sails similar to those on yachts. The primary difference is that a kite's lift is vertical, supporting its weight, while a yacht sail's lift is horizontal in order to propel the boat forward. The aerodynamic effects are the same whether the sails are used on kites or yachts, and each use has benefited from research on the other.

Air flowing over the convex surface of a sail increases in velocity and decreases in pressure. This difference in pressure between the bottom and top of the sail provides lift and maintains the shape of the fabric airfoil. To operate effectively, sails must pass through the air at a high angle of attack, so the concave surface is presented to the wind. Sails operate effectively at very high angles of attack, including those that produce stalling. When the angle of attack of the sail becomes too low, the dynamic pressure on the top of the sail exceeds that on the bottom and the sail loses the shape that makes it an effective airfoil. On a kite this is disastrous, resulting in an irrecoverable loss of control that has sometimes led to fatal accidents with man-lifting kites. Thus there is a minimum safe angle of attack for the sails of a kite. This, combined with the strength of materials and structural design, places limits on the range of wind speeds within which a particular kite can operate. For nearly all sail kites this range is rather narrow, the maximum rarely exceeding two times the minimum. On man-lifting kites the range is even narrower. Within the limits of the angle of attack and speed range of the sails, the Rogallo kites have proved to be aerodynamically excellent.

Other limitations of both flat kites and Rogallo sails are in the areas of stability and control. Like those on yachts, the sails on kites should be trimmed for subtle variations in the operating conditions. On a yacht this is done by the crew, but adjustment of sails during operation on most kites is difficult if not impossible. Even so, the trim of sails for some kites is more demanding than for yachts, because the right and left sails of kites must be balanced in their lift and drag to maintain stability. These difficulties with sails have probably been the greatest limitation to the use of kites when alternatives, such as balloons, are available. Skilled manual control has made Rogallo kites useful for the shows at Cypress Gardens and as hang gliders.

One of the early uses of kites was to pull carriages called char-volants. *This technique was invented in the early 1820s by George Pocock of England.*

The third design era of man-lifting kites centers on kites with wings like those on airplanes. With their thick airfoils, these wings overcome the limitations of thin-fabric sails. The airfoil holds its aerodynamic shape at all speeds and angles of attack, resulting in consistent and predictable performance. Modern plastic films stretched over wing ribs and spars of

THE BETTMANN ARCHIVE

Alexander Graham Bell (seated) displayed some of his experimental man-carrying kites and tetrahedral designs at an exhibition in St. Louis, Missouri, in 1904.

new high-strength, lightweight materials make these new kite structures possible. These designs are making possible new uses for kites, the most important of which are measuring and extracting the kinetic energy of the wind.

Wind-energy Research

The wind is a major energy resource, and kites are unique instruments for measuring the detailed structure of the wind. Air density and wind speed combine to determine the power density available from the wind. Although air density decreases at high altitudes, wind speed increases; therefore, power density increases continuously from the Earth's surface to an altitude of about ten kilometers (six miles). There the jet stream provides the maximum wind speed and, therefore, the maximum power density. In regions where there is no jet stream an increasing power density is common, but it does not reach as high a level.

The drag of the rough surface of the Earth dissipates the energy of the wind, but high-altitude winds replenish the power near the surface. These high-altitude winds, driven by the differences in solar heating of the Earth in the tropic and arctic regions, are a much greater energy resource than the surface winds. As a consultant to the Mitre Corp., M.

R. Gustavson of the Lawrence Livermore National Laboratory in California evaluated the potentially available global wind power of the atmosphere as being 20 times the world's power consumption, and he estimated the potentially available wind power over the United States as being 75% of that nation's power consumption. Wind power is available on a massive scale. The problem is to tap it effectively.

Conventional tower-mounted windmills are at present the most effective means of tapping wind power. Each windmill is designed to operate within a specific range of wind speeds. Slow changes in wind speed may result in windmill power variations. Wind gusts and turbulence excite vibrations in windmill structures that contribute to fatigue stress, limiting the life and power output of the machine. Individual windmills are limited to a capacity of a few megawatts, and most produce less than one megawatt. To produce the thousands of megawatts needed to contribute substantially to utility power production, thousands of windmills are being spread over hundreds of square miles in California. Effectively siting such windmills depends on a detailed understanding of variations in the wind.

The information gained from extensive measurements of the wind flow in potential wind-energy production sites contributes directly to the selection of appropriate windmills and their location and also helps scientists increase their understanding of the structure of the wind. The basic instrument in wind-flow measurements is a meteorological tower that uses a cup-type anemometer. These towers are fixed in position, and they provide accurate, long-term records of wind speed and direction. These records permit the identification of basic wind-flow patterns at the tower. The wind flow at a nearby windmill depends on these systematic winds and the way the flow is modified by the local topography. However, neither the meteorological tower nor other standard instruments provide adequate spatial data on the variation of wind speed and direction as a function of altitude or lateral location. Instead, kites have proved to be uniquely suited for making measurements of this kind.

TALA kites have been developed into refined instruments for wind measurements. TALA is an acronym for Tethered Aerodynamically Lifting Anemometer. Produced by Stephen Keel of TALA, Inc., these kites are made of Tyvek, a DuPont Co. plastic that holds its shape for a long operating life under a wide range of conditions. Essentially, these kites are sails that fly at a carefully controlled, high angle of attack. They are stable and consistent in winds between 4 and 40 meters per second (9 and 90 miles per hour). The aerodynamic performance of these kites produces a precise tether tension that is directly related to the wind speed. The drag of the tether is negligible for practical purposes, so the wind speed at the kite is determined from the tether tension at the ground.

Measurements of wind conditions at a particular

location are made by flying the kite at various altitudes and recording the wind speed and direction. Moving the location of the ground unit along a line perpendicular to the general direction of the wind and repeating the altitude variations provides detailed data on the wind flow through a two-dimensional surface at that site. Earl Davis of U.S. Windpower, Inc., employed an entire high school mathematics class to fly arrays of TALA kites to make such measurements simultaneously for extended periods.

TALA kites are stable yet responsive to turbulence. By keeping the kite at a constant altitude and making periodic measurements, one per second, for example, scientists can measure the frequency spectrum of wind turbulence. Relating these spectral data to the vibration resonances in the windmill structures identifies potential weaknesses and enables the selection of appropriate windmills for that site. The portability and simple operation of the kite make it possible to measure the details of wind characteristics for the major wind patterns at any site.

TALA kites are used by research workers throughout the world. Robert Baker at Oregon State University employed them for ten years in his studies of wind fields throughout the western United States. Anders Daniels performed extensive analyses of wind data at the University of Hawaii and developed automatic data-recording equipment for TALA kites. Such kites are versatile instruments, providing either detailed data for research on airflow and turbulence or quick checks on local conditions in evaluating potential sites.

Future Kites

Future kites for large-scale wind-power production can make the kinetic energy of the atmosphere more available to humans. Wind that is strong enough to generate power can easily support a windmill on a kite. While the wind blows, a kite and tether replace a tower. In the early 1900s meteorological kites were routinely flown at altitudes of four kilometers (two and one-half miles). New kite designs can reach the jet stream, at an altitude of ten kilometers. Although the local surface winds may be inadequate, the wind-power density at altitudes of a few kilometers is adequate for commercial power generation over much of the Earth.

Several kite designs have been studied and tested at the University of Sydney in Australia, by a team including Bryan Roberts, John Blackler, and Alan R. Fien. Based on operational simplicity, Roberts considers the gyromill superior to other designs he has considered. This is a large autogiro kite with generators driven by the rotors. It is flown into the upper atmosphere as a helicopter if the surface winds will not lift it as a kite. When the kite reaches an adequate wind stream, power to its rotors is reduced. As the kite continues to rise on the power of the wind, further increases in wind-power density

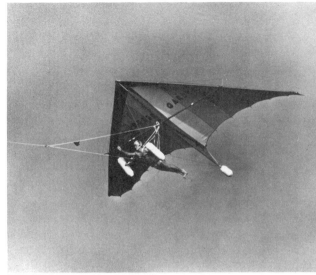

COURTESY, FLORIDA CYPRESS GARDENS INC.

(Above) The Rogallo kite has been adapted to recreational use and renamed the hang glider. Towed by motorboats, hang gliders have been used in waterside entertainment. (Below) The Tethered Aerodynamically Lifting Anemometer (TALA) is essentially a stable sail that is used to accurately measure wind conditions at various altitudes.

COURTESY, U.S. WINDPOWER, INC.; PHOTOGRAPH, ED LINTON

COURTESY, BRYAN ROBERTS, JOHN BLACKLER, AND ALAN FIEN;
UNIVERSITY OF SYDNEY, AUSTRALIA

*The gyromill, an autogiro kite with generators driven
by the rotors, is towed during a ground test to
confirm that flight and power generation are possible.*

are converted to electricity that is conducted down
the tether. During any short calm periods power is
supplied to support the gyromill as a helicopter. For
long calm periods and maintenance the gyromill
is landed. Roberts has tested model gyromills in
wind tunnels and in flight. The power produced at
the scale tested was five kilowatts. Scaling to larger
sizes, a gyromill with twin rotors 16 meters (52 feet)

*Looking very much like airplanes, large, winged kites
for generating electricity have been investigated by
engineers for the Solar Energy Research Institute.*

© 1983 JAMES BALOG

in diameter operating at an altitude of ten kilometers would produce one megawatt.

In addition to the gyromill Roberts and his colleagues studied both large winged kites and stream-
lined balloons. Both can support turbine-driven
generators. The general operation of each of these
is similar to that described for the gyromill. Exceptions are that the winged kite presents added
problems of landing and launching, and balloons
require continuous addition of helium to make up
for losses. The balloons are also limited in altitude
to about eight kilometers (five miles). Willibald
Riedler and others at the Institut für Angewandte
Systemtechnik, Research Center Graz, in Austria
consider a balloon operating at five to eight kilometers (three to five miles) and producing two to seven
megawatts to be better suited to their local conditions. In the United States Okitsugu Furuya and
Shin Maekawa analyzed large winged kites for the
Solar Energy Research Institute. They concluded
that kites generating two megawatts at an altitude
of ten kilometers are appropriate to the wind conditions over New York City. The capacity of such
kites is limited to two megawatts by existing aircraft
electrical generators, but these can be substantially
improved. High-altitude kites extracting the wind
energy from the upper atmosphere appear to be
scientifically and technically feasible.

Most kites are designed to hang benignly in the
sky. The common exception, controlled kites flown
for recreation, demonstrate a method of concentrating the power of the wind. By flying in a horizontal
figure-eight pattern, the most efficient of these kites
fly across the wind at two to five times the speed of
the wind. For a kite to be propelled at that speed
the power consumed by drag must be taken from
the wind. A theoretical limit to the power that such
a kite can extract from the wind is determined by
the square of the ratio of lift to drag. In practice the
power consumed supporting the kite in its dynamic
motion reduces the power extracted to somewhat
below the theoretical limit. Experiments have determined that the net power extracted from the wind
by recreational kites is increased by a factor of 20.
This increase in power extraction is accomplished
by substituting this crosswind motion and complexity of control for the stability and simplicity of an
ordinary kite.

To experiment with this crosswind method, researchers built model kites to resemble airplanes
with wings. They were made of strong materials
that would hold their aerodynamic shape. Such
kites developed speeds of 30 to 45 meters per second (67 to 100 miles per hour) in winds of five to
eight meters per second (11 to 18 miles per hour).
The dynamic pressure averaged over the surface of
the wing reached 1.2 kilonewtons per square meter.
(The force exerted by one newton would cause a
body with a mass of one kilogram to experience an
acceleration of one meter per second per second.)
This dynamic pressure is two to three times that on

manned airplanes that fly at those speeds but, unlike airplanes, kites need little margin of increased lift for safety. This crosswind motion extends both the maximum and minimum operating wind speeds of the kites. Excessive air speed may produce aerodynamic forces exceeding the strength of the kite. With only directional control of the kite's path, the air speed is maintained below the safe limit. In winds of half the speed required to support the kite if it were static, these model kites are easily kept airborne with continuous crosswind motion.

Computer simulations of flight dynamics have been used in combination with analysis to estimate the potential of large crosswind kites. Using existing technology, a kite the size of a C-5A jet aircraft can extract 13 megawatts from the wind. Considering less conservative designs made of such materials as kevlar and graphite composites, the maximum power extracted is somewhat greater. As observed with model kites, large power-production kites can operate over a broad range of wind speeds. The kite design depends on the minimum wind speed for peak power production, which is selected on the basis of wind characteristics and economics. As wind speed falls below this minimum, the kite continues to produce power at lower output until all power extracted from the wind is required to keep the kite airborne. At lower wind speeds power provided to the kite keeps it airborne. At wind speeds higher than that required for peak power production, the path and trim of the kite are adjusted to stabilize the power produced and avoid destructive stresses. Although final designs may produce less, a kite extracting 15 to 20 megawatts is scientifically feasible.

The future of these power-production kites is primarily an economic issue. The wind power exists, and the kites can be made. To capture a major part of the useful wind power, a capacity to generate millions of megawatts is needed worldwide. This would require millions of kites the size of medium to large airplanes exploiting the winds of the upper atmosphere. Also necessary would be hundreds of thousands of conventional windmills exploiting the usable surface winds. An economic analysis of the high-altitude kites indicates that they would be marginally competitive with present power-generation costs. That does not include economies resulting from advancing technology or from large-scale production of such kites. The comparative economics of this and other sources of energy is much more speculative than the scientific and technological issues, but it is likely that some combination of these kites will substantially contribute to power production in the future.

In his research on spaceflight applications, Jerome Pearson of the United States Air Force Wright Aeronautical Laboratories proposed a sail flying in the outer atmosphere that is tethered to the space shuttle. As the shuttle orbits 185 kilometers (115 miles) above the Earth, this kite would fly at 25 times the speed of sound through the thin air at

OFFICIAL U.S. AIR FORCE PHOTO

U.S. Air Force engineers have proposed a sail tethered to a space shuttle orbiter as a fuel-efficient way of making alterations in the craft's orbit.

an altitude of 93 kilometers (58 miles). Pearson's primary objective is to enable the shuttle to make larger changes in its orbit with the available fuel. Overcoming the degradation of the shuttle orbit due to the kite drag would require only one-third the fuel that would be required if only the shuttle rockets were used to make the maneuver. A secondary objective is the use of this hypersonic kite as a research vehicle in high-altitude aerodynamics. This combination of operational and scientific values may further extend the usefulness of the shuttle.

Kites have been vital instruments in wind-energy research for the past ten years. This work has contributed to both effective siting of commercial windmills and scientific understanding of wind-energy resources. In addition to the surface winds presently being harnessed by windmills, much greater resources are available in the upper atmosphere. New kites are being designed to use these winds for power generation.

Miles L. Loyd is Technology Leader for Applied Computational Engineering at the Nuclear Energy Systems Division of the Lawrence Livermore National Laboratory, Livermore, California.

The New Asia-Pacific Era:

A Perspective from an International Nation Building for the 21st Century

by Yasuhiro Nakasone

When I first entered the Japanese Diet in 1947, I was 28 years old. My country was still in ruins from the total defeat of World War II, a disaster brought upon us by the arrogance of our militarists and our shortsightedness in following them. I shall never forget threading my way to the corridors of the National Diet in Tokyo, past the rubble and the black-market peddlers outside. Large areas of Tokyo, like most of our cities, remained blackened moonscapes, with people still digging in the ruins. But even at that time I was encouraged by the vigor and resilience of our people. Freed at last from military imperatives and long constraints on their liberties, they set out from their makeshift shacks to rebuild a country based on the ideals of a shared culture and dedicated to the welfare of all.

Through almost 40 years since then, I have been honored to serve Japan's people as a Diet representative from my home prefecture of Gumma and, in addition, to have had the privilege of holding Cabinet office. I first entered the Cabinet, as minister of state for science and technology, at the age of 41. Through most of these years I was caught up with my fellow citizens in the work of rebuilding a peaceful, prosperous, and democratic Japan. I shared the excitement and sense of achievement in our country as we grew into the world's second-largest economic power. But in the midst of our affluence, newly found and hard won, I was worried and concerned that our very zeal to "catch up" with the world's economic leaders would distort our view of the future. As early as 1957, after a visit to Europe, Southeast Asia, and the Middle East, I wrote: "If we are complacent and leave things as they are, the time will surely come when we shall be criticized for building a new economic empire to replace our military empire of the war years."

Since I became prime minister in November 1982, I have dedicated myself not merely to furthering Japan's own peace and prosperity but to contributing positively to the peace and well-being of other nations and the construction of an abiding world order. These are not merely laudable goals

for Japan; they are necessities. There are no options among them. For today a vast gap still exists between the Japanese reality and what the rest of the world expects of Japan. Japan is no longer "catching up." We have, as they say, arrived. There were times when Japanese merely adopted a low posture in the face of outside criticism. That attitude is no longer possible for us. We must make policy, not merely reflect the policy of others. We must see that our enormous economic strength is more effectively and responsibly displayed and mobilized in the international arena.

Much of the criticism directed at Japan by the international community today is unfair. But fair or unfair, it demands our concern, our reflection, our action. The world balance of power has shifted. This is true not merely in a narrow economic sense. That is why one of the first things I did on coming to office was to address the Japanese people on Japan's need to become an "*international* nation"; that is to say, a nation that must bear a heavy share of international responsibilities, in keeping with its international position.

Just as life was hard for us Japanese in the immediate postwar days, it has become rather easy for us today—too easy, one might say, in the sense that it is easy for prospering people to avoid thinking of their responsibilities. I consider it my role, as prime minister, to communicate to the Japanese people our goals and challenges. In a democracy, leadership is ineffective without good communication. As I once said about my own government's reform program: To announce a new and difficult program in a democracy is rather like launching a glider. As long as the winds of public opinion and mass media blow, it can fly. If the supporting winds diminish, the glider will stall and crash. Thus, when we advocate a program, it must be made easily un-

The shell of Hiroshima's old city hall is preserved as a peace monument in the heart of the vibrant new city that has grown up since World War II, epitomizing Japan's determination to build toward a secure future.

derstandable. We must communicate directly and graphically—with charts, pictures, with whatever aids to understanding our advanced information society can provide—for true popular consensus in Japan is not lightly achieved.

It is in this spirit that I set forth an outline of Japan's policy as an international nation, as well as some guidelines on how our domestic structure must also change, both to better our own condition and the better to play our international role.

A Foreign Policy for Tomorrow

For Japan's foreign policy to be effective, it should have a basic philosophy, which we might express as follows:

The Active Pursuit of World Peace. This is not the mere abstract expression that it may seem. To maintain and secure world peace, nations as well as individuals must actively work at it. Thus Japan pledges itself to a national policy of supporting nuclear nonproliferation and working for the ultimate elimination of all nuclear weapons. We must work for the reduction of conventional armaments as well. Japan's own armament is purely defensive and will remain so. We do not wish to be thought of as a menace to any other country.

The Advancement of Science and Technology. The accomplishments that man has registered in this area must be used to extend prosperity and to enhance human dignity on this planet. The dramatic betterment of communications and information distribution, in particular, should encourage constant dialogue among the nations. International disputes should be discussed and solved, in a cooperative spirit, by democratic means.

Aid to the Developing Nations. It is still not so long since Japan's sobering defeat in World War II. We should remember also that Japan has only recently—as history's slow clock reckons—risen from the status of a developing nation to rank with the industrially advanced powers. Therefore, we shall endeavor to contribute to the welfare of international society by helping the developing nations.

Planning for the 21st-Century World. We see a new vision of this world. We shall do everything in our power to bring it to reality. For almost a century Japan has worked to bring about a fusion of Eastern and Western civilization. We feel that our country is uniquely situated to promote cooperation between the Pacific and the Atlantic regions in a spirit of harmony.

Japan can best further these objectives by dealing with several pressing global issues in a practical, realistic, and constructive way.

First, Japan will do its collective best to combat protectionist tendencies, wherever they may occur, by strengthening the free trade system and enlarging the perimeters of world trade. In the course of my administration we have already enacted a series of "market-opening" initiatives and have made a great effort for the promotion of the new round of multilateral trade negotiations. Whatever difficulties this may cause our own producers at home, I am determined to continue on this course until all vestiges of past protectionist thinking among us have been erased.

Second, Japan will seek to prevent war by our commitment to the concept of deterrence and the balance of power. Under present conditions these are the best guarantees of peace. In addition, we will work toward reducing the present level of armaments, nuclear armaments in particular.

Finally, Japan hopes to enhance peace by promoting a spectacular increase in the exchange of both people and information across international borders. The more exchanges we have, the further the world can move in the direction of a truly international culture.

The prospects for world peace are, of course, influenced by developments in the Soviet Union. Since Mikhail Gorbachev assumed the leadership in Moscow, we have heard much speculation about new or altered policies. Without seeming to be too optimistic, I believe that a Gorbachev regime is worth watching very closely, for several reasons. In the first place, it is obvious that Soviet policy is stagnating, not only in the domestic area but also in international relations. Gorbachev is under heavy pressure to take some action. The Soviets have observed with keen interest the policy reorientation of China, where a general opening of the market, economic liberalization, and the widespread appointment of younger leaders have taken place under a Communist Party leadership.

As a young leader himself, Gorbachev must inevitably regard older "classic" Communists as outdated—almost medieval—people. He seems to be paying more attention to long-range strategic considerations in his planning, as well as showing a talent for a more flexible handling of problems. This is, after all, in the Leninist tradition. The key factor here is age. Compare his age with that of Andrei Gromyko, for example. He may well stay in power for 20 years. Thus he has enough time to introduce innovations in Soviet Communism—in the short, the intermediate, and the long term. For any significant kind of innovation, however, he needs peace. That is what makes me think that nuclear arms negotiations between the Soviet Union and the United States will make some partial progress.

Japan must reexamine and establish a policy toward the Soviet Union in the light of this analysis. We may have before us an excellent opportunity to promote nuclear disarmament, thereby expediting the improvement of East–West relations in general. For this policy to succeed, however, it is of paramount importance to consolidate further the unity of the West. It is Western unity that has, thus far, brought about the amelioration of relations with the Soviet bloc.

This statement may sound paradoxical. It is quite

In October U.S. ambassador to Japan Mike Mansfield (center) helped kick off a two-month campaign, sponsored by the Japanese government, aimed at encouraging Japanese consumers to buy more imported goods.

HITOSHI FUGO

logical and understandable, however, in view of the Soviet Union's international political activity, as it has unfolded over the years. The Soviets, as a matter of consistent policy, have tried recurrently to drive a wedge between the Western allies, as witness their recent unsuccessful efforts to mobilize Western European opinion against the United States. It is only when such efforts are shown to have failed that the Soviets seem more amenable to peaceful discussion and constructive negotiation.

The key role in building Western security is played by the United States, and we must take into account Japan's long-standing ties with the United States as we formulate our policy. It is no exaggeration to say that the relationship with the United States—an alliance in every sense of the word—is the cornerstone of Japan's foreign policy. The Mutual Security Treaty between the United States and Japan is a key pillar in the global defense strategy of the free nations. To implement the goals of the treaty properly, Japan must, on its own, build up a defense capability sufficient to discourage any hostile action against us. By assuming its fair share of the burden for the defense of the free world, Japan will be the more readily recognized as a full, responsible partner of the alliance, able to offer advice when it is desirable to do so. Another stabilizing influence, particularly in an Asian context, is the presence of the United States on the Korean Peninsula. Strengthening the present cooperation between Japan, the Republic of Korea, and the United States is another indispensable condition for keeping the peace in East Asia.

Let me make one additional point about Asia. The security of Asia is not merely a matter of pacts and defense commitments, important though these are. Asia is different from Europe. Rich in their diversity, its peoples nonetheless share a common heritage. There are many cultural common denominators among the Asian peoples. Not least among these is a bent toward mysticism and the transcen-

dental that gives Asians the patience to wait for events, in a sense, even as we are moving them. This is in contrast to the legal and determinedly historical mind-set of the West.

These differences of viewpoint and tradition inevitably affect even such concrete matters as our requirements for security and defense. Europe is divided between the NATO alliance and the Warsaw Pact in a geometric balance, so to speak. Europe is like an oil painting with no portion of the canvas unpainted. Asia, by contrast, is like a *sumie* (black ink) picture, which has a great deal of white space. This is partly due to Asia's poverty and the widely different stages of development among Asian nations, but it is also due to Asia's "nongeometric" way of thinking.

Asian psychology is different. In Asia it is common practice to contain water that overflows riverbanks in a pond or makeshift reservoir and to leave the water there until it recedes or eventually dries up. We have time. We do not try to expedite this process. Much the same is true of Asian attitudes toward strategy and diplomacy. Unlike Europeans, Asians do not put a high priority on adversarial discussion or military threat. This adversarial attitude produces confrontation, even when it is used only as a bargaining chip. Asians prefer to use dialogue, whether direct or indirect, as a means of easing tension. One might call this a tactic of "wait and see and talk." The style of "wait and see and talk" may seem, in the short run, a waste of valuable time. Some Westerners may feel that such diplomacy by dialogue wastes time. It blurs the edges of controversy and reduces the sharp opposition of issues. Yet this is often not a bad thing. It often prevents the aggravation of disputes and indeed can work toward their settlement.

Trade Friction: Prosperity Versus Protectionism

On some economic problems, however, pressing decisions must be made. The postwar world economy owes much to the open and outward-looking policies developed within the framework of the International Monetary Fund and the General Agreement on Tariffs and Trade (GATT). In this climate, the free-market economies achieved an unprecedented level of material wealth. Serious economic dislocation, however, has become manifest in recent years. We have had a growth recession, fiscal deficits, high interest rates, unemployment, and inflation. Under pressure to solve these thorny problems, many nations are tempted to adopt the inward-looking policies of protectionism.

Protectionism is the most direct threat to a stable and growing global economy. If unchecked in time, it may bring down the entire postwar economic order. We must put new life into the free-market economic system for the 21st century, therefore, by continually expanding free economic exchange.

At their meetings in London (1984) and Bonn (1985), the leaders of the seven major industrialized democracies did not merely reaffirm their resistance to protectionist pressures, but they also acknowledged the importance of the open multilateral trading system to the economies of both developed and developing nations. They agreed to consult with their partners in GATT on beginning a new round of multilateral negotiations for trade liberalization.

At this point, I would like to refer briefly to the trade friction that is currently disturbing our relations with the United States and the EC. Since Japan lacks natural resources, we must import the essential sinews of industry—our energy and key raw materials—as well as food in great quantities. To pay for these vital imports, we must export a variety of manufactured goods. Otherwise, we cannot feed the 120 million people on this densely crowded, narrow archipelago, which is smaller than France or the single U.S. state of California.

In 1984, however, our export surplus with the United States amounted to $36.8 billion (nearly one-third of the total U.S. import excess). That with the EC amounted to $10.8 billion. Such large surpluses are both unnecessary and undesirable. They have brought on a storm of criticism from America and Europe, giving rise to a fierce outbreak of protectionist sentiment. The U.S. Congress, in particular, has become highly emotional on this issue. Its members have put intense pressure on the White House to move against Japan. Only the statesmanship of Pres. Ronald Reagan has thus far kept the so-called trade war under control. For my part, I have done my best to cope with the situation by instituting the series of sweeping market liberalization measures already mentioned. I will continue my earnest efforts to eradicate all traces of any so-called unfair practices in Japan. Nothing is more derogatory to the national honor of Japan than to be accused of being unfair.

Ultimately, I am optimistic about alleviating trade frictions. Economic disputes, however sharp, are generally amenable to solution, provided the parties concerned keep mutual goodwill alive. The United States and Japan are the largest and the second-largest economies in the free world. Together we account for over one-third of the total world gross national product. We are each other's largest overseas trading partner. In a way, we are responsible for the economic welfare of mankind. The importance of our relationship, however, lies not only in the economic dimension but also in our shared values of freedom and democracy. The twin pillars of stability in the Pacific edifice cannot afford to fall out. If we indulge in recriminations, it would only please our political antagonist, the Soviet Union, which is constantly scheming to separate us.

As the world moves toward a postindustrial society, it behooves Japan, as a leading industrial power, to contribute toward shaping a reformed international order, economic and monetary, to serve the requirements of the 21st century.

A New Asia-Pacific Era

One often hears predictions that the 21st century will be the Japanese century. While such predictions may be flattering to my country, I would prefer to think of these decades just ahead of us as the Pacific century, the advent of a new Asia-Pacific era. History teaches us that civilizations not only expand their frontiers but tend to produce new civilizations and cultures on what were once the peripheries of the old. European civilizations constantly extended their frontiers, from Greece to Rome, from Rome to England, France, and Germany, and from Europe itself toward the American colonies. Gradually the compass needle of history swung from Mediterranean civilization to Atlantic civilization. Now it is pointing toward the Pacific.

The Pacific region, as we know, is endowed with a rich variety of natural resources and vigorous, industrious peoples. Once remarkable for its sheer diversity, the Pacific region has been drawn together— in part by the rapid development of communications, transportation, and shared technology—so that what was once thought of as an oceanic Great Divide has become a Great Connector. The Pacific peoples also share a faith in the market economy. We now see an interplay of aggressive free-enterprise economies in this area.

The French historian Fernand Braudel wrote eloquently about how Western capitalism was nurtured first in the Mediterranean Basin, then moved outward to the Atlantic. In the Pacific we are witnessing the birth of a new kind of capitalism. Here the vigor and competitiveness of Western—particularly American—capitalism has been enriched by the Asian cultural heritage, in a culture that values harmony over adversarial procedures, conciliation over confrontation, and circumspection over assertion. We might call this our Confucian heritage. It is, I believe, an extremely useful shock absorber for a modern society with its tendencies toward abrupt division and sudden conflict.

Yet Asian free enterprise has fostered a competitive dynamism of its own. The distinguishing mark of the Pacific Basin countries has been their commitment to free enterprise. The past growth record of the newly industrialized countries (NICs)—the Republic of Korea, Taiwan, Hong Kong, and Singapore—has been extraordinary. The ASEAN countries—Thailand, Malaysia, Singapore, the Philippines, Indonesia, and Brunei—have forged a unique and harmonious community, also dedicated to a free market system. The developed countries in the Pacific area—the U.S., Canada, Australia, New Zealand, and Japan—have welcomed their increasingly important trading partners. And, indeed, trading patterns among the industrial nations have shifted correspondingly. By 1979 U.S. trade with the Pacific already topped its Atlantic trade. This trend has continued. The ASEAN countries as a group have become the fifth-largest trading partner of Canada and the U.S.

The growth records bear eloquent testimony to the vitality of the Pacific Rim nations. For the past two decades, Pacific area growth has averaged 6.7% per year, as compared with 3.7% for the European Communities (EC), for example.

The future also looks promising. According to a study (dated July 24, 1985) conducted by Japan's Economic Planning Agency, real economic growth for the 15-year period 1985–2000 is estimated as follows: world at large 3%; EC 2.5%; Pacific region 4%; Japan 4%; U.S., Canada, Australia 3%; China 7%. Among the ASEAN countries, Malaysia, Thailand, and Indonesia are expected to reach 7%, which is equal to the growth rate of NICs like the Republic of Korea and Taiwan. Such expansion in the Pacific region economy cannot help but have a salutary effect on the rest of the world.

Since assuming the office of prime minister, I have shaped our policies to further enhance Japan's economic cooperation with the nations of the Pacific Basin. We are mutually dependent. There can be no security and prosperity for Japan without security and prosperity for the other Pacific nations, and vice versa.

To render constructive assistance to the nation building of Pacific developing countries, Japan has been expanding our program of official development assistance (ODA), despite an extremely tight fiscal situation. In 1984 Japan's ODA amounted to $4,319,000,000, an amount inferior only to that spent by the United States. Following our new medium-term target, our government aims to provide total ODA during the seven years starting in 1986 of more than $40 billion, ultimately doubling the annual amount. The ASEAN countries, in particular, will remain the highest priority area for our programs of assistance.

The transfer of industrial technology and the dissemination of managerial know-how are of the utmost importance in promoting productivity in the developing nations. As such transfers are primarily undertaken by private enterprise, it is necessary to make full use of the initiative and vitality of our private sector.

Japan participates in a wide variety of international cooperative enterprises in science and technology. We want to share the fruits of such international research with other Pacific countries as much as possible. When I visited the ASEAN nations in the spring of 1983, for example, I ventured a suggestion that we begin consultations for the promotion of Japan-ASEAN science and technology cooperation. The ASEAN leaders responded favorably to my suggestion. In areas like agricul-

Scenes in Tokyo's Tsukiji wholesale market (right) and Yokohama's dockyards (left) illustrate the making of a favorable balance of trade: raw materials and commodities, such as fruit from the U.S., New Zealand, and the Philippines, in; manufactured goods, such as electronics components bound for New York City, out.

PHOTOGRAPHS, MILT & JOAN MANN—CAMERAMANN INTERNATIONAL

ture, engineering, and medicine, such consultations have now become routine.

My government has long stressed the importance of personal contacts with other Asian countries. In my address at Kuala Lumpur, Malaysia, on May 9, 1983, I proposed to invite a total of 3,750 young people in education and other fields from the ASEAN countries to Japan over the next five years. An increasing number of Japanese youth will visit the ASEAN countries for similar opportunities and experiences. When these people take their rightful places at the centers of their respective societies, the amicable relations between Japan and the ASEAN countries will be truly consolidated.

In 1984 "human resources development" projects were agreed upon anew at the ASEAN ministerial meeting with the "dialogue countries"—Australia, New Zealand, the United States, Canada, and Japan. Recently, the same partners chose 32 urgent projects to bring together specialists for the promotion of trade, the construction and management of industrial ports, airport and highway construction, maritime training, and other areas. Of these, Japan will take part in 15. As the idea of human resources development was originally advanced by Japan, we shall do our best to ensure its success. Such joint ventures will provide the countries concerned with social infrastructures that will serve them as master keys, so to speak, in exploiting their potential.

In this and other areas, notably international investment and the development of energy and communications resources, Japan has participated with enthusiasm in the meetings of groups from the 12 nations represented in the Pacific Economic Cooperation Conference. Here Japan and the United States play consistently supportive—although not the leading—roles.

The success of such activities justifies U.S. Secretary of State George Shultz's comment that "a sense of Pacific Community is emerging." The growing awareness of the approaching Pacific era not only excites our imagination; it calls upon us to refine our global perspective as an Asian nation. For example, Japan must be prepared to change its industrial structure to meet the requirements of Asian solidarity. As the NICs enlarge their trade volume, they shift the content of *their* exports from primary products to manufactured goods. The challenge that confronts the industrialized nations is to accept increased imports from the NICs. This necessitates sometimes painful domestic adjustments. Yet, unless the nations of the North accept their exports, we can hardly expect the developing nations of the South to contribute to our own export growth. Nor, in the absence of expanding two-way trade, can other heavily indebted NICs (such as

The competitiveness of Japanese goods in the world market has relied in part on Japan's leadership in research and development in primary industries, such as the Hitachi-built experimental hydrogen fusion power plant.

MILT & JOAN MANN—CAMERAMANN INTERNATIONAL

Brazil, Mexico, and Argentina) earn enough money to repay their debts and thus preserve the viability of the financial institutions on which both North and South rely.

Unfortunately, I must mention one discordant note in the chorus of Pacific collaboration: the Vietnamese occupation of Kampuchea. Japan has supported the proposal put forward by ASEAN for a negotiated solution of the Kampuchean problem. That proposal is based on the restoration of Kampuchea's sovereignty and the right of its people to choose their own government, free of Vietnamese occupation. So far Vietnam refuses to respond, but Japan will continue its efforts to develop a climate conducive to a political settlement.

The Broader Pacific Perspective

We must bear in mind that Pacific cooperation should not acquire too political a character. In particular, it should not develop a militaristic posture. I once proposed the concept of a Pacific Economic and Cultural Enclave (PEACE). In that proposal, I stressed the wisdom of enlarging cooperation in the economic and cultural spheres, on the assumption that our interests converged most obviously in these fields.

It is 30 years since the historic conference of Asian-African nations was held in Bandung, Indon., in 1955. Eighty-two nonaligned nations participated in a ceremonial commemoration of the conference in April 1985 and reaffirmed the original Bandung Declaration. The first Bandung Declaration was proposed by the Japanese delegation. Its ten points are still valuable in regulating the international conduct of nations. It was therefore natural that participants in the 1985 ceremony pledge adherence to them.

Let me add one caution on the Pacific relationship, however. We should not perceive this as the establishment of an exclusive regional bloc. The dynamic Pacific Basin economy should serve as a stimulus to the global economy. We should on no account think in terms of the Pacific *versus* the Atlantic, or Asia *versus* Europe. It is not a question of confrontation, one arrayed against the other. Far from it. We should look forward to an era of Atlantic-Pacific collaboration. It is my earnest hope that cooperation between the Atlantic and Pacific, a strong Europe and a developing Asia-Pacific linked together, will inspire mankind in the coming century.

Already the trilateral consultations of North America, Western Europe, and Japan have scored great successes. They demonstrate the truth that the industrialized democracies, sharing the common values of freedom and democracy, can combine their genius for the common good. My visit of July 1985 to Western European countries convinced me anew that there exists among the people of Europe an untapped reservoir of goodwill toward Japan, despite the current trade friction. With Great Britain,

EIJI MAYAZAWA—BLACK STAR

Japanese research and development in consumer goods, such as Honda's computerized automobile navigation system, has also advanced the nation's competitiveness.

our historic ally, we have revived a particularly close relationship. The many new Anglo-Japanese business ventures underline this fact.

Finally, in advancing Pacific cooperation, we should work to develop overall interdependence and mutual reliance. It remains the role of the more advanced nations to respect and support fully the initiatives of other countries in establishing a foundation for regional cooperation. I think "realistic gradualism"—to borrow a phrase from Prime Minister Robert Hawke of Australia—is a good principle to guide the Pacific adventure. My visit to Oceania in January 1985, incidentally, served to reinforce the growing friendship that binds Japan with Australia and New Zealand.

A Vital Power Balance

The peace and stability of Asia are maintained by the balance of four major powers: Japan, the United States, the Soviet Union, and China. Of these, only Japan is a lightly armed, nonnuclear nation. In the old days of rampant power politics, such a balance would have been unthinkable. Military force alone counted. That Japan, although militarily vulnerable, is now regarded as a major stabilizing force attests to the decreasing influence of mere military strength. This is a welcome trend for Japan, since we are determined to remain militarily small but economically great.

If other powers followed Japan's example, the world would become a much safer place. Not only would humanity be freed from the nightmare of a nuclear holocaust, but we would also all be spared the burden of military expenditures. It is estimated that all nations, great and small, spend roughly $800 billion a year on armaments. Think what we could achieve if this money were diverted to peaceful uses.

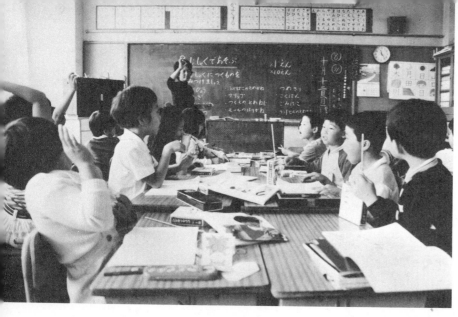

The Meika school is the oldest public primary school in Tokyo, but it has been a leader in introducing new and informal teaching methods, as in this language class. Much is hoped for in moving away from rigidly traditional methods and curricula.

I would like to examine Japan's relations with the United States, the Soviet Union, and China. We cannot overstate the vital importance of the United States for Japan. A decade has passed since the United States withdrew from Vietnam in April 1975. A period of drift and debate over the American role in Asia followed, but now the United States is reasserting its presence as a Pacific power, renewing its commitment to the peace of the Pacific region. The U.S. military presence is the great deterrent to Soviet encroachment.

Over the past 20 years, the Soviets have continued a relentless military buildup, nuclear and conventional, far surpassing the legitimate needs of self-defense. This buildup is particularly notable in the Asia-Pacific region. The Pacific Fleet, the largest of the Soviet Union's four fleets, has grown steadily since the mid-1960s, from about 50 major surface combat vessels to over 80, including two carrier task forces. Soviet submarine forces are also impressive. Moreover, the Soviets have deployed a number of missile systems with the capability of reaching targets in much of Asia. The mobile SS-20s, deployed since 1977, now number around 170. Soviet ground forces are also formidable. Totaling some 50 active divisions, they are mainly deployed along the Sino-Soviet border.

Evidently, the Kremlin calculates that if the Soviets are perceived as enjoying military superiority, any enemy can be intimidated without firing a shot. They are adept at employing military force as an instrument of coercion. The buildup of forces on Japan's Northern Territories—the four islands off the northeastern coast of Hokkaido which the Soviet Union occupies illegally—is a case in point. This Soviet military presence in Asia, however, has not been translated into political or economic gains. This is due, I think, to the renewed commitment of the United States to its allies and friends. Our mutually supporting positions on major international issues ensure peace, the prerequisite of prosperity.

This is especially apparent with regard to Japan, which the United States regards as the cornerstone of its Asian policy. Indeed, the United States now treats Japan as a major partner in world politics. Our relationship has doubtless been strengthened by the personal trust which President Reagan and I have established since early 1983, when I first visited the White House immediately after becoming prime minister. I would like to take this opportunity to express my admiration for the president's vision and leadership, stating also my deep gratitude for the warm kindness he so generously bestowed on me. "Ron" and "Yasu" will see to it that our two nations continue to work in unison as the vanguard of peace in Asia and elsewhere.

It was under President Reagan's guidance that the U.S. Defense Department took a firm position not to link the trade and defense issues. Japan's sole rationale for increasing defense capability is to maintain effective deterrence against military attack. The failure of an increasingly prosperous Japan to assume greater defense responsibilities, however, is inexcusable. We should do more for our self-defense not because the United States demands it but because we deem it necessary. What counts, above all, is the national will to defend our own fatherland. Unless we demonstrate this will, our allies and antagonists will not respect our independence.

I have already mentioned the Soviet attitude toward Asia. Although it is difficult to ascertain the ultimate design of the Soviet leadership, I am inclined to think that, generally speaking, the Soviet posture is defensive toward Europe and offensive toward Asia. In the West the Soviet Union wants to preserve the status quo by maneuvering the NATO nations into recognizing and respecting the postwar boundaries bequeathed to it at Yalta. In the East, however, it tries to expand the Soviet sphere of influence by challenging the status quo. Confrontation with China—although mitigated recently—is one, but not the only, reason for an aggressive Soviet policy. The massing of Soviet military forces in

(continued on page 402)

Japan's Presidential Prime Minister

Rarely has a nation needed a spokesman as badly as pre-21st-century Japan, the economic superpower whose extraordinary postwar achievement has been almost canceled out by the chronic inability (or unwillingness) of its political and business leaders to tell the rest of the world what the Japanese are up to. In Yasuhiro Nakasone they have finally found one. Since he took office in November 1982, Japan's 15th postwar prime minister has used every means available to him—high visibility summit meetings with his international peers, a tireless round of overseas visits and a barrage of books, well-hyped public relations events and TV interviews—to describe his mission and dramatize a new role for his island country: as a responsible, active leader in the world's political as well as economic decision making.

Japanese newspapers have called Nakasone—less than half admiringly—their "presidential" prime minister. In fact, his ringing statements, keen sense of showmanship, and highly developed personal style represent a sharp break from Japan's postwar tradition of bureaucrat-politicians. Nakasone has not hesitated to go to the people over the heads of his own faction-ridden majority party. Faced with protectionism in both the United States and Europe brought on by Japan's swollen trade surpluses, he has given his countrymen some hard choices. He has jolted Japan's complacency on, among other things, the idea of restricting defense expenditures to a token level while relying on U.S. protection. He has appealed, bluntly and forcefully, for Japanese to import more and build up their domestic economy, instead of relying on exports for so much of their growth. And at home he has tackled major sociopolitical problems like educational reform.

For all his nagging about their responsibilities—perhaps because of this—the Japanese like him. Over his first two two-year terms in office, he has done better in the public opinion polls than any of his predecessors. A handsome activist who gives out an air of youthful dynamism belying his 68 years, Nakasone embodies a happy combination of internationalism and homely "Japanese" virtues. Well traveled and widely read—and, typically, a graduate of Tokyo University's Law Faculty—he is also a small-town boy whose father was a lumber merchant in the mountain-girt prefecture of Gumma. Nakasone's favorite recreation away from the political pits is writing the elliptical, impressionistic, and intensely private haiku verses—an interesting characteristic in a man given to blunt language and often sharp expressions.

Nakasone's inability to suffer fools gladly has made him many enemies among his own consensus-loving party faithful. A man of scholarly tastes, Nakasone has an extremely lively mind capable of digesting complex issues quickly. He is an excellent listener, with an unceasing curiosity. The titles of the 16 books he has written—covering topics from revisionist capitalism to the creation of a postwar culture—suggest the almost bewilderingly wide range of his interests.

The difference, however, between Nakasone and his thoughtful contemporaries elsewhere is that he has spent virtually all of the past four decades in public office. He has accumulated the sort of political experience only rarely enjoyed by politicians in a working democracy. With 14 terms as a member of the lower house behind him, he has served, variously, as head of the Defense Agency and the Science and Technology Agency, minister of transport, minister of international trade and industry, and secretary-general of the Liberal-Democratic Party. An incurable traveler, he has negotiated with Andrei Gromyko, visited with Jawaharlal Nehru and Zhou Enlai (Chou En-lai), started a close "Ron and Yasu" friendship with Ronald Reagan in English, and greeted the president and people of Japan's closest neighbor with a few well-chosen words in Korean.

In Japan he has been called the "Weathervane" (*Kazamidori*). For no Japanese politician could ever hope to climb to political power without long experience in faction-mending, opposition-placating, and teahouse power brokering. What is distinctive about Nakasone still, however, is a kind of engaging brashness and personal assertiveness. The present-day proponent of "easy to understand politics," who dramatizes the trade imbalance by televised shopping expeditions for foreign goods, is the same man who shocked Gen. Douglas MacArthur by sending him a 7,000-word memorandum explaining what MacArthur was doing wrong during the U.S. occupation.

After almost four years in the top job, Nakasone's self-confidence remains massive. Whether his party will allow him a third term as prime minister—against recent precedent—remains to be seen. But whether or not he remains in office, Yasuhiro Nakasone has already changed the nature of that office, possibly permanently. More important than that, beneath his assertiveness and showmanship, Nakasone has given to his fellow-Japanese a coherent view of their nation's character and role, a sense of leadership and mission, as it were, that the Japanese have not known for a long time.

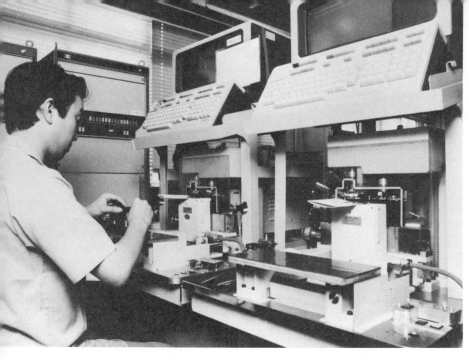

An example of a U.S. product in the Japanese market is a computer designed by Hewlett-Packard used to test and adjust Nikon cameras as they come off the assembly line.

MILT & JOAN MANN—CAMERAMANN INTERNATIONAL

(continued from page 400)

the Far East is clearly beyond the requirements of normal defense.

The menace of the Soviet forces has not been felt sufficiently by the Japanese people. This is because the Japan-U.S. Security Treaty, concluded in 1960 to replace the former Security Treaty of 1951, has functioned so effectively. Accustomed to the protection they have long received from the United States, the Japanese take it for granted that they need not worry about the security of their country. There is nothing so dangerous, however, as this kind of *self-deception.*

As I noted earlier, I am not at all pessimistic about the possibility of improving relations with the Soviet Union. Indeed, I am quite hopeful that the U.S.S.R. will eventually see the wisdom of friendly coexistence with Japan. We have a prior condition, however, for any such rapprochement: the Soviet Union must return the Northern Territories, which it has occupied forcibly. This will be a proof of the Kremlin's repeatedly avowed desire to promote neighborly relations with Japan. If the Soviet Union demonstrates its sincerity through deeds, not words, then a peace treaty can finally be concluded. In that event, Japan's cooperation in developing Siberian economic resources will also be forthcoming, to the immense benefit of the Soviets.

As for China, that giant country is in the throes of a bold industrial and social experiment known as the Four Modernizations, intended to push China's economy to the front rank. The goal is to raise per capita income from $250 in 1978 to $1,000 by the end of the century. Over a decade has elapsed since the late Premier Zhou Enlai (Chou En-lai), a statesman of great vision, enunciated this policy in 1975. After many trials and tribulations, the present leadership under Deng Xiaoping (Teng Hsiao-p'ing) is confidently carrying out the task. In Deng's words:

"The purpose of revolution, after all, is to liberate and develop the productive forces of a country." In implementing his unprecedented plans, Deng has sought the cooperation of the developed countries, notably Japan and the United States.

We in Japan have pledged to extend our utmost help. Japan and China both face formidable challenges as we lay the foundations for the 21st century. We must strive together to achieve our goal of ensuring common peace and prosperity.

On my visit to China in March 1984, I was overwhelmed by the enthusiastic welcome accorded me by its government and people. I took this as a token of goodwill toward Japan. During my sojourn, I again met Premier Zhao Ziyang (Chao Tzu-yang) and General Secretary Hu Yaobang (Hu Yao-pang) and reaffirmed the principles that guide the relationship between our nations: (1) peace and friendship; (2) equality and reciprocity; (3) long-term stability; and (4) mutual trust. I suggested the addition of this fourth principle, to which the general secretary wholeheartedly agreed. In this way this statement is a compass that will guide us through all weather, fair or foul.

It was to symbolize this newfound harmony between China and Japan that the two countries have inaugurated the Japan-China Friendship Committee for the 21st Century. It is my conviction that the development of a friendly, peaceful relationship between Japan and China is vital not only to both countries but also to the peace of Asia and the whole world. Improvement of relations, now evident, between China and the United States adds to the stability of the Pacific region. The United States justly regards a nonaligned, secure China striving for modernization and pursuing an independent policy as a stabilizing factor in Asia. Thus, the United States is cooperating with China in selected defense areas.

Three Major Domestic Initiatives

Japan must act upon all these pressing issues if we are to realize our aim of building a new "international nation." Yet we cannot succeed without a most intensive review of our domestic policy. The people of Japan have seen major changes not only in their economy but in their thought, their lifestyle, their social patterns. People want spiritual enrichment and the satisfaction of achievement as well as the externals of a stable society. In short, we must prepare for the 21st century here at home.

To this end I have dedicated myself to making Japan a nation of resilient culture and welfare. What do I mean by "resilient"? I mean a society that can absorb change without succumbing to it, that can leave itself open to all outside influences without losing its inner harmony and integrity—a society that can teach and contribute as much as and more than it has learned.

Thus we are working on three major areas: administrative, fiscal, educational.

Administrative. I came to office pledged to review Japan's whole administrative structure. This includes rationalizing the organization of government ministries and agencies, in accordance with guidelines set for us by a distinguished national commission. During the high-growth years, Japan's body politic managed to accumulate a good bit of excess administrative fat. We are now, of necessity, slimming down. Many functions that government performed for us during our rise to a higher stage of economic development now seem better given into the hands of private business.

We have already reorganized two large institutions that were government monopolies, the Nippon Telegraph and Telephone Public Corporation (NTT) and the Japan Tobacco and Salt Public Corporation. They are now private joint stock companies. Plans for separating, streamlining, and ultimately privatizing the huge network of the Japanese National Railways are now well advanced. We feel that new operating methods and private ownership will get at the root causes of JNR's massive deficits.

Administratively, our government is tightening its belt. And the drive toward privatization should surprise those foreign critics of a mythical creature called Japan, Inc., who believe everything in Japan is run by the government.

Fiscal. Our government has worked intensively to reduce government spending. By consistent cost cutting and better planning, we have set out to escape from our dependency on deficit-financed government bonds, which now amount to some 40% of Japan's gross national product! Income and residence taxes have been cut, while we seek to gain revenue from other forms of taxation.

But the goal of fiscal reform is not merely to balance the government's books. Here also we seek a wider objective. By reviewing the modalities of government finance, we hope to respond better to emerging economic and social trends. In so doing we will forge new relationships between the national and local governments and between the public and private sectors. This whole process will stimulate the private sector and take full advantage of its vitality. It is the same with our administrative reforms. With NTT's privatization, for example, more competitors will appear, involving many smaller businesses in related fields. Such changes will generate substantial private demand throughout the entire economy.

Educational. Of all these renewal projects, education is the most important in the long run. Nothing matters more to the Japanese public. Of course I am not underrating the progress already made. Japan's prosperity to date can be said to represent the achievement of our outstanding educational system. More than a century ago education was the imperative on which Japan's modernizing Meiji Restoration based its success. Our grandfathers built schools before they built steel mills, with a keen sense of priorities. The uniform system of education we developed was designed for the "catch-up" era in Japan's development and best suited to it.

Now, however, we are entering an age of higher technology. We are living in an information society that demands questing and creativity from its students. Education is the foundation of the nation's

Another U.S. product in the Japanese market is a familiar American design that figures prominently in a Tokyo display of telephone equipment.

TOSHI MATSUMOTO—SYGMA

future. Thus I believe the time has come for sweeping reforms across the entire educational spectrum, in preparation for the 21st century.

Postwar education, I believe, has been too narrowly and exclusively dependent on the basic school curricula. We have tended to neglect the importance of comprehensive education from a broader perspective, including family and social education. This imbalance lies behind the explosive increase in juvenile delinquency and violence in our schools, problems that in past years were of no consequence. Thus educational reform cannot be content with education of the intellect alone. We must aim at education of the whole person by making our curricula more diverse and flexible. We must expand freedom of choice for people seeking education; we must emphasize home and social education and make more practical, hands-on training available outside the school.

I intend to push for discussion and reform in a broad range of fields. We must review theories of child development, educational theory, teacher education, preschool education, language instruction, education for Japanese nationals overseas, as well as the whole system of entrance examinations. To do this we have set up a special council on educational reform. And I am asking for the advice of people from all walks of life and the cooperation of all political parties.

In a spirit of public morality, we should seek a humanism that will foster respect for the individual. We wish also to internationalize education in Japan, in a way befitting the people of a truly international state. To that end, incidentally, we have set up a joint study group of the Japanese Ministry of Education and the U.S. Department of Education to examine the educational systems of both countries and to make recommendations, each in its home country, for improvement. This study grew out of a conversation between President Reagan and myself two years ago about the urgency of educational problems in both our countries. It is a good example of a new kind of international cooperation.

Japan's Role in a 21st-Century World

In these pages I have been advocating the concept of Japan as an international nation. This means, as I have said, that we shift from a passive attitude of merely responding to events to an active effort to influence events positively. We have been a beneficiary of peace. We must become a creator of peace. As we move into the information society, not only Japan but most of the world's nations are in the midst of a search for new identities. It is at this crucial point that we hold the Tokyo summit in May 1986. In the past these summit meetings of the industrial powers have focused primarily on economic issues but, inevitably, economic and political issues are linked. Recent international developments have again made clear the need for preserving and ensuring our common security as the basis for economic prosperity.

It is hard to foresee the extent of our conversations—or the problems that may suddenly come upon us. As a famous Japanese political leader once noted, "In politics, one inch ahead of you it is pitch dark." But at least, on the eve of the Tokyo summit, I would like to offer some thoughts about our future goals.

The most important thing in our world today is for all peoples and nations to affirm some common principles and premises for establishing the 21st-century world and to discuss concrete means for attaining them. These tasks must be shared among the nations, depending on their circumstances, so that while we cope with today's problems, we can build our hopes for tomorrow's world.

We are passing another milestone in 1986. On April 29 we shall celebrate the 85th birthday of Emperor Hirohito and the 60th year of his reign. The first 20 years of this reign were extremely turbulent. While the emperor endeavored strenuously to save peace, he could not avert war. Finally, in August 1945, he took the momentous decision to terminate hostilities by accepting the Potsdam Declaration. On that day, the emperor composed the following poem:

Entirely regardless of what may happen to myself, I commanded the cessation of hostilities. Thinking only of my people who were dying in that conflict.

We are all grateful to the emperor for his courage in that dark hour of our history.

All nations are trying to cope with a variety of grave problems. They should share these burdens as much as possible, relying not merely on themselves but on the work of the United Nations and of various regional and functional world organizations. We should urge the existing organizations to invite all the members of the international community to a global discussion on the theme of "A Better World in the 21st Century." Such a discussion should draw up a blueprint for the world culture and the world environment that we seek.

These should be items for such a discussion:

- How to preserve human dignity in an era of rapid scientific progress.
- Amelioration of East-West and North-South relations.
- The reduction of nuclear and conventional armaments; population policy; environmental policy.
- The exchange of cultures, of peoples, of information.
- Policy for handling youth problems, drug addiction, and terror.

This is not a complete list, but it is to grapple with such major problems and to solve them that mankind must bend its concerted efforts. Such problems transcend national boundaries and cultures. The efforts of all nations, united, are required if we are to hope for solutions.

The Center of the Milky Way

by Gareth Wynn-Williams

In the days before streetlights lit up the urban sky and television provided an alternative distraction for insomniacs, the Milky Way was an endless source of speculation for those who would ponder the heavens. Early Greeks theorized that the band of light was formed from milk that spilled from the breast of a sleeping goddess, while the Javanese thought it represented the outspread legs of a giant straddling the Earth.

Although the Greek philosopher Democritus had speculated that the Milky Way consisted of millions of stars appearing too close together to be resolved by the eye, it was not until the 20th century that the three-dimensional distribution of those stars was worked out and that the Milky Way was seen to be actually one of millions of galaxies in the universe. Since that time it has become common, if confusing, practice among astronomers to spell the name of the Milky Way Galaxy with a capital G, and all other galaxies with a small g.

The Galaxy in Spite of Itself

The problems faced by early galactic astronomers resemble those of a lost hiker trying to establish the boundaries of a thick forest from a single vantage point. First, because of our fixed location, we have no access to anything resembling an "aerial photograph" of our Galaxy; we know more about the shapes of many distant galaxies than we do about our own. Second, thick clouds of interstellar gas and dust in the plane of the Galaxy block the view of all but the Earth's immediate neighborhood.

By the beginning of the 20th century, it was generally accepted, correctly, that the Milky Way appears as it does because the Sun sits in a vast flat disk of stars. However, because it was not realized how seriously dust clouds limit our view of distant stars, it was assumed, incorrectly, that the Sun was at the center of this disk, a misconception based on the observation that the Milky Way has roughly the same brightness all around the sky. The idea that the disk of stars, including the Sun, is actually rotating about a distant center gained strength in the 1920s with several crucial developments. First, astronomers found that certain large groups of stars, the globular clusters, have a strong tendency to lie in or near the constellation of Sagittarius. Second, they saw that their observations of minute changes in the relative positions of stars in the vicinity of the Sun were best explained by rotational motions about a point that lies in the same constellation. Third, the appreciation that the "spiral nebulae" seen with large telescopes are distant star systems on a scale comparable to the Milky Way encouraged astronomers to look for evidence that our Galaxy might also be a rotating spiral.

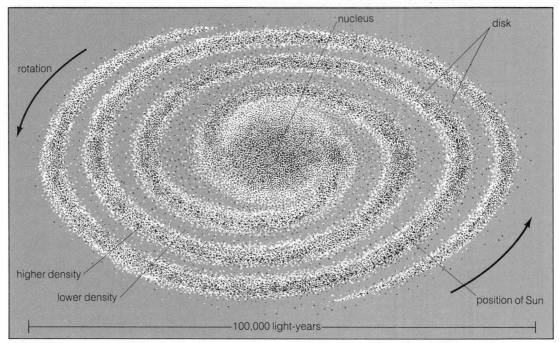

A simplified representation of our Galaxy shows it to be a rotating disk with spiraling arms of regions higher in their density of stars and other matter separated by regions lower in such density. The disk bulges near the nucleus.

Our current understanding of the structure of the Milky Way Galaxy is that it consists mainly of a disk of some 100 billion stars that is about 100,000 light-years across but only a few hundred light-years thick. (A light-year is the distance that light travels in one year, about 9.5 trillion kilometers [5.9 trillion miles].) Its shape is the result of the interaction of gravitational and rotational forces. Different parts of the disk revolve at different speeds; the Sun, which lies 30,000 light-years from the center, takes 250 million years to make one revolution. Some of the stars in the Galaxy are as old as 15 billion years, but new stars are continually being formed out of the clouds of gas and dust that also inhabit the disk. The gas clouds and the youngest stars are found in spiral arms; the older stars are more uniformly spread throughout the disk and in a fatter bulge surrounding the central regions of the Galaxy.

Prior to the 1960s, astronomers knew nothing at all about the center of the Galaxy except that the logic of geometry required it to have one. The reason for this ignorance was the thickness of the intervening barrier of dark clouds. This obscuration is so severe that light from the center of the Galaxy is dimmed by a factor of about a trillion in its 30,000-light-year journey to the Earth. Fortunately, not all kinds of radiation are blocked by the dust clouds. Infrared radiation is progressively less affected as its wavelength increases, while radio waves pass through interstellar space virtually unimpeded. Knowledge of the inner regions of the Galaxy has therefore progressed hand-in-hand with the technical development of infrared and radio astronomy over the past 20 years. Nowadays astronomers derive just as much information from observations of radiation that is invisible to the human eye as from telescopes that collect visible light.

Formulating a clear picture of the center of the Galaxy requires more than accessibility to infrared or radio images of the region. To interpret the data one must take account of the fact that different kinds of radiation are produced by quite different processes, and some forms of matter in the Galaxy are much easier to see than others. Whereas most visible light comes from hot stars, infrared radiation is generated mainly by cool stars and by dust grains heated by starlight. Radio waves result from the motions of electrons in interstellar space or from the rotation of small molecules in interstellar clouds. Generally speaking, our understanding of the distant parts of the Galaxy is based on observations of the gas and dust that permeate interstellar space, rather than on direct viewing of the stars themselves.

In Search of the Center

Astronomers now know the position of the center of the Galaxy in the sky to within one three-thousandth of a degree, a precision similar to that required to score a bull's-eye on a dartboard two miles away. This precision was achieved in stages. In the 1930s the first radio astronomers traced a faint, persistent noise heard in their instruments to the newly recognized galactic center in Sagittarius. In the 1950s radio telescopes made it possible to study the motions of hydrogen-gas clouds in the Galaxy. It was found that at the center of rotation of these clouds there is a very strong, well-defined radio source. This region has since become known as the nucleus of the Galaxy. Measurements of the position of the nucleus were refined as radio tele-

A more realistic representation of our Galaxy, viewed face on, shows its three prominent spiral arms. The gas clouds and the youngest stars are located in the spiral arms. Older stars are spread more uniformly throughout the disk and in the nucleus.

DAVID PARKER—SCIENCE PHOTO LIBRARY

scopes improved. By 1968 the position was known with enough accuracy that infrared astronomers were able to turn their newly developed detectors onto the region. Early infrared measurements were made at 2.2 micrometers (millionths of a meter); dust obscuration is still a problem at this wavelength, but 10% of the radiation survives the journey through the Galaxy and provides enough information to pinpoint the nucleus with great precision. Besides revealing the location of the galactic center, 2.2-micrometer observations have shown that the Galaxy is heavily concentrated toward its center. In the vicinity of the Sun, stars are generally a few light-years apart. Toward the center of the Galaxy, the stars are more crowded together; at a distance of three light-years from the center, their concentration is ten million times greater than it is in our part of the Galaxy, and distances between stars are measured in light-days. At the very nucleus itself, in a region less than a half light-year across, is a cluster of infrared sources called IRS 16, where the star density is even higher.

In 1983 a satellite known as IRAS (Infrared Astronomical Satellite) mapped the entire infrared sky for the first time. These images have provided us with the clearest impressions to date of what the Milky Way would look like if the obscuring dust clouds were absent. This remote-controlled space telescope, a joint venture by scientists in the United States, The Netherlands, and the United Kingdom, was designed to collect and analyze infrared radiation with wavelengths between 12 and 100 micrometers. Such radiation travels almost unimpeded through the Galaxy; unfortunately, however, it is absorbed by water vapor in the Earth's atmosphere and can be observed only by telescopes carried aloft by satellites, balloons, or aircraft.

The IRAS images do not show the stars themselves at the galactic center. What the telescope actually detected was the radiation from countless tiny grains of cosmic dust in the spaces between the stars. These are the same grains that obscure the view of distant stars. When a dust grain intercepts light from a star, it becomes warmer; in the vicinity of the galactic center, there is enough starlight to heat each dust grain to about 25 degrees above absolute zero. Although this temperature is colder than liquid air, it is high by astronomical standards and sufficient to make the dust grains glow with infrared radiation.

While IRAS gave us the clearest large-scale view of the Milky Way to date, the most detailed pictures of the heated dust in the central few light-years have been obtained in 1982 from the Kuiper Airborne Observatory, a telescope-carrying jet aircraft, at an altitude of about 12.5 kilometers (41,000 feet). Several distinct regions of infrared emission have been found. Most of these are very dense clouds of hydrogen molecules, helium atoms, and dust grains. Similar clouds have been found in the spiral-arm regions of the Galaxy; they frequently contain extremely young stars and are believed to be the "nurseries" within which new stars are born.

The strongest infrared source seen by the airborne astronomers, however, has a quite different character. By studying how the temperature of the region varies with its thickness, astronomers have deduced that there is a doughnut-shaped ring of gas and dust about 12 light-years in diameter surrounding the nucleus of the Galaxy and tilted slightly from the galactic plane. The total infrared power radiated by this ring is more than ten million times the power of the Sun. This power must derive from an object or objects within the ring.

The gas in the space between the nucleus of the Galaxy and the surrounding ring differs from that in

407

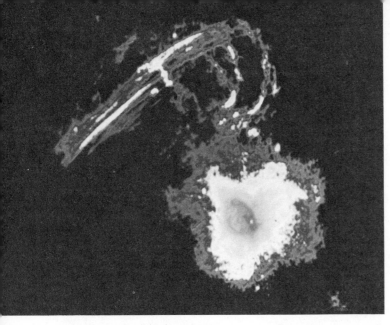

Continuous threadlike arcs rise above the center of our Galaxy. The arcs are about 150 light-years long, and each one is about 3 light-years across. These features are images of radiation in the radio region of the electromagnetic spectrum.

OBSERVATIONS MADE BY FARHAD YUSEF-ZADEH, MARK R. MORRIS, AND DON R. CHANCE; THE NATIONAL RADIO ASTRONOMY OBSERVATORY, OPERATED BY ASSOCIATED UNIVERSITIES, INC., UNDER CONTRACT WITH THE NATIONAL SCIENCE FOUNDATION

the ring in two important ways. First, it has a much lower density. Second, the hydrogen in the gas is ionized rather than molecular. In other words, each hydrogen atom in the gas is split into its component nucleus and electron, rather than paired with another hydrogen atom. Ionization in the Galaxy is usually caused by ultraviolet radiation from hot, young stars; this might be the case in the galactic center, but there is no obvious explanation of why young stars should exist there. Whatever is causing the ionization, however, is probably also the same immense power source that is heating the ring.

The clearest view of the ionized gas within the central 12 light-years is provided by the Very Large Array radio telescope. This instrument works by combining signals from 27 antennae spread over a 30-kilometer (19-mile)-diameter dry lake bed in New Mexico. In 1983 radio maps made from the collected signals showed that the gas comprises a series of arcs and filaments, one of which is probably the inner edge of the 12-light-year ring. Also evident on the maps is a compact radio source that is unlike anything else in the Galaxy.

A Strangeness Within

The discovery of a very compact source of radio emission was a signal to astronomers that something distinctly unusual is going on in the center of the Galaxy. Ordinarily, galactic radio emission has a nebulous appearance on images obtained by radio telescopes, indicating that the electrons that produce the emission are spread thinly in space. This is not the case for the source in the galactic center. By combining observations made simultaneously by several observatories around the world, astronomers have found that the compact radio source in the galactic center is no larger than the diameter of Saturn's orbit but radiates microwaves as though it had a temperature of more than 700 million degrees. It has been named Sgr A* ("Sagittarius A star") after the constellation Sagittarius, in which it is found, and it lies almost exactly at the most

likely position of the galactic nucleus. The radio emission is probably produced by the motions of fast-moving electrons in a region of strong magnetic field. This process, called synchrotron emission, is ubiquitous in space, but nowhere else in the Galaxy is there found such highly concentrated radiation. Only in quasars and in certain other, rare galactic nuclei have astronomers detected radio emission of comparable intensity.

There is a second, entirely independent piece of evidence for a very compact source of power at the center of the Galaxy, namely, the detection during the early 1970s of gamma rays having a characteristic energy of 511 keV (511,000 electron volts). Gamma rays of this energy are well known to physicists because they arise as a result of the mutual annihilation of an electron and its antimatter counterpart, the positron. Since antimatter is very quickly destroyed even in the most vacuous regions of the Galaxy, the presence of 511-keV gamma rays, which was confirmed in 1978, is a sure sign that creation of antimatter must be taking place very close to where the gamma rays are seen. The most efficient way of creating positrons is by pair production, whereby two colliding gamma-ray photons are transformed into an electron and a positron. The photons used to produce the matter-antimatter pairs do not have to be exactly 511 keV each, so long as their total energy is more than 1,022 keV. Very high temperatures are needed to produce cosmic gamma rays; astronomers have deduced that they must originate from an object that is at least 200,000 times more powerful than the Sun but has less than 0.001% of its volume.

While the 511-keV gamma rays provide powerful evidence for the existence of a strange object near the center of the Galaxy, they fail to provide some information that astronomers would like very much to have. Particularly troublesome is the fact that it is hard to pinpoint precisely where these gamma rays are coming from. As of the mid-1980s it was known only that their point of origin is within four

The center of the Milky Way is visible in an image produced from data collected by the Infrared Astronomical Satellite (IRAS) in 1983. The image does not show any stars themselves. What IRAS detected was the radiation from cosmic dust present in the spaces between the stars.

NASA

degrees of the direction of the galactic center.

There is no certainty that the radio waves and the gamma rays come from the same object, since the two kinds of radiation are produced in different ways. The uniqueness of each, however, strongly encourages astronomers to look for a single cause for the two phenomena. What is needed is an object that can liberate extremely large amounts of energy in a very small volume. Many astronomers consider that the only kind of object capable of doing this is an accretion disk around a black hole.

Black Holes

The bizarre properties of black holes have frequently caught the imagination of science fiction writers, who are fascinated by the opportunities for concealment and destruction that the objects offer. In both fiction and astrophysical theory, black holes are regions of space where the force of gravity is so overwhelmingly strong that neither matter nor light is able to escape. In the vicinity of a black hole time runs slowly and space itself becomes distorted. Any matter that is pulled from the outside world into the interior of a black hole is forever hidden from the view of those outside. It is the absence of emergent light, or of any other kind of signal, that gives black holes their "blackness."

Despite their racy reputation, black holes are far more than outlandish scientific speculation. They are a logical consequence of Einstein's general theory of relativity, which, despite its mathematical complexity, is the simplest self-consistent theory of gravity that physicists have. A theory such as relativity is necessary because Newton's classical theory of gravity, although immensely successful at predicting the motions of stars, planets, and smaller bodies, gives logically inconsistent results when it is applied to regions of space where gravity is strong enough to influence the propagation of light. Gravitational fields this strong cannot be generated in a laboratory, so physicists must look elsewhere in the universe to test their theories. Black holes, if they can be found, provide such an opportunity.

Relativity theory says that black holes *can* exist; it does not say that they *must* exist. It is, in fact, extremely difficult to make one. Matter must be squeezed together so tightly that something the size and mass of planet Earth would be compressed to the size of a golf ball. The circumstances under which this can happen are rare, a fact that partly accounts for why so few, if any, black holes have been found. The only circumstance under which astronomers are reasonably confident that a black hole can form is as the result of the final collapse of certain burned-out stars. Once a black hole is formed, however, it can grow to many times its original size by accreting any matter that strays too close to its surface. The more matter there is in the vicinity of a black hole, the more rapidly it will grow. Since the concentration of gas and stars generally is greatest at the center of a galaxy, it is at the nucleus that a massive black hole is most likely to be found. It is for this reason that astronomers are looking very hard at the evidence for a black hole at the center of our Galaxy.

Despite the enormous gravitational field around a black hole, matter rarely falls directly into it. Because of the law of conservation of angular momentum, if an object has any sideways motion as it falls, it will first go into an orbit around the black hole. If matter is falling inward in a steady stream, it will tend to pile up in a rotating accretion disk centered on the black hole. In the accretion disk collisions occur between particles moving in slightly different directions. Because the particles have been accelerated to enormous speeds by their fall toward the black hole, these collisions can generate a great deal of heat and energy. This energy may appear in several forms, including gamma rays and radio waves. In this way the accretion disk, which lies just outside of the black hole, may become very bright at certain wavelengths. In all but the strictest sense, therefore, a black hole may belie its blackness and become an intense source of energy.

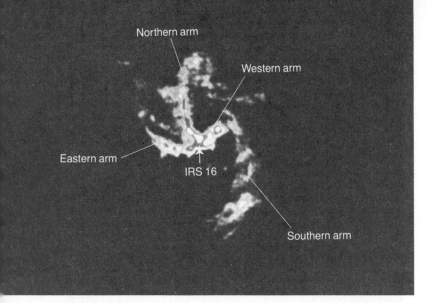

Northern arm

Western arm

Eastern arm

IRS 16

Southern arm

A radio image of Sagittarius A West contains, within a region less than a half light-year across, a cluster of infrared sources called IRS 16, Much recently collected information seems to identify IRS 16 as the very center of the nucleus of the Milky Way.

OBSERVATIONS MADE BY KWOK-YUNG LO AND MARK J. CLAUSSEN; THE NATIONAL RADIO ASTRONOMY OBSERVATORY, OPERATED BY ASSOCIATED UNIVERSITIES, INC., UNDER CONTRACT WITH THE NATIONAL SCIENCE FOUNDATION

A Black Hole in Our "Front Yard"?

Although radio and gamma-ray observations have provided the important clue that there is an unusual, compact power source in the galactic center, most astronomers want more direct evidence before concluding that a black hole must be responsible. This evidence is hard to obtain; since black holes give off no light and cast such a minute shadow, there seems to be no hope of ever directly seeing one, at least from the vicinity of our solar system. A much better strategy is to look for the strong gravitational field that must accompany a black hole. Stars and gas near the black hole move around it in circular or nearly circular orbits. If these orbits can be measured, the amount of mass in the black hole can be estimated in much the same way that the mass of a planet of the solar system can be determined from observing its moons.

It is not possible to follow an individual star in its orbit around the galactic center, because such orbits take many human lifetimes. Instead, astronomers take a statistical approach; rather than looking at one object extensively, they analyze the motions of many objects at one point in time. The technique they use is the Doppler effect; by measuring the difference in the wavelength of the same spectral line (a prominent, narrow brightening within the spectrum) as seen in a celestial object and in the laboratory, the speed with which that object is moving away from the Earth can easily be calculated.

In the case of the galactic center, it is easier to measure the velocity of the gas than of the stars, because the gas has brighter spectral lines at the wavelengths that can penetrate the Galaxy's obscuring dust clouds. Interstellar gas is a mixture of many species of atoms, ions, and molecules; hydrogen is always by far the most common element, but depending on the temperature and density of the gas, its spectral lines are not necessarily always the easiest ones to observe. Data on different regions of the galactic center are obtained from different gases; in the 12-light-year ring, where the gas is cool,

the strongest lines are produced by oxygen atoms, carbon ions, and molecules of carbon monoxide. In the case of the arcs and filaments of hot ionized gas inside the ring, the 12.8-micrometer line of neon is the most revealing. In the central region, with a diameter of one light-year, where the gas density gets very high, hydrogen and helium atoms provide the most velocity information. Measuring these infrared spectral lines is not easy; to overcome problems caused by absorption in the Earth's atmosphere, astronomers must observe using telescopes on top of Mauna Kea, a 4.2-kilometer (13,800-foot) dormant volcano in Hawaii, or, in the worst cases, using a 90-centimeter (35-inch) telescope flown at high altitude in the Kuiper Airborne Observatory.

The observations of the gas in the 12-light-year ring indicate that it encloses an amount of matter equivalent to four million Suns. Theory predicts that if the matter that is holding the gas in orbit is highly concentrated, as in a black hole, the gas closest to the nucleus will be moving much faster than the gas in the ring. If, on the other hand, the matter is in the form of millions of stars spread out over the whole 12-light-year region, the velocities close to the nucleus will not be so large. The necessary observations were made and reported in 1985; they indicate that the gas velocities do increase toward the nucleus in the way predicted for a black hole, and that this black hole has a mass equivalent to about four million Suns.

Not all astronomers accept this conclusion, and there are two observations that confuse what is otherwise a rather simple picture. One is the discovery, made in 1984, of a region of unexpectedly hot gas at the inner edge of the 12-light-year ring, the heating apparently caused by the impact of a strong wind blowing from somewhere near the nucleus itself. This wind is in some ways a help to astronomers, since it may provide an explanation for the existence of the ring itself. But, if some of the gas in the nucleus is blowing outward instead of moving in orbits around the center, then the observations of the spectral lines from the gas are much more difficult to interpret, and the evidence for the existence of the four million-Sun black hole is weakened.

The other problem results from astronomers' refining their determinations of the precise positions of the star cluster IRS 16 and of the compact radio source Sgr A*. To their distress they now find that the two do not coincide but are separated from each other by about one two-thousandths of a degree. According to some theories, if a four million-Sun black hole exists it must be at the center of the star cluster. Possible explanations for the discrepancy are that the theory is inadequate, that no black hole exists, or that Sgr A*, despite its uniqueness, has nothing to do with the black hole. It will be hard to resolve these difficulties, but if current plans to develop very sensitive infrared spectrometers for use in space are realized, it should be possible to do so by measuring the velocities of the stars in IRS 16 itself.

Other Galaxies

How does our Galaxy compare with others? The next nearest spiral galaxy nucleus, that of the Andromeda galaxy M31, is 70 times farther away than the nucleus of the Milky Way. At that distance both the 511-keV gamma rays and the Sgr A* radio source would be too faint to be detected, and everything within the 12-light-year ring would be just a dim blur. Whatever it is that is going on in the center of the Milky Way could be happening in millions of other spiral galaxy nuclei, but with present technology we are not able to find out.

What we do know is that there are certain galaxies, perhaps 1% of the total, that have extraordinarily bright, active nuclei. These objects, which include Seyfert and quasar galaxies, can be thousands of times more powerful than the Milky Way's nucleus, can fluctuate in intensity in hours, can accelerate gas clouds to speeds of thousands of kilometers per second, and can eject beams of radio-emitting plasma (hot ionized atoms) hundreds of thousands of light-years into space. Astronomers are struggling with satisfactory explanations for these objects, although black-hole accretion disks figure prominently in many theories. Because of the enormous amounts of "fuel" required by these galaxies, it is fairly certain that their violent activity takes the form of a comparatively short-lived outburst. What triggers these outbursts is not clear, although near-collisions with other galaxies seem to be involved in some cases.

Can galaxies have violent outbursts more than once? Are some galaxies predisposed to having active nuclei? Do all galaxy nuclei go through periods of violent activity at some time in their lives? These questions remain unanswered but have fueled speculation that the nucleus of the Milky Way could one day be or could once have been much more prominent than it is now. A tantalizing hint of the latter possibility comes in a finding made in 1971

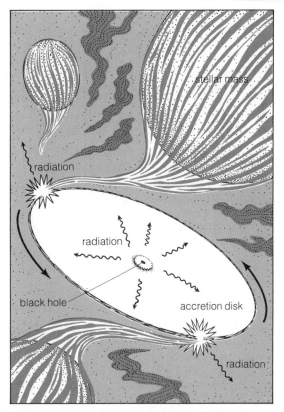

Matter falling into a black hole first tends to assemble into a rotating accretion disk centered on the black hole. In the accretion disk collisions occur between particles moving in slightly different directions. Because the particles have been accelerated to enormous speeds by their fall towards the black hole, these collisions can generate vast amounts of high-energy radiation. It is in its role as the central force controlling an accretion disk that a black hole becomes an intense source of energy.

that the motions of certain hydrogen clouds in the disk of the Galaxy could be the result of a prehistoric explosion in the nucleus. According to this theory, enough gas to form at least 30 million Suns was expelled from the nucleus about ten million years ago and is now falling back into the disk. How so much gas got to the nucleus and what caused the explosion are a mystery. The nucleus as we see it now gives little hint of such a violent episode.

Astronomers' lack of understanding of what is taking place in the nucleus of the Galaxy will no doubt lessen as their theories and measurement techniques improve. Meanwhile, their current frustrations are echoed by the words of the poet Robert Frost:

> We dance round in a ring and suppose,
> But the Secret sits in the middle and knows.

Gareth Wynn-Williams is Professor of Astronomy at the University of Hawaii, Honolulu.

The Soviet Union Under Gorbachev

by Arkadi N. Shevchenko

For the U.S.S.R. it is the best of times and the worst of times. Both aspects of this paradox bear importantly on what the Western world can anticipate from the first leader of the Soviet Union born after the Bolshevik Revolution, Mikhail S. Gorbachev.

It is the best of times for the Soviet military, which has developed the mightiest war machine in history. For the first time, Soviet armed forces have overcome the challenge of trying to catch up with the West. The Soviet Union has now achieved its long-cherished dream of strategic nuclear parity with the United States and has firmly secured superpower status. The conventional forces of the United States and NATO combined are inferior to those of the U.S.S.R. In certain categories of its nuclear arsenal, particularly in heavy, land-based ICBM (intercontinental ballistic missiles), the Soviet Union is superior to the United States. Deployment of the newest medium-range SS-20 missiles has drastically altered the military balance in Europe in favor of the U.S.S.R.

The Soviet military buildup has been attained, however, at the expense of the civilian economy. The emphasis on the military has created structural economic imbalances that preclude development and modernization of civilian industries, services, agriculture, and general technological innovation. It has become increasingly obvious that, in addition to old economic and social ills, new and more serious ones have appeared.

The U.S.S.R. is at a crossroads. If pressing economic and social problems are not alleviated in the near future, further erosion in its economic system is inevitable, thus endangering, in the long term, its very survival. Gorbachev and his followers in the Kremlin understand the urgent need to mitigate the worst of the Soviet Union's domestic problems better than their predecessors. I say "mitigate" and not "solve" because many of the worst of these problems are beyond solution, barring a radical departure from the present Soviet economic model.

Typically, Gorbachev has blamed his predecessors for the U.S.S.R.'s current economic and social ailments and has promised a new beginning. Although there is nothing new in his tactics, there is some truth to Gorbachev's recriminations. For many years the ancient Kremlin oligarchs promoted a doctrine of "continuity and stability" for Soviet leadership and society. In fact, their main purpose was a futile attempt to hold back the clock—to retain power as long as possible. Because the Soviet political structure is conservative in the extreme, for a time they actually appeared to accomplish their goal, but at great cost to the nation. Their *après nous le déluge* philosophy led to stagnation and worse.

Gorbachev has definitely initiated a new style; he is dynamic and relatively young. Barring unforeseen crises, he could remain in power for a long time. But whether his stewardship will open a new era for the U.S.S.R. remains to be seen. Even if he should receive the goodwill and cooperation of all his subordinates, he faces problems that are almost insurmountable, given the U.S.S.R.'s economic system. And that is the crux of the Soviet dilemma.

The Agriculture Gap

As Gorbachev himself has stated publicly and repeatedly, both the old and new problems afflicting the Soviet Union are tremendous. Soviet agriculture remains a perennial disaster. Food shortages are worse than they were in the 1960s, even in Moscow, except for the very heart of the city, where such a situation would be too embarrassing to tolerate. Supplies of milk and dairy products, meat and meat products, and other staple foods are always meager to nonexistent. In many provincial regions of the Soviet Union, food rationing has been established, as it was during World War II.

The catastrophic failure of Soviet agriculture is a direct result of the collective farm plan so long celebrated in Soviet propaganda. It simply does not work. Considerable human resources and machinery were allocated to the collective farming experiment and squandered on the theory's doctrinaire application. The Soviet Union, finally, had to rediscover that incentives borrowed from capitalism could move farmers to produce and market crops, while Marxist theory and Stalinist enforcement could only breed agricultural failures. Even in the U.S.S.R. there is no denial of the fact that the minuscule private sector of Soviet farming, which utilizes something like 3 to 4% of the land under cultivation, produces more than half of the country's vegetables, fruit, and meat. But not many Soviet citizens can afford to shop in the private

(OPPOSITE PAGE) WALLY MCNAMEE—WOODFIN CAMP & ASSOCIATES

market, where prices run from 2 to 20 times the official prices set for the same items in government-run food stores. The Catch-22 to this situation is, of course, that the government stores rarely, if ever, have such items as grapes, melons, peas, or lettuce.

In many areas, not just in their eating habits, the Soviet people are denied the ordinary accompaniments to living that most people in the West take for granted. In any country of the West, you can buy literally anything you want, as long as you can pay for it. In the Soviet Union you cannot. Money is not enough; one must belong to the ruling class, the party and government elite, to obtain the luxuries that in the West are mundane conveniences.

In typical Soviet farming country, where the best land may be little better than marginal, living conditions border on the primitive. Houses typically lack running water and other modern facilities. Public transportation, generally adequate in Moscow and Leningrad, is sporadic at best outside these cities, inadequate in many parts of the country. Cars and trucks are in short supply. There is almost no public entertainment, and life is dull. But as people have become better educated, they are less and less satisfied with the farmer's lot. Young people move to the cities as soon as they are old enough.

The Economy's Clogged Arteries

The entire Soviet economy lags far behind what its leaders call "normal international standards." By this they mean the way all the rest of the industrialized world lives. The U.S.S.R. is behind in heavy industry, in light industry, and in every aspect of the consumer economy across the board, from vital medicines to children's toys. In all they aspire to, except in military strength, the Soviets trail the United States, France, Japan, West Germany, the United Kingdom, and other industrialized countries.

The balance of achievements is lower than all expectations. The population is frustrated over unfulfilled promises of abundance and high living standards; a lack of incentive has led to apathy.

There is a lot of truth in the old joke that there is no unemployment in the Soviet Union but nobody works. The leadership simply cannot ignore the situation any longer. Soviets are long-suffering but not infinitely so.

Soviet industry desperately needs modernization. In many factories one can still see machine tools of '20s and '30s vintage. Rigid central planning, poor management, the absence of competition, and artificial pricing policies make inefficiency the norm rather than the exception. Labor productivity is far below any Western standards. Factory workers' salaries and standards of living are the lowest among the industrialized nations. But the workers' lack of initiative cannot be overcome unless the existing egalitarian salary system is abandoned. For example, a man who wants to make extra money may work overtime, but no matter how many additional hours he puts in, he is paid no more than 5 to 10% above his regular salary. Therefore, in order to make more money, he resorts to "moonlighting," selling or trading his skills according to what others are willing to pay. This creates, in effect, an underground free market system operating in the same way as do the private farmers' markets.

Another problem vitally affecting all economic sectors is transportation. There is no general network of paved highways, such as exist in Western Europe or the United States. In a country much less than half the size of the Soviet Union, the United States has nearly seven times as much paved highway. The absence of a first-class road system helps explain why Soviet trucks are out of service almost half the time. Vehicles are worked for long periods at a time, and routine maintenance is often neglected.

The Soviet Union has no advanced passenger railway system comparable to those of Western Europe. The ordinary Soviet citizen must often wait for weeks even to buy a ticket to go anywhere in the country. This is a permanent condition of Soviet life, true at any time of the day or year, but

A military parade in Moscow celebrates the 1917 Bolshevik Revolution. Two decades of military modernization and buildup have debilitated the Soviet civilian economy. Can Gorbachev shift gears?

WALLY MCNAMEE—WOODFIN CAMP & ASSOCIATES

during rush hours or holiday seasons the difficulty is compounded. Except, of course, for the upper elite, the *nomenklatura,* who can get tickets easily at any time. Railroad trains have special cars for them where no one else may enter, even if only one member of the ruling class—or no one at all—is using these accommodations.

Rail freight facilities suffer from maintenance problems, equipment shortages, heavy use, and the vast distances of the country. The United States, with only 42% of the area of the Soviet Union, has twice the railroad track. But Soviet freight trains haul two and one half times as much freight.

Soviet airliners fly about two-thirds of the passenger-kilometers and not quite one-third as much freight as those in the United States, but fewer than 50 airports in the U.S.S.R. have scheduled flights, as against more than 12,500 in the United States. Soviet airliners have the equivalent of first-class sections, and these, like the first-class railroad cars, are for the elite. (Naturally, special hotels cater only to the same class.)

Westerners accustomed to dialing an area code and a number and almost instantly talking with the desired party, even in some distant state or country, would find it difficult to believe what the ordinary Soviet citizen must put up with in the way of telephone service. In many areas Soviet telephone exchanges are operated just as they were a half century ago in the advanced countries of the West. It is frustrating enough to telephone within a city; intercity calls take hours or days to complete.

The latest economic woes are those regarding energy conservation (oil production has begun to drop) and, even more important, the widening gap between East and West in the field of high technology. The U.S.S.R. has not yet mastered the production of high technology that is now largely yesterday's news in the West. In computers, microprocessors, fiber optics, robots, ceramics, and many other elements of advanced technology, the Soviet Union is so far behind Japan and the West that the specter of losing the economic competition with them is beginning to haunt the Kremlin leadership.

Facing the Problems

Gorbachev's first statements as general secretary of the Communist Party of the Soviet Union vividly reflected this concern. He hinted at substantial changes to come regarding policy in this area. Indeed, some experiments in planning and management in industry and agriculture have been initiated during his first year as Soviet leader, but most of these moves were not really innovative. In somewhat different form, similar measures have been tried in the past. As of now, Gorbachev's "reforms" are essentially palliatives, not cures, for the economy. More recently, his policy emphasis has shifted from the idea of "restructuring the economy," and he has fallen back on the tired techniques of sloganeering about the need to in-

DE KEERLE—GAMMA/LIAISON

Mikhail Gorbachev has displayed a grasp of public relations and a talent for gaining favorable media coverage that his predecessors conspicuously lacked.

crease the role of party organizations in supervising economic management, the introduction of strict working discipline, the replacement of inefficient personnel, and a vigorous campaign against alcoholism. Each and every one of these measures has been called for by the last several leaders, with little effect on overall economic performance. I am sure Gorbachev realizes that even strict adherence to these exhortations cannot substantially improve the situation. I am just as sure that he realizes what the real problem is and that he recognizes that not much can be done about it without changing the economic system that keeps him and many others in power.

Gorbachev elucidated his ambitious economic blueprint in the documents "Basic Guidelines for the Next Five-Year Plan and Beyond to the Year 2000" and in the "Food Program," announced under Leonid Brezhnev and endorsed by Gorbachev. It will be interesting to follow his activities in this area because the introduction of truly new management is Gorbachev's only option if he is serious about improving Soviet economic performance.

Why, then, has he not launched such new methods immediately? There is no single answer to this question. I would like to emphasize that Gorbachev's numerous recent statements on economic problems and other matters leave no doubt that he is a product of the Soviet system or, more precisely, of the Communist Party apparatus. It would be totally wrong to conclude that he would want to alter the existing system substantially or to ease ideological indoctrination of the people. Gorbachev was selected as the new Kremlin leader not to change the system but to make it function better.

It is also certain that the inert but still powerful old men of the party and government elite would resist absolutely any meaningful changes in the U.S.S.R. Gorbachev and the Soviet mass media do not even try to hide the fact of that resistance.

Finally, Western speculation that Gorbachev has already solidified his power and authority to the

On a wheat farm near Stavropol in Mikhail Gorbachev's native region the mechanization of agriculture is still rather primitive, compared with that of the United States and other Western industrialized nations.

point where he has assumed the mantle of the autocratic and infallible Kremlin ruler are considerably exaggerated. In my opinion, Gorbachev has not achieved the level of authority among his peers that either Nikita Khrushchev or Brezhnev had in his heyday. Things simply do not move that quickly in Soviet politics.

Gorbachev needs more time to consolidate his power, a power that he now shares with other members of the Politburo and party Secretariat. He must enlarge his base of support at the regional level. One reason the misunderstanding in the West about Gorbachev's authority came about was that he began weeding out aging bureaucrats from high party and government ranks so swiftly that it surprised Western analysts of Soviet affairs. I would caution those who follow Soviet affairs not to inflate Gorbachev's gifts and effectiveness too quickly. The old party apparatchiks he removed from the bureaucracy would have left soon anyway, for natural causes if for no other. It is also important to remember that Gorbachev, unlike his predecessors, did not have very strong rivals to overcome in the final contest for the post of party leader. Grigori Romanov, the former party chief of Leningrad—young by Politburo standards at 62—and considered a possible rival for the top post, has been easily and unceremoniously retired by Gorbachev. That, however, was not a true test of strength; Romanov did not have enough time to consolidate an effective support base among leading Moscow politicians. Nor did he enjoy the necessary support of the majority in the Politburo.

The New Generation

The most important thing Gorbachev has done to solidify his authority has been his policy of replacing the old party and government cadres by new party apparatchiks. These functionaries are men of Gorbachev's generation who have been waiting a long, long time for their turn at higher posts. They can and will resist serious reforms in the U.S.S.R., but there is no doubt about their hearty enthusiasm for Gorbachev's cadre policy. Well before I broke with the Soviets, I knew that influential elements of the party and government elite were increasingly concerned about the need to infuse fresh blood into the ruling gerontocracy.

Gorbachev is rapidly bringing a new generation to power with him. The composition of the Politburo is changing. More than one-third of the first secretaries of the regional party bodies have been replaced. About 40 Cabinet ministerial positions—about half of them—have been filled by younger men.

Gorbachev is dismissing many older bureaucratic managers, who were often poorly educated and conspicuously unqualified for their jobs, with better educated and abler, younger technocrats who have more imagination and ingenuity. He is also firing some of the most corrupt elements of the elite.

Bureaucratic corruption is endemic in the Soviet Union. There is an unwritten law that the perquisites of the ruling class must be enjoyed discreetly; they must not be flaunted before the working class, and they must not be traded for money, goods, or favors. Over the years many in Brezhnev's elite coterie violated this rule openly, lulled into complacency by the longevity of Brezhnev's tenure. Gorbachev is now making an example of the more profligate abusers.

Replacements in the ranks of the elite should not be viewed as a new party purge, however. Neither are they in any way meant to undermine or curtail the dominant status and privileges of the party and government apparatus. There is no indication that Gorbachev is trying to encroach on the perquisites and prerogatives of the *nomenklatura* class. He, himself, is the embodiment of that class and is, above all, the representative of its interests. The *nomenklatura* elite will continue as the ruling class isolated from the people.

Gorbachev is merely attempting to eliminate the worst excesses committed by some. It should be clearly understood that he does not want to change one of the fundamental cornerstones of the Soviet system. Moreover, even if he should wish to do so, the *nomenklatura* elite would never permit anything to undermine its power, and it has the power to prevent anything it opposes from happening. At the moment, however, it is a good political move, as a sop to the people, that the elite should suffer some inconveniences for a while as it relearns the necessity for circumspection in exercising its privileges.

To revitalize economic performance, Gorbachev must first of all convince the apparatchiks and managers that their jobs are not necessarily lifetime sinecures. That pernicious belief has fostered laziness and an arrogant confidence that they may behave with impunity in any matter. The illusion of lifelong security as a matter of right in matters of position and privilege was primarily a legacy of Brezhnev's rule. And what Gorbachev is doing now is not something new in Soviet history. The *nomenklatura* have experienced troubles many times in the past. During my time as a member of the elite, I remember that we were much more afraid of being removed from our positions than were ordinary workers, because with loss of position would come loss of privilege. Under the *nomenklatura* system, emoluments are attached to the job, not the person. At the same time, the elite views these partial losses of fortune and favor as the inevitable price it must render periodically for its advantages.

Changes in top Kremlin leadership and in the party and government apparatus under Gorbachev have had only a marginal effect on the power structure's essential character or on the Soviet system in general. I am sure that Gorbachev has never considered making any changes whatever regarding the latter. The Soviet government is not a government of the people; power in the U.S.S.R., as in the past, is concentrated in the hands of a small group composed of members of the Politburo, the Central Committee of the Communist Party Secretariat, and a few top government officials. They are in no way controlled by or answerable to the people or even to the party's rank and file. In the U.S.S.R. there are no free elections at any level, no freedom of religion, speech, or the press; Soviet people have no right to assemble freely, nor do they have free access to information available to all in the West. If the people do not like such conditions, it is of no consequence, for they also have no right to emigrate, nor do they have the right to be properly protected from injustice. Gorbachev would be the last man in the U.S.S.R. one might expect to contemplate bringing democracy to the Soviet people. To control a people it can no longer inspire, the Kremlin under Gorbachev continues to rely upon security police and informers, coercion and intimidation.

Like each of his predecessors, Gorbachev has utilized the support of the KGB and the Army to gain the pinnacle of Soviet power. To obtain military secrets and advanced technology it cannot develop efficiently at home, Gorbachev's leadership continues to employ KGB and GRU (military intelligence) espionage abroad. One should not, however, overestimate the influence of the KGB and the Army in the Soviet Union, as some Westerners are prone to do. While their influence is important, they are only the instruments of the ruling party group. Gorbachev's policy line in this connection is clear: firm control by the party apparatus over the Army and the KGB.

The Military Paradox

As things stand in the Soviet government and the Communist Party, the military establishment, for all its strength of arms, is perhaps at its weakest point politically. There are several reasons for this. One is the depth and scope of the modernization and buildup that went on during the 1970s. That was so effective that the Soviet Union now has the strongest military structure on Earth. No longer can Soviet marshals demand new weaponry to "catch up with America." In fact, the buildup was so successful that, to some degree, it immobilized the military politically. In addition, the critical economic problems facing the country make heavy military spending impossible without enormous and possibly intolerable effort.

Finally, all the great Soviet military heroes, such as the late Marshal Georgi Zhukov, are dead. There are none left who are universally known and respected and whose voice for military spending would carry compelling weight. The current Soviet defense minister, Marshal Sergei Sokolov, is, at 74 years of age, an obscure figure, little known even in the Soviet Union and without substantial political importance. Unlike his two immediate predecessors, he is not even a full Politburo member but only a nonvoting candidate member.

The relative political impotence that characterizes the military is to an extent true also of the KGB. Although Gorbachev has made the KGB chairman, Viktor M. Chebrikov, a full Politburo member, he is still a bureaucrat, not a politician. The difference between being a politician and a bureaucrat in the Soviet Union is that the former has a base of support that allows him to exert some political weight. A bureaucrat is usually someone who has no such support beyond his immediate circle in his own branch of the government and may, therefore, be dismissed by the leadership with no repercussions. Chebrikov is 62 years old and has spent his entire career in the KGB, where he was deputy chairman under Brezhnev, Yuri Andropov, and Konstantin Chernenko.

Western Illusions

In recent times, some Western Soviet watchers have predicted an imminent collapse of the Soviet system, followed by the fall of the Soviet empire within a few years. The "problems" fueling such predictions are, in fact, exaggerated. For example, the dissident movement in the U.S.S.R. has been decapitated. It now represents no serious threat to the Soviet regime. In the same vein, suggestions that rising ethnonationalism and the burgeoning population in Soviet Central Asia (much exceeding the growth of the Slavic population) will soon cause destabilizing effects for the future of the U.S.S.R. are also overstated. It is true that there have been protests against the denial of national rights in the Baltic republics; in fact, Lithuania, Latvia, and Estonia would probably secede from the U.S.S.R. if they could. There has also been protest and discontent for the same reason in parts of the Ukraine and among the Crimean Tatars. These are problems of concern for the Kremlin, and Soviet leaders do not deny the existence of nationally related prejudices, tensions, and other difficulties. But the Soviet state with its enormous arsenal of coercive, organizational, and ideological resources is capable of dealing with any demonstrations of nationalistic fervor that might become too vociferous.

The Central Asian republics—and others—have quite a number of devoted Communist Party members, for there has been considerable economic and social progress there under Soviet rule. The standard of living in some of the non-Slavic Soviet republics is higher than it is in central Russia. The women of Soviet Asia, though many of them are Muslims, are not in the position of women in much of the Arab world. They have opportunities for education and work, and they no longer wear the veil.

As to population growth in Soviet Central Asia and some other parts of the U.S.S.R., the Russians will still rule the roost for a long time to come. In a total population of some 270 million, there are almost 140 million Russians and more than 50 million Ukrainians and Byelorussians. The Central Asians will not soon lose their minority status.

The Soviet government has tried since 1917 to eradicate religion, and if eradication is the test, the effort has failed. Diligent antireligious propaganda and atheist indoctrination in the schools were not without effect, however. The majority of Soviet citizens have no religion, and so to that extent the effort to root out religion has succeeded.

During World War II the Russian Orthodox Church did a great deal to rally patriotism and the determination to fight the Nazi invader, and this, coinciding as it did with a wartime upsurge in religious faith, greatly slowed the antireligious campaign, at least for Orthodoxy. Out of this wartime détente emerged an accommodation between state and church. The Orthodox leadership pledged that it would not engage in any political activity whatever. In return, Stalin agreed to the restoration of some churches that had been closed and allowed the clergy to work more or less openly among the population. This agreement was honored by Stalin's successors and describes the general situation today. The Russian Orthodox leaders became active in the World Council of Churches and especially in its peace initiatives, which coincided precisely with Soviet foreign policy. But the Kremlin has consistently refused cooperation with Roman Catholicism, whose spiritual leadership came from Rome instead of Moscow, as well as various other religions with connections abroad.

Islam has been more or less tolerated in Soviet Central Asia, primarily because it is not as militant and fanatical as the Ayatollah Khomeini's brand of Shi'ah. As its part of the unwritten arrangement with its Muslims, the government allowed restoration of some of the mosques that were converted to movie theaters in the early days of antireligious zeal under Lenin.

The situation of Jews in what is now the Soviet Union has been a troubled one since the days of the tsars. Anti-Semitism has been a fact of Russian life, and it has never eased significantly. Gorbachev recently asserted that Jews fare better in the Soviet Union than outside it, but this is ridiculous nonsense.

When the state of Israel was established, the Soviet Union was the first nation to recognize it. Any friendly implications of this move quickly turned sour when it became apparent that many Soviet Jews wanted to immigrate to the new Jewish homeland. Party leaders were suspicious of any Soviet citizens who wanted to leave the country. Even Jewish members of the Communist Party, and there were quite a few at that time, wanted to go to Israel. At times Jews have been allowed to leave for various reasons, political or economic. When the situation of Soviet Jews became an issue in international politics, the Soviets found they could sometimes trade Jewish exit visas for advantages in trade or economic deals with the West.

Outside the Soviet Union, its six-year-old aggression in Afghanistan is a nagging problem for the Kremlin. For the West this situation, sometimes referred to rather smugly as the Soviets' Vietnam, is another frequently misunderstood situation. Embarrassing and frustrating as this seemingly endless war is for the Kremlin, it is not a Soviet Vietnam. For one thing, the United States in Vietnam had major problems of logistics and transport fighting a war on the other side of the world. The Soviet transport problem is trivial by contrast; the war is next door. In Vietnam the U.S. war effort was finally undermined and disabled by hostile American public opinion. There is, of course, no informed public opinion in the Soviet Union. Public perception of the war is whatever the leadership tells it: "Our troops are helping the friendly government against the bandits." Soviet casualties in Afghanistan are apparently still at a level acceptable to the Kremlin and, finally, the military is most likely willing to continue the war there because the country has become a testing ground for Soviet weapons. The war in Afghanistan also provides a perfect opportunity to train soldiers for future combat operations.

Afghanistan is not the only headache facing the U.S.S.R. beyond its borders. There are even more difficulties and troubles in Poland and other parts of the Soviet bloc, as well as in the Kremlin's relations with pro-Moscow regimes in the third world. Nevertheless, to any careful scholar, it is obvious that the Soviet empire is far from collapse.

Foreign Policy Leadership

Gorbachev's appointment of Andrei A. Gromyko (76), the venerable former Soviet foreign minister, to the largely ceremonial post of chairman of the Presidium of the Supreme Soviet (the nominal chief of state), as well as his replacement as foreign minister by Eduard A. Shevardnadze (57), surprised most Soviet analysts. At the time of Gorbachev's elevation to party leader, Gromyko was solidly entrenched as master of Soviet foreign policy. As a senior and most powerful member of the Politburo and one of the few Soviet statesmen of international as well as domestic repute, he nominated Gorbachev for the post of general secretary of the party. Gorbachev needed Gromyko's assistance because the latter could deliver the support of the older leaders (they still held the majority in the Politburo at the time of Gorbachev's selection). Without his aid, Gorbachev might well have had difficulty in winning the power struggle.

Although Gromyko no longer directs the Foreign Ministry, it is unlikely that he has lost Gorbachev's confidence, nor is it likely that he has been shunted away from the inner group of Kremlin policymakers. Gromyko is a man whose experience and expertise are invaluable. His advice is sure to be sought and respected in Gorbachev's Politburo.

Gromyko is no longer foreign minister, but he played the leading role in Soviet foreign affairs for so long, enjoying prominence under so many Soviet leaders, that he became an institution, acquiring a degree of independence that is all but unique in the U.S.S.R. Gromyko would not easily accede to Gorbachev's bidding if he did not agree with it. Gromyko, probably alone among Soviet leaders, would be capable of taking Gorbachev by the arm and saying: "No, you're wrong!" This the new leader would not be likely to countenance. Naturally, Gorbachev would not want a stern and patronizing personality like Gromyko permanently intervening in the conduct of foreign policy. Nevertheless, Gromyko certainly has not disappeared from the centers of power. He is quite aware of his influence, and although he probably misses his former role, in sum, it is likely that he is pleased with his new appointment. His health is not the best, and for that reason he has had to reduce his accustomed work load drastically in recent years.

It is significant that Gorbachev's party and government housecleaning left Foreign Ministry officials practically untouched. Except for a few new faces, most Soviet diplomatic personnel, both in Moscow and abroad, remain the same as before. It is quite possible that experienced Foreign Ministry experts have even more influence now than in the past.

Eduard A. Shevardnadze is Gorbachev's choice to succeed Gromyko as foreign minister. Shevardnadze spent most of his career in Georgia, where he was first secretary of the Georgian party's Central Committee for many years. Earlier he had been a Komsomol (Young Communist League) leader there, and he is an old friend of Gorbachev, who is a native of the neighboring territory of Stavropol. Gorbachev saw to it that Shevardnadze was quickly made a full voting member of the Politburo, and he has joined the group of key personalities in the new Kremlin leadership.

Would-be customers in Moscow line up (left) on learning that a store in the regulated market has something for sale. Meanwhile, at a private open-air food market (right), a relative abundance awaits those few with the means to buy.

Faces in the Politburo

Unlike Gromyko, Shevardnadze came up through the Communist Party ranks instead of the government bureaucracy. Gorbachev also found his way to power through a party career. It is true that he came from a peasant family, that he worked on a collective farm for several years in his youth, and that he took a correspondence course from an agricultural institute at Stavropol—after he had earned his law degree at Moscow University. But it was his party credentials (including membership in the Komsomol from 1946 and the CPSU since 1952) and his later service as a party apparatchik, both in Stavropol and in Moscow, that made it possible for him to become the general secretary.

One of the most significant replacements of the old guard is that of Nikolai A. Tikhonov (80) by Nikolai I. Ryzhkov. As chairman of the Council of Ministers, Tikhonov was the oldest member of the Politburo. Ryzhkov is an ethnic Russian, 56 years of age, with an impressive executive career in industry but without any conspicuous party background. In 1982 he joined the Secretariat of the Central Committee as secretary for economic affairs. Ryzhkov is obviously a close ally of Gorbachev's since his new position puts him in charge of implementing the leader's economic programs and plans for technological innovation. With little visibility either at home or abroad, Ryzhkov was rapidly advanced over more senior party officials and has become one of the most powerful figures in the new leadership.

Yegor K. Ligachev, a 65-year-old Russian and a Gorbachev appointee to voting membership in the Politburo, is another party apparatchik who is one of the leader's closest associates. Ligachev is, in fact, number two man in the Central Committee Secretariat. He deals with ideological affairs and with cadre policy in the party apparatus. Ligachev provides Gorbachev a useful link with the older generation of party elite, who may still harbor suspicions about Gorbachev's intentions.

Vitali I. Vorotnikov (60), a voting member, is also considered close to Gorbachev. He is chairman of the Council of Ministers of the Russian Soviet Federated Socialist Republic (R.S.F.S.R.), the largest of the 15 republics, which stretches from the Baltic Sea to the Bering Strait.

Another voting member of the Politburo who predates Gorbachev (he was brought in under Andropov) is Geidar A. Aliyev (62), a non-Russian from the Azerbaijan Soviet Socialist Republic. He is first deputy chairman of the Council of Ministers of the U.S.S.R. and is responsible for managing major segments of Soviet industry. Though he was once considered a rising star with prime ministerial potential, Aliyev's influence has apparently faded.

Mikhail S. Solomentsev (72) is chairman of the Party Control Committee. He is one of the older Politburo members and also predates Gorbachev.

Vladimir V. Shcherbitsky (67), the Ukrainian party chief and a professional apparatchik, is also one of the older Politburo members. Dinmukhamed A. Kunayev (74), another non-Russian, is party secretary of the Kazakh Soviet Socialist Republic, the largest of the Central Asian republics and a major agricultural region. Kunayev, like Shcherbitsky, has little involvement in foreign affairs. Both men go to Moscow infrequently, spend most of their time in their republics, and, although they are both voting members, do not attend all Politburo meetings.

Viktor V. Grishin (71), another of the older generation, was retired at the end of 1985 from his important post as Moscow party boss. He will inevitably lose his Politburo membership in the near future.

Among several candidate (nonvoting) members of the Politburo, Boris N. Ponomarev (80) deserves special attention. He is a longtime party secretary and chief of the Central Committee's International Department. Ponomarev is responsible for the guidance and oversight of Communist parties in capitalist countries. He is also in charge of liaison with the Social Democrat parties. He oversees the World Peace Council and a number of similar movements.

Further personnel changes in the top Kremlin leadership and in the provinces were expected at the Communist Party congress scheduled for February 1986. This would be the first congress under Gorbachev. A revised party program and statute was expected to win approval, along with Gorbachev's economic plan.

The Struggle with Capitalism

To implement the present economic program, the Soviet leadership needs, first and foremost, a climate of international stability and normal relations with Western industrialized nations. Only this will allow Gorbachev to devote proper attention to the U.S.S.R.'s pressing domestic problems. At the same time, such an atmosphere will facilitate Soviet economic cooperation and trade with the West. Gorbachev's only real option in this respect, if he is to begin the massive efforts required to keep the U.S.S.R. from sinking further into its economic morass, is to avoid any major confrontation with the West in the near future.

But the revised party program, along with a number of Gorbachev's speeches—most of which have drawn amazingly little attention—indicates with absolute clarity that his calls for normalization or détente with the West are merely tactical maneuvers and do not represent a change in strategic policy.

In no way will this latest Gorbachev tactic supersede the Marxist-Leninist idea of final victory through a worldwide Soviet-style revolutionary process. Although the Kremlin is committed to the ultimate vision of a world under its control, the leaders are realistic enough to understand that at the present time this is impossible. But they are patient and take the long view. They wait and work

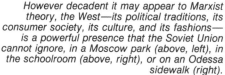

However decadent it may appear to Marxist theory, the West—its political traditions, its consumer society, its culture, and its fashions— is a powerful presence that the Soviet Union cannot ignore, in a Moscow park (above, left), in the schoolroom (above, right), or on an Odessa sidewalk (right).

toward a clear goal. To be sure, the notion held by some in the West that the Soviet leaders have a secret master plan, a timetable for conquering the world's nations one by one, is pure fiction; but while no such specific plan exists on paper, the idea of expanding Soviet power to the point of world domination is a fundamental long-range aspiration. Whether through ideology, diplomacy, force, or economics, Soviet leaders believe that eventually they will be supreme—not necessarily in this century but certainly in the next—in the competition between socialist and capitalist systems, and that such a struggle will be progressively intensified and is historically inevitable. In other words, those goals cannot be comprehended as the mere continuation of historical Russian imperialist designs or as simple power politics. Those goals are much broader

than simple imperialism and are deeper ideologically than common politics.

It is essential to understand the nature of this international struggle that is so central to our time, and to which Gorbachev is as committed as were any of his predecessors. In the West, unfortunately, not only do some of the general populace trust the Kremlin's repeated protestations that it wants only to coexist peacefully with the West, but there are also quite a few politicians, Kremlinologists or Sovietologists, and journalists who place their hopes before considerable evidence to the contrary. Of course, such voices carry weight and are therefore often profoundly misleading to the public. Such wishful thinking on the part of many otherwise hardheaded realists in the West flows from confusion about Soviet tactics and strategy.

To be sure, the Soviet tactic is to avoid any reference to the general, ultimate objectives of world Communism. Addressing the West, Soviets deliberately create the impression that they no longer believe in certain old goals left over from Marx. The Soviet leadership does not hesitate to employ mendacity in its efforts to gull the Western public. I remember a meeting at which both Brezhnev and Gromyko reminded us that it was advisable to avoid any direct references to "inevitable socialist revolutions" in our conversations with people in the West. But inside the U.S.S.R. Soviet leaders and ideologists have never tried to hide their true convictions. In his speeches in the Soviet Union, Gorbachev boldly declared: "Capitalism has no future.... We are convinced that social progress cannot be stopped, that the historic process of mankind's transition to socialism cannot be impeded."

It is an old message that has been restated at every party congress, but perhaps because it is old it does not strike the ear as forcefully or as alarmingly as it did earlier in the century. Nevertheless, it is meant today as it was meant in 1917. Some of the methods and styles of implementation have changed, but the underlying desire of the Soviet Union's leaders to dominate the Earth remains ever fresh. For our survival, we in the West must understand that, despite our intention to live peacefully together forever, the Soviet intention is to conquer.

In order to widen their zone of control or influence, Soviet leaders are focusing their attention on support of various national liberation movements in Asia, Africa, and Latin America while pursuing subversive activities in the West through Commu-

nist parties and other organizations. They provide matériel and military help, training, and ideological indoctrination.

For the time being, the Soviet Union needs the West. It has used détente successfully before to get what it wanted: amicable relations with the United States and Europe, trade credits, and substantial economic aid. The U.S.S.R. realizes that it can obtain that assistance only from the West. How would the leadership provide bread for its citizens if not for American and other nations' grain sales? Where else can the Soviets secure advanced technology that they are incapable of producing in sufficient quantity or of adequate quality for themselves? In this connection, it does indeed seem that Lenin was right: capitalists are willing to fight for the privilege of selling Communists the rope that the Communists will use to hang them.

But I believe that Gorbachev and his followers, like his predecessors, do not intend to achieve victory by resorting to nuclear war with the U.S. and its allies. As long as the strategic nuclear deterrent of the U.S. is strong enough, nuclear war is something Soviet leaders might contemplate only in the most extreme circumstances, if they were absolutely convinced that the country was in mortal peril and they could see no alternative. They consider the prospect of worldwide nuclear war unthinkable, to be avoided at all costs, even at the expense of Soviet prestige. All Soviet leaders, the old as well as the new generation, understand perfectly that nuclear world war could bury Communism and capitalism in the same grave.

(continued on page 424)

Gorbachev and his Politburo, pictured along a boulevard in downtown Moscow: some old, some new, all facing serious problems but deeply reluctant to initiate thoroughgoing reforms.

WALLY MCNAMEE—WOODFIN CAMP & ASSOCIATES

Shevchenko

Arkadi Nikolaevich Shevchenko, the Soviet ambassador who was under secretary-general of the United Nations for political and Security Council affairs, startled the world when, in April 1978, he made public his decision to seek asylum in the United States. He was (and is to date) the highest ranking Soviet official ever to defect from the U.S.S.R., and he had reached his high position at the age of 42 after one of the most rapid series of career advances in Soviet history.

Shevchenko was born on Oct. 11, 1930, in Gorlovka, Ukrainian S.S.R. His father, a well-connected physician, moved the family in 1935 to the Crimean resort town of Yevpatoriya on the Black Sea, where he managed a hospital. Arkadi grew up there in generally comfortable circumstances.

Upon his graduation from secondary school in 1949, his father's political influence helped win him an appointment to the Moscow State Institute of International Relations, a much-coveted route to a life of luxury and foreign travel. When he graduated in 1954, he was offered a job with the KGB. He declined in favor of graduate studies and was surprised that there were no repercussions.

One of Shevchenko's fellow graduate students was Anatoli Gromyko, the son of the foreign minister, whom Arkadi first met when he and Anatoli were preparing a paper for joint publication and young Gromyko asked his father to read it and comment.

On the completion of his graduate work in 1956, Shevchenko was posted to the department of UN and disarmament affairs in the Foreign Ministry. In 1958, having been a faithful Komsomol member throughout his youth, he joined the Communist Party—a prerequisite to any hope of career advancement and foreign assignments. He was a staff member at a London disarmament conference and for three months a disarmament specialist with the Soviet UN delegation. There, despite the brevity of his visit and his constant strict surveillance by the KGB, he was greatly impressed by the openness of U.S. society.

When Nikita Khrushchev visited the United States in September 1960, Shevchenko was a member of the Soviet leader's party, and the visit and the sea voyage afforded an opportunity to become well acquainted with him. Three years later the rising young diplomat was assigned to the Soviet UN Mission as chief of its Division of Security Council and Political Affairs.

A few months before the maximum time that Soviet diplomats were allowed to spend in foreign posts was to expire for Shevchenko in 1970, Andrei Gromyko offered to make him his personal political adviser, with the rank of ambassador. The experience of regular meetings at the side of the powerful Gromyko enormously increased Shevchenko's familiarity with the very top level of Soviet leadership. One of the realizations this exposure brought him was the isolation of the ruling class from the Soviet people. In December 1972 Gromyko told Shevchenko that the UN job would be vacated and that he could have it. He accepted promptly.

The job was no bed of roses. Like all Soviet UN staff members, he was directly ordered to consider himself an agent of the Soviet government and to turn every opportunity to the advantage of the Soviet Union. His chief assistant and his chauffeur were both agents of the KGB. A number of Soviet employees on the UN staff were too busy as KGB operatives to do the UN's work. Also like all other Soviet UN personnel, he had to kick back a substantial portion of his generous UN salary to the Soviet mission. All this added to Shevchenko's growing disaffection with his government.

Throughout his meteoric rise in the Foreign Ministry, he had been oppressed by the fundamental contradiction between theory and practice at the top of the Soviet hierarchy, which condemned Western consumerism while immersing itself in luxury. He considered resigning and going home to fight the system from within but quickly realized that would take him to prison or a mental institution for the rest of his life. Although his wife made it evident that she would not defect, and although it probably meant never seeing his son and daughter again, he concluded that he could not continue his life of hypocrisy.

Through an American acquaintance he trusted, he sent word of his intentions in 1975. He was then contacted by the U.S. Central Intelligence Agency, at whose urging he agree to stay in place for a time and supply information that could enable U.S. analysts to understand Gromyko's thought processes, how Soviet policies are arrived at, and the like.

He remained in his double role until April 1978, when he was suddenly summoned home for consultations, a message he was sure meant he was under suspicion. After his defection he used his experience to further Western understanding of Soviet objectives and methods. He now resides in Washington, D.C., and is a consultant and lecturer on Soviet affairs. He is the author of the recent best-selling memoir *Breaking with Moscow*.

(continued from page 422)

Soviet political and military chiefs also realize that, even if the U.S.S.R. were to launch a pre-emptive nuclear strike, the American second-strike capability could still virtually wipe out most of the heart and brain of the Soviet Union. The Soviets cannot accept such a risk. At the same time, however, by projecting its military might over the globe, the U.S.S.R. does invite the risk that conventional conflicts and confrontations with the West could escalate out of control. Among the militant ideologues and the military, there are those who are willing to take such a gamble.

Gorbachev and the West

As far as the new Kremlin's foreign policy direction under Gorbachev is concerned, one can arrive at only one conclusion: except for style and some active tactical maneuvering, Gorbachev will essentially continue the foreign policy line of his forerunners. Since World War II Soviet-U.S. relations have occupied a special place in Soviet foreign policy. They were and are not just dealings between two powerful states but complex ties between the two poles of power in the world, between the mightiest forces of two opposite and competing sociopolitical systems.

Gorbachev appears to have embraced broadly Gromyko's attitude in this regard, which was that Soviet-U.S. relations are central and crucially important. I disagree with some Western analysts' assertions that Gorbachev is shifting the focus of foreign policy to relations with Europe and the third world. Those areas have been highly important centers of Soviet foreign affairs activity for a long time. Gorbachev's latest gambits in those regions do not represent something substantially new. There are also strong indications that Gorbachev, like Gromyko, assesses the United States in terms of its might and its potential as a Soviet rival in world affairs. It is likely that he believes the United States to be not only the Soviet Union's main adversary but also its partner as long as the interests of both nations—whether temporarily or in the long term—are parallel or coincide.

In October 1985 Gorbachev said that the Soviet leadership is "firmly committed to returning Soviet-American relations to a normal track, back onto the road of mutual understanding and cooperation."

During the early 1980s, when superpower relations worsened, the Kremlin lost more than it could afford. Soviet leaders want to avoid the risk of nuclear catastrophe. They are concerned about U.S. military programs. They have also had to adjust to the reality of the deployment of U.S. Pershing II and cruise missiles in Western Europe. They understand that poor relations with Washington have backfired in Western Europe, created strains among the Warsaw Pact countries, and given China a trump card to play against Moscow.

All these things have led the Kremlin leadership back to the necessity of resuming arms control negotiations with the United States and of adopting a somewhat more flexible position in those talks. The Soviet leaders have also indicated more willingness to compromise on some other issues, and they agreed to the summit meeting held in November 1985 in Geneva. That meeting was disappointing to many because no substantial agreements were reached. But resumption of such meetings between leaders after a long interval is in itself a success. If nothing else, the summits seem to help these partner/adversaries avoid misunderstandings that could easily bring on dangerous confrontations.

The joint statement of Pres. Ronald Reagan and General Secretary Gorbachev that emerged from the Geneva summit to the effect that nuclear war must never be initiated and their recognition that there can be no winner in such a war constitute a positive step toward preventing the possibility of a nuclear holocaust. The two leaders also agreed that neither side would seek military superiority.

Is the Soviet declaration that the Kremlin is not now seeking military superiority over the United States credible? My own experience tells me that, at least for the time being, Soviet leaders understand that, even if they should wish such superiority, it is beyond their ability because of their domestic economic problems, as well as the present U.S. administration's determination not to permit it. I

On the other side of the propaganda coin, the May Day festival in Moscow featured signs pinning the blame for the arms race and international tensions on the United States and its NATO allies.

APN/GAMMA/LIAISON

The International Festival of Youth and Students, the 12th of its kind, opened in Moscow in July 1985. The festival ran heavily to political and ideological propaganda aimed chiefly at convincing the world of the Soviet Union's dedication to peace.

remember Gromyko once telling me that if in the past one or another American president did not have such resolve, another would work to revitalize American strength.

The Kremlin feels comfortable with the present strategic nuclear balance. Soviet political leaders as well as military chiefs have openly expressed their satisfaction with the current state of affairs. Obviously, the Kremlin's paramount aim is to preserve the existing balance before embarking on any agreements about reducing nuclear arsenals. That is why it vehemently opposes the U.S. Strategic Defense Initiative (SDI), dubbed "Star Wars." But the U.S.S.R. is the only nation that has an operational ABM (antiballistic missile) system in place (the Galosh around Moscow) that can possibly stop over half of any incoming missiles. Despite U.S. assurances that the SDI design is purely defensive, Soviets portray it as a weapon meant to be used for a first-strike attack. At the Geneva summit and afterward, Gorbachev continued his vigorous campaign against SDI, stressing that pursuit of that program might wreck the fresh start in U.S.-Soviet relations and that it "will not only lead to a further arms race but it will mean that all restraints will be blown to the wind."

Strategic parity has cost the Kremlin dearly in the course of a relentless and unprecedented military buildup that has continued for many years. It is true that the SDI program, if it is possible to implement—and if some important elements of it can be carried out before the Soviet Union can follow suit—would drastically alter the balance between the two superpowers to U.S. advantage. The Soviet Union's greatest fear is that it will be left behind in an uncontrollable competition for more and more technologically sophisticated strategic and, particularly, space-based weaponry. Moscow is alarmed over the astronomical expenses that would be in-

evitable in a new armaments-in-space race. Such expenditures would strain the U.S.S.R.'s economic resources more than ever at a time when Gorbachev is desperately trying to improve Soviet economic performance.

In the United States there is heated debate on all sides regarding SDI. However, if we talk not about the deployment of strategic defensive systems but about research in this field, we should understand that research is essential for national security. It is also inevitable, since the Soviet Union has been engaged in the very same kind of research for a long time. If the U.S. curtails its SDI research, we might face a situation in which the Soviet Union secretly continued its own SDI program while we did nothing. The West and the United States cannot simply watch what might happen; we must proceed with SDI research. Gorbachev's ability to charm the people should not encourage the West to trust the Soviet Union. While the Soviets are not at present becoming more aggressive, they assuredly are not becoming less aggressive.

The U.S. and the Soviet Union seem to be moving to a new period in their relations in the aftermath of the Geneva summit, but it will be quite different from the détente of the Nixon and Carter years. Although a Soviet-U.S. dialogue at the highest level is to be resumed, with Gorbachev scheduled to visit the U.S. in 1986 and Reagan set to go to the U.S.S.R. in 1987, the present administration has no doubts about the nature of the Soviet system. The administration's key policymakers realize that many basic Soviet-U.S. differences are irreconcilable and will remain so. In his address to a joint session of Congress upon his return from Geneva, President Reagan stated: "The United States cannot afford illusions about the nature of the U.S.S.R. We cannot assume that their ideology and purpose will change. This implies enduring competition."

Similarly, Gorbachev declared that "our differences [with the U.S.] are tremendous." Yet both President Reagan and General Secretary Gorbachev agreed Geneva that the search for arms control agreements must be accelerated. Arms control is a complex matter, and the protracted deadlock in the Geneva talks will not be easy to break.

Gorbachev's Kremlin will certainly continue to attempt to split NATO and put the president, the Congress, and the American people at odds on this issue. Soviet leaders know that negotiations tend to have a calming effect. In the West there are already demands to stop some or all military programs because some people believe that we have to make unilateral concessions even before coming to the negotiating table. This theory is dangerous; it is the wrong way to approach the Kremlin. Moscow sees this attitude very clearly and has become expert at playing upon fears that feed, so naturally, upon other fears. On the other hand, we should not be discouraged or misled by Soviet attacks against U.S. policy in arms reduction. Regarding foreign policy generally and disarmament in particular, the Soviet Union has always taken a double-track approach: propaganda bluster on the one hand, coupled with realistic talks on the other.

The 1985 proposals from the U.S.S.R. to reduce U.S. and Soviet nuclear arms capable of reaching each other's territory by 50%, along with Gorbachev's new plan to eliminate nuclear weapons by the end of the century, should be welcomed. But is the Soviet Union serious in suggesting complete elimination of nuclear arsenals?

For a long time the Kremlin has publicly espoused the ultimate elimination of such weapons. However, I am sure that the Soviet leadership does not consider that goal achievable or even desirable. There should be no illusions that the Kremlin would agree to liquidate all nuclear weapons. Without them the U.S.S.R. would cease to be a real superpower capable of influencing world developments as it now does. Moscow enjoys the deference power invariably fosters and would never voluntarily strip itself of the cornerstone of that power. Beyond that, the Soviets would never trust their adversaries in the "imperialistic camp." There is also the matter of Moscow's relationship to China. The Soviets would never be willing to rely solely on conventional forces in case of military confrontation with Peking. Gorbachev once pointed out that: "While attaching great significance to the normalization of relations with the United States and to honest talks with it on all the topical problems of international life, at the same time, we never forget for a minute that the world is not limited to that country alone, but is a much bigger place."

Nevertheless, Kremlin interest in reducing the risk of nuclear war and the enormous burden of the arms race should not be underestimated. An unrestricted arms race and new weapons technology could introduce new instabilities and uncertainty.

There is also the urgent necessity of reallocating resources from the military to the civilian economy if there is to be any hope of improving the civilian economy's performance. In proportion to its gross national product, the U.S.S.R. spends more than the U.S. does on its military machine. Therefore, under Gorbachev's leadership, the Soviet Union might eventually be willing to go further in nuclear arms reduction and make more serious concessions than many people in the West are inclined to believe. Any chance to achieve that—and there are such opportunities now—should not be missed.

Dealing with the Kremlin

The West must deal with the Soviet Union, like it or not. There is more than enough rationale for this: the Soviet Union and the United States occupy unique positions of power that will inevitably affect mankind's future. Although East and West apply different rules of the game to their competition, it is imperative, if we are to avoid cataclysm, to maintain a dialogue with the U.S.S.R. to seek reasonable and practical accommodations—even cooperation—where our interests are in alignment. This cooperation is essential to resolving global problems, such as preventing accidental nuclear war and nuclear proliferation, reducing the level of military threat, and achieving progress in arms control. It is required to handle the crisis situations that will inevitably appear from time to time, irrespective of the status of Soviet-U.S. relations.

The faltering economy and other afflictions besetting the Soviet Union should not mislead anyone about the durability of its regime. There is no doubt that the U.S.S.R. is experiencing serious domestic and other difficulties, but it has overcome worse troubles in the past. It has both tremendous natural wealth and vast human resources. In their ability to withstand centuries—not decades—of hardship and privation and yet persevere, the Soviet people are unmatched by any nation on Earth, with the possible exception of the Chinese. The West, therefore, should not delude itself by focusing its attention exclusively on Soviet flaws and shortcomings. There have also been successes. It is premature to predict the imminent decline of the U.S.S.R. and its empire; matters must worsen considerably before this idea can be entertained realistically.

The United States sometimes lacks the steadiness needed to deal persuasively with the Soviets. Its policy toward the Soviet Union seems to jump from extreme to extreme. Yet I have never doubted that America's strength makes it the one power capable of forcing Moscow to restrain itself. This is something that can be achieved if American leaders do not forget an old and still true lesson: what the men in the Kremlin understand best is military and economic might, energetic political conviction, strength of will. If the West cannot confront the Soviets with equal determination, Moscow will continue to play the bully around the globe.

Asides

Not all the news events of 1985 made prominent headlines. Among items reported less breathlessly in the worldwide press were the following:

Mike Alley returned to his new Evansville, Ind., apartment and found it more spacious than he remembered. Perhaps that was because all his furniture was gone. Alley had only recently arranged a bed, couch, chair, and other items in his new home when the Salvation Army stopped by to pick up a donation left by the previous tenant. In Alley's absence, they assumed the furniture was the generous contribution and hauled it off. Alley's furnishings were to be returned. Meanwhile, the furniture originally meant for the donation remained nicely packed on the porch.

It wasn't April Fool's Day, but the gag stopped students at Greenwich (Conn.) Country Day School dead in their tracks. It was rumored in October that the ninth-grade biology class would be dissecting a human cadaver. It arrived a few days before Halloween, looking greenish-gray and with a tag at the toe. Instructor Peter French had the foresight to make the first incision himself—and when he did the corpse began to bleed. Suddenly it lunged forward, grabbed for one of the students, and then sat straight up, knocking over bottles and vials. Students screamed and dived for cover before they realized that the corpse was an actor and alumnus of the school, Ricky Ford. The blood was merely a prop, and the freshmen were treated to the trick by school headmaster Peter Briggs.

Jimmy Carter memorabilia is going for peanuts these days. In fact, much of it is being thrown away. Archivists planning the Jimmy Carter Library in Atlanta are sorting through 26 million pages of documents, 1.5 million photographs, and 40,000 objects from Carter's presidency. A lot of those objects aren't keepers. It seems that during his term in office, a number of Carter's well-wishers made him gift items from peanuts, and now the peanuts are rotting. One staffer described the smell as "god-awful." But if you were one of the gift givers, don't despair; your peanut project is gone but perhaps not forgotten. A photo is snapped of each one before it is popped into the trash.

Firefighters rescued Liz Villagomez by the skin of her teeth. And she was burning with embarrassment. Villagomez was stuck in a pair of designer jeans. She had tried on her cousin's jeans, and the zipper caught her skin a few inches below the navel. The cousin tried to free her to no avail, so they called the fire department. San Jose (Calif.) Capt. Bob Edwards ever so delicately secured her release, one tooth at a time.

It'll all come out in the wash, especially if alcohol loosens your tongue. Austin, Texas, entrepreneur Robb Walsh has opened the first combination laundromat and bar. For health code reasons, a glass wall divides the bar from the machines, enabling patrons to take a load off while still keeping an eye on their loads. Walsh sees it as a solution to the problem of boring hours spent idling in conventional laundromats. He also sees it as a great way for young singles to meet, and perhaps his romantic hunch is right. After less than a year in operation, Barwash was distinguished as the first American laundromat to be rented out for a wedding reception.

Looking for that special someone? Women who refer to the book *Outstanding Young Men in America* should beware. They could end up with a real dog. California resident Arthur Bernstein delights in signing up his dog, Jefferson M. Bernstein, for credit cards, charitable contributions, and lists such

You can lead a horse to water . . . *and if you don't, he may improvise. After five consecutive days of temperatures above 100° F (38° C) in Augusta, Georgia, Earl Porterfield's horse, Slick, wanted some refreshment. So he stationed himself next to a rotating lawn sprinkler and, encountering no nay-sayers, slurped a mouthful each time the water came around.*

AP/WIDE WORLD

A penny saved is a penny earned, and 1.1 million pennies saved is a new car. At least that's how it turned out for 16-year-old Penny Stevens of Kentucky. Her father began to save her namesake coin when she was born, and that sentimental gesture blossomed into 7,633 pounds of change. It took four trucks to get the pennies to a car dealer, where she exchanged them for a 1984 Chevrolet.

AP/WIDE WORLD

as "Outstanding Men." Mobil Oil was one of the companies nice enough to issue Jefferson a charge card. How does the pooch feel about his success? He seems to think it's a gas.

As any wedded couple can tell you, marriage can be a taxing experience. That is literally true in a West Java village, where officials have imposed a tax on getting married. The fee: ten rats. A horde of rats is plaguing area farmers, and the tax is a form of pest control. Any sparring spouses there should think twice about separation—the surcharge for a divorce is 20 rats.

When Timothy Ford shot a wild turkey, he found it was already stuffed. And he ran afoul of the law. A game warden saw Ford in the woods with a gun at a time when hunting is illegal and stealthily placed a phony bird under a bush. Minutes later, Ford's bullet sent its plastic head flying. Ford was brought up on charges of illegal wild turkey hunting, but the case was dismissed. Fake game is fair game in Massachusetts, ruled Judge Clement Ferris.

"How high is up?" is a question that has yet to be answered. But Chinese shoe manufacturers have taken a step in the right direction by deciding on "How high is high?" It's 2½ in (6⅓ cm) for women and 1½ in (3⅘ cm) for men. These are the maximum heights set by the manufacturers for the heels of shoes, reported the *China Daily*. This was decided upon "out of consideration for health," but it may well put the manufacturers on the wrong foot with China's youth, with whom high heels are the rage.

Truth in advertising takes on new meaning in the town of Hines, Ore., where a thriving local restaurant calls itself "The Worst Food in Oregon." Signs outside entice passersby with such catchy slogans as "Come in and sit with the flies!" and "Food is terrible—service is worse." The special of the day is usually leftovers from the day before, and the owner, Bernie Hannaford, claims to be a lousy cook brought up to tell the truth. But is it really the worst food in Oregon? One wouldn't think so from the volume of business done at the restaurant, but then many of the customers are one-time visitors—tourists and people who are just plain curious. And besides, the prices are probably the lowest in Oregon; Hannaford hasn't changed them since the diner opened in 1970.

An Indonesian villager named Tohiran takes a lofty view of bill collectors. To avoid paying a debt, he shinnied 65 ft (19.8 m) to the top of a coconut tree, and there he stayed . . . for 19 months at last report. Local officials have ordered him down to no avail. His wife is none too pleased. His stunt has made him a cult figure and now, in exchange for food and drink, he passes the time by singing songs and giving advice—including lottery predictions—to his admirers. Can anything persuade him to come down? The same thing that got him up there—as he says, "divine inspiration."

Think your co-worker is out of this world? He or she may be a space alien, says a supermarket tabloid that claims extraterrestrials are common in the United States. The ever helpful paper supplied ten signs to help us recognize aliens. They include: bizarre sense of humor (an alien might laugh during a serious company training film, for example), strange eating habits (eating French fries with a spoon), talking to oneself (to practice "foreign" Earth languages), and mood swings initiated by high-tech hardware (reacting emotionally when a microwave oven is turned on). Surprisingly, the major news services didn't pick up on this story. Perhaps they were afraid of alienating their audience.

Make a fashion statement and you may become a fashion victim; that is, if you are an American airman in Europe. The United States Air Force's European headquarters recently announced that the wearing of earrings by airmen on base is forbidden, even off duty. Air force brass have always prohibited the wearing of earrings by men in uniform because it is not consistent with the military image. But now it seems that understated accessories are the key for off-duty dress as well.

Saved by the beep. Who at some time hasn't longed to extricate himself from a tedious conversation or tiresome situation? Well, now you can, and maybe enhance your image at the same time, with the Timely Beeper. The Timely Beeper sounds just like the beepers that doctors, executives, and others carry when they are on call or are awaiting important information. But unlike the conventional beeper, which is activated by a distant party wishing to convey a message to the beeper wearer, the Timely Beeper is secretly activated by the wearer. The False Alarm, as it is also called, allows you to pretend urgent business awaits. You free yourself from an uncomfortable position and seem indispensable at the same time. Evidently this gimmick is working; since its introduction, sales of the beeper have taken off at an alarming rate.

More than one family has had a figurative skeleton in the closet, but a family in Tennessee had a literal head in the attic for over a hundred years. During the 1850s an amateur explorer named Archibald Marvine brought a red-haired mummy head home from Egypt. It was passed down from generation to generation and stored in the attic until it reached Claire Austin, the present owner. She is loaning it to Memphis State University, where 17 scientists are studying it to determine whether it originally belonged to a male or female, what that person's social status was, and how long ago that person lived. The relic may be 2,000 years old, and it is one of the best preserved mummy heads discovered to date. The head has been exposed to academic environments many times before; Austin claims that children in the family used to take it to school for show and tell.

A policeman in India enjoyed a "conscience-ness"-raising experience. The officer, Bevara Samuel, had never forgotten an incident from his childhood. He had taken a train from one city to another and neglected to buy a ticket. So, 20 years later, he assuaged his nagging conscience and sent the railway company what he recollected to be the price of the ticket: 30 rupees. The railway collection office was grateful but felt obliged to indicate that the actual fare was 71 rupees. The scrupulous Samuel sent the balance a week later.

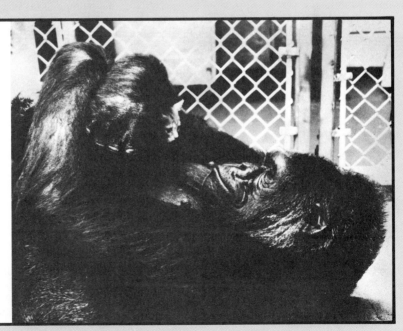

Love struck twice for Koko, the famous gorilla who knows about 500 words in American Sign Language. Koko was given a pet kitten in 1984, and the two became fast friends. When the cat, whom Koko named All Ball, was killed by an automobile, the primate was miserable. Koko recovered enough to indicate that she wanted a replacement, and she chose an orange Manx cat. Manx cats have no tails, and look very similar to the late, also tailless All Ball. The new kitten, pictured here, found a place in Koko's heart, and the happy gorilla signed "Baby" and "My cat good." Koko's neighbor, a gorilla named Michael, evidently thinks the kitten is cute enough to eat; he suggested the cat be named Banana.

AP/WIDE WORLD

AP/WIDE WORLD

Look who's hogging the ice! Engineering students at Quebec's Laval University tried to win a contest for best campus joke by casting this pig in a referee's shirt and other swine onto the ice during a hockey match at Quebec Coliseum. Game officials thought the students were out of bounds and quickly tossed the pigs out of the game.

It was a dream come true for 1,651 Shelton, Conn., students. Their report cards were mailed out but miraculously did not arrive in their parents' mailboxes. They did arrive at the Shelton post office two weeks later, mysteriously bearing Oakland, Calif., postmarks—well after unamused school officials had reprinted and remailed the cards.

Fidel Castro's government is revolutionizing the naming of children. Havana radio announced that in the future, babies must be registered with no more than two names, and that those names must be easy to read and pronounce and must correspond with the tradition and cultural development of the Cuban people. Many Cubans have long, seemingly complicated names that honor relatives, patron saints, or historical figures, and the government (which discourages religious practices) wants to make life simpler for the children of the future. The government also wants to make life less embarrassing for them. One other stipulation of the name law is that children must be given the names of persons rather than the names of things. This comes too late to help, for example, Biela and Propela, twin Cuban girls whose names in English are Connecting Rod and Propeller.

It is never advisable to leave money lying around. In California it's illegal. The state has determined that money is a health hazard. The Federal Reserve Bank of San Francisco shreds and must dispose of two tons of old paper money each day. Greenbacks contain relatively large amounts of lead and copper, and if they were taken to a common garbage dump, those elements could leach into the ground and trickle down to contaminate drinking water. So to waste money, workers seal the shredded bills in containers and transport them to a special dump for highly toxic materials.

Years ago, residents of Asia might have thought "junk food" referred to meals prepared on a boat. Now they know better. Urban Koreans and Taiwanese can purchase such Western delicacies as pizza and hamburgers and are doing so at a rapid rate. Fast-food chains, such as McDonald's, Pizza Hut, and Kentucky Fried Chicken, are scrambling to expand their operations in Asia, especially with an eye toward the 1988 Seoul Olympics. Fast food is the cheapest Western food available, and teenagers seem most willing to sample such oddities as hambogus, chicken *hurai,* and *pija* (hamburgers, fried chicken, and pizza). At last report, Mrs. Fields and Famous Amos were looking toward Taiwan with hopes of amassing cookie fortunes.

Lincoln the cat is keeping pace with medical advances. In December the 11-year-old Siamese survived an operation to implant a human pacemaker. A laboratory experiment? No, Lincoln is a housecat who was given only a month to live with his failing heart. So his loving owner gave doctors at New York State College of Veterinary Medicine the OK to implant the pacemaker. The cat's owner, Douglas Thompson, is delighted with the results, and he says that Lincoln looks less than regal but is again king of the household, bounding about the rooms. And it's no wonder; Lincoln's pacemaker is set not to a sluggish human rate of 72 beats per minute but to a kittenish 130.

Traffic was light as 87-year-old Jack Comiskey and his wife, Winifred, drove down a Florida thruway at a comfortable and safe 50 mph (81 km/h). There was almost a snarl, however, when that airplane headed their way, but things had really come to a halt by the time the waters of Tampa Bay began seeping through their floorboards. The two took a wrong turn onto an airport runway and, unconcerned, drove on though an airplane cleared for landing there barely managed to avoid them. Comiskey came to the end of the runway and blazed a trail through a grassy strip, right into Tampa Bay. Firefighters who happened to be training nearby rescued the unhurt but very surprised couple.

New Words

Language constantly changes. New words and word meanings are forever coming into the vocabulary; old ones die out. Some new words are only passing fads and are forgotten as soon as the group that originally used them gives them up. Others gain wider acceptance and become part of the living language.

The following list of new words and meanings is a sampling of the continuing change and growth of our language. Some of these entries may be forgotten next year; some may last as long as the English language itself.

air guitar: an imaginary guitar played in imitation of rock musicians, especially to recorded music

chill out: to relax, calm down, take it easy; similar to the relatively ancient slang term cool out

closed caption: describes a service by which a hearing-impaired individual can receive visual captions of television program dialogue on his or her screen by means of a decoder in the television set

computer orphan: a computer model that has been discontinued; the owner of such a computer, who faces difficulties in finding service, extra parts, and programs

courseware *n:* computer software, whether on cartridges, tapes, or disks or accessed on-line, that is especially designed for use in school classrooms

crack *n:* highly concentrated cocaine

croissantization *n:* the inclusion of croissant rolls in a previously croissantless diet, sometimes as a direct result of Yuppification

ethnotherapy *n:* psychological therapy expressly for persons of an ethnic group who have trouble adjusting to the unfamiliar culture that surrounds them

flap word: a word or phrase that elaborately states a plain fact or is used to hide the fact that nothing of import is being said at all; *e.g.,* a government might use the flap word escalation of military activity to sugarcoat the announcement that war has broken out

hothousing *n:* the attempt, sometimes inappropriate, to accelerate early intellectual development in infants, toddlers, and young children through formal programs inside and outside the home

involuntary smoker: a nonsmoker who is forced to inhale the smoke—and the tar, nicotine, carbon monoxide, and other toxic substances—exhaled by nearby smokers

legs *n:* endurance or staying power, as a film deplored by the critics that achieves popularity through word of mouth, thereby acquiring "legs," and enjoys a long run

JACQUES M. CHENET/NEWSWEEK

Hothousing of infants and toddlers has become a hot new trend among certain U.S. parents, especially among older, more affluent, and more competitive ones. Many child psychologists deplore the trend, urging parents to play with their kids instead.

Pray TV is the electronic pulpit of televangelists. Pray TV is also big business: In 1985 televangelists purchased between $1 billion and $2 billion worth of television and radio time just for advertising fund-raising appeals.

STEVE LISS—GAMMA/LIAISON

lock box: a device, often used for the protection of children, that prevents the unauthorized use of equipment such as televisions or thermostats

manny *n:* a male nanny; like a nanny he cares for children in their homes and performs many tasks normally taken on by parents

network *v:* to interact socially with large groups of acquaintances, co-workers, or total strangers with the intent of forming friendships that may also provide good business connections

Paideia *n:* a proposal for public education that would educate children up to the age of 12 in a uniform manner, focusing on knowledge, skill, and aesthetics; also called **core curriculum**

pray TV: television programming with a religious format, found most commonly on special cable stations, presided over by a televangelist

puzzle palace: a large, bureaucratic government organization, the operation and functions of which are confusing to the outsider and, sometimes, even to the insider

rad *adj:* (pronounced more like "rod") slang for with it, acceptable, admirable, very good, right, or aware; neither Yuppies nor croissants are rad

readathon or **read-a-thon** *n:* a reading marathon; a large amount of reading performed in a relatively short amount of time, or sustained over a specific period of time, usually as a group endeavor, sometimes to raise money for charity

Silicon Valley: a concentration of companies, especially electronics companies, in one geographical area; taken from silicon, an element used in computers and other electronic devices

soapcom *n:* a daily or weekly television show that combines comedy with the plot lines of a soap opera. Note: Comedy is intentional, not to be confused with unintentional comedy to be found in pure soap opera

speedboard *n:* a sailboard, or surfboard fitted with mast and sail, designed especially for racing

sunrise industry: an industry with a bright future, having good potential for growth and steady increase in profit

sunset industry: an industry with dim prospects for the future

techno-bandit *n:* a person who purchases high-technology products for delivery to countries to which the United States has banned the sale of such technology, of special concern when the sale of militarily useful technology is involved

technophobe *n:* a person who fears the adverse effect technology may have on society, the environment, or himself or herself

televangelist *n:* a star of pray TV; Protestant minister who uses television as his or her preaching medium

time compression: the speeding up of a television program with little or no perceivable effect on sound or action quality, to shorten its playing time; used primarily to fit more commercial time into syndicated reruns

time shifting: the recording of a television program on tape for viewing at a later time

yuplash *n:* rebellion against the Yuppie (young urban professional) life-style; includes rejection of the ideal of conspicuous consumption and, perhaps, of croissantization

JOHN SEVERSON/WIND SURF MAGAZINE

Speedboards, like the one piloted by Jenna de Rosnay, the 1982 women's world speed record holder, have become popular leisure craft.

Silicon Valley, centered in Santa Clara County, California, is a high-technology spawning ground for the electronics industry. The term Silicon Valley is becoming generic, applicable to any concentration of companies, especially electronics companies, anywhere.

JAMES D. WILSON/NEWSWEEK

Biographies

The following is a selected list of men and women who influenced events significantly in 1985.

Alexander, Lincoln

On Sept. 20, 1985, Lincoln Alexander was installed as the 24th lieutenant governor of Ontario. Thus he became the first black person to hold a vice-regal office in Canada. Upon assuming the position, he was entitled to a 15-gun salute as the chief executive officer of Ontario and the representative of H.M. Queen Elizabeth II in the province.

Alexander began his career in public office in 1968, when, in the face of the Liberal Party's sweep of that year's general election, he became the first black member of the Canadian Parliament and the only member of the Progressive Conservative Party to be elected from an Ontario urban center. As member of Parliament for Hamilton West, he earned a reputation for honesty and directness. In the House of Commons he served his party as spokesman on such subjects as housing, labor, manpower, unemployment, immigration, and welfare. He was also designated observer to the UN (1976, 1978). When the Conservatives formed a government after the 1979 general election, Prime Minister Joe Clark appointed him minister of labor in his short-lived Cabinet.

Born Jan. 21, 1922, in Toronto, Lincoln Mac-Caulay Alexander served as a radio operator in the Royal Canadian Air Force during World War II. In 1949 he received his B.A. from McMaster University in Hamilton, Ont. After his graduation from Osgoode Hall Law School in Toronto (1953), Alexander practiced as a criminal lawyer in Hamilton. In 1965 he was given the honorary title of queen's counsel by the Ontario government. His law partners helped engender in him an interest in politics that led to his running for Parliament.

In 1980 Alexander resigned his parliamentary seat to become chairman of the Ontario Workers' Compensation Board. He received the Man of the Year Award from the Ethnic Press Council of Canada in 1982, and the following year he was made a Commander of the Order of St. John. As lieutenant governor, Alexander became the chief of state of the province of Ontario. His duties included summoning and dissolving the provincial legislature, giving assent to legislative bills, and reading the speech from the throne at the opening of each legislative session.

Bacon, Francis

A major retrospective held at London's Tate Gallery during May–August 1985 provided ample opportunity to study the art of Francis Bacon, widely considered one of the finest and most relevant artists of the mid-20th century, perhaps even the greatest living painter. Bacon's timeless, haunting, anguished images were totally individual yet firmly within the tradition of Michelangelo, Rembrandt, and Velázquez.

Bacon's paintings, whether portraits or religious or literary subjects, were characterized by a vivid central image, rendered often with a thick impasto of paint and in minute detail, set against a bleak background that isolated the image from its surroundings. This formal juxtaposition, combined with the often-disturbing central image, reinforced the sense of alienation. The images themselves were recognizable yet somehow disjointed and disturbing—familiar elements were distorted and recombined in frightening yet vivid ways. The screaming mouth, the bloody carcass, or the haunted veiled visage were characteristic Bacon images; few artists

TERENCE SPENCER—CAMERA PRESS, LONDON

had managed to convey such a powerful message of horror and decay.

Bacon was born in Dublin on Oct. 28, 1909, the son of an English horse trainer working in Ireland. Lacking formal schooling, he moved to London in 1925 and a few years later traveled to Berlin and Paris, where he was impressed by the work of Picasso and inspired to start drawing and painting. For a few years he worked as an interior decorator and designer of furniture. In 1929 he began, entirely self-taught, to paint in oils, and by 1931 he had begun to concentrate exclusively on painting. His first major work was "Crucifixion 33," which gained public attention when it was published in critic Sir Herbert Read's *Art Now* (1933). In 1934 he had his first one-man show in London.

After 1962, when Bacon had his first major Tate Gallery retrospective, his work was widely shown in Europe and the U.S. Themes to which he frequently returned included portraits of popes, the Crucifixion, and portraits of friends. His central images were usually human or animal.

Baker, James

In February 1985 Donald Regan succeeded James Baker as chief of staff at the White House, and Baker succeeded Regan as secretary of the treasury. In their new roles both men continued to be influential in the administration of Pres. Ronald Reagan. Baker, a respected political strategist who had never before worked intensively in finance, remained a designated member of the National Security Council. In April President Reagan instructed heads of departments and other ranking officials to meet as the Economic Policy Council, with Baker as chairman, whenever economic policies were to be formulated.

In June, at a meeting in Tokyo of officials of 11 of the most economically important non-Communist nations, Baker successfully advocated floating exchange rates for national currencies. But later, on September 22, Baker, never a free-trade ideologue, met officials of four of those same nations in New York City and secured from them promises of help in reducing the exchange rate of the U.S. dollar.

In October, at a meeting of the International Monetary Fund in Seoul, South Korea, Baker presented a plan to help the heavily indebted governments of several less developed countries. The plan called for the Fund to offer assistance, for the World Bank to guarantee private loans, and for the assisted governments to follow free-market policies.

Baker was born in Houston, Texas, on April 28, 1930. In 1952 he received a B.A. from Princeton University. After serving as a lieutenant in the U.S. Marine Corps from 1952 to 1954, he received a law degree from the University of Texas in 1957 and joined the law firm of Andrews, Kurth, Campbell & Jones in Houston. In 1970 he worked on George Bush's campaign for the U.S. Senate from Texas and first publicly declared himself a Republican.

He became an undersecretary in the Department of Commerce in 1975. In 1976 he resigned that job, worked on Gerald Ford's campaign for the presidency, and then rejoined Andrews, Kurth, Campbell & Jones.

In 1980 Baker managed George Bush's presidential campaign and then campaigned for the Reagan-Bush ticket. As chief of staff to President Reagan from 1981 to 1985, he ran the White House staff in close collaboration with two long-time aides to Reagan, Michael Deaver, the deputy chief of staff, and Edwin Meese, counselor to the president.

Ballard, Robert

At two o'clock in the morning on Sept. 1, 1985, in the North Atlantic some 560 mi (900 km) south of Newfoundland, the U.S. Navy research ship *Knorr* slowly cruised the dark swells. About 13,000 ft (4,000 m) beneath the *Knorr,* tethered to it by a thick steel cable and skimming the ocean bottom in icy darkness, was a 16-ft (5-m) submersible robot sled christened *Argo.* Suddenly *Argo*'s video cameras, working in the glare of searchlights, sent to television screens aboard the *Knorr* images of the greatest shipwreck of all time. Resting upright on the edge of a submarine canyon, shorn of its stern and two of its four smokestacks yet otherwise beautifully preserved after 73 years, lay the ocean liner *Titanic.* Robert Ballard's search was over.

As head of the Deep Submergence Laboratory of the Woods Hole (Mass.) Oceanographic Institution, Ballard designed *Argo* and was in charge of testing it for the Navy. He chose the *Titanic* as his goal because it had sunk in a depth ideal for testing the deep-sea explorer. Teaming up with the French vessel *Le Suroit,* which until late June conducted its search for the ocean liner by towing an unmanned submersible equipped with side-scanning sonar for mapping the ocean bottom, the *Knorr* began combing the site of the disaster in early August. After *Argo*'s cameras picked up pictures of a large riveted metal cylinder (a *Titanic* boiler), the *Titanic* was located by the *Knorr*'s 25-year-old sonar system. *Argo* and an older Woods Hole sled, *Angus,* snapped 12,000 color photos. Mission accomplished, Ballard and his team returned home to worldwide acclaim.

Robert Duane Ballard was born in Wichita, Kan., on June 30, 1942. In 1966, a year after graduating with a degree in chemistry and geology from the University of California at Santa Barbara, he joined the U.S. Navy and was assigned as liaison officer for the Office of Naval Research at Woods Hole. He became a civilian researcher there three years later, at first working with *Alvin,* a three-man submersible. In 1973–75 he dived 9,000 ft (2,750 m) in *Alvin* and in a French submersible to explore the Mid-Atlantic Ridge. In 1976 he took *Alvin* 12,000 ft (3,660 m) down into the Cayman Trench in the Caribbean, and in 1977 and 1979 he joined an international team exploring hydrothermal vents in the Galápagos Rift and the East Pacific Rise.

CAMERA PRESS, LONDON

Becker, Boris

He looked reckless, dashing and diving around the tennis court. But Boris Becker became the darling of professional tennis in 1985 by coolly channeling that energy, imposing Björn Borg's self-control on John McEnroe's fury. "He never thinks about the pressure," said Henri LeConte, whom Becker defeated in the Wimbledon quarterfinals. "He just plays, hits the ball, wins, says 'Thank you' and 'goodbye.' "

Becker won the Wimbledon final 6–3, 6–7, 7–6, 6–4 over Kevin Curren. He thus became the first West German, the first unseeded player, and, at 17 years, 7 months, the youngest male to win Wimbledon in its 99 years. He was the youngest to win any Grand Slam tournament. Becker's style made his youth all the more remarkable. Tennis's precocious children most often are conservative baseline players, but Becker was a serve-and-volley man. He served 21 aces against Curren.

Becker was born Nov. 22, 1967, in Leimen, West Germany, a bedroom community of 17,300 near Heidelberg. His father, architect Karl-Heinz Becker, designed and built the tennis center where Boris learned the game. He was 12 when he chose to forgo his promise in soccer and concentrate on tennis. He was 16 when his long-time coach Gunther Bosch introduced him to manager Ion Tiriac.

That summer, 1984, Becker won his third consecutive West German junior championship. He won 11 of 22 matches in 13 tournaments, climbing from 200th to 65th in the world rankings. Tiriac put him on a rigorous winter training program, ignoring advice that it would wear out the youngster. Becker responded by vaulting to sixth in the rankings at the end of 1985.

Becker won his first professional tournament the week before Wimbledon, the Queen's Club men's grass court championship in London. After his Wimbledon triumph he defeated third-ranked Mats Wilander for the Association of Tennis Professionals championship and led his country past the United States to the Davis Cup final. There he did well—again beating Wilander—although his team lost to Sweden 3–2.

Berri, Nabih

Minister of state for southern Lebanon and justice minister in Lebanon's national unity government formed in April 1984, Nabih Berri was better known as the leader since 1980 of Amal (the Movement of Hope), a militia organization representing the Shi'ite community in Lebanon (about 40% of the nation's population). Its role in the 1985 hijacking of a Trans World Airlines aircraft and Berri's role in the negotiations to release hostages propelled Amal into international prominence. Amal was considered a more moderate organization than more fundamentally religious Shi'ite groups such as Hizballah ("Party of God") and Islamic Amal (influenced by the Islamic regime in Iran).

Born about 1938 in Sierra Leone, then a British colony, Berri was the son of a Lebanese merchant there. He moved to Lebanon as a boy, studied law at the Lebanese University in Beirut (graduating in 1963), and subsequently studied in France. He practiced as a lawyer in Beirut and joined Amal when it was formed in 1974. Four years later he became its leader. His first wife was a U.S. citizen, and he held a "green card" entitlement to residence in the U.S., enabling him to visit his children there.

Berri became known for his moderate secular views. His influence on Amal changed it from a rel-

JAMES MEECHAN—CAMERA PRESS, LONDON

atively obscure movement to a structured politico-military group. Amal was opposed to the partition of Lebanon, urging greater civil rights for the Shi-'ites, who saw themselves as the most deprived sect in the nation. As a minister in the government, Berri participated in talks aimed at persuading Israel to withdraw from Lebanon in 1985, although many Shi'ites believed that Lebanon should not even talk to Israel. He and his Amal militia helped to secure the release of one American and a Frenchman kidnapped by extremists in early 1984.

Under Berri's leadership Amal was involved in armed clashes with Israeli forces, Maronite Christians, Palestinians, Sunnite Muslims, and even the Druze, with whom Amal was allied. Despite his credentials as a moderate, Berri was forced to take responsibility and criticism for the radical actions of his militia. His contacts with Western diplomats resulted in his becoming a valued intermediary on Lebanon's increasingly unstable political scene.

Boesak, Allan Aubrey

With most leading black nationalist politicians under detention or in exile, two South African church leaders assumed an increasingly important role in the struggle against apartheid (racial separation). Protected both by their religious calling and by their high international standing, Bishop Desmond Tutu, the 1984 Nobel Peace Prize winner, and the Rev. Allan Boesak were able to establish themselves as two of the most influential spokesmen of non-white South Africans. In 1982 Boesak became president of the World Alliance of Reformed Churches (WARC), which spoke for 70 million Protestants around the world. He was also patron of the United

Democratic Front (UDF), which he helped establish. A loose federation of several hundred social, political, civic, and religious associations, the UDF tried to fill the vacuum in national politics caused by the banning of the black political parties.

Ordained in 1968, Boesak was a clergyman in the Dutch Reformed Church (DRC), which was closely identified with the apartheid system. Racially, he was himself classified as Coloured, a person of mixed-race descent. Boesak was persuaded that he could be more effective by remaining within the DRC. Having influenced the WARC (with which the DRC was affiliated) to denounce apartheid as a heresy, Boesak tried to persuade the DRC to endorse this stand. His career in the church was briefly threatened when the police leaked documents alleging that he was engaging in extramarital relations with a white church worker; however, he was cleared by the church authorities. He was arrested in August 1985 when he attempted to lead a mass march to Pollsmoor Prison near Cape Town to protest against the continued detention of Nelson Mandela. He was released on bail, and his passport was later withdrawn.

Boesak was born in 1946 in Kakmas, an isolated village in arid northwestern Cape of Good Hope, the seventh of eight children. His father was a teacher and his mother a seamstress. With the help of scholarships he was able to complete his theological studies at the Calvinist theological seminary in Kempen, Neth. As a student he was inspired by the anti-Nazi German theologian Dietrich Bonhoeffer, by Martin Luther King, Jr., and by the dissident DRC Afrikaner clergyman the Rev. W. C. Beyers Naude.

Botha, P(ieter) W(illem)

A miscued speech by Pres. P. W. Botha in August 1985 tumbled South Africa into an unprecedented financial crisis during which the value of its rand currency was cut in half. His speech had been given a lengthy buildup, leading Western governments and international bankers, as well as domestic critics of apartheid (the policy of racial separation), to expect a major pronouncement about a program of reforms that would bring hope of peaceful political change in South Africa and restore international confidence in its long-term future.

Explaining later why he made the kind of speech that he did, Botha said that he was determined to show that he would not be "pushed around" (one of his favorite phrases) by his critics. Throughout a long political career spanning over half a century, Botha had invariably reacted negatively and aggressively to any action or suggestion that he believed to be hostile. Prickly and choleric, he was, nevertheless, a formidable politician—unquestionably the strongest white leader in South Africa.

Botha was committed to phasing out apartheid laws and to a policy of negotiating with representative black leaders about a new constitution for

JAN KOPEC—CAMERA PRESS, LONDON

showing that a high concentration of cholesterol in the bloodstream is a sign of a defect in the cells rather than the blood.

Brown was born on April 13, 1941, in New York City. He attended the University of Pennsylvania, receiving a bachelor's degree in 1962 and a doctorate from the School of Medicine in 1966. After spending two years at Massachusetts General, he and Goldstein moved to Bethesda, Md., to join different components of the National Institutes of Health. Brown became affiliated with the National Institute of Arthritis and Metabolic Diseases and the laboratory of biochemistry of the National Heart Institute; he concentrated on gastroenterology and the functions of the enzymes involved in the digestion of food. As he and Goldstein gained clinical experience with patients suffering from disorders of cholesterol metabolism, they began to formulate a program in which their complementary skills could be brought to bear on the study of these ailments.

In 1971 Brown accepted an appointment to the faculty of the Southwestern Medical School of the University of Texas at Dallas. In 1977 he was named Paul J. Thomas professor of genetics and director of the Center for Genetic Diseases at the university's Health Science Center. When Brown and Goldstein were reunited in Dallas in 1972, they set their plans in motion. Within a year they were able to announce a major discovery: that the process by which the cells absorb cholesterol from the bloodstream depends on the presence of specific receptors on the cell surface, and that the absence of those receptors results from a genetic defect. In children inheriting this defect from both parents, the cells are almost completely incapable of removing cholesterol from the blood. During the first few years of life the circulation to the heart can become so severely impaired that the child suffers a crippling or fatal heart attack.

South Africa, but in implementing those policies he found himself trapped between two opposing forces: conservative elements within the Afrikaner (majority white) electorate who were totally opposed to abandoning apartheid, and an increasingly militant black opposition, angry and frustrated by the failure to move faster toward ending the discredited system. Even such a skillful politician as Botha found it difficult to steer his way between those conflicting forces.

Botha was born in a village in the Orange Free State on Jan. 12, 1916. After college he became an organizer of the Cape Province National Party at the age of 20. Twelve years later he entered Parliament with an established reputation as a shrewd party organizer. After holding several Cabinet posts, he became defense minister in 1966 and set about building his power base. He became known as the spokesman for the Army, and under his leadership the South African Defence Force grew into what might be the strongest and best armed in Africa. He became prime minister in 1978 and was elected executive president in September 1984.

Brown, Michael Stuart

As fellow interns at Massachusetts General Hospital in Boston, Michael Brown and Joseph Goldstein began a friendship that eventually developed into a close, lasting, and unusually successful scientific collaboration. Their discoveries about the metabolism of cholesterol were recognized in 1985 by the Nobel Prize for Physiology or Medicine. In the words of David Baltimore, an earlier winner of the Nobel Prize, "They changed a whole way of thinking about how cells and blood interact" by

AP/WIDE WORLD

Buthelezi, Gatsha Mangosuthu

As the leader of six million Zulus—much the largest of all the ethnic communities in the country—Chief Gatsha Buthelezi was one of South Africa's most significant politicians. He was also one of its most controversial figures, increasingly out of step with most other black and white leaders except for the Progressive Federal Party. As chief minister of the KwaZulu homeland from 1972, he continued to defy the union government by refusing the kind of independence it offered, despite acceptance of similar terms by four other homelands. As leader of Inkatha, a movement claiming about one million members (almost exclusively Zulus), he tenaciously fought the government over its constitutional reform introducing a tricameral parliament (excluding blacks) and campaigned for a fully democratic constitution based on universal suffrage.

Buthelezi also quarreled with most other black political movements, especially the African National Congress (ANC). Two serious points of conflict concerned his campaign against economic sanctions and his criticism of armed struggle and other forms of political violence.

Buthelezi was born Aug. 27, 1928, at Mahlabatini, where his father was chief of the Shenge tribe. Through his mother he was a descendant of the Zulu royal line. His grandfather, King Dinizulu, had founded Inkatha as a Zulu cultural movement in 1924. Buthelezi revived it in 1974 as a mass political movement open to all Africans, but few non-Zulus joined. He therefore established the South African Black Alliance, to which nonwhite political groups other than Inkatha were invited to belong. However, when its important affiliate, the Labour Party, agreed to support the tricameral parliament, the Alliance declined in importance.

While still a student at the University College of Fort Hare, where he graduated in history and native administration, Buthelezi showed himself to be a rebel. As a member of the ANC Youth Wing, he was expelled during his final year in 1950 over his boycott of a visit by the governor-general (South Africa was then a Commonwealth of Nations dominion). At the age of 25 he was made acting chief of his tribe and in 1957 full chief.

Chiyonofuji

In the fifth of Japan's six annual sumo *basho* (tournaments), *yokozuna* (grand champion) Chiyonofuji ("Chiyo") won his 13th title in September with a perfect 15–0 record. It was the third straight victory for Chiyo in Kokugikan, the new sumo stadium that opened in Tokyo in January. When he won his fourth title of the year in November, Chiyo tied Wajima, a retired *yokozuna,* for third place on the list of all-time winners. In June the 30-year-old *rikishi* won the Pres. Ronald Reagan Cup during a tournament in New York City's Madison Square Garden. Chiyo was one of 38 wrestlers who participated in the rugged three-day event. He also performed *dohyoiri,* the impressive *yokozuna* ring-entering ritual, before members of the U.S. Department of State. Chiyo was featured in an advertisement that read "The Biggest Thing to Ever Hit New York," even though he was only 6 ft (1.83 m) tall and weighed 264 lb (120 kg); the tallest *rikishi*

in competition was 6 ft 6½ in (1.99 m) and the heaviest 506 lb (230 kg). It was Chiyo's speed and skill that set him apart. He was also noted for his intense prefight stare and swift attack that earned him the nickname "Wolf." In a sport where fat is beautiful, he had manly good looks. When Chiyo married in September 1982, he may have lost some of his female supporters, but his earnings continued to climb steadily. In 1984 he reportedly earned more than 80 million yen (about $320,000). His monthly salary later reached 750,000 yen (about $3,750), but he earned extra money with each victory and advertising contract.

Chiyonofuji was born Mitsugu Akimoto on June 1, 1955, in the district of Matsumae, Hokkaido. As a boy he swam, played baseball, and ran track, but he did not wrestle. When he was 15 he graduated from junior high school and, encouraged by a retired *yokozuna* from Hokkaido, joined a sumo stable. In September 1970 he made his sumo debut and four years later became *juryo,* a full-fledged wrestler. By his fifth year Chiyo had reached the *makuuchi* division. He won his first *basho* in January 1981 with a 14-1 record and was promoted to *ozeki* (champion). After winning his second title in July, he was promoted to *yokozuna.* His trainer believed Chiyo could win five more championships before competition from younger men forced him to retire. Wolf promised only to try to win as many *basho* as he could.

Cosby, Bill

For black comedian Bill Cosby, star and executive producer of the hit television series "The Cosby Show," comedy need not always be a laughing matter. Unlike his contemporaries Richard Pryor and Eddie Murphy, Cosby eschewed aggressive humor—the kind that leaves audiences shaking with laughter. Instead, Cosby's comedy was indirect and gentle; his wry observations on life coaxed audiences into knowing smiles.

In 1985 his television series induced so many smiling faces that it regularly ranked number one in the Nielsen ratings. The show featured the humorous adventures of the Huxtables, an upper-middle-class black family that closely resembled Cosby's real-life clan. Appropriately, Cosby played father: the witty, wise, and sometimes harried obstetrician, Heathcliff Huxtable. Cosby kept the show free of the conventions of television comedy; as he put it, "I told the writers I don't want sit-com jokes. I don't want jokes about behinds, or breasts, or pimples." The series also avoided racial stereotypes. In developing the story line, Cosby explained, his guiding philosophy "is to be true rather than funny." This serious approach to comedy won him major honors: a People's Choice award, a Golden Globe award, and first place on the TVQ index, the industry's most important measure of a star's popular appeal.

Cosby, who was born in Philadelphia on July 12, 1937, first became recognized as a comedian in the

NBC PHOTO

sixth grade. His teacher wrote, "William is an alert boy who would rather clown than study." Those words proved prophetic. In 1962 Cosby quit his studies at Temple University to tell jokes for $60 a week at the Gaslight Cafe in New York City's Greenwich Village. He soon graduated to such clubs as The Flamingo in Las Vegas and to appearances on "Tonight" and "The Jack Paar Show."

Cosby's act impressed producer Sheldon Leonard, who in 1965 cast the comedian as CIA agent Alex Scott in "I Spy," the first television series to feature a black costar. In "I Spy" Cosby showed he could be funny in a serious milieu; he received Emmys for that effort in 1966 and 1967. He later starred as teacher Chet Kincaid in "The Bill Cosby Show," costarred in such films as *Uptown Saturday Night* (1974) and *Let's Do It Again* (1975), performed in concert halls across the U.S. and Canada, and appeared in numerous television commercials, including those that offered viewers "a Coke and a smile"—Cosby style, of course.

Cossiga, Francesco

Francesco Cossiga was inaugurated as Italy's eighth president on July 9, 1985. At 56 he was the youngest person ever to be chosen head of the Italian state. He was also the first man to occupy the Quirinale Palace since World War II who had played no role in the resistance movement during the German occupation. In fact, Cossiga's career had been devoted almost exclusively to his Christian Democrat Party since his university days. He was elected on June 24 by the combined houses of Parliament on the first ballot, something that had not happened since

Ditka, Mike

At Mike Ditka's first team meeting as the Chicago Bears' coach, he talked about going to the Super Bowl. It was a pipe dream no one had dared mention in recent years. Four years later, with two-thirds of the roster changed and the youngest team in the National Conference of the National Football League (NFL), the Bears beat New England in the 1986 Super Bowl 46–10. It was the highest score and biggest winning margin in the game's 20 years. Ditka was voted NFL coach of the year for 1985.

Ditka had always regarded the Bears with special pride. Even during Ditka's 13 seasons with the Dallas Cowboys, including 9 as an assistant coach, Cowboys coach Tom Landry told him he was a Bear at heart. He had played with the Bears in 1961–66 but left after saying owner-coach George Halas "tossed nickels around as if they were manhole covers." Halas forgave him and rehired Ditka in 1982 to restore the Bears to their prominence of the 1930s and 1940s. Ditka's comparative inexperience made him a surprising choice, but he did what Halas wanted. He convinced the Bears that they had as much right as anyone to win and that they should play harder simply because they were Bears.

Ditka was an all-star tight end for five of his six Bears seasons. He was NFL rookie of the year in 1961 and set a professional football record with 75 catches at tight end in 1964. He battled opponents to the last inch and challenged teammates who were not living up to his lofty standards. As coach he told the players, "Put a chip on your shoulder in July, and don't take it off until January."

Ditka designed an imaginative offense around

the election in 1946 of Enrico de Nicola, Italy's first (provisional) president. The message to the nation was that the two major parties, Cossiga's Christian Democrats and the Italian Communist Party (PCI), had come to an agreement beforehand, and the smaller parties fell into line. At the time of his election Cossiga was serving his second year as chairman of the Italian Senate. To that post, the second highest in the country, he had also been elected on the first ballot by the senators.

Cossiga was a Sardinian, born July 26, 1928, in Sassari. He was a second cousin of Enrico Berlinguer, leader of the PCI until his death in 1984. Cossiga joined the Christian Democrat Party in 1945 and three years later gained a law degree at Sassari. After holding minor party offices, he was elected to Parliament for the first time in 1958.

In 1976 Prime Minister Aldo Moro offered Cossiga the post of minister of the interior. "But I am a man of doubts," was the reserved Sardinian's response. "Precisely why I thought of you," said Moro; "doubts and imagination are necessary for the job." Two years later Cossiga had the sad challenge of supervising the state police when Moro was kidnapped by terrorists. A few hours after Moro's body was found, Cossiga resigned his Cabinet post. He was later called by his party to be prime minister in two successive Cabinets in 1979–80, for a total of 418 days.

Before being sworn in as president, Cossiga visited his native Sardinia, had a private audience with the pope, and formally resigned from the Christian Democrat Party. The last gesture was without precedent, and its message was understood and applauded throughout Italy.

the Bears and did not interfere with an innovative defense that threatened to revolutionize the game. After a 3–6 strike-shortened season in 1982 and a 3–7 start in 1983, the Bears won 30 of their next 38 regular-season games, including their first 12 in the 15–1 1985 season. They won division championships in 1984 and 1985, their first since 1963.

Michael Keller Ditka was born Oct. 18, 1939, in Carnegie, Pa., and grew up nearby in the steel-mill town of Aliquippa. His high-school coach had to talk him out of quitting because he thought he was too small. That problem solved, he became an All-America college player at nearby Pittsburgh and a first-round NFL draft choice.

Fisher, Mel

On July 20, 1985, Mel Fisher's diving crew found a treasure hunter's dream; stacked on a reef 50 ft (15 m) underwater, in the Straits of Florida 40 mi (65 km) west of Key West, lay hundreds of silver bars. They were from the cargo of the *Nuestra Señora de Atocha,* a galleon bound for Spain that sank with several sister ships in a hurricane on Sept. 6, 1622. Colonial records indicated that the *Atocha* had gone down with about 1,200 silver ingots weighing 70 lb (31.5 kg) each, 160 small gold bars and disks, and more than 250,000 silver coins. Long sought by colonial Spanish as well as modern American hunters, the trove was finally discovered after a 19-year effort by Fisher's own firm, Treasure Salvors, Inc. Often near bankruptcy and locked in legal disputes, Treasure Salvors was little more than a tourist museum and a fleet of second-hand tugs, barges, and pleasure boats. But if estimates of the find's value proved true (anywhere between $200 million and $400 million), Fisher, his crew, and the investors in his enterprise would be rich.

Melvin A. Fisher was born Aug. 21, 1922, in Gary, Ind. He graduated from Purdue University and served in the Army Corps of Engineers during World War II. In 1950 he moved to California to work on his parents' chicken farm, but his love of underwater exploring led him to open a scuba shop. In 1963 he moved to Florida, where he incorporated Treasure Salvors the next year. During the next 20 years his firm found more than 100 shipwrecks.

In 1966 Fisher began to search the Florida Keys for the *Atocha* fleet, using such devices as high-speed magnetometers, side-scanning sonar, and his own invention, called the "mailbox"—a pipe that blows away sand cover by directing jets of water from the boat's screws to the seafloor below. In 1971 his crew found the *Atocha*'s anchor. In 1980 they came across a sister ship, the *Santa Margarita,* and began salvaging an estimated $20 million in gold chain and bullion, much of which was distributed to outside investors. Then, following a trail of scattered gold and debris, they worked back to where the *Atocha* lay, five miles (eight kilometers) from where they had found the anchor.

The riches came at a great cost to Fisher and his family (his wife and children all dived for the firm); in 1975 his eldest son and daughter-in-law drowned with another crewman while searching for the *Atocha.*

Fox, Michael J.

In 1985 many people in the United States continued to protest the country's trade policy, but at least one import proved beyond criticism: the subcompact Canadian actor Michael J. Fox, who became an American superstar. The 24-year-old, 5-ft 4-in (1.6-m) Fox won recognition as both a matinee idol and a talented comic for his work in "Family Ties," a television series that climbed to the number two spot in the Nielsen ratings, and *Back to the Future,* a film that outgrossed every other 1985 release, including *Rambo.*

The keys to Fox's success lay in his slight build, apple-pie face, and engaging, laid-back manner, which together gave him the look of a pleasantly ordinary American teen. In his role as 18-year-old Alex Keaton in "Family Ties," Fox's conventionality took on an additional twist: he played the ultraconservative son of two fortyish liberals, both former flower children. In *Back to the Future* Fox became the hip, small-town youth Marty McFly, who journeys 30 years into the past, meets his parents as teenagers, and accidentally changes the course of their lives. To capitalize on his new fame, Fox in 1985 also starred in *Teen Wolf,* a low-budget comedy in which he breaks out with something more unfortunate than acne: werewolf hair.

Fox was born in Edmonton, Alta., on June 9, 1961. The son of an army man, he moved often—changing schools, friends, and personalities as often as he changed addresses. In high school Fox studied drama and discovered he could look and act

441

younger than his years. During a screen test for the Canadian Broadcasting Corporation, the 15-year-old Fox struck officials as the brightest ten-year-old they had ever seen. A star was in the making.

Despite appearing with Art Carney in *Letters from Frank* (1979), a film made in Vancouver, B.C., Fox soon concluded that he faced a dim future as an actor in Canada, so he accepted jobs in the United States, eventually appearing in the 1980–81 television series "Palmerstown, USA," the movie *Midnight Madness* (1980), and then "Family Ties" (September 1982). Reflecting on his move, Fox said that "the only way to success for a young person in Canada is to be a hockey player." And though he enjoyed playing his country's national sport, he preferred to make people laugh, a service in great demand in a humor-hungry United States.

García Pérez, Alan

The conclusive victory won by Alan García Pérez in the April 14, 1985, presidential election was widely seen to mark a watershed in modern Peruvian history. García narrowly missed winning outright with 48% of the vote, but the runner-up, Alfonso Barrantes Lingán of the Marxist Izquierda Unida party, conceded defeat, thus saving a second round of voting. García, who was sworn in on July 28, became the first elected president to succeed another democratically chosen candidate in Peru in more than 40 years. He was also the first Alianza Popular Revolucionaria Americana (APRA) leader to take office as president, despite APRA's being the country's oldest political party.

Alan García, born May 23, 1949, in Lima, had risen fast. A lawyer educated in Lima and in Spain and France, he won his first political victory in 1980 when he gained a seat in the lower house of Congress. Two years later he became general secretary of APRA. His opponents criticized his lack of political experience, and certainly he had no experience of governing. To his supporters, however, this very weakness became a strength, and certainly he did not bow to the customary pressures of the military and (more recently) the international bankers.

An imposing figure (heavily built and 6 ft 4 in [1.9 m] tall), García was compared to Spain's Prime Minister Felipe González Márquez as one who wanted to put ideology to one side and aimed to make politics practical. After taking office García became extremely visible both at home and abroad. In his maiden speech to the UN General Assembly, he was critical of the role that the wealthy industrialized world (especially the U.S.) played in relation to less developed debtor countries. This outspokenness won him many supporters at home but served to raise eyebrows internationally.

Probably the most politically destabilizing problem that García faced was that of the Maoist Sendero Luminoso (Shining Path) guerrilla movement. One of his most fervent campaigns was to alter the imbalance between Lima and the rest of Peru because he believed that this would be the way to cut off support for Sendero and also would slow the uncontrolled migration to the cities. García's strongest impact, however, was to change the demoralized mood of the country to one of tentative hope.

Geldof, Bob

Bob Geldof, pop star in decline, was prompted by television reports of the famine in Ethiopia in October 1984 to turn crusader in the cause of reawakening the pop music world's social conscience. He established the Band Aid charity, which in turn inspired USA for Africa in the U.S., to raise money for famine victims. He then employed his energies in organizing the hugely ambitious and successful

Live Aid concert, which took place in London and Philadelphia on July 13, 1985. In its wake Geldof was nominated for the Nobel Peace Prize.

At intervals he trained the spotlight of his obsessive candor on governments and institutions. In October, during a tour of six sub-Saharan countries to assess their need for famine relief, he did not flinch from asking African leaders embarrassing questions about corruption and repression in their countries. On his return he castigated members of the European Parliament for the existence of food surpluses in Europe in the face of extreme need in Africa.

Robert Frederick Xenon Geldof was born on Oct. 5, 1951, at Dun Laoghaire, County Dublin, Ireland. After leaving school he held a succession of jobs, ranging from bulldozer operator to pop-music journalist. In 1975 he and several friends formed a "new-wave" pop group called the Nightlife Thugs, soon renamed the Boomtown Rats; their performances involved releasing live rats among the audience. In 1976 the group moved to London, where it enjoyed a heady but brief success. Two singles— "Rat Trap" and "I Don't Like Mondays"—topped the record charts in Britain in 1979 and 1980, respectively. The group failed to make an impact in the U.S., though the latter song, which concerned a real-life shooting incident in San Diego, Calif., brought notoriety by being banned.

At a time when pop lyrics were largely preoccupied with the deprivation of unemployment, Geldof made enemies when he accused the punk movement of hypocrisy. Nevertheless, his sincerity silenced suggestions that his fund-raising efforts were aimed at reviving his own career. In fact, the record-buying public continued to all but ignore the Boomtown Rats, while Geldof's film career—he had taken starring roles in *Pink Floyd—The Wall* (1982) and *Number One* (1985)—was no more than moderately successful.

Goldstein, Joseph Leonard

Of people suffering heart attacks before they were 60 years old, about one in 20 had a disorder called familial hypercholesterolemia, or FH. Two medical geneticists, Joseph L. Goldstein and Michael S. Brown, made striking progress toward understanding FH; their discoveries earned them the Nobel Prize for Physiology or Medicine in 1985.

Most of the cholesterol in the blood is present in low-density lipoprotein (LDL), which exists in the form of tiny globules. These are coated with a detergentlike compound that keeps them suspended in the watery blood serum. The rest of the surface is occupied by a specific protein by which the LDL attaches itself to a complementary protein on the cells of the body in the first step in the transfer of cholesterol from the blood into the cells. The structure of the receptor protein is controlled by a single gene, and any of several defects in the gene leads to failure of the cells to absorb LDL.

About 500,000 U.S. residents, the victims of FH,

UPI/BETTMANN NEWSPHOTOS

carry one such gene; these people have about twice the normal concentration of LDL in their blood, and many of them fall prey to heart disease before they are 35 years old. The identification of the LDL receptors by Goldstein and Brown in 1973 led to a radical change in the way biologists viewed the interaction between cells and blood. It opened the way toward a series of further discoveries by the two Nobel laureates about the fate of LDL within the cell and rational methods for influencing the course of FH.

Goldstein was born in Sumter, S.C., on April 18, 1940, and graduated from Washington and Lee University, Lexington, Va., in 1962. He received his M.D. from Southwestern Medical School of the University of Texas in Dallas in 1966, then spent two years as an intern and resident at Massachusetts General Hospital in Boston, where he and Brown became close friends. They both went next to the National Institutes of Health (NIH) at Bethesda, Md., where Goldstein became a clinical associate in the laboratory of biochemical genetics of the National Heart Institute. In 1972 Goldstein returned to Dallas and the University of Texas as a member of its faculty, which Brown had joined a year earlier.

Gooden, Dwight

When Dwight Gooden had two strikes on a batter, the stands started buzzing and the K signs started dancing. K is the baseball scorecard symbol for strikeout, and to the fans in the stands, Gooden was the 6-ft 3-in (1.9-m), high-kicking New York Mets right-hander who had struck out more batters at a younger age

he was 14 Gooden was so superior to his contemporaries that a local writer nicknamed him "Doc," explaining that "what Dr. J is to basketball, Dwight Gooden is to baseball." The nickname became "Dr. K" in Gooden's rookie year. His 11.39 strikeouts per nine innings shattered the previous major-league record of 10.71. His 32 strikeouts in two consecutive games tied a National League record. His won–lost record was 17–9, with a 2.60 earned run average that ranked second in the majors.

In 1985 Gooden led both leagues with a 1.53 earned run average, 268 strikeouts, and 24 wins (against 4 defeats). He won 18 of his last 19 decisions and kept his team in the pennant race until the last weekend. Perhaps most amazing was the scarcity of walks he allowed: 3.01 per nine innings as a rookie and 2.24 in 1985.

Gorbachev, Mikhail Sergeyevich

Before his December 1984 visit to the U.K. as leader of a Soviet parliamentary delegation, few people in the West knew anything of importance about Mikhail Gorbachev. Eleven months later, however, he was U.S. Pres. Ronald Reagan's opposite number at the summit meeting that opened in Geneva on Nov. 19, 1985. The extraordinary rapidity of Gorbachev's progress was due, first, to the unusual mortality that between November 1982 and March 1985 claimed three Soviet leaders and, second, to his personality and his disciplined intellect.

When Konstantin Chernenko died on March 10, there was little doubt either in the Kremlin or in Western foreign ministries that Gorbachev would succeed him. However, when the Politburo of the Communist Party of the Soviet Union (CPSU) met the following day, Grigori Romanov, an adversary of Gorbachev, proposed that Viktor Grishin succeed Chernenko—as the latter had himself proposed in a deathbed message to the Politburo. But no one seconded Romanov's motion, and so Andrei Gromyko proposed Gorbachev to the CPSU Central Committee (CC), which unanimously elected him as CPSU general secretary.

Gorbachev's most urgent task was to reinforce his position within the Politburo. Six weeks after he became the most powerful man within the Soviet Union, the CC elected as Politburo members Viktor Chebrikov, head of the State Security Committee (KGB); Yegor Ligachev, responsible for cadres in the party Secretariat; and Nikolai Ryzhkov, who on September 27 was appointed chairman of the Council of Ministers (premier). On July 1 Eduard Shevardnadze became a full member of the Politburo and the following day was appointed foreign minister. Also on July 1 the CC accepted the "request of Comrade Romanov to be freed from the duties of a Politburo member." Then in October former premier Nikolai Tikhonov retired from the Politburo, which now had 12 members, on 8 of whom, at the very least, Gorbachev could rely for political support.

than any other pitcher in major league history. But to opponents in the dugouts Gooden's 96-mph (155-km/h) fastball and nearly 80-mph (129-km/h) curve were only the beginning. They marveled at his poise, at the way he controlled his pitches and knew how to use them. Chicago Cub manager Jim Frey called Gooden "the best pitcher I've ever seen at his age."

In 1984 he was the youngest ever to be voted rookie of the year; the youngest to play in an All-Star game, where he struck out his first three batters; and the youngest to lead a league in strikeouts. He led both leagues with a rookie-record 276. In 1985 he was the youngest to win 20 games and the youngest to win the Cy Young Award, which he received the week of his 21st birthday.

"Things have moved pretty rapidly in my career," Gooden said. "You just try to do a little bit better each year." After his rookie year he went to the Instructional League, usually for minor leaguers, to develop a change-up pitch and improve his pick-off move. He had rarely needed to hold runners on base during high school and 1½ seasons in the minor leagues because batters rarely had reached base against him.

Dwight Eugene Gooden was born Nov. 16, 1964, the youngest of four children, in a predominantly black, working-class section of East Tampa, Fla. His father, Dan, played semipro baseball and started taking him to games when he was three. By the time

Gorbachev was born March 2, 1931, at Privolnoye, Stavropol territory, into a peasant family. After working on a state farm, as a promising Komsomol (Young Communist League) member he was sent to Moscow State University, where he graduated in law. A CPSU member from 1952, he advanced steadily in the Stavropol city and territorial party organizations. In 1971 he was elected to the CC, in 1979 to candidate membership of the Politburo, and in 1980 to full Politburo membership.

Gregory, Cynthia

On June 4, 1985, American Ballet Theatre (ABT) accorded Cynthia Gregory an unusual honor for an individual dancer—a gala—to celebrate her 20 years with the company. One feature of the gala was "Memories," in which Gregory illustrated her outstanding versatility and brilliant technique in excerpts from several of the 70 works she had performed with ABT, works that ranged from the classical *Swan Lake* to contemporary solos created for her by Alvin Ailey (*The River*), Eliot Feld (*At Midnight*), and Twyla Tharp (*Bach Partita*). The exhilarating program carried a sense of poignancy, too, for the evening was dedicated to the memory of John Hemminger, her husband of nine years, who had died within the previous year.

Gregory was born July 8, 1946, in Los Angeles. She began her study of ballet at the age of five and was on the cover of *Dance* magazine at seven. In 1961 she enrolled at the San Francisco Ballet School. She officially joined the San Francisco Ballet in late 1961 and was promoted to soloist a few months later.

In 1965 she and Terry Orr, another soloist, moved to New York City and auditioned for ABT. Orr was accepted immediately, but Gregory was thought too tall—at 5 ft 6 in (1.68 m) tall, she stood nearly 6 ft (1.8 m) on pointe—and had to audition three times before she was accepted. She and Orr were married in 1966.

Gregory advanced rapidly in the company. She was promoted to soloist in 1966 and to principal dancer in 1967. The role that brought her to prominence was that of Odette/Odile in *Swan Lake,* which she first danced in the summer of 1967. She continued to work on the dramatic nuances of the role and made her interpretation one of the most memorable in ballet history. Other notable roles were in Antony Tudor's *Undertow* and *Lilac Garden,* José Limón's *The Moor's Pavane,* and Birgit Cullberg's *Miss Julie.* In 1975 she won a *Dance* magazine award.

There were, as she put it, "some rough spots along the way"—the two times she resigned from ABT. The first time, in 1975, followed her divorce from Orr, and she stayed away nearly a year. In 1979 she left ABT for six months, during which she made guest appearances around the world. The rough spots were far outnumbered by the triumphs, however, and she continued to dazzle audiences with her daring and her ability to bring new dimensions to familiar roles.

Hauptman, Herbert Aaron

When the three winners of the Nobel Prize for Physics in 1979 were announced, many commentators found it remarkable that two of them, Sheldon Glashow and Steven Weinberg, had been members of the same college class (Cornell University, 1954). Eyebrows rose even higher when Herbert Hauptman and Jerome Karle won the Prize for Chemistry in 1985; not only had they both graduated in 1937 from City College (now City University) of New York, but a third member of their class, Arthur Kornberg, had shared the Prize for Physiology or Medicine in 1959.

Hauptman and Karle were the principal architects of the most general procedure yet introduced for deducing the molecular structure of crystalline chemical compounds from the patterns formed on photographic plates when narrow beams of X-rays strike the crystals and give rise to secondary beams. The directions and intensities of those beams are strictly governed by the regular spacing of the atoms in the crystal, but the relationship is complicated, and no method had been devised for the direct translation of the X-ray patterns to crystal structures. Hauptman and Karle developed a procedure for dealing with this problem, publishing their first results by 1950. It required extensive calculations but only a single treatment of the experimental data.

Hauptman was born in New York City on Feb. 14, 1917. After completing his undergraduate education, he went on to Columbia University, also in New York City, to obtain a master's degree in 1939. He worked as a statistician for the U.S. Bureau of the Census in 1940–42 and served two two-year terms as a radar instructor in the U.S. Army Air Forces before beginning his scientific career as a physicist at the Naval Research Laboratory, Washington, D.C., in 1947. While at the laboratory Hauptman collaborated with Karle in developing a new technique for interpreting X-ray diffraction patterns. He also studied advanced mathematics at the University of Maryland and was awarded a Ph.D. in 1955.

In 1970 Hauptman moved to Buffalo, N.Y., taking a position as mathematician at the Medical Foundation, a small private organization specializing in endocrine research, and also accepting a research professorship in biophysical sciences at the State University of New York. In 1972 he was named director of research and vice-president of the Medical Foundation.

Howard, John Winston

On Sept. 5, 1985, John Howard became leader of the Liberal Party of Australia during an extraordinary and unexpected crisis in confidence caused by mistrust in the relationship between Howard and his chief, Andrew Peacock. Peacock, who, in the words of the Australian Broadcasting Commission, turned himself from a rooster to a feather duster in two hours, caused his own ouster by demanding from Howard an unrealistic assurance that he would in no circumstances challenge for the position of party leader. Misjudging the mood of his party, Peacock called a special meeting to settle "once and for all" the leadership question. Unconvinced by Howard's protests of loyalty, Peacock put the matter to the vote and was dumbfounded to find that the outcome was that the parliamentary party (*i.e.,* Liberal Party members of Parliament) chose Howard to lead them, at the same time moving the Liberal Party's power base back to Sydney from Melbourne. Howard, who was called back from a skiing holiday to face his leader's wrath, was magnanimous in victory and allowed Peacock to pick the shadow portfolio of his choice—that of foreign affairs.

Howard posed a considerable new threat to Prime Minister Bob Hawke's Australian Labor Party (ALP), which, despite successes with labor relations and the unemployment problem, failed to check inflation or contain the decline in the value of the Australian dollar. Howard's expertise and parliamentary reputation stemmed from his relative success as federal treasurer in Malcolm Fraser's Liberal Party-National Party coalition. With public opinion polls presaging a Liberal victory in the event of a federal election, Howard thus seemed a likely successor to the post of prime minister.

John Howard, born July 26, 1939, in Sydney, was a law graduate of the University of Sydney and practiced as a solicitor to the Supreme Court of New South Wales. He moved through the Liberal Party machine as a member of the party executive (1963–74) and vice-president (1972–74) of the New South Wales division of the party. In 1974 he was elected to the House of Representatives as member for Bennelong, New South Wales. He held several portfolios in the previous conservative administration, including being minister for business and consumer affairs (1975–77), and, most importantly, federal treasurer from 1977 until the Fraser ministry fell in March 1983. He then became deputy leader of the opposition.

Hughes, Ted

When Ted Hughes was appointed Britain's poet laureate in 1984, he announced: "For me the crown is the symbol of the unity of the tribe." This was different from the rather shy, unashamedly suburban respect for the British monarchy that had been expressed by his predecessor, Sir John Betjeman. The use of the word tribe provoked another poet, Tom Paulin, to parody Hughes's statement with a verse written in a sort of pidgin English. Undeterred, Hughes published a long, exuberant poem about the force of water, rainstorms, and swollen rivers of West Britain, to celebrate the christening of Prince Harry, under the title "Rain-Charm for the Duchy."

THOMAS VICTOR

This too was quickly parodied by a British poet; but an American critic, David Bromwich, was rather "impressed by the dexterity" with which the poem brought "a subject of state" into the precincts of Hughes's work, drawing from the elemental world of nature "a pleasant, handsome, rousing compliment to a Prince."

The open-air world of nature, in its most harsh and challenging aspects, had long been dominant in Hughes's work, ever since *The Hawk in the Rain* (1957), his first volume of verse. Edward James Hughes was born Aug. 16, 1930, at Mytholmroyd, Yorkshire. Long industrialized, although in its time a part of the last Celtic kingdom to fall to the invading Angles, Mytholmroyd inspired a sort of mythic tribalism. As a youth, son of a local shopkeeper, Hughes was much influenced by the mythology of Robert Graves's *The White Goddess.* When he went to Pembroke College, University of Cambridge, after his military service, he studied archaeology and anthropology, interests that were reflected in his works. A naturalist and an enthusiastic fisherman, Hughes took his son to Alaska in 1980 to fish for giant salmon. The experience inspired some of the poems in his most recent volume, *River* (1983).

Hughes married the American poet Sylvia Plath in 1956; the couple had two children. They were already separated when, in 1963, Plath committed suicide. For nearly three years after her death, Hughes stopped writing poetry. When he returned to it, his verse was not autobiographical or confessional, but it was recognized that in such laments as "The Howling of Wolves," in such books as

Wodwo (1967; named after an old English "wild man of the woods"), and in the sinister *Crow* poems of 1970–71, an element of dark autobiography might be discerned. Energy, violence, and perhaps even cruelty were often recognized as disconcerting elements in his work. He edited *Sylvia Plath: Collected Poems* (1981), and his own *Selected Poems 1957–81* appeared in 1982. In 1977 he was made an Officer of the Order of the British Empire.

Jobs, Steven Paul

Steven Jobs, who cofounded Apple Computer, Inc., in his parents' garage in 1975, almost single-handedly promoted the personal computer and built Apple into a multimillion-dollar corporation. On Sept. 17, 1985, Jobs resigned as chairman of Apple; it was the end of an era and a symbol of the growing conservatism in the personal computer industry.

Steven was adopted in February 1955 by Paul and Clara Jobs. The family moved from Mountain View, Calif., to Los Altos, Calif., because of Steven's problems in school. In Los Altos young Jobs, always a loner, showed more interest in studying electronics at Hewlett-Packard Corp. in nearby Palo Alto than in attending high school. While working summers at Hewlett-Packard he met Stephen Wozniak, who was applying his engineering wizardry to his own electronic gadgets. Jobs briefly attended Reed College in Portland, Ore., and then worked on video games at Atari, Inc., before traveling to India in 1974. In 1975 he was reunited with Wozniak. Jobs was intrigued by the marketing possibilities of the gadgets that Wozniak had developed and encouraged him to design a small computer for home use. While Jobs sought marketing strategies and financing from his bedroom office, Wozniak worked in Jobs's garage to build the prototype computer that was to become the Apple I. Jobs's name for the new company was inspired by a summer job he held in an Oregon orchard; he insisted that the new computer be lightweight and user friendly.

In 1977 Jobs and Wozniak introduced the improved Apple II, and in 1980, when the company went public, it had sales of more than $130 million. Later products failed to do as well, however, and after IBM's entry into the field with its IBM PC, Jobs's belief that Apple's computers should remain incompatible with IBM's further eroded company prospects.

In 1983 Jobs lured John Sculley, then president of Pepsi-Cola USA, to Apple to solve the marketing problems. In May 1985 (shortly after Wozniak left Apple) Sculley reorganized the firm so that Jobs continued to have creative input but had no say in daily company operations. Jobs, increasingly dissatisfied, resigned in September, announcing that he would form a new, small company. A week later Apple filed suit against its former chairman, alleging that he had "secretly schemed" to steal Apple employees as well as proprietary information on Apple's future developments.

NBC PHOTO

Johnson, Don, and Thomas, Philip Michael

When "Miami Vice" made its television debut in September 1984, many people dismissed it as an extended rock video. Within a year, however, the show had converted most of its critics, garnered 15 Emmy award nominations (it won four), and brought fame and fortune to its two stars, Don Johnson and Philip Michael Thomas.

Filmed entirely on location in Florida, "Miami Vice" was in some ways a morality play about undercover police—more concerned with nuance than dialogue and emphasizing atmosphere over plot. The show's real originality lay in its innovative use of techniques rarely seen in a television series, including night filming, wide-angle and distance shots, and slow motion. The gritty—if vividly imagined—world of drug dealers, smugglers, and organized crime contrasted sharply with the Art Deco beauty of Miami, the Italian silk and linen designer wardrobes for the stars, and the overwhelming use of pastel, ice-cream colors such as pink and turquoise (no earth tones allowed). The original rock music, which cost as much as $10,000 per episode, frequently served to advance the plot or comment critically on the action rather than as simple background music.

Don Johnson (Detective James ["Sonny"] Crockett) was born on Dec. 15, 1949. His father, a farmer in Flat Creek, Mo., moved the family to Wichita, Kan., where Johnson began acting in high school.

He attended the University of Kansas on a drama scholarship for two years before joining the American Conservatory Theater in San Francisco. He starred in Sal Mineo's Los Angeles production of *Fortune and Men's Eyes,* but he chose not to go to New York City with the play in order to star in the film *The Magic Garden of Stanley Sweetheart* (1970). During the next 15 years Johnson made many television appearances and several unsuccessful films, including *The Harrad Experiment* (1973) and *A Boy and His Dog* (1975), which later became a science-fiction cult classic. With the success of "Miami Vice" and of a new television production of *The Long, Hot Summer* (based on William Faulkner stories), Johnson was one of the hottest actors of 1985.

Philip Michael Thomas (Detective Ricardo Tubbs) was born in Columbus, Ohio, on May 26, 1949, but his family soon moved to southern California. He studied theology at the Oakwood Theological Seminary in Huntsville, Ala., and philosophy at the University of California before joining the road company of the musical *Hair* in San Francisco. He made his Broadway debut in 1971 in *No Place to Be Somebody* and then appeared in *The Selling of the President* (1972). He made several movies, notably *Sparkle* (1976), and television appearances until success struck with "Miami Vice." In 1985 he released an album of his own music, *Living the Book of My Life.*

Johnston, Lynn

First appearing in 1979, the comic strip "For Better or for Worse" was an instant success and soon became a fixture in the comic sections of more

than 500 newspapers around the world. The family of Elly Patterson, a bewildered modern housewife, made Lynn Johnston, Elly's creator and alter ego, one of Canada's most popular cartoonists. Johnston based the Pattersons on her own family. Her dentist husband, Rod Johnston, who fired her imagination by giving her useful one-liners for the strip, was the model for Elly's husband, John.

"For Better or for Worse" originated in a series of cartoons that Lynn Johnston drew for her obstetrician during her first pregnancy. The doctor badgered her to have the cartoons published. They appeared in 1973 as the book *David, We're Pregnant!* This was followed by another book of cartoons, *Hi Mom! Hi Dad!* (1975). Universal Press Syndicate saw Johnston's third book, *Do They Ever Grow Up?* (1977), and asked her to create some sample characters for a continuing series. The result was a ten-year contract to detail the life of the Patterson family.

Born Lynn Beverley Ridgway in Collingwood, Ont., on May 28, 1947, Lynn Johnston grew up in Vancouver, B.C. Her earliest inspiration as a cartoonist came from the work of Len Norris, whose cartoons appeared on the *Vancouver Sun*'s editorial page. After attending the Vancouver School of Art (1964–67), Johnston began her artistic career as a medical illustrator at McMaster University in Hamilton, Ont. She also illustrated two books by *Toronto Star* columnist Gary Lautens, *Take My Family . . . Please!* (1980) and *No Sex Please, We're Married* (1983).

After her second marriage in 1977, she moved to her husband's hometown of Lynn Lake, Man.—a community she described as "eight hundred miles from everywhere." There she created the saga of the Patterson family. Never a person to do only one thing at a time, she also started Lynn Johnston Productions, a contact and resource agency for northern Canadian touring performers, and was a contributor to the *Canadian Children's Annual,* a yearly collection of original stories and poems for children.

Johnston was always serious about art and considered her job as a medical illustrator as the best position she had had. Her true delight, however, was making people laugh. The title of the 1984 National Film Board of Canada documentary about her, *See You in the Funny Papers,* would seem to describe Johnston's greatest ambition. Through the Patterson family, she succeeded in amusing and delighting a worldwide audience.

Kampelman, Max

Appointed in January 1985 by Pres. Ronald Reagan as the chief U.S. arms control negotiator and leader of the delegation discussing with the Soviets strategic defense systems and space-based weapons, Max Kampelman was a Democrat who strongly supported the president's research program on missile defense but did not advocate the use of weapons in space. He had impressed the Reagan administration in 1983 when he worked out an especially difficult agreement with the U.S.S.R. at the 35-nation conference convened in Madrid to review compliance with the 1975 Helsinki Accords.

Kampelman was born in New York City on Nov. 7, 1920. He graduated from New York University in 1940 and received a law degree there in 1945. During World War II, a conscientious objector, he volunteered to be part of an experiment at the University of Minnesota studying the effects of semistarvation on humans. When the war was over, Kampelman continued his education, earning a master's degree and a doctorate in political science at Minnesota. He then became politically active for Hubert Humphrey. Kampelman served as legal counsel for Senator Humphrey in Washington from 1949 to 1955. His strong ties to Humphrey and to Democratic conservatives led to his participation in the formation of the Committee on the Present Danger, a group organized to warn against what it considered to be a growing Communist threat. In 1956 Kampelman became a partner and Washington director for a law firm based in New York City.

At the three-year Madrid conference Kampelman was credited with managing an extremely delicate compromise with the Soviets regarding human rights. Not long thereafter, demonstrating what was described as his ability to cut to the realistic core, he denounced the Soviets for their human rights abuses.

Acknowledging the difficulty of the ongoing Geneva arms control talks, Kampelman insisted that there was a formula to be found under which the U.S. and the Soviet Union could "live together in dignity." The first round of negotiations, held in March, was a "first step" forward in the abolition of nuclear weapons. The second round of talks began at the end of May.

Karle, Jerome

Co-winner with Herbert Hauptman of the Nobel Prize for Chemistry in 1985, Jerome Karle, with Hauptman, developed a general method for determining the three-dimensional structure of crystalline chemical compounds from the patterns formed on photographic plates when narrow beams of X rays strike the crystals and generate secondary beams. Their method required extensive calculations but only a single treatment of the experimental data and, with later improvements, made it possible to carry out an X-ray crystallographic analysis in a day or two instead of the period of several years that was formerly required.

Karle was born in New York City on June 18, 1918, and graduated from City College of New York in the class of 1937, which also produced Hauptman and Arthur Kornberg, two other Nobel Prize winners. Karle undertook postgraduate study at Harvard University, receiving a master's degree in 1938, and at the University of Michigan, where

AP/WIDE WORLD

he earned a second master's degree in 1942 and a Ph.D. in physical chemistry in 1943.

Karle joined the Chicago research staff of the Manhattan Project, which developed the atomic bomb, and then that of a U.S. Navy project at the University of Michigan. In 1946 he moved to Washington, D.C., and a position at the Naval Research Laboratory; in 1967 he became chief scientist of its laboratory for the structure of matter. From 1951 to 1970 he also served as a professor at the University of Maryland in College Park.

Kasparov, Garri

On Nov. 9, 1985, in the final game of their 14-month-long contest, Garri Kasparov defeated the defending champion, Anatoli Karpov, to become the world champion of chess. At 22 Kasparov was the youngest person ever to win the title.

The first phase of the competition between the two Soviet grand masters began in late 1984 in Moscow, with the first man to win six games to be crowned champion. Karpov quickly took a 5–0 lead, easily dominating his young challenger. But Kasparov rallied and by February 1985, after 48 games, had narrowed the gap to 5–3. At that point the head of the International Chess Federation called off the match on the grounds that both players were too exhausted to continue. Kasparov protested that the decision was made to benefit Karpov, who appeared to be tiring.

The contest resumed in September under new rules. The previous score was canceled, and a 24-game match was established. One point was to be awarded for a victory, and ½ point was to be given to each player for a draw; the first player to reach

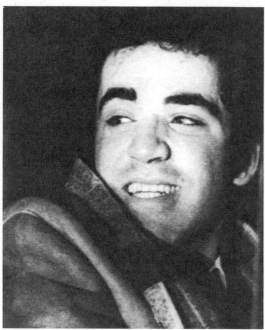
AP/WIDE WORLD

the score of 12½ points would be the winner.

Karpov again took an early lead, but Kasparov fought back. Going into the final match Kasparov led 12–11 and needed only a draw to win the title. Karpov attacked aggressively, but Kasparov was equal to the challenge and won the game and the championship. At the year's end Karpov challenged the new champion to a rematch in 1986. Kasparov responded that such an early resumption of their competition would be "nonsense," but Karpov was supported by the chess federation.

Kasparov was born Garri Weinstein on April 13, 1963, in Baku, U.S.S.R., to a Jewish father and an Armenian mother. His father died when Kasparov was seven, and he was later persuaded to drop the name Weinstein and replace it with a Russianized version of his mother's name.

Kasparov demonstrated his remarkable chess-playing ability at an early age. In 1980 he won the world junior championship, and during the next year he took the Soviet title. He defeated veteran grand masters Viktor Korchnoi and Vassili Smyslov in 1983 and 1984 to earn the right to challenge Karpov.

Keillor, Garrison

With *Lake Wobegon Days,* his second book, Garrison Keillor brought the upper Midwest into the great tradition of American regionalist humor. A fictional reminiscence of growing up in the small town of Lake Wobegon, Minn., the book jumped to the top of best-seller lists within a month of publication in September 1985.

Keillor's success in print capped the rising popularity of his radio show, "A Prairie Home Compan-ion," broadcast live from St. Paul, Minn., on Saturday evenings over American Public Radio. Since 1974 he had presented a motley assemblage of folk music, ragtime, short skits, and comic monologues, stopping the music once each evening to deliver, with deadpan sincerity, the latest news from "the little town that time forgot and the decades cannot improve." The charm of Keillor's news reports, and of his book as well, lay in his obvious affection for Lake Wobegon's 900 souls and their local institutions: their monument, the Statue of the Unknown Norwegian; their churches, Lake Wobegon Lutheran and its Roman Catholic counterpart, Our Lady of Perpetual Responsibility; their watering holes, the Sidetrack Tap and the Chatterbox Cafe; and their market, Ralph's Pretty Good Grocery ("If you can't find it at Ralph's, you can probably get along without it").

Gary Edward Keillor was born Aug. 7, 1942, in Anoka, Minn. (He invented the pen name Garrison in the eighth grade when submitting poems to the school paper.) As a schoolboy he had two ambitions, radio and writing, and at the University of Minnesota (1960–66) he edited the college literary magazine and worked at the campus radio station. In 1968 he became an announcer for Minnesota Public Radio, and in 1970 he began a long association with *The New Yorker,* which published many of his humorous sketches and tales. During that period, as host of a morning show on a public radio station in a small town near St. Cloud, Minn., Keillor introduced Lake Wobegon as the location of the show's "sponsors." The idea for a live show, modeled after the Grand Ole Opry and the classic radio programs of the pretelevision era, came to him in 1974. On July 6 of that year, the first performance of "A Prairie Home Companion" was broadcast over Minnesota Public Radio. By 1985 its national audience had grown to an estimated 2.5 million. Keillor's blend of nostalgia and wry humor won the show a George Foster Peabody Broadcasting Award in 1981. His first book, *Happy to Be Here* (1982), is a collection of his magazine pieces.

Kim Dae Jung

One of the milestones of South Korean politics in 1985 was the homecoming in February of leading dissident Kim Dae Jung from the U.S. after two years of exile. Timed just four days before elections to the National Assembly, Kim's move helped galvanize support for the newly formed oppositionist New Korea Democratic Party (NKDP). Later, under the combined behind-the-scenes leadership of Kim Dae Jung and Kim Young Sam, the country's other top opposition leader, the NKDP merged with the older Democratic Korea Party to create a formidable parliamentary opposition bloc that commanded 102 of the National Assembly's 276 seats. Although in March the government formally lifted its ban on Kim's participation in politics, he was still prevented from taking part in such activities by virtue of his being under a 20-year suspended jail sentence for sedition.

After the parliamentary elections Kim Dae Jung and Kim Young Sam shared the leadership of a broad coalition of opposition forces. That significantly furthered the cause of the opposition, but signs had emerged by July of a renewal of the personal rivalry between the two Kims. Suggesting that Young Sam and himself "divide their political roles," Dae Jung said that the pair should agree on a running-mate formula for the presidential elections promised by Pres. Chun Doo Hwan for 1988. The proposals, seen as an attempt by Dae Jung to gain an advantage over his rival, were widely criticized, and Kim withdrew them.

Kim Dae Jung was born in 1924 in the port of Mokpo, southwestern Korea. During the Korean War he was jailed as a "reactionary" by Communist forces after they took Mokpo. He escaped and joined the resistance. Before his 40th birthday he had gained a reputation as one of the country's most polished orators and charismatic politicians. He narrowly lost the 1971 presidential election to Park Chung Hee. His kidnapping in 1973 by South Korean intelligence agents while he was in self-exile in Tokyo dealt a heavy blow to relations between Japan and South Korea. Kim became a leading presidential contender after Park's assassination in 1979. However, when General Chun came to power after a military coup in 1980, Kim was arrested and later sentenced to death for sedition. The penalty was subsequently commuted.

Klitzing, Klaus von

After a lapse of 22 years, the Nobel Prize for Physics returned to Germany in the hands of Klaus von Klitzing, director of the Max Planck Institute for Solid State Physics in Stuttgart, West Germany. He was recognized for his discovery that under appropriate conditions the resistance offered by an electrical conductor to the passage of current is quantized; that is, it varies by discrete steps rather than smoothly and continuously. The size of these steps is directly related to one of the fundamental quantities of atomic physics, the so-called fine structure constant.

The significance of Klitzing's discovery, made in 1980, was immediately recognized. His experiments were repeated and refined in many laboratories, not only in studies of the properties of semiconductors and other solid materials but also in determining the precise value of the fine structure constant and establishing convenient standards for the measurement of electrical resistance.

Klitzing was born on June 28, 1943, in Schroda in the province of Posen, a part of Poland that had been annexed to Germany during World War II. (The region later reverted to Poland, and the Polish spellings Sroda and Poznan were restored.) At the end of the war Klitzing was taken by his parents to West Germany. He attended the Technical Uni-

CAMERA PRESS, LONDON

versity of Brunswick, graduating in 1969, and then earned a doctorate in physics at the University of Würzburg in 1972. In 1980, when he made his prizewinning discovery, he was a Heisenberg fellow teaching at Würzburg. Later in 1980 Klitzing was appointed to a professorship at the Technical University of Munich. He also taught at the University of Marburg before being named director of the institute at Stuttgart at the beginning of 1985.

Klitzing's research dealt with the Hall effect, named for the U.S. physicist who first observed it in 1879. It denotes the voltage that develops between the edges of a thin current-carrying ribbon placed between the poles of a strong magnet. The ratio of this voltage to the current is called the Hall resistance. When the magnetic field is very strong and the temperature very low, the Hall resistance varies only in the discrete jumps first observed by Klitzing.

Kohl, Helmut

Public opinion in 1985 gave poor marks to Helmut Kohl for his performance as West German federal chancellor. The polls found him to be the least esteemed of all the country's senior politicians, his standing having declined steadily since the federal election in March 1983. His style of political leadership—to sit out problems until they somehow solved themselves—had many critics in his own party, the Christian Democratic Union (CDU), and was especially lamented by its Bavarian sister party, Franz-Josef Strauss's Christian Social Union (CSU).

Factors contributing to this downward slide were the spy scandal that erupted in August with numerous defections to East Germany (including a member of Kohl's personal staff) and the backlash of the "Bitburg affair" in May, when Kohl induced U.S. Pres. Ronald Reagan to lay a wreath at a cemetery that contained graves of soldiers of the Waffen SS, which had administered Hitler's concentration camps. In the election for the state parliament of North Rhine-Westphalia soon after the Bitburg ceremony, the share of the vote won by the CDU fell almost seven percentage points, to 36%. The Social Democratic Party (SPD) won a remarkable 52% of the vote, and subsequent opinion polls showed that the SPD in the country as a whole had not been so popular for 13 years.

Kohl was born in Ludwigshafen on April 3, 1930, and studied at the Universities of Frankfurt and Heidelberg. He was prominent in the youth organization of the CDU and was elected to the state parliament of his native Rhineland-Palatinate in 1959. He became state chairman of his party in 1966 and three years later was elected state minister president (premier), a position he held with considerable success for seven years. He was elected to the Bundestag (federal parliament) in Bonn in 1976.

Kohl contested the chancellorship in the 1976 federal election, losing to the SPD's Helmut Schmidt, and at the 1980 election he was forced to hand over the chancellor candidature to Strauss, who lost to Schmidt decisively. The decision of the Free Democratic Party to switch coalition partners in midterm brought Kohl to power in October 1982. The switch gave him the opportunity to become chancellor on a parliamentary vote, and this was confirmed by the 1983 federal election.

Leonard, Elmore John

Elmore ("Dutch") Leonard had been called "the finest thriller writer alive," and in 1985, after 23 novels, dozens of short stories, and several screenplays, he finally gained the recognition that had eluded him for more than 30 years. Although Leonard's crime fiction was often called "hardboiled," it bore little resemblance to most other detective novels. Leonard rarely used the same character in more than one book, and his protagonists were frequently "good guys" only in the sense that they were more nearly ethical than their enemies. He never planned his complicated plots in advance, preferring to watch them grow out of his characters. That, combined with his uncanny ear for dialogue, his effective use of sometimes grisly violence, and his unforced use of satiric wit and ironic plot twists, gave his books a natural sense of reality. "If it sounds like writing," he once said, "I rewrite it."

Leonard was born in New Orleans, La., on Oct. 11, 1925. His father, who worked for General Motors, moved the family repeatedly until they settled in 1935 near Detroit, where Leonard remained. An avid athlete in high school, he was nicknamed for Dutch Leonard, a pitcher for the Washington Senators. Leonard served in the U.S. Navy during World War II, received his Ph.D. from the University of Detroit (1950), and then went to work for a Detroit advertising agency, where he wrote copy for Chevrolet trucks. He wrote Western stories for pulp magazines in his spare time and then began writing novels. He quit advertising after his fifth novel, *Hombre* (1961), was published, but he earned extra money writing educational films for Encyclopædia Britannica, Inc.

With the release of the film version of *Hombre* (1967), Leonard could finally devote himself to fiction. He wrote several novels and screenplays for *The Moonshine War* (1970), *Joe Kidd* (1972), and *Mr. Majestyk* (1974) before switching to urban crime novels in the mid-1970s. In the 1980s he shifted his locales from Detroit to the seamier side of Miami. With *Stick* and *LaBrava* (both 1983) Leonard began to gain notice. The film version of *Stick* (1985) was a critical and box-office failure, a fact that Leonard blamed on its divergence from his original screenplay. *Glitz,* his 1985 novel based mainly in Puerto Rico and Atlantic City, was a best-seller almost from its publication, however.

Lightner, Candy

When an automobile swerved out of control and took the life of her 13-year-old daughter in May 1980, Candy Lightner discovered the nightmare of losing a child. Soon she also discovered that she had to do something about the drunk-driving problem in the United States, where every year 28,000 Americans were being killed by intoxicated drivers. Clarence Busch, the 46-year-old cannery worker who had killed Cari Lightner in Fair Oaks, Calif., had a long arrest record for drunk driving and indeed only the week before had made bail on an intoxicated driving charge after a hit-and-run accident.

On the eve of Cari's funeral, Lightner learned of Busch's record and how unlikely it was that he would spend time in jail for killing her daughter. Infuriated, the 33-year-old divorced real-estate agent resolved to change the way drunk driving was handled by courts. She had in mind no programs or methods, only an unstoppable determination to get drunks off U.S. highways.

Lightner's first step was to urge Gov. Jerry Brown of California to appoint a task force to deal with the problem. At first Brown refused to meet with her, but her repeated visits to his office attracted newspaper coverage of her crusade, eventually persuading him to appoint a task force that included her. Thus was Mothers Against Drunk Drivers (MADD) officially launched.

Within a year after MADD's establishment, California had passed tough new legislation that included mandatory imprisonment for repeat offenders and initial fines of $375. (Clarence Busch eventually served 21 months in jail for killing Cari Lightner.) By 1985 all 50 states had tougher laws against drunk driving, and in July 1984 Lightner was at the side of U.S. Pres. Ronald Reagan when he signed into law a bill reducing federal highway grants to states that failed to raise the legal drinking age to 21.

Lightner's goals included establishing an indemnity fund and bill of rights for victims as well as automatic imprisonment in every state for repeat offenders. However, late in 1985 she was stripped of much of her power in MADD, losing her titles of chairman and chief executive officer though remaining as president and chief spokesperson. Critics of her administration said that it had placed too much emphasis on fund-raising and not enough on programs.

Li Peng

Li Peng (Li P'eng) became prominent in 1985 as one of the young Chinese leaders obviously being groomed to succeed such aging veterans as Deng Xiaoping (Teng Hsiao-p'ing) and Chen Yun (Ch'en Yün), whose roles in party and government were inevitably coming to an end. Elected to the Secretariat of the Central Committee of the Communist Party and the ruling Politburo, Li was being prominently mentioned as a potential successor to Premier Zhao Ziyang (Chao Tzu-yang). Li traveled to Moscow in March 1985 to represent China at Konstantin Chernenko's funeral and was well received by the new general secretary of the Soviet Communist Party, Mikhail Gorbachev. The meeting attracted much attention and was said to have resulted in a better understanding between the two Communist giants. His July visit to the U.S., during which he toured major industrial plants and energy complexes and held extensive discussions with leading industrialists and economic experts, received equal attention.

Li Peng was born in Chengdu (Ch'eng-tu), Sichuan (Szechwan) Province, in 1928. A foster son of the late premier Zhou Enlai (Chou En-lai), Li joined the Communist Party in 1945. During 1946–48 he held several minor posts in factories in northeastern China. In 1948 he went to Moscow, where he attended the Moscow Power Institute and became president of the Chinese Students' Association. After his return to China in 1955, he held posts with electric power agencies in the northeast until his transfer in 1966 to Peking, where he was named to similar positions. His rapid rise began in 1979 when he was appointed vice-minister of China's power industry. Elected to the party's Central Committee in 1982, he became vice-premier in 1983 and chairman of the State Education Commission in 1985. With responsibility for education, energy, transportation, and economic development, Li continued to grow in power and prestige. A technocrat known for his pragmatic approaches to China's domestic problems, Li appeared destined to play an important role in the post-Deng era.

McTaggart, David

Among the founders of the environmentalist group Greenpeace was David McTaggart, the organization's chief spokesman and chairman of Green-

ALAIN NOGUES—SYGMA

peace International since 1979. The Canadian businessman had become involved with the issue of French atmospheric nuclear weapons testing in New Zealand in 1971, and his life was tied to environmental issues from then on.

McTaggart was born in Vancouver, B.C., on June 24, 1932. As a youth he was an outstanding athlete. Moving to California in the 1960s, he became a successful building contractor and developer. He was deeply affected when two of his employees were seriously injured in an explosion at a resort lodge built by his firm. In 1971, emotionally recovered and with a new political focus, he helped found Greenpeace International in New Zealand. The group's purpose was to campaign for a "green peace," working with rather than against natural forces, carrying out peaceful but uncompromising actions in defense of the environment.

The following year McTaggart attracted attention by sailing his 38-ft (12.6-m) sailboat, formerly the *Vega* and renamed *Greenpeace III*, to French Polynesia, where, near Mururoa Atoll, France was about to conduct another in a series of atmospheric nuclear tests that had been occurring since 1966. *Greenpeace III* observed international law in establishing its anchor position, and the presence of the single small boat forced the French government to halt the testing. A French Navy vessel eventually rammed the boat to end the embarrassing situation. McTaggart repaired his boat and returned a year later, this time with an escort composed of antinuclear members of the Australian Labor Party and the New Zealand Labour Party. He was physically beaten by French military personnel, who denied the charge, claiming that McTaggart's ship had already left the area. Published photographs of the battered environmentalist, however, ultimately proved them to be lying.

McTaggart entered into lengthy litigation against the French. In 1977 he began organizing new support throughout Europe for Greenpeace, by then established in 17 countries and headquartered in Lewes, England, where McTaggart lived. The growth of the organization was hampered by internal disputes, but McTaggart resolved these problems in 1979 and was elected chairman of the newly established International Greenpeace Council.

In July 1985 another Greenpeace vessel, the *Rainbow Warrior,* a 160-ft (48.8-m), 30-year-old converted trawler, sailed toward Mururoa Atoll to protest once again against the French. While moored in Auckland [N.Z.] Harbour, the rainbow-painted ship was ripped apart by an explosion, causing it to sink and killing a Greenpeace photographer. Two persons arrested in connection with the blast proved to be members of the French secret service. They were tried by a New Zealand court and convicted in November, while in France the affair was acutely embarrassing to the government, which dismissed two high-ranking officials in an effort to limit the political fallout.

Mamet, David

Perhaps the most successful U.S. playwright during the last decade, David Mamet brought to the stage a unique intellectual sensibility that enabled him to explore the working-class world through the mind of the average man. The 37-year-old Pulitzer Prize-winning Mamet was fascinated by the male psyche, and he wrote in an inimitable stark style, playing variations on the theme of exploitation. Indeed,

though writing in another genre, it was remarked by many critics that Mamet bore a deep resemblance to Ernest Hemingway.

Mamet was born in Chicago on Nov. 30, 1947, to Jewish parents who divorced when he was ten. The playwright seemed to have been profoundly affected by his broken home. Although he moved to the suburbs when he was 13, Mamet often spent weekends in Chicago on his own, unconsciously gathering material for the poignant dramas he would eventually create. During his late teens he worked at Second City, Chicago's well-known comedy club. He attended Goddard College in Vermont and later taught there and at New York University.

An aspiring actor, Mamet at 20 began writing scenes for himself and his friends to act out together. Within four years, he had formed a Chicago theater company, the St. Nicholas, and installed himself as the resident playwright. He was self-taught and initially had no clear or fixed ideas about writing technique or philosophy. It was perhaps for this reason that Mamet emerged as a popular and prolific author of plays that were characterized by their calculated use of stage action and stark, uncomplicated dialogue.

By 1975 Mamet had written and produced, to critical acclaim, *Sexual Perversity in Chicago* and *American Buffalo.* He followed those early successes with such highly regarded dramas as *The Water Engine, Edmond,* and *Glengarry Glen Ross* and the screenplay for *The Verdict.* For *Glengarry Glen Ross* he won both the Pulitzer Prize and the New York Drama Critics Circle Award for the best play of 1984.

Mandela, Nelson Rolihlahla

During the 21 years he had served as a life prisoner, Nelson Mandela had become black South Africa's folk hero. Opinion polls showed that 70% of the country's 23.9 million blacks regarded him as their leader. His importance in the republic's changing political system was recognized by Pres. P. W. Botha when he offered to release Mandela provided he first renounced violence. As the initiator of the armed struggle, Mandela refused the offer of personal freedom. However, when the British human rights campaigner Lord Bethell was allowed to visit him in Pollsmoor Prison, Mandela said he was ready to call a truce in the armed struggle if the authorities would "legalize us, treat us like a political party, and negotiate with us."

Mandela was given his life sentence in 1964 after admitting responsibility for having started Umkonto We Sizwe (Spear of the Nation) to wage an armed struggle against South Africa's system of apartheid (racial separation). While in prison he was elected president-general of the banned African National Congress (ANC), the country's oldest black nationalist organization, founded in 1912. His wife, Winnie, also gained prominence by her defiance of the authorities despite a banning order restricting her to

Brandfort, a small village in the Orange Free State.

Nelson Mandela was born in July 1918 at Umtata in Tembuland, Transkei. After completing his education at a Methodist missionary school in Transkei, he took an arts degree at the black University College (now University) of Fort Hare, the nursery of black nationalist politicians. In 1941 he hurriedly left home to avoid a traditionally arranged marriage; instead, he began to study law at the University of the Witwatersrand in Johannesburg. After qualifying he entered into a law partnership with Oliver Tambo, and both founded the ANC Youth League in 1944.

The Sharpeville shootings in 1960 followed by the banning of the ANC and the Pan-African Congress led to Mandela's decision to break with the ANC's traditional policies of nonviolent resistance. He clandestinely went abroad in 1962 to seek support elsewhere in Africa and in Britain. On his return home he was arrested, and in November 1962 he was sentenced to five years in prison for subversive activity and leaving the country illegally. While still in jail he was prosecuted along with other ANC leaders in the celebrated Rivonia trial of 1963–64, which led to his life sentence.

Mitterrand, François Maurice

As 1985 drew to a close and the legislative elections to be held in France in March 1986 loomed closer, the time had come to take stock of what Pres. François Mitterrand had accomplished as chief of state since 1981. The year had been a testing one, marked in particular by the "Greenpeace affair" and later in the year by Prime Minister Laurent Fabius's public disavowal of his president's decision

to receive the Polish leader, Gen. Wojciech Jaruzelski, at the Élysée Palace. Nevertheless, at year's end Mitterrand projected a confident image in defending the record of his Socialist government.

Certainly mistakes had been made in the first year of the president's seven-year term: too many reforms in too little time, the complete nationalization of several major private concerns, the 39-hour workweek with a fifth week of paid vacation, and the mishandling of a dispute over education. However, by appointing Fabius prime minister in 1984, Mitterrand made restraint the new central theme of his policy, asserting then that modernization of the economy was the top priority. While unemployment had not fallen during the five-year period, inflation was going down and at the end of 1985 reached 5%, the average for members of the European Communities. At the same time, the franc was strong and the stock market flourishing.

Mitterrand was the first president of the Fifth Republic to have reached the presidency directly from the leadership of a major political party. The contradictions of the man, with his right-wing culture and his left-wing conscience, made for a rich and complex personality. He might well be inclined to accept a sharing of responsibilities that would allow "cohabitation" between a left-wing president and a right-wing parliamentary majority—something that had never occurred before but might well come about after the 1986 elections. Tested in power, Mitterrand had given priority to realism and had undertaken the modernization of the left and of society.

Born into a bourgeois family on Oct. 26, 1916, at Jarnac (Charente), Mitterrand trained as a lawyer in Paris and in 1946 was elected deputy for the Nièvre. A member of several governments under

the Fourth Republic, he became first secretary of the Socialist Party in 1971. Thenceforth he devoted himself to making the Socialists, at the expense of the Communists, the majority party of the left.

Modigliani, Franco

Citing the practical applications of his work as well as his enormous influence in the field of corporate finance, a five-member selection committee awarded the Nobel Memorial Prize in Economic Science to Franco Modigliani, a professor at the Massachusetts Institute of Technology. The 67-year-old laureate economist pioneered research both in the analysis of household savings and in the determination of the effects of various types of national pension programs.

At the news conference announcing the prestigious prize, Modigliani wasted no time in criticizing the United States' "disastrous" federal deficit, stating that the debt "offsets savings by people and leaves less money for investment." The MIT professor called on Pres. Ronald Reagan to raise taxes and reduce defense spending.

Modigliani was born in Rome on June 18, 1918. While a law student at the University of Rome, he entered an essay contest on the topic of price controls. After he won first prize, the contest judges urged him to consider a career in economics. After he earned his law degree, he and his wife fled Italy's Fascist regime, arriving in New York in 1939. Modigliani enrolled at Manhattan's New School for Social Research, where he received his Ph.D. in social sciences in 1944. After teaching at several colleges he went to MIT in 1962.

Modigliani's research in the area of savings was first published in 1954 and was labeled his life-cycle theory. It linked household savings to demography, economic growth, and individual behavior, holding that people save for their retirement and not to pass savings on to offspring. He and a colleague then went on to develop the theory that a company's market value is unrelated to the size and structure of its indebtedness; that, rather, stock market values are basically determined by a business's expectations of future earnings. While this had become conventional 1980s wisdom in economics classrooms, on Wall Street, and in corporate boardrooms, when it was first presented in 1958, little attention was paid to the idea that investors should focus on the future. "His work in the late '50s provided the basis for modern corporate finance," according to one Nobel committee member.

Morishita, Yoko

Prima ballerina Yoko Morishita was slower to achieve recognition in Japan than abroad, but on Oct. 14, 1985, Prime Minister Yasuhiro Nakasone honored her with a special commendation for improving the status of Japanese women. Morishita had been an inspiration through her dedication to classical dance and her success as Japan's only inter-

SANKEI SHINBUN

national ballet star. In 1971 she won the prestigious gold medal in the Varna International Competition in Bulgaria, and within two years she was dancing all over the world. *Giselle, Sleeping Beauty, Romeo and Juliet, The Nutcracker, Swan Lake,* and *Don Quixote* were included in her repertoire, as well as modern works by Maurice Béjart and George Balanchine. Partnered by Rudolf Nureyev, Fernando Bujones, Jorge Donn, or her husband, Tetsutaro Shimizu, Morishita gave about 100 performances a year in Japan and abroad. In 1985 she performed with Nureyev in the tenth Nureyev Festival in London. The two appeared together again in Greece and Japan dancing *Swan Lake* and *Don Quixote*.

The 37-year-old ballerina began dancing at age three in Hiroshima, where she was born on Dec. 7, 1948. In 1956 she went to Tokyo to train with dance pioneer Akiko Tachibana. At 13 she performed in *Coppelia;* at 15 she danced Odette/Odile in *Swan Lake*. After studying for a year in the U.S. when she was 20 and after dancing with the American Ballet Theatre, she returned to Japan via Europe. Though she was invited to join the Stuttgart (West Germany) Ballet and Maurice Béjart's Ballet of the Twentieth Century in Brussels, she declined. She joined Tokyo's Matsuyama Ballet in 1970 determined to make her career in the company that was directed by her father-in-law.

Because Morishita was only 5 ft (1.5 m) tall, she had to develop elegance without the advantage of height. "It all depends on how you use your muscles," she once explained. She believed she possessed a sensitivity and delicacy that was unique among Japanese ballerinas. She called it "the beauty of tranquillity," and with her subtle acting skills she astounded audiences and charmed the critics. Terry Trucco, one such critic, spoke for many when he called attention to the ballerina's "elegant line, inherent musicality, and formidable technique." Morishita said that a ballerina's physical strength declines after 40, but she insisted she wanted to continue dancing for 20 more years.

Pendleton, Clarence

Clarence Pendleton attracted few friends during his tenure as the first black chairman of the U.S. Commission on Civil Rights—but he drew a wealth of new labels. The media variously called him "controversial," "irrepressible," "outspoken," "combative," and "sharp-tongued" for his statements antagonizing civil rights leaders. In 1985 Pendleton seemed determined to live up to every last adjective; he called upon civil rights advocates to "drop their divisive, unpopular, and immoral insistence" on quotas; he accused black leaders of fostering a "new racism" with their demands for "preferential treatment" for blacks; and he advised black leaders to petition Congress for "reparations" if they believed the U.S. owed a debt to blacks for past injustices.

Ironically, Pendleton's early history resembled that of a civil rights leader. Born on Nov. 10, 1930, he grew up in a Washington, D.C., ghetto. He overcame that environment to graduate from Howard University in 1954 and later served as a swimming coach and gym instructor there. In 1968, because of a strong belief in government help for blacks, he became recreational coordinator for Baltimore's Model Cities program, a federally funded effort to revive poor, mainly black neighborhoods.

UPI/BETTMANN NEWSPHOTOS

In 1972 Pendleton moved to the West and veered to the right. As director of the Model Cities program in San Diego, Calif., he found that hope for progress for blacks lay with private industry rather than in public assistance, a discovery encouraged by two new friends, Republican Mayor Pete Wilson and Edwin Meese, a confidante of then-governor Ronald Reagan. With their backing he became head of the San Diego Urban League, where he initiated business development projects that, according to Pendleton, created 8,000 jobs for the poor. Some critics later contended that his programs for economic progress came at the expense of social service programs.

In 1981, wanting a conservative to head the U.S. Commission on Civil Rights—an advisory body that monitored the enforcement of civil rights laws—President Reagan gave the job to Pendleton. Three years later Pendleton joined other Reagan appointees in ending the commission's long-standing support for racial quotas. Under Pendleton's leadership the commission also opposed the concept of "comparable worth," which would require employers to pay equally for different jobs judged to be similar by various criteria. Pendleton outraged some women's groups by calling the concept of comparable worth "the looniest idea since 'Looney Tunes' came on the scene."

Perry, William

After William Perry's rookie season turned into a living cartoon show, his Chicago Bears coach explained why he used the 305-lb (138.5-kg) defensive tackle as an offensive fullback. "Morale," said coach Mike Ditka. The poor guy was not getting to play on defense, so Ditka put him on the goal-line offense to make him feel more a part of the team. "I never intended to make him a national hero," Ditka said.

But he did. By the time Perry scored his fourth touchdown of the season in the Bears' Super Bowl victory, he may have been the most adored athlete in the world. He made U.S. football a booming fad in England. In the United States, people who barely followed football were suddenly fascinated by "The Refrigerator," or (less formally) "The Fridge." He was on the covers of national newsmagazines and the couches of nightly talk shows. He did commercials for a car, a fast-food restaurant, a soft drink, and even a brokerage house. His likeness was sold on everything from T-shirts to drinking glasses. In a word, Perry was big.

"Every underdog in America identifies with him," Ditka said. "And everyone who's two or three pounds overweight." Perry was at once a hero and a national pet. He might have come off as a bully when his block bent 226-lb (102.5-kg) Green Bay linebacker George Cumby backward like a sapling on his first goal-line play, but Perry was too clearly a nice, gentle, innocent country kid who turned the big city on its ear.

JOHN BIEVER/SPORTS ILLUSTRATED

William Perry was born Dec. 16, 1962, in Aiken, S.C., the tenth of 12 children. He weighed 13½ lb (6.1 kg). "I was big when I was little," he said. He weighed 220 (100) in seventh grade and 315 (143) as a college freshman at Clemson University, when teammate Ray Brown saw him fill an elevator door, decided he was as big as a refrigerator, and called him G.E. As a senior, he led the country with 27 tackles behind the line and was Atlantic Coast Conference player of the year.

The Bears drafted him in the first round and were promptly criticized for gambling on someone who had weighed 370 lb (168 kg). "We'd rather have him for us than against us," personnel director Bill Tobin said. The team's defensive coordinator, Buddy Ryan, called him "a waste of money and a wasted draft pick" after he showed up at training camp out of shape. But he trained hard, lost weight, and finished the season playing defense fairly well; he was a starter from the eighth game on and sacked five quarterbacks, a thrill he preferred even over scoring touchdowns.

Perry first carried the ball in the sixth game. He scored a touchdown and blocked for two more in the seventh game, against Green Bay. Two weeks later he caught a touchdown pass. When he was not scoring, he kept Fridge Fever alive by trying to lift a teammate into the end zone and lumbering 59 yd with a recovered fumble. The incongruity of it all was a refreshing delight in a league so preoccupied with pretentious dignity. "The publicity and success he's had is unbelievable," Ditka said. "The one thing that shows above all others is the kid is one heck of an athlete."

Peterson, David

When David Peterson was sworn in as the 20th premier of the province of Ontario on June 26, 1985, he became the first leader of the Liberal Party to hold that office since 1943. Following the provincial election of May 2, 1985, the Progressive Conservative Party held a tenuous four-seat plurality in the legislature. The Liberal Party and the New Democratic Party (NDP) then joined forces to topple the minority government of Premier Frank Miller and, with the support of the NDP, David Peterson formed a government.

Born Dec. 29, 1943, in Toronto, David Robert Peterson was raised in London, Ont., where his family owned an electronics distributing firm. After obtaining his B.A. in political science and philosophy from the University of Western Ontario in London (1964), Peterson attended the University of Toronto Law School, graduating in 1967. Although called to the bar in 1969 and given the honorary title of queen's counsel by the Ontario government in 1981, Peterson never practiced law. He preferred instead to work as president of his family's business, for which he obtained the lucrative exclusive national distributorship rights for Japanese-made Sharp electronic equipment. As a businessman, Peterson established a solid record of community service. He was a member of the London Chamber of Commerce and the honorary patron of the 1984 Free Olympiad. The youngest president of the London Canadian Club, he was also the first to admit women as members.

The Petersons were a political family. David Peterson's father was a city alderman in London, and his brother Jim was a member of the Canadian Parliament. Peterson's wife, the former Shelley Matthews (whom he married in 1974), was the daughter of a former national president of the Conservative Party. Although he was successful in his business, Peterson too was interested in a political career. In 1975 he was elected to the Ontario legislature, where he was made Liberal Party finance critic. Running on a reform platform, Peterson was elected leader of the Ontario Liberal Party in February 1982. He proved his reputation for organizing and fund-raising skills when he succeeded in raising $350,000 toward the party's debt in only three months. In the 1985 election he ran a methodical and carefully planned campaign. As premier, Peterson vowed to conduct an open and accessible government, sealing this promise by becoming the first premier of Ontario to take the oath of office in a public, outdoor ceremony.

Pickens, T(homas) Boone, Jr.

In 1985 the biggest story in U.S. business was corporate takeovers. The most successful and controversial of the "corporate raiders" involved in these takeovers was T. Boone Pickens, the founder, president, and chairman of the board of Mesa Petroleum Co. During 1982–85 Pickens led Mesa Petroleum in several takeover battles with oil companies many times larger than Mesa. In every case Pickens lost the takeover attempt while gaining enormous profits. Pickens's critics accused him of applying corporate "greenmail" (buying a block of stock to force a buyout without a genuine desire to acquire the target company). Pickens, however, claimed to be "the champion of the small stockholder," and his supporters contended that his targets were poorly managed companies with undervalued stock and entrenched managements.

Pickens was born into the oil business on May 22, 1928, in Holdenville, Okla., where his father worked for Phillips Petroleum and speculated in oil leases. After receiving a degree in geology from Oklahoma State University in 1951, he worked for Phillips Petroleum until 1955, when he launched Petroleum Exploration (incorporated as Mesa Petroleum in 1964). During the 1960s and '70s he built Mesa into a thriving exploration and production firm, but in 1979 he created Mesa Royalty Trust to divest Mesa Petroleum of its production properties. His seemingly unerring instincts led him to sell Mesa holdings in Canada and the North Sea just before the industry in those regions slumped.

In 1982 Pickens made his first takeover assault, on Cities Service. When Occidental Petroleum bought out Cities Service instead, Pickens and Mesa made a pretax profit of more than $30 million. He lost out to Phillips Petroleum in a bid for General American Oil in 1983 for a profit of more than $43 million. Similar attacks on Superior Oil, Gulf Petroleum, and Phillips itself led to other financially advantageous "losses." In 1985 Pickens took on Unocal Corp., which put up the toughest fight yet, with lawsuits, proxy fights, and other antitakeover measures. Once again, Mesa's "loss" resulted in a pretax profit. Pickens announced in late 1985 that Mesa would soon be converted into a limited partnership with himself as the largest general partner, allowing him more time and money to pursue his raids.

Reagan, Ronald Wilson

Inaugurated for a second term as president of the United States on Jan. 20, 1985, Ronald Reagan celebrated his 74th birthday on February 6 with an optimistic state of the union message to Congress. Later in the year his optimistic attitude served him well as he faced severe criticism for certain travel plans and underwent major surgery. He remained outwardly undaunted by the inability of Congress to act on the budget or on his proposal to reform the federal income tax and by indications of economic problems in the future.

In January Reagan's itinerary for a trip to Europe in May was released. A projected trip to the Nazi prison camp at Dachau was excluded a few weeks later, and in April plans made with West German Chancellor Helmut Kohl to lay a wreath at a cemetery for German soldiers of World Wars I and II near Bitburg, West Germany, were announced.

AP/WIDE WORLD

Organizations of Jews and of war veterans objected vehemently to the choice of the cemetery because members of the Waffen SS, the group that operated Nazi Germany's prison camps, were buried there. On May 5 Reagan visited both the site of a Nazi prison camp at Bergen-Belsen and the cemetery near Bitburg.

On July 13 Reagan transferred all of his authority to Vice-Pres. George Bush and underwent surgical removal of more than one and a half feet of his colon. A polyp in the removed tissue was found to be cancerous, but physicians saw no threat to his life. Released from the hospital on July 20, Reagan jauntily joked about sending his surgeon "up to Capitol Hill to do some cutting." A patch of skin removed from Reagan's nose on July 30 was also found to be cancerous but not threatening.

On November 19 in Geneva Reagan for the first time met an incumbent general secretary of the Communist Party of the Soviet Union, Mikhail Sergeyevich Gorbachev. By November 21 the two leaders had agreed to plan future meetings and to work to reduce their arsenals of strategic nuclear weapons by 50%.

Ronald Reagan was born in Tampico, Ill., on Feb. 6, 1911. He received a B.A. from Eureka College in 1932 and then became a broadcaster in Iowa. In 1937 he became an actor under contract with Warner Brothers. He served as president of the Screen Actors Guild from 1947 to 1952 and 1959 to 1960 and was a host of dramatic television shows from 1954 to 1965. He was governor of California from 1967 to 1975 and was inaugurated for his first presidential term in 1981.

Reeves, The Most Rev. Sir Paul Alfred

When Paul Alfred Reeves, Anglican bishop of Auckland, was elected by the General Synod of the Church in 1980 as primate and archbishop of New Zealand, he said he was prepared to live with two possibilities as a 47-year-old facing a long and unique appointment: that he should give it a term and get out or stay and see out his useful life in the job. He also said he would not dismiss the possibility that "God may say one day, 'Reeves, I want you to do something else.' " God apparently did call again, in 1985, to ask him to represent his temporal leader, Queen Elizabeth II, as governor-general of New Zealand.

His excellency the Most Rev. Sir Paul Reeves (he was knighted in the queen's birthday honors) succeeded Sir David Beattie at Government House, Wellington, in November. He was the first clergyman and the first New Zealander of Maori descent to be so appointed. Reeves was born Dec. 6, 1932, the son of a Wellington tram (streetcar) driver. His Maori blood derived from his maternal grandmother. Reeves saw no significance in that background during his upbringing in one of Wellington's less pretentious suburbs and his primary schooling at Wellington South. He went on to Wellington College and then to the Victoria University of Wellington.

Reeves supported himself through his university years with vacation work in a wool store, on the wharves, in the Post Office, and as a waiter at a mountain resort. With a master of arts degree he changed course from training for teaching to theology. He had cause to appreciate his Maori background when the Maori Affairs Department assisted him to a scholarship at St. Peter's College, University of Oxford, England. He had already been ordained a deacon in the diocese of Waikato and had been curate in the timberland town of Tokoroa. He served as curate in English parishes and was ordained priest by the bishop of Oxford in 1960—the year after he married Beverley Watkins, a Wellington schoolteacher who was to bear him three daughters.

From 1964 to 1966 Reeves was back in New Zealand as vicar of St. Paul, Okato, on the Taranaki coast. While on the Taranaki coast, the region from which his Maori grandmother came, Reeves became aware of this part of his heritage and of Maori grievances. He started to identify with Maoris and their causes and went on to develop some notoriety as a commentator on social issues. During 1966–69 he lectured on church history at St. John's College, Auckland, was then director of Christian education (1969–71) for the Auckland diocese, and later was chairman (1974–76) of New Zealand's Environmental Council.

Regan, Donald Thomas

In February 1985, when James Baker succeeded Donald Regan as U.S. secretary of the treasury, Regan succeeded Baker as chief of staff to Pres. Ronald Reagan. Regan, who had a strong background in both administration and finance, quickly assumed control of the staff in the White House. Baker, more of a political strategist than an administrator, had cooperated closely with Michael Deaver, the deputy chief of staff, and Edwin Meese, counselor to the president. The departure from the White House of Meese (who became attorney general in February) and of Deaver (who returned to the private sector) left Regan alone at the staff's apex. In April the president instructed department heads and other ranking officials to meet as the Economic Policy Council, with Baker as chairman, when formulating economic policy and as the Domestic Policy Council, with Meese as chairman, when formulating noneconomic domestic policy. As the official liaison between the president and the two councils, Regan was in a position to influence the final form of all domestic policies. In May, after a public-relations debacle involving the president's visit to a German cemetery that contained graves of elite Nazi troops, Regan also assumed full control over the president's schedule.

Regan was born in Cambridge, Mass., on Dec. 21, 1918. He graduated from Harvard University (1940) and entered Harvard Law School but left to join the U.S. Marine Corps as an officer candidate. In 1946, after service in the Pacific, he retired from the military and became a stockbroker trainee for Merrill Lynch, Pierce, Fenner, & Beane. He worked in the firm's offices in Washington, Philadelphia, and New York City, becoming its president in 1968 and serving as chairman of the board and chief executive officer from 1971 to 1980. In 1973 he assumed the same titles at Merrill Lynch and Co., Inc., a holding company formed as a result of his diversification program. A strong believer in the free market system, he defended his company's increasing competition with banks and persuaded the directors of the New York Stock Exchange to abolish fixed fees for brokers.

Appointed secretary of the treasury by President Reagan in 1981, Regan favored deregulation of banking. In 1984 he proposed a plan to reform the federal income tax by reducing the number of brackets and abolishing most deductions. The Reagan administration continued to advocate a modified version of his plan in 1985.

Riddles, Libby

The Iditarod Trail dogsled race had been a 1,135-mi (1,826-km) endurance test, dedicated to masochism and machismo. It went from Anchorage to Nome, Alaska, across two mountain ranges, a river, and two time zones, retracing the main winter supply route to Nome during the turn-of-the-century gold rush, a monument to a time when men were men. But on March 20, 1985, Libby Riddles drove the first dogsled across the finish line at Nome's tavern-lined Front Street. She was the first woman winner

JAMES MAGDANZ—SYGMA

Rose, Pete

Pete Rose always played baseball with enough energy to light up Cincinnati. In 23 seasons his energy lit up more hit signs on the scoreboard than any other major-league player. He broke Ty Cobb's legendary record of 4,191 hits on Sept. 11, 1985, after a national countdown. The Cincinnati Reds' player-manager finished the season with 4,204 and was aiming for 4,300. The 1986 season would begin shortly before his 45th birthday, April 14.

When he was the National League's rookie of the year in 1963, Rose was regarded as a marginally talented switch-hitter who got the most out of his ability. He was an instant fans' favorite, running to first base on walks and sliding head-first, but players nicknamed him "Charlie Hustle" with a sneer. Like Cobb, Rose was vilified for his exuberant play, but unlike Cobb, Rose became a grand old man, not a bitter one.

He set 34 major and National League (NL) records. He was the NL most valuable player in 1973, the World Series most valuable player in 1975, and the *Sporting News* NL player of the decade for the 1970s. He played in six World Series, was an All-Star 16 times, and led the league in batting average three times. He was 37 when he had hits in 44 consecutive games in 1978, a modern NL record. The next year he had 200 hits for the tenth time, a major league record.

Rose's record sparked controversy as people defended Cobb's unrivaled .367 average in 24 seasons, .063 higher than Rose's. Rose always gave him his due. In 1984 he named his baby son Tyler, the modern version of Cobb's Tyrus. Many Cincinnatians never forgave the Reds for letting Rose get away in a salary squabble in 1979, and they savored

in the race's 13 years, finishing 2½ hours ahead of runner-up Duane Halverson. She had raced the Iditarod only twice before, finishing 18th in 1980 and 19th in 1981.

Fifteen of the 61 entrants already had dropped out. One was Susan Butcher, a two-time runner-up who had been the only woman to finish in the top five. A moose had torn through her team, killing two dogs. Other hazards in the frozen wilderness were frostbite, hypothermia, icy trails, fatigue-induced hallucinations, and blinding blizzards. Conditions were worse than usual for the 1985 race. It lasted 18 days, compared with the record of a little more than 12. Winds were 70 knots, leaving trail markers virtually invisible, when Riddles crossed the ice of Norton Sound for her stretch run. "I just decided I was going to go out and try it," she said. When she won, Riddles added, "I'm just pretty glad to have it over with."

Elizabeth Nell Riddles was born April 1, 1956, in Madison, Wis. She moved to Alaska in 1974 after living in Bellingham, Wash., where she fell in love with the ocean and mountains and surmised, "Alaska would be the same, only more so. I was ready for an adventure." She settled in Teller, on the Seward Peninsula, and began dogsledding after a year in Alaska. Dogsled racers spend as much as $20,000 on their sport, mostly buying and caring for the dogs. Riddles raised $7,000 by sewing and selling fur hats and garments and trained by demonstrating sledding to tourists. "I thought I had the team to do it," she said of her 15 mixed-breed huskies, 13 of which finished the race. First prize was $50,000. Riddles's plans? "Maybe Hawaii," she said. "And a box of dog biscuits for each of the dogs."

HEINZ KLEUTMEIER/SPORTS ILLUSTRATED

his return as player-manager on Aug. 16, 1984, after stints in Philadelphia and Montreal. The city renamed a street Pete Rose Way for the hero who grew up on the West Side. Peter Edward Rose eclipsed the legend of his father, Harry, who played semipro football until he was 42.

He broke the career hitting record 57 years to the day after Cobb's last at bat, with a first-inning single to left against San Diego pitcher Eric Show. After the cheers subsided, Rose raised his index finger, looked toward heaven, and said he saw his father there, with Cobb right behind him. Then, as his 15-year-old son Petey ran to join him, Rose put his head on the shoulder of first-base coach Tommy Helms and cried.

Rostenkowski, Daniel

On May 28, 1985, he came on national television with a friendly growl, looking and sounding like a real-life version of Tony the Tiger, the popular cartoon character from TV commercials. But the burly political animal, Daniel Rostenkowski, was not selling cereal but offering a horse trade; if Americans pledged their support, his House Ways and Means Committee would pass a version of Pres. Ronald Reagan's tax-reform program. Rostenkowski's offer drew tens of thousands of enthusiastic letters. The Democratic congressman from Illinois then faced the hard part of his political bargain—maneuvering tax reform past 35 independent-minded committee members and countless privilege-seeking interest groups.

Rostenkowski approached that challenge with skills shaped by years of experience in Chicago's political jungle. He was born on Jan. 2, 1928, the son of a Polish-American family on the city's Near Northwest Side. His father long dominated the neighborhood as alderman and ward committeeman. During the 1950s, while serving in the Illinois legislature, the young Rostenkowski nurtured a close relationship with Mayor Richard Daley, the boss of Chicago's political machine; in 1958, with Daley's help, he won election to the U.S. House of Representatives, where he became known as a forceful wheeler-dealer who unabashedly spent all his time seeking aid for Chicago and tax breaks for its businesses. Rostenkowski's efforts pleased his largely ethnic, middle-class constituents, who reelected him each term by a large majority.

But the same kind of political brashness that impressed so many Chicagoans almost ended his climb to power in the House. At a tumultuous session of the 1968 Democratic convention, Rostenkowski mortified Chairman Carl Albert by stripping the gavel from his hand and quickly restoring order. Albert never forgave him and, as speaker of the House in 1970, Albert opposed Rostenkowski's bid to become majority whip.

Rostenkowski's next chance for a major promotion did not come until 1980, when Democratic leaders persuaded him to assume the chairmanship of the Ways and Means Committee. A year and a half later the *Washington Post* accused the new chairman of taking long golfing vacations that were paid for by groups having an interest in bills before his committee. But that allegation failed to tame Rostenkowski and his fierce ambition. He later indicated that he would still pounce on the chance to become speaker of the House or mayor of Chicago.

Sartzetakis, Christos

Christos Sartzetakis, a respected Supreme Court judge, was installed as president of Greece on March 30, 1985, for a five-year term following his election by the Greek Parliament. He succeeded Pres. Konstantinos Karamanlis, the conservative statesman who resigned after the Panhellenic Socialist Movement (Pasok) majority, in a surprise move, withdrew its support for his reelection. Sartzetakis was elected on the third round with the help of the Communist Party. The conservative New Democracy Party challenged the legality of the election, but after Pasok's victory in the June 2 general elections, the defeated conservatives withdrew their reservations.

Sartzetakis was born in Salonika, northern Greece, in 1929, the son of a Cretan gendarmerie officer. After law studies at the local university he was called to the bar in 1954 and became a justice of the peace in 1955. It was while serving as a judge of first instance that he first achieved prominence. Appointed magistrate to investigate the death of left-wing deputy Gregorios Lambrakis in Salonika in May 1963, he disproved the police version that it had occurred in a traffic accident and boldly exposed collusion between the police and right-wing hooligans in a political assassination. His courage, integrity, and determination inspired the novel *Z* by Vasilis Vasilikos, which later became a prizewinning film.

After the military coup in Greece in 1967, Sartzetakis, who was in Paris for postgraduate studies, was recalled and posted to Volos, in central Greece, as a misdemeanors judge. Barely a year later he was dismissed from the judiciary during a wholesale liquidation of senior judges hostile to the military regime. He was twice arrested and held without charge. He himself said he was tortured during his detention. He was set free during an amnesty in 1971 and, after the restoration of democracy in 1974, was reinstated and promoted to appeal court judge. In 1982 he was elected to the Supreme Court.

Shevardnadze, Eduard Amvrosiyevich

When, in July 1985, Andrei Gromyko was elected president of the Presidium of the Supreme Soviet—chief of state of the Soviet Union—the man appointed to replace him as foreign minister was Eduard Shevardnadze. Whereas Gromyko had held the post since 1957 and had been in the Soviet diplomatic service for many years before that, Shevardnadze was an apparatchik from Georgia

with no previous experience of foreign affairs and was virtually unknown outside the Soviet Union. His appointment was taken as an indication that Mikhail Gorbachev, the new general secretary of the Communist Party of the Soviet Union (CPSU), intended to play the leading role in foreign affairs himself.

Shevardnadze was born on Jan. 25, 1928, in the Mamati Lauchkhutsky region of Georgia, into a well-to-do family. Educated at the school of the Central Committee of the Communist Party of Georgia and at the Kutaisi Pedagogical Institute, he joined the Georgian Komsomol (Young Communist League) in 1946 and the CPSU in 1948. He held various posts in the Komsomol administration, advancing to first secretary (1957–61). Subsequently, he was first secretary (1961–63) of the Mtskheta district committee of the Communist Party of Georgia.

In 1964 Shevardnadze moved to the Georgian capital, Tbilisi, as first secretary for Pervomaysky district. The same year he was appointed first deputy minister and the following year minister of internal affairs of the Georgian S.S.R. In 1972 he was elected first secretary of the Tbilisi city committee and of the Central Committee of the Georgian party. As internal affairs minister he gained firsthand knowledge of high-level corruption and, as head of the Georgian party apparatus, he applied himself to the task of putting the house in order.

Shevardnadze became a member of the CPSU Central Committee in 1976 and two years later a candidate member of the Politburo and a deputy to the Supreme Soviet. His close association with Gorbachev secured his July 1985 election to full membership of the Politburo and his appointment as foreign minister. Shevardnadze's first appearances on the international scene outside the Soviet bloc were at the Helsinki meeting (July 30–August 1) marking the tenth anniversary of the Helsinki Accords, when he met U.S. Secretary of State George P. Shultz, and at the UN in September and October.

Simon, Claude

In awarding the Nobel Prize for Literature to 72-year-old Claude Simon of France, the Swedish Academy emphasized his novels' "deepened awareness of time in the depiction of the human condition." Although Simon was a leading writer in the genre known as the new novel, or *nouveau roman,* he was not well known outside literary circles. The term new novelist is applied to a wide spectrum of writers who develop their novels unconventionally, moving away from continuous plot and character development and drawing instead on narrative techniques not unlike those of William Faulkner and James Joyce.

Varied reactions to the announcement regarding Simon emerged. A former Nobel literature prizewinner, commenting on the unorthodoxy of Simon's style, predicted that "in the future, all the so-called experiments will disappear. All those books which tell a story and describe character will remain alive." On the other hand, another well-known author called the choice one of the "best in years," saying that Simon was a bold writer who had "forged" his own style. Simon himself was said to be very moved by the award, but he issued no public statement.

Claude-Eugène-Henri Simon was born on Oct. 10, 1913, in Tananarive, Madagascar. He grew up in Perpignan, a town in the south of France, where he still resided. His early education was in Paris, followed by brief periods of study in England. As a young man he tried his hand at painting and traveled extensively. He fought in the Spanish Civil War on the Republican side but became disillusioned with that cause. As a cavalryman in World War II he was taken prisoner in May 1940. He managed to escape and joined the French Resistance. It was during the war that he wrote his first novel, *Le Tricheur* ("The Trickster").

None of Simon's first four novels was translated into English. The turning point in his career, according to the Swedish Academy, was the publication of *Le Vent* (1957; *The Wind,* 1959) and *L'Herbe* (1958; *The Grass,* 1960). With these two novels he won critical acceptance of his idiosyncratic and sometimes difficult narrative style. In 1967 his novel *Histoire* (*History,* 1968) won the Prix de Medicis.

Springsteen, Bruce

A gold album and cover photos on two of the U.S.'s major news magazines ten years earlier did not bring Bruce Springsteen the kind of spectacular fame he achieved in 1985. With 13 million copies of *Born in the USA* sold throughout the world (the best seller in Columbia Records' history), "The Boss" became the most popular U.S. rock star since Elvis Presley. A 15-month tour completed in October took him to 62 cities around the world with every show sold out.

Springsteen was born in Freehold, N.J., on Sept. 23, 1949. A quiet and independent boy, he developed in his early teens an infatuation with the guitar and joined his first band when he was 14. He took a few courses at Ocean County (N.J.) Community College, but despite pressure from family, school, and church to abandon a musical career, he knew what he wanted to do with his life. He signed a contract with Columbia Records in June 1972, but it was not until autumn 1975 with *Born to Run* that Springsteen first received popular and critical attention.

A fuller sound than most bands of the 1970s plus Springsteen's high level of energy contributed to the enormous success of the album. On tour he made certain that no two performances were the same, offering an element of freshness and surprise to each audience.

But there were drawbacks to the extensive publicity of 1975. Springsteen saw himself becoming a commodity rather than a talent—he saw the danger of people not hearing his messages about faith and hope in a better world and the value of friendship. As he had said publicly many times, rock music brought purpose to his life, and he considered the trappings of fame to be distractions.

In the early 1980s Springsteen released *Nebraska,* an album that was described as a history lesson, a social outcry, a recognition of the anguish of the human spirit. Much of this sense of desperation also emerged in *Born in the USA.* The album's title song, about hopes put on hold, has a chorus that many took, out of context, to be a statement of pride in America. One music critic described this phenomenon as a classic case of people hearing what they wanted rather than what was really being said.

Stallone, Sylvester

In 1985, in movie theaters across the United States, Americans refought the war in Vietnam—and won. Their designated warrior was actor-writer Sylvester Stallone, whose Vietnam veteran in *Rambo: First Blood Part II* rescues American soldiers from a Vietnamese prison while shooting and slashing his way through hundreds of enemy troops. The film, appealing to a public that was increasingly receptive to rethinking the Vietnam experience, grossed more money in its first two weeks than any other R-rated film ever released. It succeeded despite negative reviews; a *Washington Post* critic compared *Rambo* to the Nazi cinema of the 1920s and 1930s, remarking, "Here's a movie that wears its brown shirt on its sleeve." That failed to perturb Stallone, who said, "I'm not political. . . . I stand for ordinary Americans, losers a lot of them."

Stallone belonged to that group of ordinary Americans in 1975, when, with $106 in the bank and a pregnant wife, a starving dog, and an unpaid landlord hovering around him, he sat down to write *Rocky.* Three and a half days later he completed the

SIPA/SPECIAL FEATURES

script, and by early 1977 *Rocky* had catapulted him into elite company; he joined Charlie Chaplin and Orson Welles as the only artists ever to win Oscar nominations for both best screenwriter and best actor. Though Rocky resembled a typical Hollywood underdog—the tenderhearted, down-and-out boxer who unexpectedly gets the chance to compete for the title—critics praised Stallone for the energy and freshness he brought to the role. He later directed himself in *Rocky II* (1979), *Rocky III* (1982), and *Rocky IV* (1985).

In 1982 he first appeared as John Rambo in the original *First Blood*. Coscripted by Stallone, the film focuses on an unappreciated war hero who is goaded into laying waste an Oregon town. Stallone played Rambo as a mumbling, musclebound warrior, a cross between Marlon Brando and Arnold Schwarzenegger.

Stallone was born in New York City on July 6, 1946. He was a sickly child but as a teenager took up weight lifting. He studied drama at the University of Miami, but the aspiring actor could never have imagined what lay ahead: that by late 1985 he would be fighting the cold war on the big screen, saving ordinary Americans from a runaway Soviet boxer in *Rocky IV*.

Takakura, Ken

One of Japan's most popular film stars, Ken Takakura marked his 30th year in movies in 1985. The handsome actor, whose close-cropped hair was his trademark, gained fame playing *yakuza* (gangster) roles during the 1960s. He generally portrayed outlaws whose impatience with hard luck finally drives them to seek revenge. Because they dared to attack the establishment, Takakura's characters were doomed to die or to rot in prison.

For audiences, emotional identification with Takakura's characters was more important than the films' message that society cannot tolerate vindictive outlaws. Moviegoers seemed to respond when the characters defied convention or manifested *giri* (obligation to the group) or *gaman* (stoic endurance). Takakura's riveting eyes, his stoic features, and his preference for silence over words seemed to strike a responsive chord in the hearts of those who also had to endure in silence.

Takakura became a cult hero to student radicals, notably those who occupied the Tokyo University campus buildings in 1969, because his movie roles had made him the *yakuza* par excellence of that era. When Japanese gangster films began to lose their box-office appeal in the early 1970s, Takakura joined U.S. film star Robert Mitchum in the Tokyo-Hollywood production *The Yakuza* (1974). In 1976 Takakura left the Toei Motion Picture Co., his home since 1955, to become a freelance actor. Characteristically, he was generally cast as a loner with a complicated past, in search of love and peace; he combined masculine toughness with equally believable tenderness. A series of successful films, including *The Yellow Handkerchiefs of Happiness* (1977) and *A Story of the Antarctic* (1983) proved that durable tough guys finish first. Takakura won the Japan Academy Award for outstanding male actor in both 1980 and 1981 for two other films in this same tradition: *The Call of Distant Mountains* and *Station*.

Takakura was born Goichi Oda in Kita-Kyushu City in Fukuoka Prefecture on Feb. 16, 1931. His

TOHO

mother was a schoolteacher, his father a mining company employee. He graduated from Meiji University, Tokyo, in 1954 and in 1956 made his first film. Takakura once confided to director Yoji Yamada that he felt uneasy when he first became an actor. Having to wear a costume and makeup made the macho star from Kyushu worry that acting was not a proper job for a man.

Takeshita, Noboru

One of the strongest contenders for the post of prime minister of Japan when Yasuhiro Nakasone's term expired in late 1986 would almost certainly be his minister of finance, Noboru Takeshita, whose surprisingly bold political moves served to obliterate his former image as a baby-faced lightweight in the ruling Liberal-Democratic Party (LDP). Polls, nonetheless, indicated that Takeshita faced an uphill battle for the party presidency, which had long been a guarantee of the prime ministership. Shintaro Abe, Japan's foreign minister, and Kiichi Miyazawa, chairman of the LDP executive council, were both considered potent rivals.

Some critics accused Takeshita of making a career out of avoiding commitments that could turn against him. Others, however, pointed out that under the iron rule of Kakuei Tanaka, the long-time strongman of Japanese politics and the leader of the pivotal LDP faction to which Takeshita belonged, the finance minister had little opportunity to assert himself. Events, however, took a dramatic turn in February 1985 when Takeshita inaugurated his own study group, Soseikai. Although this same ploy had previously been used by Tanaka to establish a personal power base within the ranks of the

SANKEI SHINBUN

Sato faction, Takeshita's move reportedly infuriated Tanaka and, some speculated, brought on the stroke he suffered in February 1985; the perennial power broker was out of action thereafter.

Takeshita's outspoken support for currency intervention at a meeting of five leading industrial nations in New York City in September 1985 was also uncharacteristically bold. He also promoted more liberal financial policies, but he chose to project the image of a team player by insisting there was no such thing as an independent Takeshita policy. The only political policy the aspiring party leader had clearly set forth was a call for speedier development of the backward countryside, a policy long espoused by his political mentor Tanaka.

Takeshita's links to rural Shimane, a poor mountainous area where he was born Feb. 26, 1924, remained strong. Before being elected to the lower house of the Diet (parliament) at the age of 34, Takeshita served seven years on the Shimane prefectural council. He appeared to have upset the political balance within the LDP and said he believed that when the votes for party president were tallied, personal relationships and political luck would prove to have been decisive factors in the outcome.

Thatcher, Margaret Hilda

In 1985 Britain's Prime Minister Margaret Thatcher celebrated her tenth anniversary as leader of the Conservative Party and at the same time indicated in a newspaper interview that she had "about another five years" to go "before someone else will carry the torch." She became prime minister in 1979, the first woman to hold the office, and in a landslide victory in 1983 became the first incumbent since World War II to win a second election after a full term. Throughout her terms of office she exercised an unusual dominance over her Cabinet colleagues, the governmental machine, and the public, but in 1985 opinion polls for the first time reported her to be less popular than the leaders of the three opposition parties.

With the defeat of the miners' strike that had begun in the previous year, she might have expected to have been buoyed to new heights as she had been following Britain's victory in the Falklands Islands/ Islas Malvinas conflict of 1982. But instead it was the Labour Party and its leader, Neil Kinnock, who benefited chiefly from the ending of the strike. After the government had done badly in local elections in May and had lost an important by-election in the Welsh seat of Brecon and Radnor in July, it became the widely held view that Thatcher, temporarily at least, had become an electoral liability to her party. The government softened the tone of its pronouncements and so did she; she even softened her hairstyle. By the end of the year, both the government's popularity and her own personal standing appeared to be recovering.

Born Oct. 13, 1925, in Grantham, the daughter of a shopkeeper, Thatcher won her way to the Uni-

PHILIPPE ACHACHE—CLICK/CHICAGO

versity of Oxford, where she studied chemistry. She later became a lawyer, was elected to Parliament in 1959, became a Cabinet minister under Edward Heath in 1970, and seized the party leadership from him in 1975. Her career was a mixture of persistent hard work and bold opportunism. As prime minister she personified the virtues of self-help and enterprise—the roots of a free-market philosophy nearer to that of classical Liberalism than to traditional Toryism. Her ambition, she declared, was to save Britain once and for all from socialism.

Thomas, Philip Michael
See Johnson, Don.

Tian Jiyun
When Tian Jiyun (T'ien Chi-yün) was elected to both the Secretariat of the Central Committee of the Chinese Communist Party and the Politburo in September 1985, he became a potential successor to such aging leaders as Deng Xiaoping (Teng Hsiaop'ing) and Li Xiannian (Li Hsien-nien). An economic specialist and chief deputy to Premier Zhao Ziyang (Chao Tzu-yang), Tian became involved in foreign affairs and in the implementation of practical reforms designed to achieve China's goal of modernization.

Born in Feicheng (Fei-ch'eng) County, Shandong (Shantung) Province, in 1929, Tian received little formal education and joined the Communist Party in 1945. In the late 1940s he was involved in violent Communist-led land reforms. After the

People's Republic was founded in 1949, he held a number of middle-level financial posts in Guizhou (Kweichow) Province, where he remained until his transfer to Sichuan (Szechwan) Province in 1969. In the late 1970s he assisted Zhao Ziyang, then governor of Sichuan, in carrying out experimental economic and agricultural reforms in the province. As Zhao's right-hand man, Tian played an important role in bold and flexible programs that deviated from Marxist principles but significantly increased industrial output and agricultural production. These results were achieved through such innovative policies as rewarding workers on the basis of work rather than need and providing incentives based on free enterprise and market forces rather than on rigid quotas established by central authorities. In addition, factory managers were given much greater autonomy, and peasants were allowed to benefit from individual initiative.

These approaches soon attracted national attention, and both Zhao and Tian were transferred to Peking, where they were appointed premier and deputy secretary-general of the State Council (Cabinet), respectively, in 1980. After being elected to the party's Central Committee in 1982, Tian became an important member of a team that successfully introduced to the entire nation Zhao's Sichuan reforms, which markedly speeded up China's economic development, especially in the agricultural sector. For these achievements Tian was promoted to vice-premier and secretary-general in 1983. Capable, energetic, and self-taught, Tian was noted for his down-to-earth approaches to China's agricultural and economic problems. An efficient administrator, he demonstrated his organizational ability by coordinating various agencies in China's massive bureaucracy.

Turner, Tina
Literally bouncing her way back to fame, Tina Turner underwent a revival in 1985 like no other rock star in recent memory. She rose to the top of the entertainment industry during the year with a multiplatinum album, *Private Dancer;* two Grammy awards for the gold single "What's Love Got to Do with It?" and one for the single "Better Be Good to Me"; and a leading role opposite Mel Gibson in the motion picture *Mad Max: Beyond Thunderdome.* Long known as one of entertainment's most spectacular performers, she created a unique persona through her youthful appearance, her kinetic energy, and her strongly individual taste in clothing and hairstyle.

Born Annie Mae Bullock in Nutbush, Tenn., on Nov. 26, 1938, to a cotton plantation manager and his wife, she dreamed as a girl of transcending the plight of a poor rural black family and becoming a Hollywood entertainer. As a schoolgirl she sang and danced in every available talent show. In the 1950s, after moving to St. Louis, Mo., she and her sister frequented nightclubs; in 1956 they met Ike

Turner and his band in one of the clubs. After hearing Annie sing, Turner used her occasionally in band engagements. In 1959 she filled in for a vocalist at a recording session, and the result was Ike's 800,000-seller entitled "A Fool in Love." Ike named his new lead singer Tina and transformed his band into the slick Ike and Tina Turner Revue, with a female dance and vocal backup trio and a nine-piece instrumental section. Ike and Tina married and launched the first of many cross-country tours. They created a unique blend of country, gospel, rock and roll, and blues that by 1969 had filled 15 albums and 60 single recordings.

But the rewards of success for Tina Turner were overshadowed by her husband's sometimes brutal domination of her life. In July 1976 she left him. Independent for the first time, she slowly began to develop her own style and to rebuild her career. In 1983 her single "Let's Stay Together" earned her the prestigious British Silver Disc Award. A 1984 tour with Lionel Richie cemented her comeback.

Ullmann, Liv Johanne

True to her reputation as the world's most noted Scandinavian actress after Garbo and Ingrid Bergman and also as a caring mother who was actively concerned for the well-being of the Earth's suffering and starving millions, Liv Ullmann in 1985 was one of the many artists and writers who signed an appeal to the signatories of the 1975 Helsinki Accords at the tenth anniversary Conference on Security and Cooperation in Europe to "construct a cultural bridge across all conceivable borders." Five years earlier the United Nations Children's Fund (UNICEF) had appointed Ullmann as its "goodwill ambassador" to tour the third world countries most seriously affected by famine and allied scourges. What she saw affected her profoundly, as she revealed in an impassioned talk on the BBC's "The Light of Experience" series, transmitted at the end of the UNICEF 1985 World Children's Week.

Liv Ullmann was born on Dec. 16, 1939, in Japan to Norwegian parents, who took her first to Canada and then home to Norway and sent her to drama school in Britain at the age of 17. Some 30 years later, in 1985, she returned to London for her British stage debut, in a highly acclaimed revival of Harold Pinter's *Old Times.*

Since 1957, the year of her first Norwegian film, Ullmann had made 32 large-screen or TV films, the best of them with Swedish director Ingmar Bergman. Her stage debut was in Stavanger, Norway (in *Anne Frank*), in 1957, but her breakthrough performance was in Peter Palitzsch's 1960 production of Bertolt Brecht's *The Caucasian Chalk Circle* at the New Norwegian Theatre in Oslo. She was seen in Jean Cocteau's monodrama *The Human Voice* in Australia and in New York, both on stage and in a Public Broadcasting Service TV special. Ullmann's Broadway parts ranged from her 1975 debut as Nora in Ibsen's *A Doll's House* to the lead role in the 1979 musical *I Remember Mama.* The youngest person to receive the Order of St. Olav from the king of Norway, she also held six honorary doctorates from U.S. universities as well as numerous acting and other awards. She wrote two volumes of autobiography, *Changing* (1976) and *Choices* (1984), the first revealing her personal dilemmas and the second her public concerns.

Walker, John

The espionage activities of John Walker were described by some officials as among the gravest security breaches in the history of the U.S. Navy. Walker, a private detective and retired navy communications officer, was arrested by the FBI on May 20, 1985, on a charge of attempting to pass classified documents, mostly navy reports on movements of Soviet submarines and surface ships, to unidentified agents of the Soviet Union. Walker had obtained the documents from his brother, Arthur, a retired navy lieutenant commander, and from his son, Michael, a navy petty officer assigned to the aircraft carrier USS *Nimitz.* During most of his 21-year naval career John Walker had had access to detailed information about the movements of both U.S. and Soviet fleets.

John Anthony Walker, Jr., was born in 1937 in Washington, D.C. His family was a troubled one. John dropped out of St. Patrick's Roman Catholic high school in West Scranton, Pa., during his junior year after attempting a burglary. He was threatened with jail unless he joined the armed forces.

Walker was assigned to the submarine *Simon Bolivar* between August 1965 and April 1967. In March 1967 he was promoted to warrant officer. Federal prosecutors said that he began selling secrets to the Soviets in 1968. Walker was stationed in California in the late 1960s and 1970s between cruises on the *Andrew Jackson,* a nuclear-powered submarine on which he served as a radioman. That assignment allowed him access to large amounts of navy sensitive material.

Walker's son, Michael, was arrested on May 22 on charges of passing navy secrets to Soviet agents. Arthur Walker admitted that in September 1980 he had begun turning secret documents over to his brother, knowing their destination.

In October Walker indicated his willingness to cooperate with military officials in their investigation of the espionage operation. In return for a reduced sentence for Michael, John agreed to plead guilty and to provide a detailed accounting of the material passed by him to the Soviets. He received a life sentence, his son 25 years, and his brother the stiffest penalty of all—a $250,000 fine and life imprisonment.

Walters, Vernon Anthony

On May 16, 1985, the U.S. Senate confirmed Pres. Ronald Reagan's nomination of Vernon A. Walters to be the country's chief delegate and ambassador to the United Nations. Walters acknowledged the appointment as the greatest honor in his long career of military and diplomatic service. As chief delegate he was expected to be less outspoken than his sometimes controversial predecessor, Jeane Kirkpatrick.

Walters was born in New York City of British parents on Jan. 3, 1917. He was educated abroad, becoming fluent in several European languages, but, because of family financial problems, he was

VIOUJARD—GAMMA/LIAISON

unable to finish high school. He enlisted in the U.S. Army as a private in 1941, and the following year, because of his language skills, he was accepted in Officers Candidate School. During the 1943–44 military campaign in Italy, Walters was promoted to major. He served as an aide to Lieut. Gen. Mark W. Clark and as liaison to a Brazilian unit under Clark's command. From 1945 to 1948 he was assistant military attaché to Brazil.

Assigned to the Paris headquarters of NATO in 1951, Walters was reassigned to a NATO post in Washington, D.C., in 1954 after being severely injured in a skiing accident. During his long recovery he served as an interpreter for Pres. Dwight D. Eisenhower at Geneva (1955) and for Vice-Pres. Richard M. Nixon on his 1958 tour of South America. During the Nixon presidency, Walters made the arrangements for Henry Kissinger's many secret trips to Paris during negotiations to end the Vietnam war.

Between 1960 and 1971 Walters advanced from colonel to major general. In 1972 he was promoted to the rank of lieutenant general and became deputy director of the CIA. At the request of presidential assistant H. R. Haldeman, Walters advised the FBI not to investigate the burglary that was at the heart of the Watergate affair, on the grounds that it would jeopardize a CIA operation. Later, convinced that Haldeman had deceived him, Walters refused to interfere with the FBI inquiry. He retired from the Army and resigned from the CIA in 1976.

In his autobiography, *Silent Missions* (1978), Walters denied that when he was with the CIA he had taken part in any attempts to overthrow governments that posed a threat to the United States.

He also expressed his belief that Communist governments are more dangerous to U.S. interests than are right-wing dictatorships.

Williams, Lynn

As president of the United Steelworkers of America, Lynn Williams became the first Canadian to head a major U.S.-based international union. International secretary of the union since 1977, Williams was named temporary acting president by the union's executive board in November 1983, following the death of Pres. Lloyd McBride. On March 29, 1984, Lynn Williams was elected president in his own right by the members of the union. Since Williams joined the Steelworkers in 1947, his career had been a steady climb from organizer to president.

Born in Springfield, Ont., on July 21, 1924, Lynn Russell Williams was the son of a United Church minister. Early in life he was attracted to the labor movement, seeing it as an expression of the social-gospel ideal of service. He attended McMaster University in Hamilton, Ont., and obtained a B.A. in liberal arts in 1944. Discovering that the only way to enter the labor movement was by working in a factory, Williams took a blue-collar job in Toronto and joined the Steelworkers in 1947.

From 1947 to 1973 Williams was a successful union organizer. He was an integral part of the Steelworkers' biggest success in Canada, in the late 1960s when the United Steelworkers of America replaced the Mine, Mill, and Smelter Workers as bargaining agent for the Sudbury, Ont., employees of International Nickel. Williams headed the Steelworkers' first bargaining team at Inco, and this led, in 1971, to his coordinating the first World Nickel Conference, attended by unions from nine countries.

Williams believed in political action by the labor movement. In 1956 he made an unsuccessful bid for a seat in the Canadian Parliament. He was one of the founders of the New Democratic Party in Canada and served on its Ontario executive. In 1973 he was appointed to the Ontario Economic Council.

In 1973 Lynn Williams was elected director of District 6 of the Steelworkers, based in Toronto. Elected international secretary in 1977, he moved to Pittsburgh, Pa. Upon assuming the presidency, Williams determined to use his organizing skills to rebuild union membership, which had fallen by half since 1979. As a Canadian, winning the office was important to him, since it affirmed that the United Steelworkers of America was an international union in which both nations could play a role.

Yurchenko, Vitali Sergeyevich

On Aug. 1, 1985, Vitali Yurchenko, a Soviet diplomat who was in Rome on what was purportedly an assignment for the Soviet Ministry of Foreign Affairs, walked away from his colleagues, saying that he wanted to see the museums in the Vatican. Yurchenko never rejoined the group. Soviet offi-

CAMERA PRESS, LONDON

cials in Rome apparently searched for him for an entire week before asking Italian authorities to investigate his disappearance.

On September 25 the *Washington Times* reported that Yurchenko had defected to the U.S. and was being debriefed in a suburb of Washington, D.C., by the CIA. The *Times* said that Yurchenko's job at the ministry was a cover for his real position as a high-ranking agent of the KGB in charge of espionage operations in the United States and Canada.

On November 2, while visiting Washington, D.C., Yurchenko quietly walked away from the U.S. intelligence official accompanying him. Two days later he called a press conference at the Soviet embassy in Washington and said that CIA agents had kidnapped him in Rome, drugged him, and held him prisoner for "three horrible months." The CIA denied the accusations, maintaining that Yurchenko had come to them voluntarily. After the press conference, State Department officials interviewed Yurchenko with no Soviet officials present; the U.S. authorities reported they were satisfied that Yurchenko had chosen freely to return to the U.S.S.R. He immediately flew to Moscow, where he repeated his accusations against the CIA.

Yurchenko was born on May 2, 1936. Before a stint as a security officer at the Soviet embassy in Washington, D.C., he served in the Soviet Navy. At the time of his defection in Rome, he was counselor to the Ministry of Foreign Affairs.

Yurchenko's return to the Soviet Union stirred a number of speculations: that he had become concerned for the safety of family members left behind; that his defection in Rome had been staged so he could accuse the CIA of kidnapping, thus embarrassing the U.S. on the eve of a major East-West summit conference; and that a love affair with a Soviet woman living in Canada had gone sour. Whatever the truth, his accusations against the CIA could deter other Soviets from trying to defect.

OUR FAMILY RECORD

1986

THIS SPACE FOR FAMILY GROUP PHOTO

WHAT WE DID
AND
HOW WE LOOKED

*Each year important events highlight the life of every
family. Year after year these events may be noted
in the Family Record pages of your yearbooks.
You will then have a permanent record of your family's
significant achievements, celebrations, and activities.*

OUR FAMILY TREE

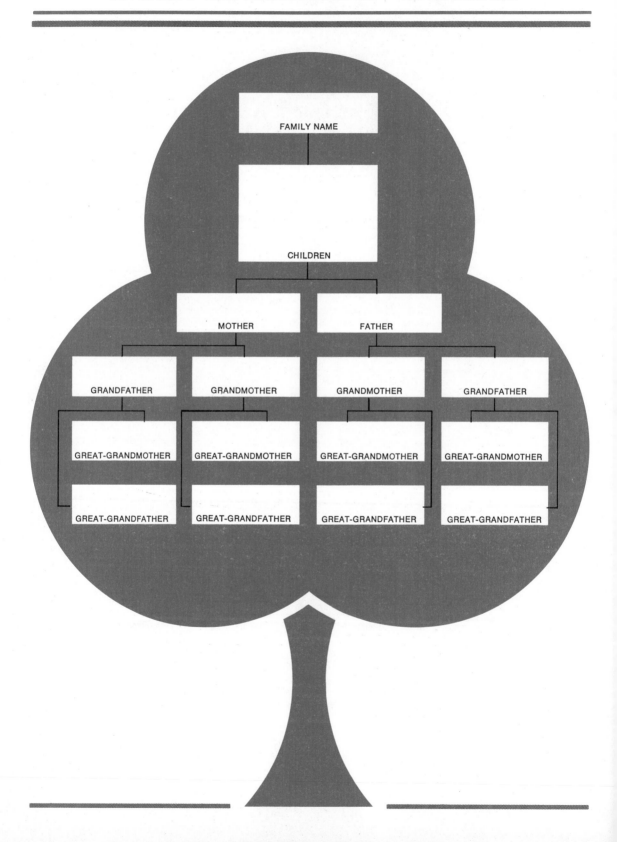

DATES TO REMEMBER

JANUARY

_____
_____
_____
_____
_____
_____

FEBRUARY

_____
_____
_____
_____
_____
_____

MARCH

_____
_____
_____
_____
_____
_____

APRIL

_____
_____
_____
_____
_____
_____

MAY

_____
_____
_____
_____
_____
_____

JUNE

_____
_____
_____
_____
_____
_____

JULY

_____
_____
_____
_____
_____
_____

AUGUST

_____
_____
_____
_____
_____
_____

SEPTEMBER

_____
_____
_____
_____
_____
_____

OCTOBER

_____
_____
_____
_____
_____
_____

NOVEMBER

_____
_____
_____
_____
_____
_____

DECEMBER

_____
_____
_____
_____
_____
_____

Birthdays, weddings, anniversaries, graduations, gifts sent

FAMILY CELEBRATIONS

BIRTHDAYS

NAME

DATE

NAME

DATE

NAME

DATE

NAME

DATE

NAME

DATE

ANNIVERSARIES

NAMES

DATE

NAMES

DATE

NAMES

DATE

WEDDINGS

NAMES

DATE

NAMES

DATE

NAMES

DATE

NAMES

DATE

NAMES

DATE

BIRTHS

NAME

DATE

PARENTS

NAME

DATE

PARENTS

NAME

DATE

PARENTS

PROMOTIONS

NAME

FIRM

TITLE

DATE

NAME

FIRM

TITLE

DATE

HOLIDAYS

OCCASION

OCCASION

OCCASION

SPIRITUAL MILESTONES

NAME _____

MILESTONE _____

_____

_____

NAME _____

MILESTONE _____

_____

_____

NAME _____

MILESTONE _____

_____

_____

NAME _____

MILESTONE _____

_____

_____

NAME _____

MILESTONE _____

_____

_____

OTHER EVENTS

_____

_____

_____

_____

_____

_____

_____

_____

_____

PASTE PHOTO HERE

PASTE PHOTO HERE

PASTE PHOTO HERE

VACATION

WHEN AND WHERE WE WENT

_____
_____
_____
_____
_____
_____
_____
_____
_____
_____
_____
_____
_____
_____
_____
_____
_____
_____
_____
_____
_____
_____
_____
_____
_____
_____
_____

FAVORITE SIGHTS

_____
_____
_____
_____
_____
_____
_____
_____
_____
_____
_____
_____
_____
_____
_____
_____
_____
_____
_____
_____
_____
_____
_____
_____
_____
_____

WHAT WE DID

_____
_____
_____
_____
_____
_____
_____
_____
_____
_____
_____
_____
_____
_____
_____
_____
_____
_____
_____
_____
_____

DRAW MAP OF TOUR

PASTE PICTURE HERE

SCHOOL ACTIVITIES

NAME _____

SCHOOL _____

GRADE _____

NAME _____

SCHOOL _____

GRADE _____

NAME _____

SCHOOL _____

GRADE _____

NAME _____

SCHOOL _____

GRADE _____

SCHOOL PARTIES

DATE _____

OCCASION _____

_____

DATE _____

OCCASION _____

_____

DATE _____

OCCASION _____

_____

DATE _____

OCCASION _____

_____

DATE _____

OCCASION _____

_____

DATE _____

OCCASION _____

_____

DATE _____

OCCASION _____

_____

DATE _____

OCCASION _____

SPORTS

NAME _____

SPORT _____

ACHIEVEMENT _____

NAME _____

SPORT _____

ACHIEVEMENT _____

NAME _____

SPORT _____

ACHIEVEMENT _____

NAME _____

SPORT _____

ACHIEVEMENT _____

NAME _____

SPORT _____

ACHIEVEMENT _____

NAME _____

SPORT _____

ACHIEVEMENT _____

NAME _____

SPORT _____

ACHIEVEMENT _____

NAME _____

SPORT _____

ACHIEVEMENT _____

CLUB ACTIVITIES

NAME _____

CLUB _____

ACHIEVEMENT _____

NAME _____

CLUB _____

ACHIEVEMENT _____

NAME _____

CLUB _____

ACHIEVEMENT _____

NAME _____

CLUB _____

ACHIEVEMENT _____

NAME _____

CLUB _____

ACHIEVEMENT _____

NAME _____

CLUB _____

ACHIEVEMENT _____

NAME _____

CLUB _____

ACHIEVEMENT _____

NAME _____

CLUB _____

ACHIEVEMENT _____

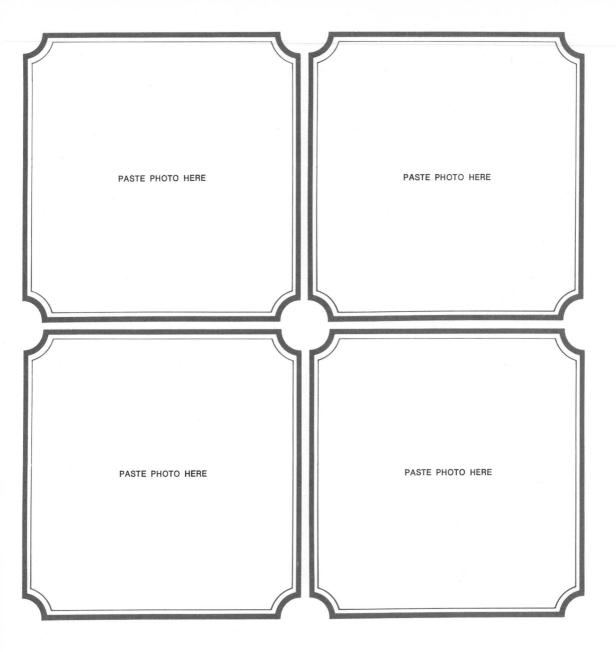

PASTE PHOTO HERE

PASTE PHOTO HERE

PASTE PHOTO HERE

PASTE PHOTO HERE

AWARDS, HONORS, AND PRIZES

NAME _____

GRADE _____

HONOR _____

NAME _____

GRADE _____

HONOR _____

NAME _____

GRADE _____

HONOR _____

NAME _____

GRADE _____

HONOR _____

NAME _____

GRADE _____

HONOR _____

NAME _____

GRADE _____

HONOR _____

GRADUATIONS

NAME _____

SCHOOL _____

NAME _____

SCHOOL _____

NAME _____

SCHOOL _____

NAME _____

SCHOOL _____

_____

PETS

NAME AND BREED

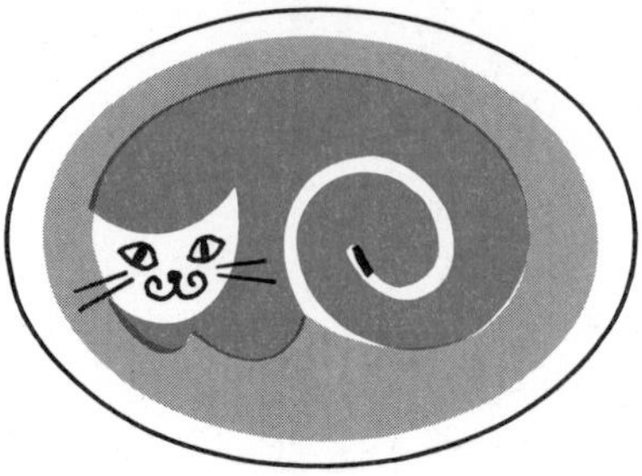

VET'S RECORD

BEHAVIOR AND TRAINING

PASTE PHOTO HERE

LEISURE HOURS

FAVORITE MOVIES

_____
_____
_____
_____
_____
_____
_____
_____
_____
_____
_____
_____
_____

FAVORITE BOOKS

_____
_____
_____
_____
_____
_____
_____
_____
_____

FAVORITE TELEVISION PROGRAMS

_____
_____
_____
_____
_____
_____
_____
_____
_____
_____
_____

FAVORITE RECORDS

_____
_____
_____
_____
_____
_____
_____
_____
_____
_____
_____
_____
_____

_____
_____
_____
_____
_____
_____
_____
_____
_____
_____
_____

HOBBIES

_____
_____
_____
_____
_____
_____
_____
_____
_____
_____
_____
_____

OUR HEALTH RECORD

RECORD OF HEIGHT

FEET   DATE   NAME

6

5

4

3

2

1

Check Height on
This Scale.
Write Name and
Date Opposite It.

RECORD OF WEIGHT

POUNDS DATE   NAME

225

200

175

150

125

100

75

50

25

Check Weight on
This Scale.
Write Name and
Date Opposite It.

DOCTORS' NAMES

NAME

ADDRESS

TELEPHONE NUMBER

NAME

ADDRESS

TELEPHONE NUMBER

DENTISTS' NAMES

NAME

ADDRESS

TELEPHONE NUMBER

NAME

ADDRESS

TELEPHONE NUMBER

VISITS

NAME

DATE

ILLNESS

NAME

DATE

ILLNESS

NAME

DATE

ILLNESS

NAME

DATE

ILLNESS

NAME

DATE

ILLNESS

INOCULATIONS

NAME

DATE

TYPE

NAME

DATE

TYPE

OPERATIONS

NAME

DATE

TYPE

NAME

DATE

TYPE

calendar for 1986

JAN

1 New Year's Day. Japanese New Year 2646. National Volunteer Blood Donor and Birth Defects Prevention months begin. Mummers Day parade. United Nations: International Year of Peace begins. Anniversary of U.S. Emancipation Proclamation (1863).

2 Earth at perihelion.

3 99th Congress (2nd session) assembles.

6 Armenian Christmas. Epiphany, or Twelfth Day.

9 Worldwide Kiwanis Week begins.

11 Alexander Hamilton's birthday, 1755?

14 Julian New Year 6699. Treaty of Paris ratified, 1784.

15 Martin Luther King, Jr.'s birthday, 1929. Adult's Day in Japan.

17 Benjamin Franklin's birthday, 1706. Poland Liberation Day, 1945.

19 Edgar Allan Poe's birthday, 1809.

20 Martin Luther King, Jr.'s birthday (observed). Aquarius begins.

23 National Handwriting Day.

25 Robert Burns's birthday, 1759. Tu Bi-Shevat, or Jewish Arbor Day.

27 Mozart's birthday, 1756.

FEB

1 National Freedom Day. American Heart, American History, American Music, Black History, and International Friendship months begin.

2 Candlemas Day. Groundhog Day.

6 Halfway point of winter.

7 Charles Dickens's birthday, 1812.

8 Anniversary of founding of Boy Scouts of America, 1910.

9 Chinese New Year 4684, Year of the Tiger. Halley's Comet: Perihelion. National Crime Prevention and Cardiopulmonary weeks begin.

11 Thomas Edison's birthday, 1847. Day to Commemorate the Founding of the Nation, Japan, 660 BC. White Shirt Day.

12 Ash Wednesday—Lent begins. Abraham Lincoln's birthday, 1809. Thaddeus Kosciusko's birthday, 1746.

14 St. Valentine's Day. Race Relations Day.

15 Susan B. Anthony's birthday, 1820.

16 Brotherhood, International Friendship, and Health Education weeks begin.

19 Pisces begins.

23 George Frederick Handel's birthday, 1685. Lantern Festival in China and Taiwan.

MARCH

1 National Nutrition, Red Cross, and Youth Art months begin. Water-Drawing Festival begins, Japan.

2 American Camping and Save Your Vision weeks begin.

8 International (Working) Women's Day.

9 Girl Scout Week begins.

10 Commonwealth Day, Canada.

11 Johnny Appleseed Day.

14 Storytelling Weekend begins.

15 Ides of March. Buzzards return to Hinckley, Ohio.

16 Passion Week and National Poison Prevention and National Wildlife weeks begin.

17 St. Patrick's Day.

19 Swallows return to San Juan Capistrano, Calif.

20 Spring begins. Earth Day.

21 National Agriculture Day. Aries begins. Johann Sebastian Bach's birthday, 1685.

25 Purim.

28 Good Friday.

30 Easter Sunday.

31 Franz Joseph Haydn's birthday, 1732.

APRIL

1 April Fools' Day. Cancer Control and National Humor months begin.

2 Hans Christian Andersen's birthday, 1805. International Children's Book Day.

6 National Cherry Blossom Festival. National Library and Young Child weeks begin.

7 Muslim Festival: Lailat al Miraj. World Health Day.

8 Flower Festival (Hana Matsuri), Japan.

11 Halley's Comet passes closest to Earth.

13 Thomas Jefferson's birthday, 1743. National Building Safety and Pan American weeks begin.

15 Anniversary of the sinking of the *Titanic,* 1912.

16 Charlie Chaplin's birthday, 1889.

20 Taurus begins. Bike Safety, Consumer Protection, National YWCA, and Keep America Beautiful weeks begin.

23 William Shakespeare's birthday, 1564.

24 Passover begins.

27 Daylight Savings Time begins, U.S.

29 Emperor's birthday, Japan.

30 World YWCA Day.

MAY

1 May Day. National High Blood Pressure and Older Americans months begin.

3 Constitution Memorial Day, Japan. Constitution Day, Poland. Kentucky Derby.

4 Be Kind to Animals and National Music weeks begin.

5 Children's Day in Japan and Korea. Halfway point of spring.

6 Yom Hashoah (Holocaust Day). National Nurses' Day.

8 Ascension Day. VE Day.

10 Muslim holiday: Ramadan. National Windmill Day, The Netherlands.

11 Mother's Day.

12 National Salvation Army Week begins. Edward Lear's birthday, 1812. Limerick Day.

14 Gabriel D. Fahrenheit's 300th birthday, 1686.

17 Armed Forces Day. Preakness Stakes.

18 Whitsunday, or Pentecost.

21 Gemini begins.

25 Trinity Sunday. National Missing Children's Day. Indianapolis 500-Mile Race.

26 Memorial Day, U.S.

JUNE

1 June Dairy, National Rose, and National Adopt-a-Cat months begin. International Mothers' Peace Day. Day of the Rice God, Japan. Central Pacific Hurricane season begins (through October 31).

5 World Environment Day. Anniversary of the first balloon flight, 1783, France.

6 D-Day anniversary, 1944.

8 National Flag Week begins.

9 Muslim holiday: Id al-Fitr (fast of Ramadan ends). National Little League Baseball Week begins.

13 Shavuot, or Feast of Weeks.

14 Flag Day. Birthday of Univac, 1951. Rice Planting Festival, Japan.

15 Magna Carta Day. Edvard Grieg's birthday, 1843. Father's Day.

16 Bloomsday.

21 National Hollerin' Contest, Spivey's Corner, N.C. Summer begins. Cancer begins.

23 Midsummer Day.

25 Custer's Last Stand, 1876. Festival of American Folklife begins, Washington, D.C.

30 Leap second adjustment time.

JULY

1 Canada Day. Anniversary of first U.S. postage stamps, 1847. National Hot Dog, National Baked Bean, National Ice Cream, and National Peach months begin.

2 Halfway point of 1986.

3 Dog Days begin.

4 U.S. Independence Day.

5 Earth at aphelion.

6 John Paul Jones's birthday, 1747.

7 Star Festival (Tanabata), Japan.

11 John Quincy Adams's birthday, 1767.

12 Henry David Thoreau's birthday, 1817.

13 Feast of Lanterns (Bon Festival), Japan. Anniversary of Live Aid concerts for famine relief, 1985.

14 Bastille Day, France.

21 Dedication Anniversary of the National Women's Hall of Fame, 1979.

23 Leo begins. Wild Horse Chasing (Soma No Umaoi), Japan.

24 Commonwealth Games XIII begin, Edinburgh, Scotland.

28 Terry Fox Day.

AUG

1 Francis Scott Key's birthday, 1779. Herman Melville's birthday, 1819.

4 Coast Guard Day. National Smile Week begins. All-American Soap Box Derby begins, Akron, Ohio.

6 Anniversary of first wartime use of atomic bomb, Hiroshima, Japan, 1945. Peace Festival, Hiroshima, Japan. Alfred Tennyson's birthday, 1809.

7 Halfway point of summer.

9 Anniversary of second wartime use of atomic bomb, Nagasaki, Japan, 1945.

13 International Lefthanders Day.

14 Tisha B'Av. Atlantic Charter Day. Victory, or VJ, Day. Intertribal Indian Ceremonial begins, Gallup, N.M.

15 Napoleon Bonaparte's birthday, 1769. Sir Walter Scott's birthday, 1771.

16 Muslim festival: Id al-Hajj.

19 National Aviation Day. Little League Baseball World Series, Williamsport, Pa.

23 Virgo begins.

26 Women's Equality Day. World Cycling Championships.

SEPT

1 National Sight-Saving, Wood Energy, Emergency Care, and Be Kind to Editors and Writers months begin. Labor Day.

3 Anniversary of declaration of World War II, 1939. Anniversary of Treaty of Paris, 1783.

6 Islamic New Year 1407. Jane Addams's birthday, 1860.

7 Grandma Moses Day. Grandparents Day.

8 International Literacy Day. Anniversary of the pardon of former U.S. president Richard M. Nixon, 1974.

12 Jesse Owens's birthday, 1913.

15 Mexican Independence Day. Old People's, or Respect for the Aged, Day, Japan.

16 International Day of Peace.

17 Citizenship Day. Constitution Week begins.

18 Harvest Moon.

23 Autumn begins. Libra begins.

25 Anniversary of the first American Newspaper, Boston, Mass., 1690.

26 Native American Day. George Gershwin's birthday, 1898.

29 Michaelmas.

OCT

1 World Vegetarian Day. National Sudden Infant Death Syndrome Awareness, Spina Bifida, and National Adopt-a-Dog months begin.

3 Annular total eclipse of the Sun. Korea founded, 2333 BC.

4 Rosh Hashana.

5 National Employ the Handicapped and Fire Prevention weeks begin.

6 Child Health Day. Universal Children's Day.

8 Chicago Fire Anniversary, 1871.

9 Leif Erikson Day.

13 Yom Kippur, or Day of Atonement. Columbus Day (observed). Thanksgiving Day, Canada.

15 White Cane Safety Day.

16 Dictionary Day. World Food Day.

17 Hunter's Moon.

18 Sukkot, or Feast of Tabernacles, begins.

19 Cleaner Air Week begins.

23 Scorpio begins.

25 National Higher Education Week begins.

26 Simchat Torah. Return to Standard Time, U.S.

31 Halloween. National Magic Day. National UNICEF Day.

NOV

1 All Saints' Day. Sadie Hawkins Day. National Authors' Day. Aviation History, Good Nutrition, National Diabetes, National Epilepsy, and National Stamp Collecting months begin.

2 All-Souls' Day.

5 Guy Fawkes Day.

6 Halfway point of autumn.

7 Madame Marie Curie's birthday, 1867. Anniversary of the Great Socialist Revolution, U.S.S.R., 1917. World Community Day.

11 Veterans, or Armistice, Day. Martinmas.

15 Children's Shrine Visiting Day (Shichi-go-san), Japan.

16 American Education Week begins.

17 National Eating Disorders and National Children's Book weeks begin.

22 Sagittarius begins. St. Cecilia Day.

23 Labor-Thanksgiving Day, Japan. Adoption and Latin America weeks begin.

27 Thanksgiving Day, U.S.

30 St. Andrew's Day. First Sunday in Advent. Samuel Clemens's (Mark Twain's) birthday, 1835.

DEC

1 Rosa Parks Day. Human Rights month begins.

2 Pan American Health Day.

3 Joseph Conrad's birthday, 1857. Anniversary of first heart transplant, 1967.

5 Anniversary of Prohibition's repeal, 1933.

6 St. Nicholas's Day.

7 Pearl Harbor Day.

9 John Milton's birthday, 1608.

10 Human Rights Day. Emily Dickinson's birthday, 1830.

15 Bill of Rights Day.

16 Ludwig van Beethoven's birthday, 1770. Anniversary of Boston Tea Party, 1773.

17 Wright Brothers Day—anniversary of first airplane flight, 1903.

18 Audubon Christmas Bird Count begins.

21 Winter begins.

22 Capricorn begins.

25 Christmas Day. Isaac Newton's birthday, 1642.

26 Boxing Day. Kwanza begins.

28 Childermas, or Holy Innocents Day.

31 New Year's Eve. Namahage, Japan. Leap second adjustment time.

Contributors and Consultants

These authorities either wrote the articles listed or supplied information and data that were used in writing them.

Stener Aarsdal, Journalist, *Børsen*, Copenhagen, *Denmark*

Joseph C. Agrella, Correspondent, *Blood-Horse* magazine; former Turf Editor, *Chicago Sun-Times, Horse Racing* (in part)

Michael Allaby, Free-Lance Writer and Lecturer, *Biology SPECIAL REPORT: Inhumane Treatment of Animals* (in part); *Environment*

J. A. Allan, Reader in Geography, School of Oriental and African Studies, University of London, *Libya*

Michael Amedeo, Writer, Encyclopædia Britannica Educational Corporation, *Biographies* (in part)

Peter J. Anderson, Assistant Director, Institute of Polar Studies, Ohio State University, Columbus, *Antarctica*

John J. Archibald, Feature Writer, *St. Louis Post-Dispatch,* Adjunct Professor, Washington University, St. Louis, Mo., *Bowling* (in part)

George Armstrong, Rome Correspondent, *The Guardian, Biographies* (in part); *Italy*

Guy Arnold, Free-Lance Writer and Author, *Nigeria*

Mavis Arnold, Free-Lance Journalist, Dublin, *Ireland*

Robert L. Ashenhurst, Professor, Graduate School of Business, University of Chicago, *Computers SPECIAL REPORT: The Homeless Computer*

Alan J. Auerbach, Professor of Economics, University of Pennsylvania, *Economic Affairs SPECIAL REPORT: A Field Guide to Corporate Mergers*

Cyril J. Ayton, Editor, *Motorcycle Sport,* London, *Motorcycle Racing*

Ines T. Baptist, Free-Lance Writer, *Belize*

Paul A. Barrett, Contributing Editor, *Financial Times' New Media Markets* newsletter and *TV World* magazine, London, *Television and Radio* (in part)

Howard Bass, Journalist and Broadcaster, Former Editor, *Winter Sports, Ice Skating; Skiing*

David Bayliss, Director of Planning, London Regional Transport, *Transportation* (in part)

Roger A. Beattie, Member of Secretariat, International Social Security Association, Geneva, *Social Services* (in part)

David C. Beckwith, National Correspondent, *Time* magazine, Washington, D.C., *United States: Developments in the States*

Reginald Ian Beyer, Deputy Curator, Royal Botanic Gardens, Kew, England, *Zoos and Botanical Gardens* (in part)

George Blooston, Writer, Contributor to *Publishers Weekly* magazine, *Book Publishing* (in part)

William C. Boddy, Editor, *Motor Sport,* Full Member, Guild of Motoring Writers, *Automobile Racing* (in part)

Dick Boonstra, Assistant Professor, Department of Political Science, Free University, Amsterdam, *The Netherlands*

Jeffery Boswall, Producer of Sound and Television Programs, BBC Natural History Unit, Bristol, England, *Biology* (in part)

Ben Box, Free-Lance Writer and Researcher, *El Salvador; Honduras*

Roger Boye, Coin Columnist, *Chicago Tribune, Stamps and Coins* (in part)

Henry S. Bradsher, Foreign Affairs Writer, *Philippines*

Robert J. Braidwood, Professor Emeritus of Old World Prehistory, the Oriental Institute and Department of Anthropology, University of Chicago, *Archaeology* (in part)

R. J. Brazee, Geophysical Consultant, *Earth Sciences* (in part)

Kenneth Brecher, Professor of Astronomy and Physics, Boston University, *Astronomy Sidebar: The Return of Halley's Comet*

Joel L. Burdin, Professor of Educational Administration, City College of the City University of New York, *Education* (in part)

Ardath W. Burks, Emeritus Professor of Asian Studies, Rutgers University, New Brunswick, N.J., *Japan*

Frank Butler, Former Sports Editor, *News of the World,* London, *Boxing*

Sarah Cameron, Economist, Group Economics Department, Lloyds Bank PLC, London, *Argentina*

Alexander Johns Campbell, Latin-American Economist, Lloyds Bank Group Economics Department, *Colombia; Paraguay; Uruguay*

Robert W. Carter, Free-Lance Journalist, London, *Horse Racing* (in part)

Christine Patton Chapman, Writer, *International Herald Tribune,* English Lecturer, Tsuda College, Tokyo, *Biographies* (in part)

Kenneth F. Chapman, Former Editor, *Stamp Collecting* and *Philatelic Magazine, Stamps and Coins* (in part)

Robin Chapman, Senior Economist, Group Economics Department, Lloyds Bank PLC, London, *Brazil; Haiti; Latin-American Affairs*

Duncan Chappell, Professor, Department of Criminology, Simon Fraser University, Vancouver, B.C., *Crime and Law Enforcement*

R. O. Clarke, Writer on Industrial Relations, Paris, *Labor and Employment* (in part)

William A. Cleveland, Editor, Britannica World Data and *Britannica Atlas, Mines and Mining*

Stanley H. Costin, British Correspondent, *Herrenjournal International* and others, *Fashion* (in part)

Rufus W. Crater, Senior Editorial Consultant, *Broadcasting,* New York City, *Television and Radio* (in part)

Norman Crossland, Former Bonn Correspondent, *The Economist,* London, *Biographies* (in part); *Germany*

Robert Curley, Editorial Researcher, Encyclopædia Britannica, Inc., *Biographies* (in part)

K. F. Cviic, East European Specialist, *The Economist, Yugoslavia*

Tudor David, Managing Editor, *Education,* London, *Education* (in part); *Education Sidebar: The Education of Ethnic Minorities*

C. R. M. Davies, Research Lecturer in Criminology and Penology, University of Liverpool, *Prisons*

John B. Deam, Technical Director, National Machine Tool Builders Association, McLean, Va., *Machinery and Machine Tools*

Philippe Decraene, Head, Center for Advanced Studies on Modern Africa and Asia, Paris, *Tunisia*

Kenneth de la Barre, Director, Katimavik, Montreal, *Arctic Regions*

Robin Denselow, Rock Music Critic, *The Guardian,* London, Current Affairs Reporter, BBC Television, *Music* (in part)

Elfriede Dirnbacher, Austrian Civil Servant, *Austria*

Bernard Dixon, Science Writer and Consultant, Former Editor, *New Scientist, Medicine* (in part)

Jan R. Engels, Director, Centre Paul Hymans, Brussels, Editor, *Vooruitgang-Progrès,* *Belgium*

Harold Evans, Editorial Director, *U.S. News and World Report, Newspapers SPECIAL REPORT: Freedom of Information*

W. D. Ewart, Marine Consultant, London, *Ships and Shipping*

D. M. L. Farr, Professor of History, Carleton University, Ottawa, *Canada*

Joan Lee Faust, Garden Editor, *New York Times, Flowers and Gardens* (in part)

Bruce L. Felknor, Editorial Consultant, Encyclopædia Britannica, Inc., *Feature Sidebar: Shevchenko*

Robert J. Fendell, Auto Editor, *Science & Mechanics, Automobile Racing* (in part)

Peter Fiddick, Media Editor, *The Guardian,* London, *Magazines* (in part); *Newspapers* (in part)

Donald Fields, Helsinki Correspondent, BBC, *The Guardian,* and *The Sunday Times,* London, *Finland*

David Fisher, Civil Engineer, Freeman Fox & Partners, London, *Engineering Projects* (in part)

Anthony H. Gaddum, Chairman, H. T. Gaddum and Co. Ltd., Silk Merchants, England, *Textiles* (in part)

Dilip Ganguly, Special Correspondent, Agence France Presse, South Asian Bureau, New Delhi, India, *Afghanistan; Bangladesh; Burma; Pakistan; Sri Lanka*

Raymond Duncan Gastil, Director, Comparative Survey of Freedom, Freedom House, New York City, *Human Rights*

J. Whitfield Gibbons, Research Ecologist, Savannah River Ecology Laboratory, Aiken, S.C., *Biology* (in part)

Frank Gibney, Vice-Chairman, Board of Editors, Encyclopædia Britannica, Inc., *Feature Sidebar: Japan's Presidential Prime Minister*

Hugh M. Gillespie, Director of Communications, International Road Federation, Washington, D.C., *Engineering Projects* (in part)

Fay Gjester, Oslo Correspondent, *Financial Times, Norway*

Arthur Goldsmith, Editorial Director, *Popular Photography*, New York City, *Photography*

Harry Golombek, British Chess Champion, 1947, 1949, and 1955, Chess Correspondent, *The Times,* London, *Biographies* (in part); *Chess*

Noël Goodwin, London Correspondent, *Ballet News,* Contributor, *Dance & Dancers, Dance* (in part)

Martin Gottfried, Drama Critic, New York City, *Theater* (in part)

A. R. G. Griffiths, Senior Lecturer in History, Flinders University of South Australia, *Australia; Biographies* (in part)

Joel W. Grossman, Archaeologist, *Archaeology* (in part)

Robert S. Grumet, Research Associate, Museum of the American Indian, Heye Foundation, New York City, *Anthropology*

Peter Geoffrey Hall, Professor of Geography, University of Reading, Professor of City and Regional Planning, University of California at Berkeley, *Social Services SPECIAL REPORT: Homelessness*

Richard E. Hallgren, Assistant Administrator for Weather Services, National Oceanic and Atmospheric Administration, *Weather*

Nicholas Harper, Music Journalist and Writer, Deputy Editor, *Classical CD,* England, *Music* (in part)

P. Havard-Williams, Professor and Head, Department of Library and Information Studies, Loughborough University, Leicestershire, England, *Libraries* (in part)

William D. Hawkland, Chancellor and Professor of Law, Louisiana State University, Baton Rouge, *Law* (in part)

Peter Hebblethwaite, Vatican Affairs Writer, *National Catholic Reporter,* Kansas City, Mo., *Religion Sidebar: Liberation Theology*

Myrl C. Hendershott, Professor of Oceanography, Scripps Institution of Oceanography, La Jolla, Calif., *Oceanography*

Robin Cathy Herman, Free-Lance Journalist, *Ice Hockey*

Fitzgerald Higgins, Editor and Reviewer, *Literature* (in part)

Harvey J. Hindin, Vice-President, Hi-Tech Editorial, Inc., Dix Hills, N.Y., *Telecommunications*

John Howkins, Director, International Institute of Communications, London, *Television and Radio* (in part)

Neville M. Hunnings, Editorial Director, European Law Centre, London, Editor, *Common Market Law Reports, Law* (in part)

Kenneth Ingham, Professor of History, University of Bristol, England, *Angola; Kenya; Mozambique; Tanzania; Uganda; Zaire; Zambia; Zimbabwe*

International Economic Information Services, London, *Economic Affairs; International Exchange and Payments; International Trade*

Ingrid Iversen, Economist, Group Economics Department, Lloyds Bank PLC, London, *Biographies* (in part); *Bolivia; Costa Rica; Ecuador; Guatemala; Mexico; Mexico Sidebar: The Mexican Earthquake; Peru*

Adrian Jardine, Company Director, Member, Guild of Yachting Writers, *Boating* (in part)

Peter Jenkins, Political Columnist, *The Sunday Times,* London, *Biographies* (in part); *United Kingdom*

George Joffé, Journalist and Writer on North African Affairs, *Algeria; Morocco*

D. A. N. Jones, Novelist and Critic, *Biographies* (in part); *Literature* (in part)

William A. Katz, Professor, School of Library Science, State University of New York, Albany, *Magazines* (in part)

John A. Kelleher, Group Relations Editor, INL (newspapers), Wellington, N.Z., *Biographies* (in part); *New Zealand*

Richard M. Kennedy, Agricultural Economist, Economic Research Service, U.S. Department of Agriculture, *Agriculture*

John V. Killheffer, Associate Editor, Encyclopædia Britannica, *Biographies* (in part)

Jon Kimche, Former Editor, *New Middle East; Afro-Asian Affairs,* London, *Israel*

Joshua B. Kind, Professor of Art History, Northern Illinois University, De Kalb, *Museums* (in part)

Jean Knecht, Former Assistant Foreign Editor, *Le Monde,* Paris, *Biographies* (in part); *France*

Richard A. Knox, Technical Author, Former Editor, *Nuclear Engineering International,* London, *Nuclear Industry*

Gina Kolata, Writer, *Science* magazine, Washington, D.C., *Medicine* (in part)

Sali Ann Kriegsman, Correspondent, *Ballet News, Washington DanceView, Dance* (in part)

Louis Kushnick, Lecturer, Department of American Studies, University of Manchester, England, *Race Relations; Refugees and Migrants* (in part)

William E. Laberis, Managing Editor, *Computerworld, Computers* (in part)

Kevin M. Lamb, Sportswriter, *Chicago Sun-Times, Biographies* (in part); *Football* (in part)

Timothy J. Larkin, Director, TL Communications, *Drugs*

Roy Larson, Former Religion Editor, *Chicago Sun-Times, Religion*

Gerd Larsson, Tokyo Correspondent, *Dagens Industri, Biographies* (in part)

Benedict A. Leerburger, Science Writer and Editorial Consultant, *Biology SPECIAL REPORT: Inhumane Treatment of Animals* (in part)

Martin Legassick, Coordinator (honorary), Southern Africa Labour Education Project, Former Senior Lecturer in Sociology, University of Warwick, Coventry, England, *South Africa*

Colin Legum, Editor, *Middle East Contemporary Survey, Third World Reports,* and *Africa Contemporary Record,* London, *African Affairs; Biographies* (in part); *South Africa SPECIAL REPORT: South Africa's Apartheid Policy*

Peter Lennox-Kerr, Editor, *High Performance Textiles,* Oxford, England, European Editor, *Textile World,* New York City, *Textiles* (in part)

Eric J. Lerner, Free-Lance Writer on Science and Technology, *Astronomy; Mathematics; Physics*

Robert G. Logan, Sportswriter, *Chicago Tribune, Basketball* (in part)

Virgnia R. Luling, Social Anthropologist, *Somalia*

Martin McCauley, Senior Lecturer in Soviet and East European Studies, School of Slavonic and East European Studies, University of London, *Union of Soviet Socialist Republics*

Trevor J. MacDonald, Manager, International Affairs, British Steel Corporation, *Iron and Steel Industry*

Keith S. McLachlan, Senior Lecturer, School of Oriental and African Studies, University of London, *Iran*

H. M. F. Mallet, Editor, *Wool Record Weekly Market Report,* Bradford, England, *Textiles* (in part)

Andrew Mango, Orientalist and Broadcaster, *Turkey*

Martin E. Marty, Fairfax M. Cone Distinguished Service Professor, University of Chicago, *Religion SPECIAL REPORT: As the "New Religions" Grow Older*

James L. Mateja, Auto Editor and Financial Reporter, *Chicago Tribune, Automobile Industry* (in part)

Charles McC. Mathias, Jr., Retired U.S. Senator from Maryland, and Former Representative in Congress, *International Trade SPECIAL REPORT: The Case Against Protectionism: A U.S. View*

Björn Matthíasson, Economist, Central Bank of Iceland, *Iceland*

David M. Mazie, Associate of Carl T. Rowan, Syndicated Columnist, Free-Lance Writer, *Social Services* (in part)

Edward Mark Mazze, Dean and Professor of Marketing, School of Business Administration, Temple University, Philadelphia, *Advertising; Consumer Affairs* (in part)

Suzy Menkes, Fashion Editor, *The Times,* London, *Fashion SPECIAL REPORT: The Street Scene—Pop, Glam, Androgyny*

T. W. Mermel, Consultant, former Chairman, Committee on World Register of Dams, International Commission on Large Dams, *Engineering Projects* (in part)

Paul Millgate, Economist, Group Economics Department, Lloyds Bank PLC, London, *Cuba; Dominican Republic; Nicaragua*

Sandra Millikin, Architectural Historian, *Architecture; Art and Art Exhibitions; Biographies* (in part); *Museums* (in part)

Mario Modiano, Athens Correspondent, *The Times,* London, *Biographies* (in part); *Greece*

Dan M. Morgenstern, Director, Institute of Jazz Studies, Rutgers University, New Jersey, *Music* (in part)

Jacqui M. Morris, Editor, *Oryx* magazine, *Wildlife Conservation*

Donald Morrison, Senior Editor, *Time* magazine, *Newspapers* (in part)

Chris Mosey, Associate Editor, *Sweden Now,* Stockholm, Nordic Correspondent, *The Observer* and *Worldwatch,* Swedish Correspondent, *Daily Mail* and *The Times,* London, *Sweden*

Joan Mullen, Vice-President and Manager of the Law and Justice Area of Abt Associates Inc., a public policy research organization, *Prisons Sidebar: Private Means to Public Ends*

Elspeth Napier, Editor, Royal Horticultural Society publications, London, *Flowers and Gardens* (in part)

Ernest Naylor, Lloyd Roberts Professor of Zoology, University College of North Wales, Bangor, *Biology* (in part)

John Neill, Consultant, Submerged Combustion Ltd., President, British Mountaineering Council, *Mountaineering*

Bert Nelson, Editor, *Track and Field News, Track and Field*

Bruce C. Netschert, Vice-President, National Economic Research Associates, Inc., Washington, D.C., *Fuel and Energy*

Geoffrey J. Noblett, Tunnelling Division Manager, Tarmac Construction International, Wolverhampton, England, *Engineering Projects* (in part)

H. S. Noel, Editor, *World Fishing,* London, *Fish and Fisheries*

Bonnie Oberman, Free-Lance Writer, *Biographies* (in part)

Thomas O'Dwyer, Director, Levant Bureau, Writer on East Mediterranean Affairs, Nicosia, Cyprus, *Cyprus*

P. J. Olney, Curator of Birds and Reptiles, Zoological Society of London, Editor, *International Zoo Yearbook, Zoos and Botanical Gardens* (in part)

Carter C. Osterbind, Professor Emeritus of Economics, University of Florida, *Building and Construction*

John Palmer, Former European Editor, *The Guardian,* London, *European Affairs* (in part)

Robert P. Patterson, Jr., Partner, Patterson, Belknap, Webb & Tyler, New York City, *Crime and Law Enforcement Sidebar: Reflections on the Bernhard Goetz Case* (in part)

Charles Robert Paul, Jr., Special Assistant to the Secretary General, U.S. Olympic Committee, Colorado Springs, Colo., *Gymnastics*

Robin C. Penfold, Free-Lance Writer on industrial topics, Editor, *Shell Polymers, Plastics*

Irving Pfeffer, Attorney, *Stocks and Bonds* (in part)

George Philip, Lecturer in Latin-American Politics, London School of Economics and Political Science and Institute of Latin-American Studies, University of London, *Latin-American Affairs SPECIAL REPORT: The Swing Toward Democracy*

Geoffrey M. Pinfold, Director, NCL Consulting Engineers, London, *Engineering Projects* (in part)

Arthur Plotnik, Editor, *American Libraries* magazine, American Library Association, *Libraries* (in part)

Thomas Hon Wing Polin, Assistant Managing Editor, *Asiaweek,* Hong Kong, *Biographies* (in part); *Indonesia; Kampuchea; Korea; Laos; Malaysia; Southeast Asian Affairs; Thailand; Vietnam*

Jonathan D. Pollack, Senior Staff Member, Political Science Department, the Rand Corporation, Santa Monica, Calif., *China; Taiwan*

John Poppeliers, Chief, Section for Technical Cooperation and Training, Cultural Heritage Division, Unesco, Paris, *Landmarks and Monuments*

H. Y. Sharada Prasad, Information Adviser to the Prime Minister, New Delhi, India, *India*

Rod Prince, Journalist specializing in Caribbean matters, *Antigua and Barbuda; Bahamas, The; Barbados; Dominica; Grenada; Jamaica; Saint Christopher and Nevis; Saint Lucia; Saint Vincent and the Grenadines; Trinidad and Tobago*

Margaret H. Quinn, Free-Lance Writer, *Baseball* (in part)

Robin Ranger, Associate Professor, Defense and Strategic Studies Program, School of International Relations, University of Southern California, *Defense and Arms Control; Defense and Arms Control SPECIAL REPORT: Intervention and Defense in Central America and the Caribbean*

Anthony A. Read, Director, Book Development Council, London, *Book Publishing* (in part)

Edward Redlich, Associate, Patterson, Belknap, Webb & Tyler, New York City, *Crime and Law Enforcement Sidebar: Reflections on the Bernhard Goetz Case* (in part)

Philip D. Reid, Professor of Biological Sciences, Smith College, Northampton, Mass., *Biology* (in part)

David Robinson, Film Critic, *The Times,* London, *Motion Pictures*

Yrjö Sarahete, General Secretary, Fédération Internationale des Quilleurs, Helsinki, Fin., *Bowling* (in part)

Albert Schoenfield, Former Publisher, *Swimming World,* Vice-Chairman, U.S. Olympic Swimming Committee, Honoree, International Swimming Hall of Fame, *Swimming*

George Schöpflin, Lecturer in East European Political Institutions, London School of Economics and School of Slavonic and East European Studies, University of London, *Czechoslovakia; European Affairs* (in part)

Nancy Seeger, Science Editor, Compton's Encyclopedia, *Dentistry; Mental Health*

Peter Shackleford, Chief of Studies, World Tourism Organization, Madrid, *Tourism*

Mitchell R. Sharpe, Science Writer, Historian, Alabama Space and Rocket Center, Huntsville, Editor, *Journal of the British Interplanetary Society, Space Science and Exploration*

Melinda Shepherd, Copy Editor, Encyclopædia Britannica, Inc., *Biographies* (in part)

Martin A. Sherwood, Author, *New Worlds in Chemistry, Chemistry*

Noel Simpson, Managing Director, Sydney Bloodstock Proprietary Ltd., Sydney, Australia, *Horse Racing* (in part)

Sid Smith, Entertainment Writer, *Chicago Tribune, Theater Sidebar: Raw Power on the Stage*

K. M. Smogorzewski, Writer on contemporary history, Founder and Editor, *Free Europe,* London, Honorary Member, Foreign Press Association, London, *Albania; Biographies* (in part); *Bulgaria; Hungary; Poland; Poland Sidebar: The Popieluszko Trial; Romania*

Hilary R. Spittle, Publications Editor, American Power Boat Association, *Boating* (in part)

Melanie Staerk, Former Executive Editor, *Swiss Review of World Affairs,* Zurich, and *Unescopress,* Berne, *Switzerland*

Charles Sternberg, Executive Director Emeritus, the International Rescue Committee, *Refugees and Migrants Sidebar: The Sanctuary Movement*

Zena Sutherland, Professor, Graduate Library School, University of Chicago, *Literature for Children*

Thelma Sweetinburgh, Fashion Writer, Paris, *Fashion* (in part)

Richard N. Swift, Professor Emeritus of Politics, New York University, New York City, *United Nations*

Charles J. Taggart, Free-Lance Writer, *Biographies* (in part)

Lawrence B. Taishoff, President, Broadcasting Publications, Inc., Publisher, *Broadcasting* magazine, *Television and Radio* (in part)

Jean van der Tak, Senior Editor, Population Reference Bureau, Inc., *Population*

Norman M. Tallan, Chief, Metals and Ceramics Division, Materials Laboratory, Wright-Patterson Air Force Base, Dayton, Ohio, *Ceramics Industry*

Theodore V. Thomas, Free-Lance Journalist and Press Consultant, *Toys and Games*

Lance Tingay, Former Lawn Tennis Correspondent, *Daily Telegraph,* London, *Tennis*

Edward T. Townsend, National Labor Correspondent, *Christian Science Monitor,* Editor and Consultant, Manpower Education Institute, New York City, *Labor and Employment* (in part)

Robert H. Trigg, Assistant Vice-President, Economic Research, New York Stock Exchange, *Stocks and Bonds* (in part)

Ossia Trilling, Vice-President, International Association of Theatre Critics (1956–77), Coeditor and Contributor, *International Theatre,* Contributor, BBC, *The Times,* London, *Biographies* (in part); *Theater* (in part)

UNHCR. The Office of the United Nations High Commissioner for Refugees, *Refugees and Migrants* (in part)

Robert William Verdi, Sportswriter, *Chicago Tribune, Baseball* (in part)

Ruth Vermeer, Development Officer, International Organization of Consumer Unions, The Hague, Neth., *Consumer Affairs* (in part)

Peter Ward, Owner and Operator, Ward News Services Canada, Parliamentary Press Gallery, Ottawa, *Canada SPECIAL REPORT: A Mood for Change*

Louise Watson, Staff Editor, Encyclopædia Britannica, Inc., London, *Biographies* (in part)

Diane Lois Way, Free-Lance Historical Researcher, *Biographies* (in part)

John R. Weinthal, Writer specializing in automobiles, *Automobile Industry* (in part)

Melvin D. Welch, Secretary, English Basket Ball Association, Former Editor, *Basketball Magazine, Basketball* (in part)

John Whelan, Publisher, *Middle East Economic Digest* and *Africa Economic Digest,* London, *Bahrain; Biographies* (in part); *Egypt; Iraq; Jordan; Kuwait; Lebanon; Middle Eastern and North African Affairs; Oman; Qatar; Saudi Arabia; Syria; United Arab Emirates*

Barbara Whitney, Senior Copy Editor, Encyclopædia Britannica, Inc., *Biographies* (in part)

John R. Wilkinson, Sports Writer, East Midland Provincial Newspapers Ltd., U.K., *Cycling*

Michael E. J. Williams, Golf Correspondent, *Daily Telegraph,* London, *Golf*

Trevor Williamson, Chief Sports Subeditor, *Daily Telegraph,* London, *Football* (in part); *Football Sidebar: The Soccer Riot in Brussels*

Michael Wilson, Editor, *Avionics,* Jane's Publishing Company Ltd., *Aerospace Industry*

Elizabeth Woods, Writer, *Literature* (in part)

Anthony Woollen, Editor, *Food Industries Manual* (20th ed.), *Food Processing*

Michael Wooller, Economist, Group Economics Department, Lloyds Bank PLC, London, *Chile; Portugal; Spain; Venezuela*

David Woolley, Air-Transport Editor, *Interavia,* London, *Transportation* (in part)

Richard L. Worsnop, Associate Editor, Editorial Research Reports, Washington, D.C., *United States*

Almon R. Wright, Retired Senior Historian, U.S. Department of State, *Panama*

Peter John Wyllie, Chairman, Division of Geological and Planetary Sciences, California Institute of Technology, *Earth Sciences* (in part)

Winston L. Y. Yang, Professor of Chinese Studies, Seton Hall University, South Orange, N.J., *Biographies* (in part)

Yasushi Yuge, Staff Writer, *The Japan Economic Journal,* Tokyo, *Computers* (in part)

Stephen Zollo, New Products Editor, *Electronics,* McGraw-Hill, Inc., *Microelectronics*

Index

This index is arranged in alphabetical order. Words beginning with "Mc" are alphabetized as "Mac," and "St." is alphabetized as "Saint."

The figures shown in brackets [83, 84] indicate earlier editions of **Compton's Yearbook** in which the topic has appeared since 1982.

Entry headings in boldface type indicate articles in the text.

Cross-references refer to index entries in this volume.

a

Abbas, Abul 183
Abbey Theatre (Dublin, Ire.) 337 [82, 83]
ABC: *see* American Broadcasting Cos.
Abdel-Aziz ibn Baz 292
Abdul-Jabbar, Kareem 42, *picture* 43 [82, 83, 85]
Abe, Kazuhisa 366
ABM treaty: *see* Anti-Ballistic Missile Systems, Treaty on
Aborigines (Australia) 118
Abortion 223, 276 [82–85]
 religion 288
 Spain 313
Abraham, F. Murray 235
Abruzzo, Ben 259
ABT: *see* American Ballet Theatre
Abu Dhabi 353 [82–85]
Abu Nidal (Palestinian leader) 231
Academy of Motion Picture Arts and Sciences 235 [82–85]
Academy of Television Arts and Sciences 328 [82, 83, 85]
Accidents 99, 103 [83–85]
 aerospace 2
 population 276
 transportation 343, 345
 see also Safety
Accutane (isotretinoin) 105 [83, 85]
ACGB: *see* Arts Council of Great Britain
"Achille Lauro" (Italian ship) 83, 364
 Egypt 120, 230
 international law 203, *picture* 202
 Italy 183
Acid rain 124 [82–85]
 Canada 64
 United States 361, 368
Ackroyd, Peter 211
ACLU: *see* American Civil Liberties Union
Acne 105 [83, 85]
A. C. Nielsen Co. 326 [85]
Acquired immune deficiency syndrome: *see* AIDS
Acyclovir (Zovirax) 106
Adams, J. M. G. 39 [82, 83]
Aden: *see* Yemen (Aden)
Admiral's Cup (boating) 51 [84]
Advertising 2 [82–85]
 newspapers 245
"Advertising Age" 2 [83–85]
Aerodynamics 386
Aerospace industry 2 [82–85]
 defense and arms control 94
 disasters 81, 99
 kites 386
 mergers 114
 strikes, *picture* 194
 textiles 332
 transportation 343
Affirmative-action programs 281

Afghanistan 4 [82–85]
 Pakistan 256
 United Nations 357
 U.S.S.R. 95, 352, 418
AFL–CIO: *see* American Federation of Labor-Congress of Industrial Organizations
African affairs 5 [82–85]
 agriculture 7
 Asian affairs 399
 engineering projects 123
 human evolution 45
 human rights 162
 intervention and defense 97
 libraries 207
 North African affairs 228
 population 275
 refugees and migrants 283
 religion 287
 weather 376
 wildlife conservation 378
 see also African countries
African National Congress (ANC) 6 [84, 85]
 race relations 282
 South Africa 302, 305
Aga Khan, Yasmin 258
Agca, Mehmet Ali 184 [82–84]
Agee, William 257 [83]
Agriculture 7 [82–85]
 biology 47
 botanical gardens 383
 economic affairs 110
 fish farming 137
 Iowa 368
 textiles 331
 see also Drought; Famine; and countries by name
Aguilar *v.* Felton 202
A. H. Robins Co. 82
AI: *see* Artificial intelligence
AIA: *see* American Institute of Architects
AIDS (Acquired immune deficiency syndrome) 219 [83–85]
 chemistry 68
 drug treatment 104, *picture* 105
 education 118
 prisons 279
 United Nations 358
 United States 364
Airbus Industrie 3 [82–85]
Aircraft: *see* Aerospace industry
Air Force, United States 94 [82–85]
 aerospace 3
 crime and law enforcement 85
Air-India 83, 100, 167, 343
Airlines: *see* Aerospace industry
Air Mali 100
Air pollution: *see* Pollution
Akimoto, Mitsugu: *see* Chiyonofuji
ALA: *see* American Library Association
Alabama 367 [82–85]
 education 116
 governor, *list* 367

 prayer in public schools 202, 286, *picture* 204
Alaska 20, 107, 149, 367 [82–85]
 governor, *list* 367
Albania 10 [82–85]
 Yugoslavia 378
Alberta, Can. (prov.) 61, 66 [82, 83, 85]
Alcoholic beverages 2, 367 [82–85]
 homelessness 299
 mental health 224
 prisons 279
Alexander, Lincoln 433
Alexander, Pamela 211
Alfonsín, Raúl 21, 200 [84, 85]
Alford, Edna 213
Algeria 10 [82–85]
 engineering projects 122
 human rights 162
 Middle East and North Africa 231
 Tunisia 347
 U.S.S.R. 96
Ali, Kamal Hassan 119 [83–85]
Alia, Ramiz 10 [83, 85]
Aliens, illegal 162 [82, 83, 85]
 Sanctuary Movement 285, 286
Aliyev, Geidar A. 420 [83]
Allen, Woody 233 [83, 84]
Alps (mountains) 238
Alusuisse (Swiss corp.) 165 [84]
Alvin Ailey Dance Theatre 91 [82, 83, 85]
Alzheimer's disease 366 [84]
"Amadeus" (motion picture) 235
Amal (militia) 205, 357
Amalgamated Clothing & Textile Workers Union 195 [82]
Amateur radio 328
Ambrose, Stephen E. 210
Amdahl Corp. 78
Amelia Frances Howard-Gibbon Award 215 [85]
American Ballet Theatre (ABT) [82–85]
 dance 90, *picture* 92
American Book Award 210
American Broadcasting Cos. (ABC) [82–85]
 corporate mergers 114, 326, 363
American Civil Liberties Union (ACLU) 279 [83–85]
American Federation of Jazz Societies 243
American Federation of Labor-Congress of Industrial Organizations (AFL-CIO) 193 [82–85]
American Federation of State, County & Municipal Employees 194 [83]
"American Health" (magazine) 216
American Heart Association 223 [83]
"American Heritage" (magazine) 216
American Home Products Co. 2
American Indians: *see* Indians, American
American Institute of Architects (AIA) 19 [82, 83, 85]
American Library Association (ALA) 207 [83, 85]
American Motors Corp. 34 [82–84]

490

American Radio Relay League 328 [85]
American Stock Exchange (Amex) 316 [82–85]
American Telephone and Telegraph Co.
 (AT&T) 77, 324 [82–85]
 advertising 2
 building architecture 18
"American Violence and Public Policy" 84
America's Cup (boating) 51 [84]
Amex: *see* American Stock Exchange
Amiga (microcomputer) 78
Amis, Kingsley 212 [85]
Amnesty International 161, 279 [82–85]
 Peru 267
 Uganda 348
Amphipithecus mogaungensis
 fossil 46, *picture* 13
Amsterdam, Neth. 25
ANC: *see* African National Congress
Anders, Edward 106
Anderton *v.* Ryan (U.K.) 202
Androgyny 133, 135
Andromeda (galaxy) 27
Anemia 222
Angola 11 [82–85]
 Africa 5, 304, 380
 agriculture 7
 engineering projects 122
 intervention and defense 97
 refugees and migrants 283
 United Nations 357
 U.S.S.R. 96
Anheuser-Busch Co. 2
Animal Liberation Front 49
Animals 49, 376, 382 [82–85]
ANS: *see* Armée Nationale Sihanoukist
Ansa Software, Inc. 78
Antarctica 11 [82–85]
Antarctic Treaty System 11 [83]
Anthropology 13 [82–85]
Anti-Ballistic Missile Systems, Treaty on
 (ABM treaty) 96
Anti-Cult Movement 290
Antigua and Barbuda 14 [82–85]
Aouita, Said 340, *picture* [85]
Apartheid 281 [82–85]
 opposition 131, 243, 357, 360
 South Africa 5, 301, 305, *map* 306
  education 118
  human rights 162
  religion 286
Apeldoorn, Neth. 139
Appel, Willa 290
Apple Computer Inc. 77 [84, 85]
Aquino, Benigno S., Jr. 267 [84, 85]
Aquino, Corazon C. 267, *picture* 268
Arab-Israeli conflict: *see* Middle Eastern and
 North African affairs
Arab Revolutionary Organization 83
Arafat, Yasir 183 [82–85]
 Middle Eastern affairs 182, 188, 229, 322
Archaeology 15 [82–85]
Architecture 17 [82–85]
 botanical gardens 384
 landmarks and monuments 196
Arctic regions 20 [82–85]
 Canada 64
 international law 204
Ardito Barletta Vallarina, Nicolás 256 [85]
Argentina 21 [82–85]
 disasters 100
 government 200
 human rights 161
 India 168
 international law 204
 international trade, *picture* 170
 Latin America 71, 198
 motion pictures 236
 refugees and migrants 283
 transportation 345
Arizona 367 [82–85]
 governor, *list* 367
Arkansas 365 [82–85]
 governor, *list* 367
Armed forces, United States 94 [82–85]
 airline crash 2, 100, 343
 crime and law enforcement 85
 medicine 220
 Vietnam MIAs 374

Armée Nationale Sihanoukist (ANS) 189 [85]
Armero, Colombia 103, 108
Arms: *see* Nuclear weapons; Weapons
Arms control: *see* Defense and arms control
Armstrong, Louis 215
Army, United States 95 [82–85]
Arrow Air 343
Arson: *see* Fires and explosions
Art and art exhibitions 22 [82–85]
 photography 270
Artificial breeding techniques 383
Artificial heart 220 [84, 85]
Artificial insemination 383 [85]
Artificial intelligence (AI) 78 [83, 85]
Art Institute of Chicago (Ill.) 239, 270 [82–85]
Arts Council of Great Britain (ACGB)
 335 [85]
Asbestos 82 [83, 85]
Ascii Corp. 78
ASEAN: *see* Association of Southeast Asian
 Nations
Ashbery, John 211
Ashcroft, Dame Peggy 235
Ashford, Evelyn 257 [82, 83, 85]
Ashley, Laura 259
Ashton, Sir Frederick 91
Asian affairs 392 [82, 83]
 agriculture 7
 engineering projects 121
 human evolution 46
 population 275
 see also Asian countries
Asians (U.K.) 117, 282, 284
Asia Society (New York, N.Y.) 25 [82]
Asides 427 [82–85]
Asimov, Isaac 215 [83]
Aspirin 104, 223 [83, 85]
Assad, Hafez al- 321 [82–85]
 Jordan 189
 Lebanon 205
Assad, Rifaat al- 321 [85]
Assam, India 167 [84]
Assassinations 168, 192 [82, 83, 85]
Association football: *see* Soccer
Association of Southeast Asian Nations
 (ASEAN) 189, 307 [82–85]
 Asia 187, 397
 Australia 30
Astronomy 26 [82–85]
 Earth sciences 106
 Milky Way Galaxy 405
 "Return of Halley's Comet, The" 28
AT&T: *see* American Telephone and
 Telegraph Co.
Atari Corp. 78
Athens, Greece 156, 338 [82]
"Atlantis" (space shuttle)
 space exploration 310, *picture* 311
Atoms 272 [85]
Attenborough, Richard 234 [83, 84]
Atwood, Margaret 213 [82]
Aulby, Mike 55
Australia 29 [82–85]
 Antarctic exploration 12
 automobile industry 33
 consumer affairs 82
 education 118
 engineering projects 123
 environment 125
 fuel and energy 149
 mines and mining 231
 motion pictures 235
 refugees and migrants 285
 Southeast Asia 307
 sports: *see* individual sports
 stamps and coins 315
 zoos and botanical gardens 383
Austria 32 [82–85]
 engineering projects 124
 space exploration 308
 tourism 338
Automation: *see* Computers
Automobile industry 33 [82–85]
 state governments 368
 transportation 345
Automobile racing 36 [82–85]
Avedon, Richard 270
Avery, Margaret, *picture* 236

Aviation: *see* Aerospace industry
Avon Publishers 54
Awards and prizes [82–85]
 architecture 19
 dance 93
 Earth sciences 107
 flowers and gardens 139
 literature 208
  children's literature 215
 motion pictures 235
 music 242
 photography 270
 publishing 54, 216, 245
 sports: *see* individual sports
 theater 333
 see also Nobel Prizes; Pulitzer Prizes

b

Babangida, Ibrahim 250
"Back to the Future" (film) 233
Bacon, Francis 433
 art 26
Bacteria 48 [83]
Badinter, Robert 280
Bahamas, The 38 [82–85]
 crime and law enforcement 84
 Earth sciences 106
Bahrain 38 [82–85]
 Middle East 229, 293
Bailey, Sir Donald Coleman 259
Bailey, Robin, *picture* 327
Baker, James 434
 Baker Plan 172
 Latin America 199
Baker, Kathy 155, *picture* 154
Baldwin, James 210
Ballard, Robert 434
Ballet: *see* Dance
Ballet West 91, *picture* [83]
Baltimore, Md. 24 [82, 83, 85]
Baltimore Stars (football) 142
Bananas 83 [84]
Band Aid (relief fund) 243
Bandung Declaration 169, 399
Bangladesh 38 [82–85]
 disasters 101, 376
 India 168
 landmarks and monuments 196, *picture* 197
 refugees and migrants 284
Bankruptcies 9 [83–85]
Banks, Willie 341 [83]
Banks: *see* Financial institutions
Banning (S. Africa) 302 [85]
Banzer Suarez, Hugo 52
Barbados 39 [82–85]
Barbuda: *see* Antigua and Barbuda
Barnala, Sirgit Singh 168, *picture* 167
"Barracks Thief, The" 210
Barrah, Muhammad Siyad 301 [83–85]
Bartholomew, Pablo 270
Baryshnikov, Mikhail 90 [82–85]
Barzani, Masoud 178
Baseball 39 [82–85]
Basel, Switz. 26 [82]
Basie, Count 242 [82, 84, 85]
Basketball 42 [82–85]
Basque Country 313 [85]
Bastid, Suzanne 205
Battaglia, Letizia 270
Baudouin I 44 [82, 85]
Baxter, Anne 259
Bayreuth Festival (W. Ger.) 240 [83]
BBC: *see* British Broadcasting Corporation
B-Capsa I (Hemophilus b polysaccharide) 106
Beagle Channel 71, 204 [82, 83, 85]
Beard, James Andrews 259
Beatrice Companies Inc. 316 [85]
Beatrix 244 [83, 84]
Beattie, Ann 208
Becker, Boris 435
 tennis 328, *picture* 329
Beckley/Myers 18
Beirut, Lebanon 206 [82–85]
Belaúnde Terry, Fernando 200, 267 [82–85]

Belgium 44 [82–85]
  automobile industry 33
  defense and arms control 96
  food processing 139
  race relations 281
  soccer riot 101, 143
  sports: *see* individual sports
  Zaire 380
Belize 45 [82–85]
  archaeology 16
Bellevue, Wash. 18
Belmont Stakes 159 [83, 85]
Benatar, Pat 257 [83]
Bendjedid, Chadli 10 [82, 84, 85]
Bennett, William J. 116, 363
  race relations 281
  religion 286
Benson, Ezra Taft, *picture* 288
Benthem, Evert van 244
Benzene 69 [84]
Bergen, Candice 258
Bern, Switz. 26
Berri, Nabih 435
  Lebanon 205, 230
Bestemianova, Natalia 166
Betancur Cuartas, Belisario 76, *picture*
    199 [83–85]
Bevilacqua, Joseph A. 366
Bhutto, Benazir 256
Bible 287
Biebach, Herbert 46
"Big River" (musical) 333
Bilingualism 116, 281 [84]
"Biloxi Blues" (play) 333
Biographies 433 [82–85]
  literature 210, 214
Biology 45 [82–85]
  "Inhumane Treatment of Animals" (special
    report) 49
Biondi, Matt 319, *picture* 320
Bird, Larry, *picture* 43 [82, 85]
Birds 46, 50 [82–85]
  wildlife conservation 376
Birmingham, U.K. 282
Birth control 277 [82, 83, 85]
  advertising 2
  animal rights 50
  Dalkon Shield 82
  Ireland 179
Birth defects 276 [84, 85]
  drugs 105
  environment 126
Births 257 [82–85]
  birth statistics 276
  infertility treatment 223
Bishops, Extraordinary Synod of 287
bissett, bill 213
Bissoondath, Neil 212
Bitburg, W. Ger. 151, 288, 359
Bitner, Nathan, *picture* 339
Black Americans 276, 281 [82–85]
  crime 84, 85, 279
  education 117
  labor and employment 196
  music 242
  religion 288
  social services 298
  U.S. literature 209
Black holes 409, *picture* 411
Black robin 377
Blaize, Herbert 156 [85]
Blanc, Mount 238
Blood (human) 106, 219 [83, 85]
BNFL (British Nuclear Fuels Ltd.) 127
Boating 51 [82–85]
Boat people 101, 283
Boe, Anette 296
Boeing Aerospace Corp. 2, 292 [82–85]
Boesak, Allan Aubrey 436
  South Africa 286, 302, 360
Boff, Leonardo 287 [85]
Bogaert, Ronald van den 380
Bogdanovich, Peter 234
Boggs, Bill 257
Bokhan, Sergei 156
Bolivia 52 [82–85]
  government 200
  Latin America 87, 197

refugees and migrants 283
  wildlife conservation 377
Böll, Heinrich Theodor 259
Bollingen Prize in Poetry 211
Bombings 83, 100, 204 [82–85]
  Afghanistan 4
  Belgium, *picture* 44
  Burma 60
  India 167
  Indonesia 169
  Iran 177
  Iraq 178
  Italy 184
  Kuwait 192
  Lebanon 206
  Middle East 228
  Mozambique 238
  New Zealand 249
  Portugal 278
  Saudi Arabia 292
  South Africa 303
  Tunisia 347, 183, 356
  United Kingdom 208, 355
  see also Terrorism
Bonds: *see* Stocks and bonds
B-1 (aircraft) 3
Bonner, Yelena 350
Book publishing 53
  Halley's comet 28
  literature 208, 213
Borg, Bjorn 258 [82, 83]
Borg-Warner Chemicals 273
Borrowing: *see* Credit and debt
Bosporus (strait, Turkey) 121
Boston, Mass. 19, 23, 220 [82–85]
Boston Celtics 42 [85]
Botanical gardens: *see* Zoos and botanical
    gardens
Botha, Pieter Willem 436 [82, 83, 85]
  South Africa 282, 301, 305, *picture* 304
Botswana 7, 304, 357 [82, 83, 85]
Bourguiba, Habib 346 [82–85]
Bowling 55 [82–85]
Bowman, Scotty 164
Boxing 56 [82–85]
  world champions, *table* 57
Boycotts 232 [82, 83, 85]
  Poland 273
  South Africa 302, 305, *picture* 161
Bradford, U.K. 100
Bradley, Bill, *picture* 111
Bradley, Thomas 288 [83, 85]
Brandt, Willy 153, *picture* 151
Braudel, Fernand 259
Brazil 57 [82–85]
  Antarctic exploration 11
  disasters 102
  education 116, *picture* 115
  government 200
  international exchange 172
  Latin America 198
  motion pictures 237
  prisons 279
  transportation 345
  zoos 382
Breast cancer 221
Breeders' Cup 159 [85]
Brennan, William C. 366
Breuer, Marcel 17, *picture* 239 [82]
Bridges 121 [82–85]
Brinkley, Christie 258
Brisco-Hooks, Valerie 342, *picture* 343 [85]
Britain: *see* United Kingdom
British Airtours 343
British Airways 3 [83]
British Broadcasting Corporation (BBC)
    217 [82, 85]
British Columbia, Can. (prov.) 61, 66
    [82, 84, 85]
British Columbia Lions 144
British Museum 26, 239 [82–84]
British Nuclear Fuels Ltd. (BNFL) 127
British Open (golf) 153 [85]
Brixton, U.K. 282
Broadcasting: *see* Television and radio
Broadway, New York, N.Y. 333
Brock, David 222
Brock, William E. 195 [82]

Bromine 125
Bronx Zoo (New York, N.Y.) 383
Brooklyn Academy of Music 91 [82, 84, 85]
Brooks, Gwendolyn 211
Brooks, Louise 259 [83]
Brooks, Thomas N. 366
Brown, Michael Stuart 437
  medicine 221
Browning, Edmond L. 288
Brussels, Belgium 44, *picture*
  riot 101, 143, 184, 355, *picture*
Brynner, Yul 259, 333 [84]
Bubka, Sergei 341, *picture* 342 [85]
Buckley, William 207
Budapest, Hungary 127
Budapest Cultural Forum 90, 132
Budd, Zola 342, *picture* 341 [85]
Buddhism 196, 373 [82, 83]
Budget, U.S. (Federal budget) 112, 361
    [82, 83, 85]
Buhari, Mohammed 250 [84, 85]
Buick 35
Building and construction (Housing)
    59 [82–85]
  botanical gardens 384
  engineering projects 122
  homelessness 299
  libraries 207
  Mexico 226
  museums 238
  race relations 282
  United States 111
  see also Architecture
Bukin, Andrei 166
Bulgaria 59 [82–85]
  anthropology 14
  European affairs 132
  human rights 161
  Turkey 347
Burgee, John 18
Burma 60 [82–85]
  disasters 103
  fossil 45
Burnet, Sir Frank MacFarlane 259
Burns, James McGregor 210
Burrows, Abe (Abram Solman Borowitz) 259
Buses 103, 346 [82–85]
Bush, George 75 [82–85]
Business and industry: *see* Economic affairs
Buthelezi, Gatsha Mangosuthu 438 [83]
  South Africa 303, 305
Byblos (fashion studio), *picture* 134

C

Cable television 325 [82–85]
  advertising 2
CACM: *see* Central American Common
    Market
Cadillac 35
Caldecott Medal, *picture* 214 [82–85]
Caldwell, Taylor (Janet Miriam Taylor
    Holland Caldwell) 260
Calendar for 1986 483
California 366 [82–85]
  consumer affairs 81
  crime 84, 279
  earthquakes 108
  education 117
  environment 126, 128
  governor, *list* 367
  refugees and migrants 284
  social services 297
California condor 376 [82–85]
Calvino, Italo 260
Camarena Salazar, Enrique 86
Cambodia: *see* Kampuchea
Cameras 268 [82–85]
Cameron, Mark James Walter 260
Cameron, Michelle 320
Camorra (Italian organized crime) 184
Campbell, Glen 257
Campbell Soup Co. 2
Campomanes, Florencio 69
Cam Ranh Bay naval base 308 [85]

Canada 60 [82–85]
　Arctic regions 20
　arts 25
　　dance 92
　　literature 212
　　motion pictures 235
　　music 240
　　theater 334
　automobile industry 33
　building and construction 59
　Cabinet, *list* 62
　crime 86, 280
　defense and arms control 96
　disasters 100
　environment 124
　fuel and energy 148
　international affairs 174, 204
　　Latin America 199
　　Saint Christopher and Nevis 291
　　United States 360, 368
　machinery and machine tools 216
　mines and mining 231
　"Mood for Change, A" (special report) 65
　newspapers 245
　nuclear industry 253
　oceanography 253
　population 276
　sports: *see* individual sports
　stamps and coins 314
　transportation 346
　wildlife conservation 376
Canadian Football League (CFL) 144
Canadian Library Association 215 [82–85]
Canadian Pacific Air 83
Cancer 106, 221, 224, 276 [82–85]
Cannabis: *see* Marijuana
Capa, Robert 270
Cape Verde 7
Capital Cities Communications Inc. 114, 326, 363
Capitalism 111, 175, 280
　Africa 6, 301
　China 72
　Japan 187
　Saudi Arabia 293
　U.S.S.R. 351, 412
Capital punishment 192, 279 [82–85]
Caravaggio 25, *picture* 24 [83]
Carbon dioxide 125, 376
Cardinals (religion) 288
Carew, Ron 40
Carey, Rick 319 [84]
Caribbean Basin Initiative (CBI) 38, 198 [83–85]
Caribbean Community (Caricom) 198 [83–85]
　Barbados 39
　Saint Lucia 291
Caribbean States 97 [82–85]
Cars: *see* Automobile industry
CART: *see* Championship Auto Racing Teams
Cartagena Group 199
Carter, Benny 242
Carvalho, Otelo Saraiva de 278 [85]
Cassettes: *see* Record industry
Castro, Fidel 87, 97, 199 [82–85]
Castro, Raúl 87 [83]
Catholicism: *see* Roman Catholicism
Cato, Milton 292 [84]
Cats 49 [82–85]
Cavaço Silva, Aníbal 277, *picture* 278
CBI: *see* Caribbean Basin Initiative
CBS: *see* Columbia Broadcasting System
CCC (Cellules Communistes Combattante) 45
CD: *see* Compact disc
CDC: *see* Centers for Disease Control
CdF Chimie 273
Ceausescu, Nicolae 291 [82–85]
Cellules Communistes Combattante (CCC) 45
Censorship 247 [82–84]
　Brazil, *picture* 58
Census Bureau, U.S. 118, 275 [82, 83]
"Center of the Milky Way, The" (feature article) 405
Centers for Disease Control (CDC) 104, 219, 364 [82, 83]
Central African Republic 283[82]
Central America: *see* Latin-American affairs; countries by name

Central American Common Market (CACM) 198 [82, 83]
Central Intelligence Agency (CIA) 352, 423 [84, 85]
Ceramics industry 67
Cereals 7 [82–85]
Cerezo Arévalo, Marco Vinicio 157, *picture*
"Certain Mr. Takahashi, A" 213
CFCs: *see* Chlorofluorocarbons
CFL (Canadian Football League) 144
Chagall, Marc 24, 260
"Challenger" (space shuttle) 309 [83–85]
Chambers, George 346 [82–85]
Championship Auto Racing Teams (CART) 36 [82–85]
Chappell, Fred 211
Charles, Eugenia 103 [83–85]
Charter 77 (Czech.) 90 [84, 85]
Cheese 139
Chemistry 67 [82–85]
Chernenko, Konstantin Ustinovich 260, *picture* 349 [84, 85]
Chess 69 [82–85]
Chevrolet 35
Chiang Ching-kuo 322 [83–85]
Chicago, Ill. 18, *picture* 36 [82–85]
　futures and options 317
　museums 239
　photography 270
　theater 334
Chicago Bears (football) 141
Chicago Religious Task Force on Central America 285
"Chicago Sun-Times" 245 [84]
Children 277 [82–85]
　drugs 104
　education 115, 117
　literature for children 213
　mental health 224
　prisons 279
　social services 297
　United States 367
Chile 70 [82–85]
　Antarctic exploration 12
　disasters 102, 108
　engineering projects 123
　fish and fisheries 137
　government 200
　human rights 161
　international law 204
　social services 298
Chin, Larry Wu-tai 364
China (People's Republic of China) 72 [82–85]
　agriculture 7
　Antarctic exploration 11
　birds 46
　computers 78
　crime 279
　defense and arms control 93
　disasters 101, 108
　education 118
　engineering projects 121
　fish and fisheries 137
　international affairs
　　Antigua and Barbuda 14
　　Bangladesh 39
　　Bolivia 52
　　Burma 60
　　Europe 131
　　India 169
　　Indonesia 169
　　Japan 188, 402
　　North Korea 192
　　Pakistan 256
　　Romania 291
　　Southeast Asia 189, 308, 374
　　South Korea 191
　　Taiwan 322
　　U.S.S.R. 352, 426
　motion pictures 237
　mountaineering 237
　nuclear industry 253
　population 276
　sports: *see* individual sports
　stamps and coins, *picture* 314
　textiles 331
　tourism 338
　transportation 344

　weather 376
　wildlife conservation 376, 382
China, Republic of: *see* Taiwan
Chirac, Jacques 146 [84]
Chiral boranes (chemistry) 68
Chiyonofuji (Mitsugu Akimoto) 438
Chlorofluorocarbons (CFCs) 125, 254
Cholera 101 [84]
　Somalia 301
Cholesterol 220 [82, 83, 85]
Christianity 286, 287, 290 [82–85]
　race relations 281
　Vietnam 373
　see also Roman Catholicism
"Christianity Today" 289
Chronology of 1985 pp. viii–xxxi
Chrysler Corporation 34 [82–85]
Chun Doo Hwan 190 [82–85]
Church and state 116, 286
Churches: *see* Religion
Churchill, Winston 212
Church of Satan 290
Chute, Carolyn 209
CIA: *see* Central Intelligence Agency
Ciccone, Madonna Louise: *see* Madonna
CITES: *see* Convention on International Trade in Endangered Species of Wild Fauna and Flora
Cities and urban affairs 299 [82–85]
　population 275, *table* 276
　United Kingdom 355
Civil rights and liberties: *see* Human rights
Claire, Ina (Ina Fagan) 260
Clarke, Austin 212
Clarke, Kenny ("Klook"; Kenneth Spearman Clarke) 260
Classical music 240 [85]
Claytor, Robert B., *picture* 345
Cleveland, Ohio 25 [82, 83]
Clothing: *see* Fashion; Textiles
Coal 101, 149, 232 [82–85]
　ships and shipping 295
　United Kingdom 353
Coca-Cola Co. 2, *picture*
Coffee 380 [82, 85]
Coins: *see* Stamps and coins
Cold (illness) 224
Cold Lake, Can., *picture* 148
Cole, Lester 260
Coleco Industries 339
Colleges and universities 118, 117 [82–85]
　libraries 207
Collins, Joan 258
Collins, Phil 243
Colmar, Fr. 239
Colombia 76 [82–85]
　archaeology 16
　disasters 100, 108, 328
　engineering projects 123
　fuel and energy, *picture* 149
　government 201
　Latin America 198
　sports: *see* individual sports
Colon cancer 221
Colorado 365 [82–85]
　governor, *list* 367
　pornography 54
Colorado, University of 16, *picture* 15
"Color Purple, The" 234
Columbia Broadcasting System (CBS) 326, 363 [82–85]
　magazines 216
Columbia Glacier, Alaska 107, *picture* 109
Colville, Sir John 212
Comecon: *see* Council for Mutual Economic Assistance
Comedy 209, 233, 327 [85]
Comegys, Fred 270
Comet 26 [83–85]
Commission for Racial Equality (CRE) 281, 284
Commodore International Ltd. 77
Communications: *see* Telecommunications
Communications Workers of America 194
Communist movement 161 [82–85]
　Afghanistan 4
　Albania 10
　Angola 11

Bulgaria 59
  Chinese education 118
  Eastern Europe 132
  East Germany 153
  France 145
  Hungary 163
  Philippines 267
  U.S.S.R. 422
  Vietnam 373
  see also Marxism
Compact disc (CD) 241 [84, 85]
Compton, John 291 [83–85]
Computers 76 [82–85]
  animal rights 49
  anthropology 14
  "Homeless Computer, The" (special
    report) 79
  industry, *picture* 402
  libraries 208, *picture* 207
  mathematics 218, *picture*
  microelectronics 227
  publishing 54, 214
  telecommunications 324
Concorde 3 [83–85]
Condor 376, *picture* 378 [82–85]
Cone Collection (Baltimore, Md.) 24
Congress, U.S. 360, 365, *list* 369 [82–85]
  Africa 5, 303, 306
  agriculture 8
  Canada 63
  China 75
  corporate mergers 114
  economic affairs 112
  education 116
  homelessness 299
  international trade 176
  intervention and defense 98
  Jordan 189
  Nicaragua 249
  refugees and migrants 284
  social services 297
  Southeast Asia 189, 308
  Taiwan 323
  see also Legislation
Connecticut 367 [82–85]
  governor, *list* 367
  religion 286
Connors, Jimmy 329 [82–84]
Conservation
  book 208
  flowers and gardens 139
  land 127
  wildlife 376, 382
Constitution, U.S. 202, 326 [83, 84]
Construction: *see* Building and construction
Consumer affairs 81 [82–85]
  Austria 32
  building and construction 59
  Canada 60
  economic affairs 110
  state governments, U.S. 368
  U.S.S.R. 133
Consumer Interpol Program 81 [83, 84]
Consumer price index 111, 316 [82–85]
Consumer Product Safety Commission (CPSC)
    339 [82, 84, 85]
Contadora Group 198, 205 [84, 85]
Contraceptives: *see* Birth control
Contras 97, 158, 249, 360 [85]
Control Data Corp. 77
Convention on International Trade in
    Endangered Species of Wild Fauna
    and Flora (CITES) 377 [82, 84]
Convention on the Transfer of Sentenced
    Prisoners 280
Copeland, Al 52 [83, 85]
Copper 380 [82–85]
Cordero, Angel, Jr., *picture* 159 [83]
Cordovez, Diego 4 [83, 84]
Cordrey, John 281
Corn (maize) 9, 46, 140 [82–85]
  Zimbabwe 382
Cornoyer-Hedrick (architecture) 19
Corporations: *see* Economic affairs
Corruption: *see* Scandals and corruption
Cosby, Bill 439 [85]
"Cosby Show, The" 242, 328 [85]
Cosmology 28 [83]

Cossiga, Francesco 439
  Italy 184
Costa Rica 82 [82–85]
  Latin America 198, 250
  refugees and migrants 283
Cotton 8, 331 [82–85]
Council for Mutual Economic Assistance
    (Comecon) 131 [83, 85]   •
Counterfeiting 315, 339 [85]
Coups d'état 5, 250, 348 [82–85]
  Thailand 332
CPSC: *see* Consumer Product Safety
    Commission
Cram, Steve 340, *picture* [84]
Cranes 376, 383, *picture* 378
Crapanzano, Vincent 14
Craxi, Bettino 183, *pictures* 131, 184 [84, 85]
Cray Research, Inc. 78
CRE: *see* Commission for Racial Equality
Creationism 117, 366 [82, 83]
Credit and debt 110, 169, 175 [82–85]
  African affairs 5
  automobile industry 35
  education 119
  farm crisis 8
  Latin America 199, 200
  see also countries by name
Crenna, Richard 328
Crime and law enforcement 83 [82–85]
  Australia 29
  counterfeit money 315
  death statistics 276
  human rights 161
  Italy 184
  law 202
  museums 240
  prisons 278, 280
  "Reflections on the Bernhard Goetz
    Case" 85
  religion 286
  state governments, U.S. 365
Crocker National Bank 85
Crocodiles 377, 383
Crozier, Lorna 213
Crystals (physics) 272
Cuba 87 [82–85]
  Antarctic exploration 12
  international affairs 172
    Africa 5, 11, 357
    U.S.S.R. 95
  intervention and defense 97
  motion pictures 237
  sports: *see* individual sports
  tourism 339
  weather 375
Cults 86, 289
Cunningham, Mary 257 [83]
Cunningham, Merce 91 [82, 83]
Cuomo, Mario 299, *picture* 368 [83, 85]
Curtin, Jane 328
Custer, George 16
Cycling 88 [85]
Cyclones [82, 83, 85]
  Bangladesh 38, 102, 376
Cyprus 89 [82–85]
  Turkey 348
Cystic fibrosis 222
Czechoslovakia 89 [82–85]
  European affairs 132
  international law 204
  mines and mining 231
  sports: *see* individual sports

d

Dairy products 9, 139 [82–85]
  see also Cheese; Milk
Dalkon Shield 2, 82
Dallas, Tex. 19, 238 [83, 85]
Daly, Tyne 328
Dams 122 [82–85]
Dance 90 [82–85]
  ice skating 165
Dance Theatre of Harlem 91 [82, 84, 85]
"Dangerous Moves" (film) 235

Daniels, William 328
Danny (hurricane) 374
Danube (riv., Eur.) 127
Data General Corp. 77
Data processing: *see* Computers
Datsun: *see* Nissan
Davies, Robertson, *picture* 212
Da Vinci, Leonardo: *see* Leonardo da Vinci
Davis, Anthony 242
Davis Cup (tennis) 328 [82–85]
Dawa, al- (Iraqi terrorist group) 192
DC-3 (aircraft) 3
DDT 48 [82, 83, 85]
DEA (Drug Enforcement Administration) 86
Dearborn Center (Chicago, Ill.) 19
Death penalty: *see* Capital punishment
Deaths 276 [82–85]
  accidents 99, 343
  see also Obituaries
Debt: *see* Credit and debt
Decker, Mary: *see* Slaney, Mary
Deer 50 [83]
Defections
  Lebanese 357
  Soviet 156, 352, 423
Defense and arms control 93 [82–85]
  aerospace 3
  Asia 168, 308, 394
  Canada 64
  Europe 131, 147
  "Intervention and Defense in Central
    America and the Caribbean" (special
    report) 97
  Middle East 188, 228
  United States 112, 358
  U.S.S.R. 352, 417
  see also Nuclear weapons; Weapons
Degas, Edgar 23
Deinstitutionalization (community care)
    299 [85]
De la Madrid Hurtado, Miguel: *see* Madrid
    Hurtado, Miguel de la
Delaunay, Robert 23
Delaunay, Sonia 23
Delaware 114 [82–85]
  governor, *list* 367
Delors, Jacques 130 [84]
Delta Air Lines 100, 343
Delvalle, Eric Arturo 256
Democratic Kampuchea (DK) 189, 307
Democratic People's Republic of Korea:
    see Korea
Demography: *see* Population
Demonstrations and riots [82–85]
  Algeria 10
  Argentina, *picture* 170
  Australia, *picture* 30
  Belgium 44, 143, *pictures* 143, 244
  Chile 71
  China 75
  Czechoslovakia 90
  Dominican Republic 104
  Egypt, *picture* 120
  farmers, *pictures* 7, 9
  Finland 137
  France, *picture* 147
  Greece 156
  Guatemala 157
  human rights 162
  Israel, *picture* 181
  Jamaica 185
  Kenya 190
  Mexico 225
  Pakistan, *picture* 255
  Panama 256
  Poland 275
  prisons 279
  race relations 282
  South Africa 301, 305
  Spain 312
  United Kingdom 86, 355, *picture* 281
  United States 360, *pictures* 231, 361
  West Germany 151
Deng Xiaoping (Teng Hsiao-p'ing) 72,
    402 [82–85]
Denktash, Rauf 89 [85]
Denmark 99 [82–85]
  death statistics 277

defense and arms control 96
music 240
race relations 282
transportation 345
Dentistry 99 [82–85]
Denver, Colo. 23 [82, 84]
Deoxyribonucleic acid: *see* DNA
Deregulation 81, 114, 149, 325 [82–85]
Design: *see* Architecture; Fashion
Deutsche Mark: *see* Mark
Devaluation and revaluation [82–85]
  Argentina 22
  Australia 31
  Israel 182
  Nicaragua 250
  United States 110, 362
  Zambia 381
Developing countries 110, 170 [82–85]
  agriculture 7
  engineering projects 122
  Europe 130
  Gorbachev's policy 424
  homelessness 299
  international trade 176
  Latin America 199
  Middle East 192, 229
  population 275
  see also countries by name
Devine, Grant 66 [83]
DeVito, Danny 257 [84]
DeVries, William C. 220 [83, 85]
DEW Line: *see* Distant Early Warning Line
Diet: *see* Nutrition
Dioxin 48, 128 [84]
Diplomatic Club (building, Saudi Arabia)
  122, *picture*
Dire Straits 243
Disarmament: *see* Defense and arms control
Disasters 99 [82–85]
  Colombia 76, 108
  Italy 184, 232
  Mexico 226, 227
  transportation 343, 346
    air 2, 4, 81, 83, 167, 187
  weather 376
    Africa 7, 129
    Bangladesh 38
  see also Drought; Earthquakes; Floods;
    Hurricanes; Storms; Tornadoes;
    Volcanoes
"Discovery" (space shuttle) 309, *pictures* 309,
  310 [85]
  Saudi Arabia 292
Discrimination [82–85]
  Romania 132
  U.S. 279
  see also Apartheid; Human rights;
    Minorities; Race relations
Disease 219, 276
  drug treatment 104
  mental health 224
Distant Early Warning Line (DEW
  Line) 64, 361
District of Columbia: *see* Washington, D.C.
Ditka, Mike 440
  football 141
Diving 319 [82–85]
Divorce 277 [82–85]
Djibouti 283 [82, 84]
DK: *see* Democratic Kampuchea
"DM" awards ("Drama Magazine"
  awards) 335
DNA (Deoxyribonucleic acid) 222 [83, 84]
Dobrynin, Anatoli 349
Doctorow, E. L. 210
Doctors: *see* Medicine
Doe, Samuel 6
DOE: *see* Energy, U.S. Department of
Dogs 49 [82–85]
Dole, Elizabeth 368, *picture* 345 [85]
Dollar (Australian) 31
Dollar (U.S.) 110, 362 [82–85]
  international affairs 170, 173, 175
  iron and steel industry 179
  stocks and bonds 316
Dominica 103 [82–85]
Dominican Republic 104 [82–85]
  Cuba 97

Donahue, Thomas R. 193
Donovan, Raymond J. 363 [82, 83, 85]
Don Quixote Pond (Antarctica), *picture* 12
Dos Santos, José Eduardo 11 [82, 83, 85]
Dotson, Gary E. 84
Douglas, Paul 366 [85]
Douglas-Home, Charles Cospatrick 260 [83]
Dow Jones Industrial Average 315,
  362 [82–85]
D'Oyly Carte, Dame Bridget 260
Dozier, Therese Knecht, *picture* 116
Draize test 49
Drama: *see* Theater
"Drama Magazine" awards ("DM"
  awards) 335
Drawings 23
Drechsler, Heike 341
Drexel Burnham Lambert Inc. 316
Drought [82–85]
  Africa 5, 129, 190, 238, 283, 376, 381
  Canada 66
  Galápagos 376
  Romania 291
  United States 138
Drozhzhin, Nikolai 320
Drug Enforcement Administration (DEA) 86
Drugs 104 [82–85]
  Bahamas, The 38
  Belize 45
  Burma 60
  Colombia 76
  crime 84, 279
  homelessness 299
  medicine 68, 223
  Paraguay 256
  United States 41, 49, 364, 367
Drummond, Michael 220, *picture* 222
Drunk driving 2, 367 [83–85]
  see also Alcoholic beverages
Druze 206 [84]
Duarte, José Napoleón 121, *picture*
  [82, 83, 85]
  intervention and defense 97
  Latin America 200
Duarte Durán, Inés Guadalupe 121
Dubai 353 [82–84]
Dublin, Ireland 23 [82, 83, 85]
Dublin Festival 337 [85]
Dubuffet, Jean 261
Duchenne muscular dystrophy 222
Duvalier, Jean-Claude 158 [82, 83, 85]
Dylan, Bob 243 [82, 84, 85]

e

Eagles 377 [82]
Eanes, António dos Santos Ramalho 278
  [82, 83]
Earth 106 [85]
  astronomy 26
  space exploration 309
Earthquakes 102 [82–85]
  Chile 71
  Mexico 108, 226, 227, 311
  engineering projects 124
Earth sciences 106 [82–85]
Easter Island, Chile (prov.) 72
East Germany: *see* Germany
Eastman Kodak 269 [83, 84]
Eastwood, Clint 233
EC: *see* European Communities
Eclipse Awards (horse racing) 159 [85]
Ecology: *see* Environment
Economic affairs (Business and industry)
  109 [82–85]
  advertising 2
  aerospace 3
  Africa 6
  agriculture 7
  Asia 308, 396
  automobile industry 33
  book publishing 53
  building and construction 59
  ceramics industry 67
  computer industry 76

defense and arms control 94
engineering projects 122
Europe 130
"Field Guide to Corporate Mergers, A"
  (special report) 113
fish and fisheries 137
flowers and gardens 138
food processing 140
fuel and energy 148
international exchange and payments 169
international trade 172
Latin America 197
law 202
libraries 207
microelectronics 227
Middle East and North Africa 231
mines and mining 231
plastics 273
prisons 280
ships and shipping 293
stocks and bonds 315
television 326
textiles 331
tourism 338
toys and games 339
transportation 344
  see also International trade; Labor and
    employment; countries by name
Economic Community of West African States
  (ECOWAS) 6 [84, 85]
ECSC: *see* European Coal and Steel
  Community
Ecuador 115 [82–85]
  archaeology 16
  government 200, 376
Edinburgh, U.K. 24, 26 [84]
Edmonton Oilers (ice hockey team)
  163 [84, 85]
Education 115 [82–85]
  computers 14, 80
  "Education of Ethnic Minorities, The" 117
  Japan 403
  law 202
  libraries 207
  medicine 220
  race relations 281
  religion 286
  United States 366
Education, U.S. Department of 118,
  363 [83–85]
"Education for All" (Swann Report) 117
Edwards, Edwin W. 365
EEZ: *see* Exclusive Economic Zone
EEZ-SCAN program 109
E. F. Hutton and Company, Inc. 85
Egypt 119 [82–85]
  "Achille Lauro" hijacking 83, 183, 204, 364
  archaeology 15
  fuel and energy 148
  human rights 162
  Middle East and North Africa 178, 183, 230
  religion 288
EgyptAir (hijacking) 231
Eisenhower, Milton Stover 261
Elections 281 [82–85]
  Africa 6
  Latin America 197, 200
  see also countries by name
Electricity 149, 252 [82–85]
Electroconvulsive therapy (shock treatment)
  224 [83]
Elephant 377
Elfstedentocht (ice-skating race) 244
Elizabeth II 45, 156 [82–85]
Elkin, Stanley 209 [83]
"Elle" (magazine) 217
Elliott, Bill 36
El Niño (current) 47 [84, 85]
El Salvador 120 [82–85]
  government 161, 200
  intervention and defense 97
  Latin America 198
  refugees and migrants 283, 285
Emigration: *see* Refugees and migrants
Emmy awards: *see* Academy of Television
  Arts and Sciences
Employment: *see* Labor and employment
EMS: *see* European Monetary System

Endangered species 139, 376 [82, 83]
Endorphins (biol.) 224
Energy: *see* Fuel and energy
Energy, U.S. Department of (DOE) 148 [83]
Engineering projects 121 [82–85]
England: *see* United Kingdom
Environment 124 [82–85]
  animal rights 49
  biology 45
  engineering projects 123
  United States 368
Environmental Protection Agency (EPA) 125,
    368 [82–85]
  automobile industry 35
  biology 48
  fuel and energy 149
Enzymes 139
Episcopal Church 288 [83]
Equal rights: *see* Human rights
"Equality and Excellence: The Educational
    Status of Black Americans" 117
Erdrich, Louise 209
Ershad, Hussain Mohammed 38 [83–85]
Ervin, Samuel James, Jr. 261
ESA: *see* European Space Agency
Eskimos (Inuits) 20, 50, 64 [82, 83]
Espionage
  India 168
  Israel 183
  Norway 252
  United States 30, 364
  U.S.S.R. 352
  West Germany 151
Esquivel, Manuel 45 [85]
"Essence" (magazine) 216
Ethiopia 129 [82–85]
  Africa 5, 301, 382
  agriculture 7, *picture* 8
  disasters 103
  engineering projects 122
  human rights 162
  Israel 182
  refugees and migrants 243, 283
  transportation 345
  U.S.S.R. 96, 97
Etna, Mt. (Italy) 109
Eureka project 130
European affairs 130 [82–85]
  aerospace 3
  botanical gardens 383
  consumer affairs 82
  dance 92
  defense and arms control 93
  economic affairs 110
  engineering projects 121
  labor and employment 193
  libraries 207
  nuclear industry 253
  plastics 273
  population 275
  prisons 280
  race relations 281
  refugees and migrants 283
  ships and shipping 293
  textiles 331
  toys and games 339
  see also European countries
European Champions' Cup (soccer) 101, 144
European Coal and Steel Community (ECSC)
    179 [83, 84]
European Communities (EC) 130 [82, 84, 85]
  agriculture 7
  automobile industry 33
  consumer affairs 82
  environment 125
  fish and fisheries 137
  fuel and energy 149
  iron and steel industry 180
  Latin America 198
  Middle East 229, 293
  South Africa 304
  see also European countries
European Court of Human Rights 131, 285
European Free Trade Association 131
European Monetary System (EMS)
    130 [83, 84]
European Parliament 130, 282 [82–85]
European Space Agency (ESA) 28, 308 [82, 83]

EVD (Extended voluntary departure) 285
Everest, Mount 237
Evert Lloyd, Chris 330 [82–85]
Evolution 45, 106, 117 [82, 83, 85]
Evren, Kenan 60 [82–85]
Ewing, Patrick 42 [85]
Exchange rate 112 [82–85]
Exclusive Economic Zone (EEZ) 109 [84, 85]
Execution: *see* Capital punishment
Exhibitions: *see* Art and art exhibitions;
  Museums
Explosions: *see* Fires and explosions
Exports: *see* International trade
Extended voluntary departure (EVD) 285
Extraordinary Synod of Bishops: *see* Bishops,
  Extraordinary Synod of

FAA: *see* Federal Aviation Administration
Fabius, Laurent 146 [85]
  East Germany 152
  Morocco 233
Fabrics: *see* Textiles
Fadeev, Aleksandr 166
Fahd ibn 'Abd al-'Aziz al-Saud 293 [82–85]
Fairness doctrine 325
Fair Price Provisions 114
Falkland Islands (Islas Malvinas) 22,
    198 [82–85]
  fish and fisheries 137
Falwell, Jerry 286 [82, 85]
Family record 471
Famine [82, 83, 85]
  African affairs 5, 7, 129
    human rights 162
    refugees and migrants 283
    United Nations' aid 358
FAO: *see* Food and Agriculture
  Organization, UN
Farabundo Martí National Liberation Front
    (FMLN) 120 [84]
Farm Aid 243, *picture* 7
Farming: *see* Agriculture
Farmland value 8
Farrakhan, Louis 288, 289 [85]
Farrell, Suzanne 91
Fashion 133 [82–85]
  "Street Scene—Pop, Glam, Androgyny,
    The" (special report) 135
Fathy, Hassan 19
Fawcett, Farrah, *picture* 257
FBI: *see* Federal Bureau of Investigation
FCC: *see* Federal Communications
  Commission
FDA: *see* Food and Drug Administration
Febres Cordero, León 115 [85]
Fed: *see* Federal Reserve Board
Federal Aviation Administration (FAA)
    81 [82, 85]
Federal budget: *see* Budget, U.S.
Federal Bureau of Investigation (FBI)
    83 [82–85]
Federal Communications Commission (FCC)
    244, 325 [82–85]
Federal Election Commission *v.* National
    Conservative Political Action
    Committee (U.S.) 202
Federal Republic of Germany (W. Ger.): *see*
  Germany
Federal Reserve Board (Fed) 112 [82–85]
  stocks and bonds 316
Federal Trade Commission (FTC) 2 [82–85]
Fédération Internationale des Quilleurs (FIQ)
    55 [82, 83, 85]
Feld Ballet 91, *picture* 90 [83]
Feminism: *see* Women
Fermi National Accelerator Laboratory 272
Ferrare, Christina 258
Ferraro, Geraldine 54 [85]
Ferrato, Donna 270
Fertility 276 [82–85]
  medicine 223
Festival of India 25, *picture*
  dance 92

Fiber, synthetic 331 [82, 83]
Fiber optics 324 [82, 84]
Field, Sally 235 [82, 85]
Field events: *see* Track and field
Fiesta Bowl (football) 142 [85]
Figini, Michela 295 [85]
Figure skating 165 [84, 85]
Film (photography) 268 [84, 85]
Films: *see* Motion pictures
Finance, international: *see* International
  exchange and payments
Financial institutions 169, 203 [82–85]
  stocks and bonds 318
  United States 9, 81, 362, 368
  see also World Bank
Finland 136 [82–85]
  infant mortality 277
  international law 204
  social services 298
  United Nations 357
FIQ: *see* Fédération Internationale des
  Quilleurs
FIRA: *see* Foreign Investment Review Agency
Firearms: *see* Weapons
Fires and explosions 100, 127 [82–85]
  British Airtours 343
  crime and law enforcement 86
  Galápagos Islands 376
  weather, *picture* 375
Fish and fisheries 137 [82–85]
  Arctic regions 20
  biology 47
  food processing 140
  Iceland 165
  medicine 221
Fisher, Mel 441
Fisher, William F. 309, *picture* 310
FitzGerald, Garret 179, *picture* [82–85]
Flick affair 151 [85]
Floods 101 [82–85]
  Austria 32
  Bangladesh 38
  Italy 184
  weather 375, *picture* 376
Florida 365 [82–85]
  governor, *list* 367
  weather 374
Flowers and gardens 138 [82–85]
  botanical gardens 383
Fluoride 99
Flutie, Doug, *picture* 258 [85]
FMLN: *see* Farabundo Martí National
  Liberation Front
FOI Act (Freedom of Information Act) 247
Food and Agriculture Organization, UN
    (FAO) 7 [82–85]
  Africa 5
Food and Drug Administration (FDA) 49,
    104 [82–85]
Food processing 139 [82–85]
  fish and fisheries 137
  lead 128
Food production 7
Food Security Act (1985) 9
Football 141 [82–85]
  "Soccer Riot in Brussels, The" 143
Force 17 (terrorism) 83
Ford, Gerald R. 216 [82–84]
Ford Motor Co. 34 [82–85]
"Foreign Affairs" (book) 211
Foreign Investment Review Agency (FIRA) 60
    [83, 85]
Forests 125, *picture* 126 [82, 83]
Forman, Milos 235
Formosa: *see* Taiwan
Fortier, Laurie, *picture* 258
Fort Worth, Tex. 24, 270 [82, 83]
"Fort Worth Star-Telegram" (newspaper) 245
Fossils 45 [82–85]
Foster, Greg 341
Fowles, John 211
Fox, Michael J. 441
  motion pictures 233, *picture* 234
FP-25 (Popular Forces of April 25) 278
France 145 [82–85]
  aerospace 3
  agriculture, *picture* 9
  arts 17, 23, 208, 235, 239, 240

automobile industry 33
building and construction 59
defense and arms control 93
disasters 102
fuel and energy 150
homelessness, *picture* 300
international affairs 112, 172, 174, 204
  Africa 6, 10, 120, 347
  Europe 130, 152, 275
  New Zealand 83, 249
  Qatar 281
mass media 217, 247
oceanography 253
population 276
prisons 280
race relations 282
refugees and migrants 284
social services 298
sports: *see* individual sports
transportation 124, 345
Franklin, Jon 246
Freedom of Information Act (FOI Act) 247
Free enterprise: *see* Capitalism
Freons: *see* Chlorofluorocarbons
Frogs 45
Frustaci, Patti 223
FTC: *see* Federal Trade Commission
Fuel and energy 148 [82–85]
  aerospace 3
  automobile industry 35
  international trade 172
  nuclear industry 252
  wind energy 388, *picture* 390
  see also Coal; Nuclear industry; Petroleum;
    countries by name
Fugard, Athol, *picture* 333
Fuji Photo Film 269 [84]
Fujisawa Municipal Sports Center 19, *picture*
Fujitsu Ltd. 78 [85]
Fundamentalism [82, 83]
  Christian 13, 117, 288
  Islamic 10, 288
Fund for Animals 50
Furniture 23 [82–84]
Furnstahl, Stephen 18
Futrell, Mary Hatwood 115 [84]

g

Gaddis, William 208
Galápagos Islands 376 [83]
Galaxies 27 [83–85]
  Milky Way Galaxy 405
Gallagher, Norman 29
Gallo, Robert 219
Gallup Poll [84]
  education 115
  religion 290
Gambling 368 [85]
Games: *see* Toys and games
Gamma rays 408
Gandhi, Indira 168 [82–85]
Gandhi, Rajiv 167 [82, 85]
  environment 126
  Japan 188
  religion 288
Ganges River 126 [83]
Gannett Co. 245 [84]
García Pérez, Alan 442
  Peru 267, *picture*
Garcia v. San Antonio Metropolitan Transit
  Authority 365
Gardens: *see* Flowers and gardens; Zoos and
  botanical gardens
Garn, Jake 309 [82]
Gas: *see* Natural gas
Gasoline: *see* Petroleum
GATT: *see* General Agreement on Tariffs
  and Trade
Gaultier, Jean-Paul 135
GCC: *see* Gulf Cooperation Council
GDP (Gross domestic product) 109
GE: *see* General Electric Co.
Geldof, Bob 442
  music 243

Gemayal, Amin 205 [83–85]
Gemsbok 383
General Agreement on Tariffs and Trade
  (GATT) 175
  Asia 396
  Europe 131, 152
General Dynamics Corporation 85
General Electric Co. (GE) 85, 316, 363 [83]
General Foods Corp. 2, 316 [83]
General Motors Corp. (GM) 33 [82–85]
  advertising 2
  stocks and bonds 316
Genetics 45 [82–84]
  food processing 139
  medicine 222
Geneva Convention 357
Geneva summit (U.S.-U.S.S.R.) 93, 131, 351,
  358, 424
"GEO" (magazine) 217
Geological Long-range Inclined Asdic
  (Gloria II) 109
Geological Survey, U.S. (USGS) 107, 232
  [82, 83]
Geophysics 108
Georgetown Hoyas (basketball team) 42 [85]
Georgia 366 [82–85]
  governor, *list* 367
Geothermal energy 150 [82, 84, 85]
Geriatrics: *see* Senior citizens
Germanium 69
Germany 150 [82–85]
  East (German Democratic Republic)
    Europe 90, 132
    music 240
    population 277
    sports: *see* individual sports
  West (Federal Republic of Germany)
    Antarctic exploration 13
    archaeology 15
    arts 26, 236, 240
    business and industry 110
      construction 59, 122
      manufacturing 33, 216
    crime and law enforcement 83
    defense and arms control 96
    environment 125, *picture* 126
    fuel and energy 150
    international affairs 169, 173, 204
      Bitburg 288, 359
      Europe 130, 147
      Paraguay 256
    magazines 217
    population 276, 284
    space exploration 310
    sports: *see* individual sports
    transportation 345
Getty, Donald 66
Getty, J. Paul, II 239
Getty Museum: *see* J. Paul Getty Museum
Getty Oil Co. 316 [85]
Ghana 231 [82, 83, 85]
Giacobini-Zinner (comet) 26
Gibraltar, Strait of 253
Gilchrist, Ellen 210
Gilliam, Terry 235
Ginsberg, Allen 210
Glaciers 107 [83]
Glass 67
Gloria (hurricane) 138, 149, 374, *picture* 375
Gloria II (Geological Long-range Inclined
  Asdic) 109
GM: *see* General Motors Corp.
GNP: *see* Gross national product
Godard, Jean-Luc 235
God in liberation theology 287
Godoy, Luis Alfonso 372
Goetz, Bernhard H. 84, 85, 278
Gogh, Vincent van 25
Goizueta, Roberto 2
Gold 68 [82–85]
  Albanian-British dispute 10
  mining 101, 231
Goldberg, Whoopi, *picture* 236
Golden lion tamarin 382
Golden Parachutes 114
Goldstein, Joseph Leonard 443
  medicine 221
Golf 153 [82–85]

González Márquez, Felipe 312, *picture*
  131 [83, 84]
Gooden, Dwight 443 [85]
Goodman, Benny 242
" 'Good War, The': An Oral History of World
  War Two" (work by Terkel) 211
Gorbachev, Mikhail Sergeyevich 444 [85]
  Asia
    China 75
    India 168
    Japan 188, 394
  children's literature 214
  defense and arms control 93
  Europe 131
    Bulgaria 60, *picture* 59
    Finland 137
    France 147
    Hungary 163
    Poland, *picture* 275
    Yugoslavia, *picture* 379
  Middle East 230
    Syria 322
  Nicaragua, *picture* 250
  United States 358
  U.S.S.R. 349, 412, *picture* 415
Gordievski, Oleg 352
Gordon, David 90 [83]
Gordon, Ruth (Ruth Gordon Jones) 261
Göteborg, Sweden 384
Gould, Chester 261
Government [84, 85]
  education 116
  human rights 161
  prisons 278, 280
  public information 247
Graham, Martha 91 [83, 85]
Grains 8 [82–85]
  see also specific grains by name
Grammy awards 242
Grand Prix (auto racing) 36 [83–85]
Grand Prix (tennis) 328 [83]
Grand Rapids School District v. Ball
  (U.S.) 202
Grands Ballets Canadiens, Les 92
Grasshoppers, *picture* 8
Graves, Michael 17 [82–85]
  museums 238, *picture* 239
Graves, Robert Ranke 261
Great Britain: *see* United Kingdom
Greece 155 [82–85]
  archaeology 15
  international affairs 204
    Australia 30
    Bulgaria 60
    East Germany 152
    India 168
    Turkey 347
  sports: *see* individual sports
  tourism 338
Greek Cypriots 89 [83]
Greene, Graham 211 [83]
Greenhouse effect 125
Greenhouses 384 [82]
Greenland 130 [82, 83, 85]
Greenmail 114
Greenpeace 12, 83, 147, 204, 249 [84]
Gregory, Cynthia 445 [85]
  dance 90
Grenada 156 [82–85]
  intervention and defense 97
Grenadines, The: *see* Saint Vincent and the
  Grenadines
Gretzky, Wayne 163, *picture* 164 [82–85]
Griffin, Peter 210
Griffith, Melanie 257
Gromyko, Andrei A. 349, 419, 423 [82–85]
  United States 359
Gronowicz, Antoni 54
Gross, Michael 319, *picture* [83–85]
Gross domestic product (GDP) 109
Grossfeld, Stan 270, *picture* 269
Gross national product (GNP) 110 [83–85]
  building and construction 59
  stocks and bonds 315
Group of Five 112, 172, 362
Guarnieri, Johnny 261
Guatemala 157 [82–85]
  government 200

human rights 161
landmarks and monuments 196
Latin America 45, 197
refugees and migrants 283, 285
Guerrillas 97 [82–85]
Africa 357
Angola 11
Ethiopia 130
Mozambique 238
Somalia 301
South Africa 304
Uganda 348
Zaire 380
Asia
Afghanistan 4, *picture*
Burma 60, 103
Kampuchea 189, 307
Pakistan 256
Philippines 267
Sri Lanka 313
Latin America 198
Colombia 76
El Salvador 120
Honduras 158
Nicaragua 249, 360
Peru 267
Middle East 206, 230, 352
Portugal 278
Guggenheim Museum (New York, N.Y.) 18,
238, *picture* [83, 84]
Guillaume, Robert 328
Guinea 204 [82, 84, 85]
Guinea-Bissau 204
Guinness, Sir Alec 212
Gulf and Western Industries 53
Gulf Cooperation Council (GCC) 228,
292 [82–85]
Gulf of Mexico: *see* Mexico, Gulf of
Gulf war: *see* Iran-Iraq war
Gum disease 99 [83, 84]
Guns: *see* Weapons
Gush Emunim 182
Gutiérrez, Gustavo 287
Gwathmey Siegel & Associates 18, *picture*
Gymnastics 157 [82–85]

h

Hagler, Marvin 56, *picture* [82–85]
Haid, Charles 258
Haiti 158 [82–85]
mines and mining 231
Hajj (Islam) 292
Hall, Jerry 257 [85]
Halley's Comet 28 [83]
astronomy 26
children's books 215
space exploration 312
Hamilton, Margaret 261
Hamnett, Katharine 135
Ham radio: *see* Amateur radio
Hanauer, Lee ("Chip") 52 [83–85]
Hanford, George 117
Hang glider, *picture* 389
Hanoi, Vietnam 374
Hardy Holzman Pfeiffer Associates
(architects) 18
Hare Krishna 290
Harlow, Robert 213
Harness racing 160 [82, 83, 85]
Harper & Row *v.* National Enterprises
(U.S.) 202
Harris, Patricia Roberts 261
Hartford, Conn. 25
Hartling, Poul 283
Harvard University 25 [82]
Hassan II 233, *picture* [82–85]
Hatfield, Richard 65 [83]
Hauptman, Herbert Aaron 445
Havel, Vaclav 90
Hawaii 365 [82–85]
governor, *list* 367
Hawke, Robert James Lee 29 [83–85]
Hayden, William 30, 307 [83, 85]
Hayward Gallery (London, U.K.) 23 [85]

Health 82, 219, 366
Heard, Anthony 246, 283, 302, *picture*
Hearns, Thomas 56, *picture* [82, 83, 85]
Heart disease 105, 220, 276 [82–85]
Heckler, Margaret 223, 363 [83, 84]
Heisman Trophy (football) 142 [82–85]
Helsinki Accords 162
Hemophilia 223
Hemophilus b polysaccharide (b-Capsa I) 106
Hemophilus influenzae, type b (Hib) 106
Hereditary disorders 222
Hermannsson, Steingrimur 165 [84]
Hernandulcin (sweetener) 67
Hernu, Charles 147, *picture* 146
"Hero and the Crown, The," *picture* 215
Herpes, genital 106 [83]
Herstigte Nasionale Partij (HNP) 283, 303
Hewlett-Packard Co. 78
Hib (*Hemophilus influenzae,* type b) 106
Hijackings: *see* Terrorism
Hillier, Sir Harold 139
Himalayas 237 [85]
Hinduism 288
Hines, Gregory 91
Hiroshima, Japan 26 [85]
Peace Memorial Park, *pictures* 186, 392
Hispanic Americans 116, 196 [82–85]
Hitachi Ltd. 78 [84, 85]
Hitler diaries 217 [84, 85]
Hizbollah (Party of God) 288
HNP: *see* Herstigte Nasionale Partij
Hockey, Ice: *see* Ice hockey
Hogan, Hulk 336, *picture*
Holmes, Larry 56, *picture* 57 [82–85]
Home computers: *see* Personal computers
Homelessness 299, 366 [85]
"Homelessness in America: A Forced March
to Nowhere" 299
Homes: *see* Building and construction
Homo erectus 45 [85]
Homosexuality [82–85]
AIDS 219, 279, 364
Honda 34 [82, 84, 85]
Honduras 158 [82–85]
government 200
intervention and defense 97
Latin America 197, 249
refugees and migrants 283
Honecker, Erich 152 [82, 84, 85]
Hong Kong 338, 339 [83–85]
Hood, Christopher 212
Hood, Hugh 213
Hormones (plant) 47
Horse racing 159 [82–85]
Hospital, Janette Turner 212 [84]
Hospitals 279 [82–85]
Hostages: *see* Terrorism
House of Representatives, U.S.: *see*
Congress, U.S.
Housing: *see* Building and construction
Housing and Urban Development, U.S.
Department of (HUD) 299 [83]
Houston, Tex. 23 [82–85]
Howard, Edward 364
Howard, John Winston 445
Australia 29
Howard, Ron 233 [82]
Howker, Janni 215
Hoxha, Enver 10, 261, *picture* [84, 85]
HPA-23 (drug) 104
HUD: *see* Housing and Urban Development,
U.S. Department of
Hudson, Rock (Roy Sherer Fitzgerald, Jr.)
219, 262, 364
Hu Feng 262
Hughes, John 233
Hughes, Ted 446 [85]
literature 212
Human growth hormone 105
Human rights (Civil rights and liberties)
161 [83–85]
Afghanistan 4
Canada 61
crime and law enforcement 83
prisons 278, 280
Latin America 201, 287
Argentina 21
Chile 71

Colombia 76
Paraguay 256
Uruguay 372
law 202
Nigeria 250
Pakistan 255
public information 247
race relations 281
South Africa 301, 305
Southeast Asia 307, 373
United States 117, 363, 368
U.S.S.R. 417
Humphrey (whale), *picture* 377
Hungary 163 [82–85]
environment 127
European affairs 132
motion pictures 236
sports: *see* individual sports
tourism 338
wildlife conservation 383
Hunting 20, 50 [83]
Hurley, Denis 286
Hurricanes 374, *picture* 375 [82–85]
Gloria 138, 149
Husak, Gustav 90
"Hussar" (ship) 15
Hussein I 188, *picture* [82–85]
Middle East and North Africa 182, 229,
322, 356
Hussein At Takriti, Saddam 177 [82–85]
Iran-Iraq war 228
Huston, John 233
Hu Yaobang (Hu Yao-pang) 192 [82, 83]
Hydroelectric power 150 [82–85]
Hydrofoil, *picture* 96
Hydrogen 406
Hydroxylapatite (plastic) 99 [85]

i

IABG: *see* International Association of
Botanic Gardens
IAEA: *see* International Atomic Energy
Agency
IATA: *see* International Air Transport
Association
IBF: *see* International Boxing Federation
IBM: *see* International Business Machines
Corp.
ICE (International Cometary Explorer) 26
Ice hockey 163 [82–85]
Iceland 165 [82–85]
infant mortality 277
international law 204
whaling 377
Ice skating 165 [82–85]
Netherlands, The 244
Idaho 365 [82–85]
governor, *list* 367
ILGWU: *see* International Ladies' Garment
Workers' Union
Illegitimacy 276 [82, 83]
Illinois 365 [82–85]
automobile industry 34
crime and law enforcement 84
governor, *list* 367
salmonella outbreak 366, *picture* 140
IMF: *see* International Monetary Fund
Immigration: *see* Refugees and migrants
Imperial Chemical Industries Ltd. 273 [84]
Imperial Choice (racehorse) 159
Imports: *see* International trade
"Impression, Soleil Levant" (painting) 240
IMSA: *see* International Motor Sports
Association
India 167 [82–85]
arts 25, 92, *picture*
defense and arms control 93
disasters 101
engineering projects 123
environment 126
international affairs
Afghanistan 4
Burma 60
Pakistan 256

Sri Lanka 313
mountaineering 237
refugees and migrants 284
Sikhs 162, 288
transportation 345
wildlife conservation 376
Indiana 54, 365 [82–85]
governor, *list* 367
Indianapolis 500 (race) 36 [82–85]
Indian Ocean 308 [82]
Indians, American 14, 21 [82–85]
Indochina: *see* Southeast Asian affairs
Indonesia 169 [82–85]
disasters 103
human rights 162
Southeast Asia 307
wildlife conservation 378
Industry: *see* Economic affairs
Infant mortality 277 [82–85]
Infertility: *see* Fertility
Inflation 111, 200, 315 [82–85]
see also countries by name
Information: *see* Telecommunications
Information processing: *see* Computers
Infrared Astronomical Satellite (IRAS) 407,
picture 409 [84, 85]
Infrared radiation 406 [85]
Inkatha (movement, South Africa) 303, 305
Institute, W.Va. 127, 368, *picture*
Insurance 296, 324 [82–85]
Integrated services digital network (ISDN) 324
Integration: *see* Discrimination; Race relations
Interest rates 59, 110, 315 [82–85]
Interferon (drug) 104
International Air Transport Association
(IATA) 344 [83–85]
International Association of Botanic Gardens
(IABG) 383 [85]
International Association of Machinists &
Aerospace Workers 194
International Atomic Energy Agency (IAEA)
253 [82]
International Boxing Federation (IBF)
56 [84, 85]
International Brotherhood of Teamsters
194 [83, 84]
International Business Machines Corp. (IBM)
76 [82–85]
International Cometary Explorer (ICE) 26
International Conference on the Health of
Miners 232
International Convention Concerning the
Protection of the World Cultural and
Natural Heritage 196 [85]
International Court of Justice (World Court)
205, 360
International exchange and payments
(International finance) 169 [82–85]
European affairs 130
international affairs 109, 173
see also Financial institutions; International
Monetary Fund; World Bank;
countries by name
International Exposition-Tsukuba (Expo
'85) 187
International Ladies' Garment Workers'
Union (ILGWU) 194
International Mineworkers Organization 196
International Monetary Fund (IMF)
170 [82–85]
Africa 6, 119, 190, 233, 250, 301, 324, 348,
380, 381
Asia 187, 374, 396
Caribbean States 104, 185
Latin America 22, 58, 72, 115, 199, 225,
226, 250
Lebanon 206
Saudi Arabia 293
International Motor Sports Association
(IMSA) 36 [85]
International Museum of Photography
238 [85]
International Organization of Consumer
Unions (IOCU) 81 [82–85]
International Publishing Corporation (IPC)
217 [85]
International Reading Association 215
[82, 83, 85]

International trade (World trade) 172 [82–85]
Africa 6
agriculture 7
Asia 307, 395
"Case Against Protectionism, The: A U.S.
View" (special report) 175
consumer affairs 81
Europe 130
fuel and energy 148
international exchange and payments 169
iron and steel industry 179
Latin America 198
machinery and machine tools 216
microelectronics 227
Middle East 229
ships and shipping 294
toys and games 339
see also Economic affairs; Labor and
employment; countries by name
International Union of Architects 19
International Whaling Commission (IWC)
377 [82–85]
International Year of Peace (1986, UN) 356
International Year of Shelter for the
Homeless 299
Interstate highway system, U.S. 123
[82, 83, 85]
Inuits: *see* Eskimos
Investment newsletters 216
Investments: *see* Stocks and bonds
IOCU: *see* International Organization of
Consumer Unions
Iowa 365 [82–85]
governor, *list* 367
IPC: *see* International Publishing Corp.
IRA: *see* Irish Republican Army
Iran 177 [82–85]
engineering projects 122
fuel and energy 148
human rights 162
Middle East 177, 228, 322, 357
punishment 278
Iran-Iraq war (Gulf war) [82–85]
chemical and biological weapons 93
fuel and energy 148
Middle Eastern affairs 177, 228, 292,
322, 357
Iran-U.S. Claims Tribunal 205
Iraq 177 [82–85]
archaeology 15
fuel and energy 148
human rights 162
Middle East 177, 228, 293, 322, 357
transportation 345
U.S.S.R. 96
IRAS: *see* Infrared Astronomical Satellite
Ireland, Ann 213
Ireland 178 [82–85]
medicine 220
prisons 279
theater 337
United Kingdom 356
Irish Republican Army (IRA) 356 [82, 83, 85]
Iron and steel industry 179 [82–85]
Irrigation 122 [82, 83]
Irving, Amy, *picture* 257
ISDN (Integrated services digital network) 324
"Isenheim Altarpiece" 239
Islam 288 [82–85]
Algeria 10
Bahrain 38
crime and law enforcement 83, 278
education 118
Egypt 119
Farrakhan 289
Indonesia 169
Israel 182
landmarks and monuments 196
Lebanon 205
Pakistan 255
Saudi Arabia 293
U.S.S.R. 418
Islamic Jihad (Islamic Holy War) 192, 207,
292 [84, 85]
Isotretinoin: *see* Accutane
Israel 180 [82–85]
archaeology 15
crime and law enforcement 83

defense and arms control 93
fuel and energy 150
human rights 162
international affairs 204
Ethiopia 130
Middle East and North Africa 120, 188,
205, 229, 322, 347
United Nations 356
United States 364
U.S.S.R. 350, 418
West Germany 152
Zaire 380
money 315
religion 288
tourism 338
Italy 183 [82–85]
archaeology 15
art 24
automobile industry 33
defense and arms control 96
disasters 101, 232
Brussels soccer riot 143
engineering projects 121
international affairs 174, 204, 364
Zaire 380
prisons 280
religion 288
sports: *see* individual sports
tourism 338
Ivory 377 [82]
IWC: *see* International Whaling Commission

J

Jackson, Bo 142
Jackson, Jesse, *picture* 282 [84, 85]
Jackson, Mich. 281
Jacob's Pillow, Mass. 18
Jacoby, Susan 279
Jaffree, Ishmael, *picture* 204
Jagger, Mick 257 [85]
popular music 243
Jails: *see* Prisons
Jalisco Mexican Products 101
Jamaica 185 [82–85]
intervention and defense 97
wildlife conservation 383
Japan 185 [82–85]
arts 92, 237, 270
business and industry 110
advertising 2
automobiles 33
building and construction 19, 59, 121
ceramics 67
fish and fisheries 137, 140, 377,
picture 138
iron and steel 179
machinery and machine tools 216
ships and shipping 294
textiles 331
tourism 338
development since World War II 392
disasters 100, 376
education 115
environment 126
international affairs 169, 174, 176, 204
Antarctic exploration 12
Australia 149
Canada 62
China 74
Europe 130
Latin America 199
North Korea 192
Qatar 280
Southeast Asia 308
United States 20
Nakasone 401
social services 298
space exploration 28, 308
sports: *see* individual sports
technology 77, 227, 324
transportation 345
Japan Air Lines 100, 343
Jaruzelski, Wojciech 60, 273, *picture*
275 [82–85]

Jarvik, Robert 220 [83]
Jayawardene, Junius R. 313 [82, 83, 85]
Jazz 241 [82–85]
Jews and Judaism 288, 290 [82–85]
  female rabbi, *picture* 286
  Israel 182, *picture* 181
  Netherlands, The 244
  Sanctuary Movement 285
  United Nations 356
  United States 360
  U.S.S.R. 350, 418
  West Germany 151
Jobs, Steven Paul 447
  computers 77
Jobs: *see* Labor and employment
Joel, Billy 258
Joffrey Ballet 91 [82–85]
John, Patrick 103 [83]
John Henry (racehorse) 159 [82, 85]
John Paul II 286, 287 [82–85]
  Beagle Channel pact, *picture* 198
  visits
    Belgium 45
    Morocco, *picture* 233
    Netherlands, The 244
    Venezuela, *picture* 373
    Zaire 381
Johnson, Don 447
Johnson, Kenneth 366
Johnson, Philip 18
Johnston, Lynn 448
"JOIDES Resolution" (ship) 106
Jones, Jo (Jonathan Jones; Kansas City Jo
    Jones; Papa Jo Jones) 262
Jones, Philly Joe (Joseph Rudolph Jones) 262
Jones, Thad 242
Jordan, Michael 42
Jordan, Stanley 241
Jordan 188 [82–85]
  Middle East 181, 229
  United Nations 356
  wildlife conservation 383
Jorge Blanco, Salvador 104 [83–85]
Josephson, Sarah 320
Journalism: *see* Magazines; Newspapers;
    Television and radio
J. Paul Getty Museum (Malibu, Calif.) 239
    [83, 85]
Juan Carlos I, *picture* 312 [82, 83]
Judaism: *see* Jews and Judaism
Junk bonds 114, 316
Jupiter (planet) 26
Justice, U.S. Department of 82, 84 [82, 83, 85]
  race relations 281
  Sanctuary Movement 285
Juveniles: *see* Children

k

Kabul, Afghanistan 4
Kadar, Janos 163, *picture* [82–85]
Kahnweiler, Daniel-Henry 23
Kakapo (parrot) 377
Kampelman, Max 448
Kampuchea 189 [82–85]
  Asia 307, 373, 399
  Australia 30
Kanak (people) 146
Kansas 366 [82–85]
  governor, *list* 367
Kansas City Royals (baseball team) 39 [85]
Karamanlis, Konstantinos 155
Karami, Rashid Abdul Hamid 206 [85]
Karle, Jerome 449
Karpov, Anatoli 69, *picture* 70 [82–85]
Kasdan, Lawrence 233
Kasparov, Garri 449 [83–85]
  chess 69, *picture* 70
Kate (hurricane) 375
Kaunda, Kenneth D. 381 [82–84]
Kawai, Toshinobu 167
Keating, Paul 31
Keillor, Garrison 450
  literature 209, *picture* 211
  marriage 258

Kelbaugh & Lee (architectural firm) 19
Kelp 47
Kemp, Jack, *picture* 111 [83]
Kennedy, Edward Moore 360 [83]
Kentucky 366 [82–85]
  governor, *list* 367
Kentucky Derby 159, *picture* [82, 83, 85]
Kenya 190 [82–85]
  agriculture 8
  fossils 45
  population 276
  wildlife conservation 378
Kertész, André 262, 270, *picture*
Khaddam, Abdel Halim 206
Khalifah ibn Hamad ath-Thani, Sheikh 281
    [83, 85]
Khamenei, Hojatoleslam Sayyed Ali 177 [82]
Khark Island, Iran 177 [85]
  Iraq 177, 228
Khmer People's National Liberation Front
    (KPNLF) 307 [84]
  Kampuchea 189
Khmer Rouge 307 [82–85]
  Kampuchea 189
Khomeini, Ayatollah Ruhollah 177 [83, 85]
Kidnappings [82, 83, 85]
  Chile 71
  Colombia 76
  El Salvador 121
  Lebanon 206, 352
"Killing Fields, The" (film) 235
Kimball, Spencer, W. 262
Kimbell Art Museum (Fort Worth,
    Tex.) 24 [83]
Kim Chong Il 192 [83–85]
Kim Dae Jung 450 [82–84]
  Japan 188
  South Korea 191
Kim Il Sung 192 [83–85]
Kim Young Sam 191 [84]
King, Betsy 155
King, Coretta Scott, *picture* 282 [85]
"King and I, The" (musical) 333
Kinnell, Galway 210
Kirkland, Joseph Lane 193 [82, 84, 85]
Kirkpatrick, Jeane J. 364 [82, 85]
Kistler, Darci 91
"Kites: New Designs for New Uses" (feature
    article) 386
Kizer, Carolyn 211
Klein, Mr. and Mrs. Eugene 159
Klinghoffer, Leon 83, 230
Klitzing, Klaus von 451
Knots 219
Knudson, Thomas 246
Koalas, *picture* 383
Koch, Marita 341 [83–85]
Kodak Co. 238 [85]
Kogawa, Joy 213 [82]
Kohl, Helmut 451 [83–85]
  France 147
  Germany 150
Kohlenberg, Philip 289
Koivisto, Mauno Henrik 137 [82–85]
Komarek, Valtr 90
Korea 190 [82–85]
  North (Democratic People's Republic
    of Korea)
    international law 205
    Japan 188
    sports: *see* individual sports
  South (Republic of Korea)
    business and industry
      automobile industry 34
      fuel and energy 20, 149
      toys 339
      whaling 377
    international affairs
      Canada 62
      Japan 188
      Zaire 380
    ships and shipping 294, *picture* 293
    sports: *see* individual sports
Korsakoff's syndrome 224
KPNLF: *see* Khmer People's National
    Liberation Front
Kreisky, Bruno 168 [82–85]
Krisch, Alan 271

Kristiansen, Ingrid 343
Kroetsch, Robert 213
Krone (Danish currency) 99
Kronos String Quartet 242
Krugerrand 232, 314
Kuiper Airborne Observatory 407
Kunayev, Dinmukhamed A. 420
Kurds 162, 178 [85]
Kurosawa, Akira 237, *picture* 235
Kuwait 192 [82–85]
  Middle East 228
    Syria 322
    United Arab Emirates 353
  U.S.S.R. 352
Kuznets, Simon (Smith) 262
Kyprianou, Spyros 89 [82–85]

l

Labor, U.S. Department of 195 [82, 83, 85]
Labor and employment 193 [82–85]
  anthropology 13
  computer industry 76
  Europe 130
  homelessness 300
  international trade 176
  newspapers 246
  race relations 281
  ships and shipping 293
  social services 297
  state governments 365
  textiles 331
  see also Economic affairs; International
    trade; countries by name
Labor unions 193 [82, 83, 85]
Lady's Secret (racehorse) 159
Lafleur, Guy 164
Lagerfeld, Karl 135
Lambsdorff, Otto 85, *picture* 152 [83, 85]
Lander, Toni 262
Landmarks and monuments 196 [82–85]
Landscaping 17 [84]
Landslides 101, 375 [84, 85]
Lane, Patrick 213
Lange, David Russell 249, *picture* [84, 85]
Langer, Susanne Knauth 262
Laos 197 [82–85]
  Southeast Asia 307
  U.S.S.R. 96
Lapine, James 211
Larkin, Philip Arthur 263
Larroquette, John 328
Lasers 272, *picture* 271
Latin-American affairs 197 [82–85]
  evolution 46
  human rights 161
  international trade 175
  intervention and defense 97
  liberation theology 287
  population 275
  refugees and migrants 283
  religion 287
  "Swing Toward Democracy, The" (special
    report) 200
  wildlife conservation 377
  see also Latin-American countries
Latin American Bishops, Conference of 287
Latinequip 198
Laurel, Salvador, *picture* 268
Laurence Olivier awards (LO awards) 335 [85]
Law 202 [82–85]
  advertising 2
  corporate mergers 113
  Goetz case 85
  prisons 279
  public information 247
  religion 286
  state governments, U.S. 367
  see also Congress, U.S.; Crime and law
    enforcement; Legislation; Prisons;
    Supreme Court, U.S.; Trials and
    lawsuits
Law enforcement: *see* Crime and law
    enforcement
Lawns 138

Lawrence Livermore National Laboratory 272
Lawsuits: *see* Trials and lawsuits
LD50 (Lethal Dose 50) 49
Lead 50, 128, 149 [82–85]
Lebanon 205 [82–85]
  human rights 162
  Middle East 182, 230, 321, 352, 356
  religion 288
  TWA hijacking 83, 364
Le Duan 373 [82, 83, 85]
Lee Kuan Yew 308 [83]
Legislation [82–85]
  animal rights 50
  farm crisis 8
  see also Congress, U.S.; countries by name
Le Guin, Ursula K. 209, *picture* 213 [83]
Lemieux, Mario 164 [85]
Lendl, Ivan 328 [82, 83, 85]
Leonard, Elmore John 452
  literature 209, *picture*
Leonardo da Vinci 24
Lesotho 6, 357 [83, 85]
Less developed countries: *see* Developing
  countries
Lethal Dose 50 (LD50) 49
Leveraged buyout 114
Lever Brothers Co. 2
Lévesque, René 65 [82, 83, 85]
Lho Shin Yong 191
Liberation theology 287
Liberia 6 [82–85]
Libraries 207 [82–85]
Libya 208 [82–85]
  Middle East and North Africa 231
    Egypt 120
    Iran 177
    Iraq 178
    Morocco 233
    Tunisia 347
    U.S.S.R. 352, 96
"Life" (magazine) 216
"Life and Times of Cotton Mather, The" 211
Life expectancy 277 [82–85]
Ligachev, Yegor K. 349, 420
Lightner, Candy 452
Lignase 48, *picture* 47
Li Hsien-nien: *see* Li Xiannian
Lincoln Center (New York, N.Y.) 334
Lindbergh, Pelle 164, *picture*
Linh, Nguyen Van 373
Li Ning 157, *picture* [83]
Li Peng (Li P'eng) 453
Liquor: *see* Alcoholic beverages
Listeria monocytogenes (disease) 101
Literature 208 [82–85]
Literature for children 213 [82–85]
Little, Jean 215
Little League (baseball) 41 [82–85]
Liu, Henry 323
Live Aid (concert) 243, 327, *picture* 240
Livestock 49 [83–85]
Living will 366
Li Xiannian (Li Hsien-nien) 75, *picture*
  360 [84, 85]
  Burma 60
Li Yihua 320
Lloyd, Christopher, *picture* 234 [83]
Loans: *see* Credit and debt
LO awards: *see* Laurence Olivier awards
Lodge, Henry Cabot 263
London, U.K. [82–85]
  arts 23, 93, 239, 240
  newspapers 246
  race relations 282
  tourism 338
London Festival Ballet 93
London Standard awards (LS awards) 335
Long, Shelley 257
Long Island City, N.Y. 238
Longowal, Sant Harchand Singh 167, 263, 288
Lon Nol 263
Lopes, Carlos 343 [85]
Lopez, Nancy 155
Los Angeles, Calif. [82–85]
  arts 18, 24, 334
Los Angeles County Museum of Art
  24 [83, 85]
Los Angeles Lakers (basketball team) 42

Los Paseos, Calif. 126
Lottery 368 [85]
Louganis, Greg 320 [83–85]
Louisiana 365 [82–85]
  governor, *list* 367
  weather 374
Louison, George, *picture* 156
Louvre (Paris, Fr.) 17, *picture*
"Love Medicine" (novel) 209
Loyd, Miles L.
  "Kites: New Designs for New Uses" (feature
    article) 386
LP: *see* Record industry
LS awards (London Standard awards) 335
Lubbers, Rudolphus Franciscus Marie (Ruud
  Lubbers) 244 [83–85]
Lukas, D. Wayne 159
Lukas, J. Anthony 210
Lunar and Planetary Science Conference
  106 [84]
Lurie, Alison 211 [85]
Lusinchi, Jaime 372 [84, 85]
Lutfi, Ali 119
Lutherans 286 [82, 83, 85]
  Sanctuary Movement 285
Lyle, Sandy 153, *picture* [83]

m

McAuliffe, Sharon Christa 309
"McCall's" (magazine) 217
McCraw, Thomas K. 211
McCurry, Steve 270
McEnroe, John 329 [82, 85]
Machel, Samora 238 [82, 83, 85]
Machinery and machine tools 216
  mines and mining 232
MacInnes, Helen Clark 263
MacLeod, Gavin 258
McMahon, Jim, *picture* 144 [82]
Macmillan Inc. 53
MacNelly, Jeff 246
McTaggart, David 453
Madonna (Madonna Louise Ciccone) (rock
  star), *picture* 258
  popular music 243
Madrid, Sp. 239 [83]
  art 24
Madrid Hurtado, Miguel de la 225 [83–85]
Magazines 216 [82–85]
  United States 2, 362
Magpies 46
Mahathir bin Mohamad, Datuk Seri 217
  [82, 83, 85]
Mailer, Norman 210 [84, 85]
Maine 365 [82–85]
  governor, *list* 367
Maize: *see* Corn
Major Indoor Soccer League 145
Makeup (fashion) 134, 136 [85]
Maki, Fumihiko 19, *picture*
Malawi 8 [84, 85]
Malaysia 217 [82–85]
  anthropology 13
  Southeast Asian affairs 307
  transportation 345
Malden, Karl 328
Mali 100
Malle, Louis 258
Maltz, Albert 263
Maluf, Paulo Salim 58 [85]
Malvinas, Islas: *see* Falklands Islands
Mamet, David 454 [83, 85]
Mammography 221
Mandela, Nelson Rolihlahla 454
  South Africa 283, 302, 305
Mandela, Winnie 302, *picture* 301
Mandlikova, Hana 330, *picture* [82]
Mandrell, Barbara 257 [82]
Manfred, Mighty 336
"Manhattan, inc." (magazine) 217
Manitoba (prov., Can.) 66 [82, 84]
Man-made fiber: *see* Fiber, synthetic
Manso, Peter 210
Manufacturing: *see* Economic affairs

Manufacturing automation protocol
  (MAP) 324
Manville Corp. 82 [83]
Maori 249 [84, 85]
Marcos, Ferdinand E. 267 [82–85]
Marijuana 45 [83, 85]
Marine Corps, U.S. 94 [83–85]
Marine disasters 101 [82–85]
Marino, Dan 258 [85]
Maris, Roger Eugene 263
Mark (Deutsche Mark) (Ger. currency)
  112 [82–85]
Marks, Bruce 91
Marriages 258 [82–85]
  population 277
Marriott, Anne 213
Marsalis, Wynton 242 [84, 85]
Martens, Wilfried 44 [82, 83]
Martin, John Joseph 263
Martini, Simone 25
Martins, Peter 91 [82–85]
Marxism 287, 412
  see also Communist movement
Maryland 368 [82–85]
  governor, *list* 367
Maserati (automobile) 34
Mason, Bobbie Ann 210
Massachusetts 366 [82–85]
  archaeology 15
  governor, *list* 367
Mass media 247
  advertising 2
  archaeology 16
  Israel 182
  South Africa 283, 302
  United States 85, 359
  U.S.S.R. 350
  see also Magazines; Newspapers; Television
    and radio
Mass transit 123, 346 [83–85]
Mastectomy 221
Materials science 386
Mathematics 218
Mathers, Jerry 258
Matsuyama Ballet 93
Mauritius 339 [82–84]
Maxwell Starkman Associates (architects) 18
Mayan culture 16 [83]
Mayo Clinic (Rochester, Minn.) 221
Mazda Motors Corp. 34 [83]
Meagher, Mary T. 319 [82, 83]
Mecca, Saudi Arabia 292 [83]
Media: *see* Mass media
Medicine 219 [82–85]
  drugs 104
  mental health 224
  space experiments 309
  see also Disease; Health
Meese, Edwin, III 281, 363 [82, 85]
Meier, Richard 18 [84, 85]
Melton, J. Gordon 290
Mengele, Josef 58, 256
Meningitis 106 [85]
Mennonites 285
Mental health 224 [82–85]
  homelessness 299, 366
Mercury (automobile) 35
Mergers, corporate 113 [82, 83, 85]
  labor unions 193
  publishing
    book 53
    magazines 216
    newspaper 245
  stocks and bonds 316
  television and radio 326
  United States 362
Merrill, James 210
Mersey estuary (Irish Sea, U.K.) 125
Messina, Strait of (Italy) 121
Messner, Zbigniew 273
Meteorology: *see* Weather
Methane 150 [85]
Methodists 285 [83]
Methodius, St. 90, 379
Metromedia Inc. 244, 363 [82]
Metropolitan Museum of Art (N.Y., N.Y.) 25,
  270 [82–85]
Metropolitan Opera (N.Y., N.Y.) 240 [82–85]

Mexico 225 [82–85]
  archaeology 16
  art 23
  crime and law enforcement 86
  earthquake 103, 108, 226, 328
  engineering projects 123
  fish and fisheries 137
  fuel and energy 148
  human rights 161
  India 168
  international exchange and payments 172
  intervention and defense 97
  Latin America 198
  machinery and machine tools 216
  refugees and migrants 283, 285
  sports: see individual sports
Mexico, Gulf of 374 [82]
Mexico City, Mex. [83–85]
  earthquake 103, 108, 226, 227, picture 107
  museum theft 240
Meyers, Jeffrey 210
MFA (Mobilization for Animals) 49
"Miami Vice" 328, 447
Michigan 365 [82–85]
  automobile industry 34
  education 202
  governor, list 367
Microcomputers 77, 79 [85]
Microelectronics 227 [84]
Microprocessors 78, 227 [82]
Microwaves 140 [83]
Middle Eastern and North African affairs
    228 [82–85]
  crime and law enforcement 83
  human rights 162
  plastics industry 273
  United Nations 356
  U.S.S.R. 352
  see also Middle Eastern and North African
    countries
Midwest Express 343
Migrants: see Refugees and migrants
Migration, human: see Refugees and migrants
Military: see Armed forces, U.S.; Defense and
    arms control; Wars
Milk 9, 81, 139 [84]
Milky Way Galaxy 27, 405 [85]
Mines and mining 231 [82–85]
  disasters 101
  labor and employment 196
  United Kingdom 353
    music 243
Miniatures (art) 23
Minicomputers 77 [85]
Minimal surface (mathematics) 218, picture
Mining '85 (exhibition) 232
Minnesota 365 [82–85]
  governor, list 367
Minolta (camera) 268
Minorities
  Arctic regions 20
  education 115, 117
  homelessness 299
  human rights 161
  prisons 279
  Romania 132
  South Africa 305
  Sri Lanka 313
  United States 194, 363
  U.S.S.R. 352
  see also Discrimination; Human rights;
    Race relations
Miranda decision (law) 363 [85]
Missiles 94, picture 93 [82–85]
  Australia 30
  Belgium 45
  Finland 136, picture
  Netherlands, The 244
  U.S.S.R. 412
Mississippi 366 [82–85]
  governor, list 367
Missouri [82–85]
  governor, list 367
Mitchell, James 292 [85]
Mitchell, Michele 320
Mitchell/Giurgola Architects 20 [83]
Mitochondrial DNA 45
Mitsotakis, Konstantinos 156 [85]

Mitsubishi Motors Corporation 34 [82, 83]
Mitterrand, François Maurice 455 [82–85]
  European affairs 130
    France 145, 282
    Poland 275
    West Germany 152
  Tunisia 347
Miyake, Issey, picture 133
Miyazawa, Kiichi 185 [85]
MNR: see Mozambique National Resistance
Mobilization for Animals (MFA) 49
Mobutu Sese Seko 380, picture [82–85]
Mochtar Kusumaatmadja 307
Modigliani, Franco 456
Mokae, Zakes, picture 333
Moloise, Benjamin 282
Mom's Command (racehorse) 159
Moncreiffe of that Ilk, Sir Rupert Iain
    Kay 263
Money: see Devaluation and revaluation;
    Economic affairs; Financial
    institutions; International exchange
    and payments
Mongolia 382
Monoclonal antibodies 222
Montana 365 [82–85]
  Custer's last battle excavation 16
  governor, list 367
Montazeri, Hussein Ali 177
Monuments: see Landmarks and monuments
Moon, Sun Myung 289 [82, 83, 85]
Moon 106
Moore, Lilian 215
Moore, Mary Tyler, picture 326 [84]
Moore, Robert L. 290
Morales, George 52 [84, 85]
Morgan, Lucy 246
Morishita, Yoko 456
Morocco 232 [82–85]
  Middle East and North Africa 230
    Algeria 10
    Syria 322
  oceanography 253
Mortality: see Deaths; Life expectancy
Moshe Safdie & Associates (architects) 19
Most-favored-nation principle 175, 198
Mota Pinto, Carlos 277 [85]
Motion pictures 233 [82–85]
  television 327
Motorboating 52 [83-85]
Motorcycle racing 237 [85]
Motorola Inc. 77
Mountaineering 237 [85]
Mouré, Erin 213
Mouse 49 [84]
Moussavi, Mir Hossein 177
Move (cult) 86
Movies: see Motion pictures
Mozambique 238 [82–85]
  African affairs 5, 304
  agriculture 7
  intervention and defense 97
Mozambique National Resistance (MNR)
    (Renamo) [85]
  African affairs 5, 238, 304
Mubarak, Muhammad Hosni 119,
    picture [82–85]
  Jordan, picture 188
  religion 288
Mugabe, Robert 381, picture 382 [82–85]
Mukherjee, Bharati 212
Mullins, Gay, picture 2
Mulroney, Brian 257 [84, 85]
  Canada 60, 65
  crime and law enforcement 86
  environment 124
  shamrock summit 360, picture 61
Munch, Edvard 26
Murders 83 [82–85]
  "Achille Lauro" 204
  Chile 71
  Colombia 76
  East Germany 153
  India 167
  Middle East and North Africa 205, 230
  Peru 267
  Poland 274
  South Africa 282, 302

Taiwan 323
United Kingdom 208
U.S.S.R. 352
Venezuela 372
Vietnamese refugees 101
Zimbabwe 381
see also Assassinations
Murdoch, Iris 211
Murdoch, K. Rupert 244 [82–84]
Murphy, Lionel 29, picture 31
Murray, Charles 210
Mururoa Atoll, French Polynesia 147, 204
Museum of Fine Arts (Boston, Mass.)
    23 [82, 83]
Museums 238 [82–85]
  art 22
Music 240 [82–85]
  radio 328
Musicals 333 [85]
Music videos 135 [85]
Muslims: see Islam
Mutual funds 316 [82–85]
Mutual Security Treaty 395
Mwinyi, Ali Hassan 323 [85]
MX missile 94 [82–85]
  Australia 30
  see also Missiles
Mydans, Carl 270
Mzali, Mohammed 346 [83]

n

NAB (National Association of Broadcasters) 2
Nader, Ralph 81 [84]
Naipaul, Shivadhar Srinivasa 263
Nairobi, University of 190
Nakasone, Yasuhiro 401 [83–85]
  China 75
  Japan 185, picture 187
  "New Asia-Pacific Era, The: A Perspective
    from an International Nation
    Building for the 21st Century"
    (feature article) 392
  United States 20
NAL (New American Library) 54
Namath, Joe 258
Namibia (South West Africa) 5 [82–85]
  Canada 64
  South Africa 304
  United Nations 357
Naples, Italy 25 [82]
Narcotics: see Drugs
NASA: see National Aeronautics and Space
    Administration
NASCAR: see National Association for Stock
    Car Auto Racing
Nash, Clarence ("Ducky") 264
NASL: see North American Soccer League
"Nation, The" (magazine) 216 [84]
National Aeronautics and Space
    Administration (NASA) 3, 26, 309
    [82, 83, 85]
National Association for Stock Car Auto
    Racing (NASCAR) 36 [82, 83, 85]
National Association of Broadcasters (NAB) 2
National Ballet of Canada (NBC) 92 [84]
National Basketball Association (NBA)
    42 [82–85]
National Bipartisan Commission on Central
    America 98 [84]
National Book Critics Circle 209
National Broadcasting Co. (NBC) 326,
    363 [82–85]
National Building Museum (Washington,
    D.C.) 238 [82]
National Bureau of Standards (NBS) 272
National Cable Television Association 326
National Center for Plant Conservation 139
National Coal Board (NCB) 353 [85]
National Collegiate Athletic Association
    (NCAA) 42, 142 [82–85]
National Convention Alliance 303
National Council of Teachers of English
    215 [82, 83]
National Crime Intelligence Center 86

National Endowment for the Arts 18
National Football League (NFL) 141 [82–84]
National Gallery (London, U.K.) 239 [83, 85]
National Gallery of Art (Washington, D.C.) 22, 239, *picture* [82–85]
National Gallery of Canada (Ottawa, Can.) 25 [85]
National Gallery of Ireland (Dublin, Ireland) 23
National Gallery of Scotland (U.K.) 24
National Hockey League (NHL) 163 [82, 83]
National Institutes of Health (NIH) 222 [83]
National Jazz Service Organization 242
National Labor Relations Board (NLRB) 194 [82, 85]
National Semiconductor Corp. 77
National Theatre (NT) (U.K.) 335 [82–85]
National Union for the Total Independence of Angola (UNITA) 5, 11, 304 [82–85]
National Union of Mineworkers (NUM) 196, 353 [85]
National Urban League 281 [84, 85]
Nation of Islam 289
Native Americans: *see* Indians, American
NATO: *see* North Atlantic Treaty Organization
Natural gas 149 [82–85]
Navratilova, Martina 330 [82–85]
Navy, United States 94 [82–85]
Naylor, Gloria 209
NBA: *see* National Basketball Association
NBC: *see* National Ballet of Canada
NBC: *see* National Broadcasting Co.
NBS (National Bureau of Standards) 272
NCAA: *see* National Collegiate Athletic Association
NCB: *see* National Coal Board
Neale, Harry 165
Nebraska 365 [82–85]
  governor, *list* 367
Needleman, Jacob 289
Neely, Richard 366
Negroes, American: *see* Black Americans
Nelson, Willie 243 [82]
Neofascism 32, 282
Neo Yee Pan 217
Nepal 237 [82, 85]
Netherlands, The 244 [82–85]
  defense and arms control 96
  gardens 139, 384
  international trade 174
  medicine 221
  music 240
  population 276
  race relations 281
  religion 287
  social services 298
  sports: *see* individual sports
Nevada 367 [82–85]
  governor, *list* 367
Nevado del Ruiz (volcano, Colombia) 76, 103, 108, *picture*
Neves, Tancredo de Almeida 57, 200 [85]
New American Library (NAL) 54
"New Asia-Pacific Era, The: A Perspective from an International Nation Building for the 21st Century" (feature article) 392
Newbery Medal, *picture* 215 [82–85]
New Brunswick, Can. (prov.) 65 [82, 83]
New Caledonia (I., Pacific Ocean) 146
  mines and mining 232
New England Patriots (football team) 141
Newfoundland, Can. (prov.) 61 [82, 83]
New Hampshire 365 [82–85]
  governor, *list* 367
New Jersey 365 [82–85]
  governor, *list* 367
Newman, Graeme 279
New Mexico 366 [82–85]
  governor, *list* 367
  prisons 280
New Orleans, La. 141 [83, 85]
New People's Army (NPA) 268 [84]
New Religions 289
News: *see* Magazines; Newspapers; Television and radio
"Newsday" (newspaper) 246 [85]

Newspapers 244 [82–85]
  advertising 2
  "Freedom of Information" (special report) 247
New words 431 [82–85]
New York 365 [82–85]
  archaeology 15
  governor, *list* 367
  museums 238
  social services 297
New York, N.Y. [82–85]
  arts 17, 23, 90, 238, 240, 270, 333
  flowers and gardens, *picture* 139
  homelessness 299
  law 202
    Goetz case 84, 85
  libraries, *picture* 207
New York City Ballet (NYCB) 91 [82–85]
"New Yorker, The" (magazine) 216, 362 [85]
New York Stock Exchange (NYSE) 316, *picture* 317 [82–85]
New Zealand 249 [82–85]
  Antarctic exploration 12
  book publishing 55
  education 119
  fuel and energy 150
  "Rainbow Warrior" 83, 147, 204
  tourism 339
  wildlife conservation 377
NFL: *see* National Football League
Ngor, Haing S. 235
NHL: *see* National Hockey League
Nicaragua 249 [82–85]
  government 200
  human rights 161
  international affairs 205
    Latin America 82, 158, 198, 225
    United States 360
  intervention and defense 97
  religion 286
Nichols, Kyra 91
Nicholson, Arthur 153, 352
Nicholson, Jack, *picture* 234 [85]
Niekro, Phil 40
Nielsen, Erik 60
Nigeria 250 [82–85]
  Africa 5
  engineering projects 122
Night Stalker (murderer) 84
NIH: *see* National Institutes of Health
Nihilator (racehorse) 160 [85]
Nissan 34 [82, 83, 85]
Nitrogen oxides (pollutants) 124
Nkomati accord 5, 238, 304 [85]
Nkomo, Joshua 381 [83, 85]
NLRB: *see* National Labor Relations Board
NMR spectroscopy: *see* Nuclear magnetic resonance spectroscopy
Nobel prizes [82–85]
  economic science 456
  literature 90, 208, 463
  chemistry 445, 449
  physics 451
  physiology or medicine 221, 437, 443
Noguchi, Isamu 238
Nolan, Lloyd Benedict 264
Nomura Securities Co., *picture* 316
NORAD: *see* North American Aerospace Defense Command
Noriega, Manuel Antonio 256, *picture*
Norris, Chuck 233
North, Andy 153
North American Aerospace Defense Command (NORAD) 94 [82]
  Canada 64
North American Soccer League (NASL) 145 [85]
North Atlantic Treaty Organization (NATO) 96 [82–85]
  Europe 131, 244, 312
  U.S.S.R. 350, 412
North Carolina 365 [82–85]
  governor, *list* 367
  race relations 281
North Dakota 365 [82–85]
  governor, *list* 367
Northeast Bancorp, Inc. *v.* Board of Governors (U.S.) 203

Northern Ireland: *see* United Kingdom
North Korea: *see* Korea
North Rhine-Westphalia, W. Ger. (state) 127
North Sea 138, 149 [82, 83]
Northwest Passage 21, 64, 204, *picture* 63
Northwest Territories, Can. (region) 21 [82, 83]
North Yemen: *see* Yemen (San'a')
Norway 251 [82–85]
  defense and arms control 96
  fishing industry 138, 377
  fuel and energy 149
  international law 204
  ships and shipping 294
  space exploration 308
Nova (laser) 272, *picture* 271
Nova Scotia, Can. (prov.) 25 [82, 83]
NPA: *see* New People's Army
NT: *see* National Theatre
Nuclear industry (Nuclear energy) 252 [82–85]
  fuel and energy 149
Nuclear magnetic resonance spectroscopy (NMR spectroscopy) 69 [84, 85]
Nuclear Non-Proliferation Treaty 352
Nuclear reactors 252
Nuclear weapons 93 [82–85]
  Canada 64
  France 147
  India 168
  Japan 394
  New Zealand 249
  United States 358
  U.S.S.R. 352, 412
  see also Defense and arms control; Weapons
NUM: *see* National Union of Mineworkers
Numismatics: *see* Stamps and coins
Nureyev, Rudolf 93 [82–84]
Nutrition 137, 220, 223 [82–85]
  see also Food processing
NYCB: *see* New York City Ballet
Nyerere, Julius Kambarage 5, 323 [82, 83]
NYSE: *see* New York Stock Exchange

OAS: *see* Organization of American States
OAU: *see* Organization of African Unity
Obesity 224
Obituaries 259 [82–85]
Obote, Milton 348 [82–85]
O'Brien, Edmond 264
O'Brien, John 25
Ocean Drilling Program (ODP) 106
Oceanography 253 [82–85]
  archaeology 15
  biology 47
  Earth sciences 106
Oda, Goichi: *see* Takakura, Ken
OECD: *see* Organization for Economic Cooperation and Development
Official Secrets Act (U.K.) 247
Ogarkov, Nikolai 349 [83, 85]
Ogilvy, James 289
Ohio 365 [82–85]
  automobile industry 34
  financial institutions 81
  governor, *list* 367
Oil: *see* Petroleum
Okello, Tito 348
Oki Electric Industry Co. 78
Oklahoma 365 [82–85]
  governor, *list* 367
Oklahoma Sooners (football team) 142, *picture*
Okomato, Kozo, *picture* 182
Old age: *see* Senior citizens
Oldsmobile 35
Oligosaccharins 48
Oliver, Al, *picture* 41 [83]
Olmec culture 16
Olmos, Edward James 328
Olsen, Donald 220
Olympus (photographic co.) 268
Oman 255 [82–85]
  Middle East 229
  U.S.S.R. 352

Onassis, Christina 257 [85]
O'Neal, Ryan, picture 257
Ontario, Can. (prov.) 65 [82, 83]
On The Road Again (racehorse) 160
OPEC: see Organization of Petroleum Exporting
    Countries
Opera 240 [82–85]
Orange Bowl (football) 142 [85]
Oregon 365 [82–85]
    governor, list 367
Organic chemistry 67
Organization for Economic Cooperation
    and Development (OECD) 109,
    172 [84, 85]
Organization of African Unity (OAU) 5,
    picture 6 [82–85]
    Morocco 232
Organization of American States (OAS)
    162 [82–84]
Organization of Petroleum Exporting
    Countries (OPEC) 148 [82–85]
    international trade 173
    Middle East and North Africa 120, 231
Ormandy, Eugene (Jeno Blau Ormandy) 264
Ornithology: see Birds
Ortega Saavedra, Daniel 97, 250, picture [85]
Oryx 382 [85]
Oscar: see Academy of Motion Picture Arts
    and Sciences
Osmond, Donny 257
OTB (jazz group) 241
Ottawa, Can. 25 [83, 85]
Ouko, Robert 190 [85]
"Out of Africa" (film) 234
Oxford, U.K. 26
Ozal, Turgut 347 [84, 85]
    Saudi Arabia 293
Ozone 125 [82, 85]

p

"P&P" awards: see "Plays and Players" awards
Pacific region 396
    weather 376
Packaging 140 [84]
PACs: see Political action committees
Page, P. K. 213
Paharpur Buddhist Monastery (Bangladesh),
    picture 197
Painting: see Art and art exhibitions
Pakistan 255 [82–85]
    archaeology 15
    defense and arms control 93
    disasters 103
    human rights 162
    international affairs 357
        Afghanistan 4
        Burma 60
        India 168
    refugees and migrants 284
    wildlife conservation 383
Palestine Liberation Organization (PLO)
    229 [82–85]
    Israel 181
    Jordan 188
    Syria 322
    Tunisia 204, 347, 356
Palestinians 229 [82–85]
    crimes 83, 183
        "Achille Lauro" 203, 364
    human rights 162
        Israel 182
        Jordan 188
        Lebanon 205, picture 206
        Syria 322
    United Nations 356
Paley, Grace, picture 211
Palme, Olof 318 [82–84]
Panama 256 [82–85]
    government 200
    Latin America 198
Pan American World Airways 344 [82]
Pancasila (Indonesian ideology) 169 [85]
Pandas 383 [82–85]
    conservation coin, picture 314

Papandreou, Andreas 155, picture [82–85]
    Bulgaria 60
    East Germany 152
Papua New Guinea 204 [85]
Paraguay 256 [82–85]
    government 200
Paris, Fr. [82–85]
    aerospace 3
    arts 17, 23, 93, 239, 240
Parochial schools 116, 202, 363 [85]
Particle accelerator 272
Party of God (Hizbollah) 288
"Passage to India, A" (film) 235 [85]
Patton, Will, picture 337
Paul VI 287
Pawley, Howard 66 [83]
Payton, Walter 141 [84, 85]
Paz Estenssoro, Víctor 52
PBS: see Public Broadcasting Service
PC: see Personal computer
PCBs (Polychlorinated biphenyls) 48, 128 [83]
Peacock, Andrew Sharp 29 [82–85]
Pebbles (racehorse) 159
Pei, I. M. 17, picture [82–85]
Pendleton, Clarence 457
PEN/Faulkner award 210
Penn, Irving 270 [85]
Penn, Sean, picture 258
Pennsylvania 365 [82–85]
    animal rights 50
    governor, list 367
    religion 286
Pennsylvania Ballet 91 [83]
Pennzoil Co. 316
Penology 278, 280
Pentam 300 (pentamidine) 104
People 257 [82–85]
People Express 344 [85]
People's Democratic Republic of Yemen: see
    Yemen (Aden)
People's Republic of China: see China
Pepsi Cola Co. 2
Perdue, Frank 258
Peres, Shimon 180, 230 [85]
    religion 288
    United Nations 356
Pérez de Cuéllar, Javier 356 [82–85]
Periodontal disease: see Gum disease
Perkins & Will (architects) 19
Perlman, Rhea 257 [84]
    television 328
Perriand, Charlotte 23
Perry, William (The Refrigerator) 457
    football 141
Personal computer (PC) 77, 79 [84, 85]
Pertini, Alessandro 184 [84, 85]
Peru 267 [82–85]
    archaeology 16
    disasters 101
    fish and fisheries 137
    government 200
    human rights 161
    international exchange and payments 172
    Latin America 197
    motion pictures 236
Peso (Bolivian) 52
Pesticides 81, 126 [82–85]
Pests 46
Petersen, William, picture 334
Peterson, David Robert 458
Petroleum 148 [82–85]
    aerospace 3
    Arctic regions 20
    automobile industry 35
    corporate mergers 114
    economic affairs 110
    international trade 172
    Middle East 228
    plastics 273
    see also countries by name
Pets 49 [82–85]
Petunias 139
PGA: see Professional Golfers' Association
PGR (plant growth regulator) 47
Phenylketonuria 222
Philadelphia, Pa. 86 [82–84]
    arts 24, 239, 270
Philadephia Flyers (ice hockey team) 163

"Philadelphia Inquirer" (newspaper) 246
Philately: see Stamps and coins
Philip Morris Inc. 316 [83]
Philippines 267 [82–85]
    disasters 100
    human rights 162
    weather 376
    wildlife conservation 383
Phoenix, Ariz. 19
Phosphorus 69
Photography 268 [82–85]
Physics 271 [82–85]
Picasso Museum (Paris, Fr.) 239
Pickens, Thomas Boone, Jr. 458 [85]
    corporate mergers 114
Pincay, Laffit, Jr. 159
Pindling, Sir Lynden O. 38, 84 [82–85]
Pinochet Ugarte, Augusto 70 [82–85]
Pinter, Harold 334
Pipelines 344 [82–85]
    Arctic regions 20
    Colombia, picture 149
    Iraq 178
    Libya 208
    Mozambique 238
    Saudi Arabia 293
Piracy 204
    refugees and migrants 101, 283
    television 327
Pituitary dwarfism 105
"Places in the Heart" (film) 235 [85]
Planinc, Milka 378, picture 379
Plant growth regulator (PGR) 47
Plants: see Agriculture; Flowers and gardens
Plaque (dental) 99
Plastics 273 [82]
    dentistry 99
"Plays and Players" awards ("P&P" awards)
    335 [85]
PLO: see Palestine Liberation Organization
Plummer, Amanda, picture 337
Poetry 210, 212, 213 [82–85]
    children's 213
Poison 48, 49 [83]
Poison Pill 114
Poland 273 [82–85]
    crime and law enforcement 86
    environment 125
    Europe 60, 132
    human rights 161
    Popieluszko trial 274
    sports: see individual sports
"Polar Sea" (U.S. ship) 21, 64, 204, picture 63
Police 86, 203, 282 [82–85]
Polisario Front: see Popular Front for the
    Liberation of Saguia el Hamra and
    Río de Oro
Political action committees (PACs) 202
    [83, 85]
Political parties: see countries by name
Political prisoners 161 [82–85]
    Afghanistan 4
    Pakistan 255
    Poland 275
    South Africa 87, 282, 302
    Uruguay 372
Pollack, Sydney 234 [83]
Pollard, Jonathan Jay 364
Pollution 124 [82–85]
    animal rights 50
    biology 48
    Canada 64
    fishing industry 138
    state governments 368
    see also Acid rain
Pol Pot 190, 307 [82, 83]
Polychlorinated biphenyls: see PCBs
Polyethylene 273
Polynomial 219
Ponomarev, Boris N. 420
Poor: see Poverty
Pope, Harrison, Jr. 289
Popieluszko, Jerzy Aleksander 86, 274,
    275 [85]
Popular Forces of April 25 (FP-25) 278
Popular Front for the Liberation of Saguia el
    Hamra and Río de Oro (Polisario
    Front) 10, 232 [82–85]

Popular music 243 [82, 83, 85]
  fashion 135
Population 275 [82–85]
  education 118
  Ethiopia 129
  urban areas, *table* 277
Porcelain enamel 67
Pornography 54, 237 [83, 85]
Porsche 36
Portraiture 25
Portugal 277 [82–85]
  disasters 102
  European Communities 130
  Mozambique 238
  social services 298
  tourism 338
  transportation 345
Pound sterling (British currency) 112
  [82, 83, 85]
Poverty 296, *picture* 297 [82–85]
  education 117
  homelessness 299
  liberation theology 287
  race relations 281
POW camps (prisoner-of-war camps) 357
Power: *see* Fuel and energy; Public utilities
Prado (museum, Madrid, Sp.) 24, 239
Prayer 116, 202, 286, 363 [83, 85]
Preakness Stakes 159 [82, 83, 85]
Pregnancy 276
  drugs 104
  mental health 224
Presbyterians 285 [83]
Preservation: *see* Landmarks and monuments
Preservatives 139
Price, Larry C. 270, *picture* 269 [82]
Price, Leontyne, *picture* 241
Prices 110, 173 [82–85]
  agriculture 8
  fuel and energy 3, 148
  international exchange and payments 169
  iron and steel industry 180
  microelectronics 227
  ships and shipping 294
  stocks and bonds 315
  textiles 331
  see also countries by name
Primates 49
Prime rate 316 [82, 83]
Principal, Victoria 258
Prisoner-of-war camps (POW camps) 357
Prisons 278 [82–85]
  privatization 280
  state governments 367
Pritikin, Nathan 264
Private enterprise: *see* Capitalism
Prizes: *see* Awards and prizes
Proconsul africanus 45 [85]
Procter & Gamble 2 [82–84]
Professional Golfers' Association (PGA)
  154 [83–85]
"Prophets of Regulation, The" (book) 211
Prost, Alain 37 [83–85]
Protectionism 112
  Asia 396
    China 75
    Japan 187
    Southeast Asia 308
    Taiwan 323
  Canada 63
  Middle East 229
  United States 175, 360
Protestantism 288 [82–85]
Protests: *see* Demonstrations and riots
Prudhoe Bay, Alaska 20 [83, 85]
Przewalski horse 382 [82, 83, 85]
Psychology 224 [82, 83]
  animal rights 49
Psychotherapy 224 [85]
Public Broadcasting Service (PBS) 328 [82–85]
Public utilities 125, 149 [82–85]
Publishing: *see* Book publishing; Literature;
  Literature for Children; Magazines;
  Mass media; Newspapers
Puchala, Linda 193
Puerto Rico 103, 375 [83]
Puerto Rican Americans: *see* Hispanic
  Americans

Pulitzer Prizes [82, 83, 85]
  literature 210
  newspapers 245
  photography 270, *pictures* 269
Punaglandin 3 68
Punishment 278, 280
Punjab, India (state) 167 [84, 85]
Purple, Adam, *picture* 139

q

Qabus ibn Sa'id 255 [83–85]
Qadhafi, Muammar Al (Muammar
  Muhammad al-Qaddafi) 208,
  352 [82–85]
Qatar 280 [82–85]
  Middle Eastern affairs 229
Quakers 285
Quantum chromodynamics (QCD)
  (physics) 272
Quark (physics) 271 [82, 85]
Quasi crystals (physics) 272
Quebec, Can. (prov.) 61, 65 [82–85]
Quimbaya culture 16

r

Rabbit 49
Race relations 281 [82–85]
  crime and law enforcement 84
    capital punishment 279
    Goetz case 85
  education 117
  human rights 162
  refugees and migrants 284
  South Africa 14, 118, 301, 305, 357, 360
  see also Apartheid; Black Americans;
    Discrimination; Minorities
Radiation 27, 406 [82–85]
Radio: *see* Television and radio
Radioactive waste: *see* Waste disposal
Radio Martí 87 [84]
Radio waves 406, 408
Radke, Trina 319
Railroads 121, 344 [82–85]
  disasters 103
"Rainbow Warrior" (ship) 83, 147, 204, 249,
Rajneesh, Bhagwan Shree 289
Ramirez, Richard 84, *picture* 86
Rat 49 [84]
Rau, Johannes, *picture* 151
RCA Corp. 316, 363
Reagan, Ronald Wilson 459 [82–85]
  crime and law enforcement 86, 278
  defense and arms control 93
  education 118
  environment 124
  international affairs
    Canada 63, *picture* 61
    Cuba 87
    Europe 131, 147, 151, 156, 183, 275, 278,
      picture 312
    India 168
    Japan 20, 187, 400
    Middle East and North Africa 188, 205,
      230, 347
    South Africa 6, 303, 306, 314
    Southeast Asia 308
    U.S.S.R. 351, 424
  labor and employment 195
  medicine 221
  public information policy 248
  race relations 281
  religion 288
  social services 297
  space exploration 308
  television and radio 325
  United States 358, 365
Recession 112, 200 [82–85]
  see also countries by name
Recombinant DNA: *see* DNA
Record industry 241 [82, 83, 85]

Red Cross 190, 301 [85]
Reder, Walter 32
Redgrave, Sir Michael Scudamore 264
Redox chemiluminescence detector 69
Reduced instruction set computer
  architectures (Risc architectures) 78
Reed, Jack 246
Reef 47
Reeves, Paul Alfred 460
  New Zealand 249, *picture* 249
Refrigerator, The: *see* Perry, William
Refugees and migrants 283 [82–85]
  Costa Rica 82
  education 117
  Europe 282, 321
  human rights 162
  India 167
  Korea 190
  Laos 197
  Libya 208
  Nicaragua 249
  Palestinians 205, 322, 357
  population 276
  Sanctuary Movement 285, 286
  Somalia 301
  South Africa 304, 305
  Southeast Asia 189, 307
  Tunisia 347
  Uruguay 372
Regan, Donald Thomas 460 [82, 85]
  United States 363
Regulation: *see* Deregulation
Relativity (science) 409
Religion 286 [82–85]
  "As the 'New Religions' Grow Older"
    (special report) 289
  human rights 161
  liberation theology 287
  race relations 281
  Sanctuary Movement 285
  United States 116, 202, 363
  U.S.S.R. 418
Rembrandt 25
Renamo: *see* Mozambique National
  Resistance
Renoir, Auguste 24, *picture* 23
Republic of Korea: *see* Korea
Revaluation: *see* Devaluation and revaluation
Reye's syndrome 104, 223 [83]
Rhinoceros 378 [82, 84]
Rhode Island 366 [82–85]
  governor, *list* 367
RIBA: *see* Royal Institute of British Architects
Rice 9 [85]
Richards, Keith 257 [84]
Richter, Charles Francis 264
Riddles, Libby (Elizabeth Nell Riddles) 460
Rigby McCoy, Cathy 257
Rigg, Diana, *picture* 327 [83]
Riots: *see* Demonstrations and riots
Risc architectures (Reduced instruction set
  computer architectures) 78
R. J. Reynolds Industries 2
Roads and highways 123, 345, 365 [82–85]
  Middle East 229
Robinson, David 212
Robinson, Eddie 144
Rock music 243 [82, 83, 85]
Rogers, Richard 19
Rollins, Sonny 242
Rolls-Royce 35
Roman Catholicism 286, 290 [82–85]
  Czechoslovakia 90
  Haiti 158
  liberation theology 287
  Netherlands, The 244
  Nicaragua 98
  Paraguay 256
  Poland 274
  Sanctuary Movement 285
  U.S.S.R. 418
  Vietnam 373
  Yugoslavia 379
Romania 291 [82–85]
  European affairs 60, 132, 163
Rome, Italy 15, 231, 287 [83]
Rose, Pete (Peter Edward Rose) 461 [85]
  baseball 40

Rose Bowl 142 [85]
Rosenblatt, Joe 213
Roses 139 [82, 84]
"Rosita" (ship) 101
Ross, Bill D. 210
Ross, Diana 258
Rostenkowski, Daniel 462
    United States 361
Roszak, Theodore 289
Roth, D. Douglas 286
Roth, Philip 210 [82, 84]
Rothenburger, Christa 167 [82, 85]
Roy, Maurice Cardinal 264
Royal Academy (London, U.K.) 24 [83, 85]
Royal Botanic Gardens (Kew, U.K.)
    384 [83, 85]
Royal Institute of British Architects (RIBA) 19
    [82, 83, 85]
Royal Museum of Scotland 239
Royal Shakespeare Company (RSC)
    335 [82–85]
Rumania: see Romania
Russia: see Union of Soviet Socialist
    Republics
Russian Orthodox Church 418 [83, 84]
Rwanda 283 [83, 84]
Ryder Cup (golf) 153 [84]
Ryskind, Morrie 264
Ryzhkov, Nikolai I. 420

S

Sabah, Malaysia (state) 218
Sabah, Jabir al-Ahmad al-Jabir Al 192, picture
Saberhagen, Bret, picture 40
SAC: see Strategic Air Command
Sacred Congregation for the Doctrine of the
    Faith 287
SADCC: see Southern Africa Development
    Coordination Conference
SADR: see Saharan Arab Democratic
    Republic
Safety 232, 332, 343, 368 [82–85]
    consumer affairs 81
    ice hockey 165
    labor and employment 195
    toys 339
    see also Accidents
Sagittarius (constellation) 405
Sahara Desert 46
Saharan Arab Democratic Republic (SADR)
    232 [83–85]
    see also Western Sahara
Sahel (region, Africa) 7, 376
Sailing: see Boating
Saint Christopher and Nevis (St. Kitts-Nevis)
    291 [84, 85]
St. John, Bernard 39
St. Louis, Mo. 240 [84]
St. Louis Cardinals (baseball team) 39
Saint Lucia 291 [82–85]
Saint Vincent and the Grenadines 291 [82–85]
Sakharov, Andrei Dimitriyevich 350
    [82, 83, 85]
Salaries: see Wages and salaries
"Salem" (ship) 85
Sales: see Economic affairs
Salmonella 81, 366, picture 140 [85]
Salomon Brothers Inc. 316
SALT (Strategic Arms Limitation Treaty)
    96 [82–85]
"Salyut" (space station) 310 [82–84]
SAMA (Saudi Arabian Monetary Agency) 293
Samsung Group 34
San'a': see Yemen (San'a')
San Andreas Fault, Calif. 108
Sanctuary Movement 285, 286
San Diego, Calif. 23, 145, picture 383 [83]
Sandinista National Liberation Front 161,
    249, 287, 360 [82–85]
San Francisco, Calif. 18, 240 [82–85]
Sanguinetti Cairolo, Julio María 372,
    picture [85]
"Santa Ana Register" (newspaper) 270
Sarandon, Susan 257

Sarney, José 58
Sartzetakis, Christos 462
    Greece 155
Saskatchewan, Can. (prov.) 61, 66 [82, 83]
SAT: see Scholastic Aptitude Test
Satellite-dish television antenna, picture 325
Satellites (artificial) 26 [82–85]
    space science 311, 325, 407
Saturn (automobile industry) 33
Saud, Sultan Salman ibn Abdel-Aziz as- 292
    space exploration 309
Saudi Arabia 292 [82–85]
    engineering projects 122
    fuel and energy 148, picture 150
    Middle East 178, 189, 206, 229
    transportation 344
    U.S.S.R. 352
    West Germany 152
Saudi Arabian Monetary Agency (SAMA) 293
Saudi Fund for Development 293
Saunders, Norman 84
Savimbi, Jonas, picture 11 [83, 85]
Savings and loan associations: see Financial
    institutions
Scandals and corruption 83 [83–85]
    Canada 60, 66
    China 75
    Czechoslovakia 90
    France 147
    Mexico 226
    Paraguay 256
    United States 365
    U.S.S.R. 349, 416
    Venezuela 372
    West Germany 151
Scargill, Arthur 196, 353 [83, 85]
SCCA: see Sports Car Club of America
Schaufuss, Peter 93
Schlossberg, Stephen L. 195
Schlüter, Poul Holmskov 99 [83–85]
Scholastic Aptitude Test (SAT) 118 [83, 85]
Schöne, Andrea 166, picture [85]
Schools: see Colleges and universities;
    Education
Scientology (religion) 290
Scorsese, Martin 258
    motion pictures 233
Scotland: see United Kingdom
Scott, Francis Reginald 265
Scottish National Gallery of Modern Art
    (Edinburgh, Scot.) 24 [85]
Scourby, Alexander 265
SDI: see Strategic Defense Initiative
Seaga, Edward 185 [82, 83, 85]
Seal First Novel Award 213
Seals 50, 378 [84, 85]
Sears, Roebuck and Co. 2, 368 [82–85]
Seat belts 368 [84, 85]
Seaver, Tom 40
Sea World (Orlando, Fla.), picture 384
Sea World (San Diego, Calif.) 383
Securities: see Stocks and bonds
Securities and Exchange Commission (SEC)
    318 [82–85]
Segal, Walter 265
Segregation: see Apartheid; Discrimination;
    Race relations
Seidelmann, Susan 233
Seifert, Jaroslav 90 [85]
Semiconductors 77, 227 [82–85]
Senate, U.S.: see Congress, United States
Senegal 204 [82, 83]
Senior citizens 63, 297 [82–85]
Service Employees International Union 194
Sessions, Roger Huntington 265
Seth, Roshan, picture 335
747 (aircraft) 2
Sewage disposal: see Waste disposal
Sexual behavior 220, 279
    assault 84
Seymour, Jane 257 [82, 83]
Sgr A* (star) 408
Shaffer, Peter 235
Shah, Eddie 246
Shamir, Yitzhak 180 [83–85]
"Shamrock summit" 63, 86, 361, picture 61
Shange, Ntozake 209 [83]
Shanker, Albert 115

Sharon, Ariel 216 [82, 83, 85]
Shcherbitsky, Vladimir V. 420
Shell Oil Co. 316 [85]
Shenuda III 288 [83, 84]
Shepard, Sam 334
Shevardnadze, Eduard Amvrosiyevich 462
    U.S.S.R. 136, 165, 419
Shevchenko, Arkadi Nikolaevich 423
    "Soviet Union Under Gorbachev, The"
        (feature article) 412
Shi'ah (Shi'ite): see Islam
Ships and shipping 293 [82–85]
    crime and law enforcement 85
    intervention and defense 97
    Middle Eastern affairs 228
Shishii, Eiko 167
Shock treatment: see Electroconvulsive
    therapy
Shorter, Wayne 242
Shriver, Pam 330 [83–85]
Shultz, George P. 136, 165, 359, picture
    372 [83, 85]
Sicily (I., Italy) 109 [83]
Siena, Italy 25
Sievers, Robert E. 68
Signoret, Simone 265
Sihanouk, Norodom 189 [82–85]
Sikhs 162, 167, 288 [82–85]
Siles Zuazo, Hernán 52 [83–85]
Silicon 69
Silk 331 [82–85]
Sill, Aleta 55
Silverman, Kenneth 211
Silvers, Phil 265
Simon, Claude (Claude-Eugène-Henri
    Simon) 463
    literature 208
Simon, Neil 333
Simpson, O. J. 258
Sims, Zoot (John Haley Sims) 265
Singapore 308 [82, 83, 85]
Singh, Nagendra 205
Singh, Sant Ajit 168
Singletary, Mike 141
Sinn Fein 356 [84]
Skidmore, Owings & Merrill (architects)
    19 [82–84]
Skiing 295 [82–85]
SLA: see South Lebanon Army
Slabbert, Frederick van Zyl 303
Slaney, Mary (Mary Decker) 258
    track and field 342, picture 341
Smith, Ian D. 381 [83, 85]
Smith, Page 210
Smith, Samantha 265
SmithKline Beckman Corp. 82
Smithsonian Institution (Wash., D.C.) 47,
    picture 48 [82]
Smog alert (W.Ger.) 127
Smoking 81, 223, 366 [83–85]
    see also Tobacco
Soares, Mário 238, 277 [84, 85]
Soccer 144 [82–85]
    disasters 100
    Brussels 44, 143, 184, picture 143
Socialism 421 [82–85]
Social Security 112, 296 [82–85]
Social services 296 [82–85]
    "Homelessness" (special report) 299
    United States 366
Sodium suramin (Suramin) (drug) 104
Software 78, 79 [84, 85]
Solar energy 150 [82, 83, 85]
Solidarity (Solidarnosc) 273 [82–85]
Somalia 301 [82–85]
    disasters 101
    engineering projects 122
    Ethiopia 130
    refugees and migrants 283
Sondergaard, Gale (Edith Holm
    Sondergaard) 266
Sondheim, Stephen 211 [85]
Soto, Gary 210
South Africa 301 [82–85]
    anthropology 14
    defense and arms control 93
    disasters 103
    education 118

international affairs 172
Africa 5, 11, 238
Canada 64
Europe 32, 131
United Nations 357
United States 314, 360
mines and mining 231
newspapers 246
race relations 87, 162, 281
musical opposition 243
religion 286
"South Africa's Apartheid Policy" (special report) 305
South America: see Latin-American affairs; countries by name
South Asian Association for Regional Cooperation 169
South Carolina 366 [82–85]
governor, list 367
South Charleston, W.Va. 128
South Dakota 366 [82–85]
governor, list 367
Southeast Asian affairs 307 [82–85]
refugees and migrants 283
see also Southeast Asian countries
Southern Africa Development Coordination Conference (SADCC) 6 [82]
Southern Baptist Convention 288 [82, 83]
South Korea: see Korea
South Lebanon Army (SLA) 205
United Nations 137, 356
South West Africa: see Namibia
South West Africa People's Organization (SWAPO) 5, 11, 357 [82–85]
South Yemen: see Yemen (Aden)
Soviet Union: see Union of Soviet Socialist Republics
"Soviet Union Under Gorbachev, The" (feature article) 412
Soybeans 8 [82–85]
"Soyuz" (space vehicle) 310 [84, 85]
Space probes: see Satellites (artificial)
Space science and exploration 308 [82–85]
astronomy 26
chemistry 68
"Discovery" 292
Halley's comet 28
kites 386, picture 391
see also Satellites (artificial)
Spain 312 [82–85]
automobile industry 33
disasters 100
European Communities 130
fish and fisheries 137
international affairs
Algeria 10
international trade 174
Morocco 233
Netherlands, The 244
oceanography 253
tourism 338
Spanish Americans: see Hispanic Americans
Spear of the Nation (Umkonto We Sizwe) 305
Speed skating 165, 166 [84, 85]
Spencer, Freddie 237 [85]
Spend a Buck (racehorse) 159, picture
Spender, Stephen 212
Spielberg, Steven 234, picture 257 [83]
Spina bifida 222 [84]
Spinks, Michael 56, picture 57 [82, 83, 85]
Sports Car Club of America (SCCA) 36 [83, 85]
Spring Hill, Tenn. 33
Springsteen, Bruce 464 [83, 85]
marriage 258
music 243
Spying: see Espionage
Sri Lanka 313 [82–85]
human rights 162
India 169
tourism 338
Ssemogerere, Paul 348
Stallone, Sylvester 464
marriage 258
motion pictures 233
Stamps and coins 313 [82–85]
Standard & Poor's Index 317 [82–85]
Stanford University 238

Stanley, Charles 288
Stanley, Kim 328
Stanley Cup (ice hockey) 163 [82–85]
Starkey, Zak 257
Stars 27, 405 [82, 83, 85]
START: see Strategic Arms Reduction Talks
Star Wars program: see Strategic Defense Initiative
State governments, U.S. 365 [82–85]
crime and law enforcement 86, 278
education 117, 118
State of Illinois Center (Chicago, Ill.), picture 18 [84]
Statue of Liberty 215, 315 [84]
Steel industry: see Iron and steel industry
Steinbach, Alice 246
Steinberg, Saul 114
Steinseifer, Carrie 319 [85]
Stephan, Robert T. 366
Stephen Lepp Associates' (architects) 19
Steppenwolf Theatre Company (Chicago, Ill.) 334
"Stern" (magazine) 217 [84, 85]
Stethem, Robert 83
Stewart, Potter 266
Sting (rock star) 243
Stockman, David 54, 364 [82–84]
Stocks and bonds 315 [82–85]
United States 113, 362
Stores: see Economic affairs
Storms 100, 374 [82–85]
Strategic Air Command (SAC) 94 [85]
Strategic Arms Limitation Treaty: see SALT
Strategic Arms Reduction Talks (START) 96, 359 [83–85]
Strategic Defense Initiative (SDI; Star Wars) 94, picture 95 [85]
Australia 30
Europe 131, 147, 152, 356
Japan 187
United States 359
U.S.S.R. 352, 425
Stratford Festival (Ontario, Can.) 334 [82–85]
Strikes 195, pictures 193, 194, 195 [82–85]
Bolivia 53, picture
Costa Rica 83
Denmark 99
Greece 156
Iceland 165
Ireland 178
Jamaica 185
Panama 256
Portugal 278
South Africa 302
Spain 312
Sweden 318
Tunisia 346
United Kingdom 149, 232, 353
United States 41, 115
Uruguay 372
Stroessner, Alfredo 256 [82–85]
Strokes 220, 276 [82, 83]
Suazo Córdova, Roberto 158 [82–85]
Suburban areas: see Cities and urban affairs
Subways 346 [82–84]
Sudan, The 5, 7, 283 [82–85]
Sugar 9 [82–85]
Cuba 87
Saint Vincent and the Grenadines 292
Trinidad and Tobago 346
Sugar Bowl (football) 142 [85]
Suharto 169, 308 [82–85]
Suicide 224, 276 [82–85]
Suknaski, Andrew 213
Sulfur dioxide (pollutant) 124
Sullivan, Danny 36
Sultan ibn Abdel-Aziz 292 [85]
"Sun City" (music) 243
"Sunday in the Park with George" 211
Sunnah (Sunni, Sunnite): see Islam
Super Bowl (football) 141 [82–85]
Supercomputers 78
Supermajority Rules 114
Superstring theory (physics) 271
Supreme Court, U.S. 202, 363, 365 [82–85]
advertising 2
education 116
media 216, 325

race relations 281
religion 286
Suramin (Sodium suramin) (drug) 104
Surface (math.) 218
Surgery: see Medicine
Surrogate motherhood 383 [85]
Svan, Gunde 296 [85]
Swann Report ("Education for All") 117, 282
SWAPO: see South West Africa People's Organization
Sweden 318 [82–85]
automobile industry 33
botanical gardens 384
ceramics industry 67
engineering projects 124
India 168
international law 204
medicine 220
population 276
tourism 338
Sweeteners 67
SWET: see Society of West End Theatre
Swimming 319 [82–85]
Switzerland 321 [82–85]
art 26
engineering projects 124
international law 205
motion pictures 235
race relations 282
Synthetic fiber: see Fiber, synthetic
Synthetic fuels 150 [82–85]
Syria 321 [82–85]
archaeology 15
Middle East and North Africa 177, 181, 189, 205, 230
U.S.S.R. 95

t

Tabouis, Geneviève 266
Tahara, Keiichi 270
Taiwan (Republic of China) 322 [82–85]
Asia 75, 191
human rights 162
machinery and machine tools 216
toys 339
Takakura, Ken (Goichi Oda) 465
Takeover (business) 113, 362
Takeshita, Noboru 466
Japan 185
Tambo, Oliver 283, 303
Tamil 162, 169, 313 [84, 85]
Tanaka, Kakuei 185 [83–85]
"Tango Argentino" 91, 334, picture 92
Taniguchi Masaharu 266
Tan Koon Swan 217
Tan Liangde 320
Tanzania 323 [82–85]
Africa 190, 380
India 168
refugees and migrants 283
Tariffs 63, 175, 198, 229 [82]
Tate Gallery (London, U.K.) 26 [82, 83, 85]
Taxation [82–85]
Australia 31
Ireland 178
United States 114, 118, 361, 365
Taylor, James 258
Taylor, Paul 91 [82, 83]
Teacher of the Year (U.S.), picture 116
Teachers: see Education
Tears for Fears (rock group) 243
Technology 78, 227, 324 [82–85]
aerospace 3
ceramics industry 67
Europe 130
food processing 139
kites 386
machinery and machine tools 216
mines and mining 232
newspapers 246
photography 268
space exploration 407
textiles 331
tunnels 124

Teeth: *see* Dentistry
Telecommunications (Communications) 324 [82–85]
  space exploration 309
  see also Television and radio
Telephones, *picture* 324 [82–84]
Television and radio 325 [82–85]
  acquisitions 244
  advertising 2
  Poland 274
  United States 363
Teng Hsiao-p'ing: *see* Deng Xiaoping
Tennessee 365 [82–85]
  automobile industry 33
  governor, *list* 367
  law 203
  state prison disturbance, *picture* 279
Tennessee Valley Authority 253
Tennis 328 [82–85]
Tenpins 55
Terkel, Studs 211 [83, 85]
Terrorism 356 [82–85]
  Europe
    Belgium 45, *picture* 44
    Greece 155
    Italy 183
    Portugal 278
  hijackings
    "Achille Lauro" 203, *picture* 202
    TWA aircraft 83, 288, 328
  India 167
  Middle East and North Africa 228
    Egypt 120
    Israel 182
    Kuwait 192
    Lebanon 205
    Libya 208
    Saudi Arabia 292
  United States 364
  see also Bombings; Kidnappings
Tetra Pak (Swedish co.) 140 [85]
Texaco Inc. 316 [85]
Texas 366 [82–85]
  governor, *list* 367
"Texas Monthly" (magazine) 216
Textiles 331 [82–85]
  fashion 136
TGV (Train à Grande Vitesse) 345 [84]
Thailand 332 [82–85]
  archaeology 15
  Australia 30
  engineering projects 122
  Southeast Asia 189, 197, 307, *picture*
  wildlife conservation 377, 383
Tharp, Twyla 91 [82, 83, 85]
Thatcher, Margaret Hilda 466 [82–85]
  Africa 6, 119, 303
  Ireland 179, *picture*
  Middle East 188, 292
  prisons 278
  United Kingdom 353
Thayer, Paul 85
Theater 333 [82–85]
  wrestling 336
Theme parks 339
"Theology of Liberation, A" (book) 287
Third World: *see* Developing countries
Thomas, Betty 328
Thomas, Lorry 286
Thomas, Philip Michael 447
Thomas, Pinklon 56 [85]
Thompson, James 84 [82, 83, 85]
Thoreau, Henry 214
Thornburg *v.* Gingles (U.S.) 281
Threatened species 139
Three Mile Island, Pa. 149 [84]
  nuclear industry 253
Thuy, Xuan 266
Tian Jiyun (T'ien Chi-yün) 467
Tiedge, Hans Joachim 151
Tillstrom, Burr 266
"Time" (magazine) 216, 359 [83, 85]
"Times, The" (newspaper) 246 [82–85]
"Times of Harvey Milk, The"
  (documentary) 235
Tissue plasminogen activator (TPA) 106 [85]
"Titanic" (ship) 253, *picture* 254
TMA (Toy Manufacturers of America) 339

Tobacco 81, 366 [83, 85]
  see also Smoking
Tobago: *see* Trinidad and Tobago
Todd, John 366
Tokyo, Japan 83 [83]
Tomasson, Helgi 91
Tomatoes 139 [82, 85]
Tomko, Jozef Cardinal 90
Tomlin, Lily 334 [82]
Tong Hui 320
Tony awards 333 [83, 85]
Topology 218
Tornadoes 102 [82–85]
Toronto Stock Exchange 316
Torrellas, Maryanne 342
Tortoises 376
Torture 161 [82, 83, 85]
  Afghanistan 4
  South Africa 87, 302
  Uganda 348
Toshiba 67
Tour de France (cycling) 88 [85]
Tourism 338 [82–85]
  Caribbean 38, 156, 291
  gardens 139
  ships and shipping 294
  United Arab Emirates 353
Toxic waste: *see* Waste disposal
Toy Manufacturers of America (TMA) 339
Toyota 34 [83, 85]
Toys and games 339 [82–85]
Toys "R" Us 340 [85]
TPA: *see* Tissue plasminogen activator
Track and field 340 [82–85]
Trade: *see* International trade
Traffic accidents: *see* Accidents
Train à Grande Vitesse: *see* TGV
Trains: *see* Railroads
Transcendental Meditation 289
Transportation 343 [82–85]
  see also Aerospace industry; Automobile
    industry; Railroads; Roads and
    highways; Ships and shipping
Transputer 227
Trans World Airlines: *see* TWA
Travel: *see* Tourism
"Treasure Houses of Britain, The" (exhibition)
  22, *picture*
Treholt, Arne 252, *picture* 251 [85]
Trials and lawsuits 83 [82–85]
  animal rights 50
  Argentina 21, 161, *picture*
  Australia 29
  British Nuclear Fuels Ltd. 127
  Canada 66
  France 147
  Grenada 156
  Indonesia 169
  Italy 184
  Nicaragua 205, 360
  Norway 252
  Philippines 268
  Poland 274, 275
  Portugal 278
  South Africa 246
  Taiwan 323
  United States 366
    Alaska 20
    baseball 41
    book publishing 54
    consumer affairs 82
    corporate mergers 114
    football 142
    magazines 216
    medicine 223
    Sanctuary Movement 285, 286
    social services 297
    West Germany 151
    Zaire 380
Trinidad and Tobago 346 [82–85]
  Caribbean affairs 39, 291
  transportation 346
Tripoli, Lebanon 206 [84]
Tritium 254
Troutman, Philip 366
Trucking industry 33 [82–85]
Tsirulnikova, Zhanna 320
Tsukuba, Japan 187, 270

Tubbs, Tony 56
Tucson, Ariz. 285, 286
Tunisia 346 [82–85]
  Middle East and North Africa 231
    Israeli bombing 183, 204, 356
  tourism 338
  zoos 382
Tunnels 123 [82–85]
Turbay Ayala, Julio César 76 [82]
Turkey 347 [82–85]
  archaeology 15
  human rights 162
  international affairs 204
    Bulgaria 59
    Saudi Arabia 293
Turkish Cypriots 89, 348 [83, 84]
Turks and Caicos Islands 84
Turner, Kathleen, *picture* 234
Turner, Big Joe (Joseph Vernon Turner) 266
Turner, Ted 114, 363
Turner, Tina 467
Turner Broadcasting System 326
Tutu, Bishop Desmond Mpilo 286 [83, 85]
  United States 360
TV: *see* Television and radio
TWA (Trans World Airlines) 344
  hijacking 83, 156, 205, 230, 288, 364
Twentieth Century-Fox Film Corp. 363
Tyler, Anne 208, *picture* 209 [83]
Type A behavior 221
Typhoons 102, 376 [82, 83, 85]
  Vietnam 374

u

U.A.E.: *see* United Arab Emirates
UAW: *see* United Auto Workers
UDF: *see* United Democratic Front
Ueberroth, Peter V. 41 [85]
Uganda 348 [82–85]
  Africa 5, 190
  refugees and migrants 283
UIAA (Union Internationale des Associations
  d'Alpinisme) 237
Uitenhage, South Africa 302
Ullmann, Liv Johanne 468 [82]
  marriage 258
Umkonto We Sizwe (Spear of the Nation) 305
UMW: *see* United Mine Workers
UN: *see* United Nations
Underdeveloped countries: *see* Developing
  countries
Unemployment: *see* Labor and employment
Unesco (United Nations Educational,
  Scientific, and Cultural Organization)
  196, 358 [82–85]
UNHCR: *see* United Nations High
  Commissioner for Refugees
Unification Church 289 [83]
UNIFIL: *see* United Nations Interim Force in
  Lebanon
Union Carbide Corporation 127, 168, 368 [85]
Union Internationale des Associations
  d'Alpinisme (UIAA) 237
Union of Soviet Socialist Republics (U.S.S.R.)
  349 [82–85]
agriculture 7
business and industry
  automobile industry 33
  engineering projects 123
  machinery and machine tools 216
  textiles 331
defense 93, 97
disasters 100
government 412
international affairs 204
  Africa 5, 120, 208, 301
  Asia 4, 72, 168, 188, 192, 256, 394
    Southeast Asia 189, 197, 308, 373
  Canada 64
  Europe 10, 131, 136, 147, 153, 156, 163,
    165, 244, 252, 274
  Latin America 87, 250
  Middle East 189, 206, 229, 255, 292,
    322, 353

United Nations 356
United States 358
motion pictures 236
mountaineering 237
science and technology
  aerospace 3, 28, 309
  Earth sciences 108
  environment 46, 127
  nuclear industry 253
  polar research 11, *picture* 20
  wildlife conservation 377
sports: *see* individual sports
transportation 344
Union Oil Co.: *see* Unocal Corp.
UNITA: *see* National Union for the Total
  Independence of Angola
Unitarian/Universalist Church 285
United Air Lines 344, *picture* 194 [82, 83]
United Arab Emirates (U.A.E.) 353 [82–85]
  Middle East 229
  U.S.S.R. 352
United Automobile Workers (UAW) 63, 194,
  picture 193 [82–85]
United Church of Christ 285 [83]
United Democratic Front (UDF) (S. Africa)
  282, 302 [84]
United Farm Workers 284
United Kingdom (U.K.) (Great Britain)
  353 [82–85]
  arts 22, 211, 235, 238, 240, 335
  business and industry 110
    automobile industry 33
    ceramics industry 67
    construction 59, 122
    fishing industry 138
    food processing 139
    labor and employment 196
    machinery and machine tools 216
    tourism 338
    toys and games 340
  defense 93
  disasters 100, 143
  flowers and gardens 139
  fuel and energy 148
  international affairs 172, 173
    Africa 6, 119, 208, 238, 304, 306, 348
    Europe 10, 60, 130, 163, 179, 275, 291
    India 168
    Latin America 22, 198
    Middle East 188, 229, 255, 292
    United Nations 358
    United States 362
    U.S.S.R. 352
  law 202
  mines and mining 232
  publishing 54, 217, 246
  science and technology
    Antarctic exploration 12
    Earth sciences 109
    environment 125
    medicine 219
    microelectronics 227
    space exploration 308
    wildlife conservation 46, 377, 382
  social issues 298
    animal rights 49
    crime and law enforcement 86, 278
    education 115, 117
    homelessness 300
    human rights 162
    population 276
    public information 247
    race relations 281
    refugees and migrants 284
  sports: *see* individual sports
  stamps and coins 314
  transportation 3, 344
United Methodist Church: *see* Methodists
United Mine Workers (UMW) 194 [83–85]
United Nations (UN) 356 [82–85]
  Afghanistan 4
  Africa 5
  consumer affairs 81
  crime and law enforcement 85
  engineering projects 123
  Europe 275, 321
  homelessness 299
  human rights 161

international law 204
Middle East 229
population 275
United States 359
U.S.S.R. 352
United Nations Educational, Scientific, and
  Cultural Organization: *see* Unesco
United Nations High Commissioner for
  Refugees (UNHCR) 283, 285 [82–85]
United Nations Interim Force in Lebanon
  (UNIFIL) 356 [82–85]
United Rubber Workers 194 [82, 83]
United States (U.S.) 358 [82–85]
  agriculture 8, *picture* 7
  anthropology 14
  archaeology 15
  arts 17, 22, 90, 208, 238, 240
  business and industry 110, 113
    advertising 2
    automobile industry 33
    ceramics industry 67
    construction 59, 123
    fish and fisheries 137
    food processing 140, *picture*
    iron and steel industry 179
    labor and employment 193
    machinery and machine tools 216
    stocks and bonds 315
    textiles 331
    tourism 338
    toys and games 339
  defense 93, 97
  disasters 99
  flowers and gardens 138
  fuel and energy 148, 253
  government
    executive departments, *table* 364
    state governments 365
  international affairs 169, 173, 175
    Africa 5
      Algeria 10
      Angola 11
      Egypt 120
      Libya 208
      Morocco 233
      Mozambique 238
      Somalia 301
      South Africa 303, 305
      Tunisia 347
    Asia
      Afghanistan 4
      China 72
      India 168
      Japan 187, 395
      Kampuchea 189
      North Korea 192
      Pakistan 256
      Philippines 267
      South Korea 190
      Taiwan 322
      Vietnam 373
    Australia 30
    Canada 61
    Caribbean
      Antigua and Barbuda 14
      Bahamas, The 38
      Belize 45
      Grenada 156
      Saint Lucia 291
    Europe 130
      Belgium 45
      East Germany 153
      France 147
      Greece 156
      Hungary 163
      Iceland 165
      Italy 183
      Netherlands, The 244
      Poland 275
      Portugal 278
      Romania 291
      Spain 312
      Sweden 318
      West Germany 151
    Latin America 198, 200
      Argentina 22
      Chile 71
      Colombia 76

      Costa Rica 82
      Cuba 87
      El Salvador 121
      Honduras 158
      Nicaragua 249
      Paraguay 256
    Middle East 229
      Iraq 178
      Israel 181
      Jordan 188
      Lebanon 205
      Oman 255
      Saudi Arabia 292
      Turkey 347
    New Zealand 249
    United Kingdom 356
    United Nations 356
    U.S.S.R. 350
  law 202
  mass media 53, 216, 244, 325
  religion 285, 286, 289
  science and technology
    biology 45
    computers 77
    drugs 104
    Earth sciences 106
    environment 125
    medicine 219
    oceanography 253
    polar exploration 12, 20
    space exploration 28, 308
    telecommunications 324
    wildlife conservation 376, 382
  social issues 296
    animal rights 49
    consumer affairs 81
    crime and law enforcement 83, 278
    education 115, 117, 207
    homelessness 299
    human rights 162
    population 275
    public information 247
    race relations 281
    refugees and migrants 283
  sports: *see* individual sports
  stamps and coins 313, *picture* 314
  transportation 3, 344
  weather 374
  see also Congress, U.S.; Reagan, Ronald;
    Supreme Court, U.S.
United States Congress: *see* Congress, U.S.
United States Football League (USFL)
  142 [83–85]
United States Supreme Court: *see* Supreme
  Court, U.S.
United Steelworkers (USW) 194 [83–85]
Universities: *see* Colleges and universities
Unocal Corp. (Union Oil Co.) 114 [82, 83, 85]
Unser, Al, Sr. 36 [84]
Updike, John 210 [82, 83, 85]
Urban affairs: *see* Cities and urban affairs
Uruguay 372 [82–85]
  Antarctic exploration 11
  government 200
  refugees and migrants 283
U.S.: *see* United States
USA for Africa 243
USFL: *see* United States Football League
USGS: *see* Geological Survey, U.S.
U.S. Open (golf) 154 [83–85]
U.S. Open (tennis) 329 [82–84]
U.S.S.R.: *see* Union of Soviet Socialist
  Republics
USW: *see* United Steelworkers
Utah 367 [82–85]
  governor, *list* 367
Utilities: *see* Public utilities

V

Vaccines 106
Valova, Elena 166 [84, 85]
Van Gogh, Vincent: *see* Gogh, Vincent van
Van Hoften, James 309, *picture* 310
Vasiliev, Oleg 166 [84, 85]

Vatican 288 [82, 83, 85]
Vatican II 287
VCRs: *see* Videocassette recorders
"Vega" (space probe) 311
Vegetables 139 [83–85]
Venereal disease 220
Venezuela 372 [82–85]
 international exchange and payments 172
 Latin America 97, 198
 motion pictures 236
Venus (planet) 311 [82, 83, 85]
Ver, Fabian C. 268 [85]
Vergeer, Hein 166
Vermont 365 [82–85]
 governor, *list* 367
Very Large Array radio telescope (VLA radio
 telescope) 408 [85]
Victoria and Albert Museum (London, U.K.)
 239, *picture* [82, 83]
Victory in Europe Day (World War II)
 151, 359
Videocassette recorders (VCRs) 327
 [82, 83, 85]
Vienna, Austria 231 [82, 83]
Vietnam 373 [82–85]
 Pacific-Asia 30, 189, 197, 307, 399
 refugees and migrants 283
 U.S.S.R. 95
Vigilantism 84, 85
"Village Voice" (newspaper) 245
Violence 83, 101, 161, 278, 281 [82, 83, 85]
 Bangladesh 39
 Colombia 76
 Indonesia 169
 Mexico 225
 Mozambique 238
 New Caledonia 232
 Pakistan 255
 Portugal 278
 Turkey 347
 United Kingdom 355
 Zimbabwe 381
 see also Assassinations; Demonstrations and
 riots; Murders; Terrorism
Virginia 54 [82–85]
 governor, *list* 367
Virus 68, 104, 219, 224 [82, 83, 85]
Vitamins 221 [82, 83, 85]
VLA radio telescope: *see* Very Large Array
 radio telescope
Volcanoes 76, 103, 108 [82–85]
Volkswagen 34 [82, 83, 85]
Vonnegut, Kurt 209 [83]
Vorotnikov, Vitali I. 420
Voting: *see* Elections
Voting Rights Act (1965, U.S.) 281 [83]

W

Wages and salaries 194, 365 [82–85]
 see also countries by name
Waite, Terry, *picture* 355
Waldenbooks 54
Waldo, Carolyn 320
Wales: *see* United Kingdom
Walesa, Lech 258, 273 [82–84]
Walker, John (John Anthony Walker, Jr.) 469
 espionage 364, *picture* 86
Walker, Laura 319
Wallace, Ian 215
Wallace v. Jaffree (U.S.) 202, *picture* 204
Walters, Vernon Anthony 469
 United States 364
Waltrip, Darrell 36 [82, 83]
Wang Laboratories Inc. 77 [84]
Warriner, Kenneth, Jr. 18
Wars 97, 356 [82, 83, 85]
 Asia 4, 256, 352, 418
 Southeast Asia 189, 197, 307, 373
 Latin America 120, 249
 Middle East 177, 182, 205, 228
Warsaw Pact 97, 132, 291 [83, 85]
 U.S.S.R. 350, 424
Washington 365 [82–85]
 governor, *list* 367

Washington, D.C. 22 [82, 83, 85]
 museums 238
"Washingtonian, The" (magazine) 216
Waste disposal 48, 125, 127, 368 [82–85]
Water 122, 126 [82–84]
Water pollution: *see* Pollution
Wayte, Mary 319
WBA: *see* World Boxing Association
WBC: *see* World Boxing Council
WCC: *see* World Council of Churches
Weapons 93, 350, 359, 412 [82–85]
 see also Defense and arms control; Nuclear
 weapons
Weather 374 [82–85]
 disasters 100
 flowers and gardens 138
Webb, Cathleen Crowell 84
Weizsäcker, Richard von 151 [85]
Welfare: *see* Social services
Welland, Colin, *picture* 239
Welles, George Orson 266
West Bank (region, Middle East) 182 [82–85]
West Berlin, W. Ger. 26, 147, 152
Westerberg, Bengt 318, *picture*
Western Accord 62
Western European Union (WEU) 131 [85]
Western Sahara 10, 231, 232 [82–85]
 see also Saharan Arab Democratic Republic
West Germany: *see* Germany
Westmoreland, William C. 216 [85]
West Virginia 366 [82–85]
 environment 127
 governor, *list* 367
WEU: *see* Western European Union
Whales 377, *picture* 384 [82–85]
Wheat 9 [84, 85]
Wheatland Corp. 53
Whitbread Prize 211
White, Ryan, *picture* 221
White collar crime 85 [82, 83]
White rot fungus, *picture* 47
Whitney Museum of American Art (New
 York, N.Y.) 17, 238, *picture*
 239 [82–84]
WHO: *see* World Health Organization
Whooping cranes 376 [83, 85]
"Whydah" (ship) 15
Wiesel, Elie 288
Wilander, Mats 328 [83]
Wildlife conservation 376 [82–85]
 flowers and gardens 139
 zoos and botanical gardens 382
Williams, Cootie (Charles Melvin
 Williams) 266
Williams, Joe 242
Williams, Lynn Russell 470 [84]
Willoch, Kåre Isaachsen 251 [82, 83, 85]
Wilson, A. N. 211
Wimbledon 328 [82–85]
Wind energy 150, 388
Winds 26, 375 [82, 83, 85]
Wine 32
Winston v. Lee (U.S.) 203
Wisconsin 365 [82–85]
 governor, *list* 367
Witt, Katarina 166, *picture* [85]
WOCE: *see* World Ocean Circulation
 Experiment
Wolff, Tobias 210
Women 276 [82–85]
 advertising 2
 drugs 104
 human rights 162
 Iceland 165
 India 168
 labor and employment 194
 literature 208, 214
 medicine 223
 mental health 224
 Norway 252
 refugees and migrants 285
 religion 288
 Saudi Arabia 292
 state governments, U.S. 368
 stocks and bonds, *picture* 316
 U.S.S.R. 418
Woodward, Joanne 328
Wool 331 [82–85]

Workfare 297
World Bank 5, 71, 172, 198, 226 [82–85]
World Boxing Association (WBA) 56 [82–85]
World Boxing Council (WBC) 56 [82, 83, 85]
World Consumer Rights Day 81
World Council of Churches (WCC)
 286 [83–85]
World Court: *see* International Court
 of Justice
"World Cultures" (electronic journal) 14
World Health Organization (WHO) 126,
 358 [83–85]
World Heritage Committee 196 [82–85]
World Ocean Circulation Experiment (WOCE)
 254 [85]
World Series (baseball) 39 [82–85]
World trade: *see* International trade
World War II ending: *see* Victory in
 Europe Day
Wrestling 336
Wygant v. Jackson (U.S.) 281
Wynn-Williams, Gareth
 "Center of the Milky Way, The" (feature
 article) 405
Wyoming 368 [82–85]
 biology 45
 governor, *list* 367

X

X chromosome 222
X-ray laser 272
X rays 27 [82, 83, 85]
X-29 (experimental plane), *picture* 3

Y

Yachting 51 [83–85]
Yamaha 34
Yeager, Chuck 54
Yemen (Aden) (People's Democratic Republic
 of Yemen; South Yemen) 96, 255
 [82, 83, 85]
Yemen (San'a') (Yemen Arab Republic; North
 Yemen) 96 [82, 83, 85]
Yen (Japanese currency) 112 [83, 85]
"Yin" (book) 211
Yugoslavia 378 [82–85]
 automobile industry, *picture* 34
 international exchange and payments 172
 motion pictures 236
 sports: *see* individual sports
 tourism 338
Yukon Territory 66 [82]
Yurchenko, Vitali Sergeyevich 470
 U.S.S.R. 352

Z

Zaire 380 [82–85]
 refugees and migrants 283
Zambia 381 [82–85]
Zebras 383
Zeidler Roberts Partnership 19
Zhelezovski, Igor 167
Zhivkov, Todor 60, *picture* 59 [82, 83, 85]
Zia-ul-Haq, Mohammad 60, 255 [82–85]
Ziegler, Philip 212
Zimbabwe 381 [82–85]
 Africa 6, 238
 agriculture 8
 tourism 339
 wildlife conservation 378
Zimbalist, Efrem Alexandrovich 266
Zoology: *see* Animals; Biology
Zoos and botanical gardens 382 [82–85]
Zovirax (acyclovir) 106
Zurbriggen, Pirmin 295, *picture* [85]
Zürich, Switz. 26 [83]

N ow there's a way to identify all your fine books with flair and style. As part of our continuing service to you, Britannica Home Library Service, Inc. is proud to be able to offer you the fine quality item shown on the next page.

B ooklovers will love the heavy-duty personalized embosser. Now you can personalize all your fine books with the mark of distinction, just the way all the fine libraries of the world do.

T o order this item, please type or print your name, address and zip code on a plain sheet of paper. (Note special instructions for ordering the embosser). Please send a check or money order only (your money will be refunded in full if you are not delighted) for the full amount of purchase, including postage and handling, to:

Britannica Home Library Service, Inc.
Attn: Yearbook Department
Post Office Box 6137
Chicago, Illinois 60680

(Please make remittance payable to: Britannica Home Library Service, Inc.)

IN THE BRITANNICA TRADITION OF QUALITY...

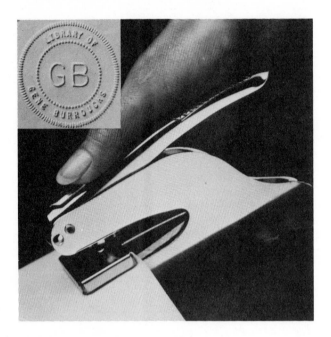

PERSONAL EMBOSSER

A mark of distinction for your fine books. A book embosser just like the ones used in libraries. The 1½″ seal imprints "Library of _____" (with the name of your choice) and up to three centered initials. Please type or print clearly BOTH full name (up to 26 letters including spaces between names) and up to three initials.
Please allow six weeks for delivery.

Just **$20.00**

plus $2.00 shipping and handling

This offer available only in the United States.
Illinois residents please add sales tax

 Britannica Home Library Service, Inc.